DATE DUE

DEC 17 2004		

THE GREAT
CONTEMPORARY
ISSUES

RELIGION IN AMERICA

THE GREAT CONTEMPORARY ISSUES

THE GREAT CONTEMPORARY ISSUES

RELIGION IN AMERICA

𝕮𝔥𝔢 𝔑𝔢𝔴 𝔜𝔬𝔯𝔨 𝕮𝔦𝔪𝔢𝔰

ARNO PRESS

NEW YORK / 1977

GILLIAN LINDT

Advisory Editor

GENE BROWN

Editor

Library of Congress Cataloging in Publication Data

Main entry under title:

Religion in America.

   (The Great contemporary issues)
   Articles, dating from 1870, taken from the New
York times.
   Bibliography: p.
   Includes index.
   SUMMARY: A compilation of articles from The New
York Times documenting the emergent character of
religion in the United States and highlighting the
major points in its development in an increasingly
industrialized and urbanized society.
   1. United States—Religion—Juvenile literature
—Addresses, essays, lectures. [1. Religion—
Addresses, essays, lectures] I. Lindt, Gillian.
II. Brown, Gene. III. New York times. IV. Se-
ries.
BL2530.U6R42   200'.973   75-54571
ISBN 0-405-09865-0

Manufactured in the United States of America

The editors express special thanks to The Associated Press,
United Press International, and Reuters for permission to
include in this series of books a number of dispatches
originally distributed by those news services.

Book design by Stuart David

Contents

Publisher's Note About the Series

It would take even an accomplished speed-reader, moving at full throttle, some three and a half solid hours a day to work his way through all the news The New York Times prints. The sad irony, of course, is that even such indefatigable devotion to life's carnival would scarcely assure a decent understanding of what it was really all about. For even the most dutiful reader might easily overlook an occasional long-range trend of importance, or perhaps some of the fragile, elusive relationships between events that sometimes turn out to be more significant than the events themselves.

This is why "The Great Contemporary Issues" was created—to help make sense out of some of the major forces and counterforces at large in today's world. The philosophical conviction behind the series is a simple one: that the past not only can illuminate the present but must. ("Continuity with the past," declared Oliver Wendell Holmes, "is a necessity, not a duty.") Each book in the series, therefore has as its subject some central issue of our time that needs to be viewed in the context of its antecedents if it is to be fully understood. By showing, through a substantial selection of contemporary accounts from The New York Times, the evolution of a subject and its significance, each book in the series offers a perspective that is available in no other way. For while most books on contemporary affairs specialize, for excellent reasons, in predigested facts and neatly drawn conclusions, the books in this series allow the reader to draw his own conclusions on the basis of the facts as they appeared at virtually the moment of their occurrence. This is not to argue that there is no place for events recollected in tranquility; it is simply to say that when fresh, raw truths are allowed to speak for themselves, some quite distinct values often emerge.

For this reason, most of the articles in "The Great Contemporary Issues" are reprinted in their entirety, even in those cases where portions are not central to a given book's theme. Editing has been done only rarely and in all such cases it is clearly indicated. (Such an excision occasionally occurs, for example, in the case of a Presidential State of the Union Message, where only brief portions are germane to a particular volume, and in the case of some names, where for legal reasons or reasons of taste it is preferable not to republish specific identifications.) Similarly, typographical errors, where they occur, have been allowed to stand as originally printed.

"The Great Contemporary Issues" inevitably encompasses a substantial amount of history. In order to explore their subjects fully, some of the books go back a century or more. Yet their fundamental theme is not the past but the present. In this series the past is of significance insofar as it suggests how we got where we are today. These books, therefore, do not always treat a subject in a purely chronological way. Rather, their material is arranged to point up trends and interrelationships that the editors believe are more illuminating than a chronological listing would be.

"The Great Contemporary Issues" series will ultimately constitute an encyclopedic library of today's major issues. Long before editorial work on the first volume had even begun, some fifty specific titles had already been either scheduled for definite publication or listed as candidates. Since then, events have prompted the inclusion of a number of additional titles, and the editors are, moreover, alert not only for new issues as they emerge but also for issues whose development may call for the publication of sequel volumes. We will, of course, also welcome readers' suggestions for future topics.

Introduction

The documentary materials brought together in this volume—spanning the past one hundred years—provide a kaleidoscopic glimpse into the unfolding of the emergent character of American religion. Religious diversity was both cause and consequence of the forging of a pluralistic American society out of successive waves of transoceanic migrations, abetted by the westward expansion of communities of variant national, racial, ethnic, cultural and class origins.

Even a cursory reading of these selections from *The New York Times* serves to explode the myth first propagated in de Crèvecoeur's *Letters of an American Farmer* and popularized over a century later in Zangwill's evocative drama *The Melting Pot* that in the United States "all the races of Europe are melting and reforming...God is making the American." If God was indeed creating "the American" he was endowing him with no single creed, confession or church. Strewn across the pages of *The New York Times* are accounts, monumental and trivial, of an extraordinarily varied assortment of religious leaders and their followers, from Madame Blavatsky and Mrs. Mary Baker Eddy to the devotees of Father Divine, Abdul Bahá'i and Hare Krishna; from the ranks of Seventh Day Adventists, Mormons, Unitarians, Ethical Culturalists and Black Muslims to the hustling revivalism of Dwight L. Moody, Billy Sunday, Aimee McPherson and Oral Roberts. Even the triple melting pot thesis with its assertion of a process of acculturation occurring within rather than across the membership boundaries of Protestant-Catholic-Jew, advanced most forcefully by the late Will Herberg, receives scant support from these news stories and commentaries of *The New York Times*. The exclusively Christian cast of characters that had created the "Holy Commonwealths" of the early American Colonies has long since been joined both by

Jews and by followers of most of the other major world religions including those of Islam, Buddhism and Hinduism. Yet like their Christian counterparts, these faiths—once rooted in American soil—produced hybrid religions of a distinctively American character, asserting their fundamental identity with fellow believers in other parts of the world while simultaneously celebrating the distinctiveness and uniqueness of the American offshoot of that tradition.

The theme of a peculiarly American religion that "wears a garment of American weaving and American adornment", and thus differs from religions subsumed in other parts of the globe, is itself rooted in America's persistent search for national identity, and contributed in strategic ways to the shaping of that collective consciousness. Sidney Ahlstrom's eloquent *Religious History of the American People* documents how that "mythic theme of America as a beacon on a hill and exemplar for the world" became a constitutive element of most American religious traditions as well as of their historiography. The power and pervasiveness of this theme—mirrored in *The New York Times*—are attested to by the fact that it has survived to this day with only minor modifications and still fewer retractions.

To this beaconesque motif, with its manifest overtones of elitism, must be added another theme, that of individualism, which became another distinguishing mark of most American religions. Ideologies of individualism with their assertions of "certain inalienable rights" formed not only the cornerstone for constitutional guarantees of individual rights and freedoms, including the freedom of religion, but in the historical period covered in this volume, continued to provide an essential impetus for repeated challenges to the religious "establishment" of succeeding generations, culminating in numerous religious revivals, renewals and innovations. At times this theme of individualism became allied to highly utilitarian notions of self-help reflected, for example, in *The New York Times'* description of a religious guide to "Heaven, Where it is, Who is There and How to Get There."

While the eighteenth century's constitutional guarantees of religious freedom represented a necessary prerequisite for the subsequent flowering of religious pluralism in nineteenth and twentieth century America, freedom of religion—even in practice—in no way guaranteed the equality of those divergent religious groups. Some religions were in George Orwell's pithy aphorism clearly "more equal than others." Protestantism, and Puritan Protestantism in particular, played a dominant role in colonial America both with regard to the number of its adherents and in its influence in shaping the prevailing spirit of America as a newly emergent nation. Similarly, in the antebellum period it was Protestantism again, though of a more enthusiastically evangelical cast, which sought to transfrom America into the world's greatest republic—a showcase for a distinctively Protestant democracy. Adherents to non-Protestant faiths—Judaic, Mormon or Catholic—were viewed at best as being outside the pale of that elect company of 'true' Americans, at worst as Sabbath breakers, enemies in the service of 'foreign potentates', heretics and infidels. American Indians, similarly excluded, were generally regarded as foes to be driven from that promised land, destined to become outcasts from that showcase of God's kingdom on earth. Idealized by an intellectual minority as the cultural vestiges of a race of 'noble savages' doomed to extinction, American Indians, even in this more positive portrayal, were occasionally depicted as practitioners of magic or creators of myths but never of religion. Black Americans, having been for the most part condemned to the status of slave, were relegated to the category that by definition marked them as something less than fully human. Such a status precluded their playing a significant role in sharing, let alone shaping, the religious traditions of the country to whose shores they had been among the first to immigrate. *The New York Times'* coverage of the religious life of Black Americans is informed by many of these same prejudices. For the most part the religions of "Negroes" are dealt with, if at all, as reflecting the patterns and beliefs that prevailed among white Protestants and Catholics, notwithstanding the fact that the overwhelming proportion of them belonged to separate congregations. Only in the aftermath of World War II does one begin to get an inkling of the existence and development of Black religions—Christian and Islamic—as reflecting distinctive traditions and perspectives peculiar to the Black experience in America, and thus not automatically reducible to a presumed common identity with the religions of white Americans.

This collection of *The Times'* articles on religious events in America actually dates from 1870, at a time when the hegemony of mainstream Protestantism over American society was being challenged from without as well as within. From the outside, Roman Catholics and Jews, who had proven to be remarkably resistant to conversion or "religious assimilation," and whose ranks had been swollen by rapidly rising waves of immigration, were increasingly making their presence felt not as aliens but as citizens of the new nation. Internally, a new breed of Lutherans and Reformed, whose membership had been similarly enlarged by immigration, had become more and more outspoken in their criticism of the strands of revivalism, evangelicism and nativism that had for so long defined the essence of mainstream Protestantism in America. Protestant evangelicism in short had ceased to provide, or more accurately evoke, that overarching and definitive synthesis once regarded as quintessentially American. Yet Protestantism, as this volume documents, continued to play a vital role both in shaping the American religious experience and in influencing the important political and social issues of the day. In 1926 Al Smith—the first Roman Catholic to campaign for the Presidency as a major party's candidate—was widely attacked. The absence of religious toleration is clearly reflected in *The New York Times'* coverage of the Smith campaign, epitomized in Bishop Leonard's declaration that "The United States is a Christian and a Protestant nation, and as long as the English language is infused with the hand of God, America will remain Protestant." John F. Kennedy's successful bid for the Presidency in 1960 evoked similar fears. The events of his term of office demonstrated, however, that even a Catholic President in America can lead a predominantly Protestant nation.

The New York Times' chronicling of the religious life of the U.S. also reflects the diverse efforts of a people seeking to understand, accept and enjoy life in a rapidly changing and increasingly unpredictable world. It is in this broader humanistic context that *The New York Times'* articles on religion can be seen as neither exclusively nor even primarily a documentation of the rise and fall of religious ideologies or practices, patterns of institutional growth and decline, or statistical accounts of clergy and laiety, missions and money. The story that unfolds from these newspaper clippings centers rather on religion as a dependent phenomenon—and portrays a series of religious reactions by individuals and organizations to specific socio-economic crises. It is the issues of urbanization and industrialization, immigration and ethnic identity, science, technology and the changing bases of human knowledge, that largely shape and evoke the responses of diverse religious traditions.

By the last quarter of the nineteenth century, Jefferson's dream of American life as an agrarian idyll clearly could no longer be maintained in the face of the growth of cities and the proliferating concentrations of men and women employed in industries of increasing size and complexity. The castigations by the churches of the disorderliness, immorality, lasciviousness and drunkenness among the 'lower orders', so prevalent in the heyday of eighteenth century Puritan thought and frequently reiterated in subsequent religious revivals, came to make way for a serious, soul-searching examination of the role of religious organizations in an increasingly urbanizing and proletarian setting. A *New York Times'* article of 1881 on "Christianity in the Cities" raises a question that may still be found on the agenda of contemporary religious organizations, though the rhetoric and imagery have been altered: "How are the masses of people who own no homes, who move every month of year, whom nobody is interested in...to feel the sunshine which the Gospel of Christ and a professedly Christian civilization ought to bring?" Increasing numbers of this new urban proletariat remained outside the sphere of influence of organized religions; substantial numbers of nineteenth century immigrants even brought with them a vehement anti-clericalism. To their ranks must be added a new breed of migrants who came to the cities not from overseas but from the American countryside; men and women who spoke the English language but who had severed their earlier ties to rural Protestantism. Ironically, the very churches which had the economic resources to reach out to the unchurched were by virtue of their middle and upper class Protestant background least able to do so. The 'elective affinity' between religious ideology and class position noted by Max Weber in his American travels had been rigidified into a social barricade. Rooted in the intellectual, emotional and social life of more affluent congregations, this affinity was mirrored in their sermons, hymns and prayers, and the niceties of their sewing circle and men's club conversations. As urban growth spread, the churches also moved, following their upwardly mobile members to socially and economically more desirable suburban locations. While continuing to address problems of urban dislocation and inner city decline, these suburban congregations, by virtue of their geographical separation, perhaps inevitably came to see these problems in increasingly abstract and morally less compelling terms. The urban unchurched thus remained outside the sphere of influence of the establishment churches.

In seeking to adapt themselves to the changing needs of an urbanized society, however, the major religious traditions had to clarify their responsibilities to the working classes. Protestant and Catholic leaders, while ready to admit that the roots of labor unrest and strikes were moral rather than material, on the whole gave only tepid support to the rights of organized labor. They would condemn "the tyranny and turbulence of the labor union" while simultaneously upholding the legitimacy of the workingmen's grievances that had given rise to such protest. The Social Gospel Movement, led with such moral fervor by Walter Rauschenbusch, demanded that men must "snap the bonds of evil and turn the present unparalleled economic and intellectual resources of humanity to the harmonious development of a true social life."[1] Yet the moral thrust of the Social Gospel movement remained ameliorative, seeking to modify but never directly to challenge the doctrines of laissez-faire capitalism of the Gilded Age. Its tactics of moral persuasion were incapable of transforming the character of employer-employee relationships from conflict and brutality to compassion and mutual respect. The dominant religious institutions failed, in short, to follow through on the radical implications of their critique of the de-humanizing consequences of life in a capitalist industrial society. By contrast the churches of the downtrodden, the disinherited, the itinerant and the immigrant sought, often with considerable success, to alleviate the suffering of their members by providing them with richly embroidered and articulated visions of a future world in which injustice, suffering and evil "shall have no dominion," and with opportunities for kinship and community of interests within a shared religious tradition. It should be noted that the life histories of these "store-front" churches are largely absent from the pages of *The New York Times.*

These *Times'* articles do vividly document some of the major turning points in the complex relationships between religion and science. They provide a dramatic reminder of the embittered and divisive battles fought both within religious organizations—witness the furor of the heresy trials of prominent Protestant theologians in the eighteen-eighties—and between religious institutions and the State over their respective power and influence in shaping the character of American education. The issues, personalities and publicity surrounding those "American teachings of Darwinism...which make the Bible a scrap of paper" bear reexamination in the context of the events which culminated in the trial of John Scopes in Dayton, Tennessee, in 1925 for teaching evolution "contrary to the laws of the State." *The New York Times'* accounts of the verbal confrontations between William Jennings Bryan and Clarence Darrow are strangely reminiscent of Fundamentalist controversies currently dividing community opinion in some parts of this country.

A volume devoted to the subject of religion in America is unlikely to be informative on matters of irreligion or a-religiousness. The selections which follow do address some of the broader issues concerning the changing role of religion in the United States, and thus, indirectly at least, speak to the secularization of American thought and institutions. The influence of

[1]*Christianity and the Social Crisis* (New York: Macmillan, 1907) p. 422.

science on religious thinking, for example, is reflected in reports on the nature and consequences of the Higher Criticism and other methodological innovations in Biblical scholarship in the closing decades of the nineteenth century. Theological debates on the doctrine of the Virgin Birth or, more recently, lay and clerical reactions to the Papal position on birth control, suggest that many matters once accepted on the basis of faith were coming increasingly to be subjected to searching inquiry, rational debate, and dissent. More concrete, albeit crude indications of the secularization of religious behavior are to be found in *The New York Times'* reports on declines in gifts to Protestant churches in the twentieth century. Reports on membership losses and declining congregations, frequently coupled with discussions of the inability of churches and synagogues to attract and retain young people, similarly attest to some of the problems confronting established religious organizations competing for men's souls in the marketplace of an increasingly secularized society. These data need, however, to be evaluated alongside information (also to be found in *The New York Times*) on many young people's search for and creation of new religious traditions—including those of the Hare Krishna movement, the Jesus People, the followers of Meher Baba and the Reverend Sun Myung Moon's Unification Church.

Meanwhile, the established churches have continued to define themselves in relation to broader societal issues both new and old. One of the consequences of industrial technology—the rise and proliferation of the mass media, especially radio and television, evoked both fears of secularization and hopes that these new media would provide more effective means for religious leaders to reach out to the community of believers and would-be believers. In the nineteen-twenties *The New York Times* chronicled the fears voiced by many congregations that the spread of radio listening would lead to "rampant commercialization and paganization" of American homes and decrease church attendance—a concern reiterated two decades later in the face of the rise of television viewing. Religious optimists meanwhile extolled the benefits of these new technologies as a novel and promising means of extending religious worship into the privacy of the home. Techniques of modern advertising, far from threatening the religious life of the nation, were to be adopted in order to more effectively sell the story of Christ as the greatest "success story" the world has ever known! Similarly, while many fundamentalist religious groups were decrying the rise of the movies as further proof of the increasing Godlessness of America, others were determined to take advantage of this new technology. Methodists, for example, hired D.W. Griffith to advise them on the selection of films that could be used to fill their church pews.

The pages of *The New York Times* also document another problem impinging upon the religious life of twentieth century America, which, unlike that of the mass media, reaches back to man's earliest settlements—the problem of sexual identity and the proper role of men and women in the overlapping domains of the sacred and secular spheres of their day-to-day activities. Religious traditions have always played a critical role in defining and, more crucially, legitimating sex roles. Christianity and Judaism provided some of the most powerful and enduring sex role models and stereotypes of ideal male and female conduct which consistently extolled the virtues and benefits of a patriarchal society. The repercussions of these religiously-inspired role definitions for American men and women have not gone unremarked. Yet by the second half of the nineteenth century, the very point at which *The New York Times* began its chronicling of events, the traditional religious images of male and female behavior were being questioned by women who found themselves, in Herbert Spencer's words, "fitted in an unfit fitness," bound by models of sexual conduct and decorum increasingly at variance with the living conditions and opportunities open, at least in principle, to people living in this "new world." Elements of the ensuing struggle for sexual equality are captured in *The New York Times'* recounting of efforts by women to gain recognition and parity in the very religious denominations of which they had always formed a large but relatively powerless component. One learns of the Episcopal vestries giving the vote to women in 1915, but with the proviso that women could, of course, only vote for men! Methodists are reported to have accepted women as Preachers in 1925. When the Southern Baptists admitted women to their Executive Committees and Boards in 1927, the *Times* quotes one of their leaders, as remarking glumly, "We have started on the downgrade." The demand for a more active voice in the religious activities of their congregations is similarly echoed by women of the Jewish and (more recently) Roman Catholic faiths. These shifts in the *de jure* positions of women within their own religious organizations have undermined the influence of religious traditions in providing viable sex role models for the larger society. Yet, as *The New York Times'* coverage of the events of the nineteen-seventies indicates, the search for new and more appropriate sex role images continues to be pursued within the religious traditions as well as outside them. But the old sex stereotypes do not yield ground easily, attesting to the continued power and vitality of the religious legitimations that imbued them for centuries with attributes of the sacred.

These *Times'* articles on religion, precisely because they deal with religion not simply as theology or moral ideal, but as an integral element of human behavior, provide a valuable corrective to the stereotypical image of America as *the* land of religious freedom and liberty. The ensuing pages do indeed document some milestones in the transition from religious toleration to religious freedom. But they also etch clearly the dimensions of religious intolerance, prejudice and bigotry that survived and flourished intermittently in various parts of the country in the form of anti-Semitism, anti-Catholicism and anti-Protestantism. Members of religious congregations are often those least ready to grant to people of other religious persuasions the very freedom of belief and practice that they take for granted in their own. Religious intolerance, moreover, is frequently exacerbated by racial, ethnic and class prejudices that further restrict the sense of "moral community" that Emile Durkheim defined as peculiar to the sociological character of religion. America's civil religion, whether in the original Rousseauian vision or in Robert Bellah's more recent refinements,[2] remains a remarkably thin and transparent veneer, imposing a superficial gloss of unity on the underlying multifarious character of American religions often bitterly opposed to one another. Religion in this sense is, according to Marx, "no longer the essence of community but the essence of division."

Finally, a brief word of caution on the matter of omissions. *The New York Times'* coverage of historical events has inevitably to be selective; its commitment to publish "all the news that's fit to print" has led at times to curious sins of omission as well as commission. The present volume, as noted earlier, is inadequate in its coverage of the religious traditions of a number of important groups, notably Black Americans and American Indians. It should come as no surprise to readers of C. Wright Mills' *The Power Elite,* that *The Times* gives disproportionate coverage to the religious establishment, particularly the mainstream Protestant denomi-

nations. But the major Jewish and Catholic religious organizations still get far more attention than do churches of the poor, the storefront congregations of inner cities, the Pentecostals and Holy Rollers of rural religious revivals, and many other groups. To ignore the force of religion in the lives of the culturally and economically underprivileged not only neglects a critical illustration of Marx's thesis of the role of religion as an "opium of the people" but, more crucially, risks a failure to understand the signal importance of the religions of Richard Niebuhr's "disinherited" in sustaining the American dream.

On the matter of church-state relations, this book does not contain the kind of detailed reporting of Supreme Court decisions that might have been expected. Similarly, the positions of various religious groups on a number of other important political issues—Nazism and the Holocaust, Communism (especially in the McCarthy Era), race relations and civil rights, war (notably the Spanish Civil War and Vietnam)—are rarely addressed in depth in these selections from *The Times*.

As a selective portrait of the religious life of America from the aftermath of the Civil War to the end of the Vietnam War, these pages nevertheless serve to highlight some major turning points in the development of religion in an increasingly industrialized and urbanized society. They permit one to raise anew certain questions concerning the determinants of and influences on the definition of what constitutes "religious news." Their analysis of these questions, however, is beyond the scope of this Introduction. It is time to let the pages of *The New York Times* speak for themselves.

GILLIAN LINDT

[2] *The Broken Covenant* (New York: Seabury Press, 1975).

CHAPTER 1

The Major Faiths

The baptizing of a Jehovah's Witness at Orchard Beach
in the Bronx.

Hausner/NYT Pictures

The Duty of the Churches to the Indians.

The letter addressed by the Secretary of the Interior to the Indian Convention which recently adjourned in this City, contained some very frank statements which our religious bodies would do well to consider. Mr. COX urged very justly that President GRANT and the public expected, on the appointment of a commission of Friends and well-known philanthropic citizens upon Indian affairs, that the powerful religious bodies of the nation would co-operate with these Commissioners and the Government to educate and Christianize the Indians; but that thus far the churches had done almost nothing, being so much occupied with the foreign heathen that they have almost utterly neglected these wards of the nation. The Secretary and the President esteemed these private philanthropic and religious efforts so highly, that the former asserted the alternative before the public to be, a vigorous attempt by the Christianity of the country to educate the Indian, or to witness the consummation of extermination in a general plundering and massacre of the wild tribes. Those officials both attach the highest value to the combined efforts of the churches and humane bodies of the nation in rendering justice to our own barbarians.

We may have overlooked the report, but we cannot recall in any missionary convention or church synod for the year, any important action originating new missionary and Christianizing efforts in harmony with the new Commission for our heathen at home. Action enough there has been about the Zulus, the Sandwich Islanders, and the Hindoos: but the American Indians, for whose miseries and crimes we are so largely responsible, have been mainly forgotten.

And yet any ordinary mission operation, such as might be started in South Africa or India, is not what is wanted. A solitary missionary, with Bible and prayer-book, going among the Comanches or the Sioux, can accomplish little in solving this great problem. Sufficient means should be raised to enable a missionary or band of missionaries to purchase and convey to some reservation all the material necessary for simple agriculture. There the mission should commence —as the old Spanish Catholic missions did, which were so successful with the Indians of the Pacific Coast—with teaching the rudiments of civilization, without which even the truths of Christianity will be of little avail to save them in this world. Beginning thus with instructions in planting crops, using farming tools, and tilling the ground, accompanying those lessons with the teachings of morality and the Divine truths of the Christian faith, material advancement will go hand in hand with moral and spiritual conversion. The wild nomadic Indian will get the rudiments of the great lesson of civilization ; he will learn to labor for a result beyond the immediate moment ; he will acquire the art of providing for his wants when game has disappeared or is scarce ; he will possess a settled home and become accustomed to a steady occupation. This wise plan has already been tried with eminent success by an experienced Indian superintendent, Mr. DENT, Gen. GRANT'S brother-in-law, among the wild tribes near the Lower Colorado. He has proved what an advance in civilization can be made among the most nomadic tribes by a system of reservations, and the teaching of agriculture.

But the Church missionary would have an advantage in these labors possessed by no agent of the Government. The heart of every wild people is especially open to the sentiment of religion. A missionary comes as if from above. He has no selfish aims. He teaches the truth for all men and all times. No doubt agriculture will be easier learnt from a religious teacher, and religion from one who has the physical means to raise the neophyte above starvation and barbarism. No other system will at all succeed with aborigines, except this combination. And our Indian Commission, with its members, so influential among the churches, is especially the one to recommend and carry out such a suggestion. As fast as the wandering tribes are placed on reservations, the religious bodies should establish agricultural missions, with chapels, schools, plows and seed, with farmer missionaries, and teachers of the Bible who know how to plant corn. We fear, however, that the routine of the churches is too much fixed in the old method to allow of this innovation. And we dread that the fatal apathy of our religious bodies, wherever the heathen at home are concerned, may disappoint all hopes of any widespread missionary work for the Indians.

May 30, 1870

Missionary Work of the Protestant Episcopal Church among the Indians.

BOSTON, April 16.—It appears from the report of Rev. Dr. Thwing, Secretary and general agent to the Protestant Episcopal Delegate Convention, representing the Board of Missions, now in session in Boston, that the Domestic Board have six missionary Bishops and 210 missionaries laboring in the field, which needs 3,000 or 4,000 times as many workers. The sum of $120,000 was expended last year, and $200,000 will be required for next year. Col. Kemble, Secretary of the Indian Commission, traced the labors of the missionaries from those who went among the red men nearly 200 years ago down to the time of the present Commission, which has fifty clergymen and laymen now in this work. These missionaries have labored among the Indians with great success. Col. Kemble animadverted with considerable severity upon the policy of our Government toward the Indian tribes, and spoke warmly in praise of the peace policy suggested by Bishop Whipple.

April 17, 1872

AN ENTHUSIASTIC MISSIONARY.

HIS HOME AND HIS MODE OF LIFE AMONG THE INDIANS IN DAKOTA.

The Auburn *Advertiser* prints a private letter from Rev. Hackaliah Burt, of that city, who is now stationed by the Protestant Episcopal Church at White River, Dakota Territory. It is dated Jan. 5, 1876, and reads thus:

"I said I would write again soon, therefore I will keep my word, and try and give you an account of how I am situated this Winter, for my life is a peculiar one. I am taking a retreat, as it were, for a few months. I do not see any white people sometimes for weeks at a time. Occasionally one or more pass by on a hunting expedition or the like. My sole companions are the Indians. I have my log house, which is not very large, (twenty by fifteen feet,) very pleasantly arranged and ornamented with pictures, which together with my books make the room very pleasant. The floor is not very good. You can hardly imagine how my quarters look unless you think of a barn or shed very low, about seven feet on the inside, with rough boards for a floor, and very poor ones at that, with white cloths tacked up against the walls filled with pictures of all kinds, mostly colored, representing horses, cows, a man hauling logs, making hay, a barn-yard scene, and two pictures of Joseph Brans, the chief of the Six Nations, taken from those two books, his life, which no doubt you remember. There are also some colored pictures representing David killing the lion, Noah coming out of the ark, the shepherds at Bethlehem; and also a picture representing the Good Shepherd, numerous scriptural texts in the Dakota dialect. I have also a picture of St. Peter's Church of Auburn, as it was before the last repairing. These, with my A B C chart from which I teach, quite fill up the walls. On my table, which is home-made, is my lamp, the old student's lamp which I had at Middletown, picture books, a slate and a lot of stereoscopic views, with a glass, and my long Indian pipe with a box containing tobacco. I have a writing desk besides, which I keep locked, except, of course, when I am using it. My book-shelves are made out of the boxes in which I brought my books. I have three chairs, and when these are filled the people sit on boards extending from one box to another. These are my benches for the children at school and on Sundays. When these benches are filled the remainder sit on the floor, which seems very natural to them. They often prefer that to a chair. On Sundays I change my abode into a church by putting a blue spread on the table, which then serves as an altar or kneeling-desk, and place a small bit of carpet before, which sister Anna gave me to put before my bed. There is but one window, and this is a small one, a single sash containing six panes, 8x10. The roof is of hay and dirt, like the roofs of all log houses. The house is chinked (as they term it) with a yellow mud, so that at a distance it has the appearance of a painted house. It stands all alone in a large open space or bottom land as we call it. But in front at a distance of about twenty rods in the large field where the Indian plants beyond this, in the timber, are the Indian tupees, among which is Little Pheasants', where I board.

I must give you some idea of how I live, that is, eat. My bill of fare, as a rule, consists of coffee, no milk, bread, and boiled meat. These they receive from the agent. When these rations run low, which always occurs every two weeks, just before the time for issuing, we live on boiled corn. If the coffee is used up and plenty of sugar is had, we have wild cherry bark or rosebuds steeped for a drink. I like both of them very much. We have plenty of venison. I always keep some crackers, canned fruit or dried, and a few such things on hand as a resort in case the Indian fare runs very low. In fact I steep some dried fruit, such as cherries, currants, or apricots every day, from which I eat.

When I go to my meals I always find a blanket or pillow placed for me in the honorable position opposite the door of the tupee. On my right is Little Pheasant and wife, and on my left his little boy, who is lame, and his daughter, a young and quite pretty Indian maiden. I have a six-quart tin pan from which I eat my meat and bread, and two pint pans for the coffee or tea. These, with my butcher-knife and fork, constitute my dishes. I always enjoy my meals very much. They always wait for me and we all eat together, after which I smoke with Little Pheasant and talk, he telling of the old days when there were no white men, and I in turn telling the customs of our white people. He is a very pleasant and agreeable host.

This is my mode of living; although in many respects rather agreeable, it will probably continue only until Spring, at which time the agency will be moved at or very near this place. It was necessary to live in this way this Winter, if any work was to be done among these Indians, which was very desirable. I, too, was anxious to live for a time, at least, just like the Indians, for the sake of learning their language and their ways. Although I miss the society of white people, yet I am not sorry that I began this Winter's retreat. The Indian question is a great one, at least to the Indians and those whites living near them, and I am desirous of being well informed as to the real condition of affairs."

February 6, 1876

THE UNITARIAN CONFERENCE.

Opening Sermon by Rev. W. G. Elliot, D. D.—Loyalty to Christ Above Loyalty to Church.

The introductory sermon before the National Conference of the Unitarian Church was delivered last evening, at the Church of the Messiah, corner of Park-avenue and Thirty-fourth-street, by Rev. Dr W. G. ELLIOT, of St. Louis, Mo., before a large and appreciative congregation. The chief points of his address were as follows:

It is well that in the first formation of this conference of Unitarian Christian churches, notwithstanding the exaggerated fear of creeds, the clear confession of Christ as the Son of God and Savior of men was made in our preamble, and is thereby implied in all we do. If the force of that plain avowal has been impaired by subsequent action, I regret it, and certainly that was not the intention of the Conference in the changes made. The ninth article of the Constitution was, in my opinion, a mistake of liberality with good intention, but without the desired result. It was intended to express no more than is true in all associated religious bodies, even with those who sign the strictest creed, that differences of opinion may exist to whatever extent the honest interpretation of words may allow, and that the proceedings of the Conference, from time to time, are binding only upon the churches that voluntarily consent to them. This had already been expressed, to some extent, by a resolution adopted before the Conference was organized, and it was only desired by the majority of the Conference to emphasize the same principle of congregational independence by incorporating the substance of the resolution into the constitution itself. Unfortunately, in the last hurry of action, after a long and excited discussion, the article was adopted in a form which seems to do a great deal more, and almost to neutralize our platform, and to make this Conference of Christian churches as open to those who reject Christ as those who receive Him. If we could take out of the ninth article the words "including the preamble and constitution," it would certainly be improved. This would leave our congregational liberty, as members of the Conference, unimpaired, while the Conference itself would remain where it was first placed, upon a distinctive Christian basis—an organization into which none but Christian believers would desire to come. But if this method is impracticable or unwise, perhaps some equally efficacious way may be found of expressing our unshaken purpose to stand where we have always stood, as Unitarian Christian churches, as disciples of the Lord Jesus Christ, and "having done all, to stand;" for this, most certainly, at all times and in every place, it is our bounden duty to do. As a Conference of churches, and as members of it, the first and indispensable requisite to Christian success is to place ourselves openly, earnestly and unequivocally on Christian ground. Standing there, we may welcome those who believe more or who believe less, to work with us, but we cannot either remold our faith or bring contempt on our Christian allegiance for the sake of working with them. A firm and steady adherence to our proper place, in defense of Christ and liberty, without turning either to the right hand or left, going straight forward to do the work of evangelists, "in the cause of Christian faith and works," is the only rightful course for us to pursue. It would be a sad mistake to court the favor of those called orthodox by any language but that which most plainly conveys the faith we really hold. We desire their fellowship and affection, but only on equal terms. Still greater would be the mistake and the sin to lower the Christian standard for the sake of attracting those who cannot submit themselves to the Gospel claims of Jesus Christ. It is sometimes thought that the way to reach worldly men, and to commend our preaching, is to meet them half way; to preach doctrines that do not require too much faith, and are not strict enough to arouse their fears. No blunder could be greater than that. Faithfulness to Christ is the way to the sinner's heart. Irreligious men are not attracted by skepticisms and denials, but rather amused or disgusted. In the midst of their sins and neglect of God, they have sense enough to know that the fault is not in Christ's Gospel, but in their own waywardness and guilt. If they come to the religious life at all, they ask for a Savior in whom they can trust. In one of our Western cities the attempt was made to establish a religious society upon what was called the broadest possible foundation, and a convenant was prepared in which no allusion to God was made. The attention of the "clergyman" was called to the omission, and he explained it by saying that there were a great many infidels and atheists in the community whom he wished to reach! Instead of conciliating them, they laughed him to scorn. Among "philosophers, so-called," such refinements and evasions of truth, to use no stronger terms, may answer, and ministers in their studies, who know little of the world's throbbing, suffering heart, may imagine that the speculative difficulties which trouble them are the same which keep men from righteousness and truth. But when we come to the working-day world, neither a religion without God nor a Christianity without Christ will do. This is the final explanation of the discouraging reports from so many of our churches. All over the Western States, where the call for liberal Christianity has been so often heard, little bands of earnest men and women have gathered, with every hope of success, and for a time the cause of Christ and liberty has promised well, but too often it has ended in dulness and decay and death. I could name many instances of this, and more that will soon be added to the list. And why? Because neither Gospel preaching nor Christian institutions have been the agency employed. Dispensing with the Christian ordinances, with prayer-meetings and Bible instructions to the young, speaking of Jesus Christ as seldom as possible, and never, by any chance, calling him Lord or Master, the pulpit has sunk into insignificance and the pews into emptiness. Young men who had been educated for the Christian ministry, without ever having professed faith in Christ, and unable to profess it, with a fair amount of talent, with a general good purpose, and with a vague impression that the whole community would be anxiously waiting to hear their gospel of deliverance, have come to those Western outposts with great expectations to leave them with great chagrin. and why? Because they have had nothing to say of their own which was permanently worth hearing, and they could not say "Thus saith the Lord." They have worked bravely from their own brains to spin the spider web of ethical instruction and metaphysics, until it has proved too weak to hold the attention of their hearers, and then, having no deeper treasury to draw from, have given up in despair, leaving their fields of work not only unimproved, but unfit for subsequent culture, as if the life and heart had been taken from the soil. I have seen it so often that I am heart-sick at the sight. We have had enough of it. If we would gain Christian success we must send missionaries who believe in Christ. Send men who love Him and would die for Him, as their Savior and friend, and we shall soon see the difference of result. There is something in personal love and allegiance which overpowers all abstractions. When we impersonate religious zeal by "standing up for Jesus," we feel a fervor of self-sacrifice such as He himself manifested, and which no discouragement can repress. Without it, there is no missionary zeal, almost no missionary success. We have erred in this. We refuse the cross and yet expect the crown. Instead of bringing men up to the Gospel, we lower the Gospel to them, and so dilute its instructions with worldly morality and skeptical philosophy, that those whom we court complain of its weakness, and go elsewhere to hear the needed rebuke and receive the desired strength. We want John the Baptist to preach repentance and John the Apostle to preach self-consecration and love. Dear brethren, consider these things. I know nothing of "right wing and left wing," and have lived too far from the strife to feel their flapping, though I have heard the noise. Let my thirty-six years of hard experience entitle me to speak plainly, and my whole testimony will be given in one word, Be faithful to Jesus Christ. Hold fast to freedom, but equally, nay, more earnestly, to our allegiance. Without it we are nothing, and can do nothing, and all our fancied progress and success will prove to be a delusion and a snare. Stand up with Jesus Christ to do his work. Do not say that such words are a "slogan" of religious cant. They are the battle-cry against sin and wrong. They are the heart-felt expression of loyalty to our Leader and Prince. To our young men especially, whose love of freedom is impatient of authority, whether human or divine, I would earnestly appeal to reconsider their premises, that they may better understand their work and how to do it. Is your object practical usefulness? to redeem men from sin? to bring them to the knowledge and love of God? And can you hope to be sufficient to yourselves in such a work? Compare your actual success with that of men not half as strong in education and knowledge as yourselves. Why are they doing twice as much work? Because they work with stronger and more definite faith. They have an authority to lean upon to which you dare not appeal. There is no use in your going forth as missionaries unless you have a positive and clearly-defined religion to teach. Take your Bibles with you, and argue from them as the sufficient rule of faith and practice, if you would hope to make converts or to hold your own. To preach ourselves is the poorest of all preaching. Especially in the stirring and practical West, youthful lucubrations and Hegelian researches are not what men go to church to hear. They want plain preaching founded upon the word of God. In this respect our American Unitarian Association has been severely blamed, as lending aid and comfort to those who preach a gospel of their own, and thus as perverting the funds intrusted to its care. Whether or not its officers have laid themselves open to this censure, it is not for me to say. Probably, in the exercise of their discretion they have sometimes erred, as which of us has not. I am not here in their defense, but I am sure that many

things have been lately said on this subject which had better have been unsaid and unwritten. Unjust and ungenerous words recoil upon those who use them, and we can find

no excuse for some words that have been spoken. We can see no good to come from such severity, nor from the equally severe recrimination that has thus been provoked. "Let all bitterness and wrath, and anger and clamor, and evil speaking, be put away from you, with all malice; and be ye kind to one another, tender hearted, forgiving one another, even as God for Christ's sake hath forgiven you." The truth is that the faults found, so far as they exist, lie at the door of the denomination, rather than of the agents who have administered its affairs. Carelessness about Scriptural truth too much prevails, so that when men of positive beliefs are wanted they cannot always be found, and when found are not always wanted. We have been trying the experiment for thirty years past with how little belief Christian ministers, or ministers in Christian pulpits, can get along. Like the famous horse that was reduced to one straw a day, some have come down to very low diet, and the same result has in some cases, spiritually, been seen. Seriously and sadly, we

have been drifting away from Christ in many of our churches, and forgetting the old landmarks. Drifting, we say; not deliberately deserting or denying Him, though sometimes betrayed even into that extreme. "Who cares for what a man believes," is freely asked. "What kind of a man is he? That is what we want to know. We are satisfied with Christ's own test, 'by their fruits ye shall know them.'" But did Jesus choose men who rejected him to preach His Gospel? If Peter had continued to deny him, and Thomas had refused to believe, would they have been made his apostles? "Not every one who saith unto me, Lord, Lord, shall enter into the kingdom of heaven, but he that doeth the will of my Father who is in heaven." Yes; but Jesus was speaking only of the true and false professors of His name, and the test of truth was obedience. We may go yet further, and admit that the unbeliever in Christ who is a good man, is better than the believer who is a bad man; but we want neither one nor the other as Gospel ministers. Why can we not use a little logic and common sense in religious as well as secular affairs? For the want of it, and for want of closer study of the Bible, we have doubtless been drifting away from our proper moorings, and imagined it was progress when it has been the reverse. It is much easier to go away from the Christian religion than to improve upon it. I have sometimes thought, "so foolish was I and blind," that this is becoming the settled and determined tendency of our Unitarian body and of this Conference, that the banner upon which "Christ and Liberty" is inscribed is to be pulled down and another set up on which liberty alone is written. Such thought, whenever it has come, has filled me with grief, for I love the Unitarian Church as I love my own family and home. But loyalty to Christ comes first. Speaking for myself, and I can speak only for myself, however dear to me the associations of the present and past, I could never consent to remain in any Church or commission which is ashamed of Jesus Christ and his gospel. The act which strikes that name from the banner would strike my name from the roll. The christianity without Christ is no christianity for me. With my convictions of duty I should have no right, and should feel no wish to be the member of any Church, however refined and cultivated and liberal, where the name of Jesus Christ is held in doubtful honor, for I believe his words, "He that is ashamed of me, of him will I be ashamed." But, thank God, we have no abiding fear that the Unitarian body, or any part of it, will take such suicidal course. The love of peace and liberty, or tenderness for the feelings of hesitating and doubting brethren, may at times

betray us into weakness or inconsistency, but the heart of the denomination is and will remain true. Its allegiance to Christ has never for a moment been lost, and will be yet more fully indicated. Let us not be impatient with each other, or with ourselves. This love of liberty is a Christian impulse, and those who have escaped from the house of bondage may be pardoned for exaggerated fears. We must suffer long and be kind, forbearing one another, forgiving one another. Be not too great sticklers about words and phrases. The letter killeth, the spirit giveth life. Let us not be discouraged. We have our troubles and internal conflicts. No Church in Christendom is without its own. Look into them more closely, and we shall find that other denominations, even those that make the greatest boast of union, are torn with schisms and disputes. Our Church has its faults, and we speak freely of them without disguise; but, after all, it is a dear mother Church to us, in which we have found and kept Christian freedom and Christian faith. We sometimes hear it said that Unitarians can never become a strong organization. Rebuke every such word. Let us rather heartily unite upon our two acknowledged principles—Christ and liberty, the Gospel and the freedom of the Gospel, and thus place ourselves in the vanguard of human progress, devoting ourselves, as our Christian profession declares, "to the service of God and the building up the Kingdom of his Son." Finally, yet more than all, we have insisted upon allegiance to Jesus Christ, and upon its full and open avowal, not chiefly because it is the doctrinal truth and the only basis on which a Christian church can rightly be built, but because it is also the only standard under which we can successfully resist the encroachments of sin, and establish the principles of Christian civilization. For this reason, chiefly, we Unitarians have done so little in proportion to our means. "One thing thou lackest; come and follow me." Christian faith is the great effective force of Christian philanthropy, of Christian work. As in our struggle for national life and freedom, the flag of our country, which some called a painted rag, with its stars and stripes, was the rallying cry, and the sight of it made our hearts beat quick, and filled our eyes with tears, and inspired our souls with heroic courage; so, in the harder struggle against the enemies of God, and in defense of His truth and righteousness, and for the rescue of the downtrodden and oppressed, the cross of Jesus Christ, which is to some no more than a piece of dead wood, is the standard under which alone we conquer. Let us never desert it! "Be faithful unto death, and thou shalt obtain the crown of everlasting life." Amen.

October 19, 1870

THE AMERICAN UNITARIAN ASSOCIATION.

BOSTON, May 26.—At the meeting of the American Unitarian Association to-day there was a long debate on the status of Rev. W. J. Potter, of New-Bedford, whose name had been dropped from the rolls on account of his assertion that, though a Unitarian so far as his relations to trinitarianism were concerned, he no longer considered himself a Christian. The controversy was carried on in a pleasant way, and many resolutions were presented. The following, offered by Rev. Dr. Cordner, of Montreal, was finally adopted:

Inasmuch as the term Unitarian, as used in the title of this association and in its publications, has always been held to carry a distinctively Christian meaning, our Unitarian ministers being held and regarded by us as public teachers of the Christian religion, and as the action of the Assistant Secretary, sustained by the Executive Committee, in omitting from the catalogue the name of a minister who says he is no longer a Christian has been in harmony with the common usage of the term among us,

Resolved, That the said action be now and hereby is approved and ratified.

May 27, 1874

'Repent and Believe'

Dwight Moody began, 100 years ago, to 'reduce the population of hell by a million souls.'

By PIERCE G. FREDERICKS

JUST one hundred years ago the members of Chicago's Plymouth Congregational Church gaped as young Dwight Moody led a motley crew of men and boys down the aisle. A new member, Moody might have been expected to rent one pew as a contribution to the church. Instead, he had rented four and was now filling them, not with family, but with riffraff from Chicago's street corners. To any who questioned him, Moody explained that he had purposely gathered those in greatest need of the gospel.

Plymouth Congregational marveled and could not know that they were seeing the first converts of the man who was

Evangelist Dwight L. Moody.

to become the greatest evangelist of the nineteenth century, a man later to address some 2,300,000 persons at a series of London meetings, "six acres of Irishmen" in Belfast and 1,500,000 in New York. During one of the latter meetings, a St. Patrick's Day Parade marched with bands silent from Thirty-fourth to Twenty-third Street rather than disturb Moody's sermon in the old Hippodrome.

HE was born into a poor family of Northfield, Mass. If his education was scanty and his interest in it scantier, a biographer could rejoice that "many an educated man is timid by reason of his knowledge, while ignorance is bold. To Mr. Moody blunders are nothing * * * efficiency is the only thing he cares about." Sent to Boston to learn the shoe business, he attended church because his employer demanded it. A more fervent goer, Edward Kimball, later "the champion church debt raiser of the U. S.," determined

to make him a genuine convert. Sensing a propitious moment one spring afternoon, Kimball "made a dash for it to have it over at once," found Moody sorting stock in the back of the shoe store and converted him on the spot.

Moving to Chicago as a shoe salesman, Moody devoted increasing time to "the greater firm of Christ and Church." He was "Crazy Moody" who proselytized among "the poor and vicious" and offered to read Tom Paine if some infidel saloonkeeper would read the Bible. Encountering a non-believer on a street car, he said, "I am to get off at the next station, but if you will kneel down right here I will pray the Lord to make you a Christian." The man knelt.

UNABLE to find a Sunday school class to teach, he formed his own of street urchins. By 1859 he had North Market Hall used on Saturday nights for the Devil's Revival, dancing converted to a Sunday school with 600 students receiving instruction, charity and recreational programs. Suddenly, he was "the Lightning Christian of the Lightning City," and a visitor from Peoria observed, "If Pandemonium were accessible, Mr. Moody would have a mission started there within a week." The Civil War found him preaching to the troops.

His voice was shrill, but in an age rich with intricate theologians he preached "the old fashion gospel, square, without rounding the corners." A man converted by Moody reported that as he walked away "one foot cried 'Glory' and the other responded 'Hallelujah.'" A reporter felt he called "a spade a spade. You are going to hell, but Jesus Christ can save you right now. What though Mr. Moody sometimes mispronounces a word or gets a singular verb with a plural nominative if he makes men feel that *religion is business*."

To this talent was added, at a Y. M. C. A. convention in 1870, that of the "sweet singer," Ira Sankey. "The harp of David was the prototype of the harmonium of Sankey," said one admirer; "a red-hot singer," declared a New York reporter. His voice was so fine that he is reputed to have converted an entire family of atheists a mile off when a favoring wind carried his rendi-

tion of "Shall We Gather by the River" their way. With Moody, he would lead choirs of 500, insisting on both "Christian deportment" and "clear enunciation of the words sung."

THEIR reputation was confined to Chicago when, in 1873, they determined to advance upon (revivalist language was much flavored by military terms from the Civil War) England. They opened before 3,000 at York, then advanced upon Glasgow to appear before 15,000 a night for a week. Soon they were careening through Scotland and Ireland, holding as many as five meetings a day. When they returned to Liverpool at the end of a two-year tour of the Isles, a $20,000 hall seating 8,000 was raised to receive them, and "Mighty London" waited.

THE traditional prayer meeting of the age featured "a long, slow hymn * * *," then the two elders with two long prayers in which they go from Jerusalem and round to Illyricum and a good deal farther * * *." The new team commenced instead with Sankey delivering a "sure-fire" — a hymn like "Pull for the Shore," "Dare to Be a Daniel," or "Hallelujah, He Is Risen."

Moody's sermons wasted no time on ecclesiastical hairsplitting — the direct self-help of a talk like "Heaven, Where Is It, Who Is There, How to Get There" was his specialty. He gave it a cozy sound: "I like to locate heaven and find out all about it I can. I expect to live there through eternity. If I was going to dwell in any place in this country, if I were going to make it my home, I would want to inquire all about the place, about its climate, about what kind of neighbors I was going to have, about the schools for my children."

An observant critic noted that "he has not one word of solace or light for the honest cultured doubter * * * but the masses of men are not philosophic disputants * * *. These masses Mr. Moody reaches because he is one of them. He is driving a bargain with them and he 'talks sense.' There they sit and listen — life becomes pleasanter for them. The future assumes a more hopeful aspect."

In London, where $150,000 had been raised for the meetings, Moody preached before the Princess of Wales, spent a week-end with the Duke of Sutherland and was dined (but not wined—he was an abstainer) by the Lord Chancellor. America clamored for him.

The return to America was adroitly plotted as a series of meetings to reach a climax in

New York. He went first to Brooklyn, then connected to Manhattan only by ferry. The building was the Rink; additional car tracks were laid to its door by the trolley company, and, as the hour of the meeting approached, cars were run at intervals of only a minute. Moody began "as though his audience were stockholders of a bank to whom he was about to make a report." Later he worked up to 220 words a minute, exhausted the stenographers and "raised religious fervor to its highest pitch."

He appeared in Brooklyn for a month, then, letting the excitement mount, advanced upon Philadelphia, where the freight depot had been fitted out to seat 12,000. The meetings were such a success that a deputation from Washington, including President Grant, Cabinet members, Supreme Court justices, Senators and Congressmen came to listen. Moody stuck to his usual combination of the dramatic and the colloquial. He was capable of melodrama. On drunkenness he would trumpet, "Go, go to some hovel where a drunkard reels every day. See the children run away and hide in terror when the besotted father staggers up the hill; the haggard-faced wife tremble."

HIS forte, however, was a more conversational tone: "Egypt was so troubled with frogs that the king couldn't stand it any longer — it was frogs, frogs, nothing but frogs everywhere, he couldn't move his foot without treading on a frog. He called Moses and says he, 'Moses, I want you to get rid of those frogs for me.' Moses says, 'When?' 'Why-a-a—tomorrow,' says the king." He often opened meetings with, "The sight of you is enough to make a dumb dog bark."

Most popular of all were the anecdotes which filled his sermons and were collected into books. Starting with a fireman ascending a ladder to rescue a child from a burning building, he went on: "The brave man faltered and a comrade at the bottom cried out, 'Cheer!,' and cheer upon cheer rose from the crowd. Up the ladder he went and saved the child because they cheered him. If you cannot go into the heat of the battle yourself, if you cannot go into the harvest field and work day after day, you can cheer those that are working for the Master."

After Philadelphia, he paused briefly at Princeton to convert 100 of that school's 500 students, then went at last to Manhattan to be received by 15,000 at the Harlem railroad depot on a howling winter night. The depot had been divided into two halls, local clergymen beguiling one side, while Moody and Sankey labored on the other.

THE New York revival lasted three months as Moody "kept firing heavy guns into the immense masses gathered to be saved." Moved from the depot to the Hippodrome, his sermons seldom failed "to move a large part of his audience to tears." Some 5,000 were converted—a figure considered good, since a large part of the audience was bound to be previously converted believers in spite of Moody's preference for infidels.

He was now a national figure, his sermons translated even into Cree Indian, and when he concluded intensive campaigning in 1879, ending six years which revivalists call "The Mighty Six," admirers estimated that he had "reduced the population of hell by a million souls."

Until his death in 1899, Moody concerned himself more and more with training suc-

AT THE HIPPODROME—Eleven thousand crowded in to hear Moody while thousands more stood outside.

cessors. First, he founded Northfield Seminary for young women, then Mount Hermon School for boys, then the Bible Institute at Chicago, which is today the Moody Bible Institute with nineteen buildings and radio station WMBI. He still preached extensively, but

the last return to anything like "The Mighty Six" came during the Chicago World's Fair of 1893.

There, under Moody's direction for six months, eighty meeting places — tents, theatres, churches—were kept operating, as many as seventy

being used in a single day. Doubters were astonished when the revival outdrew Forepaugh's Circus. "Why," cried Moody with all his old fervor, "we've got something better than Buffalo Bill!"

December 2, 1956

REVIVALISTS.

The work of Messrs. MOODY and SANKEY in producing a religious excitement in London and other English cities is daily reported to us by ocean telegraph. A somewhat similar, though more quiet, effort is going on here, under Mr. VARLEY. The close of Winter and beginning of Spring is the ordinary season for these religious excitements, and a year of depression in business, or of public calamity, is the one in which they are most likely to thrive. There is much that is absurd and extravagant about these outbreaks of popular sympathy in regard to religion. They seem to belong to another world from the ordinary world of business around us, or from the thought which moves the scientific part of the community. The speakers and movers in them have conceptions of religion or philosophy which have long ceased with thinking persons. They resort to means of popular excitement, which reason condemns. The persons who are affected by the epidemic of sympathy often die or profess what afterward disgusts them in cold sobriety. Sometimes they react from religious fervor into skepticism and immorality. The soul of man seems sometimes after these "revivals," as they are called, to have been surfeited and overladen with unnatural stimulants, and finally to reject even healthy truth in its morbid condition.

Yet, with all these defects, we are inclined to believe that "revivals" have their uses. It cannot be said of this age that it has too much religious belief. On the contrary, it is an age of skepticism and indifference. The trouble with the majority of

people is that they care nothing about the unseen realities. Science is gradually sapping faith, especially among the "professors" on one hand, and the thoughtless and uneducated on the other. Materialism is eating away earnestness. The interests of the day are so absorbing that most persons do not trouble themselves with what is intangible and invisible. They may even go through with religious forms and ceremonies, but it is with scarcely more sense of their real meaning than had CICERO's augurs of the rites of Roman worship. It is not so much unbelief—with the masses—as indifference, which kills religion. Now, the veriest skeptic who still believes in the eternal principles of morality, must rejoice at anything which can arouse the cold and dull sense of this age to "things not seen and eternal." Whatever touches the religious sentiment and conscience touches the whole moral nature of the man. Religion, if it have the faintest semblance of its appropriate and natural power, must make men better parents and more faithful children, truer in all relations of the family, more honest as business men and public spirited as citizens. Men are moved to realize all other grand sentiments and principles by great waves of sympathy. Our public meetings and orations and addresses at the beginning of the war were efforts at a "revival" of patriotism. Temperance has at times been equally impressed on a whole community by such excited efforts. Many men are exceedingly torpid and almost dead to truths which do not affect their everyday interests. Even the extravagances of a revivalist may be useful in arousing them.

Moreover, the refined and fastidious classes are too apt to judge of the masses of men by their own feelings. The truth is, the great majority of mankind are neither refined nor fastidious. But they have a dumb sense of their great wants, and they hear gladly anything which will arouse them from torpor and indifference. Mr. MOODY's theological extravagances, Mr. VARLEY's sentimental appeals, or Mr. BEECHER's epigrams do not offend them. They care little about manner, if the truth reaches them. The reformers of the world have never been nice and fastidious scholars and elegant orators. They have been rough men often, using plain words and making extravagant statements. The cultured Roman scholars of the time of NERO must have regarded the diction and manners of PETER and PAUL much as many of us regard MOODY, VARLEY, or BEECHER. History holds manners as of small account. The only thing which will be hereafter considered will be: How much truth did these men inculcate, and what moral effects did they leave behind? For a permanent influence, the action of these revivalists would be very much to be deprecated. It is too sensational, garish, and stimulating. It appeals too little to reason. But as a temporary tonic to a public mind made torpid and inactive through long devotion to material interests, it may be useful. Anything is likely to be useful which summons man from the worship of dollars and cents to the consideration of the vast questions which affect his future state.

March 29, 1875

RELIGIOUS WORK.

WHAT THE CHRISTIAN ASSOCIATIONS ARE DOING IN AMERICA.

At the World's Conference of Young Men's Christian Associations held in Geneva, Switzerland, Aug. 30, 1878, the second Sunday in November, 1879, and the week following were set apart as a season of special prayer for young men and Young Men's Christian Associations. The International Convention held in Baltimore, Md., in May last, confirmed the action of the Conference, and last evening special services were held in several of the churches in this City, in accordance with the arrangements. In the Fifth-Avenue Baptist Church, in Forty-sixth-street, near Fifth-avenue, the Pastor, the Rev. Dr. Armitage, conducted the proceedings, and brief addresses were made by Mr. William E. Dodge, Jr., Dr. Nathan Bishop, Mr. Boomer, a student in Yale College, and Mr. Richard C. Morse, the General Secretary of the National Young Men's Christian Association. Mr. Dodge briefly showed the necessity of the work, and its growth and progress within the past few years in the West and South, in the colleges, and among the Germans and the railroad men. Mr. Boomer gave an account of the progress of the work in the colleges. Of the 60,000 students in these institutions, divided among 400 colleges in the United States and Canada, not more than one-half were members of churches, and many of these were not consistent members. The college branch of the work was started in 1876, by a few young men in Princeton College. Now there were 60 associations, and the result of their labors had been the conversion of 500 students, and a great improvement in the lives of a great many more. Mr. Morse gave a history of the work accomplished since 1868, when the Western work was organized. The German branch was established in 1872, and the Southern branch in 1874. Last year the association had nine workers in the field who traveled over 30,000 miles, and visited 500 different places, from Nova Scotia to Texas. That portion of the work cost $17,000. When the Western work was organized, there were but 27 associations there, and the people of the section contributed only from $25,000 to $30,000 annually. Now there are 250 associations in the West, and the contributions amount to $175,000 annually. When the work among railroad men was organized there were but 14 associations, now there are 116. The Southern work was organized with only three societies in the section from Virginia to Texas. Now there are 155. Six years ago the International Association had local Secretaries in only 11 city centres. Now it has 17, and 12 railroad Secretaries.

Similar meetings were held in the Central Methodist Episcopal Church, Seventh-avenue, near Fourteenth-street; the Rutgers Presbyterian Church, Madison-avenue, corner of Twenty-ninth-street, and the North Presbyterian Church, Ninth-avenue, corner of West Thirty-first-street.

PETERSBURG, Va., Nov. 9.—In accordance with the recommendation of the International Convention of the Young Men's Christian Association held at Baltimore last May, and the World's Convention, at Geneva, Switzerland, the present week is to be observed here as a season of thanksgiving and special prayer for God's blessing upon young men, and upon the work in their behalf. Sermons addressed especially to young men were preached at the different churches here to-night.

November 10, 1879

AMERICAN SUNDAY-SCHOOL UNION.
From the St. Paul (Minn.) Pioneer-Press.

The American Bible Society, Tract Society, Sunday-School Union, and Young Men's Christian Association are the great union religious organizations of this country. To none of them is Minnesota more indebted than to the Sunday-School Union. Thousands of dollars have been expended, thousands of schools established, many thousands of children protected from ignorance and saved from vice by this grand old society, whose missionaries in Minnesota have from the first been men of noble character and great devotion to the work. Two of them, at least, deserve pensions from the State. They have no need of any monuments at death other than the schools they have founded and the churches that have grown from them in so many instances. The work of the union is entirely undenominational, and is broad, charitable, and Christian in all respects. There is no denomination in the State which has not received benefits from its work, and none which ought not to indorse and aid the union. In its North-western departments alone, the American Sunday-School Union has established 408 new Sunday-schools during the last year, with 1,559 teachers and 12,610 scholars. Other Sunday-schools in the same department have in 1,566 cases been aided, in which 5,756 teachers were giving instruction to 52,045 scholars. Three thousand and forty-seven destitute persons have been supplied with Bibles or Testaments; 6,145 families visited, over 2,000 addresses and sermons delivered, and 116,125 miles journeyed over by their missionaries during the year. Surely a noble record, and one of which even the old union may be proud. Thus far, Minnesota has received $10 from the Sunday-School Union where she has given one. Is it not about time to reverse this order, and ourselves aid in giving to more remote and newer settlements the blessings of schools and churches, once brought thus to us through this same agency?

February 6, 1880

THE SALVATION ARMY.

ARRIVAL OF THE PIONEER BAND IN THIS COUNTRY—THEIR PECULIARITIES.

The Australia, which arrived from London yesterday, landed 27 steerage passengers at Castle Garden, among them seven women and one man, constituting the advance guard of "The Salvation Army," an organization of lay exhorters founded in England fourteen years ago by William Booth, a Dissenting clergyman, and now numbering over 100,000 persons. They created quite a sensation in the Garden and subsequently in the streets as they proceeded to the lodging-house that had been provided for them. They were all attired in a uniform of dark blue cloth, with bright yellow binding, and around their hats were broad bands of scarlet ribbon, inscribed with the words, "The Salvation Army," in large gilt letters. One of the women, who holds the rank of Captain, the other six being Lieutenants, carried a flag of blue and red, staff, with a large yellow sun in the centre and bearing the title of the association. The male member of the band, whose name is George Railton, is known as a Commissioner, and will have charge of the future organization in the United States. He said that the "army" owed its foundation to a visit made by Mr. Booth to London in 1865. He was struck with the vast number of persons there who never attend divine service and resolved to devote himself to remedying the evil. Gathering around him a band of earnest Christians, he commenced a series of open-air meetings, and thus formed the nucleus of what was at first known as the Christian Mission. In 1878 the title of "The Salvation Army" was adopted as being less calculated to repel the persons whom it was designed to gather, and who do not like to be spoken of as needing mission effort. In September last, according to a circular furnished by Mr. Railton, there were in England 122 corps, under the command of 195 officers, using for services weekly 148 theatres, music halls, warehouses, and other buildings, holding at the annual rate of 45,000 open-air services and 60,000 in-door services and preaching to 74,000 persons in-door every Sunday evening and to 2,000,000 in the streets every week. Through its instrumentality 257 persons have become wholly employed in religious work, and 3,256 others stand ready to speak or labor in the cause whenever called upon. The "army" is said to be approved by 23 Mayors and magistrates, 17 Superintendents of Police, and 129 clergymen. Its funds are raised mainly by collections taken at the services. Last year there was raised in this way £12,000, while the general fund only amounted to £4,540. Mr. Railton says that he and his colleagues will depend on what they can collect. Their passage was paid to this country by the home association, and this they are expected to refund. They will endeavor to secure a hall, so as to begin indoor services on Sunday. Mr. Railton said that he had written ahead to Mr. James Gordon Bennett to get out some posters for him, and he was then about to call upon that gentleman in regard to them. He was much put out when informed that Mr. Bennett is in India. They will also preach in the streets to whoever will listen to them. The band gave a service of song in the Garden yesterday. It was noticeable that some of their hymns were set to American tunes, such as "Way down on the Suwanee River" and "Old Kentucky Home." They are all fresh, strong-looking young persons of about 30 years of age. A gentleman who was formerly a member of the army in England, and who emigrated to Philadelphia, started an organization on a similar principle in that city some time ago, but this is the first genuine delegation that has ever come to this country. They intend to spread themselves throughout the principal cities of the Union. Mr. Railton explained that the colors of the flag—red and blue—signify the blood and purity of Christ, and he was extremely anxious to have the fact published that the yellow had nothing to do with Orangeism.

March 11, 1880

PRESENT THOUGHT IN RELIGION.

Before a thunder-storm on a Summer's day, while the clouds are still gathering, the air is often oppressively calm, as if one were in the realms of death. Such is the religious atmosphere at this moment in the American churches. They have not yet, to any visible extent, broken with their theological past, and there is an ominous silence in the air as if religion were dead or had disappeared from the face of society, and at the same time it is known to any observant person that perhaps at no period since the Reformation have the theological positions established by LUTHER and CALVIN been so thoroughly discredited by thoughtful religious people as at the present moment. There is a wide-spread antagonism to the old theology in all the Protestant churches. The younger men in the Christian ministry everywhere are enlisted in the new thought, and vital changes of opinion are being wrought out silently in many a parsonage and rectory all over the land.

These changes are chiefly in two directions. They involve the giving up of some beliefs about the supernatural part of Christianity which have never commended themselves to the reason of men, and have been maintained for the most part through the tyranny of religious opinion in ecclesiastical organizations. They are also concerned with the attempt to broaden out Christian beliefs so that they shall be coextensive with all the interests of life. Literature to-day points out the pathway for religious development. It is comprehensive of all that concerns human life, and has largely turned upon the elevation of conduct to a higher place in the social economy. Religion cannot do less than it is doing, and ought to do vastly more. It is precisely here that the Christianity of the day is parting company with much in its theological past, and is entering, under the guidance of the broadening instincts of men, into a closer alliance with what is best in present life. This does not mean that it is to be confined to this world, though there is unquestionably a yielding in some degree to the demand of the agnostic that men's faith shall be better established upon the basis of actual knowledge, and that they shall do less skylarking, in the name of religion, than they have formerly done. This is due in part to a reaction from a too celestial kind of religion in which a larger knowledge of GOD was claimed than could be vouched for, but it is also due to the fact that men demand to-day that religion shall deal with the homely and plain things of their lives, and that it shall recognize their secular necessities as truly as their religious aspirations. Such are the thoughts which hold the minds of those who think in the channels of ordinary experience, and the working of clerical thought is not much different, though it may express itself in more logical propositions. The feeling of the multitude, not less than the conviction of the thoughtful, is that religion of men must help them to live better, to work better, to think better, to serve GOD better in their daily experience. It is to this end that the present activity of religious thought in this country is chiefly directed.

There is needed not so much the casting of a new creed as the looking at each man's life in its integrity as a concrete personality and the doing of what is best for its growth. This is the thought that is changing the atmosphere at the present time. Men begin to feel refreshed. Certain universal convictions that had been practically denied in the attempt to express the whole of the supernatural side of religion have risen to men's consciousness and found expression. Day by day they are finding larger expression. This is the process now going on without a formal and outward change of religious creed or organization. And the wonderful thing to be noted is that the movement widens in the way of affirmations. The new theology, as it is called, is not negative, neither is it afflicted with the narrowness of breadth. It is more and more positive as it advances in its sweep and comprehensiveness to a conception of the possibilities of life. It lays hold of all the forces existing in the world by which the new life may be developed. There is not a religious body in the land that is not undergoing the change of its religious beliefs. The entire religious life of the Nation is in a process of change from the beliefs of the fathers to the beliefs of a larger civilization and development. Not a man now stands still; not a doctrine now goes unchallenged; there is a universal effort to incorporate the best of life into practical religion and to give it adequate expression.

April 29, 1883

THE SECOND ADVENTISTS.

THEIR BELIEF AND HOW THEIR CHURCHES ARE ORGANIZED.

From the Springfield (Mass.) Republican.

This is the last day of the Adventist campmeeting of 1885. For eight days the woods round about the camp have re-echoed the hymns of praise. In the seclusion of the growing forest, with the leaf-checked blue in lieu of a church dome and a tent for a shrine, these plain seekers after the truth have prayed and led others to the service of God. Adventism is advancing. The former prejudice against the mere idea of a second personal coming of Christ is fast giving way, and many a minister and fairminded man of other denominations is investigating the claim that these men are daily expounding. It became a theme of discussion last week at Northfield in the Moody convention. Briefly summed up, the belief of the modern Adventist is in a personal second advent of Christ; his reign in a literal new earth, and the resurrection of the dead bodies of the saints. Man's death on this earth is not the only death he will meet; his life is but a probation, a preparation, as it were, to determine the worthiness of his entrance into the next world, which God will give et nally to the faithful alone. Therefore, it is absolutely necessary to accept the Lord in this world; it is the only hope to enter the next. As to resurrection and immortality, the views of the Adventist are different from the popular understanding. Men die, and from that time till the judgment day they are in a sleep, unconscious of all things. At the judgment they are waked up, and before the bar of divine justice are dealt with according to their actions during earthly life. Those who have accepted Christ will then receive eternal life and live with him on the new earth; the unbelievers die a second and eternal death. There is no such thing as eternal torment or eternal misery; but there is external punishment, that punishment being the second and eternal death. Strictly speaking, the popular religious feeling toward Adventism to-day is the same as it was in 1844 or 1854. The doctrinal chasm between them and popular theology is as broad and deep as between Protestantism and Catholicism. There can be no agreement between a spiritual and personal second coming of Christ. One must be wholly Adventist or not at all. A mediate line is impossible. Yet this doctrine of a personal, real, and visible Christ, set against a spiritual, ethereal, and impersonal one, far from being distasteful to the mass of the people, is eagerly received.

The American Advent Missionary Society was organized in 1866. To-day Adventism in the United States alone reckons 200,000 among its converts. They are organized into churches, Sunday schools, conferences, and associations. The churches are self-regulated, self-governed bodies who elect of their own free will their Pastor and whatever officers they desire. A general association meets yearly, formed of the representatives of the several churches in the different states. There is no Bishop, and the church is responsible to itself for everything. Yearly there is a conference in each State of all the churches in that State made up of its own church delegates. From these State conferences representatives are chosen, the number varying according to the churches in the State, to attend the advent association. Besides these State conferences are the State camp meetings. The general convention one year is held in the West, the next in the East. It takes place this year at Chelsea. The society has publishing houses, weekly papers, Sunday school papers and quarterlies. During the past year 5,873 volumes have been published and tracts to the amount of 1,844,000 pages. Besides the books and tracts, 500,000 copies of the *World's Crisis*, a weekly, have been issued. The circulation of the *Blessed Hope*, quarterly, has been 7,000, and the quarterly *Journal of Prophecy* 7,000. The work of evangelizing has been especially pushed among sailors. A missionary in Boston has visited 2,000 families and 1,400 vessels, distributing tracts and copies of the society's publications.

Two and one-half years ago the foreign movement was started. The method of reaching the people is very much the same as that of the Salvation Army. The Adventists in England are working in co-operation with the Blue Ribbon Gospel Society, the Salvation Cavalry, and a half dozen other similar organizations. Those especially sought are the poor and destitute, those whom wealthy English society scorns to notice. Elder Miles Grant, who has been working there the past year, tells pitiful stories of the utter hopelessness and helplessness of miserable wretches yearning for the truth of the Gospel.

The work accomplished on the camp grounds this year has far surpassed the hopes entertained. Three hundred families have camped there—100 more than came in former years- and in harmony and unison have carried on their work daily. The early dawn holiness meetings, under the charge of Elder Miles Grant, have proved a source of great encouragement. At the ministers' meetings general subjects pertaining especially to the way in which the mission work should be carried on, both abroad and at home, have been discussed. This meeting is a new thing and has become a fixture. The children, as usual, have been under the direction of Mrs. Abbie Wood, the Portsmouth Sunday school teacher, who for years has been actively engaged in the training of young minds. Every one on the tented ground, in fact, is imbued with the true spirit of holiness and is fully convinced of the doctrine he believes. Consequently each is doing his best to sound the warning of the near approach of Christ. "We do not care to make many converts to our faith," said one of the preachers yesterday; "all we desire is to turn the people to accept their Saviour." In Bristol, Conn., the Rev. J. C. St. John has been accomplishing great things in a blacksmith shop. A number of men gathered who had never thought of entering a church, much less of listening to sermons. In England, likewise, the masses are reached by striving first to interest them by preaching the Gospel right in their midst, sometimes with the most repulsive and filthy surroundings. Once touched, time and patience will accomplish the rest.

The ways of life of the Adventist are plain and unpretentious. They hold in the strictest veneration any place once consecrated to the service of God. No fair, festival, or oyster supper is tolerated in their churches. They believe in the primitive simplicity and sacredness of Divine worship. Hence their camp meetings and outdoor conferences.

August 25, 1885

MODERN CHURCH BUILDING

AN AMERICAN IDEA IN TO-DAY'S ARCHITECTURE.

THE EVOLUTION BROUGHT ABOUT BY CHANGES IN CEREMONIAL, BY NEW USES, AND BY SOCIAL CUSTOMS.

In the evolution of American architecture no class of buildings more impressively emphasizes the native style than the later church edifices. There has come to be recognized a distinctively American style in the architectural treatment of non-Episcopal churches more pronounced even than that of the American dwelling house. This style has come through the natural channels of evolution, required and compelled by the changes that the systems of worship in the various denominations have undergone.

Under the old dispensation, when the mother church was the supreme and undisputed authority in all ecclesiastical matters, the laity had little or nothing to say or do about the construction of churches. Then the ceremonial idea in public worship was paramount and the church architecture was made to conform to it. When, however, man began to assert his proclivities as a social and freedom-loving animal the ecclesiastics were among the first to suffer from his new ideas. The early Pilgrims scouted the suggestion of sacredness in wood and stone, and their first "meeting houses" were not confined to religious ceremonial and public worship, but were also frequently used for secular assemblies and for magistral courts. Later, under the influence and leadership of the Presbyterian Church, the ancient reverence for the edifice was for a time restored.

In the Presbyterian Church the struggle of the factions over the introduction of instrumental music into their services is still fresh in the memory of the people. The organ came, and to provide for this change the interior arrangements of the churches had to be changed. Room for the pipe organ had to be found, and a choir gallery had to be constructed. Until the decision of the question which made these changes necessary the Presbyterian Church had been about as severe in its style of architecture as well could be. Where the Scotch influence predominated the English cathedral type was held in disdain, as something too palpably ritualistic in spirit, if not in design, and the square brick church, with a single low spire, characterized the Presbyterian church in this country. The interior arrangement was severely plain and uninviting. Of course there were exceptions to this rule, at least in the matter of the external appearance of the edifice, and there exists in this city to-day, at Fifth-avenue and Eleventh-street, in the First Presbyterian Church, a brownstone structure that is a small reproduction of Westminster Abbey, built over 30 years ago.

But the spirit of transcendentalism has been at work in the pews, and both clergy and laity have learned that even bricks and stone, woodwork and stained glass and tapestry can be so molded and arranged as to express something of the divine, and to exert an uplifting influence upon the people.

The church has furthermore taken on pronounced social features, and to provide accommodations for social gatherings and entertainments still other changes in the architecture of the church have become necessary. No church edifice with pretensions to completeness is now built without its kitchen and china closet, reception room and dining hall. The social requirements have been more effective in drawing the money to provide them from the pockets of the congregation than have the religious requirements.

Baptism by immersion has also produced requirements of interior construction and has given opportunity for artistic and ornamental arrangement of the pulpit platform presented by no other ritualistic adjunct. This is not now confined altogether to the Baptist denomination, as it used to be, but is provided for those who desire it by many of the Methodist and Congregational churches as well. Humane sentiments and more luxurious tastes have almost abolished the old custom, and in its stead the churches have been provided with baptismal tanks or pools. At first of crude construction, hid away under the pulpit platform and reached by a short flight of steps through folding trap doors like the descent from a house kitchen into the cellar, their value as architectural ornaments has come to be recognized, and principles of art have come to be employed in their construction and arrangement. The ceremony of baptism by immersion has now become as impressive and dramatic as any ceremony of the church.

A church library and Pastor's study have become marked features of the church's later construction. In some of the churches in this city and Brooklyn these rooms or offices are as elaborately constructed and fitted as artistic taste and plenty of money could make them. Sometimes they form a sort of vestibule or connection between the adjoining pastoral residence and the church building, but for the most part, as in the Calvary Baptist Church, in Fifty-seventh-street, and the Emmanuel Baptist Church in Brooklyn, they are altogether within the church building and separate entirely from the Pastor's residence. In the Roman Catholic and Episcopal churches and here and there in some of the non-Episcopal churches all these extra-religious rooms are provided for in a clergy house or Episcopal residence, as is now the case with St. George's Protestant Episcopal Church, in East Sixteenth-street, and as will be with the Roman Catholic Cathedral, in Fifth-avenue at Fiftieth-street. Plans are now in course of preparation for a clergy house, to adjoin the cathedral at the rear, in which provision will be made for all the requirements of attendant and visiting clergymen and such social and literary entertainments as may from time to time require appropriate accommodation.

All these several changes in and departures from the strict ceremonial of the ancient church have brought with them requirements for room, which have been availed of to extend and broaden the precincts of the church edifice and to completely change the style, if not the order, of architecture of places of public worship in this country. They have made light and ventilation matters of necessity, and these, in turn, have provided the architects with opportunity for artistic combinations and ornamentation. In many of the new churches clear stories or domes of stained glass rise over the main auditorium, and furnish at the same time pure air and more than "dim" religious light. Stained glass has also been employed with striking effect in the reconstruction of some old interiors where there has not been room or opportunity for exterior improvement without tearing down the entire edifice, as in the Universalist Church of the Divine Paternity, at Fifth-avenue and Forty-fifth-street.

In these churches therefore there has come to be recognized a style of architecture that has grown out of the requirements of modern systems of worship and religious and social observance that is found nowhere else in the world, and that is called American. Throughout all this, however, the Gothic order of architecture has been pretty generally adhered to. A few years ago there was a Queen Anne departure from the prevailing style, but that soon ran its day, and is now employed only where the means are limited and the structure is small and of wood. Paint and pigment will make even a Queen Anne church look pretty—in the country.

Nothing has yet been decided about the Cathedral of St. John the Divine, except that it must not be over 400 feet long. Some time ago the committee on plans for the new Episcopal edifice invited plans from 14 American architects, with a view to obtaining an expression of the ideas of these artists regarding the projected work. For these plans they offered $500 each, regardless of value, but without obligation to accept any of them. Besides these, however, some 60 or 70 other architects of less renown than those invited have undertaken to express their ideas upon the great architectural subject, for there is a chance that is open to all volunteers that any one may become the designer and first of the line of supervising architects of the great edifice. It will take more than one generation to complete the building, if the intentions of its projectors are even approximately carried out.

One of the most noted of New-York architects, who has designed many of the churches of this and other American cities and who is one of the invited competitors for the new cathedral, said to a TIMES reporter:

"There will no doubt be a large number of novel designs submitted for the new cathedral, and some of them are extremely likely to be fantastic to the verge of ridiculousness. Some of the volunteer competitors are actuated by a positive contempt for the old orders and an actual craze for novelty of design, and will try to formulate their ideas, which are still very vague, in some composition that shall have the merit of novelty at least, and will therefore be American. But the idea is impracticable. The cathedral is not designed for a church, in the ordinary acceptation of that term, and is not amenable to any such freedom of treatment as may with propriety and true artistic effect be given to an edifice calculated for a greater variety of uses and more limited expression. A cathedral differs from a church in that it is required more for high ceremonies and exclusively religious expression. In this respect its external effect must be singular, and that religious, and its internal arrangement must suggest as far as possible the grand and majestic attributes of Infinity. You will find, therefore, a general conformity among the preferred plans to the Gothic order of architecture, with perhaps considerable variety in the elaboration and a greater freedom of treatment than is apparent in any existing edifice; but every plan will be suggestive of features already employed in the cathedrals of the Old World.

"There may be some new features—indeed, there is no doubt that every leading set of plans will contain some new ideas, made necessary by the demand for better light and ventilation than are provided in the older structures and by our more rigorous climate. The cathedral, I am inclined to believe, will be, when completed, as perfect an exemplification of the Gothic order as the world has ever seen. If it should prove to be so, that will be glory enough for America, for there is no nobler architectural pile possible than the perfected Gothic cathedral."

The reporter was shown the plans of a new Methodist church, for the foundations of which ground has recently been broken in Brooklyn. It is of the Gothic order, treated in the Roman-esque style. Over the main auditorium rises a dome, with a clear story all of stained glass in iron frames. The floor arrangement is amphitheatrical. A baptismal pool of rough hewn stone occupies a place in front of the pulpit when in use, but is covered by the pulpit platform on ordinary occasions. The choir gallery is arranged behind the pulpit, and the organ occupies both corners of the room back of the pulpit. Plate-glass and stained-glass partitions back of the choir gallery separate this auditorium from the Sunday school room, which is built in semi-circular form, with a gallery around the half circle. The space below and above this gallery is divided into Bible class rooms by large paneled and ornamented doors, that, for the lower tier, drop into the basement when it is desired to throw all the rooms into one, as for the opening exercises or an exhibition, and, for the upper tier, rise into the attic.

In the basement are the reception and class rooms and in the sub-basement the kitchen, china closet, heating apparatus, hot-air engine for supplying the organ with air, and storerooms. The Pastor's study adjoins the Sunday school and social department of the building, and opens upon the opposite side into the Pastor's residence, which is externally finished in harmony with the architectural style of the church. This is probably the most complete exponent thus far erected of the new American style of church building, and indicates an undoubted intention to employ social and intellectual and artistic means, as well as the distinctively religious, to keep its members while in the world free from worldliness.

December 23, 1888

DR. BRIGGS'S SCRIPTURAL VIEWS.

HIS CHAIR IN THE UNION THEOLOGICAL SEMINARY IN DANGER.

CINCINNATI, Feb. 18.—"One of the most interesting matters that will come up before the General Assembly of the Church at Detroit will be the approval or disapproval of Dr. Charles A. Briggs's appointment to the Chair of Biblical Theology by the Board of Directors of the Union Theological Seminary of New-York," said Dr. T. R. Monfort of the *Herald and Presbyter* to-day. "Dr. Briggs has been attracting the attention of the Church for some ten years by his peculiar rejection of the supreme authority of the Holy Scriptures, but it was his inaugural address in his new position that brought down upon him the adverse criticism of the Church press. In his address Dr. Briggs questioned the inspiration of the Scriptures and uttered many thoughts which the great body of the Church does not believe respectful, to say the least.

"The General Assembly has the veto power over the election of professors, and unless Dr. Briggs modifies the stand he has taken it is not likely that the Assembly will approve the action of the Board of Directors of the Union Theological Seminary. It would have been better for Dr. Briggs, perhaps, had he remained Professor of Hebrew and Cognate Languages in that institution. He is, I think, about forty-five years old—old enough, in fact, to know better than to put himself so far out of the line of the Church as to excite grave fears of his usefulness in it, and especially in the position where he will have such a marked influence upon the great body of the theological students and coming ministers of the Church. The delegates to the General Assembly will not be elected until Spring, and so it is too early to state their attitude in the matter; but there is no question that Dr. Briggs will get a shaking up in an assembly of 700 delegates representing 213 Presbyteries."

February 19, 1891

A TALK BY DOCTOR BRIGGS

SECOND DAY OF THE CONVENTION AT PLYMOUTH CHURCH.

THE PROFESSOR MAKES A PLEA FOR HIGHER CRITICISM—HE SAYS THAT THERE IS A BLESSING IN SCIENTIFIC STUDY OF THE BIBLE.

The fact that Prof. Charles A. Briggs was to speak at yesterday's session of the General Congregational Association of New-York State, now in convention at Plymouth Church, Brooklyn, attracted very many people to that familiar old edifice. Every pew was filled.

The routine business was transacted and Gen. C. T. Christensen conducted a devotional service. Then the Rev. Dr. William A. Robinson read an appeal from the Central Association urging that some concerted action should be taken looking toward the repeal of certain obnoxious laws of this State, special mention making of that section which provides that no person having a wife, husband, child, or parent, shall bequeath more than half of his or her estate to charity. A committee was appointed to consider the matter.

Several reports from Sunday schools were presented, and then the way was clear for Prof. Briggs. He was introduced by the Moderator, and was received with enthusiastic applause. After remarking that ten years ago an address on "Bible Study" would have emptied a house, Dr. Briggs talked in a colloquial way for nearly an hour. He was frequently interrupted by applause.

"Perhaps it is hardly becoming in me," he said, "to be here to-day under the circumstances in which I am placed, and I should not have come were it not for my promise to Dr. Abbott not to fail if I could possibly avoid it, and were it not for the fact that I am to stand in the pulpit that has been consecrated by that great man, Henry Ward Beecher, [applause,] whose broad-mindedness, whose nobleness of character have here disclosed that calm, clear vision of truth that some men call heresy. [Applause.] I believe, in the first place, that the Holy Scriptures of the Old and the New Testament are the word of God. That is the Puritan doctrine. That is the doctrine I hold to-day, which I always have held, and which I always expect to hold. There are many different interpretations of the phrase, the word of God. The interpretation of the Westminster Confession of Faith varies greatly from that of the shibboleths of the eighteenth century. And yet all this variance hinges on the question as to whether the Bible is entirely inspired or inspired only in parts. One says the Bible contains the word of God, the other that the Bible is the word of God. There cannot be perfect harmony of belief while one interpretation says it is and another says it contains the word of God. We cannot contain a broad term in a narrow one. The narrow term must accord with the broader one."

After comparing the Bible at some length to a lantern containing a light that shone forth for the help and guidance of man and pointing out that as lanterns were of various kinds, so the Word of God came to man in many languages and many inscrutable forms, he added: "I think I have said enough now to enable you to see that, no matter what the interpretation or what the form, the Scriptures contain the Word of God. I do not mean to say that a part of the Bible is inspired and another part is not, but I do mean to distinguish between the lantern, which is form, and the substance, which is light. The study of the Bible in modern times has assumed vast dimensions. It is one thing to study it for practical purposes, that is, for the Church and the Sunday school, and another to study it with a view to getting at the proof texts, to study it as a Christian scholar, to examine it in all its varieties of meanings, and to get at the exact truth of the Scriptures. In the olden times it was common to study it for practical purposes only. It is true that if the Bible is put in the hands of the most humble and ignorant man, he will be enlightened by it and will be enabled to see the light of God shining from it, for that light shines into the hearts of the most ignorant and the most degraded men. But in order to meet the questions which are thrust upon scholars and Christians of these modern days, we must study the Bible as a science. In the first place, we want to know what is the Bible? What parts shall we believe and what shall we not believe? For instance, why was the book of Maccabees excluded, and why do we not still offer up sacrifices for the dead? Of course, for all practical purposes, the word of your pastor may be taken in explanation of these questions and he may answer them in a way that quells all doubt and that may be perfectly satisfactory, but that is not science.

"Science alone can show and prove the reasons and interpret the various settings of the light which we have called the Word of God. Unless science can answer these questioners and fortifies your faith, your foundations are knocked from under your feet by the questions themselves. The next question to consider is a most difficult one—the question of text. It is a question that can only be determined by specialists in the study of the Bible. By specialists I mean men who study every word, every accent, and every letter of certain text, in order that they may get at their original meaning. Investigation discloses errors, and the result of investigation may tend to undermine some of the traditional opinions regarding the inspirations of the Bible. As I have said, I believe it does. The oldest texts are the ones which contain the most errors and are the most inconsistent.

"Of course, many hold that the Bible, being inspired, is inerrant, but in the face of the inconsistencies which science discloses, how are you going to prove it? We cannot see the original manuscripts, and there can be no doubt that textoral criticisms and investigations and study may enable us to find errors in the Bible. What good does it do anybody to hold that such cannot be found and that the Bible is inerrant? And what harm does it do if errors are found? Here is a text which we know contains errors. But they are trivial errors—verbal errors, chronological errors, scientific errors, and so on, and they do not affect the doctrine of Christianity nor any principle of its practice. So, even though science discloses errors in the text, we may still hold that the Word of God is the word of faith and practice. [Applause.] It is not the infallible rule of science or of chronology, or even of literary style that we search for and we discover in the Bible, but for the faith and practice, and no error has ever been discovered that at all disturbs the faith and practice which constitutes the Word of God. [Applause.]

"The next department is the department of higher criticism. Why higher? Because it is a study pursued by men who devote the most of their lives to the study of the Bible. The study of the text comes first and the study of the literature, perhaps, next. And then the higher criticism. It is higher simply because it is a high branch of biblical study. There is the question of authorship and the question of when the Bible was written, and there are many other questions to be examined and studied and answered, and it is the branch of high criticism that tries to solve them. We must delve into and behind these questions with strictly impartial feeling—irrespective of sanctity and all religious beliefs. The most touching question that I can take for example is: Did Moses write the Pentateuch? Some people say if he didn't it wasn't inspired. Now, if I know anything about Moses he didn't write the Pentateuch. [Laughter.] And if I know anything at all about inspiration it was inspired. [Applause.] The only place where we get evidence that Moses did not write the Pentateuch is in the Bible itself. Outside of that we do not go.

"What matters it whether Moses wrote the Pentateuch? How does it affect our faith and morals? Not in the slightest degree. Do you not see that there are four parallel accounts of the history and legislation of Israel, and that by having them the Divine authority is increased fourfold? It gives us four Bibles instead of one. Four parallel narratives are there, not one. This scientific investigation, or higher criticism, strengthens the Divine authority instead of diminishing it." [Applause.]

In closing his argument, Dr. Briggs said: "Men pry into everything, and we cannot leave the Bible where it has been left—where dogmatic theology reigned supreme. There was a time when an audience could not be secured to listen to a discussion of the Bible. Now no question excites more interest. The result will be that the lantern will be raised and that the light of the Scriptures will be shed over sea and land. All men will see it; all men will know it. Another point is biblical theology. It puts aside creed and all minor principles, and deals with the whole system of Christianity. We take the Old Testament and we take the New. There are points at variance in both. When we study separately the various parts and bring them all together, we have the whole truth. That is Biblical theology. Without regard to minor principles, we endeavor to find out the truth contained in the Bible. Through biblical theology everything is shown to us, not in the abstract, but in the concrete word. The Bible is the rule of faith. What does that mean? Not dogmatic faith, surely. There is, underlying it all, a rule which shows that the interpretation of the Bible is to be found in the Bible itself.

"Let me illustrate. You go up into the Adirondacks and climb a lofty peak, and stretched out below is a great variety of woodland and lakeland. How are we to reduce it to system? How are we to find out the principle that is there? We study the minor parts separately, and when we combine them we discover the one great principle which underlies it all, the unity in nature. The same thing is true of the Scriptures. There is every form and color, but beneath it all there is the essential principle of harmony and unity. It underlies the whole of the Scriptures. Biblical theology will show to us in time what is faith and what is truth, what is right and what is not right. Do not fear that scientific study of the Scriptures will do any harm to the Church or to the Bible. There is a blessing in it. It will result in ultimate harmony. It will prove God as the Divine author, and his Divine light will shine brightly in the end as the result of all this biblical study."

The Rev. Dr. William R. Harper of Yale was to have followed Dr. Briggs, but he was ill, and the Rev. Dr. A. J. F. Behrends took his place.

His argument was an indorsement of Dr. Briggs's.

At the afternoon session the Rev. Dr. E. P. Ingersoll read an essay on "The Federation of Churches: Its Nature, Possibility, and Advantages." Dr. Ingersoll believed that there should be a union of all churches. Ex-President McCosh of Princeton said that a union of churches was practicable at this time. He thought cooperation in work was possible, however, and expressed a belief that in time it would lead to a union.

The Rev. A. E. Dunning of Boston and the Rev. Dr. R. R. Meredith occupied the rest of the afternoon in discussing "Church Extension in Country and City."

The evening session was given up to the nineteenth anniversary of the New-York State Home Missionary Society. There was an address by President William A. Robinson, a report from the Treasurer, and a sermon by the Rev. Dr. R. R. Meredith. Then these officers were elected: President—The Rev. Dr. W. A. Robinson; Vice President—The Rev. Dr. S. H. Virgin; Secretary—The Rev. Ethan Curtis; Trustees—The Rev. Dr. W. E. Park; Prof. E. Y. Hamilton, the Rev. E. N. Packard, the Rev. A. F. Pierce, the Rev. Frank A. Fitch, David Thompson, and Herbert M. Dixon.

The Treasurer's report showed receipts for the year of $73,191.03. Of this sum $39,201.80 was derived from legacies, and $33.983.33 from contributions. The expenses during the same time were only $30,223.45, leaving the comfortable balance of $42,967.58.

To-day's sessions will be devoted almost entirely to reports and other routine work, and in the afternoon addresses will be made by the Rev. Dr. Rainsford and the Rev. Thomas K. Beecher.

May 21, 1891

Briggs and Anti-Briggs

As oft of yore, old Tweedledum
Falls out with Tweedledee
Concerning how to "split a hair"—
Agrees to disagree.

Plain people shake their puzzled heads—
It seems in vain to try
To settle "which is which," or what,
The "wherefore" or the "why."

'Tis Briggs or anti-Briggs, and *that*
Is all there is about it;
Some *think* that what Briggs *thinks* is right,
And some *think* that they doubt it.

But what Briggs *thinks*, or says he *thinks*,
Some *think* he doesn't *think*;
But *think* he *thinks* a lot of things
From which the godly shrink.

And so the matter standeth thus:
With all that Briggs may say
The anti-Briggsites all agree
To think the other way.

Now, what *will* happen unto Briggs?
What unto him befall?
That question puzzles us plain folks—
The laymen—most of all.

PEWHOLDER.

June 3, 1893

PROF. BRIGGS NOT MOURNING

HE WILL NOT LEAVE THE PRES-BYTERIAN CHURCH.

The Deposed Minister Declines to Discuss the Action of the General Assembly—An Officer of the Union Theological Seminary Says He Will Not Lead a Split in the Church—The Seminary Not Harmed by the Verdict—Dr. Parkhurst Says the Majority Acted in a Highhanded and Vindictive Way.

Prof. Charles A. Briggs, whom the Presbyterian General Assembly has pronounced a heretic, has returned to his home in this city. A reporter of THE NEW-YORK TIMES who called at his house yesterday failed to find any signs of mourning about the premises. There was no crape on the door and the window shades were up. Even Dr. Briggs seemed cheerful.

"But," said he, "you must excuse me from speaking about the case. I have heretofore maintained strict silence upon the subject and shall continue to do so. I have nothing to say of the past, the present, or the future."

"Dr. Briggs will not leave the Church," said a prominent officer of the Union Theological Seminary to a reporter for THE NEW-YORK TIMES last night. "He has no intention of heading a split. He will stay where he is, and will remain the leader of the liberal party within the Church, fighting for liberty of thought until the Church acknowledges the truth of his views. The next three years will witness a wonderful revolution in the religious world. The liberals are gaining strength every day, and

this heresy trial has knitted them together more firmly than they were before.

"This is the policy adopted by the liberals in Washington immediately after the verdict was announced. They are determined now to fight to the bitter end. It would be impossible to split the Church because of one man, even though that man be Dr. Briggs. Prof. Smith may also be convicted next year, but that will not result in a split. In order to create a split it would be necessary for the General Assembly to convict and suspend an entire synod. Then a large body would be cut off, and naturally they would band together and form a new Church. But no such condition exists now. Our battle will be fought inside the lines.

"The Synod meets next October in Rochester, and Dr. Briggs's case will be brought before it. It has never been brought before the Synod, though it should have been heard by that body before it went to the General Assembly. The General Assembly ignored this, and thus the trial and the conviction were both irregular, and, as I believe, of no legal force. If the Synod does not act the civil courts may be appealed to.

"As a matter of fact, Dr. Briggs is not affected by the verdict of suspension, because he is pastor of no church, and a layman may preach.

"The General Assembly has no right in a heresy trial to fix the faith of the Church. Conservatives never leave a Church, but they try to force the liberals out. But they can only accomplish this by heresy trials, one at a time, which are always long and expensive. The Briggs trial has cost the General Assembly $50,000, and the Presbytery here was bankrupted by it.

"The seminary will be in nowise affected by the boycott declared against it. The General Assembly students will not receive aid from the Presbyterian Board of Education; but, on the other hand, those churches which sympathize with us will not turn any money over to the Board of Education, but will send it to the seminary, so that the seminary will really benefit by the boycott. A number of wealthy churches have already promised this."

Mr. Ezra M. Kingsley, the Secretary and Treasurer of the Union Theological Seminary, was also inclined to be non-communicative when the reporter asked him what would be the future policy of the seminary Directors.

"The Directors do not meet till November," he said, "and until then nothing definite can be known. Of course I have my own opinions, but I do not care to express them publicly.

"I will say this, though," he added. "The action of the General Assembly in withdrawing the support of its Board of Education from our students places us exactly where we want to be—in an independent position. The seminary has always wished to be independent, but the General Assembly insisted upon a right to dictate our appointments to professorships and the transfers. We resisted that pretension and paid no heed to the General Assembly's complaints. Now we shall be under no actual or moral obligation to the General Assembly.

"The withdrawal of the support of the Board of Education will not hurt us in the slightest. I do not think any students will leave the institution in consequence of the General Assembly's action."

"The suspension of Dr. Briggs was to be expected," said the Rev. Dr. Parkhurst. "The proceedings of the majority of the General Assembly were high-handed and lacked the slightest trace of brotherly love, which is to be considered paramount to any mere dogma. They showed no disposition to be conciliatory, but were determined to push matters to the furthest extreme against the enlightened men whom they dread, but whom they dominated by numbers.

"The vindictive boycott against Union Seminary particularly pains me. The teachers of that seminary in the past have stood for all that is best and enlightened, and among them were some of the most loving, the most Christian men and teachers whom the Church has had the privilege of calling her own. It is nothing but a blind act of spite, for a boycott is ineffectual. More students and a better class of scholars will flock to the seminary now. I believe the liberal party in the Church will grow in numbers and strength."

June 3, 1893

FOREIGN MISSIONS.

The columns of THE TIMES yesterday gave some of the results, in sermons from Presbyterian pulpits, of the concerted revival in the Presbyterian Church of an interest in foreign missions. There can be no doubt that the interest in foreign missions is languid among the laity not only of the Presbyterian Church, but of all Protestant churches. It does not seem that the results in the way of conversions compensate for the cost and the trouble. Of course, in one sense, the conversion of a single soul is worth not only all the money that has been spent upon foreign missions, but all the money in the world. Humanly speaking, however, the object of ecclesiastical expenditures ought to be to get the most for the money, and in this respect investment upon the heathen abroad is less productive than investment upon the heathen at home.

In truth, the consequences of the literal following of the injunction to go into all the world and preach the Gospel to every creature have not been encouraging. Many devoted men and devoted women, of whom it would be an outrage to speak otherwise than with the utmost respect, have given up their lives to the conversion of the heathen, and the heathen have not been converted. Not a nation or a tribe of men, not even upon an island in the sea, can be said to have been Christianized by missionary efforts; and the reports of lay travelers, of whom it is quite absurd to say that all are disposed to make a mock of religion, are pretty uniformly unfavorable to the missions. Where, as in the Sandwich Islands, the tractableness of the people makes a promising field for mission work, it is inevitable that self-seeking men should enter the ranks of missionaries and should give more attention to their own physical welfare than to the spiritual welfare of the natives.

In all mission fields where more than one sect has operated the effort is not of co-operation, but of competition. The natives must find themselves grievously puzzled to choose among the missionaries who call themselves Christians, and also profess to love all men, but who evidently do not love each other. This jealously sometimes goes not only to un-Christian, but to inhuman lengths. Nobody who has read ROBERT LOUIS STEVENSON'S letter to the Protestant missionary in Honolulu who undertook to defame the memory of a Christian hero and martyr because he was also a Catholic missionary, will believe that missionary enterprises carried on in the spirit of the defamer can conduce to the real Christianization of any country.

But there is another reason why missions in some countries are foredoomed to failure, and that is the necessary ignorance of the missionaries of what they are undertaking. In India, for example, in China, and in Japan there are ancient and settled civilizations of which the religious opinions of the people are a necessary part and outcome. For a European or an American to understand one of these civilizations is the study of a lifetime. Yet a young man or a young woman from Vermont, let us say, or from Indiana, will go out, fearing nothing and knowing nothing, to convert to the Vermont or Indiana view people whose traditions are rooted in an immemorial past. To the people concerned is it wonderful that these attempts should be regarded as illustrations of a stupefying impudence. To an entirely disinterested observer, say from Mars, it is questionable whether the civilization of Vermont and Indiana would approve itself as clearly and at every point superior to the civilization of China, or of India, or of Japan. To the Hindoo, the Chinaman, or the Japanese there is no question at all. The missionary is unable to manage his susceptibilities, because in the first place he does not know what they are, and in the second he may feel it his duty to outrage them. The Congregational Board has lately held that any unsoundness on the point of the damnation of heathen or any reticence upon that comfortable doctrine is a disqualification for missionary labor. The young missionary who would be faithful must begin by explaining to the worshipper of ancestors that it has been decided in Boston that his ancestors are undoubtedly damned. Is it any wonder that the untutored ancestor-worshipper should resent what seems to him a combination of impudence and sacrilege, and should resent it even to the shedding of blood?

A main objection to foreign missions, in the present state of the world, is the enormous wastefulness of the method. There are in this country a great many thousands of Chinese and of Japanese, upon whom a great deal of the preliminary missionary work has already been done. They have been actually brought into contact with Christian civilization. They at least know more about it than their countrymen at home can know, and they know more about their countrymen at home than a foreigner can ever learn. If they can be converted to Christianity they will make the most effective missionaries. If they cannot be converted it seems quite hopeless to try converting those they have left behind. The true sphere of Chinese missions, for example, is Mott Street in New-York and Chinatown in San Francisco, rather than the rural parts of China.

November 12, 1895

THE CHRISTIAN SCIENTISTS

ADDRESS OF MRS. EDDY READ

BOSTON, June 4.—The annual communion service of the mother church of Christian Science here, the First Church of Christ, Scientist, was held to-day. The service was on the subject of the sacrament, and in accordance with the usual method prevailing in the Christian Science churches the sermon consisted of alternate references from the Bible and the Christian Science textbook, "Science and Health, with Key to the Scriptures," by Mary Baker G. Eddy, these selections bearing upon the subject of spiritual communion, which is the communion believed in by Christian Scientists.

There were four services, in order to accommodate the great number of Christian Scientists present, amounting to upward of 6,000, who came from all parts of this country, and a number from England, Australia, and Canada. At each service the auditorium was filled to overflowing, and many hundreds were unable to obtain entrance. Thousands flocked into the edifice merely to kneel in silent communion for a few moments. As fast as each service was concluded and the congregation had departed another great concourse streamed into the church, and the simple service was repeated.

The communion was devoid of symbols. At each of the services the worshippers knelt for a few moments, after which the first reader, Septimus J. Hanna, invited those present to join in the communion. His words of invitation were: "I now invite all present, whether members of this Church or not, and communicants of other churches, if there be any present, to enter with us into the inner sanctuary of Saul for a brief moment, into the holy of holies, into the secret places of the most high, for there is nothing as near as infinite love."

In addition to the communion service the fact that the annual church meeting of the mother church is to be held on Tuesday also attracted many who might not otherwise have been in attendance. This annual church meeting is held for the purpose of electing the various officers of the mother church, readers, and some auxiliary officers, such as members of the Board of Lectureship and the Board of Education. The present membership of the mother church is about 13,000, and judging from present indications fully 50 per cent of the membership will be present. About 2,500 new members were admitted to membership in the mother church at this communion.

MRS. EDDY'S ADDRESS.

The following address of the pastor emeritus of the mother church, the Rev. Mary Baker G. Eddy, was read at each communion service by John W. Reeder:

"My Beloved Brethren: Looking on this annual assemblage of human consciousness, health, harmony, growth, grandeur, and achievement, garlanded with glad faces, willing hands, and warm hearts, who would say to-day, 'What a fond fool is hope?' The fruition of friendship, the world's arms outstretched to us, heart meeting heart across continents and oceans, bloodless sieges and tearless triumphs, the 'well done' already yours, and the undone waiting only your swift hands are enough to make this hour glad. What more abounds and abides in the hearts of these hearers and speakers pen may not tell.

"Nature reflects man and art pencils him, but it remains for science to reveal man to man, and between these lines of thought is written in luminous letters, O man, what are thou? Where art thou? Whence and whither? And what shall the answer be? Expressive silence, or with finger pointing upward—thither! Then produce thy records, time table, log, traveler's companion, &c., and prove fairly the facts relating to the thitherward—the rate of speed, the means of travel, and the number en route. Now what have you learned? The mystery of godliness—God made manifest in the flesh, seen of men, and spiritually understood? And the mystery of iniquity—and how to separate the tares from the wheat—that they consume in their own fires, and no longer kindle altars for human sacrifice. Have you learned to conquer sin, false affections, motives, and aims—to be not only sayers but doers of the law?

"Brethren, our annual meeting is a grave guardian. It requires you to report progress, to refresh memory, to rejuvenate the branches, and vivify the buds, to bend upward the tendrils and incline the vine toward the parent trunk. You come from feeding your flocks, big with promise; and you come with the sling of Israel's chosen one to meet the Goliaths.

PROGRESS OF CHRISTIAN SCIENCE.

"I have only to dip my pen in my heart to say all honor to the members of our Board of Lectureship connected with the mother church. Loyal to the divine principle they so ably vindicate, they earn their laurels history will record their words, and their works will follow them. When reading their lectures I have felt the touch of the spirit of the Mars Hill orator, which always thrills the soul. I have the great pleasure to report that within the last month there have been added to this board the talent, influence, and experience of the distinguished Hon W. L. Ewing of Chicago and Judge J. R. Clarkson of Omaha, Neb.

"The members of the Board of Education, under the auspices of the Massachusetts Metaphysical College, have acquitted themselves nobly. The students in my last class in 1898 are stars in my crown of rejoicing.

"We are deeply grateful that the church militant is looking into the subject of Christian Science, for Zion must put on her beautiful garments, her bridal robes; the hour is come; the bride (Word) is adorned, and lo, the bridegroom cometh! Are our lamps trimmed and burning?

"The doom of the Babylonish woman referred to in Revelation is being fulfilled. This woman, 'drunken with the blood of the saints and with the blood of the martyrs of Jesus, drunk of the wine of her fornication'—would enter even the church, and retaining the heart of the harlot and the purpose of the destroying angel, pour wormwood into the waters—the disturbed human mind—to drown the strong swimmer struggling for the shore—aiming for truth—and if possible poison such as drink of the living water But the recording angel, standing 'with right foot on the sea and his left foot on the earth,' has in his hand a book open (ready to be read;) that uncovers and kills this mystery of iniquity and interprets the mystery of godliness—how the first is finished, and the second is no longer a mystery or miracle but a marvel, casting out evil and healing the sick. And a voice was heard, saying, 'Come out of her, my people' (hearken not to her lies) 'that ye receive not her plagues, for her sins have reached unto heaven, and God hath remembered her iniquities.'

"'Double unto her double, according to her works; in the cup which she hath filled, fill to her double, * * * for she saith in her heart, I am no widow. * * * Therefore shall her plague come in one day, death and mourning and famine, for strong is the Lord God who judgeth her.' That which the revelator saw in spiritual vision will be accomplished, the Babylonish woman is fallen, and who should mourn over the widowhod of lust, of her 'that hath become the habitation of devils, and the hold of every foul spirit and the cage of every unclean bird'?

THE ONE THING NEEDFUL.

"One thing is eternally here; it reigns supreme to-day, to-morrow, forever. We need it in our homes, at our firesides, on our altars, for therewith win we the race of the centuries; and we have it only as we live it. This is that needful one thing, divine science, whereby thought is spiritualized, reaching outward and upward—to science in Christianity, science in medicine, in physics, and in metaphysics.

"Happy are the people whose God is all in all; who ask only to be judged according to their works; who live to love. We thank the Giver of all good for the marvelous speed of the chariot wheels of truth, and for the steadfast, calm coherence in the ranks of Christian Science.

"On comparison, it will be found that Christian Science possesses more of Christ's teachings and example than all other religions since the first century. Comparing our scientific system of metaphysical therapeutics with materia medica we find it completely overshadows and overwhelms it, even as Aaron's rod swallowed up the rods of the magicians of Egypt. I deliberately declare that when I was in practice out of 100 cases I healed 99 to the 10 of materia medica.

"We should thank God for persecution and for prosecution if thereby ensue a purer Protestantism and monotheism for the latter days of the nineteenth century. A siege of the combined centuries, culminating in fierce attack, cannot demolish our strongholds. The forts of Christian Science, garrisoned by God's chosen ones, can never surrender. Unlike Russia's armament, ours is not costly as men count cost, but it is rich beyond price; stanch and indestructible on land or sea; it is not curtailed in peace, surrendered in conquest, nor laid down at the feet of progress through the hands of Omnipotence. And wherefore? Because it is 'Peace on earth, good will toward men'; a cover and a defense adapted to all men, all nations, all times, climes, and races. I cannot quench my desire to say this, and words are not vain when the depth of desire can find no other outlet to liberty. 'Therefore * * * let us go unto perfection; not laying again the foundation of repentance from dead works.' Heb. vi., 1.

THE RECENT PROSECUTIONS.

"A Coroner's inquest, a Board of Health, or class legislation is less than the Constitution of the United States, and infinitely less than God's benign government, which is no respector of persons. Truth crushed to earth springs spontaneously upward, and whispers in the breeze man's inalienable birthright—Liberty! 'Where the spirit of the Lord is there is liberty.' God is everywhere, nor crown nor sceptre nor rulers rampant can quench the vital heritage of freedom—man's right to adopt a religion, to employ a physician, to live or to die according to the dictates of his own rational conscience and enlightened understanding. Man cannot punish a man for suicide—God does that.

"Christian Scientists abide by the laws of God and the laws of the land, and following the command of the Master they go into all the world preaching the Gospel and healing the sick. Therefore be wise and harmless, for without the former the latter were impracticable. A lack of wisdom betrays truth into the hands of evil men as effectually as a subtle conspirator; the motive is not as wicked, but the result is as injurious. Return not evil for evil, but overcome evil with good. Then whatever the shaft aimed at you or your practice may be, it will fall powerless, and God will reward your enemies according to their works. Watch and pray daily that evil suggestions in whatever guise take no root in your thought or bear fruit. Ofttimes examine yourselves and see if there be found anywhere a deterrent to truth and love, and hold fast that which is good.

DANGERS OF THE NATION.

"I reluctantly foresee great danger threatening our Nation—imperialism, monopoly, and a lax system of religion. But the spirit of humanity, ethics, and Christianity sown broadcast—all concomitants of Christian Science—is taking strong hold of the public thought throughout our beloved country and in foreign lands, and is tending to counteract the trend of mad ambition.

"There is no night but in God's frown; there is no day but in His smile. The oracular skies, the verdant earth—bird, brook, blossom, breeze, and balm—are richly fraught with divine reflection; they come at love's call. The nod of spirit is nature's natal.

"And how is man, seen through the lens of spirit, enlarged, and how counterpoised his origin from dust, and how he presses to his original, never severed from spirit! O ye who leap disdainfully from this rock of ages, return and plant thy steps in Christ, truth, the stone that the builders reject. Then will angels administer grace, do thy errands, and be thy dearest allies. The divine law gives to man health and life everlasting—gives a soul to soul, a present harmony wherein the good man's heart takes hold on heaven—whose feet can never be moved. These are His green pastures beside still waters, where faith mounts upward, expatiates, strengthens, and exults.

PRACTICAL ADVICE.

"Lean not too much on your leader; trust God to direct your steps. Accept my counsel and teachings only as they include the spirit and letter of the Ten Commandments, the beatitudes, and the teachings and example of Christ Jesus. Refrain from public controversy; correct the false with the true, then leave the latter to propagate. Watch and guard our own thoughts against evil suggestions, and against malicious mental malpractice, wholly disloyal to the teachings of Christian Science. This hidden method of committing crime—socially, physically, and morally—will ere long be unearthed and punished as it deserves. The effort of disloyal students to blacken me and to keep my works from public recognition—students seeking only public notoriety, and whom I have assisted pecuniarily and striven to uplift—has been made too many times, and has failed too often for me to fear it. The spirit of truth is the lever which elevates mankind. I have neither the time nor the inclination to be continually pursuing a lie—the one evil or the evil one. Therefore I ask the help of others in this matter, and that, according to the Scriptures, my students reprove, rebuke, and exhort. A lie left to itself is not so soon destroyed as it would be with the help of the truthtelling. Truth never falters or fails; it is our faith that fails.

"All published quotations from my works must have the author's name added to them; quotation marks are not sufficient. Borrowing from my copyrighted works without credit is inadmissible. But I need not say this to the loyal Christian Scientist—to him who keeps the commandments. 'Science and Health, with Key to the Scriptures,' has an enormous strain put upon it, being used as a companion to the Bible in all your public ministrations as teacher, and as the embodiment and substance of the truth that is taught—hence my request that you borrow little else from it should seem reasonable.

"Beloved, that which purifies the affections strengthens them, removes fear, subdues sin, and endures with divine power; that which refines character humbles, exalts, and commands a man; and obedience gives him courage, devotion, and attainment. For this hour, for this period, for spiritual sacrament, sacrifice, and ascension we unite in giving thanks. For the body of Christ, the life that we commemorate and would emulate—for the bread of heaven 'whereof if a man eat he shall live forever'—for the cup red with loving restitution, redemption, and inspiration—we give thanks. The signet of the great heart, given to me in a little symbol, seals the covenant of everlasting love. May apostate praise return to its first love, above the symbol seize the spirit, speak the 'new tongue,' and may thought soar and soul be."

What the Great Metropolitan Churches Are in Business

Five Typical Religious Organizations with Memberships Running Into the Thousands and How They Manage Millions of Dollars Worth of Property

HOW would the internal management of a modern church impress a business man? With the rise of the large church in the last few decades, the question has ceased to be an excuse for comparisons of material and spiritual things. The noteworthy modern churches hold millions of dollars' worth of property. They count their membership by thousands. Many have become actual as well as spiritual guardians of their followers, with the rise of the parish and church clubs, the day nurseries, schools, and settlements. Such developments mean an elaboration of details, larger working forces, and a business system worthy of a large commercial concern.

Not many people know how these great religious institutions are managed. So five of the larger churches were selected, each as a type, in its way and the administration of each was considered, as well as the management of their dollars and cents. The results are embodied in the following articles:

ST. PATRICK'S CATHEDRAL.

One of the Greatest Catholic Parishes and How It Is Run.

WITH half a million people attending Sunday masses every year, and a parish comprising between 8,000 and 10,000 Catholics, St. Patrick's Cathedral offers one of the most remarkable examples of church organization in the city.

John D. Rockefeller has been cited as the author of a remark that Catholics had learned the lesson of making a little money count for much in a way superior to the methods of any other religious denomination. The thoroughness of the Catholic business organization has frequently been commented upon. Both statements are worth repeating here, not only because the conditions at the cathedral are typical, but they show the system in operation on a very large scale.

The revenues of the cathedral parish from all sources amount to between $50,000 and $75,000 a year. This revenue does not quite pay the expenses. The estimated number of Catholics in the parish—between 8,000 and 10,000 persons—is conservative. With the floating population it is said to be nearer 10,000 than 8,000. On the former basis, and with the revenues amounting to $75,000 a year, the cathedral costs each parishioner $7.50 a year, or a trifle more than 14 cents for each Sunday he worships there.

In some ways, however, St. Patrick's Cathedral is unique. The boundaries of the parish suggests the outlines of a great cross. They extend from Seventh Avenue and Fifty-ninth Street down Seventh Avenue to Forty-sixth Street, to Sixth Avenue, to Forty-second Street, to Madison Avenue, to Forty-seventh Street, to Third Avenue, to Fifty-eighth Street, to Fifth Avenue, thence along the latter thoroughfare to Seventh Avenue. Within these lines are some of the finest hotels, apartment houses innumerable, the heart of the new Tenderloin, a number of the city's costly residences, and the tenement houses of the east side. The difference between 10,000 parishioners and the 500,000 worshippers at the Sunday masses may be explained, in part, at least, by the presence of the hotels and apartment houses

and the fame of the cathedral among the visitors.

The parish schools cost $18,000, and the choir nearly $10,000 a year. Curiously, the choir of a Catholic church is as expensive to-day, with Gregorian chants by male voices solely, as it was when composed of men and women before the recent propaganda of Pope Pius advocating the simpler music.

Two policies contribute to the remarkable results obtained with comparatively small expenditures. One is the modest pay of the priests, the other the organization of the parishioners into societies which conduct much of the detailed work of the parish. In this, also, St. Patrick's is typical of all Catholic parishes, though remarkable in numbers.

The minister of a noted church of another denomination is not infrequently paid a salary of $10,000 a year. The estimate was made that Archbishop Farley and his ten priestly assistants at the cathedral combined, were not paid more than that sum per annum. The salaries of the assistants are about $600, of the more important dignitaries $800 each, a year. Being unmarried, they all live together in community. The perquisites of the ministers of other denominations, such as the fees for funerals, marriages, and baptisms, are in Catholic churches all turned into the general treasury.

Among the other noted city churches visited, the staffs were often found to include curates, deacons, sisterhoods, and trained nurses, who were responsible for much of the visiting and nursing and the relief of the poor. The church societies at the cathedral largely fill these needs. The care of the poor falls to twenty laymen in the Society of St. Vincent de Paul, which divided the parish into sections and visit in these in turn, and distribute about $50 a week in alms. The Holy Name Societies, with 900 men on the membership lists, the Society for the Propagation of the Faith, the League of the Sacred Heart, and the Children of Mary, the latter composed of over 500 young women, concern themselves purely with the spiritual needs and duties of the parishioners.

GRACE CHURCH.

A Typical Episcopal Church and Its Activities.

OF the Episcopal parishes, Grace Church is typical of that denomination, and at the same time carries on her work with all the elaborate organization, the manifold charities, and school system which go into the making of a great metropolitan institution.

The services are held every week day from October until June. The annual attendance at these is between 25,000 and 29,000 people. The church counts as her parishioners people who go there regularly, from points as distant as the New Jersey suburbs, Long Island, and the Bronx. As for resources, the offering last Easter day amounted to $168,000, including a thankoffering of $116,500 and an anniversary gift of $40,000 to the rector.

These facts and figures, however, serve as hints rather than a detailed description of the administration of the church. The last report of Grace Parish showed that the church had an annual income of $166,434. Of this, about 36 per cent, or $50,000, in round figures,

was spent for benevolences outside of the parish, and 48 per cent, or $80,000 for church purposes, parish institutions, and work among the poor. Approaching the church from Fourth Avenue, there are found the choir house, costing nearly $8,000 a year to maintain, and the day nursery, requiring as much more, where an average of 125 little children are cared for every day while their mothers work. As an adjunct, there is the new Neighborhood House adjoining.

The centre of the more active work of the parish, however, may be said to be the chapel, school, and club buildings in Fourteenth Street, near Second Avenue. Six hundred pupils in the industrial schools are taught by nearly fifty teachers. The parish kindergartens have approximately five teachers and 150 pupils. The baptisms, confirmations, and deaths in the parish average more than two a week for each class, and those at the chapel, according to the last report, outnumber those at the church two to one. The marriages average nearly 200 a year, or four a week. The Sunday schools offer religious instruction to more than 700 persons. The ailing may find a refuge in ten free beds and three endowed cots in the larger hospitals. Funds for the parish work are provided by the income from trust, memorial, and scholarship funds, now aggregating about $800,000. The total resources of the church earn for it something like $460 for every day in the year.

These figures would mean little did they not suggest the large scale on which a modern church is conducted and the elaborate system which their size makes necessary.

The working forces of Grace Parish, for instance, might be compared to a well-trained army. Besides Dr. William R. Huntington, the rector, Grace has a working staff of three assistant clergy, seven deacons, nine deaconesses, and five organists, besides headmasters, house mothers, a trained nurse, and a lay reader. The rector and his staff number at least forty persons.

The modern church also borrows from business houses hints for reducing their work to a system. Many of the large churches have card catalogues of the parishioners' names, with records of their good works and derelictions. The parish is divided into sections, and members of the staff are assigned to visit, aid, and possibly, investigate. A professional nurse is employed to visit the sick. Scores of societies, composed of laymen, assist in less pressing duties. In Grace Parish, for instance, there are three educational societies, three for missions, as many more for the care of the sick and needy, three for the promotion of temperance, and fifteen organizations or brotherhoods for social and educational work. The daily calendar for settlement work averages fifteen engagements every day.

TEMPLE EMANU-EL.

A System of Co-operative Work in Use for Twenty Years.

AMONG the Jewish congregations a system of co-operative work is followed which had its origin about twenty years ago at Temple Emanu-El, at Forty-third Street and Fifth Avenue, and where it has reached a stage of development which makes the conditions typical.

The ritual of the synagogue requires the services of a minister and a reader. The other official is the Superintendent of the Sunday school. The philanthropic work is carried on by a sisterhood, composed of women, and a brotherhood, with a membership of men from the congregation. The sisterhood at Emanu-El, now about twenty years old, occupies a house in Eighty-second Street, near Second Avenue. They concern themselves largely with moral and religious questions, and dispense about $25,000 a year in charities.

The brotherhood was organized about five years ago, and has a house in East Third Street, near Second Avenue, where the members provide lectures and a library and facilities for athletics. They use for this work about $30,000. These societies are affiliated with the Educational Alliance and with the United Hebrew Charities, and arrange their work in harmony.

These committees formed the basis of many similar organizations, the movement extending to a number of the smaller synagogues, and enrolling thousands of members. Twenty of these societies formed a federation. The reports it receives show that the smaller organizations distribute from $5,000 to $20,000 each in charities. The more orthodox Jews do not take kindly to the plan.

THE CALVARY BAPTIST CHURCH.

An Interesting Study in the "Mixing" of Men.

NEW YORK, the polyglot, a city of many tongues and all sorts and conditions of men, has been for years the inspiration of Dr. Robert S. MacArthur and his associates in the Calvary Baptist Church, in Fifty-seventh Street, near Sixth Avenue. As the church organization has become, in consequence, the symbol of the "mixing" of men, it offers an interesting study from that viewpoint.

Calvary Church suggests a religious institution on the commonwealth plan. Dr. MacArthur, chatting of the organization, based his argument on the idea that there were no such things as social distinctions or rich and poor.

"I have men on my committees," he continued, "whom some might class among the wealthiest and most influential people in the city. I have others who are anything but wealthy in a worldly way, and work, perhaps, in obscure positions. We make them believe that there are no distinctions among them. So the members meet on church business at each other's houses, and make no distinctions. In this church, side by side, are lawyers physicians, business men, mechanics, working men, the rich and the very poor."

There are men and women of many nationalities, too. Years ago, members of the congregation began to work among Armenians and Chinese; then Persians were added to the list, and services were held in Calvary Church in all of these tongues. In recent years, Spanish-speaking peoples have been included in the plan, and the services in Spanish and the congregations which attend them are considered ample recompense.

With such an experiment, the first question a stranger asks is: "Can a church be universal in such a way?" and "Has the plan succeeded in a material way—in numbers of parishioners and financial prosperity?

Here is the reply that was given: When Dr. MacArthur took the church thirty-eight years ago, there were 238 parishioners; since then about 5,000 new members have been admitted. The present church was built in 1882 and 1883 at a cost of $525,000, and during the present pastorate more than $2,000,000 has been raised for mission work.

THE MADISON SQUARE CHURCH.

Where the Charities Are Far in Excess of Expenses.

IN the Presbyterian denomination the Madison Square Church is one of the most interesting in its charities.

The church spends approximately $55,000 a year for its parish work and $75,000 a year for charities. The activities in the latter centre around the Church House at Twenty-ninth Street and Third Avenue, where ten clubs or bureaus minister to the poor of the neighborhood.

Among these, the alien is given much attention. There are classes and lectures for Germans, Italians, Greeks, and Armenians. Religious services are given in Greek every week. A library of books written in that tongue has also been provided for the 200 Greeks who visit the house.

There is a colony of fully 500 Armenians in the neighborhood, and visitors to the Church House almost any afternoon will see fifty people of this nationality seeking to learn English or joining in religious exercises.

January 10, 1909

PLACE 6,000 BIBLES IN CHICAGO HOTELS

Each Carrying Six, 1,000 Y. M. C. A. Youths Distribute Them Through the City.

GIDEONS BEHIND THE PLAN

In a Year They Have Given More Than 50,000, Increasing Electric Light Bills.

Special to The New York Times.

CHICAGO, Jan. 2.—A thousand earnest young men marched through the principal streets of the business district this afternoon, each carrying six Bibles under his arm. The street crowds gaped in wonder at this unusual spectacle, and gathered around in curious throngs when the thousand came to a halt in Madison Street.

At a few words of command the paraders separated into groups and moved off in different directions. Each division was followed by a crowd of its own until it disappeared into one of the city's well-known hotels.

The purpose of all this was to place in the bedrooms of these hotels copies of the Bible, for the use of transient patrons. The distribution was arranged by the Christian Commercial Travelers' Association, better known as the Gideons. Through this means, they believe, travelers will be brought into touch with religious influences, whereas they generally cannot be reached by routine church and society work.

The Gideons enlisted the Y. M. C. A. and many churches in their plan. Funds were raised for the purchase of the books, which were strongly bound in cloth by the American Bible Society and sold to the Gideons at one-third below cost. Each Bible cost 35 cents.

It was decided to make the distribution on the last day of the year, that on New Year's Day they might be at the disposal of patrons. They will not be chained down.

The Y. M. C. A. was asked to supply men to make the distribution, which was in charge of W. E. Henderson, National Secretary of the Gideons. All hands gathered to-day in the auditorium of the Central Y. M. C. A., where addresses were made by some of the leading ministers of the city. Then the volunteers filed up to the platform, where the 6,000 Bibles had been piled. Each took half a dozen and marched out.

None of the hotel proprietors objected to the Bibles being placed in their rooms. The distribution, as arranged, was as follows: La Salle Hotel, 1,000; Congress Hotel and Annex, 600; Great Northern, 400; Stratford, 210; Auditorium, 365; Grand Pacific, 200; Lexington, 300; Saratoga, 265; Majestic, 200; Kaiserhof, 260; Windsor-Clifton, 165; Deming, 109; Wellington, 200; Palmer House, 635; Grant, 184; Brevoort, 300; Morrison, 200, and smaller hotels, from 100 down.

The following legend is pasted within the cover of each volume:

This holy book, whose leaves display the life, the light, the truth, and the way, is placed in this room by the Gideons, the Christian Commercial Travelers' Association of America, aided by the churches and the Young Men's Christian Association of this city, with the hope that by means of this Book the reader may be brought to know the love of Christ, which passeth knowledge.

At their headquarters here several thousand letters have been received from hotel proprietors, ministers, traveling men, and other hotel guests commending the organization for its work and telling of benefits derived from the presence of the Bibles. One woman, who owns a little hotel west of the Mississippi River, writes:

The change I noticed first after the Bibles were placed in the bedrooms of my hotel was that my electric light bill doubled. These men get hold of a Bible, read the references you cite, and then are not satisfied. They go on reading, and my light bill goes on getting bigger. But I don't care in the least. I would just as soon have it get bigger yet if Bible-reading makes the increase.

In the last year the Gideons have placed more than 50,000 Bibles in hotels throughout the country.

January 3, 1911

15

OFFER OLIVE BRANCH TO UNION SEMINARY

Presbyterians Ask for a Conference to Restore Harmony with the Assembly.

COMMITTEE IS APPOINTED

Dr. Grant Convicted of Heresy and Suspended Until He Recants, by Unanimous Vote of the Commission.

Special to The New York Times.

ATLANTIC CITY, May 26.—The Presbyterian General Assembly voted to-day to hold out the olive branch to the Union Theological Assembly, in an endeavor to end the theological warfare that has disturbed the church for fifteen years.

This action is regarded by Presbyterians as far more important than the finding of the Rev. Dr. William D. Grant guilty of unorthodox views and suspending of him for an indefinite period. Dr. Grant is a graduate of Union, and his views are those which have caused all the criticism of the seminary, and one ex-Moderator exclaimed when the peace offering was extended:

"They have chastised the pupil, but allowed the teacher to go free."

The Grant verdict was approved by the Commissioners, most of them holding that nothing else could be done. Charles S. Cairns, Moderator of the judicial commission, presented its report, which stated that Dr. Grant's teachings denying the mediatorial office of Jesus Christ and his statements impugning the credibility of the Scriptures had led to a reversion of the findings of the lower court and to his suspension.

"The commission finds that he taught in a manner that impugns the authority of the Old and New Testaments," announced Mr. Cairns. "In doing this he is guilty of an offense against the standards of his Church, as no minister is entitled to maintain his status in the Presbyterian Church who takes such a position."

The applause which greeted this announcement brought a sharp reproof from the Moderator, Dr. Carson, who reminded the Commissioners they were sitting as a court. Mr. Cairns announced Dr. Grant's suspension "until such time as he shall make manifest to the satisfaction of his presbytery renunciation of the errors he has been found to hold, and to promise to teach them no more."

Friends of Dr. Grant pointed out that there is nothing to prevent him from appealing to his Presbytery at its next meeting, and by recanting any views that might be taken to attack the basic doctrines of the Church be reinstated within a short time.

Dr. Grant was present when the report of the commission was read. Before the vote his counsel wanted to read a statement for Dr. Grant, but his request was refused. The statement, which was in the nature of an affirmation of faith in the great doctrines of the Church, follows:

Few men have suffered as much for their beloved church as I have suffered for the church of my fathers. I reverently and lovingly bow to its decision. I do now affirm, as I have many times affirmed during these proceedings, my unqualified faith in my blessed Lord and Saviour Jesus Christ, in His Deity, Virgin Birth, resurrection, and mediatorial work, and in the Scriptures of the Old and New Testaments, as the infallible rule of faith and life. I have never knowingly taught anything contrary to the above declarations.

Some of the statements I have made in my articles I can now see are subject to misconstruction, but if I cannot preach the great doctrines of grace, as given us in the New Testament, in the Presbyterian Church, I ought to leave her ministry, but I trust it shall be my privilege and joy to continue to proclaim those doctrines as long as God shall give me strength to do so.

The findings of the judicial commission were by unanimous vote.

The Union Theological Seminary resolution was by far the most important business of the day. As a result of long conferences by the Presbyterian leaders in the Hotel Chalfonte last night, and steam roller methods by the Moderator, the expected onslaught upon the seminary was converted into a love feast.

The Rev. Edwin J. Reinke of Philadelphia opened the proceedings by withdrawing his resolution presented yesterday, in which the assembly was asked to express its disapproval of "recent utterances of the Rev. Dr. William Adams Brown of Union Seminary," and admonish him to desist from disseminating such views.

"With the consent of the assembly, I shall offer a substitute," said Dr. Reinke. "I believe this whole matter can be harmoniously adjusted." And he read as follows:

Resolved, First, that the former doctrinal deliverance of the General Assembly be affirmed.

Second, that all ministers of the Church be admonished to refrain from utterances calculated to disturb its peace or contradict its doctrines.

Third, that no further action be taken on the overtures in question.

After these were passed the Rev. Dr. David Wylie of New York offered this resolution:

Whereas, the Union Theological Seminary in the City of New York was founded by the Presbyterian Church and has been largely endowed from Presbyterian sources; and

Whereas, for some years past there has developed a condition which led to the severing of the relations which have existed from the organization of the seminary between it and the General Assembly; and

Whereas, we are persuaded that there are in the Faculty and Directorate of Union Theological Seminary men who are in accord with evangelical Christianity as expressed in the standards of doctrine of the Presbyterian Church, and who are zealous in all good works for the growth of the kingdom of our dear Lord Jesus Christ and the world; and

Whereas, we believe that it would be a signal manifestation of the spirit of our Lord and Saviour Jesus Christ, Who prayed that they all may be one, for Christian brethren under the gracious guidance of the Holy Spirit to remove all misunderstanding, alienation, and antagonism, and to become vitally and aggressively united in the doctrine and fellowship of our beloved Church in the work of bringing the Nation and the world to Christ; therefore be it

Resolved, That this General Assembly authorizes the Moderator to appoint a committee of nine to consist of five ministers, of whom he shall be one, and four ruling elders, none of whom shall be connected with Union Seminary, to confer with the Directorate and Faculty of said seminary with a view to the re-establishment of harmonious relations between the seminary and the General Assembly on the basis of the standards of the Presbyterian Church, this committee to report to the next General Assembly.

In the midst of the assembly's deliberations a wave of applause drowned every other sound as William Jennings Bryan, escorted by the Rev. Dr. H. Trumbull Lee, was seen going down the aisle. The Nebraska statesman was greeted effusively by the Moderator, who introduced him as "one of the honored Elders of the Presbyterian Church." Mr. Bryan briefly addressed the Commissioners, saying:

"Of late I have been planning to attend such meetings more frequently. I recognize the importance of these gatherings and the opportunity of speaking to leaders of Christian thought, the men who set up the standards of morality as well as the standards of our faith."

May 27, 1911

SUNDAY'S 19 AIDS DRAWTRAIL-HITTERS

Their Payroll Runs Close to $1,000 a Week and They Work 15 Hours a Day.

PASTOR 'DOUBLES IN BRASS'

From Wife of Evangelist Down to the West Indian Butler, Each Has a Part to Play in Revivals.

When Billy Sunday, the evangelist, comes to New York for the three months' campaign which begins next April, he will bring with him one of the ablest and most efficiently organized groups of Gospel workers that has ever been gathered together. Including Mr. Sunday himself, there are nineteen in the evangelist's army in the campaign that has just closed in Boston, and practically all these are sure to take part in the New York campaign. It is a compact body that has grown up gradually during perhaps the last dozen years, until now it includes men and women who can handle every sort of work connected with a revival. Other evangelists have had their singers, their Bible teachers, their assistant evangelists to conduct outside meetings, but nobody has had the scientifically-organized expeditionary force that Sunday carries with him.

It is a body of experts. Though the evangelist himself and his wife exercise command over the party, each worker is left much in control of his or her particular sphere. And, strangely enough, while each is expert in one thing, nearly all can turn to in a pinch and perform with a reasonable degree of expertness in something else.

Family Heads Organization.

At the head of the organization are three members of the Sunday family—the evangelist, his wife, and his son. The ability and power of Billy Sunday are remarkable enough in themselves; what is still more remarkable is that this man of great talent should have married the particular woman who could best supplement his own abilities. For "Ma" Sunday is a woman of remarkable executive capacity, remarkable talent in the management of people and affairs. And by the law of averages it is still more remarkable that these two persons of exceptional ability should have a son who seems to be on the way to becoming an executive genius himself.

George Sunday, the 25-year-old son, who with his family lives near his father at Winona Lake, Ind., is the Treasurer and business head of the organization. He handles much of the advance work, and has for some time past been spending most of his time in New York in preparation for the campaign here, while Sunday's other advance man, the Rev. James E. Walker, handled the preliminary work for the Buffalo campaign. Another of George Sunday's duties is the chief supervision over seating arrangements. He has the final word on the allotment of groups of seats to delegations from suburban churches, from lodges, from factories, from stores, or from any other organization where the gang instinct is strong enough to be seized on by the Sunday workers and made an asset in the campaign.

The value of this work has been shown again and again, for it is likely to be easier to get a man or woman to go with a crowd of associates and friends than alone; and sometimes whole parties of this sort have "hit the trail" in a body.

George Sunday also handles his father's charities. Sunday receives enormous sums of money in the free-will offering at the end of each campaign. Twice, at Philadelphia and at Boston, he has received more than $50,000 for a campaign of less than three months. Out of this he pays one-third of the salaries of his assistants, but this is a comparatively small sum. He owns a modest shingle bungalow at Winona Lake, Indiana; he wears good clothing and drives an automobile, but it is said the motor car and his fur overcoat were gifts. His friends say he gives most of the money that comes in through the free-will offerings to charitable and religious work.

His enemies tell stories of his wealth; but despite the many and influential enemies whom he has made nobody has ever been able to get anything on him. If he has wealth nobody has ever found it. So far as the external evidence available is concerned, he gives most of it away.

Some of the Staff.

Most prominent outside the Sunday family is undoubtedly Homer A. Rodeheaver. "Rody" is usually one of the most popular members of the party. Schoolboys like him tremendously; so do grown men; nor are the ladies backward. Rodeheaver is musical director. He leads the singing, "lining out" the hymns, getting the left half of the house to sing the first line of a stanza, the right half the second line, the choir the third, and the whole congregation the fourth. He can sing himself, in an oily, resonant voice—a good voice, as gospel singers go. And he plays the trombone to lead the choruses with devastating effect. Rodeheaver is a man of immense value. Whatever he gets for his services, he is worth it. A man with his mixing ability and his capacity for molding a crowd into just the right state of mind in preparation for Sunday's arrival would be worth a fortune to a political leader.

Rodeheaver was the son of a Tennessee miner. He worked in the mines, then in a sawmill. He served in the Spanish-American war, worked his way through Ohio Wesleyan University, and has been with Sunday for several years.

The Rev. James E. Walker is the advance representative of the party. When he and George Sunday work together on the preparation for a campaign George handles the business side and Walker the spiritual part of the work. He was pastor of United Presbyterian Churches in Pittsburgh and Chicago, and came under Sunday's notice while the evangelist was living in the latter city. Walker is married, and lives in Carnegie, Penn., a town chiefly known as the home of "Honus" Wagner, the ball player.

The Rev. Isaac Ward handles the shop work—the noon meetings at factories by which the Sunday party designs to get everybody in an industrial organization in a frame of mind to come to the meetings. Like several of the other members of the party, Mr. Ward performs the act known in theatrical circles as doubling in brass. He can play the organ, the cornet or the trombone, the latter instrument being one particularly valuable to an evangelist. He got his start as a worker among laboring men when he was pastor of a Dutch Reformed Church in Jersey City, and worked with dock laborers and workmen in the railroad yards. He now lives in New Brunswick.

George A. Brewster is another of the musical staff. He can do almost anything, and does. He sings well and often and does part of the work of playing the piano for the hymns. Brewster has been a reporter, a vaudeville actor and professor in an Iowa college. He now lives at Joliet, Ill.

Women Play Major Parts.

The Rev. Miss Frances Miller, an ordained clergywoman of the Congregational Church, has been with Sunday for eleven years. She has charge of the work among business women—shop girls, stenographers, and clerks, and also does most of the work of arranging the parlor prayer meetings in drawing rooms of the socially prominent which Sunday usually conducts once or twice in every city where he preaches. She lives in Los Angeles.

Mrs. William Asher handles the work among factory girls, nurses, and housemaids, and also supervises the extension work among women in their homes who are unable to get together for meetings. Her husband is an independent evangelist. For several years she was with J. Wilbur Chapman, under whom Sunday learned a good deal of his profession, and while with Chapman she specialized in conducting prayer meetings in saloons. She is another who lives at Winona Lake.

Miss Alice M. Gamlin handles the work among boys and girls. She was with the New York State Sunday School Association for some years, and became connected with the Sunday party during the Philadelphia campaign early in 1915.

Another who joined the party at Philadelphia was Miss Florence Kinney, who was a teacher in a girls' school in Ohio. In the Sunday party she is one of the Bible teachers and handles a considerable part of the work among college students.

Miss Grace Saxe, head of the Bible teachers of the party, was once a court stenographer, and later a writer for a newspaper syndicate. She, too, lives at Winona Lake. Miss Jean B. Lamont, a former Y. W. C. A. Secretary at Evansville, Ind., is another of the Bible teachers who handle the numerous classes organized during a Sunday campaign.

Miss Rose Fetterolf is engaged in the work among young people, particularly high school students. She was a drawing teacher in Pennsylvania before joining the Sunday party. Robert Matthews, a former reporter on a Chicago newspaper, is Mr. Sunday's private secretary, and plays the piano on the side.

Evangelists Live in One House.

Besides these regular workers in the party there are a number of auxiliaries who are equally essential to its success. Chief among these is Mrs. Rose M. Foutts, the housekeeper—for the Sunday party of late years has been living together during each campaign in a house hired for the three months; and to look after a group of anywhere from twelve to twenty people who are too busy to be bothered with the details of looking after themselves is perhaps as hard a job as the Sunday organization has to offer. But Mrs. Foutts deserves a separate story all to herself, and she is going to get one.

Joe Spiece builds all of Sunday's tabernacles. He says he found the evangelist when he was preaching in cow sheds. Spiece is not an architect—he was interested in various businesses be-

fore he became converted and joined the Sunday party; but without the technical education he became a practical expert in fire hazards and acoustics. He has perfected the sounding board which is used to throw the evangelist's voice to every part of the huge auditorium— a flower-like flat instrument that hangs over the platform with six huge arched petals of fluted wood, carrying the waves of sound with amazing clearness, and all centring on a cup in which high-powered lights throw their illumination straight down on the speaker. Spiece is now in New York superintending the construction of a tabernacle of wood which will seat 23,000 persons with full regard to the requirements of the Building Department and the Bureau of Fire Prevention.

Albert Peterson is the tabernacle custodian. When not custodianing he acts as Sunday's masseur, and plays the piano for the services in a pinch. Indeed, it is the boast of members of the Sunday party that everybody from the janitor up can lead a prayer meeting, sing, talk, or expound the Scriptures.

Fred Buse, who has been with the party for the last two or three campaigns, is the tabernacle Postmaster. It is his duty to sort out the cards signed by the repentant trail-hitters in which they express their religious preference, and keep them in a set of pigeonholes for the clergymen of the various churches to receive at their convenience. And perhaps another member should be included in the person of Dan, the West Indian butler, who has been with the party since the Trenton campaign, and has probably earned a permanent post.

The Sunday organization takes July and August off, and after each campaign there is an interval of a week or so in which those who live near enough have a chance to make a hurried visit to their families. When they collect in a new city which is to be the scene of a campaign they find much preliminary work done according to their directions, and frequently after their personal visits and suggestions, and on the basis of this preliminary work the organization pitches in for ten weeks of campaigning, during which most of its members work fourteen or fifteen hours a day.

The Payroll.

The payroll of this organization is approximately a thousand dollars a week, of which Mr. Sunday pays one-third and the local committee of his supporters two-thirds. But this thousand a week does not include board, lodging, automobile hire, or railroad fare to and from their homes, all of which is paid by the local committee. Moreover, all of the party share in lesser degree the attraction which Sunday possesses so prominently, of drawing presents from local admirers. And, since most of the expensive pleasures of life are condemned by the creed to which they all give earnest adherence, they make a good deal of money. No one who has seen a Sunday campaign will deny that, from the point of view of cold efficiency, they are worth it.

January 28, 1917

The Two Billy Sundays   Preacher and Artist

"Gets No Boost from His Face," Says Observer of His Attempts to Reform Wicked New York, but Is "as Natural as a Monkey"

By Charles H. Grasty.

NEW YORK is going through the process of getting interested in the Rev. William A. Sunday. That seasoned veteran is not frightened at a few empty benches in the tabernacle on a raw, windy afternoon. That, or the like thing, always happens in the early stages. Also, there is the

discussion as to whether "our city" isn't different and therefore capable of resisting Sunday's wiles. New York is too big, or too wicked, or too lacking in the power to focus; but New York will do just what smaller cities have done.

The truth is that Mr. Sunday possesses the qualifications of a successful popular evangelist. He has certain abilities, and he is adept in their use. The fact that he is an artist makes many people question

his sincerity. That is, he calculates and discriminates in the use of his powers. When he addresses an audience of society women in a private drawing room he shows a rare decorum and restraint. At the tabernacle he lets himself go. He knows the difference in the tastes of those two audiences. In other words, there are two Billy Sundays—one may be likened to the automobile, embracing horse power and mechanism; the other

to the chauffeur. Neither would be useful without the other, but the two make a good combination.

It often strikes me as to a great actor like Forbes-Robertson that he has trained naturalness. Sunday in his tabernacle performances is as natural as a monkey. It has always seemed to me that herein lies a peculiar difference between man and the lower animals, and in some respects it is in favor of the latter. One

A Billy Sunday Meeting in Full Swing.

(Times Photo Service.)

meets few really interesting people, but who ever met an uninteresting dog? The one has, and the other lacks, self-consciousness.

But a man must have something more than naturalness to draw and hold such crowds as flock to Sunday's meetings. To be natural is merely to be transparent; there must be something inside to shine through the transparency.

Sunday has two very positive qualities. He can make a good sermon. He has zeal and energy that fairly burn. There, then, is my diagnosis: Good ability as a preacher, fire, and naturalness, the latter two to a remarkable degree.

Goethe once gave some such advice as this to a young man: "Whenever you feel discouraged all you have to do is to spit on your hands." That's Sunday's spirit, only he applies the metaphor literally. I saw him stoop down and grab up an imaginary handful of dirt and sling it at his audience as he cried out in notes like pistol shots: "You are cowards! I throw it in your face! You are cowards!"

He is eager for his job. He can't wait quietly for his turn to come, but prowls like a jaguar up and down and around while the preliminary song service is on. The minute that is over Sunday "goes to it." He goes to it like the Fire Department to a fire. He slides metaphorically down the polished pillar with his clothes in his hands and puts them on while the truck tears up the street.

Of course any man who speaks movingly gets the help of some kind of emotional uplift from within. He does better than he knows. Sunday is carried along by an intense excitement. Without using the word in the way of criticism at all, I should say that he develops a sort of hysteria that doubtless relieves him of the necessity of much conscious effort. He has the stuff in his intellectual barrel all ready for use. His subconscious mind seizes it and hands it out.

Meantime that baseball body carries the strain. It runs up and down the platform, mounts a chair, scales the pulpit, lies prone on the floor. It is never still an instant. Every muscle is in action. Many of his physical mannerisms smack of the diamond. A man playing out in centre field gets few chances, but must always be on his toes, ready. He thus forms the habit of hitching up his breeches. Sunday does it a score of times

in the course of a sermon. Then, too, he often runs back, looking forward, one hand high in the air, as if reaching up for a high, hot line ball. His running back and forth on the platform reminds me of McGraw in his playing days when he would go to the coaching line to rattle the pitcher. Perhaps Sunday is trying the same tactics on the devil.

One would hardly realize from reading the reports of Sunday's sermons how words and action, manner and matter, fit in. He talks in torrents. Forbes-Robertson, to take the best exemplar, gets his effects through the subtle use of emphasis. Sunday holds thousands under his spell just the other way. He has no reserve whatever. He will shout until his voice is gone, but when you begin to feel sorry for him it comes back.

With all his fifty-odd years Sunday is an athlete still. His muscles are steel, his throat brass. He is finely built, without an ounce of surplus flesh. He brags of being a jay, and looks the part. With all Sunday's boasting of his being a "hayseed of hayseeds," and from "Ioway," with the accent on the last syllable, I thought I noticed a vibration of pride in his voice when he admitted that he had two great-grandfathers in the revolutionary war.

Sunday gets no particular boost from his face. If he were on the Yankees' players bench it would be a fair bet of ten to one that he could not be picked out as the preacher player by a stranger. His wide open eyes speak amiability and innocence rather than power. His nose is small and turns up. He has a mouth that might belong to an orator.

Far be it from me to disparage Billy's face. Perhaps it is just the face to help him most with his crowd. For his appeal is to the average man.

Now the average man doesn't like complexities or abstractions. He doesn't take them in. Sunday's sermonizing is strictly simple and concrete. Most ministers try to cram down too many ideas at one time. It can't be done with the average man. I have said that Sunday preaches well. Stripped of its slang his sermons would be rated good by almost any critic. He sticks to his text. Or, rather, he never goes far away and always comes back. When he takes a mental excursion he buys a round-trip ticket.

He never leaves his audience in doubt as to what he is driving at. That is the justification, if any there be, for his slang. He brings the gospel right home to "the folks." He makes it concrete and personal. When from the pulpit one hears Mary and Martha spoken of as "these two girls" we flinch a bit at the irreverence of it. When, in alluding to some Bible character, he says that he "was so low down that he had to climb up in a tree to look a snake in the eye," the average man out there in the crowd makes a mental picture that is both amusing and unforgettable.

Perhaps, after all, we who more or less take our standards of taste from transatlantic sources would come to know and serve this great democracy of ours better if we rubbed elbows more with Billy Sunday's crowd. This country is not run entirely by the men who know what to do with their hands in a drawing room, but to some extent by those who would think themselves sufficiently elegant if in such circumstances they toyed with their watch chains, if they were so fortunate as to have them to toy with.

It is not on our seaboard, but in Billy Sunday's country, that the ruling classes are produced, for in that great plain which stretches from the Alleghanies to the Rockies, men and things, the animal and the vegetable, grow rankest, richest and strongest. Think what you will about his ethics, say what you will about his manners, you must admit that Billy Sunday is vital and life giving. He stirs the waters. He rattles the dry bones. And, remember, it is from stagnation and not agitation, that rot and death proceed.

Billy Sunday Arriving at the Tabernacle to Conduct a Meeting.
(Times Photo Service.)

April 22, 1917

Trail-Hitters Not Converts, Church Test Shows

Many Signers of Cards at Billy Sunday's Meetings Were Church-goers Who Needed No Revival, According to Investigator

By George MacAdam.

THE first test of the real results of the three-month revival campaign recently conducted in this city by the Rev. Billy Sunday has just been completed. According to that test, the campaign was not the success it appeared to be. The evangelist departed from New York after he had succeeded in packing his huge tabernacle twice a day during his long stay. The free-will offering, which he turned over to charity, was imposing. The number of his "trail-hitters" was legion. But systematic inquiries among the "trail-hitters" has indicated that the campaign did not accomplish what its backers claimed for it.

Sunday's campaign was launched and kept at fever heat for the sole purpose of bringing about a religious awakening. And so the real test of the revivalist's success is to be found in the "trail-hitters." Sunday himself accepted this as the test. The invitation to "hit the trail" was the spiritual climax of each service. There were certain men appointed to keep tally of those who accepted the invitation, and the numbers were regularly given out to the representatives of the newspapers after each service. They were dwelt upon and advertised as the visible, tangible results of the revivalist's efforts.

Every person who "hit the trail" was asked to put upon a card, under the inscription "I now accept Jesus Christ as my personal Saviour," his name and address, also the church and minister preferred, if any. After the campaign was over and Sunday had departed, these cards were sorted by a committee and distributed in packets to the ministers who were respectively designated as preferred, or, if no preference was stated, then to the minister whose church was most convenient to the given address. This was for "follow-up work"—to get into the churches the people that Billy Sunday had awakened to religion, to make lasting the work that the revivalist had initiated.

The first church in New York to complete this "follow-up work" is the Fort Washington Presbyterian Church, of which the Rev. Dr. Daniel Hoffmann Martin is pastor. This church was the nearest to the Sunday tabernacle, and it may therefore be said to have been in the storm centre of the campaign. Billy Sunday, like other evangelists before him, has complained that his work has

not had as lasting results in communities as it should, because the clergymen have failed to do "follow-up work." Before his first communion service in July, Dr. Martin had made the effort to see, or have seen, all card-signers in his district. To assist him in this big task he engaged the services of the Rev. Dr. John S. Allen, for many years connected with the Marble Collegiate Church as "the pastor for strangers." Dr. Allen is recognized as an expert in this field of ministerial activity, and it is the result of his "follow-up work" on 273 card-signers that is here given. When Dr. Allen was asked for his estimate of the gain to the church and religion due to the great Billy Sunday drive, he said:

"Before giving a direct answer I should say a few words of the Fort Washington Church district. Previous to this 'follow-up work' I had made a special survey of this district for the New York Federation of Churches, and as a result of that survey I can say that this district is thoroughly typical of New York City; its population, their intelligence, their occupations, their financial standing, are all typical of those of the great mass of New York's inhabitants. So I believe that a cross-section from the Fort Washington Church district, as given by the 'follow-up' of 273 card-signers, is equivalent to a cross-section of the entire city. The results of Billy Sunday's work that I found here I believe will be representative of the entire city.

"Now, when you ask for an estimate of the results of the sensational revival conducted here for three months, everything depends upon your definition of 'results.' If the object was to secure 'trail-hitters' Sunday's work was a tremendous success: the official figures show that there were 98,000 of them. This is colossal. But what a good many pastors, men who put the vast influence of their church organizations behind the Billy Sunday campaign, are now asking is, not how many 'hit the trail,' but how many converts were made, how many were induced, to use the terminology of the church, 'to lead a new life'?

"In the daily reports of the twice-a-day meetings at the tabernacle the 'trail-hitters' were often spoken of as 'converts.' In fact, the newspapers used these two terms as though they were equivalent and interchangeable. This was accepted by the general public, and also by many of the churches that had brought Billy Sunday to New York and were standing back of him. The big daily batches of 'trail-hitters' that mounted up to the final total of 98,-000 gave the impression that a religious

revival of splendid proportions was taking place.

"But there were experienced workers who suspected that these 'trail-hitters' were not indicative of real results. There were those who suspected that many of those who trod the sawdust path were mere card-signers and handshakers; that they were not people who had experienced any genuine spiritual awakening.

"Many of these experienced workers felt that the Sunday Tabernacle ought to have been provided with a place like the old-fashioned 'inquiry room,' where the 'trail-hitters' would have been brought in contact with religious workers. In genuine cases of spiritual awakening, this would have served to further, to clinch—if I may use the expression—the work done by Sunday, and it would have eliminated the mere handshaker, the curiosity-seeker, and sensation-seeker.

"This inquiry room has always been a feature of evangelical and revival work. It characterized the work of the great Dwight L. Moody. But in the Billy Sunday meetings the only invitation was to 'hit the trail,' shake hands with Sunday, sign a card if they would, (an usher assisting if necessary,) and then pass out. The official figures, I am told, show that of the 98,000 that 'hit the trail' only 65,943 signed cards. That reduces by almost one-third the apparent actual results of the Sunday campaign.

"I say 'apparent actual results,' for the only line that can be got on the actual results is by an investigation of these card-signers; we must learn who they are, what kind of a life they have been living, and what change the Sunday campaign has made in their lives. It is the follow-up that puts the acid test to the profession made in the enthusiasm of the moment, and under the stimulus of the crowd. It is the quiet talk in the home that applies what I may call the diamond screen to the work of any revivalist.

"Now let us see how the work of Billy Sunday stands up under this test.

"Of the 273 cards that I investigated, 20 signers were out, though in each instance I called two or three times, or they had moved away and left no address. As we do not know what their attitude is, this 20 should be eliminated from our calculations, reducing our basic figure to 253.

"Of this 253 I found that 174, or more than 68 per cent., were church members, regularly attending religious service. Many of these people said that they had enjoyed the Tabernacle services, but of course they could not be considered as 'results' of the Sunday campaign.

"The next largest numerical division of the card signers I investigated is rep-

resented by those who were not known at the address given, or who had obviously given a fictitious address. There were 19 'not known,' (though I made earnest effort in each instance, inquiring of Superintendent, janitor, and tenants,) and 12 who unquestionably gave fictitious addresses. One of these addresses, for instance, was a storehouse, another was a Catholic church, others were vacant lots, or street and avenue numbers that do not exist. This class of card signer, therefore, represents over 12 per cent. of the total.

"I found 8 who were connected with Sunday schools and attending regularly.

"I have now accounted for more than 84 per cent. of the card signers that I 'followed up,' and it is not until now that I come to results of the Sunday campaign.

"There were eleven who were church members, but who, because they had moved away from their home town or for some other reason, had fallen off in church attendance. All of these promised to send for their letters and to become active church members in the Fall. These eleven cannot be considered as 'converts,' but it was the Sunday campaign that gave us their names and that enabled us to bring them back into the church.

"There were twelve who were non-church members, but who had attended church services more or less frequently. Three of these gave definite promises to join the church. The remaining nine shaded in their attitude from the woman who said, 'I believe every one should have a church connection—I'll talk to my husband about it,' to the woman who said, 'I never signed a card at the Billy Sunday meetings. I must have been impersonated.'

"But of people who had never been to church, who had never felt any religious influence, there were just seventeen, or not quite 7 per cent. of the total. Of these, four promised to join the church, six promised to come to 'some service,' four were noncommittal, and of the three remaining, one said, 'I signed the card simply as a courtesy to Billy Sunday'; another, 'I didn't know the object of signing the card,' and the last, 'I am not a church member and have no wish to become one.'

"In my entire work I did not come across a single case of a person leading, or who had been leading, a vicious life. No woman told me of a husband or son who was leading such a life. If Billy Sunday succeeded in reaching and awakening to a 'new life' any of the 'booze fighters,' gamblers, and other bad characters that he so often exhorted, they signed no card that passed through my hands."

August 12, 1917

LUTHERANS ELECT NEW CHURCH HEADS

The new organization of the Lutheran Church in North America was officially founded yesterday, when the General Synod, the General Council, and the United Synod of the Lutheran Church in the South were merged at a meeting of delegates of the three organizations

in the Engineering Societies Building, 25 West Thirty-ninth Street. Last night a meeting was held in the ballroom of the Hotel Astor to celebrate the union of the three religious bodies.

At the early meeting, at which all legal requirements necessary to chartering the new organization under the laws of the State of New York were arranged, the Rev. Dr. F. H. Knubel, pastor of the Church of the Atonement, 140th Street and Edgecombe Avenue, was elected President of the new body. He has been Chairman of the National Lutheran Commission for Soldiers' and

Sailors' Welfare. The Rev. Dr. M. G. G. Scherer, formerly President of the United Synod of the South, was elected Secretary, and Clarence D. Miller of Philadelphia was made Treasurer.

Following a speech by Captain Eugene L. Swan, representing Secretary of War Baker, who urged the support of the ministers in the crusade against social disease, a resolution was passed pledging support to the Government in meeting moral and social issues now confronting the nation.

The meeting last night was addressed by the Presidents of the merging bodies, the Rev. V. G. A. Tressler speaking for the General Synod, the Rev. M. G. G. Scherer for the United Synod of the

South and the Rev. T. E. Schmauk for the General Council.

Dr. Schmauk said that Martin Lutheranism was democracy," since its founder, Martin Luther, had rebelled against autocracy at the time that the theory of the divine right of Kings was at its height.

Dr. Schmuck said that Martin Luther was "the first American."

Property valued at more than $53,000,-000 will be turned over to the United Lutheran Church in America through the merging of the three constituent bodies. The membership of the Church in America is 800,000.

November 16, 1918

CHURCH ON WHEELS

THE Pilgrim Fathers established the right of man to worship as he pleases. Since then a whole lot of other fathers have assumed the right of man to worship when he pleases. And that is very seldom, indeed. Kansas City, Mo., has its church problem like every other American city. It has been estimated conservatively that about one-third of its population of more than 300,000 attend normally.

It was to raise such low averages that the Rev. Charles E. Draper came forward with a scheme of "The Church on Wheels." He is pastor of the Martha Slavens Memorial Methodist Church, which stands in a thickly populated part of Kansas City's residence district. His active congregation, even his Summer congregation, is by no means the smallest in town. But it wasn't large enough for the Rev. Mr. Draper.

Motor cars—Sundays—touring—church attendance. There was the association of ideas and a possible solution! Dr. Draper assembled the men of his congregation and expounded his idea. They were all for it. At the morning service the important part motor cars were to play in the evening prayer meeting was explained.

At 8 o'clock that night the members of the congregation drove up to the church in their motor cars. They didn't park and alight, for they beheld Dr. Draper, their pastor, standing erect in the tonneau of his car, which was stationed beside the church in a large vacant lot. The pastor smiled and bowed his greeting, signaled and a corps of assistants suddenly were changed into temporary traffic patrolmen, directing the cars into a semi-circular formation about the automobile of the pastor.

The families sat, obviously delighted with the comfort of their mobile pews. The dignity of the assemblage was perfectly preserved and there were no late comers. More than fifty cars were parked in the lot and at the curbs. Their occupants accorded close attention as the preacher launched into his sermon.

"To serve a modern world, so must a church be modern," Dr. Draper began. "This is my 'Church on Wheels.' Many churches, you know, have been racing their engines and just burning up gas," he continued. "It's time to stop this."

"The Church on Wheels" appears to be an established institution. Services were announced immediately for the succeeding Sunday. And it is planned that they continue until indoor weather comes on.

September 5, 1920

BISHOPS 'SOFTEN' BURIAL SERVICE

Cut Out References to "Worms" and "Beasts" in the Episcopal Ritual.

INSERT PRAYERS FOR DEAD

Vote to Permit Reading of Service at Funerals of Suicides and Unbaptized Adults.

Special to The New York Times.

PORTLAND, Ore., Sept. 14.—The House of Bishops of the general convention of the Episcopal Church rescinded today the age-old law that the church's burial service cannot be read by an Episcopalian clergyman at the funeral of a suicide, an unbaptized adult or one who has died " ex communicate." If the House of Deputies concurs, hereafter a suicide can be buried with the same ritual as the person who dies a natural death.

The rubric, eliminated by a vote of 47 to 43, reads:

" Here is to be noted that the office ensuing is not to be used for any unbaptized adult, any who die ex communicate or who have laid violent hands upon himself." The chief argument in favor of the change was that the man who took his own life was out of his mind and God alone was his Judge.

Two prayers for the dead in the funeral service were agreed to almost unanimously. The only opposition expressed was that of Bishop Reese of Georgia, who said that some of the Bishops did not want to have to pray for the dead. It was explained that the prayers were to be " permissive."

If the House of Deputies concurs, this will put prayers for the dead into the prayer book for the first time since the sixteenth century.

Reference to Worms Cut Out.

On the ground that it was not a comforting thought, the phrase, " and though after my skin worms destroy this body " was omitted from the second sentence in the burial ritual. Some of the Bishops wanted to cut out the whole sentence, which begins, " I know that my Redeemer liveth," but it was finally voted, 54 to 34, to substitute the following:

" I know that my Redeemer liveth and that he shall stand at the latter day upon the earth, and, though this body shall be destroyed, yet shall I see God, whom I shall see for myself and mine eyes shall behold."

It was voted to change the words, " Thou fool," in I. Corinthians, xx., which is a part of the service, to " Thou Foolish Man," which is the language of the American revised version.

All reference that it was " pleasing " to Almighty God to take any one out of this world was cut out of the burial service.

The verses in First Corinthians, Chapter XX., which mentions " Beasts," were eliminated.

The predominating aim throughout the burial service revision has been to soften what are considered harsh parts of the service and make it more comforting to the bereaved.

A memorial from the women's auxiliary of the diocese of Pennsylvania asking that the Episcopal Church inaugurate work for the conversion of Jews was referred to the Council of the Episcopal Church. Suffragan Bishop Garland of Philadelphia said the Episcopal Church was the only one which did not do such work.

The report of the joint commission on faith and order was adopted by the House of Bishops, after Bishop Anderson of Chicago, who for nine years was President of the commission, had declared there was need of a man to devote all his time to its work.

Sees Need of an Executive.

Bishop Anderson said the work of preparing for the World Conference to be held in Washington in May, 1925, was being retarded because there was not such an executive. He added that he had in his mind the right man, whereupon Bishop Manning of New York said he had no hesitation in mentioning the right man for the office, and that man was Bishop Brent of Buffalo, N. Y. No action was taken.

Robert H. Gardiner, Secretary of the Commission on Faith and Order since its organization, was praised by Bishop Brent, who said that when the commission was hampered in arranging for the Washington conference because of lack of money Mr. Gardiner had made up a deficiency of $14,000 out of his own pocket.

Among the resolutions passed was one asking the Episcopal Church for $25,000 a year for the next three years. This was referred to the Committee on Finances. Another resolution passed was that each Bishop should organize prayer groups in his diocese of Christians of all faiths to pray for the Washington conference.

The Executive Committee will meet in London in 1924. The Bishops authorized the joint commission to appoint delegates from the Episcopal Church.

Bishops Adopt Divorce Canon.

The House of Bishops adopted late this afternoon the canon prohibiting any divorced communicant of the Episcopal Church from remarrying, or any communicant from marrying a divorced person, the one exception being the innocent party where the divorce was granted for infidelity.

Bishop Mann of Southern Florida introduced a resolution which would deprive such persons as knowingly break this canon of the sacraments of the Episcopal Church, except in case of imminent death. The resolution was referred to the Committee on Canons.

At a great mass meeting this evening Bishop Rowe of Alaska, was presented with a purse of $71,000, the income of which is to be used for missionary work in Alaska. The presentation was in honor of his silver anniversary as a missionary in the frozen North.

The House of Deputies adopted today a resolution condemning the Ku Klux Klan.

The deputies late this afternoon threw out the word " obey " in the marriage ceremony. This makes this revision final, the House of Bishops having taken similar action yesterday. All women, however, who get married by Episcopal ministers in the next three years will have to take the vow of obedience to their husbands, as none of these changes in the Prayer Book becomes effective until the next triennial convention.

The Rev. Dr. George Craig Stewart of Evanston, Ill., reminded the deputies that this was the twentieth century, and that the idea of a wife obeying her husband had no place in life today. One deputy remarked that the Lord did not take a bone out of the man's head or his foot to make the first woman, but out of his side, thereby showing that the wife was to be a helpmate, with full equality.

September 15, 1922

Mr. Barton Makes a "Success Story" of the Life of Christ

"Stripped of All Dogma," He Says, "This Is the Grandest Achievement Story of All."

THE MAN NOBODY KNOWS: A Discovery of Jesus. By Bruce Barton. 220 pp. Indianapolis: The Bobbs-Merrill Company. $2.50.

ONE of the high priests of modern advertising has written a book about Jesus Christ. It is a book different from any other that has been written about Him. Mr. Barton's interpretation is certain to shock many readers, though it is reverent; it will convince many, though others will find it often dropping into absurdity. But it will interest everybody. "The Man Nobody Knows" was written out of sincere conviction. That much is evident from the first page to the last. It is the product of a revolt that began, Mr. Barton tells us, in Sunday school. As a boy he could not see why his teacher repeatedly told him that he must love Jesus. He was not attracted by the frail figure, the sad face that looked down on him from the wall. He liked the pictures of Daniel and David and Moses, but this Jesus was "the lamb of God." He was "meek and lowly," he was "a man of sorrows" and went around telling people not to do things. As he grew up he began to wonder about Jesus.

He said to himself: "Only strong, magnetic men inspire great enthusiasm and build great organizations. Yet Jesus built the greatest organization of all. It is extraordinary."

He decided to go back to the original sources, to free his mind from old conceptions and to see what the Gospels said. And Mr. Barton "was amazed."

A physical weakling! Where did they get that idea? Jesus pushed a plane and swung an adze; He was a successful carpenter. He slept outdoors and spent His days walking around His favorite lake. His muscles were so strong that when He drove the money-changers out nobody dared oppose Him!

A kill-joy! He was the most popular dinner guest in Jerusalem. The criticism which proper people made was that He spent too much time with publicans and sinners and enjoyed society too much. They called Him a "wine-bibber and a gluttonous man."

A failure! He picked up twelve men from the bottom ranks of business and forged them into an organization that conquered the world.

From those three paragraphs you can catch the outlines of the picture Mr. Barton builds up. It is a picture which when finished portrays Jesus not so completely as it does those manly characteristics enshrined in the creed of American salesmanship. It is a picture in which the go-getter, the worshiper of "personality" and of the "human dynamo," the mixer, the man who can "sell himself" and who can "put his message across" will take comfort. Says Mr. Barton: "Stripped of all dogma this is the grandest achievement story of all!"

Bruce Barton.
© Pirie MacDonald.

It is, of course, entirely reasonable to suppose that Jesus was of a different physical type than the religious painters have habitually pictured Him. The very conditions of His life give support to that belief. He must have done hard manual labor in His youth, for, as Mr. Barton points out, a carpenter's work was more exacting then than now; and during the years of His ministry His life was of the sort to keep Him in robust physical condition.

Nor does one need any more evidence than the Gospels provide to see that Jesus enjoyed the company of men. He was no recluse like John the Baptist. Mr. Barton is sure that He laughed, and probably He did.

So far, well enough. But Mr. Barton is not content to emphasize the healthy humanity of Jesus. He must defend Him from the charge of being a failure, and one wonders why the author feels the necessity of that. But spiritual triumph, apparently, is not enough; there is a "success story" here in terms which the twentieth century can understand. Jesus was a born executive, unerring in His perception of how to pick His subordinates and how to get the most out of them; a born organizer; the founder of modern advertising, who knew how to make the front page every day.

In filling out that side of his picture Mr. Barton, without at all

meaning to, belittles the meaning and purpose of his subject's work. Possessed by this Rotarian vision of his, he swings the Gospels forcibly into line with the commandments of the business world. What did Jesus mean, he asks, when He said: "And whosoever shall compel thee to go a mile, go with him twain?" Why, this is the very gospel of achievement; this is admonition for the clock-watchers; Jesus is telling us to work after hours. Had Mr. Barton so soon forgotten that this was part of the Sermon on the Mount, that the sentence he quotes was immediately preceded by these:

But I say unto you, That ye resist not evil; but whosoever shall smite thee on thy right cheek, turn to him the other also.

And if any man sue thee at the law and take away thy coat, let him have thy cloak also.

And all three of these admonitions led up to the counsel that followed:

But I say unto you, Love your enemies, bless them that curse you, do good to them that hate you and pray for them which despitefully use you and persecute you.

There was the incident of the stilling of the tempest. As the story is told in the Gospels, Jesus was awakened by the frightened disciples, who feared their boat would sink.

And He saith unto them, Why are ye fearful, O ye of little faith? Then He arose and rebuked the waves and the sea, and there was a great calm.

Faith may be all very well, but the picture of an unflurried executive, with "2 o'clock in the morning courage," issuing "a few quiet orders" so that "presently the menaced boat swung around into the smoother waters of safety" is better suited to Mr. Barton's purpose. Even his emphasis on the physical characteristics of Jesus becomes distorted when he makes Pilate, "his cheeks fatty with self-indulgence" and with "the colorless look of indoor living," exclaim in admiration when he brought Jesus out before His accusers, "Behold the man!" Those were Pilate's words, but in their context they are perfunctory, a mere identification.

The reasons why Mr. Barton recommends to the attention of sales managers every one of Jesus' conversations, "every contact between His mind and others," are fairly obvious. Jesus knew how to secure attention, how to work concisely and simply toward His point, how to drive it home by repetition. He knew the value of homely illustration, the worth of a story. But it is a bit hard to reconcile Mr. Barton's belief that He was consciously an advertiser in the modern sense, "the greatest of His time," with Jesus' own repeated instructions to those whom He healed to "let no man know of this."

Mr. Barton's book, it may be added, is itself a model of crisp advertising English.

AIMEE M'PHERSON TELLS LIFE STORY

Big Crowds Weep and Shout as Evangelist Sways Them With Revival Spirit.

Switches to Allegory In Referring to "Kidnapping," Saying Satan Sought to End Her Work.

Mrs. Aimee Semple McPherson told the story of her life yesterday afternoon at the Glad Tidings Chapel in West Thirty-third Street. She told it in detail up to a certain point and then reverting to the sermon form she told how Satan and his satellites planned her destruction, entered the hearts of men, persuaded them to kidnap her and then framed up the story of her ten days with Kenneth Ormiston, radio operator of Angelus Temple, in a bungalow at Carmel, Cal.

"I was always interested in radio," she said early in her talk. "I can reach so many souls broadcasting. I was interested in its mechanical end, its batteries and tubes and antennae and wave lengths, but," and then she cried out, "I never was interested in radio operators."

Cheers Greet Her Words.

Cheers, hand-clapping, "Hallelujas," "Praise the Lords" and "Amens" resounded through the auditorium crowded to capacity for this meeting. Inside the altar rail people sat on the floor. Men sat cross-legged on the stage around the feet of the speaker. Downstairs in the chapel another crowd heard the evangelist through amplifiers and her story was carried to hundreds in the street who stood in the storm and the driving wind for more than an hour to listen.

"I've heard 'em all," said one old man who hadn't missed a meeting, "and she's up to Beecher. She's the only one of the lot can touch Henry Ward Beecher."

In the narrative of her life the evangelist worked in a sharp attack on evolution.

"It nearly ruined me," she said as she talked of her early years on a farm in Canada, "and now it's trying to ruin America. It is making our young men murderers."

Then she told how her mother dedicated her to God as Hannah did Samuel; how instead of Cinderella and Mother Goose she "went to sleep with Jonah and the Whale and Daniel in the Lions' Den." She read Paine, Darwin and Ingersoll, she said, and questioned her mother about her reading. The mother was a Salvationist, she asserted, a confirmed attendant at revivals, and it was at a revival that Aimee turned to this work.

Describes Her Marriage.

A vigorous young evangelist came to the little town, and his name was Robert Semple, she said. "He had curly brown hair and a beautiful face, and he upset me. I said to my father, 'Daddy, let's go'."

The evangelist went away, and three days later as she was driving home alone "the fire came down" and she was "saved." She corresponded with the tall young man with the curly hair and he came back. Then followed the engagement, the wedding, a revivalist trip across the country, and then to China. For two years her husband preached, "while I boosted and admired." Next came sickness for both and her husband's death in the ward of a Hongkong hospital.

Without money and with two children, the 20-year-old widow started home. Evangelism was all she knew, Mrs. McPherson said, and with $65 from her first real meeting she bought a tent. Now, she continued, she had a great temple with scores of meetings a week built from the proceeds of collections. A college for evangelists is almost completed, and "until last Spring there seemed no possible limit to the work of the Lord."

Sways Audience by Recital.

In this recital Mrs. McPherson held her audience, took them with her to China, to the deathbed of her husband. Tears appeared in her eyes and tears answered from the audience. The sotto voce of a camp meeting accompanied her, swelled and died down and swelled again. When it became too strong—almost up to "moanin' meetin'" pitch—she told a funny story, playing on her hearers like an organist at his instrument.

"Then Satan—I can see him down in hell, hearing reports from his captains. One came and said he had bad news: a great revival in Los Angeles, saving souls by the thousand. The revivalist cannot be stopped.

"'What, a woman!' exclaimed Satan. 'That's easy, we'll prick her reputation and we'll destroy her like a bubble.'"

Then, she went on, the Tower of Babel was built of lies and plots and kidnapping and innuendo until it reared its top so high that all the country saw it, read the story in the papers. But God finally took notice, she said, and with His little finger turned over this tower and it fell with a crash.

"And how did He do it?" cried the speaker.

"He spread confusion of tongues," answered a hundred listeners.

"A confusion of tongues it was," Mrs. McPherson responded. "They told so many stories about this woman, gray hair, brown hair, gold hair, red hair." She touched her own blond head. "They couldn't stick together on their story. They thought with me out of the way Angelus Temple would collapse, and it didn't, and it's going bigger than ever before. The 'Four-Square Gospel' carries on! Hallelujah!"

Magnetism Sweeps Crowd.

The auditorium rang with hallelujahs. Women wept and men shouted. She had told nothing about her kidnapping, but the fact of her presence, her magnetism and her enthusiasm was convincing enough for even the skeptical—and few of them were present.

A collection was taken to help pay the expenses of Mrs. McPherson's trip. As the Rev. Robert A. Brown explained this, the evangelist interrupted to tell the potential givers that the janitor of the church had handed her a $10 bill as she came in, and she waved it for all to see.

In her night meeting Mrs. McPherson again preached to a large crowd on "The Great Triangle," a sermon relating to the beheading of John the Baptist and in which she dwelt at length and with variations on the fate of John the Baptist. She again asked for converts to "come and be saved" and more than 200 men and women went forward. There was another collection, an announcement by Mrs. McPherson that she wanted the godly present to pray for her return next Summer and the rental of Madison Square Garden for another revival of the "Four-Square Gospel."

The collection seemed quite generous. Mrs. McPherson would not indicate the amount, but admitted it would be "enough to pay expenses."

Following the night meeting Mrs. McPherson paid a visit to Paul Whiteman, orchestra leader at his new night club at Broadway and Forty-eighth Street. She had met Mr. Whiteman's father during a recent visit to Denver and had promised him that she would call on his son when she came to New York. She had a short talk with the orchestra leader, watched the dancing for a time and then left for her hotel.

There is a possibility, Mrs. McPherson said last night, that she may return to New York next Summer and conduct a revival campaign in Madison Square Garden. Her call for a show of hands on the desire of her audience to have her conduct such a campaign revealed a unanimous sentiment in favor of it.

From New York Mrs. McPherson goes to Syracuse and Rochester, thence to Florida and back to California.

ASSAILS MRS. McPHERSON.

Attacking Mrs. Aimee Semple McPherson's evangelistic movement as "fanatical and fraudulent," and declaring that it should not "engage the attention of those who are really listening for the voice of a prophet," the Rev. Frank H. Nelson, formerly of the Los Angeles Presbytery, delivered as a "prologue" to his sermon yesterday morning before the Chelsea Presbyterian Church a brief talk entitled "Why Aimee McPherson Is All Wrong." The Chelsea Presbyterian Church is meeting in the auditorium of the Twenty-third Street Y. M. C. A. while its new building is being erected.

"Only gullible people who give credence to every fad and fancy are led astray by Mrs. McPherson," he said. "The facts about her movement should be known and people should not allow themselves to be fooled by sentimental piffle and press-agent tommyrot." Mrs. McPherson can well make her boast that she is "keeping up to the amusement world," he said, adding, "Mrs. McPherson has lived too near to Hollywood to keep from the movies' pet trick of getting publicity through moral scandal."

February 21, 1927

100 Evangelists Admit Their Work Has Failed; Radio, Auto, Sports, Commercialism Blamed

Evangelism has failed, and commercialism, radios, automobiles and sports are among the reasons, according to Charles Stelzle, publicity representative of various religious and semi-religious organizations. In a statement yesterday he declared he had arrived at this conclusion after examining replies to questionnaires he sent to 100 prominent evangelists.

"It was the almost unanimous opinion of the evangelists," he said, "that men are more spiritually minded than women when once they are 'converted'; that it is increasingly difficult to interest women in religion, and that the interest of women in religion is comparatively superficial.

"Nearly all of those questioned admitted that evangelistic work is becoming more difficult, that the number of 'converts' is distressingly small, and those who are still doing evangelistic work professionally are not engaged more than half the time. Thirty others who did not reply to the questionnaire in detail said they had given up evangelism because they could no longer make a living in this field.

The average income of evangelists was about $3,000 yearly, with "free-will offerings" much smaller than ten years ago, he said.

Few churches employed evangelistic methods today, he went on, while many evangelists "could be counted uneducated," but "some of them are men of high scholastic standings; about 90 per cent are ordained ministers." He found evangelism more prevalent in the Middle West and South than in the East, and least popular in the West. The "effectiveness" of evangelism, he reports, "has decreased from 80 per cent down to 10 per cent, although it is claimed by many that while there are fewer 'converts' those who are converted are of a better type."

"It was generally admitted," he continued, "that the present unpopularity in the churches regarding evangelism and evangelists has been brought on by the evangelists themselves.

"There is a strong feeling that nothing but the 'old-time religion' will ever change conditions. By this is meant the message which they have been preaching for a generation and which, apparently, has not succeeded in winning audiences."

July 28, 1930

GAMES AND AWARDS AID SUNDAY SCHOOLS

Survey by Dr. N. C. Harner Shows Most Members Are Gained by Varied Activities.

RURAL GROWTH MORE RAPID

All-Day Auto Trips Among the Worst Sunday Offenses Listed in Inquiry, He Declares.

An elaborate program of superficial activities greatly aid the membership growth of Sunday schools, Dr. Nevin C. Harner, research worker at Teachers College, Columbia University, said yesterday in announcing the results of his survey on "Factors Related to Sunday School Growth and Decline."

Taking the data based upon an analysis over a period of eight years of 468 Sunday schools in the Eastern Synod of the Reformed Church in the United States, having a membership of approximately 150,000, Dr. Harner found that Sunday schools were attended with a greater degree of regularity if an orchestra were present or if a system of special awards and prizes were given as inducements.

Sunday schools in the rural districts gained members considerably faster than those in the city, according to Dr. Harner. Although this fact carries "encouragement" for ministers and workers in the country, it contains a "note of seriousness" concerning the future influence of the Sunday school, he declared.

"The rate of growth is small in the type of community in which the population and the life of the nation are concentrating more and more," he pointed out, adding that "it is probable that the peculiar problems of the city—counter attractions, paucity of contacts during the week, and loss of neighborhood consciousness—retard the growth of its Sunday schools."

Studying four of the schools inten-sively, Dr. Harner discovered that "paying admission to parks, games and the like" was regarded as the most serious offense that could be committed on Sunday. Making all-day automobile trips came next, followed by missing Sunday school once a month, taking part in games, watching games for which no admission is charged, swimming, and singing songs other than hymns."

The outstanding means for accomplishing the purpose of the Sunday School are "Bible study" and "worship," which caused Dr. Harner to remark that "the Bible is given a prominent place as a means to an end, rather than as an end in itself." "Games, hikes, socials" are considered to have the least value for the pupils of the Sunday School.

"Teachers well trained for their work," he said, "and a program attractive and worthwhile commend themselves as stimulants of growth, although their effect probably will be manifested more slowly than that of many meetings and activities. Also, contests for new members and attendance, the giving of awards for perfect attendance and similar devices may be expected to play their part in obtaining growth."

August 24, 1931

NEED OF A RELIGIOUS REVOLUTION

Bishop Rhinelander's Idea of What Is Required to Stem the Rising Tide Toward a "Pagan America"

HAS the United States, as a nation, turned away from the Christian religion? Bishop Philip M. Rhinelander of the Episcopal Diocese of Pennsylvania says there is not only a definitely anti-Christian drift but that it seems to be increasing in rapidity of force and movement. He startled the recent Church Convention in Philadelphia by his frank statement that the Church must meet this new condition squarely. When asked the other day to elaborate his views, he said:

"I believe that we, as a nation, have turned away from Christ. I would not consciously nor willingly exaggerate. Hysteria is a miserable ally in a great cause. But is there exaggeration in this statement? If we look for gauges or tests of civilization we are on the right track in taking as decisive signs education, in its ideals and results; literature, as popularly current, and the favorite amusements of the people. Apply these tests to our world—that is, to the world

as we know it—and see how in each case there is evident a definitely anti-Christian drift, which seems to be increasing in force and rapidity of movement.

"Phobia" of Unbelief.

"A current book by a brilliant and discerning essayist speaks of 'a collective and hereditary phobia against all belief' which characterizes 'not merely individuals but the universal modern mind.' No one, I think, familiar with the general trend and outcome of school and college education, or with the spirit of contemporary culture, would question this judgment. There is a 'phobia' of unbelief."

"Do you mean there have been changes in the curriculum of a number of schools? That theology is not taught as it was formerly or that it has been discarded altogether?" the Bishop was asked.

"This is what I mean," he answered. "The almost universal tendency is to teach ethics or morals without any direct relation to the Christian faith, so that the average boy or girl comes out of school or college with the notion that Christianity is an interesting but outworn philosophy and that even its ethical and moral standards are not final and of no particular authority. I know of no great university in this country where even among the elective courses the student can find any definite instruction in the historic Christian faith, as though it were today a living reality with a claim on modern intelligence and thought. It is probably a fact that at any of our leading colleges the student can get more definite instruction in Mohammedanism or Buddhism or almost any other of the ethnic religions than he can in Christianity.

"In literature," he continued, "the highest place is, for the first time in history, freely given to the novelists. Writers of fiction are hailed as prophets of the truth and the best guides of conscience. In the pages of these 'best sellers' and high priests of public morals you will find the most sacred Christian institutions treated with scorn and ridicule. And in particular the ideals of purity and continence and holy marriage are frankly thrown in the dust heap.

Modern Literature's Tendency.

"One cannot help but be struck by the undoubted fact that there has been and may be still a certain refinement of taste which shrinks from the brutal frankness characterized by earlier ages. But along with that frankness there was present and was recognized a very definite idealism and an influencing recognition of Christian standards as being of unquestioned validity and requiring the homage of all rightminded men and women. Shakespeare himself is coarse beyond the limits of modern prudery, but there is no question of the splendid spiritual power that speaks all through Shakespeare and vindicates with the whole force of his genius the truth and elevation of Christian ideals. What one feels about modern literature is that most of the popular writers frankly lay the axe at the root of all modern standards and advocate the right of each man to be a law unto himself and to be governed by his own unbridled passions. That is the chasm which separates our literature from the literature of every classic age in the past.

"As for amusements, immodesty in dress, looseness in sexual relations, bestiality and crime as chief attractions in theatrical shows and photoplays, unbridled license and extravagance in all things, are so much the established order of the day that the most respectable among us have ceased even to shrug our shoulders. What makes the situation so infinitely tragic is the fact that the worst of it has happened since the war. Fighting stopped, and reconstruction is supposed to have begun, eighteen months ago. We won the war, but seemingly we lost all that we were fighting for.

"Since the armistice it is universally agreed that there has been a loosening of moral fiber, a determined, almost defiant, turning away from work and discipline and sacrifice; a draining off of our scanty spiritual supplies till there is little left save animal selfishness and crude materialism. 'Bolshevism,' reduced to simplest terms, means reversion to type. It is an outlandish and newfangled name for the most ancient and most dreadfully familiar fact in human history. When men revert to type, when they turn Bolshevist, the ape and the tiger in them come to the surface and assume control.

"That is what is happening in these days of peace. Dr. Sturgis, from the Department of Missions in New York, at a memorable meeting here in Philadelphia the other night, prophesied that as the result of a careful and impartial

PHILIP M. RHINELANDER

survey a book would be written shortly, entitled 'Pagan America.' The phrase sticks in my mind. I commend it to you because it puts the whole matter in two words—Pagan America.

The Church's Position.

"Does the Church see it? See it not as a passing spectacle, but as a vision of truth which lays hold of and possesses those who see? Is the Church prepared to become a genuinely missionary body, an army on campaign, driven by the single impulse to make Christ known and loved throughout the length and breadth of our land, to bring America into God's kingdom?

"Speaking humanly (and I want to speak humanly), nothing seems more improbable. The facts, past and present, of our history do not warrant the belief that we are ready for a spiritual revolution. For it would mean just that. Call it a 'revival' if you will. 'Revolution' seems to me a better name because a more dynamic word. It suggests more sharply that an inward change is impotent and futile without corresponding outward action. It reminds us that the verbal acknowledgments of Jesus Christ as Lord and King are sheer hypocrisy unless He really has the government of us and our goods.

"And in addition, 'revolution' is a timely word. It is in the air. It is the threat which those we call our enemies are holding over us. It is always good strategy to outguess and anticipate the enemy. A spiritual revolution in the Church might be the sure and certain way to remove all danger of a political revolution by the Soviets. It would mean, first, a revolution in our expenditure. The 'expenses of the kingdom' would come at the head of our personal budgets, not at the tail. The list of items would not run as now: rent, food, fuel, wages, clothes and recreation, with a certain part of the remainder, if there be any, given to God. It would run: first, the Kingdom, its maintenance and increase, reserving what is necessary, not for luxurious

comfort or indulgence but for the greatest bodily and spiritual efficiency and happiness of me and mine. That would be, indeed, a turning upside down of settled habit. Is there the least chance of it?

"But such a revolution involves more, much more. There would be definite and sustained personal service of the Lord on the part of every one. The schedule of each business, professional and working man and woman would reserve certain hours in each day for the work of the campaign. Each would serve according to his gift: by teaching, visiting, protecting, feeding, healing, watching, helping, saving—personally going about doing good where good is waiting to be done. This again would be a revolution. For at present there is only a handful out of the whole who, if you leave out Church-going and check-drawing, do anything at all in the name of the Lord Jesus. Is it possible or thinkable that the whole body of us should be willing to sign on for service?

"But even that would not be all. The most essential, and the most difficult, thing remains. There is prayer: prayer not for ourselves, not even for our own salvation; but for the Kingdom and its coming: prayer that shall be believing prayer, conscious and confident of the power it is wielding: prayer that shall be intelligent, knowing what the needs are and how to meet them: prayer that shall be so definite an obligation that we keep to it as we keep our promises to our friends. To get us all at prayer who pray so seldom and so feebly now: that were a miracle indeed. To get $1,300,000 out of our people annually would be child's play compared to the extraordinary difficulty of getting all our people on their knees each day for fifteen minutes. That really is the heart of the whole matter. Prayer will convert America. Nothing else will. But how to win us all to prayer is a problem which staggers the imagination."

BAPTISTS ATTACK 'INFIDEL' TEACHING

Stormy Debate Leads to Vote for Inquiry Into Denomination's Seminaries.

Special to The New York Times.

BUFFALO, June 23.—After a stormy debate, the Northern Baptist Convention, which opened its thirteenth annual session today in the Broadway Auditorium here, voted this evening to appoint a committee of nine members to investigate all the theological seminaries, colleges and secondary schools of the Baptist denomination, and, "so far as is possible, to cleanse them of all infidelic teaching." The convention will continue through next Tuesday.

The resolution adopted today was offered originally by the Rev. Dr. Herbert J. White of Hartford, Conn., but was amended considerably by Judge F. W. Freeman of Denver, Col. It was, indeed, a substitute for a more searching resolution offered by the Rev. Dr. George E. Massee of the Baptist Temple, Brooklyn, who until recently was pastor in Dayton, Ohio.

Dr. Massee's resolution was drawn up at a preliminary conference on "Fundamentals of the Christian Faith," which was held Monday and Tuesday, and which was called by 150 prominent ministers and laymen throughout the United States.

The committee officially agreed upon is to consist of nine members, and they were nominated by Dr. Massee. The Rev. Dr. William B. Riley, Pastor of the First Baptist Church and President of the Northwestern Bible School, withdrew and asked that the President of the Convention have power to fill his place.

The Rev. Dr. Frank M. Goodchild, Pastor of the Central Church, New York, heads the committee. The other members are: I. W. Carpenter, Omaha, Neb.; the Rev. Dr. J. W. Brougher, Los Angeles, Cal; Henry Bond, Brattleboro, Vt.; C. R. Brock, Denver; Judge Edward B. Cinch, New York City; the Rev. A. K. Dubois, Boston, and the Rev. J. J. Ross, pastor of the Second Church, Chicago.

No Baptist institution of learning was called by name. At first there was a disposition to have the convention or the presiding officer appoint the committee, but finally, on motion of the Rev. Dr. Milton G. Evans, President of Crozier Theological Seminary of Philadelphia, the committee recommended by the "fundamentals conference" was elected.

June 24, 1920

Church Assembly Condemns Modern Women's Dress

GREENFIELD, Mo., May 21.—The Cumberland Presbyterian Church today recorded unalterable opposition to card playing, dancing and Sunday baseball, and condemned modern women's dress and immoral motion picture films.

"Too many in the pulpit and people are looking with some degree of allowance on the card table, the dance and the miserable debauching modern dress, Sunday baseball and obscene motion picture shows," said a resolution adopted by the General Assembly of the denomination.

The next Assembly will meet at Greenville, Tenn.

September 19, 1921

Both Jazz Music and Jazz Dancing Barred From All Louisville Episcopal Churches

Special to The New York Times.

LOUISVILLE, Ky., Sept. 18.—The death knell of jazz music and dancing, so far as the Episcopal Church is concerned, was sounded officially this morning before fourteen Episcopal congregations in Louisville and as many more in the environs. This is the result of resolutions adopted by the Clericus of the Episcopal Church of Louisville and its vicinity in Christ Church Cathedral.

The resolutions, prepared by the Very Rev. Richard L. McCready, Dean of the cathedral, were unanimously received by the body and sanctioned by the Right Rev. Charles E. Woodcock, Bishop of the Diocese of Kentucky.

Stating that such forms of pleasure lead to jazz manners and jazz morals among the younger members of the Church, the organization declared that "under no circumstances should they be permitted in any church or parish house under Episcopal control."

Couples retiring to automobiles and remaining there during dances were frowned on also by the body, which held that property appointed persons should have authority and ought to, at least every half hour during the continuance of the entertainment, to examine rigorously to ascertain that the practice was not being followed.

Members of the Clericus said that the body always had taken a liberal position toward dancing as a form of recreation, but conditions having progressed to such an extent, "a reasonable check must be made for community good."

Dean McCready, in presenting his resolutions, said his study began a year ago.

"Louisville must take some means of protecting the younger members of society," he said, "and there is no better agency to advance this work than the church."

"The Episcopal Church, unknowingly, by its lenient attitude has fostered the present tendency, and must command all facilities within its power to right the wrong."

Referring to all dances in parish houses, the body stated that "These, either when under the direct control of the congregation, or when rented to other organizations, should be chaperoned adequately and wisely by competent and reliable men and women of sound judgment and discretion, approved by the Clergy, who should have full authority to exclude and eject any persons whose presence or actions shall by them be deemed objectionable.'"

May 22, 1921

METHODISTS LIFT AMUSEMENT BAN

Dancing, Theatre Attendance and Cards Left to Conscience of Church Members.

MAY STILL BE EXPELLED

Pastor or Class Leader May Punish Those Persisting in Forbidden Diversions.

Special to The New York Times.

SPRINGFIELD, Mass., May 27.—Despite the expressed fears of Judge W. M. Short of Fort Worth, Texas, that Methodist young people would be tempted to try the "bunny hug," "tango" and "the shimmy" we hear about, the Methodist General Conference today adopted the majority report of the Committee on State of the Church, radically modifying the ban on amusements. Not more than 100 delegates opposed the change.

The rigid law adopted fifty-two years ago, holding a member liable to expulsion from the church for attending theatres, dances, horse races, circuses, &c., has been dropped. In its place a provision has been adopted leaving indulgence in such amusements to the conscience of the individual member, with the proviso, however, that he still may be tried and expelled if he persists in going to entertainments of which his pastor or class leader does not approve. In judging the character of the entertainments, the individual member and the pastor are to consider whether they are "diversions which cannot be used in the name of the Lord Jesus." This is a phrase written into the church constitution by John Wesley.

To check any idea among Methodists in general that amusements, previously banned, are openly approved by the Church, the Conference promulgated special advice against frequenting various types of amusement and also authorized the Board of Temperance, Prohibition and Public Morals to lead the Church in a campaign of education and publicity against "the dangers lurking in entertainments against which we warn."

Delegates in favor of the amendment said that dance hall proprietors and theatre managers would find little comfort in the new provisions for they merely mean that the Church has dropped an old law, which was frequently disobeyed because it was not workable, and has substituted an appeal to the conscience of the church members, to be supplemented by a campaign that should hold the members in line much better than the law did. In no way, it is asserted, does the new amendment open the way to approval of dancing in churches such as is indulged in by several other denominations.

Dr. George Elliott, Chairman of the Committee on the State of the Church, in arguing for the adoption of the majority report, said:

"We know that theatres are immoral, that dances are indecent and that there is an immense amount of social immorality. Commercialized amusement debauches everything. Dancing has ceased to be esthetic and has become acrobatic and athletic. The theatres are vile in that they breath the smell of sex.

"But instead of a law against these things, we should have a religion that appeals to the conscience of a man and keeps him away from these things. We will change the minister standing in the pulpit with a police club in his hand to a minister standing there with a shepherd's crook."

The paragraph in the discipline on amusements as adopted today will read:

"In cases of neglect of duties of any kind; imprudent conduct; indulging in sinful tempers or words; taking such diversions as cannot be used in the name of the Lord Jesus; or disobedience to the order and discipline of the church; on the first offense, let private reproof be given by the pastor or class leader, and if there be an acknowledg-

ment of the fault and proper humiliation, the persons may be borne with. On further offense, the pastor or class leader may take with him one or two discreet members of the church. On continued offense, let him be brought to trial, and if found guilty and there be no sign of real humiliation, he shall be expelled."

The special advice that has been altered by the change reads as follows:

"Improper amusements and excessive indulgence in innocent amusements are serious barriers to the beginning of religious life and fruitful causes to spiritual decline. Some amusements in common use are positively demoralizing and furnish the first easy steps to the total loss of character. We therefore look with deep concern on the great increase of amusements and on the general prevalence of harmful amusements and lift up a solemn note of warning and entreaty, particularly against attendance upon immoral, questionable and misleading theatrical or motion picture performances; against dancing and against such games of chance as are frequently associated with gambling, all of which have been found to be antagonistic to vital piety, promotive of worldliness and especially pernicious to youth. We affectionately admonish all our people to make their amusements the subject of careful thought and frequent prayer to study the subject of amusements in the light of their tendencies and to be scrupulously careful in this matter to set no injurious example. We adjure them to remember that often the question for a Christian must be not whether a certain course of action is positively immoral but whether it will dull the spiritual life and be an unwise example."

The Rev. David D. Forsythe of Philadelphia, was re-elected secretary of the Board of Home Missions and Church Extensions.

The conference voted to put unification of North and South Methodist Churches, already approved, before the Northern Conference in 1925, if the South Church accepts the plan at its special meeting in July.

An old-time custom was broken this afternoon when a woman delegate was nominated for an important office. The honor went to Mrs. Peter F. Stair of Detroit, who received twenty-five votes on the first ballot for secretary of the Board of Education. The first ballot resulted in no election and another ballot was taken, the result of which will be announced tomorrow.

May 28, 1924

THE "FUNDAMENTALISTS."

The Northern Baptist Convention at Indianapolis will hardly be an example of brethren dwelling together in unity, but it may mark an important point in the history of American Protestantism. A powerful and well-organized movement in favor of "the fundamentals of the Christian faith" is endeavoring to take control of the denominational machinery away from the liberal wing. The Fundamentalists believe in the literal inspiration of the Bible, "its "history, its miracles, its doctrine "and its prophecies." They imported that eminent Presbyterian layman Mr. BRYAN on Tuesday to fortify Baptist faith with a sermon about DARWIN and the Zoo. Hitherto the Baptists have had no formal written creed, and within certain vague but extensive limits the individual congregation could do as seemed good to it. The Fundamentalists, or some of them, are talking of setting up an exact and unalterable confession of faith, so that thereafter heresy will no longer be tolerated.

Freedom of conscience has certainly been one of the "fundamentals" of Baptist doctrine, and it is now seriously threatened. Baptists of the South, more numerous than their Northern brethren, are almost all Fundamentalists. They are against church union or church co-operation, and many of them are cold to the religion of works. Premillennial beliefs are widely spread among them; of what use to spend money on social service if the end of the world is at hand? It is a critical week at Indianapolis for the Baptists.

June 15, 1922

BAPTISTS REJECT A FORMAL CREED

Great Majority at Indianapolis Declares the New Testament Enough.

FUNDAMENTALISTS BEATEN

They Fail to Commit Baptists to Belief in Millennium—Dissatisfied With Nominations.

Special to The New York Times.

INDIANAPOLIS, June 16.—The Baptists who form the Northern Baptist Convention will have no man-made creed. The only creed they will assent to is the New Testament. The committee nominated for three hours' debate, the convention this evening voted by a great majority against the New Hampshire Confession of Faith. The vote was 1,264 in favor of the New Testament as the only statement of belief, and 637 for the confession.

This was the fourth victory won today by the liberals over the fundamentalists and was considered the greatest.

This morning the Committee on Nominations presented a ticket which will be acted on tomorrow morning. Because the nominees are not acceptable to the fundamentalists the latter will present a rival ticket. The committee nominated for President the Rev. Dr. Frederick E. Taylor, pastor for the last sixteen years of the First Baptist Church of this city and a native of Newark, N. J. On the rival ticket the fundamentalists will nominate the Rev. Dr. Frank M. Goodchild, pastor of the Central Baptist Church, New York, who has been the candidate of that group from the first.

Another nomination of the Conventions Committee which the fundamentalists will attempt to scrap is that of the Rev. Dr. William C. Bitting of St. Louis, who has been the corresponding secretary of the convention since it was organized.

A resolution calling upon the convention to sell The Baptist, the official organ of the denomination, to an individual or a group of individuals, which was offered by the Rev. Dr. J. C. Massee, pastor of Tremont Temple, Boston, and the recognized leader of the fundamentalists, was referred to the executive committee with instructions to report back at this convention. The Baptist is a weekly and is published in Chicago. It was established several years ago and received $20,000 on which to operate. Dr. Massee and his followers charge that, although it is the official organ of the convention, it is a supporter of the radicals.

The convention against expectations adopted the report of the Board of Promotion. This was presented by the Rev. Dr. Clarence E. Barbour, President of Rochester Theological Seminary. The marked changes made were the cutting of its budget for operation during the year $200,000 and the reduction of its Administrative Committee from twenty to seventeen members.

There have been loud rumors for months that the convention would split over this report, as the leaders in the Board of Promotion are credited with being largely radicals.

This board administers the $60,000,000 fund which has been subscribed during the last three years.

A speech of greeting was made by the Rev. Dr. E. Y. Mullins of Louisville, President of the Southern Baptist Convention, which has a membership of 7,000,000. Dr. Mullins, who is President of the Southern Baptist Theological Seminary, said that his convention had recently raised $35,000,000, and that in the last year it had received 250,000 new members. He said that Southern Baptists believed in the New Testament "from recently to end."

So great was the confusion after D. Massee offered his resolution to sell The Baptist that Mrs. Helen Barrett Montgomery, who is the President, had to pound again and again for order. One man from the floor shouted: "I have been in political conventions, but this has been the worst steam-rolling I ever saw!" There were yells and screams, and Mrs. Montgomery shouted: "Sit down and be quiet."

The report of the nominating committee was presented by its chairman, the Rev. Dr. A. M. Bailey, pastor of the First Baptist Church of Seattle. He said he had kept the committee in session for two days "and practically all of last night." Dr. Bailey said its membership represented all shades of opinion: "We did try to do our best," he added, "and angels could not do more."

Although there is a fair sprinkling of Fundamentalists on the ticket, the Fundamentalists feel that in the main it is a radical one. One fact which immensely pleases the Fundamentalists is that Judge F. W. Freeman of Denver is nominated for the Presidency of the American Baptist Home Mission Society.

The first speaker this morning was the Rev. Dr. W. B. Riley, pastor for the last quarter of a century of the First Baptist Church, Minneapolis. Instead of reading a proposed new creed Dr. Riley astonished the vast audience by presenting for adoption by the convention the doctrinal deliverance known as "the New Hampshire Confession of Faith." It was drawn up in the year 1832 and for many years has been used by many individual Baptist congregations as a statement of belief.

This document contains, in addition to the main articles of most Protestant creeds, declarations that "We believe the Christian form of Baptism is immersion" and "We believe the end of the world is approaching," and adds that Jesus Christ will return to reign on earth.

Dr. Riley closed his speech by moving the adoption of the New Hampshire Confession of Faith, with a recommendation to the Baptist Churches to use it for their creed. This was greeted with loud applause and whistling, men jumping up from their seats. Thereupon Mrs. Montgomery ruled that she would allow no kind of applause except handclapping.

Next to appear on the platform was the Rev. Dr. Cornelius Woelfkin, pastor of the Park Avenue Baptist Church, New York, commonly referred to as "the Rockefeller Church." Dr. Woelfkin got as much applause as did Dr. Riley, but from a different crowd. He moved as a substitute resolution the following:

"That the Northern Baptist Convention affirm that the New Testament is the all-sufficient ground of faith and practice, and that we need no other."

From that moment on it was the New Hampshire confession against the New Testament. When the question was finally called for, Mrs. Montgomery ruled that before the vote was taken the conference should proceed to a period of prayer. With perfect stillness over the vast tabernacle, Mrs. Montgomery herself prayed that "we may accept the decision of this body as the decision of the great Head of the Church Himself."

Dr. Woelfkin said he would speak out of experience. He said that his father, who had come to America from across the seas, had been mobbed and stoned in the streets of New York because he was a Baptist, and that his mother had likewise suffered for her faith.

"I was baptized just fifty years ago last February," said Dr. Woelfkin. "Had my sainted mother read to me from the New Hampshire confession I should not have understood it, but she read to me out of the New Testament. Gentlemen, the New Testament does not need a reduction. It needs no guard about it. Brethren Baptists have never been strong on statements. Why, brethren, will you put a yoke upon others which our fathers or we were not able to bear?" Dr. Woelfkin closed by offering his substitute, which was the resolution eventually carried.

June 17, 1922

FORM NEW CHURCH BODY.

Baptist Fundamentalists Hope to Win Other Conservatives.

Special to The New York Times.

INDIANAPOLIS, Ind., June 21.—Just before leaving this city the Fundamentalist delegates to the Northern Baptist Convention, which ended last night, organized themselves into a permanent body, with the Rev. Dr. J. C. Massee, pastor of Tremont Temple, Boston, as Chairman. They voted to have a "steering committee" of 150 members, with offices in Boston, New York, Chicago and Los Angeles.

The Fundamentalists voted not only to line up as many Baptists as possible on their side, but to try to win to their support the conservatives in theology of the Presbyterian, Methodist, Baptist, Congregationalist and other denominations. They claim they are fighting a battle which is going on in a quieter way in every communion.

June 22, 1922

DR. GRANT DENIES THE VIRGIN BIRTH IN REPLY TO CRITICS

"What Has the Virgin Birth to Do With Christianity?" He Asks.

SAYS HE IS MISUNDERSTOOD

Wants Religion as Little Bound by Dogmatic Barriers as Chemistry or Physics.

PLEADS FOR LIBERALISM

Should Be Generally Taught—All Departments of Thought Should Pull Together.

Preaching again yesterday on religious liberalism, Dr. Percy Stickney Grant, rector of the Church of the Ascension, made a direct denial of the virgin birth of Christ, one of the fundamental doctrines of the Protestant Episcopal Church. His view on the virgin birth came toward the close of his sermon, when he said:

"I get letters saying 'You are undermining Christianity. You are denying our Lord,' and so forth. What a crude misunderstanding of me to say because I don't believe that Christ was born of a virgin that I am destroying Christianity! What has the virgin birth to do with Christianity?"

The pulpit utterances of Dr. Grant which brought Bishop William T. Manning's first letter and suggestion of a heresy trial were more general than the statement made yesterday. The controversy seemed at an end a little more than a week ago, when the Bishop in a second letter informed Dr. Grant that his formal exposition of his views in a communication to the Bishop had been couched in ambiguous terms, and that "for the present" the question of trying him for heresy would rest.

The Apostles' Creed, recited in Episcopal churches by minister and congregation, or intoned by the choir as in the Church of the Ascension, clearly sets forth the doctrine of the Virgin Birth, as follows:

"I believe in God the Father Almighty, Maker of heaven and earth: And in Jesus Christ His only Son our Lord; Who was conceived by the Holy Ghost, born of the Virgin Mary * * *."

The Nicene Creed in the Episcopal Book of Common Prayer carries this passage:

"And was incarnate by the Holy Ghost of the Virgin Mary, and was made man."

"Dogmatic Barriers."

"I hope to see religion as free to thought as chemistry or physics, and as little bound by dogmatic barriers," Dr. Grant declared in beginning his sermon.

"I hope to see all departments of thought and expression, whether religious or scientific or artistic or economic, pulling together and helping each other. Think of the terrible schisms in the nature of Henry Adams, who was a son of Charles Adams, Minister to England through the Civil War, and who wrote that book, 'The Education of Henry Adams.' He said he had received an eighteenth century education but that he had to live in the twentieth century.

"As anybody who has read that book sees, there is a continual pulling and hauling between the facts of life as he had to meet them and the education given to him. A lot of people living to-day have been given an eighteenth century education, or worse, particularly in religion, a medieval education * * *

"When an automobile breaks down you want somebody who knows the machinery of automobiles; you don't want somebody who comes along and discourses pleasantly on literature or philosophy or the manners of the Greeks; you want to have somebody who understands the machinery and can put that automobile in order to go ahead. That is what we want today, people who understand the facts of life, the laws governing these facts, and we don't want these schisms in our nature that are pulling against each other.

"We want all this pulling to cease, so that whatever we get in church on Sunday is a joy and delight and imiginative power behind everything we do in the course of the week, whether in work, study, painting or music, or whatever it may be. That is what religion ought to be."

Dr. Grant said he hoped to see the time when religious experience and thought are based on such reliable foundation "that we don't have to live in fear of being robbed in our religion by scholars and men of science." Dubiousness, fear and concealment, he said, had been pretty much the attitude of intellectual men who also had a profound religious consciousness during the last 100 years; "that is, ever since we have paid a greater attention to scholarship and science as they affected the Christian religion."

"I hope to see the time when all mankind will have a sensitiveness toward life such as Jesus showed, and will have the feeling of its beauty that he had, and a soul to obey its profound and wonderful laws."

Liberalism.

Arguing that liberalism should be generally taught, the preacher said that the country would not be celebrating Lincoln's Birthday if America did not believe in teaching liberalism.

"And do you think that with such an example as that man before us who today is probably the supremest model that the spirit of America has produced in spite of those great immortal fathers of the Revolution and Constitution—do you suppose with a man such as that as our model American, we do not have to go ahead in every direction of freedom and challenge and insist that freedom shall win.

"And do you suppose there is any answer in a country like this to the question should liberalism be generally taught, except the answer 'Yes, by all means and of necessity.'

"Liberalism is not liberalism that is afraid of its own speeches," Dr. Grant said at another point in his sermon. "Rather it was founded upon great hopes as to the future and great confidence as to the present inner goodness of human nature and its desire to get ahead.

"Today liberals, so far as the church is concerned, are being unified. That is a good thing. These recent discussions have unified liberalists as nothing has done in a long time. They are getting together. They are going to be a bunch of sticks very difficult to break, and then there certainly is a great appreciation of freedom and a greater knowledge of what justifies in a clergyman of experience and teaching very wide freedom of expression.

"Now the real difference between the traditionalists and myself is something like this: They regard religion, and especially the Christian religion, as a transaction. I regard it as a process. They are satisfied to have a theory of the world which involves the fall of man, a stern judge, a redeeming son, whose death on the cross has vicarious value for them, so we are saved by beliving in His name.

Standing by the Miracles.

"Now that theology has been organized into all the parts of the Catholic Church, with its doctrine of the mass and doctrine of penance, confession, absolution and so forth. In order to justify their belief in God and man, they stand by the miracle as authority. That is all they care about the miracle. It enables them to say the thing is right. If you say 'How do you know this is so?' they say, because the miracle said Jesus has this power. I care about the miracle as a possible equipment for man. They care for the miracles only as testing the authority they demand for such a scheme of things, government, transactions as I have just described.

"Now, I care nothing about the miracles as authority, because the laws of the soul are their own authority. They are laws that can carry themselves without your help, or my help. The laws of the soul, in that phrase I have quoted from Milton, are laws that can enforce themselves. The authority of today has got to be that kind of authority—an authority from within that can enforce itself.

"Everything you know comes into everything you are thinking about religion, or it ought to. So these good people who consider religion a transaction think they must therefore fall into that particular organization and be part of that transaction that is an Old Testament idea, a part of the sacrificial idea that the pagans formulated. God promised to do certain things if you do certain things you promise, and if you don't do what you promise, why, then, God doesn't do what he says, and if you'd do certain things you get punished for those things. That to me is absolutely unethical as well as unscientific. Religion to me is a process of expansion, enlightenment and joy of the spirit of mankind, and today we are understanding as never before what all that means, and as never before we are able to so proceed and obey these laws.

The Virgin Birth.

"I get letters saying: You are undermining Christianity. You are denying your Lord, and so forth. What a crude misunderstanding of me to say because I don't believe that Christ was born of a virgin that I am destroying Christianity. What has the virgin birth to do with Christianity? The evolution of the profound spirit content of life as we get it in the Sermon on the Mount or wherever Christ spoke or acted.

"That is what I am trying to do—to fasten attention on that and not fritter away by misunderstanding the seeds of Christianity generally now presented, the biographic, the historical and the spiritual, seeing these are going to be changed as relationships change; but the spiritual is more clear, more impressive, more helpful and more wonderful every day we live. We cannot get away from it, and I am trying to show this so it is of a piece with modern psychology and by our science and by Jesus Christ's revelation of life to us. So we will be stronger and purer and merrier than ever we have been in our experience before.

"I possess one particular sort of temperament. Certain aspects of truth are dear to me and I necessarily lay great emphasist on these aspects, which meet my own needs more than others; but I recognize very fully that human nature is not cast into a single mold; if I am not helped by what may be called the Catholic point of view, I most gladly acknowledge that there are other kinds of people whose religious life becomes most real through such an outlook. And I rejoice that the Episcopal Church is large enough to include both.

"Again I can give no kind of worship or semi-worship to the mother of Christ. Another type of mind is helped by such devotion. The modern mind has no wish to reject such from the Church, but if these men rightly claim liberty for themselves to interpret, may not the liberal be accorded equal privileges? And may we not hope both that we will cast off that spirit of unchristian exclusiveness and worship together in the bond of fellowship?"

February 12, 1923

RABBI WISE DEFENDS GRANT.

Says for Himself He Doesn't Believe the Decalogue Came From Heaven.

Dr. Stephen S. Wise, rabbi of the Free Synagogue, yesterday morning at Carnegie Hall, during his sermon on Dr. Percy Stickney Grant, under the topic of "Recant or Resign," said: "I do not believe, and I never pretended to believe, that the Decalogue (the Ten Commandments), written on those two tablets of stone, came out of the heavens to those people of Israel. If that is heresy, banish me; but you know that it is not heresy. I believe that the Decalogues were wrought out of the divine potentialities of humanity, from God in man."

Dr. Wise said, "What has this threatened heresy trial in the Protestant Episcopal Church to do with the Jewish faith? I will give you my answer. It is so vital, and of fundamental concern to all religions, because when religion is imperiled our liberty is at stake. Liberty is interdenomination."

He said that it would mean death to the moral and spiritual life of the Christian Church for Dr. Grant to recant. "A man, especially a man of God, never recants," Dr. Wise said. "Recantation under coercion or threat is death to the spiritual and moral life of the Church.

"Cannot liberty be within the Church? Cannot truth be spoken in utter freedom? Dr. Grant does not believe in the metaphysical nature of Christ, but he does not deny the fundamental teachings of Jesus, the Galilean Jew. He has not denied one word Jesus taught."

Dr. Wise said that he did not note any equivocation or evasion in the reply of Dr. Grant to Bishop William T. Manning. "I do not find," he said, "a word of evasion or a scintilla of equivocation in his answer, but I do find evasion, temerity, threat or warning in the communication addressed to Dr. Grant by Bishop Manning."

February 12, 1923

PRESBYTERIANS BAN VIEWS OF FOSDICK, BRYAN LEADING FOES

By 80 Majority Fundamentalists Reject Report Referring Matter Back to Presbytery Here.

MINORITY PROPOSAL WINS

This Calls on New York Presbytery to See That Preachers Hold to Church Tenets.

5-HOUR STRUGGLE PRECEDED

Bryan Forced the Roll-Call That Brought the Issue to a Head.

Special to The New York Times.

INDIANAPOLIS, May 23.—By a vote of 439 to 359, the Presbyterian General Assembly condemned this morning the pulpit utterances of the Rev. Dr. Harry Emerson Fosdick in the First Presbyterian Church of New York City, and directed the New York Presbytery to take action to require the preaching and teaching in that church "to conform to the system of doctrines taught in the Confession of Faith."

This action, which came after a long and sharp struggle between the liberals and the fundamentalists, was a distinct victory for the latter, who were led by William J. Bryan. In the first roll-call that the assembly has had to take in this year's session the conservatives polled a majority of eighty for rejection of the report of the Committee on Bills and Overtures, which proposed to leave the Fosdick matter to the judgment of the New York Presbytery, and for the adoption of the minority report condemning Dr. Fosdick.

This minority report bore only the signature of the Rev. Dr. A. Gordon Mac-Lennan of Philadelphia. The other twenty-one members of the committee joined in the majority finding.

Text of Report Adopted.

Dr. MacLennan's report read as follows:

"The 135th General Assembly of the Presbyterian Church of the United States of America, in answer to the petition of the overture presented by the Presbytery of Philadelphia regarding the public proclamation of the Word in the pulpit of the First Presbyterian Church of New York City, expresses its profound sorrow that doctrines contrary to the standards of the Presbyterian Church proclaimed in said pulpit have been the cause of controversy and division in our Church, and therefore would direct the Presbytery of New York to take such action (either through its present committee or by the appointment of a special commission) as will require the preaching and teaching in the First Presbyterian Church of New York City to conform to the system of doctrines taught in the Confession of Faith; and that said Presbytery reports its action in a full transcript of its records to the 136th General Assembly of 1924.

"Furthermore, the General Assembly calls the attention of the Presbyteries to the deliverance of the General Assembly of 1910, which deliverance is hereby affirmed and which is as follows:

"'1. It is an essential doctrine of the Word of God and our standards that the Holy Spirit did so inspire, guide and move the writers of Holy Scripture as to keep them from error.

"'2. It is an essential doctrine of the Word of God and our standards that our Lord Jesus Christ was born of the Virgin Mary.

"'3. It is an essential doctrine of the Word of God and our standards that Christ offered up himself a sacrifice to satisfy divine justice and to reconcile us to God.

"'4. It is an essential doctrine of the Word of God and of our standards concerning our Lord Jesus Christ that on the third day He rose again from the dead with the same body with which He suffered, with which also He ascended into Heaven, and there sitteth at the right hand of His Father, making intercession.

"'5. It is an essential doctrine of the Word of God as the supreme standard of our faith that our Lord Jesus showed His power and love by working mighty miracles. This working was not contrary to nature, but superior to it.'"

The report which the Assembly turned down was as follows:

"The Bills and Overtures Committee presents the following report to the General Assembly as its recommendation in reply to Overture No. 1 from the Presbytery of Philadelphia: 'On the public proclamation of the Word in the pulpit of the First Presbyterian Church of New York City.'

"This committee has made definite inquiry and has been officially informed that the Presbytery of New York has taken cognizance of matters whereof the Presbytery of Philadelphia has lodged complaint; and has received assurances that the Presbytery of New York, upon the request of the pastor and session of one of its own congregations, has already instituted a formal study of the situation in the said First Church, as respects both the ecclesiastical relations of its ministerial staff and the preaching of the Gospel in its pulpit; and that this study is being diligently prosecuted by a committee of able and trusted Presbyters.

"Therefore, we would recommend to the 135th General Assembly that it reply to the petitioners that it deems it to be needless, if not unfairly intrusive, to transmit to the Presbytery of New York any instructions as to the manner and methods of this now pending investigation. Still less would the Assembly assume to indicate the conclusion to be reached by this inquiry.

"In view, however, of the general interest in this matter throughout our church, this assembly requests the Presbytery of New York to convey to the 136th General Assembly in the year 1924 a copy of whatever report its committee of inquiry may submit and its own action thereupon, and authorizes the stated clerk of the assembly to lay such request officially before the Presbytery of New York; and in order that the allegations in the present overture from the Presbytery of Philadelphia may be fully compared with the findings of the investigators representing the Presbytery of New York, this assembly of 1923 leaves the said overture of the Presbytery of Philadelphia in the hands of the stated clerk, to be included with overtures to be considered by the General Assembly of 1924 for such action as may then appear most effective in promoting the proclamation of the good tidings of salvation through Jesus Christ.

Renews Its Confession of Faith.

"Desiring, however, amid present theological controversies to utter no uncertain sound respecting the doctrines of truth revealed by the spirit of God in the Holy Scriptures of the Old and New Testaments, this assembly declares its full content with the ordination vows assumed by all its teaching and ruling elders, solemnly affirming that Westminster Confession of Faith and the other doctrinal standards of our church do 'contain the system of doctrine taught in the Holy Scriptures'; and the assembly here declares itself assured that the representative teachers, pastors and office bearers of the Presbyterian Church have in good conscience taken that ordination vow and in good conscience continue everywhere honorably faithful thereunto.

"Moreover, the General Assembly here bears witness that neither in modern philosophy, nor in Biblical criticism, nor in any just claim of unfettered thought, is the Presbyterian Church aware of any shadow of reason why it should alter, abate, or obscure its corporate testimony to any article of faith characteristic of Apostolic Christianity or integral to our 'reformed theology.'

"Nevertheless, remembering the constant New Testament emphasis which magnifies the spirit of love above the letter of doctrine, the General Assembly bids all, ordained and unordained, who belong to the Lord Jesus Christ in the fellowship of our Church to be ever mindful that, not by the perfection of word but by the power of life, shall Christ's Kingdom come and God's will be done among men, and that in unity of the spirit and in the bond of peace it is ever the paramount obligation of the Church to proclaim more and more widely the one essential message of our sacred saving gospel: 'God so loved the world that He gave His only begotten son that whosoever believeth in Him should not perish, but have everlasting life.'

Hugh K. Walker, Chairman; W. W. Wylie, Charles Holman, W. O. Williams, James W. Bean, D. H. Ellis, Clarence F. Turner, W. H. Ryan, M. D., R. G. McGregor, Edward D. Emerson, J. W. Claudy.

Ward W. MacHenry, O. R. Williamson, Harvey G. Mathias, David W. Phillips, William Bryant, Nolan R. Best, William H. Hopkins, Hugh T. Gary, Clare S. Adams, Harry W. Gill, M. W. Cunningham.

The roll call occupied an hour and a quarter, and before the four tellers had completed their work it was seen that the anti-Fosdick resolution had won.

Bryan Forces Roll-Call.

Mr. Bryan made a speech in favor of the minority resolution and was credited with a large share in swinging the vote. He insisted on a roll-call when there were repeated demands to take the vote by the twenty-two election sections, declaring it was "the most important issue before the assembly and it would be well for history to have a record of how each commissioner voted."

Out of fifteen votes cast by commissioners from the Presbytery of New York twelve were against the anti-Fosdick resolution and three were in favor of it. The latter were cast by Elders R. C. Tinninghast, B. F. Vankannel and George Schryver.

The Rev. Dr. Frederick W. Evans, pastor of Harlem Church, who was the sixteenth Commissioner, had to leave for home several days ago because of a recent operation on his throat. It was Dr. Evans and the session of his church who succeeded in having the Presbytery of New York appoint the committee to consider a resolution against the First Church having Dr. Fosdick as its special preacher.

The first name of the New York Presbytery called was that of the Rev. Dr. George Alexander, pastor of the First Church, who responded with a decisive "No." The others who voted "no" were William P. Merrill, Theodore F.

Savage, George M. Duff, William H. Foulkes, William Neely Ross, George Mair, Dr. C. I. Fisher, George H. Richards, George B. Dill, H. M. Humphrey and Judge Norman J. Mack.

Dr. Wishart Votes "No."

An emphatic "No" was voted by the Rev. Dr. Charles F. Wishart, the Moderator. Another "No" came from the Rev. Dr. Calvin C. Hays of Johnstown, Pa., the last Moderator.

In the big delegations from the Philadelphia and Philadelphia North Presbyteries only one voted "No"—S. Spencer Chapman of Germantown, Pa., Vice Moderator of the assembly.

Just before the final vote the Rev. Dr. Thomas V. Moore of San Francisco offered a resolution that the assembly request Dr. Fosdick, as a Christian gentleman, to sever his relations with the First Presbyterian Church, inasmuch as he belonged to a different denomination, and thereby bring the contention to an end. This was not seconded.

The Rev. Dr. Clarence E. MacCartney made the final speech for the minority report. He is pastor of the Arch Street Church, Philadelphia, and the author of the Philadelphia overture. He is moderator of the Philadelphia Presbytery.

Calls Majority Report "Whitewash."

"Fathers and brethren," began Dr. MacCartney, "this majority report is a masterpiece of whitewash. The man who wrote it ought to get a job as an expert interior decorator. This was only a skirmish—a whispering in the mulberry trees. The storm is coming, and you can't keep it back with pusilanimous compromises. If you adopt this majority report you allow the New York Presbytery to escape by a technicality.

"The Rev. Dr. Evans, pastor of the Harlem Church, who was the father of the overture sent by its session to the Presbytery asking for action against Dr. Fosdick, sat in my study two weeks ago, and he was a most depressed pastor because the resolution he had introduced was being used to whitewash the New York Presbytery.

"I could not vote for the majority report because it contains a statement which is not true. Outrageous error has appeared in one of our pulpits, and has been defended by some of our pastors.

Dr. MacCartney quoted passages from Dr. Fosdick's sermon which started the whole controversy, and compared the preacher to Thomas Paine, adding:

"There has been more orthodox praying, singing and preaching and less orthodox voting in this assembly than in any assembly for years."

Sums Up for Committee.

The Rev. Dr. James Wilson Bean of St. Paul, Minn., who summed up for the majority of the committee, took Dr. MacCartney to task.

"This is not a whitewash report," he said. "If we adopt the minority report we are deciding on a judicial case without hearing from the other side."

Dr. Bean said that Dr. Alexander, pastor of the New York church, had appeared before the Committee on Bills and Overtures, "and after that it would not have been possible for our committee to have adopted what now comes before you as the minority report."

A motion to send both the minority and the majority report to the New York Presbytery, with the suggestion that it study them, was lost.

Most of those who spoke in favor of the majority report argued that it ought to be adopted "to have peace and harmony in the church."

Mr. Bryan declared this was not the kind of peace and harmony that was desired. He asked where in the life of Christ could be found peace, adding that "these men disbelieve in the Virgin birth, the resurrection of the body of Christ, the inspiration of the Scriptures and the miracles."

General Council Elected.

One hundred and fifty-three Presbyteries out of 301 Presbyteries having voted for what is known as "Overture E," a General Council was elected to take over all the duties of the former Executive Commission and the New Era movement. Its members were nominated by a committee made up of one member from each of the twenty-two voting sections. The council organized tonight and its membership is as follows:

Terms to expire 1924—G. P. Barty, D. D., Kansas City, Mo.; J. A. Dunkel, D. D., Indianapolis; A. E. Moody, D. D., Muskogee, Okla.; A. R. Nicol, Summit, N. J.; G. G. Barber, New York City; John T. Manson, New Haven, Conn.

Terms to expire 1925—W. H. Foulkes, D. D., New York City; S. S. Estey, D. D., Topeka; S. T. Wilson, D. D., Marysville, Tenn.; George Nicholson, Wilkes-Barre, Pa.; R. W. Harbison, Pittsburgh; H. C. Glenn, Temple, Texas.

Terms to expire 1926—J. T. Stone, D. D., Chicago; F. W. Hinitt, D. D., Indiana, Pa.; W. R. Taylor, D. D., Rochester, N. Y.; J. W. Smith, Philadelphia; J. W. Baer, Pasadena, Cal.; N. H. Loomis, Omaha.

Ex-officio members are: The Chairman of the General Council, to be elected by the Council; the Stated Clerk of the General Assembly, the Rev. L. S. Mudge; the Moderator of the General Assembly, the Rev. C. F. Wishart; the retiring Moderator, the Rev. C. C. Hays; his nearest living predecessor, the Rev. H. C. Swearingen, and one representative chosen from each of the four boards of the Church and elected by his board.

The Assembly is expected to adjourn late tomorrow night.

May 24, 1923

DENY SCIENCE WARS AGAINST RELIGION

Forty Scientists, Clergymen and Prominent Educators Attack "Two Erroneous Views."

SEE DEITY TWICE REVEALED

Science Shows His Work in Nature, Religion Develops Spiritual Ideals, They Assert.

WASHINGTON, May 26.—A joint statement holding that there is no antagonism between science and religion was issued here tonight as representing the conclusions of a group of forty distinguished Americans on a subject which recently has aroused bitter and widespread controversy.

The names of two Cabinet officers, Secretaries Hoover and Davis; three Bishops and many others in positions of leadership in the political, business, scientific and religious world, are attached to the declaration, which was prepared by Dr. R. A. Milliken, director of the Norman Bridge Laboratory of Physics, at Pasadena, Cal.

"The purpose," said an accompanying explanation, "is to assist in correcting two erroneous impressions that seem to be current among certain groups of persons. The first is that religion today stands for medieval theology, and the second that science is materialistic and irreligious."

The statement itself reads:

"We, the undersigned, deeply regret that in recent controversies there has been a tendency to present science and religion as irreconcilable and antagonistic domains of thought, for, in fact, they meet distinct human needs, and in the rounding out of human life they supple-

ment rather than displace or oppose each other.

"The purpose of science is to develop, without prejudice or preconception of any kind, a knowledge of the facts, the laws and the processes of nature. The even more important task of religion, on the other hand, is to develop the consciences, the ideals and the aspirations of mankind. Each of these two activities represents a deep and vital function of the soul of man, and both are necessary for the life, the progress and the happiness of the human race.

"It is a sublime conception of God which is furnished by science, and one wholly consonant with the highest ideals of religion, when it represents Him as revealing Himself through countless ages in the development of the earth as an abode for man and in the age-long inbreathing of life into its constituent matter, culminating in man with his spiritual nature and all his Godlike powers."

Besides Secretaries Hoover and Davis, those whose names were attached to the statement included Bishops William Lawrence and William Thomas Manning of the Episcopal Church, and Bishop Francis J. McConnell of the

30

Methodist Episcopal Church; Dr. Charles D. Walcott of the Smithsonian Institution, who is President of the National Academy of Sciences; President Angell of Yale, President Burton of the University of Chicago, Dr. William J. Mayo, David F. Houston, Frank O. Lowden, John Sharp Williams, Rear Admiral William S. Sims, Julius Kruttschnitt, Frank A. Vanderlip, William Allen White, Victor F. Lawson, Henry van Dyke, President Barber of the Rochester Theological Seminary, President King of Oberlin Theological Sem-

inary, Dr. John D. Davis, Princeton Theological Seminary; Professor Henry Fairfield Osborn, President of the American Museum of Natural History, New York; Professor John Merle Coulter, University of Chicago; Professor Michael Pupin, Columbia; Professor George D. Birkhoff, Harvard; Director Noyes, Gates Chemical Laboratory, California Institute of Technology, and Professor William W. Campbell, Director of Lick Observatory; H. B. Thayer, President American Telephone and Telegraph Company; Henry S. Pritchett,

banker, New York; John C. Shedd, Chicago; Dr. James I. Vance, Nashville, Tenn.; Rev. Dr. Robert E. Brown, Waterbury, Conn.; Rev. Dr. Peter Ainslie, Baltimore; President Poteat, of Wake Forest College, N. C.; Professor Edwin G. Conklin, of Princeton University; John J. Carty, New York; Professor William H. Welch, Johns Hopkins University; President John C. Merriam, Carnegie Institution, Washington; Gano Dunn, Chairman National Research Council, and Dr. Millikan.

May 27, 1923

PRESBYTERIANS ASK LIBERTY OF THOUGHT

An affirmation, "designed to safeguard the unity and liberty of the Presbyterian Church in the United States" and signed by 150 Presbyterian ministers from all parts of the country, was issued yesterday by Dr. Murray Shipley Howard of the Lafayette Avenue Presbyterian Church, Buffalo. Dr. Howard is chairman of a committee of ministers appointed as a result of the action of the Presbyterian General Assembly in Indianapolis last May, in connection with the charges of unorthodoxy made by the Philadelphia Presbytery against Dr. Harry Emerson Fosdick, preacher at the First Presbyterian Church, New York.

The document, which has been circulated to 10,000 clergymen of the Presbyterian faith, affirms the Apostles' Creed, including the Virgin Birth and the resurrection of the body as contained in the Westminster Confession of Faith, but at the same time avows that no general assembly or individual has the right to interfere with a minister's liberty of conscience. The affirmation further criticizes the attitude of the Presbyterian General Assembly of 1923 in the Fosdick case, and asserts that in no place in the Westminster Confession of Faith is a minister called upon to "assent to the very words of the confession."

Ask Latitude in Preaching.

Latitude of thought and preaching is demanded and attempts to dictate doctrine, "except that of the Scriptures through God," is condemned. In making the document public, Dr. Howland said that the committee had been in consultation with ministers from all parts of the country, and those who have signed have been chosen as representative men. The number, it is pointed out, was limited to 150. Dr. Howland also drew attention to the fact that the affirmation was signed both by conservatives and liberals, and is, therefore, an appeal for tolerance and liberty and for the cessation of theological controversy.

The affirmation, which has been in the hands of the newspapers for several days on the understanding that it was not to be published before today, is headed "Submitted for the consideration of its ministers and people." It says:

We, the undersigned, ministers of the Presbyterian Church in the United States of America, feel bound, in view of certain actions of the General Assembly of 1923 and of persistent attempts to divide the Church and abridge its freedom, to express our convictions in matters pertaining thereto. At the outset we affirm and declare our acceptance of the Westminster Confession of Faith, as we did at our ordinations, "as containing the system of doctrine taught in the Holy Scriptures." We sincerely hold and earnestly preach the doctrines of evangelical Christianity, in agreement with the historic testimony of the Presbyterian Church in the

United States of America, of which we are loyal ministers. For the maintenance of the faith of our Church, the preservation of its unity, and the protection of the liberties of its ministers and people, we offer this Affirmation.

Presbyterian History.

I. By its law and history, the Presbyterian Church in the United States of America safeguards the liberty of thought and teaching of its ministers. At their ordination they "receive and adopt the Confession of Faith of this Church, as containing the system of doctrine taught in the Holy Scriptures." This the Church has always esteemed a sufficient doctrinal subscription for its ministers. Manifestly it does not require their assent to the very words of the Confession, or to all of its teachings, or to interpretations of the Confession by individuals or Church courts. The Confession of Faith itself disclaims infallibility. Its authors would not allow this to Church councils, their own included: "All synods or councils since the apostles' times, whether general or particular, may err, and many have erred; therefore they are not to be made the rule of faith or practice, but to be used as a help in both." (Conf. XXXI, iii). The Confession also expressly asserts the liberty of Christian believers, and condemns the submission of the mind or conscience to any human authority: "God alone is lord of the conscience, and hath left it free from the doctrines and commandments of men which are in anything contrary to His word, or beside it, in matters of faith or worship. So that to believe such doctrines, or to obey such commandments out of conscience, is to betray true liberty of conscience; and the requiring of an implicit faith, and an absolute and blind obedience, is to destroy liberty of conscience, and reason also." (Conf. XX, ii).

The Westminster Confession.

The formal relation of American Presbyterianism to the Westminster Confession of Faith begins in the Adopting Act of 1729. This anticipated and provided for dissent by individuals from portions of the Confession. At the formation of the Presbyterian Church in the United States of America, in 1788, the Westminster Confession was adopted as the creed of the Church; and at the same time the Church publicly declared the significance of its organization in a document which contains these words: "There are truths and forms with respect to which men of good characters and principles may differ. And in all these they think it the duty, both of private Christians and societies, to exercise mutual forbearance toward each other." (Declaration of Principles, v.)

Of the two parts into which our church was separated from 1837 to 1870, one held that only one interpretation of certain parts of the Confession or Faith was legitimate, while the other maintained its right to dissent from this interpretation. In the Reunion of 1870 they came together on equal terms, "each recognizing the other as a sound and orthodox body." The meaning of this, as understood then and ever since, is that officebearers in the Church who maintain their liberty in the interpretation of the Confession are exercising their rights guaranteed by the terms of the Reunion.

A more recent reunion also is significant, that of the Cumberland Pres-

byterian Church and the Presbyterian Church in the United States of America, in 1906. This reunion was opposed by certain members of the Presbyterian Church in the United States of America on the ground that the two churches were not at one in doctrine; yet it was consummated. Thus did our Church once more exemplify its historic policy of accepting theological differences within its bounds and subordinating them to recognized loyalty to Jesus Christ and united work for the Kingdom of God.

With respect to the interpretation of the Scriptures the position of our Church has been that common to Protestants. "The Supreme Judge," says the Confession of Faith, "by whom all controversies of religion are to be determined, and all decrees of councils, opinions of ancient writers, doctrines of men, and private spirits, are to be examined, and in whose sentence we are to rest, can be no other but the Holy Spirit speaking in the Scripture." (Conf. I, x.) Accordingly our Church has held that the supreme guide in the interpretation of the Scriptures is not, as it is with Roman Catholics, ecclesiastical authority, but the Spirit of God speaking to the Christian believer. Thus our Church lays it upon its ministers and others to read and teach the Scriptures as the Spirit of God through His manifold ministries instructs them, and to receive all truth which from time to time He causes to break forth from the Scriptures.

Scripture Silent on "Error."

There is no assertion in the Scriptures that their writers were kept "from error." The Confession of Faith does not make this assertion; and it is significant that this assertion is not to be found in the Apostles' Creed or the Nicene Creed or in any of the great Reformation confessions. The doctrine of inerrancy, intended to enhance the authority of the Scriptures, in fact impairs their supreme authority for faith and life, and weakens the testimony of the Church to the power of God unto salvation through Jesus Christ. We hold that the General Assembly of 1923, in asserting that "the Holy Spirit did so inspire, guide and move the writers of Holy Scripture as to keep them from error," spoke without warrant of the Scriptures or of the Confession of Faith. We hold rather to the words of the Confession of Faith, that the Scriptures "are given by inspiration of God, to be the rule of faith and life." (Conf. I, ii.)

II. While it is constitutional for any General Assembly "to bear testimony against error in doctrine" (Form of Govt. XII., v.), yet such testimony is without binding authority, since the constitution of our church provides that its doctrine shall be declared only by concurrent action of the General Assembly and the presbyteries. Thus the church guards the statement of its doctrine against hasty or ill-considered action by either General Assemblies or presbyteries. From this provision of our constitution, it is evident that neither in one General Assembly nor in many, without concurrent action of the presbyteries, is there authority to declare what the Presbyterian Church in the United States of America believes and teaches; and that the assumption that any General Assembly has authoritatively declared what the church believes and teaches is groundless. A declaration by a General Assembly that any doctrine is "an essential doctrine" attempts to amend the constitution of the church in an unconstitutional manner.

III. The General Assembly of 1923, in asserting that "doctrines contrary to the standards of the Presbyterian Church" have been preached in the pulpit of the First Presbyterian Church of New York City, virtually pronounced a judgment against this church. The General Assembly did this with knowledge that the matter on which it so expressed itself was already under formal consideration in the Presbytery of New York, as is shown by the language of its action. The General Assembly acted in the case without giving hearing to the parties concerned. Thus the General Assembly did not conform to the procedure in such cases contemplated by our Book of Discipline, and, what is more serious, it in effect condemned a Christian minister without using the method of conference, patience and love enjoined on us by Jesus Christ. We object to the action of the General Assembly in this case, as being out of keeping with the law and the spirit of our church.

General Assembly's Action.

IV. The General Assembly of 1923 expressed the opinion concerning five doctrinal statements that each one "is an essential doctrine of the Word of God and our standards." On the constitutional grounds which we have before described, we are opposed to any attempt to elevate these five doctrinal statements, or any of them, to the position of tests for ordination or for good standing in our church.

Furthermore, this opinion of the General Assembly attempts to commit our church to certain theories concerning the inspiration of the Bible, and the Incarnation, the Atonement, the Resurrection, and the Continuing Life and Supernatural Power of our Lord Jesus Christ. We all hold most earnestly to these great facts and doctrines; we all believe from our hearts that the writers of the Bible were inspired of God; that Jesus Christ was God manifest in the flesh; that God was in Christ, reconciling the world unto Himself, and through Him we have our redemption; that having died for our sins He rose from the dead and is our ever-living Saviour; that in His earthly ministry He wrought many mighty works, and by His vicarious death and unfailing presence He is able to save to the uttermost. Some of us regard the particular theories contained in the deliverance of the General Assembly of 1923 as satisfactory explanations of these facts and doctrines. But we are united in believing that these are not the only theories allowed by the Scriptures and our standards as explanations of these facts and doctrines of our religion, and that all who hold to these facts and doctrines, whatever theories they may employ to explain them, are worthy of all confidence and fellowship.

V. We do not desire liberty to go beyond the teachings of evangelical Christianity. But we maintain that it is our constitutional right and our Christian duty within these limits to exercise liberty of thought and teaching, that we may more effectively preach the gospel of Jesus Christ, the Saviour of the World.

VI. Finally, we deplore the evidences of division in our beloved Church, in the face of a world so desperately in need of a united testimony to the Gospel of Christ. We earnestly desire fellowship with all who like us are disciples of Jesus Christ. We hope that those to whom this affirmation comes will believe that it is not the declaration of a theological party, but rather a sincere appeal, based on the Scriptures and our standards, for the preservation of the unity and freedom of our Church, for which most earnestly we plead and pray.

In appening the names of the 150 signatories, Dr. Howland remarks:

"These names are as of Dec. 26, 1923. No general appeal for signatures to this affirmation has been made. It was at first intended to publish it with 100 signatures, and this was announced on Nov. 20, 1923. In response to a limited amount of personal approach, more than this number of names were offered. The committee in charge then decided that only 150 names should be attached. More than this number have been offered, and a certain selection has been made from these for this publication, in order to show that the affirmation expresses the opinions of ministers from all parts of the Church.

"It is intended to publish in the near future other signatures that have come in or may come in. Correspondence regarding the affirmation should be addressed to the Secretary of the committee, Dr. Robert Hastings Nichols, Auburn Theological Seminary, Auburn, N. Y."

The signers of the affirmation are as follows:

Charles Craroll Albertson, Lafayette Avenue Church, Brooklyn.

Albert J. Alexander, First Church, Beaver, Pa.

H. B. Allen, Presbyterian Church, Marengo, Iowa.

Robert W. Anthony, First Church, Schenectady, N. Y.

Charles A. Austin, College Hill Church, Cincinnati, Ohio.

George Emerson Barnes, Overbrook Church, Philadelphia.

Ira W. Barnett, Calvary Church, Riverside, Cal.

James W. Bean, Dayton Avenue Church, St. Paul, Minn.

R. B. Beattie, First (Munn Avenue) Church, East Orange, N. J.

William Russell Bennett, First Church, Morristown, N. J.

Barton B. Bigler, Memorial Church, St. Augustine, Fla.

Philip Smead Bird, First Church, Utica, N. Y.

William H. Black, President of Missouri Valley College, Marshall, Mo.

John Allan Blair, Tabernacle Church, Philadelphia.

H. Alford Boggs, Princeton Church, Philadelphia.

J. Gray Bolton, Hope Church, Philadelphia.

L. Byron Boozer, Collegiate Church, Ames, Iowa.

Harold Leonard Bowman, First Church, Portland, Ore.

George A. Buttrick, First Church, Buffalo, N. Y.

Charles L. Candee, Westminster Church, Wilmington, Del.

John Lyon Caughey, First Church, Glens Falls, N. Y.

James E. Clarke, Editor Presbyterian Advance, Nashville, Tenn.

L. Mason Clarke, First Church, Brooklyn, N. Y.

James J. Coale, Executive Secretary Presbytery of Baltimore, Baltimore. Md.

Henry S. Coffin, Madison Avenue Church, New York City.

J. P. Cotton, Inglenook Church, Birmingham, Ala.

Ralph Marshall Davis, Hyde Park Church, Chicago, Ill.

Walter S. Davison, Arlington Avenue Church, East Orange, N. J.

William J. Dawson, First Church, Newark, N. J.

Dayton A. Dobbs, Russell Street Church, Nashville, Tenn.

William J. Du Bourdieu, Jefferson Park Church, Chicago, Ill.

Carl H. Dudley, Presbyterian Church, Silver Creek, N. Y.

J. N. Ervin, First Church, Dayton, Ky.

William R. Farmer, professor in Western Theological Seminary, Pittsburgh, Pa.

Lawrence Fenninger, Chaplain of Hampton Institute, Hampton, Va.

Walter Rockwood Ferris, Park Central Church, Syracuse, N. Y.

William H. Fishburn, West Adams Church, Los Angeles, Cal.

J. F. Fitchen Jr., Fourth Church, Albany, N. Y.

Frank Fitt, Highland Park Church, Highland Park, Ill.

R. W. Frank, assistant professor in McCormick Theological Seminary, Chicago.

George Arthur Frantz, Presbyterian Church, Van Wert, Ohio.

Robert Freeman, Presbyterian Church, Pasadena, Cal.

Calvin H. French, Madison Avenue Church, Albany, N. Y.

George S. Fulcher, First Church, Okmulgee, Okla.

Albert C. Fulton, First Church, Syracuse, N. Y.

M. L. Gillespie, Central Church, Fayetteville, Ark.

G. M. Gordon, Brick Church, East Orange, N. J.

W. K. Guthrie, First Church, San Francisco.

Matthias L. Haines, pastor emeritus, First Church, Indianapolis, Ind.

Jesse Halsey, Seventh Church, Cincinnati, Ohio.

Martin D. Hardin, Presbyterian Church, Ithaca, N. Y.

Reuben Haines Hartley, Presbyterian Church, La Jolla, Cal.

T. M. Hartman, First Church, Paul's Valley, Okla.

Joel B. Hayden, Fairmount Church, Cleveland, Ohio.

John Grier Hibben, President of Princeton University, Princeton. N. J.

Paul R. Hickok, Second Church, Troy, N. Y.

A. P. Higley, Calvary Church, Cleveland, Ohio.

Edward Yates Hill, First Church, Philadelphia, Pa.

George Clifton Hitchcock, Presbyterian Church, Bowling Green, Mo.

Charles T. Hock, Professor in Bloomfield Theological Seminary, Bloomfield, N. J.

B. H. Hodges, Grace Church, Temple, Texas.

Walter J. Hogue, First Church, York, Pa.

Samuel V. V. Holmes, Westminster Church, Buffalo, N. Y.

William F. Hoot, Presbyterian Church, Peotone, Ill.

William Herman Hopkins, First Church, Albany, N. Y.

James M. Howard, South Street Church, Morristown, N. J.

Murray Shipley Howland, Lafayette Avenue Church, Buffalo, N. Y.

Arthur S. Hoyt, Professor in Auburn Theological Seminary, Auburn, N. Y.

George E. Hunt, Christ Church, Madison, Wis.

Graham C. Hunter, Church of the Covenant, New York City.

Joseph Hunter, Fifth Avenue Church, Newark, N. J.

Stanley Hunter, St. John's Church, Berkeley, Cal.

Charles K. Imbrie, Presbyterian Church, Penn Yan, N. Y.

Edwin H. Jenks, First Church, Omaha, Neb.

Wendell Prime Keeler, First Church, Yonkers, N. Y.

L. C. Kirkes, Hillsboro Church, Nashville, Tenn.

Ira Landrith, Moderator of the General Assembly of 1906 (Cumberland Branch), Winona Lake, Ind.

John J. Lawrence, First Church, Binghamton, N. Y.

William Philip Lemon, Andrew Church, Minneapolis, Minn.

Robert Little, First Church, Fort Wayne, Ind.

Davis W. Lusk, Superintendent, Presbytery of Newark, Newark, N. J.

Robert J. MacAlpine, Central Church, Buffalo, N. Y.

J. A. MacCallum, Walnut Street Church, Philadelphia, Pa.

George L. MacClelland, First Church, Jamestown, N. Y.

Alexander MacColl, Second Church, Philadelphia, Pa.

Joseph B. C. Mackie, Northminster Church, Philadelphia, Pa.

Malcolm L. MacPhail, First Church, Auburn, N. Y.

John A. MacSporran, Hillside Church, Orange, N. J.

Benjamin T. Marshall, President of Connecticut College, New London, Conn.

Edwin A. McAlpin Jr., Presbyterian Church, Madison, N. J.

Daniel Spencer McCorkle, Sheldon Jackson Memorial Church, Clark, Wyo.

Alexander McGaffin, Church of the Covenant, Cleveland, Ohio.

Robert Gardner McGregor, North Avenue Church, New Rochelle, N. Y.

John McNab, Third Church, Trenton, N. J.

Andrew B. Meldrum, First (Old Stone) Church, Cleveland, Ohio.

William P. Merrill, Brick Church, New York City.

George D. Miller, First Church, Warsaw, N. Y.

Jean S. Milner, Second Church, Indianapolis, Ind.

John J. Moment, Crescent Avenue Church, Plainfield, N. J.

Andrew Mutch, Presbyterian Church, Bryn Mawr, Pa.

Robert Hastings Nichols, Professor in Auburn Theological Seminary, Auburn, N. Y.

Owen D. Odell, First Church, Sewickley, Pa.

Silas E. Persons, First Church, Annapolis, Md.

R. L. Phelps, Synodical Superintendent, West Point, Miss.

Darwin F. Pickard, First Church, Watertown, N. Y.

George D. Prentice, Presbyterian Church, Berwyn, Ill.

Harry Lathrop Reed, Professor in Auburn Theological Seminary, Auburn, N. Y.

Robert R. Reed, First Church, Iowa City, Iowa.

Charles Lee Reynolds, Park Church, Newark, N. J.

Arthur L. Rice, Presbyterian Church, Klamath Falls, Ore.

Charles Gorman Richards, Rogers Park Church, Chicago, Ill.

Henry A. Riddle Jr., Westminster Church, Greensburg, Pa.

James S. Riggs, Auburn Theological Seminary, Auburn, N. Y.

Edwin F. Rippey, First Church, Sioux City, Iowa.

J. C. Russell, Presbyterian Church, Oneonta, N. Y.

J. Elmer Russell, North Church, Binghamton, N. Y.

Alfred J. Sadler, First Church, Jersey City, N. J.

Theodore F. Savage, Secretary, Church Extension Committee, Presbytery of New York, New York City.

William L. Sawtelle, First Church, Scranton, Pa.

William F. Scoular, Glen Avon Church, Duluth, Minn.

O. R. Sellers, Professor in McCormick Theological Seminary, Chicago, Ill.

Charles G. Sewall, Presbyterian Church, Rye, N. Y.

Louis W. Sherwin, Second Church, Oil City, Pa.

Herbert Booth Smith, Immanuel Church, Los Angeles, Cal.

Matthew F. Smith, First Church, Indianapolis, Ind.

A. G. Sinclair, First Church, Bloomfield, N. J.

Clarence A. Spaulding, Presbyterian Church, Santa Barbara, Cal.

Willard P. Soper, First Church, Stamford, Conn.

George B. Stewart, President of Auburn Theological Seminary, Auburn, N. Y.

Warren S. Stone, First Church, Rochester, N. Y.

Paul Moore Strayer, Third Church, Rochester, N. Y.

Paul F. Sutphen, Church of the Covenant, Cleveland, Ohio.

Alfred W. Swan, Forest Lawn Church, Marion, Ohio.

William R. Taylor, Pastor Emeritus, Brick Church, Rochester, N. Y.

H. Sears Thomson, Presbyterian Church, Fairfield, Iowa.

Rasmus Thomsen, Central Church, Amarillo, Texas.

Henry van Dyke, Moderator of the General Assembly of 1902, Princeton University, Princeton, N. J.

Tertius van Dyke, Park Avenue Church, New York City.

Joseph H. Varner, First Church, Bear Creek, Mont.

Charles Wadsworth Jr., Philadelphia, Pa.

Harold C. Warren, Trumbull Avenue Church, Detroit, Mich.

Henry J. Weber, Dean of Bloomfield Theological Seminary, Bloomfield, N. J.

Frank M. Weston, Brighton Church, Rochester, N. Y.

Clyde Randolph Wheeland, Irving Park Church, Chicago, Ill.

Edward A. Wicher, Professor in San Francisco Theological Seminary, San Anselmo, Cal.

Thomas A. Wigginton, Washington Avenue Church, Evansville, Ind.

W. Owen Williams, First Welsh Church, Wilkes-Barre, Pa.

Gilbert L. Wilson, MacAlester College, St. Paul, Minn.

Charles Wood, Church of the Covenant, Washington, D. C.

Edmund M. Wylie, Central Church, Montclair, N. J.

PRESBYTERY INQUIRY CLEARS DR. FOSDICK AND FIRST CHURCH

Praises "Our Baptist Brother" as an Impressive Advocate of Christianity.

CRITICIZES ONE SERMON

"Shall the Fundamentalists Win?" Says the Report, Was Ill-Chosen and Provocative.

DOUBTS ASSEMBLY'S POWER

Recommends Inquiry Into Its Right in Relation to Doctrine—Vote on Report Feb. 4.

The special committee of the Presbytery of New York charged with the investigation of the Rev. Dr. Henry Emerson Fosdick's Sunday morning sermons at the First Presbyterian Church, made a report yesterday which exonerated Dr. Fosdick and the Session of the First Church of all charges and implications that Dr. Fosdick had preached heretical sermons from the First Church pulpit. The report was made to the Presbytery at a meeting in the auditorium of the First Church, Fifth Avenue and Eleventh Street. It will be discussed at a special meeting of the Presbytery on the afternoon of Feb. 4.

Despite his vindication on the larger questions involved, Dr. Fosdick was adversely criticized in the report for the sermon he preached in 1922 under the title of "Shall the Fundamentalists Win?" This was the sermon that precipitated the present situation and caused the General Assembly of the Church meeting at Indianapolis last May to direct the New York Presbytery to make the preaching at the First Church conform to the doctrine taught in the Confession of Faith. The report found that Dr. Fosdick's discussion of the virgin birth was objectionable and open to misconstruction and that the title of his sermon tended to contention and strife."

Asks Conformation to Vows.

The report also called upon Dr. Fosdick, as a Baptist minister invited to preach in a Presbyterian Church, to voluntarily conform to the obligations of Presbyterian ministers to live up to their ordination vows.

Statements from Dr. Fosdick and from the pastors and elders of the First Church were included in the report. Dr. Fosdick in his statement stated his creed, affirming his belief in the Deity of Christ. The pastors and elders strongly supported Dr. Fosdick in their statement, saying that the arrangement by which he came to the church five years ago had been a great success, but they, like the committee, criticized his sermon on the Fundamentalists.

Both the committee and the session of the First Church declared that the loss of Dr. Fosdick's preaching would injure the church, and testified to the number of persons, especially young people, who had been won back to the church through his sermons.

Powers of General Assembly.

The committee suggested the appointment of a commission "to investigate the powers of the General Assembly in relation to doctrine" in the manner provided by the Form of Government of the Church. Requiring no adherence by Dr. Fosdick to the "five points" of faith reaffirmed by the General Assembly last May, the report said that the constitutional questions involved in the "five points" issue belonged under the proposed investigation. While there were many in the Church who feared for the purity of doctrine, the committee pointed out, there were also many who feared the abridgment of accustomed liberties. This phase of the report was regarded as a back-fire against the General Assembly.

The report was read by the Rev. Dr. Edgar W. Work, retiring pastor of the Fourth Church, who is Chairman of the special committee. It was signed by all the members of the committee—Dr. Work, the Rev. Dr. Charles L. Thompson, retired senior secretary of the Board of Home Missions; the Rev. Dr. A. Edwin Keigwin, pastor of the West End Presbyterian Church; George B. Agnew, an elder in the Fifth Avenue Church, and Alfred E. Marling, an elder in the Brick Church.

The committee enclosed in its report a copy of a formal statement made to it by the pastors and elders of the church. The statement was signed by the Rev. Dr. George Alexander and the Rev. Thomas Guthrie Speers, the pastors, and by Henry N. Tifft, Clerk of the Session; was dated Dec. 11, 1923, and was addressed to Dr. Work as Chairman of the Committee.

The Session said in part:

"To the specific question asked, among many others, by your committee—'How were the elders of the First Presbyterian Church impressed by the sermon entitled, "Shall the Fundamentalists Win?"'—it is not easy to make definite answer. The members of session are in the habit of doing their own thinking and their reactions to the sermon in question were not identical. We can only indicate their general consensus of opinion.

"1. We applaud the motive which prompted this sermon and its purpose, which was, as indicated by the text, to inculcate the duty of mutual tolerance while waiting for God in His providence and by His spirit to decide questions in dispute.

"2. It seemed to us, however, that the title of the sermon was ill-chosen and provocative. It sounded more like a challenge to battle than a plea for harmony and peace. Nevertheless, we made due allowance for the fact that the preacher had been aroused by a theological controversy then acute in another communion.

"3. The sermon itself seemed to us open to misunderstanding and criticism, for the reason that while the preacher presented two extreme views on several points of Christian doctrine and did not clearly define his own position with regard to them, his hearers might not unreasonably infer that he was personally committed to all the advanced opinions for which he asked toleration.

"4. As a session, and individually, we disclaim any responsibility for the wide circulation of the sermon in slightly altered form and with a challenging foreword inviting attention to the fact that such a sermon could be preached in the First Presbyterian Church. This was done without the knowledge of any of us and by a person to us unknown.

"The members of session deeply deplore the distress thus given to many devout souls who had to judge the preacher by the printed sermon instead of judging the sermon by what they knew of the preacher. To the elders and congregation of the First Church it was not an isolated utterance, but a regrettable incident in the ministry of one whom they had learned to love and honor for his loyalty to Christ and his spiritual power.

"5. In expressing, as we do, our sorrow that occasion has been given for unrest and conflict in the Church which is dear to us, we desire to emphasize the fact that the sermon in question was exceptional. The preaching in the First Church is ordinarily uncontroversial, but searching, inspiring and full of the spirit of the Gospel. It is devoid of sensationalism and deals almost exclusively with the great themes of evangelical religion—the reality of God, the Deity of Christ, His incarnation, sinlessness and vicarious sacrifice, His resurrection from the dead and His indwelling in believers; the sinfulness of sin, the call to repentance, the necessity for a new birth and the beauty of the new life in the Spirit."

Dr. Fosdick's Statement.

The committee also included in its report the following statement from Dr. Fosdick, dated Dec. 28, 1923, and addressed to Dr. Work:

"I welcome the opportunity which the appointment of your committee affords me to express my attitude toward the theological controversy in the Presbyterian Church which, in part at least, has centred in me.

"For many months now I have been the object of attack and until this letter I have made no public reply. Nor do I write this in a controversial mood. Any gentleman dislikes to be a cause of disturbance in a neighbor's household, and as an ordained minister of another denomination preaching in a Presbyterian pulpit I am profoundly sorry that contention has arisen because of me. For this reason I already have resigned my position there only because of the unanimous desire of the church's session and their insistence that withdrawal would do more harm than good.

"In spite of sharp differences of opinion between two prevalent schools of theological thought, and in spite of the unmistakable fact that I am committed to the side called 'liberal,' I confess that I have been suprised at the misinterpretation of my position which has been spread broadcast. If I did not regard myself as an evangelical Christian, I certainly should not be preaching in an evangelical pulpit. Nor was there ever a day when one in earnest about his faith would wish his unqualified Christian allegiance to be more manifest than now. These are days when the Christian faith is being resolutely assailed, when materialistic naturalism is presenting a perilous problem, when many are in doubt, when Christianity faces alike one of its supreme crises and supreme opportunities. These are days when every man who seriously and deeply believes in the gospel of Jesus Christ wants to be counted on that side and not on any other. It goes hard with me, therefore, to find myself and whatever influence I may possess rated as against things I really am for and for things I really am against.

"I am in the ministry of the evangelical churches because I belong there and nowhere else—reared in evangelical Christianity, converted in it, convinced of it, and ready to live and die for it. The liberty I claim to think through the gospel in terms real and cogent in our own time is, I am sure, not a denial of the gospel, but one of the most precious and sacred privileges and responsibilities which our evangelical forefathers claimed for themselves, fought for and gloriously used.

"Personally I have no patience with an emasculated Christianity that denudes the Gospel of its superhuman elements, its redeeming power, and its eternal hopes. I believe in the Personal God revealed in Christ, in his omnipresent activity and endless resources to achieve his purposes for us and all men; I believe in Christ, his deity, his sacrificial saviorhood, his resurrected and triumphant life, his rightful Lordship, and the indispensableness of his message to mankind. In the indwelling Spirit I believe the forgiveness of sins, the redeemed and victorious life, the triumph of righteousness on earth, and the life everlasting. This faith I find in the Scriptures and the objective of my ministry is to lead men to the Scriptures as the standard and form of religious experience — the progressive self-revelation of God in the history of a unique people, culminating in Christ. To the proclamation of the Gospel with such elements of abiding experience at the heart of it I am giving myself—trying to translate it into terms that will penetrate the intelligence and challenge the conscience of the oncoming generation.

"I am not, therefore, an enemy of the Gospel of Christ, a denier of the profound experiences and convictions which in all ages have been the glory of the Church, the substance of her creeds, and the source of her power. Nor, as I understand it, are those who like me are called Liberals. We are men at the centre of whose life is a profound faith in God revealed in Christ for man's salvation, and we are facing with passionate earnestness the needs of this disturbed, doubting and often wistful generation, endeavoring, as our fathers did in their days, to interpret the everlasting Gospel to our own time in terms that our own time can understand.

"The joy of my ministry is now, as it always has been, to lead men into vital relationship with Jesus Christ, to bring them under the spell of his Mastership, and to inspire them to make Him and all that He stands for dominant in the life of the world. Never did this ministry seem so much worth while, never were its fruits more manifest, and all my days I hope to give myself to it in the freedom with which Christ set us free."

Found Letter Impressive.

The committee said that it found "a certain solemnity and impressiveness about the confession of a man's faith" in Dr. Fosdick's letter.

Study of the preaching and teaching in the First Church, the committee went on, has convinced it also that Dr. Fosdick is proclaiming "the doctrine of grace" regularly from that pulpit.

"We believe," the report went on, "that they (doctrines of grace) are being proclaimed with power and in a manner that is producing an unusual impression upon the part of many persons who have grown careless as to the claims of the Christian religion. * * * It is our conclusion that these doctrines of the Grace of God through Christ are receiving new force and urgency for times like ours. * * * The committee is deeply impressed by what we have learned of the effect of the public proclamation of the Word in the First Church.

High Praise For Dr. Fosdick.

"Few such challenging voices have ever been heard in this city in defense of religion. There is no hint of sensationalism in the sermons. They are serious, studied, affirmations of religious truth, intended to convince men that they cannot live rightly in this world without God and Christ and the Holy Spirit. * * * In our judgment there can be no mistake concerning the tremendous challenge of this voice in the pulpit to a generation that tends to play fast and loose with religion. The arrest of thought that has been produced on religious subjects in this great and careless city is a fact that cannot be gainsaid."

Regretting that it had to qualify its praise of Dr. Fosdick with adverse criticism, the committee went on:

"It is inevitable that mistakes of judgment and emphasis will occur in a ministry such as we have described. It is the belief of this committee that mistakes have occurred."

The committee said it agreed with the session of the First Church that Dr. Fosdick's sermon, "Shall the Fundamentalists Win?" was "captioned by an objectionable and challenging title, that tended to contention and strife, and that it was open to wide misunderstanding. It also regretted the wide circulation given to the sermon.

"We go further to say," went on the committee, "that while we are sure that the preaching and teaching in the First

Church has never spoken any denial of the Church's doctrine of the virgin birth of our Lord, it is our judgment that the manner in which this subject was dealt with in the sermon mentioned, is open to painful misconstruction and just objection.

"The real crux of this situation, the committee feels," its report continued, "lies in the fact that the Presbyterian Church is accustomed to a ministry that recognizes the obligation of ordination vows. This is the genius and method of our system of government, and it cannot safely be ignored. * * * It is natural that a church, constituted as the Presbyterian Church is, should insist upon the recognition of this fact.

"It is therefore the judgment of this committee that this conception of an obligation to the denomination must be fairly met by a member of another denomination who is invited to minister statedly in one our pulpits."

Committee's Recommendations.

Stating that it would continue its work and would make a further report if the Presbytery wished, the committee closed its report with the following recommendations:

"First—The Presbytery states that it believes in the purpose and character of the preaching and teaching in the First Church of New York, and that it expresses its confident expectation that our brother of another denomination who enjoys the freedom of this pulpit will labor unceasingly and in all good conscience to promote the gospel and the spread of evangelical truth.

"Second—The Presbytery expresses its confidence in the loyalty of the Session of the First Church, and particularly in the wisdom and devotion of our beloved brother, the Rev. George Alexander, D. D., pastor of the First Church. The Presbytery further records it satisfaction with the statement of the Session as to its understanding of the duty of Sessions in safeguarding the preaching and teaching of the pulpit, in accordance with the doctrinal standards of our church.

"Third—The Presbytery holds itself in readiness to receive further reports on this subject, and to take further steps in relation to it, as occasion may require.

"Fourth. The Presbytery affirms its belief in the Bible as the only infallible rule of faith and practice, and in all the doctrines of grace and salvation that belong to evangelical Christianity. The Presbytery further declares that it sorrows deeply over controversy and strife, and that it is its desire and intention to address itself to prayer and the ministry of the Word, to the building up of our churches, to the work of evangelism, soul-winning and social welfare in this great city, and to the propagation of the gospel of Jesus Christ at home and abroad.

Discussion Postponed.

Decision to postpone discussion of the report to Feb. 4 was made in a motion by the Rev. Dr. David G. Wylie, which was unanimously adopted. The meeting yesterday was so large that it had to be held in the church proper instead of the chapel. It was the first time in seventeen years that the Presbytery had had to meet in the church itself. About 200 ministers and fifty elders participated as voters, while about 150 persons, mostly ministers from neighboring presbyteries, sat in the galleries. The Rev. Dr. Howard Duffield, moderator of the Presbytery and a pastor-emeritus of First Church, presided.

If the Presbytery adopts the Fosdick report it will go to the next General Assembly, in Grand Rapids, Mich., next May. Before the report was read yesterday the Presbytery approved an overture handed down from the last General Assembly, permitting ministers from other denominations to be stated supplies in Presbyterian churches when the Presbytery approves such a course. This overture was aimed at Dr. Fosdick when originally introduced at Indianapolis, but was amended to its present form by making the retention of such "stated supplies" dependent on the approval of the Presbytery. The Presbytery yesterday postponed action till its next meeting on an overture from the Presbytery of Larned, Kan., asking that the Presbyterian boards and agencies be moved away from New York because of the New York Presbytery's "willful disregard of the direct command of the last General Assembly."

January 15, 1924

ASSEMBLY CENSURES NEW YORK LIBERALS; SPLIT THREATENS

Presbyterian Fundamentalists Win Affirmation of Doctrine of the Virgin Birth.

HOLD IT TO BE ESSENTIAL

Judicial Commission Is Upheld in Ruling Against Licensing Ministers Who Reject It.

Special to The New York Times.

COLUMBUS, Ohio, May 26.—A momentous decision that it is feared by many Presbyterians may be a wedge for a wide split in the Church was made today by the Presbyterian General Assembly, which, sitting as a high court, upheld the complaint of the Rev. Albert D. Gantz, who challenged the right of the Presbytery of New York to license ministers who did not affirm positive belief in the virgin birth.

The sweeping victory of the extreme Fundamentalists stunned the commissioners from the New York Presbytery. Tense and nervous with excitement, Dr. Henry Sloane Coffin, a liberal leader of the New York commissioners, hurried to the platform and firmly declared that the Presbytery of New York would continue its policy of licensing candidates, standing upon the constitution of the Church, "which forbids the Assembly to change or add to the conditions for entrance upon or continuance in the holy ministry without submitting such amendment to the Presbyteries for concurrent action."

Dr. Coffin's virtual defiance of the General Assembly's authority to rule that a candidate for the ministry must positively affirm the truth of the virgin birth was followed by the announcement of the Rev. Joel Hayden of Cleveland that he would circulate a petition of protest against the decision.

One hope for the avoidance of a split in the Church, which it is admitted by the commissioners would have tragic consequences, rests in a commission of fifteen, which Dr. Charles R. Erdman, the Moderator, will appoint "to study the present spiritual condition of our Church and the causes making for unrest and to report to the next General Assembly, to the end that the purity, peace, unity and progress of the Church may be assured."

The appointment of this committee, it was said, would automatically suspend the carrying out of the decision in the Gantz case until next year's General Assembly. In the meantime, the extreme Fundamentalists and the liberals will line up for what will be a historic battle next year in the General Assembly at Baltimore, the outcome of which will determine the future of the Church, whether it will be united or whether it will split into Fundamentalists and liberals.

Dr. Macartney Explains Decision.

Dr. Clarence E. Macartney, the retiring Moderator, praised the work of the Judicial Commission in the Gantz case and said that everything for which the extreme Fundamentalists had been contending had been decided in their favor.

"The Judicial Commission, in its decision concerning the complaint against the Synod of New York, has done a great service to the Presbyterian Church and the cause of evangelical Christianity throughout the world," said Dr. Macartney. "It is impossible to overstate its far-reaching and profound significance. It establishes the following disputed points—that is, disputed by the Modernists and Liberalists in Presbyterian churches:

"The absolute right of the General Assembly as to review and control over the actions of the Presbyteries. It establishes the fact that the Presbyterian Church is a constitutional church and not a loose federation of Presbyteries.

"Those who upheld the action of the New York Presbytery in licensing men who refused to affirm certain doctrines have maintained that the Presbyteries are not subject to review and control by the assemblies, so long as they license within the bounds of their interpretation of the constitution of the Church. The decision of the Judicial Commission now determines that we have not several hundred creeds and governments corresponding to the number of our Presbyteries, but one creed and one government.

"The decision makes it clear that it is

irregular and unconstitutional for a Presbytery to license men who say they cannot affirm certain doctrines. The decision points out that the constitution of the Church requires complete and enthusiastic affirmation of the doctrines of the Confession of Faith.

"The virgin birth of our Lord Jesus Christ by decision of the highest court of the Presbyterian Church is declared to be an essential doctrine of the confession of faith. No Presbytery anywhere can dare to license men who refuse to affirm their faith in the doctrine of the virgin birth after this decision of the judicial commission. The decision has splendidly pointed out that the Confession of Faith rests upon the Holy Scriptures, and that no man can deny the narratives of St. Matthew and St. Luke and the incarnation of God in Christ without denying also the confession of faith.

"The other two complaints now go back to the Synod of New York, and in view of this decision the Synod of New York cannot do otherwise than condemn the Presbytery.

"All that we have been hoping, striving and praying for and witnessing to in the face of widespread ridicule, misrepresentation and opposition, has been magnificently vindicated. The great doctrines of the Presbyterian Church and of all evangelical churches are thus solemnly set forth by the decision as necessary portions of the Christian faith.

"There is still a God in Israel and the government and doctrines of the Presbyterian Church in the United States of America still live, praise God from Whom all blessings flow!"

Liberals Defeated After Victory.

The defeat of the New York liberals followed a victory for them over the extreme Fundamentalists in three less important cases. The first was that of Dr. Walter D. Buchanan of the Broadway Presbyterian Church and a group of extreme Fundamentalists against the Presbytery of New York, alleging failure by the First Presbyterian Church to dispense with the ervices of Dr. Harry Emerson Fosdick, Baptist "guest" preacher, promptly upon last year's decision of the General Assembly that Dr. Fosdick should subscribe to the Presbyterian creed or leave the First Church. The complaint, considered by the Permanent Judicial Commission, was dismissed on the ground that there was nothing to show that the Presbytery of New York was guilty of "contempt of court" or that there was any intent by the Presbytery to defy the General Assembly.

Two complaints by Dr. Buchanan and his associates against the Presbytery of New York for licensing Cameron Parker Hall and Carlos G. Fuller, on the ground that they failed to affirm belief in the virgin birth, were dismissed by the Judicial Commission and the General Assembly on the ground that the petitioner did not appeal first to the Synod before carrying the case to the General Assembly.

The disposition of the three cases against the New York Presbytery served to work up the greatest interest in the outstanding case—that of Dr. Gantz against the Synod of New York, opposing its right to license Henry P. Van Dusen and Cedric A. Lehman as ministers. Although they failed to affirm the Virgin birth, the candidates did not deny it. This complaint originally was made against the Presbytery of New York and was appealed by Dr. Gantz to the Synod of New York, which upheld the action of the Presbytery.

Judge Henry D. Burr of the Permanent Judicial Commission, the supreme court of the Church, in outlining the decision in the Gantz case said that representatives of both sides admitted that the candidates for the ministry named in the complaint stated that they could neither affirm nor deny the virgin birth.

Church Constitution Involved.

The case presented two serious questions involving the constitution of the church, said Judge Burr, "the right of the General Assembly to review the action of a Presbytery in licensing candidates for the ministry and the necessary requirements for licensure."

Judge Burr said the Church's form of government gave the Presbytery the power to examine and license candidates for the ministry; but this power was subject to review, else "each Presbytery would be a law unto itself."

In 1910, he said, the General Assembly took action on complaints against the Synod of New York in licensing and ordaining candidates.

The Permanent Judicial Commission, Judge Burr continued, held that Section 5 of Chapter 12 of the form of government gave to the General Assembly "the power of deciding in all controversies respecting doctrine."

Having ruled on the constitutional power of the General Assembly in the case, the decision discussed the next question, the candidates' belief in the virgin birth.

"It is not a question as to the character of the applicant, his education, his amiable qualities, or even his piety," the decision continued. "The candidate was not required to state his views as to the mystery therein contained. He was not required to attempt to explain it. He was asked whether he believed in the virgin birth, his attention being called to the narratives as contained in the gospels of Matthew and of Luke, and he declined to affirm, stating he could neither affirm nor deny. He was in doubt as to the truth of these portions of the Holy Scriptures. Hence, he was unable to affirm his belief in positive, definite statements in the gospels regarding the virgin birth.

Defines Meaning of Questions.

"Constitutional question 1, regarding belief in the Scriptures of the Old and New Testament, means the Scriptures as defined and described in Chapter 1 of the Confession of Faith. Constitutional question 2, requiring the candidate to receive and adopt the confession of faith of this Church as containing the system of doctrine taught in the Holy Scriptures, means the Confession of Faith, including Chapter 8 thereof, dealing with the Incarnation.

"Thus, while he answered these constitutional questions in the affirmative, his affirmation is qualified by his doubt hereinbefore set forth. He gave his assent knowing he could not affirm his belief in the Virgin Birth and the narratives thereof, as contained in the gospels and as declared and defined in the confession of faith, and knowing the Presbytery knew he could not so affirm.

"The General Assembly, under the constitution of the Church, has the power, and it is its duty, to review the action of lower judicatories. In the discharge of his duty, in a case regularly brought before it, the General Assembly is exercising its power as a court and as the highest judicatory in the Church, and its decisions regarding doctrinal matters in such a case is therefore binding until modified or reviewed, or until the constitution is amended.

"In 1910 the General Assembly, in an action on a complaint against the Synod of New York in sustaining the action of a Presbytery in licensing candidates who, while not denying the Virgin Birth of our Lord, failed 'to affirm it with the same positiveness as for some other doctrines,' said that 'no one who is in serious doubt concerning this doctrine should be licensed or ordained as a minister.'

"The General Assembly has repeatedly passed upon the importance of clear and positive views regarding this doctrine. It is the established law of the Church. The Church has not seen fit to alter it and your Judicial Commission sees no reason for amending the Constitution by judicial interpretation.

Holds the Presbytery Erred.

"The aplicants being each uncertain as to his belief, and being unable to affirm his belief in the virgin birth of our Lord as set forth in the Gospels and declared in the Confession of Faith, the Presbytery erred in not deferring the licensing until the candidates were certain and positive, no matter how amiable, educated or talented the candidates may have been.

"The action of the synod in failing to sustain the complaints against the Presbytery is reversed and the complaint against the Presbytery is sustained.

"This matter is remanded to the Presbytery for appropriate action, in conformity with the decision herein rendered."

The decision was put before the General Assembly by the Moderator and was adopted, only the New York commissioners and a few others voting in the negative. It was pointed out that the action of the Assembly was its only recourse unless it wished to try the case itself.

The severe blow to the Presbytery of New York took the New York commissioners by surprise. Although they had prepared themselves for any contingency, they did not believe, they said later, that the commission would reach such an extreme decision.

New York Presbytery Protests.

Pale and trembling with excitement, Dr. Coffin mounted the rostrum and read the following protest:

"The sixteen Commissioners of the Presbytery of New York, on behalf of the said Presbytery, respectfully declare that the Presbytery of New York will stand firmly upon the constitution of the Church, reaffirmed in the reunions of 1870 and 1906, which forbids the Assembly to change or add to the conditions for entrance upon or continuance in the holy ministry, without submitting such amendment to the Presbyteries for concurrent action.

ROBERT W. BOYD,
THOMAS GUTHRIE SPEERS,
GEORGE B. AGNEW,
EDWARD H. KROM,
T. N. PFEIFFER,
GEORGE M. DUFF,
LEE W. BEATTIE,
D. W. WYLIE,
HAROLD S. RAMBO,
JOHN H. FINLEY,
REGINALD L. McALL,
WILLIAM P. MERRILL,
NORMAN J. MARSH,
A. EDWIN KEIGWIN,
GEORGE H. RICHARDS,
HENRY SLOANE COFFIN.

The protest threw the Assembly into a fever of excitement. A score of voices were raised demanding the floor and Moderator Erdman, confronted by the crisis which he had used all his means to avoid, rapped for order.

Dr. John F. Carson, an extreme Fundamentalist, of Brooklyn, declared that Dr. Coffin's statement was out of order, as the Assembly still was sitting as a high court.

Synod Also Files Protest.

The court was adjourned, and then J. V. Oldenhauser, for the Synod of New York, hurried to the platform and filed the following protest against the decision:

The committee appointed by the Synod of New York to defend its action before the General Assembly based its argument upon the constitutional power of the Presbytery to determine the fitness of candidates for the gospel ministry.

We, the members of that committee, hereby respectfully voice our disagreement with the Assembly's decision, and our conviction that the Synod of New York and its constituent Presbyteries must continue to maintain the rights of Presbyteries in all matters of licensure and ordination.

J. V. OLDENHAUSER,
ROBERT HASTINGS NICHOLS,
RALPH HICKOK,
T. N. PFEIFFER,
HENRY SLOANE COFFIN.

Protests filled the air against the action of Dr. Coffin and Mr. Oldenhauser.

Moderator Erdman then tried to pour oil on the troubled ecclesiastical waters by suggesting the appointment of a commission of fifteen to look into the whole matter of the spiritual condition of the Church. A New York commissioner made a special point of seconding the proposal, which was adopted unanimously.

Dr. Joel Hayden of Cleveland offered a protest against the decision of the Supreme Judicial Commission. It bore his name alone, and he said he would circulate it among the commissioners tomorrow.

The body then tabled permanently the Chester overture, calling for the exscinding of the New York Presbytery and the demand of the Presbytery of New York for vindication of its stand in the Fosdick case.

Dr. Coffin Explains Liberals' Attitude.

After leaving the floor Dr. Coffin made the following statement to reporters in explanation of the attitude of the New York liberals:

"We interpret the decision of the Supreme Judicial Commission as an attempt to add to the Constitution by judicial decision, and thus to alter the requirements for entrance into the holy ministry. This we hold to be a violation of the Constitution.

"If they wish to make categorical acceptance of the virgin birth a requirement for entrance into the ministry, it must be submitted to the Presbyteries for concurrent action, as it is an addition to our standards, which, neither in the Scriptures nor in the Confession of Faith, mention the virgin birth as essential.

"The Scriptures and the Confession mention many things which are not regarded as essential; for example, the creation of the world in six days. If the virgin birth is to be made essential because it is mentioned in both the Scriptures and in the Confession, then it follows that the creation of the world in six days is also essential. Thus the Church would be made ridiculous in the eyes of the world.

"While the Presbytery of New York has been singled out for complaint in this matter, it is common knowledge that many Presbyteries have licensed students from various seminaries who do not categorically affirm the virgin birth. It is a well-known fact that many clergymen of the Church hold the same position.

"We will continue to assert our rights, and there will be no weakening in the assertion of our rights."

"The Commission of Fifteen is in the nature of an attempt to prevent the evil consequences which might ensue on the rendering of the Judicial Commission's report."

Dr. Coffin was asked whether the Presbytery and the Synod of New York would "bolt the decision."

"Not until the last door is closed to us," he replied.

So far as the two ministers named in the Gantz complaint are concerned, it was said that since they had been ordained licensed ministers there was no way of revoking their licenses unless they were tried for heresy or false teaching subsequent to their ordination.

Two Reports on Chester Complaint.

A majority and a minority report on the overture of the Presbytery of Chester, which asked that the Presbytery of New York be exscinded, was reported by the Committee on Bills and Overtures this morning. The majority vindicated the Presbytery, recommending that no action be taken, on the ground that there had been no sustaining testimony presented. The minority called

for the appointment of a special judicial committee to investigate the charges, as well as all the unrest in the Church, the committee to have power to summon witnesses and to make a complete investigation "of the alleged unrest based upon the alleged acts of the Presbytery of New York."

The minority report was signed by A. Gordon MacLennan, R. D. Wilson, A. Wildberger, M. M. Morelock, George S. Patterson, John McLellan, R. E. Williams and A. G. Patterson.

In a report on his mission to the Jews, Paul L. Berman of the Department of Jewish Evangelism of the Board of National Missions declared that the articles published by Henry Ford in The Dearborn Independent made it difficult for those who were engaged in the work of carrying the message of the Presby-

terian Church to the Jews in the United States.

"You cannot succeed in solving the Jewish problem by persecution and anti-Simitism," he declared. "The Egyptians tried by attempting to drown the Jews, but they found they were waterproof. They threw some of them in the fiery furnace, but they soon found they were also fireproof. In the days of Haman they thought the best solution was to hang the Jews, but they found that they were stiff-necked.

"The only way to solve the Jewish problem in America and the world is through Christ. Today 4,000,000 Jews are stretching out their arms to you, pleading that you help them. Please don't neglect them."

May 27, 1925

TWO CHURCH BODIES AGREE ON MERGER

Congregationalists and Christian Groups Complete Union With 3,000,000 Adherents.

ADOPT ONE CONSTITUTION

It Sets Forth That Differences in Interpretation of the Bible Are Not Obstacle to Union.

SEATTLE, June 25 (AP).—Formal action which merged two major church bodies, the Congregationalists and the Christian Church, with a combined membership of more than 1,000,000, was taken at a joint convention late today.

A new constitution providing for the union was approved at separate assemblies.

At the outset the united body will have the Congregationalist moderator and the Christian president as co-moderators.

The majority of the Christian churches are located in the States of the Mississippi Valley and the Southeast. Churchmen said the merger was the largest ever taking place between denominations entirely distinct in origin in history.

The churches affected total 6,670 in this country, with a communicant membership of 1,050,000 and a constituency, including adherents, of about 3,000,000.

Missions Previously Merged.

The foreign missions of the two groups already have been merged under the American Board of Commissioners for Foreign Missions. The missions are in sixteen foreign countries, where 850 American missionaries and more than 6,000 nationals are employed.

Those who led the negotiations for the union believed it was the beginning of a new trend in church life and will be followed by other mergers. They hoped other denominations will join with them to form a group large enough to warrant the use of the name the United Church of Christ in America.

The Rev. Dr. Carl H. Patton, proctor of the First Congregational Church, Los Angeles, was elected moderator of the National Congregational Council and thereby becomes co-moderator of the newly formed union.

An announcement said the union would consider current world problems from a religious standpoint and afford churchmen "opportunity for free discussion of religious problems without fear of being unorthodox."

"The Church and the New Internationalism" will be discussed by the Rev. Fred B. Smith of New York, moderator of the national council.

First seminars will be held tomorrow, devoted to problems relating to the individual, the church, the community, the national and international relations. The council will meet Thursday and Friday next week to consider the findings of the seminars.

The Rev. S. Parkes Cadman of Brooklyn will address the convention on "The Mission of the Republic" tomorrow night.

Text of Constitution Adopted.

The principles of the Church union as set forth in the preamble to the constitution adopted are:

"We hold sacred the freedom of the individual soul and the right of private judgment. We stand for the autonomy of the local church and its independence of ecclesiastical control. We cherish the fellowship of churches, united in district, State and national bodies, for counsel and cooperation. Affirming these convictions, we hold to the unity of the Church of Christ and will unite with all its branches in fellowship and hearty cooperation, and we earnestly seek that the prayer of Our Lord for the unity of His followers may be speedily answered.

"We find in the Bible the supreme rule of faith and life, but recognize wide room for differences in interpretation. We therefore base our union upon the acceptance of Christianity as primarily a way of life and not upon uniformity of theological opinion or any uniform practice of ordinances."

The constitution specifies that the new General Council shall have two Moderators, one from the Congregational group and one from the Christian group, until 1935, after which there shall be only one Moderator. There shall also be assistant Moderators. The council shall have a secretary, an assistant secretary and departmental secretaries. Bureaus of evangelism, of ministerial supply, of stewardship and of Christian unity, and two permanent commissions on social relationships and good citizenship, and on international and interracial relations are to be established by the council.

In 1930 The Christian Herald in its annual tabulation gave the Church of the Disciples of Christ a membership of 1,573,245 and the Congregational Church a membership of 930,130.

June 26, 1931

Unemployment Hits the Lutheran Clergy; Seminaries Are Asked to Weed Out Students

Because there are so many unemployed Lutheran clergymen with slight chance of getting church posts in the immediate future, the Rev. Dr. Samuel Trexler, president of the United Lutheran Synod of New York, wrote a letter yesterday from his office, 39 East Thirty-fifth Street, to all the theological seminaries of the United Lutheran Church in America asking them to weed out students who lack the qualifications to become first-class pastors.

This letter said:

"At the recent meeting of the executive committee of the synod a study was made of the men at present on our roll who cannot be placed in pastorates because of their defect in the qualities that make for a successful ministry.

"I was asked to communicate to you our conviction that higher standards should be exacted of men who enter our seminaries with a view to the ministry, and that throughout their course study be made of the students so as to eliminate from the candidates for the ministry such as seem to be lacking in the needed qualifications.

"The work of the Church is demanding constantly higher standards, and we would kindly ask you to assist us in reaching these standards."

In some churches where there has long been an assistant pastor the pastor is now doing the work alone and in many new missions where a young man just graduated from a seminary was in charge the services have been suspended until better times.

In commenting at his home on the situation, Dr. Trexler said: "Our executive committee has decided that the thorough method of dealing with the problem is to tackle it at its source—the seminary. If all candidates for the ministry are eliminated save those with the highest qualifications there will no longer be more men than churches, more pastors than pastorates."

March 7, 1931

BAPTISTS SEEK JOBS FOR IDLE MINISTERS

Conference Names Committee to Bring Congregations and Pastors Together.

CHURCH MERGERS ARE FELT

Many Organizations Also Have Dropped Assistants of Clergymen to Cut Expenses.

After the question of unemployment among ministers had been called yesterday to the attention of members attending the weekly meeting of the Baptist Ministers' Conference in the parish house of the Madison Avenue Baptist Church, the Rev. Dr. Mark Wayne Williams, pastor of the Hanson Place Baptist Church in Brooklyn and president of the conference, authorized the Rev. Dr. George Caleb Moor, pastor of the Madison Avenue Church, to form a committee of five, with himself as chairman, to "consider a definite plan for bringing together unemployed ministers and churches seeking a minister."

Dr. Moor appointed the following: The Rev. Dr. John Falconer Fraser, pastor of the Central Church; the Rev. Will H. Houghton, pastor of Calvary Church; the Rev. Francis W. O'Brien, pastor of the Greenwood Church, Brooklyn, and the Rev. George McKiernam, pastor of the Wyckoff Avenue Church, Brooklyn.

The Baptists are the second large denomination to take official cognizance of ministerial unemployment in the last four days. Last Saturday the Rev. Dr. Samuel Trexler, president of the United Lutheran Synod of New York, sent a letter in the name of the synod's executive committee to the presidents of Lutheran theological seminaries in the United States, asking them to weed out all but the best candidates for the ministry, since there are already too many ministers for the number of churches.

In discussing the action of the conference yesterday, Dr. Williams explained that a great many ministers have come to New York recently in search of churches. Some of them, he said, have been pastors here and are now out of work.

"It is hard to place them." he said, "and to make matters worse, the wives of some of these men are ill and they have small children to take care of."

Dr. Williams explained also that, because of mergers, there are fewer churches here nowadays, while the colleges and seminaries are turning out new ministers faster than the churches can assimilate them. "There are, however," he said, "many new communities developing on Long Island where Baptist congregations are being established.

"Of course a man of unusual ability can nearly always find a church. But then we have many hard-working men whose abilities are limited. We want to help them to get adjusted. I know a dozen now, looking for churches, and I can't help them. Many churches that employed assistant ministers have let their assistants go because they have only enough money to pay the pastor."

Dr. Williams said it was more difficult for Baptists to place unemployed ministers because they have no Bishops or presidents of synods.

March 10, 1931

CHURCH SCORES BREADLINE

Episcopal Social Service Body Considers It Demoralizing.

Breadlines and the giving of relief on the streets have a demoralizing effect and involve a waste of money, according to a message to all the parishes in the Protestant Episcopal Diocese of New York from the Diocesan Social Service Commission.

The message, sent out by the Rev. Floyd Van Keuren, suggests various ways in which the parishes should undertake relief work and urges close cooperation with local community organizations, social agencies and other churches.

The commission suggests that there be no relief without "case work," clearing through a soocial service exchange, a visit in the home and an interview with some one who knows the family. Parishes are urged to help their members.

October 25, 1931

MEMBERSHIP WANES IN RURAL CHURCHES

Survey Reveals Protestants in Many Centres Are Fewer Than Twenty-five.

LEADERS HELD AT FAULT

Social and Religious Research Institute Says "Stereotyped Methods" Are Used.

Protestant churches in six widely different kinds of rural American territory, comprising more than one-third of the area of the United States and containing 3,500,000 persons, are exceedingly weak and have relatively few members, according to a report made public yesterday of a survey conducted by the Institute of Social and Religious Research, 230 Park Avenue. The report, written by Elizabeth R. Hooker, has been published by the institute under the title "Hinterlands of the Church."

The general tendency in the territory studied, according to the report, is toward a further loss of power to attract and hold the people. It is stated that the ineffectiveness and continuing decline of the Protestant churches in the regions studied are attributed in part to the policy of using sterotyped methods in the rural districts.

Four of the areas are of comparatively recent settlement. They are the grazing section, the dry-farming section, the high mountain districts of the Far West and various cut-over lands. The two other areas include the old hilly sections of New England and many counties on long-settled country of the Middle West.

In the four new areas the average membership of the Protestant church was sixty-eight, against 161 in Roman Catholic churches and 370 in Mormon churches. The average Protestant membership for the individual areas ranged from seventy-three for the dry-farming regions to forty-six in Vermont rural territory.

Lack Proper Equipment.

"The churches of small centres and open-country districts average much smaller than this," continues the report, "and a large number of them have fewer than twenty-five members apiece. Being small, the Protestant churches cannot afford a modern church building, or much fuel, or light, or music, or any of the many other things utilized in a modern church program."

The report says that "the responsibility for affording religious ministry to the people of these vast hinterlands of the church is largely a Protestant responsibility." Topography, climate and rainfall, it is asserted, profoundly affect the church situation and create different problems in different localities.

"Considering, on the one hand, the obstacles to church work presented by the areas studied," the report states, "and, on the other hand, the lack of adaptation to such conditions displayed by organized Protestant Christianity in the United States, it is only to be expected that the churches of these areas should be ineffective.

"Within all the counties surveyed the open-country districts and the smaller centres have relatively fewer church members than have the large centres.

Many Churches Abandoned.

"In the old level areas the abandonment of country churches is progressing at an accelerating speed. In Vermont, the proportion of families to churches has declined a third in fifty years.

"In the old days of intense denominational activity it could be assumed that every district would have a church within reach. But in the new lands, in the absence of comprehensive interdenominational policies, hundreds of hamlets and many thousands of square miles of hinterland are without religious services; and in other localities attempts at ministry have soon been abandoned.

"If evenly spaced, the churches of the grazing lands would be eighteen miles apart and those of the mountain sections thirteen; while the distance between neighboring churches in the old hilly areas would be four miles, and in the old level areas only three and a half miles.

"In the old level areas the number of constituents of country churches has been diminished by the superior attractions of churches in neighboring towns and cities. The same tendency is at work in the old hilly sections in country neighborhoods from which large centres are readily accessible. Even in the newer regions, many churches in districts connected with large centres by improved roads are feeling the effects of a similar withdrawal of adherents. The tendency is particularly marked in the Columbia Basin and near Seattle, Denver and other large cities."

June 7, 1931

THE STUDENT GROPES FOR A FAITH
In the Colleges and Universities, an Inquirer Discovers, There Is, Amid Many Doubts, a New and Deeper Curiosity Concerning Spiritual Truth

By GEORGE W. GRAY

Is the student of today turning to the religion of his fathers or is he striving on his own account to discover spiritual truth? The question is suggested by the external fact that new and costly chapels have recently been built on college campuses, and by the deeper fact that a groping for reality in terms of religious experience is noteworthy among college students. The article that follows is the report on an inquiry made at the source.

"YOU are all a lost generation," said Gertrude Stein to Ernest Hemingway, and the phrase became the motif for his first novel and a sort of label for the disillusioned and cynical youth that emerged from the World War years. But meanwhile another generation is coming of age which does not accept the label. Especially in the universities and colleges one meets a new attitude of inquiry and hopefulness, quite in contrast with the shoulder-shrugging rejections and blatant denials of the hard-boiled '20s.

And perhaps the most characteristic expression of the new mood is the undergraduate attitude toward religion. "Dreiser, Mencken, Sinclair Lewis, Hemingway and the others of that school we have put aside as too destructive," said a student at Harvard, editor of one of the undergraduate publications, an outstanding senior. "We want to build up. Among my associates, the literary group, I haven't met a student who is an atheist. They all believe in God, but the problem is the approach to God. We don't find it in the existing churches, and we want it. If some men would show us the way, we'd run to him."

An official at Columbia, who makes it a practice to entertain freshmen in his home, was describing the characteristic course of such a gathering. "The boys are all new, most of them strangers to one another. Talk is tentative and slow at first. It drifts along for half an hour perhaps, but soon some fellow asks a question on religion. Then they all snap to attention, and the rest of the evening is spent in the most animated discussion. I know no other subject that is of such sure-fire interest."

38

Times Wide World Photo

"All the Currents of Thought That Are Running Strong in the World Meet in a University."

An official at Yale, in no way connected with the religious activities of the university, volunteered this report: "Yale students will talk about religion, discuss it seriously, even eagerly and inquiringly, but they don't go to church—not much."

At other universities one hears much the same report. "Bull sessions" on religion are of common occurrence. Groups that meet for some other business have been known to linger, after their business has ended, in a discussion of religion. Announcement of an address on religion by some eminent authority, particularly if he is a scientist, will crowd the lecture hall.

But "they don't go to church—not much," except in those institutions where compulsory chapel is still the rule, and forced attendance hardly counts as a test or as evidence of the interest we are examining.

To the loyal churchman, whether he be Catholic, Protestant or Jew, it may seem a contradiction that persons seriously interested in religion should ignore the places where it is traditionally centred. Of course, worship is not wholly ignored. In each of the colleges there is a group that habitually attends chapel—though the faithful sometimes sink to the irreducible minimum. I dropped in at the chapel service of the University of Pennsylvania one Wednesday last May and found that the morning's congregation consisted of one student.

• • •

SINCE then Pennsylvania has installed a new chaplain; Yale has placed one of its gifted graduates in charge of its chapel; Harvard has opened an $800,000 university church, and at several other centres similar and even more expensive efforts have been made to provide for the religious nurture of students. Indeed, some of the finest ecclesiastical architecture of recent years has lately been erected on college greens. Thus, Trinity College, in Connecticut, dedicated a $1,000,-000 chapel last June. And Duke University (that former Trinity in North Carolina) has just added a towering centre-piece to its freshly hewn Gothic quadrangles in the form of a $2,000,000 chapel—perhaps the most expensive church in the South.

These collegiate shrines are "in character" with the medieval grandeur of the great pile completed at the University of Chicago four years ago at a cost of $2,000,-000, with an additional $1,000,000 as endowment, and the equally impressive university chapel at Princeton dedicated in 1928—each of them spacious enough and decorative enough to enthrone a bishop.

There is an uneasy feeling among educators that religion has been neglected, and that it is needed. Even in State universities, where official religion is banned, one feels this attitude; and here denominational churches are encouraged and even solicited to provide chapels, sacraments, prayers and other aids to devotion. Gifted preachers and pastors have resigned their city parishes to become deans of chapels, chaplains to university groups, and religious advisers and counselors to students.

These efforts have met with some favorable response, and with more in some places than in others. There have been increases in attendance at the new chapels, and students are resorting to their religious advisers in greater numbers than was the case six years ago. But even if the Sunday chapel congregation of 400 students is double the former attendance of 200, this does not mean in a university of 8,000 enrolment that the students are flocking back to church. For the great majority of undergraduates the attitude toward organized religion is one of indifference.

So widespread is this indifference that many of their elders are inclined to doubt the seriousness of the reputed intellectual interest of students in the subject. Are not those "bull sessions" on religion just "bickerings"? as Dr. Bernard Iddings Bell suggested in a recent paper in The Atlantic Monthly, or mere "chatter" that is "for the most part vague and uninformed, and gets nowhere"?

Perhaps it is vague and uninformed, but so is much of the religious discussion outside college walls. And if it gets nowhere, do not many of our adult spiritual searchers and metaphysical researchers also find themselves "coming out by the same door where in they went"?

• • •

PART of this student interest in religion may be just talk, part of it may be pose, but there is a deep seriousness in many of the questions, a great deal of honest asking for a way, and the quest for certainty is not discredited by the fact that its seekers are young and perhaps not so reverent as their forebears, and insist on rationalizing that which aforetime was accepted on faith.

"Unusual intellectual honesty,"

Ewing Galloway Photo.

"We Students Don't Claim to Be Deep Thinkers."

is the way Dr. Brooke Stabler, chaplain of the University of Pennsylvania, characterized the present student mood. "Receptive, but not easily fooled," said Dr. Irving Berg, chaplain of New York University. "Wistful," Dr. Henry Sloane Coffin called it.

Dr. Robert Russell Wicks, dean of the Princeton Chapel, said he thanked science for the modern student's passion for truth. "The scientific attitude has taught students to seek the facts and to found opinion on facts. A boy said to me the other day, 'Underneath everything, the thing I want most to know is what is true.'"

This attitude leads to some very fundamental questions, for today's undergraduate is more mature than his fellow of twenty years ago. He meets in the university all the currents of thought, discovery and opinion that are running strong in the world, and his perplexities and questions reflect these wider contacts.

"From 1900 up to the time of the World War," tabulated Dr. Charles W. Gilkey, dean of the University of Chicago Chapel, "the usual religious problem raised by college students related to some dogma: the virgin birth, the physical resurrection, the Bible. I rarely hear these mentioned now. Today the typical question is a variant of the cosmic problem: 'Why are we here?' 'Has life any meaning?' 'Is there evidence of purpose in the world?' 'What good does it do to pray?' They don't ask, 'Is there a God?' but their questions amount to that."

The interviews with students themselves confirm this and put responsibility for the change on science. Not entirely on science, for history, too, is a great upsetter, and at Columbia a group of undergraduates told me in detail of the course in Contemporary Civilization and its influence on students.

"You go through a cycle," said one of the editors of The Columbia Spectator. "You come to college with a certain body of beliefs that have been pounded into you in home and school. The course throws you against a stone wall of doubts and disillusionments. It shows the church in ugly compromises; you become dubious about that which was taken for granted; you are forced to think your way out, and generally emerge with belief again—though it is different. Most of us go through that cycle."

But in the history courses, in the study of contemporary civilization, it is the history of the sciences that poses the deepest questions and raises the most serious doubts. The exploration of the cosmos through the telescope, the microscope and those other magic casements of the laboratory has tended to depersonalize religion. It has opened questions that were never raised by our parents, or if raised were quickly brushed aside as wicked impertinences or swallowed as part of that bitter exercise known as accepting the universe.

Duke University News Service.

The New Chapel at Duke University.

BUT the student of today reads that Eddington, Millikan, Compton, Henry Norris Russell, Henry Fairfield Osborn and other supermen of science are also believers in religion. If scientists can be religionists there must be some mistake about the so-called conflict between science and religion. The student in 1933 therefore is heartened to look for something beyond the decrees of mechanism and materialism and to wonder if his appropriate mentor in this search is not the scientist.

A leading editorial in The Yale Daily News, written by a student who is to be graduated in June, put the case thus:

There are increasing millions of people looking for a scientific answer to the life riddle. They place their hopes more and more in an Einstein, an Eddington, or a Jeans. * * * The universe, modern science reveals, is an appalling immensity in which human existence seems hopelessly purposeless and insignificant. * * * Is

there any purpose or hope? That is the ultimate question. Philosopher as he may be at this point, the college man of today cannot forget the awful truth. Subconsciously, maybe, he dreads the scientific fact and the eternal suspicion that there is no purpose.

On science, then, college men build their lives—some to a greater extent than others, but almost all make life endurable by creating aims, illusions and objectives. The spark of life is unquenchable. Many have great ambitions, dream of future projects and success and aim to be leaders. They earnestly seek to make life purposeful. This is their religion.

At Yale I talked with the undergraduate editor who wrote this editorial and found him serious, sensitive, ardent, baffled by the perplexities, impatient with the established religion of the campus. The sermon he had heard in chapel the day before, delivered by a visiting minister, irritated him. He got out files of The News, showed me past editorials bearing on religion at Yale, the eddies of opinion, criticism, action, reaction, readjustment.

"We students are young, and know it," he said. "We don't claim to be deep thinkers. But," he added, "we are sincere. We are looking for guidance. Today, in the midst of all the uncertainties of the depression and the muddle of thought, the main question with the thinking student is this: 'What am I to live for?' If you show us the thing that will answer that, rationally, we'll go to it—whether the thing be chapel, or the history lecture room, or the science laboratory, or Professor Billy Phelps."

It was the identical thought that had been expressed the day before at Harvard by that senior whom I quote at the beginning of this paper: "If some man would show us the way, we'd run to him."

* * *

AUTHORITY is the goal of much of the more intellectual student thinking—some norm, some hitching post in a universe of change, some acceptable oracle imbued with wisdom and power to say "yea, yea" and "nay, nay."

The New Chapel at Harvard.

Rittase Photo.

"It is surprising," said a responsible official at Harvard, "how many really able students prefer to find some authority in religion rather than work the thing out for themselves. It is true in politics; the present-day disgust with democracy is deep-rooted among the more intellectual students. There is a feeling that we must have competent authority in statesmanship; Hitlerism and fascism are discussed, not as perfect solutions, but as significant and symptomatic tendencies. The same thing crops up in their thought and discussion of religion."

Two tendencies toward religious reorientation have been observed at Harvard, and while they are too slight and affect too few persons to be called in any sense movements, nevertheless they do perhaps have some directional significance.

The first of these tendencies is a revival of interest in or curiosity about sacramental religion. This was first called to my attention by a prominent member of the senior class, the editor-in-chief of The Harvard Advocate, who said: "Some of us have been attending Catholic churches. The symbolism is very valuable. James Joyce's acceptance of Romanism and T. S. Eliot's of Anglo-Catholicism, have had an influence on students. I think Willa Cather is tending that way, too. Thomas Mann's 'The Magic Mountain' is making its contribution."

I did not learn of any of the group who has actually gone over, or become a convert, to Catholicism in any of its branches. One boy said he went to St. John's Roman Catholic Church occasionally because "they put on a good show." Another said the high Episcopal ritualism of the Church of the Advent in Boston was "esthetically satisfying"—but that he went as a visitor, not as a member.

It chances that T. S. Eliot arrived from England last Fall and is temporarily in residence at Harvard as lecturer on poetry. Every week he gives a tea in his rooms in Eliot House, to which flock his admirers. Perhaps his presence in Cambridge has given some additional strength to his following. His religious pilgrimage, from the wastelands of agnosticism to the security of Anglo-Catholicism, is cited by his group as a road which may satisfy others who are dissatisfied alike with modernism and with "science, strutting like a fat rooster in the sun."

BUT there is a second tendency. It heads up in the teaching of Dr. Albert North Whitehead, the distinguished mathematician, scientist and philosopher, who has succeeded William James as the bright star of the Harvard philosophical firmament. Whitehead appeals to the scientifically minded, as Eliot's appeal is to the literary and esthetic group. Whitehead seeks to fit the new developments of science into a philosophy of life which re-interprets and re-emphasizes the old Platonic principles that underlie Christian philosophy.

Both of these tendencies are influencing a new attention to historical Christianity. I am told by the Rev. Thomas L. Harris, religious adviser at Harvard, that there is more respect for and a much more intelligent appreciation of traditional Christian thought among students today than ten years ago.

One comes upon individual attachments, deep-seated springs of loyalty. I remember a brilliant young Phi Beta Kappa man who said he could not follow Eliot into supernaturalism and that Whitehead's philosophy was to him a befogging mysticism. Then I showed him the article by the Yale senior in a recent New Outlook which said: "We are not swinging back to religion, but to the philosophical, artistic, cultural influences which are bound up with it."

"The only thing we can surely expect is that we shall swing back to religion," hotly answered this student. "The idea of material progress held us in the past, but now that is being exploded in our midst. We cannot help but turn to religion—though it can't be the same."

It would be a mistake to assume that this article is a majority report or a comprehensive survey. I have omitted many expressions of profound impatience with the whole subject of religion. I have not attempted to include the intellectual senior who told me that at the age of 13 years, at Groton, he had settled all his religious difficulties. Nor have I attempted to portray the attitude of the ordinary or average student.

⋯

THE ordinary student is a sheep, and follows the fashion of the times—which are fed up on the church—to sneer at spiritual values, to class religion as nursery stuff, too soft for growing boys. What really matters is what the small group of thinkers are about, in what direction their thoughts are moving, with what mood they color their choices.

Their mood, if I may attempt in conclusion to characterize it, is frankly a groping, a groping for reality in the experience of religious truth—and this is true not only of those described at Harvard, but also of the scattered, yearning, inquiring individuals one finds in colleges throughout the land. "Religion," to quote one of them, "must not insult intelligence and experience."

Much of the revolt against the church derives from a feeling that it is other-worldly, outside of and foreign to daily life, away from the work and achievements of humanity. "I'd like to make a suggestion for chapel speakers," said a boy at one of the Eastern colleges. "Let us have more scientists, and instead of having them talk on such subjects as 'the religion of a scientist,' let them tell us of their laboratory explorations, their scientific adventures and discoveries that's religion to us.

Not all would agree. There are those who see in science the infernal dynamo that has usurped the Virgin's place on the altar—and reality to them is a return to the sacramental symbolisms, or at least a wishing to return.

February 5, 1933

CHURCH BANKRUPT, CLERGYMAN SAYS

Protestant Programs Cannot Be Upheld, He Writes in Current History Article.

BLAMES COSTLY BUILDING

Recovery, Roosevelt 'Revolution' and Britain's Future Among Topics in October Issue.

The Protestant church in America is bankrupt, the Rev. Charles J. Dutton declares in October Current History.

"Widely extended denominational programs," he asserts, "can no longer be supported upon their present basis. Thousands of local churches are finding it almost impossible to keep their plants operating. Many churches are closed. pledges to both church and denominational budgets are not being paid. Money for missionary work is running low, and missionaries by the hundreds, their stations closed, are being called home.

"Church publications have been forced, because of the terrific financial strain, to change from weekly publications to fortnightly or monthly; many have been discontinued. Though denominational activities as a whole are being kept alive, their vitality is low, and there is not a church leader that does not face the future with a heart filled with dismay and fear."

Scores Past Extravagance.

While admitting that the depression is responsible for much of the churches' plight, Mr. Dutton, who is pastor of the Unitarian Church in Des Moines, Iowa, insists that many of their difficulties might have been avoided if warnings against extravagant expenditures had been heeded. In this connection he says:

"The expansion of church debt resulted largely from the absurd and stupid building mania which from 1924 to 1930 afflicted nearly every congregation in the American cities.

"The blame for the building orgy cannot be laid to the ministers. Every minister has been told, time and again, by his trustees, 'You are not a business man.' The trustees, on the contrary, qualify as 'business men'; they admit it themselves. But these lawyers, bankers, shopkeepers, the so-called successful members of the congregation, were the church trustees who believed speculation would last forever, who rushed ahead in a wild effort to outstrip some rival denomination by building an enormous church. Nor should it be forgotten that there was an element of profit in building churches.

"Instead of waiting and hoping for a return of past prosperity, the churches should be asking themselves three questions: How many unnecessary functions have the churches assumed? Are there too many churches? Has the time not arrived to admit that the duplication of churches in most communities has lessened the effectiveness of all churches and brought them to the point of financial ruin?"

September 17, 1933

Rockefeller Drops Baptist Gifts In Favor of Non-Sectarian Aid

Finding Emphasis on Church Denominations a 'Divisive Force' in Christianity, He Will Limit Support Now to Religious Activities That Subordinate Creeds.

John D. Rockefeller Jr. has informed the Northern Baptist Church that hereafter he will not contribute to its unified budget and that his future donations to religious work will be made to "specific projects, chiefly interdenominational or non-denominational in character."

Mr. Rockefeller, who has given millions in the past to the Baptist denomination, also has avowed his determination "to use such influence as I have in emphasizing the basic truths common to all denominations, in lowering denominational barriers and in promoting effective cooperation among Christians of whatever creed."

Reared in the Baptist faith, the philanthropist advised the Northern Baptist Convention of the cessation of his annual contributions to its unified budget in a letter dated March 7 of this year. The letter was made public last night by his representatives.

In that letter Mr. Rockefeller said he felt that denominational emphasis in religion was "a divisive force in the progress of organized Christian work."

The letter follows:

March 7, 1935.

To the Northern Baptist Convention.

Gentlemen:

Some months ago I sent you my contribution for the current fiscal year, and in doing so stated that it would be my final annual gift to the unified budget of the Northern Baptist Convention. Hereafter, such sums as I may donate to general religious work, it is my present thought to contribute to specific projects, chiefly interdenominational or non-denominational in character, which interpret the Christian task in the light of present day needs and which are based not so much on denominational affiliation as on broad, forward-looking principles of cooperation.

Any of your specific undertakings, either in the home or foreign field, that fall within this category I shall be glad to have presented for consideration along with other enterprises.

After so many years of cooperation with your organization I naturally regret taking this action, the more so because, following the footsteps of my father, I have always been identified with the Baptist denomination, working with and supporting its various organizations.

I believe in denominations—in so far as they make necessary provision for individual variation in religious experience. I recognize the significance, the beauty and the helpfulness of ritual and creed as developed by different denominational groups. What gives me pause is the tendency inherent in denominations to emphasize the form instead of the substance, the denominational peculiarity instead of the oneness of Christian purpose. I have long felt that this denominational emphasis is a divisive force in the progress of organized Christian work and an obstacle to the development of the spirit and life of Christ among men. My faith is increasingly centred on the few fundamental principles of Christ's life and teaching as set forth in the Four Gospels. I believe these principles can be applied with practical vision and spiritual power.

If the church is to go forward, if it is to hold the young people of today, who, generally speaking, are not greatly concerned about denominational distinctions and have a decreasing interest in sectarian missions, and if their support of its activities is to replace that of older givers who pass on, the denominational distinctions are bound to fade in the forward movement of a great united church open to all who seek to follow Christ and to find in Him the abundant life.

Such a church will, I believe, meet the needs of young people and enlist their support of its missions at home and abroad. We of the older generation should not discourage them or be instrumental in lessening their interest by passing on the divisive elements of our present-day religion. Rather should we work with them in relegating the non-essentials to a place of secondary importance and stand with them for the fundamentals of Christian unity, feeling confident that on such a foundation they will rear a church far better adapted to the requirements of their day and generation than any we could build for them.

"Unity in Christian Service."

Relating this statement of my personal view and interest to present general trends, I am sure you will understand the action which I have taken. It does not indicate any lessening of my interest in religion and the Christian church. On the contrary, it springs from a deeper and growing desire to encourage and further those united and non-sectarian activities and agencies which emphasize above all else unity in Christian service, love for God as He is revealed in Christ and His living spirit, and the vital translation of this love into Christ-like living. I am, therefore, seeking to use such influence as I have in emphasizing the basic truths common to all denominations, in lowering denominational barriers and in promoting effective cooperation among Christians of whatever creed. Definitely to support such cooperative movement seems to be the next step for me to take in that direction.

Lest this explanation of my position be construed as a criticism of any who think differently, let me hasten to say that I concede to others the same right to freedom of thought and action that I cherish for myself. The Baptist denomination was founded upon principles of religious tolerance and freedom that permit the fullest cooperation with all groups in sharing the Christian experience and teaching. I am simply acting in accordance with the principles of that denomination with which I have all my life been so happily associated.

With the assurance of my deep appreciation of the consecrated, devoted service which the officers of your organization and the many organizations which it represents have rendered through the years, I am,

Very sincerely,
JOHN D. ROCKEFELLER Jr.

Aided Interchurch Movement.

In connection with Mr. Rockefeller's communication, it was recalled that he has been a stanch supporter of the Interchurch World Movement, having taken an active part in the launching of a drive for $336,000,000 on behalf of that movement in the Spring of 1920.

The Riverside Church, Riverside Drive and 122d Street, in which its pastor, the Rev. Dr. Harry Emerson Fosdick, works for his ideal of a communal place of worship "for all the disciples of Jesus," was built at a cost of more than $4,000,000, chiefly with Mr. Rockefeller's support.

In previous years Mr. Rockefeller has made lavish gifts to Baptist Church activities. In 1932 he contributed $300,000 to the Northern Baptist Convention's unified budget. In 1928 he donated $500,000 toward the convention's campaign to raise $6,000,000 for its budget requirements.

In 1929 a gift of $2,000,000 to further Baptist missions was announced by the Laura Spelman Rockefeller Memorial, which was established in October, 1918, by the elder Mr. Rockefeller as a tribute to his wife and which was consolidated with the Rockefeller Foundation on Jan. 3, 1929.

For many years Mr. Rockefeller conducted a Bible class at the Fifth Avenue Baptist Church.

November 15, 1935

42

GIFTS TO CHURCHES CUT 43% IN 7 YEARS

Contributions in 1935 Slightly Above Those of Year Before, Protestant Survey Shows.

Annual gifts to twenty-five Protestant church bodies dropped 43 per cent in the seven years from 1928 to 1935, according to an analysis made by the research department of the Federal Council of Churches.

Contributions for 1935 slightly exceeded those for 1934, however. The contribution per capita for all purposes in 1934 was $12.07 and in 1935 it was $12.10. The contribution per capita for congregational purposes only was $9.92 in 1934 and $9.98 for 1935.

Total gifts declined from $532,368,714 in 1928 to $304,692,499 in 1935, while total gifts for congregational purposes declined from $402,683,861 to $251,347,435. The per capita contribution for all purposes declined from $23.30 in 1928 to $12.10 in 1935. Per capita contribution for congregational purposes declined from $17.30 in 1928 to $9.98 in 1935.

The report says that nearly all the communions maintained their per capita contributions for congregational expenses better than those for benevolences. The Protestant Episcopalians were the only group to lose proportionately less on benevolences than on contributions for congregational expenses.

March 20, 1936

SERVICE PROCLAIMS UNITED METHODISM

KANSAS CITY, May 10 (AP).—In worshipful ceremony the Methodist Church was proclaimed one united body tonight by the 900 delegates and 56 Bishops who have spent two weeks in perfecting its government.

"The Methodists are one people" was the key phrase repeated time after time by Bishop Edwin Holt Hughes of Washington in the service symbolically sealing the schisms which have divided the American followers of John Wesley for more than a century.

Ten thousand persons watched the ceremony completing twenty-three years of unification work by bringing the 8,000,000 members of the Methodist Episcopal Church, the Methodist Episcopal Church, South, and the Methodist Protestant Church into one organization.

Every delegate and Bishop rose with raised hand as Bishop John M. Moore of Dallas put the final motion for approval of the plan of union. No one stood on the call for opposition votes.

"We do so declare," chanted the delegates in unison, as Bishop Moore read:

"The Methodist Episcopal Church, the Methodist Episcopal Church, South, and the Methodist Protestant Church are and shall be one united church."

The chant was repeated as Bishop Moore read the five formal sections of the declarations of union. Then the entire delegation joined with the Bishops in pledging:

"To the Methodist Church thus established we do solemnly declare our allegiance, and upon all its life and service we do reverently invoke the blessing of Almighty God. Amen."

Bishop A. Frank Smith of Houston, Texas, led the meeting in the formel "Hallowing of Worship," closing with all joining in the declaration:

"We do here and now consecrate the Methodist Church to the worship of God and the establishment of His Kingdom among men everywhere through Jesus Christ our Lord. Amen."

The benediction officially bringing to a close the ceremony was pronounced by Bishop John L. Nuelsen of Geneva, Switzerland.

In first business sessions during the day the conference adopted a peace resolution recognizing "honest difference of opinion" on action to secure peace and defeated, by 384 to 371, the closest vote of any session, a proposal to grant women full clergy rights.

The peace resolution merely pledged the church to "undivided opposition to the spirit of war," to "exert every possible influence" for peaceful settlement of international differences, to urge Congress and the President to "take every possible step to avoid the entanglement" of this nation in war, and to provide for peace education of children.

The conference also pledged allegiance of the new church to the Federal Government.

The conference shelved a resolution that it go on record opposing the shipment of munitions to Japan.

May 11, 1939

CHRISTIAN PACIFISTS ESTIMATED AT 450,000

U. S. Movement Stronger Now Than in 1917, Study Indicates

The Institute for Propaganda Analysis made public yesterday results of a study showing that organized pacifism in the church is "much stronger today" than it was in 1917. Virtually every church body in the country, the study found, is on record as favoring non-combatant duty for the conscientious objector.

"Up to the present time," the statement said, "the Protestant churches have registered 6,000 conscientious objectors." The three faiths — Protestant, Catholic and Jewish—have organized peace movements among their congregations, it was reported.

"Churches in America which stress pacifism as a central part of their faith have a membership of about 365,000," according to the report, "divided as follows: The Friends, about 125,000; the Mennonites, about 100,000, and the Church of the Brethren, about 140,000. Allowing for members of some pacifist churches who are not pacifists and for members of non-pacifist churches who are pacifists, the total number of Christian pacifists in the country may be about 450,000, less than 1 per cent of this country's total church membership but a dynamic minority moved to high zeal by a faith which flourishes under adversity."

The report commented that the anti-war position of religious pacifists "tend to be constant, no matter what happens in the present conflict," and should be distinguished from the position of church groups opposing the war for political reasons or because of the racial background of their members.

January 20, 1941

Congregationalists Vote Merger, 757-172, Despite Schism Threats

By GEORGE DUGAN
Special to THE NEW YORK TIMES.

CLEVELAND, Feb. 5—In the face of threats of interchurch schism and secession, the General Council of the Congregational Christian Churches today overwhelmingly approved a proposed merger with the Evangelical and Reformed Church. The vote was 757 to 172.

As the deadline ending debate that started early yesterday drew near, the Rev. Dr. James Fifield of Los Angeles, spokesman for an aggressive anti-merger minority, told the 929 accredited delegates that in the event of action favoring the merger he would "use every energy at my command to lead my congregation apart from the new church."

Dr. Fifield is pastor of the First Congregational Church of Los Angeles, one of the largest Protestant churches in this country. He is the brother of the Rev. Dr. L. Wendell Fifield of Brooklyn, N. Y.

Emphasizing his reluctance to advocate separatism, Dr. Fifield said, however, that he had no al-ternative and that "we will present to the United States and the world the spectacle of a wide open schism."

He predicted that "500 to 1,000" churches would follow his lead. Litigation to contest the merger is now being prepared, he added.

Action of the General Council today culminated a long period of negotiation with the Evangelical and Reformed Church beginning in 1942.

Both bodies have already approved a plan of union. The present two-day session was called because final ratification of the merger hinged on obtaining a 75 per cent affirmative vote from local Congregational Christian churches by Jan. 1. The affirmative percentage on that date totalled 72.2. Today's vote was taken to determine whether the percentage attained is sufficient to warrant consummation of the merger.

The Congregational Christian action will be referred to the Central Council of the Evangelical and Reformed Church, scheduled to meet here Feb. 9 and 10. This body will, in all likelihood, recommend favorable action by its thirty-four synods. Thirty-three of the thirty-four Evangelical and Reformed groups had previously endorsed the plan of union.

The new denomination formed by the merger is to be called the United Church of Christ. It would have a potential combined membership of nearly 2,000,000 persons, representing more than 8,500 local churches.

Both the Congregational Christian Churches and the Evangelical and Reformed Church are the result of an earlier union of two separate church bodies, the former in 1931 and the latter in 1934.

According to the union plan, the general synod of the united church must assume the initiative in setting up a constitution for the new church.

The plan stipulates that the basic organization of the new denomination will be the local church and that each congregation, association and conference has the right of retaining or adopting its own charter, constitution, by-laws, and "other regulations which it deems essential and proper to its own welfare."

Local Autonomy an Issue

The Congregational Christian Churches hold property valued at more than $167,000,000, while the Evangelical and Reformed Church owns property valued at about $91,000,000.

One of the principal points of divergence between the two communions is that in general there is greater centralization of assigned authority in the Evangelical and Reformed Church.

It is this emphasis upon the local autonomy of the church and the fear that it will be lost in a merger which has aroused opposition within the Congregational Christian constituency.

Late this afternoon a spokesman favoring the merger asserted that there might be "a few scattered instances of withdrawal" but that these would constitute only "a handfull." He said that threats of legal action by dissidents had been carefully considered and that legal advice indicated that the merger steps were in full accordance with the rules of both denominations.

An anti-merger advocate, however, countered with the charge that the General Council had no legal power to consummate the merger and declared that legal action would be promptly instituted on national, state, and local levels "to protect the Congregational Christian properties and other assets for the continuing fellowship, making them not available to the proposed united church."

February 6, 1949

PROTESTANTS FORM NEW CHURCH GROUP

29 Denominations of 32 Million Members Knit Together Into National Council

By GEORGE DUGAN
Special to THE NEW YORK TIMES.

CLEVELAND, Nov. 29—A new era in American Protestantism began here this morning when 600 church leaders representing twenty-five denominations and four Eastern Orthodox bodies brought into existence the new National Council of the Churches of Christ in the U. S. A.

The solemn Act of Constitution, which knit into one cooperative unit an estimated 32,000,000 churchgoers, came precisely at 11 A. M. when the Rev. Dr. Franklin Clark Fry, president of the United Lutheran Church and convention chairman for the opening session, intoned the constituting words to a hushed assembly of almost 4,000 delegates, consultants, observers and guests.

"I declare," he said, "that the National Council of the Churches of Christ in the United States of America is officially constituted. Let us now dedicate it to the glory of God and to the service of mankind."

Secretary of State Dean Acheson was to have been present tonight to address the church leaders, but was forced to cancel his engagement because of the Far Eastern situation. Mr. Acheson's speech, broadcast from Washington over four networks, was brought to the session by amplification.

Formation of the new council followed nine years of planning. It represents the consolidation of eight major interdenominational agencies, including the Federal Council of the Churches of Christ in America.

A Cross of Tables

The colorful ceremony of constitution, held in Cleveland's public auditorium, began at 9:30 A. M. with a procession of church dignitaries garbed in clerical vestments.

As the procession approached the front of the auditorium the first group of denominational delegations took their places at a huge white-cross formed of tables directly in front of the stage. The delegations that followed were at red-covered tables flanking the cross. The heads of the twenty-nine church bodies and the eight agency representatives proceeded onto the stage.

As the processional music faded, Bishop John S. Stamm of the Evangelical United Brethren Church and former president of the Federal Council of Churches, called for a moment of silent prayer "for the United Nations, for our nation, and for those now engaged in the critical Korean struggle."

After the call to the meeting had been read by the Rev. Dr. Hermann N. Morse, secretary and acting chairman of the council's Planning Committee, Dr. Fry asked each denominational head to sign the constituting document, which had been placed on a white-draped rostrum in the center of the stage.

When the last church leader had signed, the representatives of the merging groups handed to Dr. Fry papers merging their identity into the National Council.

Oxnam Asks Message

As one of the first items of business, Bishop G. Bromley Oxnam of the New York area of the Methodist Church proposed that the new council send a message to President Truman and Trygve Lie, Secretary General of the United Nations, assuring them of the prayers of the convention "in this critical time."

Bishop Oxnam also moved that the chairman of the assembly appoint a committee to consider the advisability of drafting a statement on the present international situation for submission to the delegates. Both proposals were referred to the business committee for later floor action.

Prior to the Acheson broadcast, the Rev. Dr. Edward H. Pruden of Washington, president of the American Baptist Convention and chairman of the evening session, led the assembly in a prayer of intercession for the United Nations and the people of the United States.

The merging agencies were the Federal Council of the Churches of Christ in America, the Foreign Missions Conference of North America, the Home Missions Council of North America, the International Council of Religious Education, the Missionary Education Movement of the United States and Canada the National Protestant Council on Higher Education, the United Council of Church Women and the United Stewardship Council.

The constituting denominations were the African Methodist Episcopal Church, the African Methodist Episcopal Zion Church, the American Baptist Convention, the Augustana Lutheran Church, the Church of the Brethren, the Colored Methodist Episcopal Church, the Congregational Christian Churches, the Danish Evangelical Lutheran Church, the Disciples of Christ, the Evangelical and Reformed Church.

Also the Evangelical United Brethren, the Evangelical Unity of Czech Moravian Brethren in North America, the Five Years Meeting of Friends, the Friends of Philadelphia and Vicinity, the Methodist Church, the Moravian Church (North and South Provinces), the National Baptist Convention, United States of America, Inc., the National Baptist Convention of America, the Presbyterian Church in the U. S., the Presbyterian Church in the U. S. A., the Protestant Episcopal Church, the Reformed Church in America.

Also the Rumanian Orthodox Episcopate of America, the Seventh Day Baptists General Conference, the Syrian Antiochian Orthodox Church, the Ukrainian Orthodox Church of America the United Lutheran Church in America, the United Presbyterian Church of North America and the Russian Orthodox Church in America.

November 30, 1950

MODERN CHURCHES GAINING IN FAVOR

Some Architects Find Gothic and Colonial Styles Now Are 'Artistically Archaic'

By GEORGE DUGAN
Special to THE NEW YORK TIMES.

KNOXVILLE, Tenn., Jan. 5—The churches of America are putting up a bold new front, architecturally speaking.

An on-the-spot survey conducted here today at the opening session of the National Joint Conference on Church Architecture disclosed that one out of every four new churches now under construction was modern in design rather than conventional. On the West Coast, it was estimated that for every "standard" church being built, four modernistic ones were going up.

The three-day conference is being held under the joint sponsorship of the Church Architectural Guild of America and the Bureau of Church Building of the National Council of the Churches of Christ in the U. S. A. Nearly 200 architects are attending the meeting.

Gothic and Colonial styles, the architects agreed, have become for the most part "artistically archaic."

According to Dean Henry L. Kamphoefner of the School of Design of North Carolina State College at Raleigh, traditional church architecture is a victim of the high cost of living, and a growing desire for strength, simplicity and utility.

Dean Kamphoefner presented a series of awards for church design on behalf of the guild and emphasized that the winning entries in all categories reflected a search for new structural forms that at the same time enhanced underlying religious motifs.

He noted that not one first prize went to a Gothic or Colonial structure styles in which most of the competing architects were trained. Top honors in the category that included completed churches with seating capacity of 300 or more went to the Mount Zion Lutheran Church of Minneapolis. Armstrong and Schlichting of Minneapolis were the architects.

First prize in the fewer than 300 class was awarded to Christ the King Lutheran Church of Reseda, Calif. Culver Heaton of Pasadena was the architect. Both of these churches are modern of these churches are modern.

In a keynote speech this afternoon, Walter Taylor of Washington, urged the architects to discard "Gothic pointed arches," which he said, had become a trade mark of church architecture." Mr. Taylor is the director man of the Commission on Architecture of the Department of of research and education of the American Institute of Architects editor of its bulletin, and chairman Worship and Arts of the National Council of Churches.

Twentieth century architecture, he added, "must be an expression of enduring values and this will not be found in regurgitated Gothic of the seventeenth century."

Mr. Taylor told his colleagues that both history and geography challenge the 100-year-old concept that Gothic is the special Christian architecture.

"There is a real Christian architectural tradition but it is not expressed in style," he asserted. "It is expressed in terms of proportion, of plan, of height and length of harmony and unity, of color and form."

According to Mr. Taylor, church construction today ranks fourth in dollar volume. It is exceeded only by housing, schools, and hospitals.

Another speaker, Dr. C. Harry Atkinson of New York, executive director of the Bureau of Church Buildings of the National Council of Churches, predicted that 1954 would be the "greatest year" in church building.

January 6, 1954

MERGER DEFEATED BY PRESBYTERIANS

Southern Votes Block Plan for Unity of Three Major Branches in the Nation

Special to The New York Times.

ATLANTA, Ga., Jan. 18—Southern Presbyterians rejected today a plan to merge the three largest Presbyterian groups in the country.

These have a membership of 3,500,000.

Fourteen presbyteries in the Southern states voted against combining the Presbyterian Church in the U. S. (Southern) with the Presbyterian Church in the U. S. A. (Northern) and the United Presbyterian Church.

Twelve negative votes already had been cast by Southern presbyteries. A three-fourths vote of the eighty-six presbyteries in the South was required for approval. That is now impossible in view of the twenty-six votes against the plan.

Negative votes were recorded from these presbyteries, among others:

Savannah, Ga.; Concord, N. C.; Charleston, S. C., and Cherokee, Ga.

Several Presbyterian spokesmen believed that the failure to obtain the necessary votes did not mean defeat but only a delay in eventual unity.

Voting in the South is expected to continue into the spring but would not affect the result. Northern presbyteries have been voting for the merger.

The General Assembly of the Southern church opened the merger negotiations in 1937. The General Assembly of the Northern church responded. In 1951 at the joint invitation of these groups the United Presbyterian Church entered the negotiations. Last year the General Assembly of the Southern church endorsed the merger plan, as the General Assemblies of the two other denominations had done. The final decision was up to the presbyteries.

Opponents of the union plan voiced the fear that the U. S. A. church, with 2,500,000 members, would "engulf" the smaller Southern body, with 750,000 members. They also charged that the Northern church was tainted with "modernism."

Advocates of unity maintained that a "sectional" church no longer could command maximum moral and spiritual resources.

The Southern church arose in the Civil War out of differences over slavery.

The United Presbyterian Church was formed in 1885 through a merger of the Associated Presbyterian Church and the Associate Reformed Presbyterian Church. These groups go back to the Presbyterian dissenting movement in the Church of Scotland in the Eighteenth Century.

January 19, 1955

NEW TACTICS USED BY MISSIONARIES

Protestant Work Abroad Declared Greatly Changed in the Last Half Century

By GEORGE DUGAN
Special to The New York Times.

DAYTON, Ohio, Dec. 4—The Protestant foreign mission enterprise of 1955 would be unrecognizable to the old line missionary of fifty years ago.

This was made evident here today in a series of reports prepared for the sixth annual assembly of the Division of Foreign Missions of the National Council of the Churches of Christ in the U. S. A.

The four-day meeting of delegates representing sixty-seven denominations and mission agencies opened this afternoon. Some of the chief changes that have taken place in the last five decades were revealed in the reports as follows:

¶A steady increasing use of native Christian leadership in key positions on the mission field.

¶Establishment of study centers on non-Christian religions "to enable Christian leaders to meet these revivified faiths with intelligent understanding."

¶Development of psychological and psychiatric evaluations of candidates for foreign mission work.

In surveying points of "tension" a committee report on Southeast Asia found "the continuing threat to the principle of separation of church and state". a "serious problem" in the Philippines.

"The immediate concern is religious instruction in public schools which has been activated by the Roman Catholic Church with governmental sanction," the document said.

A committee report on India described the "burning problem" there as whether Christian missionaries would continue to be welcomed by the Government.

At one of six missionary rallies held tonight in various Dayton churches the Rev. Dr. Erville E. Sowards of New York, secretary for Burma of the American Baptist Foreign Missionary Society, asserted that very few Burmese would be won over to the Communist cause through the recent visit there of the Soviet Premier, Nikolai A. Bulganin, and the Soviet Communist party secretary, Nikita S. Khrushchev.

Dr. Sowards gave as his reasons the growing strength of the Government over the Communist rebels, the nationalistic solidarity of the Burmese Buddhists and the influence of the Christian minority.

December 5, 1955

PROTESTANTS FIND SIMILARITY GROWS

Study by New Yorkers Notes Churches Are More Alike in Governing Systems

By GEORGE DUGAN

Special to The New York Times.

OBERLIN, Ohio, Sept. 5—Traditional differences in the organizational structure of Protestant churches in this country are gradually evaporating, it was reported here today.

The report, resulting from an intensive two-year study, was presented by a group of twelve prominent New York clergymen and theologians. They noted that theories and practices of church government and administration "which to an external view seem widely divergent and even divisive, disclosed, to a more interior examination, many striking correspondences and similarities."

The thirteen-page document was prepared for the first full-scale conference on church unity to be held on the North American continent.

Three hundred official delegates representing twenty-nine Protestant denominations, five Eastern Orthodox bodies and five Canadian churches are attending the conference. It is being held under the auspices of the World Council of Churches, the National Council of the Churches of Christ in the U. S. A. and the Canadian Council of Churches.

The chairman of the New York clergy group was the Rev. Dr. Truman B. Douglass, executive vice president of the Board of Home Missions of the Congregational Christian Churches.

Categories Losing Validity

According to the New York report, the traditional classification of Protestant denominations into three main categories — the episcopal, presbyterial and congregational — is losing its validity.

The episcopal form of government imposes a central authority, the presbyterial places authority in groups of churches such as presbyteries and synods, and the congregational provides autonomy for the local church.

Such "standardized terminology," the New Yorkers reported, are no longer accurate.

They noted that there were bishops "with very great administrative authority and little ecclesiological significance" as well as bishops "who are regarded ecclesiologically as constitutive of the church yet are given relatively little administrative power."

At the same time, it added, important similarities — even identities—of administrative authority and practice may be concealed by diversities of terminology and title.

Depends on Consent

"Effective power in most churches in North America is dependent largely on the voluntary consent and support of the constituency," the report declared, "no matter what authority is assigned to a particular office by the constitution or policy of the denomination.

"Let an ecclesiastical official discipline a clergyman more popular than himself in the church and community, and then see what effective power is."

Members of the New York group, in addition to Dr. Douglass were:

The Rev. Dr. Roswell P. Barnes (Presbyterian), associate general secretary of the National Council of Churches; the Rev. Dr. Robert T. Randy (Baptist), Professor of Church History, Union Theological Seminary; the Rev. Dr. Ralph D. Hyslop (Congregational), director of advanced religion studies at Union Seminary; the Rev. Dr. Hampton Adams (Disciples of Christ), pastor of the Park Avenue Christian Church; the Rev. Dr. John Knox (Methodist), Professor of New Testament at Union Seminary.

Also, the Rev. Dr. Paul Hoon (Methodist), Professor of Pastoral Theology at Union Seminary; the Rev. Dr. John Mellin, pastor of the First Presbyterian Church; the Rev. Dr. Robert F. Capon, rector of Christ Protestant Episcopal Church, Port Jefferson, L. I.; Prof. Alexander Schnemann (Russian Orthodox), of St. Vladimir's Theological Seminary; the Rev. Paul W. S. Schneirla, pastor of St. Mary's Syrian Orthodox Church in Brooklyn, and the Rev. Dr. George F. Harkins, assistant to the president of the United Lutheran Church.

The eight-day meeting began on Tuesday on the campus of Oberlin College.

September 6, 1957

FOREIGN MISSIONS ENDED BY CHURCH

Role Now 'Fraternal,' New United Presbyterians Say, and Change Board Name

By GEORGE DUGAN

Special to The New York Times.

PITTSBURGH, May 30—The new United Presbyterian Church in the U. S. A. has dropped the phrase "foreign missions" from its ecclesiastical lexicon on the ground that it is obsolete.

Twenty or thirty years ago, church leaders pointed out today, the concept of a missionary sailing off to foreign parts to convert the heathen was perfectly valid. The missionaries accomplished their task so well, however, it was added, that self-supporting, self-governing and self-propagating churches have been established on every continent.

Thus, the denomination leaders explained, new churches in many overseas areas have become sufficiently strong to become a part of the "world church" and no longer require aid from this country.

In this context, the traditional picture of the Western, white missionary bringing the Bible to the less privileged has been wiped out.

'Fraternal Workers'

Missionaries will always spread the Gospel to non-Christian areas, the churchmen emphasized, but when their goal of an indigenous church is achieved they then become "fraternal workers" instead of foreign missionaries.

In line with this thesis the new 3,000,000-member United Presbyterian Church in the U. S. A. formally changed this afternoon the name of its Board of Foreign Missions to the Commission on Ecumenical Mission and Relations. The new body, in addition to its overseas activities, will handle the church's relationship with other denominations.

A separate commission was set up to deal only with negotiations for Protestant unity.

The word "ecumenical" is derived from the Greek "oikoumene," or inhabited world.

Ecumenical mission, therefore, has been defined as the "mission of the church to the whole family of man dwelling in the whole inhabited earth."

In the area of interchurch cooperation the word "ecumenical" is increasingly being used to describe such movements as the World Council of Churches and the National Council of the Churches of Christ in the U. S. A.

In an address tonight to its general assembly the Rev. Dr. Willem A. Vassert Hooft, general secretary of the World Council, called on the new church to learn to distinguish between "false and true unity."

The official of a world body composed of 170 Protestant and Eastern Orthodox churches said that church history recorded innumerable conflicts between those "who desire first of all the renewal of the church and those whose major interest was in its unity."

These conflicts find their climax in the opposition between those who claim the heritage of the Reformation and those who claim the heritage of the Roman Catholic Church, he continued.

View on Catholic Attitude

"The very names of the Catholic and Reformed churches have added to this great confusion," he declared. "The impression was created that one part of Christendom had monopolized one aspect of the Gospel and another part had specialized in presenting a different part of the Divine Truth."

This impression was not wholly wrong, he commented, for "it is a fact that the Roman Catholic Church has been so much concerned with unity that it has neglected the great and fundamental truth of the church's constant need of renewal." He added:

"We have reason to admire that church for its insistence that the oneness of the church must be manifested in the world, but we cannot accept a unity which is not based on renewal of the mind of the church and uses too often means which belong to the old age rather than the new.

"But it is also a fact that the churches which have grown out of the Reformation have neglected the truth of the unity of the church and not taught sufficiently clearly that there is one body in Christ."

May 31, 1958

Episcopal Church Stresses Old Ritual

By JOHN WICKLEIN

The Protestant Episcopal Church is becoming more catholic in its forms of worship, its leaders believe—but not Roman Catholic.

By "becoming more catholic" they mean that Episcopal clergymen are re-emphasizing the ritual and ceremonial of the ancient Christians and asking their people to play a greater role in the public prayer of the church.

This trend will be in evidence in many churches today, the first Sunday of Advent.

Traditional Anglicans of city and suburb think the shift implies that the worship is going "High Church." A woman in a New Jersey suburb, asked what she meant by that, said vaguely: "Oh, you know—the rector wants to be called 'Father and the people cross themselves during the prayers, and so on."

A new group of Episcopalians, Puerto Rican migrants on the lower East Side, find a similarity to the Roman Catholic mass in the service that has developed out of the revived interest in liturgy. They say it makes them feel at home in their new spiritual surroundings.

Today, in St. Augustine's Chapel of Trinity Parish, a number of Puerto Rican migrants on the lower East Side will be among those attending the men and boys corporate communion and breakfast.

They will take part in a service—designated by their priests as early mass—and have breakfast together. Then, at 10 A. M., they will hear their Presiding Bishop talk on television about the role of the laymen in the worship of the church.

The Bishop, the Most Rev. Arthur C. Lichtenberger, is to appear on "Lamp Unto My Feet" over WABC-TV Channel 2. In a recent interview here he said that the Episcopal trend toward liturgy had nothing to do with High Church, Low Church or Roman Catholicism.

"It's not concerned primarily with ceremonial, but with the formal worship of the church and particularly with lay participation in the service," he said. The trend, he added, has been spreading to other Protestant denominations as well.

"There has been a concern that all the services of the church express the best liturgical form and ceremonial which is consistent with the Anglican tradition," the Bishop said. "This doesn't mean the Episcopal Church is moving toward Rome—that isn't it at all."

In Britain, recently, a controversy erupted over "Roman" practices in some parishes of the Church of England, with which the Episcopal Church is in communion.

The liturgy used in the American church today, Episcopal theologians say, is not a translation of the modern Roman Catholic mass into English, but a recovery of Christian liturgies that existed before the Middle Ages.

Explanation by the Vicar

At St. Augustine's, the Rev. C. Kilmer Myers, vicar of Trinity's Lower East Side Mission, asserted that the primitive Roman rite was more like the Anglican Eucharist than the present Roman Catholic rite. Father Myers formerly taught liturgics at the General Theological Seminary here.

"Seeming similarities in worship can lead to confusion," Father Myers said, "and we are very careful about that, so the Puerto Rican people won't be misled. They must understand they are being confirmed in an Episcopal Church."

Father Myers was asked why his chapels sometimes held ceremonial processions through the streets of the lower East Side, a practice that might seem more in keeping with Roman Catholic than Anglican tradition.

"Our reason for processions is that they are a witness to what we believe," he replied. "We've got a lot of kids who are in street gangs to march along with us."

The inside of the old stone St. Augustine's Chapel at 292 Henry Street looks in many ways like a Roman Catholic church. A statue of the Virgin and Child, with lighted candles beneath it, stands at one side. A free-standing confessional is at the rear. The Stations of the Cross line the walls.

At a coffee hour after the Spanish service one Sunday this month, the Puerto Rican parishioners appeared convinced in their Episcopalianism. One man in the forty who attended service said this about the statuary:

"We have statues because in Puerto Rico the people are used to seeking a church filled with statues. So we bought the Statue of the Sacred Heart. It's very beautiful."

Understanding the Mass

Another man expounded on why he though some Puerto Ricans changed their religion when they came to New York:

"I think many of the Spanish-speaking people come into the Episcopal Church from the Roman Catholic Church because the church here speaks the language of the people—the mass is in the language of the people—and we can understand it."

"If I was in the Catholic Church, I would follow what the priest was doing, but I wouldn't know what he was saying."

A woman was asked if she thought the service in the Episcopal Church was like the service in the Catholic Church.

"Oh yes," she said, "it's almost the same as the Catholic mass, but it's in English."

The priests of the mission are concerned that all communicants understand the mass. From time to time, they dispense with their sermons and spend the hour explaining the service to the congregation, step by step.

The Rev. M. O. Young, priest in charge at St. Augustine's, and, as he put it, "a product of Berlitz," sang mass in Spanish at the early service. Then, at the English service that followed, he provided the commentary while an assistant acted as celebrant.

Wearing robes of white with green and standing in a pulpit off to the right, he addressed a congregation of 100, half white and half Negro:

"There are people in the church today who disapprove heartily of ceremonial. Maybe they have a point. You can get so interested in 'how to do it' that you can lose sight of what you are doing.

"Ceremonial helps us to realize the great importance of what we are doing—celebrating the mass. In the mass, heaven and earth are joined. The ceremony indicates that all are one in Jesus Christ—all are censed with the same censor that censed the holy altar."

Near the end, as the people prepared to go to the altar rail and take communion, the priest told them they had reached the central act:

"Candles are brought to glorify the communion, the sanctus bell is rung to call the people's attention to an important part of the mass."

A procession of the congregation (a revival to increase their participation) brings to the altar the bread and wine, symbolically "offering to God the body and blood of Christ."

This corporate communion of the congregation, called the Holy Eucharist, re-enacts the Lord's Supper. The Anglo-Catholics' belief in its paramount place in the worship divided them from Reformation-minded churchmen in the past.

The latter valued more the free form of the traditional Protestant service and stressed the sermon from the pulpit, with its emphasis on the individual's direct relationship to eternal truth.

But Father Young believes the new interest in liturgy is a uniting force within the Episcopal Church and throughout the Christian Church. It gets behind the medieval formulations of doctrines, which are the things the Reformation was fought over, he said.

"I think the Episcopal Church is a temporary expedient—ultimately it ought to disappear in the reunion of the whole church," Father Young commented. "But the separation is justified in that some group should be loyal to the whole catholic tradition while not having to adhere to the rigidity of Roman Catholic forms."

Father Young, who looks tall in his long black robes of a parish priest, said he would be considered "Romish" by liberals in the church. But, among other things, he pointed out, he believes in marriage of the clergy (he and his wife and their 2-year-old twins live in an apartment near the chapel).

In the city the extremes of churchmanship are found in the Church of St. Mary the Virgin, 139 West Forty-sixth Street, which uses a High Church form of mass derived from Roman Catholic worship, and St. George's, 207 East Sixteenth Street, which one priest described as "practically Presbyterian." The clergy there wear neckties, not clerical collars.

There is place in the church for all graduations of churchmanship, an Episcopal seminary dean remarked.

He and other leaders think "High Church" and "Low Church" are inexact labels today because the church parties they referred to are no longer clearly defined, nor extreme in their partisanship.

"High Church" began 100 years ago in the Oxford Movement of the Church of England. It began, the dean said, in a revulsion against Puritan iconoclasts who whitewashed the stained-glass windows, shrank from sense and sense objects and restricted the worship to that which appealed to the cerebrum. It led to a new appreciation, he said, that spiritual appeal does come to man through the senses as well as the mind.

But the trend toward ritual and ceremonial will continue, the dean believes, although the cerebral will still get important stress.

Asserting that "catholic" and "evangelical" are better terms than "High Church" and "Low Church" for the differences today, the dean added:

"Both emphases belong in the church—the catholic emphasis on formal aspects of worship and the evangelical emphasis on the Protestant heritage and concern for the individual's conscience and the individual relationship to God.

"We ought to live happily together."

November 29, 1959

LUTHERANS UNITE 3 DENOMINATIONS

Rift Along Nationality Lines Is Closed in Merger of 2¼ Million Members

MINNEAPOLIS, April 22 (AP) — American Lutherans, who avow mutual beliefs but who have maintained a multiplicity of denominations through the years, today combined three of them into one.

The merged group will be The American Lutheran Church.

It was created here in a moving convocation of prayer and pageantry, the climax of more than a decade of planning.

The new church elected the Rev. Dr. Fredrik A. Schiotz, 58 years old, of Minneapolis, to be president. He was named on a third ballot.

First Union in Century

The merger is the first in the century to bring together Lutherans of different national background — an element that gave rise to most of the original divisions. It creates a church of 2,225,000 members.

Church leaders from around the world sent greetings, hailing the step as strengthening the cause of the gospel and as a prelude to still wider unity among the nation's 8,000,000 Lutherans.

"What we have here is a gathering-up of those that were ripe for the step at the present," Dr. Schiotz told a news conference. "I see it as one step in something greater."

The high point of the ceremonies came when presidents of the three denominations, standing before a candlelit altar, joined hands, while the 1,000 church representatives bowed in prayer:

"We beseech thee, good Lord give to thy church a new vision of her glory, new wisdom and fresh understanding, the revival of her brightness."

Backgrounds Differ

The merger combines the 1,153,566-member Evangelical Lutheran Church, of Norwegian origin; the 1,034,377-member American Lutheran Church of German background; and the 70,149-member United Evangelical Lutheran Church, of Danish origin.

Dr. Schiotz, a Chicago-born former school teacher, missionary executive and church administrator, has been president of the largest of the groups, the Evangelical Lutheran Church, since 1954. It has contributed ten of thirteen departmental executives of the new church.

In the election, Dr. Schiotz led from the start over the Rev. Dr. Norman Menter of Detroit, a leader of the American Lutheran Church, and the Rev. Dr. William Larsen of Blair, Neb., president of the United Evangelical Lutheran Church.

Later, the convention elected Dr. Menter as vice president and Dr. Larsen as secretary.

Dr. Larsen, head of the Joint Union Committee that has worked ten years on the merger, presided over the founding session.

The union sets the pace for another one in the making, a four-way merger of the Augustana, American Evangelical and United Lutheran Churches and the Suomi Synod, scheduled for 1962, with a total membership of more than 3,000,000.

This step will bring 95 per cent of American Lutherans, previously scattered in eight denominations, into three large bodies—the church formed today, the union set for 1962, and the Lutheran Church-Missouri Synod.

It also will reduce the total number of Lutheran denominations to eleven, compared with the Eighteen Eighties when there were more than seventy.

April 23, 1960

METHODISTS EASE RIGIDITY OF CODE

Members of Church Found Relaxing Rules of Conduct

Methodists have relaxed the rigid code of behavior that once characterized members of the church, a survey conducted by the Boston University School of Theology indicates.

Much less attention, the study showed, is paid to rigid attitudes on drinking, diligent church attendance and personal conduct.

The sampling indicated that nearly one-third of all Methodists see no harm in moderate drinking of alcoholic beverages. Abstinence has been a basic tenet of the denomination over the years.

Four out of ten Methodists attend church less than half the Sundays in the year, and one out of five expects little or no pastoral or church guidance on social concerns, according to the report.

The findings were outlined in an article, written by Hartzell Spence, in the forthcoming July issue of Together, a Methodist magazine published in Chicago. The Methodist Church, with 10,000,000 members, is the largest Protestant denomination in the country.

The study, Mr. Spence commented, shows that "a good many Methodists have relegated God to the perimeter of their lives instead of giving Him the center."

One difficulty in translating Methodist beliefs into everyday action, he said, is the looseness of Methodist theology. However, he observed, the church has preserved from its past the emphasis on the teachings of Jesus.

Today it is not so concerned with preparation for immortality, he said, as with "a practical service to God and man in personal and social relations under the power and the guidance of the Holy Spirit."

The chief place where this concern breaks down is in race relations. Only about one-half of American Methodists, the study showed, believe in equal opportunity for all races, and only seven out of ten favor the abolition of segregation.

June 3, 1961

LUTHERANS FORM A 4-CHURCH UNION

Merger, Reached at Detroit Session, Binds Together 3,200,000 Members

COMPLETE UNITY ASKED

By GEORGE DUGAN
Special to The New York Times.

DETROIT, June 28—A new Protestant church was born today in the ultra-modern setting of the huge Convention Arena in this industrial city.

Some 7,000 persons joined in prayer and worship as four Lutheran bodies were united into one—the Lutheran Church in America.

The climactic moment of merger came when four segments of a mammoth candle were brought together to form a single flame, symbolizing the goal of Christian unity.

The new church, with a membership of 3,200,000, was composed of these formerly separate bodies:

¶The United Lutheran Church, with a membership of 2,500,000. Chiefly of German background, it had more than 5,000 pastors and 4,671 congregations.

¶The Augustana Lutheran Church, predominantly Swedish, with 630,000 members, 1,400 ministers and 1,269 churches.

¶The 36,000-member Finnish Evangelical Lutheran Church, served by 102 ministers in 153 congregations.

¶The American Evangelical Lutheran Church, founded by Danish missionaries. It had 25,000 members, sixty-four pastors and seventy-nine congregations.

New York Pastor Elected

The new Lutheran Church in America is the largest of the three main bodies of Lutheranism in this country. The others are the Lutheran Church-Missouri Synod, with 2,600,000 members, and the American Lutheran Church, with 2,400,000 members. These three bodies comprise 95 per cent of the Lutherans in the United States.

This afternoon the delegates to the convention elected the Rev. Dr. Franklin Clark Fry of New York as the new church's first president. Dr. Fry was president of the United Lutheran Church. He is also president of the Lutheran World Federation and chairman of the Central Committee of the World Council of Churches.

The entire floor of the arena in Cobo Hall was transformed into a sanctuary for the uniting communion service. A large altar draped in red stood at one end, with three smaller altars placed at equal intervals between the main altar and the opposite end of the arena.

Church Unity Is Theme

A parallel communion rail and forty administrants made it possible for the Communion to be administered to some 6,000 in forty-five minutes.

The sermon was preached by the Rev. Dr. P. O. Bersell, president-emeritus of the Augustana Lutheran Church.

"We rejoice that at long last the four Lutheran bodies have come together because they belong together, they have one Lord and one faith," he said.

The theme of full church unity was emphasized in all of today's addresses.

The Rev. Dr. Malvin H. Lundeen, president of the Augustana Lutheran Church and chairman of a joint commission of forty-six churchmen that brought the new church into existence in five and a half years, declared:

"Unless and until Lutherans are sitting on the same side of the table in inter-denominational conversations, and Lutheran contribution to the ecumenical movement is seriously compromised."

June 29, 1962

Busy 7th-Day Adventists

By EDWARD B. FISKE

One of the more curious bits of American folklore claims that on Oct. 22, 1844, great numbers of Christians in the eastern United States, convinced that Biblical prophecy called for the return of Christ to earth on that day, sought out graveyards or mounted housetops and hilltops dressed in "ascension robes" to await the appearance of the Lord in the clouds.

If pressed on the matter, most orthodox churchmen today would acknowledge belief in the doctrine of the Second Coming. But most regard it as hardly essential to their everyday faith and, as one theologian said of the doctrine of the Virgin Birth, "hardly a reason to convert to Christianity."

Some denominations, however, regard belief in the imminent return of Christ as a touchstone of Christianity. Last week the leaders of the largest of these—the 1.6-million-member Seventh-Day Adventist Church—assembled in Detroit for their 50th World Conference.

The denomination is one of the most rapidly growing in the world, more than four-fifths of its growth having occurred in the last decade. The latest figures show 380,870 members in the United States, with the biggest concentration in the Western states.

Unusual Doctrine

They became a denomination in 1863 after a small group in New England concluded that the 1844 error was the result not of false prophecy but of incorrect interpretation. This date, they said, initiated not the return of Christ to earth but the beginning in heaven of a period of "investigative judgment" that would end with a future Second Advent.

They also added a second unusual doctrine to their list of essentials for the faith, observance of the seventh day, Saturday, as the Sabbath. On this point they differ even from other adventists.

The Adventists are unique in several other ways:

War—Seventh-Day Adventists are noncombatants, and the denomination runs training units to prepare its young men for duty in the Army medical services. One of its members, Cpl. Desmond T. Doss, survived some of the fiercest fighting in the Pacific during World War II to become the only conscientious objector ever to be awarded a Congressional Medal of Honor.

Diet—Church doctrines require members to abstain from alcohol and tobacco, and most Adventists are also vegetarians.

Spiritual Temple

One of the best-known early Adventists was corn flake king John Harvey Kellogg, a surgeon and food faddist who became superintendent of the church's sanitarium in Battle Creek, Mich., in the 1870's. Partly for doctrinal reasons, partly because it was a cheaper way of feeding his patients, Dr. Kellogg invented more than 100 nut and cereal products and founded the cereal company that made Battle Creek a household address to generations of box-top-clipping American youngsters.

Health—Adventists regard the human body as the temple of the Holy Spirit and place great emphasis on the inner-relatedness of spiritual, mental and physical health. The denomination publishes a magazine called Life and Health, manufactures and markets health foods, and sponsors courses for non-Adventists who want to give up smoking and drinking. The church's New York Center, 227 West 46th Street, is currently winding up a 16-week weight-reducing course.

Piety—Like other ultra-conservative Protestants, Adventists frown on the theater, movies and card playing.

Last week the delegates to the quadrennial meeting began the routine task of electing leaders and hearing reports of the church's activities from Peru to Borneo. Robert H. Pierson, a 55-year-old missionary, was elected president.

Delegates also planned a major expansion of the campaigns against smoking and drinking.

"Recent publicity about the harmful effects of smoking and drinking has made us realize that the time is ripe for a large expansion of our activities in this area of public service," said W. R. Beach, secretary of the denomination.

Plans call for 10,000 five-day anti-smoking courses in 50 countries in the next four years and the launching of a similar effort to combat alcoholism.

June 19, 1966

The Sunday School Fights for Survival

By EDWARD B. FISKE

The Sunday School—long the symbol of American Protestant education—is going through a major crisis.

An increasing number of churches and religious educators across the country are finding that Sunday Schools are inefficient and irrelevant in relating religion to modern life.

Some churches in Manhattan have abandoned Sunday Schools entirely. Others have tried to revive them with paid teachers, arsenals of audio-visual equipment and bold new curriculums.

Some churchmen see part of the solution in the transfer of some aspects of religious education from the churches to the public schools.

Almost every major Protestant denomination in the country is involved in a multimillion dollar effort to develop new program materials. One is experimenting with a "new church education" somewhat along the lines of the "new math."

While Protestant Sunday School attendance is at a new high—41,635,130 in 1964, according to the National Council of Churches—leaders are disturbed by recent signs of a lag in growth.

From 1960 to 1964, for instance, adult membership in the United Presbyterian Church in the U.S.A. rose by 100,000, while church school enrollment dropped by 120,000 in the same period.

Educators are more concerned, however, with the apparent ineffectiveness of Sunday Schools than with sagging attendance.

Church schools suffer, they say, from a serious shortage of trained teachers, the impossibility of offering a balanced program of religious education in one-hour, once-a-week sessions, and the inefficient use of materials and facilities.

Aston Glaves, who teaches junior high school-age classes at the Broadway United Church of Christ, at 56th Street, cited the "irrelevancy" of traditional Sunday School methods, such as the memorizing of Bible verses.

A Matter of Relating

"Kids stop coming at the age of 14 or 15 if you can't show them how religion relates to their own experience," said Mr. Glaves, who added that in his own classes he had begun to supplement curriculum materials with newspaper stories to show that relation.

Gail Petty, a 15-year-old student at the Convent Avenue Baptist Church, Convent Avenue and 145th Street, complained that teachers were "too concerned with driving teachings into us," and not concerned enough with teen-age problems.

"What we want is really to discuss questions that I don't think anyone has all the answers to—like how man was created," she said.

The Rev. Jack A. Worthington, in a recent article in the journal, Religious Education, reported on a recent Presbyterian survey that found Sunday School graduates only slightly more literate in religious matters than nongraduates.

Teachers Out of Date

The survey, which tested the effects of the denomination's Faith and Life Curriculum after it had been used 18 years, found that of all major groups in the church, Sunday School teachers were "the most out-of-date in their biblical, theological, historical and ethical understanding."

Mrs. Grace Alexander, a teacher at the Convent Avenue Baptist Church, said that the illustrations and stories available in Sunday School materials reflected few of the experiences of urban and nonwhite children.

"We continually have to adapt them to our own situation," she said. "You can hurt a child trying to show him the meaning of love, for instance, if the book shows a nice family scene and he doesn't have a family."

Religious educators recognize that there are also some long-run social forces at work that will make the Sunday School crisis even more severe in the future.

Prof. Ellis Nelson of Union Theological Seminary observed in a recent address to religious educators that Sunday Schools, which were founded in the 19th century period of "Protestant pluralism," were not designed to carry the whole burden of religious education.

It was assumed that public schools would "generally reinforce" the Protestant religious outlook and that the churches had only to provide "one hour of sectarian teaching a week in a church school."

"Radical pluralism" and other modern developments have since forced religious neutrality on public schools, he continued, and the 19th century reliance on Sunday Schools must be modified to coordinate Protestant education with what contemporary general education can and cannot do. One result is that Protestant churches have begun to pool their resources.

Cooperation Undertaken

In New York City, for example, most Protestant Sunday School teachers receive their training at interdenominational schools sponsored in cooperation with the Protestant Council.

The United Church of Christ and the United Presbyterian Church in the U.S.A. have plans for joint curriculum materials, and the National Council of Churches is engaged in a Cooperative Curriculum Project that will provide any denomination with scientifically designed curriculum outlines.

Educators look forward to the day when Roman Catholics and Protestants will publish common texts in relatively nonsectarian areas such as ethics. Plans for a "new town" to be built in Columbia, Md., call for Protestant, Catholic and Jewish groups to build common facilities for shared-time programs.

In its 1963 decision banning prayers and Bible readings from public schools the Supreme Court specifically left the door open for—and, indeed, encouraged—the "objective" teaching of religion as an academic subject.

Protestant educators have since noted that much of the instruction traditionally offered in Sunday Schools—church history, comparative religion, even the content of sacred writings—falls into this category.

Some have suggested that Protestant strategy in the future should encourage the teaching of religion on an objective basis in the public schools. This would free existing church resources to handle the subjective side of faith.

"It stands to reason that a child will learn much more about church history from a trained professional teacher—no matter what his faith, if any—than he will from an untrained volunteer," said the Rev. Eli F. Wismer, executive director of the Department of Educational Development of the National Council of Churches.

"More than 150 state universities now have departments of religion," he said. "There's no

God Made Us a Beautiful World

God made us a beautiful world,
Meadow and field and hill.
What can His children do
To make it more beautiful still?

These things we can surely do:
Day after happy day
We can be gentle and kind,
At home and at school and at play.

Each one can be good to all;
Work with a cheerful will.
God made us a beautiful world,
We'll make it more beautiful still!
—Nancy Byrd Turner

Literature commonly provided for Sunday school gives scant attention to city children, especially nonwhite ones, a teacher at a Baptist church here remarked in discussing problems of Sunday school. This is a page from book published by American Baptist Convention's Board of Education and Publication, with a hymn by Nancy Byrd Turner from "Hymns for Primary Worship," copyright 1946 by Westminster Press. It is used here.

50

reason why this shouldn't be extended to high schools too."

Educators still realize, however, that the burden of religious teaching will continue to rest on the local church, and they have set off in a number of directions to try to ease this burden.

Most major denominations, for instance, now incorporate into their programs where possible the latest developments in secular education. Several experiments are being conducted in programed religious instruction.

Basic Research Going On

Millions of church dollars are going into basic educational research. The Lutheran Church in America, for example has developed a detailed scale of what religious concepts can be assimilated at each state in a child's growth.

A primary reason for the widespread willingness to de-emphasize and even abandon Sunday School is the view of most educators that effective religious education must be considered in the totality of a child's experience—of which Sunday morning is only a small part.

The curriculum now being developed by the Lutheran Church in America at a cost of $7.5-million plus printing costs will offer coordinated materials for use on Sunday morning, after school, in the family, during summer vacations and at church camps.

In 1969 the National Council of Churches expects to publish materials coordinated with public school subjects such as history, science and sociology. These will enable church leaders to take up questions such as the relation between religion and science at the same time they are being raised in the public schools.

Such a philosophy of education, however, does not necessarily require Sunday Schools. The Rev. Howard R. Moody of the Judson Memorial Baptist Church on Washington Square South, who says he has "given up" on Sunday Schools, observed recently: "We figure we can communicate more to kids by including them in the life and social action of the church than we can by trying to teach them Christianity through

books."

To make better use of the time available for religious education, almost every major denomination is now involved in a multi-million dollar effort to develop modern curriculums.

The Presbyterians, having discovered their 1948 curriculum was ineffective, have adopted the "new math" approach. It begins by analyzing what a first-rate mathematician does and then presents these principles in increasingly difficult forms at each grade level. The emphasis is on the discovery of principles rather than the solving of problems.

Adapting these principles to religious education, the Presbyterian leaders began by defining the skills they felt an adult Christian ought to have, such as the ability to interpret the Bible and handle personal and social problems. They then wrote them into their new curriculum, due in the fall of 1968, in increasingly complex forms.

Religion and Problems

In contrast to this adult-oriented approach, most other denominations are developing

functional or child-centered curriculums.

The United Church of Christ organized its recent curriculum around the cyclical consideration of problems that the child will face in different forms throughout his life, such as "Christian living with one another."

The Seabury series of the Episcopal Church, on the other hand, specifies special problems for each age. The tenth-grade curriculum, for example, revolves around the conflict between conformity to popular values and the demands of religious faith.

Protestant leaders realize that Sunday Schools are not providing the churches with the educated laymen they require to function in today's world. But it is unlikely, however, that they will disappear for some time.

"We must not weaken them," said Dr. Nelson, "until we have something better."

July 24, 1966

Bishop Pike Is Cleared of Heresy

By United Press International

GLACIER NATIONAL PARK, Mont., Sept. 9— Bishop James A. Pike of San Francisco was absolved today of any heresy by the Episcopal House of Bishops. But he was given a mild rebuke on the subject of deaconesses in the church.

"The Bishop of California is not on trial in this house nor does the present accusation against one of our members have standing among us," declared a statement drafted by a special theology committee appointed to review the charges against Bishop Pike.

The heresy accusation was brought by a group of conservative Arizona clergymen. They contended Bishop Pike had denied the doctrines of the Trinity, Virgin Birth and Incarnation.

Bishop Pike, cleared for the third time since 1961 of heresy accusation, replied in a statement:

"I am deeply moved by the concern of my brothers in this house. I have never had any desire to damage this brotherhood, which is precious to me. All of us are working in difficult times in painful situations and if my witness has made your task more complicated, I am truly sorry."

The Bishops, in convention at the Glacier Park Lodge, gave a

ringing endorsement to freedom of theological inquiry but warned it must be exercised within the authority of Christ's ministry and not as an individual. Bishop Pike accepted this.

The committee report said:

"An individual may well claim freedom to think aloud, to discuss, to explore. But when he does, whatever his station, he does so as one member of Christ's body. Only the whole body, speaking maturely and corporately, can officially define the faith it confesses before its Lord. Individual speculations are just that."

Replied Bishop Pike: "No man has authority who is not under it and I reaffirm my loyalty to the doctrine, discipline and worship of the Episcopal Church."

Bishop Pike had maintained there was no basis for heresy charges in his attempts to restate ancient doctrine in terms intelligible to modern men.

The committee report encouraged inquiry into the faith. It said the sincerity of Bishop Pike's faith was not questioned, then said, "Nor will we limit the historic disciplined liberty of the theological inquiry and the necessary devoted testing of the vessels of Christian belief. Language changes [and] the concepts of men's minds change. The faith given in the

mighty acts of God does not change."

"I must be faithful to the task to which I believe God has called me—that of seeking to distinguish the earthen vessels from the treasure and in the hope of setting forth with integrity and dedication more contemporary carriers of the reality of the catholic faith," Bishop Pike said.

"I assure you that for my part I shall try always to be responsible in the written and spoken word in concern for the brotherhood and in the promotion in today's world of the mission of Our Lord Jesus Christ."

The House of Bishops adopted the report, which said it was a good thing to responsibly explore alternate ways of stating unchanging faith and to press for amendments in church order.

"Continuity and change are both facts of life to be held in fruitful tension," the report said.

Bishop Pike was warmly applauded by the bishops after he read his reply to the committee report, which was read by the chairman, Bishop Richard S. M. Emrich of Michigan. Presiding Bishop John E. Hines commended Bishop Pike for "his candid, forthright, honest, warm, encouraging statement.'

Among most of the clergy there was no desire for a heresy trial for fear of the damage it would do the church. Signatures of at least three bishops would have been required to start the machinery of a heresy

trial and not one would sign charges against Bishop Pike.

As the Bishops concluded the convention, however, Bishop Pike was overruled on the question of the role of deaconesses in the church.

He said he would abide by the decision and cancel plans to ordain Mrs. Phyllis Edwards of San Francisco and allow her to administer communion.

Nature of the Charges

The charges brought against Bishop Pike by 14 Arizona Episcopal priests covered various doctrinal points.

The first was that Bishop Pike had repudiated the Virgin Birth of Jesus.

To this the Bishop has replied that that doctrine is in the classification of other Nativity narratives and that the Episcopal Church does not require its communicants to accept these narrations as the literal truth.

The other charges, all denied by the Bishop, were as follows:

¶He denied the doctrine of the Blessed Trinity.

¶He maintained that Jesus was divine only as all men are divine and that the sole difference between Jesus and the others is that Jesus was completely conscious of his divinity.

¶He maintained that Jesus was not the only incarnation of God and that incarnation had occurred in other religious leaders before Christ.

Lastly, he denied the empty tomb and the bodily Resurrection and Ascension.

September 10, 1965

Episcopal Bishops Set Up Council to 'Renew' Church

By EDWARD B. FISKE
Special to The New York Times

WHEELING, W. Va., Oct. 27—The Episcopal House of Bishops voted today to form a council of laymen and clergymen to "help rethink, restructure and renew the church for life in the world today."

The action was generally interpreted as a response to the view of the Right Rev. James A. Pike, the Resigned Bishop of California, that the church's theological thinking is out of date.

However, the Right Rev. John E. Hines, the Presiding Bishop, described the move as a way of dealing with "ferment that exists in the church today quite independently of Bishop Pike."

He indicated that some such plan of study would have been started even if Bishop Pike had not put focus on the issue.

The Bishops, in ending a four-day meeting, adopted a resolution observing that "Christian truth requires constant rethinking and restaging in every age."

'Major Re-examination'

Modern times, it stated, "call for a major re-examination by our church not only of its theological stance but also of its structure, worship and total life."

In an allusion to the recent Ecumenical Council in Rome, the resolution said that "the Roman Catholic Church has shown that a great church can rethink publicly and with freedom not only the expressions of its faith, but also its total life and vision in our day."

The procedure that was adopted calls for the Presiding Bishop to appoint a committee to develop a council made up of "a cross-section of the church's lay and clerical membership." The committee was instructed to report to the House a year from now.

The Right Rev. Anson Phelps Stokes, Bishop of Massachusetts, who proposed the action, said that the council, once it was formed, "will produce documents of various kinds to help us understand our faith and make it relevant for today."

He said that it would take up such questions as the impact of modern science on religious belief, new forms of the ministry, the role of laymen, peace and other issues widely being discussed in the church.

No council documents will have official status, he said, unless they are formally adopted through the normal procedures of the House of Bishops or the denomination's triennial general convention.

This week's meeting was dominated by the possibility of heresy charges against Bishop Pike, who has questioned the adequacy of traditional doctrines such as the Trinity to express Christian truth in today's world.

Bishop Pike was censured for "irresponsibility" in some of his statements, but the heresy charges were dropped.

The Right Rev. Henry I. Louttit, who led the campaign against Bishop Pike, said that he and the other Bishops had agreed that the church must find new means of expression if it was to speak to modern society.

"The formation of a council," he said, "is a way of saying, 'Let's have a group do what Bishop Pike has been trying to do all by himself.'"

Bishop Pike said he was "delighted" with the move.

"I've been trying to get us talking about theology all along," he said.

In another action, the House granted autonomy to the missionary district of Cuba, whose 52 churches have since 1901 formed a constituent jurisdiction of the Episcopal Church.

The Right Rev. Stephen F. Bayne Jr., director of the Overseas Department, explained that the purpose of the move was "to set them free from any relationship with the American church which could be potentionally harassing and even dangerous for them."

After twice tabling resolutions dealing with the war in Vietnam the Bishops adopted a 150-word statement calling for "continual prayer for our country, for the people of Vietnam, for all engaged in military action, for the peace of the world and for the reconciliation of all God's people."

Ecumenism Denounced

CHARLESTON, S. C., Oct. 27 (AP)—The American Council of Christian Churches renounced today the ecumenical movement, "new morality," the principles of the National and World Councils of Churches and UNICEF.

The resolutions were unanimously adopted by delegates attending the council's 25th anniversary convention.

A resolution on ecumenism termed the movement "Satan's counterfeit and a perversion of the word God."

The only unity supported by the Scriptures is spiritual in nature, producing genuine Christian cooperation among individual believers and churches, the resolution said.

The resolution urged "believers" to separate from the National Council of Churches and the ecumenical movement.

The council denounced "the new morality" as a human attempt by liberal theologians and ecumenical leaders to justify immorality and lawlessness.

The American Council, which was organized in opposition to the National Council of Churches charged that the National Council and the World Council of Churches were "in disobedience to God's clear command" by emphasizing the "rebuilding of the world as opposed to the evangelism of individuals."

The American Council, comprising some 15 "Protestant, Bible-believing churches," was organized in 1941. The group has headquarters in New York and is affiliated with the International Council of Christian Churches.

The council further protested "the use of tax money to promote the religious interest of theological liberalism."

A resolution expressed the council's concern over books critically attacking the Bible being accepted into the curriculums of state universities and public schools "under the guise of the objective study of the Bible as literature."

In a resolution attacking the United Nations Children's Fund for its assistance to Communist countries, the council charged that most of the UNICEF money received by Communist governments "does not go to the children as they claim i does, but rather is used by these governments to further the worldwide Communist conspiracy."

October 28, 1966

---

2 CHURCHES VOTE FOR MERGER PLAN

By EDWARD B. FISKE
Special to The New York Times

CHICAGO, Nov. 11 — The general conferences of the Methodist Church and the Evangelical United Brethren Church voted today to merge into the nation's largest Protestant denomination.

Formation of what would become the United Methodist Church was approved at a suspense-filled meeting of delegates from the 750,000-member Evangelical United Brethren Church in the rococo Grand Ballroom of the Conrad Hilton Hotel.

The 413 delegates approved the merger plan by a standing vote of 325 to 88 — 15 more than the three-quarters vote required.

Representatives of the 10.3-million - member Methodist Church approved the plan earlier this morning by an overwhelming vote of 749 to 40 with five abstentions.

The merger is scheduled to take place in 1968 in Dallas. Duplicate agencies of the governing units of the two churches will then be assimilated into the new structure during a 12-year transition period.

The United Methodist Church will have a membership of slightly more than 11 million. The Southern Baptist Church, with 10.6 million members, is currently the nation's largest Protestant body.

The merger of the two denominations must still be approved by the aggregate vote of two-thirds of the members of the annual conferences, the equivalent in the two denominations of a diocese or a presbytery.

Jubilant leaders of the two churches expressed confidence, however, that this approval would be forthcoming by late spring or summer.

Bishop Lloyd C. Wicke of New York, the Methodist chairman of the committee that drew up the merger proposal, called it "inconceivable" that members of the annual conferences would reject a proposal that 95 per cent of their representatives to the general conference, the highest policy-making body, had approved.

Bishop Reuben H. Mueller, president of the Board of Bishops of the Evangelical United Brethren Church, said, "I have every confidence that we will bring it [the merger plan] through the annual conferences."

Opposition to the plan centered in the conservative Western and Border state delegations to the Evangelical United Brethren General Conference. Many of them regard Methodists in their areas as too "modernist" in some of their theological beliefs and their understanding of Christian piety.

'We Made It'

Leaders of the denomination were visibly tense as delegates voted in the ornate gilted ballroom with large crystal chandeliers, mirrored door and decorative iron balcony railings.

High above the clusters of flags and the large "United in Christ" sign that had been added for the convention were 26 painted panels that depicted scenes of courtly rather than divine love in the pastel tones of 18th century French style.

Following the announcement of the vote, one of the participants in the negotiations sank back into his chair on the dais, and said "we made it."

Opposition within the Methodist ranks came primarily from those who believed that the denomination should eliminate all racial segregation from its ranks before uniting with the Evangelical United Brethren Church.

The Rev. L. L. White, a Negro from the Southern California-Arizona Annual Conference, for instance, told the assembly that priority should be given not to merger but to "bringing our actions more in line with the beliefs in Jesus Christ that we profess."

The Rev. Roy Nichols, pastor of St. Mark's Methodist Church in Harlem, said in an interview, however, that he supported the merger in part because he believed the addition of the other denomination, which has no Southern membership, will "aid future integration efforts."

Six Methodist bishops from the South met late last night with about a dozen Negro ministers to assure them of their commitment to merge the 12 all-Negro annual conferences with the 26 predominantly white conferences that they now overlap.

During last night's session the Methodist conference over-

came the threat that the race issue had posed to approval of the merger. The Methodists did this by writing into enabling legislation for the merger a voluntary target date of 1972 for desegregation of the all-Negro annual conferences.

Such a provision had previously been adopted for the Methodist Church, but it would not have extended past 1968 in the merged denomination.

Both churches have their historical roots in the evangelical revivals that swept the eastern seaboard during the late 18th century.

Their articles of faith are orthodox, and their programs have traditionally emphasized missionary activities. Both churches frown on drinking and gambling, and preaching is central to their worship services. Clerical collars are a rarity among their ministers and bishops.

Where differences existed in the practices of the two denominations, the merger plan tended to reflect those of the larger Methodist body.

The Methodist policy of electing bishops for lifetime terms, for instance, was adopted rath-

er than that of their new partner, which elects them for four-year—but almost always successive—terms.

Likewise, it was decided to continue the Methodist practice of having bishops appoint the district superintendents who assist them in the work of their episcopal districts.

A Question Unanswered

In a gesture to the smaller denomination, which elects its district superintendents, this question was left open for possible revision by delegates to the 1968 constituting conference.

A provision for calling the new denomination simply "the Methodist Church" in unofficial documents was also stricken from the new constitution.

The Methodist Church came into being when John Wesley's renewal movement within the Church of England was imported into the Colonies. The American counterpart of the British Methodist Church was formed by 60 ministers at the Christmas Conference in Baltimore in 1784.

By the middle of the 19th century the Methodists had become the largest Protestant group in the country, primarily because of the efforts of hundreds of circuit riders, who roamed the Western frontiers with John Wesley's call to repentance and faith.

The Evangelical United Brethren Church resulted from the 1946 merger of the Church of the United Brethren in Christ and the Evangelical Church. Both denominations had their origin among German-speaking immigrants in the Middle Atlantic states.

The United Brethren Church was formed in Frederick County, Md., in 1800; the Evangelical Church, in Kleinfettersville, Pa., in 1807.

Merger between the Methodists and the two groups that combine to form the Evangelical United Brethren Church has been a subject of conversation for more than a century. The latter groups' widespread use of German in the past was a major obstacle to such unions.

November 12, 1966

Episcopal Body Assails Idea of Heresy

By JOHN LEO

A special committee of the Episcopal Church termed the concept of heresy "anachronistic" yesterday and called for a "drastic revision of canon law" to make heresy trials almost impossible.

"Any risks the church may run by fostering a climate of genuine freedom," the committee said in a report, "are minor compared to the dangers it surely will encounter from any attempts at suppression censorship or thought control."

If a church member voices theological opinions that others in the church consider seriously subversive, the committee said, they should be able to dissociate themselves from those opinions without attacking the motivations or character of the dissenter.

The committee, set up last January in the wake of heresy charges against Bishop James A. Pike, was headed by Bishop Stephen F. Bayne Jr., and made up of three bishops, five theologians, two social scientists and a journalist.

The 20-page report went to the Episcopal Church's Presiding Bishop, John E. Hines, who is expected to pass it along to the church's

triennial general convention in Seattle Sept. 17.

The committee stopped short of recommending a total ban on heresy trials for tactical reasons. It was thought that a total ban could not be maneuvered through the general convention but that the current report stood a good chance.

The committee called heresy trials "a last resort" and urged that 10 bishops be required to file a presentment for a trial instead of the present three. It also urged that no trial go forward without a two-thirds vote of the House of Bishops. Under current canon law, the bishops vote after such trials, to approve or reject the court's findings.

Bishop Pike, who has been under attack from conservative bishops for his repudiation of such traditional Christian doctrines as the Trinity and the Virgin Birth, is not mentioned in the report, although it obviously was written with him in mind.

Heresy proceedings against Bishop Pike were called for at the annual House of Bishops meeting last October, but forestalled by a resolution rejecting the whole idea of heresy trials as a throw-

back to the Dark Ages.

However, because the resolution also rebuked Bishop Pike for "irresponsible" flippancy, the controversial prelate demanded a heresy trial because he felt his name had been impugned.

Yesterday the Bishop said that he had not seen the committee report, but that it appeared to be "a breath of fresh air." He said that if the Seattle convention approved it, he would withdraw his demand for a heresy trial.

This presumably would settle the entire Pike case, which has been a major source of anxiety —and unfavorable publicity— for the Episcopal Church for several years.

Bishop Pike stepped down as Episcopal Bishop of California during the controversy and is now a theologian in residence at the Center for the Study of Democratic Institutions in Santa Barbara, Calif.

The Bishop appeared before the committee last April as an adviser. One of his recommendations was that the committee not propose a ban on all heresy trials because, he said, the church must retain the ultimate means to protect itself.

This was reflected in the committee's statement that "the church may feel it must maintain a last-resort power to deal juridically with bishops or priests who publicly engage in persistent and flagrant contra-

diction of its essential witness."

In calling for "a climate of genuine freedom," the committee said that "the Church should not only tolerate but should actively encourage free and vigorous theological debate, application of the Gospel to social wrongs, and restatement of Christian doctrines to make them intelligible to contemporary minds."

It called for the continuing education of both the clergy and laymen to provide a wider and more vigorous theological inquiry.

Advisers to the committee included the Rev. Dr. J. V. Langmead Casserley of Seabury-Western Theological Seminary; the Rev. John Courtney Murray, the Roman Catholic theologian, and John A. T. Robinson, Bishop of Woolwich, England, and author of the controversial best-seller "Honest to God."

The report and the papers of all advisers will be published as a book by Seabury Press in November.

Members of the committee, called the Committee on Theological Freedom and Social Responsibilities, in addition to Bishop Bayne, were:

George W. Barrett, Bishop of Rochester.
Louis Cassels, religion editor of United Press International.
The Rev. Dr. Theodore P. Ferris, rector of Trinity Church in Boston.
Everett H. Jones, Bishop of West Texas.
The Rev. Dr. John Macquarrie, Union Theological Seminary.
The Rev. Dr. Paul S. Minear, Yale Divinity School.
The Rev. Dr. Albert T. Mollegan, Virginia Theological Seminary.
The Rev. Dr. Charles P. Price, Memorial Church, Harvard University.
Prof. George A. Shipman, University of Washington.
Dr. David L. Sills, editor of the International Encyclopedia of the Social Sciences.

August 15, 1967

PRESBYTERIAN GROUP REJECTS MERGER BID

ATLANTA, Feb. 22 (AP)— Presbyteries of the Presbyterian Church in the U.S. have rejected a proposal to merge their presbyteries and synods, regional and state governing bodies, with those of other Presbyterian and Reformed churches.

The denomination announced yesterday that the vote against merger was 39 to 35. Three presbyteries have not voted, but their decisions could make no difference in the outcome.

Although the presbyteries rejected the proposal to merge their governing bodies with those of the other church groups, they approved a proposal permitting individual congregations of the Presbyterian Church in the U.S. to merge with congregations of the other sects.

The vote on the congregations uniting was 55 to 19.

A vote on a third proposal, to unite the Presbyterian Church in the U.S. with the Reformed Church in America, stood at 52 for and 18 against, with seven presbyteries still to vote. Twenty negative votes could defeat the proposal.

February 23, 1969

LUTHERAN CAUCUS SEEKS NEW POLICY

By GEORGE DUGAN
Special to The New York Times

DENVER, July 15—A newly organized Free Lutheran Caucus defied today the rules of the three-million-member Lutheran Church-Missouri Synod by declaring its intention to share the sacrament of holy communion "with all Christians," Protestant or Roman Catholic.

The caucus, a self-styled coalition of "activist" Negroes, youth, clergy and laity within the denomination, described the church's traditional prohibition against intercommunion as "irrelevant" in a time of worldwide hunger, war and racial tension.

Strict sacramental rules of the theologically conservative Missouri Synod forbid its members to receive communion not only in other Christian churches, but also in other Lutheran churches.

Issue Causes Concern

The issue of intercommunion if of much concern to most of the 900 delegates attending the church's biennial convention in Denver's Convention Hall.

A move to permit Missouri Synod Lutherans to receive communion at the altars of the 2.6-million-member American Lutheran Church has raised a controversy.

It is expected to be defeated after vigorous floor debate.

Historically the conservative Missouri Synod holds to the position that it cannot admit worshippers with whom it disagrees in doctrine to the Lord's table. Nor does it permit its pastors to preach in or exchange pulpits with other churches.

The Rev. George Hrbek, a Chicago minister and coordinator of the Free Lutheran Caucus, said:

"It is our intention to continue to celebrate openly our unity in the body of Christ by deliberate acts of ecclesiastical disobedience if necessary."

Mr. Hrbek said the caucus was formed last night by about 75 persons representing a cross-section of the younger church members.

'Blatantly Unrepresentative'

He said the Missouri Synod was "blatantly unrepresentative" of modern Christianity, racist and unconcerned with the world around it.

With Mr. Hrbek at a news conference were nine members of the caucus steering committee, including the Rev. Ken Sherman, who wore a gas mask to "protect my identity."

Mr. Sherman said he was "worried" about his safety because "whenever I enter the hall with my black friends I am stared at with obvious animosity."

He complained about too many policemen in the vicinity of youth services outside the hall and said that the presence of a helicopter flying over the convention's opening service last Friday at the Red Rocks Amphitheater near here constituted a hidden threat of the use of tear gas.

A petition being circulated among the delegates by the caucus declares its intention to share communion with others and adds:

"We feel this way because we follow the life style of our buddy Jesus Christ and declare with Him that we are one in spirit, one in the Lord, as well as with all Christian bodies."

July 16, 1969

CHURCH POLITICS APPEARS ON RISE

By GEORGE DUGAN

Wide-open politicking for high church office is the newest trend in religion.

Traditionally, America's Protestant denominations elected their presidents or chief executive officers without overt political campaigns. Quiet behind-the-scene maneuvering was frowned on but generally accepted. But the day of the decorous election may soon be over.

The new technique was again demonstrated in Denver last weekend when the three-million-member Lutheran Church-Missouri Synod named as its new president the Rev. Dr. Jacob A. O. Preus. Dr. Preus wasted no time in disavowing the tactics used in his behalf and publicly repudiated those supporters who had resorted to them.

Newspaper Ad Deplored

He said he "deeply deplored politicking in the church." He was alluding to an advertisement in a local daily newspaper, well-organized blocs of delegates pledged to vote for him and the distribution of campaign buttons.

Similar techniques were used last month at the biennial assembly of the United Church of Christ in Boston. There, a three-way contest was conducted in a hotel plastered with pictures of the candidates.

Shortly before his election, Dr. Preus said a paid ad in The Denver Post had appeared without his knowledge and that an endorsement in a church paper had also been printed without his consent.

On the eve of the election, the Rev. Dr. Walter F. Wohlbrecht, executive director of the Missouri Synod, denounced open politics in a religious group. He took particular exception to the formation of delegate electioneering blocs, comparing them to "cells" run by "gauleiters" in Nazi Germany.

Dr. Wohlbrecht said that in spite of synod regulations requiring that delegates come to the convention uninstructed, there had been meetings before and since the convention "to orient, acquaint, instruct or inform."

"Here and there," he said, "delegates have felt pressured or even threatened."

Dr. Wohlbrecht said that one voting delegate had declined to come to Denver because he "resisted the effort to bind his conscience to participate in bloc voting or collective voting on behalf of his district."

Two weeks ago, he said, "my attention was called to a new synodical first—a systematic home visitation of lay and pastoral delegates from congregations of one district to laymen and pastors in another district." They bore a list of voting "directives," he said.

Dr. Wohlbrecht told the 1,000 delegates that "by virtue of my office I am duty-bound to call the attention of this convention to a series of serious breaches of the democratic processes we so easily take for granted even in the church, to say nothing of badly bruised brotherly relationships within the synod, which, if unexposed and unchallenged, can develop into a malignancy and lead to deadly wounds in the body synodical."

This week in Boston at the eighth annual assembly of the Unitarian Universalist Association, the Rev. John O. Fisher, minister of the First Parish Church of Brewster, Mass., charged that some delegates under 21 years of age had taken the floor in debate and later voted.

Mr. Fisher said this was contrary to Massachusetts law governing the conduct of business of corporations. The Unitarian Universalist Association is incorporated under state law.

July 19, 1969

PROTESTANTS GIVE ON A LOCAL BASIS

National Programs Suffer First Cutback in Funds Since Depression Days

The national programs of the major Protestant churches are suffering their first cutback in funds since the Depression.

A study of the budgets of the country's large Protestant denominations and the National Council of Churches discloses that although total donations to churches continue to increase slightly, church members are beginning to keep a higher proportion of their contributions at the local level.

The new pattern has important implications for American Protestantism because it constitutes a reversal of the massive build-up of large national bureaucracies that has characterized Protestant religious life for the last two decades.

One probable effect, according to Protestant leaders, will be significant changes in the pattern of church involvement in social action. The national agencies that are now being forced to cut back on expenses have poured millions of dollars into such controversial areas as civil rights, community organization and the peace movement.

Some Key Aspects

According to church leaders, the following key developments are emerging from the serious decline in financial support of Protestantism's national administrative and policymaking organizations:

¶National budgets are being cut back on existing social-action programs, staffs are being reduced and experiments in new forms of activism are being eliminated.

¶The national bodies are reshaping their roles as planners and administrators and are becoming consultants on social-action projects increasingly being initiated and administered on the local church level.

¶In part, such decentralization is the apparent result of a backlash among conservative local congregations against the liberal policies of the national denominations and the National Council of Churches in such areas as race and opposition to the war in Vietnam. But liberals are also beginning to withhold contributions on the ground that decentralized social-action programs are more efficient.

"Our budget difficulties," said the Right Rev. Stephen F. Bayne, a bishop of the Episcopal Church, in summing up the situation, "are signaling the end of a long period of cheap and easy popularity for the church."

Many churchmen see the problems encountered by the national church bureaucracies as a reflection of the concern for decentralizing all sorts of large bureaucracies, from anti-poverty agencies to school systems.

Welcomed by Some

Many Protestant leaders welcome the growing tendency of local churches to keep more money for the development of their own social-action programs.

They contend that such a development provides opportunities for more creative handling of problems affecting their congregations. One such advocate is the Rev. Ross W. Porter, pastor of the Westminister Presbyterian Church of Steubenville, Ohio.

Mr. Porter's church is keeping a larger percentage of its total budget for "doorstep" missions in Steubenville, a steel town of 32,000. These programs include day-care work, tutoring for slower learners and the investment of church money in low-income housing.

"With decentralization," Mr. Porter said, "we will have more laymen involved and a less clerical church. People who took a dim view of progressive programs handed down from the national office will support them now because they can see where their money is going."

The Right Rev. Paul Hardin, who supervises the collections of the United Methodist Church, believes the decline in funds for national programs "is all part of our revolution against excessive authority."

"There is a cry from the laity in the local congregation for the authority to make decisions," he said.

Other churchmen are fearful, however, that the decline in the power of the national organizations may foreshadow a period of regionalism and rigidity for the Protestant church.

According to the Rev. Richard E. Moore, executive of the Ohio Synod of the United Presbyterian Church in the U. S. A., there is little hope for avoiding "stagnation" in the programs undertaken by the church as long as contributions continue to shrink on the national level.

Without direction from a central office, he argues, a local agency could well decide that "the best thing to do for a starving man is to buy him a coffin."

If the redistribution of wealth and power is to be successful, most denominational executives believe, the money collected at the local level must be circulated through the national office to avoid "insularity and provincialism."

The United Presbyterians have strongly discouraged the synods from keeping money at their level for home-grown projects without circulating it through the national office for even distribution to both wealthy and poor areas. There is no procedure, however, for enforcing this policy.

"As the money settles on the local level," said the Rev. Eugene Huff, chairman of the church's division of strategy and development, "the rich synods will hold it for themselves without any equalizing machinery."

Gifts Lag Behind Costs

But the national offices are not only hurting because of the decline of contributions coming their way from the local churches. Although church donations, which reached $3.6-billion in 1967, continue to grow, they are not keeping pace with growing costs.

The financial picture of American Protestantism also reflects a relative ebb in the growth of church membership. Although more people are joining the church, affiliation fell 1.2 per cent in 1968 to 63.2 per cent of the population, according to the Yearbook of American Churches.

The yearbook, which compiles these figures for the National Council of Churches, estimated total church membership in the United States at 126.5 million people.

The American Association of Fund-Raising Counsel, an organization of private fund-raising agencies, has compiled another indicator of the decline in religious philanthropy.

The counsel reported that $15.8-billion was contributed to all philanthropies in 1968. Of that, $7.4-billion, or 46.8 per cent, was for religious purposes. In 1960, religious contributions amounted to 51 per cent of the total.

Jewish and Roman Catholic experience in raising funds from memberships is more difficult to measure because no central accounting agency exists.

According to the counsel, Jewish collections, estimated at $900-million a year, do not appear to be suffering.

Although collections by the Roman Catholic Church, in the view of professional fund-raisers, are keeping pace with the cost of living, the higher rate of increase in educational costs is putting a severe strain on the church's parish budgets.

Last year 485 parochial schools were reported closed because of financial problems, among which were demands for higher salaries for lay teachers brought in to replace nuns.

Precise over-all figures for the Protestant churches are not maintained by any central agency. The National Council of Churches has attempted to follow financial trends, but has found the accounting systems of the denominations so divergent that accurate averaging is impossible.

Records of the major denominations, however, clearly indicate a decline in giving, particularly to the national agencies.

The United Presbyterian Church in the U.S.A., for example, reported a drop in donations to the national mission program — which includes health, education and antipoverty endeavors—of 4.2 per cent, to about $30-million. A decline of 2 per cent—to $50-million—also was recorded in gifts to mission work on all levels. The church has 3.3-million members.

The Episcopal Church, with 3.4 million members, fell 3 per cent short of reaching an already pared-down national budget for 1969 of $14-million. The number of dioceses failing to meet their pledges doubled.

This financial situation is attributed by many church leaders to the demands for decentralization of powerful hierarchies made by both liberals (who think social action would be more effective if conceived at the grassroots) and conservatives (who would prefer that many current social-action programs conceived by the national offices be curtailed or ended).

A representative conservative viewpoint was expressed by Roger Hull, chairman of the board of the Mutual of New York Life Insurance Company and head of the Presbyterian Lay Committee in the United Presbyterian Church.

"I don't think the church has any competence to make judgments on social and political issues," he said. "And it is in no position to be speaking with one voice."

Just as some liberals have denounced the church as a bulwark of the Establishment, Mr. Hull, looking at it from the opposite end of the spectrum, sees national leaders as "trying to make a political power bloc out of the church."

Many observers trace this kind of feeling, and the drop in giving by conservatives, to the forthright positions in support of civil rights and in opposition to the war in Vietnam taken by many major churches in the early nineteen-sixties.

Backlash Feared

Some church leaders are fearful that a backlash will develop over the issue of "reparations" that James Forman demanded be paid by the churches to black Americans for their suffering under slavery.

So far, no denomination has acceded to Mr. Forman's demand but a flood of mail to the national offices criticizing officials for even negotiating with him has been widely interpreted as presaging a shaper fall-off in gifts for 1970.

Many liberals are also calling for the dilution of power at the national level. They believe the programs developed by progressives in local churches can be more effective.

Richard E. Moore, an official of the Ohio Synod of the United Presbyterian Church, believes, for example, that local ministers are gaining new confidence and that their response to social problems can be "real and gutty, not abstract and theoretical as in the national offices."

Effect on Budget

"People are saying they don't like what's going on in New York," he said, "but they are getting excited by what's happening in their own backyard."

The impact of the drop in giving is evident in the budget plans of the major denominations and the National Council, which depends on the denominations for its funds.

The National Council, for instance, reported that it dropped 20 to 30 workers from its 675-member New York staff because of a decline in contributions from the denominations of several hundred thousand dollars.

The Council also has been forced by lack of funds to leave vacant the post of Associate General Secretary for Christian Unity, which was established to further ecumenical cooperation, a major council objective.

Six programs of the National Council, which has a total budget of more than $25-million, have had their 1970 budgets reduced substantially. These include the Department of Social Justice and the Department of Church Renewal.

Even the theologically and politically conservative Southern Baptist Convention, the largest Protestant denomination with 11-million members, has been prevented from expanding its budget because state conventions are reducing their contributions—a situation that has persisted for five years.

Specific Donations

Similar difficulties are being experienced in the Lutheran Church in America, the United Church of Christ and the American Baptist Convention.

The only area not feeling the pinch is that of donations for specified purposes, such as aid to Biafra. The reason, in the view of Bishop Hardin of the United Methodist Church, is that "people are still responsive when told in a clear way how their money will be spent."

The answer to these problems in most national offices has so far been to continue as before, only at a slightly lower pitch, with leaders hoping the situation will not worsen.

But some churches and agencies, such as the National Council and the United Presbyterian Church, are trying to adjust their roles to the new conditions.

The Presbyterians have, for

the last decade, been moving slowly toward dismantling their powerful national hierarchy and rebuilding it as a strategy and planning agency for programs initiated by synods and presbyteries, the local subdivisions of the church structure to which laymen send elected representatives.

The national office, for example, recently turned over the operation of a community-development center in Cordele, Ga., to the local synod. The local church is now in the process of creating new approaches to guidance services, family counseling and general "community improvement."

According to officials in the United Presbyterian's New York headquarters, only a handful of programs, hospitals and colleges remain under their control. Instead, headquarters is developing methods for evaluating locally developed programs, ranging from orphanages to community-actions projects, and is providing expert guidance where needed.

The National Council of Churches also is relinquishing its influence in a number of projects.

The Council's Delta ministry, a $575,000 civil rights project in Mississippi, was originally administered in New York. But the national office turned the program over to the 30-member staff of the ministry. Now they are in turn relinquishing their authority to the poor residents of the Delta, who will run the operation "instead of highly

publicized outsiders," as a staff consultant put it.

Although the Protestant denominations are hoping that their acceptance of more decentralization will encourage contributions, they have also begun exploring other channels of fund-raising.

In most churches there is no strict requirement for contributions to the national headquarters. The money dropped into the plate as it is passed Sunday mornings makes up 90 per cent of church income—the rest is derived from investment and endowment.

Buildings and Salaries

Over the last 30 years, most churches have generally kept 80 per cent of this money for construction programs and salaries and passed on the rest to the national organizations. It is this money that has enabled the church to set upambitious social-action programs.

In the quest for more sources of income, Bishop Bayne of the Episcopal Church has recommended "the enlisting of the designated support from non-ecclesiastical sources like foundations for unfunded or under-funded projects."

The National Association of Church Business Administrators even suggested, at its meeting last month, that the use of credit cards for making contributions be considered as one means for alleviating the problem.

August 10, 1969

Homosexuals in Los Angeles, Like Many Elsewhere, Want Religion and Establish Their Own Church

By EDWARD B. FISKE
Special to The New York Times

LOS ANGELES — The Rev. Troy D. Perry burst forward from his seat to a makeshift pulpit shouting, "If you love the Lord this morning, say 'Amen'." With one voice, the congregation of more than 400 persons roared back its response.

Such is the style of worship every Sunday at the nondenominational Metropolitan Community Church, a style that resembles that of

just about any Protestant church with a revivalist flavor.

The Metropolitan Community Church is no ordinary Church, however. It is the first congregation in the country to identify itself openly as a church for male and female homosexuals.

Its founding 16 months ago reflects both the growing willingness of American homosexuals to assert themselves as a distinct minority group and the emergence of a more

liberal attitude toward homosexuals among religious bodies.

In recent months, regional and national church bodies, especially those connected with the United Church of Christ, have begun to call for more dialogue between homosexuals and churches and to support drives to legalize homosexual relations between consenting adults.

In 1964, following a police raid on a dance, the Council on Religion and the

Homophile was formed in San Francisco to work in this field. About half a dozen such groups now exist in other cities.

In addition, officials have estimated that across the country there are as many as 100 to 200 churches that are quietly known as congenial to homosexuals. One small denomination is also reported to have an exclusively homosexual clergy and a predominantly homosexual membership.

The New York Times (by Edward E. Fiske)

The Rev. Troy D. Perry in front of the Encore Theater where he now holds church services

Mr. Perry is a dark-haired, 29-year-old preacher with a charismatic manner, a Pentacostalist theological orientation and no compunction at all about admitting that he is an active homosexual.

He convened the first service in his home in October, 1968, with nine friends and three persons drawn by an advertisement in a local homosexual newspaper. Since then the congregation has grown to 348 members, most of whom are in their mid-20's to mid-40's.

Seventy per cent of the members are male homosexuals, including a number of clergymen. Fifteen per cent are lesbians. The rest are relatives of members or other "straight" persons, who, in Mr. Perry's words, "like the friendly atmosphere around here."

Mr. Perry, who was forced out of the Church of God of Prophecy, a Pentacostalist group with headquarters in Cleveland, Tenn., because of his homosexuality, attributes the rapid increase in membership to at least two factors.

One is the reluctance of most mainline congregations to integrate known homosexuals fully into their programs, with the corollary attitude of most clergymen that their task is to persuade the homosexual to alter his behavior rather than to come to terms with it as part of his condition.

The second factor is the need of homosexuals to have

places where they can relate to each other in a congenial and low-pressure social setting.

"In the gay bars the emphasis is too much on sex," said Fred Conwell, a 32-year-old writer and a church member from Dayton, Ohio. "There aren't many places like this, where to be friendly to someone doesn't mean you're trying to go to bed with him."

The 17-room parsonage of the Metropolitan Community Church is thus the center of a large program of activities ranging from job counseling and alcoholism groups to a forthcoming Valentine's Day dance and well-attended coffee hours before church on Sundays.

Services are held in the 385-seat Encore Theater, a Hollywood movie house that donates its facilities. But the congregation has outgrown this facility and is now seeking to purchase a church building. Plans are also under way to establish related congregations in San Francisco, San Diego, Phoenix, Ariz., and nearby Orange County.

Members of the congregation reject the idea that homosexuality, per se, is either sinful or sick. Rather, they argue that it is a condition that offers the same possibilities for love or sin as heterosexuality.

This attitude is in sharp contrast to the long-standing Jewish and Christian teaching that homosexuality is a sinful perversion of the nat-

ural order created by God. This is still the unquestioned attitude of the overwhelming majority of churchgoers.

Recently, however, some church leaders have begun to reconsider the rigidity of this position.

At the social level, some Protestant church leaders and some Roman Catholic priests, acting unofficially, have begun to argue that holding to a heterosexual ideal is no excuse for the ostracism that church and society as a whole have imposed on homosexuals.

Some theologians have also gone beyond the civil liberties area to question whether the traditional condemnation of homosexuality is compatible with the love ethic of Jesus. One argument is that the harshness of the past position was largely the result of historical circumstances, such as the desire of the ancient Hebrews to disassociate themselves from the Canaanites, who made homosexual acts part of their polytheistic worship.

The controversial New Cathechism of the Roman Catholic Church in the Netherlands asserted that homosexuality is morally neutral. Among the individuals who have taken this position is Norman Pittenger, a prominent Anglican, who wrote that homosexual acts are "good" acts "insofar as they contribute to the movement of the persons toward mutual fulfillment and fulfillment in mutuality, with all the accompanying characteristics of love."

But the vast majority of thinkers, especially Catholics and conservative Protestants, have remained firm in rejecting such thinking. Carl F. H. Henry, an American evangelical leader, for instance, recently called for a "compassionate" view of homosexuals but declared that acceptance of their condition as beyond their control would "strip all sexual behavior of moral significance."

Mr. Perry acknowledges that tolerance toward homosexuality raises new and complex ethical problems, including those associated with "marriages" between homosexual couples.

The preacher has officiated at 18 such weddings, eight of them involving lesbians. He uses the regular marriage rite of the Episcopal Church, substituting words such as "spouse" for "husband" or "wife."

He encourages marriages on the ground that society, by its laws and practice on matters such as the renting of housing, keeps homosexuals in an insecure and unhealthy situation. "I am a great believer in homosexuals settling down like anyone else," he said.

Most clergymen of all faiths would still reject the idea of homosexual marriages, however, and even some involved in work with homosexuals prefer to devise means of "blessing" a relationship rather than performing a "wedding."

Mr. Perry himself was married to a woman at the age of 19 and fathered two children. When his homosexual tendencies "came out" at the age of 23, he said, a divorce followed. He now lives with a 21-year-old college student, whom he has not yet "married."

Many homosexuals oppose the idea of a strictly homosexual church. The Rev. Harvey Beach, a 34-year-old Methodist clergyman in Chicago who was forced out of the ministry because of his homosexuality, declared in an interview that such a congregation in his area would "isolate homosexuals who attended even more than they are now."

But members of the Metropolitan Community Church argue that they must stand as a judgment on the church in the same way that other movements, such as Christian Science, have called attention to the failure of mainline churches to express all elements of the Christian faith.

"The churches have closed their doors on a whole group of people," said the Rev. Richard Ploen, one of two unpaid assistant pastors of the church. "That's the only reason we exist."

February 15, 1970

Lutheran Synod's Conservatives Win New Power

Special to The New York Times

NEW ORLEANS, July 14 — Conservative factions led by the Rev. Dr. Jacob A. O. Preus took firm control of the Lutheran Church-Missouri Synod this week after more than four years of fierce struggle with church moderates.

The balance of power shifted dramatically to conservatives who pushed through the church's biennial assembly a package of new legislation for tight doctrinal and administrative controls.

In a week-long session marked by spirited debate and emotional protest, convention delegates accepted as official church theology a document issued last year by Dr. Preus. They gave his administration new powers to enforce it as the standard for seminary professors, for the church's 6,000 pastors and for teachers in the church's approximately 2,000 parochial schools.

By a 60-40 majority that held throughout the week, the assembly also condemned as heretical the prevailing theological views of professors at Concordia Seminary of St. Louis, the church's principal seminary and the largest Lutheran theological school in the country.

Conservatives swept into office all but five of their candidates for 150 positions on key church boards and agencies, and gained majority control on the 11-man governing board at Concordia Seminary. The incoming board is expected within the year to oust the school president, the Rev. Dr. John H. Tietjen, and perhaps eight other theologians and Bible scholars

on grounds of heretical teaching.

The actions provide a platform for a crackdown on dissenters in the moderate faction, who say they fear the worst but are not planning to leave the denomination in large numbers. They say they will continue to give open witness to their positions, but add that some may eventually align themselves with other Lutheran bodies.

"We've told Dr. Preus that we could live with him, but that we were uncertain whether he could live with us," said the Rev. Bertwin L. Frey of Fairview Heights, Ohio, a leader in the moderate coalition. "The next few years will tell whether any reconciliation is possible."

Conservatives hailed the assembly's actions as a desperately needed bulwark against confusion and subversion of the principle of the absolute authority of Scripture that they contend the moderates have promoted for the last 15 years.

Moderates respond that the new legislation changes the nature of national church structures, including the office of president, from supportive and advisory agencies to enforcement agencies.

Moderates organized two demonstrations that pulled them together in tears and embraces, but which irritated the conservatives. On Wednesday immediately after the assembly elevated the Preus document to the status of a doctrinal standard, about 500 delegates and advisers disrupted the proceedings by marching single file to the podium to register their individual protest. During the

solemn 20-minute procession they sang "The Church's One Foundation," a traditional Protestant hymn.

On Friday, after the assembly formally censured Dr. Tietjen, his followers rushed around him in a show of support and held an hour-long liturgical service.

The Missouri Synod, founded 125 years ago by Saxon immigrants fleeing forced merger of German churches, has 2.8 million members. It is the second largest of three major American Lutheran denominations and has traditionally been the most conservative in theology and church discipline.

Until the mid-nineteen-fifties, the Synod, which maintains its predominantly Middle Western base, resisted any movements toward the mainstream of American Lutheranism. Since then it has inched closer to the theology and discipline of the American Lutheran Church and The Lutheran Church in America, the two other major Lutheran bodies.

The tone of the convention, which ended last night, was set on the first day when Dr. Preus, a 53-year old former Latin and Greek professor, won easily a second, four-year term as president.

"It was all over after the election," said the Rev. Dr. Robert D. Preus, brother of the president, and one of five conservative members of the 48-man Concordia faculty.

For the next several days, the moderates delayed final voting on key issues, but their efforts were futile. By late Tuesday conservatives had pushed through the first of the new legislation, which established the church's right to define doctrine by majority of con-

vention votes, and to make those definitions "binding upon all members" so long as the definitions were in accord with Scripture.

This measure, the moderates contended, establishes the principle of a radical departure from the church's traditional requirement of commitment only to the Bible and to the Lutheran Confessions, a set of documents that include the Reformation Book of Concord. The new measure, critics contend, will permit the church to bind its members to theologian interpretations voted by a convention majority.

Next the assembly elevated Dr. Preus's document, which calls for literal interpretation of the Bible and insists that the Gospel of Jesus Christ is preached and taught correctly only if there is adherence to the very words of the Bible.

The convention also gave Dr. Preus new powers in administration of church seminaries and colleges, and nullified the veto power of faculties in the selection of presidents for these institutions.

The only major conservative proposals defeated during the last hours of the convention were a call to draw back from liturgical fellowship with the American Lutheran Church and to cut back participation in the Lutheran Council in the U.S.A., an inter-Lutheran cooperative agency.

The Rev. Dr. Karl L. Barth of Milwaukee, a leading conservative, appeared to express the consensus. "We have declared repeatedly our decision that the theology of Jack Preus is the only theology we have held for 125 years, and we want to keep it," he said. July 15, 1973

SEMINARY STRUCK OVER SUSPENSION

Special to The New York Times

ST. LOUIS, Jan. 21—All academic activity at Concordia Seminary of St. Louis was halted today by a student strike in protest over the suspension of the school's president, the Rev. Dr. John H. Tietjen.

By a 3-to-1 vote, an assembly representing more than 500 resident students adopted "a moratorium on all class attendance" until the institution's board of control either dismisses or exonerates 43 of 48 professors accused of teaching false doctrine.

Although it had been expected for some months, the suspension of Dr. Tietjen last night for alleged advocacy of false doctrine and for assert-

ed administrative malfeasance brought Concordia, the largest Lutheran theological school in the country, to a standstill. The majority of the faculty called an emergency session last night and spent most of today in trying to determine possible unified protest moves.

The Rev. Dr. Martin H. Scharlemann was named acting president. Most of the professors said they would find it impossible to work effectively with Dr. Scharlemann, now a vigorous conservative whom the Concordia community rallied around more than a decade ago when he himself was accused of heresy.

The developments were the latest in a long and bitter theological confrontation between conservatives and moderates in the 2,800,000-member Lutheran Church-Missouri Synod, the St. Louis-based denomination with

congregations in all states.

After a decade of moderate progress that brought the traditionally conservative church closer to the mainstream of American Lutheranism, conservatives and fundamentalists began a systematic effort to regain control of the denomination after the election as president in 1969 of the Rev. Jacob A. O. Preus.

After decisive victories at the synod governing assembly last summer, including blanket condemnation of the 43 professors for allegedly undermining the authority of the Bible, the conservatives intensified their battle for control of Concordia. The board recently dismissed four dissenting professors, canceled 19 courses scheduled for next fall, and enacted policy changes to monitor all Biblical courses and professors.

Dr. Tietjen, who was sus-

pended by the Concordia board last fall but reinstated because of procedural questions, charged today that "agents" of Dr. Preus had recently offered him "an immoral deal" to end the Concordia dispute quietly.

He said he had been offered a pastorate and assurances that further actions against professors would cease in exchange for his resignation. The seminary board knew and approved of this arrangement, he said.

The Rev. Dr. Ewald J. Otto, board chairman, said he knew nothing of this alleged deal, and denied that he had discussed such an arrangement with Dr. Preus. He acknowledged, however, that various compromise proposals to settle the dispute had been quietly floating recently in the church.

January 22, 1974

Seminary's Students Walk Out, Will Continue Studies 'in Exile'

Special to The New York Times

ST. LOUIS, Feb. 19—Most of the students at the Concordia Lutheran Seminary here abandoned the institution today and said that they would continue theological studies at a "seminary in exile" at St. Louis University Divinity School, which is run by Jesuits.

The seminary in exile, is a kind of Lutheran theological college certified by the Catholic institution and two other Protestant seminaries. All classes will be taught by 40 Concordia faculty members who were dismissed yesterday after they had rejected an order to end a month-long class boycott.

Until recently, Concordia, the major ministerial training school for the Lutheran Church-Missouri Synod, was the largest Lutheran and the third largest Protestant seminary in the country. Its total enrollment last fall was 680. A long and bitter struggle for control of the school is part of a wider controversy in the 2.8 - million - member church over doctrine.

Conservatives contend that the church's doctrine is violated unless all Biblical passages—except for The Psalms and The Book of Revelation—are interpreted as literal and historical truth. Moderates, which include dismissed Concordia professors, contend that many books in the Old Testament convey truth symbolically.

The battles political control of the denomination have been going on since the mid-nineteen hundred sixties, with conservatives now in control of all church agencies and commissions.

The Rev. Dr. Martin H. Scharlemann, acting president of Concordia, said today that he expected 100 students to enroll for the next quarter, beginning March 4. He acknowledged, however, that it would take at least three years to rebuild the student body.

February 20, 1974

United Press International

Students at Concordia Lutheran Seminary in St. Louis boarding up archway yesterday

43 DISSIDENTS GET PASTORAL OFFERS

One-Third of Graduates of Seminary Are Placed

Special to The New York Times

ST. LOUIS, June 22—About one-third of the graduates of the dissident Lutheran seminary in exile, which calls itself Seminex, have been offered pastoral positions in Congregations of the Lutheran Church-Missouri Synod.

But because ordination of the graduates violates church rules on certification and is being viewed by an increasing number of congregations as too divisive, Seminex officers remain uncertain how many graduates will eventually get pastoral positions.

The first ordination and installation as pastor of a Seminex graduate took place last Sunday in Chicago. Several more are scheduled in coming weeks, including an ordination tomorrow in St. Louis, where the church's national offices are situated.

About 400 students and 40 professors split from Concordia Seminary of St. Louis in February, protesting actions by conservatives who assumed majority control of church institutions last summer. The dissenters established their own program at St. Louis University, a Roman Catholic institution, and Eden Theological Seminary, affiliated with the United Church of Christ.

14 Are Rejected

The ability of Seminex to recruit new students, to attract churchwide support and, ultimately, to survive, depends on whether its graduates can obtain pastoral positions.

The Rev. Carl H. Reko, Seminex director of placement, said that 43 of the graduating class of 109 now had firm calls from congregations. Forty-one are negotiating, and 14 have been rejected.

The pastoral calls have come from congregations in 19 of the 38 regional districts of the 2,800,000-member denomination. So far, however, only five of these districts have formally supported acceptance by their congregations of the dissident graduates.

Meanwhile, Concordia, which was left with four active professors and fewer than 100 students, has begun rebuilding efforts with virtually unlimited financial backing of conservative church officials.

Earlier this month, the institution was granted an 18-month probation period on its academic accreditation by a commission of the American Association of Theological Schools.

June 23, 1974

Mainline Protestantism on Decline

Mainline Protestantism is losing membership, while the theologically conservative or strongly evangelistic denominations are gaining members, according to the 1974 Yearbook of American and Canadian Churches.

The heaviest losses were recorded by the American Baptist Churches in the U.S.A., down 78,243 (5 per cent) from 1,562,-636; the Episcopal Church, off 154,631 (4.8 per cent) from 3,217,365; the United Presbyterian Chrch in the U.S.A., down 104,850 (3.5 per cent) from 3,813,808 and the United Methodist Church, down 174,-677 (1.7 per cent from 10,509,-128.

Among the gainers were the conservative Southern Baptist Convention, the nation's largest Protesant denomination, which reported a membership increase of 240,657, up 2 per cent from 11,824,676.

Also reporting gains were the Mormons (Church of Jesus Christ of Latter-day Saints), up 52,738 (2.5 per cent) from 2,133072; the Jehovah's Witnesses, up 14,390 (3.9 per cent) from 416,789; the Seventh Day Adventists, up 15,282 (3.5 per cent) from 433,906 and the Assemblies of God, up 21,274 (2 per cent) from 1,078,332.

Total Up 35,000

According to the 197 edition of the yearbook, church and synagogue membership in the United States stands at 131,424,564 about 35,000 more than the figure reported a year ago.

A rough breakdown of the total gave Protestants 71,648,-000, Roman Catholics 48,460,-000, Jews 6,115,000 and Eastern Orthodox 3,739,000.

The yearbook reported that Sunday School enrollments — chiefly Protestant—continued a downward drift from 38,487,453 in 1971 to 36 697,785 in the latest year covered (1972), a decline of 4.3 per cent.

While church membership figures remained at a virtual standstill, the yearbook noted, contributions of money increased.

With 39 Protestant bodies reporting, the latest total of giving for all purposes was $4,615,607,162—an increase of $229-million, or 5.2 per cent, reported by a comparable number of churches the previous year.

The 1974 yearbook will be published May 13 by the Abingdon Press, Nashville, and will be available in bookstores at $9.95 a copy.

May 5, 1974

Protestant Churches Returning to Basic Beliefs

By KENNETH A. BRIGGS
Special to The New York Times

CHICAGO, March 8—A decade ago, many liberal Protestant denominations were reeling under the impact of the God-is-dead movement, theologies that were triumphantly secular and a flurry of social activism.

Since then, as the national mood has changed, the style and tone of the churches have undergone a major adjustment as well, gradually turning toward a "back-to-basics" approach that stresses the need for sound beliefs and personal faith.

Among other things, church leaders say, the shift signifies a growing uneasiness over what is considered a lack of clarity about such conventional beliefs as God's transcendence, the divinity of Jesus and the promise of eternal life. Spurred in part by the wave of spiritual revival that swept the nation in such forms as the "Jesus movement," the established, historical churches are seeking to restore fundamentals.

Spokesmen insist, however, that the swing does not indicate a rejection of social consciousness but rather a combining of social awareness with stronger Biblical and theological bases.

This week's meeting of the governing board of National Council of Churches revealed certain aspects of the trend. Though the agenda was characteristic of the council, consisting largely of pressing crises such as hunger and civil rights, the meeting was the most subdued that some staff workers could remember. Absent were the intensity and urgency that marked such meetings a few years ago. Instead, delegates talked quietly of finding new religious and socially responsible directions.

Significantly, the council during the last year reactivated a long defunct study group on evangelism, normally not a high council priority. The group hopes to provide what many on the council regard as an overdue program to promote spiritual concerns. Many feel the council has strayed too far from the religious pulsebeat of its 42-million constituents among 30 Protestant and Orthodox groups.

"The more liberal denominations," notes the Rev. Dr. Sterling Cary, president of the council, "have been seen as being activist. They are now trying to relate action to the faith and to theological reflection." Dr. Cary warns, however, that the new emphasis could obscure what he holds to be a legitimate commitment to social issues.

Evangelism and spirituality have been upgraded not only by the council but by several member Protestant bodies. For instance, the 1.3-million-member United Church of Christ, one of the most liberal groups, instituted a serious theological study called "Faith Crisis" in 1971 after dismissing its social action staff for budgetary reasons.

The Episcopal Church has appointed the first evangelism officer in its history, the Rev. A. Wayne Schwabb.

And the most liberal branch of Lutheranism, the Lutheran Church in America, recently engaged in a "Theological Affirmation" study on baptism that became a leading item on its annual convention schedule last summer.

Decade of Turbulence

One explanation for this search for roots is the reaction to the turbulence of the last decade. "There was a profound dissatisfaction with the theologies of the mid-nineteen-sixties such as the God-is-dead or liberation theology that turned people off and scared them," says Dr. Schubert Ogden, professor of theology at the United Methodist Perkins School of Theology in Dallas. "These fads came and went quickly because they didn't get hold of the issues the church cared about."

Having been faced with such passing movements, Dr. Ogden says, the climate was ready for an attempt to "recover an identity that was lost."

A pervasive feeling is that such a recovery is essential to the well-being of the church. "Churches that are serious in what they are doing and can make life meaningful to people will attract people," says the Rev. Dean Kelley, author of "Why The Conservative Churches Are Growing." "After all, that's their business."

Dr. Kelley also says that because many liberal Protestants simply did not know how to discuss evangelism, they tended to regard it as an embarrassment, and thereby "sold it short."

Most of the groups to which these Protestants belonged, he notes, have continued to lose membership while "stricter" churches have gained.

"We need to know what the church stands for," adds the Rev. Dr. Robert Marshall, president of the Lutheran Church in America, "and we want to hear it again and clearly." Dr. Marshall says Christians cannot expect that their faith is understood by non-Christian society.

"We have come to the time when these assumptions about Christianity are so eroded that there is increased need both for clarity and simplicity," he says.

At the same time that a reassertion of certain traditional convictions seems in order, there is caution against lapsing into forms of fundamentalism or private religion that ignore the questions of social justice. If a new style of orthodoxy is emerging, observers say, it has been tempered by the heightened awareness of human needs brought about by social involvement.

Shift of Emphasis

"We must not give the impression," says the United Church of Christ president, the Rev. Dr. Robert Moss, "that we are backing away from social action even though we badly need more theological grounding."

To a large degree, then, the shift is one of emphasis rather than radical departure. The Episcopal Diocesan Bishop of New York, the Right Rev. Paul Moore, discussing the swing, says he encouraged the impulse among his fellow Christians "to go to Selma" during the civil right activity of the nineteen-sixties but had to remind them to "say their prayers." Now, he says, the inclination is to "say the prayers, but to need reminding of the 'urgent human concerns around us' outside the church."

Symptomatic of the effort to strike a proper balance was the recent meeting of 18 ecumenical thinkers in January of this year at the Hartford Theological Foundation in Hartford, to define the essentials of the faith.

At the conclusion of a weekend seminar convened by two Lutherans, the Rev. Richard J. Neuhaus and Peter Berger, a sociologist, the group drew up a manifesto that asserts orthodox concepts of God against the supposed threats of radical or secular theology and urges Christians to apply their faith to social problems.

The document, called "An Appeal for Theological Affirmation," refuted 13 theses believed by its authors to be dangerous. Among them: That Jesus can be defined in human terms alone and that God is simply a creation of mankind and that all religions are equally valid. The document also rejects the implication that an emphasis on "God's transcendence" removes the obligation to be socially involved.

According to the Hartford consensus, the "false and debilitating" heresies never made deep inroads among Protestantism's rank-and-file but captured a small but influential segment of the church's leadership. Flirtations with unorthodox ideas sometimes gained wide media attention.

Secular Theology

Though not mentioned by name, the Hartford participants presumably took aim at particular targets, most of which have not been in evidence for some time. They included, apparently, the expired God-is-dead movement (one of whose original proponents, Dr. Paul Van Buren of Temple University, did an about-face last spring by renouncing his former views during an Easter sermon); various "liberation" theologies that center on social revolution, and various thinkers such as Harvey Cox who, through a best-selling book, "The Secular City," called for a celebration of the secular world.

Secular theology, as it became known, urged Christians to see God's will not so much in spiritual terms as in the social movements for racial justice and peace that were swirling about at the time. Belief that man had "come of age," no longer needing a dependent relationship with God, encouraged an attitude of human self-sufficiency and a theology based on the ability of mankind to solve problems by himself.

But as troubles have beset national economic and social life, conventional theology, with its emphasis on a loving God who forgives and renews hope, has again come to the surface to replace these concepts. Also, as the churches have fallen on hard times, the basics of faith have become to many the source of strength and identity.

Dr. Ogden says that many more students at Perkins "think of themselves as evangelicals," than in the past, and that they tend to be "occupied by a Biblical agenda." Much of the change, he says, is a result of the "evangelical revivals" that have recently swept many of the nation's young people.

For the majority of non-evangelical Protestants, however, the shift has been somewhat less pronounced. It is expressed more as a subtle imperative than a dramatic conversion.

"There is real interest on the part of people active in the church," says William T. Thompson, Stated Clerk of the United Presbyterian Church in the U.S.A., "to understand the beliefs that motivate what they do. In times of stress people go back to types of permanence. The church is part of that."

March 9, 1975

CATHOLICS

ROMANISM IN AMERICA.

From the London Times of Sept. 6.

Archbishop McCloskey, of New-York, was chosen for the honor (of the Cardinalate) because he stood at the head of a vast organization of the Roman Catholic Church, the resources of which, undervalued and hardly understood hitherto by the powers that rule at Rome, have come to be known and prized and made the foundation of towering hopes. Half the Old World has been lost to the Church, and of the remaining part that still holds formally to its allegiance many sections are mined by scepticism or shaken by discontent. But, if the Old World be lost, may not the New be gained? It is at least possible that this is the inner thought of Rome in these dark days. The destinies of the human race seem to move westward, and in a relative sense, if not absolutely, the star of America waxes as that of Europe wanes. But if a century hence the Western Continent will outweigh in wealth and power the divided societies of Europe, will not the dominion of the younger civilization compensate for the loss of authority over the original Empire of the Church? The beginnings of the conquest have been made, and the campaign is carried on with energy, subtlety, and perseverance. It Rome is to profit by these enterprises, she must encourage her champions with approving notice, and dignify them, alike in the sight of followers and foes, with appropriate rewards.

Thus it comes to pass that at length the spiritual adolescence of Catholic America is recognized by the papacy. The bestowal of a Cardinal's on the Archbishop of New-York is not simply a token of the Papal gratitude for individual services: it rewards a powerful reinforcement, now, for the first time, formally arrayed among the champions of the Holy See. In this sense it is understood in America, and, though Rome is reticent by habit, her actions make confession of her objects. The growth of the Roman Catholic faith on the American Continent, not only in the countries where it was planted by Spanish colonists and by others of the Latin races, but in the very heart of the society which boasts of its Anglo-Saxon individualism, is a remarkable fact, but it is not a novel one. The novelty is that Rome has recognized it with every sign of delight and hope. Twenty years ago, when the Roman Catholic Church was fighting its way vigorously against formidable enemies in the United States, when the continuous influx of Irish immigrants alarmed the States of the Atlantic seaboard as much as the Chinese immigration has surprised and embarrassed the Pacific States, when "Knownothingism," a mere outburst of splenetic and jealous bigotry, was raised to the rank of a political creed, the Court of Rome would have scouted the notion of looking for aid, save in that humble pecuniary form in which aid is always acceptable to it, from its spiritual subjects in America. The followers of the Church in that distant world were to hear and to obey when Rome spoke, but that they should influence Roman policy, should be represented in the Sacred College, should be directly governed by a Prince of the Church—these were pretensions utterly inadmissible. The Holy

Father, if he no longer set his foot on the neck of secular sovereigns, still leant on emperors, and was courted by kings. The Great Powers of the European Continent competed for the honor of protecting him, and though the yoke of their protection sometimes pressed heavy in the form of influence, the pressure was not manifest. Implicated in these monarchical relations, enthroned on a vast and compact system of ecclesiastical establishments, the Holy See was disdainful of mere Republicans, who could promise no intervention of diplomatists or armies, and whose religious endowments consisted solely in voluntary gifts. But the whole scheme of policy constructed by the sacerdotal statesmen of the Vatican after the events of 1849 has in our days crumbled to atoms. The Pope has ceased to be a temporal ruler; the Empires on which he leaned have withdrawn their supporting hands—the one fatally weakened, the other no longer loyal. But the strength of the Church in the West has gone on increasing, and its possibilities of growth now fill the minds of devoted Romanists with splendid imaginations of victory. To bring the official chief of a hierarchy from whom so much is expected within the innermost circle of the Papal policy is, as the Roman Curia now perceives, not only advisable, but inevitable. So Archbishop McCloskey, an American of Irish descent, has been, to the delight of all the Roman Catholics of North America, raised to the Cardinalate. He is now on his way to Rome to be admitted to his new dignity by the Pope himself, and he brings with him an "offering of gratitude and sympathy" from the faithful in New-York, which, besides a solid contribution of some twenty-thousand pounds sterling, includes an address describing the enormous progress of Catholic doctrine among the people of the United States.

We do not doubt that a great part of these boasts is true, or that the hopes based upon them may be,

61

to some extent, well founded. The Papacy is resolved, as it appears to establish closer relations than those of mere homage and condescension with its multitudinous and wealthy subjects beyond the Atlantic. This fact is demonstrated not only by the elevation of Archbishop M'Closkey to the highest rank in the Church below the Chair of St. Peter itself, but by the report current at Rome that Monsignore Roncetti, who was lately sent to New-York to present the Archbishop with the *berretta*, "will be appointed to a high ecclesiastical dignity in America." In truth, the course of events on the other side of the Atlantic is well worth observing, and if Rome had been accustomed to study popular movements as she has been used to watch the policies of courts, she would long ago have done what she is doing now. In all the countries of the American Continent, there is already a numerous and powerful Roman Catholic population, and nowhere, except, perhaps, in Brazil, has the supremacy of the Popedom been threatened as it has been in every part of Europe. The Spanish-American Republics will never be of much account in the world, but, such as they are, they are true to Rome. The descendents of the Freech settlers in Canada and in Louisiana are equally loyal and equally useless as allies. But the great English-speaking communities of the Continent, and especially the United States, inherit the destinies of America. Is it, then, certain that, as Rome now believes, the Catholic Church will extend its dominion and flourish under new conditions among the people of the United States? The problem is a difficult one, for there are opposing forces at work, and the triumph of Catholicism, were it as complete as the Papacy anticipates, would involve the defeat and destruction of that spirit of individualism which is characteristic of the English race in every land, and which has nowhere asserted itself more vigorously than in the Federal Union. On the other hand, the forces working for the Roman Church are both strong and ingeniously directed. Irish immigration has poured some four millions of Catholic Celts into the Union, and the descendants of the earlier exiles who have preserved their faith possibly number as many more. This vast mass, it is melancholy to confess, is for the most part at the lowest level of intelligence. The Irish, unlike the English, the Scotch, and the German immigrants, herd together in the large cities, and are there subject to sacerdotal discipline. They move at command and in a body, and their influence in politics is out of proportion even to their large numbers. In many of the towns they are dominant in local affairs, and wherever this happens, there are attempts, sometimes in part successful, to secure an indirect endowment for the Church of Rome. But it is not alone on the ponderous body of superstitious zeal which the Irish immigration has placed at the command of the Church that Cardinal McCloskey and his fellow-workers rely. At all the centres of American society they carry on an untiring and not fruitless propaganda. In a democratic community the baldness of life becomes very apparent to the rich and idle, and, as social distinctions are few and uncertain, the attractions of a creed which carefully cultivates the æsthetic side of religion, and which claims the inheritance of a grand historical tradition, are almost irresistible to a large class of minds. In every society there are those "faint hearts and feeble wings that every sophister can lime," and in America, where, in spite of the diffusion of elementary education, a high and thoughtful culture is rare, the same influences which here tempt many to the distractions of ritualistic vanities, or even across the border-land, are very potent with a certain superfine class who would gladly ape the externals of an aristocracy. Rome, then, may hope to command the masses in the United States by her power over Irish superstition, and to win the allegiance of a section of the wealthier class by the splendor of her ritual and the immensity of her pretensions. Will this be enough to make her in the course of years the dominant influence in America? We believe it will not, for, strong as the forces on her side may be, the strength of manly and intelligent individuality, nowhere wanting among men of English blood, is, we are convinced, greater, healthier, and more enduring.

September 19, 1875

THIRD PLENARY COUNCIL

A GREAT GATHERING OF AMERICAN CATHOLIC CHURCHMEN.

ARCHBISHOPS, BISHOPS, AND EMINENT THEOLOGIANS TO MEET IN BALTIMORE ON SUNDAY—PREVIOUS COUNCILS.

BALTIMORE, Nov. 6.—The third Plenary Council of Baltimore, which meets on Sunday, Nov. 9, will form the largest gathering of Catholic prelates that has assembled since the celebrated Council of Trent in the sixteenth century, except the Council of the Vatican, which adjourned in 1870 before completing its labors. Councils are as old as the church, and are either Provincial Plenary, or General. A Provincial Council is composed of the suffragan Bishops subject to the jurisdiction of a Bishop; for instance, a Provincial Council of Baltimore includes the Bishops of Richmond, Wheeling, Charleston, Savannah, and St. Augustine, who are the Bishops belonging to the Archdiocese of Baltimore. A Plenary Council is composed of the entire hierarchy of a country. The present Plenary Council of Baltimore includes all the Archbishops, Bishops, and mitred Abbots in the United States—from Maryland to California and from the Gulf of Mexico, in the South, to the great lakes of the North. Cardinal McCloskey, of New-York, and Archbishop Alemany, of San Francisco, will be prevented from attending on account of infirmities and advanced age. The former will be represented by his Coadjutor, Archbishop Corrigan, and the latter by Bishop Riordan, of San Francisco. A General Council is composed of the Catholic hierarchy of the whole world, such as the Council of Nice, in the fourth century, which was composed of 318 prelates; the Council of Trent, which numbered 255, and the Vatican Council already mentioned. The first Plenary Council of Baltimore met on May 2, 1852, and was composed of 6 Archbishops and 26 Bishops. Archbishop Francis Patrick Kenrick presided, and prepared a beautiful pastoral letter addressed to the clergy and laity of the United States. One of the immediate results of this Council was the creation of the Archdiocese of San Francisco and 14 other dioceses. Of the prelates attending the first Plenary Council only four are alive to-day, viz., Cardinal McCloskey, Archbishop Alemany, of San Francisco; Archbishop Amat, of Santa Fé, and Archbishop Peter Richard Kenrick, of St. Louis. Of these the latter only will probably attend the present Council.

The second Plenary Council assembled in Baltimore on Sunday, Oct. 7, 1866, and included 7 Archbishops, 38 Bishops, and 3 mitred Abbots. Archbishop Martin John Spalding, of Baltimore, was appointed the President and Apostolic Delegate. The Council sat for two weeks, holding two sessions every day. Its object being entirely spiritual, individual political opinions were forgotten, and not an allusion was made to the exciting topics which at that time agitated the country. The principal decrees passed at this Council were in relation to faith, the primacy of the Roman Pontiff, the relations of Church and State in this country, the power, rights, and duties of Archbishops, Bishops, and clergy; the sacraments, the education of Catholic youth, the rights of church property, the Catholic press, the spiritual welfare of the blacks, secret societies, &c. In calling this Council Plenary the Holy See followed a precedent established 1,400 years ago, when the title of Plenary was given to the General Council of the African Church held in the days of St. Augustine. As each of the 75 prelates attending the third Plenary Council will have two theologians, and as there will be present a large number of Vicars-General, heads of religious orders, (such as the Jesuits, Redemptorists, &c.,) and Superiors of seminaries, it may be safe to say that there will be present at this Council at least 300 prelates and priests.

There will be four separate meetings of the council—private congregations, public congregations, private sessions, and public sessions. The private congregations will be composed of theologians, each having a Bishop for its President, with a Vice-President and a notary. The duty of the latter will be to keep the minutes of the meetings of the congregation and prepare the final report. The public congregations will be held in the cathedral, and will include all the "synodales"—that is, all who are entitled to be present at the Synod, from the most reverend President down to the youngest theologian. At these public congregations the theologians will have the floor, the prelates simply asking questions or proposing difficulties. The private sessions are attended only by the prelates, the Secretary and other officers of the Council being present merely to record the proceedings. The chief work of the Council will be done in these private sessions, for in them the acts and decrees proposed will be searchingly investigated and closely scrutinized. The public sessions are the solemn ceremonies in the cathedral, in the presence of all the prelates, priests, and laity that will be able to get in the church. After the pontifical high mass the decrees of the Council already passed in private will be solemnly read and promulgated. But they do not become a law until they are approved by the Holy See, just as the acts passed by Congress require the approval of the President of the United States. One of the most interesting questions to come before the Council is that of introducing the canon law into the government of the church in the United States. At present the Bishop of a diocese has the power of removing a priest at pleasure, but for some time there has been a disposition among the clergy to bring the church in this country under the canon law, when a parish priest would hold his position during life or good behavior. The parish priests would then have the right to nominate their own Bishop.

The present distinguished Archbishop of Baltimore, the Most Rev. James Gibbons, is one of the youngest members of the American hierarchy. He was born in Baltimore on July 23, 1834. His parents were Irish, and at an early age he was taken to Ireland, where he was partially educated. In his nineteenth year he returned to Baltimore and entered St. Charles College, Maryland, to study for the priesthood. He was ordained by the late Archbishop Kenrick, June 30, 1861, and, after several unimportant missions, was made Secretary to Archbishop Spalding and stationed at the cathedral, where he soon became marked for future promotion. When Pope Pius IX., at the request of the prelates composing the Archdiocese of Baltimore, gave notice of his intention to appoint a Vicar Apostolic for the State of North Carolina, Archbishop Spalding, who was well aware of the virtues and talents of his secretary, recommended Father Gibbons to the new See. He was consecrated in the Baltimore Cathedral on Aug. 16, 1868, the late Bishop Foley, of Chicago, preaching an eloquent sermon on the occasion. The new Diocese of North Carolina numbered only 1,000 Catholics out of a population of 1,000,000, and Bishop Gibbons had only a half dozen priests to attend this vast field, so that upon him fell all the responsibility and a full share of the work. Bishop Gibbons displayed such marked ability in North Carolina, that upon the death of Bishop McGill, of Richmond, in January, 1872, he was raised to that vacant See, and consecrated in the following October by Archbishop Bailey, of Baltimore. He soon infused new life into the Catholic Church in Virginia; new churches were erected in various places, schools and other public institutions established, and throughout the whole State everything manifested the presence of an active, zealous, and hard-working Bishop. While he was thus engaged in building up the Diocese of Richmond, the health of Archbishop Bailey, of Baltimore, (who had succeeded the lamented Spalding in October, 1873,) began to decline, and at his special request Pius IX. appointed Bishop Gibbons his coadjutor, with the right of succession to the Archepiscopal See of Baltimore, May 20, 1877. On the 3d of October of the same year, by the death of Dr. Bailey, Archbishop Gibbons succeeded to the See of Baltimore. During his administration five to six Catholic churches have been built in the city of Baltimore, St. James's Home for Boys has been established, St. Elizabeth's Home for Colored Infants has been opened, a home founded for servant girls out of place, a Young Men's Lyceum established, a Catholic hall erected, (which was a want long felt in Baltimore,) besides numbers of churches and public institutions built throughout the archdiocese. Archbishop Gibbons and other leading Catholic prelates were summoned to Rome in the Autumn of 1883 for the purpose of taking into consideration the affairs of the church in America. The result of that conference was the convoking of the third Plenary Council of Baltimore. At first the Pope was disposed to appoint an eminent Italian clergyman to represent him at the council, but upon further advising with the American Archbishops this idea was abandoned, and Archbishop Gibbons was appointed Apostolic Delegate and President of the Council. Leo XIII. has a high appreciation and great personal friendship for Archbishop Gibbons, and as a special mark of his favor presented him with his last painted portrait, which will occupy a conspicuous place in the Council Chamber. Archbishop Gibbons is 50 years old, and although he has the appearance of delicate health he never fails to attend to all the duties of his exalted position. He is slightly above the medium height, has light hair and blue eyes, and has the most winning manner. His principal work is the "Faith of our Fathers," of which in less than 10 years 150,000 copies have been sold in the United States, Great Britain, and Australia.

The Most Rev. William Henry Elder, the successor of Archbishop Purcell in the Archiepiscopal See of Cincinnati, was born in Baltimore on March 22, 1819, and was named after his great-grandfather, William Elder, the ancestor of the American branch of the family. At a very early age he showed a studious disposition and an inclination toward piety. At the proper age he was placed at Mount St. Mary's College, Emmitsburg, Md., where in a few years he passed successfully through the classics and entered upon his philosophical studies. Finding that he was called to the ecclesiastical state, he went to Rome and became a student of the famous college of the Propaganda Fide. Here he pursued his theological studies and was ordained priest in 1846, just before the accession of Pius IX. to the papal chair. Immediately after his ordination Father Elder returned home and was made Professor of Theology at his old Alma Mater, Mount St. Mary's College. He filled the chair of theology very acceptably for 10 years, until he was appointed to the See of Natchez, made vacant by the death of the Right Rev. J. O. Van de Velde, who had been transferred from the Bishopric of Chicago in 1853. Natchez being a more important See at that time than Chicago. Bishop Elder was consecrated May 3, 1857, and filled the duties of the episcopacy for nearly a quarter of a century, during which time he was several times in danger of death during the prevalence of yellow fever in Natchez. Once he was actually reported dead, and had the unusual pleasure of reading his own obituary. In 1879 Bishop Elder was nominated as Coadjutor of San Francisco, and resigned the See of Natchez, but before his resignation was accepted he was induced to withdraw it, and he remained for two years longer among his beloved people. In 1881 Bishop Elder was nominated Coadjutor Bishop of Cincinnati, with the right of succession in the event of the death of Archbishop Purcell, whose health was at that time rapidly declining, both from his four-score years and the great financial troubles which had clouded the last lustrum of his long and eventful episcopate. The venerable Archbishop died on July 5, 1883, and Archbishop Elder, who had administered the affairs of the archdiocese for nearly three years, was officially installed by receiving the pallium, the gifted young Bishop Watterson, of Columbus, Ohio, preaching an eloquent sermon on the occasion. During the civil war Bishop Elder was sent out of his diocese by the Federal commandant of Natchez because he refused to have prayers said for the President of the United States. He based his refusal upon the grounds that in this country Church and State were distinct, and he was bound to "render to Cæsar the things that are Cæsar's and to God the things that are God's." When another Federal General was sent to Natchez he revoked the order and Bishop Elder returned once more to his flock.

Most Rev. Peter Richard Kenrick, the Archbishop of St. Louis, is the oldest member of the American Catholic hierarchy. He was born in Ireland early in the present century, and, having shown a disposition toward the ecclesiastical life, he was carefully educated in the classics and afterward in philosophy. At the seminary his learning and piety went hand in hand together. After his ordination he was stationed in Philadelphia, of which diocese his elder brother, Right Rev. Francis Patrick Kenrick, was Bishop. It was here that he was consecrated Bishop of Drasa, *in partibus infedelibus*, and Coadjutor of St. Louis on Nov. 30, 1841, by Bishop Rosati, of the latter See, whom he succeeded Sept. 25, 1843. In 1843 the Diocese of St. Louis was elevated to an archdiocese, and Bishop Kenrick was appointed its first Metropolitan. While possessing great learning and a profound knowledge of theology, he has splendid business talents, and by wise and judicious investments of the church property has managed to place the many religious establishments in his archdiocese in a flourishing condition, and to keep them free from debt; although by the laws of Missouri all such property, not held by corporations, is subjected to taxation. Archbishop Kenrick will probably be the only prelate at the present council who sat in the two previous Councils of Baltimore, and his wisdom and experience will have great weight in its deliberations.

The Most Rev. John J. Williams, the fourth Bishop and first Archbishop of Boston, was born on April 27, 1822. After the usual classical education he was elevated to the priesthood in 1843. Among other missions was that of the chapel on Beach-street, Boston, (January, 1852,) which had been built in 1850 to meet the increasing Catholic population in the vicinity of the South Cove. Under his ministration the congregation grew so rapidly that in one year it was found necessary to erect a large Gothic church, which was dedicated in 1855 by Bishop Fitzpatrick. The Very Rev. J. J. Williams was Vicar-General and Pastor of this church at the time he was made Coadjutor Bishop of Boston, having also been Rector of the old cathedral in Franklin-street, which was pulled down in the Fall of 1860, the last mass being celebrated on Sunday, Sept. 16, of that year, on which occasion the present Archbishop acted as assistant priest. In 1866 the Very Rev. John J. Williams, on account of the failing health of Bishop Fitzpatrick, was appointed Coadjutor Bishop of Boston, with the right of succession. Bishop Fitzpatrick died on Feb. 13, 1866, and on March 11 of the same year Bishop Williams was consecrated at St. James's Church, of which he had been so long the Pastor. From Oct. 19, 1869, to June 27, 1870, Bishop Williams was in Europe attending the Vatican Council. On May 2, 1875, the ceremony of conferring on Bishop Williams the Pallium, which is the insignia of an Archbishop, took place in the new cathedral of Boston, in the presence of an immense concourse of people, representing every station in life and several other religious denominations. The solemn high mass was celebrated by Bishop McNierny, of Albany; Bishop Goesbriand, of Burlington, Vt., preaching the sermon, and the Pallium, which Pius IX. had sent from Rome by an Ablegate, was conferred by Cardinal McCloskey.

The most gifted pulpit orator in the American Catholic Church is generally conceded to be Archbishop Ryan, recently elevated to the See of Philadelphia. The Most Rev. P. J. Ryan is a native of Thurles, Ireland, and was born on Feb. 20, 1831. He was educated at Carlow College in his native country, and, coming to America, was raised to the priesthood in the St. Louis Cathedral on Sept. 8, 1853, when less than 23 years old. Though the cannonical age is 24, an exception was made in his case on account of his brilliant talents. His first mission was at the cathedral of St. Louis, and for 19 years he was stationed there, and at the Church of the Annunciation, and St. John's Church, all in St. Louis. Archbishop Kenrick, who had watched the career of Father Ryan very carefully, saw in him a worthy successor for the See of St. Louis, and while attending the Vatican Council he asked Pius IX. for his appointment as Coadjutor with the right of succession. The request was granted, and on April 14, 1872, he was consecrated in the Cathedral of St. Louis by Archbishop Kenrick. But he was not destined to fill that See, for upon the death of Archbishop Wood, of Philadelphia, he was appointed by Leo XIII., on June 8, 1884, to that archdiocese, but he has not yet been invested with the Pallium. During the Council his eloquent voice will be heard in the venerable cathedral of Baltimore, whose walls have resounded with the eloquence of Spalding, Hughes, England, and other famous prelates.

Francis Xavier Leray, Archbishop of New-Orleans, is a native of France, and was born at Chateaugiron, (Ille-et-Vilaine,) April 20, 1825. He was educated in the classics at Rennes, at the Eudistes. In 1843, he came to America, being at the time 18 years old. He entered St. Mary's College, Baltimore, where he studied philosophy and theology; was Professor at Vincennes, at Spring Hill, and at Baltimore. He was ordained priest at Natchez, March 19, 1852, by the Right Rev. Dr. Chanche, first Bishop of Natchez, and was successively Rector at Jackson and at Vicksburg, having charge of all the Catholics living in the upper part of Mississippi, Alabama, and Tennessee. He passed through all the epidemics of yellow fever and cholera since 1853. During the civil war Father Leray acted as Chaplain, having charge of several hospitals, and was afterward Vicar and Dean of Natchez. He was Vicar-General during the Vatican Council in 1870, and was consecrated Bishop of Natchitoches, La., April 22, 1877; appointed Coadjutor of New-Orleans Oct. 23, 1879, and became Archbishop of New-Orleans Dec. 27, 1883. Mgr. Leray brings to the Plenary Council a ripe experience, elegant scholarship, and profound knowledge of theology. Although in his sixtieth year his active missionary life has preserved him from the infirmities of approaching age.

The Most Rev. Patrick A. Feehan, the fifth Bishop and first Archbishop of Chicago, was born in the year 1829, in County Tipperary, Ireland. He was educated at Maynooth College, in County Kildare, about 14 miles from Dublin, and came to America immediately upon completing his studies for the priesthood. He arrived in St. Louis in the Fall of 1852, where he was assigned to duty as Superior of the Ecclesiastical Seminary for boys at Carondelet, near St. Louis. He was soon after transferred to the Church of the Immaculate Conception in St. Louis, where he remained for several years. In the Fall of 1865 he was consecrated Bishop of Nashville, with jurisdiction over the churches and other Catholic institutions of Tennessee, succeeding Bishop Wheeler, who was the successor of Bishop Miles, the first Bishop appointed for Tennessee. Under his guidance the church began to grow in wealth and numbers, his influence being felt from the first. New churches were established in all the important cities and towns, and missionary stations in many of the more remote districts of the State. In personal appearance Bishop Feehan is unusually striking. He is over 6 feet in height, with black hair and a pleasing, intellectual countenance. His voice and delivery are good, his language is well chosen, graceful, and easy, marked by a natural avoidance of complicated utterances. His sermons are brief, to the point, and of a kind which always attracts and holds the attention of his auditors. He is regarded as a man moderate in his views, never engaging in controversies, but devoting his whole time to church duties. He is a financier of marked executive ability. In December, 1879, the Papal See at Rome appointed him to succeed the late Right Rev. Thomas Foley as Bishop of Chicago, the appointment being at once approved by the Pope.

November 7, 1884

GRIEVANCES OF GERMAN CATHOLICS.

CHICAGO, Aug. 2.—An invitation has been issued to all the German-American Catholics to meet at Chicago Sept. 6. There was a meeting of about 40 Catholic priests held in this city a few weeks ago, at which it was decided to issue the call for the convention, and Rector William Tappert, of Covington, Ky.; Friedrich Arendes, of St. Louis, and William Casper, of Milwaukee, were authorized to issue it. These national Catholic conventions (Katholikentage) are an old custom in Germany, but the one to be held next September will be the first one in the United States. The objects of the convention will be, it is said, a consideration of the differences existing between the German and Irish Catholics. It has often been the complaint of German Catholics in this country that they are neglected, or even intentionally slighted, by the highest dignitaries of the church. Complaint has been made at Rome, and the Propaganda has recently decided that the German Catholics in the United States must be treated as equal to the Irish. The object of the convention is to demonstrate the strength of the German Catholics and take steps to secure recognition. It is said that there are about 2,000,000 German Catholics in the United States. In respect to the cultivation of the German language in the schools and the church the convention will not advance any new demands. It is also intended that the convention shall take some position with reference to the labor problem to encourage respectable organizations of laborers and keep them from dangerous influences.

August 3, 1887

ARCHBISHOP IRELAND WINS

*CATHOLICS MAY BE TAUGHT IN
SECULAR SCHOOLS.*

THE CONCLAVE OF PRELATES DECIDES
THAT THE FARIBAULT EXPERIMENT
MAY BE EMULATED—ARCHBISHOP
CORRIGAN YIELDS TO A LARGE MA-
JORITY.

The conclave of the Archbishops of the Roman Catholic Church in the United States held its last executive session yesterday at the house of Archbishop Corrigan, Madison Avenue and Fiftieth Street.

After three days' deliberations the Archbishops have vouchsafed to make public the result of Wednesday afternoon's discussion in relation to the parochial versus the public school. In compliment to Archbishop Corrigan, who seems to have been on the wrong side of the question, but to have been the host of the prelates assembled, the conclave gave out last night two written resolutions of an apparently ambiguous character.

These resolutions really carried within themselves a triumph for the principles advocated by Archbishop Ireland. He advocated the tolerance of the public-school system so long as the parents of the children taught would cause them to attend Sunday school or to receive at home tuition in their religious faith or in the principles of the same.

Until now a number of priests in the different cities of the Union have been accustomed to condemn the public schools as ungodly, and to state from the pulpit that they would hold parents under the ban of mortal sin if they took the opportunity to refuse to send their children to the parochial schools and, instead, have them educated by the means provided by the State.

Archbishop Corrigan has laughed to scorn the report that the Vatican approved in any way the experiment tried by Archbishop Ireland in the West in amalgamating the secular and the parochial schools. He has prophesied the condemnation by the Pope of the Faribault system, but, owing to pressure, he is one of the advocates to-day of the very system which he so vainly sought to condemn.

Archbishop Ireland is triumphant. The resolutions which were yesterday made public read as follows:

First—Resolved, To promote the erection of Catholic schools, so that there may be accommodation in them, if possible, for all our Catholic children, according to the decrees of the third Plenary Council of Baltimore and the decision of the Holy See.

Second—Resolved, That as to children who at present do not attend Catholic schools, we direct, in addition, that provision be made for Sunday schools, and, also, by instruction, on some other day or days of the week, and by urging parents to teach their children the Christian doctrine at their homes.

Sunday and week-day schools should be under the direct supervision of the clergy, aided by the intelligent lay teachers, and, when possible, by the members of religious-teaching orders.

The first section of the body of these resolutions is simply a "sop to Cerberus." Of course, every prelate will try in his diocese to improve the condition of his parochial schools. But the public schools have had a long start ahead, and it will be some time before those of the Catholics will be in a condition to compete with them.

Archbishop Ireland, in the famous and much discussed Faribault experiment, advised that public and parochial schools, in districts where the existence of one would be a detriment to the other, amalgamate. In this little town in Minnesota the experiment was tried with favorable results. The public schools had money, but no teachers; the parochial schools had experienced and well-trained teachers, but no money. By combination the money of the one was set against the experience of the other. The religious teachers consented to remove all emblems of their faith from the schoolhouse, and not to refer to religious matters during school hours. The State provided the buildings, and the children of Faribault obtained the advantages of experienced teachers and cultured instructors.

Archbishop Corrigan, leading the Eastern Archbishops, bitterly opposed any compromise between Church and State. Pope Leo XIII., whose ideas are advanced, leans somewhat toward the views of Archbishop Ireland, on whom, it is understood, he intends eventually to bestow the scarlet hat of a Cardinal. He sent to America at first Mgr. O'Connell, once President of the American College at Rome, whose opinions coincide with those of Archbishop Ireland and Cardinal Gibbons, who is opposed to the ultra-Cahenslyism of the Archbishop of New-York.

Both the Gibbons-Ireland and the Corrigan factions have powerful friends at Rome. The Pope was pleased with the excessive loyalty of Archbishop Corrigan, and in reward for his allegiance gave to his secretary, Mgr. McDonnell, the wealthy Bishopric of Brooklyn, but Leo XIII. was too clever a diplomat to estrange the American faction headed by Cardinal Gibbons and Archbishop Ireland. He knew that the great West, with its almost unlimited territory and its numerous large cities, was pregnant with Catholicism, and should not be discouraged in the propagation of the faith by any exhibition of even suggestive intolerance.

The Pope tolerated the Faribault experiment of Archbishop Ireland, and heaped honors upon the Western prelate. There is no doubt that a Cardinal's hat awaits "the consecrated Blizzard" of Minnesota.

Archbishop Ireland last night refused to express any opinion upon the resolutions adopted by the American hierarchy in conclave. But the second resolution speaks for itself. It means that where before parents not sending their children to Catholic schools were condemned, under pain of mortal sin, for doing so, they are now "tolerated so long as they consent to teach their children Christian doctrine at home after school hours, or to send them to the catechism class at the parish church on Sundays." This means that Archbishop Ireland's Faribault experiment should be emulated in other parts of the United States in which the Church has a foothold.

The public school system of the United States, instead of being condemned, is at least tolerated. Parents can send their children for secular education wherever they choose. Church and State are separated.

Last night it was said that Mgr. Satolli and Mgr. O'Connell, who had been sent from Rome by the Holy Father to attend this conference and to examine into the school question, were closeted with Cardinal Gibbons and Archbishop Ireland. It was also said that all the Southern and Western Archbishops, and even two from the East, sympathized with the views expressed by Cardinal Gibbons and Archbishop Ireland at the Wednesday conclave, and the adherents of Archbishop Corrigan suffered an overwhelming defeat.

With his customary diplomacy the Archbishop of New-York has gracefully bowed to the decision of the majority.

The question of tolerance of secret societies is still in doubt. The conclave will meet again in Chicago next September, just a week after the holding of the Catholic Congress.

There will be a short session this morning, but no important business will be transacted. Cardinal Gibbons and Archbishop Riordan of San Francisco left for their homes last night. Archbishops Feehan and Ireland will leave this morning.

Although Archbishop Ireland would express no opinion of the conclave last night, he seemed entirely satisfied with its work.

November 19, 1892

POPE'S RULING FOR AMERICA.

Parishes Made Up of Foreigners Will Be Absorbed Gradually.

CHICAGO, May 22.—Information was obtained to-day that Rome has just transmitted to the Catholic Church in the United States the most significant ruling of recent years, bearing on ecclesiastical matters in America.

The decision, which has reference to parishes made up of foreigners, is literally as follows:

First—Children born in America of foreign parents, whose native language is not the English, are not obliged, when of age, to become members of the parish to which their parents belong; but they have the right to join a parish in which the language of the country—that is, English—is used.

Second—Catholics not born in America, but knowing the English language, have the right of becoming members of the parish in which English is in use, and they cannot be compelled to submit themselves to the jurisdiction of the rector of a church built for people who continue to speak the language of a foreign country.

The evident purpose of Rome is to make English the language of the American Church as speedily as possible, and thus to encourage the development of a spirit of more perfect union among members of the Catholic faith. Parishes in which a foreign language is used are tolerated as temporary institutions, which will disappear as soon as the conditions making their erection expedient will have passed away. The present ruling is perfectly consistent with the enlightened general policy adopted and followed by Leo XIII.

May 23, 1897

BISHOP'S HOUSE BESIEGED.

CLEVELAND, Sept. 22.—In civilian dress and in the uniforms of various church and military organizations fully 5,000 Polish Catholic members of the seceding societies, sixteen in number, which have left St. Vitus's Church to-day marched on the Episcopal residence, and there demanded of Bishop Ignatius F. Horstmann that they be permitted home rule in St. Vitus parish, and that the Rev. Casimir Zakrekac be assigned to that parish.

The siege of the episcopal residence was the second in the sixth months' warfare of the parish, which has been accompanied by the stoning of the parish house and the arrest of scores of parishioners, accused by the Rev. Vitus Hribar with attempting his life.

The latter, who had been sent to take the old priest's place, was forced to ask removal, and has left.

After threats and demonstrations before the episcopal residence for three hours this afternoon, which brought no response, the delegation served notice on Bishop Horstmann that an answer to their request for the old pastor must be had before next Sunday, or "ten thousand of us, aggrieved, will bivouac before the residence and no one will move in or out until our demand has met with a reply, favorable or unfavorable."

September 23, 1907

FOR CATHOLIC DAILY PAPER.

Chicago Publication Said to Have Strong Financial Backing.

Special to The New York Times.

CHICAGO, Feb. 15.—Chicago is to have a Roman Catholic daily newspaper, to be published by the Nuncio Publishing Company of 79 West Monroe Street. The first number will appear in about sixty days, according to Daniel McAlister, Secretary of the publishing company.

The new daily will be published every afternoon and on Sundays. The evening edition will consist of sixteen pages and the Sunday edition from twenty-four to thirty pages. The paper will be independent in politics and will cost 2 cents. All the other Chicago morning and afternoon papers are sold at 1 cent.

The movement was launched last June and the company was incorporated last September. Pledges of $400,000 have been made for the enterprise, it is said. The promoters say when the list of stockholders is published it will be found that the new paper has the strongest financial backing of any Catholic venture ever launched in this country. The name of the editor has not yet been disclosed, but it is announced the newspaper will be conducted by a board of five, which will censor the publication. This board will be headed by Father John Noll of Huntingdon, Ind., editor of The Sunday Visitor. The announcement further states that the paper is to have all the news of the world and all the features of a metropolitan daily.

February 16, 1915

ONE DEAD, TWO DYING AFTER CHURCH RIOT

Pennsylvania State Troopers Charge Into a Mob of 1,000 Persons.

Special to The New York Times.

PITTSTON, Penn., Jan. 16.—In a clash today between State troopers and a mob of 1,000 members of the Polish Catholic Church at Du Pont, a suburb of this town, one rioter was shot dead and another was probably mortally wounded. One State trooper, Ross Sumer of Carlisle, is dying with a fractured skull.

Of the rioters George Greizor, aged 50, was shot dead. Joseph Tinh, aged 45, was mortally wounded. Scores of other rioters were badly hurt. Several of the State police were injured, including Corporal Carlson and Troopers Ira Stephenson, Ralph Tipton, Robert Tipton, Albert Heath, and Thomas Bettner.

The riot occurred because one faction of the Catholic Church objected to Bishop Hoban's appointment of the Rev. Francis Sowsnowski as pastor. Trouble arose when the pastor first attempted to take charge, and the matter has been in the courts.

When Sheriff Buss, accompanied by Captain Pitcher and a squad of twelve State mounted troopers, arrived at the church this morning escorting the pastor, they found the edifice occupied by the militant faction and surrounded by a mob of 1,000 men and women.

The men were armed with clubs, many of which were studded with small nails. Several of the women had boxes of pepper and mustard.

Sheriff Buss called upon the mob to disperse. A yell and a shower of stones was the reply. Captain Pitcher sent for reinforcements and twenty troopers responded. Captain Pitcher then ordered the rioters to leave the church, and another shower of stones followed.

The police then charged into the mob. The rioters held their ground, meeting the charge of the police with clubs, stones, mustard, and pepper, but they were finally dispersed and seventy-eight were arrested.

A special Grand Jury will be summoned next week to act on the cases.

January 17, 1916

TO AMERICANIZE SCHOOLS.

Chicago's Catholic Institutions Will Drop Foreign Textbooks.

Special to The New York Times.

CHICAGO, May 11.—Archbishop Mundelein of Illinois has decided upon a radical departure in the education in parochial schools of children of foreign parentage, which in substance means Americanization. There are 115,000 children in the parochial schools of Chicago—Italian, Polish, German, and others—with 2,500 teachers.

The old textbooks printed in the native languages of the children on Sept. 1 will be discarded, and the only books used will be printed in English, thus unifying and Americanizing the teaching in the schools which come under the control of the Roman Catholic Church.

May 12, 1916

MUST OBEY CHURCH, SAYS MGR. HAYES

Archbishop Sets Forth Catholic Doctrinal Allegiance to Constituted Authority.

'DOES NOT ENSLAVE WILLS'

"Until the End of Time," He Declares, "No Essential Doctrine of Christ Can Be Changed."

Archbishop Patrick J. Hayes, preaching yesterday at St. Patrick's Cathedral on "The Duty of Obedience to Properly Constituted Authority," set forth the attitude of the Roman Catholic Church toward the teachings concerning which the Protestant Episcopal Church is in controversy. "Thank God," he said, "our Catholic Church is such that it is not the opinion of the preacher; it is the teaching of Christ Himself. It is always the same truth, the same sacramental system until the end of time."

In his sermon the Archbishop said:

"The picture presented in the gospel for the day, which I have just read, furnishes to my mind food for thought, especially at this present hour. I would like to call your attention to the remarkable obedience of Christ Himself. And yet how little we know of that word obedience today. Obedience seems to have belonged to the past. Obedience is going very fast. Consequently lawful authority is suffering.

"There should be obedience in the family. Christ became subject to His parents. He did what they told him although He was their very God. Christ was obedient to the synagogue. He met all the laws of the synagogue because it represented lawful authority. Christ was obedient to death, 'even the death of the cross.' So we have this marvelous example of obedience on the part of the Lord Himself. And how necessary it is for us all to learn that lesson today and to practice it in our daily lives.

Source of Authority.

"There are such wrong notions of what authority is. All authority which is lawful comes from God. St. Paul tells us there is no power except from God. The sanction of that human authority which is lawfully exercised is the sanction of God Himself.

"Remember that we are not enslaving our intellects or wills when we simply obey constituted authority. Every righteous man when exercising authority does it for service. The man in authority is the slave or servant of those whom he is appointed to rule. So a minister of God is a servant of God.

After discussing the duty of obedience to the State, Archbishop Hayes took up the duty of obedience to the Church. He said that because today so many are crying out for "freedom of thought" in theology, that fact does not change things.

"So we have to be very careful," he continued ,"that we do not attach too much importance to our own viewpoint. Men ought to have the right to discuss and explain themselves, but that is not, therefore, final authority.

"I remember being impressed very much a few years ago during the war, when it was my duty to visit some of our camps. We were in Mobile Bay and a dense fog came up. The pilot had to watch a small light to guide his boat, and then to pick up the next light. It made no difference what I thought about the situation. We had to come up against hard facts. So all through our life we are accepting authority and acting accordingly.

"We have to give our obedience to ecclesiastical authority. If we do not consent to be governed by it, we are excommunicated by it. The Church is the body of Christ. He is the head and we are the members. He is the vine and we are the branches. The head controls the body. This hand of mine must obey my brain. If my brain is working, there is no choice. We cannot remain with the living church if we are dead through disobedience and sin. The Church does not depend on the Bible or on tradition alone. We have the visible head of the Church in the person of our Holy Father, the Pope.

"Our Lord did not say He would build the Church on the sacred Scriptures or on tradition. He said: 'And I say to thee, thou art Peter; and upon this rock I will build my church, and the gates of hell shall not prevail against it.

"And until the end of time no essential doctrine of Christ can be changed. If the world continues for a thousand years there is no doctrine of divine revelation that can be changed. It is our duty to keep it intact, and we will do this to the end of time. So, my dear friends, we have authority in the Church, and that authority must be obeyed."

December 31, 1923

CHURCH SCHOOLS TO STAY.

Michigan Attorney General Holds Amendment Is Unconstitutional.

Special to The New York Times.

GRAND RAPIDS, Mich., July 9.—Attorney General Groesbeck today held that the anti-parochial school amendment is unconstitutional and cannot go on the November ballot. This decision, however, did not completely spike the guns of those who are trying to close all Catholic schools in Michigan and force the Catholic children into the public educational institutions. It is announced that Groesbeck's ruling will be carried to the State Supreme Court in an effort to get the amendment on the ballot to make it a part of the State Constitution.

For years unsuccessful efforts have been made in the Michigan Legislature to pass laws forcing the closing of Catholic schools, by making it unlawful for any child between the ages of 5 and 16 years to attend a private school. The licenses of teachers in private schools would also be revoked.

This year an amendment to the State Constitution was initiated by petitions which were filed with the Secretary of State.

The Rev. L. A. Linn, pastor of the Holy Cross Lutheran Church of Saginaw, asked the Attorney General if the amendment as initiated was constitutional. Answering Mr. Linn, Groesbeck tells the Secretary of State that the anti-parochial school amendment is grossly unconstitutional and should not be submitted to the electors. He says:

"The police power of the State to promote peace, health, order and education does not permit the closing of private schools or making idle millions in school property. The Fourteenth Amendment to the Federal Constitution prohibits the State from abridging the privileges or immunities of citizens, or depriving any person of life, liberty or property."

The Catholics have won the first round in what may yet become a long, bitter struggle to force Catholic children into the public schools.

July 10, 1920

GIBBONS A LEADER IN AMERICAN LIFE

For a full third of a century James Cardinal Gibbons had been ranked without question as one of the immortals whom America has given to the world. Millions of his fellow countrymen revered him as the pattern of the Christian patriot and sage. Europe accepted him as a faithful interpreter of America who boldly bespoke the spirit of her institutions before President Wilson undertook the task, and who left no antagonism in the doing of it. A master helmsman of the Catholic Church during the social and political evolution of the last fifty years, he was rated as one of a small group, including Leo XIII., Rampolla, Newman and Manning, who were most potent in guiding her external policies in the direction of liberalism.

The friend and counselor of Popes and Presidents, neither Rome nor Washington questioned his single-minded sincerity or the penetrating quality of his vision of public needs and rights. In all things he sought to observe as a rule of life: "Render unto Caesar the things that are Caesar's and unto God the things that are God's."

Called All Men "Brethren."

His career was coextensive with the marked decline in religious prejudice in this country from "Know Nothing" days to the present time, and many acclaimed him as the foremost factor in that change. A Catholic of Catholics in his own religious career, he was never known to speak uncharitably of any church group, but called all men "brethren." Some of his closest friends and advisers were Protestants or Jews. He spoke without compunction at civic meetings in Protestant houses of worship, and on one occasion even preached in a Masonic hall, thanking the Masons cordially for the use of their building, there being no other to be had in the little town where he happened to be.

His habit of mind on this subject may be illustrated by the following true story:

In 1911 the celebration of the Cardinal's fiftieth anniversary as a priest and twenty-fifth anniversary as a Prince of the Catholic Church evoked two remarkable demonstrations, a civic celebration at his ecclesiastical seat in Baltimore in June and a church celebration in the following Ocober. On June 6 a public meeting in his honor attended by 20,000 persons was held in the Fifth Regiment Armory in that city at which tributes to him as a great American and a great churchman were voiced by President Taft, Vice President Sherman, ex-President Roosevelt, Chief Justice White of the United States Supreme Court, Speaker Clark of the House of Representatives, Elihu Root, the Senators and Congressmen from Maryland, the Governor of the State, the Mayor of Baltimore and others. A more distinguished group of speakers could scarcely be assembled in this country for any purpose.

The day of the civic celebration was made a municipal holiday by the Mayor and City Council of Baltimore. As the time of the ecclesiastical observance approached a resolution was introduced in the City Council to decree a municipal holiday on that occasion also. Soon afterward, at a meeting of Protestant ministers who assembled in Baltimore periodically for discussions, objection to this step was made and several speeches on the subject were delivered, without, however, referring disrespectfully to the Cardinal—such a thing was practically unknown in Protestant gatherings. It was held to have been sufficient to have the holiday on the day of the civic observance and that a purely Catholic celebration should not be similarly marked.

The Cardinal read of this action in a newspaper and immediately summoned to his residence one of his close friends, who happened to be a Protestant.

"What do you think of this view?" he asked when the friend entered his modest little study.

The friend expressed the opinion that it was at least in bad taste.

"I think it is right," said the Cardinal, firmly.

Through this friend he sent at once for the author of the City Council resolution and had him withdraw it, at the same time handing to him a prepared statement agreeing with the stand of the Protestant ministers. Then he called the principal ministerial objector to his residence and commended him for what had been done.

A man who could rise to heights such as this must have possessed extraordinary traits of character. In fact, the Cardinal's gifts of character and personality were as striking as his gifts of intellect, and helped him to win many battles. He was all things to all men in the best sense of the word. He habitually romped with altar boys in his study, afterward giving them little presents to show his affection for them. At a social gathering he was the one brilliant figure to whom all eyes turned, possessing unexcelled drawingroom graces and having at his command a fund of good stories that delighted old and young. On public occasions he was looked up to as a leader by men of all creeds or no creed. In the great arena of the Catholic Church he stood for fifty years as the American champion of the liberal element, the defender of progress in the Church and free institutions in the State.

Some of His Accomplishments.

Some of the principal accomplishments of his long life may be summed up thus:

As Apostolic Delegate for the Third Plenary Council of Baltimore in 1884 and presiding officer of that body, whose decrees placed the Catholic Church in this country on the basis that it occupies today, he showed such marked ability in a lasting constructive work that Leo XIII. decided to elevate him to the Cardinalate. He demonstrated then for the first time and often afterward his talents as a leader and harmonizer of men in difficult undertakings marked by clashes of opinion.

He fought and won against heavy odds in 1886-87 the battle within the Catholic Church for a liberal attitude toward organized labor, which was then in great disfavor throughout the world. In this struggle he caused the Congregation of the Holy Office (the former "Inquisition") to reverse itself for the first time in history. The congregation had declared the Knights of Labor a forbidden organization in Canada and was about to pronounce against it in the United States, when Cardinal Gibbons threw all his daring and resourcefulness into the fight. Not only did he prevent a ban on the Knights in this country, but the prohibition was lifted in Canada, and the famous encyclical on labor by Leo XIII. followed, establishing among Catholics throughout the world the rights of the workers for which the Cardinal had so valiantly contended.

Cardinal Gibbons's "Knights of Labor Letter" addressed to Cardinal Simeoni, then the prefect of the propaganda in Rome, in which he presented his plea with powerful logic and great foresight, has been considered ever since as one of the charters in the labor movement.

In his speech at his installation as Cardinal in 1887 in his titular church in Rome, that of Santa Maria in Trastevere, he startled his venerable colleagues by the then revolutionary avowal that the American system of separation of Church and State was the best for both, and made a general defense of the American system of government, declaring that "our country has liberty without license and authority without despotism." Some of the Cardinals whose views were rooted in an older school of thought almost gasped at his assertion that "I belong to a country where the civil government holds over us the aegis of its protection without interfering with us in the legitimate exercise of our sublime mission as ministers of the Gospel of Christ." The new Cardinal's boldness was explained by some on the ground that it was "characteristically American." But he never wavered in his stand and his view has since been tacitly accepted, so far as America is concerned.

Won Fight Against Foreign Nationalism.

In the memorable controversy over the "Cahensly question," so-called from a German Catholic who figured in the agitation, he threw the whole weight of his office, his statesmanlike skill and his unceasing labors into a struggle against foreign nationalism in the Catholic Church in America and won again. He carried his fight direct to Rome, striving for years against obstacles that proceeded from European influences, and at length received complete pontifical endorsement of his stand. This verdict stopped in 1891 the rapidly increasing tendency in the Catholic Church in the United States to preserve the permanent grouping of immigrants based on foreign nationalities and has made the church ever since an influence of immeasurable power in the gradual Americanization of foreigners. President Harrison warmly congratulated him for his victory, but for which the "hyphen" menace during the World War might have been infinitely more formidable than it was.

At the height of the controversy he voiced his views in a strong sermon Aug. 20, 1891, in the Cathedral at Milwaukee, a centre of Cahenslyism, in which he said:

JAMES CARDINAL GIBBONS.

From Photo Copyright by Bachrach.

"God and our country—this be our watchword! Next to love of God should be love of our country. Let us glory in the title of American citizen. To one country we owe allegiance, and that country is America."

Early Supporter of Peace Movement.

Cardinal Gibbons was one of the strongest inspirations of the peace movement throughout the world in the days when it was regarded as almost wholly Utopian, and he continued his labors in that cause to the end. On Easter Sunday, 1896, soon after the Venezuela controversy had rocked the English-speaking world, he joined Cardinals Vaughan of England and Logue of Ireland, the representatives of the English-speaking peoples in the College of Cardinals, in an appeal in behalf of a permanent tribunal of arbitration. This had a decided moral effect throughout the world.

He hoped and strove for mediation to prevent the Spanish-American War, and believed that there could be a settlement on the basis of Cuban independence, but the blowing up of the Maine had aroused feeling in this country that could not be calmed. In the course of the recent political campaign he warmly indorsed the principle of the League of Nations.

He brought about a settlement of the Friar Lands question in the Philippines when an impassé on the subject had been reached by the Government at Washington. Later he was an active agent in the Americanization of the Catholic Church not only in the Philippines but also in Cuba and Porto Rico.

When a deadlock had been reached in the College of Cardinals over the election of a successor to Leo XIII. in 1903, Cardinal Gibbons exercised a decisive influence in negotiations which caused the choice of Cardinal Sarto, who was elevated to the pontifical throne as Pius X. He was the first American to take part in the election of a Pope.

Arrayed Church Against Socialism.

He firmly arrayed the Church in this country against socialism, and the spread of that creed among disaffected elements which could be reached by the Church was stifled. His heaviest blow in this cause was timed when it would be most effective. The centenary in 1906 of the Baltimore Cathedral, in the primatial see, whence so many Catholic influences had radiated, was made the occasion for a large gathering of American prelates, and Cardinal Gibbons gave it the aspect of a mass demonstration against socialism with all the weight of the Church behind it.

Preaching in the Cathedral a short time before the celebration began, he declared his own position with force and sustained it with clarity. On the centennial day Archbishop Glennon of St. Louis, in a sermon in the Cathedral, powerfully arraigned socialism and declared the Church's ability to withstand its tide. The influences thus set in motion have been a powerful help to the anti-radical movement in this country.

Overthrew Louisiana Lottery.

Cardinal Gibbons overthrew the Louisiana lottery when its intrenched power had defied all other assaults. When a renewal of its State charter was under consideration in 1892, he wrote a vigorous letter which arrayed the Catholic influence, potent in Louisiana, against the lottery, and the fight was soon won. The Rev. Lyman Abbott, preaching in Plymouth Church, Brooklyn, said of this accomplishment:

"Thank God for Cardinal Gibbons! Long may he wear his red cloak and his red cap; and, if there should be an election now, and you and I could vote, I would vote to make him Pope. His word, flung out with courage and with strong significance, has done more than any other word in this country, by press, by politician or by preacher, to make the leaders of that Louisiana abomination call a halt."

His Early Struggles.

Cardinal Gibbons had no small share of vicissitudes and struggles in early life before he entered the priesthood. He was born in Baltimore July 23, 1834, his parents being Irish immigrants. When the future Cardinal was 3 years old the health of his father, Thomas Gibbons, failed, and he took the family back to Ireland, settling at Westport, where James was sent to school in due time. The father died when James was 13, and the energetic mother, whose piety left a deep and lasting impress on her six children, returned with them to America, landing in New Orleans after a shipwreck in which they had a narrow escape from death.

James obtained employment as a clerk in a grocery store in that city, but attendance at a Redemptorist mission when he was 20 years old turned his thoughts to the priesthood, and he went to St. Charles College, Ellicott City, Md., to begin his classical studies for his future vocation. After several years there he entered St. Mary's Seminary, Baltimore, and on June 30, 1861, was ordained a priest at the Baltimore Cathedral.

The Civil War, with its accompaniment of fierce passion in Maryland, a border State, was in progress when he served his first and only pastorate, at St. Bridget's Church in Canton, then a suburb of Baltimore, now a part of the city. In those stirring days he repeatedly proved his courage. On one occasion he was attacked by a vagrant soldier, who seized a piece of timber and aimed a murderous blow at him. The young priest knocked down his assailant before the club could fall and thoroughly subdued him. With no other weapon than an umbrella he worsted an intruder who tried to take possession of his modest parochial residence. During the war he took no part on either side, ministering to Federal and Confederate alike when duty called him.

But no pent-up Utica could confine the talents and scope of the young priest. Despite the modesty which was one of his characteristics, he soon attracted the attention of Archbishop Spalding of Baltimore, and when he had been at St. Bridget's only three years the Archbishop called him to be his secretary. Two years later the Second Plenary Council of Baltimore met and Father Gibbons, as its Assistant Chancellor, made so deep an impression upon its distinguished members that, although but 32 years old and only five years removed from the seminary, he was unanimously nominated as Vicar Apostolic of North Carolina and was elevated to the titular bishopric of Adramyttum.

His Labors in North Carolina.

In North Carolina his labors were purely apostolic and it was a chapter in his life on which he loved afterward to dwell. There were then but 800 Catholics in the State and his real task was to win a hearing from a Protestant community. He traveled over the State, preaching in court houses and public halls, confirming on one occasion in a garret, and obtaining the favor of Protestants to such an extent that some of them subscribed money for new churches that he established. These experiences, coming at an impressionable period of his life, implanted or increased in him the broad tolerance which remained one of his chief traits throughout his life.

He was the "boy bishop" of the Vatican Council of 1870 which declared the doctrine of the infallible teaching office of the Pope, being but 36 years old when he was called to sit in that memorable body, every member of which was his senior. Projected thus into the Olympian atmosphere of the Church, he felt that his youth imposed upon him a discreet silence, but he gained a world outlook that served him signally when the greatest undertakings of his life opened before him.

Soon after his return from Rome, Bishop Gibbons was sent to the See of Richmond, Va., and in turn became coadjutor with the right of succession to Archbishop Bayley of Baltimore, who had met him at the Vatican Council and been impressed by his strong and winning personality. In 1877 he succeeded to the Archiepiscopal See in the city of his birth.

From that time on his life was interwoven almost ceaselessly with a succession of important labors and accomplishments in behalf of his church and his country, the principal ones of which have already been narrated. Perhaps it was partly because Washington was in his diocese that he was the friend of so many Presidents, particularly Cleveland, Harrison, McKinley, Roosevelt and Taft. Of these he was closest to Cleveland and Roosevelt, who intensely admired him and consulted him on important problems of State in which, they bore testimony, he spoke only as a citizen and a patriot. Cleveland consulted him on the famous tariff message of 1888, and on that occasion the Cardinal indicated almost prophetically the course of future events growing out of it. When Cleveland proposed to send a present to Leo XIII. in honor of that Pope's golden jubilee, the Cardinal suggested that it be a handsomely bound copy of the Constitution of the United States, and the President eagerly accepted the proposal. Roosevelt obtained valuable advice from the Cardinal about the settlement of problems growing out of the Spanish War.

During the World War the Cardinal co-operated with whole-hearted energy in the various campaigns to help the Government's financial and humanitarian projects. His unceasing task was to support and help the constituted authorities of his country.

His Writings.

Into the prodigious labors of his life he crowded the authorship of several books that have a world-wide vogue. "The Faith of Our Fathers," a defense of the Catholic religion on a basis of the broadest charity, has had a circulation of fully 1,500,000 copies, its limpid English style appealing to the purely literary taste, in addition to its ecclesiastical value. His other books are "Our Christian Heritage," "The Ambassador of Christ," "Discourses and Sermons," and "A Retrospect of Fifty Years."

Throughout his life the Cardinal was frail of frame. It was predicted when he was a seminary student that he would not live to do the work for which he was preparing, and while he was serving in his first and only pastorate it was declared by some of his parishioners at one time that he could not live two months. A French observer much later said that he had just enough body to contain the soul. But the Cardinal was sparing in his diet, was devoted to outdoor exercise, always took a short nap after his 1 o'clock dinner and, above all, never allowed the condition of his health to cause him worry.

On one of his most recent visits to New York, when he was past 85, he insisted on walking from the Pennsylvania Station to the Archiepiscopal residence, though a motor car was waiting to convey him. Almost every afternoon he took a stroll, going from two to four miles, and returning invigorated for new duties.

The Cardinal's life in the quaint and charming residence in Baltimore which was his home so long was simplicity itself. It was said that he was the only Bihop in the world who kept no private livery. He denied himself all luxuries and would accept no personal gifts of considerable value. The income from his books was large, and wealthy friends were more than ready to provide any amount of money he wished, but all that he received was devoted to good works for others. What was his, he gave. That was part of the code of his life.

March 25, 1921

BALTIMORE PRIESTS BARRED FROM DANCES

Special to The New York Times.

BALTIMORE, Md., Oct. 31.—Roman Catholic priests of the Archdiocese of Baltimore may no longer attend or take any part in the organization of dances under an order of Archbishop Michael J. Curley, it was learned today.

The Baltimore Catholic Review has barred advertisements of dances from its columns. The Very Rev. Albert E. Smith is the editor. Announcement of the order will be made by Archbishop Curley in The Review. It was explained that it will apply to priests only, and not to the laity.

Regulations prohibiting the presence of priests at dances were adopted by the Third Plenary Council, composed of Archbishops and Bishops in Baltimore Cathedral in 1884, but were not strictly enforced. They read as follows:

"No priest may organize or assist in the organization of a dance, no matter for what benefit the dance may be, and no matter how laudable the purpose may be.

"No priest may be present at a dance, no matter by whom organized. Many priests have acted in the capacity of advisers of reading clubs, study clubs and other organizations composed of both men and women and some have attended dances given by such organizations.

"No announcement of a dance may be made from the altar or pulpit of any church in the Archdiocese of Baltimore.

"No dance may be held in the basement of a church."

November 1, 1927

LAVELLE PRAISES ITALIANS OF CITY

Americanizing the Immigrants Is Scarcely a Problem Any Longer, He Declares.

HE AIDED THEM 25 YEARS

Tells How It Was Difficult at First to Accustom Them to Our Church System.

The problem of Americanizing the Italian immigrants has corrected itself to a very marked degree, in the opinion of Mgr. Michael J. Lavelle, rector of St. Patrick's Cathedral. Mgr. Lavelle has been in charge of the Italian parishes in the arch-

diocese of New York for nearly twenty-five years, having been appointed to this task by the late Cardinal Farley and reappointed by Cardinal Hayes. There now are fifty-eight parishes for Italians in the archdiocese.

"There is scarcely any Italian question today," said Mgr. Lavelle yesterday. The situation with regard to Italian immigrants is excellent. They are becoming good Americans, good Catholics and good citizens. They follow the American ways of observing the laws of the Church and are thrifty, industrious people who settle down, found homes and raise large families.

"For some time past a gradual improvement has been apparent. Like every other immigrant the Italian came here to better his condition. His first need was to get work and learn the language. Elder immigrants found the language hard and were slow, in consequence, in adapting themselves to American ways and customs. They kept together a great deal in colonies and for quite a while were somewhat aloof.

"With regard to the support of the Church the immigrants were somewhat perplexed. They did not under-

stand our way of doing things, and it required much care to make them feel at home. Some of the Italian priests who came here accustomed only to the ways of the old country found it difficult to understand American customs, especially the practice of the people supporting the Church and being responsible for it. In their country the State supports the Church without taxation. It was with patience and care in building up the work with the immigrant that the problems of adjustment have been largely perfected."

It was to the women that Mgr. Lavelle gave much of the credit for what he called the improved conditions. "The earlier immigrants were mostly men and boys, largely musicians and artists," he said, "and for quite a while they did not take permanent root. But once the women began to come and establish homes and raise families the Italians settled down and became a substantial part of our population. They are supporting themselves and are becoming stronger every day. They are building their churches, beginning to build their schools, and are thinking of hospitals and orphan asylums."

October 26, 1930

PRAYERS FOR IDLE URGED BY CARDINAL

Pastoral Letter Asks Churches to Hold "Crusade of Charity" on Oct. 22, 23 and 24.

SEEKS SPECIAL SERVICES

Wants Children of All Schools to Assemble Friday Afternoons From Oct. 30 to Dec. 18.

Cardinal Hayes issued a pastoral letter yesterday asking a "crusade of charity" to aid the present depression, to be held on Oct. 22, 23 and 24, in all the churches; also a diocesan "crusade of prayer," to begin on Oct. 30 and to continue through Dec. 18. The prayer will be for "the spirit of fortitude to bear patiently the present, with the lifting in the near future of the burden of sorrow that weighs so heavily on our common humanity."

The Cardinal has taken this action following the recent letter of Pope Pius XI on behalf of the unem-

ployed. The pastoral letter will be read on Sunday in all the 452 churches of the archdiocese of New York, at all masses.

Cardinal Hayes directs that a public service be held in every church each Friday evening between these dates, or on Friday afternoon. He directs also that the young people be assembled each Friday afternoon for prayer and that this assembly shall include those in the public as well as the parochial schools, also those in colleges, academies and charitable institutions. The letter follows:

"In compliance with the Holy Father's suggestion, I direct that a triduum be held in all our parish churches on Oct. 22, 23 and 24, in preparation for the feast of Christ the King, Sunday, Oct. 25. The purpose is to implore God to spread abroad thoughts of peace and its gifts (Pope Pius XI).

"Please arrange for a short instruction, followed by benediction of the blessed sacrament, with the act of consecration of the human race to the sacred heart and litany to the sacred heart—Coram sanctissimo.

"For some time past I have been feeling that, in addition to the Oratio Imperata 'Pro quaqumque necessitate,' which, in view of the present crisis, is recited daily by the clergy of the diocese during holy mass, there should be solemn public prayer on the part of the faithful. I may add that I have been urged to do so by a goodly number of our people.

"We, therefore, shall conduct a diocesan crusade of prayer, publicly expressed, on each Friday evening (or afternoon if more convenient) from Oct. 30 to Dec. 18. The service will consist of exposition of the blessed sacrament, during which the rosary and litany of the saints are

to be recited, closing with benediction.

"Furthermore, since the Supreme Pontiff refers so tenderly to the children, I also direct that on each Friday afternoon, at the close of school, from Oct. 30 to Dec. 18, the children be assembled for exposition of the blessed sacrament and benediction as above. This solemn prayer is prescribed for colleges, academies, parish schools and charitable institutions caring for children.

"Kindly explain to the children and students the purpose of this crusade of prayer, exhorting them to a sense of their own extraordinary power of intercession with our Lord.

"Please read this letter at all the masses on Sunday, Oct. 18, and make reference to the crusade of prayer on each Sunday following, to remind the people of the Friday devotions. Your own zeal, I am sure, will prompt you to urge the flock to frequent holy communion.

"The Vicar of Christ, our beloved Holy Father, imparts his Apostolic Benediction to all who respond, by prayer and aid, to his paternal appeal.

"(1) Exposition of the blessed sacrament is permitted for one or more hours, if the number of adorers should warrant it.

"(2) If local difficulty should arise preventing observance of the prescriptions of this letter, confer with the Very Rev. Chancellor.

"(3) Children attending the public schools are expected to be present, and the children of parishes without parish schools are also to assemble at convenient hours."

October 16, 1931

CATHOLICS URGED TO WIDEN POWER

Newman Clubs Are Told They Should Take Leadership in Political Life.

A plea to Catholic manhood and womanhood to meet the economic, social and political problems of the times and join in efforts "to make the Catholic influence felt" was made yesterday by William D. Cunningham of White Plains, N. Y., former judge of the New York State Court of Claims and former District Attorney of Ulster County. He spoke at the annual meeting of the province council of the New York Province of the Federation of College Catholic Clubs at the Hotel Biltmore. The meeting was part of the annual convention of the federation which is being attended by delegates from twenty-eight Newman Clubs.

"Are we only out for political place," he asked, "political place which so many of us bearing the Catholic tag have disgraced by corruption and venality? Have we no program? Do we aim no higher?"

"Catholics in America," he said further, "particularly those of Irish extraction, appear to put a premium on political office. I ask, what gain was ever brought to the great cause of the church in the United States through the medium of politicians in places of power?"

"We have not even the capacity to protest," he added, asserting that if the Jews in Poland or Czechoslovakia had experienced the condition imposed upon Catholics in Mexico and Spain, "the halls of Congress would ring with Jewish protests, and American diplomacy would not long be silent under the impact of the Jewish appeal to American public opinion."

"My hat is off to the Jewish-American," he continued. "He and his co-religionists may suffer, but he does not take it lying down. What Catholics, except a few priests, care that a subversive, Communistic government in Mexico is doing all that is possible to destroy the Catholic Church in Mexico?"

Thomas J. F. Pinkham, chairman of the province and a student at the Washington Square centre of New York University, presided, and announced that there would be held here, in the latter part of March, an economic conference under the auspices of the Newman Clubs of the province.

The convention closes today with a corporate communion at St. Patrick's Cathedral, at which Cardinal Hayes is to be the celebrant and is to make an address. A communion breakfast will be held at the Hotel Commodore, at which Colonel William J. Donovan, Mgr. Michael J. Lavelle, rector of St. Patrick's, and John Moody, the financial expert, are expected to speak.

January 8, 1933

FINDS MISSIONS FAIL FOR CATHOLIC ALIENS

Survey Shows Huge Outlay by Protestants to Proselytize Immigrants Is Futile.

Although Protestant churches in America have expended between $50,000,000 and $100,000,000 in the past fifty years on missions for proselytizing Catholic immigrants, this work has been largely ineffective, according to a survey made by Professor Theodore Abel of Columbia University for the Institute of Social and Religious Research. The findings of Professor Abel's inquiry, published in book form under the title of "Protestant Home Missions of Catholic Immigrants," were made public yesterday.

After all this mission effort, Professor Abel finds that the present membership of such mission churches is 50,000 or 60,000 and said that this estimate total includes, besides converts from Catholicism, the children and grandchildren of converts who have not themselves been brought up in Catholicism, and also persons of Protestant stock.

Practically none of the foreign-language churches is self-supporting, Professor Abel finds, and in some cases the annual cost of maintaining them is as high as $30 a member.

June 26, 1933

MUNDELEIN OFFERS TRUCE TO MOVIES

Chicago Cardinal Asserts That Catholics Will Give Producers a Chance to Clean Films.

CELEBRATES ANNIVERSARY

Reports to Pope on Activities of His Diocese, Stressing Aid Amid the Depression.

Copyright, 1934, by The Associated Press.
ROME, Sept. 21.—Catholics are willing to "suspend their decent movie campaign now to see what the movie producers will make of themselves," Cardinal Mundelein of Chicago said here today.

The visiting prelate, who today celebrated the twenty-fifth anniversary of his episcopal consecration by a mass at the tomb of St. Peter and receiving the felicitations of Pope Pius, said he did not discuss the campaign with the Pope.

"We are going to give the movie producers a chance to see what they can do," he declared. "We do not want to put the movies out of business."

The visiting prelate emphasized, however, that there would be no truce with indecency on the screen.

"We are not taking any chances," he said. "We are going to remain organized. In my diocese we have 650,000 signatures of adults without asking promises from the youths."

Bars "Mae West Type."

The Cardinal continued:

"We don't like the Mae West type. We do not ask the movie producer to bring out the "Pollyanna' type of films. The kind of film in which Will Rogers, Janet Gaynor and Victor Moore appear is what we have in mind."

Cardinal Mundelein said Reich Bishop Ludwig Mueller, head of the official German Protestant church, was merely "talking for the headlines" when he said the German Catholic Church should be separated from the Vatican. There is no possibility of this being carried out, he declared.

The report Cardinal Mundelein presented to Pope Pius, that conditions in the United States were improving gradually, greatly encouraged the Pontiff, he said after his audience.

The Chicago prelate early today said mass before the tomb of St. Peter and then motored to Castel Gandolfo, where the Pope felicitated him and expressed the hope he might live to celebrate his fiftieth anniversary.

Cardinal Mundelein said the Pope praised President Roosevelt, with whom the Chicago visitor had an interview before coming to Rome.

Reports on Chicago Churches.

The Cardinal said he informed the Pope that his archdiocese during the economic crisis had been able to continue its educational and charitable works, indicating his people thought as much of their church as of their bread and butter.

He further told the Pontiff that 865,000 persons in Chicago had made a special spiritual mission in honor of the anniversary of his consecration, more than 2,000,000 receiving communion, at which the Pope remarked: "Splendid!"

He found the Pope in excellent health, he continued.

The Cardinal received today more than 200 cablegrams of congratulations on his anniversary, among them one from Cardinal Pacelli, Vatican Secretary of State, who is en route to the Eucharistic Congress at Buenos Aires.

September 22, 1934

Pope Assails Communism as 'Enemy' of All; Holds Prayer Must Fight 'Immense Peril'

Wireless to THE NEW YORK TIMES.

VATICAN CITY, May 11.—Pope Pius made a vigorous attack on communism today in reply to an address by the Primate of Hungary, Cardinal Seredi, in introducing Hungarian pilgrims.

The Cardinal recalled the help given to the Hungarians by Pope Innocent XI to free Buda from the Ottoman menace, and Pope Pius responded by drawing a parallel between those distant times and today.

"It is, alas, true," he said, "that a common enemy exists also today, an enemy that threatens everything and every one: communism, which seeks to penetrate everywhere and unfortunately has already penetrated many places—some by violence, others by stealth and still others by fraud.

"It is highly deplorable that many people should allow themselves to be so far deceived that they do not see, or pretend not to see, the common peril, and even help—sometimes with negative connivance and sometimes with positive favors—this destructive force, which menaces everything and has a program of social ruin.

"You confide in the Holy See, and we confide in Divine Providence. When we see such blindness in face of this immense peril, when we see the defection of all those who should be united to defend, if not religion, at least the cause of civilization itself, we turn to God, in whom we place our trust.

"It is for this reason that we invite all those who visit us to pray, and today we address this invitation to Hungary. Pray, pray, pray because truly it is only by the intervention of God that we may hope to see better days and days free of a threat against everything we hold most sacred and most dear.

"It is only by praying that we may hope to see and enjoy the benefits of order and peace, that true peace of Christ, which He announced to the world—the peace of truth, of justice and of charity."

May 12, 1936

CHURCH-LABOR TIE FOR RED WAR URGED

Smith and Woll Join in Attack on Communism as Foe of Religion and Liberty

LA GUARDIA'S NAME BOOED

Catholics at Rally Are Urged to Set Up Counter-Activity to Atheistic Propaganda

Former Governor Alfred E. Smith joined Matthew Woll, vice president of the American Federation of Labor, last night in an attack on communism as the enemy of the church, of human liberty and the well-being of the working men and women of America.

Speaking under the auspices of the American Association Against Communism, Inc., and the International Catholic Truth Society, both of which were founded by the Rev. Edward Lodge Curran of Brooklyn, Mr. Smith declared there was "no room in America," a Christian country, for a social philosophy that denied the existence of God.

About 4,000 men and women, who booed the name of Mayor La Guardia, filled the Hippodrome, where the mass meeting was held, to two-thirds of its capacity. Borough President George U. Harvey, an aspirant for the Republican Mayoralty nomination, who spoke before Mr. Smith, told the wildly cheering audience that if he controlled the New York Police Department he would rid the city of Communists in two weeks with the aid of a liberal supply of rubber hose.

Smith Wins Laughs

The former Governor made his audience laugh as he discussed the purchasing power of the ruble in Soviet Russia, where, he said, an average man's earnings for a month would enable him to buy twenty pounds of sausages but would not leave him enough to buy a nightshirt. The commissars, however, are Russia's "economic royalists," he declared.

He ridiculed Earl Browder's statement that the Communist manifesto was a twentieth-century version of the Declaration of Independence, asserting that one might as well "compare the Holy Bible and The Police Gazette."

Before Mr. Smith addressed the audience, which responded liberally to appeals for funds to carry on a crusade against the Reds, Mr. Woll sounded a call to organized labor to join the church in fighting their common enemy of Marxism. Father Curran, in a plea for more recruits, said he hoped to defeat the Reds by peaceful means, but he warned that "if they wanted it the way it was in Spain, we'll let them have it."

Seated with Mr. and Mrs. Smith upon the platform was Raoul Desvernines, a member of the law committee of the American Liberty League, who accompanied the former Governor on his speaking tour in behalf of Alf M. Landon in the last campaign.

"A Wild Theory"

"I spent years of my life in a neighborhood where we heard crackpots, Socialists and all kinds of agitators," Mr. Smith said, "but we paid no attention to them. What is the need for such a gathering as this tonight, these contributions, this impassioned argument; it must be because communism is dangerous.

"I never read any intelligent explanation of the Communist government other than that it was a wild theory. It is supposed to do something for the worker. It is making headway because it is supposed to obliterate class."

First, Mr. Smith said, he would deal with the claim that communism eliminated classes. It does nothing of the kind, he said, but instead sets up two classes, the tyrants and the tyrannized, which "are the rank and file under communistic government."

He quoted Karl Marx's Communist manifesto as saying that the proletariat would use its power to seize wealth and centralize the means of production in the hands of the State. That means by force and bloodshed and despotism, said Mr. Smith.

"Let's see what Earl Browder, the Communist candidate for President, says about it," he continued. "Nobody voted for him. I'm not sure that he even voted for himself."

Mr. Smith then quoted the Communist leader as saying that "revolutions must be made by armed forces."

"The Communists do not really understand the government of this country," the former Governor added. "This country belongs to the rank and file of the American people. We went through a struggle in 1776 to get away from despots and from those who sought to make inroads on private property."

He "Looks at the Record"

The way to test claims of the benefits communism would confer upon the workers is to "look at the record," said Mr. Smith, admitting that he never had been to Russia and "just about know where it is on the map."

Here he quoted a Russian writer as having said that the "poorest worker in a capitalist country was better off than a member of the privileged class in Russia."

"Huh?" laughed Mr. Smith, removing his glasses. "Done away with the aristocracy. Yes, by taking everything away from them. But in taking it away they set up another aristocracy of privilege—the commissars. The commissars have become the princes of business—the economic royalists of Russia."

Citing the case of a certain large manufacturing industry in Russia, employing 18,000 men and women, he said that the monthly salary of these workers would not buy twenty pounds of sausage in Russia, "and that would allow him nothing for rent or taxes."

"I also wonder," he said, "what the poor Russian does for a nightshirt when a pair of pajamas costs him two-thirds of a month's salary."

As for Communists in this country, he said, he agreed with Mr. Harvey that they "should be sent back to the country from which they came."

"There is no room in this country for communism," he said. "Ours is a land of opportunity. The gateway to that is open to everybody. The poorest man or woman in America can rise to the place of greatest distinction. More than that, this is a Christian country, the only one which stamps on its money 'In God We Trust.'

"This country, given by God himself as a haven of refuge for the very people who make up the rank and file of communism, where the gateway of opportunity is swung open, is a land of equal opportunity. We propose to keep it a land of equal opportunity, and we will keep it this way free from nazism, communism, fascism or any other ism."

Mayor's Name Booed

The name of Mayor La Guardia was booed vigorously when Father Curran, in an address bitterly assailing the "unwashed liberals" of New York, announced that the Mayor had not troubled to reply to an invitation to address the rally. The priest told the crowd that the meeting had the endorsement of Cardinal Hayes, Bishop Thomas E. Molloy of Brooklyn, Archbishop Michael J. Curley of Baltimore, Bishop Ernest M. Stires of the Protestant Episcopal Diocese of Long Island and Rabbi Isaac Landman of Brooklyn.

Among the letters read by Father Curran was one from Postmaster

71

General James A. Farley, National Chairman of the Democratic party, who wrote that an equitable distribution of wealth was the best guarantee against communism. Senator Royal S. Copeland wrote that he did not know how far the menace of communism had progressed, but that it was one of the most important issues of the time.

Grover A. Whalen and District Attorney William F. X. Geoghan sent their regrets. Governor Harold G. Hoffman of New Jersey wrote expressing sympathy with the aims of the organization. Father Curran said he also had received a letter from Bishop William T. Manning attacking the communist menace.

After reading the endorsements Father Curran said:

"We are opposed to communism because it teaches only that man is for this life alone, that the end justifies the means and that any form of faith is unnecessary under the Communistic State. We are not Fascists or capitalists in the association, and we will not allow the Communists to draw the red herring of fascism across our banner. Fascism is not our problem today, but communism is.

"We are firmly resolved to match the Communist with strength for strength, and we want every American, every Protestant, every Catholic, every Jew to go along with us. We know every religious man is with us because we are fighting for faith, every working man should be with us because we are keeping such slavery away from him. We hope we haven't waited too long, as they did in Spain, where tonight they are fighting it out. If the Communists want it that way, we will give it to them. We cannot fail."

At 8:30, when the meeting was scheduled to open, only half of the 5,000 seats were occupied. There was an admission charge of 25 cents. Inspector Louis Schilling of the Third inspection district, had a hundred patrolmen and detectives on duty in and around that Hippodrome.

While the band of the Catholic War Veterans played a marching song, a guard of honor escorted the colors to the platform, where 300 priests and laymen were seated. The Rev. Edward J. Higgins, pastor of the Immaculate Conception Church of Astoria and national chaplain of the Catholic War Veterans, Inc., delivered the invocation, after which the audience joined in singing the national anthem.

Dr. Michael F. Walsh, New York

State deputy of the Knights of Columbus, and permanent chairman of the mass meeting, declared in his address that never in history had there been "a more godless, more treacherous enemy than communism." If there was need for heroes in the past, he said, there was need for them now to preserve democracy from the threat of communism.

Woll Sees a Crisis

Mr. Woll, the next speaker, told the audience that they were meeting on "the threshold of a crisis which is so grave that it stands as a challenge to both church and labor, and to the ideals of social justice to which both are committed."

Under the name of communism and fascism or nazism, Mr. Woll added, there has been established a hostility to religion and the practice of the church. Wherever the totalitarian State has come into existence, he continued, it has attacked and destroyed not only the free institutions of labor but the freedom of religion.

"Both by principle and precept, as well as by promptings of self-preservation, it is essential, therefore, that the church and labor should strive side by side for the enhancement and enrichment of liberty and freedom, personal as well as industrial, religious and social," he asserted.

Reviewing the conditions of labor in Russia, Italy and Germany, Spain and Mexico, Mr. Woll warned that agents of dictatorial philosophies were actively seeking converts in the United States. Red leaders, realizing that the American people would resist communistic tenets, place their reliance upon "extra-parliamentary measures, coercive means outside of the political field," Mr. Woll declared.

"Their instructions are they must follow the way shown by the Russian revolution of 1917 and that they must be 'on their guard' at every turn of events and to exert every effort without losing a moment for the revolutionary preparation of the proletariat for the impending battles for power.

"They have succeeded in organizing groups of unorganized workers in unskilled and semi-skilled employments. They are making persistent efforts to organize the unemployed and groups of workers on public relief rolls. They are penetrating recognized unions affiliated with the American Federation of Labor, endeavoring to organize what are known as rank-

and-file movements within those bodies. These latter constitute a serious and disturbing element in industrial relations.

"Their object, primarily, is to stir up disputes where none exist and to make it difficult, if not impossible, to adjust disputes which had legitimate origins. These tactics have already cost many lives throughout the United States and untold loss to the wage-earners and employers of the country.

"Nor is this the only field in which the Communists constitute a threat to our institutions. Their activity in schools and colleges, particularly in certain cities, has already begun to make itself felt."

Counter-Propaganda Urged

W. Lawrence Darrow, treasurer of the anti-Communist organization, who followed Mr. Woll, said he hoped the mass meeting would result in a definite program for eradicating Marxism from the United States. The first step, he said, was the establishment of a propaganda machine at least as efficient as that of the Communists. Calling for volunteers to spread "decent American anti-Communist propaganda in the shops, the schools and wherever else the seeds of communism are being spread," he said he hoped that for every Communist shouting, "There is no god!" there would be "10,000 of us shouting, 'Glory to God!' Communism is poison.'"

Nikolas Michailoff, émigré attorney, who came here in 1931 to "escape the nightmares of communism," described conditions in Soviet Russia, where, he said, the conditions among workers were five times worse than in such capitalist countries as Finland.

Cornelius V. Coleman, director of the speakers' bureau of the association, declared that throughout history any nation that attempted to eliminate religion brought oblivion on itself. The anti-religious war is not for Russia alone, but must be carried on throughout the world, according to the catechism of the modern communistic Russia, he charged.

Mr. Coleman also attacked the American Civil Liberties Union, which, he said, has admittedly advocated the overthrow of American institutions.

After Father Curran's talk E. Bruce Heath, vice president of the association, announced that the ushers would collect funds to carry on the work of the organization. Among the first contributions was one of $1,000 from Martin J. Gillen of 12 West Forty-fourth

Street. The gifts, many above $100, were reported as rapidly as Mr. Heath could read them off.

Harvey "Enlists" for War

Borough President Harvey, who spoke after the collection had been taken up, said that Father Curran was "raising an army" to drive the Communists out. As for himself, Mr. Harvey said, he was "enlisting for the duration of the war."

When he described the New York Police Department as "the finest body of men in the world, but the poorest directed," and said he would like to have control of it for about two weeks, several in the audience shouted: "Maybe you will!"

If he had, Mr. Harvey went on, he would guarantee there would be not one Communist left in New York. He would give each policeman three feet of rubber hose, he said, swinging his arm to illustrate what he would have the police do with it.

"Our next Mayor!" shouted an enthusiastic woman.

Mr. Harvey declared that in Jamaica deserving poor folk could not get on relief without paying a quarter to a Mr. Popoff of the Workers Alliance.

"You said it, I ought to know," screamed a woman in the balcony.

"How long will we tolerate a situation like this—to take relief money and devote it to the Communist party?" demanded Mr. Harvey.

"I have had experience with sit-downers, and it is nothing new, for they did it in Italy and they did it to me. I had a bunch pull a strike on the Federal Government and then try to take over Borough Hall. I called the police and they said there was no way of getting them out. I threatened to get fifty of my truck drivers and clear them out. So I drew up a warrant for fifty-five John Does and put them under arrest. When some one takes over some one's else property it is nothing more or less than everyday stealing.

"There is something that should be done about the Communist situation. Some are afraid to antagonize them, as they have votes. The Communists don't vote for me; I don't want them to vote for me, and if they ever do I will go to Maine or Vermont and live like a gentleman. They should be put on a leaking steamer and started for home. They should be taken off the ballot as a political party."

April 14, 1937

SPANISH PRELATES JUSTIFY REBELLION

By The Associated Press.

VATICAN CITY, Sept. 2.—Prelates disclosed tonight that the Holy See "sympathizes" with a long pastoral letter signed by two Spanish Cardinals and forty-six other prelates of Insurgent Spain, which declares the revolt of General Francisco Franco to be a "legitimate" one.

No official declaration has come from the Vatican concerning the letter, but it was noted that the first signatory was Isidoro, Cardinal Goma y Tomas, the Vatican's representative with the Insurgent regime, and prelates said he scarcely would have so acted without first consulting the Vatican.

It may be stated, the prelates added, that "there is nothing in the pastoral letter that is in contradiction with the view of the Vatican."

The letter contains a foreword, five principal arguments and four conclusions. There is a description of "outrages" against the church

under the Government regime, and, finally, a rebuttal of three accusations.

Reason for Issuing Letter

"False opinions created abroad," particularly by a certain group of Spanish Catholics, necessitated the letter, the foreword states.

This is apparently a reference to protestations against General Franco's methods of war by Catholics in the Basque country prior to the fall of Bilbao and Santander to the Insurgent forces.

The five principal points made in the letter are:

1. The church did not want the civil war in Spain, although thousands of her sons have taken arms on their personal responsibility to save the principles of religion and Christian justice.

2. Since 1931 [when the Spanish Republic was proclaimed] the legislative and executive power in Spain had changed Spanish history in a sense contrary to the needs of the national spirit.

3. The elections of Feb. 3, 1936 [which placed a Leftist coalition in power] were unjust. Although the Rightist-Center parties received more than 500,000 votes

more than the Leftists, they got 118 fewer Deputies because of the arbitrary annulment of votes in all provinces.

4. The Communist International had armed a "revolutionary Spanish militia," with the result that at the outbreak of the civil war on July 18, 1936, 150,000 Spanish Assault Guards and 100,000 "manoeuvre militiamen" were under arms.

5. The civil war is legitimate because "five years of continued outrages of Spanish subjects in the religious and social fields had endangered the very existence of public welfare and had produced enormous spiritual unrest among the Spanish people; and because when legal means were exhausted the idea entered the national conscience that there was no other recourse except to force to maintain order and peace.

"Also because interests opposed to legitimate authority had decided to overthrow the constituted order and established communism through violence;

"Finally, because, through the fatal logic of facts, Spain had only this alternative: either to perish under the precipitate assault of destructive communism, already prepared and decreed, as has happened in the areas where the Nationalist Government has not triumphed, or to attempt with titanic force to get rid of this frightful enemy and save the fundamental principles of its social life and national characteristics."

The Four Conclusions

The four conclusions follow:

1. "The church could not remain indifferent in a fight in which, on one side, God was renounced, while on the other side, notwithstanding human defects, the fight was for preservation of the old Spanish and Christian spirit."

2. "The church, however, does not associate herself with acts, tendencies and intentions that figure in the noble physiognomy of the Nationalist movement."

3. "The civic-military uprising deepens in the people's consciousness two roots; one of patriotism, the other of religious sentiment."

4. "For the moment there is no other hope for Spain's again acquiring justice and peace except the Nationalist movement."

The letter, detailing Leftist crimes against the church, states that 6,000 of the secular clergy were killed.

It also rebuts these three accusations: First, that the church in Spain owned a third of the nation's land; second, that priests were chosen from the upper classes and were removed from the people, and, third, that the people did not want their children baptized because they had to pay heavy fees for administration of the Holy Sacrament.

September 3, 1937

SPANISH HIERARCHY IS DENOUNCED HERE

Charging that the recent pastoral letter of the Catholic hierarchy in Spain showed its "open hostility" toward the principles of popular government, freedom of worship, and the separation of church and State, 150 Protestant clergymen and educators and laymen made public here yesterday an open letter in reply.

They asked whether the views set forth in the document have the approval of the Vatican and of the Catholics in America. They characterized as "alarming" the hierarchy's "attempt to justify a military rebellion against a legally elected government." In so doing, they charged, the hierarchy was acting as "the apologists for reaction and fascism."

"Certainly the hierarchy can hardly expect to gain sympathy here either for itself or for the Catholic religion with a declaration that treats with contempt principles that are the precious heritage of the American people," the letter said.

Two Bishops Among Signers

Among the signers of the letter were Bishop James Chamberlain Baker of San Francisco, a Methodist; Bishop Robert L. Paddock of New York, of the Protestant Episcopal Church; the Rev. Harry Emerson Fosdick of the Riverside Church and John Haynes Holmes of the Community Church.

Professors George S. Counts, John Dewey, Robert S. Lynd and Franz Boas of Columbia University, President William Allen Neilson of Smith College, President Walter Dill Scott of Northwestern University, Dr. Stephen Duggan, director of the Institute of International Education, and Dr. John A. MacKay, president of Princeton Theological Seminary, were others who signed the letter.

Bishop Paddock, who is president of the American Friends to Aid Spanish Democracy, made public the letter yesterday afternoon at the office of Dr. Guy Emery Shipler, editor of the Churchman, an Episcopal publication. He said that Dr. Shipler, who had left earlier in the day for Cincinnati, had prepared the letter.

Bishop Paddock said that the letter was "a responsible and friendly" attempt to induce the leaders of the Catholic Church in the United States to set forth their own political views. Many of the signers, he said, felt confident that American Catholics did not share the opinions of the Spanish hierarchy.

The letter said its signers were "disturbed by the fact that no leaders of the Catholic Church in America have raised their voices in repudiation of the position taken by the Spanish hierarchy" and added that "they too seem to have given their blessing to General Franco and his Fascist allies."

The signers of the letter charged that the pastoral appeal approved of resort to violence; rejected not only the Popular Front government in Spain but the Spanish Republic itself; stigmatized every form of parliamentary government as "irresponsible autocracy" and condemned in principle democratic institutions.

"It is hard to believe that this pastoral letter was written in the twentieth century," they said.

"We think it is extremely regretable that religion should have been made an issue in the rebellion," they stated. "It is clear that the Spanish conflict is between the forces of democracy and social progress, on the one hand, and the forces of special privilege, and their Fascist allies, on the other."

Conceding that there have been excesses on the Loyalist side, the letter asserted that the Madrid regime had made every effort to prevent such occurrences and to punish those responsible, while on the Rebel side General Franco had encouraged violence.

The letter charged that the Spanish hierarchy was "indifferent to the actual facts" of systematic brutality and religious persecution on the Rebel side. It asserted that priests and nuns had been murdered within the Rebel lines and that Protestant missions within the Insurgent areas had been systematically destroyed.

October 4, 1937

175 CATHOLICS BACK AID TO INSURGENTS

Charging that the recent open letter of Protestant clergymen and laymen "misrepresented the facts and issues in Spain," and calling for the end of all foreign intervention on both sides in the Spanish civil war, a group of 175 Roman Catholic clergymen and laymen in the United States made public yesterday a statement defending Catholic support of General Francisco Franco's rebellion and attacking the Loyalist Government of Spain.

The statement supplied an answer to the question raised by the Protestants' open letter as to whether American Catholics supported the Spanish Bishops who had taken General Franco's side in a pastoral letter. The 175 Catholics defended the Spanish hierarchy as having acted on behalf of the preservation of religious and civil liberties and of all the functions of democracy.

The Catholics denied that the Spanish Bishops had aligned themselves in support of Nazi or fascist ideas or policies. They charged that if General Franco were defeated the Loyalist Government would end democracy in Spain and establish a dictatorship like that of Soviet Russia.

The Catholic reply was made public by the Rev. John La Farge, associate editor of America, national Catholic weekly magazine.

Among the prominent Catholic laymen who signed it are former Governor Alfred E. Smith, Chancellor James Byrne of the University of New York, Martin H. Carmody, Supreme Knight of the Knights of Columbus; John Moody, publisher; Michael Williams, editor of The Commonweal; Professor Carlton J. H. Hayes of Columbia University and former Supreme Court Justice Daniel F. Cohalan.

Others are John M. Dealy, national commander of the Catholic War Veterans; John E. Fenton, national president of the Ancient Order of Hibernians; Louis Kenedy, president of the National Council of Catholic Men; Patrick Scanlan, managing editor of The Brooklyn

Tablet; Charles H. Ridder, publisher of The Catholic News, and I. M. Wilkinson, Dean of Fordham University Law School.

Help to Loyalists Is Cited

In urging the end of foreign intervention in Spain, the Catholic statement said that those who criticized the Moors, Italians and Germans in General Franco's army ignored the Russians, French, Americans and other foreigners in the Loyalist forces. If all foreign volunteers and all outside Government aid were withdrawn from both sides, it predicted, the war will end quickly, and Spain "would then be able to right itself and express itself."

Appealing to the American democratic concept of civic and religious liberties for all, the statement charged the existence of a "campaign of misrepresentation, errors and deliberate lies" against the In-surgents. It challenged American Protestants to say whether they accepted and approved a régime "which has carried on a ruthless persecution of the Christian religion since February, 1936."

Holds Catholics Act as Citizens

Characterizing the Loyalist Government as a mixture of Socialists, Communists, syndicalists and anarchists, the statement asserted that Catholics supporting General Franco did so as citizens and not as Catholics. It said that the Catholics of Spain had accepted the republic after the fall of the monarchy in 1931 and had tried to work for a liberal and progressive form of government, but that the Leftists now controlling the Government had not.

The statement charged that Communists had seized power illegally, had started to build a Soviet dictatorship and had begun to violate the civil and religious rights of Catholics and other citizens before the Franco revolt broke out.

According to the statement, the Communists had begun to abolish freedom of speech and press and were preparing for a military coup to seize absolute power when the murder of José Calvo Sotelo in July, 1936, caused Spanish patriots to realize that there was "no alternative except recourse to arms."

The reason the Catholics supported the revolt, the statement said, was "to save themselves from destruction and annihilation," not only as Catholics but also as citizens. It asserted that the Spanish rebellion was as much justified as the American Revolution of 1776, and that it was against a "malign power" that would have destroyed free Spain.

Denying charges of Insurgent atrocities, the statement asserted that Communists had set fire to all the Spanish churches in the areas they controlled, had destroyed all religious objects and had massacred virtually all priests in a deliberate attempt to destroy the Catholic religion. It charged that 14,000 Catholics had been executed by the Loyalists. It denied that the Communist movement was a result of the revolt or a result of "deep social resentment created by social abuses."

The Negrin Government now ruling Spain, the statement held, does not represent the will of the people, whereas two-thirds of the people have "freely and enthusiastically acclaimed loyalty and allegiance to General Franco."

October 14, 1937

COMMONWEAL ASKS CALM VIEW ON SPAIN

Urges Americans to Maintain 'Positive Impartiality' and 'a Sanity of Judgment'

EX-EDITOR IN OPPOSITION

Michael Williams Sees Revolt of Franco Forces Justified Under the Circumstances

A plea to Americans to be neutral in the Spanish civil war is made in a statement by the editorial directors of The Commonweal in the coming issue of that periodical, published next Friday. In the same issue Michael Williams, former editor, takes issue with this point of view.

Under the heading of "Civil War in Spain and the United States" the editorial board's statement says in part:

"Most discussion of the Spanish question to date in the United States by supporters of both sides has been distinguished more for its heat than for any light cast upon the significance of events. Those directly responsible for the conduct of this magazine have believed that anything said, however temperate and however qualified as their own opinion, might add rather to the heat than to the light. We have hoped for peace, and the opportunity to comment upon the better problems which peace proposes.

"But the war continues, and the manner of waging it, both in Spain and here in our own country, seems to change very little with the passage of time. As long as 'total' war continues on the Spanish peninsula, it will continue to torment all of us, both in America and in Europe.

View Shared by Thousands

"We do not for an instant pretend that what is said below is the only proper position for Catholics in the matter; we only affirm our belief, subject to correction, that our position is perfectly compatible with Catholic principles and that it is a view shared by many thousands of American Catholics.

"First of all we feel that some distinction must be made between the Spanish problem in Spain and the Spanish problem in the United States. In Spain there is an active civil war which is being fought by both sides in order to achieve, from the point of view of each political group, a better social order. The same struggle to achieve a better social order exists in every country but not in the form of an armed struggle, of a civil war.

"The general problem exists throughout the world, but the war in Spain relates to Spaniards acting in their immediate struggle and allegiance; outside Spain it relates to non-Spaniards observing a more remote armed struggle and engaged in the general problem in a different way.

"We do not feel qualified to discuss the problem as it is in Spain in any detail because the information available is so generally characterized by propaganda that we do not have any sufficient knowledge of the whole situation. Two reports on a single event emanating from the opposing camps will be in complete contradiction to each other. The official principles of each side must be taken into account, but the actions of each side, when they can be known, speak louder than words.

Views of Governments Cited

"A Spaniard, unless he is one of the few who are determined—and able—to make the 'double refusal,' seemingly must choose between two governments whose characters are mixed and are impossible to know from here with any comprehensiveness.

"One government, or part of it, has instigated, or at least permitted, the murder of priests, nuns and lay people; has utilized ruthless methods of accomplishing social and political and economic ends, and chosen, as far as it is possible to see, many objectives in all these fields that should be condemned. Its alliance with Russia implies some, if an unknown degree, of identification with the evils of the Soviet regime.

"The second government, which gives the church open support, yet, in its conduct of warfare, repeatedly, and despite protests from the Holy Father, destroys defenseless civilians, particularly by its air raids upon cities. Air raids made by one side cannot cancel out those made by the other. Many of its leaders give utterance to totalitarian views very similar to those which have been condemned by the church in other countries.

"The system of government it utilizes and favors, so far as can be seen, contains elements that should be sharply rejected. Its alliance with the fascist and Nazi nations implicates it to some, if an uncertain, extent in the evils of those regimes.

"In this country there has been violent partisanship either for the Spanish Nationalists or for the Madrid-Barcelona Government. We feel that violent American partisanship on either side with regard to the Spanish question is bad, not only because the facts are obscure but chiefly because both sides include elements that no American wants imported into this country. Neither has begun to enforce or even propound anything comparable to the Bill of Rights, which protects an individual from unbearable use of authority.

"To be strongly partisan concerning the Spanish civil war is indeed to aggravate a current intellectual disease: the conviction that we are going to be forced to choose between fascism and communism. This is a dangerous disease; sufferers from it are blinded by it to the truth that both systems are anti-Christian and secularist. (Unquestionably the greatest error is to think that the life of Christianity is bound up with the maintenance of any such temporal form of society.) The choice today is between secularism, the Hegelian State in any of its current forms, and the 'personalist' Christian State, conceived as existing for the protection and assistance of its citizens.

"The issue is, of course, never clear in any given instance; but to transfer the issue from its proper ground—the distinction between the conception of man as free and the conception of man as existing only for the State—to a totally improper ground is to further the cause of evil. The freedom that demands the constant vigilance and protection of every citizen is the freedom to pursue a person's spiritual, mental and social life without dictation by the exterior material force of a majority or a directing minority.

"We are quite frankly wholehearted partisans of the personalist, Christian State. The seeds of both fascism and communism will germinate only in the soil of injustice, and then must be fertilized by a general public conviction that the leaders of the non-totalitarian State are deficient in moral strength and do not deserve the confidence of their people.

"The problem of preserving or creating a form of State in which Christianity can truly flourish is, therefore, primarily a moral problem and one internal to the country concerned. In each instance both the government and all citizens must dedicate themselves to remedying present injustices, solving present social and economic problems and, as much as is possible, preventing future injustice. Those entrusted with the governance of the State must strive in every way to make themselves worthy of public confidence and trust.

"It is for these reasons that we believe that the wisest, as also the most charitable and perhaps the most difficult, policy for Americans is to maintain that 'positive impartiality,' a sanity of judgment toward both sides in Spain, expressing a preference, for specific ideas and actions when they are certainly known, but being an uncritical partisan of neither.

"Americans should cease labeling everything they may not like in America or elsewhere as either 'fascist' or 'communist'; they should try, instead, to study American problems not only in the hope of contributing to their reasonable and equitable solution but also in the belief that such a solution in America will constitute a part of the solution of international and world problems. Above all, we must avoid fostering the growth of totali-

tarianism and hatred of Christianity by avoiding all activities that even faintly encourage that spirit of hysterical opposition and human distrust which is the very life blood of both of those systems. Peace can come only when there is good will, and when there is good will, the road is open to peace."

Mr. Williams's Views

Mr. Williams, under the heading "News and Reviews," writes in part as follows:

"There are so many important things well said in the statement on Spain by the editorial directors of The Commonweal with which I heartily agree, that my strong disagreement with the statement as a whole becomes painful and regrettable. I dislike the necessity of being personal in what I have to say, but it seems necessary, under the circumstances.

"For of course I must suppose that the readers of this journal cannot help but recall the fact that when I was the editor, a year ago, I often and strongly expressed my belief that the armed revolt of the Franco forces in Spain, abhorrent as nearly all revolts against constituted authority must be for all who hold the teachings of the Catholic Church, was, under the circumstances existing in Spain, thoroughly justified, and that, because of those circumstances, the victory of the Franco uprising would be beneficial to the cause of Christian civilization; its defeat, therefore, disastrous to that cause in Spain itself,

and a weakening of that cause elsewhere in the world, our own country, of course, included.

"I still hold those opinions, but the present editors of The Commonweal do not.

"The one important consideration is the question whether or not the advice now tendered to The Commonweal readers, namely, to be absolutely neutral, as concerns any judgments made upon the comparative merits of the contending forces, tends to be helpful or harmful to the interests of Christian civilization. For my own part, then, I am most regretably constrained to say that such advice tends to be harmful.

"My chief reason for thinking so is the fact (as it seems to me) that The Commonweal's statement carries its suspicion, and its repudiation, of the propaganda emanating from both sides in Spain far beyond a justifiable degree, and, therefore, it seems to ignore what to my way of thinking is the determining, ultimate truth concerning the Spanish situation, namely, the fact that what I would regard as unimpeachable testimony exists which goes to prove that there was a well-planned, long-prepared, deliberate and frightfully significant effort made by the predominant forces controlling the Government of Spain, prior to Franco's counter-revolution, utterly and finally to destroy the Catholic religion in Spain—to wipe out its sacred ministry, its consecrated teachers, and its lay leaders, and in fact to

liquidate, if possible, the entire body of believers; and, thereafter, the plan was designed to proceed against the Church on all fronts, and in all the highly effective ways taught and practiced by the anti-God experts of Russia, and followed, more or less successfully, more or less radically, but always in that general direction, by other atheistic revolutionary governments and parties throughout the world.

"I am not, and I am fully satisfied that the overwhelming majority of American Catholics are not, and have no desire to be, either Fascist or Nazi, still less, of course, do we lean toward Communism; and I for one cannot agree that I lean toward any form of totalitarian political tyranny if I decide, and say, after reading what the Spanish Bishops tell the whole world, that it is true that an anti-God revolution was let loosely or at least could not be stopped by, the United Front government of Madrid. In that revolution, other values prized by vast numbers of the Spanish people were also attacked.

"And I consider that the facts, not mere propaganda, show that against that revolution, with its mixed motives, but predominantly a terrorism aimed at the Catholic Church in Spain, there was a counter-revolution, led by Franco, and validated by the adhesion of a vast number, probably the majority, of the Spanish people. The dreadful disaster of civil war ensued."

June 21, 1938

PLEA TO BE NEUTRAL ON SPAIN DEPLORED

Catholic Paper America, in Criticizing The Commonweal, Assails Loyalist 'Evil'

FINDS MANY DISSIDENTS

But Tells Them That Rebels, Despite Their 'Mistakes,' Are 'Christian and Spanish'

In an editorial sharply criticizing the recent plea by the editors of The Commonweal, Roman Catholic weekly, for an attitude of impartiality toward the civil war in Spain, another Catholic weekly, America, will take a stand "unalterably opposed" to the Loyalists in its issue to be published Saturday.

The periodical says that despite "faults and mistakes" of the Insurgents headed by General Francisco Franco, they are "Christian and truly Spanish, and are progressively eager to build a new social

order founded on justice and charity."

Referring to the bombing of cities by the Insurgents and support from Italy and Germany, the publication says that General Franco has "a tender regard for babies and mothers and non-combatants," and declares that his corporative views "are highly consistent with Catholic principles and the Papal encyclicals."

"Franco is not perfect, and the Nationalists make mistakes," the editorial declares. "But, between Franco and his Nationalists, and Negrin [Premier Juan Negrin], with his Socialist-Communist-Anarchist-Syndicalist combine, there can be no studied, smug, superior, positive impartiality. The past, present and future evil of the one side is so heavy that it tips the scales against it."

Reserves Freedom to Criticize

America adds that it reserves "its freedom and its intention" to criticize and condemn the State that the Nationalists "will eventually establish through all Spain," in the event that "justice and charity be violated."

"Truthfully, but sadly," the editorial comments, "one admits that many thousands of American Catholics profess the same inability as the Commonweal editors to see the Spanish issues clearly. They have split themselves off from the solid Catholic thought in the United States and have tended toward the

opinions of the non-Catholic majority.

"They have been deeply affected by the newspapers, periodicals, radio and other mediums of communication, as have most Americans. While they may not believe all that they read and see in favor of the Loyalists, they refuse to believe, or to credit, almost all that is reported in favor of the Nationalists.

"When confronted by Franco facts, they seek for deep reasons of mistrust or they speculate about disturbing consequences. Despite their protestations of 'positive impartiality,' they are predisposed to believe what is unfavorable to Franco and what is favorable to the Loyalists.

"Analyzing further the mind behind this attitude of thousands of dissident American Catholics, one tries to understand their appeal for nonpartisanship. A passionate and blind partisanship on any subject is irrational. To be an intellectual partisan, however, means only that a person has convictions, well-founded and well-reasoned. Lacking convictions, the mind is vapid or vacillating. In the matter of Spain, the truth is evident, or at least available."

Says Soviet Was in Preparation

The editorial asserts that it is "an established fact" that the Leftist factions in Spain "were being driven toward a Socialist State as a transitional approach to a Soviet State," and that successive Leftist governments "were preparing for a social and cultural revolution in

Spain." The periodical adds that it is "a fact beyond denial" that "few opportunities were missed by these Leftist governments to attack the traditional religion of the Spanish people."

Reiterating charges that "Communist leaders" had been plotting a military coup in 1936 and that the "fundamental rights of free speech, free press, free assembly were assailed," America declares that "no American and no Catholic who fully understands the course of events in Spain, especially during the first half of 1936, could offer allegiance or approval to the governments controlled by the Socialist, Communist, Anarchist and Syndicalist Popular Front."

"But should an American and a Catholic remain positively neutral in regard to the Nationalists?" the editorial asks.

"General Franco and his associates are a native Spanish protest to a tyranny that had become unendurable and that was becoming permanent. He did not conquer territory when he marched up to Madrid, or when the northern army marched down to join him. The territory and the populace welcomed him.

"He was a symbol of a resurgent force springing from the soul of a people. He represented what the Spaniards, in millions, wished—namely, the preservation of Spain from an aggressive and dominating idea. These observations are factual."

June 28, 1938

East Side Orphan Who Became Cardinal Won Affection of People of New York

PRINCE OF CHURCH SERVED NATION TOO

Patrick Joseph Cardinal Hayes was as much a product of the "sidewalks of New York" as former Governor Smith. He was born on the lower East Side, he was educated here, and he rose from priest to Cardinal within the Archdiocese of New York. No citizen of this metropolis took greater pride or had its welfare more at heart, nor did any churchman ever win a firmer place in the affection of its people than he did.

His influence was not bounded by the city limits, for, as leader in the richest and most influential See in the United States, if not in the world, he was looked upon also as the leader and spokesman for Catholic America. Keenly interested in world affairs at all times, he was especially interested in the country of his ancestors, being a stanch champion of the Irish cause.

Cardinal Hayes was born on Nov. 20, 1867, at 15 City Hall Place, in what was then known as the Five Points district. Left an orphan at 5, he was brought up in the neighborhood by an aunt, who sent him to St. Andrew's Parochial School and then to De La Salle Institute, conducted by the Christian Brothers. Cardinal Mundelein of Chicago was a pupil in a neighboring East Side parochial school while Cardinal Hayes was attending St. Andrew's.

His boyhood was in no way different from that of the other children who played on the streets. It was a happy time for him and one that in after life he often referred to with pleasure. He never forgot his beginnings and always kept an especially warm spot in his heart for the lowly and poor people among whom he spent the early years of his life and who were his first parishioners.

"I was born among the very poor people in the lower part of New York," the Cardinal once said, "and my thought and love have always been with these unfortunates. I made up my mind years ago that if I could do anything to give them a new start I would be merely doing what God intended all of us to do."

His Tribute to His Aunt

The strongest influence of his early life was exerted by his uncle and his aunt, Mr. and Mrs. James Egan, who were father and mother to him from his early boyhood. When Mr. Egan died, in December, 1935, Cardinal Hayes conducted the funeral service at St. Patrick's Cathedral and at the grave in Calvary Cemetery.

"My Aunt Ellen took loving care of me until 1917, when she passed away," he said. "My first priest, Father Michael Curran, has gone, too. He was a great character. If the men insisted on staying in the back of the church, perhaps in the hope of avoiding the sermon, he would not hesitate to leave the altar and lead them by the ear to seats.

"But everybody loved him. He christened me. Archbishop Corrigan confirmed me. I remember how

Times Wide World

CARDINAL HAYES IN HIS STUDY LAST MARCH

One of the latest pictures of the prelate, showing him at St. Patrick's Cathedral at a press conference on the occasion of the fourteenth anniversary of his elevation to the College of Cardinals and the official opening of the annual Catholic Charities campaign.

greatly he impressed me. He was a slender man and wore a silk hat and spectacles. I would stare at him with awe."

The future Cardinal was graduated from De La Salle Institute in 1886, when he entered Manhattan College to finish his academic schooling. From 1888 to 1892 he attended St. Joseph's Seminary at Troy, N. Y. There he has left the memory of a grave, reserved young man with a singular sweetness of disposition, a kindliness and sense of humor that were outstanding characteristics throughout his whole life. He was a good, though not unusually brilliant, student. Although too short and slight of build for any strenuous form of athletics, he made a habit of spending a certain amount of time each morning running around the campus track. In this way he laid the foundation for a physique which stood the strain of the arduous work of his later years.

After graduation from St. Joseph's he was ordained a priest by Archbishop Corrigan, but before actively taking up parish work he went to the Catholic University in Washington for two years to take a graduate course in theology. There he acquired the background which was to make him an authority as a theologian and canonist. During his years as Chancellor of the Archdiocese he was invariably consulted concerning any ruling to be made. New canon laws were submitted to him for interpretation when the text reached here from Rome, and it was said that his decisions were accepted as final.

His First Parochial Work

Parochial work began when the young priest was sent to St. Gabriel's Church here in 1894 as assistant to the Rev. John Farley, then a Monsignor and later a Cardinal. It was the beginning of an association during which the younger man rose step by step after the elder until Cardinal Farley died and his place was taken by Cardinal Hayes.

In 1903, after his preceptor had become auxiliary Bishop of New York, Father Hayes was appointed Chancellor of the Archdiocese, and in the same year was also appointed president of Cathedral College, on Madison Avenue. A year later he was made a Doctor of Divinity by the Vatican, and in 1907 Domestic Prelate to the Pope.

When Mgr. Farley became Archbishop of New York, Father Hayes was made auxiliary or titular Bishop. He was consecrated in St. Patrick's Cathedral on Oct. 28, 1914. A year after that he was appointed irremovable rector of St. Stephen's Church.

On the entrance of the United States into the World War Bishop Hayes threw himself whole-heartedly into the task of furthering America's cause. He made frequent public appeals, served as a member of the National War Council and, on Nov. 24, 1917, was made Bishop Ordinary of the United States Army and Navy Catholic Chaplains by Pope Benedict XV, the appointment carrying ecclesiastical jurisdiction over Catholics in the service wherever the American flag was raised.

As Chaplain General he obtained 900 priests to serve as chaplains, commissioned and non-commissioned, for service overseas and at home. He organized the United States into a "war diocese," in order better to control the vast organization under him. He visited virtually every army camp and naval base in the United States, and was even prepared to go to France, when the illness and death of Cardinal Farley on Sept. 18, 1918, prevented his trip overseas.

Refused an Army Commission.

Although offered a commission in the army several times, he declined because he felt that his position as Catholic Bishop would carry more influence and give him a wider scope for his work than if he were under military control. Because of his trips to camps all over the country, he soon became a national figure. He traveled about the country unannounced, sparing himself no inconvenience to reach the men in service.

In addition to speaking often in the course of the Liberty Loan drives, he was instrumental in helping to raise a fund of $500,000 to aid French Catholic victims of the war. In 1920 he was decorated with the Order of the Crown of Italy for his work on behalf of the Italians during the war. It was Bishop Hayes who worked out the details for the $2,500,000 Catholic war drive, which was so successful that nearly twice that sum was raised.

The death of Cardinal Farley having left a vacancy in the New York See, it was naturally expected that Bishop Hayes would take over, to whatever extent permissible, the work of the Cardinal. In fact, during the last years of his life Cardinal Farley had leaned heavily on his younger colleague and had come to trust him implicitly with important decisions. One well-known instance was the decision in regard to the Boy Scout movement.

This organization had become very popular in Protestant churches, and a great deal of influence was brought to bear upon the Cardinal by leaders of the Boy Scouts to permit the introduction of the movement into Catholic parishes. Cardinal Farley turned the matter over to Bishop Hayes, who, after a careful study of the by-laws, constitution and other matters bearing on the movement, gave his approval. The Cardinal then placed his seal of approval on the organization, which has since flourished in Catholic circles.

Made Archbishop of New York.

Papal recognition of his increased importance came on Feb. 26, 1919, when he was made Archbishop of New York. It was just about that time that the Irish question assumed its most serious aspect. Among the thousands of Irish-Americans in New York who agitated for the freedom of Ireland, the newly appointed Archbishop was one of the most prominent and sincerely interested. He held no brief for those who sought to attain their ends by violence, being confident the matter could be settled by peaceful means. Whenever he was asked to give his aid by voice or pen he complied.

"The Irish question cannot be dismissed summarily by shouting 'Irish politics' " he wrote in a statement. "Centuries old in time; racial and religious in character; problem for English statesmen, especially since Gladstone's day; pressing for solution in the upheaval of the world because of democracy's onward march, I should be a very sorry figure as an American citizen and as a Catholic prelate, irrespective of my Celtic blood, were I not profoundly concerned and sympathetic with Ireland's love for freedom and her struggle by every lawful means to obtain it."

At another time, in a letter made public, he said:

"The Irish sword, which has been drawn the world over for the cause of liberty, has once more borne a noble part in the defense of the weak. Many lands you have helped to liberate, though not yet, alas! the one in which, after America, you, as I myself, are most deeply interested.

"But the end, I hope and believe, is not yet. Our President has laid down the principle of self-determination for all peoples; both houses of Congress, following the fine American tradition of supporting the oppressed, have declared by overwhelming majorities their sympathy with the aspirations of the Irish people.

"The voice of hundreds of thousands, nay, of millions of men of the Irish race, who have so amply manifested their thorough devotion to our Republic by taking up arms without any consideration except the interests of the country, will be heard with assent by our fellow-citizens of every racial origin, and the united voice of America will be heard across the sea as it utters the demand that the land of our fathers should not remain the only country in all Europe to be excluded from the right of self-determination."

On Stand With de Valera.

When Eamon de Valera came to America late in 1919 the Archbishop accepted him as President of the Irish Republic. He sat in the reviewing stand with de Valera at the St. Patrick's Day parade of 1920, and in other ways showed his admiration of the man. In January of that year he gave $1,000 as his personal gift to the $10,000,000 Sinn Fein campaign.

After the Irish Free State was established Cardinal Hayes set himself to bring about peace between the government and the Republican followers of de Valera. At one time, when civil war seemed imminent, he sent a message to Archbishop Byrne of Dublin, warning both sides that such a conflict would shock America and cost Ireland the loss of many sincere friends on this side of the Atlantic.

There was little doubt in Catholic circles that in due time Archbishop Hayes would be appointed to the cardinalate left vacant by the death of Cardinal Farley. The call to Rome came suddenly in March, 1924. The Archbishop had only two days to prepare for his departure, and, it was said, had to borrow the money with which to make the trip. Another native New Yorker, Archbishop Mundelein of Chicago, was called at the same time and the two prelates made the voyage and received the red hat together.

The ceremony took place on March 24, 1924. On April 4 Cardinal Hayes assumed the pastorate of his titular church, Santa Maria in Via Lata, and shortly thereafter set out for New York with Cardinal Mundelein on the Leviathan, arriving on April 28. The welcome which Cardinal Hayes received from the Catholics of New York City was wildly enthusiastic and demonstrated vividly how warm a place he had won in the hearts of the people of his native city. Several days later a pontifical mass was celebrated, attended by foreign diplomats, Federal, State and city officials, educators, financiers and leaders of the bench and bar.

Outspoken in His Views.

Elevation to the cardinalate brought wider influence and a greater weight of prestige, but it entailed no change in the policies or convictions to which the Cardinal had held from the beginning. He continued to attack immodesty in dress, divorce, radicalism, the Ku Klux Klan, obscenity in the theatre. He was a firm friend of actors and of the drama, but often took occasion to object to what he believed to be the too great license of the modern stage. One such criticism, in which he said the theatre was misusing the stage "to glorify obscenity and filth and to exploit the degradation of the unfortunate," started a movement for cleaner plays. His denunciation of the birth-control movement, which he characterized as "pagan," was very vigorous and in 1921 he issued a pastoral condemning it.

The Cardinal's most vigorous denunciation of the tenets of birth control and its proponents came in December, 1935, when from the pulpit of St. Patrick's Cathedral, preaching his first sermon there in four years, he voiced his "measured, deliberate and emphatic condemnation of the effrontery" of those "who would fly in the face of God and bring ruin and disaster to the land." He denounced its advocates as "prophets of decadence."

Saw Church Misrepresented

His sermon, in which he explained the position of the church, was prompted by statements made by speakers, including Jewish and Protestant clergymen, at the American Birth Control League Convention here shortly before. These statements, he said, had placed the Catholic position on the subject in a false light. He charged that sponsors of birth control saw in it a palliative for the "failure of our economic order."

He never ceased to battle against obscenity on the stage and screen, and in 1934, he saw his efforts bear fruit in the organization of the Legion of Decency, through which Catholics, Protestants and Jews joined hands to purify the motion pictures. A pastoral letter in which he declared that public morals should be protected from contamination as the public health is protected from disease, gave impetus to the crusade.

Early in 1937 the Cardinal backed a drive by the Knights of Columbus against burlesque shows. With other denominations joining in the drive, it forced the closing of fourteen burlesque houses in the city.

The Cardinal then gave his support to a bill in the Legislature to empower the Commissioner of Licenses to close shows considered immoral. With a unanimity rare in the profession, the theatre's guilds and crafts opposed the bill as setting up a "one-man censorship" that would set the stage back fifty years. Governor Lehman vetoed the bill after it had passed the Legislature.

Child Labor Amendment Foe

Cardinal Hayes showed his strongest influence on a legislative question when he opposed the Federal Child Labor Amendment to the Constitution as it came up before the State Legislature for ratification in 1937. In a statement read in Catholic churches throughout the State he criticized the proposed amendment as endangering "the rights of parents" and surrendering "broad powers over the lives of children to a remote agency at Washington."

Both President Roosevelt and Governor Lehman made forceful appeals to the Legislature for ratification, but it was killed in the Assembly, where many of the members were Catholics, by a vote of 102 to 42.

In another statement on the broadening of the power of the Federal Government, the Cardinal opposed the administration of all relief and charity by the Government. Remarking that there could be no social security without spiritual security, he told a group of Catholic Charities workers that only private charities could keep alive the personal and religious spirit.

His views on prohibition were often quoted. His position as the acknowledged spokesman for America's 20,000,000 Catholics gave great weight to his pronouncements in favor of temperance and against prohibition.

"The Catholic Church stands always for temperance," he said. "There are the virtues of justice, fortitude and prudence, and temperance fits in with these three. If an individual can't be temperate, but abuses liquor, he is bound by conscience to abstain entirely. You have to avoid extremes."

At another time he said: "When the Master Himself used wine at the Last Supper, it is very difficult to avoid the evident conclusion that He might have used anything else, but that He took wine. It is not, in my judgment, the proper thing to ask our children to consider as vile, something outlawed, that which we use day after day in our worship. If immorality flows out of intemperance there must be prohibition, but that doesn't mean that such prohibition should apply to all."

Perhaps the most outstanding trait of the Cardinal was his interest in and sympathy for charitable causes. To list the efforts with which his name was connected would be to detail every major charitable campaign in which Catholics were interested for the last twenty years. What was considered by many as his most important achievement was his development and coordination of Catholic charities into a federation, which now operates in conjunction with the Jewish and Protestant federations. In this federation work he directed a campaign to raise more than $3,500,000 through the clergy and people of the archdiocese.

Work for Catholic Charities.

One of the works of his archdiocese in which Cardinal Hayes always maintained great interest was Catholic Charities, which he founded in 1920. He often described it as a means of co-ordinating more than 200 agencies and devices for charitable endeavor. From the beginning it became the central organization of Roman Catholic relief work in the Archdiocese and Cardinal Hayes continued each year to take a prominent part in its annual appeals for funds, as well as in its activities.

The importance with which the work of Catholic Charities, which stressed the principle of relief through the family as a unit, was regarded outside the archdiocese was attested in April, 1931, when Pope Pius XI sent an apostolic letter to Cardinal Hayes, praising him for having created "a new method" in charity.

Contrary to the practice usual in such cases, which is that communications of this type are signed by the Papal Secretary of State or some other high official of the staff of the Vatican, the letter to Cardinal Hayes was signed by the Pope himself. At the time it was pointed out that the personal signature constituted the only exception in the history of the Church in this country to the general rule governing such communications.

The amounts collected by Catholic Charities each year grew from the beginning. In 1932 Cardinal Hayes was able to point out that receipts in 1931 were $1,712,084, an increase of $165,000 over 1930, although poor business conditions had tended in general to decrease charitable and philanthropic activity.

When President Calles of Mexico began to enforce the rigid anti-Catholic laws of that country Cardinal Hayes was one of the first of the influential American Catholics to rise in protest. In December, 1926, he issued a pastoral denouncing what was characterized as the persecution, and about the same time asked William D. Guthrie, president of the Bar Association of New York City, to prepare a legal opinion on the Mexican Government's religious policy. Mr. Guthrie, after a study of the situation, called the Mexican laws "violations of long-established rules of international law." Cardinal Hayes on several occasions attacked the Mexican policy from his pulpit at St. Patrick's.

Every once in a while the Cardinal officiated at a marriage, among the occasions being when he performed the ceremony at the marriage of Miss Emily Josephine Smith to Major John Adams Warner on June 5, 1926, and when Miss Catherine A. Smith was married to Francis J. Quillinan on June 9, 1928. The brides are daughters of the then Governor Alfred E. Smith.

Silent on 1928 Campaign

In the Presidential campaign of 1928, in conformity with the practice of the Catholic clergy throughout the country, Cardinal Hayes abstained from any public comment or support of either candidate.

In 1929 Cardinal Hayes was called upon to present the Laetare Medal awarded annually by Notre Dame University to former Governor Smith at a dinner held in May by the Notre Dame Club at the Hotel Plaza. The medal is awarded annually to a Catholic layman for outstanding achievement, in other than a religious line, redounding to the glory of the church.

In the Fall of that year the Cardinal paid a visit to Rome. The Cardinal and four other churchmen went on a Mediterranean cruise as the guests of George MacDonald, Papal Chamberlain, making most of the journey in Mediterranean waters aboard a private yacht chartered for the purpose.

While in Rome the Cardinal paid his ad limina visit to the Pope, and took part in various ceremonies, including services in his titular church, that of Santa Maria in Via Lata. He was received by the Pope for a farewell interview on Dec. 7, and he returned to New York in January, 1930. Meanwhile the esteem in which Cardinal Hayes was held at the Vatican had been expressed through receipt at his residence here of a mosaic portrait of the Cardinal, worked out from a photograph at the mosaic factory of the Vatican, and sent as a gift expressing the Pope's best wishes.

Soon after his return the Cardinal officiated in St. Patrick's Cathedral at the wedding of Miss Veronica Curry, daughter of John F. Curry, who was then leader of Tammany Hall, to Edmund M. McCarthy, at which hundreds of notables in politics and business were among the guests.

Two major religious movements were undertaken by the Cardinal during 1930. In one, after pronouncements at the Cathedral on the subject, he directed the churches of the Archdiocese of New York to join in prayer against continuance of the atheistic activities then in full swing in Soviet Russia.

Other denominations subsequently joined in this campaign of prayer. In this second line of activity the Cardinal directed a campaign in favor of clean plays upon the New York stage, and this, in which other denominations also cooperated, ran through many months.

For a part of 1931 he was hampered by weakness resulting from an attack of influenza early in the year, which necessitated a Southern trip, undertaken also in company with Mr. MacDonald. During the journey, which took him to Texas, he was received by the Governor of that State and was invited to address the Senate of Texas from the rostrum of its chamber. The occasion was said to be the first time in the history of the South that a Catholic prelate had received such an invitation.

After his return to New York in improved health, he was nominated by the Pope in August, 1931, to be a member of the Congregation for the Oriental Church, one of the twelve congregations charged with the administration of the wide activities of the faith. During the latter part of the year he made arrangements, subsequently carried out, to head an American delegation to the Dublin Eucharistic Congress of 1932.

Before attending the Eucharistic Congress, however, he left New York for another journey, beginning in January, 1932. This took him to the Bahama Islands, which until that date had been administered as a part of the New York Archdiocese. In ceremonies at Nassau, the Cardinal inducted the Very Rev. John Bernard Kevenhoerster, who at one time had been in charge of a Bronx parish, as the first Prefect-Apostolic to the islands, and confirmed other officials of the new insular church administration.

The same political neutrality which Cardinal Hayes had exhibited in 1928 came to the fore again in 1932 after former Governor Smith, one of the most prominent members of the Catholic laity, announced that he was again a candidate for the Democratic nomination which President Roosevelt, then Governor, was seeking. Shortly after Mr. Smith had announced his candidacy and denounced Mr. Roosevelt as a demagogue, the two

sat at the left and right of the Cardinal at a Catholic Charities luncheon.

Approved of New Deal

Cardinal Hayes frequently has expressed approval of President Roosevelt and his New Deal measures and, at the closing dinner of the Conference of Catholic Charities in October, 1933, the President sat between the Cardinal and the Apostolic Delegate. It has been said that Cardinal Hayes regarded the National Recovery Act as a practical application of the tenets of social justice outlined in the two great labor encyclicals, Pope Leo XIII's "Rerum Novarum" and Pope Pius XI's "Quadragesimo Anno."

In the Spring of 1934, shortly after he had been guest of honor at a testimonial dinner marking his completion of twenty years as a Bishop, fifteen years as an Archbishop and ten years as a Cardinal, he consecrated another native son of New York, the Most Rev. Stephen Joseph Donahue as Bishop Auxiliary of New York. He was assisted in the solemn ceremony at St. Patrick's Cathedral by two Archbishops. Two other Archbishops, forty-eight Bishops and thirty-seven monsignori attended the service.

Although he abhorred war and the warlike spirit, Cardinal Hayes did not adopt the extreme pacifist position, holding that preparation for adequate defense was the best insurance against attack. In June, 1934, when the fleet visited New York for a Presidential review, he told 2,000 officers and men that the ships now at anchor, though terrifying in appearance and latent power were "the best guaranty of peace, good-will and security." A pastoral letter issued the following Spring, calling upon Christians to fight communism, deplored the saber-rattling by rulers of foreign nations. The letter said:

"Justice—social, economic, legal, international—is the cry of the hour while we witness the most terrifying warlike preparations of all history by rulers and nations who pay no attention to the mandate of the Prince of Peace, 'Love thy neighbor.' "

One of his greatest triumphs came in September, 1935, when as the personal representative of Pope Pius XI he received the homage of more than 100,000 Catholics attend-

ing the National Eucharistic Congress at Cleveland. Accompanying him to the congress were 250 distinguished clergymen and prominent laymen, including former Governor Smith.

A year later Cardinal Hayes spoke in a short-wave broadcast to many nations in celebration of the seventy-ninth birthday of Pope Pius XI. He acclaimed the Pope as "God's special gift to the church and the world, during these critical times."

"Justly may we acclaim Pope Pius XI a great Pontiff of the Most High," he said, "a far-seeing prophet of man's place in time and eternity, a heroic shepherd, a supreme leader of men in human and divine relations, spokesman of the Prince of Peace, an incomparable Father whose every thought is to promote the best interests, temporal and spiritual, of mankind."

As a preacher Cardinal Hayes was very popular. He had a strong, vibrant and perfectly modulated voice, which gave an impression of singular charm. His wide interest in and thorough grasp of public affairs the world over, his cogent, logical presentation and his unusually keen sense of humor made him one of the city's most popular preachers.

One of the outstanding features of Cardinal Hayes's character was his perfect poise. It was said that no one ever saw him angry or upset. An example of this poise, often recounted, occurred at the beginning of the war, when a bomb was exploded in St. Patrick's Cathedral. Cardinal Hayes was at work in the chancel office with a priest, who jumped from his seat in excitement. The Cardinal did not move a muscle. The priest ran out, hatless and coatless, although it was a Winter day. After some time, when all the clergy had rushed in and the police were in control, Cardinal Hayes appeared, quietly directed the closing of the cathedral to the public, arranged other details and then, with his usual calm, returned to the work that had been so violently interrupted.

Although slight of build, Cardinal Hayes made a singularly dignified appearance, and one totally lacking in hauteur or stiffness. His kindly face, with an irrepressible twinkle of humor in his eyes, inspired far more affection than it did awe. He was, indeed, considered to have been one of the most popular and beloved prelates that New York has ever known.

September 5, 1938

Mgr. Lavelle Eulogizes Cardinal Over Radio; Calls Archdiocese a 'Model of Contentment'

Mgr. Michael J. Lavelle, pastor of St. Patrick's Cathedral and Vicar General of the Archdiocese of New York, close friend and associate of Patrick Cardinal Hayes, extolled the prelate last night in a memorial radio broadcast over Station WOR.

"He was a very able administrator, with an admirable mixture of kindness, strength and resource," Mgr. Lavelle declared.

"For eighteen years he was Archbishop, and fourteen years Cardinal, and his rule was fruitful, happy and progressive. He held the

hearts of the clergy, the religious and the Catholic people and held the respect of the people at large. I don't remember having heard or seen a criticism of him in the newspapers. The diocese is a model of content, work, cooperation and happiness.

"He was a great educator, prominent in the Legion of Decency, and the establisher and completer of the great Catholic Charities of the Archbishop of New York. He was interested in public affairs but never handled politics in any way. His

life was an inspiration and his memory is a benediction."

The Rev. Dr. Joseph A. Daly of St. Gregory's Church, 138 West Ninetieth Street, paid tribute to Cardinal Hayes as "a truly great churchman and a truly great American."

Between speakers the announcer read passages from Cardinal Hayes's writings. On the subject of death, he quoted the prelate as follows:

"We should never fail to remember that time was given to us for eternal years and not for time's own sake. The end of time for each one of us is death; for the world, destruction. Nothing more certain than that the night cometh when

we can no longer live or move or have our being in time."

Of God, Cardinal Hayes wrote: "It is the sublimity of folly to deny the existence of God. The perfection, the infinity, the immensity, the incomprehensibility, the majesty, the omnipotence, the beauty and the goodness of God are engraved on the hearts of men and are proclaimed by the glory of the firmament above and the earth beneath. His name is written in indelible, clear and unmistakable letters upon all that we behold with our eyes and reflect on with our minds."

The program also consisted of the reading of tributes sent by Governor Lehman, former Governor Alfred E. Smith, Bishop William T. Manning of the Protestant Episcopal Church and others.

September 5, 1938

CATHOLIC BISHOPS PLEAD FOR POLAND

De-Christianization of It and Other States Would Be 'Ever Resented,' They Say

Special to THE NEW YORK TIMES.

WASHINGTON, Nov. 16—American Catholics would "ever resent" their countries being made a party to the de-Christianization of Po-

land, the Baltic States and neighboring Catholic lands, the Catholic Archbishops and Bishops of the United States said in a resolution adopted today at their general annual meeting at the Catholic University of America.

The resolution extended the commiseration of the Bishops of the United States to "their brother Bishops, the clergy, the religious and the faithful" of all the wartorn countries of Europe. Circumstances, it added, excited in them a particular anxiety for the fate of religion among their fellow-Catholics in Poland, the Baltic States and neighboring lands.

"Cruel, inhuman aggressors are now heaping upon them frightful

atrocities," it states, "and unprecedented barbarities. The exercise of their religion is either denied them or is so thwarted as to be practically impossible. And dark fear is now in them that when victory comes their hope of a better day with security in the enjoyment of their civil and religious freedoms will not be realized."

"To them the Bishops of the United States, with their clergy and people, extend deep sympathy with the prayerful hope that the strong, victorious nations in charity and justice will give them succor in their sufferings and the full enjoyment of their indisputable rights," the resolution says.

"American Catholics would ever

resent their country's being made a party to the de-Christianization of historic Catholic peoples."

In another resolution the Bishops expressed opposition to the "immediate passage" of legislation looking toward compulsory military training of all the male youth of the United States.

The Most Rev. Michael J. Curley, Archbishop of Baltimore and of Washington, presided at the session.

An address commemorating the twenty-fifth anniversary of the National Catholic Welfare Conference was made by Archbishop John T. McNicholas of Cincinnati.

November 17, 1944

HIGH MASS SINGING BY LAITY IS GAINING

Plain Chant Teacher-Training Began at Manhattanville in '18 Under Papal Program

A far-reaching reform in worship is gaining ground in the Roman Catholic Church, it was ascertained yesterday. It consists of progressive restoration of singing by the laity of the common parts of the high mass as was done in the early, formative years of the church.

The ideal set by papal directives lately has been that there shall be congregational singing at high mass. From the eleventh to the nineteenth century the early practice was dissipated, despite the collating of ancient chant melodies

in the sixth century attributed to Pope Gregory the Great. This labor resulted in the widespread use of the Gregorian plain chant, which reached the height of its popularity from the seventh to the tenth century.

In succeeding centuries secular usages brought in corrupt practices until papal decrees prohibited them. Pope Leo XIII in 1884 decreed against "themes from theatrical or dance music, from popular songs, love songs, comic songs" and noisy music instruments.

Restored by Benedictines

By that time Benedictine monks in Europe were searching monasteries for manuscripts of the ancient Gregorian chants and restoring them to use. With a greeting from Pope Leo for "the hoped-for betterment of divine worship" and the endorsement of Pope Pius X there arose the modern liturgical movement. This includes definite use of Gregorian chants and the promoting of practical knowledge

and appreciation of the church's liturgy.

Since 1918 the Pius X School of Liturgical Music under Mother Aileen Cohalan at Manhattanville College of the Sacred Heart, Convent Avenue and 133d Street, has taken the lead in providing teachers and conducting summer sessions to instruct in plain chant. Several demonstrations have taken place. Others are planned.

Archbishop Richard J. Cushing of Boston will pontificate at masses at 10 A. M. on May 12 and 19 in the Mechanics Building in Boston, where more than 2,700 young singers will be heard in the mass on each occasion. Children from 171 elementary schools of the archdiocese will participate in the first of these and students from eighty of its high schools will sing at the second.

First in New England

The complete program is in charge of the Rev. Cornelius T. H. Sherlock, director of the department of education of the Boston

archdiocese, and is the first extensive demonstration in New England. The project is the outgrowth of teacher training sessions of the Pius X school the past four summers at Newton College of the Sacred Heart, Boston, where a fifth will be held next August.

The project has required semimonthly sessions since September at Emmanuel College, Boston, for 500 religious school teachers under direction of the Rev. Russell H. Davis of St. John's Seminary, Brighton, Mass. He is being assisted in training these teachers to pass the instruction on to students by the Misses Margaret Gleeson and Margaret Leddy of the Pius X school.

The thirty-fourth summer session of the Pius X school will be held June 29-Aug. 10 with courses for men and women at Manhattanville College. Solemn high masses will be sung on Fridays except June 30 throughout the session.

May 7, 1950

POPE ALLOWS RITES IN ENGLISH IN U. S.

Approves Use in Sacraments of Matrimony, Baptism and Extreme Unction

By ARNALDO CORTESI
Special to The New York Times.

ROME, Aug. 17—The Vatican, through the Sacred Congregation of Rites, has granted clergy in the United States, the optional right to administer the sacraments of baptism, matrimony and extreme unction in English.

This concession, which was said in Rome to be proof of the Pope's particular goodwill toward the United States, was granted at the request of the Episcopacy in the United States. It applies only to the territory of the United States

and not to other English-speaking countries such as Canada.

Apart from missionary areas, similar concessions have been made to only three other countries: France, Germany and Italy. In 1941 and 1942 they were made to missions in New Guinea, China, Japan, Indochina, India, Indonesia and Africa. The missions received permission to translate the Roman ritual into the local languages, reserving Latin only for a few essential formulas. In 1949, moreover, the use of Mandarin Chinese was permitted in China for the whole of the mass, except the canon, which must continue to be recited in Latin.

Vatican circles noted that in practice the Roman Catholic Church often had shown an accommodating spirit where the liturgical use of modern languages was concerned but that it always adhered to these fundamental principles:

¶That the use and even the exclusive use in liturgy of languages incomprehensible to all

or many of faithful is not an error.

¶That the language used in liturgy should never become a vehicle for the expression of political or nationalist passions but on the contrary should be a supranational bond between Catholic communities, even if they belong to different racial groups and between Catholic communities and the Holy See.

¶That a special dignity and appropriateness for liturgical purposes is recognized for ancient languages that, even if more or less dead today, have been consecrated by centuries of liturgical use.

Church Here Defers Comment

Officials at the Roman Catholic Chancery here declined to comment on the new dispensation until official confirmation had been received. Msgr. Gustav J. Schultheiss, secretary to Cardinal Spellman, said the request had been sent to the Vatican after the Congregation of Bishops in Washington, D. C., last November.

Other church sources said that in the sacraments of baptism and

matrimony the use of English, or the vernacular of any particular country, had always been the tradition in the essential parts of the ceremony.

In matrimony, the two parties, who are actually the ministers of the sacrament with the priest as witness and ratifier, manifest their consent externally in the vernacular, and this is the essence of the sacrament, the sources said.

Change Sought 150 Years

MILWAUKEE, Wis., Aug. 17 (UP)—The Rev. A. F. Wilmes, secretary of the National Conference on Catholic Liturgy, said the use of English in Catholic liturgy had been discussed for about 150 years, but this was the first time permission had been granted. About 1,100 Catholic clergy and laymen are attending the fifteenth national conference on liturgy here.

A Milwaukee concern, the Bruce Publishing Co., has been selected as the exclusive publisher in the United State of the book that will contain the English version of the sacraments and blessings.

August 18, 1954

CATHOLICS HEAR AUTHOR

Many Roman Catholics are attracted to liberal political theories today only because they are embarrassed by their religious affiliation, William F. Buckley Jr. said yesterday in an address at the annual communion breakfast of the Catholic Institute of the Press.

Mr. Buckley, co-author of "McCarthy and his Enemies," a defense of the Senator, spoke on "Controversy and the Catholic." The breakfast was held at the Plaza Hotel.

Mr. Buckley condemned the attitude that seems to say: "Although we are Catholics, we are progressive." "A Catholic," he said, "should take a position only because he feels it is valid and compelling."

April 23, 1956

'CERTAIN' CLASSES BANNED BY BISHOP

By SETH S. KING

Special to The New York Times.

WICHITA, Kan., Sept. 2 — Roman Catholic students from the diocese of southeastern Kansas have been forbidden to enroll in most undergraduate psychology and philosophy courses offered at non-Catholic colleges and universities.

Bishop Mark K. Carroll, head of the diocese, has charged that many of these courses constitute a form of "brainwashing" that endangers a student's faith in his church and his loyalty to his country.

In a recent pastoral letter, Bishop Carroll directed all Roman Catholic youths in his diocese who were planning to enter non-Catholic colleges anywhere to discuss their educational plans with the local pastors and, in many instances, with the ishop himself.

"I have done this with the specific purpose of warning them against certain courses which are inimical to their patriotism and faith," he said today in an interview.

In past years students in his diocese had been told to seek advice before entering non-Catholic schools and there was nothing unusual in his position, the Bishop asserted.

His directive this year was much more emphatic, he said, because he had become alarmed by the findings of psychiatrists who had studied the cases of those American prisoners in Korea who had defected to the enemy.

The attitudes of these prisoners were the results of the educations they had received, Bishop Carroll said. Their educations, in most cases, were "non-religious or even irreligious," he added.

"Here at home we have a very sneaky, sly form of brainwashing going on in our secular colleges," he declared. "It is not approved by the boards of regents or by the college presidents. But it is due to individual professors of psychology and philosophy in particular, as well as some professors of sociology, history, and economics."

The civilized world had denounced the tactics of Communist brainwashing, he said.

"But the American public at large seems to be somnolent and totally indifferent to the brainwashers at home who are deliberately, in the name of academic freedom, destroying the potential services our educated youth must give to our country if it is to survive as a democracy," he declared.

Bishop Carroll said he had not singled out any particular course at a specific university, nor did he aim his objections at any individual professor.

"But as pastor of the Wichita area, I have a responsibility to my people to warn them against things that might take their faith from them," he said.

He said he had found some students who had gone away to secular colleges filled with high ideals and deep religious faith return "as thoroughly brainwashed as they could be."

"If you tell our young people that they have no God-given dignity or moral responsibilities," he said, "then we shouldn't arch our eyebrows if their actions emulate the antics of a barnyard."

Bishop Carroll, who for fifteen years taught in Roman Catholic high schools in St. Louis before becoming the Bishop of Southeastern Kansas, said he particularly objected to the methods employed by many teachers of psychology in secular colleges.

"The modern psychologist who regards God as a nebulous cloud instead of a person is going to consider his students in class as a veterinarian would treat sick cattle," he declared.

Bishop Carroll said too many secular colleges were stressing the wrong subjects in their curricular. It was clear, he said, from the study of the Korean prisoners that many subjects considered so important—such as physics, chemistry, foreign languages, and art—were of no avail in facing the ordeal of brainwashing.

"But the soldiers, whether Jews, Protestants or Catholics, who were well grounded in their faith were the only ones who had the intelligence and courage to remain loyal to the United States," he declared.

The advice he has given to those students who have conferred with him depended on the individual's age, his background and the curriculum he wished to follow, Bishop Carroll said. A few of the more mature students "who could separate the wheat from the chaff" would be free to take courses in psychology and philosophy or in history and sociology that might otherwise be objectionable, he asserted.

Bishop Carroll was asked what his attitude would be if it were necessary for a young Roman Catholic student to take a course in beginning psychology or philosophy in order to win a degree.

"That would be too bad," he replied. "My answer would probably be 'no.' There are some psychology and philosophy courses that Roman Catholics would fail anyway, because they could not write a passing test paper and remain true to their religious teachings."

Bishop Carroll's diocese covers the southeastern quarter of the state of Kansas, with the chancery in Wichita. About 500 Roman Catholic students in this diocese will attend non-Catholic schools this fall, he said.

September 3, 1956

CATHOLIC CHURCH HELD 'DISTORTED'

By GEORGE DUGAN

The public image of the Roman Catholic Church in the United States is 'still the view of an immigrant, even foreign, institution of growing immensity only gradually reconciling itself to the American way," Msgr. Francis J. Lally said yesterday.

This picture, he observed, "is not at all pretty and surely not an honest one." Msgr. Lally is editor of The Pilot, official newspaper of the Archdiocese of Boston. He addressed the annual communion breakfast of the Ladies of Charity of New York Catholic Charities in the Waldorf-Astoria Hotel.

Many non-Catholics, Msgr. Lally declared, see the church in terms of power rather than salvation. And beyond this, he noted, "most of our neighbors only see the Catholic Church on special occasions."

"They see our colorful processions and our dignified liturgy, which have something of the historic about them, and they are impressed and even wonder if we are not really relics of a past age, out of step with the twentieth century," he continued.

"They see us most often in our negative moods; they see us condemning and forbidding, they see us as censorious and authoritarian.

"To be sure there is a place and necessity for this in the life of the church—the Christ who drove the money-changers from the temple and cursed the barren fig tree is as real as the Christ of Bethlehem and the beatitudes.

"But to see Christ only in anger is not to see the whole Christ, and to see His church only in its disciplinary degrees is not to see the whole church either."

The church, her doctrines and her devotions are so little known, he remarked, as to make misunderstandings "almost inevitable."

An Appeal for Correction

He called on the laity to rectify the "distorted" public image of the church.

"Ask yourself in candor what your own neighbors see when they see in you the Catholic Church," he said. "Do they see a spirit narrow and interested only in itself and its own necessities; or do they see a great universal charity which knows no bounds and sets no boundaries?

"Do they see in you a life filled up with little pieties and most conscious of religious duties; or do they see a soul on fire with Pentecost and spreading that fire in all directions? In short, do we present the church, each one of us, in the manner that Christ Himself revealed it?"

In another address, Miss Jane M. Hoey, former director of the Federal Bureau of Public Assistance, Department of Health, Education and Welfare, urged the Catholic laity to become "capable, competent workers in religious activities and become able to take their places in society."

More than 1,300 women attended the breakfast. The Mayor and Mrs. Wagner were among the guests. The breakfast followed mass at St. Patrick's Cathedral.

October 4, 1959

CARDINAL RONCALLI ELECTED POPE; VENETIAN, 76, REIGNS AS JOHN XXIII; THOUSANDS HAIL HIM AT ST. PETER'S

11 BALLOTS TAKEN

New Pontiff Elevates Conclave Secretary to Cardinalate

By ARNALDO CORTESI
Special to The New York Times.

ROME, Oct. 28 — Angelo Giuseppe Cardinal Roncalli, Patriarch of Venice, was elevated to the Papacy this afternoon. He will be 77 years old Nov. 25.

He will sit on the throne of St. Peter as the 262d Supreme Pontiff of the Roman Catholic Church and will rule the Church as sovereign under the name of John XXIII. No Sovereign Pontiff has used the name John since 1334, when John XXII died.

The successor to Pope Pius XII, who died Oct. 9, was elected on the eleventh ballot by fifty-one Cardinals assembled in conclave since Saturday. He was named as the third day of the voting in a walled enclosure in the Vatican was drawing to a close.

The conclave that elevated him was one of the fifteen shortest held since the Papacy returned to Rome from Avignon, France, in the second half of the fourteenth century. Fifty-nine conclaves have been held since then.

Associated Press Radiophoto

THE NEW PONTIFF, Pope John XXIII, raising his hand in blessing yesterday on a balcony of St. Peter's Basilica. He appeared before throng an hour after he was elected.

Coronation Likely Nov. 9

Cardinal Roncalli became Supreme Pontiff at the very moment when he replied affirmatively on being asked by the Dean of the Sacred College of Cardinals whether he accepted his election. He uttered the Latin word "Accepto" ("I accept") a few minutes before 5 P. M. [11 A. M. New York time]. He was invested with the full powers of the Papacy from that instant, though his reign will be counted from the day of his coronation, expected to be Nov. 9.

One hour after his election, the new Pope appeared on the outer balcony of St. Peter's Basilica and gave his first blessing as a Pope to the thousands gathered in St. Peter's Square. Before and after the blessing the crowd sang hymns. The hymns sung were "Christus

AS PAPAL NUNCIO IN PARIS: Angelo Giuseppe Cardinal Roncalli, who became Pope yesterday, was Archbishop when, on New Year's Eve, 1947, he read diplomats' greetings to Vincent Auriol, then President of France.

Vincit" (Christ Conquers) and the Te Deum.

New Cardinal Named

As the first act of his Pontificate, Pope John XXIII conferred the Cardinal's red hat on Msgr. Alberto di Jorio, who had acted as secretary of the conclave. The new Pope did so by removing his own Cardinal's biretta from his head and placing it on that of Msgr. di Jorio.

This was a return to tradition, since in the past all Popes were wont to reward the secretary of the conclave. However, Pius XII omitted to do so.

The new Pope also asked all Cardinals to remain in conclave until tomorrow morning, which they did.

That the Catholic Church again had a head was conveyed to watchers in St. Peter's Square by the white smoke emanating from a stovepipe above the roof of the Sistine Chapel, where the voting took place. Immediately the crowd shouted "Viva il Papa!" (Long live the Pope!). Many thousands started running across the square to take up positions as near as possible to the balcony from which the new Pope was to impart his blessing. The white smoke signal issued forth at 5:08 P. M.

Fifty-five minutes after the white smoke signal Nicola Cardinal Canali, Senior Cardinal Deacon, appeared on the brightly lighted balcony of St. Peter's.

In a voice so broken with emotion that it was difficult to understand what he said, he shouted the traditional Latin phrase "Nuncio vobis gaudium magnum: Habemus Papam" (I announce to you a great joy: we have a Pope). He followed by naming the Cardinal who had been elected Pope and with the name by which the new Pontiff is to be known.

Thousands upon thousands streamed into St. Peter's Square as soon as the white smoke announced that a new Pope had been elected. Spectators from all over Rome hurried to the square though a strike had halted all streetcars and buses. Automobiles, making what haste they could toward the Vatican, caused a gigantic traffic jam for miles around. The crowd in St. Peter's Square was only moderate when the white smoke revealed that a new Pope had been chosen. It was enormous by the time Cardinal Canali announced the new Pope's name.

Night had fallen by the time the new Pope arrived on St. Peter's balcony. Street lights had been turned on half an hour before the new Pontiff's public appearance.

Excitement in the crowd grew as preparations being made inside and outside St. Peter's told the crowd that the new Pope would appear at any minute. There were cheers when a regiment of Italian Carabinieri, with its band and regimental flag, marched into the square to give military honors to the new Pope.

There was a shout when a

number of attendants hung a magnificent tapestry from the balcony of St. Peter's. It was the same as the one Pius XII had used. It has a wide red border and in the center is the coat of arms of the late Pope on a white background.

Another shout greeted the switching on of lights in the enormous Hall of Benedictions above the portico of the basilica.

Cries of "Viva il Papa" were renewed and St. Peter's Square became a sea of waving handkerchiefs when it became evident that the new Pope was on his way to the balcony.

Cardinals Precede New Pope

Pope John XXIII appeared before the crowd almost unexpectedly. The enormous door leading from the Hall of Benedictions to the balcony was thrown open and two Cardinals walked out. They were Eugene Cardinal Tisserant, dean of the Sacred College, and Clemente Cardinal Micara, the late Pope's vicar general for the diocese of Rome. Behind them came a crucifer holding aloft a golden papal cross. Behind them were surpliced ecclesiastical members of the Papal Court.

Then the new Pope walked out onto the balcony with a rapid step. He was such a simple and unassuming figure that at first he was not recognized. He stood on the balcony before a mighty cheer rent the air. The waving of handkerchiefs increased. The Pope acknowledged the applause by waving a friendly greeting.

Over his white Papal cassock the Pope wore a white rochet, a linen-and-lace vestment resembling a surplice. Over his shoulders he wore the mozzetta, a short red cape edged with ermine. Around his neck and falling down the front of his body was a Papal stole of red silk, richly embroidered with gold. He also wore a skull cap.

The wild cheering and shouting subsided and was followed by a hush. To most of those in St. Peter's Square the Pope was a tiny figure dwarfed by distance and seen over several acres of tossing heads. He stood out clearly in the floodlights shining upon him and was framed by the door leading into the Hall of Benedictions.

The new Pope raised his white-clad arms to Heaven while the people in the square dropped to their knees. The new Pope's voice, firm and strong over loudspeakers, sounded melodious as he chanted the Latin benediction "Urbi et Orbi" ("to the city and the world").

While ecclesiastical members of the papal court sang responses, the Pope recited the Litany of the Saints and prayed that God remit the sins of erring man and lead him to eternal life. He asked for "indulgence, absolution and the remission" of sin and then intoned the benediction proper.

Most of those in the kneeling crowd crossed themselves and some women held their infant children with extended arms over the heads of the crowd as though to expose them more

Associated Press

ARCHBISHOP Roncalli in 1934. From 1925 to 1944 he was a Papal representative in the Balkans and Mideast.

CREATED A CARDINAL: The future Pontiff as he received the Red Hat at Castel Gandolfo in 1953.

GENIAL ENVOY: Cardinal Roncalli at a diplomatic gathering in Paris in February of 1953. In January of that year he had been made a Cardinal at Castel Gandolfo.

AT SHRINE OF LOURDES, in France, Cardinal Roncalli took part in centennial ceremonies this year. He served as the apostolic delegate to the Marian Congress.

thoroughly to the Pope's blessing.

The Pope intoned "May the blessing of Almighty God, the Father, the Son and the Holy Ghost descend upon you and remain with you always."

The ecclesiastics attending the new Pope had hardly finished singing "Amen" when the crowd was on its feet again, cheering and shouting. The Pope watched the crowd for a brief period, making repeated gestures of salutation. Then he turned quickly and disappeared into the Hall of Benediction.

A few minutes later the tapestry hanging from the balcony was removed, the door was closed and the lights were extinguished.

It is understood that Pope John XXIII led all other candidates in the balloting that occurred during the morning in the conclave. On the second of the morning ballots he was only a few votes short of the thirty-five he needed for election. It was said to be clear to all Cardinals that he would be elected on the first afternoon ballot. As expected, he got almost all the votes cast as soon as the balloting was resumed.

Voting Results Announced

The result of the voting was announced by the three Cardinal tellers, whose task was to check the votes read out by the three Cardinal scrutineers and to keep a tally of how many votes each candidate had obtained.

When it was announced that Cardinal Roncalli had obtained

more than the required minimum of votes, Alfredo Cardinal Ottaviani, the junior Cardinal Deacon, threw open the door of the Sistine Chapel and summoned Msgr. Enrico Dante, Prefect of Pontifical Ceremonies.

Meanwhile, Cardinal Tisserant had approached Cardinal Roncalli and asked him in Latin "Do you accept your canonically performed election as supreme Pontiff?" Cardinal Roncalli made an affirmative reply and immediately acquired absolute jurisdiction over the Roman Catholic Church everywhere in the world.

At the same time as the Pope accepted the Papacy all Cardinals who had participated in the election lowered the violet canopies over the thrones on which they had sat during the voting. Only the canopy over the new Pope's throne remained in position. Thus it became his first papal throne and he remained seated on it to receive the first "obedience" of the Cardinals and the Papal Court.

Cardinal Tisserant then approached the new Pope again and asked "Quo nomine vis vocari?"

[By what name do you wish to be called?]

A record of the Pope's reply that he wished to be called John XXIII was written on parchment by the Prefect of Pontifical Ceremonies, with the Secretary of the Sacred College and two masters of ceremonies acting as witnesses.

October 29, 1958

CATHOLIC COUNCIL CALLED FOR 1962

Special to The New York Times.

ROME, Dec. 25—Pope John XXIII formally announced today the convocation in 1962 of the Roman Catholic Church's twenty-first Ecumenical Council.

The announcement was contained in a Papal Bull the Pontiff signed in Clementine Hall in the Vatican.

Later, in a Christmas address preceding his Apostolic blessing, the Pope expressed hope that the New Year would see "the end of all wars, the calming of all discord and a world united in a single cry to heaven, a cry of fraternal and filial love: 'Our Father, Who art in heaven.'"

A steady, heavy downpour held the crowd in St. Peter's Square to two or three thousand. Most of the crowd huddled under umbrellas, but others watched from automobiles. The rain also canceled plans to have the Pope speak from the balcony above the Basilica's main doors.

Second Vatican Council

The Ecumenical Council will be known as Vatican II. The Bull, "Humanae Salutis," derives its name from the first words of the Latin text.

The opening phrase reads, "humanae salutis reparator" (Redeemer of human salvation).

This council will be the second to be held in the Vatican. Pope Pius IX convoked the first Ecumenical Council to be held at the Vatican in December, 1869. The council was suspended in July, 1870, because of the outbreak of war between France and Prussia, after having defined the dogma of Papal infallibility. As a result of this dogma, when a Pope speaks as a "teacher" or "shepherd" on matters of faith and morals, the Roman Catholic Church regards him as infallible.

Pope John, in issuing his Bull, spoke to a world "lost, confused and anxious under the continual threat of new frightful conflicts." He said the Ecumenical Council was being called "to offer an opportunity for all men of goodwill to turn their thoughts and resolutions to peace: a peace that can and must come, above all, from spiritual and supernatural realities, from human intelligence and conscience enlightened and guided by God, Creator and Redeemer of mankind."

In giving his reasons for calling the Council, the Pope said:

"The Church today is watching a society in crisis. While mankind is at the threshold of a new era, grave and immense tasks await the church just as in the most tragic epochs of its history."

The Pope said it was the duty of the church to bring the modern world into "contact with the vivifying and eternal energy of the Gospel."

He described the world of today as one "that exalts its victories" in science and technology and as one that "also bears the consequences of temporal order that some people seek to reorganize without God."

Modern society, the Pope said in the Bull is characterized by great material progress without corresponding moral progress. He said this enfeebled the desire for spiritual values and gave rise to an almost exclusive search for worldly pleasures. "And there is an entirely new and disconcerting fact: the existence of militant atheism operating on a world-wide scale" the Pope said.

These reasons and "an urgent duty to call together our children to give the church the opportunity to contribute more efficaciously to the solutions of the problems of the modern age" caused him to call the Ecumenical Council, the Pope said.

Plans for the Council were disclosed by Pope John Jan. 21, 1959. The issuance of the Bull made the convocation of the Council official.

The Bull was read in the four basilicas of Rome by prelates of the Church. It was first read at St. Peter's and then at St. Paul's Outside the Walls, St. John Lateran and St. Mary Major.

The term "Bull" derives from the Latin word for lead, with which major documents of the church are stamped. Minor documents usually bear a wax seal. The term has never achieved official recognition, but has been used since the thirteenth century.

The crowds waiting in the rain for a glimpse of the Pope were rewarded when he went twice to a window of his apartment to wave.

During his Christmas day discourse, the Pope was dressed in flowing gold and white robes. He wore his triple-tiered crown.

For his Apostolic blessing, "Urbi et Orbi" to the city of Rome and to the world, Pope John put on a white skullcap.

He appeared tired, but in good health. Although he cleared his throat several times during his talk, his voice was firm. He looked grave as he spoke.

Vatican Council II will concern itself in the main with the internal affairs of the Roman Catholic Church. Considerable time will be devoted to church discipline, wider use of the vernacular in place of Latin, the Catholic missionary enterprise over the world and the possibility of additional reforms in the liturgy.

Students of the Council in the United States have predicted that requests for new definitions of dogma might consume weeks of discussion.

Overshadowing all these in terms of public interest will be what Pope John once described as a "gentle invitation" to Eastern Orthodoxy and Protestantism to "seek and find that unity for which Jesus Christ prayed so ardently to His Heavenly Father."

Church leaders here do not expect the Council to pave the way for the foreseeable reunion of the three great branches of Christendom.

What they do predict is the emergence of a warmer climate of friendship, greater cooperation in areas not directly concerned with doctrine, more discussion of basic points of agreement rather than disagreement and an increasing number of friendly contacts among Christian leaders.

In the last regard it seems certain that official observers representing the Protestant and Eastern Orthodox churches will attend an Ecumenical Council of the Roman Catholic Church for the first time. They will, in effect, return the visit made last month by five Roman Catholic priests to the third assembly of the world Council of Churches in New Delhi, India.

The Roman Catholic Church's first Vatican Council opened Dec. 8, 1869. When it adjourned seven months later the Italians had seized Rome from the Pope. By then, the Council had issued pronouncements on faith and reason, materialism, atheism and pantheism.

It also defined Papal infallibility, which is probably the principle barrier that must be crossed before Christendom can be reunited. Some Roman Catholics say that the calling of the Council is a clear indication that the Pope wishes to confer with his episcopal colleagues in a democratic manner and that, should he speak ex-cathedra, or as Supreme Pontiff, it will be after such consultation.

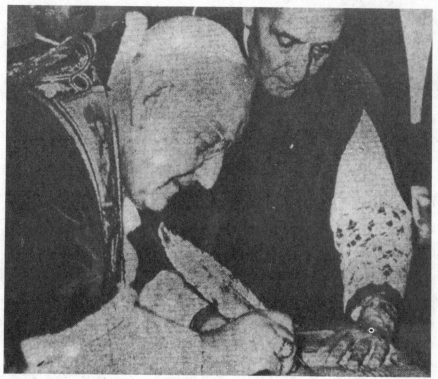

Associated Press Radiophoto

SIGNS PAPAL BULL: Pope John XXIII signs document at Vatican proclaiming that a General Ecumenical Council of the Roman Catholic Church will be held in 1962. Assisting the Pontiff at the signing is Msgr. Enrico Dante, Prefect of Vatican Ceremonial office.

December 26, 1961

Catholic Scholar Warns Church To Relax Power Over U. S. Laity

By United Press International.

HELENA, Mont., May 27 — One of America's leading Roman Catholic scholars said today that the "virus" of anti-clericalism was appearing among Catholic laymen in the United States. He said it would spread unless clergymen relaxed "some of the power and authority they have been accustomed to exercise over the laity."

The statement by Msgr. John Tracy Ellis was clearly intended to bring into the open a long-simmering dispute over the proper role of the laity. It was made in a commencement address at Carroll College. Msgr. Ellis serves as Professor of Church History at the Catholic University of America in Washington.

"It would be a disservice to the church that we love were we to deny the presence in our midst of symptoms that suggest an anti-clerical sentiment hitherto unknown to American Catholics," Msgr. Ellis said.

He emphasized that he was not speaking of "the indefensible conduct of an insignificant minority of lay Catholics in New Orleans who have gained na-

tional notoriety by their defiance of the racial integration policies of their Archbishop." This was an allusion to the order by Archbishop Joseph Francis Rummel to integrate Catholic schools next fall.

The "strain on clerical-lay relations" that causes concern, he said, results from the frustrations "educated and loyal" Catholic laymen experience when they seek to obey the injunctions of recent Popes to take a more active role in the life of the church.

Msgr. Ellis served as domestic prelate of Pope Pius XII in 1955. He is a member of the American and American Catholic Historical associations, and has served as managing editor of The Catholic Historical Review.

In his speech, he noted that the educated Catholic layman of 1962 was "a quite different person from his unlettered immigrant grandparents of two or three generations ago." Although "fundamentally respectful of authority," he is not inclined to refer all problems to his priest, or to accept uncritically every decision made by the clergy, Msgr. Ellis said.

He added that today's Catholic wanted to have a real part in the life of the church, and was

seeking "a channel through which he may contribute his talents and special skills to the apostolate of his time."

Step Called Imperative

Unfortunately, Msgr. Ellis said, "too many laymen trying to find their place in apostolic action have experienced embarrassing encounters with a certain type of churchman who seems never to have heard Pius XII's exhortation" about giving the laity a bigger role in modern Catholicism.

"The continued harmony and good order of the Catholic community makes it imperative that the clergy be persuaded that present conditions call for a relaxing of some of the power and authority that they have been accustomed to exercise over the laity in matters not directly pertaining to their divine mission," he said.

As examples of how laymen may be given an appropriate voice in church affairs, Msgr. Ellis cited the Archdiocese of Montreal, where Paul-Emile Cardinal Leger has turned the entire Catholic school board over to laymen, and the diocese of Providence, R. I., where seven of eleven members of the school board are laymen.

Richard Cardinal Cushing, Archbishop of Boston, announced recently that laymen would participate in a synod of his archdiocese, which he plans to call after the Vatican Council in Rome.

The role of the laity has been the subject of considerable com-

ment in Catholic circles recently.

Warning in Editorial

The national Catholic magazine America warned in an editorial last month that evidences of anti-clerical sentiments were beginning to appear among laymen.

Bishop George W. Ahr of Trenton, in a public statement early this month, said, "In recent months there has been a vast volume of ill-considered, badly advised and poorly defined talk about the place of the laity in the church."

This talk, he added, "has already resulted in ignorant, insolent and arrogant criticism of the bishops by certain laymen." He did not identify the laymen.

Cardinal Leger, in an interview, May 12, said the time had come for clergy "to make an act of confidence" in laymen by giving them the opportunity to engage in a "healthy collaboration" with priests in such important matters as running Catholic schools.

Anti-clericalism, or hostility toward priests, has plagued the Catholic Church in Western Europe and Latin America for centuries.

Except for one flare-up before the Civil War, there has been very little overt anti-clericalism among American Catholics. On the contrary, the warm relationships between priests and laymen in this country have often been cited by Popes as a model for Catholics everywhere.

May 28, 1962

Use of Vernacular For Part of Mass Is Voted in Council

By MILTON BRACKER

Special to The New York Times

ROME, Oct. 9 — The Ecumenical Council placed strong emphasis today on the role of the parish priest. It also approved, as expected, the reform that will eventually authorize him to say parts of the mass in the vernacular—for example, English in the United States.

The Council voted another amendment. It will require the preaching of a homily, or sermon, at masses on Sundays or holy days when a congregation is present.

In the United States, an American Archbishop explained, sermons are not widely neglected, but they tend to diminish during the summer and are sometimes replaced by letters from the bishop.

Session's Eighth Meeting

The amendment also declared that a homily should properly deal with the "mysteries of the faith and the norms of Christian life," rather than be a topical address on morality not directly associated with the scriptural content of the mass.

In its eighth meeting since the resumed session was opened by Pope Paul VI Sept. 29, the Council, officially designated Vatican II, touched more on the regular churchgoing habits of Roman Catholics than it had at any previous meeting.

The Council was again doing

two things at once. It was continuing the debate on the structure of the church—the second chapter of the schema "De Ecclesia"—concerning the nature of the Church.

At the same time it was voting on amendments to the first chapter of the schema on liturgy, or public worship. The purpose of these amendments is to simplify the mass and to awaken interest in it.

Between yesterday and today, 12 of 19 amendments to the liturgy chapter were approved—all by votes of more than 2,200 to fewer than 100.

The Most Rev. Paul J. Hallinan, Archbishop of Atlanta, a member of the Liturgical Commission, said that the voting so far had reaffirmed "the hopes of those who were encouraged last fall" by the favorable preliminary vote on the unamended schema.

Archbishop Hallinan and his associates said, however, that the new votes were not definitive.

"People must not be encouraged to think that mass next Sunday or next Christmas will be in the vernacular," the American prelate said.

Even if the amended chapter becomes part of a final schema, and is promulgated by the Pope, it will still be up to the regional Bishops to put the reforms into effect.

At most, the language change will be authorized but not required. It would apply to most of the early part of the mass.

Translations Discussed

American and other English-speaking bishops have been meeting informally outside the Council to explore the question of texts and translations, with a view to coordinating any changes should the use of English be authorized.

One bishop put it this way: "We wouldn't want to come to the point where, in exchanging Latin for English, we found that we weren't sure if we were exchanging it for English, American, Canadian, Australian or South African."

Strictly speaking, the "vernacular" use of English varies in those countries.

The surprise of the day was not the vote on the liturgy amendments, but the insistence by several speakers that the Council, in concentrating on the role of the bishops, was forgetting the presbyterate, or priests who are not bishops.

In the United States there are about 55,000 such priests to fewer than 250 bishops. Parishioners generally have far more to do with their priest than with their bishop.

Bishop Antonio Anoveros of Cadiz, Spain, declared that priests were not "merely delegates of bishops." He said it might be advisable to consider "collegial," or collective, activity of the priests in the fields of government, teaching and liturgy.

One Council expert took this to mean that the priests might constitute a collective body around their bishops in the way, urged at this session, that the bishops would constitute a collective body around the Pope.

Half-Page to Priesthood

The Most Rev. William Conway, Archbishop of Armagh, Ireland, deplored the fact that the schema on church structure gave nine pages to the episcopate and seven to the laity, but only half a page to the priesthood.

He suggested a separate chapter on the priests' undertaking, according to the official summary, "to put the dignity of the priesthood into bolder relief."

The Most Rev. Dennis Hurley, Archbishop of Durban, South Africa, agreed with the view that the priesthood was treated "too casually" in the present schema. He said the priest was in effect the hands and feet, the eyes and ears, the "very voice" of the bishop, and thus was entitled to greater attention within the church.

Indeed, Archbishop Hurley added, it is through the priest that the voice of the bishop may be communicated to the flock either like "the trumpet of an archangel—or the reading of a telephone book."

The Rev. Gustave Weigel of Buffalo, present as an expert, voiced the view that there were two "evils" in trying to place the priest in relation to the bishop.

One, he said, was to "make the priest only the altar boy of the bishop" and the other was to consider him as a "bishop slightly reduced."

Vernacular Used in Some Areas

In some regions of the world parts of the mass are already said in the language of the country.

According to the Rev. C. J. McNaspy, a Jesuit who is an authority on liturgy and an editor of the Roman Catholic weekly America, parts of the Roman Catholic mass are said in Slavic, Syrian and Chinese, among others.

Father McNaspy said the Ecumenical Council's action is really a traditional step, in the sense that Latin came into use for the mass because most people in the area of Rome understood Latin in the fourth century. Previously it had been said in Greek; Latin was the vernacular.

October 10, 1963

Vatican II Re-educates The American Bishops

By JOHN COGLEY

ROME.

POPE JOHN XXIII, who was gentle even when he dropped bombshells, first spoke of calling an Ecumenical Council one gray day in Rome late in 1958. The Pontiff was alone with his Secretary of State, the late Domenico Cardinal Tardini, listening to depressing reports from the four corners of the world. In an age seemingly bent on self-destruction, his church appeared to be increasingly irrelevant and powerless. John looked down from his window to the almost empty square below. Then, as he told the story later, he turned slowly and told the Cardinal of his decision. In time, he was to condense its import into the single word *"aggiornamento"*—i.e., a bringing up to date.

Cardinal Tardini, although polite, was not enthusiastic. Councils, he knew from history, usually meant trouble for the church. Pope John was equally aware. He knew the stormy history of the consiliar gatherings, 20 in number, which frequently had ended in schismatic movements and ecclesiastical turmoil. But the benefits to be gained from calling in his bishops to take a new look at the church seemed to him to outweigh the dangers.

Tardini reported the Pope's "in-

JOHN COGLEY is a former editor of Commonweal now on the staff of the Fund for the Republic in Santa Barbara. He covered the Vatican Council for Religious News Service.

spiration" (as John called it) to other members of the Roman Curia (literally, "court")—the bureaucracy, headed by cardinals and staffed by high ecclesiastics, which is the church's equivalent of a political executive. The Curial conservatives seem to have hoped that, if the matter was not pressed, the Holy Father might forget about it. If necessary, they felt they could outwait his "interim" pontificate. Their attitude was summed up by the Archbishop of Genoa, Guiseppe Cardinal Siri: "Popes die, councils pass; the Curia remains."

"Sono nel sacco qui [I'm in a bag here]," John once told Cardinal Cushing of Boston. But each time the aged Pope was warned that preparations for the council might take years, he advanced the date for its convocation. On Oct. 11, 1962, the first session of Vatican II, as the Ecumenical Council is properly named, opened in St. Peter's Basilica. In attendance were the 2,300 prelates, known collectively as the Council Fathers—cardinals, archbishops, bishops and heads of religious orders.

Now the third session of the council has drawn to a conclusion. There will be a fourth next year. Curial conservatives still take a dim view of it. Some say jokingly that John, who died in 1963, remains in Purgatory because no decision can be made about him until St. Peter sees how Vatican II turns out.

The trend is clear, however. The

bishops have, to their own astonishment in many cases, taken part in a revolution — an attempt to "reform and renew" a church which, as Prof. Albert Outler, an American Methodist observer at the council, remarked, was long considered "irreformable" by non-Catholics and practically "unchangeable" by Catholics themselves. "I'm almost afraid to go home," one bishop admitted. "My priests will think that I have been turned into a heretic."

NO one has been more surprised than the American bishops. From their seminary days, they had been brought up to accept the Roman Curia's view of episcopal authority. They conceived of themselves as "agents" of the Pope — as his will was expressed through the Curia — rather than as members of an episcopal "college," albeit headed by the Pope, with responsibility for the universal welfare of the church.

Obedience, rather than leadership, was the virtue stressed in their training. A generation ago, any seminarian who voiced criticism of the church such as has become commonplace in the consiliar hall of St. Peter's would soon learn that he belonged elsewhere. A few "radicals" slipped through the net from time to time, but only in the rarest cases could one of them be found later in the ranks of the hierarchy. And those few were usually destined to become "long-time-no-see" bishops,

HIERARCHY—Increasingly, American prelates at the third session of the Ecumenical Council found themselves taking liberal stands. At their head are these five cardinals: from left, Cushing of Boston, Meyer of Chicago, Ritter of St. Louis, all considered "progressives," Spellman of New York, regarded as a "middle-of-the-roader," and McIntyre of Los Angeles, a "conservative."

like the stanchly liberal Auxiliary Bishop of Chicago, Archbishop Bernard J. Sheil, who is among the senior members of the hierarchy but has never had his own diocese. His present title of archbishop, conferred by Pope John, is honorary.

Furthermore, members of the American hierarchy have rarely been chosen from among the more intellectual priests from whom fresh ideas might come. The Catholic Church in America owes its strength to generations of "brick and mortar" bishops, but there were few — at least before the Council — who could be said to have shown any special interest in ideas as such, even theological ideas.

It is not surprising, then, that the Americans, by and large, thought they were being summoned to Rome to put their seal of approval on the traditional formulas, and then to be dismissed quickly. "It turned out rather differently," Bishop Robert J. Dwyer of Reno remarked recently, but that is what they expected. Few even thought it necessary to bring skilled theologians with them as advisers. They relied, rather, on trusted stalwarts from their own chancery offices who knew their canon law and could double as chauffeurs, valets or simple secretaries.

As a result, at the first session, the American bishops were hopelessly outshone by the more sophisticated French, German, Dutch and even Italian hierarchies. Few spoke on the floor, and there was a frank feeling of confusion among them. They did not even meet together regularly, feeling that anything smacking of bloc action was unworthy of a church council.

They soon came to realize, however, that decisions would have to come from the interplay of human minds rather than the direct intervention of the Holy Spirit. As Catholic bishops, they are, of course, convinced that the Holy Spirit presides over their work, but none of them claims to have received immediate inspiration or personal infallibility.

DURING the second session, then, the Americans began to meet regularly and to call in theological *periti* (specialists) to disentangle some of the issues they would be dealing with in council. A spirit of camaraderie was built up. Old friendships were strengthened and new ones formed. In effect, the bishops went back to school under the tutelage of the church's top theologians.

They have followed this same practice at the third session, which opened in September. The discussions of religious liberty and of relations with the Jews, for example, were dominated by American spokesmen, who "caucused" and were briefed on the first topic by the Rev. John Courtney Murray, S. J., the leading Catholic authority in the United States on church-state relations. On these issues, the American bishops formed a united front and were very influential in winning the Fathers' support.

It is at this session that the Americans have found

STARTING TIME—Prelates arrive at St. Peter's for a council meeting. There has been a "day-by-day exposure to new ideas."

themselves, so to speak, and decided that, by and large, they belong with the group designated, in the catch-all categories of the council, as "progressives." More than one has admitted that he finds himself voting for changes in ecclesiastical practices and doctrinal interpretations he would have deemed totally unacceptable only two years ago.

THIS does not mean that all 240-odd American bishops (the exact number changes almost weekly with deaths and new appointments) have participated actively in the council. About one-third are missing from Rome at any given time. Some, because of age or infirmity or even lack of interest, have not attended any of the sessions. Even among the most faithful attendants, most are content to listen and to vote. Slightly more than one-tenth of the American bishops have participated in council affairs as speakers, commission members or as writers of interventions (statements of position on questions before the council). This is about the average for the larger hierarchies.

THE American Fathers include five members of the College of Cardinals. They are, from left to right, so to speak, Joseph Cardinal Ritter of St. Louis, Albert Cardinal Meyer of Chicago and Richard Cardinal Cushing of Boston, all "progressives"; Francis Cardinal Spellman of New York, a "conservative" in the first and second sessions but now a "middle-roader"; and James Francis Cardinal McIntyre of Los Angeles, the one remaining outright "conservative."

Cardinal Spellman presents an interesting case history. He was, for example, unsympathetic to the Liturgical Constitution, proclaimed at the end of the second session, which provides for the use of the vernacular in the mass and much wider participation for the laity in divine services. Similarly, he opposed the principle of episcopal "collegiality" (the notion that all the bishops of the church share with the Pope in its governance, and are no longer to think of themselves as mere legates of Rome assigned to particular dioceses). He and the conservatives lost on both issues.

Yet, on the two issues of the third session in which the American hierarchy took a special interest—religious liberty and the church's relationship with Jews — Cardinal Spellman was with the "progressives" all the way. He was not present for the discussions, but he sent in powerful written interventions. And it is known also that when the schemas (or drafts of pronouncements) on these two questions ran into Curial opposition, Cardinal Spellman used his influence to save them from evisceration.

ANOTHER case history is that of Cardinal McIntyre. He has long been hostile to the forces of "reform and renewal" — banning liberal speakers in his diocese, and outlawing critical Catholic publications such as the lay-edited Commonweal, the Jesuit America and Ave Maria, published by the Holy Cross Fathers of Notre Dame in Indiana.

Five years ago, Cardinal McIntyre would have been only the most extreme in a body of conservative American bishops. Today, he is almost alone. Not only is he considered a die-hard in the American hierarchy — and there is a grudging respect for his tenacity even among the most "progressive" Fathers of the Council — but he has been described by more than one Vatican observer as the most reactionary prelate in the church, bar none — not even those of the Curia, or churchmen like the implacable Ernesto Cardinal Ruffini of Palermo, whose opposition to any whiff of change now draws only amused sighs of resignation from most of the Council Fathers.

THE closest to a leader in the American hierarchy at the present time is Cardinal Meyer of Chicago. He is universally looked up to by his fellow Americans, and he has won the respect of all the Church Fathers for the depth of his observations on the council floor. It has been said frequently in Rome that he is not only the outstanding American but one of the most respected of all participants.

Cardinal Meyer has been hesitant to assume the kind of active leadership the bishops would be quite willing to give him. He is a gentlemanly prelate, professorial in manner, somewhat standoffish. He is not a "mixer," and is ill at ease when clerical camaraderie gets a bit boisterous, and it can when good-fellowship reigns among the Bishops and their periti.

Yet there are signs that he may be overcoming his reluctance, a matter that assumes new importance now that the principle of episcopal collegiality has been affirmed. Undoubtedly, the role of national episcopal conferences will be strengthened in future (the last time the American bishops discussed a doctrinal question in common was in Baltimore in 1884). And with that change, the traditional atomism of the American hierarchy will have to give way. The American bishops, then, will need a forceful leader, and Cardinal Meyer is the man they are looking to.

WITH some exceptions, there has been strikingly little leadership at the council from the American archbishops. The Most Rev. John J. Krol, Archbishop of Philadelphia and the first Polish-American to reach the top levels of the hierarchy, is the outstanding man in this group. There are recurrent rumors here that collegiality means that no more Cardinals will be named, but if any are Archbishop Krol is sure to be high on the Pope's list. He is one of the under secretaries of the entire council, and in that position he plays a pivotal role. It is known, for example, that he helped his close friend, Archbishop Hallinan of Atlanta, steer the historical Liturgical Decree to a safe landing—no mean accomplishment in view of the powerful opposition to it.

On the level of simple bishop, one of the most influential Americans has been the Most Rev. John Wright of Pittsburgh, a member of the Doctrinal Commission, which produced the draft "De Ecclesia [On the Church]," widely admired as an expression of Pope John's aggiornamento. Others among the "new breed" of bishops are the Most Rev. Ernest Primeau, Bishop of Manchester, N.H.; Bishop Stephen Leven of San Antonio, an auxiliary; the Most Rev. Charles A. Buswell of Pueblo, Colo., the Most Rev. Victor Reed of Oklahoma City; and Bishop Robert E. Tracy of Baton Rouge, La. The catalogue suggests that as one moves south and west American Catholicism becomes more liberal, more attuned to the restlessness of the people — until it comes to a dead stop on the outskirts of Los Angeles, where the New York-born Cardinal McIntyre presides.

The "progressive" changes wrought in the American hierarchy in the past two years are, of course, due initially to Pope John, who made aggiornamento an acceptable idea as well as a universal word. Yet other factors have played a role. One is the day-by-day exposure to new ideas. And a major one is the bishops' new concept of their own role in the church—the feeling of united responsibility for the universal church, affirmed theologically in the doctrine of collegiality. No longer need the bishops be preoccupied with anticipating the Curia's communications.

After three sessions of daily meetings with fellow bishops from other lands, a swelling confidence in their own ability to discern the good of the church, the airing of many long pent-up frustrations and doubts about traditional practices, exposure to the thought of the best and most forward-looking theologians in the Catholic world, the encouragement of two Popes, a groundswell of critical comment from parish priests, nuns and the articulate laity, the comfort of one another's company, and the privacy afforded in a city where 2,300 other prelates are gathered and one bishop more or less goes unnoticed — with all this, plus the help of the Holy Spirit, which the bishops themselves would put first, the American bishops have found themselves.

The big problem facing them now is that they are ahead of both their priests and their people. Normally, a hierarchy lags behind the intellectual leaders in the church. New ideas come from below and with great difficulty are recognized by the authorities. This process has been reversed during Vatican II. Now, new ideas have to be presented by the bishops themselves, who will certainly run into many of the same difficulties that traditionally have faced other forerunners. Some bishops, after they leave the stimulating atmosphere of consiliar Rome, will certainly slip back into the old ways. But they will be checked by those who will forge ahead, for there is no stopping the Catholic revolution they have set in motion. Like all revolutionaries, they will have to face the organizing anguish of keeping it within the bounds of orthodoxy, without losing its essential spirit of "renewal and reform."

November 22, 1964

U.S. Catholics Begin Reforms in the Mass

Switch to English for 45 Million Hailed as Successful

By GEORGE DUGAN

Revolutionary changes in the liturgy, or public worship, of the Roman Catholic Church became effective yesterday for 45 million worshipers in the United States.

The liturgical reforms, the first major accomplishment of the Second Vatican Council, were promulgated by Pope Paul VI nearly a year ago.

Yet, despite the novelty of reform and human opposition to changing lifetime habits the transformation was generally hailed as an ecclesiastical success.

Where "rehearsals" had been going on for several weeks, the faithful followed along with a minimum of trouble. In other cases the changes were accompanied by the shuffling of missal inserts and hymn sheets and by cautious whispering.

The use of the approved text, which substitutes English for Latin in many of the priest's prayers and most of the congregation's responses, proved a stumbling block to some.

Singing unfamiliar hymns also presented difficulties.

Spot checks among church-goers yesterday revealed general approval of the liturgical changes.

Miss Marie Gibbons, a parishioner at St. Catherine of Siena Church, 411 East 68th Street, said she was "all in favor" of the reform.

"It's going to force Catholics to do what they have been supposed to do all along—follow and participate in the mass," she said. "It will also cut down on day-dreaming."

A minority point of view was voiced by Miss Daisy Nieland, a churchgoer in Perth Amboy, N. J.

"I'm a traditionalist, and I miss the Latin," she commented. "It was comfortable and a form of worship that I should like to pass on to my children. My whole family agrees with me. We had a lively discussion of the subject around the Thanksgiving turkey."

An elderly man volunteered this view: "I'm so lost I don't know where I am."

Reason for Changes

The purpose of the liturgical reform is to bring the church closer to the people and to make the mass more meaningful to the man in the pew.

And churchgoers became participants rather than witnesses.

In many instances, priests faced their congregations from behind the altar. Lay persons were also called upon in some churches to escort the materials of communion to the priest for consecration.

The changes marked, in large measure, the end of a liturgical era that began 400 years ago when the Council of Trent established basic norms for the Latin mass that became outdated yesterday. The day was the first Sunday of Advent, the beginning of the liturgical year.

While the reform is worldwide, the working out of details was left to national councils of bishops and ultimately to the bishops in their dioceses.

In a number of churches yesterday, progress had not yet reached the point where the priest faced the congregation. Many churches, however, inaugurated the use of laymen as lectors and commentators.

The lector read the epistle of the day in place of the priest, and the commentator played the role of a master of ceremonies, informing the people when to stand or sit and explaining the Latin prayers of the celebrant.

To most liturgists, the reforms that went into effect yesterday were wishful dreams no more than five years ago.

Latin Prayers Explained

Their fruition, in such a short span of ecclesiastical time, is the work of one man, aided by scores of devoted followers.

The man was the late Pope John XXIII, who shattered his image as an "interim pontiff" by calling the first Ecumenical Council of the church in nearly 100 years.

He asked for an "aggiornamento," or up-dating that would let the "fresh air" of reform and renewal waft through the ancient windows of his church.

His answer came on Dec. 4, 1963, when the council approved the monumental, 15,000-word Constitution on the Liturgy.

At the time the United States Bishops Commission on the Liturgical Apostolate said the document would "affect the spiritual life of prayer and worship of all Catholics" and would make the church "more comprehensible to all men."

First Said in August

An American priest is credited with shepherding the liturgical constitution through the maze of Vatican procedures. He is the Rev. Frederick R. McManus, a professor of canon law at Catholic University in Washington and one of the world's leading liturgists.

Last August, Father McManus was accorded the honor of celebrating the first vernacular mass in this country at St. Louis under the authority of Joseph E. Cardinal Ritter.

Last March, as an outgrowth of the liturgical renewal, a number of minor changes became obligatory.

Among these were mandatory sermons at all masses on Sundays and holy days of obligation, some changes in the ceremonies of matrimony and confirmation and the easing of requirements in regard to the Divine Office said daily by priests and religious.

Later the prayer said by the priest before placing the wafer on the tongue of the communicant was discontinued. In its place the priest simply says the words, "The Body of Christ," to which the communicant replies, "Amen."

November 30, 1964

Catholic Liturgy, Gaining Acceptance, Entering a New Phase

By PAUL L. MONTGOMERY

The changes in the liturgy of the Roman Catholic Church, introduced in the country with a burst of energy last fall, are entering a new phase of quiet consolidation and long-range planning.

The consensus of liturgical experts is that the time since Nov. 29, when the vernacular mass was inaugurated, has helped to remove misconceptions and teach valuable lessons about the future of the updated church.

Now, they believe, the church is ready for the three or five years it will take for the new liturgy to become as familiar to Catholics as the Latin version once was.

Liturgical reform has come to mean more than the ostensible public worship of the church. Because the constitution on the liturgy was the first promulgated by the Second Vatican Council, it has served as a test and a model for what Pope John XXIII called "aggiornamento" — renewal — of the church.

And, because the mass is at the center of the church's life, matters such as social action, the authority of bishops in forming the teachings of the church, and the function of the individual conscience have become attached to the liturgy question.

Some Oppose Liturgy

Those close to the seats of power of the church are quick to acknowledge that there is a handful of American bishops and a number of priests who at best have been reluctant to institute liturgical reform, and many parishioners who are uncomfortable singing hymns or responding to the priest in English. But they believe these pockets of resistance are rapidly disappearing.

There appears to be no danger of a full-scale revolt triggered by liturgical matters, as has happened a number of times in the church's history.

Little observable support developed for the Catholic Traditionalist Movement, which created a flurry a few weeks ago by defending the old form of the mass and charging that a "conspiracy" had brought in the new one.

On Thursday, after an interview with his bishop, Lawrence Cardinal Shehan of Baltimore, the Rev. Gommar A. De Pauw, chairman of the group and a professor of moral theology and canon law at Mount St. Mary's Seminary in Emitsburg, Md., announced that he was withdrawing from active participation, although he expressed hope that the laity would take over the movement.

Lessons Listed

Liturgical experts have listed the following lessons as the ones that will provide a bridge between the sudden newness of the reforms last fall and the ultimate realization of them.

¶Worshipers who were at first attracted by the novelty of responding to the mass in English have begun to look for deeper significance.

¶Bishops who believed that reforming the liturgy was merely a matter of decreeing new church laws have come to place higher value on theological preparation of the people.

¶Clergymen who believed that there would only be a minimum response to the reforms—as had happened several times in the last 20 years—have found that this time the vast majority of the Catholic hierarchy is behind full implementation of them.

¶Parishioners who thought that the new liturgy was only a temporary experimental phase have learned, on the authority of Pope Paul IV himself, that the church does not intend to go back to the old methods.

¶And finally, almost everyone, including the experts, have learned that the road toward full realization of the Second Vatican Council's Constitution the kids, who love to sing the measured in Sundays but in years.

Church Has Changed

Asked about the state of liturgical reform in his church, a young priest with a parish on the West Side of Manhattan gave this answer last week:

"You look over the congregation on Sunday morning and

89

you really get an idea of what the church of 1965 is all about. All the types are there.

"First you see the esthetes who believe there has been a loss of mystery since Latin left the mass. Then there are the good Joes, the bulk of the congregation, who are trying to do the best they can with something they don't quite understand. Here and there you see th kids, who love to sing the hymns and ring out the responses. And finally the dumb re i tors, the ones who kneel whe they're supposed to sit and would rather be struck dead than sing or respond to the priest.

"But underneath all this when you talk to them, there is a wonderful spirit—really a sense of wonder at what is happening to the church as a corporate body. In a year or two. I think, I will turn around to read the Gospel and see—maybe, just maybe—what the apostles saw 1900 years ago."

By far the largest body of objections to the new liturgy comes from those who approve of the changes but believe they have not gone far enough, or been done well enough.

Varied Version Presented

One source of dissent is the quality of the English translation, which was hastily put together and contains a mixture of 17th- and 20th-century English. The members of the committee that was charged with the translation of many of the prayers in the mass, for ex-

ample, were presented with various English versions of a Latin passage and asked to check the one they thought most fitting. The result, one said, "has an I.B.M. flavor, to say the least."

The Rev. C. J. McNaspy, an associate editor of the Jesuit weekly, America, and a leading liturgist, calls the current English version "clumsy and inarticulate in part" but says that a new translation embodying modern scholarship should be available soon.

Father McNaspy also points out that when Latin was adopted as the language of the mass in the fourth century it was the vernacular, and replaced Greek because the older language had become incomprehensible to many. "People opposed to the use of English on the ground that Latin is 'traditional' have not done their homework," he says.

Another source of objection is that not all of the mass is in English. A woman from Baltimore, writing to the magazine, Jubilee, made this remark about it:

"My one great disappointment with the decree on the sacred liturgy was the stipulation that the prayers of the canon remain in Latin. I can't visualize Christ at the Last Supper with his back to those for whose unity He had just prayed, giving them Himself in a language they could not understand."

Most liturgists believe that eventually the entire mass will be in the vernacular. As it

stands now, under the Constitution on the Sacred Liturgy adopted by the Vatican Council on Nov. 22, 1963, the parts of the mass pertaining to the people can be said in the vernacular on approval of the territorial conferences of bishops. This approval has already been granted in most of the world's Catholic dioceses.

For the parts of the mass that are said by the priest, the approval of the Pope must be obtained before they can be said in the vernacular. Most of these parts occur in the canon of the mass, the central symbolic act in which the bread and wine are consecrated. As far as is known, no one as yet asked the Pope for permission to use the vernacular in these parts.

Lessons Learned

Most liturgists note that the degree of acceptance of the new mass is directly proportional to the degree that the individual parish has been prepared for it by classes and instruction. The purpose of this instruction is to effect a basic shift in the attitude of the worshiper from that of a spectator of the sacrifice of the mass to a participant in it.

Frederick R. McManus, president of the Liturgical Conference and director of the Secretariat of the American Bishops Commission on the Liturgy, says that the "doctrines of the mass need to be explained, or the effects will not be very well received."

Another pressing problem connected with the liturgy is the state of Catholic music. The Rev. Gerard S. Sloyen, head of the Department of Religious Education at Catholic University in Washington, said that because the new liturgy demands new music, sources of composers, organists and choir directors will have to be developed.

A story making the rounds at Catholic headquarters here perhaps best illustrates the effect of the new liturgy on Catholic thinking.

A traditionalist Midwestern bishop, it seems, was examining a class of boys preparing for their first communion. He explained that the church had always been conceived as a hierarchical society, ranging from the Pope through his bishops and priests down to the people. He then asked the boys for a definition of the church, hoping to hear an answer reflecting his views.

The first boy to reply, however, showed that the new concept, emphasizing the role of the congregation, had made its mark.

"The church is the people," he said.

"Certainly it's not just the people," the bishop said helpfully.

"No," another boy said, and then to the bishop's dismay added. "It's God's people."

April 11, 1965

Crisis of Obedience

Catholic Protests on Hospital Closings Are Part of Change Within the Church

By JOHN COGLEY

If they carry out a threat, a group of Roman Catholics from the Greenpoint - Williamsburg district of Brooklyn will picket the Vatican Pavilion at the World's Fair tomorrow to protest against the decision of their Bishop to close St. Catherine's Hospital. Yesterday a group of pregnant women demonstrated against the closing of St. Francis Hospital in the Bronx. Last year, James Cardinal McIntyre of Los Angeles had to cross a picket line every morning when he arrived at his office. The pickets were Catholics who objected to the Cardinal's policy of staying aloof from the racial struggle.

News Analysis

The students of a diocesan seminary in the Middle West staged a pray-in during the Ecumenical Council Vatican II to dramatize their objections to the traditional theology taught in their classrooms.

At the convention of the Catholic Press Association last month in New York, an award for the best article in a journal of opinion was given to a report highly critical of Cardinal McIntyre and the policies of the church in his archdiocese.

'The DuBay Case'

The article was called "The DuBay Case" and was an account of an incident involving the Rev. William DuBay, a young priest who came to prominence when he wrote to the

Pope and urged him to remove Cardinal McIntyre on charges of "malfeasance."

The priest's letter would never have come to public notice had he not called a news conference to be sure it did. There was no mention of the St. Catherine's Hospital case in the issue of The Tablet, official paper of the diocese of Brooklyn, delivered yesterday.

This crisis of obedience now being felt throughout the church cuts across national, political and ideological lines.

In France last month, Archbishop André Pallier of Rouen spoke openly of the possibility of a schism next year caused by ultraconservative Catholics after the promulgation of the texts on religious liberty and on the church in the modern world by the Ecumenical Council.

The average non-Catholic bystander is watching all this with wonder. Whatever happened, he asks, to the almost military discipline of Catholics, with their clear lines of authority from Pope to Bishop to pastor to layman and their superb organization that only a few years

ago even gained the public admiration of the American Management Association?

It is a good question, but not easy to answer.

Currents Converging

Several currents of changing attitudes have converged and are blowing away the tidy relationships of the past in a mighty gust of independent thinking.

The laity, without denying the special roles of the Bishop and the priest, have become convinced that they are not merely dues-paying associates of the clergy but bear a responsibility for the church's total stance in the world. The favorite formula among the new lay leaders is: "We are not just members of the church, we are the church."

Then, there is a changing view of ecclesiastical authority. The old ideal was that it was enough that an order be given. Nowadays, reasons for the order are solicited, sometimes even demanded. This is as true in certain convents and monasteries as it is in parishes and dioceses.

The Rev. Robert Johann, a

young Jesuit professor at the order's seminary in Shrub Oak, N. Y., summed up this view at a conference on authority and freedom recently at Georgetown University:

"No one subject to another can abstain from judging whether a particular directive is for the good of the community. Nor can anyone abstain from acting in accordance with this judgment."

Finally, especially among younger Catholics, there is a rebellion against "churchiness"

or "institutional-think," as some of them call it.

They see no reason why they should divide their personalities into two: one for the world and another for the church. They are given to asking why they should change their mode of thinking when they move from the ordinary rough-and-tumble of American civic life to their role as members of a religious community. "Honesty," the constant preoccupation of the present college generation, is also becoming a magic word among the young clergy and laity of

the Catholic Church.

Criticism, questioning, objecting, protesting, calling to account have long been part of American life. They are exalted by commencement speakers and canonized in the nation's patriotic scriptures. They appear now to be becoming part of American Catholic ecclesiastical life as well.

All this, of course, means taking a risk. The whole idea of authority could be wrecked if the enthusiasm for "honesty" got out of hand. This week, Paul-Emile Cardinal Léger of Montreal, one of the most

progressive bishops at the Ecumenical Council, said there was in the church today "a climate of opinion hostile to the whole idea of authority, much less its exercise."

Other bishops, progressive and conservative, to use the omnibus categories of the council, believe Cardinal Léger is right. The difference between them is that the conservatives find the situation intolerable; the progessives, in the interests of expanding freedom in the church, believe that the risk must be taken.

June 12, 1965

The American Catholic Is Changing

By JOHN LEO

WHO is the American Catholic? One speaker used to begin his lectures this way: "The American Catholic is Bing Crosby, Bob Considine, George Meany, William Buckley, Clare Boothe Luce and Senator Joseph McCarthy. He is also Sargeant Shriver, Dorothy Day, Dr. John Rock, Justice Brennan, Tom Dooley and Senator Eugene McCarthy. . . ."

All right. Catholics can be given credit for diversity—along with most other religious groups. But how different is the American Catholic from his neighbor?

The question gains immediacy both from the reverberations of Pope John's call for an *aggiornamento,* and from

the rise of American influence within Catholicism. "America," says one European bishop, "is living in the 21st century, and the experience of Catholics there will have a lot to do with how the church adapts."

Well, then, how different *is* the American Catholic from his neighbor? The sociology is a bit thin, but the answer would have to be: not much. The social, cultural and economic state he finds himself in is a better index to his thinking and behavior than his religion. This is a fairly recent development, and visiting European Catholics usually miss no opportunity to remark (often with dismay) that the U. S. Catholic cannot be distinguished from any other American.

Nevertheless, there are differences. In general, the American Catholic is less likely than his non-Catholic

neighbor to become a social activist, more likely to vote Democratic (until he moves to suburbia), less likely to excel in the academic world (particularly the sciences), more likely to have a large family, less likely to make "Who's Who."

If he reaches the top in American society, he is more likely to have made it through politics, the professions or show business. He is likely to stress order more than freedom, and more likely to favor strict laws enforcing sexual mores—though the pattern here seems to be breaking down.

SOCIOLOGISTS and historians think that the immigrant experience, not religious belief, is the key to these differences. In general, Catholics were latecomers

---

JOHN LEO is an associate editor of Commonweal, a leading Catholic publication.

Pope Paul, visiting New York, arrives at Yankee Stadium.

to America, arriving in massive waves of migration between 1840 and 1920, mostly from Ireland, Central Europe and Italy.

According to the "immigrant theory," the course of American Catholicism has been determined by the cultural base of the immigrants, who were largely impoverished peasants and villagers, cut off from the intellectual traditions of their religion and their native lands. The ordinary prejudice against newcomers was heightened by the native American anti-Catholicism which Arthur Schlesinger Sr. called "the oldest and most ingrained of American prejudices." The result was that immigrant Catholicism turned in on itself, developing deep defensive traits, and devoting its energies to parochial affairs.

ON its own terms, the young church was a sound success. Of all major branches of Catholicism, it became the only one to hold onto the working class and to avoid anti-clericalism. Its vitality—though directed inward—was high. Out of working-class salaries it built an enormous system of

schools, hospitals and religious organizations. It also kept the loyalty of younger generations in an age when Catholicism could be a costly social handicap.

But for all that it paid a price. The cost of building the schools delayed the arrival of Catholics into the great American middle class—only with the prosperity following World War II did Catholics arrive in any numbers. Separate Catholic institutions, particularly the schools, enforced Catholic isolation. The values of intellect and imagination were hardly stressed and the church lost creative people of the first rank — Fitzgerald, O'Hara, Farrell and Eugene O'Neill. What intellectualism there was, was devoted to ingenious defenses of Catholic teaching. Disinterested scholarship was rare, and generally suspect.

Part of the legacy today, is that American Catholics are dramatically underrepresented on the intellectual front. There are no great American Catholic scientists (though this seems to be true of Catholics everywhere). Neither are there Catholic philosophers, poets, theologians and writers

in any proportion to the Catholic population.

A decade ago, Msgr. John Tracy Ellis, the historian, sent tremors through the American Catholic Church with an essay documenting the lack of Catholic intellectual activity, and implying that Catholics tended to rely rather complacently on the "immigrant theory" to explain it away. Since then, Catholics have conducted a profound—and often loud—investigation of the subject in an attempt to upgrade intellectual values. The job is far from done, although a recent study by Chicago sociologist Andrew Greeley shows that now, for the first time, Catholics are in graduate schools in proportion to their numbers.

The Ellis essay ended an era of puffy self-satisfaction, when Catholics basked in the illusory glow of the so-called "religious revival" and counted success in terms of rising statistics on schools, communicants and converts. Monsignor Ellis touched off a decade of sweeping self-analysis (known in less sympathetic quarters as "the orgy of criticism"). Combined with the

reforms of the Second Vatican Council, it has brought to the fore a generation of younger Catholics vaguely referred to as "the new breed" who are committed to secular values as well as the Catholic faith. Among other things, they have taken control of the major Catholic publishing outlets, thus assuring that rigorous self-criticism will continue. During 1965 alone, there have been no fewer than 12 bristling attacks on the Catholic press by individual bishops who consider it dangerously overcritical.

EDUCATION is one of the prime concerns. The Catholic Church in America has been committed to the ideal of "every Catholic child in a Catholic school." In the 19th century, the decision was received by the laity with some reluctance and grumbling, but in the 20th century, the pressure for more and more Catholic schools has come from laymen.

Today slightly more than half of the 11 million school-age Catholics are in Catholic elementary and secondary schools. But the proportion will not rise. In the past decade, Catholics have managed to add 1,550 schools to their system; in the same period, more than 14 million babies have been born to Catholic couples. The statistics suggest that perhaps only a third of the next generation of Catholics will attend Catholic schools.

Much of the push for Federal aid to parochial schools grows from the fear that a rush of government spending on public schools will price the Catholic schools out of the market and doom them to perpetual inferiority. As it is, the Catholic schools are economically viable today only because 100,000 nuns are willing to teach for token wages, sometimes as low as $20 a month.

Under these conditions, the Catholic schools have become the center of hot debate among Catholics. There are those who favor an all-out drive for Federal aid. Others think the church should resign itself to a nonexpanding school system, cut back on construction, and throw its weight behind the public schools. This is already the policy in the St. Louis Archdiocese—which, in 1962, placed a ban on school construction and expansion, and urged parents to vote for any bond issues necessary for the expansion of the public school system.

A small minority thinks the church should get out of the school business altogether and find less expensive but more dynamic ways of instructing its children. This strain of thought surfaced last year with publication of Mary Perkins Ryans' influential book "Are Parochial Schools the Answer?" It expressed the feeling that parochial schools drain away so much money and energy needed on other fronts that they have become white elephants. Meaningful parish activities often give way to naked fund-raising affairs designed merely to keep the schools afloat.

A popular belief, among many Catholics as well as non-Catholics, is that the parochial schools are inferior, but the evidence is not at all conclusive. Whether they are or not, many Catholic intellectuals argue that the differences in outlook between the Catholic who goes to public school and the Catholic educated at great sacrifice in a parochial school are too small to justify the expense of a separate school system. Others argue that the parochial schools are divisive, although a recent study at the University of Chicago does not bear this out.

"THE DEPUTY"—Rolf Hochhuth's play attacking Pope Pius XII. "A good part of the American Catholic press agreed with its thesis."

POLITICALLY, the American Catholic has tended to be conservative, suspicious of central government. "Liberal" has been a dirty word, associated theologically with misguided attempts to make Catholicism palatable to non-Catholics by dropping a few essentials, and associated politically with freewheeling relativism and secularism. As late as 1958, a popular Catholic magazine could run an anxious article on the vexing question: "Can a Catholic be a liberal?"

In part, the suspicion of liberalism goes back to the 19th century, when the European liberal movement was firmly anti-Catholic. When many of the immigrants came over, the liberal movement was involved in a direct physical attack on the papacy. Then, too, the Irish, who were to dominate American Catholicism, came from a static, conservative society, and one with a settled tradition of regarding the central government of the British as illegitimate. Parallel attitudes toward government existed among other immigrant groups. Most of the Italian immigrants, for example, came from the south, where government officials were unhelpful at best, and usually corrupt.

That Catholics came to be regular Democratic voters was not a choice for liberalism, but more or less a historical accident. It seemed that all their enemies were Republicans, and there was nowhere else to go. While the Jews, for instance, tended to see the Democratic party as an instrument for social progress, no such vision descended upon the Irish. For them it was simply an instrument of self-interest and the leading channel of upward mobility.

In America, the inability to see government as a force for social progress is usually attributed to "rugged individualism." For American Catholics, it went hand in hand with spiritual individualism: the emphasis was on personal morality, personal devotion, personal salvation. In practice, American Catholicism did not seem to be a charter for communal concern, but a set of rules for a one-man obstacle race from earth to heaven. Episcopal thunderbolts tended to be hurled far more often at threats to personal morality, such as dirty movies, than at infractions of social morality, such as race prejudice or economic exploitation.

The tradition of individualism and social conservatism has put a strain on the traditional loyalty to the Democratic party. When Democratic Catholics from the city move to the suburbs, Republican values often seem suddenly much more congenial.

The emergence of the Communist issue hastened the process, presenting American Catholics with peculiar temptations toward superpatriotism. First of all, the Catholic Church identified the danger of Communism early. The sight of Franklin D. Roosevelt courting Stalin as late as 1945 sent resentments soaring; they were to boil over in the later investigations of "dupes" and "collaborators" who had been unsure about Communism while the church was so certain.

This spirit operated at full throttle during the McCarthy period. Precisely because they could not be found in the upper reaches of government, and had not taken part in the social causes of the thirties and forties, Catholics could

note with some satisfaction that the Communist investigations would cast no reflections on *their* loyalty. In fact, the investigations were widely taken as long-awaited proof of Catholic reliability. As Daniel Patrick Moynihan wrote: "Harvard men were to be checked; Fordham men would do the checking."

It was no accident that McCarthy reserved special gusto for his attacks on the intellectuals of Harvard and "the striped-pants set" of the State Department, which many Catholics took as symbols of their cultural oppressors in America. In a way, many Catholics, particularly the Irish, were taking the occasion to settle some old scores.

But there are signs that the reflex action of anti-Communist proconservative bias is on the wane. In 1964, for example, 70 per cent of Catholics voted for Johnson rather than Goldwater. The Catholic vote, in fact, is losing its normal distinctiveness. Catholics voted more heavily for Johnson than for Kennedy. Eisenhower's vast strength among Catholics both in 1952 and 1956 shows how feeble the once-compelling ties to the Democratic party now are. (So do the indications that both Lindsay and Buckley did extremely well among Catholic voters in the recent New York mayoral election.) Since 1960, no clear pattern has developed in Catholic voting, and aside from faith-related issues such as a birth-control referendum, none is likely to reappear.

THERE is evidence, too, that Catholic "crusades" in the public order are on the wane. Nothing resembling Cardinal Spellman's all-out attack on "Baby Doll" has occurred in the sixties, though movies have become far more explicit on sexual matters. Censorship groups are now out on the fringe of Catholic life, and, significantly, they are now more likely to be interfaith efforts than purely Catholic forays.

The Supreme Court decision on school prayer drew loud complaints from many Catholics, but no crusade. By and large, Catholics seem to have opposed the Becker amendment to reinstall school prayer. "The Deputy," Rolf Hochhuth's play attacking Pope Pius XII, brought mob scenes and violence in much of Europe, but passed without incident in America. A good part of the Catholic press agreed with Hochhuth's thesis.

On birth control, which is still a potentially divisive problem in the public order, the attitudes of Catholics are in flux. The allocation of anti-poverty funds for birth control, and the further-reaching proposals now before Senator Gruening's committee, have produced isolated protests, some of them strong, but nothing like the furor touched off in 1959 over a single veiled suggestion, in a report to President Eisenhower, that foreign-aid funds might go to birth-control programs.

CATHOLICS themselves are divided on the morality of birth control, as an average week's reading of the better Catholic journals will show. Immense pressure has been raised for a re-examination of the church's stand, and many pastors have reported birth control as the major reason for married couples' remaining away from the sacraments. What studies there are indicate that perhaps three out of 10 married Catholics practice birth control. One study in North Carolina indicated that half of the Catholics there used contraceptives.

One recent poll shows that 61 per cent of American Catholics expect their church to modify its stand on the question. A 1964 survey indicated that just 49 per cent of Catholics considered contraception immoral, and just 23 per cent thought that the practice of birth control would prevent salvation.

Many Catholics, of course, still feel strongly about birth-control laws, but the sentiment is on the wane. The debate on contraception within Catholicism has taken much of the heart out of the fight. More important, the present generation of Catholics is much more conscious of the rights of others than the last.

Kenneth Underwood's book "Protestant and Catholic," which studied Catholic-Protestant relations in Holyoke, Mass., in the years 1947-48, indicated that Catholics, given the slightest opportunity, would not hesitate to ride roughshod over non-Catholics. Yet he noted the beginning of a pattern that has since emerged: Better-educated and higher-income Catholics tended to stand apart from pressure tactics and unenlightened clerical advice. They were loyal to the church, but not to religious efforts which seemed to restrict the rights of their neighbors.

Catholic-Protestant tensions have lessened dramatically in the last five years. The leading Catholic newspapers and magazines have Protestant columnists and regular contributors — sympathetic, but critical when necessary. Catholics are

PAROCHIAL SCHOOL — A combined sixth and seventh grade. Catholic schools face a crisis.

now inclined to think that Paul Blanshard, the author of "American Freedom and Catholic Power," whose attacks sent them into a defensive frenzy in the fifties, had some real points, though failing to understand the complexity of Catholicism and the self-corrective forces within it. Blanshard, for his part, is still critical, but hardly shrill; he has been seen dining with bishops in Rome.

The polls reflect the change. A 1964 study in the U.S. asked the question: "Do you agree that both Luther and the Catholic Church were both partly right and partly wrong in the dispute that led to their split?" Forty per cent of the Catholics who answered said yes, compared with 36 per cent of the Protestants. In the last two years, Catholic scholarship has produced a number of Reformation studies sympathetic to Luther.

According to one Catholic story, the bishops at the Vatican Council were all handed cards bearing a portrait of Luther; on the other side, the card read: "In your heart you know he's right." Catholic lecturers, speaking to packed houses at $250 a throw, now open their talks with jokes that once were termed "anti-Catholic" and now are cheerfully received as "ecumenical."

The efforts of Popes John and Paul have helped spread this spirit, but it is likely that ecumenicism would have caught on in America even without them. Catholic-Protestant hostility is simply dated; on the Catholic side, the hostility and fear that go back to

the immigrant period had to be brought in line with the normal pattern of amiable business and social relationships with Protestants. The immigrant emotions could not have held on much longer.

THERE is no doubt that the social and cultural freedom of American life is having a profound effect on the emerging generation of Catholics. So are the reforms set in motion by Pope John and the Second Vatican Council.

Over the last few years, the biggest question among American Catholics has been the role of the layman, both in and out of the church. Donald Thorman's "The Emerging Layman" and Daniel Callahan's "The Mind of the Catholic Layman" have been best-sellers among Catholics. The layman is clearly restless with his traditionally minor role in his church, and theological, liturgical and political developments have given him considerable leverage.

The "new-breed" American Catholic resists any idea that he is an agent of the church operating in society; he tends to be indifferent to institutional claims. Often he will bypass even the most progressive Catholic organizations in favor of work for secular service groups. The network of Catholic interracial councils, for instance, seems to hold less appeal for him than the established nonreligious civil-rights organizations. In short, he is anxious to enter the mainstream of American life, to end Catholic separatism and to identify Catholic efforts

with the disenfranchised instead of the status quo.

No one knows how strong this movement is. Critics claim it represents only 1 per cent or 2 per cent of the Catholic population. But defenders maintain that evidence shows the new attitudes going deep into the population at large, not just the intellectual class.

At any rate, the American layman is more relaxed about his religion, particularly since Pope John and John F. Kennedy. He now thinks his Americanism is taken for granted, and his defensiveness is fading. As Catholics move in large numbers into the middle class, the temptation will be less toward putting religious strains on the public order than it will be to settle down complacently with a set of newly acquired bourgeois values. The reflex conservatism he felt, even as an outsider, might still make him an inordinately comfortable insider.

Internally, American Catholics have achieved vitality — without much expression of it in terms of social concern — and a high level of religious practice — without a very wide grasp of the implications of their faith. The Vatican Council has brought the best parts of their tradition to the fore: the American emphasis on freedom has girded them against the kind of authoritarianism that is continually a danger in a well-structured church. Their attitudes and values are very much in flux. Only time will tell which ones will prevail.

Cases of 13 'Silenced Priests' Described by Catholic Weekly

By JOHN COGLEY

The Roman Catholic weekly Ave Maria, published by the Holy Cross Fathers of Notre Dame, Indiana, has just released a special issue with case histories on "the 'silenced' priests" — 13 American Catholic clergymen who have been reassigned, disciplined or otherwise restricted in their public activities since June, 1964.

Ave Maria called on a number of Catholic church leaders to comment on the "crisis of authority" connected with priestly participation in social movements.

There is no sample of the hierarchical point of view in the magazine's special issue on "silenced priests."

"Most of these men have been restricted in their action or in their teaching because of some involvement in the struggle for civil rights or in what is loosely and carelessly called 'the peace movement,'" the magazine states.

An exception is the Rev. Gommar De Pauw, founder and former chairman of the Catholic Traditionalist Movement. The movement is primarily dedicated to repealing changes in the Roman liturgy decreed by the Vatican Council.

The Belgian-born priest was a professor at Mount St. Mary's Seminary in Baltimore when he came to national attention because of his outspoken and sometimes caustic opposition to the use of English in the mass and expanded lay participation in the liturgy. He withdrew from the traditionalist movement on the orders of Lawrence Cardinal Shehan.

In July, 1965, Father DePauw was reassigned from his teaching post in the seminary to a large Baltimore parish. Before moving into the parish he left for Rome where he attended the Vatican Council.

Opposition on Coast

Four of the priests named by the magazine ran into difficulties in the Los Angeles archdiocese whose archbishop, James Francis Cardinal McIntyre, has a worldwide reputation for being among the sternest disciplinarians and most conservative members of the Catholic hierarchy.

In June, 1964, the Rev. William Du Bay, a 29-year-old assistant pastor in a predominantly Negro parish, cabled Pope Paul VI and asked for the Cardinal's removal from the archdiocese. Father Du Bay accused the prelate of "gross malfeasance" and "abuses of authority."

Cardinal McIntyre, the priest charged, carried out a "vicious program of intimidation and repression" against priests who had assumed leadership in the struggle for racial equality.

The young priest was quickly removed from parish assignments. He is now a chaplain at St. John's Hospital in Santa Monica.

The Rev. Joel Moelter, a member of the Carmelite Order, was allegedly banned from saying mass at St. Bernadette's parish in Los Angeles after he had preached on the California Proposition 14, in October, 1964.

The proposition, which was adopted in the statewide election the next month, was assailed by Negro and civil-rights groups as putting property rights above human rights.

In December, 1964, the Rev. John V. Coffield, a Los Angeles pastor, resigned from his parish and went into a self-imposed exile from his home diocese "as the strongest protest I can make" against Cardinal McIntyre's racial and social policies. He is now living in Chicago.

The Rev. Phillip E. Berryman in May, 1965, was abruptly transferred from a busy parish in Pasadena to a girls' high school in Los Angeles, two days after he gave a sermon on racial injustices. He was later granted a leave of absence to work in Latin America.

The magazine listed the following "silenced priests."

The Rev. William Du Bay, formerly administrative assistant in a mostly Negro parish, Compton, Calif., a Los Angeles industrial suburb.

The Rev. Joel Moelter, St. Bernadette's parish, Los Angeles.

The Rev. J. Clement Burns, formerly on the faculty of La Salle College.

The Rev. John V. Coffield, former pastor of Ascension Church, Los Angeles.

The Rev. Philip Berrigan, formerly on the faculty of Epiphany College Seminary, Newburgh, N. Y.

The Rev. Phillip E. Berryman, formerly of St. Philip the Apostle Parish, Pasadena, Calif.

The Rev. Maurice Ouellet, formerly of St. Elizabeth's Mission, Selma, Ala.

The Rev. Gommar De Pauw, former teacher at Mount St. Mary's Seminary, Baltimore.

The Rev. James E. Groppi, Milwaukee.

The Rev. William Whelan, Milwaukee.

The Rev. Bonaventure O'Brien, professor of theology at St. Bernardine of Siena College, Loudonville, N. Y.

The Rev. Daniel Berrigan, poet, author and associate editor of Jesuit Missions magazine.

The Rev. Daniel Kilfoyle, another Jesuit priest formerly associated with Father Berrigan in a group called, Clergy Concerned About Vietnam.

January 4, 1966

The Catholic Cold War

Conservative Elements Becoming More Perturbed by Critics Within Church

By JOHN COGLEY

The speaker was the Archbishop of Philadelphia, the Most Rev. John J. Krol, but it might have been any one of a number of perturbed Roman Catholic bishops from any part of the United States. The scene was the installation of a new Bishop of Scranton last week. At one of the related ceremonies.

News Analysis — Archbishop Krol mounted a podium to denounce a group of unnamed Catholics whose actions, he charged, were undermining the authority of the hierarchy. "Variously inspired by eagerness for novelty, exaggerated self-confidence or illusions of prophetic charism," the Philadelphia prelate said, "they preach their own views with little concern for being united with the living and common magisterium [teaching authority] of the Church."

The Archbishop's words did not come as a total surprise. For rhetoric has become an increasingly commonplace weapon on a cold war within post-Vatican Council Catholicism.

This war is being waged between many younger leaders among both clergy and laity and the more conservative members of the hierarchy.

Meeting Canceled

Commencement time, with so many platforms available and young audiences on hand, is sure to bring on fresh bombardments of the new defensive episcopal rhetoric. The highly conservative Apostolic Delegate in Washington, Archbishop Egidio Vagnozzi, has already been heard from. He delivered an attack similar to Archbishop Krol's to a Texas graduating class last week.

A few days before Archbishop Krol's denunciation, another Pennsylvania prelate, Bishop Joseph McShea of Allentown, stirred criticism in his diocese when a meeting of a Bethlehem laymen's group was abruptly canceled because the Bishop found an invited speaker unacceptable. The speaker was John Leo, columnist for both Commonweal and The National Catholic Reporter — the leading spokesmen for Catholic liberals in the United States.

In an apparent effort to counter the criticism, Bishop McShea, in a sermon, later assailed the "audacity" of certain Catholic writers.

A spokesman for the Allentown diocese added that the Bishop "felt he should not welcome a man who has attacked the Pope, Cardinal Spellman, the Vincentian Fathers, New York chancery authorities and the Jesuits, just to name a few." Mr. Leo cheerfully admitted that in his columns over the years he had indeed criticized some of the actions and policies undertaken by the ecclesiastics named. In reply to the criticism from Allentown, he added: "This is another example of the conflict between those who think the Church should be open and analyze its faults and those who equate criticism with disloyalty or danger."

Criticized Pope

Mr. Leo is probably typical of the young Catholic rebels who upset some members of the hierarchy. And he has no intention of ceasing to present controversial views in the Catholic press.

Examples of controversial criticism can be found in columns that Mr. Leo wrote during the Ecumenical Council, Vatican II. He thought, for example, that the Pope in setting up a synod of bishops should have permitted the bishops to elect their own members and determine their own agenda.

Again, he was critical of Cardinal Spellman's handling of the papal tiara, which was given into the Cardinal's care after the Pope symbolically took it off and contributed it to the world's poor in the fall of 1964.

"Cardinal Spellman brought the tiara to the World's Fair and he wanted it venerated," Mr. Leo said last week. "Quite frankly, I don't feel very much like venerating anyone's hat. The Pope made a gesture to serve the poor, and it was used as another bit of leverage for the cult of personality in the Church. I don't think the Pope meant it this way."

In Los Angeles, home of the ultra-conservative Francis Cardinal McIntyre and a small group of liberal "new breed" priests, the atmosphere is charged with tension. Both parties, the unbending Cardinal and the progressive clergy, can depend on vociferous support from different sections of the laity.

Problem in Chicago

In Chicago, the new Archbishop, the Most Rev. John P. Cody, is not finding it easy to adjust his method of governing to the archdiocese's liberal traditions. Chicago gained its reputation as a citadel of Catholic progressiveness when its diocesan newspaper refused to support General Franco in the Spanish Civil War. Then its Archbishop, Cardinal Mundelein, furiously denounced Hitler, and its young Auxiliary Bishop, Bernard J. Sheil, assailed anti-Semitism, anti-unionism and, later, McCarthyism.

Under the recent archbishops, Cardinals Stritch and Mayer, both notably permissive in their attitude, the Chicago archdiocese further developed a reputation for encouraging liberal lay activity, freedom of action and of expression.

The Chicago Catholic community, therefore, was shocked

last March when a meeting of progressive theologians who had played important roles in the Vatican Council was canceled by St. Xavier's College supposedly at the behest of Archbishop Cody.

The incident was reported in the Chicago newspaper, and within hours, the meeting was rescheduled. The cancellation, chancery officials explained, resulted from a misunderstanding.

Archbishop Cody's response to publicity, however, was privately attributed by many observers to a growing respect among Catholic authorities for the importance of public opinion.

For with the development of an independent-minded Catholic press under editors who will not tolerate censorship, public opinion is playing an ever greater role in church affairs.

A Growing Interest

In addition, the secular papers and magazines are showing a

growing interest in religious matters. In the past, the general press frequently avoided ecclesiastical controversies and limited themselves to reports on sermons and clerical appointments or to careful descriptions of the standard cardinalatial wardrobe. This kind of immunity-by-neglect can no longer be counted on.

Catholic bishops cannot escape responsible public criticism any more. They have no choice but to make at least an informal accounting for their actions, once these actions have caught the attention of the press, religious or secular.

And although the bishops, at least a great many of them, are not used to accounting for their actions, some, including older members of the hierarchy, have adjusted to the new situation gracefully. Others, however, can be counted on to interpret any public questioning of the wisdom of their actions

as an outrageous challenge to their authority.

This week the Jesuit editors of America, who are always circumspect in their comments on the hierarchy, acknowledged in an editorial called "To Bishops With Love" that public opinion in the Catholic Church now "has a palpable reality that no one in authority can afford to ignore or minimize."

Bishops and other religious superiors, the weekly's editorial suggests, will accept the fact with greater equanimity if they consider how the same force is at work in the affairs of President Johnson.

The bishops are reminded that today the press is "more important than the pulpit" in the life of the Church — a lesson many learned at the Vatican Council, which adopted ideas sometimes found in the press but almost never heard from the pulpit before 1962.

June 4, 1966

STUDY EVALUATES CATHOLIC SCHOOLS

By EDWARD B. FISKE

Education in Roman Catholic schools has been "virtually wasted" on three-quarters of the students, so far as influencing their adult religious behavior is concerned, a study financed by the Carnegie Corporation and the Federal Office of Education has found.

The directors of the study reported that the religious devotion of an individual's family was more important than formal education in influencing religious attitudes.

There is "not much point" in admitting pupils to Catholic schools to influence their adult religious life unless their fam-

ilies are very devout, the sociologists said.

And while Catholic education has done a good job in making the already devout more devout, the study found, there is "no evidence that Catholic schools have been necessary for the survival of American Catholicism." The study did not attempt to evaluate the quality of secular teaching.

For the purposes of the study, religious behavior was determined by such factors as weekly attendance at mass, monthly communion, financial contributions, attitudes toward Papal authority and religious knowledge.

Findings to Be Published

The study will be published next month by the National Opinion Research Center in Chicago. It was directed by the Rev. Andrew M. Greeley, a leading Catholic sociologist, and Peter H. Rossi, a non-Catholic

sociologist at the University of Chicago and director of the National Opinion Research Center.

The three-year study, which cost $186,000, was sponsored by the Carnegie Corporation. The United States Office of Education contributed $50,000 under its basic research program.

The authors based their conclusions on interviews with a cross-section of 2,100 American Catholics and on supplementary questionnaires given to other Catholics and to Protestants.

The authors noted that American Catholics, as a group, had shown a "high level of minimal allegiance" to their faith and that "the absence of a Catholic education does not seem to lead to a notable decline in minimal allegiance."

The study found that Catholic education succeeded in raising religious practice above this minimal level only when it was combined with other factors, such as the influence of a par-

ent or marriage to a devout Catholic.

Limitations Are Noted

In describing the possibilities for Catholic education to increase the religiousness of those from devout backgrounds, the authors stressed several important limitations. For a Catholic education to affect religious behavior significantly, they said, it should be continuous from grade school through college.

Though not denying the possibility that there was "divisiveness" along religious lines in the United States, the study discounted the widely held theory that religious education was a divisive force.

"Catholic - school Catholics are just as likely to be interested in community affairs and to have non-Catholic visitors, friends, neighbors and co-workers as are public-school Catholics," the sociologists said.

July 25, 1966

CATHOLICS CENTER EFFORT IN SCHOOLS

Notre Dame Study Reports Education Is Major Effort

By JOHN COGLEY

The Roman Catholic Church in the United States, some of its home-grown critics have charged, is as child-centered as any other institution in American life.

A study of parochial schools issued by the University of Notre Dame yesterday shows that a vast proportion of the church's funds, most of its full-

time personnel, and an overwhelmingly high measure of its energy are devoted to maintaining its parochial school system.

There has been some discussion about abolishing the schools. According to the Rev. Andrew M. Greeley, a University of Chicago sociologist and authority on Catholic education, that would be like abolishing the Rocky Mountains.

The nation's Roman Catholic parochial grade and high schools now educate from five million to six million children, a figure that would have certainly astounded Mother Elizabeth Seton, the nun generally credited with being the founder of the system.

Mother Seton, a convert from

the Protestant Episcopal Church to Roman Catholicism, founded the Sisters of Charity, who established the first parish school at Emmitsburg, Md., in 1810.

200 Schools in 1840

By 1840, according to the Notre Dame study, "Catholic Schools in Action," there were 200 Roman Catholic schools in the United States. Three years later, Mother Seton's parochial system was endorsed by the American Bishops, who urged all pastors "to provide a Catholic school in every parish or congregation subject to them, where this can be done."

By 1884, at the Third Plenary Council of Baltimore, which was a kind of little ecumenical council, the hierarchy adopted resolutions requiring that within two years a school be built near every parish church unless the local Bishop granted a dispensa-

tion, and declaring that parents were bound to send children to Catholic schools, unless it was evident that their religious education was being satisfactorily carried out in the home.

Today, with parochial classrooms bursting at the seams, emphasis on the moral duty of parents to send their children to parochial schools is minimized by bishops, pastors and preachers.

Nothing comparable to the Catholic parochial school system in the United States is found elsewhere, even in the most traditional of Roman Catholic countries. As a private school network, the parochial schools are unmatched in size by everything except the nation's vast public school complex. And even here, in the Northern urban centers, the comparisons come to the measuring of giants.

Urban Percentage High

In a 1963 study, for example, the Rev. Neil G. McCluskey, a Jesuit educator, found that 26 per cent of the children of New York, 34 per cent of those in Chicago, 39 per cent in Philadelphia, 23 per cent in Detroit, 28 per cent in Cincinnati, 30 per cent in Boston, and a whopping 42 per cent in Pittsburgh attended Roman Catholic parochial schools.

The origins of the system are deeply rooted in American social history. Latter-day justifications for the Roman Catholic schools have frequently been elaborated in theological philosophich, and even pedagogic terms.

It is doubtful, however, that the system would have ever gotten under way or been given the initial financial support it received from a far-from-affluent Roman Catholic community, composed largely of recent immigrants, if the early public schools had been truly "neutral" on religious questions.

Horace Mann, who is now regarded as the patron saint of public education, was looked upon as something of an extremist for opposing "sectarian" teaching in the pioneering public schools of his time, the early 1800's.

However, even he welcomed the Bible into the classroom "enshielded from harm, by the great Protestant doctrine of the inviolability of conscience, the right and sanctity of private judgment, without note or interpreter."

Used Protestant Bible

The Bible in question, of course, was the King James Version. Roman Catholic children were required to join in reading from it. They were also required to recite Protestant prayers and to sing Protestant hymns.

According to a statement of the Catholic hierarchy of the time: "The schoolboy can scarcely find a book in which one or more of our institutions or practices is not exhibited for otherwise than it really is, and greatly to our disadvantage."

Today, in an era of Protestant - Catholic good feeling, Roman Catholic parochial school students are urged to recite prayers with Protestants, to read the same Bible, and, even when there are no Protestants present, they often sing hymns written by Protestants for Protestants, not only in school but in church.

In the nineteenth century, however, inter-religious frictions were often exacerbated by long-standing prejudice, ethnic differences, and a massive influx of Catholic immigrants.

Religious orders of teaching sisters and brothers, many of them strongly ethnic in character, came from Europe with the new immigrants in order to take over the mushrooming Roman Catholic school system. A few orders were founded here for the same purpose.

The parochial school system in the United States, however, was from the beginning democratic in character, attended by the sons and daughters of hod carriers and professional men, without distinction.

The Notre Dame authors admit that it is now "difficult" to answer "Why do Catholic schools exist?" To respond to the question, however, they invoke the Pastoral Letter of the Archbishops and Bishops of the United States published in 1919.

In that document the hierarchy proposed five principles as "the basis of Catholic education."

¶Education is "essentially and inevitably" a moral activity. It is fitting therefore that it be carried out under the church's auspices.

¶Human capacities must be developed harmoniously. "An education that quickens the intelligence and enriches the mind with knowledge, but fails to develop the will and direct it to the practice of virtue, may produce scholars but it cannot produce good men."

¶Education must cede first place to the knowledge of God and His law.

¶Religious instruction must keep pace with other branches of learning. "It should so permeate these that its influence will be felt in every circumstance of life."

¶An education that unites intellectual, moral, and religious elements is the best training for citizenship.

The Notre Dame study directors developed a test to determine whether parochial school students of the present-day could reason about religious questions, discriminate between proposed answers, and see the relationship between their theoretical knowledge about their religion and practical conclusions.

Did Reasonably Well

The group tested, according to the study, did reasonably well. More than half chose the desired answers. But more than a third chose the "conventional" responses; and 12 per cent responded with what the authors described as "moralistic" replies. Girls in all-girls high schools showed the best understanding of their religion, according to the findings.

The study, which was completed before the outcome of the Ecumenical Council, Vatican II, became clear, could not measure the effect of changes brought about by the Council. In the opinion of some observers, consequently, its findings may be quickly dated, for it is generally agreed that Roman Cath-

olicism is undergoing vast changes, which are being carried out with surprising speed.

For example, the Vatican Council stimulated immense ferment in the orders of teaching brothers and sisters. Many of these religious, especially the younger ones, have a new image of themselves and of their role in the church and in the world. This will affect their teaching.

Moreover, they have a new image of the laity. The more progressive are already sharing authority with their lay collaborators in the schools. The lay-religious tensions among teachers, the study notes, are almost sure to be relieved, or, where there are not, the expected changes are almost sure to be intensified.

Again, in the spirit of the Ecumenical Council and the new look given to Roman Catholicism by Pope John XXIII, the parochial schools are more and more being looked upon as being at the service of the general community rather than as citadels protecting pupils from non-Christian influences. This will result in more collaboration with secular institutions.

The post-Council emphasis in Catholicism on a Biblical, non-juridicial approach to religion, most experts in the Church agree, is certain, as time goes on, to revolutionize the spirit of the parochial institution. Not only the manner but, more importantly, the substance of religious training will be affected.

As one high school student recently put it:

"When your teacher misses class because she took time off to participate with other nuns in a civil rights demonstration, you get a different idea of religion. At least you get a different idea of why she is leading the kind of life she leads in her convent—what makes her tick."

August 28, 1966

CATHOLICS ISSUE A NEW MAGAZINE

Conservative Monthly Is Set Up by Buckley Relative

A new conservative Roman Catholic magazine has produced its first issue despite a last-minute name change and a bolt of lightning that delayed production five days.

The monthly magazine, titled Triumph, was founded by L. Brent Bozell, a former editor of the conservative National Review and brother-in-law of its editor, William F. Buckley Jr.

It is designed to counter what Mr. Bozell regards as the "liberal" tone of the Catholic press in the United States.

"Our aim is to provide a literate voice in contemporary Cath-

olic journalism that is not actively abetting the secularist revolution in the Church," he said in an interview.

The tradition-minded journal was originally entitled Future. Shortly before publication, however, the editors discovered that this word was part of the title of a Junior Chamber of Commerce publication.

5,000 Copies in Issue

"We didn't have the money to defend ourselves in court," said Mr. Bozell, "so we changed the name at the last minute."

The first issue of 5,000 copies was scheduled to be run off Aug. 17, but it was delayed five days when lightning struck the transformer of The Periodical Press in Philadelphia where it is printed.

Mr. Bozell also complained that the post office in Philadelphia had been slow in sending out the magazine and that "only a smattering of subscribers have received their copies so far." He said the magazine was filing a formal complaint with the Post Office.

The magazine's opening editorial states that the editors are concerned with "helping to earn the triumph of Christianity over secularism."

Subjects of articles in the first issue include sin, church-state relations, the authority of the clergy, the doctrine of transubstantiation and the assassination of President Kennedy.

Mr. Bozell, who was converted to Roman Catholicism at the age of 20 from the Episcopal Church, said the magazine would deal not only with religious subjects but also with related social and economic issues.

"We think that the temporal world ought to be formed by norms based on Christian truths," he said. "The institutions of society—schools, communications, governments — ought to be formed in such a way as to help individuals lead Christian lives and find their way to heaven."

Mr. Bozell said the new magazine would back such causes as strong anti-obscenity and divorce laws.

"Freedom is not the highest value," he said. "It is more important that a man be virtuous than that he be politically or economically free."

Several editors of Triumph also contribute to The National Review, but Mr. Bozell said there is "absolutely no connection, financially or otherwise" between the two publications.

Budget of $100,000

The magazine will have a budget of approximately $100,000 a year, and Mr. Bozell expects it to be self-sufficient after two years. Funds for the first issue, came after a year-long direct mail appeal, he said.

Other editors of the magazine, whose offices are in Washington, include Thomas Molnar, Frederick Wilhelmsen, John Wisner and Mr. Bozell's wife, the former Patricia Buckley.

Contributors include Philip Burnham, a former editor of Commonweal, Christopher Dawson, Otto Van Hapsburg, Dietrich von Hildebrand and Erik von Kuehnelt-Leddihn.

September 18, 1966

Catholics Form Group to Seek 'Openness' in Church Decisions

By GEORGE DUGAN

Thirty Roman Catholic laymen and priests and a nun announced yesterday the formation of a national Institute for Freedom in the Church, designed to open channels of "democratic communication and mediation."

Distressed at instances of what they termed limitations on free discussion within the church, the group said it would seek an "openness" in decisions made by church authorities, preceded "as far as possible" by regular consultation within the Catholic community.

Formation of the institute was made known at a news conference in the Roosevelt Hotel. Five of the 30 persons constituting its board of directors were present.

The five were Eugene Fontinell, chairman of the institute's board and head of the philosophy department at Queens College; Daniel Callahan, an associate editor of Commonweal magazine; William Birmingham, editor of Mentor-Omega book publishers; the Rev. William Clancy, provost of the Pittsburgh Oratory, a community of secular priests, and Richard Horchler, program director of the National Conference of Christians and Jews.

Mr. Fontinell cited as one of the reasons for organizing the group the "silencing" of the Rev. Daniel Berrigan, a Jesuit who was suddenly transferred from his post on his order's foreign missions board here. He was sent to Latin America after having criticized the role of the United States in Vietnam.

Mr. Fontinell said that in the absence of contrary evidence "people could not help but think" that Father Berrigan "was being silenced for his political activities."

The new institute, Mr. Fontinell said, will call attention to "actions and situations" within the church that "in our opinion violate the principles of freedom."

He emphasized that the group would not "frivolously seek headlines," but added that it would not "evade rendering a judgment on a controversial matter when we feel that a judgment is called for."

By the same token, he added, "we have no intention of immediately leaping into every conflict situation that now exists in the church."

The institute hopes to have an eventual membership of 25,000. Dues will be on an ascending scale of $5 general, $10 sustaining and $25 for a founding member.

A statement of purpose disclosed yesterday listed "procedures and areas of activity" that included the following:

¶Help examine existing policies in the conduct of church life with a view to offering constructive recommendations.

¶Help investigate problem areas before an explosive situation develops.

¶Examine claims of violations of freedom with the hope of ameliorating the conditions and rectifying any abuses.

¶Undertake studies of major areas where lack of freedom has been "institutionalized" within the church and recommend new approaches and procedures.

The institute's address was given as Box 1107, New Rochelle, N. Y.

The Institute's Directors

The board of directors of the institute for Freedom in the Church, in addition to the five at the news conference, consists of the following

John Bannan, associate professor of philosophy at Loyola University, Chicago.
Thomas Bird, lecturer in Russian at Queens College and editor of the magazine Diakonia.
Sister M. Charles Borromeo, of the faculty at St. Mary's College, Notre Dame, Ind.
Dennis Clark, a Temple University specialist in race relations and urban affairs.
Matthew Clarke, of the Reed Research Institute for Creative Studies.
Joseph Cuneen, founder and managing editor of the magazine Cross Currents.
The Rev. Charles Curran, professor of moral theology at Catholic University, Washington.
Leslie Dewart, associate professor of philosophy at St. Michael's College of the University of Toronto.
Thomas Hargadon, assistant to the mayor of Newton, Mass.
Richard Hinners, associate professor of philosophy at Loyola College, Montreal.
Journet Kahn, of the faculty of St. Xavier College, Chicago.
John McDermott, associate of philosophy at Queens College.
Donna Myers, a member of The Grail, an international movement of Catholic women.
John Mulholland, director of planning, National Council of Catholic Men.
Joseph Mulholland, director, Center for College Improvement at Queens College.
Michael Novak, author and faculty member at Stanford University in California.
John O'Connor, columnist and contributor to Catholic journals.
Nancy Rambusch, director of the preschool education training department of the Mount Vernon, N. Y., public schools.
The Rev. Eugene Shallert, department of sociology, University of San Francisco.
Leonard Swidler, co-editor of the Journal of Ecumenical Studies.
The Rev. John P. Vrana, faculty member at St. Francis Seminary, Oklahoma City.
The Rev. Joseph Walsh, Catholic chaplain at Brandeis University, Waltham Mass.
Richard Walsh, director of the radio-TV film department of the National Council of Catholic Men.
Garry Wills, professor of classics at Johns Hopkins University, Baltimore.
John Donnelly, president, National Council of Catholic Men.

September 22, 1966

MEATLESS FRIDAYS WILL END ON DEC. 2 FOR U.S. CATHOLICS

By GEORGE DUGAN
Special to The New York Times

WASHINGTON, Nov. 18— American Roman Catholics will no longer be required to abstain from meat on Fridays.

A pastoral statement by the National Conference of American Bishops, meeting in annual session at Catholic University, said that the abstinence requirement would end Dec. 2.

Exceptions to the dispensation are the Fridays during the 40-day Lenten period and Ash Wednesday, the first day of Lent.

The date of Dec. 2 was selected because it is the first Friday following the first Sunday in Advent, traditionally the beginning of the church's liturgical year.

The decision was announced at the headquarters of the United States Catholic Conference, the bishops' administrative secretariat that was formerly known as the National Catholic Welfare Conference. The prelates ended their five-day meeting this afternoon.

Advocated by Council

The lifting of the meatless Friday law is in accord with reforms advocated by the Second Vatican Council to bring the practices of the church in line with modern conditions.

Catholic leaders agree that in the world of the 20th century, dietary habits have become irrelevant as a means of penance. It is their feeling that penance would be more meaningful if works of charity and other forms of personal penance were substituted for abstinence and fasting.

The sin of eating meat on Friday can be abrogated by the American hierarchy because it pertains to church law or discipline and not Divine law.

National episcopal conferences have been granted the authority to determine their own forms of penance by Rome. The more than 200 bishops who attended the meeting here are the spiritual leaders of some 46 million Catholics.

The abolishment of meatless Fridays, in effect, will start next Friday as most American Catholics are traditionally dispensed from Friday abstinence on the day after Thanksgiving. The Archdiocese of New York has already declared this dispensation.

The pastoral statement issued today reflected these concepts. The statement called on Catholics to do the following:

¶Re-emphasize the importance of penitential observance in the whole life of the Christian.

¶Renew and encourage the liturgical observance of the Advent season as a season of effective preparation for the Christmas season.

¶Preserve the tradition of abstinence from meat on all Fridays of Lent. The bishops declared in this connection their confidence "that no Catholic Christian will lightly hold himself excused from this penitential practice."

"For all other week days of Lent," the statement said, "we strongly recommend participation in daily mass and a self-imposed observance of fasting. In the light of grave human needs which weigh on the Christian conscience in all seasons, we urge particularly during Lent, generosity to local, national and world programs of sharing of all things needed to translate our duty to penance into a means of implementing the right of the poor to their part in our abundance."

The bishops insisted that by abolishing Friday abstinence they had not diminished the "fact of sin" and the need of penance. Eating meat on Friday had always been regarded as a sin.

"We emphasize," they asserted, "that our people are henceforth free from the obligation traditionally binding under pain of sin in what pertains to Friday abstinence, except as noted above for Lent.

"Perhaps we should warn those who decide to keep the Friday abstinence for reasons of personal piety and special love that they must not pass judgment on those who elect to substitute other penitential observances. Friday, please God, will acquire among us other forms of penitential witness which may become as much a part of the devout way of life in the future as Friday abstinence from meat.

"In this connection we have foremost in mind the modern need for self-discipline in the use of stimulants and for a renewed emphasis of the virtue of temperance, especially in the use of alcoholic beverages.

Hospital Work Suggested

"It would bring great glory to God and good to souls if Fridays found our people doing volunteer work in hospitals, visiting the sick, serving the needs of the aged and the lonely, instructing the young in the faith, participating as Christians in community affairs, and meeting our obligations to our families, our friends, our neighbors and our community, including our parishes, with a special zeal born of the desire to add the merit of penance to the other virtues exercised in good works born of living faith."

A statement issued by Archbishop John F. Dearden of Detroit, president of the National Conference of Catholic Bishops, said in part:

"I believe that I express the sentiments of the bishops of the United States when I state that we have resolved this week to carry out the spirit of the Second Vatican Council by inaugurating the implementation of its directives in this country. With further study, reflection, prayer and God's grace, we will revitalize the church in our nation for the years ahead.

"It should not be concluded that our work is done. It is only beginning. Indeed, this is a transitional meeting, the first for the United States bishops as a group since the Second Vatican Council and, therefor, one which we do not expect to produce definitive answers but to create the machinery necessary for future progress. I am confident that such machinery now exists and has been set in motion. With the assistance of our loyal and dedicated clergy, religious and laity— the entire people of God—the goals of the Second Vatican Council will be achieved."

On Oct. 14, the Roman Catholic bishops of Canada authorized churchgoers to eat meat on Fridays throughout the year. The new ruling permitted the churchgoers to make other penance of their own choosing to replace the meatless Friday penance.

Several days later, the French bishops ruled that Catholics would be allowed to eat meat on Fridays beginning Jan. 1 except during Lent.

The Italian bishops lifted the ban last August. In addition, the hierarchies of Mexico and the African republic of Upper Volta have taken formal action to end meatless Fridays.

The Roman Catholic Church defines abstinence as refraining from eating the flesh of warm-blooded animals, including fowl. Fasting is defined as the consumption of not more than one full meal and two lesser ones in a day.

Last February, Pope Paul VI ruled in an apostolic decree that prayer or charitable works might be substituted as penance instead of fasting and abstinence.

The papal decree authorized national bishops' conferences to make their own decisions in regard to banning meatless Fridays, taking into consideration the social and economic conditions in their countries.

But the Pope insisted that fasting and abstinence were still obligatory on Ash Wednesday, the first day of Lent, and Good Friday.

He suggested that Catholics in underprivileged areas could

substitute prayer for fasting while those in highly developed countries might perform works of charity as their penance.

American Catholics have always been required to observe the law of fasting from Monday through Saturday during the 40 days of Lent and to practice abstention every Friday, the traditional day on which Jesus Christ was believed to have died on the cross.

Dispensation from Friday abstinence is normally granted in cases of extreme poverty, destitution, illness, heavy work or other "grave" reasons.

Many Roman Catholics have ignored the ban when refusal to eat meat on Fridays would embarrass their host.

Special dispensations were frequently granted by bishops in times of community emergencies, holidays or other occasions.

An automatic dispensation in effect in the United States and Canada permitted train travelers to eat meat on Friday and major airlines have been granted dispensation by the Holy See for their Catholic passengers.

Military personnel and dependents living with them were also excused from Friday abstinence.

In Spain, Catholics have eaten meat on Fridays since 1089. The

dispensation was granted in recognition of the Spanish defeat of the Moors.

Strict in Ireland

One of the earliest known papal decrees on Friday abstinence that actually established the custom as church law, was promulgated by Pope Nicholas I, who reigned from 858 to 867.

In Ireland, England and the United States the obligation of Friday abstinence has been interpreted most strictly. In these areas "fish on Friday" became almost synonomous with being a practicing Catholic. It was not so strictly interpreted in the traditionally Catholic areas of continental Europe and thus the obligation of abstinence was never so stringently practiced or applied.

The last area in the Western Hemisphere where the exemption prevailed was in the southwestern United States. Spanish conquistadors had brought the dispensation with them to the New World. It was not until 1951 that the dispensation ended for Catholics in New Mexico, Arizona and part of Texas.

Because of peculiar local conditions, temporary dispensations have been granted because the poor did not have enough money to buy fish.

November 19, 1966

Paulists Publish New Concept of Catechism

By GEORGE DUGAN

A new concept in teaching religion to Roman Catholic children, departing radically from the traditional rote of the Baltimore Catechism, was made "available for immediate adoption" yesterday by the Paulist Fathers.

The new teaching program, published by the Paulist Press, involves the use of recorded music, art work, a youngster's own drawings and teacher-parent guide books.

The method was made available, the publishers said, because of the "excellent results" it is now receiving in tests throughout the country. It was formally introduced yesterday at a reception in the Warwick Hotel.

For years the Baltimore Catechism of 1884 has been the basic method of Roman Catholic religious instruction in this country. It depends entirely on rote, with youngsters replying to questions with preselected answers committed to memory.

The Paulist Fathers, founded in 1858 by the Rev. Isaac T. Hecker as the first community of priests to originate in the United States, are primarily

An illustration from section of Paulist classbook dealing with the creation of the earth

preachers and teachers.

The new program prepared by the publishing affiliate, like the revised catechism produced by several other Catholic publishers, was undertaken largely as a result of the reforms instituted by the Second Vatican Council.

In most instances, the new catechisms are still being tested in various dioceses. Each individual diocese will study all the new catechisms and choose those they find acceptable for classes in their jurisdiction.

The new Paulist approach is regarded as more advanced than

any other catechetical program in that it makes wider use of visual materials, such as art work.

In the rote procedure used in the Baltimore Catechism, the teacher asks: "What is God?" And the well-rehearsed child replies: "God is a pure spirit,

99

infinitely perfect, creator and master of all things."

Developers of the Paulist approach agreed several years ago that no 6-year-old child could grasp the full meaning of the answer.

So, armed with the imprimatur, or go-ahead from Rome, a team of 30 catechists, theologians, psychologists, sociologists and teachers began their own reform in 1961 in Canada.

Under the new catechism, when the child is confronted with the question, "What is God?" he will, under classroom guidance, look at a brightly colored picture of the rising sun reflected in a pool of blue water.

Textual material on the facing page reads: "God says: Let there be dry land and water and there was dry land and water. Let there be in the sky a sun for the day and a moon for the night, and there was in the sky a sun for the day and a moon for the night."

Then: "We say to God: Lord, how great and wonderful you are! Who is like you in heaven and on earth?"

Other components of the program include handbooks for parents and teachers, a long-playing record with basic religious themes, and bright posters designed to provide "visual focal points."

Evaluation Deferred

Msgr. John Dougherty, Associate Superintendent of Schools for Religious Education in the Archdiocese of New York, described the new materials yesterday as "attractive and promising." He said, however, that an evaluation of their effectiveness would be premature at this time.

The archdiocese is using a series produced by W. H. Sadlier, publisher at 11 Park Place, and experimenting with several catechisms that include a movement away from the traditional question-and-answer approach.

The Paulist series, and another published recently by Benziger Brothers, a New York publishing house, are each being tested in four schools, Msgr. Dougherty said, and a new Allyn and Bacon series, pub-

'THE RISEN JESUS': In this illustration, which is part of the new Paulist teaching program, "the risen Jesus shows himself to his apostles." The picture has been designed to "help convey a spiritual attitude of faith in the risen Jesus as well as joy in the mind of the child."

lished at Rockleigh, N. J., may also be tried next year. He said a decision on which series to use permanently would be made after June, 1968. It is possible, he added, that more than one will be approved.

Another Plan Begun

The Confraternity of Christian Doctrine, the arm of the National Conference of Catholic Bishops charged with the instruction of those not in parochial schools, started a program two weeks ago to develop its own new catechism to replace the Baltimore Catechism.

A spokesman for the conference said yesterday that the new series of texts would take three to five years to complete.

As the Canadian experiment developed, the Paulist catechism was constantly tested. By the fall of 1964 a small group of schools were using it. One year later, it was being used by 125,000 students in 6,000 Canadian class rooms.

The Rev. Alvin Illig, general manager of the Paulist Press in Glen Rock, N. J., said the program was now being used in one-third of the dioceses in this country.

Father Illig was accompanied at yesterday's reception by Sister Chabanel of Toronto, a modishly dressed nun of the teaching order of the Institution of the Blessed Virgin Mary.

Sister Chabanel's light touch of lipstick, her short blue dress with white collar and carefully waved hair, caught some of the priests speechless. Later, she explained that she was just as comfortable "in or out" of her normal nun's habit.

In praising the Paulist program, Sister Chabanel pointed out that a youngster "can't be switched in midstream."

"When he outgrows the baby Jesus," she observed, "he outgrows Jesus."

Father Illig described the Paulist venture as a new concept in religious education and a "10-year leap forward in catechetics."

Although only the first-grade course is now available, the Paulist Press plans to offer new catechism materials for all grades of parochial schools over the next few years.

In the parents' guide book, a brightly colored picture of animals appears under an adaptation of passages from the first chapter of Genesis.

It begins with the words: "We praise God for our beautiful world," and then continues:
"God says,
Let the fish swim in the water,
let the birds fly in the sky,
let the animals run over the earth.
And the fish swam,
and the birds flew,
and the animals ran over the earth."

The Roman Catholic Church in the Netherlands recently published a new 600-page catechism for adults that is designed to stimulate thought rather than merely to transmit knowledge by question and answer.

It incorporates the liberal theological thinking that has characterized the Netherlands Catholic Church in recent years and emphasizes the ambiguity inherent in many religious problems and moral issues. It will be published in English next fall by Herder & Herder and is expected to create considerable controversy among English-speaking Catholics.

February 10, 1967

9 Catholic Scholars Join Move to Let Clergymen Marry

By EDWARD B. FISKE

Nine prominent Roman Catholic scholars have become advisers to a new unofficial Catholic organization seeking a change in canon law to permit priests to marry.

The organization, known as the National Association for Pastoral Renewal, was formed

at a meeting in an unidentified Midwestern city last November by 23 Catholic priests from dioceses throughout the country.

The priests drafted a specific proposal for modifying the 800-year-old requirement that priests not marry. Last month they began polling priests on their views.

Wide Support Believed

An officer of the association said yesterday that the purpose of the survey was to demonstrate that there was widespread support for a change among clergymen, and to per-

suade the National Conference of Catholic Bishops to "begin serious discussion of the celibacy problem."

The officer said that 10,000 priests in more than 25 dioceses had been reached and that about a quarter had returned the questionnaire. Of these, he said, "about 90 per cent" favored the proposal.

The leaders of the association have declined to make their names public. The only address they give is Post Office Box 584, Madison Square Station, New York, N.Y. 10010.

The officer reached yesterday said that publication of the names of the 12 members of the organization's coordinating committee "would put some of them on the hot seat and would restrict the freedom that we now have to discuss the issue frankly with various bishops."

Yesterday, however, the association announced the formation of a national advisory board consisting of nine prominent Catholic priests and laymen.

Following are the nine members of the board:
The Revs. John A. O'Brien and

John L. MacKenzie of Notre Dame University.

The Revs. Eugene Burke and Alfred McBride of the Catholic University of America.

The Rev. Joseph Fichter of Harvard University.

Thomas Neill of St. Louis University.

William Birmingham, editor of the Catholic journal Cross Currents.

The Rev. Roderick Hindery, vice rector of Immaculate Conception Seminary in Conception, Mo.

Petro Bilaniuk of St. Michael's College, the University of Toronto.

Father O'Brien described the work of the association yesterday as a "most timely movement." He said in an interview:

"Anyone who reads the paper today knows that the number of candidates for the priesthood here and in other countries is at an all-time low, and that the number of defections in many countries is reaching an all-time high.

"Common sense dictates that the question of celibacy as a necessary condition for ordination should be studied and investigaged. This should be done calmly and in light of the Vatican Council's call for a reexamination of the relevance of so many of the Church's customs, practices and structures."

Changes Sought by Group

The proposal drafted by the association calls for changes that would:

¶Make marriage optional rather than mandatory for diocesan clergy; that is, priests who are responsible to the bishop of a diocese rather than to a religious order, such as the Society of Jesus.

¶Allow members of religious orders who desire to marry to transfer to the diocesan priesthood.

¶Make it possible for priests who have already married and have been forced to seek a new occupation to return to the active priesthood.

The association's proposal does not take up the question of whether seminarians should be permitted to marry and subsequently to become ordained. The Catholic Church's requirement for its priests in this respect is a matter of discipline rather than of unalterable dogma.

The only priests of the Latin rite married now are converted Protestants. Married men are permitted to be ordained by Eastern Orthodox churches, but bishops are chosen from the unmarried clergy.

The issue of allowing marriage by the clergy attracted great attention among delegates to the Ecumenical Council when, in September, 1964, it became known that the Vatican was more lenient in granting dispensations to priests who had been suspended from their priestly duties, and who wanted to marry within the church.

Traditional Rule Stressed

In October, 1965, however, the Pope said that it was "not at all opportune" to have a public debate on the issue at the council, and reiterated the church's traditional discipline.

The New Testament describes voluntary abstinence from marriage as helpful for those dedicating themselves to the service of God. However, it speaks of this as an ideal, rather than as a requirement.

In II Corinthians, vii, 8-9, for instance, St. Paul said: "To the unmarried and the widows I say that it is well for them to remain single as I do. But if they cannot exercise self-control, they should marry. For it is better to marry than to be aflame with passion."

Priests and bishops frequently married in ancient and medieval times. After much dispute, the Second Lateran Council in 1139 then made abstention from marriage a requirement for clerics.

A change would have to come from Pope Paul VI.

The association proposes that a new "ordinariate" be formed for married clergymen. This is an ecclesiastical division for priests engaged in a particular apostolate. For example, Cardinal Spellman is the vicar for chaplains in the Military Ordinariate.

Father Fichter, who is a sociologist, made a study of 3,000 American priests last year, and found that 62 per cent of them favored making marriage optional, although only 5 per cent said they themselves wou'd

marry, if given the opportunity.

In an interview yesterday, Father Fichter emphasized that the issue was "only one aspect of the much larger question of renewal of the whole ministry."

He said that it could not be considered apart from other issues such as the status of lower-echelon clergy, seminary training and promotion systems, and "what the priest does if his superior tells him one thing and his conscience another."

An information aide of the Most Rev. John F. Dearden, Archbishop of Detroit and leader of the National Conference of Catholic Bishops, said yesterday that the agenda for the bishops' meeting in Chicago on April 10 had already been set, and that he saw "little chance" that the marriage issue would be discussed.

The officer of the Association for Pastoral Renewal who was interviewed yesterday said that unofficial priests' associations and groups of laymen and priests are planning polls on the marriage issue in other dioceses, including the Archdiocese of Chicago.

An aide to the Most Rev. John King Mussio, Bishop of Steubenville, Ohio, said that Bishop Mussio sent the association's proposal to his priests this week with an accompanying letter, which took no position on the issue but encouraged the priests to make their views known to the association.

March 24, 1967

CATHOLIC LAYMEN IN CHICAGO UNITE

By EDWARD B. FISKE
Special to The New York Times

CHICAGO, April 2.—Fifteen hundred Roman Catholic laymen from the Archdiocese of Chicago created today a new unofficial organization dedicated to "lay power."

The organization, known as the Chicago Conference of Laymen, will seek to mobilize lay opinion on current issues in the church and to give laymen new decision making power in the archdiocese.

The leaders said they would work in areas such as birth control, parochial school policies, race relations and church finance.

One goal is the development of a method whereby "Catholic laymen of Chicago can play a role in the selection of major ecclesiastical officials of their archdiocese."

The organization was founded at an afternoon meeting that filled the gymnasium of St. Ignatius High School, a parochial school operated by Jesuits.

The meeting had been previously scheduled at the University of Chicago, but the registration of 1,500 was four times

the number originally expected, and the meeting was moved.

Call For Laymen's Role

The delegates unanimously adopted a document calling for a role for the layman that is "commensurate with his capacity and with the church's need for his experience."

A spokesman for the Most Rev. John P. Cody, Archbishop of Chicago, said that he would have no comment on the new group. The archdiocese has no formal connection with the conference and was not invited to send a representative to today's meeting.

The conference is regarded as the first of its kind, although the role of the laity in church affairs has become a major concern since the Vatican Ecumenical Council of 1962 to 1965, which urged that laymen be given a greater voice in church affairs.

In Minneapolis an Association of Christians for Church Renewal was formed last summer with a reported mailing list of 600 persons. It recently published a report that, among other things, called on the Most Rev. Leo Binz, Archbishop of St. Paul, to convene a lay congress next year.

Cities Lack of Awareness

The Rev. John McKenzie, a Jesuit Biblical scholar, said at today's meeting that "the

clergy as a body are not sufficiently aware either of how the layman lives or what his potential is."

Except for Father McKenzie, the only clergymen invited to the meeting were six observers from the Association of Chicago Priests, an unofficial organization that says it has 1,300 members. It seeks to give priests a stronger voice in archdiocesan affairs.

Mr. Heyrman said that the Chicago Conference of Laymen grew out of informal conversations among Catholics who are active in existing lay groups, such as the Catholic Interracial Council.

"Following the Ecumenical Council, however," he said, "it became clear that these had reached their limits and that new forms are necessary."

A letter was sent out several weeks ago inviting laymen to today's meeting. It stated in part:

Day of Adult Layman

"It is a new day in the church. The day of the adult layman has begun. The church cannot be renewed, cannot fulfill her mission unless laymen are able to have a meaningful share in her life—in terms of their power and presence in decision making and their freedom to play a prophetic role."

Each of the 1,500 participants in today's conference, who in-

cluded many young married couples, were invited to sign up for one of 14 commissions. These will work in areas such as birth control, Catholic education, church finance, ecumenism, the Catholic press, lay-clergy relations, and war and peace. Steering committee nominations were also solicited.

Donald Heyrman, a sales manager for the Burroughs Corporation, who is chairman of the conference steering committee, said that the organization would function in part as a "pressure group" within the archdiocese.

"We hope our ideas will be listened to on their merits," he said, "but if they are not given consideration, it would be unrealistic to say that we won't take advantage of the fact that we are organized."

Mr. Heyrman said that the commissions would engage in research and that public hearings might be held on issues such as birth control.

A major goal of the association will be the addition of laymen to bodies that determine diocesan policies in areas such as finance and education. Mr. Heyrman acknowledged that laymen are now members of some advisory boards, such as school boards, but he called this "largely window dressing."

April 3, 1967

Book In the News

By JOHN LEO

THE heaviest reader response to an article on the "Speaking Out" page of the Saturday Evening Post came after a 1966 contribution by the pseudonymous Father Stephen Nash, "I Am a Priest: I Want to Marry." Angry Roman Catholics who demanded to know the identity of the author should now be satisfied. He is Father James Kavanaugh, a personable 38-year-old priest on leave from the Diocese of Lansing, Mich. He has expanded his article into a book—"A Modern Priest Looks at His Outdated Church" (Trident Press, $4.95) —that has sold 60,000 copies in the past six weeks and now ranks seventh among general books on the best seller list.

Some of the book's success may be attributed to the effective promotion given it by Father Kavanaugh and his publisher. Today Father Kavanaugh is resting in Washington in the middle of a second arduous national tour. Last Thursday he was interviewed on the "Today" television program in New York, then hurried to Washington to make bookstore appearances. Tomorrow he will be in Baltimore; leading Midwestern cities follow. Two excerpts from his book have appeared in Look magazine.

LITTLE in the book is new, fairly presented or convincingly argued. Yet it is a personal cry of anguish that goes right to the heart of the troubles currently plaguing the Roman Catholic Church.

Father Kavanaugh is a representative of "the other" Catholic Church. In the terminology of sociologist William Osborne, there are now two Catholic churches, and in America at least, they are growing ominously far apart. One is the church of ecclesiastical reform — concerned with order, committees, changes of personnel, sanctions and preservation of structures. It is more concerned with certitude than understanding, and even with the best of intentions, it is not equipped to adapt very rapidly.

The other church, which can be called the church of religious reform, is concerned with norms, values and behavior, with honesty and understanding rather than certitude. Since Pope John, this church has made irreversible changes without recourse to the ecclesiastical church.

One example is birth control —the church of religious reform has decisively changed its mind on this issue. Public-opinion polls show that Catholics now use contraceptives in about the same proportion as non-Catholics, and there are few theologians under the age of 50 who will even attempt to suggest a serious theological reason for opposing all contraception. It is no longer a theological issue, but rather a diplomatic problem for the gradual adapters of the ecclesiastical church. The church of religious reform has moved on to other matters.

Father Kavanaugh's book is a bitter brief for "the other" church. He argues that ideals have been frozen into law, abstractions have been given primacy over persons, arbitrary traditions (such as compulsory clerical celibacy) have trampled the uniqueness of the individual, and produced misery and guilt on a systematic basis.

THE fact that an unthinking and tenuous bit of theology (framed entirely by celibates) on the birth-control issue could have brought so much unnecessary agony seems an outrage to Father Kavanaugh. "Don't give me more learned arguments!" he writes. "I have read them all a thousand times. Don't tell me that I must wait patiently for a Pope to appear on a balcony before I can send [a Catholic woman] home to her husband's bed." This is a representative passage from the book; angry, oversimplified, somewhat anti-intellectual, insistent that from now on values will grow from the Christian vision of "the other" church, and not from official declarations.

The success of Father Kavanaugh's book, so mysterious to Catholic intellectuals who "knew it all along," suggests that only now is the code of the other church being articulated for its widest audience.

In sum, the traditional sanctions and bureaucratic control that prevented open discussion have decayed and are no longer credible to many Catholics. Conflict is being institutionalized, and a new Catholic ethos, formed with no relation to Rome, is growing rapidly from the bottom of the church. The somewhat panicky reaction from Rome — Pope Paul's encyclical on celibacy is an example—is to try to stem the tide by insisting on papal primacy and by suggesting that error in a lengthy church tradition is "unthinkable."

Father Kavanaugh insists that the institutional church as we know it is breaking up. I think he is correct, and that the convulsions within Catholicism are just beginning.

MR. LEO, a former editor of Commonweal, is a member of The Times news staff.

July 30, 1967

AUTHOR-PRIEST HIT BY LANSING BISHOP

LANSING, Mich., Sept. 15, (AP) — The Rev. James J. Kavanaugh, author of "A Modern Priest Looks At His Outdated Church," has been termed "a disobedient priest" by his bishop, the Most Rev. Alexander Zaleski of the Lansing Roman Catholic Diocese.

The bishop said he wanted to clarify a statement in which Father Kavanaugh said he "is a priest in good standing in the Diocese of Lansing."

"I previously have stated that he had refused to accept an assignment in the Diocese of Lansing and is absent without my permission." Bishop Zaleski said. "This obviously means that he is a disobedient priest.

"Moreover, when he departs in his public statements from the teaching of the Church, he speaks out not as its representative but as a private person.

Excerpts from the book appeared in Look Magazine. The book is critical of some of the teachings of the Catholic Church.

Father Kavanaugh wrote that he believed priests should be allowed to marry. His engagement recently was announced in California, where he is a counselor at the Human Resources Institute at La Jolla.

Father Kavanaugh, 37 years old, was ordained in June, 1954.

September 16, 1967

Laymen to Help Pick Candidates For Priesthood in a Sheen Plan

Special to The New York Times

ROCHESTER, Sept. 14—The Most Rev. Fulton J. Sheen, Bishop of Rochester, has ordered broad reforms for the diocesan seminary, including the appointment of seven lay persons to consider the fitness of aspirants to the Roman Catholic priesthood.

The board—four men and three women—will "assist the seminary authorities in the selection of fit candidates for the altar." Bishop Sheen said the board could be the first of its kind in a Catholic seminary in the United States.

Since coming to Rochester last December the Bishop has introduced a number of departures from traditional patterns in the diocese. The moves were surprising because he had been considered a conservative.

Among other innovations, announced this week, are the addition to the faculty of Protestants to teach preaching and pastoral skills.

A layman will interpret the controversial theology of the late Teilhard de Chardin. A former British Communist leader will give a course on "The Utilization of Existing Institutions and Structures for the Purposes of the Church."

Bishop Sheen also announced the start of an extensive program of psychological testing so that those who were emotionally or otherwise unfit might be "quickly removed from the path of the priesthood."

The changes were made public this week in a "pastoral letter on seminary renewal." About 150 local students are preparing at St. Bernard's Seminary for service in the diocese.

Bishop Sheen said in an interview that the changes were intended to "give the seminary some intellectual excellence" and to "increase the emotional stability of those in the priesthood."

Question Sometimes 'Late'

He regards the appointment of the board of seven lay persons as the most important change, he said.

He noted that during the ordination of a priest the bishop asks the congregation, "Do you know any reason why this candidate should not be ordained?" This question, however, Bishop Sheen said, "is sometimes asked too late."

The new consultative board will work with diocesan officials in examining candidates before they reach the point of ordination. 'Thus the whole people of God, the laity and the clergy will assist one another in forming a priesthood after the heart of Christ," Bishop Sheen declared.

In other efforts to weed out those unfit for the rigors of the priesthood, the 72-year-old prelate asserted that all seminarians would undergo psychological testing and take courses on the theme of "The Mature Man."

These courses, he said, will deal with the motivation, personality and discipline of priests as well as with pastoral problems such as mental illness, drug addiction and alcoholism.

The Bishop noted that such psychological investigations were specifically approved by the recent Ecumenical Council and by Pope Paul VI in his June encyclical on priestly celibacy.

Bishop Sheen, who has just been appointed by the Pope to participate in the forthcoming Synod of Bishops in Rome, announced other appointments to the faculty of St. Bernard's Seminary.

Dr. William Nelson of Colgate Rochester Divinity School, a Baptist institution, will lead field training for the future priests. The Rev. Conrad Massa, a Presbyterian, will teach homiletics, or preaching.

Dr. Massa was picked not because he is Protestant but because he is "skilled in homiletics, "Bishop Sheen said. "I must admit, though," he remarked, "that Presbyterians tend to know more about preaching than we do."

The former Communist leader who will teach is Douglas Hyde, a Catholic convert who was editor of The Daily Worker in Britain.

Since his move last January from the post of auxiliary bishop of the Archdiocese of New York to his own see, Bishop Sheen has made a number of highly unusual moves.

He became the first American Catholic bishop to challenge publicly United States policies in Vietnam, and he appointed a priest identified with a militant civil rights organization to be his urban specialist. He also raised the age of confirmation to the mid-teens.

September 15, 1967

Bridge Between 2 Eras

By JOHN LEO

Cardinal Spellman connected two eras in American Roman Catholic history. One era might be symbolized by William Cardinal O'Connell, young Father Spellman's mentor in Boston and the inspiration for the raffish and shrewd Cardinal in Edwin O'Connor's "The Last Hurrah." The second has already been termed the Era of John F. Kennedy. Cardinal Spellman was never on the best of terms with either of his fellow Boston Irishmen. But he combined something of the spirit of both. Like Cardinal O'Connell, he reflected a strong tradition of religious politicking and fierce tribal loyalty, combined with a suspicion of Protestants and secular culture. Like John Kennedy, but to a lesser extent, his expansive American confidence in freedom and democratic procedures broke through that tradition.

An Appraisal

At the Vatican Council, the Cardinal led a spirited fight to endorse religious liberty and scotch the ancient charge of deicide against the Jews. He also brought along as his personal peritus, or expert, the late John Courtney Murray, the theologian whose attempts to reconcile American and Catholic traditions had long been viewed with suspicion in Rome.

Outside the Midwest, Catholicism in America has had basically an Irish flavor, and Cardinal Spellman embodied the values that brought it about: financial acumen, a sense of organization and power, a closeness to his people that inspired almost total obedience.

Values Now Questioned

Since Pope John XXIII, the primacy of these values is no longer unquestioned within Catholicism. In America, they enabled a poor immigrant church, faced with the hostility of Protestants in a pre-Ecumenical era, to survive and spread. Today, they are caustically rejected by a new generation for whom Cardinal Spellman was the image of "bricks and mortar" religion, authoritarianism, and the enforced isolation of Catholics from the mainstream of American life.

Cardinal Spellman's style combined intolerance on dogma with personal tolerance. Among other things this meant rules for New York priests that were harsh by general American standards, but also great gentleness and sympathy for priests in trouble. Then, too, while ecumenical activity has been frowned on by the Chancery office almost to the present, the Cardinal enjoyed close personal relationship with Protestant and Jewish leaders as a matter of course.

The Cardinal was generally viewed as embodying another Irish Catholic trait: emphasis on the personal over the social. Personal sins of sexuality, drunkenness and uncharitableness have been declaimed far more regularly from New York pulpits than social sins of racism and exploitation of the poor.

In a gravediggers' strike in 1949 the personal affront to the unburied dead drew more of the Cardinal's sympathy than the social plights of the striking workers, and he oversaw the work of seminarians who dug graves to help break the strike.

Traditionally, the major concern of the Irish bishop has been the welfare of his own tribe. From this viewpoint, social crusades not involving direct interests of religion are often seen as peripheral or optional for Catholics.

These emphases put the Cardinal out of tune with the new ecumenical and socially dedicated spirit in Catholicism. At the Vatican Council, his role was small. Younger men with fresh ideas took the spotlight.

Back home, the primacy he once enjoyed as senior Cardinal went to the newly formed national Conference of Bishops. What was creative ferment to many progressive Catholics was viewed from the Cardinal's residence as an alien spirit of disloyalty. Visiting priests described him as baffled by many recent developments in the church.

The Cardinal's strong influence was attributed to enormous energy, affability and ability to befriend powerful men. That influence waned as the friends died and other styles of leadership overtook Catholicism.

His major contribution, perhaps, was to personalize and humanize the image of Catholicism. The public, in responding to his personal charity and gentle manner, enabled Catholics to shed the defensiveness that had long marked their social attitudes in America. That period has come to a close, though perhaps with some religious implications the Cardinal did not foresee.

December 3, 1967

YOUNG CATHOLICS ALTERING VALUES

Traditional Views Rejected by Students at Manhattan

By JOHN LEO

A campuswide survey at a Roman Catholic college here indicates a large-scale rejection of traditional Catholic practices, moral rules and pastoral leadership.

Only 7 per cent of the nearly 3,000 students polled at all-male Manhattan College considered the use of contraceptives wrong under all circumstances. Only 26 per cent opposed abortion, and only 21 per cent flatly opposed pre-marital sex relations.

Seventy-three per cent said their bishops and parish priests had no effect or influence on their daily lives; 62 per cent said they were "indifferent" to Sunday mass and 53 per cent denied the necessity of telling their sins to a priest in confession.

The students do not, however, seem to live by the views they report.

Seventy-five per cent said they regularly attended Sunday mass. Although only one student in five said he accepted the traditional distinction between mortal and venial sins, 72 per cent said they would not go to communion until they had confessed their mortal sins.

And despite the widespread acceptance of the idea of pre-marital sex, only half the seniors and one-fifth of the freshmen said they had experienced sexual intercourse.

A 'Haunting' Question

The Rev. Bruce M. Ritter, a Franciscan theologian on the Manhattan faculty and chairman of the Christian Life Council, which conducted the survey, commented:

"Though they show a radical impatience with many of the structures and procedures of the institutional church, our students generally have not yet abandoned either these structures or the traditional moral practices. Are they going to? This question must haunt and trouble the American hierarchy as no other."

The 23-member Christian Life Council, composed of faculty members and students, polled the entire student body last May and got an 83 per cent return on its 152-question survey.

The council tries to promote apostolic programs at Manhattan. The college, which is operated by the Christian Brothers, is in the Riverdale section of the Bronx.

On questions of dogma the survey turned up a high degree of orthodoxy. Eighty-seven per cent believed in the Trinity (although, strangely, only 73 per cent affirmed belief in a personal God). Only 15 per cent denied the existence of angels and devils, and 15 per cent flatly denied the belief that Jesus founded the Roman Catholic Church as "the one true church." Three-fourths said they believed in the Virgin birth—the doctrine that Jesus did not have a natural, human father.

A 'Revealed Morality'

Sixty-five per cent said they believed that the Pope could speak infallibly, at least "when he reflects the thinking of the entire church."

"There is strong evidence," Father Ritter writes in the forthcoming issue of Manhattan College Alumnus, "that while our Manhattan men may be willing to accept a revealed faith (the Trinity, the divinity of Christ, etc.) they are quite unwilling to be bound by a revealed morality—e.g., in questions or marriage and sexual conduct. They object quite violently to what they term 'indoctrination' and its burden of guilt."

However, the students were not certain about one central dogma. Fifty-five per cent said they believed that Jesus was "really and truly present" in the eucharistic bread and wine, while 30 per cent believed He was not.

To the question "Do you frequently and explicitly think of yourself more in terms of a Christian than Roman Catholic?" 48 per cent said yes, 27 per cent said no.

There was high support for Catholic schools. Of those who had attended a Catholic high school, 70 per cent would send their children to one; 73 per cent favored continuing the Catholic elementary-school system.

A majority considered parish life unsatisfying and Sunday sermons generally or always poor. More than 85 per cent reported respect for the vocation of priest or lay brother.

More than half those replying admitted some bias against Negroes, and 69 per cent termed the Vietnam war "morally just insofar as any war can be."

February 13, 1968

POPE BARS BIRTH CONTROL BY ANY ARTIFICIAL MEANS; TAKES NOTE OF OPPOSITION

Encyclical Binding on Catholics but Is Not Immutable Dogma

By ROBERT C. DOTY
Special to The New York Times

ROME, July 29—Five years of uncertainty over how the Roman Catholic Church would view modern methods of birth control ended today with the official presentation of a papal encyclical letter that upheld the prohibition on all artificial means of contraception.

The 7,500-word declaration by Pope Paul VI, "Humanae Vitae" ("Of Human Life"), reaffirmed that Roman Catholics might limit the size of their families only by the rhythm method—confining sexual intercourse to a woman's infertile period—or by abstinence.

This, it was conceded both by the Pontiff and Msgr. Ferdinando Lambruschini, the Lateran University moral theologian who presented the text at a news conference, "will perhaps not be easily received by all."

'Great Act of Courage'

But, the monsignor said, "in its human aspect the pontifical decision, which concedes nothing to popularity, is a great act of courage and perfect serenity."

In the opinion of other Roman churchmen, the Pope's decision, overruling the recommendations for liberalization by a majority of his own study commission of clerics and laymen and running counter to widespread pressure for change inside and outside the church, may produce a serious crisis of authority.

Monsignor Lambruschini said that the encyclical—a papal letter sent to all bishops of the church—was not an infallible pronouncement, that is, an immutable part of the central dogma of the church. But he insisted that it was an "authentic pronouncement" binding "the consciences of all Christians, hierarchy and faithful alike." The Pope offered his teaching to "all men of goodwill," but specifically demanded obedience only from Roman Catholics.

Marilyn Silverstone-Magnum

BIRTH CONTROL: Women receiving instruction in contraception at a family planning clinic in Calcutta, India

Pills Are Outlawed

By affirming only the rhythm method, the Pontiff outlawed, without specific mention, the use of birth control pills, intra-uterine loops, diaphragms or condoms.

In the case of women whose physicians had prescribed "therapeutic plans" to cure "diseases of the organism" the Pope ruled that it was not illicit to apply such means even if they impeded procreation, "provided such impediment is not, for whatever motive, directly willed."

The Pontiff dismissed demographers' warnings of an imminent world population explosion, holding that more effective action by governments to increase the development of resources was the proper answer, not "utterly materialistic measures"—birth control—that he said were incompatible with human dignity and natural law.

Other sections of the encyclical repeated well established church prohibitions of abortion and sterilization, "temporary or permanent," and restated the Pontiff's right to interpret nat-

ural law authentically with the aid of the Holy Spirit.

It reaffirmed the principle of "responsible parenthood"—the need to take into account the ability to provide for the well-being of offspring. But the encyclical said that this could be done only by "the deliberate and generous decision to raise a numerous family" or by deciding for "grave motives" to avoid procreation "for the time being" by the use of periodic abstinence from intercourse.

The heart of the Pope's declaration was his reaffirmation of the doctrine proclaimed 38 years ago by Pope Pius XI "that each and every marriage act [of sexual intercourse] must remain open to the transmission of life."

This was a rejection of the interpretation of the principle of totality advanced specifically by the majority of the Pope's own study commission of clerics and laymen in June, 1966, and, implicitly, by Ecumenical Council Vatican II.

Takes Issue With Council

This holds that the morality of married sexuality rests not on the significance or motive of any given sexual act but on the total approach of the couple to their obligations to God, to each other and to the

creation of a family. Within this context, it would be possible for Roman Catholic couples to exercise responsible parenthood—another aim approved by council, the commission and the Pope — spacing children properly by contraception.

But the Pope overrode the commission because, he wrote, "certain criteria of solutions had emerged which departed from the moral teaching on marriage proposed with constant firmness by the teaching authority of the church."

The Pope accepted the general principle affirmed by the council putting the uniting quality of conjugal love and its procreative function on an even plane as ends of marriage. But he denied the contention, implicit in some council discussions and explicit in the commission report, that husbands and wives could give physical expression to their love for each other in ways that eliminated the possibility of procreation.

The Pontiff also discussed fears of human population explosion. The threat should be met, he said, by "social and economic progress" compatible with human dignity rather than by adoption of "utterly materialistic" measures to limit births.

He attributed the existence of the problem to the lack of wis-

dom of governments, an insufficient sense of social justice and "indolence" in making sacrifices necessary to raise living standards.

Any relaxation of the ban on contraception, he warned, would would have the effect of encouraging marital infidelity, premarital promiscuity by the young and "dangerous" actions in the field of birth limitation by governments.

"Who," he asked, "will stop rulers from favoring, from even imposing upon their peoples, if they were to consider it necessary, the method of contraception which they judge to be most efficacious."

An Issue of Authority

In the opinion of some churchmen here, the encyclical raises a serious issue of authority. They noted that it demands of scores of Roman Catholic theologians and half a dozen bishops and cardinals a capitulation to views that are diametrically opposed to those they have publicly expressed in the past.

It runs counter to the practice of leaving the issue of contraception to the consciences of individual Roman Catholics, which is already widely sanctioned by prelates in the Netherlands and parts of Germany and Mexico, and is applied, sanctioned or not, by millions of Roman Catholic laymen.

"It can be foreseen," the Pope wrote, "that this teaching will perhaps not be easily received by all: too numerous are those voices—amplified by the modern means of propaganda—which are contrary to the voice of the church."

But, he went on, the church is merely the costodian and interpreter of moral law, not its arbiter and author, and can do nothing but maintain humble firmness in its exposition.

Problem for Christian Dialogue

Three elements of the encyclical and the manner of its announcement seemed to some informed observers to increase the problems of dialogue for Christian unity with Protestant and Anglican communities.

It complicates the resolution of the problem of marriages between Roman Catholics and other Christians because, as one student of the problem observed, "it is not so much an issue of who marries them at what altar as it is of how they live together for 50 years."

A second aspect likely to offend Protestant and Anglican sensibilities was the total reliance of the Pope on church tradition rather than scriptural revelation in his ruling. Non-Roman Christians hold, generally, that the most promising basis for restored Christian unity is supplied by revelation rather than by the interpretations and additions of successive Popes and theologians, and they note that the Bible is nowhere categorical on the subject of contraception.

Meeting this objection raised at his crowded news conference, Monsignor Lambruschini asserted that none of the faithful disputed the church's right to interpret authentically "the natural moral law even if not based implicitly or explicitly on revelation."

Finally, Monsignor Lambruschini chose the moment of the meeting of the world Anglican community in the Lambeth conference in London to criticize specifically an Anglican document taking a view of sexual problems differing from that of the Pope.

This was the 1966 report of the British Council of Churches, "Sex and Morality," which terms immoral, the Vatican spokesman said, only those sexual acts that trample on personal values such as liberty of choice and autonomy of the individual. This failed to recognize the primary evil of violations of chastity, he said.

Nowhere in the encyclical, it was noted, is there any trace of the cautious "on-the-other-hand" language that has marked many of the Pontiff's pronouncements. Such language in the past has permitted Roman Catholics to interpret encyclicals broadly enough to accommodate many divergent points of view.

"This was putting it on the line on a gut issue," said one observer, "and it poses a real problem of discipline and authority."

The five years that have elapsed since the late Pope John XXIII first raised the contraception question by appointing the study commission have divided the Roman Catholic world into three groups, this observer said. One minority has decided that past teaching is erroneous and has discarded it irrevocably. Another, he said, has anticipated the Pope's ruling and embraced the ban as immutable.

The majority in between, he continued, has remained in a state of doubt, most of them resolving the doubt conditionally in favor of the use of contraceptives.

"The crunch is going to come in the reaction of the members of this group," he said. "They are presented with a severe problem of conscience. Will they accept the ruling or drop out?"

A similar problem faces those prelates who have already loosened disciplinary bonds by telling priest confessors that they need not deny the sacraments to parishioners who had employed contraceptives. Among them are Julius Cardinal Doepfner, Archbishop of Munich, Bishop Bernhard Stein of Trier, Bishop Sergio Mendez Arceo of Cuernavaca, Mexico, and the late Bishop Willem Bekkers of the Netherlands. Bishop Bekkers's precedent of leaving the birth control issue to the individual conscience has been widely followed elsewhere in the Netherlands.

July 30, 1968

Catholic Psychologists Question Pope's Encyclical on Artificial Contraception

SAN FRANCISCO, Sept. 2 (UPI)—A group of 60 Roman Catholic psychologists strongly suggested today that Pope Paul VI's condemnation of birth control rested on a false psychology of man.

The criticism was expressed in 15 "questions" in a formal statement by persons who attended the convention of the American Catholic Psychological Association.

In effect, the questions said the Pope's recent encyclical, "On Human Life," lacked evidence for some of its conclusions and in some points was simply wrong.

"The encyclical's findings seem to be in conflict with the scientific findings of modern psychology," said Sherman McCabe of the University of Notre Dame. He announced the questions along with the Rev. Louis Gaffney of Seattle University and Vytautas Biellauskas of Xavier University, Cincinnati.

One of the challenged assumptions of the encyclical was that women are passive with little sex drive. Modern psychology holds that women have as much sexual desire as men and need sexual gratification for their personality development, the psychologists said.

The 15 questions also criticized the Pope's view of the conjugal act as mainly a physiological episode and suggested that the encyclical did not sufficiently consider the element of love.

The psychologists also indicated a belief that the Pope did not recognize the importance in human behavior of the unconscious.

Another disagreement was over psychology's view of men as an integrated organism and the encyclical's dualistic approach distinguishing between body and mind.

The Pope, the psychologists said, gave no evidence for his conclusions that contraceptives lower women's dignity and encourage immorality.

A special committee was to be appointed to study the "questions" and present papers that, it was hoped, would "assist the church to further its understanding of man." It will be headed by Paul J. Centi of the College of the Holy Cross, Worcester, Mass.

The Catholic psychologists, meeting in connection with the convention of the American Psychological Association, staged a symposium on celibacy that brought different criticism of the church.

The Rev. Eugene C. Kennedy of Maryknoll College, Glen Ellyn, Ill., told an audience including many priests and nuns that clerical celibacy, "ordered to the service of an institution rather than people, is collapsing in our day."

He called for a reform that would allow clerics a choice. Celibacy, he said, is desirable for healthy persons seeking to give of themselves fully in service, but undesirable for unhealthy persons using it as a flight from human relationships.

September 3, 1968

Catholics Found Easing Sex and Birth Curb Views

Survey by Jesuit School

By JOHN LEO

American Catholics are caught up in guilt and conflict as they move toward increasingly liberal attitudes on birth control and marriage, according to a study released yesterday by the Urban Life Institute of the University of San Francisco, a Jesuit school.

The $55,000 study, based on a national sample of 1,042 married Catholics taken by the Gallup organization in late 1966 and early 1967, was reported to be the broadest of its type. It turned up the following deeply contradictory attitudes:

¶A large majority of Catholics (71 per cent) approve the use of contraceptives, but an even larger majority of those who use them are staying away from the sacraments of the church.

¶Two-thirds of Catholics, like two-thirds of Protestants, are attempting to limit the size of their families, but Catholics fear that acting in conscience against church discipline on this issue will "open a Pandora's box" and destroy Catholic unity.

¶Although half of all Catholics agreed that their church has an unrealistically narrow view of marriage, 44 per cent also agreed that contraceptives were likely to threaten the spirit of self-sacrifice required of good Catholics.

In general, the study found Catholics fiercely loyal to their church, even as they move toward the sexual attitudes of non-Catholics.

"Catholics tend to think with the church and act with the

secular society," according to the survey.

Sixty-five per cent of those polled had used contraceptives at one time or another. Under certain circumstances (undefined) a majority of Catholics would approve divorce (62 per cent) and sterilization (53 per cent), while a minority (46 per cent) approve of abortion.

"Catholics are shedding a Puritan-flavored sexual morality," said Hazel R. Firstman, director of the study. "My own opinion, after going over all the data, is that the guilt and ambivalence will soon be rid of. The liberal attitudes will stay and grow."

The survey found that younger Catholics — those 34 and under — and inactive Catholics were far more liberal than older Catholics and those who attended church weekly.

Inactive Catholics — defined as those who go to communion once a month or less — were found to be 2½ times more likely to be using contracep-

tives. The survey did not determine whether these Catholics were inactive because of guilt over use of contraceptives, or whether liberal attitudes in general made regular church attendance less likely.

By a slight margin, rhythm is still the most used method of birth control among Catholics as well as the least effective: 75 per cent of those who had used it said it didn't work, and 44 per cent said they had had accidental pregnancies.

Catholic and Protestant attitudes show "more similarities than dissimilarities," the study reported. Almost as many Catholics as Protestants (polled as a control group for comparison) approve the spacing of births (87 per cent to 93 per cent).

One surprising finding was that fewer Catholics (57 per cent) than Protestants (71 per cent) thought they should have as many children as they wanted or could afford.

"All in all," the study asserts, "the large number of Catholics who state they reject the distinctive ethic of large families, nonuse of contraception, no divorce, no sterilization, or the superiority of celibacy speaks of a credibility gap between married Catholics and their perception of the official church teachings on practical matters of marriage."

The survey hinted that Catholics may be having less trouble accepting new sexual attitudes than in acting against authority figures in the church.

"They may have personal feelings," the study said, "that although use of contraceptives is not sinful before God, disobeying church authority is."

According to the data, Catholic marriages are remarkably stable and happy. "To me this was the most surprising finding," said John T. Noonan, professor of law at the University of California at Berkeley, and one of the Catholic scholars

who served as consultant in the study.

"Most said their marriages were not just 'happy' but 'very happy,' and infidelity turned out to be a low-level problem, compared with other countries and other times," he said.

The study, financed by the Taconic Foundation, was begun as a project of the Sir Thomas More Marriage and Family Clinics, an independent lay Catholic organization in Los Angeles.

A 200-question mail questionnaire was answered anonymously by representative Catholics selected by the Gallup organization.

The Marriage and Research Project, as it came to be called, is now an independent organization affiliated with the Urban Life Institute of the University of San Francisco. The project sociologist was Ralph Lane Jr., chairman of the sociology department at the university.

October 1, 1968

Catholic Bishops Worried by Priests Who Wed

By EDWARD B. FISKE

WASHINGTON, Nov. 13 — The American bishops of the Roman Catholic Church expressed "grave concern" today at the growing number of priests who were leaving the ministry to marry.

They expressed confidence in the Church's procedures for such cases, however, and thus appeared to shut the door, at least for the time being, on priests and religious superiors who had urged new laicization procedures that would show more respect for the men involved.

The issue of priests who marry arose this morning on the floor of the semiannual meeting of the National Conference of Catholic Bishops. The 220 prelates are holding a five-day session behind closed doors at the Washington Hilton Hotel.

While the conference as a whole debated the crisis in the priesthood, a seven-member committee labored on the second draft of a proposed pastoral letter on matters of human dignity, including birth control and selective conscientious objection.

The committee, which was closeted until 4 A.M. today and resumed its efforts five hours later, was having difficulty finding a formula acceptable to liberals and conservatives.

Full Debate Awaited

This afternoon, the Most Rev. John J. Wright of Pittsburgh, the bishops' ranking theologian and chairman of the committee, read sections of the new draft and asked for a secret vote on changes that had been made overnight in response to written suggestions by more than 60 bishops.

Leaders hope that the document, or at least the controversial sections of it, will be ready for full-scale debate tomorrow.

At a news conference this morning, the Most Rev. James P. Shannon, a spokesman for the conference, said that the bishops regarded the rising number of men leaving the priesthood to marry as "a very serious problem."

"They are doing their level best to understand the reasons and to see what can be done to handle the situation," he said.

Bishop Shannon estimated that more than 100 priests a year were laicized, or reduced to lay status, at their request.

However, a recent study by the National Association for Pastoral Renewal, an unofficial organization working for an end to the celibacy requirement for priests, estimated that more than 700 priests left the ministry last year.

The fact that many such men do not receive prompt laicization under existing procedures has led to widespread criticism of present procedures.

Under present policies, a man who seeks to leave the priesthood, whether to marry or not, applies to a local bishop, who makes his own evaluation of the situation and passes the papers on to Rome for a decision.

Critics have charged, however, that the Vatican often takes a year or two to act, and that local bishops often delay the process or impose degrading conditions on the applicants, such as demanding that they keep the matter secret or move to another section of the country.

Many priests have concluded

that the only sure way to achieve laicization is to marry first and then apply to the local bishop.

In the debate this morning, the Most Rev. Ernest J. Primeau, chairman of the bishops' Committee on the Revision of the Code of Canon Law, reviewed present procedures and reported on the suggestions for reform.

According to Bishop Shannon, however, the bishops indicated that they were satisfied with the present procedures, although there was considerable interest in expanding counseling services for those who apply for laicization.

Later this afternoon Bishop Primeau stated that the bishops did not intend to introduce any changes soon.

The conference passed a statement endorsing the rights of migrant grape pickers in California to organize.

But at the request of two California bishops it struck out a section endorsing the nationwide boycott of California grapes that had been organized in behalf of the workers and supported by numerous other religious groups, including the National Council of Churches. November 14, 1968

107

Catholic Bishops Temper Curbs on Birth Control

By EDWARD B. FISKE

WASHINGTON, Nov. 15—The nation's Roman Catholic bishops declared today that artificial birth control was an "objective evil," but that Catholics who could not in conscience follow the church's teachings should not feel cut off from holy communion.

In an 11,000-word pastoral letter adopted this morning, the bishops emphatically endorsed the conclusions of Pope Paul VI's July encyclical, "Humanae Vitae," which reaffirmed the traditional Catholic opposition to artificial contraception.

But at the same time they acknowledged that "circumstances may reduce moral guilt" and thus opened a wide door for those of the faithful who responsibly decide to use contraception to do so without guilt.

In other sections the documents also:

¶ Urged a change in the Selective Service laws to permit selective conscientious objection, or the right of an individual to decline to participate in some wars, though not necessarily all, on the ground of conscience;

¶ Encouraged consideration by political leaders of a "total review of the draft system and the establishment of voluntary military service in a professional army with democratic safeguards and for clear purposes of adequate defense."

¶ Called for "early ratification" by the Senate of the nuclear nonproliferation treaty.

¶ Approved "responsible dissent" from the church's noninfallible teachings by competent scholars in the interests of "legitimate theological speculation and research."

The pastoral letter, which was adopted by a secret written vote of 180 to 8, did not take a clear position on whether a Catholic who uses artificial birth control must go to confession before receiving holy communion.

Instead, it simply declared, "With pastoral solicitude we urge those who have resorted to artificial contraception never to lose heart but to continue to take full advantage of the strength which comes from the sacrament of penance and the grace, healing and peace in the Eucharist [holy communion]."

In presenting the document at a news conference this morning, the Most Rev. John J. Wright of Pittsburgh, chairman of the seven-member drafting committee, offered a conservative interpretation of this section.

"I cannot conceive of circumstances under which a person could use artificial contraception and not think of himself as committing a grave sin," he said.

Other bishops clearly disagree with Bishop Wright on this point, however, and in this sense the document—while conservative by the standards of some statements by European and other hierarchies—was a compromise effort.

One bishop, for instance, who preferred not to be identified, said today that the sinfulness of artificial contraception "still depends on the circumstances.'

"Tom and Mary may be overwhelmed with anxieties, sickness, poverty or concern for the welfare of their marriage," he said. "All of these can lead to a reduction of moral guilt, and if you talk about reduction you have to allow for the possibility that it could be reduced to nothing."

The pastoral letter, entitled "Human Life in Our Day," took the form of a commentary on the implications for American Catholics of the Constitution on the Church in the Modern World of the Ecumenical Council, Vatican II.

The central theme was the "doctrine and defense of life," with special reference to family life and problems of modern warfare.

The long-awaited American response to the Pope's encyclical was hammered out by Bishop Wright's committee with the help of written comments on the first draft by more than 60 bishops. Informed sources said that the care with which the bishops sought a variety of opinions was a reason for the near-unanimous vote.

The document was presented by Bishop Wright, who is the hierarchy's ranking theologian, at a crowded news conference in a conference room of the Washington Hilton Hotel, where the 220 bishops of the National Conference of Catholic Bishops concluded a five-day meeting today.

The section on family life begins with the assertion that Christian sexual morality is ultimately based on "the sanctity of life itself and the nobility of human sexuality."

Encyclical Quoted

It then quotes a statement by Pope Paul in his encyclical that there is an "objective moral order established by God," which requires that "each and every marriage act must remain open to the transmission of life."

Bishop Wright emphasized that traditional Catholic moral teaching made a distinction between evil acts and sinfulness on the part of those who committed them.

"What is evil is an objective category that can be defined by the church," he said. "Sinfulness is a subjective judgment that an individual can only make on the basis of his own conscience."

The bishop said he could tell an individual that he had committed an act that the church regards as evil but that he could not tell the individual whether this was sinful.

"I cannot enter his mind," he said.

In accordance with this principle, the 57-page pastoral letter concludes on the basis of the papal encyclical that artificial birth control is an "objective evil" that "closes the marital act to the transmission of life, deliberately making it unfruitful."

It also states, however, that the encyclical "does not undertake to judge the consciences of individuals but to set forth the authentic teaching of the church which Catholics believe interprets the divine law to which the conscience should be conformed."

In applying these principles to the question of birth control, the document emphasizes what is called the evil nature of birth control itself. It declares:

"We feel bound to remind Catholic married couples, when they are subjected to the pressures which prompt the Holy Father's concern, that however circumstances may reduce moral guilt, no one following the teaching of the church can deny the objective evil of artificial contraception itself."

It then urges those who have used artificial contraception to continue to take part in the sacramental life of the church.

Sources in the hierarchy said the key phrase as far as liberals were concerned was "circumstances may reduce moral guilt."

The pastoral letter thus opened up the possibility that even though the church teaches that birth control is objectively evil, its use by an individual under some circumstances would not necessarily be sinful.

Although the practical effect for many individuals may be the same, the American document differs substantially in tone from liberal statements issued recently by the Canadian and a number of European hierarchies.

Statements by the Austrian, German, Scandinavian, French and other hierarchies did not repudiate the "objective evil" of birth control.

The French statement, for instance, declared, "Contraception can never be a good. It is always a disorder, but this disorder is not always guilty."

The Austrian statement of Oct. 4 stated explicitly that someone who violates the encyclical may receive holy communion "without first going to confession."

The American document concentrated almost exclusively on the objective evil of birth cotrol, with only passing reference to the circumstances under which its use might not be sinful.

Because it stopped short of saying that any Catholic who uses birth control must go to confession before receiving holy communion, however, liberal bishops regarded the document as assuring that birth control could be used under some circumstances without sin.

The section of the pastoral letter on "licit theological dissent" affirms the place of "lawful freedom of inquiry" within the church.

"This is particularly true in the era of legitimate theological speculation and research," it declares. "When conclusions reached by such professional theological work prompt a scholar to dissent from noninfallible received teaching the norms of licit dissent come into play."

In the section on the rights of conscience and warfare the bishops endorsed the principle of selective conscientious objection that has already been advocated by the World Council of Churches and other religious bodies.

They stipulated, however, that "some other form of service to the human community should be required of those so exempted."

In urging ratification of the nuclear nonproliferation treaty, the bishops also warned against the dangers of escalation inherent in the building of an American antiballistic missile system.

"We seriously question whether the present policy of maintaining nuclear superiority is meaningful for security," they declared. "There is no advantage to be gained by nuclear superiority, however it is computed, when each side is admittedly capable of inflicting overwhelming damage on the other, even after being attacked first."

Reaction in the Vatican

ROME, Nov. 15 (UPI) — Vatican sources said tonight that the American Catholic bishops' statement on birth control appeared to be "less rigorous than might have been expected" after the encyclical of Pope Paul VI opposing contraception.

The sources said the statement seemed to follow the same "general tendency" as recent statements by French and West German bishops on the subject.

There was no official reaction from the Vatican.

November 16, 1968

Catholic U. Report Backs Right Of Dissent to Church Teaching

By GEORGE DUGAN
Special to The New York Times

HOUSTON, April 13 — The right of Roman Catholics to exercise responsible dissent from church teachings without fear of unjust recrimination was upheld here today in a report made public by the trustees of the Catholic University of America.

The report cleared 20 faculty members of alleged irresponsible and unprofessional conduct when they opposed Pope Paul's ban on artificial birth control last summer.

The report also recommended that no further action be taken that would question the fitness of the professors to teach at the university. All 20 have been holding their teaching posts with the proviso that they be silent during the seven-month inquiry.

The report is already being hailed by liberal Catholics as a landmark in Catholic higher education because for the first time a highly controversial dispute over theological dissent was submitted to academic rather than to the traditional ecclesiastical authorities and disciplines.

In addition, Catholic University is the nation's only institute of higher learning that is sponsored by the Pope.

In voicing their opposition at that time the professors made the broad assertion that Catholics might disagree with the authoritative, noninfallible teachings of their church "when sufficient reasons for so doing exist."

"Therefore," the dissenters' statement said, "as Roman Catholic theologians, conscious of our duty and our limitations, we conclude that spouses may responsibly decide according to their conscience that artificial contraception in some circumstances is permissible and indeed necessary to preserve and foster the values and sacredness of marriage."

This statement drew the ire of Patrick Cardinal O'Boyle, chancellor of the university, and the fear spread that the institution might summarily dismiss some of the faculty members.

Support for Statement

Subsequently, however, at the Cardinal's suggestion, the trustees met in special session and submitted the controversy to a special, six-man board of inquiry.

It was the board's 60-page report that was made public today. It came to the trustees with the board's unanimous approval as well as the unanimous approval of the university's academic senate, a 40-member body representing all of the institution's various schools. The trustees ended a two-day meeting this afternoon in the Astroworld Hotel.

The board of trustees of the university late today acknowledged receipt of the report of the board of inquiry.

It also called for the appointment of a five-man committee of its members to "examine the report of the board of inquiry and report back" to the trustees.

The board of inquiry emphasized that it was not judging the theological correctness of the professors' statement, but it insisted that the statement expressed a "tenable theological opinion."

The report flatly declared that the faculty statement of dissent was "adequately supported by theological scholarship" and that the professors' action in "composing, issuing and disseminating" the statement did not violate their commitment to the university or to the academic or theological communities.

The report called on the university to "reassure" the academic community that in the future it would not resort "even to a threat of suspension, much less actual suspension, of faculty members without first affording the professor involved academic due process."

The report also warned that, "while acknowledging the ultimate canonical jurisdiction and doctrinal competence of the hierarchy, the trustees remain sensitive to the devastating effect of any exercise of power in the resolution of academic difficulty."

A statement issued today by two spokesmen for the faculty members expressed their appreciation to the board of inquiry for its findings and hailed the report as "extremely favorable."

The report also saw no harm in the joint public release of the statement to the communications media.

April 14, 1969

U.S. BISHOPS FORM NOMINATING PANEL

Seek Influence Over Vatican Choice of Prelates—Voice Voted for Negro Priests

By EDWARD B. FISKE
Special to The New York Times

WASHINGTON, Nov. 11 — The nation's Roman Catholic Bishops voted today to set up a Committee for the Nomination of Bishops to give them a united voice and possible new influence regarding the Vatican's choice of American Bishops.

The prelates also agreed unanimously to fund a National Central Office for Black Catholics that will mean more influence for Negro priests and laymen over the activities of the church in Negro areas.

The actions were taken on the second day of a five-day meeting of the National Conference of Catholic Bishops at the Statler Hilton Hotel. More than 220 of the country's 268 Catholic Bishops are attending.

The day's deliberations were marked by a noticeable rise in tension between the Bishops and representatives of numerous lay and clerical groups seeking to make their views known.

One reason for the increasingly ugly mood in the corridors was the arrest last night of six young Catholic peace demonstrators outside the National Shrine of the Immaculate Conception while the Bishops were inside participating in a "peace mass."

In a separate incident early this afternoon, the leader of a coalition of 10 dissident groups shouted obscenities at a Bishop who was part of a committee meeting with the organization.

The layman, Donald Nicodemus, executive secretary of the National Association of Laymen, defended what he termed his "black rhetoric" as "necessary to get the cards on the table."

Because of fear of such incidents, the staff of the Bishops' Conference increased from two to three the number of private guards hired to keep outsiders out of the meeting and press areas.

The new Committee for the Nomination of Bishops will be headed by the president of the Bishops' Conference, now John Cardinal Dearden of Detroit, and include one additional Bishop from each of seven sections of the country.

The Most Rev. Mark J. Hurley, Auxiliary Bishop of San Francisco and a member of the press panel that reported on the secret deliberations, termed the new committee "a tremendous advance." He said that it had been formed in keeping with the mandate of the Second Vatican Council of 1962 to 1965 to "open up the question of the selection of Bishops."

The Nomination Process

Under current procedures the Bishops of each diocese suggest likely episcopal candidates to their Archbishop, who passes them onto the apostolic delegate, or papal representative in Washington, for forwarding to the Vatican. The final choice is the Pope's.

In recent years considerable pressure has built from the

grass-roots level to give laymen and priests a significant voice in the nomination process and to diminish the intermediary role of the apostolic delegate.

Bishop Hurley and other Bishops said that the precise relation of the new committee, both to the delegate and to the Archbishops, had yet to be determined.

It was evident, however, that if the committee took on substantial powers to "screen" nominations its selections would go to the Vatican with considerable prestige behind

them and diminish the influence not only of the delegate's recommendations but also those of individual Archbishops with considerable influence in Rome.

The National Office for Black Catholics will be established by the Black Catholic Clergy Caucus, which represents a third of the 165 Negro priests and 800 Negro sisters in the country.

The caucus had requested the support of the Bishops and $5,000 to finance the election of a 21-member board of directors by Negro priests, laymen,

nuns and brothers. The Bishops did not specify this precise sum but agreed to finance the election and provide additional operating funds in the future.

The Rev. Donald Clark, leader of the caucus, said in an interview that the new national office would take on such tasks as training Negroes for church jobs, advising whites working in Negro areas and helping Negro seminarians.

white," Father Clark said.

The Most Rev. Harold R. Perry, the country's only Negro Catholic Bishop, said later that he expected the office to func-

tion in an advisory capacity on such matters as the naming of Negro Bishops and the placement of priests but emphasized that this "will in no way infringe on the responsibilities of local Bishops."

Tonight 200 persons, including 20 former priests and their wives, attended a debate on whether priests should be permitted to marry.

The debate was sponsored by the National Association for Pastoral Renewal, a group seeking to change the church's rule on celibacy.

November 12, 1969

Catholic Bishops Approve Broad Changes in Liturgy

By EDWARD B. FISKE

Special to The New York Times

WASHINGTON, Nov. 14—The American bishops of the Roman Catholic Church approved a series of far-ranging liturgical changes today, including the English translation of a shorter and simpler order for the mass.

The changes, which are designed to implement the new liturgical concepts of the Second Vatican Council of 1962 to 1965, will go into effect on an optional basis on March 22, which is Palm Sunday.

They will become mandatory in the country's 18,000 Catholic parishes in December, 1971.

Among the innovations are an expanded Lectionary of Scripture readings and the introduction of readings from the Old as well as the New Testament during mass. The rituals for infant baptism and marriage are also revised.

The changes were announced this morning during the final session of a five-day meeting of the National Conference of Catholic Bishops. More than 220 of the country's 268 bishops attended the meeting, which was held in secrecy in the Statler-Hilton Hotel.

In another action today, the bishops attacked Government programs in the area of birth control and warned that "the element of coercion is being

openly advocated by some of the leading exponents of population control."

Specifically, the bishops charged that Government-sponsored birth control programs had made use of potentially "harmful" methods such as intrauterine devices, and that projected programs by the Government and federally supported private organizations involved the possible use of "abortion as well as other objectionable elements."

The new mass was called for by the Second Vatican Council in keeping with its general efforts to simplify church practices, emphasize involvement in current issues and give laymen a greater voice in church affairs.

Thus the new rites are generally shorter, use modern English, and emphasize the participation of the congregation in hymn singing and prayers.

The Latin text of the mass was released by Pope Paul VI last April, and the English translation was subsequently

made by the International Committee on English in the Liturgy, which includes representatives from the Catholic Church in 11 English-speaking countries. The bishops of most of the other countries have already approved at least some sections of the translation.

The translation of several sections, including the Nicene Creed, Gloria and Agnus Dei, was done in cooperation with Protestant liturgists.

The bishops rejected a number of options that were open to them. These included ecumenical translations of the Lord's Prayer and Apostles" Creed and a reduction in the number of holy days of obligation. These are feast days, such as All Saint's Day on Nov. 1, when Catholics are required to attend mass.

The new rite makes wide use of plural rather than singular forms to emphasize the communal nature of public worship. Thus the creed begins, "We believe in one God" rather than "I believe."

It introduces more options than the current order at several places. Thus, at the conclusion, the priest or deacon may say either "go in the peace of Christ," "the mass is ended, go in peace," or "go in peace to love and serve the Lord."

At the beginning of the mass, the new ritual also introduces a Penitential Rite in which worshipers pause in silence to consider their sins. Afterward they collectively ask for forgiveness and receive absolution from the priest.

The new baptismal rite is the first ever developed entirely for infants and places increased

emphasis on the importance of the faith of the child's parents.

The new marriage ceremony includes a wide variety of new prayers that focus on concrete problems that married couples face. Thus one prayer asks God, "may they be glad that You help them in their work and know that You are with them in their need."

The marriage ritual also introduces three questions that the priest must ask the couple. These include whether they have acted "freely and without reservation," will be faithful to each other and "will accept children lovingly from God and bring them up according to the law of Christ and his church?"

The only stated provision for altering any of these involves the last question, which may be omitted in the event that the couple is "advanced in years."

In other actions today the bishops approved the establishment of a National Catholic Crusade against Poverty, which will seek to raise a fund of $50-million over "the next several years." The Most Rev. Francis J. Mugavero, Bishop of Brooklyn, was named head of a committee to formulate a specific proposal.

In response to criticism by various lay and clerical groups in the corridors, John Cardinal Dearden, president of the conference, declared at a news conference that the bishops did not feel compelled to speak about the war in Vietnam or the moratorium this week because "no new moral issues" had arisen since earlier statements.

November 15, 1969

Catholic Right:

Challenge By a Small But Very Determined Band

Several months ago, a group of Roman Catholics wearing red berets was arrested on charges of breaking into a hospital clinic in Washington, D. C., to protest the performing of abortions. Contrary to what might be assumed from their style, the demonstrators were not from the militant Catholic left, but quite the opposite. Backed by an organization known as the Sons of Thunder, they spoke for a new, if still relatively small, force in American Catholicism—the militant right.

Frustrated over what they regard as over-implementation of the liberal trends of Vatican II, impatient over papal tolerance of "heresy" in the Netherlands and elsewhere and scandalized by trends toward liberal abortion laws, a hard core of Catholic conservatives has begun to adopt the tactics—and confront the problems—thus far associated only with the left.

Among recent evidence is the following:

● **Parochial Schools:** A number of conservative Catholic organizations, notably Catholics United for the Faith and the Society for the Christian Commonwealth, have begun campaigns to back parent-operated alternatives to official parochial schools. The campaigns result from a conviction that church-sponsored schools have "sold out" to sex education, doctrinally spineless catechisms and other liberal influences.

● **Financial Boycotts:** The 12,-000-member National Federation of Laymen has begun "Operation Salvation," which is aimed at withholding funds from parishes whose schools reflect humanistic and Freudian values. Among the techniques are cards to place in offering baskets, in lieu of money, and bumper stickers, both proclaiming: "No doctrine, no dollars."

● **Dropouts From the Right:** Whereas most defectors from the faith have been restless liberals, noticeable numbers of conservatives also have begun to drop out. Alphonse J. Matt Jr.,

These are some of the publications—and one of the slogans—of a militant rightist minority within American Catholicism, in revolt against the liberal reforms of Vatican II.

associate editor of the traditionalist weekly newspaper The Wanderer, reported last week that his journal was receiving numerous subscription cancellations from "readers who feel they have been betrayed by the hierarchy." Most give up on any church; others join Eastern Orthodox, Eastern Rite Roman Catholic or even Protestant fundamentalist bodies.

● **Open Criticism of the Hierarchy:** Whereas most public opposition to Pope Paul VI and other church leaders has been from the left, conservatives have now become increasingly vocal. In an interview last week, William A. Marra, a lay philosopher at Fordham University, expressed typical traditionalist frustration with the Pontiff.

"He looks at all the heresy that is rampant in the chanceries, and all he can do is weep," Mr. Marra said. "The most charitable thing you can say about him is that he is ineffectual."

Assessing the size of either the left or the right in American Catholicism is tricky business. One measure of the left is the 65,000 circulation of the National Catholic Reporter, a weekly newspaper that has been must reading for Catholic reformists. Activists on the right probably number a good deal less than that but claim, in effect, that they are the tip of the iceberg and that they have the tacit support of many non-activist laymen and priests.

Right now, both sides are probably losing ground in absolute terms because, as Michael Lawrence, an editor of the traditionalist monthly Triumph, put it, "Catholics are getting tired of religious fights."

Mr. Lawrence sees this as a boost for conservatives because "people want to cool things for a while and live with what we have." Most traditionalists, however, seem to believe that the liberal reforms of Vatican II have now become so normative that it is the liberals who have more to gain by preserving the status quo. The result has been the new militance of remaining rightist militants and widespread debate among them over how to

restore the church to past values.

One approach has been to challenge the legitimacy of church leaders and their policies. The Rev. Gommar A. DePauw, founder of the Catholic Traditionalist Movement, has gone further than most conservatives and charged that last year's revision of the Order of the Mass by the Vatican was illicit.

Criticism of the Pope

Veritas, a small-circulation publication emanating from Louisville, has sharply criticized Pope Paul and administered to him its "Whack-of-Shillelagh Award," a sort of ecclesiastical Fickle Finger of Fate prize, for, among other things, "conspiring with enemies of God." It has also demoted Archbishop Thomas J. McDonough of Louisville to "Father McDonough."

The Remnant, which broke off from The Wanderer, which has a circulation of 45,000, has publicly wondered about the legitimacy of the new mass, but some traditionalists have been wary even of raising such questions. "We sometimes wonder about Vatican policies, like the diplomatic initiatives with Communist countries," said Mr. Matt. "But with the hierarchy so much under siege these days, we try to avoid saying things that will undermine their authority even further."

The Wanderer handled the mass question by inspiring a committee to work on a new translation of the Latin original that might satisfy both the American hierarchy and rightist laymen.

In the area of morality, the greatest militancy has come from Triumph, a Washington-based monthly edited by Brent Bozell, a brother-in-law of William F. Buckley Jr., the conservative columnist. It has systematically set traditional Catholic thought against many policies of the state.

The journal, which has lost some friends by its assertion that state aid to parochial schools will destroy their Catholic character, has focused on the "life issue" — the threat of birth control and abortion to the Christian concept of the dignity of human life. Also, it has raised the question of whether a Catholic should pay taxes to Federal and state governments that give at least tacit assent to abortions.

Conscience Problem

"I would face a serious problem of conscience if I lived in a state like New York," said Mr. Lawrence.

The vanguard of civil disobedience from the right are the

Sons of Thunder. They claim a hard-core membership of 150 and are led by a strapping 24-year-old Triumph editor named Bradley Evans, who has long hair and wears a rosary and a St. Theresa medal around his neck.

In addition to demonstrations, the Sons of Thunder have begun organizing anti-abortion coun-seling clinics whose volunteer doctors are committed to convincing pregnant women to have their babies. Along with others in the Triumph circle, they are thinking of setting up communities of Catholics committed to living according to the principles of natural law, and dream of the day when the Government of the United States will be changed into a sort of modified theocracy.

How much support the various shades of Catholic traditionalism will garner has yet to be seen, but it is clear that a small but committed core is ready to challenge not only secular values in general but also the leaders of the church themselves.

"Our greatest enemies are the bureaucrats in the chanceries who still retain the lingering good will of moderately educated Catholics," said Mr. Marra. "On this point we understand the liberals very well."

—EDWARD B. FISKE

March 14, 1971

Most U.S. Priests Found To Oppose Birth Curb Ban

By EDWARD B. FISKE

Two studies sponsored by the American bishops of the Roman Catholic Church have found that a majority of the country's priests reject the church's teaching against artificial birth control and believe that priests should be free to marry.

They also found, however, that despite recent unrest in the church, priests maintain a "high degree of personal morale" and that only one priest in five would be likely to marry if given the choice.

The reports, which together constitute the most comprehensive survey of the priesthood in any country, will be formally presented to the bishops at their spring meeting in Detroit April 27 through 29.

Summaries and selected statistical tables were mailed out to the bishops in the last few days. A copy was made available to The New York Times.

The first study—from the sociological perspective — was conducted by the National Opinion Research Center, a research organization affiliated with the University of Chicago. It was based on questionnaires and some telephone interviews with 6,000 priests, former priests and bishops.

The second—from the psychological perspective — drew on in-depth interviews with 271 priests. It was conducted by the department of psychology of Loyola University in Chicago.

The findings brought into question a number of widespread assumptions about the priesthood and included the following:

¶Conflicts with bishops and other authorities are seen as a greater source of frustration to priests than restrictions against marriage.

¶Five per cent of diocesan priests resigned between 1966 and 1969, and three per cent said that they were likely to leave. These figures, the first authoritative ones to be released on the number of Americans leaving the priesthood, are lower than many previous estimates.

¶Most priests who have left are quite satisfied with their decision, and, contrary to the statements of some priests' groups, only two out of five are interested in returning.

A Budget of $500,000

¶A "large proportion" of priests are shown by psychological testing to be "underdeveloped" persons who do not make full use of the freedom they have.

The two studies are part of a seven-part report on the priesthood that was initiated by the National Conference of Catholic Bishops in the spring of 1967. It was intended as an aid to church reform following the Second Vatican Council, but was also seen by some as a way of responding to the issue of celibacy, which at the time was emerging as a major source of controversy.

The study, which has an over-all budget of about $500,-000, was supervised by an ad hoc committee of 14 bishops and priests headed by John Cardinal Krol of Philadelphia. In addition to the sociological and psychological studies, reports are being drawn up on the history, theology, spirituality, Scriptural basis and pastoral problems of the priesthood.

The sociological study, which was headed by the Rev. Andrew Greeley, a University of Chicago sociologist, drew on questionnaires from 5,000 active priests, 800 priests who had left the ministry and 250 bishops. The active priests in the sample were roughly 10 per cent of total of such priests for the country, and officials reported an 80 per cent response rate among them.

A major finding was the existence of "drastic differences" of opinion between priests and bishops on sexual morality. The survey reported, for instance, that the church's position on birth control "does not command majority support among the priests."

Stand on Divorce Shifting

Moreover, the study found that support for the official position has deteriorated considerably since Pope Paul VI's 1967 encyclical "Humanae Vitae," which reaffirmed the traditional ban on artificial contraception. Twenty-seven per cent of the priests surveyed said that they had become more "liberal" since the papal proclamation. Only 3 per cent indicated that they had become more "conservative."

According to the document, support is also waning among priests for the church's teaching against divorce, but there is "little evidence of a change in position on either premarital sex or abortion."

On the issue of celibacy, the study found that "more than half the priests are at least somewhat in favor of a change" in church policy, while bishops remain "strongly opposed" to the idea. Among priests between the ages of 26 and 35, the number favoring optional celibacy was 84 per cent.

John Cardinal Krol heads panel conducting seven-part study of priesthood.

In addition, the study found that three out of every five priests—and a majority of all priests 55 or under—"expect" the church to change its policy on celibacy, and three-quarters of them expect this to occur within 10 years.

The survey also discovered, however, that "the overwhelming majority of priests see [celibacy] as an advantage in their work" and that only one priest in five would marry if given the choice. Even among priests under 35 years of age, the number who said they "would certainly or probably marry" if given the option was only 33 per cent.

The researchers explained the apparent contradiction by stating, "Apparently, many of those who support a change do so because they are not convinced that celibacy is essential to the priesthood, and because they think that celibacy can be harmful for some priests and is keeping many men out of the priesthood."

Acceptance of Values

In general, the sociologists found that there was a "fundamental acceptance by priests of the basic religious values" of the church, that most priests enjoyed an "adequate" level of job satisfaction and that a "large majority" would become priests if they had to make the choice again.

Evaluation of the responses of both active and resigned priests indicated that loneliness was the most important cause of leaving to marry, but that a widespread sense of powerlessness and frustration in dealing with authorities was the most pervasive problem among those who remained.

In all age categories of active priests, the most common complaint was "the way authority is exercised in the church." Even among those who had left the active priest-

hood, only 15 per cent chose a change in the celibacy requirement when asked to make a single recommendation for church reform.

The problem of frustration was described as especially serious among associate pastors, whose job satisfaction was reported to be "even lower than that of unskilled manual workers."

The researchers reported that 5 per cent of diocesan priests resigned in the four years from 1966 to 1969, and that 3 per cent said that they would either "certainly or probably" leave the priesthood. The main reason, they found, was "the desire to marry."

They said that the dropout rate "may not be high in comparison with other professions" but that "it is certainly high compared to impressions about what the rate was in the past."

The Rev. Andrew Greeley of University of Chicago headed sociological study.

They also found "considerable decline in enthusiasm for vocational recruiting" among priests and said that this could be "far more serious than the resignation rate."

The sociologists said that resignees had apparently been "moderately successful" in their new occupations, and that about one-third now made more than $12,000 a year.

Fundamental Differences

The study concluded that although bishops were somewhat more liberal than priests regarding ecumenism and social action, their conservatism on matters of doctrine, church government and sexual morality had contributed to a "dangerous gap" between themselves and priests.

The sociologists warned that this gap was not merely a "disagreement between those who have power and those who do not" but also a sign of

fundamental "ideological differences about the nature of the church and religion." The result, they said, is "considerable potential for serious conflict."

The report did not contain policy recommendations but observed that the church faced two distinct problems—loneliness and conflict over centralized authority—and that "no single solution," including, presumably, a change in the celibacy requirement, would effectively meet both problems.

The Loyola study was directed at a subsample of 271 priests from the National Opinion Research Center's sample and made use of two-hour depth interviews by professional psychologists and standardized written tests.

The study was headed by the Rev. Eugene C. Kennedy, a professor of psychology at Loyola. The project director was Victor J. Heckler, a research associate in psychology at the same institution.

The most general finding of the researchers was that American priests were neither "sick" nor "supermen" but psychologically quite typical of the American male population as a whole.

They added, however, that both society and the church placed "high expectations" on priests, such as the celibacy requirement, and that "many of their conflicts and challenges arise precisely because they are ordinary men who may have to live as though they were not ordinary at all."

The psychologists divided their subjects into categories reflecting the extent of their personal growth and found that two-thirds could generally be described as "underdeveloped."

"A large proportion of priests in this cross-sectional sample,

The Rev. Eugene C. Kennedy, Loyola of Chicago, led psychological poll.

as in any cross-sectional sample of American men, have not developed to full maturity," they declared.

The researchers said that the marks of "underdeveloped" priests included passivity, self-doubt, uneasiness about intimate relations with other persons and a "tendency to identify themselves through the role of the priesthood rather than through their own personalities."

The Real Issue

While emphasizing that such tendencies are not limited to priests, the psychologists suggested that "isolation and protection from normal socially developmental experiences" often contributed to the incomplete personal growth of priests.

The Loyola study confirmed the conclusion of the opinion research center's report that a majority of priests favored optional celibacy but that most would not marry if given the choice.

"This suggests that the real psychological issue, even when it is not identified consciously as such, is greater freedom rather than the question of celibacy itself," the researchers declared.

The psychological study agreed with the other one that priests tended to think of themselves as restricted by church authorities but suggested that these restrictions were more apparent than real.

"The remarkable discovery of this study is that authority seems to impinge so little on the day-to-day activities of these priests," the authors said.

They suggested that the fundamental problem was thus not so much the way authority was exercised in the church but the fact that many priests with "underdeveloped" personalities still had an "ambivalent" and "unresolved" attitude toward it.

The researchers suggested that the problem of "incomplete growth" among many American priests could be largely solved by forcing priests to exercise more judgment and accept more responsibility. They recommended "greater freedom" in such areas as celibacy, place of residence, life-style, financial independence, and continuing education. This should be accompanied, they added, "by increased demand on their professional performance as priests."

The authors rejected the idea that more freedom for priests could only be accomplished at the expense of the institution. "Most of them want to do their best," they said, "and they would not flout the laws of God or the church if they were given a wider range of options. Indeed, they might, as a group, develop a more mature concept of authority than they now have."

April 15, 1971

Catholic Bishops Resist Changes Within Church

By EDWARD B. FISKE
Special to The New York Times

DETROIT, April 29 — The American Bishops of the Roman Catholic Church ended their annual spring meeting here today with an apparent determination to seek a restoration of order and the traditional line of authority after a period of turmoil in the church.

The mood of retrenchment persisted despite growing pressure for changes in the celibacy requirement and other aspects of the priesthood, and widespread accusations that the hierarchy was out of touch with sizable elements of the church.

In keeping with the tone of caution, the 230 members of the National Conference of Catholic Bishops in attendance elected yesterday a delegation of representatives to the forthcoming international synod of bishops in Rome that is heavily weighted toward conservatives and arch-conservatives. The delegation was ratified today by the Vatican.

The delegation will consist of John Cardinal Dearden of Detroit, John Cardinal Krol of Philadelphia, John Cardinal Carberry of St. Louis and the Most Rev. Leo C. Byrne, Archbishop of St. Paul-Minneapolis.

Although no formal announcement was made pending ratification by the Vatican, the bishops also reportedly selected the Most Rev. Joseph T McGucken, Archbishop of San Francisco and the Most Rev. John F. Whealon, Archbishop of Hartford, as alternate delegates.

At a news conference following the meeting, Cardinal Dearden, the president of the conference and the only progressive among the six, said that the primary responsibility of the delegation would be to convey the "thoughts and judgments of the American bishops" to the international forum.

He added, however, that its mandate also included an obligation to describe the "de facto situation" in the American church, including presumably the extent of disagreement among priests on sensitive issues such as celibacy.

The bishops. met for three days at the Sheraton-Cadillace Hotel here to discuss two issues: the priesthood, and world justice and peace. These are the two topics that will be discussed by bishops from around the world when the synod convenes Sept. 30 to provide counsel to Pope Paul VI.

$500,000 Study Cited

Much of the debate this week centered on documents summarizing the initial results of a seven-part $500,000 study of the priesthood by sociologists, psychologists, theologians and others.

The study, commissioned by the bishops in 1967, reported that the majority of American priests opposed church policies against artificial birth control, divorce, and marriage by priests. The theological section asserted that there were no theological reasons for not ordaining women or married persons.

As in the past, the bishops were under visible pressure from lobbying groups.

A delegation of seven women from the National Organization for Women held a news conference yesterday and charged that the Catholic Church is a "sexist institution." The women's liberation advocates, four of whom identified themselves as Catholics, called for more involvement for women in church decision-making, including the forthcoming synod.

Shortly afterward the National Federation of Laymen, a conservative organization claiming 16,500 members, held their own news conference and accused the bishops of failing to deal with "the critical matter of defective doctrinal content of catechetical texts and material."

Throughout the meeting, four representatives of the Young Priests Caucus of Chicago operated a "hospitality suite" on the seventh floor of the hotel to discuss the celibacy issue with bishops who cared to stop by. The Rev. Robert Gallie, one of the priests, said that he was "disappointed" that only one bishop did so.

Although the meetings were closed, with uniformed security guards posted outside, reports indicated that most bishops, while willing to discuss priestly dissent on matters such as celibacy, did not regard the dissent as sufficiently important to alter their own positions or to modify church policy.

The general position appeared to be that a majority of priests could be wrong and that as church leaders they were obliged to respect tradition more than polls. Several attributed dissatisfaction with the celibacy requirement, for instance, to a general corruption of moral standards in society as a whole.

"This is an age of pansexualism and materialism," said the Most Rev. John R. Quinn, auxiliary bishop of San Diego. "It's difficult to talk about celibacy, with its overtones of faith and the supernatural."

Bishop Alexander M. Zaleski of Lansing noted that sexual symbols were used to sell such products as automobiles and expressed the view that priests seeking more fundamental changes in the church had focused on the celibacy issue as one that "would get the most exposure and is the most sensitive in terms of the whole culture."

Discussion of the priesthood reflected the existence of two distinct concepts of the modern priest.

The traditional position, articulated by St. Thomas and subsequent orthodox theologians, views the priest as one who attempts to emulate the ministry of Christ and tends to emphasize the "cultic" or "sacerdotal" functions of the priest, such as the celebrating of holy communion.

The second position, which was endorsed in the theological study prepared for the bishops by the Rev. Carl Armbruster, a Jesuit theologian, tends to begin with references to the ministry of the entire church rather than that of Christ and to emphasize the role of the priest as "servant" of God and the church.

April 30, 1971

Vatican Rules Against Priests Who Disagreed on an Encyclical

The Washington Star

WASHINGTON, April 29— The Vatican has ruled that Roman Catholic priests disciplined by Patrick Cardinal O'Boyle here in 1968 over a dispute in interpreting an encyclical on birth control must comply with the teaching norms set down by the archbishop and by the church.

The landmark decision, handed down by the Vatican's Congregation of the Clergy, said that while the individual conscience of the priest and of individual Catholics was the "subjective norm" for determining rules of conduct, "objective norms" were the province of the church, as handed down by the Pope and the princes of the church.

The action comes almost 10 months after the case was taken to Pope Paul VI. The 19 priests who filed the complaint felt that they could not find adequate due process through the appropriate church courts in the United States.

John Cardinal Wright, formerly of Pittsburgh, Prefect for the Vatican Congregation, recommended that "without further delay, formality or necessity for written or oral explanations, each priest who accepts the 'findings' set forth above present himself individually at his earliest convenience, to his ordinary [O'Boyle] and declare his desire to enjoy the full faculties of the archdiocese."

The petition was filed by the Rev. Joseph Byron of St. James Church in Mount Rainier, Md., in behalf of himself and 18 others. Originally, nearly 50 priests were disciplined. Father Byron was the only pastor among them.

Father Byron, reached at his church, said, "I'm glad the decision came through and that the elements are there for solution." He said, however, that he did not "feel free" to discuss the document handed down by the Congregation "at this time."

"They have to stand on their own merits."

The document, "Theological and Pastoral Principles," establishes that the Pope and the bishops in their local churches have "the duty and responsibility to teach on matters pertaining to faith and morals." It is, therefore, incumbent on the local bishop to "instruct his priests in their pastoral ministries of preaching, teaching and counseling."

The statement said that Pope Paul VI's encyclical, "Humanae Vitae," of June, 1968, "declares without ambiguity, doubt or hesitation the objective evil of the contraceptive act, is an authentic expression of his magisterium and is to be understood in accord with the dogmatic tradition of the church.

"Conscience is not a law onto itself," the document said, "and in forming one's conscience one must be guided by objective moral norms, including authentic church teachings."

April 30, 1971

PRIESTS IN CHICAGO CENSURE A CARDINAL

CHICAGO, June 15 (AP) — The Association of Chicago Priests voted 144 to 126 tonight to censure John Cardinal Cody, Roman Catholic Archbishop of Chicago, for allegedly failing to speak out on behalf of the needs of priests.

The association, representing 900 of the 2,400 priests in the Chicago archdiocese, also voted to censure five auxiliary bishops who, with Cardinal Cody, attended the meeting in April of the National Conference of Catholic Bishops.

The action is believed to be unprecedented in the Roman Catholic Church in America.

The agenda for the bishops' meeting, held in Detroit, included hearing results of a sociological survey that reported a majority of the American priests favored optional celibacy. But the 325 bishops at the meeting did not discuss the question.

The bishops also selected four men to represent American priests at the international synod of bishops in Rome this fall. Three of them have said that they would not support optional celibacy.

The Rev. Laurance Maddack, chairman of the association's coordinating committee, which drafted the resolution, said: "We are reacting especially to our own bishops, and to Cardinal Cody. . . . We feel that when the chips were down, they let us down."

June 16, 1971

CATHOLIC DIOCESES GET FISCAL ADVICE

Bishops Tell How to Tally and Publicize Finances

By EDWARD B. FISKE

The American Bishops of the Roman Catholic Church have released a set of guidelines for local dioceses on how to record and publicize their financial status.

The guidelines, under preparation for two years by a committee headed by Cardinal Cooke of New York, are a response to growing sentiment among clergy and laymen that the church in this country should no longer conduct its financial affairs in secrecy.

In recent years groups ranging from diocesan senates of priests to liberal pressure groups, such as the National Association of Laymen, have pushed for more open financial policies.

Prior to the end of the Second Vatican Council in 1965 only four of the 156 American dioceses issued annual public financial statements. Since then about half have done so in varying detail, and a third more have indicated their intention of issuing reports in the future.

This Is a Good Thing

Bishop Joseph L. Bernardin, the general secretary of the National Conference of Catholic Bishops, acknowledged yesterday that pressure has been building for more open policies, but he said that the new guidelines were essentially a response to a "realization that this is a good thing."

"As a result of Vatican II, more and more people are aware of their responsibility in the church, and part of that responsibility is knowing how church resources are being used," he said.

"In addition Bishops are showing a greater willingness to share this sort of financial information. They don't want to bear this sort of burden alone."

The new document, entitled "Diocesan Accounting and Financial Reporting," is 141 pages long and consists primarily of technical information on how to adopt standard accounting procedures to Catholic financial affairs.

The material was prepared at a cost of about $75,000 by the accounting and consulting firm of Peat, Marwick, Mitchell & Co. in consultation with a 29-member advisory committee of Bishops, priests, businessmen and church financial managers.

Also included is a section of advice for diocesan officials on how to make public their financial reports. It emphasizes, however, that public statements are optional.

Description of Services

The document declares, for instance, that public accounting should be done on an annual basis and that financial figures should always be accompanied by interpretative material describing the "services rendered and programs carried on by the diocese."

It also provides a number of examples of balance sheets, with categories such as "marketable securities," "investment in deposit and loan funds" and "real estate."

The document states that "for practical purposes, the primary criterion for including institutions in diocesan statements is that the diocese has fiscal responsibility for the institution."

This means that while financial statements would cover the costs of diocesan administration, high schools and other programs administered by the local chancery, they would not cover more or less autonomous operations, such as a local parish or a local chapter of the Knights of Columbus.

While recommending that dioceses list the extent of such investments as stocks and bonds, the models do not provide for a listing of particular securities. Such information has been an issue among laymen and clergymen concerned with the social implications of church investment policies.

In releasing the new guidelines, the United States Catholic Conference, the administrative arm of the American hierarchy, announced that a number of regional seminars would be held throughout the country in the next few months to train diocesan fiscal personnel to implement the new accounting system.

Officials also indicated that the new procedures, assuming they are more or less universally adopted, would make it possible to put together data on national church finances that is now unavailable because of widely varying accounting system in local dioceses.

Two years ago the Archdiocese of New York released a brief financial report indicating expenses for 1968 of $21-million. Other dioceses that have issued reports include Bridgeport and Hartford in Connecticut.

September 5, 1971

Vatican II Is Reaching Grass Roots

By EDWARD B. FISKE

Special to the New York Times

WHITE PLAINS — Two hundred and twenty-five members of St. Bernard's Roman Catholic Church turned up at a parish meeting one night recently and spent 35 minutes debating whether to dismiss the physical education teacher in the parochial school and hire instead someone to teach music, art and reading.

The discussion ended in a draw between athletics and culture with a decision to have a part-time person in both areas.

The debate was a small but typical example of the changes that are occurring at St. Bernard's—and thousands of American parishes like it—as the changes of the Second Vatican Council find their way to the grass-roots level.

Laymen's Role Enlarged

St. Bernard's laymen are not only helping to set school policies but also are poring over financial records that were once a strictly clerical preserve. Living room liturgies are standard operating procedure, and a regular guitar mass at 9 A.M. every Sunday draws more adults than children.

"I love it," said William V. Cuddy, a 42-year old lawyer who is chairman of the parish's new educational committee. "I can't remember ever looking forward to going to mass before."

The changes, though, are bringing understandable strains to St. Bernard's. Older parishoners openly wonder whether the church they knew as children still exists. Attendance at mass is half what it was a dozen years ago. For a variety of reasons, the parish is rapidly approaching a financial crisis.

Moreover, six years after the close of Vatican II the clergymen and laymen at St. Bernard's are still struggling hard to discover just what it means to be a Catholic community in the nineteen-seventies.

"The council got the church moving toward the spirit rather than merely the letter of the law," said Eugene V. O'Brien, vice president of the 16-member parish council. "But we're still in the process of reacting. We don't know yet how it will affect us."

St. Bernard's, which was founded in the mid-nineteen-twenties, covers the area between Mamaroneck Avenue and the Scarsdale line. Its 900 families are almost all white, from varying ethnic origins, and economically in the middle-class or lower middle-class brackets. About half of the breadwinners commute to New York City.

The pastor is Msgr. Charles J. McManus, a tall 53-year-old priest with short gray hair and rimless glasses that give him a somewhat scholarly appearance. Before his transfer to St. Bernard's last year, he served for eight years as principal of nearby Archbishop Stepinac High School.

Like many similar parishes, St. Bernard's has moved firmly but cautiously in implementing the sweeping reforms of Vatican II.

All of the obvious changes have been made, such as masses in the vernacular, and the lay-dominated parish council, which functions as an advisory body to the pastor, will have evolved by next year from an appointed to a totally elected body.

The council's major accomplishments thus far have been a line by line study of parish finances—followed by a public report—and a series of recommendations to improve religious education.

Not surprisingly, the minority of laymen who have become active in council affairs are enthusiastic about their new sense of responsibility. Innovations such as the home masses have also been generally well received.

"The living room felt a little nicer afterward," said Mrs. Theresa Brennan, who was the hostess for one home mass.

Some parishoners, though, are less than enthusiastic. Joseph Baltz, a 62-year old lawyer, for instance, said that the format of the mass had been changed at the expense of its "essence" and declared, "You begin to wonder if God is changing, too."

Appathy Biggest Worry

Edward J. McLoughlin, who has been an usher at St. Bernard's since 1925, lamented the loss of "mysticism" in the mass and said that the parish council had made the role of the laymen too formal. "I think the priest should run the parish in the old-fashioned way," he stated.

Monsignor McManus, who has a doctorate in philosophy, doesn't agree, but he is not so much worried about criticism from either liberals or traditionalists as he is about what he called the "pressure of apathy."

"Only 110 parishoners out of the 1,500 eligible voted for the new parish council members," he said in an interview last week. "I think we're moving, but we're doing so like a fully loaded trailer truck going up an incline."

Vatican Two, which lasted

Photographs for The New York Times by LEE ROMERO

The Rev. Charles R. Giancola of St. Bernard's Roman Catholic Church in White Plains with Vernon G. Adlfinger, wearing jacket, president of 16-member parish council; Mary Sweeney of the council and Hector Saravia, usher.

from 1962 to 1965, sparked widespread international controversies among bishops, priests, and lay activists on matters such as birth control, priestly celibacy and the role of layman and lower echelon clergy in the naming of bishops.

At St. Bernard's, though, it's hard to find anyone discussing such matters. Birth control is seen as a matter for couples to decide for themselves. Despite what most bishops say in public utterances, most laymen here seem willing to accept married priests.

"It'll be a terrific burden financially," said Frederick P. Miano, a 41-year-od financial analyst, "but at least it means you have a guy with more experience in life."

The one subject parishoners at St. Bernard's do get excited about is one that Vatican Two touched on only indirectly — the problems of youths. In this area they are frankly looking to their church for leadership.

"I dread bringing kids through the next five years," said Mr. Cuddy. "It's a full-time job. The church is trying, but at this point everyone is feeling their way."

White Plains is regarded as having a good school system, and parishoners say that they no longer feel sinful if they choose to send their children to public rather than parochial schools.

Moral Training Stressed

Nevertheless, drugs and some recent racial incidents in the public schools have deepened the desire of many parents at St. Bernard's to make sure that there is a solid religious and moral— and some add disciplinary— dimension to their children's schooling.

"It's the little things like manners and grace before meals that make the parochial schools superior," said Mrs. Brennan, a mother of four. "We feel this is important and are ready to fight for it and pay until it hurts."

Despite such attitudes, though, the future of St. Bernard's elementary school is in doubt. The school ran a $36,000 deficit last year, and it is uncertain how long the parish, which is losing nearly $1,000 per month and could run out of cash reserves by the end of the year, can continue to make it up.

"I forsee the school surviving for at least three years," said Monsignor McManus, "but I don't see beyond that either way."

Even if it survives, however, the parochial school can handle only 300 of the 800 elementary-age children

Father Giancola during mass at parish where laymen have recently taken a greater role

in the parish, and the parish —acting on a recommendation from the educational committee—has hired a husband-and-wife team to develop a coordinated religious education program that would reach children in public schools and adults as well.

Priests say that the new interest of laymen in running their own affairs has forced them to develop a new style of leadership, one based on education and persuasion rather than command, and

even has led to a sense of independence from the Archdiocese of New York itself.

The latter was indicated when the parish council sent a letter to Cardinal Cooke stating that it regarded the archdiocesan plan whereby the wealthier parishes were given assessments to aid needy ones as unwise and unfair.

Whatever the roadblocks being encountered as St. Bernard's moves toward becoming the kind of church envisioned by Vatican Two,

though, most parishioners agree that there is a new sense of seriousness about the church and a new spirit of openness and freedom.

Mr. Cuddy observed that for him the most important change has been the fact that "nothing is accepted uncritically anymore."

"For our generation it's an exciting time to be a Catholic," he declared. "I don't know where it will all lead, but it's exciting."

September 8, 1971

The Catholic Church in the U.S.

Defections from Authority And the Institution Itself

The Catholic Church in New York City recently turned to Madison Avenue with $100,000 for an advertising campaign to recruit priests, and the Trinitarian Fathers have put ads in Playboy magazine for the same purpose (and received 700 bona fide inquiries). The following story examines some of the church's problems.

By JOHN DEEDY

Since the mid-nineteen-sixties, and especially since Humanae Vitae, Pope Paul's 1968 encyclical restating birth control prohibitions, the story of the Catholic Church in the United States has been full of bad news: parochial schools in financial straits; laity grown indifferent to episcopal authority; priests and nuns in flight from religious life, many in search of human fulfillment through marriage; vocations falling to all-time lows, the new generation of Catholics seemingly regarding the challenges of the secular world to be as socially demanding and spiritually redeeming as those of the ministry.

Observers obviously differ on how serious the situation is, though it seems to reflect problems of the Vatican and the church worldwide. But there is evidence that "defections" from the priesthood (placed at 3,413 in the United States alone during the years 1966-69) and institutional closings (for example, Cardinal Cushing College in Boston and Dunbarton College in Washington) may not be isolated phenomena with limited meaning for the wider church; but rather part of a pattern which, if trends persist, could eventually mean disintegration of the Catholic Church in the United States as it is presently known.

Some strong new evidence is in data collected as part of the National Opinion Research Center's General Social Survey, and recently explicated by William C. McCready and Father Andrew M. Greeley, sociologists on the center's staff. What the data document is a continued decline in church attendance among American Catholics, but one that has now reached into the previously stalwart ranks of the middle-aged, traditionally the backbone of American Catholicism.

Specifically, Mr. McCready and Father Greeley found a 13 per cent decline in Sunday mass attendance in the 30-49 age category (from 62 to 49 per cent) and a 21 per cent drop in the 50-and-over generation (from 76 to 55 per cent). The under-30 generation, which had been in sharp decline over several years, dropped only one percentage point, from 40 to 39 — the one ray of light, say the researchers, that they could locate in the statistics based on an interdenominational sampling of 1,592 persons in July, 1972, and 1,367 in July, 1973.

The two sociologists assert that the changes may constitute "the most dramatic collapse of religious devotion in the entire history of Christianity." They add that "we know of no other time in the course of human history when so many people — particularly older people — so decisively removed themselves from canonically required ecclesiastical practices." (Catholic Church law mandates Sunday mass attendance.)

With the Catholic population of the United States counted at over 48 million, it is clear that they are talking of hundreds of thousands of Catholics. Such a loss has serious financial as well as religious implications.

This is so since, unlike much of Protestantism, which operates on the annual pledge basis, the economic welfare of the Catholic Church is tied to the Sunday collection basket. Under such a system, regular Sunday attendance becomes an absolute urgency if institutional solvency is to be maintained.

Because of declines in mass attendance, income is just not keeping up with ordinary parish expenses, even in affluent communities. For instance, in Scarsdale, a Westchester County suburb of New York, parishioners of Immaculate Heart of Mary Church were informed last month that their parish was $20,000 in debt and was carrying neglected maintenance liabilities of $75,000.

No scientific study has been done on why Catholics are "turning-off" to church attendance in such large numbers, but several causes have been suggested: a feeling that the new liturgy is not rewarding; low-quality sermons in many parishes; disenchantment with some parish administrators; and, not least, an attitude that attending Sunday mass regularly just is not important anymore.

The paradox in the Sunday mass statistics is that they do not necessarily indicate a loss of belief or an abandonment of faith. Father George J. Kuhn of St. Augustine parish in Larchmont, N. Y., puts it this way: "Many older Catholics have merely caught up with the young and freed themselves of mortal-sin hang-ups with re-

Father Neil Connolly isn't out to change the world. Just the South Bronx.

Neil Connolly was assigned to St. Athanasius Church on Tiffany Street shortly after he was ordained. It's a neighborhood most people leave as soon as they can.

He's been there for 15 years.

"I can't really say we're changing things,"

There's also a storefront church where he celebrates Sunday Mass to help make Christ's presence more visible in the neighborhood.

It's obvious that whatever Neil Connolly does he does for love, not money.

But there's so much more work to do in the

A recruiting advertisement for Catholic priests

spect to Sunday mass."

Mr. McCready and Father Greeley see "a strong relationship between lack of confidence in leadership and not going to church." Leadership translates in the Catholic lexicon largely as bishops.

A year ago, Msgr. John Tracy Ellis, a scholarly church historian generally regarded as having no axes to grind, wrote in the Chicago newsletter Overview of "the virtual lack of leadership" in the American Catholic Church, and speculated that this could result in the failure of the church as a viable believing community. About the same time, Dan Herr, president of the Thomas More Association and a columnist in The Critic, a national Catholic bimonthly, wrote: "It is all too clear . . . that the bishops have lost their credibility and their power. They speak and few listen; they command and even fewer obey."

In defense, the leadership can cite certain sociological phenomena as contributing to declines in Catholic religious practices. These range from the dissolution of the American Catholic subculture, with its built-in impulses for Catholics to respond in predictable ways to directives, to the pervasiveness of the secular culture, which makes of Sunday a day of leisure and recreation.

Mr. McCready and Father Greeley believe "the worst may be far from over," particularly if the slippage they document is traceable to lack of confidence in ecclesiastical leadership. They do not see declines leveling off "until some sense of confidence is restored."

The complications in this respect are several. For one thing, the leadership of the American church is given, many think, to perpetuating its species by controlling the processes by which new leaders, bishops particularly, are raised up. For years, progressive Catholic groups have urged radical changes in the episcopal selection procedure, including a strong voice for the laity in the selections. But thus far, improvements in the system have been more token than substantive.

Another problem is what Msgr. Ellis once termed the failure of American bishops "to show initiative, creative thinking and imagination." Generally, as the McCready-Greeley report states, there is a "business-as-usual" approach to problems.

Some felt this "business-as-usual" approach was epitomized at the recent meeting in Washington. Though the bishops did protest to Rome over the arbitrary way in which the matter of Confession before First Communion was decided for the United States, some tended to minimize the show of spunk. They noted the time devoted to minor topics like receiving Communion in the hand (motion defeated, 121 to 113). And particularly they noted the annual statement brought forth by the bishops: a 55-page pastoral on devotion to the Virgin Mary.

John Deedy is managing editor of Commonweal magazine.

December 16, 1973

Religious Fund-Raising Can Be Less Than a Lofty Calling

By JOHN DEEDY

Religious fund-raising is no nickels-and-dimes proposition. With the lure of possible divine favor supplementing humanitarian satisfactions and tax-deduction advantages, religion dwarfs all other philanthropic fields as the beneficiary of individual and corporate generosity in the United States.

According to the American Association of Fund-Raising Counsel, religion received 43.1 per cent of the $25.1 billion in private funds channeled during 1974 to philanthropic causes. This is almost triple the sum that went for health and hospitals, eight times that for the arts and humanities, and five times that for social welfare. Of the total $10.8 billion, 87.7 percent came from individuals.

Unlike figures for other philanthropic areas, however, that dollar amount is an estimate. Under the "separation of church and state" clause of the Constitution, religious institutions are free from the usual laws of disclosure and accountability that regulate nonprofit organizations. Forty-four American church bodies make voluntary public reports, and their figures are the basis for the Fund-Raising Counsel's projections. The reporting churches represent some major denominations, such as the Episcopal Church and the United Methodist Church. But they do not include, among many others, the Roman Catholic and Mormon churches, or Jewish religious communities. Most of the 200 church bodies in the United States opt for privacy.

It is a situation ready-made for abuses and financial adventurism. Currently, concern centers about the Pallottine Fathers of Baltimore, who raise anywhere between $8 million and $15 million annually for such causes as

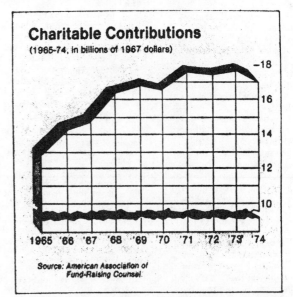

Charitable Contributions
(1965-74, in billions of 1967 dollars)

Source: American Association of Fund-Raising Counsel.

the "starving and naked" of foreign missions, but who apparently disburse only a fraction of that sum for the needy. For 1974, this was $746,685 in cash and supplies, less than half the amount used for postage on their 75 million fund-raising letters and cards. At the same time, millions have been invested in business and in Maryland and Florida real estate; $54,000 even found its way into a loan that was used to help finance the divorce settlement in 1974 of Marvin Mandel, the Maryland Governor.

Though other financial revelations have embarrassed Catholics in recent years, playing fast and loose with the moneys of religion is not a uniquely Catholic proclivity. When Rex Humbard, the evangelist from Akron, O., found himself in financial straits in 1973, he was able to ease them by selling the Real Form Girdle Co. of Brooklyn, acquired by Humbard enterprises in 1965.

Nor are Jews ready to cast the first stone. There are a few "proprietary operations" lying around, said Rabbi Paul Kushner, associate director of the Synagogue Advisory Council. "The Jewish community is doing its bloody best to police these matters internally," he added, primarily through "moral suasion and pressure."

Internal policing is also the preferred Catholic mode, and a policing action that includes Rome and the Baltimore Catholic chancery is presently taking place in the Pallottine case, alongside a Maryland state investigation. But not everyone is satisfied that such measures can suffice.

In Congress at the moment are several bills—including a charitable solicitations act, introduced by Representative Lionel Van Deerlin of California, and a truth-in-contributions act, introduced by Senator Walter Mondale and Representative Joseph Karth, both of Minnesota—that could assign to religious groups many of the same requirements as those binding upon nonreligious groups soliciting funds from the public. Among other features, the Van Deerlin bill would require disclosure of how much is paid to fund-raising agents and how much of each dollar raised actually goes to charity. The Mondale-Karth bill would have every charity that grosses more than $25,000 spend at least 50 cents of each dollar on charity.

A complicating factor is that legislation such as this runs up against the First Amendment guarantees of free exercise of religion. In their preliminary stages, therefore, neither the Van Deerlin nor the Mondale-Karth bill specifically includes religious institutions within its scope. Yet there is little doubt where the sights are set. "We'd like to include them in the final version," Richard Halberstein of Congressman Karth's office recently told The National Catholic Reporter. Representative Charles H. Wilson of California has, in fact, bitten the bullet and named religious organizations in a bill awaiting action by the House's Post Office and Civil Service Committee.

The reception from religious groups is not expected to be enthusiastic. Last November, James Robinson, director of the United States Catholic Conference's government liaison office, went on record against the Van Deerlin bill. "Potential donors who have questions or doubts regarding the charitable solicitations they receive can inquire directly of the soliciting persons or organizations," he wrote the House Subcommittee on Consumer Protection and Finance; "if they are not satisfied with the answers they are given, they have the most effective remedy of all: not making the contribution."

Even if, as some believe, there is not much disorder to begin with and religion is being held unfairly suspect, public confidence has been shaken. Already one Catholic religious group, the Missionhurst Fathers of Arlington, Va., has reported a sharp drop in donations in the wake of the Pallottine scandal. Theirs may be only a momentary drop. On the other hand, if it is not momentary, religious institutions could be playing Russian roulette in fighting measures that would require them to run tight financial ships and report fully to the public.

John Deedy is managing editor of Commonweal magazine.

March 14, 1976

Papal Birth Stand Found to Hurt Church

By KENNETH A. BRIGGS

Overwhelming rejection by the Roman Catholic laity in the United States of the 1968 papal ban on artificial birth control has led to drastic declines in religious devotion and annually costs the church nearly a billion dollars in income, according to a survey of Catholic attitudes released yesterday by the National Opinion Research Center.

The report, issued in a 483-page book entitled "Catholic Schools in a Declining Church," further shows that support for parochial schools remains strong despite the church's general retreat from that field.

The study, a 10-year followup of a 1963 survey, raises critical questions about church decisions. It calls the birth-control decision "both a failure and an organizational and religious disaster." At the same time, it notes that "Catholic schools seem substantially more important today than they were a decade ago" but that "fewer resources are allowed them."

The report says that Catholics would have given $5.5 billion to the church in 1974 if they had given at 1963 levels. But even though Catholics were more affluent than they were a decade ago, they gave only $3.8 billion.

Of the $1.7 billion difference, the researchers assert, almost a billion can be accounted for by the alienation from the church created by the Pope's encyclical, "Humanae Vitae."

"It is rare," said the Rev. Andrew Greeley, program director of the Opinion Research Center, which is part of the University of Chicago, "for a social researcher to be able to explain a phenomenom so simply. But that is what happened."

Theologians and the church authorities are expected to debate the survey's reports both on methodological and philosophical grounds.

Archbishop Joseph L. Bernadin, President of the National Conference of Catholic Bishops, called the study "valuable and important" as a source of data, but cautioned the church that "Catholic truth is not determined by sociologial data or analysis."

Archbishop Bernadin said "Humanae Vitae' contains the authentic teaching of the church concerning human sexuality and the morality of contraception."

In January, the Vatican's latest pronouncement on sexuality condemned premarital sex, masturbation and homosexuality and reaffirmed the church's stand against artificial contraception.

This stand has caused a massive defection from Catholic institutions and in personal religious behavior, interrupting a wave of church programs, according to the report.

The survey portrays the Catholic community as highly receptive to church reforms initiated by the Second Vatican Council. But it says that the salutary effects of the Council have been seriously undercut by the birth control ruling.

The encyclical "seriously impaired the credibility and authority of the papacy, leading to sharp decline in mass attendance and a sharp increase in apostasy in the years immediately after the encyclical," the survey said.

There was a decline of one-third in the indexes of religious devotion, the report concludes.

The survey was conducted from March 1, 1974, to June 6, 1974. A team of 40 researchers completed 927 in-person interviews, which averaged 84 minutes in length. Fifty-seven percent of those interviewed were women, 86 percent were white and 81 percent were betwen the ages of 20 and 59 years.

The researchers found a drop in attendance at weekly mass, from 76 prcent of those interviewed in 1963 to 60 percent in the new survey. There was a reduction from 72 to 60 percent in those who pray daily, 37 to 17 in those who attend monthly confession and 66 to 50 i nthose who would "very much" like to see a son enter the priesthood.

As an indication of the loss of papal authority, the report says that 10 years ago 70 percent agreed that it was "certainly true" that Jesus invested the church's leadership in the Pope. In the new study, the figure fell to 42 percent. Only 37 percent agree with the doctrine of papal infallibility in certain pronouncements in faith and morals.

In the same decade, the number of priests has remained steady at 58,000, the number of seminarians has dropped from 50,000 to 18,000, and the number of sisters from 180,000 to 135,000.

The research team, including Father Greeley, William C. Mc-Cready and Kathleen McCourt, reported that the Catholic public strongly backed Catholic schools.

Although enrollment in parochial schools has dwindled by a half million since 1965, the survey found 90 percent of the people questioned supported those schools. 80 percent said that they would increase their giving to underwrite them.

March 24, 1976

CATHOLIC SCHOOLS SLOWING DECLINE

New Strength Attributed to Emphasis on Spiritual and Moral Values

By GENE I. MAEROFF
Special to The New York Times

CHICAGO, April 24 — The precipitous enrollment decline that threatened the existence of this country's Roman Catholic parochial schools has eased, and the schools are now drawing new strength from an emphasis on spiritual and moral values that many parents find lacking in public schools.

After a decade in which social, religious and financial influences forced the closing of more than 3,000 schools and caused enrollments to fall from 5.5 million to 3.4 million, there is a feeling among Catholic educators that the worst is behind them.

The new mood of cautious optimism was evident among the more than 15,000 lay and religious educators who gathered at McCormick Place here this week for the annual meeting of the National Catholic Educational Association.

"We are very much on the upswing," said the Rev. John F. Meyers, president of the association. "Morale is high and this convention symbolizes it. It's no longer a question of whether we are going to be able to save the schools, but what we are going to do to improve them."

The efforts by Catholic schools to infuse the education they offer with a moral dimension at a time when many of society's traditional values are being shaken is seen as a key to enhancing the appeal of the schools.

Furthermore, while the public schools are suffering a loss of confidence, the Catholic schools find themselves being looked upon favorably by many parents for maintaining an atmosphere in which youngsters and teachers feel safe and the schools remain orderly.

"It's not that we do anything all that different in discipline," said the Rev. Michael O'Neill, the former superintendent of the Catholic schools in Spokane, Wash. "It's just that the parents have their kids there voluntarily," he said, adding that the students were not about to cause difficulty "by tearing apart the school."

Change in Quality

There is also a belief that Catholic schools, once viewed as academically inferior to public schools, have pulled even in quality and, in some cities, even surpassed public schools.

As Catholic educators reassess their position and take note of the waiting lists that have developed for admission to some of their schools, particularly at the secondary level, sentiment is growing for lifting the moratoriums on school construction that were imposed for many dioceses during the days of disastrous decline.

On the other hand, though this year's enrollment decline of 2.6 percent is the smallest since the 1960's, some Catholics are concerned that they must be careful about expansion because of the effects of the drop in the Country's birth rate.

One of the most notable changes in the thinking of Catholic educators appears to be their shift away from a preoccupation with obtaining public funds for their schools, though financing itself remains a major problem.

"After having put a lot of time and effort in to trying to get Federal aid," said the Rev. John R. Gilbert of Bloomington, Minn., chairman of the association's elementary school executive committee, "we have seen many court decisions go against us, and we have become realistic. That idea has now been put on the back burner."

The attempt to promote and justify Catholic schools on the basis of their teaching of values is a result of the revised outlook.

"People today are looking for values-oriented schools," said Sister Joseph Marie, a diocesan educational consultant in Dubuque, Iowa. "We have always had this difference, but we didn't use to emphasize it; we apologized for it."

Brother Thomas P. Draney of New York, in a speech entitled, "Time to Tell It Like It Is," told his fellow Catholic educators that in contrast to the Catholic schools, the public schools were teaching "the religion known as secular humanism—the religion recognized by the Supreme Court."

Encouraged by Book

Some of the encouragement that Catholic educators feel today is attributable to a recent book, "Catholic Schools In A Declining Church," by the Rev. Andrew M. Greeley, Dr. William C. McCready and Dr. Kathleen McCourt.

The book, based on research by the National Opinion Research Center at the University of Chicago, asserts that 90 percent of the country's Catholics support parochial schools and most want to help keep them open.

It is the author's contention that a 1968 papal encyclical reaffirming official condemnation of birth control offended many American Catholics and that the schools suffered from the resulting decline in devotion and waning of financial commitment to the church.

Dr. McCready, a sociologist, suggested at the meeting that a step toward revitalizing Catholic schools would be for the church hierarchy to withdraw from operating the schools and turn over financial and educational decision-making to local laymen and clergy.

Laymen already have become predominant on the teaching faculties, accounting for 63.1 percent of the 149,760 teachers in the nation's 9,993 Catholic elementary and secondary schools.

April 25, 1976

Conference of Catholics Supports Resolution on Ordaining Women

By KENNETH A. BRIGGS
Special to The New York Times

DETROIT, Oct 23—Roman Catholics from a broad spectrum of the church ended a three-day conference today on liberty and justice that has profound implications for pastoral theology and the way the church will govern itself in the future.

Late in the afternoon, the assembly adopted, with little opposition, resolutions of support for the ordination of women and of married men.

The United States bishops, who must pass on the proposals at a later date, were also encouraged to allow women to preach and to ease the "conflict and anguish" arising from the church's teaching on birth control by affirming the right of married couples to "form their own consciences."

The birth control proposal entailed what one participant called "a tremendous struggle" and represented a compromise that some felt was too ambiguous. Rejecting an outright call for modification of church teaching, which forbids artificial means of birth control, the delegates finally adopted a proposal that was interpreted as requesting that the bishops adopt a position that more nearly conforms to the widespread practices of Catholics.

Source of Controversy

Noncompliance with the church's strict teaching, as enunciated in the 1967 Papal Encyclical "Humanae Vitae," is thought to be one of the major sources of division in the church.

In the morning session, amid a welter of proposals dealing with a variety of economic, political and human rights issues, delegates approved amnesty for Vietnam draft evaders and illegal aliens and called for a halt to arms sales to foreign nations.

Apart from the eventual outcome of the controversial issues, it seemed certain that the movement for fuller participation in critical decision-making within the church had received a major impetus during the assembly.

The "Call to Action" conference was a result of an unparalleled effort by the nation's bishops to create dialogue on concerns of church membership. According to several leaders and delegates, the assembly exceeded most expectations, raising justice priorities and providing an extraordinary model for conducting national consultation. Already there is speculation that such an assembly might become a regular feature of church life.

Such a move would represent a fundamental change in the way the church conducts its national affairs and would mirror the advisory system introduced recently on lower levels.

"I never thought I'd live long enough to see this day come in our church," Msgr. Jack Egan of the University of Notre Dame told yesterday's plenary session. "I've never seen such superb organization, dedication to a task or such cooperation."

Another participant, Joseph Cunneen, editor of the Catholic journal Crossroads, said that the church was in a period "of very healthy ferment."

Both style and substance are taking on unusual significance.

The proposals themselves, which resulted from a two-year series of hearings, dialogues and surveys, must be submitted to the Conference of Bishops for review and possible implementation. There have already been signals that some bishops will be reluctant to affirm some of the recommendations that challenge traditional church teaching or practice, such as the suggestion that excommunication be removed from divorced Catholics who have been remarried.

The social-action agenda reminded many observers of the debates that many large Protestant groups held during the last decade. As Protestants have backed away from some of these emphases, in the wake of great internal tensions, the Catholic church has begun to raise the questions anew.

But the deliberations place the bishops in a sensitive position inasmuch as they are receiving the advice which they asked for when the program was set in motion three years ago as a Bicentennial observance. A remarkable cross-section has now spoken and, in the words of one priest, the Rev. Marvin Mottet of Davenport,

Iowa, "If they reject the proposals it will be a catastrophe for the church."

But others warned that some of the proposals would alienate many grass roots Catholics and that the 1,340 delegates, most of them chosen by diocesan bishops, failed to adequately represent the Catholic constituency.

Referring to one sensitive matter, the blanket rejection of all arms sales to foreign countries, Msgr. George Higgins of the United States Catholic Conference said it was a typical example of the assembly's apparent inability to "give sufficient nuance" to some key issues.

Birth Control Little Discussed

The conference provides a sharp contrast to the impression that the church is concentrating on abortion to the neglect of other issues. Abortion, in fact, has received relatively little attention. The abortion issue had gained strength largely as a result of meetings between the executive committee of the bishops and the two major Presidential candi-

dates. There was a strong drive to open the discussion to a broader range of issues by many members of the hierarchy and other key church people after that controversy developed.

To many Catholics, the conference, and the process it represents, is the logical outgrowth of a steadily enlarging view of the Second Vatican Council's concept of "collegiality," whereby all sectors of the church are brought into decision making. The Detroit meeting raises this process to a new level, encouraging open discussion on some subjects once considered to be the hierarchy's prerogative.

The implications of this style were especially apparent in the respectful but firm disagreements often voiced between bishops and laity. "It was amazing," said a woman delegate from Ohio, "to see a bishop take part in a group, give his views and get a single vote like everyone else. Sometimes they were outvoted."

October 24, 1976

JEWS

Imposing Cast

"OUR CROWD": The Great Jewish Families of New York. By Stephen Birmingham. Illustrated. 404 pp. New York: Harper & Row. $8.95.

By DAVID CORT

THE credentials, status and repute of American Jews, or more locally New York Jews, have long awaited the confirmation of this history, which could not have been published in other times without being taken as anti-Semitic. American Jewish histories have been written, but are still in the manuscript stage, for "our crowd" has always preferred to remain impenetrable. In this preliminary study, some trace of the sycophancy which the very rich require and can enforce is evident, but Stephen Birmingham, like William Manchester, tries to escape from it, and can, insofar as he is dealing with old and sometimes tired money. Future American histories will have to take into account Mr. Birmingham's financial and social history and imposing cast of characters.

A fact of American life is that many "old" families, whether gentile or Jew, have surprisingly brief his-

tories on this continent. On simple precedence of arrival, few can compete with the shipload of Sephardic Jews who reached Manhattan in 1654, via Spain, Portugal, the Netherlands, Brazil. Until 1800 there were fewer than 1,000 American Jews, mostly Sephardim — Hendricks, Cardozo, Baruch, Lazarus, Nathan, Solis, Gomez. Like Proust's Monsieur Swann, they had far more aristocratic talents than the gentiles, the dubious heirs of feudal paladins.

The wave of steerage Jews beginning in the 1830's was German, chiefly from Bavaria (the Guggenheims were Swiss), and family status later swung on whether the founder had peddled his wares on foot or with a wagon. The first Seligman, Joseph, a brilliant university graduate, was perfectly willing to set out on foot in Pennsylvania, with a 100-200 pound pack. The first Lehman started with a wagon. The Guggenheims, Joseph Sachs and Marcus Goldman were pedestrian. These were all poor immigrants. At first the German Jews were accepted by the New York Sephardic temple, Shearith Israel, but this hospitality soon dried up, for the German Jews of Philadelphia, Cincinnati and the South gravitated to New York, and there were simply too many "loud, aggressive, new-rich Germans."

The pattern of the Germans was to progress to a dry-goods store, then move to New York, then go into banking, a very informal line of work at the time, executed on foot. The understandable obsession of these

Germans was in making money, their luck that they had moved in on a financially naive society at the strategic moment. Later they were outmatched by European German Jews of wealth who really knew what they were doing. They also had some difficulty understanding the "roughneck" native Americans, Harriman, Hill, Fisk, Gould.

Before these later developments the Seligmans — to whom this history gives a disproportionate place —adued to their far-flung chain of stores one in gold-rush San Francisco, where it was the only general store to survive the fire of 1851. With the subsequent profits, their chief business became the import of California gold. Thus they were the first of the German Jews to go into banking. (And this became another social distinction, as against the others who remained only great storekeepers.) They learned so fast that they were the only New York commercial bank not closed by the Panic of 1857.

By the time of the Civil War they were not only in position to supply the Union uniforms but also to market the Union's treasury bonds. Though it is debated, Joseph certainly helped establish the Union's credit in Europe. Later the Seligmans became international bankers on the Rothschild model, involved in the gold corner and Black Friday of 1869 and the Panama Canal.

No other Jew at the time could follow in the swath of August Schönberg, representative of the Rothschilds, who changed his name

MR. CORT, a writer on the American scene, past and present, is the author of "Social Astonishments" and the just published "The Glossy Rats."

Nineteenth-century peddler. From "Our Crowd."

to Belmont, became a gentile, a great swell, epicure and duelist and married a daughter of Commodore Perry. He first acknowledged the Seligmans after the Civil War, for he treated even his father-in-law as a lackey. In the Jewish story he is a bewildering freak.

The story gets ever more complex. The legend on the Statue of Liberty was composed by a Sephardic aristocrat, Emma Lazarus: "Give me . . . the wretched refuse." To the German Jews, she meant them, and they would not subscribe to the statue fund. (The later Russian Jews greatly admired the legend.) The Jewish Harmonie Club, founded in 1852, revered a portrait of the Kaiser, and the members sent their sons to German universities.

The Union Club included the Sephardic families of Hendricks, Lazarus and Nathan, and refused to expel Judah P. Benjamin, a member of Jefferson Davis's Cabinet. A Lazarus was a founding member of the Knickerbocker Club. Joseph Seligman could do no better than the Union League Club, even though President Grant offered him the post of Secretary of the Treasury over Hamilton Fish, a member of the "400." Joseph refused it. When Ward McAllister's "400" excluded all Jews, the Sephardim blamed this loss of status on the German Jews.

As the former peddlers lost their grip, a wave of well-off European Jews arrived on the scene: Jacob Schiff, Otto Kahn, the Warburgs, Adolph Lewisohn. The first three

took over Kuhn, Loeb which had reached New York from Cincinnati in 1867. When the Russian Jews began arriving, the formerly poor German Jews snubbed them; the Schiffs and Lewisohns befriended them. Schiff and Kahn in particular were great men, deserving of far nobler reputations than they have left.

Much bad news was to come. Formal anti-Semitism began in 1877, when Joseph Seligman's barring from a Saratoga hotel became a national controversy. In the early 1900's, Russian and Polish Jews were reaching New York at 90,000 a year. Since many were socialist-minded, the rich German Jews led the anti-Semitism. Jacob Schiff, as well as Morgan, was blamed for Black Thursday, the Panic of 1901, triggered by the corner on Northern Pacific stock. In World War I the German Jews were unfairly accused of German sympathies ("the German bankers," Kuhn, Loeb and also Goldman, Sachs). And in the Depression all bankers, gentile and Jew alike, lost their commanding power, never to regain it.

MOST recently the most vigorous lines have been the Guggenheims ("The Googs"), the Lehmans, who came from the Deep South in 1868, and a newcomer, John L. Loeb. But the later Seligmans and Loebs produced a hothouse of eccentricities: extreme courage, extreme arrogance, extreme frivolity. I once met the elderly, very distinguished, trifling Jefferson Seligman through his 20-year-

old protégée, Kittens Leightamer, who later flowered in tabloid headlines. Here was no sign of Joseph who, with a university degree, carried a 200-pound pack through backwoods America.

Hardly a hint has been given here of the rich social tapestry, the fascinating embellishment of real American and New York history. Pictures and an extremely simplified "family-business tree" are included.

One receives the impression that these Jews, holding at first to a more tenacious memory of their origins, lost some of the volatile, free-floating strength of the American society. It was the Germanness of the German Jews that must have accounted for their rigid and haughty stratifications, modeled on the Almanach de Gotha. When this was outgrown, everything seemed to go, including their faith. "Our crowd," probably to its loss, became very largely Christian or agnostic.

Around any such history as this, of such proud and powerful people, much controversy will develop, usually in quite unexpected quarters. A very intelligent Jew said some time ago that, since Dachau, the Jewish establishment had made two final determinations: (1) from now on, a Jew is a Jew and that is final; and (2) in America, he is an American and that is final. This long overdue history serves both determinations well.

July 2, 1967

and of fortitude in affliction. That to further the recognition of these truths in word and deed is a sacred duty which they owe both to themselves and to their fellow-men, and whereby they shall best secure the common happiness, prosperity, and peace. That to insure the moral elevation of the "masses" in particular, with all the great benefits which that includes, they hold to be a lofty aim, and one well calculated to afford true satisfaction to all who behold in the work of progress the fitting accomplishment of human destiny. That it is desirable to transmit to the incoming generation the best convictions of the present unimpaired; to acquaint them in such manner as befits their years and understanding with the principles, aspirations, and consolations of the modern view of life; and thus to train them in the enjoyment of the inestimable benefits of liberty from their youth upward. That for all these purposes the necessity of united action, in which alone lies the pledge of extended usefulness, permanency, and strength, is self-evident. Any person of either sex may become a member of the society upon the approval of three-fourths of the Trustees present at a regular meeting of the board, at which the name of the candidate shall be presented and baloted for. No subscription or assent to any formula of faith, belief, or creed shall be required as a qualification for membership.

The Trustees, consisting of 15 members, shall look after and manage the affairs, financial, temporal, and social, of the organization, and shall be elected for one year. The first board consisted of Joseph Seligman, Albert A. Levi, Henry Friedman, Edward Lauterbach, William Byfield, Joseph Seidenberg, Max Abenheim, Max Landman, Emil Salinger, Meyer Jonasson, Jacob Stellheimer, Jr., Samuel V. Speyer, Samuel A. Solomons, Julius Rosenbaum, and Marcus Goldman. It was entirely re-elected last year, we believe, and at present serves.

A lecturer (or lecturers) is chosen by the society, such lecturer being ex officio a member of the Board of Trustees. He delivers a lecture each week, in which the principles of ethics are developed and advanced among adults, and in part by the establishment of a school or schools wherein a course of moral instruction is supplied.

The lecturer who has been lecturing for some time past each Sunday morning for 8 months out of the 12, at Standard Hall, is Felix Adler, late Professor of Hebrew Literature and Oriental Languages at Cornell University. He lectured to a body of Liberal Jews, or Reformed Judaists, by whom the Society for Ethical Culture was originally formed, before its foundation, coming to the City from Ithaca on Saturday, and returning Sunday evening in time to discharge his professional duties. The chair he occupied had been endowed for three years by a number of wealthy liberal-minded men, who, at the expiration of the term, offered to re-endow it, provided Adler should fill it. The Professor, although he had secured the highest esteem of the Trustees for his personal worth and personal character, and their sincere admiration for his learning and talents, had proved too liberal in his religious views to meet what they conceived to be the spiritual requirements of an orthodox establishment. His lectures here had attracted attention and unfolded rationalistic views, so that they were unwilling he should continue his connection with the University. They did not say so, however. They veiled their real sentiments by the assumption that they could not accept an endowment of a chair without naming the Professor who was to occupy it. Adler's friends, therefore, withdrew their generous offer, and he retired from the institution, which to this day remains without the Professorship of He-

brew Literature and Oriental Languages.

The endowment would probably have been tendered to Harvard University, and he would probably have occupied the same chair there as at Cornell, had he not, meanwhile, been urgently invited to be the regular lecturer before the Society for Ethical Culture, which had just been founded. Such position, though less remunerative in a pecuniary sense, and far more laborious, was in the direct line of his desires and aspirations, as well as of his intellectual equipment. Consequently, he accepted it as a solemn and conscientious trust, for upon him devolves more, especially the intellectual concerns of the society, and to him belongs the powers generally exercised by ministers of theological denominations.

Prof. Adler is a native of this City, son of Dr. Samuel Adler, a Jewish Rabbi of the more liberal persuasion—a German, long resident here, and noted for his profound learning and exalted character. The son was educated at the University of Berlin, having been for some time under the private instruction of the late Dr. Geiger, renowned throughout Europe for his mental force and ripe scholarship. He obtained at Berlin the degree of Doctor of Philosophy, and, though but 28, has shown an intellect of the highest order, and distinguished himself by his erudition and the variety of his attainments.

He is of medium stature, rather slight, but of symmetrical figure, and faultlessly, even fastidiously neat in person and attire. His face is calm, mobile, full of intelligence, indicative of a very nervous, sensitive, imaginative, idealistic temperament. He has a somewhat prominent nose, a broad, well-shaped, idea-suggesting forehead, a delicate complexion, a sensitive, pleasant mouth, blue eyes, brown hair, mustache and whiskers, the last darker than his hair. His appearance and manner evince the thinker and the scholar, and his outgiving is one of great modesty, even of shyness, despite earnest convictions, great moral courage and elevated and inflexible purpose.

Dr. Adler, like most of the original members of his society, belongs or, more properly, belonged, to the Reformed Judaists, who, as he says, arose in Germany, and whose leading members have invariably been Germans. He and his people regard Moses Mendelssohn as the deliverer of the Jews from much of their narrowness, many of their ancient traditions, and time-honored prejudices, and thus Mendelssohn became the author, in the widest acceptance, of the reformatory movement. The Jews, according to Adler, have ceased to be a national unit, and will exist hereafter as a confederation of religious societies. The present condition of Liberal Judaism is nearly related to that of Liberal Christianity. The old is dead; the new has not been born. Such changes as have occurred in the constitution of the Jewish religion have not brought them in any wise nearer to Christianity. On the contrary, since the belief in a personal Messiah has been surrendered, the hope of their conversion has become more vague and visionary than ever. Those whom the worship of the synagogue and the temple no longer attracts either become wholly skeptical and indifferent, or, as is often the case, transfer their allegiance to the new humanitarian doctrine, which is fast assuming the character of a religion in the ardor it inspires and the strong spiritual union it cements. For the great body of the Jews, however, the central doctrine of Judaism remains unshaken, and doubtless so long as Christianity exists, Judaism as a distinct creed will coexist with it. As a religious society, they desire to remain distinct. But as citizens they are eager to remove whatever distinctions still hamper their intercourse with their neighbors of other creeds.

Latterly many persons have joined the society who are not Jews, who would ordinarily be ranked as Christians, although they are not such in a theo-

logic sense, because they are not believers in any Church, creed, or dogma. They are firm adherents and vindicators of the religion of humanity, their faith being confined to practical plans and effort in its behalf. The membership, which is steadily increasing, now numbers 700 or 800, and represents as many nationalities and differences of opinion on general subjects as any organization in the City.

Adler has proposed divers plans for bettering the condition of the working classes, such as colonization, apprenticeship, and co-operation, all of which are sensible and practical. He wholly discourages appeals to passion and prejudice, strikes and trade unions, which invariably do more harm than good. His measures are of a kind to enkindle hope and inculcate patience. Though the reverse of an alarmist, he sees danger in the present condition of things—in the concentration and glut of laborers in the cities, the hostile feeling between labor and capital, the lack of intelligence on one hand and the want of sympathy on the other, the absence of recognition of the humanity and manhood of the toiling millions. He is opposed to the giving of money without an equivalent. This leads to pauperism, and pauperism is the worst form of destitution, since it destroys dignity and the spirit of independence and self-respect. The laboring classes, to be truly and permanently benefited, must feel and see that the more fortunate and prosperous have their interest at heart, and are willing to help them to help themselves. They have the right to live, meaning the right to work, the right to cleanliness, and the right to be private and virtuous, which, in the crowded and poisonous tenement-houses of the City, they can never enjoy. Material reforms must come before moral reforms can be established. It is idle to talk of good conduct, self-restraint, regard for law and order until men are enabled to live decently and stand fairly and becomingly before their fellows.

The society established, Jan. 2, a free kindergarten school at the National Assembly Rooms, West Forty-fourth-street, between Eighth and Ninth avenues, for the benefit of children from 3 to 6 years of age, whose parents' means do not permit them to spend money for their education. Children who, too young to be left alone, require the constant attention and care of their mothers, are received at the kindergarten, and their mothers, thus relieved, can earn money for their support. The school began with six, and now has near 70 children, who illustrate the excellence of the system.

What may be called a direct result of the society and of Dr. Adler's teachings and endeavors, is the foundation of a working men's lyceum, with the avowed intent to help themselves. It has no political object or significance, no spirit of, or sympathy with, trades unions. Its aim is to so educate the laborer that he may understand his best interest, and to enlighten public opinion on the mutual and interdependent relations between him and society. There are now some 80 members, men of intelligence and character, who meet Saturday, fortnightly, in the Bond-Street Bank building, corner of Bond-street and the Bowery. They have collected some 600 volumes, and it is remarkable that they read the best of them, histories, philosophies, and works of science being the most sought. They hope ere long to secure able lecturers, who shall express their views on political economy and on such topics as immediately concern their welfare. One of their projects is the foundation, ultimately, of a Mechanics' Institute, differing from the Cooper Union and like institutions in this, that it shall be under the direction of, and be entirely administered by, the working men themselves.

March 17, 1878

TROUBLE IN THE JEWISH CAMP.

A CHICAGO RABBI REFUSES TO PERMIT FELIX ADLER TO LECTURE IN HIS SYNAGOGUE AND DENOUNCES HIS DOCRINES.

Special Dispatch to the New-York Times.

CHICAGO, March 21.—There is trouble brewing in the Jewish camp. Recently, the Sinai Literary Association of this city appointed a committee to correspond with Dr. Felix Adler, of New-York, for the purpose of seeing if that famous liberal could make it convenient to lecture before the association at an early day. At a meeting of the society held at the Sinai Temple last night, the committee reported that Dr. Adler would be in Chicago on the 25th, 26th, and 27th of this month, and that he had consented to lecture. The committee also presented as a part of its report, the following protest from Dr. K. Koh-

ler, Pastor of Sinai congregation:

"To my great surprise I hear that in the Sinai Literary Association, a motion is on foot to invite Dr. Felix Adler, of New-York, to deliver a lecture before the members, he being expected to come here next week. Of what benefit to a society of Jewish young people, the lecture of a man can be who has deserted the Jewish flag and openly professes his disbelief in God and immortality, I really fail to see, unless the eradication of the Jewish faith is the object contemplated. But, I suppose, very few of your members, if any, know anything about the young Professor, who merely by his fine oratory, combined with great arrogance, created for awhile some sensation in New-York. At any rate, I shall not allow my temple to be disgraced by a lecture to be delivered within its walls by one who blasphemes God and Judaism."

The strong language of this protest has occasioned a somewhat acrimonious discussion. Dr. Adler will not be allowed to lecture in the synagogue.

March 22, 1878

THE HEBREWS FROM RUSSIA

A PROBLEM THAT PERPLEXES THE AMERICAN JEWS.

ENGLAND'S PROMPTNESS IN SENDING REFUGEES TO THIS COUNTRY — FIFTEEN THOUSAND HELPLESS PEOPLE ALREADY ARRIVED—BENEVOLENCE OF THE JEWS IN AMERICA.

The Jewish problem, which, in variously modified aspects—chiefly through brutal persecution—is seeking solution in different parts of Europe, in quite a unique form is now also added to our own stock of "burning" questions. The subject divides into two parts: One is philanthropic, and makes immediate claims upon the attention of the American people; the other is economic, and, while important in its bearing on the future of the country, does not now demand to be settled out of hand.

There are reasons for believing that the people of this country, except in special cases, are not fully alive to the importance of this Jewish influx. There is such a thing as getting too much even of the very best in this world. The American people are no doubt prepared to do their whole duty in this refugee matter, but circumstances — unless the case is kept well in hand—may compel them to do a great deal more than their legitimate share. John Bull, as represented by the Mansion House Committee, seems to have collected a large sum of money for the express purpose of increasing our population; however, what is to become of these people after they get here does not seem to concern him in the least.

The whole question should be discussed—and, if need be, settled—in the clearest lights, and without prejudice. Until now it has been left for solution with our Jewish population, as if the Nation at large had no concern in it. It is a mistake to suppose that the Jews are anxious to keep this matter in their own hands. It is rather true that they are quite willing to be relieved of all responsibilities in the case, and the most far-sighted among them view the future with alarm. They realize the peculiarity of their position most keenly. A leading Jewish merchant expressed himself to the reporter for The Times to this effect: "We are a commercial people, and the force of circumstances, as well as our traditions, confine us to a limited range of occupations. Within this sphere we are liable to establish a controlling influence—to secure a monopoly, as it were—and thus incur the danger of fanning into a flame any smoldering fires of prejudice. We are deeply concerned in this Jewish immigration—our own future well-being seems at stake in it. A pressing demand is made upon us just now, and we are bound to do our duty in the emergency; but to throw the whole responsibility upon us, by treating it as a sect question, when it is a great internatianal problem, seems to me to be not only wrong and unjust but extremely short-sighted on the part of the American people."

The importance of this problem to the whole people is, perhaps, best brought into view by the aid of some statistics. The Jew, because of his special callings, as compared with average people, seems, at the least, to triplicate himself. That is to say, he appears to the casual observer at the lowest estimate three times more numerous than the census figures warrant. Any village containing only a dozen Jews to a new-comer will appear as almost an exclusively Jewish settlement. The reason is that all Jews are in business, their signs on the principal streets are ever the boldest and most conspicuous, and they will themselves appear where the stranger can not fail to take cognizance of them. In the larger cities they divide into two classes—on the one hand shop-keepers, on the other peddlers. In any case they are peculiarly conspicuous. Their shops are generally on leading thoroughfares, and not a small part of their business is "sidewalk trade." The peddler, of course, lives on the street, and a single individual in this line easily succeeds in making himself more "numerous" than 50 mortals having ordinary callings. A thousand street vendors readily lend themselves to give the appearance of 10,000.

Except he has given this illusive aspect of the subject his attention, it will surprise the reader to learn that the entire present Jewish population of the United States does not exceed 250,000 souls. Since the 1st of January, 1882, Russian Jews have arrived at the rate of about 2,000 per month. There are said to be 3,000,000 Jews in Poland and Russia. Already 100,000 or more have fled the Czar's dominion in search of refuge. If America continues to remain an unrestricted asylum to receive whomsoever John Bull may see fit to send, the possibilities in the way of Semitic acquisitions seem almost unlimited.

Aside from the peculiar characteristics that distinguish Jews from the common run of people, and make them either desirable or undesirable acquisitions at given periods in a country, there is to be observed a wide distinction between refugees and ordinary immigrants. Thus a third and most important element is added to the problem. The average immigrant arrives on these shores with a fixed purpose, definite aims, and a disposition, as well as qualifications, that will enable him to assimilate with the body of our people. The refugee, on the other hand, is absolutely helpless when he arrives, and, what makes matters worse in this case, peculiar circumstances prevent these new arrivals from placing themselves in agreement with their new relations. In this we have still another amplification. It must be remembered that these Russian Jews are in the strictest sense orthodox. The story told by Col. Ingersoll, where a Jew imagined that the heavens thundered because he had eaten a small piece of pork, would have special application to these people, and that, too, without the addition in the case of Ingersoll's Jew, who really thought Jehovah had taken occasion to get angry over a very little matter. These people would consider the eating of pork as matter enough for a cosmic cataclysm. The average Jew in America is a Jew only from an ethnological point of view. His racial antecedents he holds an accident, and for the rest he does in New-York as New-Yorkers do. He believes no more than he is compelled to, and eats pork if he has a taste for it. From a religious point of view the Russian Jew is further from the American Jew than the American Jew is from a Christian or infidel. An orthodox Jew, who undertakes to earn his bread in a non-Jewish community, is literally confined to bread for his diet. Not only is he debarred by his creed from eating pork, but such other meats as he ordinarily permits himself to eat must be slaughtered according to certain forms, and by one specially consecrated to the office of shochet or butcher. Now it happens, unfortunately, that full-fledged shochets do not abound very numerously in American rural districts, and in consequence any isolated orthodox Jew finds it hard lines until he concludes to adapt himself to the customs of the country. "This is apparently a small, but a very serious, matter," remarked a prominent Hebrew to a reporter of The Times. "One of the first batches to arrive we colonized in Colorado. They were without a shochet, and consequently without meat, until we sent them one. Few of us care for this form, but to these people it is sacred above almost anything else. Should we undertake to persuade them that this is an empty, or at any rate minor, form, they would be horror-stricken and lose all faith in our counsels, and besides it would be cruel to disabuse their minds. It is partly, at least, for conscience's sake that these Jews have been persecuted, and to tell them after losing their all that their sacrifices meet with no appreciation among their own race brethren would be the extreme of cruelty. It may be a superstition, but we cannot overcome it, though it adds immensely to our difficulties."

Up to the present time, since the beginning of the Russian persecutions, the arrivals of Russian Jews have aggregated about 15,000. At first all were embarked to arrive at New-York, and thus came under the care of the New-York Jewish Emigrant Society. This body had about $110,000 placed at its disposal—$35,000 of which was contributed by the Mansion House Committee and the rest raised among wealthy Jews in this City—and by judicious management hoped to carry forward a systematic work, estimating that they would be able to take care of about 300 arrivals per week. For a time all went fairly well, but all of a sudden, without previous warning, several thousand were thrown upon their hands, and then the whole machinery became clogged. Lately the English committee has made direct consignments to various inland localities—to many points previously supplied by New-York with the full number that can be maintained—and the result is that the whole work is thrown into confusion. For example, Milwaukee, it was thought, would be able to care for 300, and that number were shipped to that point from New-York. Within a fortnight a party of 350 have been consigned to the same point direct from England, via Montreal. The result is that Milwaukee suddenly finds herself paralyzed. It has more than it can assimilate in any practical way, and the consequences cannot fail to be disastrous. Other places are being served in the same way. It would appear that without the least regard to the practical expedients of such a course, the English committee have adopted a sort of cast-iron census rule, by which the number consigned to any place is entirely regulated by the general population as given in the last census report—and in pursuance of this method of distribution a party of nine have been sent direct from England to Newport. Whether Summer cottages go along with this assignment is left a matter of painful uncertainty.

Various colonization schemes have been tried with varying success. One in Louisiana is an acknowledged failure. Another in Colorado presents some promising features. However, whether inherently feasible or otherwise, a lack of funds for the carrying forward of schemes of this sort will prevent the colonization of these refugees from ever becoming anything beyond an interesting experiment. In the nature of the case these people must remain where they can be best provided for. This is obviously in the established Jewish centres, and this fact is being more and more recognized by those having this refugee problem to solve. Unless immense sums of money can be placed at the disposal of the local Jewish committee for transportation purposes they will be compelled to devote all their means to the procurement of the merest necessaries of life for the people already on their hands. Under such circumstances, but one result can be looked for: These people will remain at the places to which they are originally consigned, the larger cities, and New-York must necessarily absorb the bulk.

The number any city is able to assimilate being in a measure limited or regulated by the Jewish population within its borders, it becomes a question of importance how, under this law of aggregates, the new-comers will be apportioned, and in this connectin some statistics will be of interest.

Under the auspices of the United Jewish Associations, recent efforts have resulted in a very complete Jewish census. The figures obtained are, perhaps, a trifle under the mark, but in the main sufficiently correct for a basis of estimates and calculations. With regard to the leading cities of the Union the report of the association gives the following figures:

BY CITIES.

Cities.	*Jewish Population.*	*Cities.*	*Jewish Population.*
New-York	60,000	Cleveland	3,500
San Francisco	16,000	Newark	3,500
Brooklyn	14,000	Milwaukee	2,500
Philadelphia	13,000	Louisville	2,500
Chicago	12,000	Pittsburg	2,000
Baltimore	10,000	Detroit	2,000
Cincinnati	8,000	Washington	1,500
Boston	7,000	New-Haven	1,000
St. Louis	6.500	Rochester	1,000
New-Orleans	5,000		

BY STATES AND TERRITORIES.

The following are the returns by States and Territories, covering the congregations, their membership, and the population at large:

States and Territories.	*Number of Congregations.*	*Number of Members.*	*To'l Jewish Population.*
Alabama	8	254	2,045
Arizona	..	..	48
Arkansas	4	165	1,466
California	12	613	18,580
Colorado	1	31	423
Connecticut	3	169	1,492
Dakota	..	..	19
Delaware		..	585
District of Columbia	3	144	1,508
Florida	1	..	772
Georgia	7	313	2,704
Idaho	..	..	85
Illinois	10	567	12,625
Indiana	14	398	3,381
Iowa	3	91	1,245
Kansas	2	56	819
Kentucky	4	285	3,602
Louisiana	13	495	7,538
Maine	1	..	500
Maryland	14	600	10,337
Massachusetts	9	650	8,500
Michigan	6	263	3.233
Minnesota	1	28	414
Mississippi	8	239	2,262
Missouri	5	506	7,380
Montana	..	..	130
Nebraska	1	20	222
Nevada	1	29	780
New-Hampshire	..	..	150
New-Jersey	8	229	5,593
New-Mexico	..	..	108
New-York	52	3,371	80,565
North Carolina	2	65	820
Ohio	24	1,014	14,581
Oregon	2	60	868
Pennsylvania	26	1,969	20,000
Rhode Island	2	105	1,000
South Carolina	3	110	1,415
Tennesse	7	271	3,751
Texas	7	210	3,300
Utah	..	..	258
Vermont	1	19	120
Virginia	8	291	2,506
Washington Territory	..	..	145
West Virginia	2	58	511
Wisconsin	3	95	2,559
Wyoming	..	..	46
Totals	278	13,763	230,984

Taking 250,000 Jewish inhabitants as a basis of calculation, 15,000 refugees would allot 1 to every 17 settled Jews. According to an apportionment on this basis the quotas of the larger cities would be about as follows: New-York, 3,500; San Francisco, 950; Brooklyn, 800; Philadelphia, 750; Chicago, 700; Baltimore, 600; Cincinnati, 500; Boston, 450; St. Louis, 400; New-Orleans, 300; Cleveland, 200; Newark, 200; Milwaukee, 150, (it has already received 650;) Louisville, 150; Pittsburg, 125; Detroit, 125; Washington, 100; New-Haven, 60; Rochester, 60.

But any mere abstract arithmetical rule to cover a complex problem such as this of the Russian refugees, if too rigidly applied, cannot fail to work mischief. Besides, it will come to pass that the larger cities must do far more than their arithmetical proportion. In the first place, at least one-third of the Jewish population of the country is isolated in semi-rural communities in such a way that effective co-operation is out of the question. In the second place, these refugees are evidently best adapted for city life, and it is safe to assume that fully 75 per cent. of all now on these shores or to arrive will finally settle in the larger cities, and no doubt 50 per cent. of all new-comers will, in one way or another, make their home in or about this City. The whole tendency is now in this direction. Several large appropriations by wealthy Jews here have been made with special reference to the establishment of "shelters" in this vicinity, where the women and children may be taken care of, thus placing the men at liberty to seek and procure employment. Two thousand women and children are now on the hands of the committee, and most of these will eventually find their way to the "shelters" to be erected on Ward's Island. It has been proposed to the Mansion House Committee that they pay the local committee $10 per month for all refugees under their charge. Unless something definite in the way of assistance is soon devised, the local committee at an early day will be completely stranded. About $100,000 has already been expended. Now an additional sum of $75,000 has already been subscribed by the Hebrews of this City. It was expected that at least twice that sum would be contributed, but hopes in that direction have been disappointed. There is an evident unwillingness on the part of many Jews that this should be regarded as an exclusively Jewish matter, both because the burden is more than the Jewish population can bear and because of the consequences that such exclusive responsibility may entail. If too much is done by them they argue that the American people may eventually hold them accountable for any real or imaginary surplusage. The more is done for these refugees the more they will press for these shores, and sometimes sufficient for the day is the evil thereof.

It is for reasons detailed in the foregoing, and many others equally cogent that might be suggested, that the local Jewish committees deem it wise to relieve themselves as much as possible from at least a few of the responsibilities and duties hitherto devolved upon them. They contend that in a matter of such importance, involving, perchance, great national interests in the near future, the Nation should assume all responsibility. The State of New-York has appropriated $250,000 for immigration purposes. None of this sum will go toward caring for the refugees so long as the Jewish committee remains in control of this work, and the members of the committee are of opinion that at least a portion of this fund should be devoted to the needs of Jewish refugees. The Jews of this City have always taken care of their own immigrants. It was their intention to continue doing so, but now the work has grown beyond their means, and they feel compelled to abdicate in favor of the regularly constituted authorities.

The charge of clannishness has often been set up against the Jews. It is certainly their boast and pride that no Jew has ever been allowed to suffer want in the midst of their plenty. Their labors in behalf of the needy of their race, together with their contributions in the past, have been all that the most philanthropic could wish. It will be of interest to present some statistics bearing on this subject. Given a population of 250,000, there must in turn be subtracted from this an indefinite proportion, say 50,000, living too remotely from the centres of activity to participate in any concerted action. In order to bring the benevolent work of the Hebrews of this country clearly and concretely before the readers' mind, let him suppose a city of 200,000 people and then endow it with the institutions to be enumerated.

HOSPITALS.

There are six or more hospitals supported by the Jews of the United States. All of these are extensive institutions, and models in their arrangements and management. Although maintained by Jews they are by no means confined to Jewish needs. These institutions are situated in the following places: Mount Sinai Hospital, New-York; Jewish Hospital, Philadelphia; Hebrew Hospital, Baltimore; Jewish Hospital, Cincinnati; Touro Infirmary, New-Orleans; Michael Rees Hospital, Chicago.

ORPHAN ASYLUMS.

There are 11 orphan asylums and homes distributed among the following cities of the Union: Hebrew Benevolent and Orphan Asylum, Home for Aged and Infirm Hebrews, Deborah Nursery and Child's Protectory, Sheltering Guardian Society, New-York; Foster Home and Orphan Asylum, Philadelphia; B'nai B'rith Orphan Asylum, Cleveland; Jewish Orphan Asylum, Baltimore; Pacific Orphan Asylum, San Francisco; Home for Aged and Infirm, Family Orphan Society, Philadelphia; Home for Widows and Orphans, New-Orleans. Besides these there are other benevolent institutions in almost every city in the Union for dispensing charity, for free burial, &c.

BENEVOLENT ORDERS.

There are four Jewish orders or secret societies in the United States. Their object is the moral, social, and intellectual advancement of Israelites, the payment of pecuniary benefits to members in case of sickness, and, in case of death, an endowment of $1,000 to the family of the deceased member, as well as the promotion of all benevolent undertakings. These societies are as follows:

1. Independent Order of B'nai B'rith. This has 7 Grand Lodges, 302 subordinate lodges, and 22,814 members. For the five years ending December, 1878, there were paid for sick and endowment benefits $1,007,039. Funds on hand, $570,089.

2. Independent Order of Free Sons of Israel. This has 2 Grand Lodges, 86 subordinate lodges, and 8,604 members.

3. The Order of Kesher Shel Barzel. This has 5 Grand Lodges, 170 subordinate lodges, and 10,000 members. Paid in 1878 for endowment benefits, $129,803. Funds on hand, $112,693.

4. Improved Order Free Sons of Israel. This has 1 Grand Lodge, 44 subordinate lodges, and 2,849 members. Paid in 1879 for sick and endowment benefits, $39,038. Funds on hand, $21,964.

There are several female orders attached to the above, and others independent, which pay weekly benefits to their needy members, and specific amounts in case of death.

SCHOOLS AND COLLEGES.

There are 13 free schools maintained by the Hebrews of the United States devoted to Hebrew and religious instruction. They are distributed as follows: New-York, 5; Philadelphia, 4; Cincinnati, 1; St. Louis, 1; Chicago, 1; San Francisco, 1.

There has been established besides a Hebrew Union College. This is situated at Cincinnati. It has an efficient corps of Professors, and is under control of a Board of Managers of 24 members. This college affords gratuitous instruction in Hebrew, classical, and rabbinical departments, not only to Israelites, but to students of all denominations, and is authorized by law to confer degrees.

There are in all the larger cities Young Men's Hebrew Associations for mental, moral, and social culture by means of lectures on scientific and literary topics, Jewish history, &c. Reading-rooms and libraries are attached.

HEBREW CONGREGATIONS.

The Union of American Hebrew Congregations comprises 118 congregations, and has for its object the union of the Israelites of America in all that is beneficial to their interests, and especially to establish and maintain institutions for instruction in Hebrew literature and Jewish theology, and to establish relations with kindred organizations in other parts of the world for the relief of the Jews from political oppression, and rendering them aid in their efforts toward social, moral, and intellectual elevation.

The value of the property of these societies, chiefly represented by synagogues, by States is as follows:

States and Territories	Value of Property	State and Territories	Value of Property
Alabama	$50,000	Michigan	40,000
Arizona	25,000	Minnesota	35,000
California	450,000	Mississippi	30,000
Colorado	5,000	Missouri	200,000
Connecticut	30,000	New-Jersey	75,000
Dist. of Columbia	35,000	New-York	2,750,000
Georgia	55,000	North Carolina	25,000
Illinois	400,000	Ohio	800,000
Indiana	85,000	Oregon	10,000
Iowa	20,000	Pennsylvania	825,000
Kansas	15,000	South Carolina	80,000
Kentucky	175,000	Tennessee	75,000
Louisiana	250,000	Texas	100,000
Maryland	75,000	Virginia	50,000
Massachusetts	50,000	Wisconsin	75,000
Total value			**$6,900,000**

RECAPITULATION.

Number of congregations	278
Number of members	13,763
Total Jewish population, (with recent accessions)	250,000
Hospitals	6
Orphan asylums and homes	11
Benevolent lodges	602
Funds held by above lodges	$704,646
Colleges and schools free	14
Value of synagogue, hospital, and church property	$6,900,000

"As rich as a Jew" has all the force of a proverb among the vulgar. The aggregate wealth of the Jews of New-York is supposed by many to be something quite fabulous, and the natural fondness on the part of Israelites for display goes far to give color to the supposition that every Jew has a gold mine in his back yard. Talking on this subject, a prominent Israelite remarked: "It is a mistake to credit us with extraordinary wealth as a class. A few among us possess considerable of this world's goods—are recognized millionaires—but in New-York there are not above a dozen of this class, and the rest are no richer than the average of the people among whom they reside."

Said another: "We are disappointed at the non-action, or what amounts to the same, of many of our money kings. I feel certain that the Rothschilds, with their influence at Courts, and especially at St. Petersburg, could have put a stop to these outrages. Perhaps we over-estimate their influence, but we are none the less disappointed that there has been no visible effort on their part in the direction indicated. Besides, they have not contributed from their abundance as they ought. According to the papers, several bankers at Paris and Frankfort have been large contributors—one is credited with having given 1,000,000f.—but we have reason to doubt these statements. However, sums as large as that would be none too large from people like the Rothschilds in an emergency so pressing as this."

The colonization scheme to any considerable extent being practically out of the question, the local committees are turning their attention to other means of supplying these refugees with employment. Unpleasant as the fact is to them, they are forced to admit that the bulk of these refugees must find employment in the larger cities. Many are intelligent, but few are adapted to manual labor. They lack the required physique. Under the inspiration of the institutions, a wholesome diet, and other improving forces, the native-born Jew of America fills out to excellent proportions; but the European Jew, especially of the lower order, is an animated deformity, and in Germany few are found qualified to perform military service. Taking all the circumstances detailed above into account, it is readily seen that the problem presented by the Russian Jew is by no means an easy one of solution, and at no distant day national action of some kind will no doubt be imperatively demanded by the situation and evoked.

July 16, 1882

THE PROPOSED JEWISH COLLEGE

RADICAL DIFFERENCES OF THE LIBERAL AND CONSERVATIVE HEBREWS.

PHILADELPHIA, Dec. 27.—The Rev. S. Morais, who is one of the leading spirits in the movement to establish a new college in the United States under the auspices of the conservative Jewish element, has decided to visit the rabbis and influential Jews of the conservative party in New-York and Brooklyn, to urge the importance of such a college to offset the liberal tendencies of the Union College at Cincinnati. New-York and Brooklyn form the great stronghold of the Jews in this country, there being 80,000 of that faith in New-York and 20,000 in Brooklyn. The number in Philadelphia does not exceed 15,000. Mr. Morris said to-day that there is an institution in New-York styled the Temple Emanu-El, which has assisted to some extent in educating young men by sending them to European colleges and universities. Several of these returned and filled positions as rabbis, but at the present time only one of them is so engaged. Mr. Morais favors the founding of a college where Jewish young men, destined for the various learned professions, would receive their classical training and at the same time be placed under conservative influences. A school of divinity would be attached to the college for the special education of students who intend to enter the ministry. The reverend gentleman said that the liberals wish to get near the Christians, in order to win them back eventually to the old faith, but he doubted that such would be the result. The innovations are mostly in reference to the observance of the Mosaic law and customs, the liberals firmly holding to the fundamental doctrines.

The Rev. Dr. Samuel Hirsh, the most influential liberal leader among the Jews of this city, said: "The great majority of the Jews in the free and enlightened countries of the world, as America, England, France, and Germany, are liberals. In Russia, where there are 2,000,000 Jews, they are mainly conservative, because they are kept down and not allowed to think for themselves. The proposed new college will avail nothing; people in this country think for themselves. The Rev. Mr. Morais does not fully understand this. His views on college training are all wrong. His idea is to make students receive by rote their religious training. That will do in some countries, but not here. Our young men think for themselves, and would do so in spite of such attempted training. In order to get our people down to his views, we would have to go back to the feudal ages and reinstate all the old persecutions as they were in those dark times. We would have to go back further. We would have to return to the daily bloody sacrifices and many things which our people do not carry out any more. We differ materially from the conservatives in some important respects. Their idea of a Messiah is found in Numbers, xxiii., xxix. Ours is found in Josiah ii., 12. The result of this inconsistent teaching is shown by the fact that many of their members leave their original faith and become Christians. Where it does not result in that it tends to lead to hypocrisy. No college they can found in this country will stop the flow of liberal ideas. We favor holding religious service on Sunday, not because we disregard our own Sabbath, but because we recognize the circumstances and surroundings of the times and place. Many Jews are compelled to work upon Saturday. For the benefit of such we propose to have religious services on the day when, in accordance with the customs of those whose power is greatest, no work is performed, and nearly all are at liberty to attend religious services."

The Rev. Dr. Jastrow, a conservative rabbi, said this evening that he did not believe there would be a new college. The agitation would, he thought, result in the displacement of the present Faculty, or Liberal influences, in Union College and that it would be committed to Professors and managers who would not meddle with the questions upon which the liberals and conservatives differ.

December 28, 1885

RIDICULED BY UNBELIEVERS.

Anarchist Hebrews Made Sport of Yom Kippur with Dancing.

The Hebrew Anarchists who for several years have celebrated the great Jewish fast of Yom Kippur—Day of Atonement—by balls and other entertainments instead of fasting, repentance, and prayer for forgiveness, repeated the celebration yesterday.

Last year a strong protest was made by orthodox and liberal Jews in this city against this profanation of their great fast by the unbelievers, and the owner of Clarendon Hall, where the Anarchists' ball was to have been held, refused to allow them to use it. So the ball was not held. This year, however, they succeeded in getting the hall by a sharp trick. They adopted the name of the Gruppe Proletariat, and hired the lecture room and ballroom for twenty-four hours, from 6 o'clock Tuesday evening to 6 o'clock last evening.

The police heard that they had taken the hall only after they were in possession, and so were restricted to simply watching the proceedings, which really were tame. Speeches were made in which religion in general, and the Hebrew religion in particular, was denounced. The proceedings began on Tuesday evening by a variety entertainment and speeches in the lecture room. Among those who made addresses were John Most, A. Frank, Julius Bogdansky, who recently posed as one of the unemployed leaders, and M. Katz, the editor of the Anarchist paper, Die Arbeiter Stimme.

The merrymakers of Yom Kippur made no secret that the celebration had been arranged to ridicule the Hebrew religion. One young man worked himself to a high degree of excitement and exclaimed: "There is no God for us to be afraid of, nor is there any true religion. Those fools who are spending the day in praying and fasting imagine that they will save themselves and have luck. We, however, know better. Down with religion and long live Anarchy."

John Most followed with another attack upon religion, and called the Bible a tissue of lies. Julius Bogdansky delivered a speech denouncing the Hebrew religion as a humbug.

Every one who wanted to witness the celebration had to pay an admission fee of 15 cents, and reporters of the "capitalistic press" were made to pay an additional 15 cents to go into the ballroom, because they represented the enemies of Anarchy. The reporter of the Socialists' organ was not admitted at all, "because," argued the Anarchists, "the Socialists are false friends, and that is worse than an open enemy."

It was rumored that Emma Goldman would speak. In fact it was said that she did go to the building, but she was advised to go away lest her presence might cause some disturbance, and then arrests would follow.

The "Marseillaise" was frequently played. An announcement was made that a concert would be given to raise funds to defray the expenses of Emma Goldman's trial.

September 21, 1893

DAILY LIFE AMONG POOR HEBREWS
Forced to Work in Overcrowded Rooms— Queer Customs and Ceremonies Religiously Observed.

The semi-Oriental city situated on the east side of New-York is an immense bee-hive, in which tens of thousands, and, it might be said, scores of thousands, of men, women and children toil almost incessantly, often crowded together in poorly ventilated rooms, working for wages just enough to pay for rent and to buy food and inferior clothing.

The sweating shops and the heartlessness of the taskmasters, known by the name of contractors, have been repeatedly described. Although these sweating shops have been considerably reformed since public attention was called to them, still there is a great deal of room for further improvement.

Many of these sweat shops are used also as dwelling rooms. When working hours begin, after a hurried breakfast, the bedding is put out on the fire escapes, so as to leave more room for the workers. On fine days the bedding is benefited by ventilation in the open air, but when it rains, and the bedding cannot be put out, it interferes with work, and adds to the discomfort—or rather misery—of the inmates.

The luncheon of these workers has not much variety. A salt herring, or a piece of skim cheese, such as is sold in Essex Street and vicinity, and a salted cucumber, with a cup of coffee when they can get it, about completes the bill of fare. If the worker can get a khaley, a white oval loaf which has been varnished by smearing raw egg over it before baking, the worker is very lucky. A khaley, when well made, is very good, and in Poland and Russia the Jews are said to excel in this kind of baking. Before making up the loaves for this kind of bread, the housewife must pinch off a piece of the dough and throw it into the fire as an offering.

The heartiest meal of the day is taken in the evening, when soups and cooked meats are eaten. The chickens and the beef and mutton having passed inspection by the shokhets, or butchers, and having been found good, are pronounced kosher, (clean,) and the people have the satisfaction of being sure that they commit no sin in eating.

It has been supposed by some that the word shokhet—butcher or slaughterer—is of Egyptian origin, from Shekhet, the goddess of slaughter and cruelty, and that she was the patroness of butchers. No orthodox Jew may eat even a chicken that has not been either slaughtered or inspected and pronounced kosher by him.

In slaughtering a chicken, the shokhet seizes it by the wings with the left hand, and hooks one of its feet to his little finger. The head of the chicken is then turned backward toward the wings, and the skin of the upper part of the neck is drawn back by the thumb and finger of the left hand, so that the skin over the throat is taut. A feather or two is pulled out, to enable the knife to run smooth, the throat is pressed down, and a slash or two of the sharp knife severs the upper part of the windpipe and jugular. Before killing the hen the shokhet feels it over, so as to make sure that there is no fractured bone, but if, after the slaughter, the fowl is found to have some other defect it is pronounced tarefa, (unclean,) and the owner may not eat it, but can sell it to some Gentile.

The inspection of slaughtered animals is a source of very large revenue to the shokhets and rabbis, who come from Poland and Russia and Hungary, and they have been repeatedly charged with extortion and tyranny, as were the priests of the Temple sacrifice in the days of old. Where the shokhets and rabbis are combined there is practically no appeal from them. The rebels must either abstain from meat or incur the risk of being excommunicated. And a shokhet who might break away from the fraternity that is in power runs the risk of a boycott by having all the animals that he kills declared tarefa.

Friday morning is the great marketing day, for provisions have to be bought and cooked by sunset, and all must be ready by sunset, when, according to the law of Moses, all fires have to be put out in Jewish dwellings.

The intersection of Hester and Essex Streets is a very busy provision market on such days. The stores are filled with all kinds of provisions, and hucksters, with their pushcarts, line the sidewalks, calling out their wares and trying to get the best of their customers, who crowd both the sidewalks and roadway. Fish, fruit, poultry, pickles, bread, and cakes are piled up everywhere, and men, women, and children are busy driving the closest bargains they can.

"How much do you want for this chicken?" asks a thrifty housewife of a huckster, as she picks up a fair-looking fowl from the pile in the cart.

"For you I'll sell it for 30 cents. It is an excellent hen, and is a gift at that price," says the huckster.

"No, Reb Itshok, it is too dear for me," remarks the woman.

"Well, I have something cheaper. Here is one for 18 cents," and Itshok takes up a lean hen, with a skin of a bluish tinge.

The woman makes a grimace as she shrugs her shoulders and regards the blue hen with contempt, and she adds: "And what do I want with this hen? Afkapoores? For a sacrifice? I don't want it."

After five minutes' haggling the housewife gets the good fowl for 23 cents and goes home rejoicing.

Although good fruit can be found here, yet by far the greater part is of ordinary and inferior qualities. The Board of Health has raided this district several times, and seized many cartfuls of unwholesome fruit that has been dumped into the scows. Peaches and pears at three and four for a penny can be found here in abundance.

In the evening of Friday, when everything is ready and the lamps are lighted, the women observe a peculiar devotional exercise called blessing the light. The open hands are lifted toward the lights, and then are placed over the face, while a prayer is offered. Whether this is a relic of ancient fire worship, and whether the Jews learned the custom from the ancient Persians, has not been determined. Robertson Smith says that in ancient Oriental countries, and especially among Semites, when an immigrant came into a country he had to pay reverence to the deity of that country, although he was not obliged to give up the worship of his own deity.

September 6, 1895

EAST SIDE JEWISH PROBLEM CONSIDERED

Discussion of Elevating Measures in Educational Alliance.

Prominent Speakers Deprecate the Division Among Co-Religionists Growing Out of Diverse National Interests.

Strong appeals for the outstretching of a helping hand to the unfortunate among the Jews of Eastern Europe were made last night by speakers at a public meeting held at the Educational Alliance, East Broadway and Jefferson Street. The meeting was held under the direction of Justice Lodge, No. 532, of the Independent Order of B'nai B'rith, and several hundred men and women were gathered at 8 o'clock, when the meeting was opened by Dr. Isidor Singer, President of the lodge. The big hall was decorated with a score of American flags, the largest of which was draped over the stage.

Dr. Singer, in his introductory remarks, called attention to the fact that the desire of the meeting chiefly was to discuss the topic "The East Side Problem in Its Various Aspects." "Let us not forget," he said, "that the so-called east side problem is by no means a merely local problem, as many of the most ardent Ghetto patriots and admirers seem to think. Not only we of this section, but every New Yorker and every American is interested in the problem that confronts us—the transformation of the poor, down-trodden Russian, Roumanian, or Galician Jew into a free and patriotic well-to-do American citizen."

Dr. Singer then introduced Leo N. Levi as the Chairman. Mr. Levi said he merely wished to say that the people of the east side, he felt, were capable of dealing with their own problem and of settling it, and that great steps were being made daily toward the betterment of the Jewish people there.

Cyrus L. Sulzberger of Schwarzschild & Sulzberger was the next speaker. "The Jewish tragedy of the world is being solved here on the east side," said Mr. Sulzberger, "and we of the east side must do more to let in the persecuted of Europe. To-day we are blocking the way for them. It is not so much what is needed on the east side here, but what is needed on the east side of Europe. Let us stop thinking so much of ourselves and think a bit of our brothers across the seas. Shall we block the gateway to their relief or move along and make way for the men behind?

"There are 300,000 Jews in the east side colony, and there is room for no more in the square mile of territory occupied by our people south of Houston Street and east of the Bowery. The immigrants of our people must go to their own, and our people can see but one remedy. Those who can afford it should go to Harlem, the Bronx, and to Brooklyn, where there is room. And our people also should go to the golden fields of the great Northwest of this country. This will permit the assimilation of the incoming immigrants of our race whom we must help."

Joseph Barondess, the labor leader and head of the cloakmakers' organization, said that when the Jews of Europe leave their homes, their friends, their families, and their all and come to this country for their future it is not from choice, but from sternest necessity.

"We have an east side problem." said he, "but the first thing for us to do to solve it is to cultivate self-respect and then we will have the right sort of outside help. It does not do to meet, pass resolutions to send to our Assemblymen, our Senators, our Congressmen, and then expect them to do the work. The laws are good, but there is a lack of enforcement. We have the anti-sweatshop law and the law against child labor, but if you will come with me in this city in the sweat shop district I will show you children of six years working twelve hours a day for $1.50 a week. The laws are all right, but when our people slumber and lose their respect the lawmakers and the law enforcers forget.

"We have fifty times the population to the block that there is in almost any other section of the town, and we should have spent here fifty times the amount of money that any other section gets to beautify our section, and, Heaven knows, we need the beautification."

Isidor Straus addressed the meeting very briefly, saying he had come to listen, not to speak. He said the Educational Alliance Building had been erected for just such meetings, and he hoped to go away from the meeting with many good suggestions on which to work for the benefit of his people. He said the great work of the Jews of this country is to Americanize their brothers who join them, to teach them the true uses of liberty, and to distinguish it from license.

Dr. Lee K. Frankel, President of the United Hebrew Charities, followed and deprecated the line of demarcation between the Jews of America by which there were German Jews, Russian Jews, Roumanian Jews, and Portuguese Jews, and up-town Jews and east side Jews. "We of American soil must all be American Jews," he declared, while cheers greeted the declaration, "and we must all join in the great work that is before us. The Jewish problem here has been a problem since the first Jewish immigration to this country, in 1655. The old Dutch Governor finally permitted them to land on condition that none should ever become a county charge. And to-day we have only seventeen Jews in the almshouse. That shows what we have done to date; but we are not yet started."

Nathan Bijur, Vice President of the United Hebrew Charities, said the Jews should never be content to let others solve their problems for them, but should be determined to solve them for themselves. "For centuries our people have known no country for their own, and instead of working out Governmental problems have been working out ethical problems and ideals, often at the expense of what is practical. Now let us do something practical."

Dr. David Blaustein, Superintendent of the Alliance, said that the trouble with the Jews in America is a lack of confidence in one another, and the hatred bred of their different birthplaces.

"The German Jew hates the Russian Jew," he declared, "not because he is a Jew, but because he is a Russian, thereby showing what good patriots our people are to the countries of their nativity. And the Russian Jew and the German Jew together hate the Austrian Jew; all three hate the French Jew, and all four hate the Roumanian Jew, while all together they hate the Galician Jew. This prejudice never finds full sway until they get to this country, because they never meet until here. Until this is past and confidence is restored the east side problem will, indeed, be hard to solve."

Dr. Maurice Fishberg and the Rev. H. Masliansky were the last speakers of the evening. Miss Melanie Guttman, soprano; Frederick W. Schalscha, violinist, and Eugene Bernstein, pianist, furnished music.

April 22, 1903

WANT JEWISH SETTLEMENTS.

East Siders Meet to Protest Against Christian Proselyting.

A meeting was held last night, under the auspices of an organization known as the Jewish Centres Association, in the auditorium of the Educational Alliance, to protest against proselyting as carried on in the Jewish districts of this city by Christian missionaries and settlement workers. The object of the association is explained in the following circular distributed in the hall:

"The object of the Jewish Centres Association shall be to provide as many suitable centres as possible, where the Jewish children and youths shall receive, under Jewish influence, the advantages of religious, physical and moral training. We shall attempt to offer in as wide a field and to as large a number of beneficiaries as possible those inducements to improve their condition that are now too often held out to them by Christianizing institutions only as allurements to stray from our ancestral faith."

The efforts and influence of the missionaries and settlement workers were criticised in many speeches. Albert Lucas, Superintendent of the Jewish Centres' Association, presided. He said in part:

"Don't run away with the idea that the Christian missionaries are bad men and women. They are good men and good women, but they are good Christians, and the goal of all they do for our children is to make them believe that the martyrs of our race who have been burned at the stake for two thousand years were in the wrong. We want to take the children away from such influences and place them within reach of the influences of Jewish teaching."

Mr. Lucas said he could not refrain from mentioning the Jacob A. Riis Settlement in Henry Street as one instance of "a hurtful influence." He read a letter he had received from Mr. Riis in response to one he had written him protesting against proselytizing. Mr. Riis said frankly in his letter that the work carried on in the settlement that bears his name was Christian in its tendency.

May 6, 1906

ZIONISM'S HOPE HERE, SAYS JACOB H. SCHIFF

Special to The New York Times.

ATLANTIC CITY, July 28.—Jacob H. Schiff of New York declared at the closing meeting of the Jewish Chautauqua at the Royal Palace Hotel to-day that the hope of the restoration of the Jewish nation in Palestine was not the guiding star of Israel's hope, but that the promised land of the Jew was in America.

There was instant applause, long and hearty, when the sentiment was uttered, which broke out afresh when Mr. Schiff reiterated the sentiment and said that in the free land of the United States was to be found the inspiration of the Jew for a higher citizenship.

Mr. Schiff told of the hopes, the aspirations, and the longings of the Jew. He sounded a note of warning to the Jewish people and declared that there should be a lessening of the evils of overcrowded tenement life in the great cities of New York, Philadelphia, and Baltimore, and a dispersion of Jews through the South and West.

Mr. Schiff's address was as follows:

"As I stand before you, ladies and gentlemen of the Jewish Chautauqua, there rises before my eyes a vision of coming days—the dream of an American Israel of the future, of a generation not yet born, the children's children of the men and women who, in this generation, have come from all parts of the globe to these blessed shores—of the thousands who come to free themselves from persecution, oppression, abridged civil rights, and limited liberty.

"The vision which presents itself to me shows me a people of our faith, who have thrown off the shackles, the peculiarities and the prejudices which have handicapped their fathers—a great host, Jews in faith, but one in sentiment with their surroundings, warmly attached to their country, of which they have become part and parcel—a people among the best of the land, proud of their American citizenship, thoroughly imbued with its spirit, with its obligations, with its high privileges, but just as proud of their religion—almost a new type—these descendants of Jewish Pilgrim Fathers, true Americans of the Jewish faith.

"A vision it may be to-day; a reality it is bound to become on the morrow. That the reality be not behind the vision we, whose lot it is to be the pilgrims, the fathers of coming generations of Jewish Americans, must, in our own generation, seek to do our duty in its entirety. We owe it to ourselves and to those who come after us, that we imbue our offspring with the love for our faith our fathers have implanted in us; that we demonstrate to them the beauty of our religion, the moral strength it imparts under all conditions; that we impress them with the meaning of our faith, not alone to its adherents, but with the value of its teachings to all mankind; that we teach it to our children in the word of the Law-giver: 'When we sit in our houses, when we go on our way, when we rise in the morning, and when we lay down at night.'

"Because of the duty of the Jew, thus conceived, we should give our entire support to the Chautauqua, for no other agency is so well adapted to aid in bringing about the Jewish revival which is needed, can so well assure the maintenance of our faith, of its traditions and its spirit, throughout the land, and more especially in the small communities now springing up everywhere, in which opportunities for Jewish life and learning are often wanting.

"To awake Jewish consciousness we do not need, in these United States, to have held out to us a hope of the re-establishment of a Jewish nation in Palestine, in the dim, far-away future. Not in distant lands, but here among us we need centres from which to draw love for and attachment to our religion, for the inspiration it gives to make the Jew a better man, a better citizen, wherever his home may be. Even if the origin in a common ancestry fastens upon us a responsibility which we willingly assume, it is Israel's faith, it is the feeling that something of high value is in our common keeping, which creates our unity and promotes, more than anything else, the

mutual attachment of the Jew for the Jew, wherever his home may be, and of whom he always speaks as his coreligionist.

"I can understand the causes which have brought forth Zionism, and even if not in sympathy with the movement, I have less sympathy with the attacks made upon those who, from a belief that it will bring about a quickening of Jewish consciousness, have joined its ranks, but, at best, in its last analysis, Zionism, it must be conceded, even by its honest supporters, can only be an ideal of much uncertainty of attainment in what is claimed to be its ultimate purpose. But if we cannot consistently be Zionists, we should the more recognize and live up to the duty that we do all in our power to promote the maintenance of our faith through active propaganda, never forgetting what our fathers and forefathers suffered to assure the transmission of their, of our religion, to coming generations, in all its worth and purity.

"Not Zionism, a movement impracticable of realization, should be needed to arouse our conscience as Jews; better that we recognize our duty to the Jewish educational institutions, of which, I aver, the Jewish Chautauqua can and should be made one of the most efficient agencies.

"Rapidly the Jewish population of this country is increasing. For the present, massed in the seaport towns of the Atlantic Coast, before long the new-comers are certain to seek better homes and wider quarters in the great and attractive territory which stretches from the Gulf to our Northern boundary, from the Mississippi to the Pacific.

"To-day not quite two millions; at not a distant day, double that number are certain to comprise an American population of the Jewish faith. To-day, looked upon as a foreign element, in times to come, an integral part of a race of Americans yet in the making. To-day students, to-morrow teachers; to-day pilgrims, to-morrow patriots. This is the vision, friends, which passes before my eyes. My prayer, my hope—ay, my conviction, is that in due time it become a reality."

While the applause was still heard William B. Hackenburg of Philadelphia took the floor, and, after moving a vote of thanks to Mr. Schiff, followed it with a resolution providing that 50,000 copies of the address be printed for general circulation. This was adopted amid enthusiastic approval, and at the close of the meeting funds were subscribed to

carry out this part of the Chautauqua propaganda.

Secretary Charles Edwin Fox of Philadelphia in his annual report advised that Chautauqua, the home of the parent society, be selected for the annual assembly. The suggestion was referred to the Executive Board.

Mr. Fox said that the number of circles has increased from 45 to 84, with a membership of 2,200, representing communities scattered from Texas to Seattle, and from Maine to Canada and points in the United States along the great lakes. He declared that the Jewish Chautauqua was no longer an experiment, but a success, and appealed for wider interest and participation in the movement.

Treasurer Newburger's report showed that the expenses of the Chautauqua work last year were $7,346. There is a balance of $1,400.

Officers were elected as follows:

Chancellor—The Rev. Dr. Henry Berkowitz of Philadelphia; President—George W. Ochs, Philadelphia; Vice President—Israel Cowen, Chicago; Treasurer—Frank Newburger, Philadelphia; Secretary and Director—Charles E. Fox, Philadelphia; Field Secretary—Miss Jeanette M. Goldberg, Galveston, Texas.

Honorary Vice Presidents—Adolph S. Ochs, Milton Goldsmith, New York; Albert Hessberg, Albany, N. Y.; Mrs. Jacob H. Hecht, Boston; Max Senior, Cincinnati; Mrs. S. L. Frank, Baltimore; Mrs. August S. Frank, St. Louis; The Rev. Dr. I. L. Deucht, New Orleans; Mrs. S. Lesser, Augusta, Ga.; N. Washer, San Antonio, Texas; William J. Berkowitz, Kansas City, Mo.; Mrs. George Galland, Wilkesbarre; Abraham Thalmier, Hartford, Conn.; The Rev. Dr. William S. Friedman, Denver, Col.; Rabbi Samuel Koch, Seattle, Washington; Edward Richard, Mobile.

Board of Trustees, Honorary Members—William B. Hackenberg, Jacob Gimbel, Emil Selig, Abram Simon, Miss Corinne B. Arnold, Isaac Hassler, Louis Gertsley, Mrs. Charles Heifelberger, Mrs. Fannie Muhr, Mrs. H. Berkowitz, Perry Frankel, Mrs. Joseph H. Rubin, Alfred M. Klein, Samuel S. Fleisher, Samuel Grabfelder, Philadelphia; Jacob H. Schiff, Solomon Sulsberger, Mrs. Rose Frank, New York; The Rev. Dr. Tobias Schanfarber, Chicago; Simon Wolfe, Washington, D. C.; Dr. William Rosenau, Baltimore; Mrs. Adolph Rose, Vicksburg, Miss.; Louis B. Marshall, Alfred Newburger, New York; Rabbi Henry Fisher, Atlantic City.

Educational Council—Max Hersberg, D. W. Amran, Charles Bernheimer, the Rev. Dr. Julius Greenstone, Dr. Louis W. Steinbach, Miss Ella Jacobs, the Rev. Dr. Joseph H. Krauskopf, Philadelphia; Dr. Maurice H. Harris, Prof. Richard Gottheil, Dr. Lee K. Frankel, Prof. Morris Loeb, Dr. Solomon Schechter, Miss Julia Richman, New York; Rabbi Gerson B. Levi, the Rev. Dr. Emil G. Hirsch, the Rev. Dr. Joseph Stolz, Dr. A. B. Yudelson, Chicago; Rabbi Harry Levi, Wheeling, West Va.; Dr. Kauffman Kohler, Cincinnati; the Rev. William S. Friedman, Denver, Col.; Rabbi Henry Fisher, Atlantic City; Rabbi Nathan Stern, Trenton; Rabbi Barnet A. Elias, Charleston, S. C.

July 29, 1907

ZIONISTS DEFEND THEIR AMERICANISM

Over a thousand members of the Zionist Council of Greater New York met in Cooper Union last night and passed resolutions denouncing those who have opposed the Zionist movement, which has as its object the establishment of a permanent Jewish colony in Palestine and the ultimate regaining of the entire Holy Land by the Jewish people.

It was admitted by several of the officers of the Council that the meeting was in the nature of a reply to the recent public statement of Jacob H. Schiff that Zionism was incompatible with American citizenship. Mr. Schiff's name was not mentioned by the speakers, but it was clear from the tone of their remarks and the resolutions passed that he was referred to.

Dr. Harry Friedenwald of Baltimore, President of the Federation of American Zionists and Chairman of the meeting, in his opening remarks said:

"The Zionists are charged with not being true Americans, their American allegiance is called into question, their patriotism doubted, and their loyalty impugned.

"It pains us that these charges have been made, but the pain is doubled because they have been made by those whom position and power should have made to consider the significance of the charges they were making before they heaped ignominy upon their brethren, even though they had different views, and should have made them hesitate until they had determined their truth or falsity. Men of less knowledge, less sagacity, and less wisdom, could have shown them how groundless the charges, how false in every way, how ruinous to all, and how they might become a boomerang, injuring all. We cannot call back their words; we cannot blot out the evil they have done. Let them and others beware of repeating them. Upon their shoulders will lie the guilt of creating an anti-Semitism, which has embittered the lives of our German and French brethren, but which has not darkened our country.

"Let them learn that true Americanism is in conflict with no activity which is honest, honorable and unselfish, nor

with any sentiment that is moral, righteous and noble. Let them learn that true Americanism is consistent only with high ideals and our striving toward them. Let us Jews thank God that this is true Americanism."

The resolutions, which were passed unanimously by a standing vote, read:

We Zionists of America feel compelled to give public expression to our deep sorrow at groundless accusations that have been hurled against us by men of our faith whose qualifications and whose authority to pass judgment against us we utterly deny. We Jews native born and naturalized citizens of this country, are charged by other Jews with disloyalty to our country by reason of our efforts to create a legally assured home for the Jewish people in Palestine. We denounce these accusations as fundamentally un-American in theory and false in practice.

We have shown by our actions in the past how sacredly we regard the rights and duties of American citizenship. We are therefore outraged to hear Jew repeat against Jew the pernicious calumnies resorted to by all Jew-baiters for almost 2,000 years.

We feel that our brethren who have made these charges against us have not carefully considered their words.

Be it, therefore, resolved at this meeting of Zionists, held at Cooper Union, New York, Sept. 14, 1907, to admonish our brethren to desist from a course which can but increase the heavy burden now borne by the Jews of the world and which, if persisted in, will lead to the introduction of anti-Semitism into this free country.

Various speakers told of the progress of the Zionist cause.

September 15, 1907

JEWISH COMMUNITY OF NEW YORK FORMED

Convention, After a Lively Debate, Declares All Delegates Must Be Citizens.

ALL PARTISANSHIP BARRED

Chairman Magnes Breaks His Gavel During the Warm Discussion Over National Committee's Power.

After a warm argument lasting more than four hours, in the course of which the Rev. Dr. J. L. Magnes of Temple Emanu-El, the presiding Chairman, broke his ivory gavel, the Jewish convention, in adjourned meeting at the Hebrew Charities Building yesterday afternoon, finally adopted a constitution.

The meeting had been adjourned from the night previous when at a late hour the first two articles of a constitution for the proposed Jewish Community of the City of New York were adopted. The first was passed on the motion of Lewis Marshall, as follows:

I. That it be the sense of this body that a Jewish community of the City of New York be formed.

Immediately upon its adoption Jacob H. Schiff moved the adoption of Article II., which was unanimously carried. This article read:

II. The purpose of the Jewish community of New York City shall be to further the cause of Judaism in New York City, and to represent the Jews of this city with respect to all local matters of Jewish interest. This organization shall not engage in any propaganda of a partisan political nature or interfere with the autonomy of a constituent organization.

Dr. Magnes called the adjourned meeting to order at 2:30 yesterday afternoon and after a resolution was passed on the recent death of Rabbi Adolph Radin, the Tombs Chaplain, the Credential Committee reported that 218 Jewish organizations were represented at the convention, among them being 74 synagogues.

The third article of the proposed constitution was then read in English and Yiddish. It dealt with the qualifications for membership in the Community and provoked a long discussion, in which Rabbi Joseph Silverman took an active part. The paragraphs that provoked the greatest argument were those stating that "No person shall be eligible as a delegate unless he be an American citizen." And that "No political organization shall be eligible for membership." Dr. Silverman had this to say on these points:

"I don't think any delegate should speak for uptown or downtown, because he really speaks for himself. We are neither up nor down town Jews, but Jews of New York, so let us drop the other manner of speech. We all want to be Jews and Americans. Above all things, we want to be known not only as Jews, but as Americans, who are loyal to their country. We want those who are not citizens to take out papers at once, and until this is done they are not fit to be delegates or to represent us as a body. If this community is to send representatives to the Jewish National Committee they must be Americans to do American National Jewish business. As to political organizations not being eligible, we are professedly not a political body, and do not wish to recognize any Jewish political body. This is a Community devoted to Jewish interests alone."

No Aliens Wanted, Sulzberger Says.

Cyrus L. Sulzberger, President of the United Hebrew Charities, said: "We have no business to organize ourselves for political purposes under a religious banner. There are no Protestant or Catholic political bodies and there should be no Jewish political body. Every man should be an American citizen. We want no aliens in our community. This body is not for men who care so little for their country that they are not citizens. It is their duty to become such, and let it not be said that we are a community of aliens but of Americans who know their needs and what they want."

Judge Leon Sanders moved the adoption of the article point by point, and this was done amid much discussion, in which Miss Sadie American, Dr. Silverman, H. P. Mendes, Louis Marshall, and Joseph Barondess joined. When the paragraph as to American citizenship being necessary for membership came up there was much excitement, and one man, who was not a delegate, was asked by the Chairman to leave the hall. Rabbi Rabinowitz shouted that the delegates did not know for what they were voting, but the article on membership was finally passed by a close vote.

Article IV., on meetings and officers, was then taken up and passed, and then there was a hot debate on Article V., which stated the relationship of the community to the National Jewish Committee.

Rabbi Rabinowitz declared that the community should be local and independent of the National Committee, and Albert Lucas denounced the National Committee for what he called "an illegal combination with Police Commissioner Bingham concerning the Jews' observance of the Sunday business laws." He said that the Jews could regulate their Sunday business affairs without the interference of the committee.

Judge Sanders protested that there had been no "illegal combination," and that the matter of the Jews who observed the Sabbath doing business on Sunday was in accord with the statutes of the State. Louis Marshall then said:

Disclaimer from Louis Marshall.

"As one of the criminals of the American Jewish Committee, some explanation is due you from me. This committee is not for trampling on the community of New York, and to show this the New York members have tendered their resignations to that body. When this community is organized, its quota of twenty-five members will practically control the American National Jewish Committee. Are you willing to take this power which the former New York members of the committee are offering you? New York Jews are suffering from too much individuality and independence, and it is high time that they surrendered some of this for the good of the whole.

"The Jewish National Committee had nothing to do with the Bingham arrangement. The Commissioner called certain Jews in conference and the law was legally interpreted that Jews should not have to work seven days in the week. Jacob Schiff called the committee into being because of a necessary head at the time of the Russian relief work to protect the interest of the Jews in any part of the world. Was it wrong that the committee helped Jews in distress in all parts of the world? Was it wrong to make a passport of worth and American citizenship respected in any country? Here is the organization if you please. We don't want to take you. You come and take us!"

After much applause and cheering, Rabbi Drachman said that it would be unwise to take this step at the present time. The committee was doing a different work than the community should do, as it merely belonged to the social, religious, and charitable work of the Jews. What was needed was a local city Jewish community to handle internal problems. Dr. Magnes here explained that all members of the National Jewish Committee would be elected by representative Jewish bodies in Chicago, Baltimore, and elsewhere if the New York community took the lead. He declared it a matter of jurisdiction for the committee to decide what was local and what National.

Chairman Breaks His Gavel.

At this point many of the delegates began shouting at once, a dozen men rising to a point of order, and Dr. Magnes broke his gavel in an effort to restore order. Article V., in which a Committee of Twenty-five of the community is provided for and made a part of the National Committee and which reserves the power over local Jewish matters to the Executive Committee of the Community, was finally adopted. The other articles as to dues, quorum, and amendments were quickly passed, and then on the motion of Samuel Dorf the whole constitution was adopted as amended.

Edgar J. Nathan, Chairman of the Nominating Committee, then announced the list of officers and Executive Committee nominated. The reading aroused a storm of protest, as it was asserted that partisanship was shown. A motion to postpone the election of officers was carried.

The convention voted to meet again Saturday evening for the election of officers.

March 1, 1909

APPEALS TO YOUNG JEWS.

Movement to Bring Them Back to Religion Started on East Side.

For the purpose of bringing together the congregations of the many Jewish synagogues on the east side a mass meeting, the first of its kind, was held last night under the auspices of the Sons and Daughters of Israel in Kalverier Synagogue, at 15 Pike Street. The movement is designed to bring together the younger generation of Jews and stimulate them with a stronger religious feeling. If it proves successful there will be built on the east side a large synagogue where congregations from the smaller synagogues may meet one another.

The principal speakers last night were Justice Samuel Greenbaum and Congressman Henry M. Goldfogle. Rabbi Israel Odes, leader of the movement, presided.

Justice Greenbaum announced that he was heartily in favor of the movement. Young people had come to think that, as the clothes and traditions of their parents were old-fashioned, the religion of their parents also must be old-fashioned. "They must be made to understand," he said, "that there is no fashion in religion.

"I fear, too, sometimes," he said, "that the old people do not understand the dangers that beset the young. There are temptations here that must be fought, and the young must fight them. One of the saddest of sights is to see our girls coming out of the factories, and then to see them again on Sunday on the streets with paint and powder on their faces, looking like women we cannot mention."

The home, he said, was one of the greatest safeguards for the young, and he urged that the beautiful customs of the Jewish home be preserved. He asked young people to come forward and work to bring back their companions to the synagogues, and to strive to uphold the Jewish ideals.

Congressman Henry M. Goldfogle urged his hearers to keep alive the religious spirit of the Jewish race.

March 18, 1912

ORTHODOX JEWS RESIST KEHILLAH

Plan to Form a Separate Organization if Deference Is Not Given to Their Wishes.

DR. MAGNES OPPOSES THEM

They Want Secular Affairs Left Entirely to Themselves—To Appeal to Convention.

Representatives of twenty-five congregations of Orthodox Jews met last night at the Synagogue Khal Adas Jeshuron in Eldridge Street, to organize an insurgent movement against the Kehillah, the general Hebrew Federation of Educational and Charitable Organizations.

Representatives of the Orthodox congregations voted that they would never submit control of educational matters to the general federation, neither the control of the method in which cattle are to be butchered and beef sold as kosher meat.

The meeting was in preparation for the general convention of the Kehillah which will be held on Saturday and Sunday in the Hebrew Technical School building, at Second Avenue and Fifteenth Street. There were represented last night by only 25 votes out of the 200 which will be cast in the convention, and Rabbi Judah L. Magnes, Chairman of the Executive Committee of the Kehillah, has announced that its administrative forces will oppose the demands of the Orthodox group.

After counting their strength the leaders of the insurgent movement decided to recommend that an appeal be made directly to the delegates at large, regardless of Rabbi Magnes and his Executive Committeemen, and that if this appeal fails, to withdraw from the Kehillah and found a new organization composed exclusively of Orthodox congregations.

In the Kehillah, which was organized as a general Jewish federation a year ago, the 200 delegates represent 200 different Jewish social, religious, and charitable organizations.

Dissatisfaction on the part of the orthodox congregations, each one of which was represented by a single delegate, was first raised against the general federation when a bill was introduced at Albany for its incorporation. The proposed charter gave the Executive Committee power to regulate the slaughter of animals for the kosher trade and to issue certificates to butcher shops selling genuine kosher meat. A delegation headed by Isaac Allen visited Albany to oppose the incorporation of the Kehillah and after a public hearing the bill was killed. Rabbi Magnes then raised a fund of $300,000 for a Bureau of Education of the Kehillah and commenced to grant funds to Hebrew schools which voluntarily came under the supervision of the Kehillah Board.

A protest against this practice was made by the orthodox congregations, as it was held that the schools tended to depart from orthodox teachings. At a conference with Rabbi Magnes a committee of orthodox Jews was appointed to draw up a programme for the Kehillah to follow toward orthodox congregations.

The committee's report was that the Kehillah must keep hands off all religious practices and educational policies and must leave matters wholly to do with orthodox Jews to themselves. The rejection of this report by Rabbi Magnes was what occasioned the call for an insurgent movement.

"If we are forced out of the general federation of Jewish organizations," said G. Bublick, editor of The Jewish Daily News, at last night's meeting, "then we will form a federation of our own and will treat with the general federation as a united body."

Among those who signed the call for last night's meeting were the Rev. Dr. P. Klein, Rabbi M. S. Margolies, the Rev. Dr. Bernard Drachman, the Rev. Dr. H. P. Mendes, and M. Jarmulowsky, who acted as Chairman.

April 11, 1913

APPEAL TO JEWS RESENTED.

Recent efforts by political supporters of President Wilson to line up the Jewish vote for his re-election have aroused twenty-six prominent Jews of the city to prepare and issue a protest against such mixing of religion or race and politics. The protest, which was made public yesterday, reads:

We the undersigned earnestly protest against drawing religion into politics.

Wide publicity has recently been given to a direct appeal calling upon the "Jews of America" to form a "Ten Thousand Club" and to contribute $1 each to a fund in aid of the campaign for the re-election of President Wilson. The appeal purports to recite in detail various official acts declared to have been favorable to the Jewish people. The sponsors of this appeal seem to have had some misgivings as to propriety of their course, as they later attempted to explain that the address "was prepared for publication in the Yiddish press and for the guidance of their readers."

Within the past few days a letter has been circulated which indicates a continuance of the effort to disseminate campaign literature containing a like appeal to the Jewish voters.

It is not our purpose to discuss the candidates or the principles and achievements of any political party. We differ in our political affiliations; but we are agreed in condemning any appeal for votes whether to Jews or to the members of any other race or creed, as such. We regard such methods as an insult to the intelligence of the voters who are sought to be influenced by them, and as tending to degrade them politically.

We desire to emphasize the fact that the American Jews regard their citizenship as a sacred possession and resent as a reflection upon their manhood the intimation that they can be influenced in the exercise of the right of suffrage by any considerations which do not apply equally to all of their fellow-citizens.

Leo Arnstein.
Julius Ballin.
George Blumenthal.
Joseph H. Cohen.
W. N. Cohen.
H. L. Einstein.
Henry Goldman.
D. Guggenheim.
L. J. Horowitz.
Lee Kohns.
Arthur Lehman.
David Leventritt.
Adolph Lewisohn.

Louis Marshall.
Eugene Meyer, Jr.
Leopold Plaut.
E. R. A. Seligman.
I. N. Seligman.
Louis Stern.
Oscar S. Straus.
Benjamin Tuska.
Israel Unterberg.
William I. Walter.
Felix M. Warburg.
Charles Wimpfheimer.
Henry F. Wolff.

It was understood from several of the signers of this protest that a substantial number of Wilson advocates were among them, one or two estimates placing the number as high as half of those protesting.

October 16, 1916

WANTS 50,000 JEWS TO GO TO PALESTINE

Special to The New York Times.

ATLANTIC CITY, May 16.—Dr. Chaim Weizmann, leader of the World's Zion Organization, in addressing the convention of the Independent Order of B'rith Abraham, on the Steel Pier, this afternoon, made a plea that 50,000 Jews go to Palestine from America within the next year.

Samuel Hartmann of New York, Grand Master of the order, evoked great applause at the conclusion of Dr. Weizmann's address by saying:

"It will be the Independent Order of B'rith Abraham that will blaze the path for all the Jews of the United States."

In his address, Dr. Weizmann said:

"Every 50,000 Jews placed on the soil of Palestine paves the way for another 100,000, and they in turn for another like number, and so on. We ask ourselves how are we going to find the means? Europe is sick. It is on European Jews who for fifty years have borne the brunt of the work for Palestine, that the burden has rested heaviest. They appeal to you; they don't beg. They say it is your duty to give.

"In that way we all share the common responsibility and the common opportunity. Last year we told the great

nations we were sure Jewry would do honor to them and to the new homeland. But it is impossible to convince the nations that the Jews have not the money. The nations say: 'You Jews have financed nations all over the world; you have financed many undertakings; you have made good in many fields; you cannot tell us that, when the time comes to finance your own homeland, you have not the financial means.'

"This is why we come to America: to tell you in unmistakable terms the actual situation. These are hard, solid facts. They have to be swallowed and digested. Something is happening in Jewry. A new page is turned, a new chapter is being written by the sweat and blood of our people. Will the Jews of America respond? I am sure they will. It is not the very rich nor the very poor that will build Palestine; not the very rich, because they don't want to; not the very poor, because they can't. It is the middle class and the working man that we feel will answer our appeal most readily."

Dr. Weizmann reviewed the work in Palestine industrially, commercially, from the standpoint of sanitation and with a view to making the life of the working man wholesome and comfortable. Great difficulty has been experienced, he said, because the funds at hand are not what they should be.

May 17, 1921

To a Zionist Appeal.

To the Editor of The New York Times:

I note in your issue of the 17th inst. that Dr. Weizmann desires 50,000 Jews residing in America to return to Palestine during the next year. Dr. Weizmann must have a very keen sense of humor. In the first place, the great majority of us are not "Jews residing in America," but American Jews, and in the second place, the great majority of us are proud of our American citizenship, and it is the City of Washington that inspires our loyalty, not Jerusalem. Why can't these wandering Zionists learn once for all that Americans of the Jewish faith are 100 per cent. American; that they love America with all their heart and refuse to return to the desert? I earnestly trust you will find space for this protest.

ROBERT K. GUGGENHEIMER.
Johns Hopkins University, Baltimore, May 17, 1921.

May 20, 1921

PREDICTS "AMERICAN" JEW.

Will Result From Contest Between Reform and Orthodox, Says Rabbi.

Pleas for unity among all elements of Judaism were made last night at the open exercises of the Hebrew Union College School for Teachers at Temple Emanu-El, Fifth Avenue and Forty-third Street, by the Rev. Dr. Samuel Schulman of Temple Beth-El, and Chairman of the Joint Governing Committee of the Hebrew Union College School for Teachers, and by the Rev. Dr. Julian Morgenstern, President of the Hebrew Union College, Cincinnati, Ohio.

The School for Teachers in New York City is to be administered by the Hebrew Union College in co-operation with the Association of Reform Rabbis of New York City, of which Dr. Schulman is President. Last night's exercises were opened with a prayer by the Rev. Dr. Kaufman Kohler, President Emeritus of the Hebrew Union College, of which he was for eighteen years President.

Dr. Morgenstern described reform Judaism which he said was brought to America from Germany and orthodox Judaism which came with the East European Jewry. He said that the struggle between those two phases of Judaism was not so much over theological and ritual differences as social distinctions. He predicted that the struggle for leadership between the reform and orthodox would eventually bring forth "the American Jew."

"Forth from the strife and tumult," said Dr. Morgenstern, "born as it were upon the very field of battle, will step the victor, young and vigorous, strong, looking not backward to either German or Russian ancestry, nor cherishing suspicion or grievance against his fellow Jew or differing ancestry, but looking forward proudly to the future and dedicating himself to the sacred task of building up for himself and his children a precious heritage of truth and light, 'the American Jew.'"

Rabbi Schulman said that Jewish education was the education in the heritage of the Jews. He asserted that knowledge of Jewish literature, religion and traditions would bring about unity. By unity he said that he did not necessarily mean uniformity. "Jewish education is also intended to make us feel what kind of God we are worshiping," said Rabbi Schulman.

November 5, 1923

DR. ELIOT URGES JEWS TO UPHOLD TRADITIONS

Should Keep Race Individuality and Not Be Assimilated, He Tells Harvard Zionists.

Special to The New York Times.
CAMBRIDGE, Mass., Dec. 12.—Intermarriage with Christians and abandonment of the traditions of their race are two evils seriously threatening the Jewish race today, Dr. Charles W. Eliot, President Emeritus of Harvard, told the Harvard Zionist Society here today.

Dr. Eliot said that the Jews had not in the past been assimilated by other races and that they should not be, but should keep their race individuality in America just as the Irish have done.

"I have noticed with regret, said Dr. Eliot, "the increasing tendency of Jews to marry Christians, I have had a long observation of such intermarriages between peoples who are not kindred, and I have never known them to turn out well. I hope that you Jews will consider that.

"What we want in this country is a number of races, with various gifts, each contributing its own peculiar quantities to the common welfare."

In substantiating his theories, President Eliot spoke of the emigration of the Irish to America, declaring that the Irish "have never been assimilated in America, anywhere, and that it is not desirable that they should be. So it should be with the Jews."

"Americans," President Eliot continued, "do not expect to assimilate any foreign people, even the Jews. It seems that non-assimilation is better for the future of the nation."

During several visits to New York, President Eliot said, he noticed the tendency among young Jewish people to disregard the customs of their parents. He mentioned a luncheon at Columbia where three Jewish couples ordered dishes which seemed selected for the sole purpose of showing their independence of their religion and added that their conversation partook of the same spirit.

"This tendency is unfortunate, not only for Jewish people but for all other people," he declared. "It sets a bad example for all of us."

President Eliot deplored the internal division of the Jewish race. He favored a portion of Palestine for the Jews. The physical well-being of the race there might be improved by the adoption of muscular occupations, he said.

December 13, 1924

THE JEWS IN AMERICA

Dr. Eliot's Opinion That They Should Retain Their Racial Individuality and Not Intermarry Is Attacked and Defended.

To the Editor of The New York Times:

I have read with great interest the report in THE NEW YORK TIMES of the remarks of Dr. Charles W. Eliot, President Emeritus of Harvard University, before the Harvard Zionist Society in Cambridge, Mass., a short time ago.

I have great regard for Dr. Eliot's opinion. He has on many occasions expressed himself very favorably toward the Jewish people, and only lately in a foreword in a book he wrote in a book entitled "Patriotism of the American Jew," written by the late Governor Samuel W. McCall of Massachusetts, his attitude has been most favorable toward the American Jews. But I think he is mistaken when he says that the Jews "should keep their race individuality in America just as the Irish have done," and that he has never known intermarriages between Jews and Christians to turn out well.

He goes on to say, "What we want in this country is a number of races with various gifts, each contributing its own peculiar qualities to the common welfare," and also that "the Irish have never been assimilated in America anywhere and it is not desirable that they should be." If it is not desirable that the Irish should be assimilated, the same is true of all the other nationalities. None of the others, then, should be assimilated—the English should always marry with the English, the Scotch with the Scotch, the French with the French, the Germans with the Germans, the Italians with the Italians, &c. Then we would have in America fifty or a hundred sets of nationalities, and no Americans. It is really an impossible idea and just the opposite has taken place and should have taken place.

Dr. Eliot is entirely mistaken when he complains about the tendency among young Jewish people to disregard the customs of their parents. He either forgets or does not know that the modern Jew does not believe in keeping the old dietary laws contained in the Old Testament any more than the Christians do. The dietary laws having been made more than 3,000 years ago were probably founded upon reasons of health, which was quite suitable at that time for the Eastern countries. Modern Judaism is a reform of the Old Testament, the same as is Christianity, leaving out such parts of the Old Testament as are not suitable for the present age. There are very few of the Jews whom we are apt to meet who know anything about these obsolete laws.

In my opinion there is no Jewish race.

The Persians, Arabs and even the Armenian Christians are much more Semitic than the Jews whom we generally meet here. While their coming from Semitic ancestors and having generally intermarried among themselves has left its influence upon them, their racial condition is greatly influenced by the country and climate in which they have lived for many centuries. For instance, I have a family tree showing that my ancestors in 1609 came to Hamburg from Holland, where they no doubt lived for centuries before that time. The Disraeli family came from Portugal early in the sixteenth century. The Jews commenced to arrive in the United States about 300 years ago. I know of many happy marriages between Jews and Christians, and there is no good reason why that should not be so.

ADOLPH LEWISOHN.
New York, Dec. 30, 1924.

Synod of Leipsic Is Recalled.

To the Editor of The New York Times:

I have read your comment on Dr. Eliot's remarks with regard to race coherence and the preservation of the elements in the constitution of a race. With the advance of modern science it is not at all surprising that a scholar of Dr. Eliot's personality should revive after so many years of serious and scientific thinking an adage that is as old as the Old Testament. The Volstead act of the Hebrews was prohibition of intermarriage followed by a number of amendments, and the first Jewish Synod, held at Leipsic in 1869, declared against intermarriage as being injurious to the peace of the home and to the preservation of the Jewish faith, the faith of the minority. The venerable Dr. Eliot is sounding the alarm of the fathers on the theory of the preservation of the original elements in the purity of the races.

The man whose philosophic vision is limited or who has none with regard to religion is apt to assimilate in the choice of a country, if he's so inclined, in selecting or adopting a faith outside of his own. Intermarriage evidently tends toward assimilation and disintegration of the original elements, which, when mixed, produce an alloy and is no longer the metal in its original state. Some day a learned professor may yet come along and revive another adage—"that there's nothing new under the sun"—

which science is demonstrating daily. Soon, perhaps, humanity may find itself, and when it does it'll find so many existing conclusions superficial. "The world is my country, to do good my religion," was spoken by a master mind. The world hasn't reached the stage yet to understand the meaning of the phrase.

When the mentality of the race at large is fertilized and the crop resulting therefrom is a normal crop, a crop that is neither overgrown or undergrown, our teachers of today may perhaps then qualify as pupils, and then there will be no discussion as to religious heredity.

Under present conditions, however, one must coincide with the views of Dr.

Eliot. There are very few peaceful intermarriages. One of the greatest internationally known authors, who himself happens to be intermarried, remarked a few years ago in answer to the question on intermarriage that were he to do it over again he positively would not enter into a marriage of that kind.

Light is becoming clear to some minds. All they need is just a little study. The theory of evolution has already incited the curiosity of one of its most powerful opponents. Time is a great cure, and he may yet be an evolutionist.

DR. A. C. WOLMARK.
New York, Dec. 30, 1924.

January 4, 1925

ZIONISTS AT PEACE WITH NON-ZIONISTS

Dr. Weizmann's 'Olive Branch' Accepted by Louis Marshall, Ending Friction Over Drive.

BOTH PLEAD FOR UNITY

Head of Palestine Movement Says Holy Land Cause and United Campaign Suffered by Rift.

Peace between the Zionists and non-Zionists in the United States has finally been pledged after many months of warfare, kindled by the conduct of the $25,000,000 United Jewish Campaign. The olive branch, it was disclosed in correspondence made public yesterday, was proffered by Dr. Chaim Weizmann, President of the World Zionist Organization and accepted "with profound satisfaction" by Louis Marshall, spokesman for the United Jewish Campaign. Zionists had repeatedly attacked leaders of the campaign for their alleged stress of the Russian colonization plan and their minimization of Palestinian endorsement in their campaign.

In this letter to Mr. Marshall, the Zionist leader mildly rebuked his fellow-Nationalists for their continued criticism of the United Jewish Campaign, although Dr. Weizmann said that he, too, had voiced "some misgivings as to the work planned to be done in Russia," when he had first heard of the contemplated drive.

Feared Rival Movements.

"Those in charge of Zionist activities unfortunately assumed, first, that the colonization work in Russia was a competitive movement as against Palestine," Dr. Weizmann wrote. "They also felt that a great relief campaign in America might neutralize Zionist efforts and result in their failure to obtain the necessary funds for Palestine. Realizing as they did that Palestine needed more resources at that time than ever before, they were apprehensive of any movement which might interfere with the work of upbuilding Palestine.

"On the other hand, those in charge of the activities of the United Jewish Campaign and the Joint Distribution Committee very naturally focused their interest on the problems presented by Eastern Europe, stressing the great need which existed in all parts of that region for immediate relief. They, therefore, resented an attitude which they looked upon as hampering them in their campaign.

"The result, as I see it, has been that both these great causes have suffered, for had there been harmony, had there been a clearer understanding, had the controversy respecting the United Jewish Campaign never taken place, I truly believe that a larger amount of money would have flowed into the treasuries of both these great organizations.

"The Joint Distribution Committee has during its whole existence shown a sincere interest in Palestine. At no time during its history has it ever failed to recognize the needs of Palestine, and I believe I am correct in saying that of the $62,000,000 raised previous to the United Jewish Campaign over $7,000,000 was spent in Palestine. I understand that out of the proceeds of this recent campaign approximately $2,000,000 has been appropriated for Palestine, and while this money cannot be used to meet requirements of the Zionist budget, yet it is to be used in the upbuilding of Palestine."

Recognizes Split in Opinion.

Dr. Weizmann said he fully understood the possibility of differences of opinion on Palestine and he expressed the hope that at some time American Jewry as a whole "could be helpful and participate in Palestinian development."

"We must endeavor to cooperate amicably with our non-Zionist brethren who do not concede the priority of Palestine over those of our brethren who live in other countries," Dr. Weizmann went on, "whether the help given to them be of a palliative or of a constructive nature, or whether it involve the settlement upon the land of those who desire that opportunity."

He ended with the plea that those who have labored for Jews outside of Palestine 'forget past unpleasantness" and that the imperative need now is for peace among all the forces of American Jewry, in order to achieve such unity as will advance the highest interests of all-Israel here any everywhere."

In his reply Mr. Marshall declared that the pleas for peace and unity "have struck a sympathetic chord in my heart, as they have in the hearts of those with whom I have long been associated in communal endeavors."

"Speaking for my associates and myself, I convey to you, with profound satisfaction, our acceptance of the proffered olive branch," Mr. Marshall said. "In your act we perceive convincing proof that strife has ceased in the ranks of American Jewry. Let the differences of the past sink into oblivion. Let us once more cultivate and practice the virtues of that peace upon which, as remarked by our sages, the world is built, and, it may be added, upon which the preservation of Jews and Judaism depends. With restored fellowship we may be enabled to demonstrate to friend and foe alike that with unity as the very essence of our lives and thoughts we shall continue to make significant contributions to civilization and culture and to the kelfare of mankind."

January 23, 1927

JEWS SPREADING INLAND.

Survey Shows They Are Leaving Ports of Entry and Dispersing.

A marked tendency on the part of Jews in the United States to move away from the ports of entry and disperse gradually through the country is disclosed in a survey being made by Dr. H. S. Linfield of the American Jewish Committee, according to a statement made public yesterday by the Jewish Telegraph Agency.

There is no city in the United States of 25,000 population or over, which does not have Jewish inhabitants, according to this survey, and the spread of Jews to smaller places is very considerable. The chief centres from which dispersion takes place into rural territory and small towns are New York, Philadelphia, Boston and Pittsburgh. The study brings out that there is a notable tendency of Jews to spread from the North to the West and South.

September 10, 1928

IMMIGRATION CURB HELD BLOW TO JEWS

Last Hope of Freedom Taken From Thousands Abroad, Contends New Book.

The restriction of immigration by the United States has had its telling effects upon Jewish life in America, according to Paul Masserman and Max Baker, authors of "The Jews Come to America," recently published by the Bloch Publishing Company.

Immigration restriction, the book points out, "has hastened, in a sense, Americanization and assimilation. It has disintegrated the ghetto. It has given perhaps a death-blow to the Yiddish press. It has weakened orthodoxy. It has practically destroyed the Yiddish stage. Most important of all, it has taken from thousands of Jews in Eastern Europe the last hope of freedom."

Tracing the Jewish migration to this country, the authors assert: "There were no people in the New World—and for that matter, few in the old—who were spiritually as akin to the Jews as the Pilgrims and the Puritans. The Puritans studied the Old Testament in order to better understand the New. From the former they derived their civil polity, from the latter their church discipline and ceremonials. Moses was their law-giver, the Pentatuch their code, and Israel under the Judges their ideal of popular government.

"With the rise of the Puritans came a revival of the study of the Old Testament and of Hebrew teachings. The Law of Moses was the most influential factor in the government of the New England colonies. In framing the laws of the Colonies legislatures sought to harmonize political ideas with biblical ideas. The Mosaic Law was adopted in the Connecticut Code of 1650; while half the statutes in the Code of 1655 for the Colony of New Haven contained references to the Old Testament, and only 3 per cent to the New."

Judaism was also an important factor in the formation and development of American government and democracy, according to the authors. "American democracy found its teacher and preceptor not in the Christian European state of the eighteenth century, but in the ancient Hebrew Commonwealth," they contend.

September 13, 1932

ASSERTS JUDAISM REMAINS RELIGION

Dr. S. H. Goldenson Attacks Movement Which Views It as a 'Civilization.'

TREND LAID TO ZIONISM

New Theory Offered as 'Non-Committal Category,' Rabbis Are Told at Chicago.

Special to THE NEW YORK TIMES.

CHICAGO, June 25.—A defense of Judaism as a religion rather than as a "civilization" or "system of cultural values" was stressed in the presidential address of the Rev. Dr. Samuel H. Goldenson of New York tonight before the annual meeting of the Central Conference of American Rabbis.

The conference will devote its discussions to a revaluation of the principles of Judaism in the light of the changes in Jewish and general life. Nearly 200 American and Canadian rabbis are present and meetings will run through Sunday evening.

Dr. Goldenson contended that the survival of the Jew or any other people depended upon religious faith and not upon the recently advanced concept which would make Judaism a civilization.

The secular movement referred to by Dr. Goldenson has been taken up largely among the conservative Jews, for whom Professor Mordecai Kaplan of New York is the accredited spokesman.

Dr. Goldenson warned the conference that the Jews were "faced with differences that do not derive from primary conceptions and beliefs." He also noted "an important, far-reaching and possibly revolutionary shift" in present-day discussions among Jews.

Wide Effort Is Seen.

He ascribed the tendency to picture Judaism as "a civilization" an attempt to find means to include non-religious or anti-religious Jews in that people's efforts toward nationhood, even though dispersed throughout the world.

"It is thought," Dr. Goldenson declared, "that by regarding Judaism as a civilization instead of a religion it will be easier to cope with the disintegrating forces of modern life. But the incidental result of this thought is to demote the religion of Israel from its high and exalted place that it has always occupied in the life of the Jew.

"The simple fact is that Israel, when it was most completely itself, did not produce any great art or science or speculative thinking. It was interested almost exclusively in spiritual aspects of life."

Dr. Goldenson cited the opposition of the German clergy to Chancellor Hitler's program as proof that religion exhibited greater strength for survival than any other body of sentiments.

"Witness the resistance to Hitlerism offered by the religious groups in Germany and contrast it with the resistance offered by art and science," he said. "No one will doubt that Hitlerism is inimical to genuine culture as it is to religion, and yet the only groups that have thus far found strength and courage to take some stand against the new régime have been the religious bodies.

Greater Zeal in the End.

"Similarly, I believe that in the end there would be found greater zeal to live Jewishly by regarding Judaism as it has always been, than to look upon it as a system of cultural values.

"And if the test should come, were civilization ever to be substituted for religion, it would be found that the Jew himself would inevitably express his will to live, not in terms of a civilization as it is ordinarily conceived, but rather as a way of life permeated and suffused with religious spirit."

Dr. Goldenson attributed the new interpretation of Judaism "more than anything else" to Zionism, and added:

"I doubt very much whether any one would seriously have argued for this new conception of Judaism if it had not been for the practical problems raised by the Zionist movement, constituted, as it is, of many elements that are not particularly attached to Judaism as a religion.

"It is to find a place for the secular, the racial, and the purely nationalistic, as well as the religious, aspects of Zionism that civilization is offered as a great and noncommittal category to include them all. Perhaps civilization as a sanction for the movement is nothing more than eulogistic rationalization of the mere fact that Jews as Jews want a national existence of their own.

June 26, 1935

ASKS WORLD SESSION ON RIGHTS OF JEWRY

American Jewish Congress Acts on Reports of Discrimination Here and Abroad.

DARK PICTURE OF EUROPE

From a Staff Correspondent of The New York Times.

PHILADELPHIA, Oct. 18.—The majority of the 9,785,000 Jews living in Europe face disaster because of an almost universal program of economic boycott and socio-political discrimination, according to reports read here today at the annual session of the American Jewish Congress.

The delegates, from practically every State, after listening to speeches in which discrimination against Jews in this country and overseas was emphasized, adopted a resolution approving a world Jewish conference to take up problems affecting Jews here and abroad and providing that the American Jewish Congress take part in a preliminary conference next Summer at Geneva.

In reviewing the political and economic conditions of the Jews in Europe, Dr. Joseph Tenenbaum, chairman of the executive committee, declared that the majority were engaged in a struggle of life and death, facing "economic annihilation, mass starvation and disintegration."

He referred to conditions of Jews in Russia, Poland, Germany, Austria, Hungary, Rumania, Lithuania, Latvia, Danzig, Czechoslovakia and Saloniki as being of "catastrophic dimensions."

Asserting that European Jewry was living through "the darkest hour of its history of martyrology," he said:

"The present Jewish perplexities extend beyond the peaks and valleys of economic cycles. The existence of the Jewish people is at stake."

Looks to America to Lead Way.

Stating that the solution of these problems must be found in this country, he continued:

"America must and will lead the world out of the present chaotic conditions.

"We have the power and the strength. International peace is unthinkable with the present racial strife poisoning the minds of conationals. Whatever will be the ultimate international settlement, we American taxpayers will foot the bill.

"We have a right to know for what purpose our money will be used: if the governments in Europe will spend our tax proceeds for constructive work of peace or for promotion of anti-Jewish strife, discrimination and Jew-baiting.

"A country ruled or ruined by the Nazis, the Couzists, the Hackenkreuzler and the like does not deserve our sympathy, and least of all our money."

Dr. Wise Rebukes Opposition.

Dr. Stephen S. Wise, rabbi of the Free Synagogue and president of the Jewish Institute of Religion, New York City, and honorary president of the congress, speaking in favor of convening a world Jewish congress, took cognizance of a division of opinion as to its advisability.

Declaring that destructive critics had charged "undue haste" in calling the congress, he said:

"I refuse to believe that we may never summon the representatives of world Jewry together for wise and considered action with respect to their common problems because of the danger of allegations being made such as those that are to be found in the protocols of the elders of Zion.

"There is only one problem before us with respect to a world Jewish congress: Can it help? Will it serve the highest interest of the Jewish people?

"What may falsely and absurdly be alleged against such a congress if it be deemed needful to convene it, it is for the base and the cowardly to take note of and not for those among us who believe in the right of the Jewish people as a people to defend themselves, to safeguard their hardly won rights, and to urge the best judgment of humankind in support of lawful and rightful Jewish claims."

Rise in College Bias Charged.

Dr. Mordecai Soltes, chairman of the committee on discrimination in colleges, reported finding the problem acute, particularly with regard to "obstacles in the form of entrance requirements placed in the path of Jewish applicants for admission into medical schools."

"We must disclose the facts and

134

arouse public indignation." he said. "We must educate and mobilize public opinion. We must make clear to the leaders of the medical schools that we do not intend to remain silent any longer.

"Our country does not ask questions concerning a person's religion when it grants him the privilege of citizenship. It makes no distinctions regarding religion when it admits pupils in elementary or high schools.

"And no questions regarding their religious affiliations should be asked of students applying for admission into medical schools which operate under charters granted by the respective States and which frequently receive substantial support from the State treasuries. Only one test should be applied—that of merit."

Calls Jews Too Anxious for Peace.

Bernard S. Deutsch, president of congress, in his address asserted that anti-Semitic manifestations, open and hidden discrimination and acts of violence against the Jews had been rife everywhere in the past year.

Taking issue with the statement of George Bernard Shaw that "the world has made its peace with the Jew, but the Jew refuses to make peace with the world," Mr. Deutsch said:

"The world has not made its peace with the Jews, though the Jew is but too anxious to make his peace with the world.

"Conditions in which the Jews find themselves all over the world bear this out.

"Never before has there been such a crying need for a world congress."

Rabbi J. X. Cohen of the Free Synagogue of New York City, chairman of the committee on economic discrimination, said he found that the business depression had sharply intensified the handicap against the Jewish worker.

He asserted that the employment agencies in New York City until recently had displayed placards reading, "Applications not accepted from Jews." These signs, he added, were removed after protest.

He urged the congress to insist on "fair play," and to continue fighting for "victims of un-American economic discrimination."

The delegates, convening at the Benjamin Franklin Hotel, were welcomed by Mayor Harry A. Mackey, and a message congratulating the congress was received from Governor Pinchot. Brief addresses were made by former Representative Nathan D. Perlman of New York, Dr. Max Raisin, Dr. Samuel Margoshes, Rabbi Samuel Wohl, Leo Wolfson and Z. Tygel.

Judge Julian W. Mack of the United States Circuit Court of Appeals, speaking at the annual dinner this evening, made a plea for unity among the delegates, asserting that only by whole-hearted cooperation could the fight against anti-Semitism be successfully carried on. He also stressed the importance of cooperation between the Jews of this country and those in other nations.

Other speakers included United States Attorney George Z. Medalie of New York, Judge William M. Lewis, Carl Sherman, Simon E. Sobeloff and Israel N. Thurman.

October 19, 1931

'Nazis' Attack Jews.

BERLIN, Dec. 2 (Jewish Telegraphic Agency).—A clash between "Nazis" and Jews occurred here this evening when an organized "Nazi" group invaded the Grenadierstrasse of the Jewish quarter.

Shouting "Down with Judea!" the "Nazis" fell upon Jewish passersby. A Jewish crowd soon collected, however, and offered resistance to the attackers, causing their retreat. Two "Nazis" were injured in the clash.

Indicating its belief that the Hitlerites are scheduled to take over power very shortly, German Right, the organ of the "Nazi" lawyers, today offers an elaborate treatise on the steps which the "Nazis" plan to rid German of the Jews, without arousing foreign opinion.

The Jews will be deprived of their rights, without changing the Constitution and without causing excitement abroad, the "Nazi" deputy, Ernst Heydenbrand, writes.

"When the Nazi government comes into power it will not immediately adopt the most vigorous measures against the Jews," he asserts. "It will simply prepare a list of all Jewish citizens and declare that their citizenship has been withdrawn. Thus the Jews will be unable to participate in the elections or serve in State positions.

"When the government is sufficiently strong it will introduce the fullest measures against the Jews with the customary 'Nazi' severity."

December 3, 1931

JEWS DENOUNCE HITLER.

A conference of major Jewish organizations was urged last night to consider the "alarming situation" produced by the anti-Semitism of Adolf Hitler in Germany and the "imminence" of his accession to power. The proposal was embodied in a resolution unanimously adopted by more than 500 Jews, meeting under the auspices of B'nai B'rith at Temple Emanu-El, Fifth Avenue and Sixty-fifth Street.

The resolution was presented by Municipal Court Judge Myron Sulzberger after speakers had denounced Hitlerism not only as a menace to Judaism but to the peace of the world. It is to be forwarded for action to the national headquarters of B'nai B'rith in Cincinnati.

Supreme Court Justice Albert Cohn, district president of B'nai B'rith, presided.

March 10, 1932

REASSURES JEWS HERE.

Reich Foreign Office Spokesman Bars "Unjustified Experiments."

The Jewish Morning Journal through its Berlin correspondent received yesterday a cable quoting a spokesman for the German Foreign Office to the effect that "no unjustified experiments" would be undertaken by the Hitler Government.

The statement follows:

"In order to reassure the Jews of New York City, who are anxious as to the fate of the Jews of Germany, we wish to state that the German Government is earnest and determined in its desire to guarantee safety and order for all its citizens and it has no intention of making any unjustified experiments."

February 3, 1933

250,000 JEWS HERE TO PROTEST TODAY

More Than 1,000,000 in All Parts of Nation Also Will Assail Hitler Policies.

JEWISH CONGRESS TO ACT

Four Demands to Be Presented to German Envoy Urging End of Anti-Semitism.

BERLIN JEWS IN DISSENT

National Organization There Asks That Garden Mass Meeting Be Called Off.

More than 250,000 Jews in this city and 1,000,000 throughout the country will join in protest meetings today against the persecutions and discriminations practiced against Jews by the Hitler Government in Germany, while hundreds of thousands of Jews, in response to a call from their religious leaders, will spend the day in fasting and prayer that the persecutions may cease.

The protest in this city will centre in a rally in Madison Square Garden to be addressed by leaders of Jewry and the Christian world. While more than 20,000 are expected to fill Madison Square Garden, overflow meetings will be held outside the Garden and in Columbus Circle. Meetings also will be held in Jewish temples and in halls throughout the city. At the same time protest rallies will take place in more than 200 cities in all parts of the country.

The proceedings in Madison Square Garden will be heard through amplifiers by the crowds at the overflow meetings and will be broadcast throughout the nation and to thirteen foreign countries. The doors of the Garden will open at 6:30 P. M.

Rabbi Stephen S. Wise, honorary president of the American Jewish Congress, organizer of the protest demonstration, will open the Garden meeting and will then introduce Bernard S. Deutsch who, as president of the congress, will preside. Among the speakers will be former Governor Alfred E. Smith, Senator Robert F. Wagner, who will fly from Washington to be present; Bishop William T. Manning, Bishop John J. Dunn, representing Cardinal Hayes; Bishop Francis J. McConnell, Charles H. Tuttle and Mayor John P. O'Brien. Governor Lehman was to have spoken at the meeting, but he told The Associated Press at Albany last night that State business would not permit him to attend.

William Green, president of the American Federation of Labor, will voice the protest of 3,000,000 organized workers.

Elaborate Police Arrangements.

Elaborate police arrangements for the Garden meeting and the overflow rallies have been made by Police Commissioner Mulrooney, who will be in personal command of the 700 police, including mounted and motorcycle squads, detailed to the meetings. The speakers will be escorted to the meetings by motorcycle policemen.

Speaking before his congregation in Carnegie Hall yesterday, Rabbi Wise announced that following today's meetings the American Jewish Congress will transmit to the German Government through Ambassador Wilhelm von Prittwitz four "vital demands." The demands are:

"1. There must be an immediate cessation of all anti-Semitic activities and propaganda in Germany.

"2. The abandonment of the policy of racial discrimination against and of economic exclusion of Jews from the life of Germany.

"3. The protection of Jewish life and property.

"4. There shall be no expulsion of 'Ost-Juden' Jews who have come into Germany since 1914."

"These are our demands," Rabbi Wise said. "If these demands be granted, as God knows they ought to be, there will be an end of every plan and undertaking of protest."

As Dr. Wise spoke, the executive committee of the American Jewish Congress was in session in his study a few paces away. The meeting lasted for several hours.

Every seat in Carnegie Hall was taken as Rabbi Wise and Mr. S. Deutsch, addressed the congregation. Hundreds were turned away. Mr. Deutsch read a statement in behalf of the congress.

Rabbi Wise emphasized that the protest movement against persecutions in Germany was not intended as a movement against Germany, and revealed that he had received a message from Berlin demanding that American Jews abandon their "anti-German demonstrations."

"I wish again to record my conviction that the Versailles peace treaties should have been revised long before this," he declared; "that the Allies in the last years have been guilty of deep wrongs against Germany, the German people, the German State, and that Germany has the right to demand that either the allied nations shall disarm, as they promised and covenanted that they would, or that Germany shall have the right to arm.

"Germany has the right and has had the right to demand certain things of the Allies which should have been granted long before this, and had they been granted, we might never have seen these days come upon Germany."

Mass Meeting Brings Protest.

While Dr. Wise would not reveal the source of the message received by him from Berlin, it became known that Ernest Wallach, vice president of the Central Association of German Citizens of Jewish Faith had sent him a telegram on behalf of the president of the organization urging that tonight's rally in Madison Square Garden be called off. Copies of the telegram were sent by Mr. Wallach to Governor Lehman, Mr. Smith and others scheduled to appear at the Garden meeting. Mr. Wallach is now in the United States on business. In his message Mr. Wallach urged that if tonight's meetings cannot be called off that the speakers "refrain from stirring the emotions of the audience against Germany."

The telegram said:

"The undersigned vice president

of the Central Association of German Citizens of Jewish faith has just received the following cable from the president of the association, Dr. Julius Brodnitz, in Berlin:

" 'We earnestly urge you to do all in your power in order that Monday's mass meeting be called off, or if such should, against our sincere hopes, not prove possible, to prevail upon the speakers of the evening to refrain from stirring the emotions of their audience against Germany. We can assure them that the German Government is permanently and successfully engaged in assuring peace and order to all citizens without discrimination.'

"In conveying the contents of this telegram to you, as one of the principal speakers of tomorrow's event, I beg to identify myself with the appeal therein voiced by the elected representation of Germany's Jewish population and to earnestly bespeak you to aid us in preventing any action which is liable to encroach upon the prestige of our country and thereby seriously affect our most vital interests."

Dr. Wise declared that the American Jewish Congress had not excited public opinion, but had "merely sought to channelize the high indignation and the solemn protest of America into ways that shall be orderly and effective." He then enumerated the demands to be made upon the German Government.

Denial Held "Unconvincing."

The statement of the American Jewish Congress, as read by Mr. Deutsch, follows:

"The denial of the Central Union of German Citizens of the Jewish Faith which was broadcast from Berlin on Friday is pitifully unconvincing. We know from the sworn experiences of American citizens who were brutally assaulted and tortured by the Nazis because they were Jews or looked like Jews, that it is a regular part of the Nazi technique to extort from the victims or survivors of their atrocities, under threat of further torture, or even death, a written denial that they had been mistreated or that anything untoward had happened to them. If these American citizens, knowing that the powerful government of the United States was behind them, nevertheless felt constrained to sign exculpating statements for their Nazi torturers under duress, how can we now credit

any denial emanating from the terrorized Jews of Germany, whose civil rights and very lives are in peril and may be at stake.

"But if we read this forced denial itself carefully, we find in it its own repudiation—first, from what it denies; second, from what it eloquently fails to deny; and lastly, and most important, from what it specifically admits.

"It denies just three and only three specific charges, which are strictly limited as to time and place and description. The great particularity of the charges to which the denial is thus limited at once suggests that all the other charges with which the world has been ringing for the past two weeks are true and cannot be denied. The denial fails even to attempt to deny them.

"It fails to deny or even to explain why it is that such leaders of German Jewry and German intellectual life as Theodore Wolff, Alfred Kerr, Arnold Zweig, Bruno Walter and dozens of others like them, besides hundreds and thousands of other German Jews of less prominence, have had to flee Germany for their lives and are now taking refuge in Prague, Switzerland, Holland, Belgium, France and even in Poland. It does not deny that many other German Jews, including great writers, physicians, business men and lawyers, whose only crime is that they are of the Jewish faith or race, are now languishing in German jails.

"It does not deny that the hospitals, universities and schools of Germany, and theatres, orchestras and banks have been, and are now, systematically being 'purged,' to use the Nazi phrase, of all Jewish personnel, no matter how eminent and world-famous or how lowly, to their economic ruin and to the shame and injury of German culture, science, art and finance. It does not deny that Jewish judges are being ruthlessly removed from the bench, notwithstanding their constitutional guarantee of tenure of office, and that Jewish lawyers are being driven from the bar. It does not deny that all Jewish civil servants of the State, whether in high or low position, have been, and are being, ruthlessly dismissed.

"The denial does not deny, as, indeed, it would be futile to deny in the teeth of the overwhelming evidence, the circumstantial tales of persecution and horror which the thousands of Jews and also Christian liberals who have just

escaped out of Germany are telling—tales which have justly shocked the whole of civilized mankind. It does not deny and cannot deny that the persecution, suppression and even the total expulsion of the Jews from Germany has been for years the avowed policy and boasted program of the Nazis so soon as they attained power; that the Nazi Cabinet Minister in charge of the police only last week announced derisively in a public speech that the police under his charge could not concern themselves with the protection of Jewish property, and that Hitler himself, in his speech in Potsdam at the opening of the Reichstag, intimated that the Jews of Germany were outlaws and criminals, as pointed out editorially in THE NEW YORK TIMES of Saturday (March 25). With the heads of state making public announcements of this character, what bloody excesses may one not expect from their frenzied followers?

"Official" Threat Recalled.

"Finally, the statement of the Central Union does not deny and cannot deny the news of the very day on which the statement was published here, namely, that the Jews of the Palatinate, or Rhenish Bavaria, are all being rounded up by the police, with a threat of expulsion in the offing; that their funds in banks have been impounde, so as to make escape impossible in the meanwhile, and that the foreign correspondents were ominously told Saturday by 'an official Nazi source' that 'Chancellor Hitler will take action to adjust the whole problem of Eastern Jews who had taken refuge in Germany since 1914.'

"However, most significant of all are the admissions contained in the denial of the Central Union. The denial admits that there have been 'acts of political revenge, also reprisals against Jews'; and it admits further that 'the anti-Semitic aims in the various domains of life and business which are manifesting themselves fill us, indeed, with grave concern.' The Central Union goes on to say, however, that that is 'a German domestic affair.' This we in turn deny, and deny most vehemently. It is not alone 'a German domestic affair' that anti-Semitism in the various domains of life and business is the official

policy and program of the German Government. Anti-Semitism in Germany is a challenge to civilization itself; and all civilized people and peoples have a right and a duty to protest against it. Whether the plan is to crush out the 600,000 members of the Jewish race in Germany by economic repression and a denial of civil rights or by bloodshed is equally a crime alike against God and humanity which calls for the condemnation of mankind and for the exertion of every possible means by the outside world to prevent it."

Bernard H. Ridder, editor of the Staats-Zeitung, who had been scheduled as one of the speakers at the Madison Square Garden meeting, will not address the gathering, it was said last night. A representative of Mr. Ridder explained that he had been unable to see eye to eye with the American Jewish Congress as to what he should say.

Mr. Ridder prepared a speech, the manuscript of which he submitted to the Congress, his representative said. That body did not regard it as satisfactory, and at Mr. Ridder's suggestion submitted an alternative speech. Mr. Ridder found that this contained stronger expressions than he desired to use, it was said, and consequently he rejected it.

A. H. Cohen, executive director of the Congress, denied, however, that Mr. Ridder's speech had been rejected or that a substitute speech had been prepared. He said that so far as the officials of the Congress were aware, Mr. Ridder would speak at the meeting to-night.

All holders of tickets to the Madison Square Garden meeting to-night will be admitted until 7:30 P. M., after which time, conditions inside permitting, the doors will be thrown open to the general public. Holders of reserved seats are requested to use the Eighth Avenue entrance. All others will use the entrances at Forty-ninth and Fiftieth Streets.

The Jewish Theatrical Guild, meeting yesterday afternoon at the Morosco Theatre, passed a resolution protesting against the anti-Semitic outrages. It also urged the Secretary of State to make representations to the government of Germany that the persecution be stopped. The meeting was attended by some 1,500 persons.

March 27, 1933

REICH ADOPTS SWASTIKA AS NATION'S OFFICIAL FLAG; HITLER'S REPLY TO 'INSULT'

By OTTO D. TOLISCHUS.
Wireless to THE NEW YORK TIMES.

NUREMBERG, Germany, Sept. 15.—National Socialist Germany definitely flung down the gauntlet before the feet of Western liberal opinion tonight when the Reichstag, assembled for a special session here in connection with the "Party Day of Freedom," decreed a series of laws that put Jews beyond the legal and social pale of the German nation, and in token of this act proclaimed the swastika banner to be the sole flag of the German Reich.

With this action, in the words of Reichstag President Goering, begins the next step of "National Socialist upbuilding," generally being called here the second revolution, the first part having been concluded with Germany's rearmament, in honor of which the present party conclave bears its name.

Provisions of New Laws.

The new laws provide:

1. German citizenship with full political rights depends on the special grant of a Reich citizenship charter, to be given only to those of

German or racially related blood, who have proved by their attitude that they are willing and fit loyally to serve the German people and the Reich.

This deprives Jews of German citizenship but leaves them the status of "State members" (Staatsangehoeriger), and Germans found undeserving of Reich citizenship may likewise be reduced to this status, which, among other disadvantages, entails loss of the vote

2. Marriages between Jews and citizens of German or racially related blood, as well as extra-marital sexual relations between them, are forbidden and will be punished by penal servitude or imprisonment. Jews must not engage feminine domestic help of German or racially related blood under 45 years old. Jews likewise are forbidden to show the German national flag, but may show under protection of the State the Jewish colors of white and blue. Violations of the last two provisions are punishable by imprisonment up to one year or a fine or both.

3. The Reich, or national, flag is the swastika flag, which is also the flag of commerce to be flown by German merchant ships. But a special war flag is to be fixed by Hitler and the War Minister, which is expected to follow the present black, white and red flag and will probably contain the swastika cross in place of the iron cross for a symbol.

Reichstag Is Voiceless.

Those laws, which General Goering himself called momentous, were introduced with speeches by Hitler and General Goering and adopted unanimously and with many cheers by the Reichstag, which by like unanimity and cheers rendered itself voiceless at the beginning of the session.

At the request of Dr. Wilhelm Frick, Minister of the Interior, the Reichstag abolished its own rules of procedure and placed itself "under the principle of leadership," to be exercised by General Goering. This motion is as important as any of the laws passed, for it formally abolished the Reichstag as a deliberative body and reduced it to a mere division of the National Socialist party. That, Dr. Frick explained, brought the Reichstag in step with the new epoch.

Hitler's speech, revised at the last minute, was remarkably short and was delivered in a rather weakened voice. But the Fuehrer had been under tremendous physical strain during the last few days and today. He delivered one speech this morning, and for five hours stood in the Nuremberg market place reviewing the march of 120,-000 men of various National Socialist formations, which demonstrated the physical force behind the laws passed tonight.

In his Reichstag speech Hitler motivated the laws themselves by again putting into the foreground his assertion in the early part of the Nazi conclave that Jews were propagators of bolshevism and in this connection he referred to the Bremen flag incident and the verdict of Magistrate Brodsky, saying:

"The insult to the German flag—which has been settled in the most loyal manner by the American Government—is an illustration of the attitude of Jewry toward Germany, even when it is in an official capacity, and an effective confirmation of the rightness of our National Socialist legislation, the aim of which is to prevent similar incidents in our administration and jurisprudence."

For the rest, however, he merely mentioned the alleged "provocative" efforts and new anti-German boycott agitation on the part of the Jews, and he made a specific reference to alleged Jewish demonstrations against the anti-Jewish one in Berlin, which were given at the time as a reason for the Kurfuerstendamm riots that initiated the present anti-Jewish drive, now realized.

Assails Memel "Oppression."

Most of the speech was devoted to foreign policy, in which connection, in pronounced contrast with the National Socialist treatment of Jews, he sharply protested against the "mistreatment and oppression" of Germans in the Memel territory. He demanded that Lithuania be held, "before Mussolini," to observe treaties, and suggested such action by the League as Germany had met before the problem "assumes a form that some day may be regretted by all powers."

Similarly, a strong tone was taken against Moscow and the Communist International, but at the same time Hitler also renewed his repeated protestations of "unshakable love for peace" and proclaimed Germany's neutrality in "things which do not affect her."

"The purport of the new army, which is to demonstrate its might tomorrow," he said, was not to threaten the freedom of any European nation, nor to consume the reserves of National Socialism's reconstruction work in "frivolous and insane adventures" but finally to safeguard the freedom of the German people.

Gives Warning to Jews.

In proposing the explicit laws against Jews, Hitler said the German Government was trying to avert incalculable defensive action by an indignant population, and guided by that fact "through a single secular solution a level will, perhaps, be created enabling the German people to find tolerable relations with Jewish people." But he added:

"If this hope should not be realized and if international Jewish agitation should continue, the situation will have to be reconsidered."

"If the attempt at legal regulation fails again," the Fuehrer added, "the problem will have to be transferred from law to the National Socialist party for a final solution."

This avoidance for the present of the threatened enabling act, which would have legally delivered the Jews to the mercy of individual party members, as well as the enactment of any special economic restrictions, aside from the professional restrictions imposed, was regarded here tonight as a victory, such as it is, for Dr. Hjalmar Schacht, Minister of Economics.

On the other hand, the implications of the laws and the actual status of Jews in Germany are still wholly unclear and will depend entirely on administrative enforcement of regulations still to be issued by Dr. Frick and Rudolf Hess, Minister without portfolio. If the law puts Jews in a status similar to that of aliens they may be subjected to further economic restrictions as well.

In his final declaration to the Reichstag, Hitler told the Deputies they had passed laws "whose effect would be recognized only after many centuries," and he appealed to them to take care that the nation did not leave the way of law and asserted that these laws "are enabled by unprecedented discipline of the whole German people, for which you are responsible."

For some it appeared symbolic that after a beautiful day a steady downpour of rain started just as the Reichstag let out, and it was also a fitting touch that as Hitler returned to his hotel with a drawn and unsmiling face, in spite of cheering crowds, he was greeted at the entrance by Julius Streicher, anti-Semitic leader, who on his countenance registered his victory.

In accordance with the new "parliamentary leadership principle" General Goering extended the debate by giving a lengthy speech from the President's seat. The new flag law, he said, was necessary. He ridiculed those who seek compromise with national socialism by hiding behind the old imperial emblem, and he likewise attacked Jews as "race destroyers" and asserted "German women and girls must be protected." There were no other remarks.

The Reichstag was the first called in Nuremberg in 400 years. It met in an improvised hall in the house of the Cultural Association and was attended by the entire Cabinet, with Foreign Minister von Neurath and especially General Werner von Blomberg, Defense Minister, Dr. Frick and General Walter von Reichenau, head of the War Academy, prominent among the government representatives.

Hitler in a Fiery Mood.
By The Associated Press.

NUREMBERG, Germany, Sept. 15.—Adolf Hitler's Reichstag, stung by the strictures of a New York magistrate against the Nazi emblem, tonight pronounced the swastika to be the Reich's sole flag, hurled defiance to Jews throughout the world and limited German citizenship to members of the Germanic race.

The specially summoned lawmakers acted after their Fuehrer, in a fiery mood, had opened the Reichstag session with a bitter attack on Lithuanians for their alleged tratment of Germans in the Memel territory, and had called upon the lawmakers to approve three new laws.

In a speech that lasted only twelve minutes, the Reichsfuehrer told his lawmakers in apparent reference to the Ethiopian question that Germany would take no position on "any question which does not directly affect us," but "we look with interest to Lithuania."

"Memel, which was stolen from Germany and the robbery legalized by the League of Nations, has for years tortured Germans only because they are members of the German nation and because they wanted to remain Germans," he declared. "They are treated worse than criminals in other countries just because they are Germans."

Tremendous applause greeted his statement.

The German dictator, opening the Reichstag shortly after 9 P. M., plunged immediately into foreign questions. He said he desired to make a short statement before introducing several laws. Of the Memel question he asserted:

"Protests in Kaunas of signatory powers were without results. The German Government looked upon all of this with deep regret. We hope some day these assurances will not assume forms which might be regretted by the whole world.

"Preparations for coming elections constitute a breach of the treaty. Lithuania must be admonished with all possible means to hold to these treaties."

The 600 Deputies cheered and yelled their approval as each of the three laws was presented. Frequently they raised their hands in the Nazi salute, and there was laughter throughout the chamber at the provision forbidding Jews to hire domestic help under the age of 45.

General Hermann Goering, President of the Reichstag, beginning to read out the three new laws, spoke first of the "debt of gratitude which the [Nazi] movement owes to its symbol [the swastika]."

This was greeted with such a storm of cheering that the rest of his announcement was drowned out. When the noise had died down General Goering continued, but frequently was interrupted by cheers and applause.

"The laws proposed to you today rightly belong to the Reich party convention on freedom," he said, "for they are to guarantee us our foreign and domestic freedom. Each period of German history had its special symbol. We are grateful that by the will of fate the glorious imperial colors were furled during the years when Germany endured a period of shame.

"The fact that it could be unfurled at all, after the years of Germany's disgrace, is due to the fact that the swastika restored her honor to Germany. Those who believe they have the right now to fly that flag forget that it was the trench soldier, Adolf Hitler, who pulled the cockade out of the dirt. The Fuehrer made these colors clean and honest.

"Do not forget that if the swastika had not been victorious the red flag of bolshevism would be flying today and bolshevism would have engulfed Germany in blood.

"In holding the swastika in his hand, Hitler held German fate in his hand, also. The flag was the symbol of racial purity, too. Therefore no Jew may raise this holy symbol."

September 16, 1935

200 JOIN IN APPEAL FOR JEWISH EXILES

Plea Is Made Over Signatures of Bishops, University Heads and Business Leaders.

A call to all Americans of all creeds and races to contribute to the United Jewish Appeal was made public yesterday over the signatures of 200 persons, many of them bishops, deans of theological schools, leaders of Christian organizations, university presidents and other notable laymen.

The signatories introduced the appeal with a declaration that "we unequivocally voice our protest against the program of the German Government for the destruction of the Jewish people. By her actions, Germany has compelled other nations to take notice of her policies, for the problem which she has created is presented to the world at large for solution. She has put the burden of her exiled refugees on all other nations."

Among the signatories were Bishop Ernest M. Stires of Long Island; the Rev. Dr. J. Ross Stevenson, president of the Princeton Theological Seminary; John R. Mott, president of the World's Alliance of Young Men's Christian Associations; the Rev. Dr. Charles R. Brown, Dean Emeritus of the Yale Divinity School; Charles C. Burlingham, president of the New York Welfare Council; the Rev. Dr. Samuel McCrea Cavert, general secretary of the Federal Council of Churches of Christ in America; the Rev. Dr. William H. Foulkes, vice president of the International Society of Christian Endeavor.

$3,250,000 Is Sought.

Their statement was made public by Rabbi Jonah B. Wise, national co-chairman of the United Jewish Appeal of the Joint Distribution Committee and the American Palestine Campaign, engaged in raising $3,250,000 as the minimum amount estimated for this year.

The statement of the outstanding Christian supporters of the appeal declares:

"Believing that the standards of civilized society are lowered and the security of international peace is endangered by racial and religious persecution, we unequivocally voice our protest against the continued and intensified program of the German Government for the spiritual and economic destruction of the Jewish people in Germany.

"The German Government has barred Jews from a place of honor and self-sustenance; it has forced tens of thousands of Jews to leave their country. It has added persecution to the removal of opportunity for economic maintenance. More than 80,000 refugees have been thrust out into the world during the past two years, according to James G. McDonald, League of Nations High Commissioner for Refugees. By her actions Germany has compelled other nations to take notice of her policies, for the problem which she has created is presented to the world at large for solution. She has put the burden of her exiled refugees on all other nations.

Find It Duty to Repair Ravages.

"Parallel to our obligation to protest against conditions which made their plight possible is our responsibility to the men, women and children who are being rendered homeless and hopeless by the German Government. If we have the right to condemn intolerance, we also have the duty to repair its ravages.

"We join, therefore, in the plea to the people of America to respond immediately and generously to the United Jewish Appeal, the organized effort in this country to provide for relief and rehabilitation of the Jews of Germany and of the refugees from Germany. These refugees are now at the mercy of unstable political and economic conditions in various countries. Our failure to offer them aid would totally deprive them of their remaining courage and will to persist."

"The voice of America has ever been raised on behalf of the hurt and the wronged. The heart of America has always been open to the suffering and the oppressed. In our ears there now sounds an anguished plea for help which should pierce the conscience of every American who values his own freedom of worship and his own right to live.

"Coupled with our condemnation of their wrongs must be a generous outpouring of aid which will enable the Jews of Germany to survive."

October 7, 1935

Swastikas Painted on Jewish Temple Here; City-Wide Watch Is Started by the Police

Eleven large orange-colored swastikas were painted on the outside front wall of Temple Rodeph Sholom, 7 West Eighty-third Street, between 4:30 and 6:30 yesterday morning. It was the third instance of such vandalism there.

Rabbi Louis I. Newman declared that he felt that the vandalism had a connection with the recent protest by Secretary of State Hull to the German Foreign Office. He said:

"They have done this before and undoubtedly will do it again. I believe it has a direct relationship to Secretary Hull's protest to the German Foreign Office against the abusive language used recently in the German press."

Rabbi Newman saw the vandalism about 10 A. M. when he entered the temple. The symbols, some of which had by that time been washed away, were about ten to twelve inches square and extended across the width of the building about six feet from the ground, he declared.

As a result, Chief Inspector of Police John J. Seery issued a general order later in the day directing commanding officers in all boroughs to instruct radio motor patrols and the patrol force to pay particular attention to all synagogues and temples to prevent defacing of property.

Patrolman Walter Ryan of the West Sixty-eighth Street station reported the vandalism at 6:30 in the morning. Flat house paint was used in applying the Nazi symbols, and considerable difficulty was experienced in removing them.

On two other occasions swastikas were painted or scratched on the synagogue property, officials connected with the congregation said yesterday. Once the Nazi symbol was scratched on the glass in the doors inside the building.

The last time the facade of the building was defaced the vandals used chalk and the Nazi symbols were quickly removed. This time, however, Herbert Werner, superintendent, was not able to obliterate entirely the swastikas. He used benzine and sandpaper and succeeded in removing most of the signs.

Detectives questioned residents of the neighborhood, but they were unable to locate any one who saw the defacing of the building.

In the last two or three years synagogues in various sections of the city have reported vandalism and the painting of Nazi symbols on their property.

March 15, 1937

NAZIS SMASH, LOOT AND BURN JEWISH SHOPS AND TEMPLES UNTIL GOEBBELS CALLS HALT

BANDS ROVE CITIES

Thousands Arrested for 'Protection' as Gangs Avenge Paris Death

EXPULSIONS ARE IN VIEW

Plunderers Trail Wreckers in Berlin—Police Stand Idle —Two Deaths Reported

By OTTO D. TOLISCHUS
Wireless to THE NEW YORK TIMES.

BERLIN, Nov. 10.—A wave of destruction, looting and incendiarism unparalleled in Germany since the Thirty Years War and in Europe generally since the Bolshevist revolution, swept over Great Germany today as National Socialist cohorts took vengeance on Jewish shops, offices and synagogues for the murder by a young Polish Jew of Ernst vom Rath, third secretary of the German Embassy in Paris.

Beginning systematically in the early morning hours in almost every town and city in the country, the wrecking, looting and burning continued all day. Huge but mostly silent crowds looked on and the police confined themselves to regulating traffic and making wholesale arrests of Jews "for their own protection."

All day the main shopping districts as well as the side streets of Berlin and innumerable other places resounded to the shattering of shop windows falling to the pavement, the dull thuds of furniture and fittings being pounded to pieces and the clamor of fire brigades rushing to burning shops and synagogues. Although shop fires were quickly extinguished, synagogue fires were merely kept from spreading to adjoining buildings.

Two Deaths Reported

As far as could be ascertained the violence was mainly confined to property. Although individuals were beaten, reports so far tell of the death of only two persons—a Jew in Polzin, Pomerania, and another in Bunzdorf.

In extent, intensity and total damage, however, the day's outbreaks exceeded even those of the 1918 revolution and by nightfall there was scarcely a Jewish shop, cafe, office or synagogue in the country that was not either wrecked, burned severely or damaged.

Thereupon Propaganda Minister Joseph Goebbels issued the following proclamation:

"The justified and understandable anger of the German people over the cowardly Jewish murder of a German diplomat in Paris found extensive expression during last night. In numerous cities and towns of the Reich retaliatory action has been undertaken against Jewish buildings and businesses.

"Now a strict request is issued to the entire population to cease immediately all further demonstrations and actions against Jewry, no matter what kind. A final answer to the Jewish assassination in Paris will be given to Jewry by way of legislation and ordinance."

What this legal action is going to be remains to be seen. It is known, however, that measures for the extensive expulsion of foreign Jews are already being prepared in the Interior Ministry, and some towns, like Munich, have ordered all Jews to leave within forty-eight hours. All Jewish organizational, cultural and publishing activity has been suspended. It is assumed that the Jews, who have now lost most of their possessions and livelihood, will either be thrown into the streets or put into ghettos and concentration camps, or impressed into labor brigades and put to work for the Third Reich, as the children of Israel were once before for the Pharaohs.

Thousands Are Arrested

In any case, all day in Berlin, as throughout the country, thousands of Jews, mostly men, were being taken from their homes and arrested—in particular prominent Jewish leaders, who in some cases, it is understood, were told they were being held as hostages for the good behavior of Jewry outside Germany.

In Breslau they were hunted out even in the homes of non-Jews where they might have been hiding.

Foreign embassies in Berlin and consulates throughout the country were besieged by frantic telephone calls and by persons, particularly weeping women and children, begging help that could not be given them. Incidentally, in Breslau the United States Consulate had to shut down for some time during the day because of fumes coming from a burning synagogue near by.

All pretense—maintained during previous comparatively minor anti-Jewish outbreaks—to the effect that the day's deeds had been the work of irresponsible, even Communist, elements was dropped this time and the official German News Bureau, as well as newspapers that hitherto had ignored such happenings, frankly reported on them. The bureau said specifically:

"Continued anti-Jewish demonstrations occurred in numerous places. In most cities the synagogue was fired by the population. The fire department in many cases was able merely to save adjoining buildings. In addition, in many cities the windows of Jewish shops were smashed.

"Occasionally fires occurred and because of the population's extraordinary excitement the contents of shops were partly destroyed. Jewish shop owners were taken into custody by the police for their own protection."

Excesses in Many Cities

Berlin papers also mention many cities and towns in which anti-Jewish excesses occurred, including Potsdam, Stettin, Frankfort on the Main, Leipzig, Luebeck, Cologne, Nuremberg, Essen, Duesseldorf, Konstanz, Landsberg, Kottbus and Eberswalde. In most of them, it is reported, synagogues were raided and burned and shops were demolished. But in general the press follows a system of reporting only local excesses so as to disguise the national extent of the outbreak, the full spread of which probably never will be known.

On the other hand, the German press already warns the world that if the day's events lead to another agitation campaign against Germany "the improvised and spontaneous outbreaks of today will be replaced with even more drastic authoritative action." No doubt is left that the contemplated "authoritative action" would have a retaliatory character.

Says the Angriff, Dr. Goebbels's organ:

"For every suffering, every crime and every injury that this criminal [the Jewish community] inflicts on a German anywhere, every individual Jew will be held responsible. All Judah wants is war with us and it can have this war according to its own moral law: an eye for an eye and a tooth for a tooth."

Possession of Weapons Barred

One of the first legal measures issued was an order by Heinrich Himmler, commander of all German police, forbidding Jews to possess any weapons whatever and imposing a penalty of twenty years'

confinement in a concentration camp upon every Jew found in possession of a weapon hereafter.

The dropping of all pretense in the outbreak is also illustrated by the fact that although shops and synagogues were wrecked or burned by so-called Rollkommardos, or wrecking crews, dressed in what the Nazis themselves call "Raeuberzivil," or "bandit mufti," consisting of leather coats or raincoats over uniform boots or trousers these squads often performed their work in the presence and under the protection of uniformed Nazis or police.

The wrecking work was thoroughly organized, sometimes proceeding under the direct orders of a controlling person in the street at whose command the wreckers ceased, lined up and proceeded to another place.

In the fashionable Tauenzienstrasse the writer saw a wrecking crew at work in one shop while the police stood outside telling a vast crowd watching the proceeding to keep moving.

"Move on," said the policemen, "there are young Volksgenossen [racial comrades] inside who have some work to do."

At other shops during the wrecking process uniformed Storm Troopers and Elite Guards were seen entering and emerging while soldiers passed by outside.

Crowds Mostly Silent

Generally the crowds were silent and the majority seemed gravely disturbed by the proceedings. Only members of the wrecking squads shouted occasionally, "Perish Jewry!" and "Kill the Jews!" and in one case a person in the crowd shouted, "Why not hang the owner in the window?"

In one case on the Kurfuerstendamm actual violence was observed by an American girl who saw one Jew with his face bandaged dragged from a shop, beaten and chased by a crowd while a second Jew was dragged from the same shop by a

single man who beat him as the crowd looked on.

One Jewish shopowner, arriving at his wrecked store, exclaimed, "Terrible," and was arrested on the spot.

In some cases on the other hand crowds were observed making passages for Jews to leave their stores unmolested.

Some persons in the crowds— peculiarly enough, mostly women— expressed the view that it was only right that the Jews should suffer what the Germans suffered in 1918. But there were also men and women who expressed protests. Most of them said something about Bolshevism. One man—obviously a worker—watching the burning of a synagogue in Fasanenstrasse exclaimed, "Arson remains arson." The protesters, however, were quickly silenced by the wrecking crews with threats of violence.

Warned Against Looting

To some extent—at least during the day—efforts were made to prevent looting. Crowds were warned they might destroy but must not plunder, and in individual cases looters either were beaten up on the spot by uniformed Nazis or arrested. But for the most part, looting was general, particularly during the night and in the poorer quarters. And in at least one case the wreckers themselves tossed goods out to the crowd with the shout "Here are some cheap Christmas presents."

Children were observed with their mouths smeared with candy from wrecked candy shops or flaunting toys from wrecked toy shops until one elderly woman watching the spectacle exclaimed, "So that is how they teach our children to steal."

Foreign Jewish shops, it appears, were not at first marked for destruction and were passed over by the first wrecking crews. But in their destructive enthusiasm others took them on as well and even

wrecked some "Aryan" shops by mistake.

Among the foreign wrecked establishments were three American-owned shops—the Loewenstein jewelry shop in Kanonierstrasse, near the office of THE NEW YORK TIMES, the owner of which shop is now in America; the Leipzig fur snop in Rosenthalerstrasse, owned by C. G. Schultz, who is also in America, and the Rose Bach rug shop in the Hauptstrasse.

Other Places Wrecked

Also wrecked were the Warner corset shop on the Kurfuerstendamm, which is partly American-owned; a Jewish Ford dealer's on Unter den Linden, and a large, well-known department store that has considerable British capital invested in it.

The Leipzig fur shop displayed a large American flag in its window, but the manager reported that the wreckers had shouted that they did not care whether the place was American or not and went to work. This shop reported the loss of three silver fox capes and other furs; the Bach rug shop reported the loss of goods valued at 2,000 marks.

No photographing of the wreckage was permitted and Anton Celer, American tourist, of Hamden, Conn., was arrested while trying to take such pictures, although he was soon released. Members of a South American diplomatic mission likewise got into trouble on that account.

Grave doubt prevails whether insurance companies will honor their policies. Some are reported to have flatly refused to reimburse for the damage because of its extent, and, considering the standing the Jew enjoys in German courts today, there is little likelihood of his collecting by suing. But there still remains to be settled the damage done to "Aryan" houses and other property.

November 11, 1938

U. S. LEADERS JOIN IN REBUKING REICH

Hoover, Landon, Ickes and Others Accuse Germany of Crime Against Civilization

In language of a temper and intensity seldom used in times of peace by citizens of one country in speaking of another, six distinguished Americans last night joined in a nation-wide broadcast protesting against Germany's persecution of racial and religious minorities.

The speakers were a former President, Herbert Hoover; the last Republican candidate for President, Alfred M. Landon; a Cabinet member, Secretary Harold L. Ickes; a United States Senator, William H. King of Utah; the president of a leading Catholic university, the Rev. Robert I. Gannon of Fordham, and a Bishop of the Methodist Episcopal Church, Bishop Edwin H. Hughes.

All saw in the present persecution of the Jews, assaults on Catholic Cardinals, persecution of other religious leaders and suppression of all minorities, crimes not only against the victims but against civilization itself.

King for Recalling Envoy

Senator King, a leading Democrat, said he regretted that the thirty governments which recently joined to ameliorate the condition of German refugees had not then advised the Nazi government that "continuation of its persecution of the Jews would call for a severance of all diplomatic relations with it."

"And I may add," he continued, "that so far as I am concerned, I should be very glad to see our government recall our Ambassador."

The broadcast, made under the auspices of the Federal Council of Churches, opened with the Columbia male quartet singing "O God, Our Help in Ages Past."

As Secretary Ickes, the last speaker, completed his address, the quartet began the first verse of "America:"

My Country, 'tis of Thee, Sweet Land of Liberty, Of Thee I sing.

Bishop Hughes and Father Gannon opened the broadcast from the New York studios of WABC at 485 Madison Avenue. Mr. Hoover followed from San Francisco, then Senator King from Washington, Mr. Landon from Topeka and Mr. Ickes from Washington.

The former President, in his address, said he could not believe that the German people themselves approved of the path on which their leaders were taking them and that America had more than a usual right amongst nations to protest the outrage.

It was the United States, he said, which fed the starving German population after the war, it was this country that forced modification of the Versailles Peace Treaty beyond limits planned by others, it was Americans who brought German relief from reparations payments, who sent vast sums to Germany in times of financial stress, who brought about the moratorium that saved the financial structure of the republic.

"It is our hope," he said, "that those springs of tolerance and morals of human compassion which lie deep in the German people may yet rise to control of Germany. But

in the meantime our condemnation of their leaders should be without reserve. They are bringing to Germany moral isolation from the whole world."

Mr. Landon also expressed the belief that if the German peoples were free to voice their real sentiments they would not be cruel and intolerant. He also called attention to brutalities practiced elsewhere, in Russia, Italy and Spain, adding: "These inhuman actions we read of belong to another age."

Warns on Mute Acceptance

Like others of the speakers, particularly Father Gannon and Bishop Hughes, he warned against mute acceptance of such practices, saying that, although today it was the Jews and Catholics, tomorrow it might be some one else, unless the trend were stopped.

"We are properly agonizing for the Jews of Central Europe," he said in conclusion. "Tonight let us agonize for the gentiles of the world who will be in the end destroyed by their violence."

Secretary Ickes said at the beginning of his address that he came not as a Cabinet officer nor a political spokesman, "but as a Christian and as a human being" to protest against the high crimes against civilization being perpetrated in Germany.

"America," he said, "would cease

to be true to her highest and best traditions were she to stand tongue-tied at a time of such violations of the laws of humanity, such brutal, unprovoked and un-Christian acts as we are witnessing today in various parts of the world.''

Bishop Hughes went to the Bible and Father Gannon to history to find a parallel for what is happening and a portent for the future.

The Methodist Bishop recalled the story from the Scriptures of Mordecai and Haman, the latter marking Mordecai for death because he refused to allow his religious conscience to be assimilated, and building a gallows on which to hang him.

"The final result," he continued, "was recorded in the words: 'So they hanged Haman on the gallows that he had prepared for Mordecai.'

"This story remains a spiritual parable applicable to the present debacle. We all wish to believe that the German people prefer to accept the role of Esther rather than the role of Haman, and in so doing save themselves and the world from the dreadful reaction that always follows after injustice and cruelty. All good people may pray that this may be the religious outcome.''

Father Gannon said we must go back to the days of Attila the Hun, who called himself the ''scourge of God'' to find a historical counterpart for what is happening today.

And it is even worse now, he continued, because the early Huns had always been barbarians, while the National Socialists ''were born in a civilized Fatherland, a glorious Germany, rich in cultural traditions, dotted with churches whose lovely painted windows shone with German saints—this fact gives the present campaign of frightfulness a very profound significance, a significance as profound as hell.''

In conclusion, he said:

"Pagan barbarism has again raised its head. But this time it is a barbarism that has apostatized from Christianity and thus has learned to burn and loot and slay with a malice unknown to more simple savages.''

November 15, 1938

Assails Anti-Semitic Talks

BUFFALO, Oct. 10 (AP)—Dr. Norman V. Peale of New York said today that the ''most unchristian thing that has happened in this country in a long while has been the raising of the anti-Semitic issue'' by Senators Nye and Wheeler and Charles A. Lindbergh. Addressing the Genesee Conference of the Methodist Church, Dr. Peale said that ''their attack on the motion picture industry because it is largely controlled by Jewish-Americans is unwarranted on the basis of facts.''

October 11, 1941

NAZI PLAN FOR JEWS IS A PRISON STATE

Rosenberg's Bureau in Berlin Reported Mapping Isolation Territory in the East

STRICT GHETTO CODE SET

By GEORGE AXELSSON
Wireless to THE NEW YORK TIMES.

STOCKHOLM, Sweden, Feb. 8—The biggest prison the world has even seen is one of the Nazis' plans for Jews; that half of world Jewry that the Germans estimate is still under their control will be isolated in Eastern Europe and the creation of a Jewish State, more or less enclosed by barbed wire, is being contemplated, according to Berlin dispatches reaching Stockholm today.

In this State, which will be ruled by Dr. Alfred Rosenberg as part of the gubernatorial functions of his new Ministry for the German-occupied territories of the East, the Jews will be severed from any communication with the rest of the world and left entirely to live and deal with each other.

In this State, as now contemplated, it is said, a special set of laws and decrees would be introduced, intended ''strictly to prevent the spread of Jewish influence in other parts of the world.''

The Berlin dispatches say these decrees are now in the process of being drawn up in the Department of Jewish Questions of Dr. Rosenberg's Ministry. Berlin reports that the projected Nazi code will ''realize the ultimate aim of the Nazi anti-Jewish policy, namely, of ridding Europe of the last Jew.''

Nazi Intentions Declared

If eye-witnesses' testimony, available here, of conditions already applying to Jews in the Gouvernement General of Poland may be taken as an indication of this Nazi policy, the destiny in store for Jews under German control would be particularly sombre. The present German intentions, as freely admitted by leading circles in Berlin, is to the following effect:

"Jews must be cut off from the rest of the population and return to their ghettoes. Jewish quarters must be roped off and guarded by sentries. Jews must work only inside their ghettoes.''

That is already the case with the Jews of Warsaw, who are left to live or starve to death behind barbed wire enclosing the Jewish quarter there.

At every gate of this reservation stand steel-helmeted German soldiers with fixed bayonets. If a non-Jew enters this quarter of black despair, as sometimes one may do with the permission of the Germans for sight-seeing, he will be accompanied by a German who sees to it that he does not contravene a strict ban against speaking to any of the inhabitants.

The inhabitants of the ghetto obtain the same bread ration as that granted to the Poles, but deaths from starvation are said to be particularly frequent in the Warsaw ghetto.

Warsaw Left in Its Ruins

Incidentally, the Germans are reportedly making no effort to rebuild bomb-wrecked Warsaw, so that the city may never again serve as a center of Polish independence. The Nazis, instead, are concentrating their attention on Cracow, which is much closer to Reich territory.

Although the Russian Army is daily cutting more slices from the territory under the control of Dr. Rosenberg and his ministry, deportations of Jews from the Reich eastward are proceeding steadily and ''according to plan.''

Most of the larger cities in South and Southwest Germany, for instance Frankfort on the Main, may be said to have already been evacuated by their Jews.

Not all of them have gone to Litzmannstadt, which is in the center of the new Warthegau and which the Germans have designated as the new Jewish city, where some 10,000 Jews from Belgium are already at forced labor making uniforms for the German Army.

Some have been moved to Berlin, for the Nazi plan apparently is to concentrate the Jews so that they can be kept under immediate control for such measures as may be decided upon later.

February 9, 1942

RELIEF GROUP AIDS 795,000 OVERSEAS

Joint Distribution Committee Reports $5,488,000 Outlay for 1942 Work Abroad

MANY REFUGEES ASSISTED

The American Jewish Joint Distribution Committee, Inc., appropriated $7,250,000 for relief, emigration aid, educational and reconstructive assistance to 795,000 people abroad during 1942, James H. Becker, chairman of the organization's national council, declared at the twenty-eighth annual meeting yesterday in its offices, 100 East Forty-second Street.

Mr. Becker, who gave a detailed report of the committee's relief work, said that the actual cash expenditures thus far amounted to $5,488,000 and the money was spent ''mostly under United States Treasury licenses where these were necessary.'' He reported that thousands were helped to leave Europe for the Western Hemisphere and Palestine. Regardless of the disruptions of war, the committee continued and in some cases intensified its work in Western Europe, Latin America, North Africa, Palestine, Turkey, Persia and with Polish refugees in Asiatic Russia.

Mr. Becker disclosed also that the committee was able, through the use of Portuguese vessels, to rescue more than 7,700 persons from Europe.

More than 6,000 refugees fled from France to Switzerland and several thousand to Spain, calling for increased emergency aid. He reported also that the committee appropriated $25,000 to take care of 1,200 children who moved into the unoccupied zone after their parents had been deported from France.

Help in North Africa

"In North Africa, which is today a center of vital interest to all Americans, the Joint Distribution Committee has been operating principally in behalf of refugees from France to French Morocco, Algeria, Tunis and Tangier,'' Mr. Becker said.

He pointed out that the work of the committee in eighteen Central and South American republics has sped the integration of 125,000 Jewish newcomers into their newly adopted countries.

The chairman said that the committee is cooperating with the Polish Government in Exile in a non-sectarian program on behalf of 2,000,000 Polish nationals, of whom about 600,000 are Jews. ''Arising out of the problem of Polish refugees in Rusia, has been a separate refugee problem in Teheran, Persia, where more than 25,000 Polish refugees have been transferred. Among these people are some 2,800 Jews, about half of them children, at least 450 orphaned. Palestine certificates have been obtained for 800 Jewish children and the committee has pledged itself to pay the transportation costs from Teheran to Palestine."

A special appropriation of $200,000 for war relief purposes in Palestine was made at the request of the Jewish Agency and other Zionist bodies. This was over and above the grants customarily made for cultural, religious puropses and for transportation of refugees to Palestine, Mr. Becker said. He also reported that the committee has appropriated $2,000,000 with which to repay, after the war, loans which local committees in enemy and enemy-occupied countries carry on the work.

Plan Post-War Work

Paul Baerwald, honorary chairman, pointed out that as regards post-war reconstruction, the committee was already planning for the peace.

He commended the choice of former Governor Lehman as director of foreign relief and rehabilitation.

All officers of the committee, with the exception of Mr. Lehman who resigned as vice chairman of the committee when appointed to his new post, were re-elected. Mr. Lehman became associated with the Joint Distribution Committee in 1916.

Mrs. Felix Warburg and Mr. Baerwald were re-elected honorary chairmen of the committee. Lieutenant Edward M. M. Warburg was re-elected chairman. James N. Rosenberg was continued as honorary chairman of the executive committee and Mr. Becker was re-elected chairman of the national council.

The eight vice chairmen re-elected were: George Backer, David M. Bressler, Alexander Kahn, Lieut. Comdr. Harold F. Linder, Rabbi Jonah B. Wise, all of New York; William Rosenwald of Greenwich, Conn., William J. Shroder of Cincinnati, Ohio, and M. C. Sloss of San Francisco, Calif. I. Edwin Goldwasser and Alexander A. Landesco were re-elected treasurers. .

The thirteen from New York among the thirty-one members added to the board of directors were: Ralph F. Colin, Arthur Fluegelman, D. Samuel Gottesman, Mrs. Walter A. Hirsch, Stanley M. Isaacs, Joseph J. Klein, Abraham Krasne, George Z. Medalie, Max Ogust, Nathan M. Ohrbach, Jacob Potofsky, Samuel Shore and Jerome I. Udell.

The members added to the executive committee were Ralph F. Colin, Mrs. David M. Levy, Isaac H. Levy, George Z. Medalie, Dr. A. J. Rongy, I. H. Sherman, all of New York; James H. Becker of Chicago, Ill., Joel Gross of Newark, N. J., and David M. Watchmaker of Boston. Twenty-five members of the executive committee were re-elected.   December 5, 1942

580,000 Refugees Admitted To United States in Decade

Disclosure of State Department Data to Bloom's Committee Is Linked to Its Opposing Bills for Wider Action

By FREDERICK R. BARKLEY
Special to THE NEW YORK TIMES.

WASHINGTON, Dec. 10—The United States has admitted about 580,000 victims of persecution by the Hitler regime since it began ten years ago, Breckinridge Long, Assistant Secretary of State, told the House Foreign Affairs Committee on Nov. 26 in secret testimony released today by Chairman Sol Bloom.

The release of the testimony by permission of the State Department was construed as an intimation that Mr. Long's report had swung the committee into opposing two bills providing for executive creation of a commission "to effectuate the rescue of the Jewish people of Europe."

Although the transcript contained no direct opposition to the measures, it indicated Mr. Long's feeling that such legislation would hinder future American rescue efforts and also constitute a criticism of what the State Department had done quietly to this end.

Mr. Long testified that the majority of the refugees admitted were Jews, because "we have recognized from the start that the Jews were the most persecuted and the object of more antipathy than any other sections or class of the people, although they were not the only ones."

He mentioned Poles particularly as having been "hunted down and killed like rats" by the German Army, which seized Polish properties.

While other neutral or anti-Axis countries aided in rescuing victims of German oppression, he said, the chief job of meeting the problem fell on this country and Britain, which formulated the policies making possible the salvation of so many oppressed peoples.

He added, however, that Spain, Portugal and the French National Committee cooperated with the English-speaking nations to remove 30,000 French refugees from Spain, leaving only about 1,200 for transfer to temporary shelter in North Africa, which he thought had now been completed.

All refugees from German tyranny in the ten-year period were admitted to the United States under the visa and quota regulations, Mr. Long said, except for the "awful period" of persecution when visitors' visas were used.

"We did every legitimate thing we could do," he said, "and we observed the laws of the United States."

But when this country entered the war and transatlantic transport for civilians ceased, he pointed out, the effort was virtually blocked.

Six months before this country entered the war, Mr. Long contin-

ued, it was found that Germany was attempting to send secret agents here in the guise of refugees. To thwart this practice a State Department control commission was set up as a screening agency.

Stating that only about 100 of these carefully "screened" persons were now coming into the country weekly by small Spanish and Portuguese vessels, Mr. Long added: "They are persons in whom I think the United States can have entire confidence."

Operating Agencies Are Cited

Turning to the pending bills, Mr. Long said that everyone in the State Department and everyone else with whom he had come in contact had been interested or active in "endeavoring to save the Jewish people from the terrorism of the Nazis."

"There has been an agency of the American Government actually attending to these affairs for more than four years," he continued. "There is now an international agency set up at the instigation of and cooperating with the United States.

"And I think your committee will desire to consider whether any step you might take would be construed as a repudiation of the acts of the executive branch of your own Government or a reflection upon the actions of the intergovernmental body which have been associated with the American Government in its activities."

Mr. Long here referred to the Inter-governmental Committee set up at the Bermuda refugee conference, which, financed by the United States and Britain, is now functioning in London and receiving new proposals on the problem every day.

Bermuda Undertaking Disclosed

One of the proposals adopted at the Bermuda conference, believed not to have been made public before, was given by him as follows: "The executive committee of the Inter-governmental Committee is hereby empowered by the member States to undertake negotiations with neutral and Allied States and organizations to take such steps as may be necessary to preserve, maintain and transport those persons displaced from their homes by their efforts to escape from areas where their lives and liberty are in danger on account of their race, religion or political beliefs.

"The operation of the committee shall extend to all countries from which refugees come as a result of the war in Europe or in which they may find refuge. The executive committee shall be empowered to receive and disburse for the purposes enumerated above funds both public and private."

Among other efforts to rescue victims of the Nazis, Mr. Long mentioned the offer of Sweden to take in as many as it could, the acceptance by Switzerland of probably about 60,000 Jews, Italian Army men and American citizens who were living in northern Italy, as well as Jewish people from parts of France formerly under Italian occupation.

Question of Wider Open Door

At the end of his testimony Mr. Long indicated his feeling that, while it would be unwise for the committee positively to reject the pending bills, it should hold them in suspension for further study.

"The point is that the historic attitude of the United States as a haven for the oppressed has not changed," he said. "The Department of State has kept the door open.

"It has been carefully screened, but the door is open and the demands for a wider opening cannot be justified for the time being because there just is not any transportation.

"There are vacancies on the list of quotas, and any wholesome, proper person who appears and applies for permission to enter the United States can, under the law, and under the direction of the department, enter the United States."

December 11, 1943

U. S. Board Bares Atrocity Details Told by Witnesses at Polish Camps

By JOHN H. CRIDER

Special to THE NEW YORK TIMES.

WASHINGTON, Nov. 25 — In the first detailed report by a United States Government Agency offering eyewitness proof of mass murder by the Germans, the War Refugee Board made public today accounts by three persons of organized atrocities at Birkenau and Oswiecim [Auschwitz] in southwestern Poland that transcend the horrors of Lublin. The accounts were vouched for by the WRB.

While at Lublin 1,500,000 persons were said to have been killed in three years, 1,500,000 to 1,765,000 persons were murdered in the torture chambers of Birkenau from April, 1942, to April, 1944, according to these Government-verified reports. Many thousands of other deaths by phenol injection, brutal beatings, starvation, shooting, etc., also are recounted.

"It is a fact beyond denial that the Germans have deliberately and systematically murdered millions of innocent civilians—Jews and Christians alike—all over Europe," the WRB declared.

"This campaign of terror and brutality, which is unprecedented in all history and which even now continues unabated, is part of the German plan to subjugate the free peoples of the world," it added.

"So revolting and diabolical are the German atrocities that the minds of civilized people find it difficult to believe that they have actually taken place," the board stated. "But the Governments of the United States and of other countries have evidence which clearly substantiates the facts."

After describing the nature of the reports now made public, the WRB added:

"The board has every reason to believe that these reports present a true picture of the frightful happenings in these camps. It is making the reports public in the firm conviction that they should be read and understood by all Americans."

Nationality Basis Cited

Simultaneously with Government publication of the narrative from two young Slovak Jews, who escaped last April 7—the only Jews to have escaped from Birkenau—and a non-Jewish Polish major—the only survivor of sixty Poles moved to Birkenau from Lublin—Peter H. Bergson, chairman of the Hebrew Committee for National Liberation, announced at a news conference that the United Nations War Crimes Commission had "refused to take into consideration any acts committed against persons other than nationals of the United Nations."

German atrocities against Jews and others of nationalities included in the German sphere of influence have not been recognized by the commission, Mr. Bergson said.

He added that his committee was recommending the following action to the United Nations concerned:

"1. That they issue a joint declaration proclaiming that crimes committed against Hebrews in Europe, irrespective of the territory on which the crime was committed or the citizenship or lack of citizenship of the victim at the time of death, be considered as a war crime and punished as such.

"2. That the Governments of the United Nations concerned instruct their representatives on the War Crimes Commission to see to it that the above-mentioned declaration is put into effect.

"3. That representatives of the Hebrew people be given membership on the War Crimes Commission and that temporarily, until such time as a Hebrew national sovereignty be re-established, the Hebrew Committee of National Liberation be authorized to constitute the Hebrew representation on the War Crimes Commission."

The two Slovak youths cited in the WRB reports estimated the number of Jews gassed and burned at Birkenau in the two-year period at 1,765,000 in the following table, but the Polish officer estimated that about 1,500,000 Jews were killed in Oswiecim in that fashion. Here is the recapitulation by the two escaped Jews (countries of origin in parentheses):

Poland (transported by truck)	300,000
Poland (transported by train)	600,000
Holland	100,000
Greece	45,000
France	150,000
Belgium	50,000
Germany	60,000
Yugoslavia, Italy and Norway	50,000
Lithuania	50,000
Bohemia, Moravia & Austria	30,000
Slovakia	30,000
Camps for foreign Jews in Poland	300,000
Total	1,765,000

2,000 Bodies a Day

In the report the Jewish youths described the gassing and burning technique as follows:

"At present there are four crematoria in operation at Birkenau, two large ones, I and II, and two smaller ones, III and IV. Those of Type I and II consist of three parts, i.e., (a) the furnace room, (b) the large hall, and (c) the gas chamber. A huge chimney rises from the furnace room, around which are grouped nine furnaces, each having four openings. Each opening can take three normal corpses at once, and after an hour and a half the bodies are completely burned. This corresponds to a daily capacity of about 2,000 bodies.

"Next to this is a large 'reception hall,' which is arranged so as to give the impression of the antechamber of a bathing establishment. It holds 2,000 people, and apparently there is a similar waiting room on the floor below. From there a door and a few steps lead down into the very long and narrow gas chamber. The walls of this chamber are also camouflaged with simulated entries to shower rooms in order to mislead the victims. The roof is fitted with three traps which can be hermetically closed from the outside. A track leads from the gas chamber toward the furnace room.

"The gassing takes place as follows: The unfortunate victims are brought into the hall (b), where they are told to undress. To complete the fiction that they are going to bathe, each person receives a towel and a small piece of soap issued by two men clad in white coats. Then they are crowded into the gas chamber (c) in such numbers that there is, of course, only standing room.

"To compress this crowd into the narrow space, shots are often fired to induce those already at the far end to huddle still closer together. When everybody is inside, the heavy doors are closed. Then there is a short pause, presumably to allow the room temperature to rise to a certain level, after which SS men with gas masks climb the roof, open the traps, and shake down a preparation in powder form out of tin cans labeled 'Cyklon,' for use against vermin, which is manufactured by a Hamburg concern.

Ordeal Lasts Three Minutes

"It is presumed that this is a 'cyanide' mixture of some sort which turns into gas at a certain temperature. After three minutes everyone in the chamber is dead. No one is known to have survived this ordeal, although it was not uncommon to discover signs of life after the primitive measures employed in the birch wood.

"The chamber is then opened, aired, and the 'special squad' carts the bodies on flat trucks to the furnace rooms, where the burning takes place. Crematoria III and IV work on nearly the same principle, but their capacity is only half as large. Thus the total capacity of the four cremating and gassing plants at Birkenau amounts to about 6,000 daily."

In his independent report the Polish officer described the mass extermination thus:

"The first large convoys arrived from France and Slovakia. Physically able men and women—those without children or the mothers of grown-up children—were sent to the camp of Birkenau. The remainder, i. e., old or weak men, women with small children and all those unfit for labor, were taken to the Birch Wood (Brzezinki) and killed by means of hydrocyanic gas. For this purpose special gassing barracks had been built there.

"These consisted of large halls, airtight, and provided with ventilators which could be opened or closed according to the need. Inside they were equipped so as to create the impression of bathing establishments. This was done to deceive the victims and make them more manageable. The executions took place as follows: Each death convoy consisted of some eight to ten trucks packed with the 'selectees'; the convoy was unguarded, as the whole frightful drama took place on camp territory."

Taken to Gas Chambers

Then the victims were taken to the gas chambers, according to the report, which continued:

"Everything was hermetically closed, and specially trained SS units threw hydrocyanic bombs through the ventilation openings. After about ten minutes the doors were opened and a special squad composed exclusively of Jews had to clear away the bodies and prepare for a new group of 'selectees.'

"The crematoria had not yet been constructed, although there was a small one at Auschwitz which, however, was not employed for burning these bodies. Mass graves were dug at that time into which the corpses were simply thrown.

"This continued into the autumn of 1942. By this time extermination by gas was being intensified and there was no more time even for such summary burial. Row upon row of bodies of murdered Jews, covered only by a thin layer of earth, were widely dispersed in the surrounding fields, causing the soil to become almost marshy through the putrification of the bodies.

"The smell emanating from these fields became intolerable. In the autumn of 1942 all that remained of the bodies had to be exhumed and the bones collected and burned in the crematoria (by that time four had been completed). An alternative was to gather the remains of the unfortunate victims into heaps, pour gasoline over them, and leave it to the flames to finish the tragedy. The immense quantity of human ashes thus collected was carted away in every direction to be scattered over the fields where these martyrs had found their last rest."

In addition to mass asphyxiations, the Germans resorted to executions, phenol injections and brutality to dispose of victims. Here is one eyewitness account of brutality recorded by the Polish major:

"One day a working comrade discovered a few pieces of turnip, which he carefully hid. He continued his work but, from time to time, took surreptitious bites off his treasure. Another prisoner having 'squealed' on him, the capo arrived a few minutes later.

"It must be remembered that the capo is absolute master of his commando and that everybody tries to get into his good graces. Unfortunately, this favor often had to be attained to the detriment of the well-being or sometimes even of the lives of other prisoners.

"The capo proceeded to search our comrade and, finding the pieces of turnip, knocked the weakened man to the ground, hitting him brutally about the head and face and in the stomach. He then ordered him to sit up, hands outstretched in front of him on the ground with a weight of bricks on each hand; the pieces of turnip were stuck in his mouth.

"All the men were then assembled and informed that the unfortunate man was to stay in this position for a whole hour. We were warned that this punishment would befall any member of the commando who committed a similar 'offense.' The condemned man underwent this ordeal guarded by one of the foremen, very eager to fulfill his task to the satisfaction of the capo, so that he hit our friend every time he tried to shift his position slightly.

"After fifteen to twenty minutes the man became unconscious, but a bucket of water was poured over him and he was again forced into his original position. After he had slumped over, senseless, for a second time, his body was thrown aside and nobody was allowed to pay further attention to him. After roll call that evening he was taken to the 'infirmary,' where he died two days later."

The use of the hypodermic needle for murder was described by the Polish major as follows:

"The sick were classified into two groups, 'Aryans' and Jews. These groups were again subdivided into further groups, of which

the first included the sick, who were to remain in hospital, being considered 'curable.' The second consisted of extremely rundown patients, chronic cases, and the half-starving or mutilated whose recovery could only be effected by a long stay in the hospital.

"This group was practically condemned to death by phenol injections in the heart region. Racial considerations played an important role. An 'Aryan' really had to be seriously ill to be condemned to death by injection, whereas 80 to 90 per cent of the Jews 'hospitalized' there were 'eliminated'

in this manner. Many of them knew about this method and applied for admission as so-called 'suicide candidates,' not having the courage to throw themselves on the high tension wires."

The accounts of the Slovaks and the Polish major mentioned a special "hygiene institute" at Oswiecim, which was adjacent to Birkenau, and where mysterious "experiments" were conducted on Jewish prisoners, mostly on females. The Polish major's account, which provided the only clue of what went on in the "institute," said:

"Here sterilizing by X-ray treatment, artificial insemination of women, as well as experiments on blood transfusions, were carried on."

The reports mentioned several well-known individuals, such as Witold Zacharewicz, Polish actor, and a brother of Léon Blum, former French Premier, as having been executed.

"Prominent guests from Berlin were present at the inauguration of the first crematorium in March, 1943," the reports said.

November 26, 1944

No Room In the Inn

WHILE SIX MILLION DIED. A Chronicle of American Apathy. By Arthur D. Morse. 420 pp. New York: Random House. $6.95.

By E. W. KENWORTHY

IN early January, 1944, Randolph Paul, a staid tax lawyer who was then the Treasury Department's general counsel, handed to Secretary Henry Morgenthau Jr. an 18-page document entitled "Report to the Secretary on the Acquiescence of This Government in the Murder of the Jews."

The report, the substance of which is published for the first time by Arthur D. Morse in his history, "While Six Million Died," narrated in detail eight months of inaction and outright opposition by the State Department on a proposal to license the remittance to Switzerland of some $600,000 for the rescue and support of Jews still remaining in Rumania and occupied France. The money was to be reimbursed by wealthy Rumanian Jews who had escaped.

The report, prepared by Josiah E. DuBois Jr., Paul's assistant, and John Pehle, head of the Treasury's Foreign Funds Control Division, had been ordered by Secretary Morgenthau for a meeting with President Roosevelt on January 16. Its conclusion stated: "[State Department officials] have not only failed to use the Government machinery at their disposal to rescue Jews from Hitler, but have even gone so far as to use this Governmental machinery to prevent the rescue of these Jews.

"They have not only failed to cooperate with private organizations in the efforts of these organizations to

Danzig, 1939: Banner outside a synagogue which reads: "Come lovely May and release us from the Jews."

work out individual programs of their own, but have taken steps designed to prevent these programs from being put into effect. . . .

"While the State Department has been thus 'exploring' the whole refugee problem, without distinguishing between those who are in imminent danger of death and those who are not, hundreds of thousands of Jews have been allowed to perish."

Mr. Morgenthau changed the title to "Personal Report to the President," and tempered the language slightly. But the report which the President read in his presence on January 16 still said: ". . . there is a growing number of responsible people and organizations today who have ceased to view our failure as the product of simple incompetence on the part of those officials in the State Depart-

ment charged with handling this problem. They see plain anti-Semitism motivating the actions of these State Department officials and, rightly or wrongly, it will require little more in the way of proof for this suspicion to explode into a nasty scandal. . . . The matter of rescuing the Jews from extermination is a trust too great to remain in the hands of men who are indifferent, callous and perhaps even hostile."

President Roosevelt, who had repeatedly expressed his horror at the wholesale murder of Europe's Jews by the Hitler government and its satellites but who had also given repeated instructions to officials dealing with refugee matters that it was not "desirable or

practicable to recommend any change in the quota provisions of our immigration laws," saw the looming political danger pointed out by Morgenthau. Six days later he created the War Refugee Board under Pehle.

It was late in the day, yet the Board, by zeal and imagination, succeeded in saving thousands of Jews and others from the gas chambers, and there is good reason to believe Ira A. Hirschmann, the Board's representative in Turkey, that "individual thousands of refugees could have been saved" had the Board been created a year or two earlier.

Mr. Morse, who resigned from his position as executive producer of CBS Reports to

MR. KENWORTHY covers the State Department for The Washington Bureau of The Times.

write this book, has provided a documentation of Secretary Morgenthau's charges—a documentation provided from the Government's archives, much of which has not been previously disclosed. And on the whole, the record he sets down supports his own conclusion: "One might describe the American response to Nazi racism as an almost coordinated series of inactions . . . it was one thing to avoid interference in Germany's domestic policies, quite another to deny asylum to its victims."

Mr. Morse subtitles his book "A Chronicle of American Apathy." Yet one wonders whether the apathy would have been so great had the public been privy to the attitude of State Department officials revealed in cables and memos dug up by Mr. Morse.

Item: In August, 1942, Gerhart Riegner, Geneva representative of the World Jewish Congress, sent a cable through the United States consulate in Geneva to Rabbi Stephen S. Wise, head of the American Jewish Congress, stating that he had learned from a trusted informant, a leading German industrialist, that Hitler had many months before ordered the "total solution" of the Jewish question in Europe by the extinction of all Jews. A covering memo to the State Department from Vice Consul Howard Elting Jr. endorsed Riegner as "a serious and balanced individual."

In the Department's Division of European Affairs, Elbridge Durbrow recommended that the cable not be forwarded to Rabbi Wise "in view of the . . . fantastic nature of the allegations and the impossibility of our being of any assistance if such action [by Hitler] were taken." (Rabbi Wise later got the same information from Riegner through British diplomatic channels.)

Item: On February 10, 1943, the State Department sent an order to the Bern legation or-

---

THE holocaust has ended. The six million lie in nameless graves. But what of the future? Is genocide now unthinkable, or are potential victims somewhere in the world going about their business, devoted to their children, aspiring to a better life, unaware of a gathering threat?—"While Six Million Died."

---

dering the minister not to accept any more reports for "transmission to private persons." Thus did the Department close its channels to Riegner's intelligence, from which it might have learned much.

Item: An undated memo of the Division of European Affairs on the origins of the Evian Conference of July, 1938, which created the ineffective Intergovernmental Committee on Refugees, stated that Secretary of State Cordell Hull and other officials had decided the conference was necessary, in view of the public outcry against Nazi atrocities, if the Department was to "get out in front and attempt to guide the pressure, primarily with a view toward forestalling attempts to have the immigration laws liberalized."

Item: On April 19, 1943—again largely in response to public pressure—the Anglo-American Conference on Refugees opened in Bermuda. The next day Assistant Secretary of State Breckinridge Long recorded in his diary: "One danger in it all is that their activities [the telegrams to the President by Jewish and other groups] may lend color to the charges of Hitler that we are fighting this war on account of, and at the instigation and direction of, our Jewish citizens. In Turkey . . . and in Spain . . . and in Palestine's hinterland and in North Africa the Moslem population will be easy believers in such charges. It might easily be a definite detriment to our war effort."

It is a serious question whether the United States could have saved large numbers of Jews from Hitler's ovens and firing squads, and Mr. Morse does not make due allowance for all the practical difficulties. But the burden of his indictment of the President and the State Department is that almost no effort was made until 1944, and that most proposals were met with indifference or, even worse, active opposition.

Nowhere was this opposition so open and forceful as in the refusal to enlarge immigration quotas or to provide for the transfer to Germany and its satellites of unused quotas of other countries. And even the quotas of Germany and the occupied countries were not fully used because of the severity with which consulates—on State Department orders—administered the laws. From 1933 until 1943, there were altogether 1,244,858 unfilled places, and of these 341,-567 were allotted to citizens of countries dominated or occupied by Germany.

In her "This I Remember," Mrs. Roosevelt, who urged her husband to relax the quota system, wrote: "While I often felt strongly on various subjects, Franklin frequently refrained from supporting causes in which he believed, because of political realities."

There were political realities—the campaigns of the American Legion, the Veterans of Foreign Wars, much of organized labor, and various "patriotic societies"—against admitting Jews outside quota limits, and it is true that politics is the art of the possible. Nevertheless a strong and determined leader can do much to expand the possible and make it acceptable. This Roosevelt failed to do, and it is a grievous mark against him. Indeed, altogether this is a grievous book that should rend the heart and smite the conscience of a nation that began as a refuge for the despairing, the homeless and the persecuted.

March 3, 1968

EXISTENCE OF JEWS HELD ENDANGERED

Entrance Into Power Politics Is Deplored by Professor Baron in Temple Emanu-El

The existence of the Jewish people has been endangered by their recent entrance into the realm of power politics, Dr. Salo W. Baron, Miller Professor of Jewish History, Literature and Institutions at Columbia University, declared yesterday in a lecture in Temple Emanu-El, Fifth Avenue and Sixty-fifth Street.

The Jews have survived as a people up to now, Professor Baron said, because "the inner forces of their culture, life and religion enabled them to adjust to the changing forces acting upon them," rather than because of political struggle.

Calling on the Jews to remember that their heritage was cultural and religious, not political, Professor Baron declared that, although "our present-day scene is filled with political strife, with the problems of Palestine, of Jewish rights in this country, of anti-Semitism," they have through experience developed a nonpolitical attitude toward life.

"In the past," he said, "the great evolution of the Jewish spirit was possible only because, in the sense of international politics, Palestine was in a period of pause in which several great powers of the Near East—Egypt, Babylonia and Assyria—were absent from the scene.

"Judaism has from the earliest times developed a certain enlightened self-interest in the brotherhood of people. Ambition for power was not in the intrinsic life and spirit of the people or in their interest. In the basic factors of Jewish culture, religion and intellectual life, lies the source of reconciliation. It is in these things rather than in politics that life is decided beyond the present generation.

"The forces of religion have surrendered to the forces of nationalism. But the world is now determined by regionalism, not by nationalism. There is very little danger that religion will again forget itself as it did in the era of nationalism. For a religion to nationalize itself we must have a local culture. Regional cooperation, however, is strictly in the political and economic realm.

"Judaism now has its great chance. We are politically weak but spiritually strong. Despite all frustrations we cling to our perenial hope that now at last, when facing the alternative of recklessly smashing all that it had built up for countless generations, mankind will listen to the message of Israel's ancient prophets and build a new world, not on the shifting sands of temporary imperial advantage but upon the secure foundations of religious ethics and human understanding."

December 24, 1945

ALL ZIONISTS HERE HAIL JEWISH STATE

Formal Song and Prayer Rise While Plain Folk Meet and Congratulate One Another

Leaders and the rank and file of various Zionist groups hailed yesterday the proclamation of a new Jewish state in Palestine.

Throughout the day there were spontaneous and joyous demonstrations, not only in various Zionist offices but in a majority of Jewish neighborhoods in the five boroughs.

Late in the afternoon Mayor O'Dwyer, in a cablegram to David Ben-Gurion, addressed as "Premier Designate of Israel, Tel Aviv, Israel," said: "I congratulate the new free Government of Israel. May a bright future reward you for the long fight of the past."

Fourteen-year-old Chaim Shertok, son of Moshe Shertok, the newly designated Foreign Minister of the Jewish state, standing beside his mother, Mrs. Zipporah Shertok, unfurled the American and the Zionist flags from the window of the fourth-floor offices of his father, who recently returned to Tel Aviv.

Sons of Their Fathers

The youngster, wearing a white sweater and an emblem signifying his membership in a youth movement in Palestine, grinned broadly. "Every Jewish boy," he said, "is anxious to build the Jewish state and defend it." And as both flags flapped in the gentle winds, Hayim Greenberg, a member of the American section of the Jewish Agency for Palestine, recited a short prayer.

"Blessed art Thou, O Lord, King of the Universe, that Thou hast maintained and preserved us to witness this day," was the English translation.

A moment later, a group of young men and women linked arms in the street, formed a ring, and then danced the hora, a Palestinian folk dance, singing as they whirled. Indoors and outdoors, the "Hatikvah," the Zionist anthem, was sung. The five floors of the Agency's offices swarmed with leading Zionists and employes who joyously greeted each other.

Mrs. Shertok said her daughter, Yael, 17, recently left for Palestine to undergo training in the Haganah. Her son, Yakob, 21, is also a member of the Haganah.

At the offices of the Zionist Organization of America, 41 East Forty-second Street, cups of wine were lifted in a toast to the new state, and Dr. Emanuel Neumann, president of the Z. O. A., expressed the hope that "the heavy burdens assumed by the provisional government of the Republic of Israel will be lightened by its prompt recognition by the Government of the United States."

Looks to Colonization

While the staff of the Z. O. A. danced and sung in the offices, impromptu speeches were delivered by Jacques Torczyner, a member of the organization's administrative council, and Daniel Frisch, vice president of the Z. O. A.

HAILING FORMATION OF THE NEW JEWISH STATE

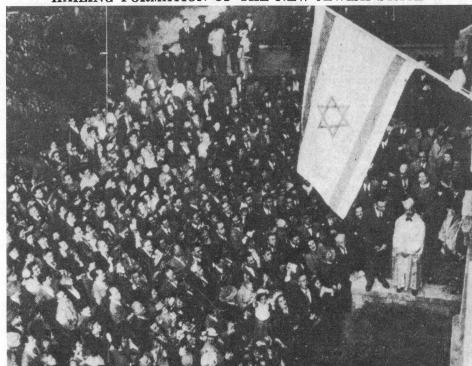

At flag-raising ceremony outside Washington office of Jewish Agency for Palestine yesterday

Celebrants dancing in the street after the flag was unfurled

The New York Times (by Tames)

Dr. Israel Goldstein, national chairman of the United Palestine Appeal, with offices in the same building, said the new government in Palestine "presents American Jews with an unprecedented opportunity to further Jewish immigration and colonization in Palestine."

Dr. Chaim Weizmann, Zionist leader, in a message to Mr. Ben-Gurion, expressed confidence "that all who have and will become citizens of the Jewish state will strive their utmost to live up to the new opportunity which history has bestowed upon them."

Dr. Stephen S. Wise, president of the American Jewish Congress, asserted that "the call for a Jewish commonwealth in Palestine came from a united American Jewry speaking through the American Jewish Congress at its first session in 1918; thirty years later that hope has been fulfilled, and the Jewish state is now in being."

While other leaders such as Henry Morgenthau Jr., general chairman of the $250,000,000 United Jewish Appeal, and officers of Hadassah, the Women's Zionist Organization of America, Meir Gross, chairman of the World Executive of the Zionist-Revisionist Organization, greeted the new state, the City Council vice chairman, Joseph T. Sharkey, announced that he will introduce a resolution at the Council meeting Tuesday embodying the city's official greeting to the new nation.

May 15, 1948

END TO ARGUMENT ON ZIONISM URGED

By WILLIAM M. BLAIR
Special to THE NEW YORK TIMES.

KANSAS CITY, Mo., June 22—A plea for the end of the political controversy over Zionism among Jews was made tonight by Dr. Abraham J. Feldman of Hartford, Conn., president of the Central Conference of American Rabbis, at the opening of the annual convention of the group.

"After all, the government of the state of Israel is not your government or mine," he said in calling for a halt to the half-century of debate in the presence of the fait accompli.

"The democracy of Israel will forge its own political destiny. We shall help them where and when we can, and rightly so.

"But the political controversy among us here should now be adjourned. We have been, we are, we shall remain Americans. As Americans, we shall continue to give our beloved United States the same full measure of devotion we have ever given it."

He said, "We must now proceed to enlarge our tent, to lengthen our cords and strengthen our stakes. We must multiply our synagogues and inhabit them, enlarge our educational endeavors, enrich the cultural life of the Jewish communities in this land, deepen our faith, Judaize our homes, remove idolatries of materialism and secularism from our midst."

The delegates were welcomed by Mayor William E. Kemp, Dr. Samuel S. Mayerberg, Rabbi of the Congregation B'nai Jehudah of Kansas City, and J. A. Altshuter, president of the congregation.

Dr. Feldman suggested the establishment of interdenominational councils of religious education for children under the auspices of the individual faiths in light of the Supreme Court decision on release-time religious instruction in public schools.

In approving the high court ruling which held the release-time instruction unconstitutional, he urged religious forces to "view the decision as a mighty challenge to proceed to constructive, affirmative and enlightened action in behalf of a more intensive, religious educational program, on weekdays, within the churches and communities, apart from the public schools."

Dr. Feldman deplored what he described as "an ominous restlessness both among Rabbis and congregational leaders" which he had found during the last year as conference president.

"I am alarmed by the tensions caused by misunderstandings, the mistakes of judgment and the errors in practice amongst colleagues and congregations, and by the strain of economic factors in the relationships between Rabbis and people."

His recommendations to meet this situation included greater use of the conference's committee on arbitration and adoption of a countrywide system by which congregations guarantee rabbinical tenure after a specified number of years.

June 23, 1948

ZIONIST GROUPINGS ARE ACTIVE IN U. S.

By IRA FREEMAN

With the fulcrum of Zionism shifted dramatically to the new state of Israel, the power arm of the international movement to settle the Jews in Palestine now definitely is in the United States.

The 5,000,000 American Jews constitute the greatest concentration of population and wealth of their co-religionists in the world today. In Eastern Europe, formerly the area of densest population, the Jews were reduced from 9,000,000 to about 3,500,000 by Nazi and Fascist extermination and incidental war deaths between 1933 and 1945.

Not all Jews in the United States are Zionists. Of the 5,000,-000, Zionists like to estimate that four-fifths are "sympathetic" to their cause, a guess that anti-Zionists strenuously contradict. In any case, only a little more than 1,000,000 Jews in America bought "shekels" (ballots) to vote in the election of delegates to the last World Zionist Congress in 1946.

The aggregate claimed membership of the eight Zionist parties in the United States is under 700,000. Each of the political parties here is an American, or American-Canadian, or, in a few cases, a Western Hemisphere affiliate of an international Zionist party. Invariably, the national headquarters of each American party is in New York, which has the largest Jewish population of any city in the world as well as the lion's share of wealth and influence possessed by Jews.

Principal Zionist Groupings

The principal Zionist groupings throughout the world now are: General Zionists, middle-class, centrist elements; Labor Zionists, divided into a dominant right-wing called Mapai and a recently organized left coalition called Mapam; orthodox religious Zionists, of which the Mizrachi is the leading party, and the Revisionists, militantly rightist, nationalist party.

While they all agree on the establishment of an independent state in Palestine, they disagree widely on what kind of state and what its policies shall be.

Comparison of the relative size of the major party groups in Israel, in the United States and on a world-wide basis shows significant differences. Based on delegations elected to the twenty-second World Zionist Congress in Basle, Switzerland, in 1946, the international parties compared as follows in percentage of delegates:

General Zionists	33
Mapai	26
Mizrachi	15
Mapam	14
Revisionists	11
All other parties together	1

At the same Congress, the major Palestine parties lined up thus in percentage:

Mapai	35
Mapam	25
Mizrachi	13
Revisionists	13
General Zionists	11

The American parties were represented this way in percentage:

General Zionists	57
Labor Zionists (both wings)	24
Mizrachi	14
Revisionists	5

From the above tables it will be seen that while the Labor Zionists control the Israeli Government, they are a minority in the United States. Conversely, the General Zionists are one of the smaller parties in Israel but the giant of American Zionism.

Money Provided from U. S.

European Zionists provide the manpower and American Jews provide the money for Israel. The displaced and needy Jews of Europe make up the vital immigration to Israel, giving to the new state its predominantly labor and moderate-Socialist character. On the other hand, American Zionists do not emigrate in any number, but supply many millions of dollars and considerable technical skills to prepare and settle the land.

There are eight Zionist parties in the United States today. The General Zionists are represented by the Zionist Organization of America and Hadassah, the women's association; Mapai is represented by the Labor Zionist Organization of America; Mapam by a coalition now being formed by the United Labor Zionist party with the Progressive Zionist League and Hashomer Hatzair. Here also are affiliates of the Zionists-Revisionists and the Mizrachi Organization.

The Zionist Organization of America is the big wheel in American Zionism. As old as the Zionist movement itself, fifty-one years, it now claims 250,000 members in 800 local branches throughout the United States.

In its commodious national offices at 41 East Forty-second Street, a large staff is employed, with experienced experts heading the various departments. Among its leaders have been such prominent Jews as Rabbi Abba Hillel Silver, chairman of the American Zionist Emergency Council, the representative body of all Zionist parties in the United States; Dr. Emanuel Neumann, international lawyer now president of the organization; Rabbi Stephen S. Wise, first secretary of the original Federation of American Zionists, and the late Supreme Court Justice Louis D. Brandeis.

According to Dr. Samuel Margoshes, Jewish journalist and public information chairman, the main activities of the organization are fund-raising for Palestine, promoting Israel's cause with the United States Government and public, encouraging private investments in Palestine and cultivation of Jewish culture in America.

Like all other Zionist organizations, the Zionist Organization of America combats assimilation lest American Jews lose their identity and thus their enthusiasm for Israel. The organization currently spends $25,000,000 a year in maintaining Jewish culture within the United States.

Hadassah, the General Zionist women's organization, is thirty-seven years old and has 270,000 members in the United States. It is a unique Zionist party in that while it has a political function in the diaspora, as the Jews call their dispersion throughout the world, in Palestine it is a non-political, welfare agency. From national offices at 1819 Broadway, the Hadassah raises more than $9,000,000 a year separately, apart from the United Palestine Appeal, for its fifty-two child centers, hospitals and other projects in Palestine.

The Labor Zionist Organization of America-Poale Zion claims 65,000 members among trade unionists and liberal Jewish elements. Organized in 1905, it is the American affiliate of Mapai, largest party in Israel, of which Prime Minister David Ben-Gurion is leader. Baruch Zuckerman, veteran Jewish writer and president of the party, says it helps "assure the labor and cooperative character of the Jewish state by supporting the Jewish worker-pioneers who are its foundation."

It has established in Palestine three colonies of American pioneers, trained at "hechalutz" youth farms at Cream Ridge, N. J., and Colton, Calif. It is a major support, also, of the National Committee for Labor Israel, which has offices in the same building at 45 East Seventeenth Street, and the chairman of which, Joseph Schlossberg a retired officer of the Amalgamated Clothing Workers, is an important member of the Labor Zionist Organization.

The National Committee for Labor Israel raised $4,600,000 in its last campaign for Histadrut, the labor federation and huge combine of producer and consumer cooperatives that dominates economic life in Palestine. David Dubinsky, president of the International Ladies Garment Workers Union, while not a member of the Labor Zionist Organization, is a heavy supporter of the Histadrut fund.

The Mizrachi Organization of America claims 70,000 members among orthodox religious Jews of the middle class. Most of its adult members are foreign-born and Yiddish-speaking. It has, however, an active youth movement, and has dispatched fifty young pioneers to Palestine from its training camp at Cranbury, N. J. It is conservative in politics, often voting with the Zionist Organization of America.

Mizrachi (meaning "spiritual center") raises funds for its thirty-six religious colonies and middle-class cooperatives in Palestine, some of which, because of exposed positions, have had bloody fights with Arab soldiers. Formed here in 1912 as a protest against separation of religious from secular functions of world Zionists, Mizrachi demands official recognition of orthodox Judaism by the Israeli Government.

Mapam Small in U. S.

Mapam, the left Socialist coalition and second largest party in Israel, is small in the United States and so new that its amalgamation is not yet complete. The groups to be merged into an American Mapam are the United Labor Zionist Party, the Progressive Zionist League and the Hashomer-Hatzair, with a total claimed membership of 10,000.

Paul Goldman, general secretary, runs affairs of the United Labor Zionist party from his law office at 305 Broadway. He claims 3,000 members among trade unionists and small shopkeepers. His group, least radical in the coalition, advocates strict neutrality in the "cold war" and demands Yiddish instead of Hebrew be the dominant language in Israel.

Both the Progressive Zionist League and Hashomer Hatzair, which have their own offices at 305 Broadway, are Marxist and oriented toward the Soviet Union, but are not Communist. The former consists of 2,000 intellectuals and white-collar workers of small means who favor a Socialist, bi-national state with the Arabs in Palestine, according to Jack Warga, member of the national executive committee.

The Hashomer Hatzair, organized in 1923, consists of 5,000 boys and girls from 12 years old to their early twenties who hope to emigrate to Israel as pioneers. Six hundred have gone already to five colonies there after having trained in groups of forty at a youth farm in Hightstown, N. J.

The Zionists-Revisionists, just moved into new offices at 675 Eighth Avenue, claim 12,000 members among middle class, youth and professional elements, according to Mordecai Katz, member of the West Hemisphere headquarters executive. He denied that the party, formed fifteen years ago on the policies of the late Vladimir Jabotinsky, was "Fascist" or "reactionary," as its enemies from the ranks of labor, including Mr. Ben-Gurion, have charged. On the contrary, the party is "liberal" and "democratic," although vigorously anti-Socialist, Mr. Katz insisted.

The principal activity of the party is propaganda for all of Palestine, including Trans-Jordan, to be given to the Jews, and for a large-scale exchange of minorities between Israel and the Arab neighboring states.

Negotiations for reabsorbing the Freedom party, which Menahem Begin, Irgun Zvai Leumi leader, split off from the Revisionists this year, were progressing hopefully, Mr. Katz said. The Freedom party, entered in the Israel elections, has no Zionist counterpart here. It is supported with funds and expert propaganda by the American League for a Free Palestine, which claims 400,000 Jewish and non-Jewish contributors, including many prominent public figures.

December 27, 1948

JUDAISM COUNCIL REBUKES ZIONISTS

By IRVING SPIEGEL

Special to THE NEW YORK TIMES.

CHICAGO, April 15—The American Council for Judaism unanimously condemned today the "frequent utilization of Israeli officials by institutions or organizations of Americans of Jewish faith as a means of mobilizing American Jews into a bloc with political or economic responsibilities" to Israel.

As the council, which is strongly opposed to Zionism, ended its seventh annual conference, the delegates adopted resolutions that denounced the policies of the Zionist movement in the United States. The three-day meeting had been devoted to round-table discussions and addresses concerned with Zionism, "Jewish nationalism" and fund-raising in this country.

The delegates unanimously re-elected Lessing J. Rosenwald of Jenkintown, Pa., retired chairman of Sears, Roebuck & Co., as council president. Henry A. Loeb of New York was elected treasurer, and Morris Wolf of Philadelphia was named secretary.

In denouncing the appearance of Israeli officials in the United States to influence the political and economic responsibilities of American Jews toward Israel, the delegates declared:

"We reject the propaganda employed by such Israeli spokesmen and by some Americans that American Jews must accept such responsibilities because of a common destiny with the State of Israel. This is an unwarranted and unauthorized invasion of the integrity of the citizenship of Americans of Jewish faith."

In one strongly worded resolution, the delegates asserted that the "most insidious aspect of Jewish nationalism is its efforts to create in our youth a separation and a 'volition to go to Israel' and to view Israel as their 'homeland.'"

Still further, the conference maintained that "the amount of Jewish nationalist history and doctrine in religious school textbooks is alarming." The resolution added:

"We call upon the Union of American Hebrew Congregations and all rabbinical and lay leaders to recognize these facts and to review the content of textbooks and to take the leadership in re-establishing religious school teaching in our synagogues worthy of the traditions of our faith.

"We particularly call upon the parents of children attending religious schools to recognize their responsibility to determine the orientation and teaching methods of the religious schools attended by their children. The concerted action of parents will quickly cure this evil."

Samuel G. Smilow of Minneapolis, chairman of the resolutions committee, called attention to the forthcoming flotation of the Israeli bond issue of $500,000,000 and denounced the bond campaign's "predominant theme" that "Americans of Jewish faith have a unique responsibility to buy these bonds of a foreign government." He asserted that "there is no such unique obligation upon Americans of Jewish faith."

Miss Bella Meiksin, who is associated with the Jewish Labor Committee and formerly did work for the International Rescue Committee, addressing the luncheon session, pleaded for liberalized immigrant legislation to extend the admission of displaced persons for at least six months longer.

Miss Meiksin, who for four years worked on D. P. resettlement and rehabilitation in Germany, asserted that "hundreds of thousands of displaced persons were still waiting for resettlement in the free countries of the world."

April 16, 1951

RABBI CITES TASK FOR JEWS IN U. S.

By IRVING SPIEGEL

Special to THE NEW YORK TIMES.

NEW LONDON, Conn., June 24—Rabbi Philip S. Bernstein, who was re-elected president of the Central Conference of American Rabbis here today, asserted that the liquidation of the problems of displaced persons in Europe and the establishment of Israel as a nation had "produced a turning point in Jewish history."

As a result, he added, "whatever institutions American Jewry will have, must be created and sustained by the American Jewish community, or there will be none."

The conference, representing the spiritual leaders of the Reform branch of Judaism, closed its sixty-second annual meeting with the unanimous adoption of a series of resolutions, including one that urged Congressional authorization of a grant of $150,000,000 to Israel "to assist the people and Government of Israel in their gigantic task of rehabilitation and resettlement."

Dr. Bernstein, spiritual leader of Temple B'rith Kodesh in Rochester, N. Y., and formerly an adviser on Jewish affairs for United States military authorities in Europe, said that the "once greater European Jewry" no longer existed. American Jews, he said, no longer can expect "European Jews to provide ideas, institutions, and personnel necessary to enrich Jewish life in this country."

The establishment of the new State of Israel, Dr. Bernstein declared, "has enabled American Jewry to settle down to its own responsibilities." He added that "this is as it should be."

Noting that the United States and Israel had the greatest Jewish communities, Dr. Bernstein said:

"Not only will they not be in conflict with each other, but they will mutually fructify each other. Israel has much to give to the American Jew—culturally and spiritually. American Jews have much to contribute to Israel, not only financially but also in democratic institutions and modern techniques."

He announced that a delegation of thirty-five Reform rabbis, headed by himself, would leave on July 4 for Israel for a five-week visit, and expressed hope that the visit would be a "symbol and an instrument of this cooperation" between Israel's population and the American Jews.

Dr. Bernstein then asserted that the "major energies of American Jewry, including the rabbis, in the last quarter of the century, were devoted to saving Jews, and that although much remains yet to be done, it is clear that we are approaching a period in which American Jewry will have the right and the duty to be concerned also with its own institutions and developing American Jewish life."

The desirability of closer cooperation between the Conservatives and Reform wings of American Judaism was discussed, and the conference authorized Rabbi Bernstein to communicate with the Rabbinical Assembly, composed of the Conservative rabbis, with a view toward setting up a joint consultative committee to work out further areas for combined activity.

The conference urged the Government to support Israel's demand for reparations from the Western German Government. In another unanimously adopted resolution, the conference asked widespread support of the combined campaign of the Union of American Hebrew Congregations and the Hebrew Union College-Jewish Institute of Religion.

Other officers re-elected here included Rabbi Joseph L. Fink of Buffalo, vice president; Rabbi Phineas Smoller of Los Angeles, secretary; Rabbi Sidney L. Regner of Reading, Pa., financial secretary, and Rabbi Isaac E. Marcuson of Macon, Ga., administrative secretary.

June 25, 1951

RABBIS ARE RESTRAINED

Highly Orthodox Unit Forbids Joint Action With Liberals

Eleven Orthodox deans of Jewish seminaries have signed a directive declaring that joint action with more liberal rabbis is "prohibited by Torah law." The rabbinic interdiction was released yesterday by the Rabbinical Alliance of America, a highly Orthodox organization with 300 members.

Specifically, the document declared that Orthodox rabbis should not participate in the activities of the New York Board of Rabbis or the Synagogue Council of America. Both are major Jewish agencies, and have been composed of Orthodox, Conservative and Reform members.

The directive, however, does not mean an end to all Orthodox participation in these groups. It expresses only the view of a group that is one of several organizations of Orthodox rabbis.

March 9, 1956

SECULAR REVIVAL IN JUDAISM FOUND

Rabbis and Scholars Believe the Trend to Social Unity May Yet Benefit Religion

By GEORGE DUGAN

American Judaism is in the midst of a major revival that is more sociological than religious, in the opinion of a group of leading Jewish scholars.

They emphasized, however, that this sociological trend — largely a result of the "flight to the suburbs"—might yet bring about a vast spiritual renascence.

The scholars, most of them rabbis and educators, presented their views yesterday at the opening session of the second annual general assembly of the Synagogue Council of America. The two-day meeting is being held at Columbia University's Earl Hall.

It was the consensus of most of the papers, and commentary on them, that there was more "religiousness" and less religion in contemporary American Judaism.

Nathan Glazer, author and sociologist, put it this way: "Jewishness," or all the activities that Jews come together to carry out without the auspices of religion, appears to be on the increase, whereas "Judaism, the historic religion of the Jew," seems to be on the decline.

In agreeing with Dr. Glazer, the Rev. Dr. Albert I. Gordon, rabbi of Temple Emanuel, Newton, Mass., found prayer and worship a "lost art" in the suburbs.

He deplored the "incidental" observance of the Sabbath and predicted that dietary laws would soon "be on the way out."

See Wives as Dominant

Dr. Gordon saw the rise of a "new matriarchate" in the suburban areas where the Jewish wife, contrary to traditional Judaism, was taking over the direction of the home.

"Her opinions, ideas and aspirations are manifest at every turn," he declared. "She has gained this new position of executive leadership, in the main, because her husband, nice pefson though he may be, has in fact defaulted."

A high point of the session was the presentation last night of the council's annual award to former Senator Herbert H. Lehman. He was honored for his "memorable career as a brilliant example of a nobly courageous spirit translating the teachings of Judaism and the synagogue through service to the people of his state and nation."

Earlier, citations for Jewish "religious statesmanship" were presented to Roger W. Straus, chairman of the board of the American Smelting and Refining Company, and to Marvin J. Silberman, a Scarsdale, N. Y., realty man.

The Synagogue Council of America represents the Orthodox, Conservative and Reform branches of Judaism in the United States.

Orthodoxy maintains the binding authority of Jewish religious law and insists upon its immutable character. Conservatism also upholds authority, but recognizes that growth and development are an essential element of its nature. The Reform branch emphasizes the evolving character of Judaism and the continuous interpretation of religious law in accordance with the needs of modern Jewish life.

Secular Relgion Seen

Yesterday afternoon, in a paper on "The Nature of Jewish Religious Commitment," Dr. Bernard Lander, acting dean of the Yeshiva University Graduate School, asserted that "at best, a large segment of the Jewish community has evolved in our contemporary America a secular religion."

He proposed that an "intensive campaign" be waged to bring more unattached Jews back to the synagogue and that both the rabbinate and the laity recognize Judaism as a genuine religion rather than a secular culture.

Last night Will Herberg, author and Adjunct Professor of Judaic Studies and Social Philosophy at Drew University, Madison, N. J., told the assembly that the United States had become a nation of "three great religions." He said that religion had replaced "ethnicism" as a means of identifying oneself as an American.

"We are confronted today," he asserted, "with the strange paradox of more religiousness and less religion; indeed, we are confronted with the possibility that, with the rapid spread of religiousness among American Jews in the form of religious identification and synagogue membership, the very meaning of religion in its authentic sense may be lost for increasing numbers. * * * This is a danger that confronts Protestant and Catholic in America as well as Jew.'"

March 25, 1957

YOUTHS SEE DEATH OF ANTI-SEMITISM

Rabbi Interviews Teen-Age Reform Jews——Finds All Content With Faith

By JOHN WICKLEIN

Reform Jewish youths across the country believe anti-Semitism is dead or dying, according to a survey to be distributed this fall by the Union of American Hebrew Congregations.

Because of this and an increase in temple training, the study indicated, Jewish teenagers are not running away 'rom Judaism as their parents

may have done twenty years ago. They feel much more secure in being Jews. They think it is all right to date boys and girls who are not of their faith. They say, however, that they are strongly against intermarriage.

The teen-agers detailed their beliefs about men, women and God to Rabbi Jerome K. Davidson at regional camps of the National Federation of Temple Youth, an affiliate of the union of congregations. He drew responses from 822 young people through questionnaires and from thirty-six more in two-hour interviews.

"Anti-Semitism doesn't threaten these kids any more," Rabbi Davidson said in an interview last week. "They're not trying to leave Judaism."

His figures showed that 95 per cent of those who answered said they would be reborn as

Jews if they had a choice and had it to do over.

One reason for this trend, the rabbi said, is that the "religious revival" has hit Jews as well as Christians in this country. A second is that the boys and girls questioned did not feel any anti-Jewish sentiment in the communities where they lived, and from that they generalized that it did not exist elsewhere.

Today in America, the rabbi said, Judaism is accepted as an American faith — if you are a Protestant, Catholic or a Jew, you are considered part of the mainstream. Twenty years ago, he said, other Americans considered Jews of a marginal faith.

In his report, Mr. Davidson, who is assistant rabbi of Temple Beth El in Great Neck, L. I., suggests that rabbis who educate children to meet anti-Semitism are dealing with a

problem of yesterday.

It would be far more significant. he said, for them to train youth to see their social responsibilities as Jews in the American community.

Rabbi Davidson found surprisingly little social idealism among the young people he talked to, and he thinks this might be an extension of their feeling of security.

"Their lack of idealism comes from being satisfied with being American teen-agers," he said. "They are not rebelling against their parents, and they are not rebelling against the world—except on the intellectual level.

"They hate segregation, and they hate the suffering of the poor. But they see little of this in their communities, so it doesn't bother them."

One point on which Rabbi Davidson found some disagreement between teen-agers and their parents was the issue of dating outside the faith. Seventy-eight per cent of those answering said they agreed with the statement "I would have no objections to going out alone on a date with a non-Jew."

Yet when it came to marrying a non-Jew, they were against that by as large a margin as they were for dating across religious lines. Some said they feared the religious problems that would arise, but most,

the rabbi said, put it more positively: "They fear intermarriage because they want to remain Jews, have Jewish spouses, Jewish children and Jewish homes."

A Jewish home to those interviewed meant a religious home, the rabbi said. Ninety-four per cent of the group said they thought all or most people believed in God.

But they were not too concerned with the divergency of belief of their fellow men. "It

may be that 'belief' is the key word, not 'God'," Rabbi Davidson said. "Probably it is the importance of believing, not the nature of that which is believed, that is significant to the young people. Twenty years ago, you didn't get invited to a party if you weren't an atheist. It's more fashionable to believe today."

The God these young people believe in, the rabbi said, proved to be an intensely personal God who rewards and punishes and

answers every prayer.

This is not the belief stressed by Reform Judaism, he said. It would be well, he said, to lead youth away from this view, so that young people might find God in the realm of nature and in the various experiences of their lives.

"The reward for living a good life is a good life here in this world," he said.

August 30, 1959

Jews Abroad Criticized

Special to The New York Times.

JERUSALEM, Dec. 28—Premier David Ben-Gurion contended today that Jews who lived outside Israel were godless and violated the precepts of Judaism every day they remained away from the country.

Addressing the twenty-fifth Zionist Congress, the Israeli Premier said that the Jewish religion was the product of the land of Israel and was therefore bound up in duties to the state. In his eyes these duties begin with migration.

"Since the day when the Jewish state was established and the gates of Israel were flung open to every Jew who wanted to come, every religious Jew has daily violated the precepts of Judaism and the Torah of Israel by remaining in the Diaspora," he said.

The Diaspora is the term used for the dispersion of Jews outside Palestine.

Citing the authority of the Jewish sages, the Premier added:

"Whoever dwells outside the land of Israel is considered to have no god."

Mr. Ben-Gurion declared that Jews concerned for the future of their people must realize that without unity and more profound Jewish consciousness they are headed for extinction one way or another.

"In several totalitarian and Moslem countries Judaism is in danger of death by strangulation," the Premier said. "In the free and prosperous countries it faces the kiss of death, a slow and imperceptible decline into the abyss of assimilation."

With an audience of 3,000 persons in a convention hall here, Mr. Ben-Gurion addressed himself sternly to the more than 500 delegates among them and demanded that they increase visits of Jews to Israel, encourage capital investments and send children to study in Israel.

"It is clear that thousands of these young people, after seeing for themselves what the Jewish state has done and what it still has to do, would willingly and enthusiastically join the builders and creative workers," he asserted.

Growing Respect Cited

"There is no doubt that the state has straightened the backs of Jews in every country where they live and enhanced the respect in which they are held by their neighbors," the Premier said.

"It would be no exaggeration

to say that apart from small groups on the right and the left there is nothing that has united the entire Jewish people, of all parties, views and sections, so much as the state of Israel.

"I have given this point pride of place because I regard the unity of the Jewish people as a primary condition for its survival—and the survival of Israel as well—and as I have said elsewhere, I am a Jew first and an Israeli afterwards. * * *

"The question that you who are sitting here must answer not by words and resolutions but by deeds is whether you have the desire, the will and the ability to work for and to insure the immigration that Israel needs in ever greater quantities, an immigration motivated not only by the burden of distress and external pressure but by the powerful impulse of the creative vision of redemption, which exalts and enriches the spirit of man."

"This is the grave and urgent challenge facing our generation," Mr. Ben-Gurion added. "This is the last generation of servitude and the first of salvation, but it might well be the last of salvation if those who are loyal to Zion do not summon up the courage to act on the conviction and inner conviction that Zionism has only one meaning today: to Zion."

Premier's Stand No Secret

Mr. Ben-Gurion has never made any secret of his scorn for Jews in other countries who

are free to emigrate to Israel but prefer to remain in the Diaspora.

Zionist leaders have accused him of taking the position that Jews outside Israel are simply a source of financial support to be tolerated only as long as necessary.

His invocation yesterday of a religious argument in criticizing Jews who choose to remain in the Diaspora appeared to be new. It appeared to be aimed particularly at Orthodox Jews who adhere strictly to traditional Jewish religious laws and who are called Religious Jews in Israel.

Mr. Ben-Gurion, who is not a Religious Jew, has often been at odds with this group because the laws and policies of Israel are at some points at odds with religious tradition.

Orthodox Jews in the United States have sometimes called for stricter adherence to these traditions in Israel. Two years ago, the president of the Religious Zionists of America said that Israel's principal task in the next ten years should be a return "to her ancient religious mission" by implementing the moral imperatives of the Talmud in her codes of law and administration.

Most Zionist leaders reject Mr. Ben-Gurion's attitude toward Jews who choose to remain in other countries. There has been considerable criticism of his position that Zionism outside Israel is obsolete.

December 29, 1960

JEWS HERE SCORE BEN-GURION STAND

Zionists Join Non-Zionists in Criticizing Demand for Emigration to Israel

By A. J. GORDON

The American Jewish Committee accused Premier David Ben-Gurion yesterday of having violated an understanding made ten years ago regarding the relationship between Israel and Jews outside that country.

The committee, a non-Zionist group, issued a statement in reply to Mr. Ben-Gurion's remarks Wednesday at the twenty-fifth World Zionist Congress in Jerusalem in which he said that Jews who lived outside Israel were "considered to have no god."

Each day those Jews remained away from Israel they violated the precepts of Judaism, the Premier said.

The committee said it was shocked by Mr. Ben-Gurion's statement that Jews throughout the world were obligated to emigrate to Israel. The committee maintains that any emigration must be an act of choice.

"As Americans devoted to democratic principles," the com-

mittee declared, "we have a deep interest in the development of a democratic society in Israel, while as Jews, we have a natural sympathy with our fellow Jews, with whom we are bound by traditional historic and cultural ties."

Accord Held Violated

However, the group said, Mr. Ben-Gurion's statement was a "violation of the explicit understanding" arrived at ten years ago with Jacob Blaustein, then president of the American Jewish Committee.

The understanding, the committee said, was that "the Government and people of Israel fully respect the right and integrity of the Jewish communities in other countries to de-

velop their own mode of life and their indigenous social, economic and cultural institutions in accordance with their own needs and aspirations."

Spokesmen for other Jewish organizations in New York also took issue with Premier Ben-Gurion. In his speech Wednesday, the Premier was particularly critical of Orthodox Jews, who follow strictly the traditional Jewish religious laws and who are called Religious Jews in Israel. Mr. Ben-Gurion is not one of the Religious Jews and has often been at odds with them.

Abraham Goodman, chairman of the National Administrative Committee of the Zionist Organization of America, said:

"It seems ironic that this denunciation should come from one who, to the best of knowledge, has most of his life not been practicing religion and is now taking upon himself in addition to his heavy burdens as Premier to usurp the functions of the rabbinate."

Assertion Called 'Fantastic'

Clarence L. Coleman Jr. of Glencoe, Ill., who is president of the American Council for Judaism, Inc., characterized as a sign of what he termed Zionism's "desperation" the assertion by Mr. Ben-Gurion that Jews outside Israel were godless. "It is fantastic nonsense,"

he said, for Mr. Ben-Gurion to imply that "in the freedom of America there has not already been developed a meaningful Judaism."

He added: "Our nationality is American, our religion is Judaism. Our homeland is the United States of America, and we reject the concept that all Jews outside of Israel are in 'exile.'"

The Union of American Hebrew Congregations, the parent body of Reform Judaism in the United States, declared that Mr. Ben-Gurion's "argument runs contrary both to the Jewish tradition and to contemporary reality." It said that "wherever

Jews choose to live their covenant relationship with God remains the same."

Rabbi David I. Golovensky of Beth El Synagogue, New Rochelle, president of the New York Board of Rabbis, declared that "the vitality and dynamism of American Judaism, which helped create the State of Israel, is a complete refutation of Ben-Gurion's gratuitous and, I believe, deplorable assertions."

The American Jewish Congress, which describes itself as "pro-Zionist," said in a statement issued by its president, Dr. Joachim Prinz:

"The wholesale indictment by Prime Minister Ben-Gurion

of all Jews who live outside of Israel must and will be completely and unequivocally rejected by the Jewish community."

The Union of Orthodox Rabbis of the United States and Canada called the Premier's statement on non-Israeli Jews "erroneous."

Others who criticized Mr. Ben-Gurion's remarks included the Central Conference of American Rabbis, a Reform group, and Rabbi Samuel M. Silver, who is president of the Association of Jewish Chaplains of the Armed Forces.

December 30, 1960

JUDAISM IS FOUND BESET BY RIVALRY

Layman, in Book, Deplores Competing by 3 Branches

By IRVING SPIEGEL

What is called "disruptive squabbling" among rabbis of the three branches of Judaism is frustrating religious growth in the American Jewish community, according to a prominent layman.

He is Philip M. Klutznick, former president of B'nai B'rith and at one time general chairman of the United Jewish Appeal. His view is set forth in his book, "No Easy Answers,"

which will be published tomorrow.

Until his appointment last February as United States representative to the United Nations Economic and Social Council Mr. Klutznick had been active in national Jewish groups for thirty years.

In his book he wrote that a competition for adherence to their respective religious affiliations was being carried on among rabbis of the Orthodox, Conservative and Reform branches of Judaism.

Puzzlement of People

As a consequence, he said, Jews groping for the fundamentals of Judaism in an American environment are perplexed by theological distinctions.

The effect, he added, is that the rabbinate's own efforts toward a religious revival are lost in "the welter of confu-

sions, rivalries and hostilities among the theologians themselves."

Mr. Klutznick was also critical of Jewish religious leaders for what he described as their "unwarranted urge" to have the synagogue dominate all of Jewish community life. This, he said, presupposes "competition rather than cooperation" between synagogue and secular organizations.

"The implication left by these exclusivists—to their own detriment—is that the synagogue comes off second best," he added.

Noting that a considerable number of rabbis, "seeking a hospitable pulpit," readily move from one denomination to another, he continued:

"Despite their scholarly thunder, most rabbis are less separated by ideological beliefs than by their loyalties to rab-

binical or denominational organizations."

To strengthen Judaism in this country Mr. Klutznick proposed that the three branches emphasize "common areas of agreement" and that the individual rabbi concentrate on his role as teacher and religious specialist instead of being "miscast as a jack-of-all services."

"I am not suggesting that rabbis submerge or compromise where their differences are compelling," he wrote. "It is their role to challenge error, even among themselves.

"But are not the rabbis and religious scholars who pursue factionalism more fervently than they exalt the common qualities of Judaism committing a graver error—that of frustrating a Jewishness in America that is striving for maturity?"

June 18, 1961

HASIDIM BOUND BY STRICT RULES

Sect Went to Williamsburg During World War II

The Williamsburg section of Brooklyn, where 10-year-old Yosef Schuhmacher apparently had been living, is populated by Hasidic Jews so Orthodox that women, when married, cut off their hair and wear wigs not deemed a temptation.

Books in English may not be read on the Sabbath. Pallid scholars, dressed in black and with side curls dangling under the brims of fur-trimmed hats, walk silently along the sidewalks.

Once this section, hard by the East River, was a resort patronized by the rich. Its hotels near the Brooklyn ferry,

in the middle of the nineteenth century, attracted such gourmets and sportsmen as Commodore Vanderbilt, Jim Fisk and William C. Whitney.

But with the opening of the Brooklyn Bridge in 1883, and the Williamsburg Bridge in 1903, great numbers of Jewish immigrants from the lower East Side moved across the river to Williamsburg.

It was not until World War II, however, that the section—founded about 1810 and named for a Colonel Williams, the engineer who surveyed it—drew the Hasidim. The sect was founded about 1750 in Poland by Rabbi Israel ben Eliezer to revive the ideals of the Hasidism of the third century B. C., which fought innovations sought by the Greeks.

The Hasidim, mostly eastern Europeans, were among the displaced persons of the second World War, and the neighborhood they inherited in Williamsburg was by then a slum, hav-

ing lost all the grandeur it once had.

The men escape the neighborhood during the day, for many of them are jewelers in Manhattan's diamond center or tradesmen elsewhere. The women, however, rarely see another neighborhood.

Members of the Hasidim, like other Orthodox Jews, may not ride in automobiles on the Sabbath, nor may they use elevators or anything mechanical. Everywhere they go, they walk.

By early Friday, the windows of most Hasidic homes have been washed, the best linen has been spread and much of the cooking has been done, because fire is forbidden on the Sabbath, from sundown Friday to sundown Saturday.

On Saturday the Hasidim are in their finest clothing, with little girls as well as women in long sockings, long dresses and long-sleeved blouses. The boys,

also with side curls and black hats fashioned in the tradition of the princes of Hasidism, may not play games.

Once the Sabbath has passed, boys and girls are back in everyday clothes, but, even throughout the week, the adherence to tradition remains.

Some members of the sect in Williamsburg feel threatened, as the area, like most poorer sections of New York, has undergone a vast change in the last few years. Puerto Ricans and Negroes also have increased their population in Williamsburg. The area is smaller than ever, and some members have already announced plans to move away to quieter areas where they can remain apart from outside influences.

Some Hasidic Jews already have moved to communities in New Jersey and Long Island, and many others plan to join them.

July 2, 1962

SOME OF OUR BEST WRITERS

JEWS AND AMERICANS. By Irving Malin. Preface by Harry T. Moore. 193 pp. Carbondale and Edwardsville: Southern Illinois University Press. $4.50.

By STANLEY KAUFFMANN

EVERY age is a Golden Age of some kind, and our era, harassed in many ways, is a millennium in at least one regard. It is, in this country, as happy a time for the cultural-intellectual life of Jews as any since 12th-century Spain under the Moors. In the last 10 years or so, we have particularly seen the increasing prominence of American-Jewish novelists. They have been there, statistically, for decades, but their rise is recent. What is more pertinent, they now form the dominant "school." There seems to be a dominant school at any given time in American fiction: in the 1920's it was realist-naturalist; in the 1930's it was proletarian; in the 1940's and early 1950's it was Southern. We live now in the time of Bellow, Malamud, Mailer, Salinger, Roth. Our literary criticism is ornamented with the work of Irving Howe, Lionel Trilling, Alfred Kazin, Stanley Edgar Hyman, Philip Rahv.

The situation has hardly gone unremarked; for at least 15 years articles have been pouring out, some happy, some amazed, some markedly wry, about the prominence of Jews in American culture. Books on the subject are overdue. Now one has arrived, and is immediately notable because it does not discuss the subject. On page 4 of "Jews and Americans" Irving Malin asks, "Why is the Jew a new culture hero?" but he never attempts an answer. Although this may seem the most interesting aspect of the matter to many of us, Mr. Malin directs himself exclusively to a thematic analysis of seven American-Jewish authors. Let us examine what he has done before we speculate about what he has not done.

His method is the one that he used in his previous study, "New American Gothic." He selects themes, devotes a chapter to each theme, and then against that theme measures each of his seven writers in turn: Karl Shapiro, Delmore Schwartz, Isaac Rosenfeld, Leslie Fiedler, Saul Bellow, Bernard Malamud and Philip Roth. No sooner have we run down the list of seven, sighting them against one theme, than we go back to the head of the line in the next chapter and start in again. The patness of the procedure is wearying and by its very rote does not serve Mr. Malin or his authors with the subtlety that a more flexible, interwoven, associative method might have provided.

The themes he has posited are, he believes, aspects of Jewishness, and he does indeed demonstrate that they are present, sometimes strongly, in his authors' works. But his successes

Mr. Kauffmann's views on both books and films are widely published. He is also a novelist and broadcaster.

are chiefly with this relatively simple analysis; when he presses further, he falters. Comments meant to be profound are often pedestrian: "Malamud has said, 'All men are Jews.' Perhaps he is right in a metaphoric way." In what other way on earth had Malamud intended the remark? "The Jewish Experience is a series of moments in the search for God." How does this differ from the Baptist or Methodist Experience?

All through the book runs the subject of Judaism — the Jewish religion as distinct from Jewish culture (or Jewishness); and this is certainly appropriate as a means of definition. But several of these authors "find little nourishment in the theology of their parents," and at least two of them (Shapiro and Roth) have explicitly disavowed concern with Judaism. Thus Malin's final comment is both a bit smug and a bit dismissive of many of the questions he has raised: "The Jewish Experience is great enough to accept our rebellious writers." The ambivalent vein of theological doubt and inherent Jewishness in these men is better represented by what Isaac Babel wrote to his mother one Passover: "Today I'll buy matzos and, for your sake, I'll intone praises to that old crook the Jewish God . . ."

Malin says that these authors are at their best when directly concerned with their Jewishness—generally true, I think; but he then ignores what he considers the weaker works and sees all the better ones as thematically Jewish. "The Natural" may be minor Malamud, but it is certainly an exponent of his life as an American Jewish author and cannot be ignored in an appraisal of his work simply because it does not fit in a Procrustean bed of Jewishness. "Goodbye, Columbus" is a trenchant picture of a certain stratum of suburban Jews, but their Jewishness is not the point of the novella any more than Catholic Irishness is the point of Frank O'Connor's "First Love."

What is radically worse, what basically weakens the book, is Malin's failure to see that his themes are equally relevant to non-Jewish American writers. Cannot Faulkner, Ellison, Styron—and many others—be put to inquiry as to Exile, Fathers and Sons, Time, Head and Heart, Irony, Fantasy, Parable? Of course most themes are universal. It would be difficult, outside of specific Jewish references, to isolate themes that applied only to Jews. Still, what is missing from Malin's book is a clear sense that these are universal themes and that what he is discussing is the response of seven individuals—conditioned by a certain heritage—to those universals.

There remains Malin's unanswered question: "Why is the Jew a new culture hero?" Two clarifications are immediately necessary. It is not only the Jewish

writer—novelist, poet, critic—who has surged to the fore; Jews are prominent in all intellectual disciplines. But their prominence does not stop there. Jews have founded and run some of the best publishing houses and are inseparably identified with the most popular art in history, the film. Jewish locutions touch our speech nationwide: in the South I heard a drawling high-school boy tease a friend: "Reginald? That's a name for a baby?" The kosher delicatessen (sometimes quasi-kosher, or *demi-vierge*) is a na-

Leslie Fiedler.

tional urban institution, and pastrami has become one of the great levelers, doing for Jews what spaghetti and pizza have done for Italian goodwill.

Among theatrical performers Jews have been favorites for a long time. Indeed, it might be argued that Jewish pioneering into American intellectual acceptance was done by the impertinences of the Marx Brothers, with their writers, George S. Kaufman, S. J. Perelman and Morrie Ryskind behind them. Today Mort Sahl and Lenny Bruce are, in two admirable senses, carrying on. A generation ago the gifted Fanny Brice was primarily a comedienne. The gifted Barbra Streisand is a comedienne, too, but she is also a sex-figure. A generation ago the attractive Miss Streisand would probably have had to have a "nose job."

Secondly, it must be emphasized that the Jew is now an acknowledged cultural hero to American Jews—and this was not always the case. Embarrassment, an urge to be indistinguishable, restrained many in an older generation and made them confine their admiration for Jews to Jewish circles. These restraints do not often apply now; and since there are now more Jews in America than there were, this accounts for some of the new eminence of Jewish figures.

Still, the question eventually comes down to the country at large and to writers in particular, because without some Gentile acceptance, this cultural event could not have occurred, and without writers we cannot be sure that culture is happening.

The chief reason for the culture-heroism of the Jew is the most obvious one: it *could* happen here. America has never been and is not now devoid of anti-Semitism (and similar uglinesses). But it would be sophomoric to deny that this country has always been concerned in theory to give maximum opportunity to minority groups and in practice has had increasing success. (Negroes are the obvious past—but not future—exception.)

Additionally, from the beginning, there have been social and other affinities between the United States and the Jews. Merle Curti notes: "Christianity had been derived from Judaism, a fact that was greatly emphasized in Puritan thought." Edmund Wilson has written: "Our conception itself of America as a country with a mission in the world comes down to us from our Mosaic ancestors"; and he has explored the philo-Semitism of some 19th-century New England intellectuals. Certainly a delusory *Schwärmerei* is possible in halcyon days. Marvin Lowenthal cites one example (" 'The character of the Jewish people always had a strong affinity to the character of the German race' —the statement is Heine's and thousands of his fellow German-Jews heartily agreed with it."

NEVERTHELESS, however strained and stained, there are certain root congruencies between Jewish and American ideas: the Chosen Land or People, the concern with social justice, and the fundamental belief,' only now beginning to erupt through the stolidity of old Europe, that the son must be "better" than the father—in education and status.

Jewish immigration to this country began in substantial numbers a little over a hundred years ago, and for about the first 20 years brought principally German-speaking Jews from Germany, Austria, Bohemia. In 1881 the assassination of Czar Alexander II started a series of pogroms in Poland and Russia that caused a great wave of immigration of Yiddish-speaking Jews. The earlier, Germanic wave of immigrants, by then well established

in America, resented the second wave and affected to look down on them as an inferior breed of Jew.

This asinine view continued

Bernard Malamud.

until Hitler's day and cannot be said to be extinguished even now. Commentators on the American-Jewish literary success have generally ignored this stratification and, more important, have neglected the fact that almost all American-Jewish writers of prominence have come from the second, originally Yiddish group. (This fact gives particular pleasure to one descended from the Germanic group who has always been unamused at its silly airs.)

One can hazard some guesses as to the reasons for the salience of the Yiddish-descended. These Jews of Russian-Polish origin come from families that were not and could not be concerned, for several generations, with assimilation, that were turned inward for sustenance. Jewishness was simultaneously the enforced and the cherished ambience; it gave these people figurative oxygen tanks to breathe from, surrounded by a world that wanted to suffocate them. It gave them secret stubbornness in everything from their mundane jobs to a grand will to survive.

Possibly a chief support to this stubbornness — the wall against which their backs were pressed—was their very powerlessness. "The virtue of powerlessness, the power of helplessness, the company of the dispossessed, the sanctity of the insulted and injured — these, finally," says Irving Howe, "are the great themes of Yiddish literature." That literature came from this Eastern European group who, among Jews, had

the most recent reminders that they were a people whose millions had been beaten, butchered and burned for centuries *before* Auschwitz. The color of this remembrance tinctures American-Jewish literature deeply. Says a friend to Bellow's troubled Herzog: "Well, when you suffer, you really suffer. You're a real, genuine old Jewish type that digs the emotions. . . . I understand it. I grew up on Sangamon Street, remember, when a Jew was still a Jew. I know about suffering—we're on the same identical network."

They grope for that network. It is to them what the sign of the fish was to early Christians. In Roth's story "Eli the Fanatic," the D. P. Yeshivah teacher says to the slick suburban Jew whom he is discomfiting: "You have the word 'suffer' in English?" It is a poignant line, dark with history; it reaches for the network.

The sum of all these experiences, plus an immanent subconscious conviction that Jews are luckier than most Americans, often gives the work of American-Jewish writers an especially vivid emotional articulation, a quality of having added European richness to a muscular American base, gives Jewish humor an irony that is part exultation unto the second and third generation ("We're alive! We made it!"), and gives to Jewish troubles the assurance that they have fallen into the right hands, as when a rough stone comes to an experienced stone-cutter. The fact that many of these writers have known bilingual homes (Yiddish and English) encourages a continuing tension of observer-participation, as if they had a viewpoint outside the community with which, gratefully, they are now inextricably involved.

AMONG these writers, in addition to those already mentioned, one can name Harvey Swados, Joseph Heller, Bruce Jay Friedman, Edward Adler, Grace Paley, Norma Stahl Rosen, Wallace Markfield, Irvin Faust. To the question as to why most of them have appeared only since World War II one answer seems to be that talent, even genius, is actuarially present at any time and that it flourishes in response to favorable climate (the surge of architectural talent in the Gothic Era, of operatic talent in 19th-century Italy). There is an additional reason, specific to our subject. In Judaism there have been, as Abraham Heschel says, three constants: worship, learning and action. The first and third are constants of most faiths, but learning, as a religious tradition, is relatively

rare. The self-applied term, the People of the Book, may be a vanity, but a vanity can become an ethic. In the course of time, with the right environment, it has probably helped many American Jews to become people of books.

For that environment, which is the current philo-Semitism among American Gentiles, clearly World War II is in some part responsible. Hitler's Final Solution created a new interest in Jews among Gentiles, out of compassion and conscience, also possibly just out of curiosity. The war also brought a new cosmopolitanism and an increased liberalism of intellectual and social view in which animus against an author merely because he is Jewish would seem freakish. The tidal spread of college education — whatever the faults of our colleges — has had at least the minimal effect of lessening prejudice and encouraging receptivity. A general and quite conscious effort to broaden our national cultural life has inevitably also embraced Jewish writers.

Saul Bellow.

Another event that has greatly helped is the Negro revolution. The civil rights movement, I think, is partially but directly responsible for the Jewish culture hero, for the immense success of Bellow's book, even for the belated success of Henry Roth's "Call It Sleep" and Daniel Fuchs's Williamsburg trilogy. The question of the acceptance of Jews is no longer on the frontier of Gentile consciousness, it is well behind the lines, has been swept — by the urgency of Negro problems — into the state of being quite *passé*. Readers feel that they ought to be well past it. If, for example, they can't identify with Moses Herzog, who is white, how are they ever going to achieve brotherhood with black men?

There no longer seems to be much tremor of daring or broad-mindedness in non-Jews at reading a Jewish novel. There is even possibly some compulsion, heightened by current racial struggles, to reach for Jewish novels as evidence of fraternal disposition.

Further, in a society hungry for large-scale emotional experienings just like other writers; are still capable of supplying it. Jews write novels of small adulteries and adolescent awakenings just like other writers; but some of them seem particularly able to see the world of plastics and computers in terms of tragic strophe. In "The Assistant" Malamud converts a little Brooklyn grocery into a pit of agonies. In Bellow's "Seize the Day" Tommy Wilhelm moves through an upper West Side hotel as through a medieval morality play, to the fixed and waiting jaws of hell.

Trailing these vital reasons are some pallid mimetic ones. A decade ago there was a joke that "Marjorie Morningstar" had made it chic to be Jewish. Today, doubtless many a coffee-table bears an unread copy of "Herzog," a casually displayed vogue symbol. But the very fact that it is such a symbol is relevant. Another extrinsic source of interest, I think, is the existence of the state of Israel which, for some Gentiles, has made Jews everywhere, through a kind of sentimental projection, seem more impressive and real.

Crowning this entire complex of reasons, there is a contributory paradox. Despite the antiquity of the Jews, their life

in the arts is relatively young. Jews have been writing novels, painting pictures, composing sonatas, for not much more than a century and a half.

Philip Roth.

Legal and social restrictions hampered them before that (as did the Second Commandment's injunction against graven images). If a cultural inheritance can be said to accumulate — as I think it can, in both ineffable and effable manner — then that store has found particularly free circumstances of use in America—by Jews being Americans as well as Jews.

Jewish writers are not exempt from the crises in materials and techniques that affect all Western artists. But one senses in the Jewish writer some convic-

tion that in his very "accumulated" Jewishness there is a weight, even an abrasiveness, that may break open the tough skin of modern life and let him in: that his Jewishness — in his own mind, at least, which is all that matters — gives him a liberty, a tangent of connection; makes him both more adaptable and more accessible.

When Walker Percy, the Louisianian author of "The Moviegoer," was asked why the South has produced so many good writers, he replied, "We got beat." Jews have something of the same sense of belated restitution and fulfillment on paper.

As to the future, the current situation will change simply because cultural situations always do. The Jewish eminence will fade, in a vogue sense, probably to be replaced by an already evident Negro vogue; which, like the Jewish one, will be aided by non-literary considerations — in this instance, the civil rights movement, jazz, international politics. The Jewish writer will have had the pleasure of being modish but will then have the greater freedom of having *been* modish. He will have greater power and responsibility, the power of belonging, the responsibility of not belonging too much.

For Jews are facing the fact that, when they are just as "good" as anyone else, they run the risk of being no different. Individual differences may be fading in all of our society, but their loss may hurt worst where their presence once caused the most trouble. (Many

Jewish intellectuals have apprehended this and, seemingly as refreshment of identity, are addicted to Jewish horseplay, private from Gentile eyes. This is acutely rendered in Markfield's "To an Early Grave.")

Benjamin DeMott has fittingly warned the Jewish writer that he cannot build his future entirely on the past: "His chance of producing a more moving book than the age as a whole deserves can be diced away in lamentation." Certainly it is not the building and maintenance of private wailing walls that is here advocated. But comprehensiveness and universality begin in self-knowledge, at least in the desire for them. The American Jew faces the faceless Age of Cybernation like everyone else, but he may have an additional strength to survive in it through the entirety of his American Jewishness, as well as by devotion to his common humanity.

Let him write off, at its apogee, his position as cultural hero, since it is doomed anyway, and let him use what he has gained from his popularity, as well as from his heritage, in the best exploitation of self. Let him thrive in post-spotlight acceptance, in what can be termed congenial unpopularity, a condition secure enough to keep him connected with society, unflattering enough to keep his edges honed, his nerves extra-sensitive. Or how, when the time comes, will the Malamud of 2065 know that he is Malamud?

May 30, 1965

JEWISH UNIT GETS APOSTASY REPORT

By IRVING SPIEGEL

Three sociologists at Columbia University's Bureau of Applied Social Research reported yesterday in a special study that 13 per cent of the Jewish students in American colleges rejected their Jewish ties by their senior year, but half of them reaffirmed their identity within three years after college graduation.

The conclusion is part of a preliminary report on apostasy among college students, prepared for the American Jewish Committee and released at the Committee's 62d annual meeting at the Americana hotel. The report, the work of David Caplovitz, Paul Ritterband and Fred Sherrow, was prepared over the last year.

In an interview, Mr. Sherrow

said that he and his colleagues defined an apostate, for their study, as one who identifies himself as having "no religion" after having been brought up within a faith.

The report showed that apostasy was about as frequent among Jews as among Protestants but was only half as frequent among Roman Catholics. The report, which was begun originally in 1961 by the National Opinion Research Center of the University of Chicago, covered 34,000 college students in 135 colleges. Of this number, 3,632, or 11 per cent, said they had been reared as Jews. The data were reappraised since then.

The Columbia sociologists reported that 13 per cent of the Jews, 12 per cent of the Protestants, but only 7 per cent of the Catholics, were apostates. They indicated that the Protestant and Catholic apostate rejected only his religion, the Jewish apostate both his religion and his ties to his Jewish community.

The researchers concluded that the forces making for apostasy during the college years tended to abate during the years after graduation.

"The fact that almost half of the original group of apostates had reaffirmed their Jewish identity three years later shows that apostasy is for many a tentative, experimental stance rather than a firm conviction. The forces making for the re-integration of apostates seems to be much more powerful than those generating new apostasy."

The authors believed that the forces making for the weakening of Jewish identity, of which religion is only one element, also contribute to the erosion of religious commitment among Christians.

In the interview, Mr. Sherrow explained that while one is at college he is exposed to the ideas and the attitudes of the intellectual community and of other students who are themselves intellectually oriented. Mr. Sherrow said that "a more selective process takes place after graduation."

On one hand, the more intellectual student who goes on to graduate school "finds himself in an atmosphere that is even more homogeneous than undergraduate school, and this atmosphere tends to strengthen former feelings of apostasy or could induce him to become an apostate," Mr. Sherrow said.

In contrast, he said that the nonintellectual student "who moves out into the general community, where identification with a religious community is the normative pattern, begins to be more influenced by middle-class, American standards that would reduce his tendency to apostatize."

The research team plans to prepare a fuller monograph on the findings by the end of this year, which will cover a number of topics not dealt with in the preliminary report.

At a dinner yesterday at Toots Shor's, the committee honored Edwin J. Lukas, who is retiring as director of the panel on civil rights and social action after 18 years.

May 26, 1968

SCHOLARS PONDER YOUNG JEWS' ROLE

Panel Finds Majority Reject Institutions of Judaism

By IRVING SPIEGEL
Special to The New York Times

WASHINGTON, Sept. 8—The sentiment of Jewish youth, including many activists in campus rebellions and other "anti-establishment" revolts, is not to withdraw from Judaism. What many of them do reject are the "corporate institutions" of present-day Jewish life.

This was a consensus view of a group of Jewish scholars and educators who, in panel sessions today and yesterday, discussed the "generation gap" in Jewish community life at the 125th anniversary convention of B'nai B'rith, the 500,000-member Jewish service organization.

About 1,200 persons are participating in the five-day meeting at the Shoreham Hotel.

Failure of the Jewish community to make many of its institutions — the synagogue, community center and competitive religious and secular groups —more relevant to Judaism's "ethical and religious distinctiveness" in place of an overemphasis on "organizational activities and apparatus" were among the conditions criticized as discouraging to young Jews "eager to apply the ethical imperatives of Judaism to the pressing social problems that afflict society."

Basis Institutionalized

The "parceling out" of Jewish culture on an institutionalized basis has "fragmentized and debased the natural Jewish community and culture of earlier generations," declared Dr. Harold Weisberg of Brandeis University.

Religion is "done" under the auspices of the synagogue, combating anti-Semitism is "done" by various community relations groups, recreation is "done" at a community-center or country club, Dr. Weisberg said.

The effect, he added, is to expose Jewish youth to a Jewish community "fragmentary in character and without a continuity of culture or organic relationships."

Dr. Weisberg, a professor of philosophy and chairman of B'nai B'rith's Adult Jewish Education Commission, contended that Jewish youth were "made into Jews rather than Jewishly educated" at Jewish schools and summer camps of the "institutionalized community."

Society Is Rejected

He scored the Jewish community for not having "paid sufficient attention to the spiritual and cultural problems of its institutions." Jewish youth today, he said, regards Judaism as "only relevant" to their parents' society—a society that they have rejected.

They have characterized their parents as "fake liberals who talk a good game but do not act."

Rabbi Jay Kaufman, executive vice president of B'nai B'rith, said that activism among Jewish college youth was "powered by a deep-felt ethic" that the adult Jewish community could ignore only at its peril.

They are part of a campus generation "rebelling against its role as the first generation of a technological society in which men have become tools of their own tools," Rabbi Kaufman said.

"They recognize and are angry about the lack of human emotions in a computerized existence in which there is no spiritual continuity and everything seems to be programed for early obsolescence," he added.

Dr. Robert Gordis of the Jewish Theological Seminary of America and Label A. Katz, a former president of B'nai B'rith, both criticized the "superficial character" of Jewish education, which, each declared, is leading to the alienation of large numbers of young Jews from the Jewish community.

A convention report showed that of 1.3 million American Jewish youth between pre-school and college age, only 540,000—about 40 per cent— were enrolled in some form of Jewish educational activity, much of it a minimal Sunday school program.

Mr. Katz made a plea for advancing Jewish education to "first priority status" in Jewish community life.

The convention's focus on Jewish youth reflected the results of a two-year study by B'nai B'rith conducted by 30 survey groups in Metropolitan and suburban areas to determine what American Jews regarded as their "community priorities" for the 1970's.

Concern for retaining the cultural loyalties of their youth was first, far outranking problems of anti-Semitism or relationships with Israel.

September 9, 1968

Who Is Calling?

By RICHARD N. LEVY

Rabbis have started growing beards in southern California. Haven't they always, you will ask, puzzled—the very word "rabbi" calling forth an ancient soul enwreathed in long, white hair.

Yet the rabbis I speak of are not ancient but relatively young, and many of their colleagues not so long ago cast beards aside lest people think them out of date. Nowadays, of course, to be shy of hair is to be out of date, but this new hirsuteness is not merely a bow to contemporary fashion. It is, on one level, an expression of a new kind of freedom: like some nuns in Los Angeles, rabbis too are throwing off their habits—the shorthaired, dark-suited fetters in which so many of their upper-middle-class congregants had kept them bound so long. In this they are echoed (or heralded) by many young Jews in southern California, whose search for new forms of Jewish identity more and more rabbis are joining:

A local synagogue has operated a basement coffeehouse for two years now, and young people weekly loom out of its black and luminescent walls with poetic or musical offerings for a Sabbath evening. . . .

During the fall, some sixty people wandered in and out of a Saturday afternoon "underground synagogue" whose name was perhaps more alluring than its final form: a free-wheeling feelingful discussion of the Biblical portion of the week followed by Havdalah, the ushering-out of the Sabbath, whose traditional spice box was replaced by incense. The "synagogue," operated under Hillel auspices, counted as its major success a young man who for the first few weeks arrived with choleric anger flaming from his voice, an Arab kefia around his head, and a gilded calf dangling from his neck. By the fourth week, kefia, calf, and choler all had melted amid this open environment where self-styled exiles from Judaism could find acceptance for their own Jewish feelings.

Such Biblical discussions should be of especial interest to readers of this Book Review, since for the young the Bible is less the Great Best Seller than it is the Great Obstacle. If so many adults for so many years have considered the Bible such a marvelous book, something clearly must be wrong with it—and many approach it with the hostile mien reserved only for the most threatening authorities. "Underground" Bible study thus becomes a kind of sensitivity training session, in which students come to accept Abraham, Jacob and Moses for what they are and for the mystical insights recorded about them.

Sensitivity training is Big in southern California, and synagogues, Hillel foundations and rabbinical schools have been utilizing it as a means to bring their students closer to each other and to the tradition from which they come — and against which many are struggling. The text for such sessions is a book at least as problematic as the Bible: the Siddur, the prayer book, whether traditional or looseleaf. Martin Buber believed that men stand in the presence of God (the Eternal Thou) when they stand in relation to each other, as subject to subject. If he was right, then the prayerbook is a useful guide for such relationships.

For people who have trouble with praying, merely to write a new service will not help — they come to any service as strangers to each other and to God. Several groups in Los Angeles have thus created a prayer service merely by sharing their feelings about the prayers—reading a sentence and talking about it, while a sensitive soul might strum a thoughtful tune on his guitar.

What is happening here? After the rush of the past 20 years to build synagogues and enlarge congregations, many young people are refusing to come in: you have grown too big, they protest; like our schools and our cities, now even the synagogues are anonymous — there is no room for me there. I need a small group to find myself, to pray with, to study in, to be silent among — I need no building, no dark hushed halls — just a little room with a rug on the floor and others sitting near me.

Readers of the Book Review will note that so far I have

mentioned only two books—and said more about relationship with them than the words in them. For to the children of the People of the Book words can be enemies too, for usually they are someone else's words, someone else's definitions; the Jew so many yearn to be exists now only in the silence, in the place to which words have not yet come. And in what language shall I speak, they ask: in English, which I know too well, whose words rain down around me every day, flooding me with meanings others have derived? Or shall I speak in Hebrew, whose translation I may not know at all, whose words I can therefore fill with my own meanings, and when I sing them, fill them not alone with meaning but with myself?

But some students can still be found at their words, poring over books of recent vintage which encourage young readers to assert their own definitions within the author's words. A blithely random sampling of Jewish students at U.C.L.A. discloses that many are drawn to the stories of Isaac Bashevis Singer, often because he creates an environment of the past in which these students can participate in no other way. Another attraction of Singer is his contention that the visible, rational world is not the only reality possible for us, a conviction which draws students also to Buber, Abraham Joshua Heschel, and the tales of the Hasidim.

Eschewing the rash of books depicting a Jewish community ready to dissolve in banality, students seem to prefer the conviction found in many of Bernard Malamud's stories and novels that somewhere there must be a profound significance in being a Jew today. In "The Fixer," Malamud's tortured protagonist declares, "We're all in history, that's sure, but some are more than others, Jews more than some." Even in the (so far) pastoral calm of U.C.L.A., every aware Jewish student knows that he is very much in history, whether he is arguing the case for Israel's survival or agonizing over his proper role in the black rebellion.

Some heretofore uninvolved Jewish students are organizing a course on "Can Jewish Identity Survive in America," including a simulation project of an ideal Jewish community. Others, a bit more radical, are planning a Jewish Urban Plunge — a weekend involvement in the day and night life of downtown and ghetto Los Angeles, with Sabbath worship and discussions keyed to the special relationships of Jews with other minority groups.

The Jewish student (most of him) stands firm inside the history his ancestors created, yet (many of him) outside the synagogue his father built. The ancient call to be a prophet people stirs his hot and very modern blood — but who is calling? Where is the ancient bush aflame with purpose, the holy ground which only his bare feet can walk? So many call — his people and his person, his nation and his vision, the graceful palm-lined drives and the burned-out hovels by the tracks — whom should he answer? Who is really calling him?

There are words and books and bearded rabbis, but ultimately only he will answer with the ancient words, in the fullness of his coming to himself: Here I am. ■

Mr. Levy is interim director of the Hillel Council at U.C.L.A.

March 16, 1969

Jewish Theologians Are Reviving an Increase in the Recovery of Traditional Customs and Teachings

By EDWARD B. FISKE

Spurred by a wide range of foreign and domestic developments — from Israel's Six-Day War of 1967 to the black power movement—Jewish theologians and philosophers are showing a renewed interest in the recovery of traditional Jewish religious customs and teacings.

This is the central conclusion that emerged from a series of recent interviews with Reform, Conservative and Orthodox leaders in this country.

"We are looking for authentic Jewish experience," said Rabbi Eugene B. Borowitz, a Reform theologian at Hebrew Union College-Jewish Institution of Religion in Manhattan. "Like others in today's existentialist revolutionu, we are seeking not to assimilate with culture as a whole but to do our Jewish thing."

Other developments noted by religious thinkers in the three denominations include the following:

¶Some Reform Jews, whose tradition has played down the idea of divine revelation and emphasis on religious law, have begun to practice stricter observance of the Sabbath and dietary laws.

¶At the other end of the spectrum, a "new left" has developed within the Orthodox movement that seeks to apply Jewish law in a more flexible way to issues such as divorce and marriage, Vietnam and birth control.

¶The passage of time and continuing conflict in the Middle East have led Jewish theologians to confront two cataclysmic events in new ways: the Holocaust, or Nazi destruction of six million Jews, and the existence of the State of Israel.

¶Because of the new emphasis on distinctly Jewish issues, theologians from the three denominations are finding greater unity among themselves and —for the first time in decades —are moving in directions distinctly different from their Christian counterparts on several vital issues.

¶Among young Jews of all traditions, a small movement has grown up that has little use for theological abstractions but that seeks to recover mystical and other aspects of Jewish religious experience.

Ferment Within Minority

Most of the authorities interviewed acknowledged that the number of Jews who are serious about religious observance is relatively small—perhaps one in six—and that even among those who attend temples and synagogues the number seeking new religious forms is a minority.

Nevertheless, there is considerable ferment within this minority that has its origins, in part, in the issues raised by the Holocaust and the continuous threat to the State of Israel.

For many years the Nazi extermination of six million Jews was the subject of considerable documentation but little religious reflection.

"The Europeans who lived through it could not think about it objectively," said Rabbi Seymour Siegel, a professor at the Jewish Theological Seminary in Manhattan. "It has taken a new generation simply to begin to confront it theologically."

The major exceptions were the late philosopher Martin Buber, who spoke of the "eclipse of God," and Elie Wiesel, the novelist, who survived Auschwitz and has had considerable influence among theologians through his treatment of the theme of Jewish persistence in the face of tragedy.

Articles and lectures on the Holocaust, however, have become frequent in recent years, especially since the 1967 war. 'In the June war I saw the Holocaust as a psychological reality for the first time," said Abie Pesses, a 22-year-old graduate student in philosophy at the University of Toronto.

The fundamental issue was pointed up by Richard L. Rubenstein, a Conservative rabbi at the University of Pittsburgh who has identified himself with the Christian "death of God" theologians. His position is that the horror of Auschwitz was "unlike any other kind of evil in the past" and that consequently it is no longer possible to believe in the traditional God of Judaism.

Debate Over Holocaust

Despite widespread agreement that Dr. Rubenstein had raised a valid issue, his conclusions received virtually no support from fellow Jewish theologians.

Except for extremists on the right wing of Orthodoxy, who have seen the Holocaust as divine punishment for the sins of Jews, and some extreme liberals, who have seen no problem because they have rejected the idea of an omnipotent God, most Jewish thinkers have followed the lead of Mr. Wiesel and Emil L. Fackenheim, a philosopher at the University of Toronto.

In brief, their position has been that while no religious explanation is possible of such a profound and horrible tragedy as the systematic destruction of six million people, a religious response is not only possible but necessary. The essence of this response is an affirmation of life and a commitment to the survival of the Jewish people.

"Most assuredly no redeeming Voice is ever heard from Auschwitz no ever will be heard," wrote Dr. Fackenheim. "However, a commanding Voice is being heard and has, however faintly, been heard from the start....Jews are forbidden to grant posthumous victories to Hitler. They are commanded to survive as Jews, lest the Jewish people perish."

If there is virtual unanimity that the Holocaust can have no religious meaning itself, however, Jewish theologians nevertheless debate whether it adds meaning to the rebirth of the State of Israel.

"I'm convinced there is a connection between the two," said Rabbi Walter S. Wurzburger editor of Tradition Magazine and rabbi of Congregation Shaaray Tefile in Far Rockaway, Queens. "I'm not saying Israel justifies such a tragedy, but its emergence in the wake of the Holocaust confirms my faith that the people

of Israel continue to play a theologically significant role as God's witnesses."

Meaning of Israel

Others, however, disagree sharply. Rabbi David Hartman, a prominent 38-year-old Orthodox leader in Montreal, for instance, declared: "The Holocaust doesn't fit in any place. It's not a religious sign. It's just a catastrophe."

The other major topic of current theological debate is the religious meaning of Israel, which Rabbi Siegel described as the "incarnation" of Judaism.

"Israel is the place where the faith was born and will ultimately be reborn," he declared. "A threat to it is a threat to the Jewish faith."

In this case also, one pole is set by some extreme Orthodox Jews, who say that Israel was established entirely by men rather than by God and thus is a trap rather than a religious sign. Others agree that it has no religious dimension, but do so for different reasons.

For instance, Alvin J. Reines, a Reform rabbi and professor at the Hebrew Union College-Jewish Institute of Religion in Cincinnati, stated, "For the first time in thousands of years, Jews abandoned a theology of simply letting God do it. They went out and acted and found that the way you derive something good from reality is to do it."

For the overwhelming majority of Jewish religious thinkers, however, the establishment of Israel—and its victory during the Six-Day War — was clearly a momentous religious event.

"For the first time in almost 2,000 years many of the holiest places in Israel were again under Jewish control," said Dr. Michael Wyschogrod, an Orthodox philosopher at the City College of New York. "It's difficult not to see the redeeming presence of God."

Some, including Rabbi Abra-

ham Joshua Heschel of Jewish Theological Seminary, even ventured to suggest that the events of June, 1967, were the "atchalta d'geula," — the "beginning of redemption."

In the course of debating these issues, some significant changes have taken place in the Jewish theological spectrum, including growing agreement and cooperation across existing Jewish denominational and institutional lines on some issues.

Modern Thought Stressed

Some members of the Reform movement, which began in Germany in the 19th century in an effort to adapt Judaism to the "spirit of the modern age," are showing a new concern for the traditional Orthodox practices against which it first reacted.

The Central Conference of American Rabbis, for instance, the Reform rabbinic body, has

The New York Times (by Edward B. Fiske)
Rabbi David Hartman
Canadian Orthodox
"The Holocaust doesn't fit in anyplace."

it is imperative to reconcile Judaism with science or anything else."

This movement to the right among Reform thinkers has has been welcomed by their Orthodox and Conservative counterparts, but not uncritically.

"They are still asking what the law will do for them," said Dr. Wyschogrod. "If the law is divine, it doesn't need this kind of justification."

More traditional Reform thinkers also resist the trend. "The halacha is outmoded," said Rabbi Reines. "It is grounded in an agricultural economy. I see something like the Sabbath as a state of being, not a requirement that you be in a certain place every Saturday."

As a counterpart to the new Reform right, a "new left" is developing among a small number of Orthodox theologians. Most are disciples of Rabbi Joseph B. Soloveitchik, the leading Orthodox thinker of the day who has, nevertheless, been considerably more restrained in his public statements.

'Scholasticism' Reaction

In negative terms, the new movement is a reaction against what its adherents regard as the "scholasticism" of most current Orthodox leaders.

"Orthodoxy sought to guarantee its survival by freezing the halacha and its theology," said Rabbi Emanuel Rackman, spiritual leader of the Fifth Avenue Synagogue and assistant to the president of Yeshiva University.

"As a result, it now cannot realize its full potential in an age when more and more intellectuals are prepared for the leap of faith but hardly for a leap to obscurantism."

In positive terms, the new Orthodox left seeks greater emphasis on social issues and wider latitude in interpreting the law as it pertains to problems like Jewish-Gentile relations, the religious capabilities

Dr. Richard L. Rubenstein
University of Pittsburgh
Auschwitz was "unlike any other kind of evil in past."

recently begun a study of prayer and made efforts to restore Sabbath observance.

Rabbi Arnold J. Wolf, a Reform rabbi in Highland Park, Ill., known for his social activism, said that he now refrains from all unnecessary activities on the Sabbath and keeps the Biblical dietary laws on pork and seafood.

"I don't observe those on meat and milk, but I'm not sure I'm right and may change," he said.

At the theological level, Reform thinkers such as Rabbi Borowitz, Dr. Fackenheim and Rabbi Jakob J. Petuchowski of Cincinnati are returning to the halacha, the entire corpus of Jewish law and practice, as a basis of criticizing secular cultural values.

"There is a new effort to talk about the supernatural and a personal God, but in the modern idiom," said Rabbi Bernard Martin, a theologian at Case Western Reserve in Cleveland. "We no longer feel

The New York Times
Rabbi Abraham J. Heschel
Jewish Theological Seminary
Events of June, 1967 were the "beginning of redemption."

of women and marriage problems.

Rabbi Irving Greenberg of the Riverdale Jewish Center, for instance, declared that in situations where the letter of Jewish law contains impediments to the remarriage of a widow or divorcee, the objective should be to work within the halacha in a creative way to allow a second marriage.

"Every effort must be made to restore the law to its original function of affirming life, of shaping, directing and enchancing life," he said. "This is especially crucial in the wake of the Holocaust and the rebirth of Israel, when Jews moved from a position of powerlessness to one of power."

This new left has been rejected as a threat to stability by Orthodox leaders and is not without internal conflict.

Middle Position

Dr. Wyschogrod, for instance, said that Rabbi Greenberg and others have gone too far in the direction of changing the law to make it acceptable. "Young people today are not necessarily attracted by a system that simply makes life easier," he declared. Rabbi Greenberg replied, however, that the point was not comfort but "taking the claims of the

present as seriously as those of the past."

In the course of these developments, Conservative theologians such as Rabbi Louis Finkelstein, chancellor of Jewish Theological Seminary; Rabbi Siegel, Rabbi Heschel and Rabbi Max Kadushin have occupied their traditional middle position of respect for the law but wide latitude for differing interpretation.

Some, however, have pushed for an increased rate of change on issues such as marriage and divorce laws and the liturgical calendar.

An important exception to the movement of the three traditions toward each other has been the recent attempts of the Reconstructionist movement under the leadership of Rabbi Mordecai M. Kaplan to break away from its Conservative base and create a fourth grouping in American religious Judaism.

This movement, which was founded in the nineteen-thirties to "reconstruct" Judaism along naturalistic and cultural lines, established its own rabbinical college last year in Philadelphia.

Despite differences, the effect of these theological developments has been to give Jewish theology a momentum and sense of identity that it has not had in recent decades.

"Jewish theology is developing its own dynamics for the first time in years," said Rabbi Wolf. "Classical German Reform theology was the Jewish version of German Protestantism. Now we are going back to our own sources."

Rabbi Fackenheim was among those who linked it to the resurgence of particularism in society as a whole. "The Jewish equivalent of 'black is beautiful' is 'Israel is alive'," he declared.

Rabbi Siegel observed that "for the first time since the Enlightenment" the major trends in Jewish thinking are in opposition to those of Christian thinkers. "Christians are moving away from religious law to the new morality while Jews are returning to it," he stated. "Christian theologians are questioning whether God exists, while we are becoming more conservative."

On this point Rabbi Borowitz added that while Christians are putting more emphasis on involvement in the "secular," Jews are becoming increasing-

ly suspicious of it. "We've been through this," he declared. "We know that in the general culture you lose your soul."

Tensions between the two groups have also been increased by the Six-Day War, when Jews felt that Christians did not show sufficient understanding of the deep theological significance the State of Israel holds for Judaism.

Despite these trends in Jewish thinking, however, some younger Jews are becoming increasingly suspicious of theology and placing more emphasis on direct religious experience.

Rabbi Hartman, for instance, has begun experimenting with liturgy in his Montreal congregation, and an experimental religious community known as the Havurat Shalom has been established near Cambridge, Mass., with an emphasis on trying to give traditional liturgical traditions new expression.

"Unless theology is very personal, it's nowhere," said Rabbi Arthur Green, one of the founders. "Theology is useful only if it provides a language for discussing experience."

November 23, 1969

The Jewish Contradiction

By ARTHUR I. WASKOW

The Jewish community in America is now living in a situation unprecedented in 2,000 years of Jewish history —but only its young people are facing the fact, and even they have just begun to.

The new situation is that after generations of prayer for a return to Zion, there is a Zion. So now the Diaspora—the "dispersion" of Jews in communities around the world—must either think and feel its way through to a new meaning for itself, or wither away. At last the Diaspora is no longer a necessary evil; can Jewish thought, then, grow to see in it a positive good?

For older Jews the importance of the Diaspora is simple enough; it supports and assists those Jews who have returned to Zion and created the State of Israel.

Arthur Waskow, a Fellow of the Institute for Policy Studies, is author of "The Freedom Seder" and the forthcoming "Against the Pharaohs."

But the Jewish youth in America is not so easily satisfied. For many young Jews, the irony—they would say "hypocrisy"—of being a "bond-buying Zionist," of supporting Israel without settling there, puts too great a strain on youthful idealism. They say that ancient chant, "Next year in Jerusalem," now rings untrue: it is always possible, if the chanter means it, to go *this* year. And if not, why keep on chanting it?

For some young Jews, this contradiction is resolved by deciding to return and build up Zion themselves. For some, it is resolved by abandoning serious connections with being Jewish —perhaps choosing an identity as a Marxist or as a citizen of "the Woodstock nation" instead. But for some it has turned into a serious re-examination of what it means to remain Jewish and to remain in the Diaspora, in America.

These last two groups are posing agonizing questions to the American Jewish Establishment.

The first group, those who "assimilate" as radicals or hippies, are not what was traditionally called assimila-

tionists, because they, too, are rejecting American society. (Some would say "Amerikan" society, and would say it with images of Germany and genocide before their eyes—even for them, a "Jewish" memory.) The older assimilationism is dead—dead because when the blacks tried to join the melting pot it cracked forever, dead because being American has come to many young people to mean being "Vietnam." But the new "outsider" assimilationism upsets parents, or B'nai B'rith, or the local Jewish Community Council, even more than the old assimilationism.

For older Jews focus on their children's fierce rejection of Israel, their contempt for bar-mitzvahs, their creation of communes instead of families, their refusal to get married at all— let alone to a nice Jewish girl or boy!— in short, their shrug at conventional Jewish life and values.

But what about the new "committed Jews" who want to create a way of staying in America and staying Jewish? You might be far less likely to expect the older Jewish community to greet them with hostility—but it does.

What are these young, committed, Diaspora-centered Jews about?

Some believe that Prophetic Juda-

157

ism requires the whole Jewish community to take on the role of Jonah warning Nineveh to turn away from its sins, lest it be destroyed—warning America to give up the war against Indochina, H-bombs, racism, and pollution of the earth, lest America be literally destroyed. Others have discovered—and adopted—the tradition of the Jewish Labor Bund, which from 1897 to 1939, first in Tsarist Russia and then in inter-war Poland, was committed to socialism and to the survival and liberation of the Jewish people, but unlike the Zionists saw that liberation was embodied in the countries where the Jews already lived.

Still others seek the revival of the ecstatic values of Hassidism, of dance and mysticism.

Some look to the Israeli Kibbutz as a model of what could be done in North America. They dream of moving beyond the Woodstockian communes.

And others have tried to create tiny chavurot or fellowships—rabbinical schools that are much more like the Talmud discussion-groups of Eastern Europe than like the formal seminaries of America. Or living-room congregations for prayer and discussion that are much more like the little *shtetel* of Eastern Europe than the imposing synagogues of America.

Why should this inspire hostility from older Jews? Because it threatens many images. One is the image that America is the Golden Land. These young Jews reject conventional American values. Another is the image that after centuries of persecution Israel is the Promised Land—and these young Jews are perfectly prepared to criticize the policies of Israel.

But if older Jews can make nothing of the new insurgencies younger ones can make nothing Jewish of anything else. Might they turn on to vigilante Judaism of the Jewish Defense League sort? Scarcely. To most young Jews it stinks of racism, repression, and reaction.

So the die seems cast. Either the American Jewish community will disappear during the next generation, or it will survive through forms and values radically different. But then, some young Jews are saying: either Isaiah's Days of Peace and Justice will be achieved on earth in the next generation, or the earth itself will be consumed by fire and poison. If that is indeed the choice, who could more joyfully work for Isaiah's vision than Isaiah's people in America?

October 21, 1970

Jewish Day Schools Becoming Important Factor in U.S.

Sponsors Call Them Good Alternative to Public Education

By FRED FERRETTI

The Jewish day school, its facilities and enrollment growing each year, is becoming an increasingly important factor in America, educationally, socially and politically.

The number of schools has grown significantly since the end of World War II when there were 69 with 10,000 students in the United States; now there are 378 schools with 75,000 students.

Their growth as viable alternative schools has been the concern of a four-day convention of Jewish day school principals and administrators in Greenfield Park, N. Y., that concludes today.

The educators have been studying ways of utilizing such modern school concepts as nongraded classes.

They have been seeking ways of applying classroom management, hitherto used in experimental secular schools, to religious teaching. And they have been outspoken in their belief that Jewish fund-raising organizations must devote greater efforts to assisting the day schools financially.

Program of Study

According to their sponsors, the day schools are providing a needed alternative to public schools, which no longer enjoy the traditional unquestioning support of the Jewish community.

Like their counterparts in Catholic schools, Jewish day school pupils study secular subjects as well as religion. The Talmud, the body of Jewish oral law and commentary, is studied, as well as the Bible, especially the Torah, which comprises the Five Books of Moses.

The curriculum also includes Hebrew language and literature; Jewish history, including the history of modern-day Israel, and the significance of Jewish holidays and ritual practice.

According to Orthodox, Conservative and Reform Jewish observers, the increasing number of Jewish day schools reflects one aspect of a shift in the social attitudes of some young American Jews.

Whereas many young people born in the United States had been devotees of the melting-pot theory—they felt that to be Jewish was to be segregated and tried to become as un-Jewish as possible—now, many are expressing an identification with their heritage and with long-discarded tradition.

All three branches of the Judaism now say they recognize the reality of cultural pluralism, and a resurgence of pride in being Jewish among the young.

Politically, the Jewish day school reflects yet another shift, though slight, in American Jewish thinking. The Jewish community used to present a solid front favoring complete separation of church and state and opposing aid to nonpublic schools.

Now, some Orthodox groups have joined Catholics to petition for Federal and state assistance funds for private schools. Most Conservative and Reform groups, however, still continue to oppose such aid.

The United Synagogue of America, a Conservative group, opposes government aid to parochial and private schools, as does the Union of American Hebrew Congregations, a Reform group. The Union of Orthodox Jewish Congregations of America favors aid.

Among secular Jewish organizations, aid is opposed by the American Jewish Congress, B'nai B'rith, the Jewish War Veterans, the National Council of Jewish Women, the American Jewish Committee and the Jewish Labor Committee.

Support by Orthodox

Favoring aid are the Rabbinical Council of America, the Agudath Israel group and Torah Umesorah (the National Association of Hebrew Day Schools)—all Orthodox organizations. The position of the Orthodox groups is not surprising, in view of the fact that almost all Jewish day schools have Orthodox sponsorship.

However, there are shades of advocacy and opposition. Rabbi Henry Siegman, executive vice president of the Synagogue Council of America, which represents Orthodox, Conservative and Reform groups, said in an interview:

"The commitment to traditional church-state separation is increasingly under attack in the Jewish community. Where before we used to present a monolithic front now we hear talk about funding for the secular portions of Jewish day school studies being acceptable.

"The rationalization is that if the schools render vital service to the nation, then they're entitled to aid.

"Even so, an ambivalence exists. The schools want the funds but they're afraid of government interference."

Rabbi Siegman's organization has invited Catholic and Protestant organizations to a national study conference on "Public Aid to Nonpublic Education" that begins today in Monsey, N. Y.

Meanwhile, he said, efforts continue to have the fundraising arms of the Jewish community devote more of their energies toward day schools.

The number of Jewish day schools continues to increase in urban areas of the country. Schools now exist in 31 states and 75 communities. In Los Angeles, for example, there were 60 day schools in 1960; now there are 75 and the enrollment is about 20,000. Two new day schools have been opened in the San Francisco-Oakland Bay area in the last two years.

Local and U.S. Figures

Boston, Cincinnati, Chicago and Pittsburgh report enrollment at Jewish day schools up. In New Jersey, there are 4,000 students attending 18 day schools and enrollment is in creasing at the rate of 3 to 4 per cent a year.

But in the area embracing the city proper and Westchester and Nassau Counties, the figures are even more impressive. Of the nation's 378 day schools, 170 are in the local area. In addition, there are 34 Jewish day nurseries, making a total of 204 day schools here.

Helping stimulate the growth of day schools, in the view of Rabbi Siegman, is the ineffectiveness of Sunday and afternoon schools, which he calls "farces." Explaining his stand, the rabbi said:

"If kids go to public school and then to synagogue in the afternoon, they know Hebrew is secondary. The all-day school establishes parity, if it does nothing else."

With more than 50 per cent of the country's schools, New York has about 52,000 day school pupils, or about 67 per cent of the nationwide total.

Unusual Development

Nationally, there are 122 Jewish high schools, 60 of which are in New York. Significantly, Orthodox schools, which for many years were the only day schools serving the Jewish community, have been augmented by 34 schools of the Solomon Schecter Day School movement, named for the founder of Conservattive Judaism.

In addition, there is now a Reform Jewish day school here, Rodeph Sholom. Scheduled to open are the Nelson Glueck Day School in Philadelphia and another school in Miami.

Spokesmen for all branches of Judaism agree that the mere existence of a Reform day school is unusual, for it has been among Reform Jews that the most resistance to traditional Jewish education arose, and has remained.

The Manhattan Day School at 110 Manhattan Avenue is a typical school. Half of its curriculum is state-mandated, half is Hebrew studies. It has 300 students, from kindergarten through eighth grade.

On a recent tour of the school, its principal, Rabbi Sholom Rephun, took a visitor to a third-grade class where 8-year-olds were learning the Book of Genesis with commentaries in Hebrew under Feivel Brill; then, next door where Mrs. Judith Bloomfield was presiding over the school's experimental mathematics lab, begun last year.

In another room, six 12-year-old girls sat around a small table talking about parents with Mrs. Norma Cybul, the school's guidance counselor.

In another class, a group of eight boys was being quizzed on the Talmud by Rabbi Jacob Pasternak.

As Rabbi Rephun walked the halls, students stopped to chat with him. He knew their names, their parents, their problems and their skills. At one point, a young lad dashed around a corner and rushed headlong into Rabbi Rephun's kneecaps. The rabbi grabbed him.

Separating Pupils

"Daniel," he said. "Daniel.

These men are touring our school. Tell them what you like."

"English," said Daniel.

"It is not exactly the answer we would want," the rabbi said, grinning. He explained later that the boy was Daniel Saguy, the son of an Israeli Consul in New York.

In the school, the boys and girls attend classes together until the sixth grade; then they are separated. Most pupils attend schools from 8:30 A.M. to 4:30 P.M.

Rabbi Rephun said that most of the school's graduates would go on to Jewish all-day high schools. Some, he said, will become rabbis. It is estimated that about 900 students graduate from Jewish high schools each year and of these, 60 go on to rabbinical studies.

At least one teacher at the Manhattan Day School is an Israeli citizen, studying here and teaching in his offhours.

Mr. Toubin of the American Association for Jewish Education, says that there are more than 100 Israeli teachers here on exchange programs under State Department auspices. "If not for them," he said, "most of the secondary schools would have to close down."

Reasons for the most recent growth of the Jewish day school are given as the winning of the six-day war by Israel, the awakening of the young Jew to his tradition and the decline in quality of the public schools. Most spokesmen agree that these factors have stimulated recent growth.

Other Reasons Offered

In addition, Rabbi Siegman said:

"If kids go to a public school and then to a synagogue in the afternoon they know Hebrew is secondary. What they develop is a contempt for Jewish education. That's changing now. The all-day school establishes parity if it does nothing else."

Dr. Morton Siegel, executive director of the United Synagogue of America, agreed. "They realize supplementary education is inadequate to give identity," he said. "They want more. On the part of some, it is dissatisfaction with the public schools. It is not an attempt to run from integration."

It is in the concept of parity that caution arises. Dr. Siegel is against parity if it means acceptance by religious schools of government funds. His concern is shared by Dr. Jack Spiro, national director of education for the Reform Jewish movement.

"We could never accept aid on any level," Dr. Spiro said. This applies to "books, lunches, milk programs, so-called aid to children," as well as direct financial assistance, he said, continuing:

"You can argue that accepting aid for secular studies is all right, that religion is not threatened, but I don't agree. We could never accept any money for anything. If you do and try to explain it, it's nothing but rationalization."

May 9, 1971

Reform Leaders Concerned Over the Lack of Awareness by American Jewish Youth of the Nazi Holocaust

By IRVING SPIEGEL
Special to The New York Times

LOS ANGELES, Nov. 7 — Spiritual leaders of American Reform Judaism expressed concern today over the attitude of American Jewish youth who view the Nazi holocaust as "ancient history" without meaning for them.

Reform rabbis, in interviews and in informal talks at a special session on this theme at the biennial convention of the Union of American Hebrew Congregations, criticized organized religious groups for their failure to instill in youth a deep-rooted awareness of what the holocaust means to contemporary Jewry.

They conceded that the problem had been compounded by the fact that most American Jewish youngsters were born after the Hitler regime had been destroyed.

Asserting that Jewish college youth "find themselves unrelated to the crucial events which shaped our contemporary Jewish consciousness," Rabbi Jack Bemporad, director of worship for the union, called it "imperative" that organized Jewligious and secular groups overcome the gap" between those who lived through the Nazi holocaust in the nineteen-thirties and nineteen-forties and those born after the end of the Nazi regime in Germany in 1945.

Along with other spiritual leaders, Rabbi Bemporad called for an intensified development of curriculum materials in religious schools and synagogues that would focus on the teachings of the holocaust. In this connection he and other rabbis urged that a day must be set aside annually by the American Jewish community to commemorate the six million Jews who were killed during the Nazi regime. Such a day, they said, would be similar to one that is observed in Israel annually and is known as "Yom Hashoh" — day of the holocaust.

Rabbi Jack D. Spiro, director of the union's commission on Jewish education, said that while material was being produced by his group on the holocaust, the "formidable challenge" was to overcome the attitudes of the Jewish youngster.

The youngsters, he said, feel that other humanitarian issues facing them surpass the remembrance of the holocaust.

Rabbi Roland B. Gittelsohn of Boston said that young Jews frequently responded to the holocaust "by asking why they should become so excited about the murder of Jews a generation ago, when the Vietnamese, Bengalese and many other peoples are being brutally killed."

In urging that a day be set aside by the Jewish community in observance of the holocaust, Rabbi Joseph B. Glaser, executive vice president of the Central Conference of American Rabbis, the rabbinic arm of American Reform Judaism, cited a remark by his 14-year-old son, Simeon, when both were in Israel at the time of the observance:

"When the siren began to blow, everybody froze—people, buses—just dead silence—no motion, I really knew then what the holocaust meant." November 8, 1971

Intermarriage

Some Jews Are Mad At Bernie

The bride was Roman Catholic and the groom Jewish. They wanted a religious wedding, so they hit on a compromise that would show that "religions can live in harmony with religions." A priest conducted the saying of vows; a rabbi led them in the giving of the rings. Both clergymen gave blessings, and, in a final gesture of bubbling interfaith good will, the entire wedding party gathered in a circle with their hands together like the New York Knicks just before game time.

The scene is from the television comedy hit, "Bridget Loves Bernie." Because of its theme—in effect, can the son of a Jewish delicatessen owner find happiness with the daughter of an Irish Catholic business magnate?—the program has become embroiled in controversy.

Leaders of virtually the entire spectrum of American religious Judaism have asked the Columbia Broadcasting System to withdraw the program on the ground that it makes intermarriage look "mod" and thus mocks a basic teaching of Judaism. "The program treats intermarriage in a cavalier, cute, condoning fashion, and deals with its inevitable problems as though they're instantly solvable," complained Rabbi Balfour Brickner, spokesman for the Synagogue Council of America. Jewish religious leaders have held several meetings with C.B.S. officials, and one rabbi is organizing a boycott of the program's sponsors.

Producers of the program expressed bewilderment at the protests. John D. Mitchell, president of Screen Gems, which supplies the program to C.B.S., called it "an entertaining comedy show," and added, "While we recognize that interfaith marriage is a reality in today's society, I don't for a single moment believe that "Bridget Loves Bernie' is advocating it or that any couple would be influenced by it."

Mr. Mitchell and the network are confronting a visible symbol of what in the last few years has come to be regarded as a major problem within American Judaism — and possibly even a threat to its continued existence.

Prohibitions against marriage to non-Jews go back to the earliest Mosaic laws, and violation has traditionally been regarded as only slightly less serious than conversion to another faith. Jewish religious law on the subject has generally been backed up by heavy informal social pressure in Jewish communities.

In the last few years, though, behavior patterns in this country have begun to shift. A study released last year by the Council of Jewish Federations and Welfare Funds found that nearly one-third of American Jews who married between 1966 and 1972 had non-Jewish spouses. This was more than double the rate of the previous five years and nearly four times the pre-1960 figures.

Moreover, the number of rabbis willing to perform mixed marriages—and willing to do so openly—has gone up sharply. Though Orthodox and Conservative rabbis remain almost unanimously opposed to the practice, the Central Conference of American Rabbis (C.C.A.R.), a Reform group, reported last year that one-fifth of its members will perform mixed marriages without conditions, and that another fifth are willing to do so when "special conditions exist" — such as a pledge to raise the children as Jews.

The reasons for the new openness toward intermarriage include the declining authority of Jewish religious law, the diminishing reluctance of Jews in an ecumenical age to enter into relationships with Christians, and the growing acceptance of intermarriage in the general population. A Gallup survey released in November reported that general public acceptance of marriage between Jews and non-Jews increased from 59 per cent to 67 per cent between 1968 and 1972.

The trend is deeply troubling to many Jewish leaders, and numerous rabbinical groups have decided that the place to start combating it is within their own ranks. Last week, the New York Board of Rabbis, whose members are Reform, Conservative and Orthodox, voted to condemn "without equivocation" members who perform mixed marriages. The C.C.A.R., which tabled a resolution against the practice two years ago, will vote on the matter in November.

Opposition to mixed marriage is generally based on the assumption that, once it reaches a certain level, the very survival of Judaism as a distinct faith and culture is threatened. "Judaism is ultimately saved in the family more than anywhere else," said Rabbi Joseph B. Glaser, executive vice president of the C.C.A.R. He said that he opposes rabbis who perform mixed marriages because "it's a signal to young kids on the way up that it's okay."

Others disagree. Rabbi Philip Schechter, a Reform rabbi who heads three small congregations in the New York City area and says that he has conducted more mixed marriages than he can remember, said, "I reject the survival argument. History shows lots of periods of extensive intermarriage, and we've survived." He also argued that refusing to conduct mixed marriages is counterproductive. "By the time a couple comes to a rabbi, they have already decided to get married," he stated. "If he refuses, then he is just driving them both away from the faith."

Some revisionist sociology has begun to question the assumption that intermarriage is tantamount to leaving Judaism. George Johnson, research director of the Synagogue Council of America, suggested that intermarriage may be "the result rather than the cause of assimilation." The basic problem, he said, is a declining sense of Jewish identity among American Jews. As a result, many Jews see intermarriage and the preservation of their Jewish identity as fully "consistent" with each other. Moreover, he added, "Jewish behavior among non-intermarried families is so minimal that intermarrieds are in many cases equally Jewish, or perhaps even more Jewish, than the non-intermarried."

—EDWARD B. FISKE

February 11, 1973

For Many Jewish Families, It's Time to Return to Tradition

By NADINE BROZAN

In Manhattan, members of Congregation Rodeph Sholom gather early on a Sunday morning to learn from their rabbis how to perform the rituals of the Sabbath.

In Greenwich, Conn., Temple Sholom organizes a program in which "host" families invite "learner" families to share Sabbath dinners in their homes.

In Albany, the Parenthood group of Congregation Beth Emeth formulates a class that will require parents to attend with their children.

And in Los Angeles, families belonging to the Leo Baeck Temple retreat for the weekend to their synagogue, camping out in sleeping bags.

As recently as last year, Jewish organizations were wringing their collective hands over the apparent erosion of the family. As the conduit of Judaism's safe passage from one generation to another, it seemed to be foundering.

Now the evidence grows that it is headed for safer shores and, in the process, is creating new institutions and revitalizing old ones.

Theories to explain the turnabout are as abundant as examples that it has indeed turned back to past strengths.

Speculations include the crisis of Israel, the failures of science and liberalism, disillusionment with materialism, the moral climate of Watergate, the isolation of the nuclear family, and, most often, the search for identity in an impersonal society.

Decade of Preoccupation

"The Jewish family has been uptight for about 20 years," said Eleanor Schwartz, head of a steering committee on the Jewish family, a joint venture of major Reform organizations. "Since the upsurge of intermarriage, the feeling was that Jews could intermarry themselves out of existence. In the last 10 years, everyone's been preoccupied with the deterioration of even the nuclear family.

"Now the more depersonalized the world becomes, the more horrible the facts of life in the news, the more important is the quest for identification and bonds," she added. "We're yearning for ways to find that our humanness has significance."

Whatever the causes, the evidence accumulates: the demand for courses in everything from challah baking to religious consciousness raising, the sales of a Union of American Hebrew Congregation manual on how to observe the Sabbath, the spreading appeal of family retreats.

It's happening both within the confines of the establishment—for example with the formation of family-oriented Reform day schools, and outside the establishment— the packed rallies of Hineni, an 18-month-old revival movement that its founder, Esther Jungreis, said bridges the gap between "pediatrics and geriatrics."

On an individual level, changing patterns can be measured by such families as the Elliot Simons of New City, N. Y., and the William Ackermans of Great Neck, L. I.

"We need to feel that we are a Jewish family, not just Jewish people," Sandra Simon said. Since last fall, the couple and their two children have regularly attended Friday evening services at Temple Beth Torah in Upper Nyack and have observed the Sabbath and other holidays at home.

Dramatic Evolution

"You get a feeling for the holidays if you celebrate them with someone you love," Mrs. Simon said.

The Ackermans have undergone a more dramatic evolution. For the last three months, they have broadened their Sabbath commemoration to include not just Friday evening temple worship but Saturday morning and afternoon, too. And they adhere to all proscriptions against work during the 24-hour period. When not at Temple Israel, a Conservative synagogue in Great Neck, they spend the time in quiet activities with their four children, ages 3 to 12.

"If anybody ever needed the concept of the Sabbath —to withdraw and renew— it is the contemporary suburban family," Linda Ackerman remarked. "Friday night is the one evening a week we all eat together. We need a day in which there are no pressures, no appointments, no car pools, a day for the family to relax, talk and read together."

Starting this week, their home will be kosher. The unanimous decision to observe the strict dietary laws "is a symbol that we mean as a family to lead a committed Jewish life," Mrs. Ackerman said.

While the Ackermans draw closer in their own nest, they have, like thousands of other families across the country, expanded their definition of family to include people who are not related. In their case, the tie was forged with a group of 19 families whose children attend an enrichment class for 5- and 6-year-olds at Temple Israel.

The Amelin (Hebrew for little toilers) class, described by its founders as a Hebrew Head Start, was formed last spring at the instigation of parents, "who felt there were deficiencies in education."

'Ritually Deficient'

"Then we realized," Mrs. Ackerman said, "that the deficiencies derived more from the home, that education can only elaborate what is taught in the home, and our homes were ritually deficient."

Parental responsibility is obligatory, and beside the classroom work, the parents, the pupils and their siblings, and grandparents get together at least once a month for services, holiday parties and such occasions as music nights.

The concept that the entire family, not just the individual child, enrolls in a school is pervasive at Rodeph Sholom, which established the first Reform day school in the country in 1969. It now has a student body of 84 in kindergarten through fourth grade; within two years it will expand through sixth grade.

Asked why Reform Jews, whose youngsters might otherwise be candidates for private schools, choose to send them to a fulltime Jewish school, Laura Gold, Parents' Educational Guild president, explained: "Because it's a family school. It provides a family other than our own."

Rodeph Sholom administrators have been astonished by the numerous requests of parents for such activities as volley ball nights, square dances and pot luck suppers.

The family unit is also grafting new branches onto the trunk of the synagogue.

The nine-month-old Parenthood of Congregation Beth Emeth, a Reform congregation of 1,100 families in Albany is one example. The group, comprised of 25 families, mainly parents in their mid-20's to early 40's, celebrate all holidays together and hold special dinners, and experimental services.

"I began to find that there was little to satisfy what I remember as the home-centered Judaism of my youth. We started this group to provide families with the opportunity to do Jewish things together," said Professor Melvin D. Urofsky, who teaches history at the State University of New York at Albany. Professor Urofsky and his wife serve as cochairmen of the group.

Like many of its counterparts, Parenthood is now planning a weekend retreat of prayer, discussion and study next month at a camp in Great Barrington, Mass.

In contrast to the retreats normally held at camp sites or in hotels, the members of the Chaverim of the Leo Baeck Temple in Los Angeles retreat in the synagogue itself. (The group is one of many havurot, or minicongregations that have sprung up across the country as a reaction against religious depersonalization. Some havurot exist within a congregation; others are independent.)

For 24 hours, the Chaverim participants live together, cook together, and compose and conduct their own services and seminars. At night, they stretch out in sleeping bags on the floors, in the pews, on the pulpit.

When the Leo Baeck Chaverim was founded three years ago, its members shied away from intense commitment.

"At first, we simply decided to attend services together," said Mrs. Mark Levy. "But what has happened is that, almost to a family, everyone has made a deep commitment that has also made us very close to one another. We regard each other with very special feeling. We celebrate all important events together— when someone moves into a new house, we arrive with special food and a mezuzah for the door."

Tree Festival

Out of that commitment has also come some ceremonial innovations. For Tu b'Shevat, the festival of trees, the group planted trees in the Santa Monica Mountains, an area hard hit by forest fires. Last week the group held a Passover picnic at a nearby ranch.

To Rabbi Leonard Beerman, senior rabbi of the temple, such activities reflect a change in the interaction between worshiper and institution, with the congregant no longer content just to listen.

"People realize that being observant is not something someone else can do for them; it's something they themselves energize. There is a strong desire to achieve authenticity in living and not just belong to a temple out of noblesse oblige," he said.

According to Rabbi Haskel M. Bernat of Chicago, director of the Commission on Worship of the U.A.H.C. and the Central Conference of American Rabbis, family involvement will alter the synagogue of the future. He foresees not only liturgical, but architectural change "to remove the pews."

"They're an antifamily, isolating experience," he said. "People will worship in small circles where they can sense and touch one another."

For the moment, he continued, "there is a recognition by the synagogue that it is not necessarily the single instrument of Jewish continuity but that, in fact, it always had a partner, the family. While the synagogue can be the instructor of Jewish values, the home is the promulgator."

April 17, 1974

RABBIS DEPLORE LOSS OF YOUTHS

Orthodox Group Concedes Failure on Alienation

By IRVING SPIEGEL
Special to The New York Times

MIAMI BEACH, June 26 — American Orthodox rabbis acknowledge that they have failed to capture what one of them described as "the hearts and minds of many of our educated, intellectual Jewish youth."

At meetings and in interviews here, the rabbis said that while they had succeeded in reaching "vast numbers who had drifted away from observant Judaism" that number was small compared with those who remain alienated from traditional Judaism.

Rabbi Fabian Schonfeld, newly elected president of the 1,000-member Rabbinical Council of America, deplored the failure of the American Orthodox rabbinate to mount a counter-attack against "corrosive forces of secularism and nihilism" that he said were markedly influencing Orthodox-trained youngsters. The rabbinical council is holding its 38th annual meeting at the Caribbean Hotel.

A recent study disclosed that about 53 per cent of American Jews were unaffiliated with any religious institution, Orthodox, Reform or Conservative—the three branches of Judaism. In some younger age groups 60 per cent were unaffiliated.

'Differs From Forebears'

Citing these figures, Rabbi Schonfeld said that the American Orthodox community had failed to develop new approaches to transmit its heritage "into a youth that differs so much from its forebears."

"As a result of this failure," he said, "many Jewish youths have turned to all sorts of new ideologies including the exotic, such as Eastern religious practices, as well as radical leftist political doctrines."

Rabbi Walter S. Wurzburger, editor of "Tradition," the council's journal of Orthodox Jewish thought, said that the number of young Jewish men and women attending college had increased sharply in the last generation to 90 per cent.

"They speak and think," Rabbi Wurzburger said, "in terms and concepts unknown to their fathers and they expect those who wish to communicate with them to utilize these same intellectual concepts."

Changing Life Style

Rabbi Joseph Grunblatt, lecturer on Jewish philosophy at Touro College in New York, said that the Orthodox community must contend with "a changing life-style that contradicts its basic values." He said that "where Judaism teaches the value of righteous living, modern life-styles emphasize obsession with sex and complete freedom from any discipline." He said that this made difficult the task of teaching and transmitting the ethical values of Judaism.

Rabbi Rafael G. Grossman of Memphis, chairman of the convention, concluded that this conflict was a major factor in an increasing rate of intermarriage, which now exceeds 33 per cent. "This danger," he said, "threatens the entire fabric of the Jewish future, let alone that of the Orthodox community."

Rabbi Bernard Twersky, public information officer of the council, said that the Orthodox body would establish a committee of scholars and rabbis to study the psychological, social and religious factors that shape the behavior and outlook of young Jews in an effort to determine reasons for the rising intermarriage of Jews with persons of other religions.

June 27, 1974

JEWS SAID TO EASE VIEW ON MARRIAGE

Study Finds an Increasing Attempt to Keep Jewish Partner in Community

By KENNETH A. BRIGGS
Special to The New York Times

WASHINGTON, May 15 — Many Jews appear to be softening their attitude toward Jews who marry outside their faith, according to researchers.

Those undertaking the study for the American Jewish Committee emphasize that there has been little apparent shift in the solid opposition among Jews to mixed marriages. Intermarriage is still viewed as a serious threat to Jewish survival.

But they say that their preliminary findings, in addition to recent discussions in Jewish periodicals, indicate that many are attempting to keep Jews who marry outside the faith within Jewish cultural, religious and family life.

Much of this reassessment seems to reflect a conviction that condemning intermarriages or declaring the Jewish partner "dead" in the eyes of his religion have been counterproductive. Despite repeated appeals and denunciations by various spokesmen, including groups of rabbis, the intermarriage rate has steadily risen in the view of the experts and will continue to do so.

Way of Responding

"If there is going to be intermarriage," says Inge Gibel, who is working on the two-year intermarriage study, "what is the most creative way of responding to make sure that there is no loss of Jewishness by the Jewish partner?"

Miss Gibel says that Jews involved in these marriages are more likely to affirm their religious heritage than in the past, largely because the family and synagogue are more open to their participation.

Thus, a mother and her children who 30 years ago might have felt rejected and unwelcome in her temple or in her parents' home would more likely be accepted and encouraged these days, Miss Gibel says.

Another sign of flexibility is the example of the Jewish father whose children are technically non-Jews because their mother is a non-Jew but who are readily accepted into the synagogue.

The prevalence of this attitude and the degree to which it has taken hold varies greatly within Jewish life. The vast majority of Orthodox Jews are unrelentingly opposed to granting concessions to Jewish law and are the most inclined to take a hard line.

More Acceptance

It is among Conservative and Reform branches of Judaism and among secular Jews that the shift toward a more accommodating view is most evident.

Among the causes cited is a feeling that a supportive response is likely to do more for Jewish survival by maintaining a positive relationship between the Jewish partner in an intermarriage and his or her Jewish background.

"From a cold-blooded point of view, it is a way of minimizing losses," says Milton Himmelfarb, the committee's director of information and research services. "Maybe we'll break even by trying to socialize the Jewish and non-Jewish partner into Jewish society. The standard way to put it is that you haven't lost a daughter but gained a son."

The prevailing conditions of pluralism and increased intergroup contact make a continuing climb in the intermarriage rate inevitable, Mr. Himmelfarb says.

Of those who do intermarry, the Jewish partner "both wants to be Jewish and also to be married to this person," says Rabbi James Rudin of the Interreligious Affairs Commission. He says Jews in these situations are more self-conscious about remaining Jewish these days and are less likely to be absorbed into the Christian community.

Pull Both Ways

"We have underrated Judaism," Rabbi Rudin says. "We used to think it was automatic that the Jews would become part of Christendom. That's not true. There is as much pull the other way toward Judaism."

Miss Gibel says: "The trend has been for the Jewish partner to work harder at being Jewishly involved."

The non-Jewish partner who is seeking conversion also appears to be benefiting from the new climate. Religious law forbids conversion solely for the purpose of marriage. It must be based on personal, religious grounds. But observers say that even some Orthodox rabbis are re-examining their attitudes toward this practice to make it easier for the non-Jewish person to be taken into the faith.

Though there is much continuing alarm over intermarriage, it would seem by the study and by other reports that it is being increasingly considered a fact of life.

"It's becoming normative," says Yehuda Rosenman, Jewish communal affairs director, "in a very matter-of-fact way."

May 16, 1976

OTHER FAITHS

'A Mighty People In the Rockies'

The Mormons reach their 125th anniversary 1,250,000 strong, and still growing.

By REBECCA FRANKLIN

SALT LAKE CITY.

AFTER a strange and tortured history, Utah's Mormons are giving abundant evidence that they have fulfilled and even surpassed the prediction of Mormon Prophet Joseph Smith that they would become "a mighty people in the midst of the Rocky Mountains." The church, which this Wednesday celebrates the 125th anniversary of its founding in Seneca County, N. Y., now has a membership of more than 1,250,000, and the message of the Mormons has been carried throughout the world by zealous, unpaid missionaries.

Mormonism, more properly called the Church of Jesus Christ of Latterday Saints, has its world capital in this beautiful high-level valley of the Great Salt Lake, encircled by the crinkled slopes of the Wasatch and the Oquirrhs. As were the Friends in Philadelphia, the Saints have been all but swamped by outsiders—"Gentiles," as non-Mormons are called. But the mountain fastness which was their refuge in a time of grievous persecution, the place they lovingly called Zion and Deseret and the New Jerusalem, is still peculiarly their own. Approximately 50 per cent of the city's population of 201,000 (and more than 70 per cent of Utah as a whole) belong to the Mormon faith.

MORMONS are not yet the richest people on earth, as Brigham Young, another Mormon prophet, said they would be, but the wealth of the church and its people is considerable. In Salt Lake City alone, the church owns banks and insurance companies, the afternoon newspaper (The Deseret News), two large hotels, two hospitals, two sugar concerns, storehouses bulging with food and clothing for its vast welfare program, and a substantial interest in the leading department store. The church also owns the $9,000,000 Brigham Young University at Provo, a business college, a music school and more than one hundred seminaries and institutes where Mormon doctrine and history are taught to grade school, high school and college students.

More than that, Mormons are respected citizens—even, in some cases, holders of high public office—in a country which once rejected them. Secretary of Agriculture Ezra Taft Benson, one of the Twelve Apostles of the church, is the great-grandson and namesake of an apostle who accompanied Brigham Young on the anguished exodus from Nauvoo, Ill. The Secretary's grandfather was born in a

REBECCA FRANKLIN (Mrs. Ward Morehouse) is a freelance writer who recently made a study of the Mormons and their history.

covered wagon as the caravan moved across the plains.

Utah's Republican Senator Arthur Vivian Watkins, a man with the resolute sense of duty which Mormons encourage in their young, last year presided over the headline-making sessions of the Special Senate Committee on the McCarthy censure. Senator Watkins' grandfather, converted to Mormonism in Great Britain, pushed and pulled a handcart across the country to Utah in 1856 with his wife and two children. Utah's junior Senator, Wallace Foster Bennett, has been treasurer of the Mormon Sunday School General Board since 1938. And J. Reuben Clark Jr., First Counselor in the First Presidency of the Church, has served the country as an Ambassador and as Undersecretary of State.

THE expanding church has an ambitious building program. A temple, larger even than Salt Lake City's famous spired edifice, is nearing completion in Los Angeles. Three other temples are planned for Switzerland, England and New Zealand. (Non-Mormons are not allowed to enter temples, but are welcome in Mormon chapels, or meeting houses.) Between 400 and 500 chapels are being built at an estimated cost of $40,000,000. And here in Salt Lake City a block of property has been bought as the site of an auditorium which will seat at least 35,000.

President David O. McKay, ninth in the line of church leaders since Founder Joseph Smith and, like his predecessors, acknowledged as "prophet, seer and revelator," says that the work of the church today is "stronger and more flourishing than ever before." Like all dedicated Mormons, President McKay has for his church all the ardor of a person newly in love. To sincere Mormons, the church is all truth, all wisdom, all beauty, the answer to all the woes of the world, the divinely appointed keeper of the revealed word of God. Moreover, they appear to have in common that rare and enviable quality, unquestioning faith.

AT 81, white-maned President McKay recently visited Mormon churches in Australia, New Zealand and several Pacific islands, speaking on an average of twice a day, shaking hands with thousands and covering 45,000 miles in forty-five days. His energy and years are not, however, unusual in the Mormon hierarchy. Except for Joseph Smith, who was slain by a mob when he was only 38, all the presidents of the church have enjoyed long lives. Brigham Young, the second president, died at 76, the shortest-lived of Smith's successors.

Indeed, Mor-

mons in general live longer than the people of the United States as a whole, a pleasant statistic they attribute largely to Joseph Smith's Word of Wisdom, which warns against use of tobacco, alcoholic beverages, coffee and tea, and urges Mormons to eat fruits, grains and vegetables with a minimum of meat. To the profound regret of the church, hard liquor is now sold in Utah in state-controlled stores, but there are no drink-by-drink sales, no open bars and no cocktail lounges.

IN other respects Mormon "liberalism" has often shocked stricter Christian sects. The Saints have always been a singing, dancing, music-loving, theatre-minded people, Brigham Young once surmising that there was more singing and dancing in Heaven than in Hell. "Men are, that they might have joy," says the Book of Mormon. Night after night in the exodus from Nauvoo, weary Saints followed prayer with singing and dancing to the music of Capt. William Pitt's brass band, a spectacle that startled many an early settler on the plains.

Even in the demanding early days in Salt Lake City, the Saints managed to produce plays and to organize choral groups and orchestras. The Salt Lake Theatre, built in 1861-62 by Brigham Young, was for many years a noted outpost of the drama, drawing to its stage such famous personalities as Charles Dickens, Sarah Bernhardt, Utah's own Maude Adams, Otis Skinner and Edwin Booth.

TODAY, virtually every L. D. S. chapel has a recreational hall with a stage. Members of the Mutual Improvement Association, to which every Mormon child over 12 may belong, use these halls almost every day in the week. Undoubtedly one of the most efficiently organized youth movements in the world, M. I. A. provides "spiritualized recreation" for its 250,000 members through music, dancing, drama, speech and athletics, a never-ending round of carefully supervised activities. For one hundred years the Saints have been "keeping 'em busy and out of mischief."

Unlike Mormon chapels, temples are used only for marriage ceremonies and other sacred ordinances, including vicarious baptism for the dead, surely the most extraordinary

Other Faiths

doctrine of the church. Holding literally to the Scripture which says, "Except a man be born of water and of the spirit, he cannot enter into the kingdom of God," the Mormons have set out to baptize, by proxy, all those who died without baptism in the Mormon faith--clear back to Father Adam. Thousands of Saints have served as proxies for more than 17,000,000 such baptisms. The church maintains that ancient knowledge of the practice is suggested by the words of St. Paul, "Else what shall they do which are baptized for the dead, if the dead rise not at all? Why are they then baptized for the dead?"

To obtain the names of the dead, specifically those who were ancestors of present-day Mormons, the church's genealogical society, headed by Archibald F. Bennett, gathers records of births, deaths, wills, deeds, and other documents from every state and from many foreign countries. The society's library, open to all faiths, now has the world's largest collection of genealogical records on microfilm, some 109,567 rolls. This, according to Mr. Bennett, is more film than the Library of Congress has. A vault for the safekeeping of film negatives will be built on a near-by mountainside.

Mr. Bennett's 22-year-old son, David M. Bennett, is one of approximately 67,000 missionaries who have represented the church since its beginning. He will spend from two to two-and-a-half years abroad, paying all his own expenses and receiving no compensation whatsoever. Most young men in the church look forward to the time, usually around age 20, when, if they meet certain qualifications, they may become missionaries.

There is no professional or paid clergy in the church and any male, beginning at the age of 12 in the lower rank, may hold the priesthood if he is worthy. Each ward (roughly the equivalent of a parish) is presided over by a Bishop who may be a physician, a lawyer or a salesman, serving without compensation. Sermons are delivered by members; a boy or girl of 12 or 13 may occasionally occupy the pulpit for a short talk. Total participation is the aim.

Today, as in the past, the Mormon Church has certain basic appeals. Foremost among them is the assertion that it is the Church of Jesus Christ "restored" by direct revelation to Joseph Smith--the one, true church. Of more universal appeal, however, is the Mormon concept that the principal object of life is happiness. Still another basic appeal is the church's philosophy of freedom, which holds that man is a free agent, free to choose between good and evil: "Force and coercion are strangers to the Gospel."

Mormons proudly claim that their religion is simple and practical. It consists, they say, of the teachings of the Bible plus modern revelation, a fundamental of Mormon theology. "We believe all that God has revealed, all that He does now reveal, and we believe that He will yet reveal many great and important things." To the Saints, Joseph Smith was no less a prophet than were the prophets of the Old and New Testaments.

The Mormon believes that the Gospel existed on earth long before Christ, and that it was rejected and restored in various "dispensations." He believes that God is a person, of form and dimension. He asserts that all men will be saved "but some will receive a higher place than others * * * for their works have been better." He believes that Jesus Christ will come again to the earth.

The church teaches that every human being lived before he came on earth, that his spirit was "in the beginning with the Father." It teaches further that people continue as living personal beings after death, and that marriage and family relationships continue in the hereafter. To this end, couples who marry in the temple are "sealed" for "time and eternity." Large families are advocated by the church (birth control is contrary to its teachings) and families of six or seven children are not at all unusual. The Mormon birth rate is about twice that of the United States as a whole.

The Mormon story begins with Joseph Smith, a farm boy born in Sharon, Vt., who in 1816 moved with his family to the vicinity of Palmyra in western New York. He later related that at the age of 15 he had a vision of the Father and the Son. Subsequently, he said, he was visited by the Angel Moroni who told him that the "everlasting gospel" had been written on gold plates and buried in the Hill Cumorah four miles south of Palmyra. Eleven witnesses signed declarations that they saw the gold plates which Joseph Smith said he uncovered and translated by means of the Urim and Thummin, the sacred instruments or "stones" mentioned in the Old Testament.

The translated records became the Book of Mormon, named for one of the prophets in it. Saints consider it complementary to the Bible but accept it as Scripture (in the Mormon - owned Hotel Utah, the Book of Mormon rests side by side with the Gideon Bible in every room). The book tells of a family who left Jerusalem about 600 B.C. and sailed to the American continent where they became the ancestors of some of the American Indians.

From the beginning Joseph Smith's new church experienced both astonishing success and frequent harassment. Joseph Smith's assertions of divine revelations, as well as other teachings contrary to beliefs then current, repeatedly incited intolerance. The Saints were closely knit, they were almost unforgivably industrious, and their ranks were being increased by a constant stream of converts from abroad. They were accused of having grandiose political aspirations.

Driven from New York, then from Kirtland, Ohio, and Jackson County, Mo., often with loss of life, always with loss of homes and property, the Saints sought refuge along a broad bend in the Mississippi forty-five miles north of Quincy, Ill. There they built Nauvoo the Beautiful, a place ever green, ever tragic in Mormon memory. Several visitors, among them Col. Thomas L. Kane, the Philadelphia lawyer - soldier noted for his anti-slavery activities, described it admiringly.

It had, said Kane, "bright, new dwellings, set in cool, green gardens, ranging up around a stately, dome-shaped hill" where stood the temple, "whose high tapering spire was radiant with white and gold."

In 1844, after Joseph Smith offered himself for the Presidency—and following the suppression of an inflammatory anti-Mormon newspaper in Nauvoo — indignation against the Mormons swept Illinois. Martial law was declared and Gov. Thomas Ford persuaded Joseph Smith and his brother, Hyrum, to go to near-by Carthage, guaranteeing their safety.

When the men arrived they were arrested for treason and committed to jail. There, on the morning of June 27, a mob in blackface encircled the building, broke down the doors and began shooting. Hyrum Smith died almost instantly. A moment later three bullets struck Joseph Smith, who had sprung toward an open window. As the dying prophet of the Mormons toppled through it, his assassins heard him cry out, "Oh, Lord, my God!"

Brigham Young, an Apostle born in Whitington, Vt., took over the leadership of the shocked and saddened Saints, and when persecution and mob threats mounted, headed the exodus from Nauvoo which began in the bitter weather of Feb. 4, 1846. They left behind them the largest city in Illinois and most of their worldly possessions. They were determined, said Brigham Young, to find a place "where the devil can't come and dig us out."

Few migrations in history have been as packed with drama, human misery and heroism. Between 1846 and 1869, some 85,000 Mormons made the journey across the plains and mountains of Utah. Six thousand died along the way. They came not only from this country but from thirty foreign nations as well. They rode in wagons, they walked and they pushed and tugged

BOOK OF MORMON

The Book of Mormon tells the story of a band of Israelites who, fearful of the prophesied Babylonian captivity, fled by boat to the Western Hemisphere more than 2,000 years before Columbus. Here they built a new civilization, but eventually fell into two warring nations—the Nephites and the Lamanites. In the Battle of Cumorah, fought in what is now upstate New York, the Nephites were annihilated, leaving control of the New World to the Lamanites or, according to Mormon belief, the American Indians. Before Mormon, the last Nephite leader, was killed in this battle he conveyed to his son, Moroni, the records which, according to Joseph Smith, were revealed to him centuries later, and dug out of the Hill Cumorah, near Palmyra, N. Y.

handcarts.

When, on July 24, 1847, the first dusty caravan entered the valley of the Great Salt Lake, Brigham Young, then ailing with mountain fever, looked down upon the treeless valley floor like Moses from Mount Nebo and murmured the historic words, "This is the place, drive on."

Two hours after the Saints arrived they were plowing and irrigating the land. The site quickly chosen by Brigham Young for "a temple to our God" is now the world-renowned Temple Square, where stand the mushroom-domed Tabernacle and the pinnacled Temple, a building of splendid magnitude. More than 1,000,-000 tourists visit Temple Square each year.

Urged by some of his flock to flee the wilderness and seek gold in California, Prophet Young began instead to fashion an empire which he wanted to call Deseret, a word from the Book of Mormon meaning land of the honey bee. Colonizers were sent out in all directions. Wherever they went they irrigated the dry land, and planted grains and sugar beet, and the fruit orchards which are the special glory of Mormon husbandry. They built towns and sturdy homes and, always, schools, for the Mormon holds that no man can be saved in ignorance.

From the beginning the Saints have always taken care of their own. Last year more than 40,000 Mormons who were in need because of illness, age or unemployment were helped with commodities, or cash, or both. Canned goods, fresh vegetables, meat, milk and wearing apparel are distributed to the needy by 116 Bishops' Storehouses. The church's welfare program owns a fleet of trucks, a grain elevator holding 300,000 bushels of wheat, a flour mill, farms, soap factories, clothing factories and sixty-five canneries. The Saints are advised not to accept unearned Government aid.

A GREAT many people know nothing of the Mormon Church except that it formerly countenanced polygamy, a subject still handled somewhat gingerly by the Saints. The doctrine of plural marriage, disclosed by Joseph Smith as a divine revelation in 1842, was not publicly announced until 1852 in Salt Lake City. Mormon leaders said the doctrine simply "restored" a practice carried on by Old Testament patriarchs under divine sanction. It was a shocker to Mormons as well as those outside the church, but not until 1862 was there a Federal law against polygamy.

Holding the law to be unconstitutional, the Saints fought it through the Supreme Court, but lost. The Federal Government then cracked down harshly. The church was disincorporated, thousands of Mormons were disenfranchised and imprisoned, and countless homes were broken. In 1890, the church president, Wilford Woodruff, proclaimed the "Manifesto," which decreed an end to plural marriage. The penalty for plural marriage today is excommunication.

Brigham Young had twenty-seven wives and fifty-six children, all of them, says the family record proudly, "normal in mind and body and with no marks or blemishes of any kind." Gaylen S. Young, a Salt Lake City attorney who is one of Brigham Young's 309 grandchildren, says that ten of the wives were wives in name only, whom Brigham Young married because they needed his financial support. Only 3 per cent of the Mormon membership is said to have entered into plural marriage.

Whatever its moral implications, the practice must be said to have achieved one practical end, that of quickly multiplying the Saints. Mr. Young estimates that his grandfather's descendants now number more than 4,000.

NEARING the end of his life, Brigham Young, in response to a request from a New York newspaper for a summary of his work, wrote:

"The result of my labors for the past 26 years briefly summed up are: The peopling of this territory by the Latter-Day Saints of about 100,000 souls; the founding of over 200 cities, towns and villages inhabited by our people, the establishment of schools, factories, mills and other institutions calculated to improve and benefit our communities. My whole life is devoted to the Almighty's Service, and while I regret that my mission is not better understood by the world, the time will come when I will be understood, and I leave to futurity the judgment of my labors. * * *"

Neither criticism nor the passing years have erased the achievements of Brigham Young and his brave band of pioneers.

April 3, 1955

What Impels Jehovah's Witnesses

By WAYNE PHILLIPS

ONE hundred and eighty thousand Jehovah's Witnesses, from every part of this country and about 130 other lands, recently gathered in New York for what they called a Divine Will International Assembly. It was the largest gathering of any kind ever held in the city, and it drew attention as never before to this group, which in recent years has been growing more rapidly than any other religious organization.

The Witnesses impressed New Yorkers not only with their numbers, but with their diversity (they include people from all walks of life), their racial unself-consciousness (many Witnesses are Negroes) and their quiet, orderly behavior (in contrast to the religious controversy, and hostility, they have often aroused). In streets, subways, buses, everywhere New Yorkers looked they seemed to see the Witnesses wearing their yellow and purple badges with the legend: "God's Kingdom Rules—Is the World's End Near?"

The Witnesses' most striking belief is that since 1914 Satan has ruled the world, but that, in the rapidly approaching Battle of Armageddon, God —whom they call Jehovah—will destroy Satan and all other evil in the world. Thereafter, they believe, God will rule the world and those who have accepted his rule will live on in life everlasting. In one of his many talks at Yankee Stadium and the Polo Grounds, both of which the Witnesses took over for eight days, their leader, Nathan H. Knorr, told them that civilization stands now "at the threshold of a peaceable, happy and life-giving world."

"THIS is the grandest news," he declared, "although it means that we are living at the end of this worry-filled, problem-wracked, insane, loveless old world. We want the new. We are eager to leave the old."

Jehovah's Witnesses, who take this name from Isaiah xliii. 10 ("Ye are my witnesses, saith the Lord, and my servant whom I have chosen * * *."), grew from a small Bible class organized at Alleghany, Pa., near Pittsburgh, in 1872 by Charles Taze Russell. As the movement spread, a printed course of Bible instruction was evolved and sold from door to door. The Watch Tower Bible and Tract Society, which printed these courses and is the organizational form of the movement, was first incorporated in 1884. The name Jehovah's Witnesses was not formally adopted until the first international meeting at Columbus, Ohio, in 1931.

IT was a small movement and most people became aware of it only obliquely—by seeing one of its members standing on a street corner offering copies of its semi-monthly publications The Watchtower and Awake! for sale at 5 cents a copy; by having one of its members call at the door and endeavor to interest them in reading the Bible; by passing the obscure Kingdom Halls that were opened in cities throughout the country, and where Bible study classes are held five days a week.

All baptized Jehovah's Witnesses regard themselves as ministers ordained to devote their lives to preaching the Bible to all men. They work at what they call "temporal jobs" only to supply their essential material needs. All their other energies are devoted to studying the Bible and the techniques of their ministry.

Repeatedly the religious beliefs of the Witnesses have involved them in controversy. They do not believe in saluting the flag, interpreting this as a form of obeisance before temporal imagery that would conflict with their spiritual loyalties. They fought a long and bitter fight up to the Supreme Court before winning the right of their children to attend schools without taking part in flag saluting ceremonies.

For somewhat the same reasons, the Witnesses do not accept military service, and during World War II draft days they claimed exemption on the ground that they were all ordained ministers preaching to the public. Draft boards sent hundreds of young men associated with the Witnesses to Federal penitentiaries.

Another Witness belief forbids blood transfusions—a position they base on the Biblical injunction against eating blood. When, as occasionally happens, one of their children lay close to death and it seemed only a transfusion could save his life, parents have firmly forbidden it, despite extreme public pressure.

The Witnesses cite references to both the Old and New Testaments for all their beliefs, using all translations of the Bible, although their interpretations of these references differ greatly from those of other faiths. They believe the true meaning of the Bible is prophetic and is constantly being unfolded to men, and they deny any possible conflicts within it. They condemn other faiths for what they consider erroneous additions to and elaborations of the teachings of the Bible. Witnesses do not believe in the immortality of the soul, or a fiery hell, or that Christ died on the cross. They believe that only 144,-000 persons will go to heaven and that all but about 15,000 of them are already there; that all others who die have no hope of life hereafter or resurrection. Such teachings have brought mob violence, imprisonment, torture and death to Witnesses in countries where other faiths are officially maintained.

IN 1942, when Mr. Knorr was chosen as their president, the organization had 115,240 adherents in fifty-four countries. This year, the number of ordained Witnesses reached 780,000 scattered over 164 countries and territories.

The extent of their influence, however, may better be measured by their publishing activity. The basic book expounding

WAYNE PHILLIPS has been a staff reporter for The New York Times for the past six years.

their doctrine, "Let God Be True," first appeared in 1946, and so far 16,167,846 copies have been published. Their magazine The Watchtower publishes 3,550,000 copies of each issue in fifty languages, including such little-known African dialects as Cinyanja, Ibo and Xhosa.

The expansion of the Witnesses has been a matter of increasing concern to other faiths. Most of their adherents are apparently being attracted from those other churches.

Following are interviews with a number of Jehovah's Witnesses who attended the International Assembly. All talked willingly and openly about their reasons for embracing what they call "The Truth," and all were apparently deeply convinced of their beliefs.

* * *

MR. AND MRS. WILFRED CHILDS had come to the convention from their home in the summer resort town of York Harbor, Me. In their late twenties, they have been married three years and have no children. Mr. Childs, who has trouble with his hearing and sight, never learned to read too well, and works as a mechanic on automobiles and trailer trucks. His wife augments his $40-a-week take-home pay by caring for an invalid woman.

Florence Childs came from a French Canadian family that had moved south into Maine. She was brought up as a Roman Catholic, but had never been a very regular churchgoer. Her first contact with the Witnesses came two years ago when one of them—Mrs. Norma Vigneau of Portsmouth, N. H.—called at her door.

"She got me interested in reading the Bible," Mrs. Childs said, "and I found that if you knew where to look there were many answers to the questions the priests always told me were mysteries and had to be accepted on faith."

FOR more than a year Mrs. Childs continued her studies under Mrs. Vigneau's direction. "I didn't dare tell my husband about it; he was death on any kind of religion," she said. "But finally I had to tell him, because I wanted to go to one of the talks at the Kingdom Hall in Portsmouth, and I couldn't get there unless he drove me."

Mr. Childs had been raised in northern Vermont as a Methodist, but long before had rejected any church. "I was shocked when my wife first asked me," he said. "But I finally agreed to take her when she told me all they did was study the Bible. I've always had a lot of respect for the Bible, but never had any use for the way the churches used it."

About a year after his wife was baptized, Mr. Childs also accepted baptism—"because I was convinced the Witnesses preached just what was in the Bible and nothing else." Although they live twelve miles from Portsmouth, they get to meetings there three times a week, work together every day on their studies of the Bible and, once a week, go out together door-to-door to try to interest others.

* * *

NORMA Vigneau, the 34-year-old Witness who first came to the door of Mr. and Mrs. Childs, had her first contact with the Witnesses in the same way—when a member of the Portsmouth group called on her. Mrs. Vigneau, brought up in a family of New England Unitarians and a graduate of Lasell Junior College in Auburndale, Mass., was shocked by what he preached.

"I felt sorry for him," she recalled. "I asked myself: 'How could anyone be so ignorant as to believe these things?' I felt it was my duty to invite him in, get out my college textbooks and show him why he was wrong."

To rebut his arguments, though, she found she had to delve deeper and deeper not only into her college texts but into the Bible, and over a period of months she found it was she, rather than he, who was being persuaded.

"I began to realize that in college I had been taught to think in circles," she said. "Nothing was black or white there; everything was the same neutral shade of gray. Finally I began to wonder what I was fighting against—here was something that was simple, straightforward, honest and beyond doubt."

The time came when she had to reveal her interest to her husband, Bob, who had been brought up in a Methodist family but had little use for any church. After the war, he and a partner had opened a gasoline station in Portsmouth, but he became fed up with that business, sold out to his partner, and was using the money to build an apartment house.

WAITING FOR ARMAGEDDON—Jehovah's Witnesses believe the climactic battle between God and Satan is rapidly approaching. Above are typical Witnesses at their recent assembly.

For quite a while he just went along, indifferently, with his wife's new ideas. But gradually he found the preachings striking a sympathetic chord.

"During the war my eyes were opened to a lot of things," he said. "I heard the politicians and preachers telling us we were fighting to create a better world. After the war I looked around and saw the United States grabbing everything she could get everywhere, and the people everywhere hating us and telling us to get out. I knew there was nothing better about the world. It became so I got sick every time I picked up a newspaper. I knew this couldn't be what God wanted in the world, and when the Witnesses got me started reading the Bible I found out it wasn't."

* * *

OTTO SMITH, who is 33, came to the New York gathering from Anchorage, Alaska, where he has lived since the war. But he is originally from a strict Baptist family in Corpus Christi, Tex. His dissatisfaction with the faith of his parents broke into the open during the war, he recalls.

"I was a gunner on B-24's stationed in England and flying over Germany," he said. "Before every mission the Protestant, Catholic and Jewish chaplains would get us together and pray. And I kept thinking how over there on the other side the ministers and priests were doing the same thing. 'Now, how can God listen to all of them?' I kept asking myself. It wasn't until I came in contact with the Witnesses that I understood that He wasn't listening to any of them."

Otto was working as an automobile salesman in Anchorage when the first Witness he ever met came to his door and, after a talk, left a copy of "Let God Be True." Otto read it and other literature, and began studying the Bible.

"My wife was dead set against the Witnesses at first," he said. "She comes from East Texas, and they don't have much use for Witnesses down there because of the flag-saluting business before the war." But gradually, Otto said, he interested his wife also, and they were baptized together in 1952.

* * *

AMONG the physicians who have accepted the beliefs of the Witnesses is Dr. F. D. Roylance of Haworth, N. J. Dr. Roylance, 48, is a graduate of the Columbia College of Physicians and Surgeons and is secretary of the medical executive committee of the Englewood, N. J., Hospital.

EN MASSE—Jehovah's Witnesses transform Yankee Stadium, above. They also filled the Polo Grounds.

"I was baptized by my parents in the Disciples of Christ when I was 12 years old," Dr. Roylance said, "but after starting our own family my wife and I began attending the Congregational Church."

For about ten years, he said, he had been studying the Bible on his own, looking for answers to spiritual questions that puzzled him. Occasionally he listened to talks by Fundamentalist preachers on his car radio as he rode between calls on patients.

"But I first learned about the Witnesses," he said, "from a patient who started bringing me Watchtower literature. 'This makes sense,' I said after I read it, and I wrote to the Watchtower. They sent a brother to see me."

In November, 1956, Dr. Roylance was baptized and began to give all the time he could spare from his practice to study and preaching. For him it meant a severe family crisis.

"My wife is very much opposed to all this," he said. "She is Italian, but her father took the family out of the Roman Catholic Church before they came to this country. She still goes to the Congregational Church, and she resents very much the time that this takes from my work and our three children."

Professionally, he said, it had not caused the problems that others might expect. "I recognize that there are cases where a blood transfusion is the best thing that can be done to save a life," he says, "and if a patient is not a Witness and wants the transfusion I don't have any hesitation about prescribing it."

AMONG the Witnesses who came from foreign countries to the New York Assembly was Max Liebster, 43, born and raised in an Orthodox Jewish home at Reichenbach, near Frankfurt, Germany. Two days after the war began in 1939 he was arrested and sent to a prison at Pforzheim. "For four months I was on my knees every day all day praying for understanding," he recalls. "'Why, why,' I asked, 'should God permit this persecution of his chosen people?'"

After four months, he was put on a prison train to be taken to the concentration camp at Oranienburg near Berlin. In the car with him was a Jehovah's Witness.

"This man was a farmer," Mr. Liebster said. "His wife had been killed, his five children taken away and sent to a Nazi training center. But he said he would go to prison rather than fight for Hitler. Never before had I seen a man who loved God's commandment more than himself or his family. For fourteen days on the train we were together and talked. He told me how Christ was proven in the Hebrew scriptures—and he quoted the scriptures to me from his head, for they had taken his Bible from him."

At Oranienburg Mr. Liebster saw this Witness tortured and finally killed rather than consent to serving in Hitler's army. "I saw it with my own eyes," he said, "and I made up my mind that I, too, would witness to the truth with my life if I were released."

Later he was moved to a succession of other camps until he reached Buchenwald. There the Germans had confined Léon Blum, the French Socialist leader, in a house set apart from the barracks, with a Witness assigned as his orderly. On May 15, 1945, just after the liberation, Mr. Liebster and two other former Jews were baptized as Witnesses in Léon Blum's bathtub.

"Altogether 10,000 Witnesses were sent to concentration camps," Mr. Liebster said. "Eight thousand came out, but 2,000 were too crippled to work. The 6,000 who were left started preaching all over Germany. Now there are a little over 60,000 of us in West Germany and another 25,000 in East Germany."

* * *

WHAT do the varied experiences of these Witnesses add up to?

It would be wrong to make any blanket conclusions about Jehovah's Witnesses and what motivates them on the basis of a handful of interviews. But through them run certain common threads: a deep yearning for religious experience, a conviction that the world is becoming increasingly worse, a desire to find some fundamental explanation of why, a wish to escape from worldly conflict and confusion, and a prayer that, somewhere in the undefined future, things will be better. In addition, and possibly more important, it seems clear that these people—who otherwise probably would have been both alienated from and outside any religious influence—have sought and found in the Jehovah's Witnesses a framework that provides them with both the purpose and strength for the kind of personal morality all religions seek to espouse.

August 10, 1958

85,319,274 LISTED IN RELIGIOUS UNITS

Members in 67 Larger Bodies in U. S. Rose From 53,397,575 Between 1926 and 1950

RATE OF INCREASE 59.8%

Report by Council of Churches Shows a Rapid Growth by 'Holiness' Sects

By GEORGE DUGAN

Membership rolls of the sixty-seven larger religious bodies in this country increased from 53,397,575 to 85,319,274 in the twenty-four-year period between 1926 and 1950, it was shown yesterday in a statistical report prepared by the Central Department of Research and Survey of the National Council of the Churches of Christ in the U. S. A.

This increase of 59.8 per cent, the report noted, compared with a population growth of 28.6 per cent over the same period.

In a breakdown, according to the three major faiths, Protestantism showed increases totaling 63.7 per cent; Roman Catholicism, 53.9 per cent, and Judaism, 22.5 per cent.

"Holiness" Sects Grow Rapidly

The report gave some startling

1926-50 Gains in Church Rolls

Figures showing the increases in membership for twenty-three of the largest religious bodies in the United States from 1926 to 1950 and the percentage rises follow:

	1926	1950	Per Cent Increase
American Baptist Convention	1,289,966	1,561,073	21
Southern Baptist Convention	3,524,378	7,079,889	100.9
National Baptist Convention U.S.A.,Inc.	3,196,623	7,091,394	121.8
National Baptist Convention of America.			
Churches of Christ	433,714	1,000,000	130.6
Congregational Christian	994,491	1,204,789	21.1
Disciples of Christ	1,377,595	1,767,964	28.3
Greek Orthodox Church (Hellenic)	119,495	1,000,000	736.9
Evangelical and Reformed	675,804	726,361	7.5
Evangelical United Brethren	583,516	717,531	23
Jewish Congregations	4,081,242	5,000,000	22.5
Church of Jesus Christ of Latter-day Saints	542,194	1,111,314	105
American Lutheran Church	474,923	692,484	45.8
Evangelical Lutheran Church of America.	496,707	813,837	63.8
Lutheran Church—Missouri Synod	1,040,275	1,674,901	61
United Lutheran Church	1,214,340	1,954,342	60.9
African Methodist Episcopal	545,814	1,166,301	113.7
African Methodist Episcopal Zion	456,813	530,116	16
The Methodist Church	6,760,642	8,935,647	32.2
Presbyterian Church in the U. S. A.	1,894,030	2,318,615	22.4
Presbyterian Church in the United States.	451,043	678,206	50.4
Protestant Episcopal Church	1,859,086	2,540,548	36.7
Roman Catholic Church	18,605,003	28,634,878	53.9

statistics in regard to the growth of the smaller "holiness" sects of Protestantism.

The Church of God in Christ, organized in Arkansas in 1895, grew from 30,263 members in 1926 to 316,705 in 1950—an increase of 946.5 per cent.

The Pentacostal Assemblies of the World, Inc., a mid-western group that originated in the early part of the century, showed a percentage increase of 536.9, rising from a membership of 7,850 in 1926 to 50,000 in the comparatively short span of twenty-four years.

Other bodies registering membership gains in excess of 200 per cent included the Assemblies of God (564.1 per cent), the Church of God (Cleveland) (652.6 per cent), and the Church of the Nazarene (256.7 per cent).

The Greek Orthodox Church

(Hellenic), the Russian Orthodox Church, the Serbian Orthodox Church, and the Syrian Antiochian Orthodox Church reported percentage gains of 736.9, 320.4, 444.5, and 714.6, respectively.

A fairly large share of these increases, however, can be attributed to the influx of refugees and displaced persons, a National Council spokesman said.

In commenting on the growth of the pentecostal bodies, the report noted that these smaller groups emphasize "intensive evangelism" and are "strongly Bible-centered."

Many religious leaders throughout the country, it added, have testified that the "holiness" sects are now bringing into their memberships "not only the socially disadvantaged" but also "considerable numbers of the more for-

tunately situated persons in the population."

At the same time, the report pointed out, in terms of large numbers of members gained, the older and larger bodies continue to make "impressive" additions to their official membership.

Southern Baptists Double

As a case in point, it singled out the Southern Baptists, who doubled their membership in the period, adding 3,500,000 members, "or in terms of numbers, many more than those added by many smaller sects."

In explaining why the year 1926 was selected as a base, the report noted that the last adequate census of religious bodies was made in that year by the Bureau of the Census. The figures compiled at that time, it said, were "generally in accord" with the reports supplied by the official statisticians of the various religious bodies.

According to the report, total church membership in 1950 was equal to about 57 per cent of the total population, the highest ever reported.

The analysis showed that, in 1950, the sixty-seven religious bodies having more than 50,000 members had about 98 per cent of all the members of the 256 religious bodies in continental United States.

The report said that interfaith comparisons give rise to questions concerning the definitions of church membership. In all cases the religious bodies make their own definitions and report accordingly, the report said.

The Roman Catholics, the Protestant Episcopal Church and many Lutheran bodies report all baptized persons, the report explained, and Jews estimate all Jews in communities having congregations. Many Protestant bodies count only persons having obtained full membership.

March 11, 1952

RELIGIOUS BODIES GROWING RAPIDLY

Church and Temple Rolls Go to 97,482,711, but Drop in Morality Also Is Noted

Interest in religion, as measured by church and temple membership, has reached new heights. This is indicated in statistics released yesterday by the National Council of the Churches of Christ in the U. S. A.

The National Council is a federation of thirty Protestant and Eastern Orthodox bodies with 35,000,000 members. The statistics are contained in the Yearbook of American Churches for 1956, to be published this month by the National Council. The figures apply only to the continen-

tal United States. They were gathered from 254 church bodies.

The new total of Americans with church or temple membership is 97,482,711—up 2,639,666 from the previous year. The new figures in most cases are for 1954. They show that 60.3 per cent of Americans are church members. This is an increase of 2.8 per cent, and compares with a population rise for the same period of 1.7 per cent.

In 1940, 49 per cent of the population was on the church rolls. A century ago the figure was 16 per cent.

Increase Since 1940

The figures show that since 1940 the number of Protestants has increased by nearly 20,000,000, while there are 11,000,000 more Roman Catholics. In 1954 35.3 per cent of the population was Protestant, and 20 per cent Roman Catholic. In 1940 the percentages were 28.7 per cent Protestant and 16.1 per cent Catholic.

Membership in six major faith groupings for the last two years is shown as follows:

	1953.	1954.
Protestant	55,837,325	57,124,142
Roman Catholic	31,476,261	32,403,332
Jewish	5,000,000	5,500,000
Eastern Orthodox	2,100,171	2,024,319
Old Catholic and Polish National Catholic	366,088	367,918
Buddhist	63,000	63,000
Total	94,842,845	97,482,711

Sunday and Sabbath schools are overflowing, with a total of 37,623,530 students and teachers—up 2,234,064 from the previous year's high. Church school teachers and officers, most of them volunteers, now number nearly 3,000,000, an increase of almost 250,000 over the year before.

There are now more than 213,000 clergymen in active charge of local churches, also an increase over the previous year's figures. Church congregations increased 2 per cent. The total number of such congregations in the United States is now 300,056, an increase of 5,597 congregations in a year.

Eighty-five per cent of the Protestant church members are on the rolls of nine general denominational groups and large denominations. These nine are Baptist, Methodist, Presbyterian, Lutheran, Protestant Episcopal, Congregational Christian, Disciples of Christ, Churches of Christ and Christ Unity Science.

This year, as for years past, the Baptists are the largest of the Protestant groups. They are divided into twenty-six bodies, with a total following of 18,448,621. The largest single Protestant church body is the Methodist Church, which has a membership of 9,202,728.

Dr. Benson Y. Landis, editor of the Yearbook of American Churches, said in a statement that "apparently people are interested in religion to an unprecedented degree in modern times."

"The awesome destructive power of atomic energy may have something to do with it," he suggested. "But beyond ascribing membership increases to such known factors as unusually high birth rates, accelerated evangelism on the part of the churches and shifting population trends from city to suburbs, it is difficult to point to the causes."

The possibility that the religious boom may be a spiritual bust was pointed out by the Rev. Dr. Eugene C. Blake, president of the council. In the current issue of Look magazine he writes that, despite the great religious upsurge, morality seems to be on the decline. He holds that interest in religion is in danger of becoming a fad, and asserts that "religion without morality is no religion at all."

One possible cause for the increase in church membership is suggested by Dr. Blake in his article. It has become fashionable, he writes, to "make an instrument of God" by using religion for selfish ends such as job security, health and peace of mind.

"Everybody seems to be interested in religion," he says. "But many people with new religious interest are attempting to turn that interest into magic—to use God for their own purposes rather than to serve God and find His purposes."

Other persons are turning to religion through a confusion of sexual and religious impulses, Dr. Blake declares, adding:

"Syncopated hymns interspersed with the multiple repetition of expressions such as 'saved by the blood' or 'ye must be born again' add up to mass hysteria. These ancient words have a specific meaning in Christian thought. But the meaning is no longer there when these phrases are used merely as stimulants for the glands."

Dr. Blake also attacks the "peace of mind doctrine." He explains that "the reason for so many attacks upon the popular purveyors of 'peace of mind' is not that the church is against placidity and in favor of anxiety,' but rather, "it is that the Christian Gospel must not be distorted to give a sense of peace to men where there is no peace and ought not to be."

He says that there is nothing wrong with wanting peace, health and security; that they become evil only when they are made man's highest concern. He concludes: "Then they become idols and their devotees fanatics. Then our faith is but a shadow, a spiritual bust."

September 6, 1955

CHURCH LEADERS SPLIT ON 'REVIVAL'

Dean Pike Dubious, Dr. Stone Optimistic in Episcopalian Discussion at Honolulu

By GEORGE DUGAN
Special to The New York Times.

HONOLULU, Sept. 5—Two Episcopalian leaders took a look here at America's religious "revival" and came out on opposite sides of the fence.

Both acknowledged a "conspicuous" upsurge of interest in religion, but disagreed concerning its validity for the future.

The discussion took place at the fifty-eighth Triennial General Convention of the Protestant Episcopal Church. The formal business sessions began this morning. The speakers were the Very Rev. James A. Pike, Dean of the New York Cathedral (St. John the Divine), and Dr. Richard G. Stone, president of St. Mary's Junior College, Raleigh, N. C.

They spoke yesterday on "America's Town Meeting of the Air," an American Broadcasting Company series, to make a program that will be heard on the mainland next Sunday.

Warns of 'Great Dangers'

Dean Pike readily agreed that more persons were going to church, that reading and writing about religion had reached new levels and that public proclamations emphasizing spiritual values were more frequent.

All this has great potentialities for good, he declared, but "great dangers" lurk in it.

As one of the dangers he cited what he described as a tendency to use God as "one of a number of resources to enable us to get what we want and enjoy life as we would." Some persons, he observed, use God to help them sleep better, to calm their anxieties and to make them more attractive and successful.

"But true religion," he went on, "puts God first and us second. Its true prayer is: 'Thy will be done with our help'—not, 'My will be done with Thy help.'"

A similar tendency is often projected in the realm of public affairs, he added.

"We are told," he proceeded, "that we should return to religion to strengthen us against communism. Of course we are against communism and if as a people we were truly devoted to God—with Him first in our lives —we would be secure and nothing would disturb our peace. But to seek to use God, who is everlasting, as a means to attain something that is earthbound— something that is part of the passing show, namely, our particular national interest—is to turn things completely around."

Urges Clear Expression

Dean Pike cited as another danger in the current religious revival that "while trumpeting our religiousness we do not in our personal and corporate action and attitudes sufficiently display that we really mean what we say."

"This," he declared, "is to put ammunition in the hands of the forces of atheistic materialism behind the Iron Curtain who would like to debunk and discount all that we profess to stand for."

Dr. Stone took the view that the revival was a "very real force."

He said that the United States had always found change to be a normal pattern and that thus it had a need for different types of religious outlets. The old-time evangelists had their place in the last century, he asserted, and Billy Sunday and Billy Graham have their places in the twentieth century.

"It would seem obvious," he continued, "that such large congregations would have listened to these revivalists only if they felt they were receiving spiritual value. These preachers are not merely prophets of doom; they tell the good tidings of God's love and redemptive power. Without their type of presentation possibly millions of people would not be awakened to a need for God.

"Evangelism may not appeal to a large number of us, but it must serve a need or people would not respond to it."

In the convention today Canon Theodore O. Wedel, warden of the College of Preachers, Washington, was re-elected president of the House of Deputies.

The Rev. Alexander Rodger, Ridgewood, N. J., was named secretary of the House of Bishops. He succeeds the Rev. John H. Fitzgerald, Brooklyn, secretary of the House of is seriously ill and was named secretary emeritus.

September 6, 1955

CAMPUS INTEREST IN RELIGION GAINS

Study Finds Less Scorn and Examination of Principles Intellectually Respectable

By STANLEY ROWLAND Jr.

There is widespread and deep interest in religion among college and university undergraduates today. This is in marked contrast to twenty years ago.

Educational and religious leaders report a surge of interest in religion among students in recent years, and to an extent among faculty members. The principles of religions, mainly Christianity and Judaism, are seriously examined and discussed. In short, religion has become "intellectually respectable."

This information on attitudes toward religion on the nation's campuses was developed in a study. Educators and clergy leaders believe it is significant for at least two reasons: young people, while in college, often start building beliefs and attitudes that will be basic to their mature thinking; and from college students of today will come leaders of tomorrow.

Twenty years ago, except for small church colleges and groups of "Christers" on the campuses of other institutions, undergraduates frequently ignored religion or ridiculed it. A college graduate of the Nineteen Thirties summed up his experiences this way: "None of us would be caught dead taking religion seriously."

A chaplain at New York University characterized his findings on campus attitudes toward religion two decades ago by giving this picture of a class exploring the Christian viewpoint: "The story of the Creation was lifted literally from Genesis, measured against the findings of geology and anthropology, and thrown out with a laugh. Out with it went all Christianity as superstition."

Inquiry Replaces Scorn

Such harsh attitudes toward religion have by no means vanished from campuses. But they are no longer as frequent. Scorn often has been replaced by objective inquiry.

Undergraduate concern for religion is reported by men close to students at Harvard, Yale, Princeton, Columbia and George Washington Universities; the College of the City of New York, Hunter College, Queens College and others. More than 1,200 of the nation's 1,900 colleges and universities now have a "religious emphasis week" of some sort.

"Live interest and deep searching in religion" was found in talks with students and faculty members at 300 colleges and universities across the country by the Rev. James L. Stoner, director of the University Christian Mission of the National Council of the Churches of Christ in the U. S. A., a federation of thirty Protestant and Orthodox bodies. Student concern for religion is "perhaps a little greater" in the Midwest, he found.

Half a dozen men close to students at Princeton University "agree whole-heartedly that today's undergraduates are deeply

169

concerned with religion, and that sincerity of purpose is characteristic of this interest. Where students of the Nineteen Thirties were wrestling with social problems, students in the Nineteen Fifties are giving more and more time to a thoroughgoing consideration of what religion is all about."

Nicholas McKnight, Dean of Students at Columbia College, summed up his impressions this way: "I've been in the dean's office here for more than twenty years, and never have I seen such a wide interest in religion among the students."

Men at New York University report a "wide and genuine concern for religious values." A student counselor at N. Y. U. reported that when someone spoke on religion his views were "at least intelligently considered, and that's all we ask."

Chapel Attendance Static

The increased concern for religion on the nation's campuses is not reflected primarily in chapel attendance, which has shown no great increase. The major evidence of the concern falls under the headings of discussion, religious activity groups and religion courses.

Exploraton of Christianty and Judaism takes place in many informal campus "bull sessions."

The questions asked by students are "often keen, but they're asked to find answers, not just to be polite or to be nasty," according to Mr. Stoner.

Religious activity groups are playing a larger and livelier role in the total life of the campus than before. Twenty years ago, a number of groups believed themselves fortunate if they could hold the few followers they had.

Mr. Stoner gives these figures: On the nation's campuses there are 3,000 student religious groups with 1,200 full-time employes. There were 200 such employes twenty years ago.

At N. Y. U., the Newman Club, a society for Roman Catholic students, doubled its membership last year and expects to do the same this year.

The Protestant adviser at Hunter reports increased membership and a "good deal of concern for relating religion to other fields of knowledge."

At Queens, a pre-college program of meetings for freshmen sponsored by the Hillel Foundation for Jewish students was "overwhelmed." At Columbia, where religious club members include men from Columbia College and women from Barnard College, the expansion of religious activities has made it necessary to turn all of Earl Hall over to the clubs.

Princeton finds that religious groups no longer use "the back door approach to religion, which emphasizes activity rather than matters of faith." Today's students "go directly to the religious organization of their own choosing because they are interested; because they are eager to test the main ideas of religion."

Some groups offer courses on their specific beliefs, such as Roman Catholicism, Protestantism or Judaism. The courses are voluntary and carry no credit. They are frequently well attended.

Religion courses in college curriculums have shown a greater percentage increase than the student body in a number of cases. Some institutions have organized departments of religion in recent years. These range from large universities such as N. Y. U. to small, liberal arts schools such as Carleton College, Northfield, Minn.

At Yale twenty years ago, some fifty students out of 2,800 were enrolled in three religion courses. A separate Department of Religion was established there in 1945. This year, 500 undergraduates out of 4,000 are enrolled in fourteen religion courses. The courses are given for credit but are voluntary, as they are at most institutions.

Forty students attended two religious courses at Columbia twenty years ago. Now more than 250 are taking the equivalent of ten full-year courses. The undergraduate body has increased less than 50 per cent.

Princeton's first undergraduate course in religion was offered in the academic year 1939-1940. It attracted twenty-one students. This year 700 undergraduates are enrolled in religion courses, and Princeton began a graduate program leading to the degree of Doctor of Philosophy in Religion.

In his visits to colleges across the nation, Mr. Stoner also has found more than 100 faculty groups meeting regularly to discuss religious principles. The National Council of Churches this summer organized a Faculty Christian Fellowship.

To sum up: There is wide concern for religion on the nation's campuses compared with twenty years ago. The emphasis is on basic principles and theology. This interest in religion is more often evidenced by objective study and inquiry than by reverence. It does not necessarily mean a turning to the church.

October 22, 1955

Religious Interest on Campuses Takes Place Outside Churches

By STANLEY ROWLAND Jr.

The wide interest in religion at the nation's colleges differs markedly from the religious revival in the nation as a whole.

The new concern for religion by some students has been characterized as a "basic re-examination of our popular assumptions." Manifestations of this concern range from increased religious activities and study to a search for religious beliefs that is sometimes combined with hostility toward the church.

Though student interest in religion has increased greatly over twenty years ago, attendance at college chapel services has increased only "some" or "a little" or "little if any," a study shows. So far, concern for religion by undergraduates has not brought them into the church in numbers.

But in the nation as a whole 60 per cent of the population are reportedly on the rolls of churches and synagogues. Other indicators of the general religious revival include the popularity of radio and television programs dealing with religion and the high sales of Bibles and such inspirational books as "The Power of Positive Thinking" by the Rev. Dr. Norman Vincent Peale.

However, some church leaders have sharply criticized the general religious revival as in some ways hollow or lacking in thought-out conviction. These critics include Billy Graham, revivalist; the Very Rev. James A. Pike, Dean of the New York Cathedral (Protestant Episcopal), and the Rev. Dr. Eugene Carson Blake, president of the National Council of the Churches of Christ in the U. S. A., a federation of thirty Protestant and Orthodox bodies.

Religious Search Prevails

On college campuses, there is not so much a religious revival as a religious search.

In rare instances, college staff members suggested that a few of the students professing interest in religion were "jumping on the bandwagon." But most suggestions that undergraduate concern for religion was superficial brought sharp reactions.

"Present-day students are too independent to climb on a religious bandwagon," in the judgment of an authority at Harvard University.

Authorities at Princeton University find that "undergraduates today, harassed by psychological, social and other hard-to-define insecurities, are genuinely interested in relating religion to thought and life and most emphatically are not being simply fashionable."

The teachings of Dr. Peale, himself a popular though not uncriticized figure in the general religious revival, do not seem popular among undergraduates. This was brought out by conversations with students and religious counselors at New York colleges.

In an informal discussion at Columbia University among students and religious advisers, Barnard College girls termed Dr. Peale a "religious Dorothy Dix." Others asserted that the clergyman "distorts Christianity, and is successful because he's a salesman who knows how to package his wares slickly."

An undergraduate at New York University declared: "Once religion promised 'pie in the sky.' Now we have Dr. Peale, who promises pie in the penthouse."

However, religious leaders point out that the nation's colleges and universities include such a variety of students that "Dr. Peale doubtless has his supporters among undergraduates."

Clergymen and educators mention a number of causes for the searching undergraduate concern for religion. Most often mentioned is "a disillusionment with the idea that science can solve all man's problems," sometimes coupled with the idea that "man alone cannot solve all problems."

Talks with educators, religious leaders and students leave the impression that undergraduates feel sharply that man with all his social and physical sciences has produced two world wars and the hydrogen bomb in less than fifty years. They feel that for all the discoveries and benefits of medical science, mankind is in a far more perilous position now than before.

Other frequently mentioned causes for the wide undergraduate concern for religion are the "accumulation of weapons of mass destruction," the "fact that the United Nations is not working properly," and the "need for individual expression." However, from talks with religious counselors and students, these would seem to be aggravating pressures in a general disillusionment with scientific or materialistically centered humanism.

Conversations with students do not bring out a desire to forego scientific achievement or live in the past. Nor do such conversations indicate, as a few educators said, that student concern for religion is a flight from reason.

Rather, students are often applying to religion and religious teachings the vigorous searching and intellectual approach found in other disciplines such as the sciences. Christianity and the teachings of the Judeo-Christian tradition, which claim to hold man's salvation, are now being searchingly investigated by students.

Aquinas, Calvin Studied

Some undergraduates are reading the works of such theologians as St. Thomas Aquinas and John Calvin. There is a serious effort to relate religious teachings and theology with sociology, psychology, the physical sciences and the concrete problems of the modern world. A five-day conference of the Student Christian Association at Princeton in December will deal with "The Relevance of the Christian Faith to the Individual in a World of Power."

A number of educators and religious counselors agree that student concern for religion is a serious attempt to find a spiritual basis for action in the modern world.

The ideas and questions of a number of students were epitomized by one when he said:

"A lot of what the church says is fine, but what's it doing about it? All my church does is give us a few parties and tell us to be good boys and think about God. Does this help solve the Negro problem? Will it prevent World War III? Will it save a single country from communism? Christianity has plenty of answers, good ones, but the people doing least about them are Christians. "If I thought my church was doing a damn thing, maybe I'd go more."

October 24, 1955

'In God We Trust'
GETTYSBURG, Pa., July 30 (Æ)—The official motto of the United States now is "In God We Trust." A Congressional resolution making that phrase the national motto was signed today by President Eisenhower.

July 31, 1956

RISE OF RELIGION IN U. S. ANALYZED

Churches Council Finds Gain in Revival, but Its Moral Effect Is Questioned

Thirty-five leaders in public life agreed yesterday that religion was "booming." But some of them questioned whether the revival was yet strong enough to improve the moral tone of the nation.

This was the essence of a survey conducted by the Na-tional Council of the Churches of Christ in the U. S. A. and published in the November issue of the council's monthly organ, The Outlook.

Leaders in government, religion, labor, industry, education and the arts were queried by the council, a federation of thirty Protestant and Eastern Orthodox church bodies.

Here's what some of them said:

President Eisenhower—"The new national figures on church membership and benevolence are impressive. * * * A growing concern for religion gives hope that our concern for the welfare, the freedom and the dignity of our fellow men in America and around the world is also growing."

Adlai Stevenson—"It is our hope that this new religious interest will not make us self-righteous, but that it will make us aware of our limitations and of our need. The test of a religious revival lies in what it produces in uprightness of personal life and justice in society."

A Test of Membership

Senator Paul H. Douglas—"The increase in church membership * * * is most interesting. But is there a real growth in the awareness of the fatherhood of God and the brotherhood of man?"

The Rev. Billy Graham, evangelist—"There is no doubt that we are experiencing the great religious renaissance in American history. However, there seems to be little evidence of increased personal morality, though there seem to be more and more encouraging signs of a deepening here and there of a willingness for total commitment to Christ."

The Rev. Dr. Norman Vincent Peale of New York—"I think there is a genuine revival of religion. * * * The revival is not complete, certainly. It has not yet been reflected in a pronounced reformation in morals."

Dr. Nathan M. Pusey, president of Harvard University — "A shift is coming. If it was only yesterday that theology was simply 'tolerated' within universities as a harmless survival from an earlier day, today it is almost universally acknowledged that the study of religion rightfully belongs."

October 21, 1956

LACK OF RELIGION FOUND IN CHURCH

A Congregationalist Survey Finds 33% of Members Belong in Name Only

By JOHN WICKLEIN

A survey conducted for the Congregational Christian Churches indicates that one-third of the denomination's members are only nominally religious.

Dr. Yoshio Fukuyama, the denomination's director of research, said yesterday that of the two-thirds who showed a stronger religious feeling, the largest number approached religion as an organizational activity rather than an intellectual, creedal or devotional experience.

The survey, he said, suggests that the churches are preoccupied with having "active, organizational members" at the expense of other expressions of religious concern.

Dr. Fukuyama's study is among the first to try to go beneath membership statistics indicating an uptrend in religious interest, to determine the quality of the members' religious commitment.

What Is Religion?

To do this, he analyzed responses from 4,095 members of twelve Congregational Christian Churches in the north-central and northeastern states. He checked these against seventy-nine interviews gathered from the respondents, to use for illustrative purposes.

Through direct questions and indirect, cross-check questions, the survey attempted to find out from the church member an answer to the big question: "What do you mean by religion?"

"If you go by the very general category of church membership," Dr. Fukuyama commented, "you can say, sure, people are more religious — there are more church members, and the percentage of church membership is going up."

To a sample census question in 1957, he pointed out, 94.6 per cent of the respondents 14 years old or over identified with some religious group. Only 2.7 per cent said they had no religion. Last year, 63.4 per cent of the American people were reported to be members of some church or synagogue.

Separate 'Styles' Noted

Many researchers think this is a continuing indication of a "surge of piety" that began in World War II. But there are those who argue, Dr. Fukuyama pointed out, that religion has become increasingly secularized —to make it a popular and so-cial activity—and therefore is of decreasing importance in the nation's life.

To study the religious attitudes of Congregational church members, Dr. Fukuyama divided them, on the basis of their responses, into four "styles." These consisted of the religiously knowledgeable church member, the organizational member, the unquestioning believer and the inward-experiencing, devotional member.

Those who had no strong orientation toward any of these styles he listed as "nominal" members. When the results were tallied the "nominals" formed a fifth category, which at 33 per cent was the largest of the five.

The responses indicated that the unquestioning believer and the devotional member were dying out within the denomination, being replaced by the "organization" type of church member, and to a lesser extent by those intellectually oriented to religion.

Among those who showed strong orientation, 44 per cent were placed in the "active organizational" category. This included regular attendance at services, participation in church activities and support of church programs through voluntary service and contributions.

The remainder included 22 per cent who were intellectually oriented, 28 per cent who were belief oriented and 23 per cent who were devotionally oriented.

The percentages total more than 100 because many persons were strongly oriented in more than one direction.

Intellectual Activity Sought

An interesting by-product of the survey was a finding that the "knowledgeable" and "organizational" members were more socially liberal than those with "belief" or "devotional" orientations.

Leaders of the Congregational Christian Churches believe that while the organizational aspect of church life is strong, the movement is toward the church member who is knowledgeable and intellectually interested in his religion.

The Rev. Dr. Truman B. Douglas, executive vice president of the denomination's Board of Home Missions, said: "I feel that the organizational should always be subordinate-instrumental and not basic. We should play down the organizational and get to the real business of religion."

Dr. Fukuyama's survey, financed by the Congregational mission board, was done in conjunction with an urban church project carried out by the Bureau of Research and Survey of the National Council of Churches.

The Congregational Christian Churches are now merging with the Evangelical and Reformed Church to form the United Church of Christ.

January 8, 1961

Belief in God Found Increasing

There is a general supposition in the U.S. that as the nation has grown more complex and urbanized, belief in God and church membership have waned. It is more likely though that both religious faiths and church affiliation are at an all-time high. That at least is the impression one takes from recent polls.

The latest of these polls was conducted this summer by the Harris Survey of Washington. Here are some of the Harris findings: 97 per cent of the adult population profess a belief in God; 72 per cent, belief in an afterlife; 83 per cent contribute money to religious causes; only 3 per cent never attend church and more than half attend weekly or oftener.

Few Atheists

Of the 3 per cent who say they are nonbelievers, only one-third regard themselves as atheists; the other two-thirds say they are agnostics.

The Harris Survey did not specify what was meant by "God." It is reasonable to presume that not all in the whopping majority who professed belief in Him meant to state that their faith was in the Personal "I Am Who Am" of the Biblical religions. Some may have had in mind an impersonal Intelligence brooding over the universe; others may hold to a pantheistic notion of divinity. For, in this regard, it is significant that only 72 per cent of those polled believe in an after-life.

Strangely enough, the persons interviewed appeared to be plagued by doubt about the depth of their religious commitment. Most felt that they were less religious than their parents and expected their children to be more religious than they. Only 27 per cent regarded themselves as "deeply religious."

The Harris Survey does not differ markedly from the findings of the Gallop Poll. Last Christmas, Gallup reported that 45 per cent of the American people attend religious services weekly, a dip from the 49 per cent peak reached in 1958, but still a formidable figure compared to the past. Just 25 years ago, Gallup figures showed only one-third of the people attending church weekly. And that was a rise over previous decades.

Last Easter, the Gallup Poll also gave another indication of Americans' concern about the hold religion has upon them. It said that 45 per cent of the adult population were persuaded that religion was losing its influence in American life; when collegians were singled out the figure on those who believed this shot up to 62 per cent.

But the shadowy statistics available from the past and historic evidence simply don't bear out the fond image of earlier generations of prayerful Americans that is a staple of Fourth of July oratory. The Yearbook of American Churches, published by the National Council of Churches, notes a continuously rising curve of church membership through the decades. The yearbook is largely dependent on figures supplied by the churches themselves (since the U.S. Census Bureau ceased to enumerate religious statistics in 1936) and some denominations make no reply to the yearbook's inquiries. Its reliability has been questioned. Still, after all the necessary qualifications as to the absolute accuracy of its figures are made, it is significant that the yearbook reports a proportionate growth of church affiliation through the years— from 16 per cent in 1850, 36 per cent in 1900, 47 per cent in 1930, 57 per cent in 1950 to 64 per cent in 1963.

Lost in Tradition

Americans have long been plagued by the idea that the living generation has wandered far from the church-going probity of its elders, it would seem. In 1686, the Rev. John Whiting, minister of the First Church in Hartford, Conn., struck a note that would become familiar when he spoke glowingly of the past as "better in Spirituals, less Sin; and better in temporals, less Sorrow: O that New England might yet say in good earnest, and do accordingly, I will return to my first Husband." Sermons in a similar vein have been preached through all the years of American life, but the statistics belie them.

There is every indication now that the long doctrinal battle against atheism and agnosticism, which took up the energy of past generations in the clergy, has been won, if the polls mean anything at all. The emphasis of contemporary theological concern, as a consequence, has shifted from defensive apologetics to a search for the relevance of religious belief to secular life. Such matters as race relations, war and peace, the quality of life in an affluent society and the problem of poverty in the midst of plenty now preoccupy leaders of all the faiths.

"It is not enough to believe in God," one of the new-breed clergymen said after studying the Harris figures. "We have to get men to believe in themselves as well. And here the 3 per cent who hold out against religious faith may have something to teach us."

August 29, 1965

Changed Atmosphere, Same Attitudes

By JOHN COGLEY

The "religious revival" was regarded as a signature of the 1950's. Massive revival meetings, best-selling inspirational books, clerical columnists in the press, crowded Sunday schools, overcrowded suburban churches, and booming Jewish temples and youth centers became as typical of the Eisenhower era as stormy internal security hearings, 3-D movies, Hopalong Cassidy, hoola hoops, the gray flannel suit, and Betty Furness standing by her refrigerator.

During these years Dr. Billy Graham became internationally famous. Bishop Fulton J. Sheen occupied prime time on a national television network. Piety bloomed like cherry blossoms along the Potomac. The President's Cabinet meetings were opened with a prayer by the Secretary of Agriculture, one of the 12 Apostles of the Mormon Church. In official addresses the Deity was invoked frequently and possessively.

Religion and patriotism became entangled in much of the political oratory of the day, and in the public mind as well. The nonreligious were loosely regarded as something less than 100 per cent patriotic by a few; and even when the charge was not made, the atmosphere of religiosity was such that many nonbelievers came defensively to their own support.

While all this official piety was in flower, religious rivalries and interfaith tensions were highly publicized. It was the era, for example, when Paul Blanshard's exposés of Roman Catholicism achieved best-seller status and many Catholics reacted to them with a blend of super-patriotism, religious defensiveness, personal resentment and hurt.

Sweet Concord

It was also an era when Protestant-Catholic clerical squabbles made frequent news. Christian brotherhood among church leaders seemed to be praised more widely than it was practiced. In the spirit of the times, some Jewish spokesmen of the period were known to observe privately that they did not mind too much that Christians were fighting among themselves because such battles kept them from forming a united Christian front against the Jews.

Today, at least on the face of it, the American religious scene has changed radically. Protestants and Catholics are not only on speaking terms, they are actually worshipping together. Christians and Jews are talking more cordially than they have for years, in spite of holdouts on both sides. At the very least, church leaders have taken to holding their tongues when speaking about one another and have learned to weigh the ecumenical effect of their words. Where there are differences of opinion, evil or power-seeking motives are not quite so readily attributed by one side to the other though it still happens.

The compliance with Governmental policy that was widely expected from the religiously affiliated in the 1950's has been almost reversed. Church protests against the war in Vietnam are now massive and sustained, for example.

The participation of ministers, priests and rabbis in the civil rights movement has grown immensely. A few years ago, the Rev. Dr. Eugene Carson Blake, who as Secretary General-elect of the World Council of Churches is the nation's most prestigious Protestant, was arrested in a Maryland civil rights demonstration. In Selma, Alabama, in 1965, 300 Roman Catholic priests and nuns signed a statement expressing their willingness to go anywhere they were summoned by the Baptist leader, the Rev. Dr. Martin Luther King, and did so even after they had been asked to go home by the local Catholic bishop.

Birth Control Gaining

In the 1950's President Eisenhower, recognizing the difficulties of getting a Federal birth control program passed, said that he could not imagine anything less suitable for Federal assistance than family-planning. Today, the Government is pouring millions of dollars into such programs. Catholic objections are minimal. The anti-birth control laws of Connecticut have been repealed, with the public compliance of Richard Cardinal Cushing, who stated that his coreligionists had no interest in imposing their view on others.

How have these changes affected popular religious attitudes and behavior? Not as significantly as recent headlines might suggest, according to a recent poll carried out by the Gallup organization for the monthly Catholic Digest. At the grass-roots no massive changes were noted.

Roman Catholics, for example, are still overwhelmingly agreed that Protestants are as patriotic as they are—93 per cent take this position. The number who believe that Jews are as patriotic as Catholics is larger now than it was in 1952—84 per cent as against 78 per cent.

Nor has the Protestant view of Roman Catholic loyalty between the Eisenhower and Johnson years, according to the poll, changed significantly. In both years, 1952 and 1966, 80 per cent of the Protestants polled considered Catholics as loyal as they were. However, twice as many (6 per cent) were sure in 1952 that Catholics were not as loyal than are willing to say the same today.

Atheism is slightly higher in the 1960's but still insignificant. Fourteen years ago, 99 per cent of those polled had some kind of belief in God. The more recent figure is 97 per cent.

Roman Catholics, the only group obliged by church law to do so, head the list for weekly church attendance — 67 per cent go to Mass every Sunday. This repre-

sents a slight upward swing from 1952's 62 per cent.

About one out of every three Protestants attends religious services weekly—a rise of about 8 per cent over the 1952 figure. Another one-third do not go to church at all, two and a half times the number of Catholic dropouts.

The most striking figure in the survey may be the dip in attendance at Jewish Sabbath services. Fourteen years ago, 12 per cent of the Jews polled attended weekly; now the figure is only 4 per cent. However, in 1952, 56 per cent of the Jews in the survey never went inside a temple; that figure has now sunk to 39 per cent.

Within Protestantism, the Gallup

figures turned these trends:

A larger number of Baptists are not going to church at all any more but the number of weekly attendants has not changed significantly. The Methodists have almost the same history—the 20 per cent who went every Sunday in 1952 is now 24 per cent while the number not going at all has increased from 37 per cent to 41 per cent.

Women in Attendance

The largest gains appear to have been made by the Lutherans —an increase of 14 per cent in weekly church attendance and a drop, from 36 per cent to 29 per cent, in total absence.

The nation's Presbyterians seem

to be divided into three equal parts, now as in 1952—one third go to church every Sunday, one third go occasionally, and one third never darken the door. Congregationalists, now incorporated into the United Church of Christ, have made significant gains. In the earlier poll, only 10 per cent were weekly church attendants. That figure has gone up to 28 per cent. The number of always-stay-at-homes decreased from 32 per cent to 31 per cent.

Not surprisingly, women are more faithful about church attendance than men, but not spectacularly so. The every-Sunday figure is 42 per cent; for men, it is 34 per cent.

August 21, 1966

70% IN SURVEY SEE RELIGION ON WANE

Gallup Poll States One in 7 Finds an Increase

Special to The New York Times

PRINCETON, N. J., May 31 —Seven adults in every 10 (70 per cent) say they think religion is losing its influence on life in this country, while only one person in seven (14 per cent) believes religion is increasing its influence.

These opinions represent almost a complete reversal of what surveys showed 12 years ago. When the issue was presented to the public in 1957, only 14 per cent of all persons said religion was losing influence, while 69 per cent held the opposite opinion.

For the first time since 1957, a larger proportion of Catholics surveyed than Protestants believe religion is on the wane. Many Catholics say they are disturbed about Pope Paul VI's birth control edict and the growing cleavage between liberal and conservative factions within the church.

The change in the views of the public between 1957 and today on the effects of religion, charted in six national surveys during this 12-year period, parallels a decline in churchgoing over the last decade. Last year's Gallup audit showed 43 per cent of adults attending church in a typical week, the low point recorded to date.

Declining Attendance Cited

Declining attendance among young adults, those in their 20's, accounts for much of the over-all decline in churchgoing. National church attendance declined 6 points, in the audit, between 1958 and 1968, but the drop has been 14 points among young adults.

Reasons for believing religion is "losing" ground include these: the church is "outdated," "it is not relevant in today's world," "morals are breaking down," and "people are becoming more materialistic."

But some persons interviewed see a growth in religion, although not of the formal variety. A youthful store manager in Santa Rosa, Calif., said: "People are becoming aware of the fact that true religion does not exist in dogmatic church policy but in the hearts and minds of men."

A 42-year-old housewife in the East says she wants organized religion to remain strong but thinks churches should "change their attitude to capture the youth," adding, "Young people today are looking for authority, but don't know where to find it."

Six Surveys Since 1957

In six surveys covering a 12-year span, the following question has been asked of a representative cross-section of the nation's adults, embracing all religions in proportion to the number of their followers:

At the present time, do you think religion as a whole is increasing its influence on American life, or losing its influence?

Here are the latest results, based on interviewing 1,521 persons between May 2 through May 5, and the trend:

	Increasing	Losing	No Diff.	No Opin.
	%	%	%	%
1957	69	14	10	7
1962	45	31	17	7
1965	33	45	13	9
1957	23	57	14	6
1968	18	67	8	7
1969	14	70	11	5

Little difference is found between the views of men and women, churchgoers and nonchurchgoers. Younger adults are far more likely to say religion is losing influence (85

per cent) than are older persons (67 per cent).

Views of Students

An even higher proportion of college students (78 per cent) than of the general population say religion is "losing" ground. And the trend charted here has also been in the same direction—four years ago, 62 per cent of college students said religion was declining in influence.

A recent study of 85 high school seniors and juniors from Westfield, N. J., conducted by the Gallup Poll, showed nine in 10 holding the opinion that religion was losing its influence on American life.

A 17-year-old senior girl who wants to teach home economics, said: "Organized religion has nothing to give me, and I have nothing to give it. The churches today have little to do with the people. They don't relate."

A 17-year-old high school student who plans to be a chemist said: "Present church systems have to cater to the older generations and this doesn't move or inspire youth. You have to please the young people today or there won't be any church in the future."

June 1, 1969

Campus Religious Fervor Shuns Standard Religions

A new religious intensity appears to be making itself felt on American campuses. It rejects the standard faiths, but some scholars and theologians say it has all the elements of a religion to go with the "counter culture" developing among a large segment of the nation's youth.

The characteristics of the movement are not being defined along lines normally understood as religious, but in terms of the younger generation's emphasis on love, celebration and the

search for meaning.

As one coed expressed it: "I think of religion as being dogmatic. If it's outside the church, it's not religion — it's faith."

"The dissenting young have indeed got religion," says Theodore Rozak, the sociologist, in a new book, "The Making of a Counter Culture."

"It is not the brand of religion Billy Graham or William Buckley would like to see the young crusading for — but it is religion nonetheless," Mr. Rozak says.

Signs of this new religious intensity appear to be taking the following forms:

¶Students are showing a heightened concern with the mystical, the symbolic and "ultimate questions."

¶Enrollments in religion courses are reaching record levels. And the course content, moving away from an emphasis on Western religions, is adjusting to student interest in Eastern faiths and religious values in general.

¶Campus ministers, in efforts to revive waning student interest in the church, are redefining their institutional ties and in many instances forsaking traditional functions to plunge into campus politics.

Changes Affect Minority

Observers generally agree that these changes, though widespread, are affecting a minority of college students. However, it is also agreed that, while no detailed statistics exist, the number of students whose religious attitudes are changing is increasing with each new class.

"They are expressing themselves in religious terms," said Michael Novak, the lay Roman Catholic theologian who teaches at the experimental Old Westbury campus of the State University of New York. "When I was at Harvard five years ago, 'moral' was a bad word—now it's the most important word on campus."

"Almost everybody tends to think of religion as an institutional structure," Mr. Novak said. "That's really not true. What's really religious is an ultimate view of self and community and doesn't necessarily have anything to do with God.

"If it is antipragmatic, and has to do with the ultimacy of life and death, then it is religious. If there is a problem in defining what the youth are doing as religious it is one of semantics."

The new religious feeling, according to some observers, has a complete set of its own symbols, ethics and rituals.

Prof. William C. Shepard, a 27-year-old member of the religion department at Smith, considers the Woodstock music festival, held at Bethel, N.Y., last August a prime example of this "new religious culture."

"Religious needs persist among the young," he said, "but none of the traditional religious alternatives have been able to satisfy them.

"I call drug-induced experiences, as well as the whole ethos built around drugs in the youth counter-culture, religious. Pot-smoking and drug-taking assume an almost ritualistic status in the lives of many, and the need-satisfaction in this situation is obvious."

Many students who might fit Mr. Shepard's description say they would resist being labeled religious.

Helen Campbell is a senior religion major at Smith, yet she rejects traditional Christian ways of describing God.

She says, religiousness is "not just doing something that others can see — if I really express religion I do it by just going into the forest."

The new religiousness is usually expressed in a private way and overt, organized displays of it are comparatively rare on campus, though Zen groups and occasional visits by gurus are not unusual.

Usual Rituals Varied

In the standard Western faiths, students sometimes add spontaneous forms to traditional worship, such as in the Pentecostal movement among Catholic students that has gained wide publicity.

At the Free University City of the University of Massachusetts this year, a hundred Jewish students who wanted to celebrate Rosh Hashanah outside the synagogue gathered for a discussion that became a "totally emotional experience."

"We ended up singing and dancing out in a field at night," said John Gerard, a 22-year-old graduate student, "and hugging each other to keep warm."

A religious nature is frequently ascribed by students and faculty to predominantly political events. Gilbert Salk, a University of Massachusetts student, delivered an emotional speech prior to Vietnam Moratorium Day that brought the audience to its feet shouting, "The war is over."

"He went into a dance, waving his arms," a campus minister said. "It was the essence of a revival meeting, where the audience makes a 'committment t Christ' at the end."

Some theologians, such as Harvey Cox of the Harvard Divinity School, are calling the communal life among groups of hippies a "new monasticism" with vows of poverty, obedience to a life style and a kind of chastity that prevents sex from creating divisions in the community.

Mr. Cox calls the hippies "neo-mystics" and describes their way of life as "contemplative," with its "loud music, bright costumes and convulsive dancing" producing an inner feeling "curiously akin to deep and pervasive silence."

The clearest evidence of this renewed religious interest on campus is in the growing enrollments in religion courses and concurrent shifts in the way the subject is treated.

At Smith, for example, the number of students selecting religion courses has grown from 692 in 1954 to 1,387 this year, with no change in the size of the student body of about 2,000.

A similar increase is being registered in graduate programs. For Columbia's graduate program in religion, there were 200 applications this year for only 20 places, with a record number of them coming from students with liberal-arts background.

"Students here are interested in myth and images and symbols," said Sam Hill, professor of religion at the University of North Carolina, where the eight department members are teaching 1,200 of the 11,000 undergraduates.

"These are the same kids who are taking sociology and English literature, and we are getting floods of them," he said. "Our courses in the psychology of religion, ethics and the religious imagination are taught by people who have always thought along these lines — now their time has come."

At Old Westbury, Tran Van Dinh, a Vietnamese writer, teaches a course called "Asian Humanism" to 50 students. Most of the students in the course, as in many of the newer courses in the field, were not thinking of it in strictly religious terms, but also as a source of "insights."

Change in Intention

Students are also being drawn into new religion courses that make a critical analysis of the subject and its role in the prevailing culture. This is a departure from the older style courses that investigate Western religions from within already accepted traditions.

"The students are becoming acutely aware," said John Pemberton, professor of religion at Amherst College, "that the sole function of a religion sometimes is simply to justify its culture."

The same kind of reasoning has produced a profound change in the campus ministry. Once the staid presence of the institutional church on the institutional campus, the ministers who find their calling in the colleges are now frequent-

ly the allies of students who would remake the university.

"The campus ministry involves advocacy," said the Rev. William Starr, a Protestant minister who is adviser to about 10 left-leaning student groups at Columbia.

"I am a co-belligerent," Mr. Starr said. "Ministers like myself see these struggles as the ones that require religious commitment. I tend to define my religiousity in terms of politics."

At Stanford University in California, the Rev. B. Davie Napier has transformed his chapel into a forum for antiwar activity.

More Influence Sought

"I came here," he said, "because it puts me in the best position to influence the church. I hope these kids will go home and bust into their congregations and tell them they are not the way they should be."

It appears, however, that most students who are unhappy with their churches and synagogues have no interest in trying to reform them. If they are religious at all, they tend to indulge in the private forms and practices of their culture.

Traditional churches are rejected even by many students who continue to profess Christianity, such as the members of the University Christian Movement, a loosely knit group of radicals who last year broke their ties with the National Council of Churches and gave up their national office.

"When you talk about Christianity," said Ruth Topham, a member at the University of Massachusetts, "you are talking to me about love for your fellow man — it's not something you give lip service to. To live it you have to overcome everything you are taught in this country."

These students would like to model their lives after the early Christians who, in Theodore Rozak's words, were a "similarly scruffy, uncouth and often half-mad lot."

Miss Topham spoke for many of her generation when she said "I'm not going away from religion, just from the church."

November 2, 1969

Young Adult Church Attendance Found Stabilized in a Gallup Poll

By KENNETH A. BRIGGS

Stabilization of rates of church-going among America's young adults has helped keep the nation's over-all religious attendance pattern at a steady level in the 1970's, according to the annual Gallup Poll on church-going released yesterday.

The survey reports that 40 percent of American adults attended church or synagogue in a typical week in 1975, a figure that has held firm since 1971. In the 18-to-29-year-old category the rate for last year was found to be 30 percent, highly consistent with rates for the last five years.

It was among the youngest adults that organized religion suffered its greatest disaffec-

tion in the 1960's when young people were generally expressing disapproval of major institutions. The latest report says that on the basis of the last five years "this disenchantment with religion among America's youth appears to have subsided."

Another significant finding was that nearly as many young people as older adults were participating in prayer groups, Bible study and other spiritual activities in addition to regular church services. The nationwide figure was 20 percent and for young adults alone, 18 percent.

Otherwise, the poll shows no dramatic changes in church attendance from the previous year for the three major faiths. Roman Catholics dropped a point to 54 percent, Protestants gained one to 38 percent, and Jews remained stable at 21 percent.

Since 1964, the most startling trend has been the steady decline in Catholic attendance from 71 percent to its present level. In the same period, the other two faith groups have remained virtually unchanged.

To estimate the average attendance during 1975, surveys

of representative samples were made in eight selected weeks to account for seasonal fluctuations. A total of more than 12,000 adults, 18 and older, were interviewed in person in more than 300 scientifically selected sampling locations. This question was asked:

"Did you yourself happen to attend, church or synagogue in the last seven days?"

Church attendance has fluctuated somewhat in different sections of the country since 1971. The latest results show that in the four-year period attendance in the Midwest rose from 40 to 45 percent while in the East, the South and the West declines were found. The West slipped from 33 percent to 28, the South from 45 percent to 42, and the East

from 39 percent to 38.

In the same time span, little change has been found in the percentages of college, high school and grade school educated people who attend church or synagogue. Each category averages about 40 percent.

Persons polled were also asked: "Do you happen to be a member of a church or synagogue, or not?" Seventy-one percent answered yes, and 55 percent said they had attended a service during the previous week.

The national pattern of church membership has been mixed over the last several years. Most large Protestant bodies have been losing members, the Catholic Church has experienced no appreciable

growth and evangelical churches have made gains.

Church leaders have been especially concerned about the attitudes of young people toward religion. During the 1960's, many young adults manifested distrust of religious establishments.

By the end of the decade, however, many of those who had been disillusioned were caught up in a spiritual wave, sometimes called the Jesus movement, which centered on young people but took place largely outside the churches.

This religious momentum, combined with a widespread search for non-material values, has engendered greater respect for religion and stemmed the attrition, in the opinion of many observers.

As measured by Gallup, 40 percent of young adults attended church in a typical week in 1967, in the midst of the downslide. By the beginning of this decade the rate had leveled off after a drop of 10 percentage points.

Other surveys have cautioned religious leaders against undue optimism over the latest apparent trend among young people. A 1974 study by the National Opinion Research Center in Chicago, for example, indicated that Catholics under age 30 were still twice as likely to fall away from the church as those over 50 and that those who have attended college were still more likely to drop out.

January 4, 1976

RESURGENT FUNDAMENTALISM

As Billy Graham Sees His Role

Bringing his crusade to New York, the controversial, crowd-drawing evangelist calls himself a 'proclaimer': 'My job is simply to proclaim the Gospel.'

By STANLEY ROWLAND Jr.

ON May 15, Madison Square Garden will open its doors for an event that has been under quiet but elaborate preparation for more than a year, that is being prayed for in groups across the world, that will continue for at least six weeks and perhaps more than four months, making exactly the same appeal night after night, six or seven nights a week, attracting people from as far as Canada and the South, building ever-increasing crowds if a dozen other cities around the world are any indication and featuring one man with a Bible.

It will be the first full-scale New York crusade of the Rev. William Franklin Graham, a 38-year-old evangelist known as Billy Graham to millions of supporters and critics. Born of a Presbyterian farm family in Charlotte, N. C., and now a Baptist who makes his home in Montreat, N. C., the evangelist is interdenominational in his preachings. The local crusade was initiated by the Protestant Council of the City of New York and is backed by churches of many denominations. Its pattern of events will be typical of all his crusades.

In action on the speaker's platform Mr. Graham loosens his tie and speaks with a clear urgency. He is a tall, commanding figure (6 feet 2 inches), and conviction seems to vibrate through his tense body. In firm, sweeping gestures, his arm goes straight out

with finger pointing, then up with the fist clenched, then down in a short arc to the Bible on the podium as he drives a point home with a Biblical quotation. Sweat begins to glisten on his face.

THE words come in a rush. Bible verses and colorful descriptions of Eve, Joe Doaks and the shenanigans of Satan tumble headlong over one another, converging on one central point: repent, believe in the Lord Jesus Christ, and be saved. Again the big arm springs out, cupped hand seeming to take in the crowd as he describes through taut lips how Christ confronts the man in the street. Then, a little abruptly, his urgent words cease. In quiet tones he invites people to come forward and "receive Christ." They come. Subsequently, local volunteers, guided by the Graham staff, route them to churches of their choice.

Why do they step forward? Some observers write it off entirely to emotion. There are cases where this is probably important. However, Mr. Graham is not extraordinarily emotional as evangelists go, at least some of his conversions do last, and a number of those who "decide for Christ" do so only after having returned thoughtfully for several nights.

Another explanation is supplied by reason and observation. Put a hand-

STANLEY ROWLAND Jr. is a religious news reporter for The New York Times and the author of many religious articles.

some, forceful speaker of obvious conviction before a crowd of 15,000 people, and it would be surprising if at least a few did not respond. Add the fact that a number go to a crusade meeting because they feel a lack in their lives, and the chances of response are increased. Then add the fact that Mr. Graham tells his hearers that they are not impersonal cogs in a machine but individuals with immortal souls cherished by God, and the chances of response are augmented once more in this "age of anxiety" or "conformity."

Mr. Graham insists that the reasons for lasting conversion are primarily religious. He says that the Holy Spirit rides with his words out to the audience. Some disagree. Others, who do agree, say that the Gospel carries within itself the power of conversion when proclaimed with real conviction, though the proclaiming may be done from various viewpoints by a priest, a theologian, or a Billy Graham.

Converts themselves usually explain in simple, personal terms of religious experience. During the London crusade, a doctor who went with binoculars to "see the circus" returned for five nights, then made his decision. "I gave my life to the Lord," was his blunt, simple explanation. A newspaper man went to "the show." After his conversion, he walked home five miles through the rain "trying to figure out what had happened to me." He and the doctor go on to tell of lives of new dedication and meaning.

Actually, Mr. Graham is simply doing with large-scale, thorough organization what other evangelists are doing with much less money and preparation. When he hits a city it is with guaranteed backing and extensive spadework beforehand. Then he digs in for a goodly stay. Big crowds make news, the publicity keeps hammering away, and gradually the crusade begins to permeate the city. In the midst of it all stands Billy Graham. Although clergymen and laymen have called him everything from a profiteering phony to a Christian knight in the shining armor of the Holy Spirit, the simplest description of him is also probably the most accurate: he is a proclaimer.

"The meaning of the word 'evangelist' is 'proclaimer,' a proclaimer of good news," Mr. Graham explained at the start of a recent interview. "My job is not to defend the Gospel; my job is simply to proclaim the Gospel, and to let the Spirit of God apply in the individual hearts."

H E returned again and again to this definition of his task in the course of a two-hour talk in his suite atop a lofty local hotel. The evangelist punctuated his remarks with brief, wholesome laughs and gestured occasionally, but rarely raised his voice. He spoke in the strongest terms of the Bible (he takes it on faith and quotes it whenever pressed) and publicity (his feelings are mixed).

His richly textured, medium dark gray suit with its narrow lapels hung with impeccable exactness; cuffs broke on shoe tops so precisely that one felt he feared lest he smack of the small town. Yet he needed a haircut; his almost blond hair was a little shaggy where it couldn't be seen in the mirror. And his formal black shoes badly needed a shine.

Glancing over the sunny rooftops, Mr. Graham explained why he considers this city the great challenge. "It's the very complexity of New York City, with all its cultural and linguistic backgrounds," he said. "Actually the whole world looks to New York as the world capital. * * * To touch a city spiritually of an area of 12,000,000 people is a tremendous thing, especially where you have 58 per cent of the people that attend no church.

"**I** HAVE found a sense of discouragement and I think frustration on the part of many ministers here that I have not felt in other parts of the United States. I have come to have a great burden and I believe a sense of compassion for this city." As for the prospects at Madison Square Garden, he admitted: "Our type of crusade may not make a dent in New York. I think the greatest thing that will be accomplished is that possibly the entire city for a brief period will become God-conscious."

Then, likening himself to the sower in the Biblical parable of the seed that fell on fruitful and unfruitful ground, he waxed earnestly hopeful. "There are people in this city that I believe that God the Holy Spirit has been preparing for this crusade. When they hear the word of God, when they hear the Gospel preached, there is going to be an automatic response." But others, he said with a philosophical shrug, will "be over it next morning. We know that happens Christ said it would happen."

H E leaned back in a low armchair and launched into a dissertation on financing.

"We have never sold anything but song books," he said, "and that is for the people right there, and we get nothing from that. The money goes to the local crusade. You see, they need $900,000 here for this crusade, and that money is handled entirely by the executive committee." He named several business men who have been signed up by local Protestant leaders and are under the chairmanship of George Champion, the president of the Chase Manhattan Bank. "They handle the money and I never see it. I don't get any of it, none of our team will receive any honorariums while here. They're entirely on salary from Minneapolis, Minn. [home of the Billy Graham Evangelistic Association, a non-profit corporation, supported by contributions, of which Mr. Graham is president]. I receive $15,000 a year as my salary." One-tenth goes as his tithe to the Baptist Church.

Hunching forward with elbows on knees, he hammered away on the subject of financial purity. He said that the "Billy Graham" buttons and whatnot that were hawked at the London crusade in 1954—and will probably appear here—were products of private firms trying to turn a fast buck. "We didn't sell them, we never had anything to do with it, in fact we never have anything to do with 90 per cent of what's made to go on," he insisted. This attitude contrasts with his approach in Los Angeles in 1949, when he first won national attention by converting a famous athlete and an infamous gambler, both of whom remain stanch Christians, and where he advertised himself as "America's Sensational Young Evangelist" in "Mammoth Tent Crusade" with "Dazzling Array of Gospel Talent."

R EMINDED of this past, Mr. Graham looked a little pained. "That was in the early

Billy Graham reads from the Bible in London's Trafalgar Square. "Conviction seems to vibrate through his tense body and sweeping gestures."

days before we had very many people coming to our meetings. And all the publicity is handled by local committees. There will be a tremendous amount of advertising here in the City of New York, for example, for this crusade, both by television and so forth, but there won't be any adjectives describing me." Then he leaned forward and blurted:

"My wife and I have lost our privacy, and I don't think anyone who has lost their privacy ever doesn't long to have it back. You don't realize what a priceless possession it is to be a private individual. To be looked at, to be stared at everywhere one goes, never to go to a restaurant without being looked at." He unfolded from the chair and took a restless turn around the room.

"**T**HAT is one of the reasons that I left England, not to go back, at least in the last two years, because I felt there was too much of Billy Graham.

I wanted the discussion to be around Christ." On his last night in London he packed Wembley Stadium with 120,000 persons. In 1955 he spoke in various cities in Great Britain and on the Continent. His wife, Ruth, whom he met while they were undergraduates at Wheaton College, in Illinois, stays home in Montreat with their four children when Billy is off crusading. Last year he toured India.

The evangelist folded back into his armchair and explained how he had changed from a blunt critic of that country's policies to something of an apologist for Prime Minister Nehru. "I was critical of India because I didn't understand India, I didn't understand why Mr. Nehru takes some of the stands he takes until I went to India and saw for myself the terrible economic and social problems he must wrestle with, and that actually Mr. Nehru represents the Indian people in his pacifism and his neutrality. That gave me an understanding."

THEN, almost in the tone of a young man who wants to share a discovery, he told what traveling had taught him about the racial issue. "I don't think it's a sectional problem at all, I don't even think it's an American problem. I think it's a world problem." He cited the caste system in India and diagnosed the Arab-Israel conflict as racial, then jumped back to his insistence upon racial integration at his meetings. Leaning forward, he warmed to the subject:

"I don't think it can be done altogether by preachments, though I shall certainly do my share of it. But it's going to have to be done by setting an example of love, as I think Martin Luther King [the leader of the Montgomery bus boycott] has done in setting an example of Christian love. * * * Paul said there is neither Jew nor Greek, nor Scythian nor barbarian in Christ."

His role, he reiterated, is to face people with Christ—an exhausting business. "I try to be in bed nine hours every night. Billy Sunday used to stay in his pajamas all the time and I used to wonder why—that he stayed in bed so much—until I understood how exhausting a thing it is to address a crowd of 15,000 or 20,000 people and try to get them to receive Christ." He continues, not because he fancies himself a preacher—"I am not a great preacher,

and people will be disappointed in my preaching"—but because "God has given me a gift, a gift of evangelism, and I couldn't deny that gift. Paul told Timothy, 'Stir up the gift that is within thee.'"

MR. GRAHAM plunged into his favorite topic: the Bible. He disowned the statement, quoted even by admirers, that at one time he was willing to give the exact dimensions of heaven, and readily admitted to passing through a period of Biblical skepticism some time ago. He declined to be classified as either fundamentalist or as anything approaching liberal, though he has sporadically been accused of both from opposite directions. At one point he declared that the Bible is the inspired word of God, but not dictated by Him; at another point he asserted that Christ was God incarnate, and at still another he asserted that if Christ should appear today He would go on television because "the Bible says that when He comes back every eye shall see Him." Then, using the method of graphic analogy that runs through his sermons, he erected a defense for his variety of Biblicism.

"Suppose I take this Bible and say there're parts of it—let's suppose this—that are not inspired of God, that are not authoritative. All right,

then I become the judge. And I sit up and I say, 'Well, this page is no good. I'll rip that one out.'" He tore one hand through the air above his open Bible. "'I can't accept that.' Then I turn over here and I rip another one out. * * * And after a while I have about ten million different kinds of Bibles because one scholar says this and one scholar says that and one scholar says another, until after a while I have no authority.

"And I've talked to scores of ministers at this very point who have lost the authority in their message and their whole ministry has gone out the window because they're not sure what they can believe any longer. Well, to me, I would far rather settle it and say, 'By faith I accept it as God's inspired word.'" Scientific theories about the origin of the universe take as much, or more, faith to believe, he argued—"I mean, it's faith either way."

TO Mr. Graham this means an act of belief, not a pat formula. "The Bible depicts the Christian life as a conflict and a battle and a warfare. I believe that when a person receives Christ and tries to live the Christian life that he immediately comes in conflict with various areas of his society and the people around about him because he is going against the current stream."

He pushed a palm through the air and forced his fist against it. "I mean, here's the stream coming this way and a true Christian is going this way. Well, immediately there's a conflict in every area"—fairly severe, it seemed from his gestures—"but Christ in the heart gives peace, and a great resource of power in the midst of these battles."

THIS is the crux of Mr. Graham's beliefs, the battle against sin and the power of Christ. His easy, analogical reasoning, full of references to "ten million" of this and "scores" of that, has drawn the charge of superficiality from Christian thinkers. In his defense, it must be pointed out that he promises no cures or worldly success. He preaches an elementary, "hard" Gospel of sin and salvation.

"There will be no emotional outbursts" at Madison Square Garden, he promised. "When I give the invitation for people to receive Christ it will be so quiet you can hear a pin drop. It will be as holy and reverent a moment as you would have in any church in the worship service. And you will see people coming forward deliberately, quietly, reverently, thoughtfully, and many of their lives—the evidence will pile up for years to come—will have been transformed and changed in that moment."

April 21, 1957

100,000 Fill Yankee Stadium to Hear Graham

Throng Sets Arena Record—Nixon Is Platform Guest

By GEORGE DUGAN

One hundred thousand persons jammed Yankee Stadium last night to hear the Rev. Dr. Billy Graham call sinners to repentance. It was the largest crowd in Stadium history.

More than 10,000 others were turned away.

At 7 P. M. when the service began, every nook and cranny in the arena was filled. Standees lined the aisles of the triple-tiered stadium.

The only open space was the carefully manicured greensward of the infield. A four-foot picket and wire fence circled the bases. It was the only barrier between

the speakers' platform and a sea of faces.

Among the 300 persons sitting on the platform with Dr. Graham was Vice President Richard M. Nixon.

Record of 1935 Eclipsed

The estimate of the crowd was made by James K. Thompson, the Stadium manager. He said it eclipsed a record set in 1935 when 88,150 sports fans watched the Joe Louis-Max Baer heavyweight fight. In 1953, a meeting of Jehovah's Witnesses drew 81,-000 in the stadium itself, with 7,500 more assembled outside.

In the heat last night about seventy persons were treated at first aid stations for fainting and dizziness.

The rally had been intended originally as the slim, blond evangelist's farewell to New York. But on Friday, thirty hours before it was to get under

way, the New York crusade committee and members of the Graham team agreed unanimously to continue the campaign at Madison Square Garden for three more weeks, or through Aug. 10. However, there will be no services at the Garden tonight or tomorrow.

The first arrivals for last night's rally began to trickle into the Stadium as early as 10 A. M., when a few choir members turned up. By 2:30 P. M. seven of nearly 400 busloads had arrived. Most of the crowd came from within the metropolitan area. While free tickets had been distributed none was required for admittance.

At 6:33 P. M. all seats in the Stadium were filled. Ten minutes later guards permitted the pressing throng to swarm out over the outfield.

The hour-and-a-half program followed, in expanded form, the

familiar pattern of the Madison Square Garden meetings.

Prayer was offered by the Rev. Dan Potter, executive director of the Protestant Council of the City of New York, and the Rev. Dr. Ralph B. Nesbitt, associate pastor of the Fifth Avenue Presbyterian Church.

The 3,000-voice choir sang the "Hallelujah Chorus" and later joined with George Beverly Shea in singing the favorite Garden hymn, "How Great Thou Art."

Pacing the platform, with his barely visible necktie microphone carrying his voice to all corners of the huge park, Dr. Graham reviewed the ills of the world from economics to moral deterioration and declared that "Christ is the only answer to our problems and dilemmas."

There were no similarities in his delivery to that of the late Billy Sunday, who never missed an opportunity to "slug it out with the devil" in a dramatic pantomime of a baseball game.

Shortly before 8 P. M., the stadium lights were turned on,

illuminating the vast assembly with a soft glow.

Five minutes later, Dr. Graham introduced the Vice President as "one of the hardest working men in the United States." He described Mr. Nixon as this country's "ambassador of good will, a young man with vision, integrity and courage."

In his reply Mr. Nixon brought greetings from President Eisenhower, whom he described as a good friend of Dr. Graham.

The Vice President said one of the major reasons for this country's progress was the "deep and abiding faith" of its people.

Mr. Nixon praised the choir and added that he appreciated music because he played the piano in a Sunday school at East Whittier in California.

The Vice President said that as he was walking in with Dr. Graham he complimented the evangelist on the crowd. He quoted Dr. Graham as saying that "I didn't fill the stadium, God did."

Mr. Nixon said he knew Dr. Graham very well, had played golf with him and had heard him speak. He added that while his golf might not have been so good, he was an eloquent speaker. He called the evangelist a sincere, humble man.

A few moments before 9 P. M. Dr. Graham made his customary appeal for "decisions."

Because of the huge crowd he said that he could only ask those that "accepted Christ" to stand or raise their hands if they were already on their feet.

Slowly, over the Stadium individuals rose, couples got up. And in the outfield hundreds of hands slowly pointed upward.

No accurate estimate could be made of the number of persons who made their decisions. There were hundreds and very likely thousands.

At the end of Friday night's rally in the Garden, the Graham crusade had been attended by a cumulative total of 1,102,600 persons spread over sixty evenings.

It appears that the New York

The New York Times

BOWED IN PRAYER: The Rev. Dr. Billy Graham and Vice President Nixon at Stadium

campaign will make the greatest number of converts of any crusade to date, overshadowing the record totals of the 1954 London crusade.

There, 34,800 persons made "decisions for Christ" at regular meetings, and another 3,667 in rallies reached by closed circuit television.

As of Friday night, the Garden campaign recorded 35,228 "decisions for Christ" plus an unknown number of others who were "saved" by watching tele-

vision on their home screens.

From opening night on May 15 through the projected closing date of Aug. 10, the New York Crusade will cost about $2,140,000, including television time.

All finances are handled by the local crusade committee. Dr. Graham and his team members are on a flat salary from the Billy Graham Evangelistic Association in Minneapolis.

The Stadium rally was televised from 7:30 to 9 P. M. by the

American Broadcasting Company, with the New York area blacked out. It was rebroadcast here at 10:30 P. M.

The Police Department's Bureau of Planning and Operations said last night that fifty patrolmen and ten officers had been assigned to the Stadium, 161st Street and River Avenue, the Bronx. An unspecified number of detectives mingled with the crowd.

July 21, 1957

GRAHAM OUTDREW PAST EVANGELISTS

By GEORGE DUGAN

The longest and biggest evangelistic crusade in modern times ended here Sunday evening when the Rev. Dr. Billy Graham wound up a sixteen-week campaign with a farewell rally in Broadway.

No one knows yet what effect the crusade had on New York. Statistics furnished by the Graham organization show that the tall, blond evangelist preached the Bible to nearly 2,000,000 persons in Madison Square Garden—many of them repeaters—convinced more than 55,000 individuals to make "de-

cisions for Christ" and on July 20 drew an attendance of 100,000 at a Yankee Stadium rally, the largest crowd in the history of the ball park.

Estimates vary greatly as to how many of the 55,000 "born again" souls will enter or re-enter the life of their respective churches.

Some of Dr. Graham's most ardent supporters say 60 per cent. Some of his most outspoken detractors say less than a percentage point.

When and if an accurate figure is produced, it will satisfy the evangelist. He has often said that the saving of one sheep is enough.

Exponent Extraordinary

Whether or not the technique of mass evangelism is to one's taste, there can be no denying that Dr. Graham is its exponent extraordinary.

He has been described as a phenomenal product of current history, a "man of the hour" who is providing a faith for the uncertain and the fearful.

He has also been criticized as an overly pietistic preacher who hews to the literal interpretation of the Bible to the total exclusion of the social gospel.

This, his supporters emphatically deny. They point to sermon after sermon in which th evangelist deplored racial segregation as contrary to the teachings of Christ, prescribed solutions to juvenile delinquency and condemned inadequate housing.

Dr. Graham probably will be ranked as one of this country's great evangelists, if not the greatest.

His predecessors were Charles G. Finney, Dwight L. Moody

and Billy Sunday. These were the giants of evangelism in their day. Unlike the free-lance practitioners of the Aimee Semple MacPherson school, these men always solicited and got the cooperation of local Protestant leaders wherever they waged their campaigns.

Appeared 40 Years Apart

Curiously, all of them appeared at approximately forty-year intervals. Except for technical refinements and variations, their approach was basically the same.

Each came to New York at the peak of his career. They preached, in the main, a straight-from-the-shoulder Gospel sermon and planned their assaults on sin with meticulous care. They were successes in a city that had been known for generations as the "graveyard of evangelism."

Dr. Finney was probably more of a theologian than his successors, but still an evangelist.

He came to New York in 1832 after several years of campaigning upstate. His crusade here consisted of a three-week revival in a remodeled downtown theater.

Dr. Finney was credited with several hundred conversions—no mean feat in the New York of more than a century ago.

In later years, he became president of Oberlin College, Oberlin, Ohio.

Forty-four years later, in 1876, Dwight L. Moody appeared on the New York scene. Like Billy Graham, he had made earlier conquests in England and Scotland.

Held Forth at Hippodrome

Short, bearded and a former shoe salesman, Mr. Moody (he was never ordained) campaigned for two and a half months in the Hippodrome. He drew a total attendance of 1,500,000 and converted some 5,000 persons.

"D. L.," as he always signed his name, seldom preached "hellfire and damnation." Instead, he told countless anecdotes and emphasized the joys of Christian living. Dr. Graham considers his evangelism closer to the Moody type than the Billy Sunday technique.

In a shrill voice, paced once at 200 words a minute, Dwight L. Moody preached what he described as the "old fashioned Gospel, square, with no round corners."

For his opening service, the vast Hippodrome, used mainly for circus performances and operas, was converted into two auditoriums, seating a total of 11,000 persons.

Both were filled, with an estimated overflow of 5,000 persons who apparently were turned away. The arena, then at Madison Avenue and Twenty-sixth Street, was the largest assembly hall in New York and had never before been used for a religious service.

Forty years ago, in 1917, Billy Sunday hit New York like a bombshell. In a ten-week stand, he broke all records. Varying reports place his total conversions from 50,000 to 98,000.

He was known as the "acronast for Jesus." But his Bible-thumping, shouting evangelistic evangelist" and the "gym-was spectacularly successful.

He preached repentance and salvation in a wooden tabernacle at Broadway and 168th Street.

The small, partly bald preacher had been a big-league baseball player for eight years in the Eighteen Eighties with Chicago and Pittsburgh in the National League. He never let his listeners forget it. Larding his sermons with sports talk and beating the devil with a baseball bat, he led his converts down the "sawdust trail."

Despite their surface differences, America's top evangelists have much in common, especially the big three—Moody, Sunday and Graham.

Gospel singing was an integral part of their operation. Dwight L. Moody had his Ira Sankey, known as a "sweet" gospel singer. Billy Sunday had his Homer Rodeheaver and Billy Graham has his George Beverley Shea and Cliff Barrows.

Singing Moved Audiences

Many persons attending the Graham rallies in the Garden were moved more by Mr. Shea's rendering of "How Great Thou Art" than by the preaching of the evangelist. Mr. Barrow's direction of a choir that filled an entire end of the arena was professional.

All three evangelists depended for a large share of their financial support on wealthy individuals. William E. Dodge, John E. Converse and Morris K. Jessup were among the contributors to the Moody campaign. Rockefeller, McCormick and Wanamaker money helped Billy Sunday. One unidentified individual in New York paid for Dr. Graham's Saturday night telecasts for one month. The bill was close to $200,000.

Each worked out a careful program of advance planning. Jerry Beavan, a born public relations man, already has his finger on Graham campaigns that are building up for 1960.

Unlike the run-of-the-mill, free-lance evangelists that crop up frequently, no one doubts the sincerity of these preachers. They were and are convinced that God was speaking through them.

September 3, 1957

GRAHAM'S IMPACT TERMED FLEETING

Ministers Here Hold Crusade Was Limited in Appeal

By GEORGE DUGAN

The 1957 Billy Graham Evangelistic Crusade gave the Protestant churches of New York a "spiritual lift," but otherwise it had little lasting impact on the city.

This is the consensus of a survey conducted by The New York Times among a cross-section of this area's ministers four months after Dr. Graham ended his summer-long campaign in Madison Square Garden.

A total of 504 Protestant clergymen in New York City and Nassau and Westchester Counties received a one-page questionnaire. They were asked to make a brief assessment of the Graham Crusade and to answer three questions:

¶How many referrals did you receive?

¶How many of these were new names?

¶How many of these referrals are now attending service regularly?

The list of ministers was picked at random from the 1957-58 directory published by the Protestant Council of the City of New York and represented about 25 per cent of all churches in the directory.

However, most Manhattan clergymen received the questionnaire.

Replies came in from 159 ministers, a little more than one-third of those queried.

Running through the vast majority of comments, almost like a theme, was this appraisal:

The Graham campaign was a sincere, highly organized effort to "mass-evangelize" a great metropolitan center. Unquestionably, many of the millions who heard and saw the evangelist got what one Lutheran clergyman described as a "spiritual shot in the arm."

But the comments also made it clear that most of those who attended the Garden rallies were already affiliated with a church.

A rector of a Protestant Episcopal Church in Westchester observed that the crusade had "very little impact—all the referrals (5) were already pillars of the church."

A "referral" is an individual who went forward to "accept Christ" at the end of the nightly rallies. Referrals were requested to give their names and church affiliation, if any for follow-up.

The 159 clergymen reported a total of 3,997 referrals, of which 2,552 were already members of their churches.

Statistics on the third question—How many are now attending service regularly?—were inconclusive because many ministers left that answer blank. Some reported that they had no way to check and others said the time was too short to give a fair figure.

Enough replies were received, however, to indicate that the "pillars of the church" stayed on, but many of the new names went to another church or dropped out of sight.

Favored by Fundamentalists

Dr. Graham was received most favorably by the more fundamentalist Baptist churches. He made the least impact on mission churches in underprivileged areas.

The Rev. George E. Calvert of the East Harlem Protestant Parish, an interdenominational project, reported that he had lost three members to Calvary Baptist Church and "two others are completely upset."

A strong demarcation was evident in the survey between the so-called conservative churches and the more liberal groups. The latter opposed what they described as the evangelist's over-simplification of the Christian gospel, his "Madison Avenue approach" and mass evangelism in general.

The Rev. Howard R. Moody of the Judson Memorial Church (Baptist and Congregational) said the Graham Crusade "set back the Christian cause by several years." Judson maintains a special ministry for juvenile delinquents in the Greenwich Village area.

Three Unitarian ministers and one Universalist were unanimous in calling the results of the Graham campaign "completely negative."

Members Aided Crusade

On the other hand, the Rev. Edward Hanson of the First Baptist Church in Tarrytown summed up the more conservative view this way:

"Since our church is in agreement with Billy Graham's theological position and evangelistic emphasis and in view of the fact that thirty or more out of a comparatively small resident membership of 150 served as counselors, ushers and choir members * * * all of whom have continued active here, our congregation, as well as myself, feels that we have been greatly benefited by the crusade."

Marble Collegiate Church, whose pastor is the Rev. Dr. Norman Vincent Peale, received the largest number of referrals—373. Of these, 184 were listed as new names.

A comment from a church spokesman said that there was no way to determine how many of the new individuals still attended church.

Riverside Church received 135 referrals, forty-seven of whom were already affiliated. Twenty-three moved away, thirty-four failed to respond to a follow-up, sixteen joined the church and fifteen are likely prospects.

Replies were received from ministers of the following denominations: Presbyterian, 30; Episcopalian, 28; Methodist, 20; Baptist, 19; Lutheran, 16; Congregational, 9; Reformed, 8; Community, 4; Unitarian and Universalist, 4; Interdenominational, 4; Collegiate, 3; United Brethren, 2, and unclassified, 12.

Efforts to reach Dr. Graham yesterday were unsuccessful. He was reported to be speaking and traveling around the island of Puerto Rico with two team members. He is scheduled to be in San Juan today.

Meanwhile, the Rev. Dan M. Potter, executive director of the Protestant Council of the City of New York, was told of the

179

results of the survey. The council was instrumental in organizing Dr. Graham's New York Crusade.

In a statement, Dr. Potter said: "From the point of view of the Protestant Council's department of evangelism, the Billy Graham New York Crusade was an unbelievable success.

"Thousands were led to a commitment to Christ, the city became God - conscious, the churches were strengthened and the Christians were urged to apply their faith fully to all aspects of life."

Mr. Potter added that Bible-study and prayer groups had been organized throughout the metropolitan area on an interdenominational basis.

Crusade Began May 15

The Billy Graham Crusade began here on May 15 and ended Sept. 1. More than 2,000,000 persons, many of them repeaters, heard the evangelist during his crusade.

The following are comments, or excerpts of comments, by Protestant clergymen concerning the crusade:

The Rev. Dr. Phillips P. Elliott, Presbyterian and president of the Protestant Council of the City of New York:

"The Graham Crusade provided a background against which many important decisions have been made and we find that those who have joined the church recently, in many cases, have been stimulated by the crusade to this action although they made no decision at the meetings themselves.

"This, it seems to me, is as effective a form of decision, if not more so, than those publicly made during a large meeting. We feel the whole life of the church toned up as a result of the crusade and some of our people have been deeply enriched by it."

The Rev. Donald Harrington, Community Church of New York:

"The impact of Dr. Graham on our parishioners was minor. Several went in groups, not because they were interested in his fundamentalism, but in him and his work as a phenomenon.

"A few of these thought he probably did some good for those who believed in his gospel. A larger number felt that he did positive harm by discrediting religion, arousing guilt feelings for which no adequate therapeutic activity was prescribed, and through a basic escapism so far as the really hard solutions which our contemporary problems require, are concerned."

The Rev. William F. Sunday, Lutheran:

"Sixty-seven referrals were received by me; all but seven communicant members of our church, mostly young people. I believe all are attending services regularly, as before.

"Except for two young people who wanted to substitute the Billy Graham hymnal for our own historic hymnal and who subsequently left us to become affiliated with a Baptist church, there were no withdrawals. Those who did sign cards I believe were genuinely helped."

The Rev. Dr. Albert A. Chambers, Episcopalian:

"Our efforts to follow up the three referrals were unsuccessful. In one instance we never could locate the young man since he gave his parents' address and since the parents were not 'on speaking terms' with him.

"I would say that the general impact of Dr. Graham's crusade interested many of our people. I am sure that much discussion of religion resulted from the crusade, but would hesitate to say that any change had been brought about in our parish life because of it. Our people are unusually devoted—a fact in which we rejoice greatly."

The Rev. Frederick Reustle, Congregationalist:

"We did not cooperate in any way, nor did we actively oppose it. Some of our people visited the spectacle out of curiosity. One man took his children 'so that they might experience a phenomenon in American life that will soon disappear.'

"If there were any validity to their supernatural claims they [the Graham team] would have converted a few rabbis, some Jewish people, a few intellectuals and artists. Since their results in this area are a total failure it throws doubt upon their entire performance.

"Conversion is a valid experience; its trouble is that this type fails to deliver on its promises. Two types were attracted—the emotional teenager and the confused, uncertain and bewildered adult who is left dangling when his life's work is done."

The Rev. Dr. Albert J. Penner, Congregationalist:

"While a good many members of our church and congregation attended one or more sessions of the crusade, I am not aware of any positive impetus to the life and work of our church as a result, nor have I observed any stimulus from it to the work of the churches through the Protestant Council."

January 26, 1958

GLOSSOLALIA WINS NEW ADHERENTS

Speaking in Strange Tongue Gains in Protestantism

By McCANDLISH PHILLIPS

A movement emphasizing a restoration of charismatic, or spiritual, gifts to the Christian ministry has been spreading speedily through the nation's Protestant denominations.

It is marked, among other things, by glossolalia, the practice of praying, singing or speaking in fluent accents whose meaning is not known to the speaker.

Though glossolalia is nearly always a stream of unintelligible sounds that no one understands, once in a while an individual is reported to utter declarations of God's love in a foreign language that is understood by others present but that the speaker has never consciously learned.

Glossolalia is not a new phenomenon. It was the peculiar mark of the very opening of the Christian era, and today is Whitsunday—a feast that commemorates the coming of the Holy Spirit upon the first disciples, who at that moment spoke in a variety of Mediterranean languages they had not learned.

Charismatic Renewal

Across the United States, hundreds of ministers and thousands of laymen in some 40 denominations have adopted this strange prayer form. Most of them have also begun to practice a variety of other spiritual "gifts," especially healing by prayer with the laying on of hands.

These and other phenomena are part of a random but pervasive movement called the Charismatic Renewal. It takes its name from the word charism, which means a divine gift bestowed upon a believer.

Long the distinguishing feature of the exuberant worship of Pentecostal churches, glossolalia has been considered alien to the proprieties of traditional Protestantism.

But its recent appearances in such august settings as the Protestant Episcopal Church and Yale University have caused Protestant circles to take a rather startled look at the phenomenon.

Last May, Bishop James A. Pike, warning of "heresy in embryo," put a virtual ban on glossolalia in his Protestant Episcopal diocese, which covers the central coast of California, the state in which the movement began. The attitude of most top church leaders is guardedly permissive.

Spiritual Gifts Stressed

The charismatic movement has brought a sudden, radical change to a broad segment of American Protestantism. It appears to be producing a new kind of minister and virtually a new mode of worship.

The movement emphasizes spiritual gifts called the charismata. The New Testament lists at least nine such charismata, or "gifts of the Holy Spirit." They are:

The gifts of prophecy; healing; tongues; interpretation of tongues; faith; the word of knowledge; the word of wisdom; exorcism, or discerning of spirits; and miracles, as outlined in I Corinthians 12:8-10.

The charismatic movement began on a minute scale about seven years ago. It appears to have gained its first adherents in two Protestant Episcopal churches—the Church of the Holy Spirit in Monterey Park, Calif., and Trinity Church at Wheaton, Ill.—and in the United Presbyterian Church of Upper Octarara, near Parkesburg, Pa.

The first public stir over the movement occurred in 1960 at St. Mark's Episcopal Church in Van Nuys, Calif., when its rector, the Rev. Dennis J. Bennett, told his congregation the story of his experience and one of the associate priests removed his vestments and stalked out of the church in protest.

Father Bennett resigned in the ensuing controversy. He became vicar of a church in Seattle that had few members and quickly turned it into a thriving congregation with a ministry that included healing and charismatic prayer meetings.

Appears in Europe

The movement has spread to every state and has begun to appear in Europe. Charismatic ministers travel a great deal from city to city, addressing meetings of interested ministers and laymen and helping them get started praying in tongues.

A group of Pentecostal origin, the Full Gospel Business Men's Association of Los Angeles, has a nationwide network of 280 chapters and hold monthly prayer breakfasts or dinners that are heavily attended by ministers of the mainline denominations.

A largely Episcopal group, the Blessed Trinity Society of Van Nuys, Calif., sponsors three-day preaching missions in churches and auditoriums under the name Christian Advance, and publishes a glossy, expensive quarterly magazine, Trinity.

The Inspirational Tape Library of Phoenix, Ariz., has eight copies each of 154 tape-recorded talks on the charismata by 90 ministers of all denominations. It lends the tapes by mail.

In November, 1962, the House of Bishops of the Protestant Episcopal Church adopted a statement warning that "the danger of all new movements is self-righteousness, divisiveness, one-sidedness, and exaggeration." Noting that "new movements have in history enriched the body of Christ," the statement counseled those not involved to take an attitude both "generous and charitably critical."

The Bishops called upon "all

180

new movements to remain in the full, rich, balanced life of the historic church" and thereby protect themselves from distortion or excess.

A person experiencing glossolalia for the first time may enjoy so vivid an apprehension of the reality of Christ that he will burst forth into an "inspired language" of adoration. This often comes as a result of the laying on of hands.

In other cases, an individual who is praying will quietly enter a new realm of worship and find himself offering prayer in unknown tongues.

After the first experience, those who continue to practice glossolalia say that praying in tongues may be engaged in anywhere at any time, silently or aloud, at will. They insist that it is entirely voluntary and they resent the suggestion that glossolalia is some kind of a "seizure."

'Tremendous Catharsis'

As utterly strange as it seems to the uninitiated, those who pray in tongues prize it as a gift of inestimable value, quickening to worship and strengthening to faith. They say it enlarges and liberates the soul in communion with God and gives them joy and release from tensions or worry.

"When you pray in tongues, you find tremendous catharsis and fulfillment," said the Rev. Harald Bredesen, minister of the First Reformed Church of Mount Vernon, N. Y.

Christians who have not experienced glossolalia are perplexed or annoyed by the phenomenon. Its appearance in a congregation sometimes causes apprehension or sharp hostility. Opponents fear that it will up-

set orderliness in worship and lead to excess.

The movement had already gained a foothold in a score of seminaries and colleges when word was published last year that 19 Yale students, including graduate students with Phi Beta Kappa keys, were praying in tongues and finding it meaningful. "In a mysterious but unmistakable way these gifts make Christ more real to the individual," David Wills, a Carnegie Teaching Fellow in history, said.

This news created a new wave of interest on campuses and in theological schools and some of the Yale men carried their new-found belief to other campuses.

At Princeton Theological Seminary, 20 students contend that they have had direct experiences with the charismata and 35 others attend prayer meetings at which they attempt to exercise spiritual gifts.

Movement Analyzed

The fullest analysis of the movement has been made by Dr. Stanley C. Plog, associate director of the training program in social and community psychiatry in the School of Medicine of the University of California at Los Angeles.

He found that a first sample of 352 persons questioned and interviewed represented "over 40 separate Christian denominations."

Dr. Plog found the charismatic movement to have "a much broader representation of various age, sex, occupation and income groups than almost any new social movement one could name." He said most such movements in the political, economic and religious spheres begin with a narrow base of people with a common interest acting in concert.

He found the charismatic movement to range in age from adolescents to the aged, in income from under $100 to considerably more than $1,600 a month and in educational levels from "persons with less than three years of school to individuals with advanced professional degrees."

He found it to have a much more "nearly equal representation of men and women" than other contemporary religious movements, in which he said "women outnumber men quite heavily."

The movement proved to have a surprisingly narrower political range. Dr. Plog found political party affiliation to be "strongly in favor of the G.O.P." One group studied was 3 to 1 Republican.

Dr. Plog described the movement as "very active, very eager, aggressive and proselytizing." It was a paradox, he said, that the charismatic movement, with its emphasis on the supernatural, was "arising at a time when our whole culture is becoming more sophisticated, urbane and urban."

To the charge of unintelligibility, which they cannot deny, charismatics answer in Biblical terms. The Apostle Paul wrote that "one who speaks in a tongue speaks not to men but to God, for no one understands him, but he utters mysteries in the Spirit." (I Corinthians 14:2).

"When a person prays in tongues, to his own ear and understanding it is simply a stream of sounds," declared the Rev. Laurance Christenson, pastor of Trinity Lutheran Church in San Pedro, Calif. "It is neither an emotional nor an intellectual act but an act of spiritual worship. According to the Bible, one's spirit is in a

state of prayer. This may or may not be accompanied by intellection or motion."

"Christians who pray in tongues witness with great unanimity that it has markedly deepened and strengthened their Christian faith," he said.

A study commission appointed by Bishop Pike found that glossolalia "stresses open vowels and a general lack of harsh gutterals, somewhat in the manner of Hawaiian or a southern Romance language."

Not 'Human Language'

Tape recordings of Mr. Bredesen speaking in tongues were played to a group of linguists in Toronto. They had, among them, done field work on more than 150 aboriginal languages in over 25 countries.

They found it to be "highly improbable that this is a human language." They found a "very high repetition of individual sounds and syllables" and a "pronounced tendency toward recurring sequences.".

The most surprising finding was that the speaker was not exercising "conscious control" of the form of the sounds he uttered. The linguists found that the minister was speaking "with nonconscious selection, on an automatic level." Their analysis said:

"The complete lack of 'paralinguistic' features, e.g. pauses, hesitations, stumbling in speech, obvious mistakes, and corrective repetitions, is interesting, for this shows quite clearly that the production of this speech is not under any conscious control—except in matters of beginning, stopping, speed of utterance and loudness."

May 17, 1964

Church Groups Protest Social Action Programs

By GEORGE DUGAN

Most church bodies in the country will embark this spring —the favored season for religious conventions—on new long-term programs, will strengthen old ones, to combat poverty, racism and injustice.

The large, mainstream denominations hold that this approach is their way to apply the Christian ethic to modern needs and problems.

Paradoxically and inevitably, the first loud cries of opposition will come from bitter critics within the denominations' own ranks.

These are the conservatives, theological and sociological, banded together in relatively small but vocal groups across the country.

They view themselves as stanch defenders of a faith dedicated solely to the saving of souls, and are convinced that

religion has no business "meddling" in secular affairs.

Arch Foe of 'Leftist'

For many, the churches' efforts to fight injustice opens the door to Communist infiltration.

The arch-enemy of such "leftist leaning" of modern Christianity is the Rev. Dr. Carl McIntire, president of the International Council of Christian Churches, which he founded in 1948 as the fundamentalist alternative to the World Council of Churches.

Dr. McIntire directs a paid-time broadcast over 600 radio stations in which he preaches a strict, literal interpretation of the Bible, distrusts ecumenism, voices a fear of a Communist take-over of American Christianity and, from time to time, exhibits a friendly attitude toward the John Birch Society.

Less specific, but by no means less articulate, are the Foundation for Christian Theology, an Episcopal group based in Texas; the Methodist Circuit Riders and the Presbyterian Lay Committee. The committee, based in New York City, is dedicated to the "adherence of our church to its primary mission—the teaching and preaching of the Gospel of Jesus Christ."

Bible Teaching Stressed

James J. Cochran, executive vice president of the Presbyterian committee and editor of its publications, said in an interview this week that his group was dedicated to restoring the "true mission of spiritual leadership" to his church.

According to Mr. Cochran, the United Presbyterian Church should stop making public pro-

nouncements on issues that have no direct bearing on religious matters. Rather, he said, it should place greater emphasis on Bible teaching and the "need for evangelism and spiritual guidance."

Recently, Kenneth Keyes, president of Concerned Presbyterians, an unofficial lay group in the Southern Presbyterian Church, told a Charlotte, N. C., audience that he feared a collision between liberals and conservatives that might split the denomination.

Mr. Keyes, an elder from Key Biscayne, Fla., put in words the thoughts of many of his conservative allies.

The control of most Protestant denominations today, he charged, is in the hands of "men who no longer believe that the primary mission of the church is to lead the lost to

181

Christ and to encourage believers to surrender themselves more fully and completely to Him."

These "liberal" leaders, he said, believe that the church's chief function is to "become involved in social, economic and political matters."

He warned that an "in-formed and aroused ruling eldership is not going to stand idly by and allow the church they love to be destroyed."

There is no accurate estimate available of the number of persons actively opposed to church involvement in social issues. The best guess of a statistician for the National Council of Churches put the number at 10 million of some 100 million churchgoers in the United States.

There are a greater number of people who are not nec-essarily active in their opposi-tion but who passively oppose church involvement. A Gallup Poll a year ago reported that 53 per cent of 1,500 persons interviewed said that churches should avoid involvement in political and social issues.

A comparable survey in 1957 showed that 47 per cent favored the expression of church views on social and political ques-tions, while 44 per cent de-murred.   April 12, 1969

The Southern Baptists, with more than 11 million members,

are the nation's largest Protestant denomination, and they preach:

'The Day of Judgment Is About to Come'

By BILL SURFACE

CLIFFORD CHANDLER and W. R. (Bob) Jones, two preachers in their 50's, have just walked into a motel near New Orleans on the eve of the Southern Baptists' annual convention this summer. Officially, there is nothing scheduled for them to do until the next morning. But as avowed God-fearing, Bible-believing, soul-saving preachers from Griffith, Ga., neither man will forget his Southern Baptist mandate to convert sinners regardless of where he may be. By the time the pastors have set down their luggage, Chandler has noticed that the nervous woman behind the desk is a chain smoker. "Brother Bob," he whispers, " 'at woman's eating cigarettes."

Staring through his horn-rimmed glasses, Jones asks the woman in a deep voice: "Ma'am, are you a Christian?"

"Y'all preachers, ain't ya?" she replies.

"Are ya a Christian?" Jones reiterates.

"Naw," she says. "Are y'all?"

"We've both accepted the Lord and was saved," Jones replies. "And he gave me the strength to quit drinkin' beer and smokin' cigar-ettes. Ya an alcoholic, too?"

"I drink a little beer, but boy, I'd sure like to quit smokin'," the woman says, her hand shaking so badly that she can barely write on the reservation card.

"If you just have faith the size of a grain ah mustard seed," Jones said, "ya can say into a mountain, 'Be ya removed' and, ma'am, it'll be removed. Makes no difference if it's a mountain or cigarettes."

"Let's ask the Lord to help ya," interjects Chandler, a tall, soft-spoken man, as he kneels beside the desk and prays.

They tell the woman, now plainly moved, that she might be comforted by telling the Lord why she is so nervous. "Y'all'll never believe me," she says.

"The Lord'll believe anything if it's true," Jones says. "I was just a sinner saved by the grace ah God."

"Me and my ol' man used to own part of this place," she begins, as tears form. "He drank it up and me and him got divorced and he got married agin. I didn't even have bus fare back to Alabama and had to ask 'em for a job back here. Three weeks ago I went down to the river to drown myself and the po-lice saw me and drug me back. 'Fore that, I took a whole bunch ah pills to commit suicide and it just make me throw up."

"The Lord's keepin' ya from killin' yourself," Jones says. He places his hands on her shoul-ders, and prays that she will go to church this evening so that God may free her from the devil's bondage and give her peace of mind. Chandler, meanwhile, has telephoned the Gentilly Baptist Church. "They got a service at 7:30," he reports, "and the preacher is gonna be lookin' for ya."

"Y'all sure good people," she says, wiping her tears with her sleeve.

"Ya give all the credit and glory to the Lord solely," Jones says, as they drive the woman to church. "He's just usin' me and Brother Cliff as feeble instruments. If He hadn't wanted ya to go, He wouldn't have worked with ya like this."

OVER-ALL church attendance in the United States has steadily declined in proportion to population for the past five years, but the 39,500 Southern Baptist pastors are proselytizing in so many homes, hotels and hollows as part of their 1969 crusade to persuade lost souls to repent that they are approaching their goal of 425,000 conversions—and seem likely to surpass their most successful worldwide campaign, entitled "A Million More in '54."

They are already the nation's largest Protes-tant denomination, with 11,332,229 members at latest count, although 31,257 of the 34,295 churches affiliated with the Southern Baptist Convention are concentrated in 12 sparsely populated Southern states, plus Missouri, Okla-homa and Texas. As Baptists migrate from rural areas, moreover, they are opening or increasing churches. One-third of their churches (and 60 per cent of the membership) are in or near cities of 50,000 or more. Southern Baptists now have churches in every state—including 1,788 with 487,947 members in the Far West. In the Northeast, they have grown sufficiently — 88 churches and chapels in New York, New Jersey and Connecticut—to schedule a meeting for next month in Syracuse to form a Southern Baptist Association for New York.

It is a demanding religion. Unless a South-ern Baptist wants to risk being considered a "backslider," he (or she) usually attends Sun-

BILL SURFACE, who frequently contributes to this Magazine, is writing a book about the rural South to be published next spring.

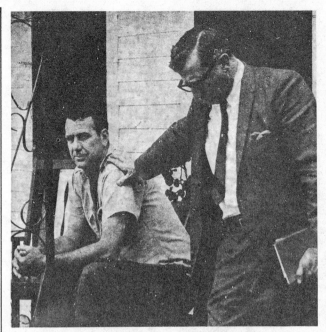

Proselytizer: Bible in hand, the Rev. Bob Jones tries to save a Griffith, Ga., man whose wife found him drinking hair tonic.

Congregation: A Sunday evening service at Jones's Baptist Tabernacle, in Griffith. Once regional, Southern Baptists now have churches in every state.

New York Times photographs by GEORGE TAMES

day school, both morning and evening services on Sunday, and prayer meeting on Wednesday evening. If he lives near a conservative small town, he often feels compelled also to attend a week-long revival meeting and send his children to Sunday school and vacation Bible school. An equally strict pattern often prevails outside the church. A devout Southern Baptist lady would not, among many abstentions, drink, smoke, dance, swear, play cards or wear shorts.

More important, no religious group has ever possessed so much influence on the morals and manners of such a large region of the United States. By virtue of their numerical strength, the Southern Baptists do not have to endorse political candidates to enforce their ideas on anything from a race track to a roadhouse. Any politician espousing a position alien to the Southern Baptists' moral beliefs is likely to find himself at the mercy of an army of doorbell ringers, the Southern Baptist radio-television network, 30 well-read state newspapers and the Baptist Press Service, which often appears to have the fastest mimeograph operators on either side of the Mason-Dixon line. Members of the Tennessee General Assembly, for example, recently found the Southern Baptists peering over their shoulders as soon as a bill to legalize pari-mutuel betting and horse racing in Tennessee cleared a House committee. The General Assembly was reminded, in a well-circulated resolution, that 850,000 Southern Baptists — enough to elect or defeat any state candidate — wanted the bill not only defeated but also

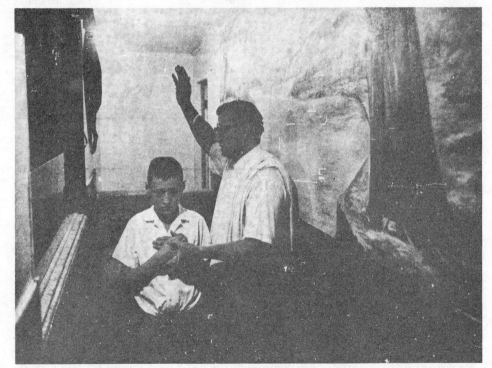

Immersion: The symbolic washing away of sin is an essential rite for Southern Baptists. Here, in a glass-fronted font behind the altar, an 11-year-old boy is received into the church by the Rev. Bob Jones.

"defeated resoundingly!"

Similarly, Southern Baptists are not reluctant to remind Congressmen, Senators and Presidents about their sympathies — and strength — on issues extending beyond state boundaries. One of the most effective methods is VIEWpoll, the Southern Baptists' equivalent of the Gallup Poll. In recent weeks, it has reported that 84.6 per cent of Southern Baptist pastors and 70.3 per cent of Sunday-school teachers would consider any appointment of a United States

representative to the Vatican an "unfortunate step backward"; that 71.8 per cent of the pastors favor Israel and 3 per cent side with the Arab countries in the Mideast conflict, and that 83.3 per cent of the pastors approve and only 7.7 per cent disapprove of President Nixon's performance. What the pastors particularly approve is Nixon's frequent meetings with the Rev. Billy Graham who, they realize, may be considered a non-denominational evangelist up North but was ordained as—

and remains—a Southern Baptist preacher.

YET, because of their strong opinions, Southern Baptists are flexible in many ways. Unlike other major denominations, Southern Baptist churches are so autonomous that their highest administrative organization, the Southern Baptist Convention, has no jurisdiction to dictate policy to any of the churches, 1,196 county associations or 32 state Baptist organizations.

Sing-in: Members of a Southern Baptist group called the MIL (Meaning-in-Life) Singers, who set the words of sermons to familiar rock tunes, perform for vacationing young collegians in Florida.

A changing church: Traditionally segregated since their break with Northern Baptists in 1845, Southern Baptists are beginning to integrate. Here the Rev. Bill Jackson, who has some 60 Negroes among the 400 members of his church in Decatur, Ga., leads a group of youngsters to a church party.

Many Southern Baptist churches are so jealous of their independence that the S.B.C. will not even join the National Council of Churches and thereby affiliate a Southern Baptist church with any of the council's positions. "We're a lot like a cafeteria to the churches," maintains Porter Routh, executive secretary of the S.B.C.'s executive committee. "They can go through the line and take or bypass any of our suggestions. If they don't see anything in the line they like, then they can go back to the kitchen and cook up something that suits them."

Not unexpectedly, such local freedom fosters considerable latitude in the interpretation of Christ's message. In most areas, Southern Baptists consider smoking to be scandalous, sinful and, for women, a virtual damnation to hell. Yet, in North Carolina and Kentucky, where many pillars of Southern Baptist churches grow tobacco for a living, most Baptists are closer to the theory smilingly offered by one preacher at this year's convention: "Smoking won't make ya go to hell but it'll make ya smell like ya already been there.

There is even greater diversity in what Southern Baptists feel the world needs. During this era of unprecedented social revolution at universities, for instance, delegates to the Kentucky Baptist Convention voted to demand that the trustees of Georgetown (Ky.) College rescind their decision to end the long-standing prohibition of dancing on campus. By contrast, Jess Moody, pastor of the First Baptist Church in West Palm Beach, Fla., preaches that churches need to "stop making ministerial mud pies because the Day of Judgment is about to come and catch

the world in its pajamas."

"We've got to stop this hot-blooded 'Gig 'em in the gut for God,'" he thundered from a platform during the convention. "It's time for Christians to let every political hopeful know that we will not elect men to office who, in order to serve their own personal egos, will disrupt the lives of millions of boys and send 50,000 of them to graves God never intended should be dug. It is time the great American eagle came off her nest where she has been hatching dollars and emits a freedom scream that will clear the air of hawks, doves and a few old buzzards."

Conservative or liberal, Southern Baptists are united on one issue: liquor. Southern Baptist women consider the use of liquor so sinful that some of them unite with local bootleggers to transport voters to the polls and defeat any referendum aimed at legalizing the sale of whisky in their county or township. Largely because of the Baptists' efforts, 58.4 per cent of Georgia's population — or nearly everyone living in a small town or rural area—cannot legally buy alcoholic beverages. Similarly, prohibition continues in most rural areas of Tennessee, Kentucky, Alabama, Mississippi, Texas and, to a lesser extent, North Carolina, Louisiana, Florida, Virginia and West Virginia. Even most Governors of Kentucky, rather than alienate the Baptists, have long refused to allow mint juleps to be served at the Kentucky Derby parties in the Governor's mansion (although drinks usually have been available on unmarked buses parked nearby).

The wickedness of liquor, Southern Baptist pastors maintain, is not even debatable. In general, their attitudes parallel the feelings of Ray

McKern, a craggy-faced pastor of Snow Creek Baptist Church in Seneca, S. C. "Lord, drinkin' liquor is one of the worst violations of God's law there is," McKern insisted. "The Bible says, 'Look not on the wine when it is red.' Says, 'At the last it'll biteth the tongue like a serpent and stingeth like an adder.'"

"Bible says lot more'n 'at," interjected Benny Johnson, pastor of Park Street Baptist Church in Esley, S. C. "It says you drink 'at stuff and your eyes'll behold strange women and the heart'll utter perverse things."

"I'd be agin hit even if hit wasn't in the Bible," McKern said. "Hit's harmful to the body. Breaks down your spirit, breaks up homes. Whisky is the major reason for all divorces in this country."

"Amen," Johnson added.

THE Bible is also the Southern Baptists' doctrine for all other issues. Strict fundamentalists, Southern Baptists have long been taught that the Bible is an infallible guide to heaven. Although about 10 per cent of the younger pastors and many theological professors now contend that parts of the Bible are subject to analysis, the vast majority of Southern Baptists seem nearly as conservative about it as Bob Harrington, who preaches in what some pastors consider the "middle of hell" —downtown New Orleans. "I not only believe every word in the Bible," he says with a smile, "I even believe the leather is genuine."

By Southern Baptists' interpretation of the Bible, everyone has been so thoroughly corrupted by Satan that he must be saved by repenting his sins and professing faith in Christ either at a Southern

Baptist church or with one of its ministers, then be immersed in water to symbolize that he has washed away his sins. Once a man has been baptized into a Southern Baptist church, he also is supposed to become, as defined in the S.B.C. constitution, "a missionary with a burning passion to lead other lost souls to God through Jesus Christ."

Except for wives pressuring husbands, there is not a particularly high percentage of new Southern Baptists who actually evangelize. But there are enough redemptive men who become crusading preachers—combined with a highly effective program for bringing people into church—to give the Southern Baptists a self-perpetuity. Southern Baptist churches have always been a social center for most white middle-class individuals from the time they began attending, at the age of 5 or 6, summer Bible schools that offer crafts, cookies and Biblical stories.

Such children, if also enrolled in Sunday school, sense that they must be saved by the time they are about 10 years old. Some children, parents insist, need to be saved at a much earlier age. Last year, Southern Baptist pastors baptized 1,463 children under the age of 6 and 36,867 less than 8 years old, although in many cases they doubted that the children actually understood the meaning of their decision.

I WAS in the sixth grade in Upton, Ky.—and attending my first Southern Baptist revival —when I heard the preacher reiterate that the old devil was holding onto lost souls so that they could join him in hell. It was an obvious cue. I felt something had held me back, although, as I

Missionaries: The Norman Harrells, Southern Baptists both, call on an Eskimo family in Alaska. The church has over 4,000 missionaries.

"Middle of hell": That's what Southern Baptists call downtown New Orleans, above, where this storefront church is located.

recall, I hadn't done anything I considered particularly sinful. Suddenly I ran down the aisle and was crying by the time I shook hands with the preacher and fell to my knees to be regarded as saved. I felt somebody bump my arm and saw that my brother Donald, two years younger, had followed me. Then I remember a woman, sitting in one of the left front pews, saying that it was wonderful that the Lord had saved two brothers at once. It was, at the time and as a child, comforting to feel that you wouldn't burn in hell. I attended the church until I left Upton for college.

Southern Baptists go beyond the usual church pattern of drawing almost entirely from one or two classes of people. A typical small-town congregation of 240 will include both the president of the local bank and the woman who sells Greyhound bus tickets in a corner of the lunchroom.

There are two conspicuous exceptions to this cross section. Most of the really wealthy people in the area will, if they attend church at all, be affiliated with the Episcopal or Presbyterian churches (which some Baptists accuse of being "uppity") or, sometimes, the Methodist churches, which offer a philosophy not substantially different from that of the Southern Baptists. (There are, of course, a few prudent millionaires who do attend Baptist churches; H. L. Hunt, the conservative oilman and perhaps third richest American, belongs to the First Baptist Church of Dallas.) The other exclusion is the lower-lower class of semi-illiterate people who live in shacks beside the railroad or up a hollow and earn meager livings as tenant farmers or part-time

or seasonal workers at saw-mills and factories. Most such people reject the Southern Baptist preachers' appeals on the ground that they don't have a decent pair of suit pants to wear to church. If these men attend church, they generally profess to being members of the more casual Church of God.

REGARDLESS of the religion, it was primarily the Southern Baptists who caused the feeling that attending church, per se, was the right thing to do, and about the only way eventually to escape the frequently harsh Southern life. Baptist philosophy, it seems, fitted rural Southerners better than all others. As conscientious Southerners struggled unsuccessfully to improve themselves, they found solace in the preaching about their glorious afterlife in heaven where they would, in effect, be free from such common worries as drought, weeds, tobacco worms, boll weevils, chicken hawks and unemployment. Disasters and deaths, meanwhile, could be more easily accepted as "God's will." The Baptists were so persuasive that many Southerners who never entered a church felt that they really should.

"The Southern Baptists created such an atmosphere that you were either a believer in the Lord or an infidel," emphasizes the Rev. W. A. Criswell, pastor of the First Baptist Church of Dallas and president of the Southern Baptist Convention. "It was as simple as being one of the good guys or bad guys and no middle ground. But so many enemies of the church—including preachers in other denominations — are saying parts of the Bible are full of myths that people don't know

what to believe. There are enough people who think they have an option today that it's getting harder to convert them. But Southern Baptists are still growing because of our great missionary zeal."

Many crusaders are women. Southern Baptist churches have more women than men and, if they have been raised as lifelong Baptists, they tend to exude such a strong sense of participation that, by Northeast standards, they might be considered "busybodies." At last count, 1,430,509 women also were members of the Southern Baptists' Women's Missionary Union, which meets regularly to conduct Biblical studies, pray for each of the Southern Baptists' 4,100 foreign missionaries on their birthdays and assist some of the poor or distressed so that they eventually may "feel God's love."

Betty Bock, a tall, articulate member of the downtown First Baptist Church of Birmingham, Ala., is a W.M.U. activist. Her group, in one recent week, took food to a family awaiting the burial of their mother; taught illiterate women to read labels, letters and parts of the Bible; took a 38-year-old grandmother who had been deserted to the appropriate Government agency, and read Scripture to a young man who, after previously fathering five illegitimate children, suddenly decided to "do right" by the latest pregnant girl.

"It'd be wonderful if people responded every time we read the Bible," says Mrs. Roy Snider, director of a W.M.U. group in Camden, Ark. "But it's just like farming. You can't haul in the corn unless you plant a field and plow it."

ONCE the women plow the fields, the pastors are seldom far behind. Cliff Chandler, the preacher from Griffith, Ga.,

makes it so difficult to avoid God's message that the membership of his Mt. Gilead Baptist Church has increased from 137 to 340 in the past eight years. Like most Southern Baptist pastors, he makes 60 per cent of his conversions among persons under the age of 17. Yet, night after night, Chandler visits the homes of recognized sinners as well. He goes back two, four, six, eight times, until, one by one, they repent—like the railroad worker said to drink a pint of whisky every weekend.

"Even the railroad man's grandboy told me he'd never give up 'at whisky," Chandler volunteers. "He's now one of our finest song leaders. Listen, we had a young man who'd sunk so low he was working in a liquor store and naturally he and his wife didn't go to church. Well, I preached the funeral when their little boy got run over by a car, and you could see they realized they couldn't go on like that. After they both were won to the Lord, he quit 'at liquor store and got 'm a good Government job. One fellow even opened his store on Sundays. Right on Sunday. It took some doing, but he's not only going to church—he's got his boy sellin' Bibles."

Bob Jones, who was saved at Mt. Gilead Church and now pastors the Baptist Tabernacle in Griffith, has similarly increased his church membership from 48 to 240 since 1965. "The answer to any problem is right here," Jones says. "This alcoholic asked me if I knew about a home in North Carolina or someplace that'd help her quit drinking. I said, 'You come here for two weeks and if you still wanta go to one of 'em homes I'll drive you myself.' Course she didn't want to go. The answer was here—getting right with God. Young people didn't go to church a lot. Like most young people of our land they were challenging the grown-ups to show 'em something. We show 'em how to find Christ."

MANY people in Griffith still don't want to find Christ, Jones concedes, if they are satisfied with their lives and jobs. Prosperity, he finds, makes it hard to convert some sinners. "People'll come more listening to God's message if they're down and out and in sin," he says. "But these people who got material things are kind of like hogs, I hate to say. Hogs go round eating acorns all day long and never look up to see where they're comin' from. People get 'em a good job and a new car and don't even realize the Lord give it to 'em."

Many of those who come to realize do so after hearing a revivalist, building up momentum, reiterate his catalogue of personal sins. For example, the avowed sins of John R. Bisagno, now pastor of the First Southern Baptist Church in Del City, Okla., have helped result in 3,250 conversions at his church alone during the past four years. A former trumpet player in a touring dance-hall band, Bisagno preaches that few men ever inhabited worse places and were still accepted by God.

"I felt like I was walking down the floors of hell when I took my bands into the dives of the South," he recalled recently. "It was a back alley into a smoky room, where the stench of cheap perfume and liquor and sweating bodies was enough to make one nauseated. I went back to a hotel to lay across a bed where a flashing light outside my room kept me awake most of the night, and as I stretched out half-drunk on those creaking springs, my head would begin to swim and reel in the wee hours of the morning. Somebody told me about Jesus. I found Christ. Oh, the appeal of sin was strong. It was: 'Come on back.' But I'm not going back. No-o-o. I'm with the Lord."

Many pastors are so adamant about keeping lost souls out of hell that they will follow a presumed sinner to his deathbed. For sheer persistence, it is difficult to surpass the efforts of the Rev. Roscoe Douglas, a white-haired, 75-year-old former coal miner who began preaching in an unpainted store near Kentucky's Black Mountain in 1934, when he reasoned that the death of his infant daughter was "God's way of punishing me for not doin' anything for Him." Now pastor of the Pansy Baptist Church, a neat, carpeted building that sits at the foot of a hollow in Harlan County, Douglas recalled recently:

"Buddy, those coal miners are hard to convert when they get old. Floyd —— was layin' 'ere in that hospital one Saturday night and wouldn't let anybody talk to 'm 'bout salvation. I found out he knew some of my kinfolks from Jellico, and told 'm: 'The Lord don't want you to go to hell, Floyd.' Didn't faze 'm. Lambert fellow who'd been saved, me and him bent down and had a prayer. Floyd's wife poked me and said: 'Floyd's listening.' Somebody else said: ''At ol' man's cryin'.' I grabbed my Testament and told Floyd: 'The Lord's workin' with ya while ya got time.' He broke down and cried like a baby."

According to Douglas, Floyd pulled his arm out from behind his head in such a way that it appeared he would shake the pastor's hand and make what would be considered his decision. Instead, Floyd laid his hand in his lap and whispered: "'Morrow."

When tomorrow came, Douglas visited Floyd. "He was groanin' something awful," Douglas said. "And his mouth was all drawed 'round the side of 'is face."

Bending over, Douglas held Floyd's shoulder while reiterating that he didn't want him to go to hell.

"'Morrow," Floyd would whisper.

"It wasn't movin' 'm," Douglas recalled. "You know who had hold of his other hand, don't ya? That old devil didn't want to give Floyd up. But I kept prayin' and talkin' for what must've been 30 minutes and he got right with the Lord. He said he believed in the Lord and made his decision and was saved. 'Morrow woulda been too late. He died the next night, and his kids just hug me 'cause I win their daddy to the Lord."

ALTHOUGH salvation is his primary purpose, a conscientious Southern Baptist pastor has an even deeper role in his community. As might be expected, he often is the first person whom families turn to if they are desperate, their children are in trouble, or they seek to place a relative in one of the 45 Southern Baptist hospitals, 28 nursing homes or 54 colleges and universities (such as Baylor and Wake Forest).

Since pastors are frequently away from home, enough problems fall upon their wives to make them often the leading local activists. "A pastor's wife can't be somebody who gets excited at Christmas and makes a bunch of cookies and Kool-Aid," says Mrs. J. A. Hogan, the pastor's wife in Sweet Rock, Ark. "We go to places that don't smell good. Sixteen of us women took some girls out of reform school and put them in Christian homes away from temptation. Three of them girls had done everything. Sex, stealing, the works. One swore she'd killed somebody. But they're all in Sunday school, and the meanest one in the bunch—she's in the choir and married and got two of the sweetest little kids."

Despite the demands, Southern Baptists do not have to advertise to attract pastors. Men become preachers, they maintain, after receiving a "call"—one that may vary from a sudden conviction they should preach to a direct communication from the Lord. Frequently it is a personal tragedy, such as a fatal automobile accident in the family.

If the call comes before or while a young man is attending college, he can go to one of seven Southern Baptist seminaries (where 8,050 are now enrolled) for three years. Older men responding to the call can apply at schools such as the Clear Creek Baptist School in Pineville, Ky., regardless of their lack of education. During the three-year course, these men practice by preaching in missions and jails, in parking lots or on street corners, and support their families by working in the school's furniture factory. Still, even today, a man is not compelled to attend a single course to preach or start a church. All he needs is a Bible and a building.

Southern Baptist pastors are never assigned. Each church hires or fires its own, and pays him what it chooses. A church with no more than 100 members may pay its pastor as little as $40 a month (25 per cent of all Southern Baptist pastors hold outside jobs). Pastors of churches with 400 to 750 members average $6,000 a year, plus a house and car, while the 288 pastors of churches listing 3,000 or more members receive an average of $13,255 and expenses.

Further calls and visions guide the course of a pastor's career. Appropriately, few visions have been more specific than the one reported by Mr. Criswell, whose Dallas church is the largest Southern Baptist church (15,111 members). When he was a young preacher in Muskogee, Okla., in 1944, Criswell told me in a whispering voice, he had a vision in which he was led into the First Baptist Church of Dallas during funeral services for the late Dr. George W. Truett (whose emotional oratory made him the S.B.C.'s best-known pastor). According to Criswell, Truett rose from the coffin, grasped his left hand and pleaded: "You must pastor at my church in Dallas." When Criswell replied: "Oh, not I," he recalled, Truett clutched his right knee and insisted: "Yes, you must go down to preach to my people."

"The church's pulpit committee had never heard of me," Criswell said, "but three weeks after the vision they asked me to preach a guest sermon and, on Sept. 27, 1944, they called me to be pastor."

ONCE called, Baptist pastors have been reluctant to change because of their allegiance to a belief that "Jesus Christ is the same yesterday, today and forever." But Southern Baptist churches,

per se, are changing. Organized in 1845 after a quarrel with Northern Baptists over the appointment of a slave owner as a missionary, the Southern Baptists are beginning to feel the breezes of integration. About 100 young people calling themselves "Baptist Students Concerned" met independently during the S.B.C.'s convention in New Orleans to debate, among other issues, why Southern Baptists send missionaries to Africa's bush country but rarely evangelize among American Negroes (whose own Baptist churches with 6.2 million members were modeled after the Southern Baptist philosophy). Although no formal motions about integration were passed, some Negroes already attend perhaps 2 per cent of Southern Baptist churches, mostly near integrated universities, but also in such surprising areas as Carrollton, Miss.

"I'd made 10 or 12 trips to this white family's house," says James C. Harvey, the seminary-trained pastor in Carrollton. "A little girl asked me to win her daddy and mom to God. It was an awful place. Kids going to the bathroom off the front porch, or running through the house when Scripture was being read. Daddy'd either be drunk or looking out the window when I'd read, and all of them aren't converted yet. Then I stopped by these two colored teachers' houses. They were hungry for the gospel and four of 'em were saved right away and come to our church. This thing could be worked out this way through the church and the Lord."

THERE has never been a greater urgency for all races, Southern Baptists insist, to work things out with the Lord. In recent weeks, an increasing number of pastors have preached that—based on the Bible—the growing dependence on nuclear bombs, missiles and drugs points to an imminent second coming of Christ. A recent light earthquake in the Midwest and upper South was considered by many pastors as God's last warning that the world had become too wicked.

"The times make it imperative that we teach what the Bible says about the great separation," Mr. Criswell said, as he held onto my arm. "The Lord will descend through the clouds and the saved—of all ages—will be caught up with him in midair and go on to heaven. The others will be shut out from the Lord and left in the darkness, brimstone and fire that make up hell. As we know, God will end the human age in his own way. Even scientists are talking about extinction of the human age. Whatever you call it, it will be God's way. I personally feel—I can scent it—that all signs point to the Lord's return sometime soon. It could be only a matter of hours." ∎

Pentecostals Gain Among Catholics

By EDWARD B. FISKE

Pentecostalism, a form of religious piety that emphasizes spontaneous and emotional outpourings of prayer and has generally been identified with Protestant Christianity, is rapidly becoming an important new force among Roman Catholics.

Catholics of all ages and from all walks of life have begun holding regular midweek prayer services ranging from intimate gatherings of a dozen persons in a Brooklyn apartment to weekly events at the University of Michigan that draw 400 to 500 persons.

In addition, the movement has spawned dozens of experiments in communal living and the rudiments of a national organization that sponsors conferences and distributes literature and tapes relating to Pentecostal Christianity.

Started 4 Years Ago

Informed estimates of the number of Catholics involved in the movement range from 15,000 to 50,000. Although this constitutes only a small minority of the nation's 47 million Catholics, authorities note that the phenomenon is not yet four years old and is still growing.

Catholic Pentecostals have been attacked by liberals, who charge that they are excessively preoccupied with personal holiness, and by traditionalists, who see the movement as a threat to doctrinal and liturgical orthodoxy. Others, including some Pentacostals, have warned that it can be divisive.

Most members of the movement, however, reply that their involvement in Pentecostal rites has enhanced rather than weakened their commitment to fundamental traditions such as the mass. They also report that it has introduced them to deep religious emotion at a time when much Catholic worship has become cold and sterile.

"The charismatic movement has given us a living experience of what Catholicism has always taught," said Daniel Giordano, a 25-year old participant in the Brooklyn group. "For me Jesus has become a living Savior right here and now. He's not just a figure out of a history book."

Pentecostal elements first entered Christianity in the first century on the day of Pentecost when, according to the Book of Acts, the Holy Spirit descended on the early Christians in the form of tongues of fire.

In his first letter to the Corinthians, St. Paul described various spiritual gifts that are imparted to those who, in the language of the present-day movement, have "received the baptism of the Holy Spirit." Among them are the gifts of prophecy, wisdom, healing and speaking in tongues.

The most controversial of these is speaking in tongues, a phenomenon whereby an individual speaks in what appears to be a coherent but foreign language. Pentecostals generally describe this as a form of divinely inspired prayer, possibly one that draws on subconscious faculties. Many also report instances in which an individual spoke in a real language that was unknown to him, but reliable documentation of such cases is rare.

"Charismatic gifts" were common in the early church but virtually disappeared in the wake of Montanism, a second-century apocalyptic movement that carried interest in the Holy Spirit to an extreme.

A modern resurgence of Pentecostal worship began in 1901 in Topeka, Kan., when a preacher named Charles F. Parham began a Bible school devoted to spiritual gifts. This led to the founding of entire Pentecostal denominations, including the Assemblies of God and numerous Holiness churches.

Andrew Sacks for The New York Times

Participants in a Pentecostal service at a Catholic center in Ann Arbor, Mich. The community there is reported the best organized among Catholics, as well as largest.

10 Million Pentecostals

Pentecostal churches, which think of themselves variously as Protestant or a separate branch of Christianity, now enroll an estimated 10 million persons, including 2 million in this country, and constitute the fastest growing Christian churches in Africa and Latin America. Today several thousand Pentecostals from 50 nations will open a six-day congress in Dallas coordinated by the Assemblies of God.

In 1960 the Rev. Dennis Bennett introduced the speaking of tongues into an Episcopal church in Van Nuys, Calif., and initiated an interest in charismatic worship in mainline Protestant denominations that has continued to the present day, especially among Presbyterians, Lutherans and Espicopalians.

Catholic Pentecostalism began at Duquesne University in Pittsburgh in February 1967, when four laymen received the "baptism of the Holy Spirit" and began speaking in tongues. The movement spread to the universities of Notre Dame, Michigan State, and Michigan and subsequently into

The New York Times (by Donal F. Holway)

A woman in the group at North Vale telling about her experience in Pentecostal movement. Group formed circle.

local parishes.

Typical of Catholic Pentecostal services was a recent Thursday prayer meeting at St. Anthony's Church in North Vale, N.J. About 150 persons, including a sprinkling of nuns and priests, gathered in a large tight circle in the school gymnasium.

At the center were a priest and a woman in a blue sweater with a guitar.

The two-hour meeting was marked by spontaneous Bible readings, prayers, speaking in tongues and pious Gospel hymns that one would normally associate with fundamentalist Protestants. Frequently a member of the group stood up and told how belief in Jesus had solved personal problems. One woman, for instance, said her husband had received a transfer he had sought from his employer.

Following the prayer meeting the participants broke up into small groups for additional prayer and instruction. In one classroom about a dozen experienced Catholic Pentecostals prayed and laid their hands on the heads of new adherents who sought "baptism in the Spirit."

Among the worshipers was Mario Guardici, a 47-year-old junior high school teacher from Maplewood who said that his discovery of Christ through these meetings had changed his whole attitude toward life. "I think of God all day, even in the classroom," he declared. "I have a real love for people that I never did before."

Peter Forbes, a student at Bergen Community College who said that before his conversion he had been a heavy user of drugs, declared, "I'm high on Jesus. I've tried everything, and there's nothing like Jesus."

The same night in Ann Arbor, Mich. several hundred persons gathered in the basement of a Catholic student center for what is reportedly the largest regular Pentecostal service now being held by Catholic Pentecostals. It, too, was marked by spontaneous singing and reading and frequent exclamations of "Hallelujah" and "Praise Jesus."

The Ann Arbor community is the best-organized of any Catholic Pentecostal group, with many of the members living together in communal fashion and some working full-time for the movement. In addition to the Thursday services it sponsors a Monday-evening meeting for a firmly committed core of 200 persons.

In South Bend, Ind., a half-dozen young Catholic Pentecostals, mainly Notre Dame graduates, live together in "True House" and run nightly prayer meetings in cooperation with other Catholic Pentecostals.

Among them is James Byrne, a 24-year old adherent who said that Pentecostalism, which many prefer to call "charismatic renewal," had helped him solve a drinking problem. "I was a mess, spiritually, morally and psychologically," he said. "Then I just gave myself over to God, and my life was changed."

Monks Adopt Method

In some cases whole convents have begun praying in a "charismatic" manner. In Pecos, N.M. a group of Benedictine monks now includes spontaneous prayer in its daily services and has begun holding weekend retreats to introduce laymen to the movement.

A seven-member committee has now been created to provide communication among 250 groups around the country, and a newsletter published by the Ann Arbor community has subscribers in 18 countries. Last June the movement held its fourth annual conference at Notre Dame and drew 1,350 delegates.

Catholic Pentecostal leaders frankly acknowledge their historical debt to Protestant Pentecostals. The Rev. John F. Randall, a priest in Providence, R.I., for instance, said that his group began when he and some young people visited the Rev. David Wilkerson, an evangelical Protestant preacher in Manhattan who used Pentecostal methods in work with gangs and drug addicts. His book, "The Cross and the Switchblade," has become must reading for Catholic Pentecostals.

At the same time Catholic Pentecostalism has developed its own unique style. The Rev. Kilian P. McDonnell, a 49-year old Benedictine who has studied it extensively, noted that Catholic meetings, while replete with fundamentalist Protestant rhetoric, tend to be "more structured and reserved" than their Protestant counterparts.

The formation of communities of Pentecostals who live and work together is also a Catholic innovation.

Catholic Pentecostals generally describe the emergence of their movement at this particular time as the work of the Holy Spirit and note that at the beginning of the Second Vatican Council of 1962 to 1965 Pope John XXIII composed a well-known prayer for a "new Pentecost."

Members also observe that the council created an atmosphere of openness for all

sorts of religious forms, and that young people today tend to be receptive to all sorts of movements that offer meaningful new types of personal experiences.

The movement has been criticized as potentially divisive and for creating circles of "elite" Catholics. The Rev. Andrew M. Greeley, a prominent Catholic sociologist, recently attacked speaking in tongues as psychologically unsound and declared, "I do not believe that God's Spirit, when He chooses to speak to us, is going to play the foolish game of speaking in foreign languages."

Woman Criticizes Movement

Josephine Massingberd Ford, an associate professor of theology at Notre Dame, was reportedly banned from participating in meetings in South Bend and subsequently accused leaders there of "not recognizing the Spirit in Negroes or women."

Members of the movement note, however, that last November the American Catholic hierarchy, in response to numerous requests for a policy statement on the phenomenon, declared that there were "legitimate reasons" for its existence and urged that it be permitted to develop under "proper supervision."

Pentecostals greeted this statement warmly, for most regard their movement as the best possible basis for the renewal of the church begun by the Vatican Council. "You can have the best theology and liturgy in the world," said Mr. Byrne, "but if a man's heart isn't touched by the fire of God's love, it's not worth very much."

November 3, 1970

Congregations:

The Appeal Of 'That Old Time Religion'

"A lot of our people are wondering whether the churches have gone too far in jeopardizing our own survival for the sake of serving society."

The speaker, Brady Fallart, an official of the American Lutheran Church, was discussing an apparent trend in American religious life: Denominations that have plunged heavily into social action and have embraced ecumenical movements are losing membership; those that have in general discouraged social action and insisted that they alone possess religious truth are gaining adherents.

The trend can be seen in the latest statistics published by the National Council of Churches. Total church membership last year rose slightly

to 131 million, but most of the major liberal Protestant denominations either lost members or barely held steady. The United Methodist Church, for instance, hit a high mark of 11.1 million members in 1965 and is now down to 10.7 million. The Episcopal Church had more than 3.4 million members during the period from 1964 to 1967 but last year dropped to 3,286,000. Similar patterns are reported for Mr. Fallart's American Lutheran Church, the Christian Church (Disciples of Christ), the United Church of Christ, the United Presbyterians and others.

On the other hand, statistics show a group of churches that are making steady gains. The Church of Jesus

Christ of Latter-day Saints, better known as the Mormons, reported recently that its membership in the United States increased 50 per cent to 2.1 million during the last 12 years. And statistics show steady increases of two to five per cent during a comparable period for Southern Baptists, Seventh-Day Adventists, the Church of the Nazarene, Jehovah's Witnesses, the Christian Reformed Church and various Pentecostal groups, including the Assemblies of God.

What distinguishes the gainers from the losers? In a new book called "Why Conservative Churches are Growing," Dean M. Kelley, the resident church-state expert for the liberal National Council of Churches, offers one explanation.

The churches that are gaining members, he observes, are generally those that have held on to old-time beliefs, shunned compromising contact with other churches or secular causes and made clear their belief that they alone have the truth. They are strong on discipline, missionary zeal, absolutism, conformity and even fanaticism.

The churches that are losing members, on the other hand, Mr. Kelley reports, are those that profess tolerance of diversity and openness to dialogue with others. Efforts to foster inter-faith cooperation "may be conducive to brotherhood, peace, justice, freedom and compassion," he writes, "but they are not conducive to conserving or increasing the social strength of the religious groups involved."

Such analysis would also seem relevant to the Roman Catholic Church in the United States, which moved during the 1960's from the absolutist to the tolerant camp. Since 1968, its membership has been leveling off and in 1970 the church experienced the first decrease since its founding, though there was a slight recovery last year.

Mr. Kelley, who is a Methodist, argues that the main reason his and other mainline churches are losing members is that they have diluted the principal product religion has to offer: providing meaning in personal life. "Man is an inveterate meaning-monger," he writes. "When churches get sidetracked into noble but nevertheless extraneous goals such as changing social structures, then allegiance falters."

Others have different theories. The Right Rev. Roger W. Blanchard, executive vice-president of the Episcopal Church, is among those who see the religious trend as a retreat from the social turmoil of the 1960's. "Many people today are looking for a kind of security that fundamentalist churches can provide," he says.

George E. Sweazey, a former moderator of the United Presbyterian Church who now teaches at Princeton Theological Seminary, takes the position that theological confusion is the major problem. "If professional theologians can't even say what to believe," he says, "what about the average person?"

Mr. Kelley says that the churches now in decline would help themselves by exercising more "strictness" in membership standards. He suggested closely-knit cells of members that reinforce each other's beliefs. And conversely there would be fewer efforts to accommodate the expectations of outsiders.

Those in churches that are growing often attribute their success to evangelism (an endeavor that invariably suffers when a church decides that others might have some of the truth). Dean Dinwoodey, representative of Mormons in Washington, said that his church is thriving because "we remain committed to the family and put a lot of effort into youth work." Porter W. Routh, executive secretary of the executive committee of the Southern Baptist Convention, said that his theologically conservative denomination has "benefited by the resurgence of interest in Jesus among young people."

Some officials in the so-called liberal churches, worrying about the effect on financial needs, church building and Sunday school attendance, are trying to reverse the trend. Bishop Blanchard said members of the Episcopal executive council will soon visit every area of the country to "hear what people are saying at the grass roots." The American Lutherans and other churches are looking to Key 73, an interdenominational evangelistic thrust planned for next year, as a help.

But some argue that all these efforts are not needed; they see the decline in membership as a healthy sign, a sort of purification. "It may be a sign of the faithfulness of the church," said Mr. Fallart. —EDWARD B. FISKE
August 6, 1972

The Oral Roberts empire

University, television programs, magazine publishing, direct mail, home for the aged, computer center and old-time religion all under one tent

By Edward B. Fiske

TULSA. The sound stage in the university sports center was set for the taping of another prime-time television special. Prerecorded orchestral music boomed from giant unseen speakers overhead. Young girls darted about under the camera lenses holding cue cards. Pianist Roger Williams, the featured guest star, waited in the wings for his slot on the program, while onstage, members of a ranking college basketball team bounced around in front of a makeshift backboard.

Soon the cue cards began to carry lines like "Jesus loves me, this I know, for the Bible tells me so." Roger Williams played "Abide With Me" and then talked with the host, Oral Roberts, about the pianist's childhood as a minister's son. And

when the coach of the basketball team was asked the secret of his team's success, he replied, "The Christian witness that the campus portrays."

The show taped at Oral Roberts University was an hour-long Christmas program, the 16th in a series of "contact specials" by one of the country's most controversial religious figures. The sophisticated combination of technology, showmanship and old-time religion that went into it is indicative of the dramatic new style of Oral Roberts.

Until several years ago Oral Roberts was known primarily as an evangelist and "faith healer"—a term he intensely dislikes because, he says, "it suggests that I'm doing the healing rather than God." He logged hundreds of thousands of miles in this country and abroad with his tent. At the end of each service he would sit on a folding chair

Edward B. Fiske is religion editor of The Times.

189

with his coat off and his shirtsleeves rolled up and, with beads of sweat rolling off his brow, lay his hands on the heads of the sick and invalids who paraded, or were brought, before him. With his hands shaking and his voice quivering with emotion, he would pray for a healing from God.

Roberts estimates that he laid his hands on more than a million heads. There is no doubt that many people for whom he prayed were not healed, as he readily admits: "I know how many I've prayed for who, when I finished praying, looked up in hurt and disappointment because nothing had happened. My failures are ever before me." There is also no doubt that he healed large numbers of them, of problems ranging from stuttering to paralysis—whether by means of divine intervention, spontaneous remissions that would have occurred anyway, or the healing of psychosomatic illness.

But while his ministry brought him fame, it earned him little acceptance outside Pentecostal fundamentalist circles. The press treated him harshly. He was the butt of humorous jokes ("Did you hear that Oral Roberts tried to make a phonograph record, but the hole in the center kept healing over?"). In his home town, Tulsans tended to regard him as only a little less embarrassing than their other well-known son, anti-Communist crusader Billy James Hargis.

Now all this has changed. Roberts has, as it were, gone straight—and made it in the big time. The tent was folded in 1968 and replaced by a television studio. His weekly half-hour program is seen on 275 stations in this country and Canada, and four times a year he sinks $600,000 into a prime-time special that is seen on more than 400 stations. Oral Roberts University, carved out of 500 acres of farmland on the southern rim of Tulsa and dismissed by skeptics as just another Bible college when he opened its doors in 1965, now boasts $55-million worth of gleaming facilities, full academic accreditation, a nationally ranked basketball team and probably the most sophisticated technology of any liberal-arts college in the country.

Roberts also runs a home for the elderly, and his Oral Roberts Association sends out 400,000 letters a month, mostly replies to personal problems and requests for prayer. The annual budget of his operations is now $17-million, and as architect of Tulsa's leading tourist attraction and one of Oklahoma's few institutions of higher education, he has been welcomed by the city fathers as one of their own. He plays his golf (handicap six) at the exclusive Southern Hills Country Club and serves on the board of the National Bank of Tulsa. Gov. David Hall, a longtime personal friend, says that "next to Will Rogers, he is the best-known person Oklahoma has produced."

HOW Roberts reached the point of overseeing such an ecclesiastical empire is already being told in terms that border on hagiography. He was born near Ada, a small town in southwest Oklahoma, on Jan. 24, 1918, and christened Granville Oral Roberts. In his latest autobiography, "The Call," he reports that while he was still in the womb his mother consecrated him to God in gratitude for the healing through prayer of a neighbor's child who was dying of pneumonia. His preacher father was barely able to support the family of four, and Roberts says that on one occasion the family was miraculously saved from hunger by the last-minute gift of food from an unknown source.

In the sermon for the Christmas special, he talked about how he rebelled against his parents and "ran out of life just like a car runs out of gas." At the age of 17, he went on to say, he was playing in a high-school basketball tournament and suddenly collapsed on the floor with blood running from his nostrils. He was taken home with what was diagnosed as tuberculosis and lay near death for six months. One night his sister packed him into a car and drove him 20 miles to hear a little-known tent evangelist named George Moncey, who laid his hands on him and "asked Jesus Christ to open my lungs.

"I remember it like it was yesterday," said Roberts. "There was warmth at first, a warmth like warm water coming over me. It went into my lungs, and I'd been breathing off the top of my lungs because if I didn't I would hemorrhage, but I took a deep breath, and I could go all the way down, and I knew that a miracle was starting. And the man talked to me a moment, and he had me talk back, and I talked without stammering [something from which he suffered as a child]. In a few moments' time I was standing straight and tall. I was breathing down deep; I was talking. I was a healed man, and in my heart God's voice was ringing, 'You are to take my healing power to your generation.' Now, I didn't know how to do that. I've gone around this world; I've preached to crowds up to 100,000, and small crowds, middle-size crowds, on television and all over. And I've made many mistakes, and I've had lots of failures. But there are a lot of people today who know Christ, and who are healed, because God spoke to a boy, raised him up and put something in his soul."

The healing of his stuttering and tuberculosis at the age of 17 was the definitive event in his life, and as a result of this experience Roberts felt called to the ministry. He was ordained in the Pentecostal Holiness Church, a small fundamentalist sect that broke away from the Methodist Church in the late 19th century when the latter lost some of its frontier zeal and became solidly middle class. Like other Pentecostal groups, the Pentecostal Holiness Church emphasizes speaking in tongues, an emotional experience in which an individual, under the influence of the Holy Spirit, appears to speak in a foreign language (it usually sounds like Russian). The sect also teaches that a true Christian pursues a rather austere existence, that the capacity to shun such things as jewelry is a sign of "sanctification."

After a brief pastorate in Enid, Okla., Roberts decided on an itinerant ministry. Soon he became convinced that, in preaching simple conversion of the soul, he was not reaching "the whole man." So he began praying for healing of the body as well, and in doing so he had no fear of being physical. "My heart is in my hands," he once told journalist Albin Krebs. "When I pray for the sick I feel something in my hands, because first of all I feel it inside myself. And my compassion comes running out through my hands, and I'm close to a person. I get out there where he is, with his afflicted child, demented relative, someone—a little afflicted child slobbering at the mouth. I put my hands upon his face, and the slobber gets all over my hands. Because that's the way I know how to help him. That's the way I express my religion." This sense of the physical persists today; while praying on television he invariably takes the hand of the person nearest him and asks viewers and members of the audience to do the same.

By the mid-nineteen-sixties, Roberts began getting uneasy about his identification with the Pentecostal Holiness Church. Small, theologically narrow and culturally on the periphery of mainstream America, it was clearly no longer an appropriate base for a man who had staked out all of Middle America as his congregation. A turning point in his life came when Billy Graham invited him to the 1966 Berlin Congress on Evangelism, organized by evangelicals in this country and abroad. It was an emotional experience, one that brought to the surface a lot of the tent evangelist's previously unacknowledged aspirations to be part of what he called "the mainstream of Christianity." Roberts depends less on the approval of those around him than most people, and respectability is not his first priority. But the hospitality he felt at Berlin meant a lot to him. Recalling the event, his wife, Evelyn, observed, "All these years Oral has been a loner. He didn't necessarily want it this way, but he just didn't know how others felt about him. At Berlin he was absolutely overwhelmed by the love he felt. He said to me, 'They are no different than we are.'"

Berlin was also important because it established his relationship with Graham, whom he likes to refer to in public as "the No. 1 evangelist in the world." Friends say that Roberts stands in awe of Graham, and there's no doubt that over the years he has measured his success in relation to him. He frankly admits, for instance, that he was bitter when Graham held a successful crusade in Australia shortly after Roberts had had to cut one of his short because of hecklers and a vicious press. Graham has been gracious in helping Roberts, though—he appeared at the dedication of O.R.U. against the advice of some of his local supporters—and the two are good friends.

Two years after Berlin, Roberts decided to join the Methodist Church. It was a logical choice, for he had been a member as a child, and it has always valued religious expedience more than coherent theology. With 10.5 million members, second in size only to the Southern Baptist Convention among American Protestant denominations, it is clearly big enough and sufficiently diffuse to offer him both mainline credentials and elbow room. On April 7, 1968, he made the switch official by joining the Boston Avenue United Methodist Church in Tulsa.

In the short run, the cost was high. Members of the Pentecostal Holiness Church accused him of selling out to secular forces, and for a period his income fell off by 20 per cent. Staff members say, though, that most of the defectors have now returned to the fold.

After several years of planning, Roberts had opened his university in September, 1965. Roberts insists that the command to start a university was part of his original call from God, and he now looks back on it as simply the logical rounding out of his earlier activities—developing the mind as well as healing the spirit and the body. There were other elements in his abrupt change of style in the nineteen-sixties. Attendance at his tent meetings had leveled off. "People were no longer attracted by its novelty," he said. Television had cut into the entertainment value of an evening of singing and preaching. Moreover, his own constituency was becoming better educated and more sophisticated in its taste. Roberts said that in the early nineteen-sixties he began developing a "gut feeling" that the old ministry had run its course.

TO find out what is behind the recent blooming of Roberts, I visited Oral Roberts University twice in recent months and talked with him at length in his comfortable modern office overlooking the campus. Roberts is just over 6 feet tall, with a stocky build that he drapes in colored shirts and fashionable suits chosen with the advice of the wardrobe people at the National Broadcasting Company and worn with low, Western - style boots. His hair is full and only slightly graying, and his sideburns are long and carefully groomed. His face is a marvel of malleability. When he talks, his eyebrows move up and down, his jaw seems to move in circles and his mouth takes a half-moon shape that results in a kind of boyish grin.

In the old days on the saw-dust circuit, Roberts was striking because of his hands, firm, sensitive, gentle—fit vehicles for the transmission of divine healing grace. Now it is his eyes. Set slightly close together, they have the same intensity as Fulton Sheen's. Yet they exude warmth. When you're speaking with him, he gives the impression that as far as he's concerned, you're the only other person on earth. "When he gets one-on-one with you, he can tell exactly what you're struggling with," said an aide.

The visitor to the university Roberts built is immediately struck by the dazzling architecture. Clean, modern and efficient, the buildings are right out of "2001," an educational and spiritual Disneyland. In the center, symbolically and geographically, is the 200-foot Prayer Tower, a space needle with gold mirrors up the stem and spikes sticking out from the observation platform to symbolize Jesus's crown of thorns. Nearby are sunken gardens and fountains, a gym resembling a giant flying saucer that has just landed, a new fine arts center with a geodesic dome, still under construction, that suggests a metallic evangelistic tent. Most impressive of all is the six-story Learning Resources Center, a combination library, classroom building and multimedia center that houses the technology that a recent Carnegie Commission report said should be the objective of other liberal-arts colleges by the end of the century. With the aid of a computer, professors put basic factual material and introductory lectures on video tape, and then spend most of their time in small group discussions.

The atmosphere on the campus of O.R.U. is as clean and pure as the architecture. There are 1,800 full-time students, mostly from conservative Protestant homes,* three-quarters from out of state,

* There are also 25 Roman Catholics and one Jewish convert to Protestantism.

and all polite. They answer visitors' questions with "yessir" and "nosir," abide by curfews and follow a dress code that mandates a shirt and tie for men and a standard of modesty for women that, as one administrator put it, "boils down to the principle that the bottom must cover the bottom." The school is coed, and students pursue about the same sort of social life as elsewhere, except that they agree not to drink or smoke, and there is no dancing on campus. Administrators are quick to point out that men and women live in separate dorms. Bulletin boards are dotted with notices of what's going on in local churches, and, despite required weekday chapel services, the most popular event of the week is usually the Sunday evening worship service on campus.

Leaders of the school have no pretensions that the Sunday-school atmosphere is for everyone, and those who don't like the rules are courteously encouraged to go elsewhere. "Only a certain kind of student will be happy here," said Roberts, "and I don't want someone to come here who doesn't fit, because I don't want him to be unhappy." Roberts is well aware of the fate of other universities, like Princeton and Harvard, that began on a religious basis but became secularized, and he is consciously committed to preserving his Garden of Eden in an unfallen condition. Dissent on matters of fundamental philosophy tends to be interpreted as disloyalty. "If students aren't living a real Christian life, he considers it an attack by the enemy, by Satan," said Timothy Barrett, a 19-year-old student from Columbus, Ohio.

O.R.U. has a financial base that is national in scope and would be the envy of any president of a financially troubled private university. All of the endowment and capital budget and 60 per cent of the $4.6-million annual operating budget comes from the Oral Roberts Association. This represents an accumulation of gifts, the average being about $3.50, sent in by the 2.5 million "partners" who subscribe to Roberts's magazines or otherwise support his ministry. The rest comes from tui-

tion and fees, which amount to only $2,100 per student a year. Administrators of the college eventually hope to reverse the operating figures so that students will pay 60 per cent of costs and the association 40 per cent. They are also three years into a 10-year plan that aims at raising the endowment from $26-million to $100-million and increasing the value of the physical plant from $55-million to $100-million. By then, they figure, O.R.U. should be able to survive even without the financial drawing power of Roberts himself.

There is no doubt who runs things around O.R.U. Roberts interviews all prospective faculty members, and while the trustees have outvoted him on matters such as a proposal he backed to liberalize curfew hours slightly, the facts of life are understood by all—so long as he brings in the money, he will decide how it is spent.

He is clearly one of the shrewdest businessmen in Tulsa. One banker who has worked with Roberts on business affairs says he has "the lowest R.C.—resistance to change — factor of anyone I've ever met." He was a pioneer in developing new techniques for bulk correspondence and has an impressive record in assessing real-estate potential. He is now part of a group seeking a charter for a new bank, and the outlook would seem bright, since, as one potential competitor put it, "A lot of people would like to have their money in an Oral Roberts bank."

In the past, he was highly vulnerable regarding his personal finances. Once a week during the crusades, in keeping with the Pentecostal tradition, he would receive a "love offering" for his support. Now he has gone the standard route of Billy Graham and others in stabilizing his finances. He receives $24,000 in salary from the university, as well as the use of a car and the president's home. He says that he takes no personal gifts, and his book royalties go into a trust fund for his children. The banker quoted above, who is familiar with his personal affairs, put his total net worth "in the low six figures."

Roberts is well-organized, has little time for small talk and little patience with people who don't get to the point quickly, and there is a certain Horatio Alger air around his offices. Walls and desks carry slogans like "Expect a Miracle," and "Something GOOD is going to happen to you." He is careful to hire builders and optimists—"He won't let negative thinkers near him," said one aide. A staff member called him "answer-oriented," something that seems to rub off on his students. A professor at a seminary that is just beginning to get O.R.U. graduates said they tend to be intelligent but unsophisticated. "When they are given a question and some suggested sources, they tend to ask which source has the right answer," he said. "They don't see that some questions simply don't have one right answer."

The quarterly prime-time "contact specials" on television are indicative of Roberts's capacity to change with the times. His former programs, like Billy Graham's to this day, were simply films of his crusades, one medium being conveyed by another. In his new ones, even the weekly programs, he takes television seriously in its own right, and in this sense they constitute a major innovation in religious television. He fills the programs, which have been filmed on locations ranging from Tokyo and Hawaii to the new sports center at O.R.U., with elaborate sets and costumes, uses popular songs as well as religious ones and draws viewers with guest stars like Jerry Lewis, Pearl Bailey, Jimmy Durante and Johnny Cash. You can watch the first half-hour of most without realizing it's a religious program. Nevertheless, he has managed to preserve continuity with the past—and to use the mass media as a way of communicating the same earthy pastoral concern that marked the old prayer lines.

ROBERTS has a down - to - earth, slightly awkward style that produces easy-going credibility. He talks with a Southwest Oklahoma accent (there are

some words that he still can't pronounce correctly, like "popular," which comes out "polper"), and when he mentions God his eyes usually roll heavenward. Billy Graham talks to masses; Roberts can talk only to individuals. He seems to see little people up the television camera. "I force them to put that camera so close to me that I can almost breathe in it," he said. "If they don't, I lose that feeling [of personal contact], and when I've lost it, boy, I'm nothing, a washout. My inner man has to touch you, or I am not the man God called."

He has no hesitation about discussing his own doubts and weaknesses. Graham exudes authority and certainty—"The Bible *says*. . . ." He once told me, "I can honestly say that I haven't had a single doubt about what I preach in 10 years." Roberts, on the other hand, seems to feel that he can help people best by showing how he solved his own problems with prayer. And he almost begs you to let him help you out.

In the Christmas special, Roberts pointed to a Bible in his hands and told his viewers, "This Bible says, 'Pray ye one for another that ye may be healed.' And healing comes in many forms. Maybe you need to give your heart to God, to repent and be forgiven of sin. Maybe you need the Holy Spirit. Maybe you need a healing. Maybe you need financial help. Maybe your home put together, or, if you are young, you have a problem staring you in the face. You need a healing. Put your hands on yourself, and let's pray. Really pray. Father, in the name of Your Son, Jesus Christ of Nazareth, Whose I am and Whom I serve, I come to Him and to You. I come to Christ in the now, and I ask You for many miracles. And now, dear friend, through Jesus Christ, Who saved my life, Who healed me, Who raised me up and gave me back my life by a miracle, I pray for you. I ask God to touch you, to heal you. . . ."

The television programs are important to Roberts's other activities because they provide both visibility, something that helps attract students, and personal contacts. Each program has a giveaway —

for the Christmas special it was a picture book of O.R.U. that cost the organization about 35 cents — and can generate as many as half a million letters. People who write in get a free three-month subscription to Roberts's magazine, Abundant Life, and begin receiving letters that introduce them to the work of the Oral Roberts Association.

The association employs 300 people in a modern two-story building with charcoal-gray glass walls, tucked inconspicuously into a hillside in a remote area of the campus. Its principal task, in addition to producing the television shows and publishing, is answering the more than 10,000 letters that Roberts receives each day. This is done by a staff of 100 carefully trained women who take sentences and paragraphs written by Roberts and assemble them into personalized responses. They are printed with the aid of a computer and sent out, at a cost of 37 cents each, over Roberts's printed signature.

Ronald Smith, director of the association, said that they get plenty of amusing letters, like one from a man who wanted prayers for the end of daylight-saving time because "his garden was burning up already, and another hour of sunlight each day would finish it off for good." Most, though, are from people with deep need, those, for example, with drinking and marital problems or chronic illnesses, and Roberts seems to be getting through to many of them. One woman, for instance, wrote that following a divorce she simply "gave up" trying to bring up her children and ended up in a hospital with an ulcer. She said that her children started watching the evangelist on television and got her to take a look. "Your message awakened hope and a stirring of faith in me for the first time in a very long while," she said. "I started praying with you on the program, and the ulcer began to heal. Jesus became part of everything in my life. I asked Him to help me keep Him in my life and restore my faith completely so I could bring up my children properly. Your prayers have changed our lives."

ROBERTS maintains the deep sense of personal piety and religious experience that is at the root of the Pentecostal Holiness tradition. He prays wherever he may be. "Sometimes I'll pass by the bathroom in the morning and hear Oral talking to God while he's shaving," said his wife, a former schoolteacher whom he met at a camp meeting in the thirties and began courting by presenting her with a copy of his first book, "Salvation by the Blood." (The couple have four children: Rebecca, 28, the wife of a Tulsa builder; Ronald, 26, a graduate student in linguistics at the University of Southern California; Richard, 24, who is regularly featured on the father's television programs and is being groomed to carry on his ministry; and Roberta, 22, a student at Oral Roberts University.)

Though speaking in tongues is hardly ever mentioned in his television programs, it remains an important part of his life—and part of what his university is all about. "When you learn to pray in tongues, you pray with more understanding," he said. "It blossoms your intellect." Praying in tongues is like opening a faucet. "You're under the pressure of the Holy Spirit," he stated. "The Holy Spirit is in you all the time." Roberts said that this capacity to turn to prayer before making any decision lies behind his creativity and decisiveness. His only mistakes, he said, have come when he listened to his staff instead of to the Almighty.

While he still accepts the fundamentalist label, meaning that he accepts traditional doctrines like the Virgin Birth and the necessity of conversion for salvation, his theology is shaped by the fact that the definitive event of his religious life was not a conversion from sin but a healing. In practice, he is more interested in people than doctrines. To the extent that he has a thought-out theology, it is a theology of grace— God is present in the world and available to make men whole. This year, for the first time, he is teaching a theology course on the Holy Spirit, but usually his ideas come across through slogans—"Expect a miracle," "Release your faith," "God is a good God," and so forth.

Roberts's relationship to the Methodist Church has been cordial but a bit unusual. He has been invited to address numerous conferences, and this year Methodist-related Emory University in Atlanta has invited him to its annual "ministers' week." But the church establishment has by and large played it cool. While virtually no one, even liberals, is willing to criticize him publicly, no one has offered him any major assignment within the denomination. As one well-known Methodist put it, "There just isn't any slot in our structure for someone with his own constituency."

His ideas have been criticized on several grounds—for oversimplification, for emphasizing personal fulfillment at the expense of social responsibility, for reducing Christianity to a new form of positive thinking. "He doesn't play fair with the mystery of suffering," said one Tulsa pastor. "Jesus didn't heal everyone. There must have been 50 people at that pool, and He only healed one. Christian tradition says there are lessons to be learned from suffering." He also accused Roberts of preaching "a new form of heresy—Christianity as entertainment. . . . When he talks about God as being available for your personal fulfillment, you have the terrible feeling that he means you'll make it financially. Send money to us, and God will prosper you." One evangelical layman called it "a new kind of indulgence."

Roberts rejects such criticism, usually by pointing to the practical consequences of his ministry. When pressed, he will acknowledge that his slogans are less than precise. But so be it. "It's adapting yourself to the thinking of the people so they can grasp what you mean, which is what Jesus did all the time," he said. "If there's a better term, I try to come up with it, because I'm not married to words and terms. 'Expect a miracle' has made people think to begin with. It's a wonder. It's an unusual happening. It's something you can't explain. Our Lord could explain it, but you and I have a hard time."

HOW significant will Oral Roberts turn out to be? No one can be sure at this time because he is still very much a figure in transition. It's clear that he has a style that is well-suited to the nineteen-seventies — experiential, more geared to personal fulfillment than to social change, concerned with the recovery of a lot of apple-pie virtues after an era of turmoil and flux, seeking to integrate the physical, mental and spiritual dimensions of man.

It's probably accurate to say that, in the wake of his plunge into prime-time television, Roberts commands more personal loyalty than any other clergyman of the nineteen-seventies. Graham is obviously the dominant figure of the era, but he is a more impersonal force. He stands as a link with the Calvinism of the past and a symbol of civil religion. Thousands of people have responded to his appeal to conversion, yet few have any continuing relationship with him. When you go forward at a Graham rally to make your "decision for Christ," you are then led into another room where you speak not to Graham but to a trained volunteer "counselor." Roberts, on the other hand, is a personally significant figure to thousands of people in Middle America. In religious terms, his constituency is not that of Graham— middle- and upper-middle-class believers, mostly to the right of center politically—but the lower- and middle-class remnants of the agrarian tradition. They are the people who got left behind, untended and unsatisfied, when the Baptists and the Methodists became wealthy and respectable.

Albert Outler, a Methodist who is one of the country's best-known theologians, called Roberts "an important phenomenon," because he has been able to bring a degree of intellectual depth to the revivalist tradition. "Most revivalism has been anti-intellectual," he said. "Roberts grew up in this environment, but has a respect for learning and is doing a better than average job in developing a university where religion is taken seriously but so is scholarship. Not since Charles G. Finney have we had anyone who had an effective revivalist spirit and a theology to match it."

Outler suggested that the popularity of Roberts, along with the growth of the Catholic Pentecostal Movement, may very well turn out to be a harbinger of a new Great Awakening. The last such outburst of religious fervor took place in the early 19th century and, with its emphasis on conversion, discipline and personal spirituality, put a lasting mark on American Protestantism. Numerous church historians, as well as Outler, believe that the conditions are ripe for another such development. ■ April 22, 1973

'God made me to win'

One of Oral Roberts's most successful ideas was to build up a nationally ranked basketball team to publicize his Oral Roberts University—something that he decided to do "when I realized that 40 million men turn first to the sports page every morning." (He rejected football because "God made me to win, and I know what it would take to win in football.") Last year, in their first year of major college competition, the blue-and-white uniformed Titans of O.R.U. had a 26-2 record, were ranked 17th in the country and made it to the second round of the National Invitational Tournament in Madison Square Garden. This year they slipped to 21-5, and fell from the grace of the top 20; they again received an N.I.T. bid, but lost to powerful North Carolina in the opening round.

Most of the basketball players are black, which gives the campus a strange look because blacks make up only 5 per cent of the student body and it seems as if every one you see is about 6-foot-6. Athletes are expected to follow the same campus code as everyone else, and even have a few rules of their own, including a ban on fighting during games. "Our Lord must be lifted up," said Roberts. "If our boys fight on the floor or anything like this, I'll stop it. I'll go right down and stop it. It will have destroyed everything I stood for."

Since most of the blacks are Southern, they usually find the religious atmosphere on the campus easy to adjust to, and most say that race relations are good. O.R.U. makes it a policy to continue their scholarships until they graduate, even if their eligibility is used up. "People here see you as a person, not just a basketball player," said Richard Fuqua, who was the No. 2 scorer in the country last year.

Roberts takes a keen personal interest in the team. He often stops by practices and travels with the players when he can, and even helps out with recruiting. David Vaughan, a 7-foot mainstay of this year's team, was all set to go to Memphis State but changed his mind when Roberts delivered on a promise to preach in the church where Vaughan's father is pastor.

It is tempting to think that Roberts also uses his powers in other ways. Going into their first-round game in the N.I.T. against Memphis State last year, the Titans were 10-point underdogs. Just before leaving the dressing room at halftime they huddled together for prayer. Roberts leaned forward with his arms outstretched across several pairs of sweaty buttocks and said softly, "Lord, we expect a miracle." They won 94 to 74.—E.B.F.

Richie Fuqua and Roberts at the '72 N.I.T.

COMPUTERS HELP BAPTISTS' GROWTH

Convention Gaining Faster in North Than in South

By J. C. BARDEN

The Southern Baptists, who are now growing at a faster rate in the North than they are in the South, are using computers to determine the most likely places for starting new churches outside their Bible Belt stronghold.

"We're coupling scientific techniques with spiritual ones," said Dr. M. Wendell Belew, the director of the Mission Division of the Southern Baptist Convention's Home Mission Board.

"By using computers we can determine what areas need churches," he said from his office in Atlanta. "Then we send in people to see if the Holy Spirit is at work. If it looks good, we send in more resources."

Many Are 'Unchurched'

The method helped to account for a growth rate last year of more than 10 per cent in Southern Baptist Churches in the North, according to church statistics. The growth rate of those in the South was 2.0 per cent. The Southern Baptists began using computers in mid-1972, when most of the information from the 1970 census became available.

The denomination took root outside the South in the early nineteen-fifties as its members began to move North. It was several years, however, before the church made a conscious effort to expand outside the South.

The church did so, Dr. Belew said, when its leaders determined that there were "a fantastic number of unchurched" people outside the South, and that there was "no need for the church to be geographically circumscribed."

Numerically, the church's membership outside its traditional area accounts for only a small portion of the total (with 12 million members, the Southern Baptist Convention is the country's largest Protestant denomination), which is partly the reason for the high growth rate there compared to that in the South. The $11-million that the church spent last year in its home mission efforts also helped.

The conversion efforts are aimed at people who are "unchurched," according to Dr. Belew, who said that the church's new members outside the South came largely from this group. A small portion switch from established churches, he said.

Computer Problems

So far, Dr. Berew estimates, computers have aided in the establishment of 50 churches. As even more census information becomes available and church workers become more adept at using it, Dr. Belew believes, computers will play a part in the establishment of nearly every new Southern Baptist Church.

If an area is highly transient, which the computers could determine from census information on housing, that fact would indicate that a church there would not be self-supporting.

Or, if the computers showed that other evangelical churches were active in an area, or that it was heavily Roman Catholic or Jewish, the Southern Baptists would probably not move in.

The computers have already presented problems, however. "We've bombed out in some area that looked good statistically," said Don F. Mabry, who heads the home mission board's survey department.

And Dr. Belew said that Southern Baptist Churches were prospering in some areas where the best advice from computers would indicate that the church should stay out.

August 19, 1973

Colson's Religious Experience: Its Significance for Evangelicals

By BOB G. SLOSSER
Special to The New York Times

WASHINGTON, June 23— When Charles W. Colson left the Federal Courthouse here Friday after being sentenced to prison for his part in the Watergate scandals, he looked, with his furrowed brow and slightly disheveled hair, like a little boy about to cry. He also looked, with his horn-rimmed glasses and sober expression, a little like an owl.

News Analysis

When he said, "I've committed my life to Jesus Christ," many of those who heard him were not sure whether they were listening to a guileless, childlike believer or a wise old bird who might be putting them on. Was it reality or a high-class con job?

Their confusion was deepened two sentences later when he said, "What happened today was the Lord's will and the Court's will, and, of course, I accept that fully." Still alive in their memories was Mr. Colson's reputation as the White House tough guy who would "walk over my own grandmother" to re-elect President Nixon.

Unreal-Sounding Words

To the large segment of society that has just about snapped free of the religious roots that once went deep in American life, the words Friday sounded unreal. To the 40 million evangelical, or Bible-oriented, Christians in the country, however—even those still uncertain as to the validity of Mr. Colson's experience — the words were a playback of one of their most familiar Scriptures:

"If any man be in Christ, he is a new creature: old things are passed away; behold, all things are become new." (II Corinthians, v, 17.)

Mr. Colson, closely supported by a small but active prayer group in Washington that includes Senator Harold E. Hughes, Democrat of Iowa, and Republican Albert H. Quie, Republican of Minnesota, has for several months proclaimed this as his experience.

Statement by Hughes

Only yesterday in an address to Presbyterian evangelists in Louisville, Ky., Senator Hughes was quoted by United Press International as saying, "I want to say to any of you that if there is a question in your mind that Mr. Colson does not believe in the word of God and Jesus Christ and that he is not willing to lay down his life for it, he is dead wrong."

Meanwhile, however, an increasingly skeptical world, including many among those identifying themselves as Christians, has found it difficult to believe in such change.

The issue, of course, is thousands of years old, and men have argued, and warred, over it.

The evangelical Christian believes that man is separated from God by sin and is spiritually dead. According to this belief, man can be reconciled with God only through acceptance of and trust in the death upon the cross of Jesus Christ, recognized as the Son of God sent for this purpose. Forgiveness of sins and reconcilation, to the evangelical, is a free gift of God that cannot be earned.

Forgiveness of Sins

Numerous passages of the Bible are cited as support for this belief. Among the best known is John iii, 16-17: "For God so loved the world, that He gave His only begotten Son, that whosoever believeth in Him should not perish, but have everlasting life. For God sent not his Son into the world to condemn the world; but that the world through Him might be saved."

Further, and driving directly to the Colson case, the evangelical Christian believes that when a person accepts Jesus Christ as his Saviour—that is, asks for and receives forgiveness of his sins—that person embarks on a new life as his spirit is touched and made alive by the Holy Spirit, the third person of the Trinity or godhead along with the Father and the Son.

This is the essence of the evangelical belief, based in

large part on the account in chapter 3 of the gospel according to John of Jesus' dialogue with Nicodemus, a ruler of the Jews. In that account, Jesus said, "I say unto thee, except a man be born again, he cannot see the kingdom of God."

This rebirth, the evangelical believes, results in the life of Christ being lived in every believer through the presence of the Holy Spirit in the believer.

This conviction was the motivation for a comment by one of Mr. Colson's closest Christian friends, Mr. Quie, after the sentencing Friday. "He has Christ in him" and he will be all right, Mr. Quie said to reporters.

As for the future, Christian and secular communities alike are waiting to see if the reported change in Mr. Colson's life is revealed in his conduct and work.

Many of the nation's evangelical Christians are still smarting from what they felt was a betrayal through Water-

gate by some in the Nixon Administration, including the President himself. The President and some of his colleagues were given to the use of "God words" in speeches and remarks; many were also frequent churchgoers; the President himself befriended such leaders as the Rev. Billy Graham, the evangelist. This had caused many Christians, many in Middle America, to rally to Mr. Nixon and his Administration, as sort of the church's representative.

The release of the White House transcripts of Presidential conversations caused many of them to rethink this loyalty and large numbers backed away, at least to a position of neutrality, from what they perceived to be a lack of fruit in a professed believer's life ("He that abideth in me, and I in him, the same bringeth forth much fruit"—John, xv, 5). Therefore, they are anxious about what will unfold in the Colson story.

They know that the Bible, which most of them take to be the inspired word of God, calls for total truthfulness and honesty on the part of the followers of Jesus. They place great stock in the 51st Psalm, in which David repents of his adultery with Bathsheba and says in the sixth verse, "Behold, thou desirest truth in the inward parts."

What will this mean to the Watergate case? This is the central question to the average American who may be giving little thought to the condition of individual souls. Will he who seemed to figure so prominently at so many critical junctures in the twisting Watergate road tell all?

In fact, Mr. Colson summarized the gleeful thoughts of many Presidential critics when he said Friday, "I'm sure there are guys in the White House sweating."

'Speak Every Man Truth'

The evangelical position in this situation seems to be exemplified in these two passages from the Bible:

"Lying lips are abomination to the Lord: But they that deal truly are his delight"—Proverbs, xii, 22.

"Wherefore putting away lying, speak every man truth with his neighbor"—Ephesians iv, 25.

To the evangelical, then, it would appear that Mr. Colson must respond truthfully to every question asked of him. He himself said it this way Friday:

"I do not intend to be an advocate. I'm not going to try to frame a case. I'm sure there are guys in the White House sweating, but I'm not going to testify that way. I've made a commitment to Christ and I really believe the only commandment I have to follow is to tell truth. I will tell the truth."

June 24, 1974

Southern Baptists Show Signs of Unrest

By KENNETH A. BRIGGS
Special to The New York Times

NORFOLK, Va., June 18—The mythical wall of theological uniformity once thought to bind Southern Baptists together is showing further signs of crumbling under the pressures of increasing diversity of thought.

As the 12.7-million-member church ended its annual convention here today, there were various indications of the differences besetting the church. Ironically, the principal cause of unrest was the challenge by a right-wing fundamentalist group to what it regards as an alarming trend toward modernism.

The group, organized in 1973 as the Faith and Message Fellowship, has expressed profound displeasure with the direction being taken in Sunday School materials and in the church's preaching. In taking a hard fundamentalist stand, it represents the old orthodoxy attacking a more recent climate of toleration for a greater variety of views.

Deep Concern

Although the actual strength of the fellowship is not known,

it has caused deep concern among those who regard it as a threat to a more favorable attitude of openness. For years the theological spectrum had been widening, but until the emergence of a visible counterforce, relatively little attention had been given to the phenomenon.

Much of the debate centered on biblical interpretation. Southern Baptists were once overwhelmingly wedded to the doctrine of biblical inerrancy, but the development of historical and literary methods of biblical criticism, long used by more liberal Christians, have been making inroads among Southern Baptists. In the last 20 years, for example, such study at Southern Baptist seminaries has given the church a slightly different perspective.

The growing trend has been to understand the Bible as revealing the truth required for salvation but to de-emphasize scriptural literalism. More than ever before, consideration has been given recently to the core meaning rather than to the accuracy of biblical details.

A similar debate between this perspective and the fundamentalist line has driven another denomination, the Missouri

Synod of the Lutheran Church, to the verge of a formal split. Such an outcome among Southern Baptists is unlikely because, unlike the Missouri Synod, no single authority can attempt to impose his will on the church.

Amid the convention's delight over a continuing pattern of church growth and pride in the Presidential candidacy of a fellow church member, former Gov. Jimmy Carter of Georgia, there were signs of theological concern. Among them are the following:

¶The election of James L. Sullivan, the retired head of the Baptist Sunday School Board, as convention president for next year. Mr. Sullivan is believed to be able to hold the church together and to blunt the impact of the faith and Message Fellowship. He once called the fellowship "a fragmenting" and "extremist" movement, adding that "in time, extremism always destroys itself."

¶A boycott of the annual preconvention pastor's conference by many ministers who were convinced that Adrian Rogers president of the pastor's group and a member of the fellowship's board of directors,

had stacked the program with ultraconservative speakers.

¶Continuing bitterness over the discovery, three weeks before the convention, that the church's school press, headed by William A. Powell, who is president of the fellowship, had been distributing fundamentalist materials not written by Southern Baptists.

¶An indirect attack on the fellowship by Arthur Rutledge, former head of the church's prestigious Home Mission Board. "One of the things that disturbs me is the group we have that has set itself up as a watchdog of orthodoxy," Mr. Rutledge said. "There may be differences in how we got the Bible, the theories of inspiration," he said. But he concluded that there was no justification for the fellowship's defensive posture.

In rebuking the fellowship, most leaders are careful to argue that Southern Baptists are not becoming more liberal. "If people are really modernists in the sense that they no longer believe the Bible, they no longer believe Christ is divine and heaven is real, they will leave the Baptist ranks in a hurry," Mr. Sullivan said. "You don't have to deal with them, they will depart from us because they can't feel at home with the conservative stance that we have." June 19, 1976

Georgia Church Believes In a 'Salvation by Faith'

By KENNETH A. BRIGGS
Special to The New York Times

PLAINS, Ga. — Clarence Dodson called on "Brother Jimmy" to open the Sunday school lesson with a prayer. Jimmy Carter, the Democratic Presidential candidate, rose to his feet, closed his eyes and asked the Lord to help "remove the obstacles that keep us from being close to Thee," for "the strength to overcome weakness" and for the gift of compassion.

When Mr. Carter finished, he took his seat and listened attentively to Mr. Dodson, a veteran of 35 years of church school teaching, instruct the 15-member men's Bible class in the basement of the Plains Baptist Church on "being set free in Christ."

The roots of Mr. Carter's faith lead to this particular country church. Among Southern Baptists, there is no such thing as "the" church. One's church is the local church. It decides its own affairs, worships as it pleases and develops it own style.

St. Paul's Distinction

Continuing, the lean, soft-spoken Mr. Dodson talked of St. Paul's distinction between those who merely go through the motions of religion and those who feel impelled by faith to "walk with Him everyday."

"A man can come down the church aisle, take the pastor's hand, become baptized and a member of the church," Mr. Dodson said. "Then he might sit back and think he's got a ticket to heaven. But it doesn't work that way."

"Being born again into the Kingdom of God is just the beginning of our Christian walk," he continued, an open Bible in his outstretched hand. "Day by day we must seek the will of God."

To Mr. Dodson and many others in this Southern Baptist congregation of 350 members, the language of salvation is the common parlance and those who understand it have been somewhat surprised to find that many outsiders are puzzled by it.

Asked About 'Born Again'

Plains Baptists have first-hand knowledge of all the fuss as reporters and visitors ask them to define the term "born again."

"It's hard to explain," says Hugh Carter, the candidate's cousin who is a clerk of the church. "The church has just always been the biggest part of my life. When a person realizes that Jesus Christ died for our sins and is willing to say it publicly, this is the rebirth."

There is great pride in the Baptist "salvation by faith" tradition here and the church that stands for it. Among other things, the presence of so many outsiders, many of whom state no religious faith, has given these Baptists an unprecedented chance to "witness," another of the familiar phrases that means to evangelize.

The Rev. Bruce Edwards, who took over the pulpit almost two years ago, says the situation is "something every preacher wants." When he first arrived, he says, "the people needed sermons that would help them grow and give them a better foundation for the faith they already had."

The church of Jimmy Carter's upbringing has evolved somewhat over the years. For one thing, the emphasis on predestination and stern repentance has largely given way to a more positive stress on salvation as a joyful answer that can be freely chosen. For another, strict Biblical fundamentalism has undergone a moderating influence to the point where few would insist that scripture cannot err.

Some Changes Among Baptists

Most rural Southern Baptists are slowly experiencing some changes. The pace is faster among those in the cities and the suburbs and some churches are more conservative than others over such matters as whether the Bible can be taken literally.

Even the term "born again" has broadened. Some still refer to its traditional definition as a moment of high emotions when an overwhelming spiritual reality engulfs one's whole being and rescues the soul from perdition. However, others — a majority in the opinion of Mr. Edwards — experience such a commitment over a long period as the cumulative impact of many smaller moments.

"For me it kind of grew," said Ernest Turner, owner of the local hardware store who posted a printed passage from Psalm 119 in his store window. "I really can't say the moment when Holy Spirit came into my life. But there's a joy that happens when you know you're saved. There's a peace."

Since Jimmy Carter was nominated at the Democratic Convention in July, the church has grown accustomed to overflow congregations—swelled by the Secret Service and members of the press, among others—and its members have had to contend with such annoyances as the pilfering of song books by souvenir hunters. For the first time

in its history, however, the church is reluctantly locking its doors to cut down on losses.

Blacks Worshipped There

The church's annals show that blacks and whites did worship together briefly at Plains Baptist in the last century, as Mr. Carter says in his autobiography, "Why Not the Best?" and it was a breakthrough. But a notation from 1866 indicates that whites considered the arrangement temporary, urging blacks to learn how to lead a church. By 1870, blacks had their own church.

But despite Mr. Carter's successful effort several years ago to persuade the church to overturn its decision to bar blacks, the victory has had little practical effect. The church remains all-white, and there is virtually no contact by the church with the black community.

The beneficiaries of the church's social conscience are often more distant. Of this year's budget of $37,000, 15 percent is designated for national and foreign missions.

For most members, the church is an intertwining of social, civic and religious purposes. Like most churches in small communities, it has an active nucleus in an inactive periphery. It is a catalyst for friendship and a gossip mill as well as a school for serious thought and study.

Church's 'Articles of Faith'

According to the church's "Articles of Faith," Plains Baptist tenets include belief in the Trinity, original sin, justification by faith, resurrection and Christ's final judgment of the world. It also holds that there is eternal punishment for wrongdoers and eternal joy for the righteous.

In the men's Bible class the other Sunday morning, Mr. Dodson, toward the close of his 45-minute explication of a portion of St. Paul's Letter to the Galatians, told a story to illustrate the value of humility.

The story concerned a man who "rose in life" to be prime minister. The man's rivals were jealous and sought to "find fault with him so they could trip him up." They could find nothing defective in his character but finally discovered that the man went into a closet for "20 minutes a week."

They complained to the king, who investigated. The prime minister explained that he went into the closet in order to put on the shepherd's clothing he had once worn.

"For he was afraid he might forget," Mr. Dodson continued, looking toward the spare walls and rows of folding chairs where Mr. Carter sat. "He said he went back to remind himself what he had been and might not be if not for the change that had come into his life."

September 28, 1976

CHAPTER 2

Religion and the Secular Realm

Religion *and* politics in the classroom. A photograph of Malcolm X under a statue of the Blessed Virgin in a New York City parochial school.

Dukes/NYT Pictures

THE BIBLE RULED OUT.

IT CANNOT BE READ IN WISCONSIN'S PUBLIC SCHOOLS.

MADISON, Wis., March 18.—One of the most important cases decided by a court in many years was that of Weiss against the District School Board of Education. Some of the public school teachers were in the habit of daily reading the Bible to their pupils, and to this some Catholic parents objected, particularly because the Bible used was the St. James edition, portions of which are repugnant to the Romish Church. The case was tried in the Circuit Court for Rock County, which overruled the demurrer of the Catholics to the answer of the School Board. The action of the Circuit Court is now in turn overruled by the Supreme Court, this giving the victory to the Catholics and declaring the reading of the Bible in public schools unconstitutional. The court says:

"In considering the question whether such reading of the Bible in public schools is sectarian instruction, 'prohibited in public schools by the Constitution,' the books will be regarded as a whole, because the whole Bible without exception has been designated as a text book for use in the Edgerton schools, and the claim of the School Board is that the whole contents thereof may lawfully be so read. This being so, it is quite immaterial if the portions thereof set out in the return as the only portions thus far read are not sectarian. Yet it should be observed that some of the portions so read seem to inculcate doctrines of the divinity of Jesus Christ and of the punishment of the wicked after death, which doctrines are not accepted by some religious sects."

The court refuses to affirm or deny that the Catholic Church is opposed to common schools. The court further says that the reading from the Bible in the schools, although without comment on the part of the teacher, is "instruction," seems too clear for argument. The court holds that the Bible contains many doctrinal passages, and that the general tendency of it is sectarian instruction. It also holds that such textbooks as are founded on the fundamental teachings of the Bible, or which may contain extracts therefrom, may be used in school. It says:

"Some of the most valuable instruction a person can receive may be derived from reading alone, without any extrinsic aid by way of comment or exposition. The question therefore seems to narrow down to this: Is the reading of the Bible in schools—not merely selected passages therefrom, but the whole of it—sectarian instruction of pupils? In view of the fact already mentioned that the Bible contains numerous doctrinal passages upon some of which almost every religious sect is divided, and that such passages may reasonably be understood to inculcate the doctrines predicated upon them, an affirmative answer to the question seems unavoidable. Any pupil of ordinary intelligence who listens to the reading of the doctrinal portions of the Bible will be more or less instructed thereby in the doctrine of the divinity of Jesus Christ, the eternal punishment of the wicked, the authority of the priesthood, the binding force and efficacy of the sacraments, and many other conflicting sectarian doctrines."

The court further says that the place where the Bible is read is a place of worship, and that as taxpayers are compelled to erect and support schoolhouses, and the children are, under the late law, compelled to attend public or private schools, the constitutional clauses forbid us to use schoolhouses as places of worship.

March 19, 1890

SABBATH A DAY OF REST

JUSTICE PRYOR SO HOLDS, BUT OF THE CHRISTIAN HOLY DAY.

He Denies Incorporation to a Hebrew Society Because It Proposed to Have Its Annual Meetings on Sunday—Hebrews Are Indignant and May Appeal.

Justice Pryor, in the Supreme Court, yesterday, denied the application of the "Agudath Hakehiloth of New York," for a certificate of incorporation, and in refusing the certificate delivered an opinion which treats of the American Sabbath.

According to the petition of the association, the objects for which the corporation was to be formed are, "to promote the strict observance of and adherence to such customs, laws, usages, and rites of the Orthodox Hebrew religion, or faith, as are not repugnant to, and inconsistent with, the Constitution and laws of the United States and the laws of the State of New York; to improve the condition of the Orthodox Hebrew congregations, and to abolish the now existing religious evils."

The clause in the petition to which Judge Pryor excepts is this one:

"The time of holding its annual meeting is to be on each and every second Sunday of January of each and every year."

In refusing the certificate Justice Pryor says:

"In the certificate submitted to me I observe that the annual meeting of the proposed corporation is appointed to be held 'on each and every second Sunday of January of each and every year.' It is not a religious corporation, and its annual meetings are for the performance of precisely such secular business as is transacted by other civil corporations.

"The question is not whether such meetings on Sunday is illegal, but whether they should be approved by a Justice of the Supreme Court. A thing may be lawful and yet not laudable.

Sabbath Protected by Common Law.

"'In the State of New York the Sabbath exists as a day of rest by the common law, and without the necessity of legislative action to establish it, and may be protected from desecration by such laws as the Legislature, in its wisdom, may deem necessary to secure to the community the privilege of undisturbed worship and to the day itself that outward respect and observance which may be deemed essential to the peace and good order of society, and to preserve religion and its ordinances from open reviling and contempt.' (Lindenmuller vs. The People, 33 Barb., 548.) 'The Christian Sabbath is one of the civil institutions of the State, and the Legislature, for the purpose of promoting the moral and physical well being of the people and the peace, quiet, and good order of society, has authority to regulate its observance and prevent its desecration.' (People vs. Moses, 140 N. Y., 215.) This sanctity of the Christian Sabbath is sanctioned and secured by repeated acts of legislation extending from the colonial period to the present year, and as well by the impressive deliverances of the Court of Appeals. As Justice of the Supreme Court, I may not approve that which the immemorial and uniform policy of the State condemns.

Aggression Upon Christian Sabbath.

"Although not explicitly stated, it is nevertheless an inference, from the face of the certificate before me, that the members of the proposed corporation are of a race and religion by which not the first but the seventh day of the week is set apart for religious observance. The fact might be of decisive importance were a desecration of their holy day contemplated; but the act intended is an aggression upon the Christian Sabbath. The law, which scrupulously protects them in the observance of their ceremonial, gives them no license, and I am sure they have no desire to affront the religious susceptibilities of others. True, to a prosecution for work or labor on the first day of the week, the defendant may plead that 'he uniformly keeps another day of the week as holy time and does not labor on that day, and that the labor complained of was done in such manner as not to interrupt or disturb other persons in observing the first day of the week as holy time,' (Penal Code, Section 264;) but otherwise the legislation of the State against profanation of the Christian Sabbath is operative and imperative upon all classes of the community.

"Because the holding of corporate meetings on Sunday is contrary to the public policy of the State, if not to the letter of its law, I decline to approve this certificate.

"Application refused."

The names of the Directors of the proposed association are Moses Singer, 426 Grand Street; Samuel Fried, 328 East Fourth Street; Leopold Weizenhoffer, 334 East Houston Street, and Aaron Weisberger, 319 East Fourth Street.

A BURST OF INDIGNATION.

Jewish Rabbis and Laymen Do Not Mince Words in Protest.

Reporters for THE NEW YORK TIMES saw a number of prominent Jewish rabbis and lawyers yesterday and asked their opinions on the decision of Justice Pryor. All were emphatic in their views that the Justice had strained the interpretation of the State law. Their views follow:

The Rev. Dr. Gustave Gottheil of Temple Emanu-El, 521 Fifth Avenue, said:

"A decision of a Supreme Court Justice ought always to be treated with becoming respect, otherwise I would not consider the decision worthy of serious criticism. It is certainly an extraordinary attempt to protect the rights of the church by the direct encroachment on the rights of another, and, worse than this, it is a return to the mediaeval principle, which we have happily outgrown, to make the courts of justice the guardians of religious institutions. It is admitted that the association which seek the right of incorporation is a purely religious one, and how one annual meeting of such a society can in any way interfere with the due observance by other people of that day as a day of rest is very difficult to see.

Dr. Gottheil Sarcastic.

"The Judge may be assured that there is no danger of its members getting drunk or disorderly at their meetings. Neither will their singing of hymns or less objectionable songs be so loud and boisterous as to disturb their Christian neighbors. It could hardly be believed, if we had been told so, that religion could be construed by a Judge of an American court as seemingly to extend its application to the Christian Church alone. I hope that in the interest of peace and good will among the various denominations the decision will not stand."

A Hebrew Lawyer's Points.

Ex-Judge M. S. Isaacs had the following statement to make:

"Mr. Justice Pryor is usually so punctilious and accurate that it is to be regretted that in this opinion he has gone just a little too far. While he may be technically correct in refusing his approval to the certificate in question, (for fixing the day of its annual meeting is not a legitimate part of a certificate of incorporation,) he is in error in holding that a corporation cannot meet on Sunday. Many charitable corporations in this State habitually meet on Sunday, and their principal business is necessarily transacted on the only day of the week which permits their officers to come together for consultation.

"The Judge's contention might apply with equal force to the publication by well-known corporations of the Sunday edition of newspapers. Besides, there is grave doubt whether the authorities quoted wholly support the contention as to the sanctity of the Christian Sabbath. The Sunday laws are substantially police regulations to secure rest and quiet for citizens who 'observe Sunday as holy time.' The exception as to works of necessity and charity would probably cover such meetings of a benevolent corporation, as, under the decision of our courts, they excuse what formerly were considered infractions of the Sunday law."

Dr. Kohler Warmly Dissents.

The Rev. Dr. K. Kohler of Congregation Beth-El, Fifth Avenue and Seventy-sixth Street, said:

"All our charitable and religious institutions, without exception, have meetings on Sunday, and we would advise Judge Pryor to close them all. The decision will not stand. It seems to me that it is the best thing people can do on Sunday, when they hold meetings of that sort. In itself the question of enforcing the Sunday law upon those who keep Saturday as their Sabbath, like the Jews and Seventh Day Adventists and Baptists, is not legal. It might be legal in Russia, but not here. Even some church institutions hold their meetings on Sunday, for that is the day a man is free from other business cares and toil, and can devote time, mind, and heart to things of a higher religious or philanthropic purpose. The decision is unreasonable, and I have little doubt but what it will be overruled. I sincerely hope that the association will not yield, but will appeal for the sake of the principle of non-interference in matters of conscience and personal liberty, upon which this decision encroaches. I also hope that it will meet with the support of all the Jews."

The Judge's Argument a Quibble.

The Rev. Stephen S. Wise of the Madison Avenue Congregation, said:

"It seems to me the argument of Justice Pryor is merely a quibble. He allows that the Jews observe the Biblical seventh day as their Sabbath. That being true, there is no alternative left them but the transaction of such nominal business as presents itself in the course of congregational life, upon that day of the week, which is legally, not religiously, a day of cessation of labor. Were Judge Pryor's decision, if decision that may be called, which, in his own words, is simply the personal expression of an unauthoritative opinion, to be retroactive in effect, it would simply efface by one fell stroke practically all Jewish congregations now existing. If I may be permitted to dissent from the opinion of the distinguished jurist, I would say that the institution for whose existence a certificate of incorporation was solicited, is distinctly a religious corporation.

"Technically, the business which it might transact at its annual meeting might be designated as business, but it is certainly correct to interpose that any business transacted by a body of men gathered according to corporate title for the purpose of religious worship partakes so largely of a religious character that the appellation, if not unjust, is none the less misleading. The transactions carried on by a religious corporation can at best but be incidental to the other more important matters for which it is primarily called into existence.

"I believe that Judge Pryor's decision will not stand the test or scrutiny of a higher tribunal, but that the right of a Jewish religious corporation to meet on the first day Sabbath will be fully vindicated by a decision which will view the question at issue in its higher and broader bearing."

Rabbi Mendes Is Emphatic.

The Rev. H. Pereira Mendes, rabbi of Shearith Israel, in West Nineteenth Street, when shown the opinion of Justice Pryor, said:

"Justice Pryor considers a meeting of a Jewish society, if held on a Sunday, improper. I fail to see the difference, however, between a Jewish society holding its annual meetings on Sunday, and providing for them in its constitution openly and publicly, and in another Jewish society which holds its meetings on a Sunday, although such meetings are not provided for in its constitution.

"A large number of our greatest Jewish societies hold their meetings on Sundays. Of course, they do not disturb the public peace. I am summoned to the annual meeting of a Jewish society that will be held to-morrow. Its annual meetings have been held on Sunday for many years, as I can remember. Nobody has ever interfered. No authority has ever said it was wrong. The President of it is a man who would be the last to permit the meeting to be held on that day, if it were in any way illegal or improper.

"It seems to me that if a meeting is held without disturbing the public peace and 'in such manner as not to interrupt or disturb other persons in observing the first day of the week as holy time,' no one need complain. To my mind, there is less wrong in holding a meeting on Sunday, if decorously conducted, to promote such worthy objects as are set forth in the constitution of the society in question, than to allow quasi-sacred concerts amid associations not at all conducive to Sabbath sanctity, and to making the Sabbath day 'a holy time.' A few weeks ago there was a six days' bicycle race. I am not aware that the hour or two preceding the start, which hours fell on Sunday, were much of 'a holy time.'

The True Christian Sabbath.

"But I take higher ground than Justice Pryor. If, as he says, the State legislates against the profanation of the Christian Sabbath, it becomes the duty of the State to find out which is the Christian Sabbath. The Christian Sabbath is the Sabbath that was observed by Jesus, the Founder of Christianity. He observed the seventh-day Sabbath, and the seventh-day Sabbath was observed by his followers until about the year 324, when, under the auspices of Constantine—who had turned Christian, but who was a murderer, a hypocrite, and one of the greatest villains that ever breathed—the first day of the week was exalted into the Sabbath Day.

"There is not a single Christian minister who can defend that change, in view of the fact that Jesus said 'not one jot or tittle of the law' was to be changed. There is not a single Christian minister but knows, if he believes in Father, Son, and Holy Ghost, that by keeping Sunday as the Sabbath he acts contrary to the spirit of the law that Jesus preached to establish, and he dishonors the Father to honor the Son; for the real reason that Sunday is observed as a sacred day is well known to be the fact that the earliest Christians met on that day in honor of their Lord, who they believed was resurrected on that day. These early Christians emphatically did not observe Sunday as the Sabbath. It was their 'Lord's Day.' They all observed the seventh day as their Sabbath.

Back to First Principles.

"It has often seemed strange to me that the Protestants, whose object has always been to get back to first principles and to reject all human accretions on their faith, should not go back to first principles as the founder of the faith established them. Among these first principles is the consecration of the seventh day as the Sabbath. Would that at some synod of Presbyterians, Episcopalians, Methodists, or Baptists—or at some Lambeth Council—some Christian prelate could have the courage to make a stand for a true Sabbath day!

"The face of their Christ is always depicted as mild and ideal, but I fancy that face would be lighted up by a flash of anger and indignation, its lips would curl in contempt, its eyes would tell of condemnation, if He should come to earth now and see how His followers outrage and insult His honor by setting aside the commands of the God whom He worshipped, and whom He wished every one to call 'Father.' I can imagine Him furiously denouncing such splitting of hairs and such forcing of camels through the eyes of needles as have been done by Christian Pharisees. I can imagine Him urging His priests to honor the God whom He honored by honoring His commands, and among them the one that says: 'Remember the Sabbath day to keep it holy; the seventh day is the Sabbath of the Lord'; and on these conferences and synods refusing, I can imagine Him wringing His hands in despair and crying out, 'Father, forgive them, for they know not what they do.'

"If this country is a Christian country, and Justice Pryor is a Christian, the law that Christ preached and practiced should be observed, and should overrule State law. The logical solution is that Hebrews should be allowed to meet on Sunday, and that the Christian Sabbath should be tranferred to the seventh day.

"If Christ came to New York, then, to be consistnet with His own teachings, He would have to attend a Jewish synagogue for Sabbath worship. It is absurd to think that He would give Himself the lie.

Praise for Christianity.

"I am one of those Hebrews who recognize the magnificent and beautiful work accomplished in the world by Christianity. It elevated all the pagan races of Europe from Olympus to Calvary. It has strewn the world with flowers of wondrous beauty. Let it now lift the world still higher, from Calvary to Sinai, and do what that race is doing, even the race in which their Christ was born 'to blossom and bud, and fill the face of the world with fruit.'

" Now what Christian minister has the courage to make the first move. He would be a Christ-ian, a follower of his Christ's example, and not a Christian, certainly not a Constantinian Christian.

Simon Sterne Calmly Critical.

Simon Sterne said: " I think that Justice Pryor has certainly strained a point in making his decision. The Jewish society in question is an organization of a wholly non-business character, and it looks like straining matters very greatly to declare that it would be against public policy to allow it to hold its annual meetings on Sunday. A great many of the Hebrew societies hold their elections on Sunday, and very

naturally, because it is an enforced holiday, and they have time to attend to such duties on that day. In the case of hospitals and charitable institutions, I feel quite certain that most of them elect their officers on Sunday. At their meetings on Sunday, besides the elections, reports are read or submitted.

" It seems a little captious in Judge Pryor, who is a learned and liberal man, and who is no Puritan. I do not suppose for an instant that he would refuse to hold as valid the election of any of these officers who had been chosen on Sunday. Many of them are among our best citizens, and some are prominent and able lawyers.

" It is one thing to prevent labor that would destroy Sunday as a day of rest, and quite a different thing to prevent a semi-religious organization from choosing its officers on Sunday. The latter would not interfere in the slightest degree with any one in the strictest observance of the day. This restraint is not put upon Hebrews in England. They meet there on Sunday without restriction.

" I am sorry that the decision of Justice Pryor is made in a case where it might be supposed to indicate some feeling against the Hebrews as a race and as antagonistic to the Hebrew religious faith."

December 27, 1896

ADVENTISTS ATTACK BLUE LAW MOVEMENT

Memorial Declares Sabbath Keeping Not a Civil Duty, so Congress Should Not Act.

WASHINGTON, Jan. 15.—Sunday blue laws are described as an encroachment of civil power into the spiritual realm by a memorial adopted by the General Conference Committee of Seventh Day Adventists, made public at its headquarters here. Opposition to all Sunday laws is declared, particularly to proposed Federal enactments.

Asserting that the complete separation of Church and State was essential to the country's well-being, the memorial declared that failure to recognize this distinction in the past had been the pri-

mary cause of religious persecutions. The present " strong organized effort " to obtain blue law enactments, it added, " are destructive both to the Church and the State, however innocent they may appear, and if successful will eventually destroy the pillars upon which our Government is founded."

" Sabbath keeping is not a civil but a religious duty," the memorial declared. " Congress therefore has nothing whatever to do with the question of its observance.

" Only those whose hearts God has changed can truly keep a holy Sabbath. As no legislation by Congress can change the human heart, to make citizens perform a religious act when they **are not religious is to enforce hypocrisy by law.**

" Honest labor is no more uncivil on Sunday than on Monday. It is religious prejudices which are disturbed by labor on this day more than on other days. But bolstering of some particular theological dogma and protecting the religious prejudices of citizens is not the business of Congress."

January 16, 1921

KING JAMES BIBLE BARRED IN SCHOOLS

High California Court Holds Protestant Book Is 'Sectarian,' Hence Forbidden by Code.

CASE FROM LOWER COURT

Originated in Purchase of Bibles for Selma High School, Which Townsman Protested.

Special to The New York Times.

SAN FRANCISCO, Nov. 1.—The King James version of the Bible cannot be used in the public schools of California, it being properly the book of " a certain religious sect," according to a ruling made by the District Court of Appeal. This opinion reverses that of the Su-

perior Court of Fresno County, which gave to the Trustees of the Selma High School the right to buy a dozen Bibles for use in school classes, after suit had been brought by a Selma resident to restrain the Trustees from buying the Bibles.

The Fresno court held that the King James Bible was not a sectarian book, but merely the " Book of all Christians," as the Trustees contended when the proposed purchase met with opposition.

The opinion of the Appellate Court, written by Justice Nourse, holds, however, that the King James Bible is really the " book " of the Protestant religion, and as such is sectarian and should not be used as a school text. It comments upon the many translations of the Bible from the earliest down to the King James version and emphasizes the point that other religious sects have their books, such as the Talmud and the Koran.

Continuing, the decision reads:

" While Protestantism may not be a ' sect ' in the strict interpretation of the term, the Protestant Bible contains the precepts of many of the Protestant denominations, and ' denomination ' is merely another term for ' sect.' Controversies have been waged for centuries over the authenticity of the various translations of the Bible, each sect insisting that its version is the only inspired book.

" As a result of this controversy, men fail to consider any Bible for its literary or historical value, but bar all from

the schools, for fear that their children might absorb some doctrine adverse to the teaching of their own denomination.

" The King James Bible, having been adopted by Protestants as their book, is objectionable to those who do not follow that faith. It is thus a book of a sectarian or denominational character within the meaning of the political code.

" The sole question for determination was whether the King James version of the Bible was a sectarian or denominational book. On this appeal it was argued that the use of school money for the purchase of Bibles is prohibited by the Constitution and statutes of California. Statutes from the political code were cited that provide ' It shall be the duty of Boards of School Trustees to exclude from school and school libraries all books, publications or papers of a sectarian, partisan or denominational character."

Also quoted were the sections of the code that provide that " no publication of a sectarian, partisan or denominational character must be used or distributed in any school or be made a part of any school library, nor must any sectarian or denominational doctrine be taught therein."

The opinion of the Court is in accordance with the findings of U. S. Webb, Attorney General of California. Several months ago he ruled that he was of the opinion that the reading of the King James version of the Bible as a religious exercise, or its use as a text book in the public schools, was prohibited by the Constitution and laws of California.

November 2, 1922

OREGON SCHOOL LAW DECLARED INVALID BY SUPREME COURT

Bench Unanimously Upholds Right of Parent to Dictate Child's Education.

STATE CONTROL REJECTED

Justice McReynolds, in Opinion, Calls Law "Standardizing Children" Unconstitutional.

PRIVATE SCHOOLS JUSTIFIED

State Law Is Characterized as Destructive of "Useful and Meritorious" Institutions.

Special to The New York Times.

WASHINGTON, June 1.—The inherent right of a parent to send his boy or girl to any school he deems best was upheld and the right of a State to insist that the children must attend certain institutions was sharply denied when the Supreme Court declared unconstitutional this afternoon, the Oregon law prescribing that children between 8 and 16 years of age must be educated in the public schools.

The Court, at the same time, declared that to sustain the Oregon law would mean the destruction of thousands of dollars worth of property belonging to the parochial and secular schools, and that this would amount to depriving them of their possessions without due process of law.

Few decisions in years have attracted as much attention as the present one which was rendered unanimously and was handed down by Associate Justice McReynolds.

Charges that the law was backed by the Ku Klux Klan and was aimed at the Roman Catholic Church have been heard on every side since the statute was enacted. The law, however, makes no distinction against parochial schools, and in the case which was decided this afternoon, the Hill Military Academy, a nonsectarian institution, joined with the Society of the Sisters of the Holy Name of Jesus and Mary in opposing the State authorities, who were officially listed as Walter M. Pierce, the Governor; Isaac H. Van Winkle, the Attorney General, and Stanley Myers, the District Attorney for Multnomah County.

The dual fight of the parochial and the secular schools had already been won in the Federal Court for the District of Oregon, but the State officials appealed from that decision to the Supreme Court, which today upheld the lower court's dictum.

Holds Child "Not Creature of State."

"The child is not the mere creature of the State," declared Justice McReynolds in that part of his opinion which dealt with the right of the parent to dictate the school to which his child should go.

"Those who nurture him and direct his destiny have the right, coupled with the high duty, to recognize and prepare him for additional obligations," he continued, speaking for the court.

"We think it entirely plain that the (Oregon) act of 1922 unreasonably interferes with the liberty of parents and guardians to direct the upbringing and education of children under their control. As often heretofore pointed out, rights guaranteed by the Constitution may not be abridged by legislation which has no reasonable relation to some purpose within the competency of the State.

"The fundamental theory of liberty upon which all Governments in this Union repose excludes any general power of the State to standardize its children by forcing them to accept instruction from public teachers only."

It could not be expected that the Supreme Court would touch on the Ku Klux Klan issue because it had not been spread officially on the records of the case, but at one point Justice McReynolds stated:

"The appellees are engaged in a kind of undertaking not inherently harmful, but long regarded as useful and meritorious. Certainly there is nothing in the present records to indicate that they have failed to discharge their obligations to patrons, students of the State. And there are no peculiar circumstances or present emergencies which demand extraordinary measures relative to primary education."

Text of the Court's Opinion.

The opinion delivered by Justice McReynolds was as follows:

These appeals are from decrees, based upon undenied allegations, which granted preliminary orders restraining appellants from threatening or attempting to enforce the Compulsory Education act adopted Nov. 7, 1922, under the initiative provision of her Constitution by the voters of Oregon, Judicial Code, Section 266.

They present the same points of law; there are no controverted questions of fact. Rights said to be guaranteed by the Federal Constitution were specially set up, and appropriate prayers asked for their protection.

The challenged act, effective Sept. 1, 1926, requires every parent, guardian, or other person having control or charge or custody of a child between 8 and 16 years to send him "to a public school for the period of time a public school shall be held during the current year" in the district where the child resides; and failure to do so is declared a misdemeanor.

There are exemptions—not specially important here—for children who are not normal, or who have completed the eighth grade, or who reside at considerable distances from any public school, or who hold special permits from the County Superintendent.

The manifest purpose is to compel general attendance at public schools by normal children, between 8 and 16, who have not completed the eighth grade. And without doubt enforcement of the statute would seriously impair, perhaps destroy, the profitable features of appellees' business and greatly diminish the value of their property.

Reviews Work of Catholic Schools.

Appellee, the Society of Sisters, is an Oregon corporation, organized in 1880, with power to care for orphans, educate and instruct the youth, establish and maintain academies or schools, and acquire necessary real and personal property. It has long devoted its property and effort to the secular and religious education and care of children and has acquired the valuable good-will of many parents and guardians.

It conducts interdependent primary and high schools and junior colleges, and maintains orphanages for the custody and control of children between the ages of 8 and 16. In its primary schools many children between these ages are taught the subjects usually pursued in Oregon public schools during the first eight years.

Systematic religious instruction and moral training, according to the tenets of the Roman Catholic Church, are also regularly provided. All courses of study, both temporal and religious, contemplate continuity of training under Appellee's charge; the primary schools are essential to the system and the most profitable.

It owns valuable buildings, especially constructed and equipped for school purposes. The business is remunerative—the annual income from primary schools exceeds $30,000—and the successful conduct of this requires long-time contracts with teachers and parents.

The compulsory act of 1922 has already caused the withdrawal from its schools of children who would otherwise continue, and their income has steadily declined. The appellants, public officers, have proclaimed their purpose strictly to enforce the statute.

After setting out the above facts, the society's bill alleges that the enactment conflicts with the right of parents to choose schools where their children will receive appropriate mental and religious training, the right of the child to influence the parents' choice of a school, the right of schools and teachers therein to engage in a useful business or profession, and is accordingly repugnant to the Constitution and void.

And further, that unless enforcement of the measures is enjoined the corporation's business and property will suffer irreparable injury.

Contentions of Military Academy.

Appellee Hill Military Academy, is a private corporation organised in 1908 under the laws of Oregon, engaged in owning, operating and conducting for profit an elementary, college preparatory and military training school for boys between the ages of 5 and 21 years. The average attendance is 100, and the annual fees received for each student amount to some $800.

The elementary department is divided into eight grades, as in the public schools; the college preparatory department has four grades similar to those of the public high schools; the courses of study conform to the requirements of the State Board of Education. Military instruction and training are also given under the supervision of an army officer.

It owns considerable real and personal property, some useful only for school purposes. The business and incident good-will are very valuable. In order to conduct its affairs long-time contracts must be made for supplies, equipment, teachers and pupils. Appellants, law officers of the State and county, have publicly announced that the act of Nov. 7, 1922, is valid and have declared their intention to enforce it. By reason of the statute and threat of enforcement appellee's business is being destroyed and its property depreciated; parents and guardians are refusing to make contracts for the future instruction of their sons, and some are being withdrawn.

The academy's bill states the foregoing facts and then alleges that the challenged act contravenes the corporation's rights guaranteed by the Fourteenth Amendment and that unless appellants are restrained from proclaiming its validity and threatening to enforce it irreparable injury will result. The prayer is for an appropriate injunction.

No answer was interposed in either cause and after proper notices they were heard by three Judges (Jud. Code Sec. 266) on motions for preliminary injunctions upon the specifically alleged facts.

Findings of the Lower Court

The Court ruled that the Fourteenth Amendment guaranteed appellees against the deprivation of their property without due process of law consequent upon the unlawful interference by appellants with the free choice of patrons, present and prospective. It declared the right to conduct schools was property and that parents and guardians, as a part of their liberty, might direct the education of children by selecting reputable teachers and places.

Also, that appellees' schools were not unfit or harmful to the public, and that enforcement of the challenged statute would unlawfully deprive them of patronage and thereby destroy appellees' business and property. Finally, that the threats to enforce the act would continue to cause irreparable injury; and the suits were not premature.

No question is raised concerning the power of the State reasonably to regulate all schools, to inspect, supervise and examine them, their teachers and pupils; to require that all children of proper age attend some school, that teachers shall be of good moral character and patriotic disposition, that certain studies plainly essential to good citizenship must be taught, and that nothing be taught which is manifestly inimical to the public welfare.

State Cannot "Standardize" Children.

The inevitable practical result of enforcing the act under consideration would be destruction of appellees' primary schools, and perhaps all other private primary schools for normal children within the State of Oregon.

Appellees are engaged in a kind of undertaking not inherently harmful, but long regarded as useful and meritorious. Certainly there is nothing in the present records to indicate that they have failed to discharge their obligations to patrons, students or the State. And there are no peculiar circumstances or present emergencies which demand extraordinary measures relative to primary education.

Under the doctrine of Meyer v. Nebraska, 262 U. S. 390, we think it entirely plain that the act of 1922 unreasonably interferes with the liberty of parents and guardians to direct the upbringing and education of children under their control.

As often heretofore pointed out, rights guaranteed by the Constitution may not be abridged by legislation which has no reasonable relation to some purpose within the competency of the State. The fundamental theory of liberty upon which all Governments in this Union repose excludes any general power of the State to standardize its children by forcing them to accept instruction from public teachers only.

The child is not the mere creature of the State; those who nurture him and direct his destiny have the right, coupled with the high duty, to recognize and prepare him for additional obligations.

Right to Protect School Property.

Appellees are corporations, and, therefore, it is said, they cannot claim for themselves the liberty which the Fourteenth Amendment guarantees. Accepted in the proper sense, this is true. Northwestern Life Insurance Company v. Riggs, 203 U. S. 243, 255; Western Turf Association, v. Greenburg, 204 U. S. 359, 363.

But they have business and property for which they claim protection. These are threatened with destruction through the unwarranted compulsion which appellants are exercising over present and prospective patrons of their schools. And this Court has gone very far to protect against loss threatened by such action. Truax v. Raich, 239 U. S. 33;

Truax v. Corrigan, 257 U. S. 312; Terrace v. Thompson, 263 U. S. 197.

The Courts of the State have not construed the act and we must determine its meaning for ourselves. Evidently it was expected to have general application and cannot be construed as though merely intended to amend the charters of certain private corporations as in Berea College v. Kentucky, 211 U. S. 45. No argument in favor of such view has been advanced.

Generally it is entirely true, as urged by counsel, that no person in any business has such an interest in possible customers as to enable him to restrain exercise of proper power of the State upon the ground that he will be deprived of patronage.

But the injunctions here sought are not against the exercise of any proper power. Appellees asked protection against arbitrary, unreasonable and unlawful interference with their patrons and the consequent destruction of their business and property.

Their interest is clear and immediate, within the rule approved in Truax v. Raich, Truax v. Corrigan and Terrace v. Thompson, supra, and many other cases where injunctions have issued to protect business enterprises against interference with the freedom of patrons or customers. Hitchman Coal and Coke Company v. Mitchell, 245 U. S. 229; Duplex Printing Press Company v. Deering, 254 U. S. 443; American Steel Foundries v. Tricity Central Trades Council, 257 U.S. 184; Nebraska District et cetera v. McKelvie, 262 U.S. 404; Truax v. Corrigan, supra, and cases there cited.

The suits were not premature. The injury to appellees was present and very real, not a mere possibility in the remote future. If no relief had been possible prior to the effective date of the act, the injury would have become irreparable.

Prevention of impending injury by unlawful action is a well-recognized function of courts of equity.

The decrees below are affirmed.

Issues in the Oregon Controversy.

WASHINGTON, June 1 (AP).— In educational and religious circles keener and wider interest was shown in the attack upon the constitutionality of the Oregon Public School law than in any other controversy which reached the Supreme Court in recent years.

Like most States, Oregon has a compulsory education law which requires children to attend school, and prescribes the course of study. The right to enforce such regulations has not been seriously questioned in the courts. But in 1922 the voters of Oregon, 115,506 to 103,685, went a step further and enacted a law under which children between the ages of 8 and 16, with some exceptions, would, after September, 1925, be required to attend "public" schools.

Summarized, Oregon's argument was that the National Government was founded upon the theory that Church and State should be maintained separate, a principle to be closely guarded in the education of its youth; that the right of a State to control a minor when public welfare required had been thoroughly established in the courts and included control over education.

That private and parochial schools are not superior to public schools, therefore the new law would not deprive them of any rights or privileges or subject them to any disadvantages; that the opposition came from those who wanted children given sectarian religious instruction; that the fight involved the survival of the public schools.

The Protestant Episcopal Church, the Seventh Day Adventists and the American Jewish Committee each filed a brief as friend of the court in support of the position taken by the parochial and private schools.

Opponents of the new law declared it a serious menace. They attributed the weakening of the moral fiber of the time to the lack of religious and moral training, particularly in children, declaring that unless present tendencies were restrained conditions here would be worse than those in Soviet Russia.

Oregon's idea of separation of Church and State would mean, they declared, no Church but only State, because if school could be prohibited from teaching religion and morality all religious instruction would be brought within the control of the State.

June 2, 1925

SCHOOLS FOCUS RELIGIOUS ISSUE

Question of Instruction Based on the Bible Has Assumed Importance in Many States— Court Test in New York

HOW and when religious instruction is to be given to school children has rapidly become a question of national importance in the United States. Shall it be part of the school curriculum or not, and, if not, shall it be given to pupils outside school confines but during time allotted to the regular study period?

California was the first State to advocate the dismissal of children from school earlier than usual, on a given day once a week, to enable them to attend religious classes on school time. Though its own Legislature failed to adopt this measure, the idea was taken up by other States and is now an established fact in many of them.

These "school time release" laws represent a new type of legislation to get around the difficulties arising from constitutional injunctions against the teaching of religion in public schools.

New York State is now testing the constitutionality of such a law, which had been in operation in White Plains. To test the legality of this "school time release" practice, the Freethinkers' Society of that city last Winter applied for a writ of mandamus to compel State Commissioner of Education Graves to put an end to the system. Justice Ellis J. Staley sustained at Albany the Board of Education of White Plains and denied the application of the society, which, however, continued the fight before the Appellate Division of the Supreme Court, and it is expected that the case will eventually reach the United States Supreme Court.

Arguments For and Against.

Advocates of the system contend that it does not interfere in any way with individual or religious freedom, since it leaves choice of religion and place of instruction with those concerned. Opponents argue that it links Church and State, for it makes religious organizations a part of the public school system inasmuch as they are permitted to give instruction to children on school time and with school credit.

But, back of much of the legislation regarding religious instruction looms the Bible, and those actively interested in the matter may be roughly divided into three groups: First, those who accept the Holy Scriptures as irrefutable and final authority on the origin and development of man and other species of life and are opposed to the "theory of evolution." Second, those who strive to put the Bible in the public schools as a subject of instruction. Third, those who desire to prevent their children from falling under the influence of religious teaching contrary to their own faith and hence demand time set apart for special instruction of the kind.

Compulsory school Bible-reading laws are now in effect in eleven States. In Ohio a law providing for the use of the Bible in the public schools was passed by both houses, but the Governor vetoed it. Delaware has a law prescribing the reading of the Bible "without comment," in public schools and colleges. It was passed in 1923, and has since been amended to provide for the fining and dismissing from service of any teacher who fails to comply with the act. Efforts are being made to obtain a test of the constitutionality of the law. A committee made up of representatives of various denominations and assisted by the American Civil Liberties Union is engaged in this task. The Trenton (N. J.) Board of Education has declared itself in favor of religious instruction in the schools

and decided to make it a part of the curriculum.

California Bill Defeated.

A State measure to include the Bible either as a subject to be studied in public schools or as a reference book in the school libraries was defeated in the recent election in California. A similar bill introduced three years ago in the Legislature was rejected. This year the measure was submitted

to the vote of the people in the form of a constitutional amendment.

The progress of anti-evolution legislation does not appear to have been as rapid as its proponents may have wished. In the campaign for the enactment of such laws during the last few months only one success has been achieved. On the other hand, there have been three failures registered.

December 12, 1926

Appellate Court Upholds Religious Teaching Of Pupils in School Time Outside Buildings

Special to The New York Times.

ALBANY, Jan. 5.—The constitutionality of the legislative act which authorized the religious instruction of pupils in public schools one hour a week during school hours outside the school buildings was unanimously upheld today by the Appellate Division, Third Department, in an opinion written by Justice Rowland L. Davis.

The decision was in the test case brought by Joseph Lewis, President of the Free Thinkers' Society, against Dr. Frank P. Graves, State Commissioner of Education, to compel him by mandamus to order discontinued the plan used in White Plains as well as in the

130 cities and villages of the State where it was being practiced.

The appeal was from an order of Justice Ellis J. Staley, who denied the application for the writ made at the Albany special term several months ago.

The attack on the law was led by Arthur Garfield Hays and John C. Mahon, of New York City, counsel for the Free Thinkers' Society, on the principal grounds that the practice violated one of the fundamental provisions of the Constitution, declaring that the Church and State shall remain separate, and that it was also in conflict with the compulsory school attendance law, which the

Commissioner of Education is required to enforce.

Ernest E Cole, counsel for Dr. Graves, argued that not to permit the absence of children from regular school classes to attend their church schools would be an interference with religious liberty and that no pupil was required to attend the church classes without the consent of the parents.

John R. Bushong filed a brief for the General Committee on week-day religious instruction of White Plains, which declared that to hold the law unconstitutional "would be a direct blow to the training of American youth, contrary to fundamental public policy, and would amount to moral anarchy."

It is expected that an early appeal will be taken to the Courts of Appeals and after that to the United States Supreme Court.

January 6, 1927

BLUE LAWS DIFFER GREATLY AMONG THE VARIOUS STATES

Sunday Observance Legislation Calls Forth Many Contradictory Interpretations

By HARRY HIBSCHMAN.

SUNDAY, or so-called "blue," laws differ widely in the various States of the Union. In Pennsylvania, for example, full and strict enforcement of a law passed there in 1794, and still technically in force on the statute books, would prohibit the selling in drug stores, on Sunday, of newspapers, cigars, soda water and ice cream; the supplying by garages of gasoline and oil; indeed, the use of a pleasure car itself, except for the purpose of going to church.

A citizen in Connecticut may, within the law, do a number of things that are prohibited in Pennsylvania. If his community so votes, he may have the chance to go to a concert on Sunday, something under legal ban in Pennsylvania; but the music played must be "standard symphonic compositions and music of a classical nature." Although a Sousa military march is thus proscribed, the State military forces and rifle clubs are permitted to use the rifle ranges on Sunday between the hours of 1 and 6 in the afternoon.

Sunday Amusements.

An act to permit Sunday amusements in South Carolina was recently vetoed by the Governor. Golf,

therefore, is still forbidden there, together with all worldly labor and business and the selling of goods of any description. Trains may be run to carry fruit or mail or to take persons to and from religious services. As late as 1921, in South Carolina, it was held that the sale of ice cream on Sunday, even where the proceeds went to the Red Cross, was a violation of the old Sunday law.

Golf has been judicially condemned in Massachusetts, as has been playing in a band on Sunday, except in a sacred concert or on Memorial Sunday. A baker may not deliver bread outside his own premises, though he may sell it in the bakery. In Maine it is technically illegal to open any place of business, to do any work, or to travel except for charity or necessity on Sunday. In New Hampshire milk, bread and drugs may be sold on Sunday, but law prescribes that there shall be no work, business or labor of a secular character; no game, no play, no sport.

In New York, "the first day of the week being by general consent set apart for rest and religious uses," the law prohibits as "serious interruptions of the repose and religious liberty of the community" the following: shootings, hunting, playing, horse-racing, gaming and other pub-

lic sports, exercises or shows, noise, unreasonable disturbances, trades, manufactures, mechanical labor. Selling is restricted to food, tobacco and things of a similar character. Baseball and motion pictures may be permitted by local ordinance.

Liberal Interpretation.

The interpretation of this statute is quite liberal; but the original blue law root may be recognized; and were the law strictly enforced, many things tolerated now would be punishable. It would certainly go hard with Coney Island.

Sunday baseball has been interdicted in some States and permitted in others. Thus in Missouri the Court declared it legal on the ground that it was not a game and in Tennessee it was permitted because it was not yet in existence when the Sunday law was passed and, therefore, does not come within purview of the law. But in Nebraska the Court held to the contrary. Originally it was also under the ban in New York.

Sunday moving pictures have been permitted without special legislation in South Dakota, but are prohibited in New Jersey, Oklahoma, Texas, Mississippi and Kentucky. In Wisconsin, as in Pennsylvania, publishing a newspaper on Sunday has been held illegal, so that there could be no recovery on a contract for advertising in a Sunday issue.

In Indiana cigars are not a necessity, the courts say; therefore, to sell them on Sunday is illegal. Baseball and newspapers are, however, permitted. On the other hand, carrying pleasure-seekers to a picnic is a violation of law.

October 2, 1927

CATHOLICISM AND POLITICS

Editor Quotes Encyclicals and Other Documents to Demonstrate That the Attitude of the Church Is One of Non-Interference

To the Editor of The New York Times:

May I say a word in answer to statements appearing in two letters in THE TIMES of Aug. 11?

Henry W. Elson says Governor Smith belongs "to a great religious organization with headquarters at Rome, which believes in the union of Church and State and would like to divide the public school fund." I am a Catholic in good standing, help edit an official Catholic newspaper and do not know of an American Catholic who wants union of Church and State. "Catholics, like all other citizens, are free to prefer one form of government to another," says Pope Leo XIII in his letter "Au Milieu des Sollicitudes." And again in his Encyclical "Sapientiae Christianae" he says:

"The Church, the guardian always of her own rights and most observant of those of others, holds that it is not her province to decide what is the best among many diverse forms of government and the civil institutions of Christian States. Amid the various kinds of State rule she does not disapprove of any, provided the respect due to religion and the observance of good morals be upheld."

Cardinal Gibbons in The North American Review, March, 1919, wrote:

"Fifteen millions of Catholics live their lives in our land with undisturbed belief in the perfect harmony existing between their religion and their duties as American citizens. It never occurs to their minds to question the truth of a belief which all their experience confirms. Love of religion and love of country burn together in their hearts. They love their Church as the divine spiritual society set up by Jesus Christ, through which they are brought into a closer communion with God, learn His revealed truth and His holy law, receive the help they need to lead Christian lives and are inspired with the hope of eternal happiness. They love their country with the spontaneous and ardent love of all patriots, because it is their country and the source to them of untold blessings. They prefer its form of government before any other. They admire its institutions and the spirit of its laws. They accept the Constitution without reserve, with no desire, as Catholics, to see it changed in any feature. They can with a clear conscience swear to uphold it."

Mr. Elson says we would like to divide the public school funds. Some Catholics, since they submit to double educational taxation, thereby saving the city great sums of money, would probably like to see the educational funds of the city divided. A number of well-known non-Catholics, such as Bird S. Coler, have made suggestions along these lines. The Church, however, is making no such request. Moreover, I know of no prelate hereabouts who "would like to divide the public school fund."

Mr. Johnstone speaks of Mr. Smith being subject to a foreign potentate. Catholics owe spiritual allegiance to the Pope, not temporal. If he says go to mass on a holy day, we go. If he would say form an army and fight Mexico, we would stay at home. We "render to Caesar the things that are Caesar's and to God the things that are God's." The way Catholic Belgium fought Catholic Austria showed that civic loyalty was separate and distinct from spiritual loyalty. To my knowledge no one protested against General Foch as leader of the allied armies because he owed allegiance to "a foreign potentate." Our Government was glad to receive and accept the support of all Catholics, not even giving consideration to the foreign potentate bugaboo.

"The spirit of the Constitution" bars Smith, argues Mr. Johnstone. Since when? The letter of the Constitution specifically says there shall be no religious test for a man aspiring to public office.

If Mr. Smith can successfully guide the greatest and most populated State in the Union without violating the Constitution or being guilty of other childish suppositions, it would seem reasonable to assert, in answer to Mr. Elson and Mr. Johnstone, the rest of the nation would be safe in his hands.

PATRICK F. SCANLAN,
Managing Editor of The Tablet.
Brooklyn, N. Y., Aug. 16, 1926.

August 22, 1926

OPPOSITION IN SOUTH WORRIES SMITH MEN

Georgia and Alabama Drys and Church Leaders Harp on Religious Issue.

PARTY OFFICIALS ACTIVE

Senator Harris Tells of Promised Defeat If He Supports the New York Governor.

By JULIAN HARRIS.

Editorial Correspondence of THE NEW YORK TIMES.

COLUMBUS, Ga., Aug. 1.—When Governor Alfred E. Smith was asked by newspapermen if he was worried about the South, his answer was "No." And by way of returning the compliment to this section, it should be put in the record that the great majority of Southern Democrats are not worried about Governor Smith. But the loyal Southern Democrats who compose this majority are frankly worried about the South on account of the bitterness aroused by the frenzied efforts of the politico-religious dry minority to defeat Governor Smith in Democracy's stronghold. For these Anti-Smith Democrats—a few politicians, the W. C. T. U., a number of ministers of the Baptist and the Methodist churches, and many Ku Klux-minded persons—are invoking religious bigotry and fear of papal control of our Government to lash the intolerant and uninformed voters into line for the Republican nominee.

The hot-bed of this fanaticism is in Georgia and Alabama, though conditions in the latter State have been somewhat cooled by Democratic statements from life-long prohibitionists like Musgrove, Samford and others. But in Georgia the politico-religious situation is actually menacing—not to the Democratic Party or Governor Smith, but to and among Southerners. The bitterness in Georgia is literally unbelievable. The leaders in this outburst of intolerance are the women of the W. C. T. U. and those Baptist and Methodist ministers who frankly stand committed to anti-Catholicism. These political parsons of the Baptist and Methodist Church have not only openly aroused religious feeling but have defied their religious leaders. The sane and tolerant advice of the Rev. Warren A. Candler, senior Methodist Episcopal Bishop, and Dr. J. D. Mell, for twenty years President of the Georgia Baptist convention, was not only rejected by the Atlanta Evangelical Ministers' Association, led by Dr. L. R. Christie, a Republican Baptist, but was dubbed "nonsense."

Soften Ministerial Statement.

Particularly violent were the Atlanta Methodist ministers. In the face of the injunction of Bishop Candler that preachers should avoid politics and preach the Gospel of Christ, they adopted resolutions in which occurred the following statement:

"You cannot nail us to a Roman cross and submerge us in a sea of rum."

When the resolutions were submitted to the political meetings of the Evangelical Ministers Association two or three demurred at stating their position so baldly. As a result, when the resolutions were given to the press, the foregoing statement had been changed to read: "You cannot nail us to a cross and submerge us in a sea of rum."

Not content with this the Evangelical ministers struck at Bishop Candler and Dr. Mell in these words: "We are told that we ministers must be smug little fellows; that we must shun the remotest suggestion of politics as the slime of the nethermost pit; but must keep clean for Sunday sermonettes and cultivate a faraway look. We are used to that nonsense."

Hoke Smith Arouses Democrats.

There is in my mind no doubt that what emboldened the anti-Smith

BISHOP DECLARES FAITH BARS SMITH FROM WHITE HOUSE

Leonard Says No Governor Who Kisses Papal Ring Can Be Elected President.

SEES HIM RULED OUT AS WET

Asserts No Nullificationist Will Ever Lead a Constitution-Loving People.

Special to The New York Times.

ROUND LAKE, N. Y., Aug. 8.—Asserting that "no Governor can kiss the Papal ring and get within gunshot of the White House and no nullification Governor ever will become a leader of a Constitution-loving people," Bishop Adna W. Leonard of Buffalo, General Superintendent of the Methodist Episcopal Church for Northern and Western New York and President of the Anti-Saloon League, today attacked Governor Smith as a Presidential candidate on the double ground that he

was a Catholic and an anti-prohibitionist.

Addressing the audience which had assembled for the morning church service at the Citizenship Conference, which has been in progress here for three days, the Bishop also attacked Senator Wadsworth. Bishop Leonard, in his sermon, said "no Methodist, unless he values lightly the vows of the Church, can remain loyal to the Church and support Wadsworth at the same time."

A large part of Bishop Leonard's address was devoted to a nation-wide call for Anglo-Saxon unity against foreigners, particularly the Latins.

Bishop Leonard's assault upon Senator Wadsworth was followed by other attacks by Franklin W. Cristman of Herkimer, dry candidate for the United States Senate against Wadsworth, and by Arthur J. Davis, New York State Superintendent of the Anti-Saloon League. Mr. Cristman attacked Wadsworth as one who had deserted his party's principles, while Davis charged he was trying to make a deal with William Randolph Hearst.

Lieut. Gov. Seymour Lowman, Republican and stanch dry, who also spoke, failed to mention Mr. Cristman or his candidacy.

Officials Who Are "Social Outcasts."

In his speech, Bishop Leonard said:

"It is true the Lord is my keeper, but we also are charged with certain obligations. We appreciate the value of human life more today than we formerly did. We realize as never before that we are keepers of our own bodies and that it is utter folly to disregard the primal physical laws.

"We are keepers of our own minds also, and no man can reach the heights of intelligence and knowledge unless he also obeys the laws which govern the conduct of the human mind and not fill it with the muck and slush so easy to find now.

We should fill our minds with unlimited knowledge concerning the prohibition question. We should build our knowledge, not on party principles, but on the truth in the Constitution of the United States. The man in public office who dares lift a finger or voice against that document should become a social outcast in the American body politic. Not only are we the keepers of our own minds, you see, but of the minds of a nation, building public opinion upon that of ourselves.

"Not only are many disregarding law, but through materialism actually forgetting God.

"The United States is a Christian nation and a Protestant nation and, as long as the English language is interwoven with the word of God, America will remain Protestant. It is of national importance that each individual should have some sort of religion or faith. A nation needs a faith in the almighty providence of a loving God.

Attacks Smith and Wadsworth.

"Liberty does not mean that we are to allow foreigners to come here and trample our flag in the dirt, flout our laws and damn our Government. The Latin people are a big problem for us today, and those officers of the Government who let these types of foreigners slip through the doors illegally should be let know the meaning of a term of imprisonment.

"Give us time, and the Anglo-Saxon will see to it that the ideals of a Latin world are not attained here, but the ideals of a free, Christian land.

"We must remember that there is an America outside of New York State, where the nation is being built about the Bible, church and open school. No Governor can kiss the papal ring and get within gunshot of the White House, and no nullification governor ever will become a leader of a Constitution-loving people.

August 9, 1926

SMITH AND THE PRESIDENCY.

Governor's Catholicism Arouses Diverse Views Among Correspondents.

To the Editor of The New York Times:

Your editorial of Aug. 2 entitled "Bigotry at Home" gives some excellent and timely points that no one can afford to ignore; but it misses the point in one very important respect, or rather omits it.

Everybody that knows Al Smith likes him. He is not only a lovable character, he is also a man of much ability and would make a strong and patriotic President. But great numbers of people who personally like him would no doubt vote against him because of the fact that he belongs to a great religious organization, with headquarters at Rome, which believes in the union of Church and State, and would like to divide the public school fund. The writer heard Governor Smith in a public address speak in favor of our system of keeping Church and State apart, but he has no evidence that the Catholic Church has ever officially made such a declaration.

But Senator Caraway talks nonsense when he says that if the Democrats do not nominate Smith, they will be at sea and will probably name some unknown man. The party has an abundance of Presidential timber. One man who has not been as prominent-

ly mentioned as he should be is Vic Donahey, Governor of Ohio. He is a man of much ability, of unswerving integrity, and has shown himself a wonderful vote getter.

HENRY W. ELSON.

Plainfield, N. J., Aug. 8, 1926.

Fears Power of Pope.

To the Editor of The New York Times:

In your editorial entitled "Bigotry at Home" you seem to have a mistaken idea. The objection to Governor Smith for President is not a matter of bigotry, but on account of his being subject to a foreign potentate, the Pope, who claims temporal power, as well as spiritual. All true Americans would naturally object to Governor Smith, or any other Catholic, on this ground, it being contrary to the spirit of our Constitution.

FRANCIS M. JOHNSTONE.

Cooperstown, N. Y., Aug. 7, 1926.

Ready to Quit Republicans.

To the Editor of The New York Times:

A week ago today your editorial reported that Senator Caraway of Arkansas noted, before sailing for Europe, that since Governor Smith of New York is not a Baptist, Methodist or Presbyterian, he will not have a chance for the Presidency. Today on the front page you report Bishop Leonard of Buffalo as stating that

"No Governor who kisses the papal ring can be elected President."

Are we ready to concede that the politics of this country is run and controlled by the Methodists, Baptists and Presbyterians? If so, vote me out of the Republican Party.

M. E. GREEN.

New York, Aug. 9, 1926.

A Methodist Is Amused.

To the Editor of The New York Times:

As a lifelong Republican who was reared a strict Methodist, the antagonism to Governor Smith of New York on account of his religion is a source of quiet amusement.

Isn't Calles, presumably a Catholic, trying to enforce the laws of Mexico as he understands them? Wasn't the Pope's temporal power shorn by Catholic Rome? Didn't Catholic France drive out certain monastic orders?

Al Smith's antagonists ignore the fact that first of all he is a man with the courage of his convictions, who has made good in every position into which he has been pushed, and can always be trusted to do what is right.

If our country, and every other country for that matter, had a few more men of Al Smith's type, the world would be better off.

WILLIAM D. KEMPTON.

Cincinnati, Ohio, Aug. 8, 1926.

August 11, 1926

Protestant Ministers in Georgia and Alabama, the vast majority of whom are Baptists and Methodists, to enter the political fight where the silence and inaction of the Democratic Party's leaders and officials, in Georgia particularly. The parsons thought that the two States were completely and supinely anti-Smith. Alabama Democrats were the first to open fire on the malcontents and bigots, and then Hoke Smith, of Cleveland's Cabinet, formerly Governor of Georgia and one-time United States Senator, stepped into the breach. Without consulting the timid leaders, Hoke Smith issued a call for a Democratic rally to be held in Atlanta the latter part of July, in order that the real Democrats could begin a campaign for the party's nominees. Newspapers throughout the State indorsed the plan, letters and telegrams of congratulations poured in on the venerable Georgian, and National Committeeman John S. Cohen and State Executive Committee

Chairman G. E. Maddox headed for Hoke Smith's office. Cohen and Maddox pleaded with the elder statesman to call off the rally, telling him that a lively campaign was under way and pledging a real fight for Democracy. The former Cabinet member yielded and called off his meeting.

Apparently the officials of the Democratic Party in Georgia are beginning to get busy. Senator George and Congressman Crisp spoke for Governor Smith last week and were heartily cheered. And this week William J. Harris, senior United States Senator from Georgia, issued what is usually called a "ringing statement." I had been told by some one who is in a position to know that Senator Harris would not make any speeches for the Democratic nominees; that he might issue a statement and let it go at that. This informant said he knew that Kluxers, W. C. T. U. members, anti-Catholics and other anti-Smith people had been putting pressure on Senator

Harris to induce him to keep hands off," if he "wanted to be re-elected two years hence."

Whether Senator Harris will make any speeches remains to be seen. I am inclined to think he will, but he has confirmed the statement that he has been "warned" he would be defeated if he advocated the election of Governor Smith. He added: "If my support of the Democratic Party retires me from the Senate, I am quite willing to make the sacrifice."

The Democratic Party will emerge unscathed, but the wounds inflicted by the lash of intolerance will be slow in healing. And the numerous Baptist and Methodist churches, with congregations divided and many members turned against political pastors who abused the Democratic nominees, will be the greatest and most permanent sufferers.

August 5, 1928

LUTHERAN EDITORS FIX ELECTION STAND

Decide to Inform Readers of Attitude of Catholic Church Toward Government.

NOT TO ADVISE ON VOTING

Resolution States Allegiance to Rome Might Cause Candidate to Clash With Country's Interests.

COLUMBUS, Ohio, Sept. 6 (P).—A resolution referring to the approaching Presidential election and declaring that "the peculiar allegiance that a faithful Catholic owes, according to the teaching of his Church toward a foreign sovereign who also claims supremacy in secular affairs may clash with the best interests of the country" was adopted here today by the National Lutheran Editors Association.

The resolution voiced support of the principle of separation of Church and State, but urged editors to take no stand either for Herbert Hoover

or Governor Smith in the campaign.

It was adopted after the association, composed of editors of publications reaching about 2,000,000 readers, had made known its attitude toward a Catholic President in a statement drawn up by Dr. C. R. Tappert of Philadelphia and adopted by the association. Dr. Tappert is editor of the Lutherischer Herald. The statement read in part:

"If the issue were purely political, the Church papers could not be particularly concerned about it. If it were a matter only of the personal religion of the candidate, it would be contrary to the spirit of our Constitution to prejudice a man because of his Church affiliations.

"The situation, however, is peculiar because of claims, teachings and principles of the Roman Catholic Church which are antagonistic to and irreconcilable with the fundamental principles set forth in the Constitution of our country concerning the separation of Church and State, such as the opposition of this Church to the toleration by the State of any religion other than the Roman Catholic; its denial of the right of individual judgment, liberty of conscience and freedom of worship; the claim that the worldly government is in duty bound not only to assist, support and protect exclusively that Roman Catholic Church but to suppress, if necessary, by force every other religion.

"Allowance may be made for the temporary suspension of the actual enforcement of such claims and principles, but they are recognized ideals, the realization of which must be the aim and constant endeavor to every faithful Catholic.

"The situation is further peculiar because of the allegiance a faithful Catholic owes, according to the teachings of his church, toward a foreign sovereign who claims supremacy also in secular affairs and who has world-wide political interests of his own which may severely clash with the best interests of our country.

"It becomes the duty of our church papers to give to their readers reliable information as to the attitude of the Roman Catholic Church toward the authority of the worldly government and especially the precious liberties guaranteed by our Constitution; to counteract misinformation and to correct false and misleading innuendoes, statements and impressions.

"The church papers, however, will not and need not advise their readers how to vote, but must leave this to their own intelligent and conscientious judgment."

Publications represented by members of the association are those of the United Lutheran Church in America, and Austana Augustana Synod (Swedish), the Norwegian Lutheran Church in America, the United Danish Church, the Danish Church, the Joint Synod of Ohio and other States and the Iowa Synod Evangelical Lutheran.

The following officers were elected for the year: the Rev. Harold Jensen of Omaha, President; Dr. C. R. Tappert of Philadelphia, Vice President; Dr. Emmanual Poppen of Grove City, Ohio, Secretary, and A. M. Sundheim of Indianapolis, Treasurer.

September 7, 1928

DRY PAPER OPPOSES SMITH AS CATHOLIC

Editorial Urges Support of Hoover to Safeguard Puritan, Protestant Traditions.

Special to The New York Times.

COLUMBUS, Ohio, Sept. 23.—The cleavage in the campaign, breaking down party lines, is ascribed to the personalities of the candidates, in an editorial in The American Issue, official organ of the Ohio Anti-Saloon League. The editorial urges opposition to Smith in part because he is a Catholic and represents the "jazz"

element in American life.

"Why are Democrats leaving their party this year, and why are Republicans temporarily going over to the Democratic Party?" the editorial asks.

"Al Smith is a new type of Presidential candidate. Neither party has offered such a candidate for Chief Executive of the nation. This is said not because Smith is a Catholic, but because he is different from any candidate of either party within the knowledge of the present generation. He appeals to the sporty, jazz and liberal element of our population. He is not in harmony with the principles of our forefathers. * * *

"The division is on candidates, not parties. Neither is the division wholly along dry and wet lines, although this issue is a factor, and a big one.

"But this is only one point of difference between the two candidates. Smith represents Tammany, and what it stands for, while Hoover is typical of the life away from New York City.

"If you believe in Anglo-Saxon Protestant domination; if you believe in the maintenance of that civilization founded by our Puritan ancestors, and preserved by our fathers; if you believe in those principles which have made this country what it is; if you believe in prohibition, its observance and enforcement, and if you believe in a further restricted immigration rather than letting down the bars still lower, then whether you are a Republican or a Democrat, you will vote for Hoover rather than Smith.

September 24, 1928

ANALYZES SMITH'S DEFEAT.

F. R. Kent Says No Democrat Could Have Won, People Wanted Hoover.

HARRISBURG, Pa., Nov. 8 (P).— Assertions that Governor Smith would have been elected had he not been a Catholic were decried by Frank R. Kent, political writer, in a speech tonight before the Pennsylvania League of Women Voters.

"There are no sound reasons for believing that if Smith had not been a Catholic he would have won over Herbert Hoover on Tuesday," Mr. Kent said. "While Governor Smith was beaten, I don't believe any Democrat could have been elected. Notwithstanding the fact that almost any other Democrat could have held the South and got more electoral votes in that way, no other Democrat could have got as large a popular vote as Smith. There wasn't any outstanding issues, the people simply wanted Hoover."

November 9, 1928

Bible Reading in Schools.

Bible reading in public schools is now expressly required by statute in eleven States (and by order of the Board of Education in the District of Columbia); it is specifically permitted by law in five States; and is generally construed as lawful in twenty of the thirty-two remaining States whose constitutions and statutes do not expressly require, permit or forbid it, says the United States Office of Education. Bible reading in public schools is now held lawful by supreme court decisions of twelve States. Six of these decisions are found in States whose laws either require or specifically permit Bible reading, and six in States whose laws are silent on the subject.

October 5, 1930

FEW STATES HELP RELIGIOUS SCHOOLS

The majority of State Constitutions forbid the use of public funds for the support of sectarian or religious education, according to a nation-wide survey of the legal provisions for State school supervision and aid under the auspices of the Institute of Catholic Educational Research of Fordham University.

The survey showed that the New York State Constitution prohibits aid to educational institutions under the control of any religious denomination, but that assistance to pupils has been held to be legal in some cases where the school does not benefit.

Provision in Pennsylvania

In Pennsylvania, however, the Legislature is permitted to appropriate public funds for the support of non-public schools. No constitutional provision is made for the aid of private or sectarian schools in Arkansas, Maine, Vermont and Maryland.

In only a few States are the provisions concerning qualifications of teachers in private schools of an express nature. In Alabama, Michigan, Nebraska and South Dakota teachers are required to hold State licenses, the requirement being the same for both private and public schools. Six other States prescribe by law that teachers shall be competent, but the laws are vague on how this competency shall be determined.

On Constitution Study

The Rev. James T. Cronin, director of the institute, who directed the survey, reported that eighteen States had laws requiring that the United States Constitution receive consideration as a special subject of study. In twelve States citizenship and loyalty are required subjects.

"Few previous attempts have been made to collect and publish such data on a nation-wide scale," Dr. Cronin said in commenting on the survey, "and our findings will undoubtedly prove of broad general interest in the educational world.

"The Constitutions of nineteen States expressly permit the Legislature to exempt private and sectarian schools from taxation. We found also that in fourteen other States the Legislature is required, under certain conditions, to exempt private school property from taxation."

Twenty-five States prescribe a basic curriculum either by specifying the list of subjects to be taught in both public and private schools, or by prescribing the list for public schools and stipulating that an equivalent list be taught in private schools.

The survey was carried on with the cooperation of chief State school officers and Catholic educators.

December 27, 1936

HIGH COURT VOIDS JEHOVAH SECT CURB

Special to THE NEW YORK TIMES.

WASHINGTON, May 20—In a unanimous opinion, delivered by Justice Roberts, the Supreme Court today reversed the conviction of three members of Jehovah's Witnesses for soliciting funds for religious purposes in New Haven without a permit and playing before Roman Catholics in the same city a phonograph record attacking the Catholic Church. The Connecticut law under which conviction was obtained was ruled unconstitutional.

Newton Cantwell, and Jesse and Russell, his 16 and 18 year old sons, all ordained ministers of the sect, could not be convicted under a Connecticut law regulating the solicitation of funds, said Justice Roberts, because the law was "a censorship of religion," and unconstitutional.

Jesse, who played the phonograph record, could not be convicted of breach of peace, the Justice added, because "however misguided others may think him," Jesse's conduct did not mean a violation of the "narrowly drawn" law.

"To condition the solicitation of aid for the perpetuation of religious views or systems upon a license the grant of which rests in the exercise of a determination by State authority as to what is a religious cause, is to lay a forbidden burden upon the exercise of liberty protected by the Constitution," Justice Roberts said.

"We find no assault or threatening of bodily harm, no truculent bearing, no intentional discourtesy, no personal abuse," Justice Roberts said of Jesse Cantwell. "On the contrary, we find only an effort to persuade a willing listener to buy a book or to contribute money in the interest of what Cantwell, however misguided others may think him, conceived to be true religion."

Throughout Justice Roberts's opinion ran the idea that, no matter how bitter religious differences might be, fundamental rights of individuals must be protected under the Constitution.

"In the realm of religious faith, and in that of political belief, sharp differences arise," the Justice stated. "In both fields the tenets of one man may seem the rankest error to his neighbor.

"But people of this nation have ordained in the light of history, that, in spite of the probability of excesses and abuses, these liberties are, in the long view, essential to enlightened opinion and right conduct on the part of the citizens of a democracy.

"There are limits to the exercise of these liberties. The danger in these times from the coercive activities of those who in the delusion of racial or religious conceit would incite violence and breaches of the peace in order to deprive others of their equal right to the exercise of their liberties, is emphasized by events familiar to all. These and other transgressions of those limits the States appropriately may punish."

The Connecticut law, said Justice Roberts, deprived the Cantwells of their liberty without due process of law in contravention of the Fourteenth Amendment.

May 21, 1940

SUPREME COURT ENDS COMPULSION OF FLAG SALUTE

Reverses 1940 Stand in 6-to-3 Decision Upholding Jehovah Sect Under Bill of Rights

By LEWIS WOOD
Special to The New York Times.

WASHINGTON, June 14—In a reversal of the Gobitis decision of June, 1940, the Supreme Court held by 6 to 3 today that under the Bill of Rights public school children could not be compelled to salute the American flag if this ceremony conflicted with their religious beliefs.

The ruling was handed down while the nation was celebrating Flag Day in commemoration of the 164th anniversary of the Stars and Stripes.

It upheld a challenge by members of the sect of Jehovah's Witnesses to a flag-salute regulation issued by the West Virginia Board of Education.

In the Gobitis case the Witnesses brought a test against similar regulations of the Minersville, Pa., School District, but the Supreme Court then sustained the flag-salute order by 8 to 1.

Protection by Constitution

Writing the majority opinion in today's case, Justice Robert H. Jackson said:

"We think the action of the local authorities in compelling the flag salute and pledge transcends constitutional limitations on their power and invades the sphere of intellect and spirit which it is the purpose of the First Amendment to our Constitution to reserve from all official control."

The First Amendment protects freedom of religion, speech and the press, and right of assembly and petition.

Specifically overruling the Minersville and similar decisions, Justice Jackson also said:

"To sustain the compulsory flag salute we are required to say that a Bill of Rights which guards the individual's right to speak his own mind left it open to public authorities to compel him to utter what is not in his mind."

Justices Owen J. Roberts, Stanley F. Reed and Felix Frankfurter all dissented, standing by their attitude in the Gobitis case, in which Harlan F. Stone, then an associate justice, alone opposed the compulsory flag salute.

Justices Hugo L. Black, William O. Douglas and Frank Murphy, who were in the majority in the Gobitis decision, written by Justice Frankfurter, switched in the new test. Justices Jackson and Wiley Rutledge were not members of the court in 1940.

Sect Wins Other Cases

Dealing with other controversies involving Jehovah's Witnesses, the Supreme Court today unanimously held invalid a Mississippi statute under which three members of the sect were convicted of sedition for disseminating teachings "tending to create an attitude of stubborn refusal to salute, honor and respect" the flag and the Federal Government.

Justice Roberts wrote this opinion, which was controlled by the West Virginia ruling. Following recent precedents, the jurists also arranged for dismissal of a case in which a Jehovah's Witness was convicted for selling literature in the District of Columbia.

In the West Virginia case Justice Jackson pointed out that children of the Jehovah's Witnesses, obeying a canon of the sect against worshiping an image, had been expelled from school and threatened with reformatory terms for refusal to salute the flag, while their parents had been prosecuted.

"Rights of the Individual"

Asserting that the refusal of the children to participate in the ceremony did not interfere with or deny the rights of others to do so, Mr. Jackson continued:

"Nor is there any question in this case that their behavior is peaceful and orderly. The sole conflict is between authority and rights of the individual.

"The State asserts power to condition access to public education on making a prescribed sign and profession and at the same time to coerce attendance by punishing both parent and child. The latter stand on a right of self-determination in matters that touched individual opinion and personal attitude."

Discussing the meaning of pledges and the flag salutes as symbols of an idea, Mr. Jackson remarked:

"A person gets from a symbol the meaning he puts into it, and what is one man's comfort and inspiration is another's jest and scorn."

More than ten years ago, Mr. Jackson recalled, Chief Justice Charles Evans Hughes "led this court in holding that the display of a red flag as a symbol of opposition to peaceful and legal means to organized government was protected by the free-speech guarantees of the Constitution."

"Here it is the State that employs a flag as a symbol of adherence to government as presently organized," he went on. "It requires the individual to communicate by word and sign his acceptance of the political ideas it thus bespeaks.

"Objection to this form of communication when coerced is an old one, well known to the framers of the Bill of Rights."

"Futility" of Compulsion

Justice Jackson also said that there was a doubt whether Abraham Lincoln "would have thought that the strength of government to maintain itself would be impressively vindicated by our confirming power of the State to expel a handful of children from school."

Dwelling upon "the ultimate futility of such attempts to compel coherence," he added:

"To believe that patriotism will not flourish if patriotic ceremonies are voluntary and spontaneous instead of a compulsory routine is to make an unflattering estimate of the appeal of our institutions to free minds.

"If there is any fixed star in our constitutional constellation, it is that no official, high or petty, can prescribe what shall be orthodox in politics, nationalism, religion, or other matter of opinion, or force citizens to confess by word or act their faith therein."

Dissent by Frankfurter

In a separate dissent, Justice Frankfurter, a Jew, said that "one who belongs to the most villified and persecuted minority in history is not likely to be insensible to the freedoms guaranteed by our Constitution."

He said that, were his "purely personal attitude relevant," he would whole-heartedly associate himself with "the general libertarian views in the Court's opinion, representing as they do the thought and action of a lifetime."

"But," he contended, "saluting the flag did not curb religious beliefs, and West Virginia had power to make the regulations without violating constitutional rights."

"It is self delusive to believe that the liberal spirit can be enforced by judicial invalidation of illiberal legislation," he stated.

Noting the existence of 250 religious denominations in the United States, he commented:

"Certainly this court cannot be called upon to determine what claims of conscience should be recognized and what should be rejected as satisfying the 'religion' which the Constitution protects.

"I cannot bring my mind to believe that the 'liberty' secured by the Due Process Clause gives this court authority to deny to the State of West Virginia the attainment of that which we all recognize as a legitimate legislative end—namely, the promotion of good citizenship, by employment of the means here chosen."

Mr. Frankfurter pointed out that the flag salute had been five times previously before the Supreme Court, and that every justice—thirteen in all—who had participated "found no constitutional infirmity in what is now condemned."

Justices Roberts and Reed said in four lines that their judgment in the Gobitis decision was still correct. Justices Black and Douglas and Justice Murphy presented special concurrences with Justice Jackson.

With three major cases still on the calendar, the court announced another decision session for next Monday.

SHUN VATICAN TIES, CHURCH GROUP ASKS

Federal Council Says Government Ought Not Give Status of 'Preference' to Catholics

Special to The New York Times.

PITTSBURGH, Nov. 29—Opposition to the establishment of diplomatic relations between the United States and the Vatican was expressed by the Federal Council of Churches of Christ in America at its biennial meeting today on the ground that such action "would confer upon one church a special preferential status in relation to the American Government" and would be "contrary to the spirit of the American tradition."

The action was unanimous and was taken on a report entitled, "Maintaining the Separation of the State and Church," previously approved by the executive committee.

The council conceded that occasions might arise when temporary contact was necessary for the sake of specific economic or political action, but on the whole "a continuing official connection between our Government and the Vatican" would compromise the American principle of separation of the church and State.

Says It Would Be Favoritism

Contending that diplomatic relations with the Vatican would be the equivalent of diplomatic relations with the Roman Catholic Church, the report cited the historic refusal of the United States to recognize one church above another, and added:

"If it is argued that it is the Vatican as a state, not as a religious institution, with which diplomatic relations are established, it must be pointed out that in practice it is impossible to separate the two. The Roman Catholic Church, according to its own conception, is a religious body and a political body at the same time."

The council emphasized that there was no intention of speaking against Roman Catholicism as a form of Christian faith. It called the Roman Catholic Church "one of the great branches of historic Christianity."

Dr. G. Bromley Oxnam, resident Methodist Bishop of the New York area, was elected president of the Council, succeeding Presiding Bishop Henry St. George Tucker of the Protestant Episcopal Church. Other officers elected were Dr. Benjamin E. Mays, a Baptist, president of Morehouse College, Atlanta, vice president and the first Negro to be elected to the post; Dr. W. Glenn Roberts, Society of Friends, Brooklyn, recording secretary, and Harper Sibley, Protestant Episcopal, Rochester, N. Y., treasurer.

Bishop Oxnam was president of De Pauw University, Greencastle, Ind., for seven years prior to his election to the episcopacy in 1936.

Sunday School Seen in Decline

A pessimistic note on the future of the Sunday school was sounded by the Rev. Philip M. Widenhouse, director of the Department of Research and Planning of the Washington, D. C., Federation of Churches. He said that a survey in Washington disclosed that at the present rate of enrollment loss, "the Sunday school will cease to be in thirty years."

Mr. Widenhouse said that while there had been a net increase of 36,000 in church membership in the District of Columbia since 1940, this represented only an 11 per cent increase compared with a population rise of 34 per cent.

A recommendation that the Department of State be urged to seek establishment of an agency on "human rights and fundamental freedoms" was approved.

John G. Ramsay of the CIO United Steel Workers addressed the meeting, saying:

"In the post-war period there must not be poverty in the midst of God-given abundance. To labor, it is logical reasoning to say, with 12,000,000 of our boys and girls who are now on the battle lines joining us on the production lines, we can produce more for peace than we have for war."

The application for membership in the Council from the American branch of the Russian Orthodox Church, with 300,000 members, was approved. The application of the Universalist Church, 50,000 members, was rejected.

November 30, 1944

Oxnam Assails Catholic 'Politics' As Aimed at Domination of State

Bishop, Federal Council's Head, Says Some in the Roman Church Even Threaten Press in Attempt at Control

Special to The New York Times.

ST. LOUIS, Oct. 28—"Some leaders" of the Roman Catholic Church in the United States were accused by the Rev. Dr. G. Bromley Oxnam, Bishop of the New York Area of the Methodist Church and president of the Federal Council of Churches of Christ in America, tonight of trying to bring about church domination of the State in this country, and of attempting to stifle religious liberty, even to the extent, he said, of threatening newspapers and radio stations with boycotts if they did not disseminate views to their liking.

Speaking at a Protestant mass meeting in observance of Reformation Sunday, Bishop Oxnam assailed what he called the "politics" of the Roman Catholic Church, causing Protestants of America to be "gravely concerned with certain practices that we believe are leading to religious strife."

He said that Protestants opposed clericalism, diplomatic representation at the Vatican, public support of sectarian schools, and what he declared was support of Franco Spain by the Roman Catholic Church.

"Protestants," said the Federal Council president, "repudiate Roman Catholic theories of church and state which lead logically to a subservient state dominated by an absolute church."

In his address Bishop Oxman said:

"Serious tension is developing between Roman Catholics and Protestants in the United States. This is regrettable and inexcusable. It is sinful. Intolerance has no place in a nation whose sons have died to free mankind from intolerant totalitarianism.

"The war of the nations must not be followed by a war of the classes. Christians who believe that a just and brotherly world depends upon the enthronement of the spiritual teachings of Jesus must be one in discovering the means to translate the ethical ideals of religion into the realities of world law and order, economic justice and racial brotherhood.

"I know Roman Catholic statesmen, jurists, industrialists, labor leaders, teachers, scientists and priests who are eager to join hands with their Protestant brothers to establish a society in which the sacredness of every personality is recognized and in which there 'hovers over all a sense of the reality of the Christ-like God, so that

worship may inspire service as service expresses brotherhood.'

"Roman Catholic and Protestant worship the same God, adore the same Christ and are inspired by the same Holy Spirit. Both know that religion is loving God and brother.

"The world desperately needs a new unifying concept. The Christian conception of brotherhood is such a concept. How can a divided church expect a world to respond to its plea for a united humanity?

"Understanding awaits plain speech. Such speech must be respectful, friendly and reveal Christian love, but it must be frank.

"Protestants are gravely concerned over what they believe to be an attempt upon the part of the Roman Catholic Church to exercise political domination here, similar to the control exercised in many nations. Protestants will fight to preserve religious liberty, not only for Protestants but for Roman Catholics and Jews and other faiths.

"The Protestant pledges himself to accept, and in humility calls upon his Roman Catholic fellow-Christian to practice, a very simple principle of religious liberty, 'Do unto others as ye would be done by.'

"Protestants have been subjected to serious misrepresentation in the Roman Catholic press. When Protestants have protested their protests have been called intolerance.

"It is not intolerance to protest against Roman Catholic activities that seek, through boycott, to threaten newspapers and therefore to control them in Roman Catholic interest. This is to endanger a free press and to destroy civil liberty.

"It is not intolerance to protest against actions of certain Roman Catholic leaders to deny Protestant ministers access to the radio by threatening station owners with the loss of consumer support of products advertised.

"It is not intolerance to insist upon the separation of church and State and therefore to object to the use of public funds for private and sectarian education.

"It is not intolerance to refuse to accept dictates that would deny Protestant churches the right to engage in missionary work in other lands at the very moment the Roman Catholic Church affirms its right to carry on missionary work in all lands.

"It is not intolerance to protest against Roman Catholic support for the fascist regime of Franco Spain when our sons die to destroy fascism everywhere and to preserve democracy for mankind.

"It is not intolerance to point out that Protestantism will oppose the clericalism that has cursed other lands.

"It is not intolerance to insist that a church must be a church, that it cannot be both church and State. Protestants, therefore, oppose the establishment of diplomatic relations with the Vatican. This is no lack of respect for the distinguished, devoted, brilliant and brotherly Christian who is the present Pope.

"It is not intolerance to point out the Roman Catholic position on religious liberty that in effect means a demand for religious liberty when the Roman Catholic is in the minority but denies it in practice where the Roman Catholic is in the majority."

October 29, 1945

SPELLMAN SEES ATTACK ON CHURCH

HE CALLS IT UN-CHRISTIAN

Archbishop Welcomes 4,000 Boy Scouts at St. Patrick's— Hails Their Godliness

Archbishop Francis J. Spellman told 4,000 Boy Scouts at solemn vespers yesterday in St. Patrick's Cathedral that the 1,600 Protestant clergymen who took a stand against any religious sect taking a part in world politics had done a "disservice to their country" and he urged the boys to "respect others and never lower yourselves to attack the beliefs of others."

The Archbishop referred to a message addressed to President Roosevelt, Prime Minister Churchill and Premier Stalin and signed by 1,600 religious leaders. The statement, which was published Saturday, declared the Vatican and any Protestant or Jewish religious establishment should "have no place at the council tables of state."

Sees Golden Rule Violated

Declaring that the signers of the statement "violated the Golden Rule," the Archbishop said:

"It is difficult to believe that there are '1,600 ordained ministers and religious leaders' in our country who would put their names to a document offering insult to 25,000,000 fellow-Americans who are at least doing their share to win the war and serve their country and whose religion teaches them to love their neighbor.

"It is impossible for us to believe that 1,600 Americans 'manifesting their allegiance to the spirit of the Nazarene' should act in contradiction to His teachings unless there had been imposition on their good faith."

Archbishop Spellman, who presided at Vespers, welcomed the Boy Scouts to the cathedral for the eleventh annual celebration of Catholic Boy Scout Sunday, which was observed in conjunction with the thirty-fifth anniversary of the founding of Scouting in the United States. Mgr. Edward Robert Moore, director of the National Catholic Committee on Scouting, celebrated the benediction.

Hails Scouts' Patriotism

The Archbishop hailed the Boy Scouts for their "love of God and love of country" and declared that the "program of the Scouts is one of the first stones on which the future of the country can be secured and insured."

The Rev. Thomas J. McNulty, area Scout chaplain for Manhattan, told the boys that future world leaders would come from their ranks, and he advised them to "let no fears keep you from staying physically strong, mentally awake and morally straight."

Archbishop Spellman awarded "Ad Altare Dei" crosses, nationally known award for Catholic Scouts, to fifty boys. Included among the delegates were refugee Boy Scouts from France and a delegation from twelve Latin-American nations.

Preceding the service the Scouts marched from the Twelfth Regiment Armory, Sixty-second Street and Columbus Avenue, to the cathedral.

February 12, 1945

TAYLOR'S JOB PEACE ONLY, SAYS TRUMAN

When His Helping to Put World Back on Feet Is Done Vatican Post Will End, He Asserts

Special to THE YORK NEW TIMES.

WASHINGTON, June 14—President Truman announced his intention today to terminate the post of Personal Representative of the President to the Pope, but said that Myron C. Taylor, presently accredited to the Vatican, would remain on the job until completion of his mission, which he defined as aiding in re-establishing the peace of the world.

The President denied to his news conference ever having consented to the "recall" of Mr. Taylor during a recent White House conference on the subject with Protestant churchmen, or fixing a termination date for his mission.

He explained that he had sent Mr. Taylor to Rome to help in making the peace, just as President Roosevelt had sent him to aid in keeping the peace, and that when his current mission was completed there would be no official representative there. Although the President showed no disposition to discuss the recent protest of the Protestant churchmen over the present arrangement or the sharp rejoinder it brought from Cardinal Spellman, he indicated to his press conference and again later today that he would overlook no opportunity to hasten the signing of the peace treaties and the restoration of order in the world.

In an impromptu talk to a small group on the White House lawn after bestowing the Congressional Medal of Honor on five war heroes, the President said:

"The war is only half won. We haven't won it until we have won a peace which makes the individual safe in his liberties the world over.

"We are going to win the peace, and the reason we are going to win that peace is because the vast majority of our young men and women are made of the same material as these young men on whom I have pinned these medals."

Mr. Truman told his press conference that he had no idea how long the completion of Mr. Taylor's mission would require, but said he would remain until it was completed.

The President had been asked whether he had in mind the completion of the Italian peace treaty in speaking of Mr. Taylor's efforts to help make the peace. In reply, Mr. Truman shook his head, saying he had in mind the peace of the world.

June 15, 1946

RELIGION IN SCHOOLS UPHELD IN ILLINOIS

SPRINGFIELD, Ill., Jan. 22 (AP) —The Illinois Supreme Court ruled today that religious education in public schools does not violate the United States or Illinois Constitutions if the classes are "purely voluntary."

The court upheld a lower court decision dismissing the suit of Mrs. Vashti McCullum, who had sought to halt voluntary teaching of religion in Champaign, Ill., public schools.

In Champaign, Mrs. McCullum, wife of a University of Illinois professor, said she planned to appeal the decision to the United States Supreme Court.

Daughter of a Rochester, N. Y., freethinker, Arthur G. Cromwell, she has described herself as an atheist and termed religion "a chronic disease of the imagination contracted in childhood." She also contended that the classes were "a mercenary business venture," and "an encroachment upon the constitutional and statutory provisions of the State and nation." Her 10-year-old son was embarrassed because he was the only one in his room not attending the classes, she said.

January 23, 1947

HIGH COURT BACKS STATE RIGHT TO RUN PAROCHIAL BUSES

By LEWIS WOOD
Special to THE NEW YORK TIMES.

WASHINGTON, Feb. 10—In a decision of far-flung interest the Supreme Court by 5 to 4 ruled today that New Jersey public school funds raised by taxation can be used to pay for transportation of children to Catholic parochial schools.

The controversy which the tribunal settled by this narrow margin revolved around the interpretation of the first amendment to the Constitution which forbids Congress to pass a law "respecting an establishment of religion, or prohibiting the free exercise thereof."

For the majority, Justice Hugo L. Black held that a New Jersey law permitting the payments amounts to religious or public benefit legislation and that no person may be barred from these benefits because of his religion. Justice Black was joined by Chief Justice Fred M. Vinson and Justices Stanley F. Reed, William O. Douglas and Frank Murphy.

Every Form of Aid Opposed

The minority view expressed by Justice Wiley Rutledge, held that the First Amendment's purpose was to separate religious activity and civil authority by forbidding "every form" of public aid or support for religion. The dissent was shared by Justices Felix Frankfurter, Robert H. Jackson and Harold H. Burton.

In an independent objection, Justice Jackson, supported by Mr Frankfurter, charged the majority with "giving the clock's hands a backward turn," because the prohibition against establishment of religion cannot be circumvented by a "subsidy, bonus or reimbursement."

The case, which required three opinions totaling seventy - three pages to dispose of, arose through a protest by Arch R. Everson, a taxpayer of Ewing Township, near Trenton in Mercer County. He contested the right of the township Board of Education to reimburse parents of Catholic children for transportation to the parochial schools on regular buses. A State court supported his protest, but was reversed by the New Jersey Court of Errors and Appeals, which was upheld by the Supreme Court today.

The Board of Education had authorized payment of $8,034 to be paid to parents of children for transportation to school, and of this $357.74 was reimbursed to the parents of the Catholic boys and girls.

Typical expressions from the three documents presented in the Supreme Court follow:

Majority, by Justice Black: "New Jersey cannot exclude Catholics, Lutherans, Mohammedans, Baptists, Jews, Methodists, non-believers, Presbyterians, or the members of any other faith, because of their faith or lack of it. We must be careful, in protecting the citizens of New Jersey against State-established churches, to be sure that we do not inadvertently prohibit New Jersey from extending its general State law benefits to all its citizens without regard to their religious belief.

"We cannot say that the First Amendment prohibits New Jersey from spending tax-raised funds to pay the bus fares of parochial schools as a part of a general program under which it pays the fares of pupils attending public and other schools. The First Amendment has erected a wall between church and State. That wall must be kept high and impregnable. We could not approve the slightest breach. New Jersey has not breached it here."

Burden of Taxes Cited

Minority, by Justice Rutledge: "No one conscious of religious values can be unsympathetic toward the burden which our constitutional separation puts on parents who desire religious instruction mixed with secular for their children. But if those feelings should prevail, there would be an end to our historic constitutional policy and command. No more unjust or discriminatory is it in fact to deny attendants at religious schools the cost of their transportation than it is to deny them tuitions, sustenance for their teachers, or any other educational expense which others receive at public cost.

"Two great drives are constantly in motion to abridge, in the name of education, the complete division of religion and civil authority which our forefathers made. One is to introduce religious education and observances into the public schools. The other, to obtain public funds for the aid and support of various private religious schools. In my opinion both avenues were closed by the Constitution. Neither should be opened by this court."

Independent dissent by Justice Jackson, with Justice Frankfurter: "Catholic education is the rock on which thee whole structure rests, and to render tax aid to its church school is indistinguishable to me from rendering the same aid to the church itself. The State cannot maintain a church and it can no more tax its citizens to furnish free carriage to those who attend a church. The prohibition against establishment of religion cannot be circumvented by a subsidy, bonus or reimbursement of expense to individuals for receiving religious instruction and indoctrination.

"It (the church) does not leave the individual to pick up religion by chance. It relies on early and indelible indoctrination in the faith and order of the church by the word and example of persons consecrated to the task. The effect of the religious freedom amendment to our Constitution was to take every form of propagation of religion out of the realm of things which could be directly or indirectly be made public business and thereby be supported in whole or in part at taxpayers' expense."

In deciding this case, Justice Black dealt with two main attacks against the New Jersey practice. These were: 1. That the State law and Board of Education resolution take by taxation the private property of some persons and bestow it upon others for private use, thus violating the due process clause of the Fourteenth Amendment. 2. That the law and resolution force persons to pay taxes to help support Catholic schools, thus violating the First Amendment.

Right Pass Beneficial Law

As to the first contention, the majority spokesman held that New Jersey must not be precluded from passing a law for the public benefit, and:

"The fact that a State law, passed to satisfy a public need, coincides with the personal desires of the individuals most directly affected is certainly an inadequate reason for us to say that a legislature has erroneously appraised the public need."

Justice Rutledge, in his forty-seven-page dissent, described in detail the fight by Madison to separate church and state. New Jersey's action, he said, "exactly fits the type of exaction and the kind of evil at which Madison and Jefferson struck." Under the test they framed, "it cannot be said that the cost of transportation is no part of the cost of education or the religious instruction given."

The dissenting justice said an appropriation from the public treasury to pay the cost of transportation to Sunday school, or weekday classes at the church or parish house or to meetings of young people's religious societies such as the Y. M. C. A., Y. W. C. A., Y. M. H. A. or Epworth League "could not withstand the constitutional attack" brought against the New Jersey bus payments.

In his lengthy objection, Justice Rutledge also stated:

"The realm of religious training and belief remains as the amendment made it, the kingdom of the individual man and his God."

Justice Jackson in his separate opinion said he originally wished to join the majority. He said he had a sympathy "though not ideological" with Catholics who had to pay taxes for public schools and also felt it necessary to support schools for their own children. But, saying he had been forced to change his mind, he criticized the majority ruling.

"The undertones (of the majority) opinion," he added, "advocating complete and uncompromising separation of church from state seem utterly discordant with its conclusion yielding support to their comingling in education matters."

The Ewing Township Board of Education resolution authorized transportation of pupils from Ewing to "the Trenton and Pennington high schools and Catholic schools by way of public carrier." The Catholic schools were St. Mary's Cathedral high school, Trenton Catholic Boys high school, St. Hedwig's parochial school and St. Francis school.

February 11, 1947

NEW BODY DEMANDS CHURCH SEPARATION

Special to THE NEW YORK TIMES.

WASHINGTON, Jan. 11 — A new organization, Protestant in name and inviting the support of the Protestant churches and other religious and non-religious bodies, proclaimed its appearance on the national scene today with a manifesto urging reaffirmation of the American principle of separation of church and state.

Calling itself the Protestants and Other Americans for the Separation of Church and State, the group declared that the Roman Catholic Church was seeking to "fracture the constitutional principle at one point after another" in a long-range campaign to "secure total support for its extensive system of parochial schools from the public treasury."

It alleged further that the Roman Catholic Church had made "ominous progress in its strategy of winning for itself a position of special privilege in relation to the state" through establishment of what it called an "ambassadorship" to the Pope.

Contending that religious freedom in the United States sprang from the separation of church and state, Protestants and Others United demanded in its manifesto that free transportation, lunches, textbooks and other aids to sectarian education be abrogated and that the Presidential representation at the Vatican be discontinued.

Says Legislatures Yield

The Protestant group said "a powerful church" flourished under the religious liberty provided by our form of government but was "committed to a policy plainly subversive of religious liberty as guaranteed by the Constitution."

"Already, the Legislatures of certain states, yielding to the political pressure of this church, have enacted legislation empowering local school boards to grant these special privileges," the manifesto said. "The Federal Supreme Court in two decisions has confirmed state legislation which sanctions the use of public school funds to provide free textbooks for parochial schools (1930), and to transport pupils to such schools (1947).

"On a bolder and more ambitious scale, this same church now demands aid for its schools from the Federal Government. A proposed Federal grant of several hundred million dollars annually in aid of public education, especially in those states whose economic resources are insufficient to provide adequate education for their children, has been before Congress for many years.

"Action on this proposal has been held up by the pressure of this church which demands that its parochial schools shall share with the public schools in any such Federal appropriation in an amount proportional to the number of pupils in each school system.

"Thus far, Congress has withstood this demand. But two bills have been introduced in that body, one of which completely yields to the church's maximum demand, while the other provides that the funds may be distributed by each state in accordance with its own statutes.

"The latter, the so-called Taft bill (S. 472), is a disguised evasion of the issue. It plays directly into the policy of the church which has already secured legislation in eighteen states permitting financial aid to parochial schools in one form or another, and in effect invites the states to violate the mandate of the First Amendment. The effect of its passage by Congress would encourage and facilitate the church's campaign in these states to widen the initial legislation already enacted in its favor, and to secure similar and even more advanced legislation in all other states.

"Protestants and Other Americans United respectfully demands that Congress shall not by such an evasion abdicate its responsibility to defend the Constitution, regardless of political pressure on the part of any sectarian interests which would thus subvert it."

While its immediate objectives, for the execution of which it hopes to raise $100,000, are directed at the Catholic Church, the new organization professed not to be anti-Catholic in a religious sense. It asserted that its opposition to the tactics of this church was confined to the political arena.

Those signing the manifesto, are all well known in Protestant affairs but the document made it plain that Jews and Roman Catholics also were invited to join in the interest of maintaining freedom of religion.

The signers were: Dr. John A. Mackay, president of Princeton Theological Seminary; Dr. Edwin McNeill Poteat, president of Colgate-Rochester Divinity School; the Rev. G. Bromley Oxnam, Bishop of the Methodist Church, New York area; Dr. Louie D. Newton, president of the Southern Baptist Convention, and Dr. Charles Clayton Morrison, former editor of The Christian Century.

Dr. Poteat is to serve as president of the organization, which will establish national headquarters in Washington.

The following program of immediate objectives was set forth:

"1. To enlighten and mobilize public opinion in support of religious liberty as this monumental principle of democracy has been embodied and implemented in the Constitution by the separation of church and state.

"2. To resist every attempt by law or the administration of law further to widen the breach in the wall of separation of church and state.

"3. To demand the immediate discontinuance of the ambassadorship to the Papal head of the Roman Catholic Church.

"4. To work for the repeal of any law now on the statute books of any state which sanctions the granting of aid to church schools from the public school treasury.

"5. To invoke the aid of the courts in maintaining the integrity of the constitution with respect to the separation of church and state, wherever and in whatever form the issue arises, and, specifically; to strive by appropriate constitutional means to secure a reconsideration of the two decisions of the Supreme Court upholding the use of tax funds (a) for providing the pupils of parochial schools with free text books, and (b) for the transportation of pupils to parochial schools.

"6. To call out and unite all patriotic citizens in a concerted effort to prevent the passage of any law by Congress which allots to church schools any portion of a Federal appropriation for education, or which explicitly or implicitly permits the states to make such allotment of Federal funds. This purpose in no wise prejudices pro or con the propriety of a Federal grant in aid of public education.

"7. To give all possible aid to the citizens of any community or state who are seeking to protect their public schools from sectarian domination, or resisting any other assault upon the principle of separation of church and state.

"8. In seeking these objectives we are determined to pursue a course that cannot be justly characterized as anti-Catholic, or as motivated by anti-Catholic animus. As Protestants, we can be called anti-Catholic only in the sense in which every Roman Catholic is anti-Protestant. Profound differences separate us in the area of religious faith, but these differences have no relevancy in the pursuit of our objectives as clearly defined in this manifesto. The issue of separation of church and state has arisen in the political area and we propose to meet it there."

Besides Dr. Poteat as president, Drs. Morrison, Mackay and Oxnam will be vice-presidents; E. H. De Groot Jr. formerly connected with the Interstate Commerce Commission, will be treasurer, and Dr. J. M. Dawson recording secretary. Dr. Dawson is executive secretary of the United States Office of Baptist Public Relations.

The executive committee will be made up of these officers and the following persons: E. E. Rogers, associate editor of the Scottish Rite Bulletin; Miss Charl Williams of the National Education Association; Dr. Newton, Dr. Frank H. Yost, an editor of the Religious Liberty Association Publications; Dr. Clyde L. Taylor, secretary of the National Association of Evangelicals, and two others. This committee will be elected annually by an advisory board of 100 members from the various parts of the country.

January 12, 1948

RELIGIOUS TEACHING IN SCHOOLS BARRED BY SUPREME COURT

8-1 Decision in Champaign, Ill., Case Holds Such Use of Public Buildings Unconstitutional

CHURCH AND STATE APART

Atheist's Successful Protest May Bring Fight Here on the Released-Time Program

By JAY WALZ
Special to THE NEW YORK TIMES.

WASHINGTON, March 8—The Supreme Court declared today that religious instruction in public school buildings was unconstitutional.

An 8-to-1 decision upheld the complaint of a mother in Champaign, Ill., an avowed atheist, who said that her son had been "embarrassed" by being the only child in his room not attending religious classes under a local plan.

The majority rejected the Champaign program because it involved use of public school buildings for classes taught once a week on school time. Justice Hugo L. Black stated for the court that the use of tax-supported property for dissemination of religious doctrines violated the Constitutional concept of separation of church and state.

Justice Stanley F. Reed, in dissent, said the decision threw into doubt all forms of religious instruction connected in any way with school systems.

Pupils Released Early Here

Such classes are now attended by thousands of pupils under programs set up in scores of communities throughout the country, including New York City, where children may be excused during specified school hours for religious classes held elsewhere.

Justice Robert H. Jackson, while joining the majority, said he believed it went too far and argued that the decision would open the gates to a flood of litigation by groups that did not like local practices.

Under the Champaign plan, set up in 1940, the school board cooperated with the local Council on Religious Education by offering the needed facilities. The Council provided outside teachers representing the Protestant, Roman Catholic and Jewish faiths. Pupils, with the consent of their parents, could attend classes taught by an instructor of their group.

School authorities insisted that the arrangement, involving no financial outlay by the taxpayers, was well within the specifications of the Bill of Rights since it was open to all sects on a basis of equality, and pupils were free to attend, or not attend, the classes.

However, Mrs. Vashti McCollum, wife of a University of Illinois professor, objected on the ground the plan discriminated against her oldest son, James Terry, then 10.

Mrs. McCollum said she was an atheist and did not wish her child to receive religious instruction. When he did not attend the classes, she contended, the boy was made conspicuous and subjected to ridicule by other pupils. Once, when it turned out he was the only pupil in his room not taking the course, he was asked to sit out in a corridor alone.

State Courts Denied Protest

The mother asked Illinois courts to stop the whole project as violating the historic concept of separation of church and state. The state courts ruled that no constitutional or statutory rights were violated by the Champaign system.

The Supreme Court today overruled these findings and sent the case back to the Illinois Supreme Court for "proceedings not inconsistent" with the high tribunal's opinion.

Justice Black said the Champaign practice was "beyond all question" using tax-established and tax-supported schools "to aid religious groups to spread their faith," and, he added, "it falls squarely under the ban of the First Amendment."

Justice Black denied that the court's view showed "a governmental hostility to religion or religious teachings," as attorneys for the school board had argued

"The First Amendment rests upon the premise that both religion and government can best work to achieve their lofty aims if each is left free from the other within its respective sphere," said Mr. Black.

The majority also charged that the Champaign system helped sectarian groups by providing pupils for their religious classes through use of "the state's compulsory public school machinery." "This," it stated, "is not separation of church and state."

Frankfurter Quotes Jefferson

Justice Felix Frankfurter, in a separate opinion siding with the majority, wrote that Thomas Jefferson in describing the church-state relationship spoke of a "wall of separation." This did not mean, the Justice added, "a fine line easily overstepped."

"In no activity of the state is it more vital to keep out divisive forces than in its schools, to avoid confusing, not to say fusing, what the Constitution sought to keep strictly apart," wrote Justice Frankfurter.

He pointedly noted, however, that the court in this decision was not ruling generally on all programs involving "released time" for religious instruction. He implied that some systems might not withstand "the test" of the Constitution, while others would.

Justice Reed's dissent noted that both the United States Military and Naval Academies had, since their beginnings, maintained "and enforced a pattern of participation in formal worship."

"When actual church services have always been permitted on Government property, the mere use of the school buildings by a non-sectarian group for religious education ought not to be condemned as an establishment of religion," Justice Reed stated.

"Devotion to the great principle of religious liberty should not lead us into a rigid interpretation of the constitutional guarantee that conflicts with accepted habits of our people," he continued.

Justice Jackson, writing that he was joining the majority "with reservations," argued that the decision against religious teaching in the schools would even make difficult the teaching of the liberal arts.

"Music without sacred music, architecture minus the cathedral, or paintings without the scriptural themes would be eccentric and incomplete," he wrote.

March 9, 1948

CATHOLIC BISHOPS HIT SUPREME COURT

Special to The New York Times.

WASHINGTON, Nov. 20 — The Roman Catholic Bishops of the United States, concluding their annual meeting here, issued a statement today on "The Christian in Action," aimed against secularism and singling out as a special target the Supreme Court decision in the McCollum case.

Urging religion in the home, in education, in economic life, and in citizenship, the statement was an even stronger declaration of policy than this same body issued last year. It declared that secularism was "the most deadly menace to our Christian and American way of living."

The McCollum case, in which the Supreme Court declared religious instruction in the public schools unconstitutional, was taken up by the Bishops as part of their discussion of "Religion and Citizenship." Impartial encouragement of religious influence on citizens was considered by the founders of this nation as "a proper and practical function of good government," the statement said.

"The American tradition clearly envisioned the school as the meeting place of these helpful interacting influences," the Catholic Bishops declared.

Terming the phrase "a wall of separation between Church and State" as merely a metaphor used by Thomas Jefferson to emphasize free choice in religion, the Bishops declared, "It would be an utter distortion of American history and law to make that practical policy involve the indifference to religion and the exclusion of cooperation between religion and government implied in the term 'separation of Church and State' as it has become the shibboleth of doctrinaire secularism."

The intent of the enactors of the First Amendment, the statement declared on the basis of an historical review, was "no official church for the country as a whole, no preferment of one religion over another by the Federal Government—and at the same time no interference by the Federal Government in the Church-State relations of the individual states."

In the McCollum case, which banned religious instruction in the schools as a violation of the First Amendment, an atheist mother complained that her son was made the object of ridicule as the only pupil in his room not taking religious instruction.

Said the Catholic Bishops: "If this secular influence is to prevail in our Government and its institutions, such a result should in candor be achieved by legislation adopted after full popular discussion, and not by the judicial procedure of an ideological interpretation of our Constitution.

"We therefore hope and pray that the novel interpretation of the First Amendment recently adopted by the Supreme Court will in due process be revised."

Organized effort to make the home more truly Christian was urged in the statement, with the suggestion that families follow the programs mapped out by the Catholic Family Life Bureau.

Regarding education, the statement said, "If we as Christians are to do our part in restoring order to a chaotic world, Christ must be the Master in our classrooms and lecture halls and the Director of our research projects."

As to economic life, the Catholic Bishops strongly urged setting up a system of "industry councils" consisting of responsible leaders of both capital and labor to work "in cooperation for the common good."

However, the prime appeal was made to the individual Christian to combat secularism "in every phase of life where individual attitudes are a determining factor," for "as man is, so ultimately are all the institutions of human society."

November 21, 1948

EDUCATION IN REVIEW

NEA Reports 73% of Nation's Public Schools Have No Religious-Education Programs

By MURRAY ILLSON

Nearly three-fourths of the public school systems in the United States did not have any program of religious education during the 1948-49 school year, according to a nation-wide survey by the research division of the National Education Association, released last week.

Questionnaires were sent to 5,100 superintendents of schools in the forty-eight states, the District of Columbia and Alaska. The poll covered 3,300 cities of more than 2,500 population; 1,500 small towns and villages, and 300 counties where an urban community formed the center of the county system.

Replies were received from 2,639 school systems, broken down as follows:

	Number	Per cent of total
Communities which have not had a religious-education program of any kind	1,621	61
Communities which have had one or more types of programs but have given them up	310	12
Sub total	1,931	73
Communities in which some type of religious instruction was given	708	27
Total	2,639	100

Public school systems in forty-three states reported there were various types of religious education available in conjunction with "released time" programs. "Released time" is a plan by which public schools allow their pupils a certain amount of time to attend religious-instruction classes.

States Without Programs

No religious-education program was reported in four states—Maryland, Nevada, New Hampshire and Wyoming—and in the District of Columbia and Alaska.

States having the highest proportion of cities with religious-education programs were Utah, New York, Minnesota, North Carolina, Rhode Island and Oregon.

The NEA study showed that of the cities responding to the questionnaire, 46 per cent of those with populations of more than 100,000 had religious-education programs in operation. As the city size decreased, the percentage of those with programs decreased progressively —only 17 per cent of the communities under 2,500 population had religious-education programs.

Of the 708 communities that reported public school cooperation in providing religious instruction, 15 per cent permitted the use of classrooms for such instruction during school hours. Most of the remainder, according to the NEA study, have "avoided the actual operation of religious-education classes but have made concessions by permitting the use of school buildings after hours or by releasing pupils from full attendance during the regular school hours."

The NEA report estimated that of a total of 5,000,000 pupils in the 708 school systems which had cooperated in religious instruction, only 700,000 actually took part in the programs.

Attitudes of Communities

The NEA asked the 2,639 school superintendents to interpret their communities' attitudes toward religious instruction in the public schools. To this,

59 per cent reported that their communities felt that no formal plan of religious education was necessary to supplement the present school curriculum; 23 per cent thought that the public schools should provide some type of religious instruction, and 18 per cent did not reply.

Broken down by categories, the answers to this question were as follows:

	Thought them unnecessary	Thought they were needed	Did not reply
Communities that never had religious-instruction classes	77%	12%	11%
Communities that had discontinued such classes	42	36	22
Communities that are now giving such instruction	27	41	32

As to the attitude of teachers in the 708 school systems which had religious instruction available, 82 per cent of the superintendents who replied to this question said their teaching staffs were favorably disposed toward the programs.

Of the 310 school systems that reported they had given up their religious-education programs, 52 per cent gave as their reason the United States Supreme Court decision in the McCollum case. Early last year the court ruled that the "released time" program in effect in the Champaign (Ill.) public schools was unconstitutional. Under that program religious instruction was given in public school buildings to pupils when parents requested it.

Other reasons given for dropping the religious-education programs were the shortage of good teachers, 13 per cent; general lack of interest, 11 per cent, and too few pupils enrolled, 8 per cent. Reasons mentioned less frequently included conflicts with school schedules, ineffectiveness of the program, disagreement among religious groups, public opposition, disciplinary problems and inadequate financial support.

August 14, 1949

President and Evangelist Pray in the White House

By The Associated Press.

WASHINGTON, July 14—President Truman and the evangelist, Billy Graham of North Carolina, stood today in the President's office and prayed for divine guidance for the nation and its Chief Executive.

The young evangelist told reporters about it after a half-hour's visit at the White House. He said he had proposed that Mr. Truman call a nation-wide day of prayer and humiliation.

The President, the evangelist said, is giving "serious thought" to going on the radio to reassure the country and to a call on church leaders to arrange a national day of repentence and prayer.

The evangelist and three of his associates, he said, stood in Mr. Truman's office and, at Mr. Graham's suggestion, prayed.

"I prayed aloud, and the President stood with his head bowed. I just prayed to the Lord, and asked God to give him wisdom."

July 15, 1950

GEN. CLARK NAMED FIRST AMBASSADOR OF U.S. TO VATICAN

Action Arouses Protestants— Recess Appointment Likely —Congressmen Silent

By WALTER H. WAGGONER

Special to THE NEW YORK TIMES.

WASHINGTON, Oct. 20—President Truman nominated today Gen. Mark W. Clark, Chief of the Army Field Forces and an Episcopalian, to be the first United States Ambassador to Vatican City. The United States thereby resumed formal diplomatic relations with the Papacy, which had been broken off in 1868.

The President's action, the White House said, was based on his belief that both the broad national interest and "the purposes of diplomacy and humanitarianism" would be served by the appointment and that a return to direct diplomatic contact with the Vatican "would assist in coordinating the effort to combat the Communist menace."

By taking this step, long under consideration but unexpected at this time, Mr. Truman has introduced a highly controversial issue into the domestic political scene. The argument is likely to be waged along both religious and regional lines, and expectations

that Protestant groups and congregations would take violent exception to formal diplomatic recognition of the fountainhead of Roman Catholicism were being promptly fulfilled this afternoon.

Hearing Planned in 1952

The President probably will send General Clark to the Vatican under a recess appointment, with the Senate taking up the nomination when the second session of Congress convenes in January. Senator Tom Connally, the Texas Democrat who heads the Senate Foreign Relations Committee, said that "undoubtedly there will be hearings" when the legislators return.

The sending of an Ambassador to a country that has not previously had one and, in effect, recognizing that country's government diplomatically, is a prerogative of the Executive office, a Government official said. No action is required by Congress except the confirmation of the Ambassador, he added.

A statement by Joseph Short, the President's press secretary, recalled the service of Myron C.

Taylor as personal representative of President Franklin D. Roosevelt and President Truman to Pope Pius XII and observed that the Taylor mission continued to perform, during and after the last war, "an extremely useful service not only in the field of diplomacy but in the amelioration of human suffering."

Mr. Taylor resigned in January, 1950, for "personal considerations of a compelling nature." Although the President praised Mr. Taylor's work highly, finding that it made "a fundamental contribution to the unity of moral conviction," there was speculation then that the post might never be filled again.

Formal Ties Apparently Favored

That speculation was strengthened when Mr. Truman recalled Mr. Taylor's assistant, Franklin C. Gowan, a career diplomat, two days after his superior's resignation had been accepted.

At that time the President said that the question of whether the United States would maintain its relationship with Vatican City was then under study at the State Department. More than a year and a half later the State Department and the White House had apparently agreed that formal, rather than personal, diplomatic relations were desirable.

The United States established consular representation in the Papal State in 1797, and that form of contact continued until the end of the Pope's temporal power in 1870.

President James Polk recommended in his annual message of Dec. 7, 1847, that formal diplomatic relations be established with the Papacy, and on April 7, 1848, Jacob L. Martin became this country's first charge d'affaires, responsible under President Polk's instructions, however, only for relations "of a commercial character."

Lewis Cass Jr. succeeded Mr. Martin as charge d'affaires and then, on June 29, 1854, became the first Minister Resident in Rome. The last Minister Resident was Rufus King, who resigned on Jan. 1, 1868, after Congress cut off all funds for representation to the Vatican.

Papal consuls remained in this country, however, until 1873, thirty years after the first consul general from the Papal State had arrived and received recognition. There has been no Papal representative with diplomatic status here since 1873, but the Holy See has been represented in Washington for many years by an Apostolic Delegate, who is charged with carrying out religious and ecclesiastical duties between the Holy See and the Roman Catholic Church in this country.

President Roosevelt made a pioneering step toward a return of diplomatic relations with the Vatican when he proposed in a Christmas message to Pope Pius XII on Dec. 23, 1939, that a personal representative of the President with the rank of Ambassador be sent to Vatican City "in order that our parallel endeavors for peace and the alleviation of suffering may be assisted."

The Pope promptly accepted the proposal in a note of Jan. 7, 1940. On Feb. 4, Mr. Taylor was appointed.

On May 3, 1946, President Truman called upon Mr. Taylor to undertake a similar mission for him.

The White House statement accompanying the nomination of General Clark placed the action again on a basis of humanitarianism, but a major consideration this time was the position and strength of Roman Catholicism in the resistance of the West to communism.

"It is well known that the Vatican is vigorously engaged in the struggle against communism," the statement said. "Direct diplomatic relations will assist in coordinating the effort to combat the Communist menace."

37 Other Nations Cited

The White House noted that thirty-seven other nations have "for a great many years" maintained diplomatic representatives at the Vatican. If diplomatic relations with the Papal State are established by the United States, it is assumed that the Pope would respond with a Papal Nuncio, the Vatican's equivalent of an Ambassador.

The range and pitch of the outcries from the ranks of the Protestants promised that Mr. Truman's action today might weigh heavily in the forthcoming political campaigns and the 1952 election.

Some veteran political observers said they could not recall such an outburst of bitterness and indignation since the peak of the campaign for the 1928 election, when the late Al Smith, a Roman Catholic, was the Democratic Presidential candidate.

The Senators who have spoken out so far, on the other hand, have favored the President's action. Senator Pat McCarran, Democrat of Nevada and a Roman Catholic, remarked that the President "is to be complimented" for the appointment.

Senator H. Alexander Smith, Republican of New Jersey and a Protestant, contributed some bipartisan praise, expressing his gratification for a "direct contact between the Vatican and the President in connection with pending international problems, especially the creeping menace of communism throughout the world."

VATICAN IS PLEASED

Much Satisfaction Expressed at Choice of Clark

Special to The New York Times.

ROME, Oct. 20—The news that President Truman had nominated Gen. Mark W. Clark as first United States Ambassador to the Holy See was received in Vatican circles this evening with deep satisfaction.

Nevertheless all official comment was withheld for the present.

The Presidential decision put an end to a situation that had caused great regret in the Vatican. High Vatican officials on many occasions have expressed their chagrin over the fact that the United States—the world's greatest nation—should have failed to maintain diplomatic relations with the center of Catholicism.

Vatican circles said they were particularly pleased that Mr. Truman had not nominated a personal representative as did President Roosevelt in 1940, when he sent Myron C. Taylor to Rome, and that his choice had fallen on so distinguished a personality as General Clark.

Among the powers that have representatives accredited to the Vatican are such Protestant countries as Britain and such Moslem states as Egypt and India.

There is no doubt in Vatican circles that General Clark's appointment will unleash strong criticism on the part of the Communists, not only on account of the appointment per se, but also because he is a

general. On the other hand, it is pointed out that the Communists had high regard for General Clark when he, as commander in chief of all Allied forces in Italy, was also commander of the Italian partisans, among whom the Communists figured prominently.

It is thought in Rome political circles that General Clark will be able to do some valuable work for the West in his capacity as Ambassador to the Holy See.

Spellman Praises Choice

Cardinal Spellman, head of the Roman Catholic Archdiocese of New York, praised President Truman's nomination of General Clark.

The Cardinal's statement follows:

"I am pleased at the action of President Truman in appointing an Ambassador to the Holy See. Certainly the United States and the Holy See have identical objectives of peace and it is most logical therefore that there should be a practical exchange of viewpoints in the search for this peace so devoutly desired by all peoples and especially 'little peoples.'

"I am also very pleased that President Truman has appointed to this post a distinguished, able and patriotic American as is Gen. Mark Wayne Clark whose contributions to our country both as a military and civic leader have been outstanding."

The Most Rev. Richard J. Cushing, Archbishop of Boston, termed the appointment "a joyful announcement," The Associated Press reported.

The prelate declared that it "means recognition of the Vatican State as one of the greatest international forces for the defeat of communism on a world-wide basis," adding: "if America is to assume a position of world leadership in the battle against communism, as she must, it is well that she be represented at the Vatican."

October 21, 1951

CLARK WITHDRAWS AS VATICAN CHOICE; ANOTHER PLANNED

Truman, at General's Request, Will Not Resubmit His Name for Envoy to the Holy See

CONTROVERSY IS BLAMED

Special to The New York Times.

WASHINGTON, Jan. 13—The White House announced tonight that Gen. Mark W. Clark had asked to be withdrawn from consideration as United States Ambassador to the Vatican, and, accordingly, President Truman was not resubmitting the general's name to the Senate.

However, the White House also stated that the President intended to submit another nomination for the post later. Thus, the controversy over the President's plans, first announced last October, to resume diplomatic relations with the Vatican after an eighty-four-year break was not resolved by General Clark's withdrawal.

The announcement was contained in a terse statement given out shortly after 7 o'clock tonight by Joseph Short, White House press secretary. Some correspondents received the information by telephone from Mr. Short.

Statement of White House

"The nomination of Gen. Mark W. Clark to be Ambassador to the State of Vatican City will not be resubmitted to the Senate," Mr. Short's statement said.

"This course is being followed at the request of General Clark.

"The President plans to submit another nomination at a later time."

[General Clark said through an aide at Fort Monroe, Va., that "the statement from the White House just about covers it," The Associated Press reported. "The controversy that has developed has impelled me to ask the White House to withdraw my name," the general added.]

The Clark nomination was sent to the Senate last Oct. 20, a few hours before Congress adjourned its session. It was not acted on, but became almost immediately a subject of controversy, and the debate appeared not to have died down during the Congressional recess.

Only yesterday, Senator Tom Connally, Democrat of Texas, who is chairman of the Foreign Relations Committee, which would consider the nomination, disclosed that his opposition to the appointment had broadened.

While previously the Senator had been against the naming of General Clark to the post, he de-

clared he was now opposed to the nomination of any one to represent this country at the Vatican State.

Military Status a Factor

Moreover, the Clark appointment was complicated by his military status. Normally, only a majority of the Senate need approve a nominee to confirm him for a diplomatic appointment. But there is a long-standing Federal law preventing a man in the military service from taking a diplomatic post, and it would require action by both the Senate and the House of Representatives to exempt General Clark from this statute.

Senator Richard B. Russell, Democrat of Georgia, recently expressed doubt that the Senate Armed Services Committee, which would have jurisdiction over such an exemption measure, would approve it. Mr. Russell is chairman of that committee.

General Clark, who is chief of the Army Field Forces and stationed at Fort Monroe, Va., was understood from the beginning to have made continued military status a condition on which he was willing to accept the ambassadorial assignment.

For this reason, the White House, shortly after Congress adjourned without taking any action on the nomination, announced that President Truman had decided against giving the general a recess appointment.

Some opposition to General Clark, personally, stemmed from orders he had given to a Texas National Guard regiment as commander of the Allied Forces that fought up the Italian peninsula during World War II. He sent the Thirty-sixth Division across the Rapido River in the face of heavy odds and many casualties were suffered. Texans, particularly, have criticized this as ill-considered.

However, the principal and most heated controversy, generally, was not over the selection of General Clark, who is an Episcopalian, but over the reestablishment of the post itself. Opposition was spearheaded by Protestant organizations and spokesmen, including the minister of the Baptist Church in Washington that President Truman frequently attends.

Their central argument was that sending a diplomatic representative to Vatican City, site of the Holy See of the Roman Catholic Church, violated the American principle of separation of church and state.

Support for the President's action was based on the thesis that the intention was not to send an envoy to the Catholic Church as a religious body, but to the Vatican as a political state.

U. S. Minister There Till 1868

The United States until 1868 maintained a minister there, and a number of leading countries still do, it was pointed out.

Supporters saw the action as strengthening the forces against communism. The Vatican hailed the prospective appointment, and Catholic leaders in this country described it in such terms as a "significant advance in the progress of international understanding," and "a step toward world peace."

White House sources would not enlarge on Mr. Short's words that the President's new nomination would be sent to the Senate "at a later time." This did not necessarily mean "in the near future," some observers believed, and there was resulting speculation as to how soon the President would act.

It was recalled that in his State of the Union Message to Congress last Wednesday, the President in an outline of the measures he thought Congress ought to act on this session in the public interest, did not mention his plans to resume diplomatic relations with the Vatican.

Protestant Opposition to Go On

Protestant leaders voiced hope last night that the President would drop the whole idea of establishing relations with the Vatican, the United Press reported.

Dr. Edward Hughes Pruden, pastor of the Baptist church President Truman attends in Washington, said his opposition to the nomination was not based on "personalities." "A change in the nominee would not alter my feelings," he added. Dr. Pruden said he had tried to talk Mr. Truman out of nominating General Clark in the first place.

In Greenwich, Conn., the head of the National Council of Churches of Christ in the U. S. A., representing 31,000,000 Protestant church members, summed up the Protestants' general attitude.

Bishop Henry Knox Sherrill, council president, said:

"The opposition of the National Council of Churches of Christ in the U. S. A. to the appointment of an Ambassador to the Vatican has had no personal relationship with General Clark.

"We are opposed to the appointment of an Ambassador on sincere principle and will continue to be so, whoever may be appointed.

"It has caused religious controversy at a time when national unity is needed and, if pressed, will do so increasingly. The happiest solution would be to hear no more about this unwise proposal."

The Rev. Dr. Robert J. McCracken, minister of the Riverside Church at Riverside Drive and 112d Street in New York commented:

"Opposition to the nomination of an Ambassador to the Vatican will still be maintained by Protestants. That opposition has not centered on the person but on the policy proposed. What the Protestants seek is an assurance that no Ambassador will be appointed for the reason that such an appointment would give political status and preferential official recognition to a particular church. For Protestants what is involved is the flouting of a basic American principle."

At his home in New Rochelle, N. Y., Dr. Franklin Clark Fry, president of the United Lutheran Church, said:

"I am grateful that the President is not pressing for the establishment of an American Embassy at the Holy See at this time. Millions of patriotic and far-seeing Americans have seen in this move a dangerous threat to the age-old American policy of equality for all religions and a healthy separation of church and state."

The Rev. Leland Stark, rector of Epiphany Church, told his Protestant Episcopal congregation in Washington:

"While it is indeed the bare truth to say that we should be entering into a diplomatic alliance with the Vatican as a sovereign state, a knowledge of the whole truth will reveal that in reality the diplomatic alliance is with the Roman Catholic Church, no matter how many careful and solemn assurances are made to the contrary."

The mere proposal of an ambassador to the Vatican, the minister said, has "driven a great wedge between the two main branches of the Christian church." He added that national unity had been threatened.

The Rev. Brunno K. Neumann, pastor of Chicago's Lutheran Memorial Church, said the White House announcement that General Clark's name would not be resubmitted to the present session of Congress "ameliorates the situation, if only temporarily."

The Rev. Mr. Neumann said even if President Truman dropped the whole idea of an Ambassador to the Vatican, "he could not completely appease the non-Catholic groups."

In Boston Archbishop Richard J. Cushing, spiritual leader of some 1,500,000 Catholics, refused to comment on the President's action.

Francis Cardinal Spellman, Archbishop of New York, still was in the Far East on a tour and could not be reached for comment.

January 14, 1952

HIGH COURT UPHOLDS RELEASE OF PUPILS TO STUDY RELIGION

6-3 Decision Says Law Here Does Not Violate Doctrine of Church-State Separation

NO COERCION SEEN IN PLAN

By LEWIS WOOD
Special to THE NEW YORK TIMES.

WASHINGTON, April 28—The constitutionality of the released time program through which New York City public school pupils may be freed from classes one hour weekly for religious instruction away from school property was upheld by the Supreme Court in a 6-to-3 ruling today.

Justice William O. Douglas, who wrote the majority opinion, held that the New York plan set up under state law did not violate the constitutional prohibitions on statutes "respecting an establishment of religion" or the "free exercise" thereof. He found, too, that there was no coercion in the program.

Justice Douglas also insisted that the New York plan was different from the religious education scheme of the Champaign, Ill., schools, which was struck down as unconstitutional by the Supreme Court March 8, 1948, on the demand of Mrs. Vashti McCollum.

In the Illinois case, he recalled, classrooms were turned over to religious instructors, and the high court accordingly opposed this use of tax-supported property for disseminating religious training. However, the New York program, he said, involved neither religious instruction in public school classrooms nor expenditure of public funds.

3 Sharp Dissents Issued

Three sharp dissents were presented by Justices Robert H. Jackson, Hugo L. Black and Felix Frankfurter. The majority, besides Justice Douglas, consisted of Chief Justice Fred M. Vinson and Justices Stanley Reed, Harold H. Burton, Tom C. Clark and Sherman Minton.

The dissenters criticized the majority for differentiating the McCollum case from the New York issue. Justice Jackson said that the New York program involved coercion and thus was unconstitutional. He attacked the majority decision as warping and twisting the fundamental "wall" between church and state.

Justice Black accused New York of "manipulating its compulsory education laws to help religious sects get pupils."

Justice Douglas' opinion discussed the scope of the First Amendment to the Constitution, which bars laws "respecting an establishment of religion, or prohibiting the free exercise thereof." He agreed that there must be complete separation of religion and state so far as interference with establishment and free exercise of religion are concerned, but he said:

"The First Amendment, however, does not say that in every and all respects there shall be a separation of church and state.

"Rather, it studiously defines the manner, the specific ways, in which there shall be no concept or union or dependency one on the other. That is the common sense of the matter. Otherwise the state and religion would be aliens to each other—hostile, suspicious and even unfriendly.

The challenge to the released time plan, which the majority rejected, was brought to the Supreme Court by two Brooklyn parents, Tessim Zorach of 15 Willow Street and Mrs. Esta Gluck of 212 East

Fourth Street. Their children respectively attended Protestant Episcopal and Hebrew Sunday schools. Although public school students, they did not participate in the released time program.

Their attack was argued in the Supreme Court on Jan. 31, along with that by two New Jersey residents against state laws requiring daily reading of five verses of the Old Testament in public schools and permitting recitation of the Lord's Prayer.

The court on March 3 ruled, 6 to 3, that the New Jersey plaintiffs had not shown sufficient injury for it to rule on the constitutionality of the state statutes. The New York case was not decided until today.

Justice Douglas held that it would take "obtuse reasoning" to inject any issue of "free exercise of religion" into the New York case. He said that no pupil was "forced" to go to a religious classroom, and that a student was actually "left to his own desires" as to his religious devotions.

As to allegations of coercion, the justice asserted that the school authorities were really "neutral," merely releasing students when their parents requested. He noted, however, that if coercion had been employed, a "wholly different" case would be presented.

The New York plan may be unwise and improvident from an educational or community viewpoint, but the individual preferences of the justices may not be taken as the "constitutional standard," Mr. Douglas said, adding:

"We [the majority] do not see how New York by this type of 'released time' program has made a law respecting an establishment of religion within the meaning of the First Amendment.

"When the state encourages religious instruction or cooperates with religious authorities by adjusting the schedule of public events to sectarian needs, it follows the best of our traditions.

"We find no constitutional requirement which makes it necessary for Government to be hostile to religion and to throw its weight against efforts to widen the effective scope of religious influence."

Jackson Sees 'Temporary Jail'

Attacking the New York program, Justice Jackson said that it actually "serves as a temporary jail for a pupil who will not go to church." He said that the day the United States "ceases to be free for irreligion, it will cease to be free for religion," except for a sect that "can win political freedom."

He also argued that the distinction "attempted" between the McCollum and New York cases was "trivial almost to the point of cynicism."

Justice Black likewise saw no significant difference between the two issues. In the McCollum case, he said, the Supreme Court held that Illinois could not constitutionally manipulate school machinery to "channel children into sectarian classes; yet that is exactly what the court (now) holds New York can do." This, he remarked, "is not separation but combination of church and state."

Justice Frankfurter agreed with Justice Black that the principles used in deciding the McCollum case had been "disregarded" by the majority in settling the New York controversy.

DISPUTE GOES BACK TO 1926

The dispute over released time first attracted attention in this state in 1926 when Joseph Lewis, president of the Freethinkers Society of America, challenged the program set up by the White Plains Board of Education. The plan, which was subsequently upheld in the courts, was similar to one now in effect in the state.

Since then the program has been tested on several occasions in the New York courts and its constitutionality upheld. In 1940, the Legislature authorized public schools to establish released time programs under rules outlined by the State Education Commissioner, and the practice gained momentum. In New York City, 105,647 pupils participated in the program last term, a decrease of 4,490 from the previous year.

The controversy flared again in 1948 after the Federal Supreme Court upheld Mrs. McCollom in her suit against the Champaign, Ill., school system.

April 29, 1952

COURT GUARANTEES FILMS FREE SPEECH; ENDS 'MIRACLE' BAN

OPINION UNANIMOUS

High Tribunal Reverses State Appeals Bench in 'Sacrilege' Case

OVERTURNS OWN DECISION

Denies, as Held 37 Years Ago, That All Motion Pictures Are 'Business Pure and Simple'

By LEWIS WOOD
Special to THE NEW YORK TIMES.

WASHINGTON, May 26—The Supreme Court today unanimously decided that motion pictures were entitled to the constitutional guarantees of free speech and a free press. In doing so, the court reversed the New York State Court of Appeals, which had banned the showing of the controversial picture, "The Miracle," on the ground that it was "sacrilegious."

The picture, which was produced in Italy by Roberto Rosselini, husband of Ingrid Bergman, is the story of a simple-minded Italian peasant woman who is seduced by a stranger she believes to be St. Joseph. She imagines her child is miraculously conceived.

The court's opinion on the constitutional protections overturned a position it had held for thirty-seven years. In 1915 the court had ruled in an Ohio case that the exhibition of movies was a "business pure and simple," and not to be included in the constitutional guarantees. Today the court announced:

"We conclude that expression by means of motion pictures is included within the free speech and free press guaranty of the First and Fourteenth Amendments. To the extent that language in the opinion in [the Ohio case] is out of harmony with the views here set forth, we no longer adhere to it."

"Sacrilegious" Held Indefinite

As to "The Miracle," the nine justices found that the word "sacrilegious" as embodied in the New York law was a vague and indefinite test, too susceptible to various meanings to constitute a satisfactory standard. The court stated:

"In seeking to apply the broad and all-inclusive definition of 'sacrilegious' given by the New York courts, the censor is set adrift upon a boundless sea amid a myriad of conflicting currents of religious views, with no charts but those provided by the most vocal and powerful orthodoxies. New York cannot vest such unlimited restraining control over motion pictures in a censor."

Both rulings for the undivided court were written in a ten-page opinion by Justice Tom C. Clark.

An extensive concurrence by Justice Felix Frankfurter, joined by Justices Robert H. Jackson and Harold H. Burton, discussed in detail the definition of "sacrilegious," and said that students would despair of finding the meaning attributed by the New York court.

Opinion Is Bounded

While censorship of motion pictures in various states may be affected by the Supreme Court decision, Justice Clark apparently took pains not to outlaw controls of all kinds.

"Since," he wrote, "the term 'sacrilegious' is the sole standard under attack here [in the New York case] it is not necessary for us to decide, for example, whether a state may censor motion pictures under a clearly drawn statute designed and applied to prevent the showing of obscene films.

"That is a very different question from the one now before us. We hold only that under the First and Fourteenth Amendments a state may not ban a film on the basis of a censor's conclusion that it is 'sacrilegious'."

Justice Clark said also that the guarantees for freedom of speech and a free press did not mean that the Constitution "requires absolute freedom to exhibit every motion picture of every kind at all times and all places."

Clothing the exhibition of motion pictures with the Constitutional pledges brought heart to film interests that had begged that the Supreme Court take advantage of the case of "The Miracle" to express itself. The impact of the Clark opinion will now be carefully studied to ascertain how far the power of state censorship boards will continue.

Argued in the Supreme Court April 24, the case of "The Miracle" has attracted wide and acute interest. The film, anathema to millions of Roman Catholics, was barred from exhibition in New York in February, 1951. A committee from the New York Board of Regents, Justice Clark related, found there was basis for the claim of "sacrilegious." Subsequently the State Court of Appeals held against Joseph Burstyn, Inc., distributor of the film.

At the outset Justice Clark described three points of appeal by Mr. Burstyn. But, the Justice proceeded, the Supreme Court needed to consider only the argument that the New York law "is an unconstitutional abridgment of free speech and a free press."

219

The justice recited the history of the Ohio case and the Supreme Court's coincident pronouncement that movies were merely "business" enterprises, with no just claim for constitutional protection. Pointing out then that the Supreme Court had constantly extended the barriers against hampering free speech and a free press, he said the case of "The Miracle" was the first affording a chance to include films.

He dismissed arguments that motion pictures could not enjoy constitutional protection because they were business enterprises. Likewise, he held that movies should not be barred from these privileges because some persons said the films might sometimes exercise evil influences.

Each Expression Different

In the opinion, Mr. Clark found that motion pictures were not necessarily subject to "the precise rules governing any other particular method of expression." Each method, he continued, tended to present its own peculiar problems.

"But the basic principles of freedom of speech and the press, like the First Amendment's command, do not vary," he declared. "Those principles, as they have frequently been enunciated by this court, make freedom of expression the rule. There is no justification in this case for making an exception to that rule."

Under such a standard as "sacrilegious," Justice Clark ruled for the court:

"The most careful and tolerant censor would find it virtually impossible to avoid favoring one religion over another, and he would be subject to the inevitable tendency to ban the expression of unpopular sentiments sacred to a religious minority."

Further on, the Justice said that from the standpoint of freedom of speech and the press, "the state has no legitimate interest in protecting any or all religions from views distasteful to them which is sufficient to justify prior restraints upon the expression of those views."

"It is," he continued, "not the business of Government in our nation to suppress real or imagined attacks upon a particular religious doctrine, whether they appear in publications, speeches, or motion pictures."

Spellman Objections Noted

The concurrence by Justice Frankfurter detailed the vigorous objection of Cardinal Spellman of New York to the showing of "The Miracle."

"The vast apparatus of indices and digests, which mirrors our law, affords no clue to a judicial definition of sacrilege," the concurrence also stated. "Not one case, barring the present, has been uncovered which considers the meaning of the term in any context."

Justice Frankfurter cited "a few examples" to show what difficulties, he said, could face a conscientious censor or motion-picture producer or distributor in determining "what the New York statute condemns as sacrilegious." These "examples" described how one religious group or another might be offended by specific details of motion pictures.

Concurring in the judgment of the court, Justice Stanley F. Reed held that the Clark opinion did not prevent states from setting up plans to deal with motion pictures.

"Assuming," he said, "that a state may establish a system for the licensing of motion pictures, an issue not foreclosed by the court's opinion, our duty requires us to examine the facts of the refusal of a license in each case to determine whether the principles of the First Amendment have been honored. This film does not seem to me to be of a character that the First Amendment permits a state to exclude from public view."

Court Fight Long

The Supreme Court's decision marks the culmination of some two and a half years of legal procedure involving the film, "The Miracle" and film censorship in general through municipal, state and Federal courts.

The Italian-made drama starring Anna Magnani as the peasant who is seduced by a stranger whom she believe to be Joseph, opened at the Paris Theatre here Dec. 11, 1950, as part of a tri-partite omnibus feature collectively titled, "Ways of Love."

Showings of the picture were banned Dec. 23 by Edward T. McCaffrey, City License Commissioner, who found the offering "officially and personally blasphemous." On Dec. 30 Mr. McCaffrey lifted the ban when warned that State Supreme Court Justice Henry Clay Greenberg was about to sign a temporary injunction.

Early in January, 1951 State Supreme Court Justice Aaron Steuer ruled that neither the commissioner nor any other municipal officer had the right to interfere with the showing of the film.

Cardinal Spellman then called on every Roman Catholic in the United States to boycott the picture and any theatre showing it. The theatre was picketed and the management was notified of several threats to bomb the house. Early in February the license to exhibit the picture was revoked in a unanimous finding by the State Board of Regents on the ground that it was "sacrilegious."

Mr. Burstyn, who was supported in his campaign by various religious and civic groups, brought the issue before the Appellate Division of the State Supreme Court, which upheld the Board of Regents' ban. Last June, the case came before the Court of Appeals, after which it was prepared by Ephriam London, Mr. Burstyn's counsel, for consideration by the United States Supreme Court.

HOLLYWOOD HAILS ACTION

Decision Called Acknowledgement of Films' Social Status

By BOSLEY CROWTHER

Special to THE NEW YORK TIMES.

HOLLYWOOD, Calif., May 26—Hollywood reacted with joy and surprise today to the decision of the Supreme Court in the case of "The Miracle."

Film producers, who had been vaguely hopeful that the court would decisively declare against the constitutionality of film censorship hailed the ruling as a major triumph for the motion picture medium and found comfort in the formal acknowledgement of the social status of films.

No one expressed anxiety that this development would result in any let-down of responsibility by producers here. Frank Freeman, chairman of the board of the Association of Motion Picture Producers, said he could make no formal statement until he had conferred with his board. However, he expressed his personal opinion that the ruling was of "broad and far-reaching importance" and that it "places upon the industry an obligation to guard its responsibilities with the same regard for the public interest that we have always assumed."

Dore Schary, vice president and head of production at Metro-Goldwyn-Mayer, saw particular inspiration in the social implications of the ruling. He said:

"I think this is such a wonderful, healthy decision because it must confound both the far Left and the far Right, which have assumed that our democracy is trembling — the far Left because it sees the rise of fascism as a menace and far Right because it fears the spread of communism. Our democracy is not trembling. It is as solid as a rock, as this decision manifests."

Stanley Kramer, a recognized leader among the younger film makers, said:

"I feel that this decision reiterates that the motion picture is an art form, which means it must be just as far removed from censorship as possible."

While Joseph I. Breen, head of the Production Code Administration, which administers the industry's own voluntary self-regulating morals code, could not be reached for comment, it was remarked by a spokesman in his office that the administration had always felt outside censorship of motion pictures to be superfluous.

Eric Johnston "Delighted"

In Washington, Eric Johnston, president of the Motion Picture Association of America, said:

"We are delighted that the United States Supreme Court in 'The Miracle' decision says that the motion picture, as part of the press, is entitled to the free speech and free press guarantees of the Constitution. * * * The decision allows us to hope that the court in a subsequent case will go all the way and make it unmistakably clear that the motion picture, like its sister medium of the press cannot, under the Constitution, be censored anywhere in our country."

The association is specifically interested in the case of W. L. Gelling, manager of the Paramount Theatre in Marshall, Tex., who was fined and jailed in February, 1950, when he defied a local board's order and exhibited the Twentieth Century-Fox film, "Pinky." The case has gone through various Texas courts and now the association, which assisted in the appeals in the case, is waiting to see if the Supreme Court will take jurisdiction.

Joseph Burstyn, president of Joseph Burstyn, Inc., 113 West Forty-second Street, distributors of "The Miracle," called the decision "a victory of the first magnitude." The decision, he declared, "clears the way for the motion picture to take its rightful place as a major and adult art form and as a medium of expression and communication of ideas on all facets of our life and society. * * * The motion picture has come a long way since 1915 when the Supreme Court first ruled that it was not part of the press."

Dr. H. M. Flick, director of the Motion Picture Division of the State Education Department, the state's official censor group, which first approved "The Miracle," felt he could make no comment on the opinion at this time. He stated, however, that there should be some form of regulatory legislation governing the exhibition of motion pictures.

"This is in no way a reflection on the self-regulation of the motion-picture industry," he declared. "It is based, rather, on our personal experience in processing motion pictures, since more than 40 per cent of the pictures processed are not submitted to the industry for Production Code approval. If the present statutes are inadequate, it would seem that immediate steps should be taken to formulate legislation which would protect the public against unscrupulous exploitation."

Mr. Burstyn said that he intended to submit petitions for showing "The Miracle" to the State Court of Appeals and the censor board as soon as possible. He had no idea how long it would take to get the necessary legal permission to display the film.

The American Civil Liberties Union, in a statement by its executive director, Patrick Murphy Malin, called the court's ruling "the most striking blow the courts have dealt censorship in years."

"The effect of the decision," the union declared, "is to recognize legally what has for many years been a reality, that motion pictures do disseminate ideas and are entitled to the protection of free speech accorded all media of expression in our Bill of Rights.

"This action in effect may well end the control over movies that state and city censorship boards exercise throughout the country and could presage a new era in the use of films in transmitting ideas on issues of public importance.

"It is also an answer to pressure groups, who in the case of 'The Miracle' sought to impose their view—against the showing of the film—on the public, which is entitled and intelligent enough to make its own decisions as to what it wants to see, hear or read.

"It should give warning to all pressure groups, whether they be racial, religious or political, that bans on expression of opinion cannot be defended in a democratic society because they run counter to the democratic concept of unfettered free speech.

"The court's decision is heartening to the American Civil Liberties Union, which has consistently fought, as in this case through 'friend of the court' briefs, to have the Supreme Court establish the principle of noncensorship and to give the motion-picture industry the full equality it deserves."

Jewish Congress Sees Vindication

Dr. Israel Goldstein, president of the American Jewish Congress, also hailed the decision as "vindicating" the organization's position. Dr. Goldstein said:

"The decision vindicates the position taken by the American Jewish Congress in its brief to the Supreme Court in this case, holding that the censorship of films on theological grounds violates the Constitutional guarantee of religious liberty and separation of church and state.

"Religious doctrines, the Supreme Court has again held, can stand up on their own and do not require the coercive arm of the Government to present what sectarian groups may consider sacrilegious."

May 27, 1952

CATHOLIC BISHOPS CHALLENGE CRITICS ON SCHOOLS ISSUE

Deny Any 'Divisive' Influence —Religion Is Called 'Most Vital National Asset'

By JOHN D. MORRIS
Special to THE NEW YORK TIMES

WASHINGTON, Nov. 15—The Roman Catholic Bishops of the United States expressed deep concern today over what they viewed as a movement to divorce religion from education in the nation's schools.

In a statement issued after their annual meeting here, the prelates suggested that the result of such a movement had been to intensify the possibility that secularism was being accepted as a way of life in America.

They termed this a grave danger, and as evidence of it they cited charges that Catholic and other private schools were "divisive" influences -- an allusion, evidently, to criticism voiced in Boston last April by Dr. James B. Conant, president of Harvard University, and other speakers at a meeting of the American Association of School Administrators.

The Bishops maintained that all differences were not divisive but sometimes "simply manifestations of our fundamental freedom." Education that is truly religious, they said, is "a unifying rather than a dividing force."

Shifting of Ground Charged

Some of the same religious leaders now lending their influence to secularism, the Bishops commented, were "loud in their praise of practically everything that came out of the realms of atheism and tyranny" in the days when communism "was posing as a new and advanced kind of democracy."

"Now that it is no longer fashionable to regard communism as other than the avowed enemy of our country," they added, "they indeed maintain a discreet silence on the subject of Communistic virtues, but they still throw the weight of their influence behind such totalitarian movements as an all-embracing state-controlled school system of education completely devoid of religion. * * *

"Consciously or unconsciously, in eliminating the influence of religion and in working for the absolutism of majority vote, they are promoting the disintegration of those social institutions whose foundations are in religion—freedom, equality, human dignity, the stable family, and that constitutional democracy which has been characteristic of this country."

The real threat to the nation, the Bishops asserted, does not come from religious differences but from "irreligious social decay." They cited a divorce rate that has become "a national scandal," rising juvenile delinquency and a lowering of moral standards that has resulted in public corruption.

The broad theme of the Bishops' paper was "Religion, Our Most Vital National Asset." They pictured the country as having been engulfed in an atmosphere of restless foreboding and deep insecurity, due largely to conditions in the world but accompanied by "a lowering of vitality in our social institutions."

The great and fundamental need, according to the statement, is a strengthening of religion in the individual, the family and the civic community.

The statement was signed in the names of the Catholic Bishops by the Administrative Board of the National Catholic Welfare Conference. The signers included Cardinal Spellman, Edward Cardinal Mooney of Detroit, Samuel Cardinal Stritch of Chicago and ten Bishops and Archbishops.

In the last analysis, the statement observed, there can be no society of free men without the creative and sustaining force of religion.

Lack of Services Decried

In stressing their belief in the importance of religion to good citizenship, the Bishops reaffirmed the church's contention that the Government should recognize the fact and "help parents fulfill their task of religious instruction and training."

"When the state fails in this help," they said, "when it makes the task more difficult and even penalizes parents who try to fulfill this duty according to conscience, by depriving their children of their right under our Federal Constitution to auxiliary services, this can be only regarded as an utterly unfair and short-sighted policy."

This criticism apparently was directed at the Government's failure to devote public funds to the purchase of textbooks and to provide transportation for parochial school pupils.

A section of the statement was devoted to the argument that the First Amendment to the Constitution, where it dealt with the separation of church and state, did not prevent, and had not been intended to prevent, the encouraging and even aiding of religion.

While deploring evidences of "social decay" in the United States, the Bishops saw some "encouraging signs" of a renewed religious interest. They mentioned the number of religious books attaining wide circulation, frequent discussions of religious topics in newspapers and other periodicals, increases in church attendance and the growing use of radio and television for religious programs.

November 16, 1952

Vatican Newspaper Deplores Absence Of Religious Training in Schools of U. S.

ROME, Dec. 14—The lack of public religious instruction in public schools in the United States was termed a "tragedy" today by L'Osservatore Romano, the Vatican newspaper.

One of the fundamentals of the United States is individual liberty, and this gives parents the right to have their children receive a religious education, the newspaper said.

"What happens in America?" the newspaper asked. "Because of misunderstood respect for the opinions of all and to avoid religious controversy (which the Pilgrim Fathers wanted to escape when they sailed for the new world), the state in its schools does not allow the teaching of any religion."

"The state thus deludes itself that it does not harm any of its citizens, while in fact it harms all citizens," the newspaper added.

L'Osservatore Romano acknowledged that religion in general was held in high esteem in the United States, whereas "cynical indifference and hatred" was shown for it in some European countries. But the treatment of some parents who send their children to private schools in the United States is "unjust," according to L'Osservatore Romano.

They are forced to spend twice for schooling, once by paying taxes to support public schools and the second time by contributing toward the creation and upkeep of church-controlled private schools, it added.

The newspaper warned Roman Catholics in the United States that "in their present position as a strong minority in a country where they are surrounded by an atmosphere of liberty and general sympathy, they ought to think twice before, hoping to win improvements, they make any move that might cause them to lose what they have."

The newspaper quoted statistics from the "Liberty of the School and Family Education" by the Rev. Lino A. Ciarlatini, published in New York this year, to prove that "religious education is denied to nine-tenths of the Protestant children and to five-tenths of the Catholic children" in the United States.

December 15, 1954

SUNDAY BUSINESS EMBROILS STORES

Town Merchants Aroused by Spread of Highway Outlets, Open 7 Days

---

SERVICE VS. TRADITION

Blue Laws Are Unenforced and Often Unenforceable, Retailers Complain

The growing trend toward Sunday business has become one of the most controversial issues in retailing.

In most Eastern states, the openings have been confined to small shops, particularly suburban highway stores. In the Middle and Far West, however, some major department stores have been opening their warehouses for "Sunday sales."

To justify such openings, shop owners contend they are offering a service to persons who work all week and can only shop on Sundays. The move attracts many customers in industrial areas, where three-shift factory operations are prevalent.

In recent months, retailers who adhere to Sabbath closings have been fighting back. They base their opposition on three points: the openings upset community traditions, they provide "ruinous" competition for stores abiding by municipal laws that require non-essential shops to be closed and they move labor and merchants a step back to a seven-day work week.

Many states have ancient blue laws on the subject. Some of these do not provide penalties for offenders. Attempts to invoke local ordinances—in the absence of state laws—have often been overruled by state courts.

Senator Is Irate

Several months ago Senator A. S. (Mike) Monroney, Democrat of Oklahoma, spoke out against some Washington merchants who violated the "American Sabbath" in an attempt to make Sunday "the big bargain day of the week."

"The very idea that the sale is being held on Sunday has a tendency to give added urgency and sales promotion impact, to the disadvantage of the regular advertisers who observe the Sabbath," he added.

In some areas, retailing associations have been attempting to enforce closings. For example, the Florida Furniture Dealers Association in Miami last week passed a resolution urging Sunday closings of furniture stores. The group expects to seek appropriate legislation when the Florida Legislature convenes in April, 1957.

Sunday openings of non-essential businesses are not a major problem in New York and Connecticut, according to retail organizations. Stringent state laws provide for fines against first offenders. Second offenders in New York may be subject to "confiscation of all merchandise offered for sale."

One of the hottest battles on the issue has been developing in New Jersey. Although there is a state law prohibiting non-essential Sunday business, retailers contend it has no teeth.

Some 500 business men have banded together to form the New Jersey Association for Sunday Closing of Non-essential Business. The group is leveling its main fire against competitors in highway shopping centers. Such stores have been cropping up in suburban areas throughout the state. Practically all of them remain open on Sundays, the association asserts.

William J. Schneider, president of the group, said it had called for action in Newark last Sunday. As a result, some fifteen summonses were handed out by the police. The city has an ordinance against Sunday openings, but it was not previously enforced, according to Mr. Schneider.

"We are prepared to fight against Sunday openings with all our power and we intend to do it by getting a state law passed that will keep stores shut tight," he said.

Mr. Schneider noted that past attempts "to put teeth" into the state law had been opposed principally by seashore entrepreneurs. They transact a large portion of their business on Sundays.

"We are willing to exempt them and other legitimate businesses—drug stores, newsstands, etc.—from closing on Sunday. We have prepared a new bill that will provide stiff penalties for offenders, and we are going to work to get it passed as soon as possible," Mr. Schneider asserted. "We are in this fight to the end."

There were indications two weeks ago that another fight might be shaping up in Cleveland. Eight owners of home furnishings stores there were told they were violating blue laws by staying open on Sundays. They told the police they would remain open as long as other stores in the area were permitted to go unpunished for the same offense.

May 20, 1956

AMISH KEEP CHILDREN FROM NEW SCHOOL

MORGANTOWN, Pa., Feb. 9 (AP)—Some members of the Amish sect, proclaiming that their faith is older than their Government, refused to send their children to a new $2,000,000 school.

The parents say they consider the spacious Twin Valley junior-senior high school too worldly for the children.

The school is ten miles from the Amish homes or "over the mountain" as they say here in the Pennsylvania Dutch country.

"We wish a good economic training for our posterity and we aim to make good citizens, self-supporting farmers and Christians of our children," an Amish spokesman wrote.

Aaron E. Beiler, replying to a school-board ultimatum to get the children in school or else, asserted:

"Our religious convictions direct us to stay away from secondary high school attendance. Examples and experience are the best teachers. Shall we ask: 'Why should we be disturbed and molested?'"

The dispute has been going on since the academic year began in September. Last night the school board here voted to give parents three days' notice before starting action under the state's compulsory school-attendance law. Eighteen pupils from nine families are involved.

February 10, 1960

POLITICAL CRITICISM OF CATHOLIC BACKED

WASHINGTON, Feb. 5 (UPI)—A non-denominational Protestant magazine said today that it was "perfectly rational" for Protestants to oppose the election of a Roman Catholic as President.

The assertion was made in an editorial by Christianity Today, a fortnightly journal published here and circulated to about 200,000 Protestant clergymen throughout the country.

The magazine is oriented toward the so-called "conservative" or "Fundamentalist" wing of Protestantism. Its editor is Dr. Carl F. H. Henry. Listed among fifty-two "contributing editors" are the Rev. Dr. Billy Graham, the evangelist; Bishop Arthur J. Moore of Atlanta, a Methodist, and the Rev. Edward L. R. Elson, pastor of the National Presbyterian Church of Washington, which President Eisenhower attends.

The unsigned editorial said Protestants who opposed a Catholic candidate for the Presidency were not guilty of "bigotry" in the sense of irrational prejudice.

"Informed Protestants believe, not at all irrationally, that the interests of the nation are safer in the hands of one who does not confess to a foreign, earthly power," the editorial said.

The editorial contended that the Vatican "does all in its power to control the governments of nations, and in the past and the present it has often succeeded."

"Where the Romanists are strong enough, they persecute; where less strong, they oppress and harass; where they are in the minority, they seek special privileges, Government favor and more power," it declared.

February 6, 1960

THE 'CATHOLIC VOTE': HOW IMPORTANT IS IT?

Analysts Disagree on What 1928 Campaign of Gov. Smith Proved

Catholic Share of the Population Varies in Different Areas

By LEO EGAN

Senator John F. Kennedy's religion appears to be becoming the dominant issue of the Democratic pre-convention campaign, to the great distress of many Democrats and of many Roman Catholics.

The prominence achieved by the religious question in the pre-convention campaign is a matter of deep concern to many Democratic leaders. Should Senator Kennedy be nominated they fear it will be said that he was chosen because of his religion. On this ground his nomination could be resented by voters of other faiths.

On the other hand, should someone else be nominated the leaders fear it will be said that the Senator was rejected because of his religion, whether this was a major consideration or not. Such an interpretation of the convention results could alienate a great many Catholics who usually vote the Democratic ticket.

Republicans, of course, do not have this problem because there is no Catholic in contention for their Presidential nomination. Nevertheless, debates are taking place among Republicans as to whether it would be politically wise to name a Catholic for Vice President, should Senator Kennedy fail to get the Democratic nomination, to capitalize on any dissatisfaction among Democrats who are Catholics.

Polls and Surveys

Involved in the debating in both parties is an assumption that there is such a thing in the United States as a "Catholic vote" and an "anti-Catholic vote." As to whether this assumption is justified is, in itself, debatable. Any number of polls and surveys can be cited to show that Catholics have divided politically, at least since 1928, just as other religious groups and for the same reasons.

Some authorities who question whether there is a "Catholic vote" as a general proposition believe, nevertheless, that Senator Kennedy, if nominated, would be the beneficiary of a barrier-breaking movement among Catholics. It is believed that many Catholics who normally vote Republican would vote this once for the Massachusan to end the theory that a Catholic cannot be elected. In subsequent elections they could be expected to return to their old voting habits.

There is reason to believe that some Catholics benefited from similar barrier - leveling votes as candidates for Governors of various states and for seats in the United States Senate in the past. After the fact that a Catholic could be elected was established, the religions of the candidates ceased to be a factor in how Catholics voted, even in states where they constituted the largest single religious group in the electorate.

Thus areas in New York where Catholics predominate were among those returning the heaviest pluralities for former Gov. Thomas E. Dewey, an Episcopalian, in 1950, when he ran against the late Walter A. Lynch, a Catholic. In Massachusetts, where Catholics constitute more than half the total population, Protestants frequently defeat Catholics for state-wide offices.

According to the relatively reliable "Official Catholic Directory," Catholics now constitute 23.6 per cent of the total population of the United States. When Alfred E. Smith ran as the Democratic candidate for President in 1928, Catholics constituted only 10 per cent of the total population. Mr. Smith, a four-term Governor of New York, has been the only Catholic nominated for President by a major party to date.

The distribution of Catholics among the states is far from uniform. In North Carolina they constitute less than .9 per cent of the total population and in Rhode Island more than 61 per cent.

In thirteen states, which have a total of 185 electoral votes, Catholics represent better than 30 per cent of the total population. In two others, with sixteen electoral votes, they constitute 25 to 30 per cent and in seven more, with ninety-eight electoral votes, they represent 20 to 25 per cent of the total population.

Thus in twenty-two states having 299 electoral votes in all, Catholics constitute 20 per cent or more of the total population. Only 270 electoral votes are needed to elect a President.

Minority Role

The other side of the picture is that Catholics constitute less than 10 per cent of the total population in fourteen states having a total of 129 electoral votes. All but two of these fourteen are Southern or Border states.

Among the fourteen are six of the seven states Adlai E. Stevenson carried in 1956. They are Alabama, Arkansas, Georgia, Mississippi, North Carolina and South Carolina. The only other Stevenson state was Missouri, where Catholics constitute 17.7 per cent of the total population.

Five of these least Catholic states were among the eight that Governor Smith carried in 1928. They were Alabama, Arkansas, Georgia, Mississippi and South Carolina. The other states carried by Mr. Smith were Louisiana, 35.2 per cent Catholic, Massachusetts, 52.8 per cent, and Rhode Island, 61.3 per cent.

Another measure of the importance of the "Catholic vote," if it exists at all, to the Democrats is the fact that large numbers of traditionally Democratic Catholics are reported in various pre-election and post-election surveys and studies to have voted Republican in 1952 and in 1956.

In this year's debates over the importance of Senator Kennedy's religion to the outcome of the struggle for the Presidency, Governor Smith's experience in 1928 is frequently cited as proof that a Catholic cannot be elected. It is likewise often cited as proof that Mr. Smith's religion had relatively little to do with the outcome.

On the affirmative side, Mr. Smith's loss of such traditionally Democratic states as Virginia, North Carolina, Florida, Tennessee and Oklahoma are regarded as "proof" that religion was the major factor in the campaign.

On the negative side, Mr. Stevenson's loss of all of these except North Carolina is given as "proof" that factors other than religion were at work in 1928 as well as 1956.

Governor Smith's religion is now generally regarded as only one of many serious political liabilities he faced in 1928. Others include the then widespread view that a Democratic national administration meant "hard times," Mr. Smith's Tammany Hall-Big City background, his brown derby hat and big cigar that helped create an image of a machine politician, and his espousal of the "wet" cause in the great debate over prohibition.

Race Issue

The race issue was also important in the loss of some Southern states. The late Senator Thomas J. Heflin's famous question linking religion and race was widely used against Mr. Smith in the South. The question went something like this: In the Catholic Church Negroes and whites worship together. Wouldn't a Catholic President therefore be bound by his religion to end racial segregation in the South?

Those backing Senator Kennedy this year contend that the differences between the Harvard-educated Senator and the former New York Governor who gave the Fulton Fish Market as his alma mater and the changes that have taken place since 1928 are such as to make any comparison between this year and then totally without application.

There are many Democrats, among them some distinguished Catholics, who would like to believe the arguments being advanced on behalf of Senator Kennedy in this debate. But, being politically timid, they are reluctant to put the issue to the test.

Their general attitude is that present political conditions are such as to favor a Democratic victory this fall on the fundamental issues confronting the country. Why, then, they ask, should all this be risked by allowing an irrelevant issue that could divert the attention of voters from these basic issues to be raised?

The answer may be that it is not possible to avoid it. All indications are that Senator Kennedy, unless he stubs his toe in West Virginia, will get more votes than any other contender when the first ballot is taken at the Democratic national convention in July.

In these circumstances the issue must be faced. If Senator Kennedy is to be turned down, those in control of the convention will be under heavy pressure to make a convincing demonstration that his religion was not responsible for the decision.

April 17, 1960

Palmer in The Springfield (Mo.) Leader
"Can't lose it."

Vatican Paper Proclaims Right Of Church to Role in Politics

Special to The New York Times.

ROME, May 17—L'Osservatore Romano, the Vatican newspaper, declared today that the Roman Catholic hierarchy had "the right and the duty to intervene" in the political field to guide its flock. It rejected what it termed "the absurd split of conscience between the believer and the citizen."

The pronouncement was in a front-page editorial described by the Vatican Press Service as "authoritative." It was presented in a special make-up that L'Osservatore Romano usually reserves for semi-official statements emanating from its Vatican superiors, as distinct from its own editorial opinion.

The article clearly referred to the political situation in Italy, where some left-of-center elements in the dominant Christian Democratic party, which enjoys Vatican backing, have recently advocated collaboration with Left-Wing Socialists, against the advice of the Roman Catholic Episcopacy.

However, L'Osservatore Romano made it plain that the pronouncement was valid for Roman Catholic laymen everywhere. It deplored "the great confusion of ideas that is spreading, especialy in some nations, among Catholics with regard to the relations between Catholic doctrine and social and political activities, and between the ecclesiastical hierarchy and the lay faithful in the civil field."

Vatican sources were uncommunicative whether the editorial was to be interpreted as having reference also to the United States, where Senator John F. Kennedy, a Roman Catholic, lately stressed in his bid for the Presidency his independence of any interference by the church in the political field.

L'Osservatore Romano condemned efforts "to detach the Catholic from the ecclesiastical hierarchy, restricting relations between the two to the mere sphere of sacred ministry and proclaiming the believer's full autonomy in the civil sphere."

The Roman Catholic religion, the editorial asserted, is a force that "commits and guides the entire existence of man." The Catholic," it went on, "may never disregard the teaching and directions of the church but must inspire his private and public conduct in every sphere of his activity by the laws, instructions and teachings of the hierarchy."

It said that in the political field the problem might arise whether to collaborate with "those who do not admit religious principles." Whether such collaboration is morally licit must always be decided by the ecclesiastical authority and never by the individual faithful, it declared.

With obvious reference to Italy, L'Osservatore Romano declared that "the unalterable antithesis between the Marxist system and Christian doctrine is self-evident."

Kennedy Aide Comments

Special to The New York Times.

PORTLAND, Ore., May 17—Pierre Salinger, press secretary to Mr. Kennedy, made the following comment tonight on the Vatican newspaper's article:

"The American officeholder is committed by an oath to God to support and defend the Constitution of the United States which includes Article 1 providing for separation of church and State.

"Senator Kennedy has repeatedly stated his support of the principle of separation of church and state as provided for in the United States Constitution. He has stated that this support is not subject change under any condition."

May 18, 1960

Anti-Catholic Views Found in the South

By JOHN WICKLEIN

"If the Presidential election were held today, Texas would go for Nixon—and the main reason would be Southern Baptist opposition to putting a Catholic in the White House."

This was the opinion, stated last week in Dallas, of a Methodist minister who is also a field general in the campaign to elect Senator John F. Kennedy, a Democrat and a Roman Catholic, as President. Across town, in the opposing camp, an editor for the Baptist forces said this:

"The vast majority of Southern Baptists in Texas will vote the Republican ticket this year, and I think the Baptist attitude on it will be decisive."

In Texas and throughout the South, the issue between the Southern Baptists and Senator Kennedy has been joined. Members of fundamentalist groups and Masonic organizations have also been speaking out, but the Southern Baptist Convention, with 9,600,000 members and 31,-000 preachers, is the most potent religious force in the campaign.

Politicians Surprised

Anti-Catholic activity is much more widespread than Southern politicians and the more liberal churchmen foresaw. Its extent became evident from interviews in the last two weeks in Atlanta, Dallas, Memphis, Nashville, Charlotte and Washington, and from reports from other areas.

In Texas, Tennessee and North Carolina, Democratic campaigners think religious feeling is running strong enough to swing these states to Vice President Nixon.

All three have heavy Baptist concentrations. So have Florida and Virginia, and anti-Catholic preaching there, combined with the civil rights issue and hand-sitting by the states' Democratic leaders, has the Kennedy forces worried.

In Washington last week, Robert F. Kennedy, lean and shirt-sleeved, prowled the newly expanded offices of the Democratic National Committee, masterminding the Senator's campaign.

"Right now," the candidate's brother said, "religion is the biggest issue in the South, and in the country."

Senator Kennedy hopes to "get the people's minds off the religious issue and on to something that is more important—our relations with the Soviet Union, the farm problem, and other serious questions that are facing them."

But, his brother added, the Senator will meet the issue head-on—as he did in West Virginia—by going out and preaching religious liberty and church-state separation himself.

A special headquarters committee, headed by James W. Wine, fromer associate general secretary of the National Council of Churches, has been appointed to answer questions on the issue. Mr. Kennedy said that local-level groups of ministers and laymen would also be established to combat religious opposition wherever it arises.

In the South, turning the street-corner talk away from religion would seem to require a master's touch.

1928 'All Over Again'

"It's the 1928 campaign all over again," said one Kennedy Protestant, ruefully.

But there is a difference.

"In '28," a Dallas political observer remarked, "the people got right up and said 'I'm just not going to vote for that Catholic, Al Smith.' Today it isn't fashionable to be a bigot. Today these same people say 'I'm opposed to Senator Kennedy because the Roman Catholic Church does not believe in the separation of church and state.'"

This time, church people who raise objections in sermons, pamphlets and editorials aren't running against the candidate, but against the Pope.

For one, the Rev. Dr. E. S. James, a grandfatherly looking man who edits The Texas Baptist Standard, says he is deeply troubled that what he feels bound in conscience to write will lose him friends among the Catholics. His feeling is this:

"I believe that Senator Kennedy is a clean, intelligent young man. His utterances show he believes in keeping church and state separate. If the Roman Catholic church itself would declare for separation, I would be for a man who is a Catholic. But the church hasn't done it; the issue remains."

No Prohibition Issue

There are other differences in 1960: today no prohibition issue arouses the "dry" Methodists to take out openly after a "wet" Democratic nominee, as Bishop James Cannon of Virginia did in '28.

The Methodists, second only to the Baptists in regional religious influence, hold the same firm views on church and state as the Baptists. But although some Methodist conferences, such as one in South Carolina, have adopted resolutions against electing a Catholic, the ministers haven't taken their views into the pulpit.

And in the whole South, no major political leader has come out publicly against Senator Kennedy because he is a Catholic. Thirty-two years ago, Senator Tom Heflin of Alabama, a violent anti-Catholic, campaigned actively to defeat Governor Smith.

That year, in the South, the Democrats carried only Alabama, Arkansas, Georgia, Mississippi and South Carolina.

As in the Hoover-Smith campaign, scurrilous anti-Catholic literature has again popped up, but it is not nearly so prevalent as pamphlets listing papal pronouncements against separation and religious freedom. Some of this is lifted from context, and none of it includes the 1948 declaration of the American Bishops supporting the Constitutional principle of separation.

Despite the differences, the two campaigns have enough similarities to make the Kennedy Democrats run scared. Many at Los Angeles figured that any possible Protestant defections in the South would be more than balanced by a Catholic surge in the big-electoral-vote states of the North.

But so large a state as Texas, with its twenty-four electoral votes, would be hard to write off to the religious issue. And Texas, as one Dallas editor remarked, has more Baptists than people. Actually the Baptists themselves claim only 1,500,000 adult adherents, out of 9,500,000.

Texas conservatives, many of them leading Baptist laymen, took the state for Eisenhower in 1952 and 1956. Carr P. Collins, a member of the First Baptist Church in Dallas, the denomination's largest, this time has organized Texans for Nixon. His pastor, the Rev. Dr. W. A. Criswell, has preached against Senator Kennedy by name.

In a sermon broadcast on a local radio station July 3, Dr. Criswell said "Roman Catholicism is not only a religion, it is a political tyranny." Senator Kennedy, he declared, would not be able to resist its pressures.

The political overtones were so strong that the Democrats asked for equal time. The station acceded: the next Sunday, the Rev. F. Braxton Bryant, a Methodist minister and a Kennedy worker "just graduated" from the Young Democrats, presented a fifteen-minute broadcast in rebuttal.

One night recently, the red-haired Mr. Bryant, flushed and enthusiastic after a party rally, leaned toward his interviewer in the lobby of the Statler-Hilton and said:

"It's such a nefarious thing, and so hard to rebut. Baptists have a fixed mind on this, not all of which you can call prejudice. But American Catholics are part of our democratic heritage—they believe in separation, despite what their church might have said in the past. Even though Jack Kennedy has a reputation for telling the truth, we are asked to believe he is a liar."

Blames Nixon Aides

Mr. Bryant felt the attacks were unjust, and politically inspired:

"Leaders of the Nixon forces, not Nixon himself, are using the religion issue against Mr. Kennedy—and you can quote me on that. They wouldn't be human if they didn't.

"Even Billy Graham—he's for Nixon—is being political every time he says 'Religion is a major issue, but I'll wait till I enter the voting booth to express my convictions.' "

A Texas Presbyterian minister, however, said he knew of no one who was not using the issue sincerely. Privately, he said he would vote for Kennedy because the Senator was only a nominal Catholic.

In Garland, sixteen miles outside of Dallas, the Rev. Tom Landers, an independent Baptist, last month gathered "Bible" Baptist pastors into a group called Christians United for a Free America. Its purpose: To oppose the election of Senator Kennedy religiously, in a "nonpolitical" way.

His Miller Road Church, a modern, yellow warehouse of a building that seats 2,000, was being readied for a Bible conference. "Time Is Short" said a banner across the dais. The pastor, a chunky man with dark-brown, slicked-back hair, smiled behind dark-brown-rimmed glasses.

"Very few people really know the reasons we're opposing Kennedy; the grounds for religious opposition," he said. "The basis is that he owes allegiance to a sovereign power over and above that of the United States."

To acquaint their people—factory workers who normally vote Democratic—with their views, the Christians United pastors are mailing out tracts such as Mr. Landers' "Can We Afford to Elect a Catholic President?" to other pastors in the area, for use in sermons and discussion groups.

"Bible-believing people look to their pastors for guidance," Mr. Landers explained.

But not far away, in Denton, three young Southern Baptists who had heard a lot preached about Baptist independence decided that now was the time to show some. Saying they were "tired of all this anti-Catholic talk from the pulpit," they set up Baptists in Texas for Kennedy. Came Sunday, and their pastor, the Rev. Leo Armstrong, chided them in his bulletin:

"We go to the polls and vote not as Baptists, but as American citizens, using our freedom and directed by our Lord to do what is best for the preservation of our nation."

The president of the Southern Baptist Convention, the 56-year-old Rev. Dr. Ramsey Pollard, expressed a similar idea: "I speak as an individual, not as an official of the convention." He spoke in the softly lighted, air-cooled study of his huge Bellevue Baptist Church in Memphis.

"I think the vast majority of Southern Baptist ministers and laymen will vote against Kennedy," he said. "Most of us feel he is a devout Catholic, a splendid young man. But we do not feel he can dissociate himself from the Roman Catholic hierarchy."

He pointed out that every Baptist state paper and eight state conventions, as well as the denominational convention, had publicly expressed fears on the election of a Catholic.

Dr. Pollard said he understood that the Masonic bodies across the South were working actively against Senator Kennedy in lodge meetings, for similar reasons.

In Atlanta, a well-known Masonic and Shrine leader said his mail had been running heavily anti-Catholic, including personal letters and throwaways attacking the hierarchy. But there is no concerted Masonic campaign to defeat the Democratic nominee, he said, and political utterances in the well of a Masonic hall would be made on an individual basis.

Dr. Pollard said he and other Baptist pastors objected to being called bigots when their views were based on principles in support of religious liberty.

Baptist opposition must be based on historical facts about Catholic attitudes and actions, he went on, "and not on absurd statements that cannot be proved."

As an example, he referred to the spurious "Knights of Columbus Oath," in circulation since 1912, which purports to require the Knights "to wage relentless war against all heretics, Protestants and Masons."

This has turned up all over the South, as it did in 1928, and some Southern Baptist clergymen have used it in sermons. Many have since been publicly retracted after protests, and threats of libel suits from the Knights of Columbus.

"Oath' Is Circulated

Recently the Southern Baptist Press, an agency that has a news wire and mailing service in the region, warned Baptist editors and pastors against using the "oath" and another spurious piece, "America is a Catholic Country," which is being mailed — anonymously—in quantity.

The Baptists in Tennessee are joined in their opposition by the Church of Christ, a 2,000,000-member Fundamentalist group centered in Nashville. This group thinks the Catholic church is schismatic. A sign on one of their sanctuaries says "Founded by Jesus Christ, A. D. 33." Its pastors and editors are more vehement than the Baptists, and they are backing their stand in newspaper ads.

Edward Ball, editor of The Nashville Tennessean, said his paper, which is pro-Kennedy, had received more letters on the religious issue than on any other in recent years.

The people of North Carolina, two airline puddle-jumps to the east, have been so stirred by their pastors that Gov. Luther H. Hodges, a Democrat, has made a public plea for an end to "politicking from the pulpit."

"Prejudices are the greatest menace facing the world today," he declared.

Last Sunday in Charlotte, worshipers from a middle-income residential area waited in the foyer of the cool and imposing Midwood Baptist Church to shake the hand of their pastor, the Rev. Wendell G. Davis.

A thin, middle-aged man wearing a Shrine emblem was asked whether he agreed with Mr. Davis that a Catholic should not be the next President.

"Being a Mason," he said, "I could not vote for a Catholic."

Ten of twelve men and women questioned—most all of them Democrats — said they would vote against Senator Kennedy because of his religion. The twelfth said he was for Nixon, but not for any religious feeling against the Senator.

A number of moderate and liberal ministers in the South expressed similar thoughts in interviews, but almost none has taken a stand in the press or pulpit. Even some conservative Baptists remarked privately that they had no "fear" of Senator Kennedy as President, but they just could not "take a chance" that if he were elected, some Catholic elected at some later time might hand the country to Rome.

"I'm heartsick and chagrined," said Harry Golden, sinking into a green contour chair in the rambling frame building in Charlotte that is his home and The Carolina Israelite office. Mr. Golden, working for the Kennedy campaign, had just collected reports on the religious issue from his correspondents throughout the region. "I did not believe it could happen. There's every bit as strong a feeling as there was in '28," he said.

"You know what one of these good church people said to me the other day? He said 'I'd even rather vote for a Jew than vote for a Catholic'. I got up and said 'Pardon me while I vomit!' When I came back, he was gone."

Kennedy backers in the South, perhaps to keep their morale up, are beginning to say they see signs of a reaction against the religious issue. Maybe, they say, Southerners will begin to feel guilt and revulsion over the anti-Catholic talk, and vote for the Senator despite their pastors.

Certainly, they point out, vocal Southern Baptist opposition in the South will be a catalyst for a large Democratic turnout among Catholics in the North —the reverse side of the religion issue.

Governor Buford Ellington, Tennessee Democrat who recently endorsed the Kennedy-Johnson ticket, put it this way: "If these preachers had waited till two weeks before the election, it would have been fatal. But the reaction has already started, and I think that before the election, this thing is going to backfire on 'em."

The Gastonia-Charlotte group has been chartered as a local committee of Protestants and Other Americans United for Separation of Church and State. Among other things, P. O. A. U., as it is popularly known, cautions against efforts of Catholic groups to get public aid for parochial schools. Its materials appear in tract racks of Baptist and other churches across the South, and its films are being widely used by church people opposed to the election of a Catholic.

September 4, 1960

Protestant Groups' Statements

Special to The New York Times.

WASHINGTON, Sept. 7—Following are the texts of separate statements issued today by Protestant clergymen and laymen meeting at the National Conference of Citizens for Religious Freedom and by the Protestants and Other Americans United for Separation of Church and State:

By National Conference

Despite efforts to ignore or to stifle it, the religious issue remains a major factor in the current political campaign. Indeed, it has become one of the most significant issues. We of this conference, ministers and laymen in Protestant churches of thirty-seven denominations, realize that the candidacy of a Roman Catholic for President of the United States has aroused questions which must be faced frankly by the American people.

We believe that this religious issue should be handled with utmost discretion; that it should be discussed only in a spirit of truth, tolerance and fairness, and that no persons should engage in hate mongering, bigotry, prejudice or unfounded charges. We further believe that persons who are of the Roman Catholic faith can be just as honest, patriotic and public spirited as those of any other faith. We believe in the same freedom of religion for Roman Catholics as for ourselves and all other people.

The key question is whether it is in the best interest of our society for any church organization to attempt to exercise control over its members in political and civic affairs. While the current Roman Catholic contender for the Presidency states specifically that he would not be so influenced, his church insists that he is duty-bound to admit to its direction. This unresolved conflict leaves doubt in the minds of millions of our citizens.

[1]

The Roman Catholic Church is a political as well as a religious organization. Traditionally, its hierarchy has assumed and exercised temporal power, unless and until that power has been successfully checked by the instruments of representative government. Today the Vatican in Rome, representing the seat of Catholic religious and temporal power, maintains diplomatic relations with the Governments of forty-two countries, exchanging Ambassadors who have official status. Spokesmen for the Vatican in the United States have repeatedly urged establishment of diplomatic relations with the Roman Catholic Church, including appointment by the President of an official representative.

The President has the responsibility in our Government for conducting foreign relations, including receiving and appointing ambassadors. It is inconceivable that a Roman Catholic President would not be under extreme pressure by the hierarchy of his church to accede to its policies with respect to foreign relations in matters, including representation to the Vatican.

[2]

The Roman Catholic Church has specifically repudiated on many occasions the principle sacred to us that every man shall be free to follow the dictates of his conscience in religious matters. Such pronouncements are, furthermore, set forth as required beliefs for every Roman Catholic, including the Democratic nominee. Binding upon him, as well as upon all members of this church, is the belief that Protestant faiths are heretical and counterfeit and that they have no theoretical right to exist.

[3]

The record of the Roman Catholic Church in many countries where it is predominant is one of denial of equal rights for all of other faiths. The constitutions of a number of countries prohibit any person except Roman Catholics from serving as president or chief of state.

The laws of most predominantly Catholic countries extend to Catholics privileges not permitted to those of other faiths.

In countries such as Spain and Colombia, Protestant ministers and religious workers have been arrested, imprisoned and otherwise persecuted because of their religion. No Protestant church or Jewish synagogue can be marked as such on its exterior.

[4]

We realize that many American Catholics would disagree with the policies of their church in other countries and would not want to introduce them here under any circumstances. But this does not altogether reassure us.

The Roman Catholic Church in the United States has repeatedly attempted to break down the wall of separation of church and state by a continuous campaign to secure public funds for the support of its schools and other institutions. In various areas where they predominate, Catholics have seized control of the public schools, staffed them with nun teachers wearing their church garb, and introduced the catechism and practices of their church. In Ohio today (a state with a Roman Catholic Governor), according to an Attorney General's ruling, Roman Catholic nuns and sisters may be placed on the public payroll as schoolteachers.

The record shows that one of the bills introduced by John F. Kennedy (HR 5838, Eighty-first-Congress), now a nominee for the Presidency, as a member of the House of Representatives from Massachusetts, had as its purpose Federal aid to education which included private and parochial schools. Representative Kennedy also sought to amend the Barden bill in the Eighty-first Congress in such a way as to provide funds for parochial schools. He was, however, the only Senator of Roman Catholic faith who voted against the Morse amendment to the Aid-to-Education Act in the Eighty-sixth Congress in 1960. The Morse amendment would have provided partial grants and partial loans for the construction of parochial schools. We are hopeful that the newer phase of Senator Kennedy's thinking on this issue will prevail, but we can only measure the new against the old.

By recommendation, persuasion and veto power, the President can and must shape the course of legislation in this country. Is it reasonable to assume that a Roman Catholic President would be able to withstand altogether the determined efforts of the hierarchy of his church to gain further funds and favors for its schools and institutions, and otherwise breach the wall of separation of church and state?

[5]

Under the canon law of the Roman Catholic Church, a President of this faith would not be allowed to participate in interfaith meetings; he could not worship in a Protestant church without securing the permission of an ecclesiastic. Would not a Roman Catholic President thus be gravely handicapped in offering to the American people and to the world an example of the religious liberty our people cherish?

Brotherhood in a pluralistic society like ours depends on a firm wall of separation between church and state. We feel that the American hierarchy of the Roman Catholic Church can only increase religious tensions and political-religious problems by attempting to break down this wall. Much depends upon strong support for this well tested wall of separation by Americans of all faiths.

Finally, that there is a "religious issue" in the present political campaign is not the fault of any candidate. It is created by the nature of the Roman Catholic Church which is, in a very real sense, both a church and also a temporal state.

By the P.O.A.U.

There is a moment for calm analysis and sober speech

Pach Bros.

SEES A FAITH ISSUE: The Rev. Dr. Norman Vincent Peale, who is heading group of Protestant ministers and laymen, formed to discuss religious issue in the Presidential race.

about the religious issue in the current political campaign. That moment has surely come. All words and actions in this moment must be devoid of bitterness and fanaticism. It should be remembered that our organization is educational and that it has a permanent aim—the preservation of the American tradition of the separation of church and state.

We have consistently criticize literature expressing religious bigotry and scandal. Warnings regarding trash of this sort have frequently gone out from our headquarters. We have opposed the formation of any political party based on religious blocs in the population. We do not support or oppose any specific candidate or party in this or any election. Our members include Republicans, Democrats and independents. We want all of them to remain loyal to our purpose regardless of their political preference in this election.

Policy Discussed

Nevertheless, we cannot avoid recognition of the fact that one church in the United States, the largest church operating on American soil, officially supports a world-wide policy of partial union of church and state wherever it has the power to enforce such a policy. In the United States the bishops of this church have specifically rejected the Supreme Court's interpretation of the separation of church and state. In their statement, the Christian I Action, Nov. 21, 1948, they declare that the Supreme Court's interpretation of the First Amendment has reduced separation of church and state to "the shibboleth of doctrinaire secularism."

They then state: "We, therefore, hope and pray that the novel interpretation of the First Amendment recently adopted by the Supreme Court will in due process be revised. To that end we shall peacefully, patiently and perseveringly work."

The bishops have further committed themselves in this pronouncement to an interpretation of the Constitution which would permit full tax support for sectarian schools.

The Roman Catholic Church is both a church and a state. It has political representatives at forty-two of the world capitals and has many church political parties. The newest of these is a Catholic party called Christian Action now operative in Puerto Rico.

Birth-Control Issue

We cannot forget that the Roman Catholic Church has forbidden its members in the most specific language to "support any public assistance, either at home or abroad, to promote artificial birth prevention," and that its canon law denies to its members the right to send their children to American public schools without special permission. Canon Law 1374 reads: "Catholic children may not attend non-Catholic, neutral or mixed schools, that is, those which are open also to non-Catholics, and it pertains exclusively to the ordinary of the place to decide, in accordance with instructions of the Holy See, under what circumstances and with what precautions against the danger of perversion, attendance at such schools may be tolerated." (Bouscaren and Ellis, Canon Law, P. 704).

These policies are clearly inconsistent with the American concept of separation of church and state, and, to the extent that any candidate supports or endorses them, he is unfitted for the Presidency of the United States. To the extent that he repudiates these policies and demonstrates his independence of clerical control, he is entitled to our praise and encouragement.

Praise for Candidate

We have repeatedly praised the candidate of Roman Catholic faith in this campaign for declaring frankly that basic government financial support for parochial schools is unconstitutional. We have likewise praised him for his opposition to the appointment of an American Ambassador to the Vatican. We are skeptical about his equivocal words on birth control. We find that he has at no time stated simply that if Congress passed a law providing for aid in this matter that he would not hesitate to sign and administer it. We are concerned, too, about his silence in regard to the official boycott of public schools contained in the canon law of his church. We remain uneasy about the persistent denial of religious liberty to non-Catholics in some Roman Catholic countries such as Colombia and Spain, for we know that the Roman Catholic Church is everywhere committed to the doctrine that "error has no rights" theoretically. We know that in Spain twenty-two Protestant churches open for worship under the republic have since been closed by police and remain closed. We know that the Protestant seminary in Madrid was closed by police and cannot obtain permission to reopen. We know that two-thirds of the area of Colombia has been "roped off" from Protestant activity and more than 200 Protestant schools in this territory have been closed by police. What effect, we wonder, would the election of a Roman Catholic as President have upon governments which practice such suppression with the knowledge and cooperation of the Vatican? To ask Protestant and Jewish people to take a light view of this matter, or to disregard it entirely, is to be unrealistic. For us this is a matter of self-preservation.

Some Papers Praised

We commend that section of the press which has forthrightly and maturely dealt with the religious issue in this campaign. We regret the evasive journalism which, in other cases, has declined to face its responsibility in this respect. Some editors do not even recognize the elementary fact that one church in the United States has for centuries pursued a policy of partial union of church and state, and that the adoption of such a policy in this country would be a calamity of the first magnitude. When a candidate belongs to an organization which champions such a policy, it is not bigotry or prejudice to examine his credentials with the utmost care and frankness, and to ask how far his commitment goes.

We leave it to our members to decide for themselves, on the basis of all the evidence, whether the election of a Roman Catholic would promote or hinder the historic American principle of church-state separation. We recognize that millions of Roman Catholics in the United States are not only loyal to this American principle, but are also patriotic citizens. We also recognize that there are other issues in this campaign beside the church-state issue, and that it is the duty of the voters to choose the man they consider best fitted to meet all the exacting demands of the office.

September 8, 1960

Clergy and Scholars Fight Religious Pleas to Voters

By WAYNE PHILLIPS

One hundred American churchmen and scholars joined yesterday in a statement opposing "all attempts to make religious affiliation the basis of the voter's choice of candidates for public office." The signers of the statements included Archbishops of the Greek Orthodox and Roman Catholic faith, Bishops of the Protestant Episcopal and Methodist churches, and many prominent rabbis.

Many of the laymen who signed the statement hold or have held important positions in religious or educational organizations. However, it was emphasized that they were signing the statements as individuals.

Circulated Earlier

It was also stressed that the statement had been circulated before one issued last week in Washington by a group of Protestant leaders led by the Rev. Dr. Norman Vincent Peale, minister of the Marble Collegiate Church in New York.

The declaration by Dr. Peale's group questioned whether a Roman Catholic President could withstand pressure from the hierarchy of his church "to breach the wall of separation of church and state."

The statement issued yesterday made no reference to this.

Dr. Peale is a supporter of the Republican Presidential nominee, Vice President Nixon, a Quaker. The Democratic nominee, Senator John F. Kennedy of Massachusetts, is a Roman Catholic.

The dean of the Union Theological Seminary, Dr. John C. Bennett, denied yesterday that he had been referring to Dr. Peale when he attributed some of the attacks on Senator Kennedy to "a kind of Protestant underworld."

Dr. Bennett denounced the Peale group's statement in an editorial he wrote for the Sept. 19 issue of Christianity and Crisis, a Protestant interdenominational journal of opinion. But he distinguished between it and the unsigned attacks he attributed to the "underworld."

The governing council of the American Jewish Congress, in a meeting here yesterday, adopted a statement declaring that the issue of separation of church and state was a legitimate one for discussion in the Presidential campaign.

But the views of the candidate, and not the views of the organization to which he belongs, should be the basis for judging him, the statement contended.

The statement issued yesterday by the 100 churchmen and scholars originated with a small group of Protestant laymen. Among them was Francis S. Harmon, a New York lawyer formerly of Hattiesburg, Miss., who is active in the National Council of Churches, the Y. M. C. A. and the Riverside Church.

The statement was circulated by mail to prospective signers. An accompanying letter was written over the names of Dr. F. Ernest Johnson, professor emeritus of education at Columbia Teachers College; the Rev. John La Farge, a Jesuit scholar; Rabbi William F. Rosenblum, past president of the Association of Reform Rabbis of New York and the Synagogue Council of America, and Dean Liston Pope of the Yale Divinity School.

To meet the pictured challenge, the signers suggested ten principles as guidelines for action in the 1960 campaign. In paraphrase they were:

¶Exclusion of the members of any faith from public office violates the Constitution.

¶The bearing of the religious views of a candidate upon his decisions in public office is a public matter.

¶If an office holder cannot reconcile the responsibilities of his oath of office with his conscience he should resign.

¶Voters should not support a candidate solely because no one of his faith has ever been elected to a particular office.

¶No religious organization should seek to influence or dominate public officials for its own advantage.

¶No religious group should be

given special advantages by the state or be allowed to use state agencies to restrict other faiths.

¶A candidate's faith should be viewed in its best light rather than its worst.

¶Appointments made by public officials should be on a non-discriminatory basis.

¶A President is not obligated to participate in purely ceremonial functions that conflict with his religious faith.

¶A public official must recognize that the values of faiths other than his own must be brought to bear on the problems he faces.

Following is the list of the 100 persons who signed the statement. They include fifty-five Protestants, twenty-nine Roman Catholics, one Greek Orthodox and fifteen of the Jewish faith.

The Rev. Dr. Hampton Adams, New York.
Rabbi Morris Adler, Detroit.
The Rev. Dr. M. Forest Ashbrook, Scarsdale, N. Y.
Rabbi Bernard Bamberger, New York.
The Rev. Prof. John C. Bennett, New York.

Herbert Berman, Queens, N. Y.
Dr. Harry J. Carman, New York.
The Rev. Dr. Clarence W. Cranford, Washington.
Richard Cardinal Cushing, Archbishop of Boston.
The Rev. Thurston N. Davis, S. J., editor in chief, America, New York.
Prof. Dan W. Dodson, New York University.
The Rev. Robert F. Drinan, S. J., dean, Boston College Law School.
The Right Rev. Angus Dun, Washington.
The Right Rev. Richard Emrich, Detroit.
Rabbi Maurice N. Eisendrath, New York.
Moses I. Feuerstein, Brookline, Mass.
Dr. George Forell, Maywood, Ill.
The Very Rev. Msgr. Timothy J. Flynn, New York.
Dr. Herbert Gezork, Newton Center, Mass.
The Rev. Dr. Gerard R. Gnade, Ridgewood, N. J.
Miss Dorothy I. Height, New York.
Francis Stuart Harmon, New York.
Carlton J. H. Hayes, New York.
Miss Jane M. Hoey, New York.
The Rev. Dr. James E Hoffman, Hasbrouck Heights, N. J.
Prof. William Ernest Hocking, Madison, N. H.
The Rev. Luther Holcomb, Dallas.
Paul Horgan, Roswell, N. M.
Mrs. Mildred McAfee Horton, Randolph, N. H.
The Rev. Dr. Fred Hoskins, New York.
Paul Hume, Washington.
George K. Hunton, New York.
Archbishop Iakovos, New York.
Rabbi Jay Kaufman, Queens, N. Y.
Rabbi Wolfe Kelman, New York.
Rabbi Israel Klavan, Queens, N. Y.
The Rev. Dr. J. H. Jackson, Chicago.
The Rev. Dr. F. Ernest Johnson, New York.
Prof. Harry W. Jones, Columbia University, New York.

Dr. Lewis Webster Jones, New York.
The Rev. Dr. John LaFarge, S. J., New York.
Dr. Charles R. Lawrence, Pomona, N. Y.
Morris Laub, New York.
The Most Rev. Robert J. Dwyer, Bishop of Reno.
Dr. Donald C. Stone, Pittsburgh.
Mrs. Wallace Streeter, Washington.
Dr. Channing H. Tobias, New York.
The Rev. Dr. Luther A. Weigle, New Haven.
Bishop Lloyd C. Wicke, New York.
The Rev. Dr. Samuel McCrea Cavert, Bronxville, N. Y.
Rabbi Arthur Hertzberg, Englewood, N. J.
The Rev. Dr. J. Oscar Lee, Brooklyn.
Miss Edith Lerrigo, New York.
The Right Rev. Arthur Lichtenberger, Greenwich, Conn.
The Most Rev. Robert E. Lucey, Archbishop of San Antonio, Tex.
Benjamin E. Mays, president, Morehouse College, Atlanta.
The Rev. Dr. O. Clay Maxwell, New York.
Dr. Millicent McIntosh, president, Barnard College, New York.

Francis E. McMahon, Chicago.
Mrs. Eugene Meyer, Mount Kisco, N. Y.
The Rev. Dr. Arthur L. Miller, Denver.
The Right Rev. Msgr. Edward G. Murray, S. T. D., Roslindale, Mass.
The Rev. John Courtney Murray, S. J., Woodstock College, Md.
The Rev. Claud D. Nelson, New York.
The Rev. Prof. John Oliver Nelson, New Haven.
The Rev. Dr. Reinhold Niebuhr, New York.
Bishop G. Bromley Oxnam, Scarsdale, N. Y.
The Right Rev. James A. Pike, Protestant Episcopal Bishop, Diocese of California, San Francisco.
The Rev. Dr. Liston Pope, New Haven.

The Rev. Dr. Frank W. Price, New York.
Mrs. Roger Putnam, Springfield, Mass.
Rabbi Sidney L. Regner, New Rochelle, N. Y.
Prof. Ira De A. Reid, Haverford, Pa.
The Rev. Dr. Frederick E. Reissig, Washington.
The Rev. James H. Robinson, New York.
Rabbi William F. Rosenblum, New York.
Rabbi Edward T. Sandrow, Cedarhurst, L. I.
The Very Rev. Francis B. Sayre, Washington.
The Right Rev. Henry Knox Sherrill, Boxford, Mass.
Dr. George N. Shuster, New Rochelle, N. Y.

Mrs. Harper Sibley, Rochester, N. Y.
Edward Skillin, editor, The Commonweal, New York.
Harold C. Stevens, New York.
Miss Thelma Stevens, New York.
Schuyler N. Warren, New York.
Dr. Samson R. Weiss, New York.
Dr. Jesse R. Wilson, Wells, Tex.
Cleveland E. Dodge, New York.
Wayne H. Cowan, New York, managing editor, Christianity and Crisis.
Porter Chandler, New York.
The Right Rev. Horace W. B. Donegan.

Protestant Episcopal Bishop of New York.
Prof. Jerome G. Kerwin, University of Chicago.
William C. Martin, Methodist Bishop of Dallas, Tex.

Joseph J. Morrow, Stamford, Conn.
Gerard E. Sherry, Monterey, Calif.
Chauncey Stillman, New York.
John B. Sullivan, New York.
James F. Twohy, San Jose, Calif.
Rabbi Charles Weinberg, Malden, Mass.
Paul D. Williams, Richmond, Va.

September 12, 1960

Transcript of Kennedy Talk to Ministers and Questions and Answers

Following is a transcription of a television broadcast in Texas last night during which Senator Kennedy appeared before a meeting of the Greater Houston Ministerial Association, read a prepared statement and answered questions from members of the association, as recorded over a telephone line by The New York Times:

Kennedy's Statement

I am grateful for your generous invitation to state my views.

While the so-called religious issue is necessarily and properly the chief topic here tonight, I want to emphasize from the outset that I believe that we have far more critical issues in the 1960 election: the spread of Communist influence, until it now festers only ninety miles off the coast of Florida — the humiliating treatment of our President and Vice President by those who no longer respect our power — the hungry children I saw in West Virginia, the old people who cannot pay their doctor's bills, the families forced to give up their farms—an America with too many slums, with too few schools, and too late to the moon and outer space.

These are the real issues which should decide this campaign. And they are not religious issues—for war and hunger and ignorance and despair know no religious barrier.

But because I am a Catholic, and no Catholic has ever been elected President, the real issues in this campaign have been obscured—perhaps deliberately, in some quarters less responsible than this. So it is apparently necessary for me to state once again not what kind of church I believe in, for that should be important only to me, but what kind of America I believe in.

Backs Separation Ideal

I believe in an America where the separation of church and state is absolute—where no Catholic prelate would tell the President (should he be a Catholic) how to act and no Protestant minister would tell his parishioners for whom to vote—where no church or church school is granted any public funds or political preference—and where no man is denied public office merely because his religion differs from the President who might appoint him or the people who might elect him.

I believe in an America that is officially neither Catholic, Protestant nor Jewish—where no public official either requests or accepts instructions on public policy from the Pope, the National Council of Churches or any other ecclesiastical source—where no religious body seeks to impose its will directly or indirectly upon the general populace or the public acts of its officials—and where religious liberty is so indivisible that an act against one church is treated as an act against all.

For, while this year it may be a Catholic against whom the finger of suspicion is pointed, in other years it has been, and may someday be again, a Jew—or a Quaker or a Unitarian or a Baptist. It was Virginia's harassment of Baptist preachers, for example, that led to Jefferson's statute of religious freedom. Today, I may be the victim—but tomorrow it may be you—until the whole fabric of our harmonious society is ripped apart at a time of great national peril.

Finally, I believe in an America where religious intolerance will someday end—where all men and all churches are treated as equal—where every man has the same right to attend or not to attend the church of his choice—where there is no Catholic vote, no anti-Catholic vote, no bloc voting of any kind—and where Catholics, Protestants and Jews ,both the lay and the pastoral level, will refrain from those attitudes of disdain and division which have so often marred their works in the past, and promote instead the American ideal of brotherhood.

That is the kind of America in which I believe. And it represents the kind of Presidency in which I believe—a great office that must be neither humbled by making it the instrument of any religious group, nor tarnished by arbitrarily withholding it, its occupancy from the members of any religious group. I , believe in a President whose views on religion are his own private affair, neither imposed upon him by the nation or imposed by the nation upon him as a condition to holding that office.

I would not look with favor upon a President working to subvert the First Amendment's guarantees of religious liberty (nor would our system of checks and balances permit him to do so). And neither do I look with favor upon those who would work to subvert Article VI of the Constitution by requiring a

228

religious test—even by indirection—for if they disagree with that safeguard, they should be openly working to repeal it.

I want a chief executive whose public acts are responsible to all and obligated to none—who can attend any ceremony, service or dinner his office may appropriately require him to fulfill—and whose fulfillment of his Presidential office is not limited or conditioned by any religious oath, ritual or obligation.

This is the kind of America I believe in—and this is the kind of America I fought for in the South Pacific and the kind my brother died for in Europe. No one suggested then that we might have a "divided loyalty," that we did "not believe in liberty or that we belonged to a disloyal group that threatened "the freedoms for which our forefathers died."

And in fact this is the kind of America for which our forefathers did die when they fled here to escape religious test oaths, that denied office to members of less favored churches, when they fought for the Constitution, the Bill of Rights, the Virginia Statute of Religious Freedom—and when they fought at the shrine I visited today—the Alamo. For side by side with Bowie and Crockett died Fuentes and McCafferty and Bailey and Bedillio and Carey—but no one knows whether they were Catholics or not. For there was no religious test there.

I ask you tonight to follow in that tradition, to judge me on the basis of fourteen years in the Congress—on my declared stands against an ambassador to the Vatican, against unconstitutional aid to parochial schools, and against any boycott of the public schools (which I attended myself)—and instead of doing this do not judge me on the basis of these pamphlets and publications we have all seen that carefully select quotations out of context from the statements of Catholic Church leaders, usually in other countries, frequently in other centuries, and rarely relevant to any situation here - and always omitting, of course, that statement of the American bishops in 1948 which strongly endorsed church-state separation.

I do not consider these other quotations binding upon my public acts—why should you? But let me say, with respect to other countries, that I am wholly opposed to the state being used by any religious group, Catholic or Protestant, to compel, prohibit or prosecute the free exercise of any other religion. And that goes for any persecution at any time, by anyone, in any country.

And I hope that you and I condemn with equal fervor those nations which deny their Presidency to Protes-

tants and those which deny it to Catholics. And rather than cite the misdeeds of those who differ, I would also cite the record of the Catholic Church in such nations as France and Ireland—and the independence of such statesmen as de Gaulle and Adenauer.

But let me stress again that these are my views—for, contrary to common newspaper usage, I am not the Catholic candidate for President. I am the Democratic party's candidate for President who happens also to be a Catholic.

I do not speak for my church on public matters—and the church does not speak for me.

Whatever issue may come before me as President, if I should be elected—on birth control, divorce, censorship, gambling, or any other subject I will make my decision in accordance with these views, in accordance with what my conscience tells me to be in the national interest, and without regard to outside religious pressure or dictate. And no power or threat of punishment could cause me to decide otherwise.

But if the time should ever come—and I do not concede any conflict to be remotely possible—when my office would require me to either violate my conscience, or violate the national interest, then I would resign the office, and I hope any other conscientious public servant would do likewise.

But I do not intend to apologize for these views to my critics of either Catholic or Protestant faith, nor do I intend to disavow either my views or my church in order to win this election. If I should lose on the real issues, I shall return to my seat in the Senate satisfied that I tried my best and was fairly judged.

But if this election is decided on the basis that 40,000,-000 Americans lost their chance of being President on the day they were baptized, that it is the whole nation that will be the loser in the eyes of Catholics and non-Catholics around the world, in the eyes of history, and in the eyes of our own people.

But if, on the other hand, I should win this election, I shall devote every effort of mind and spirit to fulfilling the oath of the Presidency — practically identical, I might add, with the oath I have taken for fourteen years in the Congress. For, without reservation, I can, and I quote "solemnly swear that I will faithfully execute the office of President of the United States and will to the best of my ability preserve, protect and defend the Constitution, so help me God."

Questions and Answers

Q—I think I speak for many that do not in any sense discount or in any sense doubt your loyalty and your love to this nation, or your position

that's in accord with our position with regard to separation of church and state. But could I bring it down to where we stand right here tonight as two men of just nearly equal age just standing facing each other. If this meeting tonight were being held in the sanctuary of my church—it's the policy in my city that has many very fine Catholics in it but the policy of Catholic leadership to forbit them to attend a Protestant service. If we tonight were in the sanctuary of my church right behind we are, would you and could you attend as you have here?

SENATOR KENNEDY— Yes, I could. Now I can attend any—as I said in my statement I would attend any service in the interest, that had any connection with my public office or in the case of a private ceremony, weddings, funerals, and so on, of course I would participate, and have participated. I think the only question would be whether I could participate as a participant—a believer—in your faith and maintain my membership in my church. That seems to me comes within the private beliefs that a Catholic might have. But as far as whether I could attend this sort of a function in your church, whether I as Senator or President could attend a function in your service connected with my position of office, then I could attend, would attend.

Q—Was the position with gard to the chapel of the Catholics * * * dedicated, which I believe * * * the invitation to attend?

A—That's right.

Q—And then the press had said I believe Cardinal Dougherty brought pressure and you refused and did not attend?

A—I'd be delighted to explain because that seems to be a matter of great interest.

I was invited in 1947 after my election to the Congress by Dr. Daniel A. Poling to attend a dinner to raise funds for an interfaith chapel in honor of the four chaplains who went down on the Dorchester. That was fourteen years ago.

I was delighted to accept because I thought it was a useful and worth-while cause. A few days before I was due to accept, I learned through my administrative assistant who was, had, friends in Philadelphia that two things —first, that I was listed— and this is in Dr. Poling's book in which he describes the incident as the spokesman for the Catholic faith at the dinner—Charles Taft, Senator Taft's brother, was to be the spokesman for the Protestant faith. Senator Lehman was to be the spokesman for the Jewish faith.

The second thing I learned was that the chapel instead of being located as I thought it was as an interfaith chapel was located in the basement

of another church. It was not in that sense in a faith chapel, and for the fourteen years since that chapel was built there has never been a service of my church because of the physical location.

I therefore informed Dr. Poling that while I would be glad to come as a citizen—in fact many Catholics did go to the dinner—I did not feel that I had very good credentials to attend as the spokesman for the Catholic faith at that dinner to raise funds when the whole Catholic church group in Philadelphia were not participating, and because the chapel has never been blessed or consecrated.

Now, I want to make it clear that my grounds for not going were private. I had no credentials to speak for the Catholic faith at a dinner for a chapel at which no Catholic service has ever been held, so that, until this day, unfortunately, no service has been held at the present time.

Queried on Labor

Q.—Mr. Kennedy, Canon Rutenbahr of Christ Church Cathedral here in Houston. I've read this platform and the planks in it with great interest, and especially in the realms of freedom. And I note that in the educational section, the right of education for each person is guaranteed or offered for a guarantee. It also says that there shall be equal opportunity for employment. In another section it says there shall be equal rights to housing and recreation. All of these speak, I think, in a wonderful sense, to the freedom which we want to keep here in America.

Yet, on the other hand, there is in another place in the platform, I read these words: "We will repeal the authorization for right-to-work laws."

Now, it seems to me that in this aspect here, and I feel that these are much more important than any religious issue, here you are abolishing an open shop. You are taking away the freedom of the individual worker, whether he wants to work and wants to belong to this union or not.

Now, isn't this sort of double talk? You're guaranteeing freedom on the one hand, and yet you're going to take it away on the other.

A.—No, I don't agree with that.

Q.—I think there's a dichotomy here in the platform.

A.—Well, that provision's been in the platform since 1948. And I'm sure there's a difference of opinion between us on that matter and between many Democrats on that matter.

But I think that it's a decision which goes to economic and political views. I don't think it involves a constitutional guarantee of freedom.

In other words, under the provisions of the Taft-Hartley Law a state was permitted to prohibit a union shop. But it was not permitted to guarantee a closed shop.

Now, my own judgment is that uniformity in interstate commerce is valuable. And therefore, I hold with the view that it's better to have uniform laws and not a law which is, in interstate commerce, and these are all—this is not intra, but it's interstate commerce—which permits one condition in one state and another in another.

This is not a new provision. It's been in for the last three platforms.

Q— * * * Bible College and pastor of First Church of God here in Houston, and I am a member of the Houston Association of Ministers.

Mr. Kennedy, you very clearly stated your position tonight in regard to the propagation of the Gospel by all religious groups in other countries, and I appreciated that much because we Protestants are a missionary people.

However, the question I have to ask is this: if you are elected President, will you use your influence to get the Roman Catholic countries of South America and Spain to stop persecuting Protestant missionaries and to give equal rights to Protestants to to propagate their faith as the United States gives to the Roman Catholic or any other group.

A.—I would use my influence as President of the United States to permit, to encourage the development of freedom all over the world. One of the rights which I consider to be important is the right to free speech, the right of assembly, the right of free religious practice, and I would hope that the United States and the President would stand for those rights all around the globe, without regard to geography or religion, or critical position.

Thank you.

Q.—Mr. Kennedy, this is V. H. Westmore, pastor of the Southmay Baptist Church here in Houston. I have received today a copy of a resolution passed by the Baptist Pastors Conference of St. Louis and they are going to confront you with this tomorrow night. I would like for you to answer to the Houston crowd before you get to St. Louis.

This is the resolution: "With deep sincerity and in Christian grace we plead with Senator John F. Kennedy, as the person presently concerned in this matter, to appeal to Cardinal Cushing, Mr. Kennedy's own hierarchical superior in Boston, to present to the Vatican Mr. Kennedy's sincere statement relative to the separation of church and state in the United States and religious freedom as represented in the Constitution of the United States in order that the Vatican may officially authorize such a belief for all Roman Catholics in the United States."

Bars Church Advice

A.—May I just say as I do not accept the right of, as I said, any ecclesiastical official to tell me what I shall do in the sphere of my public responsibility as an elected official. I do not propose also to ask Cardinal Cushing to ask the Vatican to take some action. I do not propose to interfere with their free right to do exactly what they want. There's no doubt in my mind that the viewpoint that I have expressed [applause] tonight publicly represents the opinion of the overwhelming majority of American Catholics, and I have no doubt my view is known to Catholics around the world. I'm just hopeful that by my stating it quite precisely—and I believe I stated it in the tradition of the American Catholics way back all the way to Bishop John Carroll—I feel that—I hope this will clarify it without my having to take the rather circuitous route. This is the position I think of the American Catholic Church in the United States with which I am associated.

Q.—We appreciate your forthright statement. May I say we have great admiration for you, but until we know this is the position of your church, because there will be many Catholics who will be appointed if you are elected President, we would like to know that you are free to make such statements as you have been so courageous to make. [applause]

A.—So let me say that anyone that I would appoint to any office as a Senator, or as a President, would, I hope, hold the same view of the necessity of their living up to, not only the letter of the Constitution, but the spirit.

If I may say so, I am a Catholic. I've stated my view very clearly. I don't find any difficulty in stating that view. In my judgment it is the view of American Catholics from one end of the country to the other.

Why, because as long as I can state it in a way is, I hope, satisfactory to you, why do you possibly doubt that I represent a viewpoint which is hostile to the Catholic Church of the United States?

I believe I'm stating the viewpoint the Catholics in this country hold toward the happy relationship which exists between Church and State.

Q.—Let me ask you, sir, do you state it with the approval of the Vatican?

A.—I don't have to have approval in that sense.

Gives His Judgment

A.—But my judgment is that Cardinal Cushing, which is a Cardinal from the diocese of which I'm a member, would approve of this statement, in the same way that he approved of the 1948 statement of the Bishops.

In my judgment, and I'm not a student of theology, I am stating what I believe to be the position of—by personal position, and also the

position of the great majority * * *

Q.—Today, I had a telephone conversation with Dr. Poling and received this telegram from him. I'm sure you would like to clear this matter up. Let me read briefly from his telegram.

"The memorandum on religion as an election issue prepared by Senator Kennedy's associates has a section on the Poling incident.

"This section contains serious factual errors. I believe the Senator will wish to correct the errors, or that he will wish to withdraw that section.

"The original draft of the program on the interfaith dinner held in the Bellevue-Stratford Hotel on Dec. 15, 1947, identified Mr. Kennedy, then Congressman from Massachusetts, as Hon. John F. Kennedy, Congressman from Massachusetts. Mr. Kennedy was never invited as an official representative of a religious organization nor, indeed, as the spokesman for the Catholic faith.

"No speaker on that occasion—Catholic, Jew or Protestant — was identified by his faith. When, two days before the dinner occasion, Mr. Kennedy canceled his engagement, he expressed his regret and grief, but stated that since His Eminence the Cardinal requested him not to come, he, as a loyal son of the church, had no other alternative.

"Therefore it was necessary to destroy this first program and to reprint."

A.—Now, I will state again the words that I used, or quotation from the Rev. Poling's book, spokesman for the Catholic faith. A book which was produced about a year ago, which first discussed this incident.

Secondly, my memory of the incident is quite clear. In fact, it's as good as Rev. Poling's. Because when the matter was first discussed, Rev. Poling stated that the incident took place in 1950. And it's only in the last two months that it has come forward that the incident took place in 1947.

Thirdly, I never discussed the matter with Cardinal Dougherty in my life. I've never spoken to the Cardinal. I first learned of it through Mr. Riordan who was my administrative assistant, who knew of Mr. Doyle, who worked for the National Catholic Welfare Conference, who stated that there was a good deal of concern among many of the church people in Philadelphia because the location of the chapel, and because no service would ever be held in it because it was located in the basement of another church.

It was an entirely different situation than the one that I had confronted when I first happily accepted it.

Now there were three speakers — Kennedy was one of them, Taft was the second,

Senator Lehman was the third. I don't think I've misstated that one of them was supposed to speak for the Catholic faith, as a spokesman in Mr. Poling's words, one of them for the Protestant faith, and one for Jewish faith.

Now, all I can say to you, sir, is this chapel—I was glad to accept the invitation—I did not clear the invitation with anyone. It was only when I was informed that I was speaking, and I was invited, obviously, as a serviceman because I came from a prominent Catholic family, that I was informed that I was there really in a sense without any credentials.

The chapel, as I have said, has never had a Catholic service. Iit is not an interfaith chapel. And therefore for me to participate as a spokesman in that sense for the Catholic faith, I think would have given an erroneous impression.

Now, I've been there fourteen years. This took place in 1947. I'd been in politics probably two months, and was relatively inexperienced. I should have inquired before getting into the incident. Is this the only incident htta can be shown?

A Private Dinner
[applause.]

This was a private dinner. This was not a public dinner. This was a private dinner which did not involve my responsibilities as a public official. My judgment was bad only in accepting it without having all the facts, which I wouldn't have done at a later date. But I do want to say that I've been there for fourteen years. I have voted on hundreds of matters, probably thousands of matters, which involve all kinds of public questions, some of which border on the relationship between church and state, and quite obviously that record must be reasonably good or we wouldn't keep hearing about the Poling incident.

I don't mean to be disrespectful to Reverend Poling. I have high regard for his son. I have high regard for Dr. Poling. I don't like to be in a debate with him about, but I must say even looking back I think it was imprudent of me to have accepted with more information, but I don't really feel that it demonstrates unfitness to hold a public office.

Q.—The reason for our concern is the fact that your church has stated that it has the privilege and the right and the responsibility to direct its members in various areas of life including the political realm. But we believe that history and observation indicate that it has done so, and we raise the question because we would like to know if your are elected President and your church elects to use that privilege and obligation, what your response will be under those circumstances.

A.—If my church attempted to influence me in a way which was improper or which affected adversely my responsibilities as a public servant sworn to uphold the Constitution, then I would reply to them that this was an improper action on their part, it was one to which I could not subscribe, that I was opposed to it and that it would be an unfortunate breach of —an interference with—the American political system.

I'm confident that there would be no such interference. We've had two Chief Justices of the Supreme Court who were Catholics. We've had three Prime Ministers of Canada in this century. I've already mentioned Mr. de Gaulle and Mr. Adenauer. My judgment is that an American who is a Catholic, who is as sensitive as a Catholic must be who seeks this high office, as exposed to the pressures which whirl around us, that he will be extremely diligent in his protection of the Constitutional separation.

Q.—We would be most happy to have such a statement from the Vatican.

Sources Are Quoted

Q.—Because of the briefness of the time, let's cut out the applause.

Q.—Senator Kennedy, V. E. Howard, minister of the Church of Christ. First of all I should like to quote some authoritative quotations from Catholic sources, and then propose the question.

"So that a false statement knowingly made to one who has not a right to the truth will not be a lie"—Catholic Encyclopedia, vol. 10, page 696. Quoting: "However, we are also under an obligation to keep secrets faithfully and sometimes the easiest way of fulfilling that duty is to say what is false or tell a lie." Catholic Encyclopedia, Vol. 10, page 195. "When mental reservation is permissible it is lawful to cooperate one's utterances by an oath if there be an adequate cause."—Article on perjury, Catholic Encyclopedia Vol. 11, page 696 quoting again, "The truth we proclaim under oath is relative and not absolute."—Explanation of Catholic Morals, page 130.

Just recently from the Vatican in Rome this news release was given from the official Vatican newspaper, and I am quoting that of date May 19, 1960, Tuesday, that the Roman Catholic hierarchy had the right and duty to intervene in the political field to guide its flock. The newspaper rejected what is termed "the absurd split of conscience between the believer and the citizen."

However, Osservatore Romano made it clear that its announcement was valid for Roman Catholic laymen everywhere. It deplored the great confusion of ideas that is spreading especially between Catholic doctrine and social and political activities and between the ecclesiastical hierarchy and the lay faithful in the civil field.

Pope John XXIII recently gave this statement, I quote you The St. Louis Review, date of Dec. 12, 1958, "Catholics may unite their strength toward the common aid and the Catholic hierarchy has the right and duty of guiding them." Question, sir: Do you subscribe to the doctrine of mental reservation which I have quoted from the Catholic authorities? Do you submit to the authority of the present Pope which I have quoted from in these quotations?

A.—Well, let me say in the first place I've not read The Catholic Encyclopedia and I don't know all the quotation which you're giving me. I don't agree with the statement. I find no difficulty in saying so. But I do think probably I can get a, make a, better comment if I had the entire quotation before me. But in any case, I had not read it before and if the quotation is meant to imply that when you take an oath you don't mean it or that it's proper for you to take oaths and then break them, it's proper for you to lie, if that is what this states—and I don't know whether that's what it states unless I read it all in context and then of course I would not agree with it.

Secondly, on the question of the Osservatore Romano article, once again I don't have that in full.

I read the statement of last December which was directed to a situation in Siciliy where some of the Catholics were active in the Communist party. But I'm not familiar with the one of May, 1960, that you mention. In any case the Osservatore Romano has no standing as far as binding me.

Thirdly, quotation of Pope John of 1958, I didn't catch all of that, if you'll read that again, I'll tell you whether I support that or not.

Views on Pope John

Q.—Pope John XXIII only recently stated, according to St. Louis Review dated Dec. 12, 1958: "Catholics must unite their strength toward the common aim and the Catholic hierarchy has the right and duty of guiding them." Do you subscribe to that?

A.—Well, now, I don't, I couldn't describe . . . guiding them in what area. If you're talking about in the area of faith and morals, in the instructions of the church, I would think any Baptist minister or Congregational minister has the right and duty to try to guide his flock. If you mean by that statement that the Pope or anyone else could bind me in the fulfillment of my public duties, I say, "no."

If that statement is intended to mean, and it's very difficult to comment on a sentence taken out of an article which I have not read, but if that is intended to imply that the hierarchy has some obligations, or has an obligation, to attempt to guide the members of the Catholic Church, then that may be proper.

But it all depends on the previous language of what you mean by "guide." If you mean direct, or instruct, on matters dealing with the organization of the faith, the details of the faith, then, of course, they have that obligation. If you mean that by that under that to guide me or that anyone could guide or direct me in fulfilling my public duty, then I do not agree.

Q.—Thank you, sir. Then you do not agree with the Pope on that statement.

A.—Gentlemen, now that's why I wanted to be careful because that statement it seems to me is taken out of context that you just made to me. I could not tell you what the Pope meant unless I had the entire article. I would be glad to state to you that no one can direct me in the fulfillment of my duties as a public official under the United States Constitution that I am directed to do to the people of the United States, sworn to to an oath to God. Now that is my flat statement. I would not want to go into details on a sentence that you read to me which I may not understand completely.

Q.—We have time for one more question if it can be handled briefly.

Q.—Senator Kennedy: Robert McClaren from Westminster Presbyterian Church here in Houston.

You have been quite clear and I think laudably so on this matter of the separation of church and state, and you have answered very graciously the many questions that have come up around it. There is one question, however, which seems to me quite relevant and this relates to your statement that if you found by some remote possibility a real conflict between your oath of office as President that you would resign that office if it were in real conflict with your church.

A.—No, I said with my conscience.

Q.—With your conscience?

A.—Yes.

Q.—In the syllabus of errors of Pope Leo IX which the Catholic Encyclopedia states is still binding, although it is from a different century, it is still binding upon all Catholics, there are three very specific things which are denounced including the separation of state and church, the freedom of religion other than to Catholics to propagate themselves and the freedom of conscience. Do you still feel these being binding upon you, that you hold your oath of office above your allegiance to the Pope on these issues.

A.—Well, let's go through the issues, because I don't think there's a conflict on these three issues. The first issue, as I understood it, was on the relationship between the Catholic and the state and other faiths, was that it?

Q.—No, the separation of church and state, the explicitly * * *

A.—I support that, and in my judgment the American Bishops' statement of 1948 clearly supported it. That in my judgment is the view held by Catholics in this country. They support the Constitution of separation of church and state and they are not in error in that regard.

Q.—The second was the right of religions other than Roman Catholic to propagate themselves.

A.—II think they should be permitted to propagate themselves, any faith, without any limitations by the power of the state or encouragement by the power of the state. What was the third?

Q.—The third was the freedom of conscience in matters of religion and this also in Point 46, I believe it is, extends to freedom of the mind in the realms of science.

A.—Yes, well I believe in freedom of conscience. Let me just, I guess our time in coming to an end, but I believe in it. Let me state finally that I am delighted to come here today. I don't want anyone to think because they interrogate me on this very important question that I regard that as unfair questions, or unreasonable, or that if somebody who is concerned about the matter is prejudiced or bigoted. I think this fight for religious freedom is basic in the establishment of the American system, and therefore any candidate for the office, I think, should submit himself to the questions of any reasonable man. My only objection would be (applause).

My only limit to that would be that, if somebody said, "Regardless of Senator Kennedy's position, regardless of how much evidence he's given that if what he says he means, I still wouldn't vote for him because he's a member of that church," I would consider that unreasonable.

What I consider to be reasonable and an exercise of free will and free choice is to ask the candidate to state his views as broadly as possible, investigate his record to see whether he states what he believes and then make an independent rational judgment as to whether he could be entrusted with this highly important position.

So I want you to know that I am grateful to you for inviting me tonight. I'm sure that I have made no converts to my church, but I do hope that at least my view, which I believe to be the view of my fellow Catholics who hold office, I hope that it may be of some value in at least assisting you to make a careful judgment. Thank you.

September 13, 1960

Southern Baptists Now Hail Kennedy

By JOHN WICKLEIN

ST LOUIS, May 25 — The Southern Baptists Convention, which warned last year against the election of a Roman Catholic to the Presidency, today praised the Roman Catholic who was elected.

Twelve thousand "messengers" to the convention voted unanimously to send a telegram to President Kennedy expressing their appreciation of his stand in favor of religious liberty and the separation of church and state. They assured him of their prayers.

The motion was offered and adopted without a word of opposition from the floor.

More than one of the messengers remarked that "Jack Kennedy is making a pretty good Baptist President."

They went on to adopt a resolution criticizing the Roman Catholic hierarchy for waging "an aggressive campaign to press" the President and Congress into a program of tax-support for church-operated schools.

The President has declared that across-the-board aid to parochial schools is unconstitutional. The convention resolution opposed grants, loans or other direct aid at all levels of education.

It was introduced by the Rev. Dr. C. Emanuel Carlson of Washington, executive director of the Baptist Joint Committee of Public Affairs.

Backs Public Schools

In an interview he said the chief aim of the resolution was to preserve the strength of the public schools.

"It has become very popular in some circles—in the John Birch Society, for instance—to condemn the public schools," he said.

Church schools have an important role in education and should also be strengthened, he commented. But, he went on, this should be done by the churches themselves.

At the afternoon session, the convention turned to the issue of race relations, an issue that has been skirted in the last two years.

The Rev. Foy Valentine, executive secretary of the Christian Life Commission, delivered a report in which he said that racism "is almost beyond question the No. 1 social-political-moral problem in the world today."

Although the convention has gone on record time and again against racism, he said, many of its members have ignored the problem, hoping it would go away. Still others, he went on, have found in racism "a shoddy sanctuary from the Christian responsibility of cross-bearing."

He called on the messengers to "change the current pattern of tense, bitter, fruitless, antagonistic, sinful relationships between Negroes and whites to a pattern of positive Christian love and genuine Christian brotherhood."

Mr. Valentine's appeal followed one last night from Josephine Skaggs, a Southern Baptist Missionary to Nigeria.

Appeal From Nigeria

"My heart has been chilled by Southern Baptists who invited me to come to their churches to tell them about our mission work in Africa, but who refused to permit colored people to enter," she said, continuing:

"What good can the Peace Corps do as they say in effect, 'I hate Negroes at home, but I love them in Africa'?"

In response, the convention passed unanimously a resolution that said:

"Let us commit ourselves as Christians to do all that we can to improve the relations among all races as a positive demonstration of the power of Christian love."

The resolution, in an allusion to the Freedom Riders, rejected "mob violence and unwarranted provocations" as means of solving the race problem.

Earlier, the group turned aside a resolution that urged closer fellowship and cooperation with other Protestant denominations and requested colleges of the state Baptist conventions to admit Negroes.

The convention, which has a constituency of 9,700,000 members, will continue in session at the Kiel Auditorium here through tomorrow.

May 26, 1961

HIGH COURT BACKS STATES' BLUE LAWS

Pennsylvania, Maryland and Massachusetts Are Upheld on Sunday Trading Bans

By ANTHONY LEWIS
Special to The New York Times.

WASHINGTON, May 29 — The Supreme Court upheld today the constitutionality of state blue laws prohibiting commercial activity on Sunday.

An 8-to-1 majority rejected the contention that blue laws were invalid as an "establishment of religion," barred by the First Amendment. This argument held that the laws were designed to support the general Christian day of worship.

The court was more closely divided on a second question—whether blue laws might constitutionally be applied to Orthodox Jews, Seventh Day Adventists and others whose religion requires them to rest on another day of the week.

Those opposing the blue laws argued that they interfered with the "free exercise" of religion—also guaranteed in the First Amendment—by such persons. The court rejected the argument by a vote of 6 to 3.

Four cases, involving the blue laws of Maryland, Pennsylvania and Massachusetts, were decided today. There were nine opinions altogether, totaling 220 pages.

Chief Justice Earl Warren wrote the principal opinion in all four cases. In two cases he had a majority with his opinion. In the other two he spoke for only four justices, with concurrences supplying the margin for decision.

The sole dissenter who thought blue laws were invalid altogether as an establishment of religion was Justice William O. Douglas. Justices William J. Brennan Jr. and Potter Stewart thought the statutes could not constitutionally be applied to those whose religion demanded rest on a day other than Sunday.

Chief Justice Warren made a point of saying that the court was not now upholding any conceivable Sunday law. If such a statute had the clear purpose of using "the state's coercive power to aid religion," he said it would be unconstitutional.

Nevertheless, the various opinions today, and the state laws they upheld, made it extremely unlikely that any Sunday law would be struck down.

Alaska Only Exception

Forty-nine states, all but Alaska—now have laws prohibiting some activities on Sunday. Thirty-four, including New York, have statutes broadly prohibiting all commercial labor. Of these states, twenty-one provide limited exemption for Orthodox Jews and others who celebrate another day as the Sabbath.

The four cases considered by the court today divided, in the issues they raised, into two groups.

The first case from Maryland, began with the criminal prosecution of seven employes of a highway discount store for selling such things as a can of floor wax and a toy submarine on Sunday. They were fined $5 each.

The second case came from Pennsylvania. A discount house known as Two Guys from Harrison-Allentown sought an injunction against enforcement of the Pennsylvania Blue Law. A three-judge Federal District Court refused the injunction.

In these two cases the Chief Justice's opinions were joined by Justices Hugo L. Black, Tom C. Clark, Charles E. Whittaker, Brennan and Stewart. Justice Felix Frankfurter wrote a concurring opinion joined by Justice John Marshall Harlan.

Exemptions Attacked

Those challenging the Maryland and Pennsylvania laws argued that the laws were so riddled with irrational exemptions that they denied the equal protection of the laws under the Fourteenth Amendment. For example, the laws allowed some foods to be sold but not others.

Chief Justice Warren brushed aside this equal-protection argument. He said the states had broad power to classify and could not be said to have no reason for barring hunting, for example, but allowing it if done by organized rod and gun clubs.

The Chief Justice traced the history of blue laws back to 1237, when Henry III of England forbade the frequenting of markets on Sunday. He agreed that their origins were religious.

Further, the opinion noted that both the Maryland and Pennsylvania statutes still contained such phrases as "the Lord's day." They trace back to the earliest blue laws in the two states, 1649 in Maryland and 1682 in Pennsylvania.

But Chief Justice Warren said that the purpose of Sunday-closing statutes had gradually changed over the years. Nowadays, he said, their basic purpose is to prevent overwork and unfair competition.

"It is not difficult to discern," he said, "that as presently written and administered, most [blue laws], at least, are of a secular rather than a religious character."

"People of all religions and people with no religion," he went on, "regard Sunday as a time for family activity, for visiting friends and relatives, for late-sleeping, for passive and active entertainments, for dining out and the like."

The two other cases came from Pennsylvania and Massachusetts. Both were brought by Orthodox Jews who contended that the states' blue laws were unconstitutional as applied to them.

In the Pennsylvania case, five retailers in Philadelphia sought an injunction against the laws. A three-judge Federal District Court turned them down. In Massachusetts an injunction was sought by the Crown Kosher Super Market of Springfield, three of its Orthodox customers and the chief Orthodox rabbi of the city. A three-judge Federal District Court ruled in their favor—the only one of the four lower courts to do so—and held the Massachusetts blue law unconstitutional.

In both cases those attacking the laws pointed out that, under orthodox Jewish doctrine, they had to close their places of business before sundown Friday and remain closed all day Saturday. Unless they can open Sunday, they said, they will be in operation less than five days a

week and be at a tremendous disadvantage.

Chief Justice Warren agreed that the laws would hurt Orthodox Jews and others who celebrated Saturday as the Sabbath. But he said this was only an indirect effect on religion and not a prohibition on its free exercise.

"The Sunday law," he said, "simply regulates a secular activity and, as applied to appellants, operates so as to make the practice of their religious beliefs more expensive."

"We cannot find a state without power to provide a weekly respite from all labor," the Chief Justice said, "and at the same time to set one day of the week apart from the others as a day of rest, repose, recreation and tranquilty."

Justice Frankfurter's concurrence applied also to these two cases. He and Justice Harlan agreed generally that a state could enforce blue laws even against persons who would be obliged to close shop an extra day a week because of their religion.

But Justice Frankfurter, without Justice Harlin's concurrence here, found a flaw in the

case of the five Jewish retailers from Pennsylvania.

He said their suit had been dismissed improperly without trial and they should have had their day in court. He therefore dissented, making the vote for affirmance of the lower court in this case, 5 to 4.

Justice Brennan, dissenting, said the court's decision had "exalted administrative convenience" to a constitutional principle by refusing to demand an exemption for Jews and others who believed in a Sabbath other than Sunday.

The result, he said, is to "make one religion economically disadvantageous."

Justice Stewart, agreeing with that view, wrote:

"Pennsylvania has passed a law which compels an Orthodox Jew to choose between his religious faith and his economic survival. That is a cruel choice. It is a choice which I think no state can constitutionally demand."

Justice Douglas, dissenting in all four cases, said he did not "see how a state can make protesting citizens refrain from doing innocent acts on Sunday because the doing of those acts

offends sentiments of their Christian neighbors."

"No matter how much is written," Justice Douglas said, "no matter what is said, the parentage of these laws is the Fourth Commandment [ordaining the Sabbath]; and they serve and satisfy the religious predispositions of our Christian communities."

The Maryland case was argued by John Martin Jones Jr. for the state and Harry Silbert of Baltimore for the retailer. In the first Pennsylvania case Harry J. Rubin argued for the state and Harold E. Kohn of Philadelphia for the discount house.

David Berger, City Solicitor of Philadelphia, defended the blue law against attack by the five Jewish merchants of that city, and Theodore R. Munn of Philadelphia opposed him. Joseph H. Elcock, Assistant Attorney General of Massachusetts, represented that state, and Herbert B. Ehrmann represented the Crown market.

May 30, 1961

Presbyterians Bid Churches Cut Ties To Civil Authority

By GEORGE DUGAN
Special to The New York Times

DES MOINES, Iowa, May 21—The United Presbyterian Church, at its General Assembly here, opposed devotional acts in the public schools today in a statement on church-state relations.

Denominational leaders regard the statement as the most comprehensive document on the subject ever prepared by a Christian body. It took issue with such acts as Bible reading and prayer in public schools, religious observances and displays on public property and Sunday closing laws.

The document was a result of three years of study by a special committee. The Rev. Dr. Elwyn A. Smith, professor of church history at the Pittsburgh Theological Seminary, was chairman of the committee.

After the statement was approved, Dr. Smith said that for the first time a major Protestant body "has faced up to its responsibilities in a pluralistic

society." Presbyterianism has "finally come to terms with pluralism on theological grounds," he said.

The United States Supreme Court is expected to rule shortly on two cases involving the constitutionality of Bible reading and prayer conducted by public school authorities. In essence, the question is whether such exercises are religious in nature and thus violate the Constitution's prohibition of the "establishment of religion."

In an introductory comment, the statement said, "We Presbyterians wish to live, teach and evangelize within a political order in which no church will dominate the civil authorities or be dominated by them."

The introduction made clear that the Assembly was not uttering pronouncements binding on Christian conscience. Nevertheless, it said, "No conscientious Presbyterian should ignore the guidance of the General Assembly as representative of the whole church."

Most of the debate, as expected, centered on Bible reading and prayer in the public schools. A number of the 840 commissioners, or delegates, said that the omission of such devotions would result in a "withdrawal" of all knowledge of God.

Ask Omission of Prayers

The vast majority, however,

agreed that Bible reading and prayers as devotional acts tended toward "indoctrination or meaningless ritual" and should be omitted for both reasons.

At the same time, it was asserted that Bible reading in connection with courses in the American heritage, world history, literature, the social sciences and other academic subjects was "completely appropriate" to public school instruction.

Ministers, priests and rabbis should be free to speak in public schools, provided their speaking did not constitute religious indoctrination or their presence form a part of a religious observance, the document contended.

Religious observances should "never" be held in a public school or introduced into the public school as part of its program, the statement said.

Compulsion Is Opposed

Questioned later about baccalaureate services, Dr. Smith said that if they were held in a public school and were compulsory they "don't belong there."

The Assembly also agreed that:

¶Religious holidays should be acknowledged and explained, but never celebrated religiously, by public schools or their administrators when acting in an official capacity.

¶Whenever possible, students of various religious faiths should be allowed sufficient time to permit the celebration

of their religious observances away from public school property. However, organized religious groups should avoid jeopardizing the integrity of the public educational process by unreasonable demands for time away from public schools for any reason.

¶Public officials should permit displays, pageants or services of a religious nature on public property provided there is no discrimination. All fees and rentals should be borne by the religious group involved, except for necessary police and fire protection.

¶Where a religious agency not supported by public funds ministers to the general public, it has the moral responsibility to make clear to its patients or patrons those areas in which, because of religion, its practices depart from, conflict with or prohibit certain procedures established by medical or public consensus.

¶United Presbyterians should carefully investigate the effect of existing Sunday closing laws on persons who, because of their faith, voluntarily cease economic activity on a day other than Sunday and are required by law to cease their economic activity on Sunday as well. United Presbyterians should seek amendments exempting such persons from Sunday laws as a part of an authentic concern about their fellow men.

May 22, 1963

SUPREME COURT, 8 TO 1, PROHIBITS LORD'S PRAYER AND BIBLE READING AS PUBLIC SCHOOL REQUIREMENTS

2 CASES DECIDED

Government Must Be Neutral in Religion, Majority Asserts

By ANTHONY LEWIS
Special to The New York Times

WASHINGTON, June 17 — The Supreme Court decided today that no state or locality may require recitation of the Lord's Prayer or Bible verses in public schools.

An 8-to-1 majority wrote what appeared to be a final legal answer to one of the most divisive issues of church and state. The opinion of the Court was by Justice Tom C. Clark.

Even the sole dissenter, Justice Potter Stewart, said that religious ceremonies in public schools could violate the constitutional rights of dissenters. But he found the record in today's cases inadequate and would have sent them back for further hearings.

The prayer cases were among a dozen decided today in what turned out to be the final session of the present Supreme Court term. The Court recessed until October.

Insists on Neutral Stand

Justice Clark sounded the theme that government must be "neutral" in religious matters.' His opinion ended with these philosophical phrases:

"The place of religion in our society is an exalted one, achieved through a long tradition of reliance on the home, the church and the inviolable citadel of the individual heart and mind.

"We have come to recognize through bitter experience that it is not within the power of government to invade that citadel, whether its purpose or effect be to aid or oppose, to advance or retard.

"In the relationship between man and religion, the state is firmly committed to a position of neutrality."

Seek to Soften Criticism

Today's decision was a follow-up to last year's ruling against he recitation in New York public schools of a prayer composed by the State Board of Regents. The Justices were evidently concerned to prevent, as best they could, the bitter criticism that greeted the New York case.

In his opinion Justice Clark stressed the importance of religion in this country's tradition. He took care to say that the decision did not affect the right to use the Bible for teaching purposes or did not deal with such other matters as Army chaplains.

Justices William J. Brennan Jr. and Arthur J. Goldberg, in concurring opinions, also sought to disarm potential criticism. The Goldberg opinion was joined by Justice John Marshall Harlan.

Varied Voices Speak

It was particularly noted by courtroom observers that the voices of a Protestant, a Catholic and a Jew on the Court spoke up for the principle of church-state separation.

Justice Clark is a Presbyterian active in the affairs of his church here. Justice Brennan is the Court's only Roman Catholic and Justice Goldberg the only Jewish member.

The Court's decision dealt with two cases, from Maryland and Pennsylvania. Each involved both the reading of Bible verses to the students each morning, and the recitation of the Lord's Prayer by the classes in unison. The factual settings differed slightly.

In Pennsylvania a state statute requires the reading of "at least 10 verses from the Holy Bible, without comment, at the opening of each public school on each school day."

The law was amended in 1959 to allow children to be excused at their parents' request.

A suit challenging the practice was filed by Edward Lewis Schempp, a Unitarian, his wife and two children, Roger and Donna. The children attend Abington Senior High School, near Philadelphia.

In that school the practice is for selected students to read verses from the Bible over the public address system each morning. Then the students in every classroom stand and repeat the Lord's Prayer in unison.

Find Conflict With Beliefs

The Schempps said these exercises conflicted with their religious beliefs. They did not seek to have Roger and Donna excused, feeling—Justice Clark said—that their "relationships with their teachers and classmates would be adversely affected."

The Maryland case involved a ruling of the Baltimore school board requiring the reading of a Bible chapter "and/or The Lord's Prayer" at daily opening exercises in schools.

The case was brought by Mrs. Madalyn Murray and her son, William J. Murray 3d, both professed atheists. They said that William had been subjected to taunts and physical assault in school because of his having objected to the morning exercises.

The lower courts came out opposite ways in the two cases.

A three-judge Federal District Court in Pennsylvania held the prayer and Bible-reading unconstitutional. Maryland's highest tribunal, the Court of Appeals, voted 4 to 3 to sustain the Baltimore practice.

The legal issue was the meaning of the First Amendment's religious provision—"Congress shall make no law respecting an establishment of religion or prohibiting the free exercise thereof."

'Decisively Settled'

First, Justice Clark said the Supreme Court had "decisively settled" that these two clauses —on establishment and free exercise of religion—were made applicable to the states by the 14th Amendment. He cited cases back to 1940.

Second, he said the Court had "rejected unequivocally the contention that the establishment clause forbids only governmental preference of one religion over another."

He noted that 16 years ago the Court said the clause also forbade laws aiding "one religion or all religions."

No party to the case had questioned these two "long-established" points, Justice Clark said. But he said others had, and so the court was emphasizing that any doubts about them could only be "academic exercises."

The Regents prayer opinion last year, which was written by Justice Hugo L. Black, rested entirely on the establishment clause of the First Amendment. Justice Clark eventually did so, too, but he discussed the free exercise clause at length along the way.

Both clauses, Justice Clark said, enforce governmental neutrality on religion. Of the purpose or effect of legislation is to inhibit or advance religion, he concluded, the Constitution is violated.

But in a free exercise case, the opinion continued, the citizen must show some coercive effect of government action on his religious practices. The establishment clause can be violated without coercing any individual.

Justice Clark said there was no question but that the required recitations in public schools, with children under compulsory school attendance laws, were an establishment. The logic of his opinion would doubtless apply to any teacher's undertaking a prayer exercise without official orders.

Argument Dismissed

The opinion dismissed the argument, made by both Baltimore and Pennsylvania authorities, that these were not religious exercises but were merely designed to promote "moral values."

Justice Clark said:

"Surely the place of the Bible as an instrument of religion cannot be gainsaid."

"It certainly may be said that the Bible is worthy of study for its literary and historic qualities," Justice Clark said.

Pointedly, he remarked that today's decision did not rule out any such study in public schools "when presented objectively as part of a secular program of education.

"But the exercises here do not fall into those categories," he continued. "They are religious exercises, required by the states in violation of the command of the First Amendment that the government maintain strict neutrality, neither aiding nor opposing religion."

Justice Stewart, in his dissent, conceded that the prayer and Bible-reading requirements would be "extremely doubtful" under the establishment clause of the First Amendment if they plainly insisted on a "a particular religious book and a denominational prayer."

But in fact, he said, the Maryland and Pennsylvania practice was to allow the use of varying versions of the Bible —Protestant, Catholic and Jewish. Thus he said the effect was to allow the majority of each community to exercise its religion freely in the public schools.

The real issue, Justice Stewart said, was whether in the course of such exercises minorities were being coerced in their beliefs — denied the free exercise of their religion.

"The dangers of coercion" are greater in a schoolroom than

in adult situations, Justice Stewart noted.

He conceded that religious exercises with no provision for students to be excused or to give them some "equally desirable alternative" to occupy their time would be "unconstitutionally coercive."

Says Proof Is Required

But Justice Stewart said all these factors should not be assumed. There should be proof of coercion on any complaining child, he said, and there was none in these cases. Therefore he concluded that further evidence should be taken.

There were three concurring opinions, all expressly joining Justice Clark's views but going on to elaborate personal observations.

Justices Brennan and Goldberg each dismissed as without weight the contention that those cases were somehow different from the Regents prayer because they did not involve material composed by state officials. They called that "constitutionally irrelevant."

Both opinions also went out of their way to say that other religious elements in public life would not be affected.

Justice Goldberg emphasized what he termed, here, "the pervasive religiosity and direct governmental involvement."

Some Activities Exempted

Justice Brennan listed a number of activities that he indicated would not be held constitutional violations — the provision of chaplains in prisons and military camps, the saying of prayers in legislatures, teaching about religion, uniform tax exemptions for religious institutions, public welfare benefits that incidentally aid individual worshipers.

The Brennan opinion, 77 printed pages long, canvassed the history of the church-state conflict to show long concern in this country about any breakdown of church-state separation. It concluded:

"The principles which we reaffirm and apply today can hardly be thought novel or radical. They are, in truth, as old as the republic itself."

The third concurring opinion was by Justice William O. Douglas. It briefly repeated a view he expressed in the New York case last year that any use of public funds for a church, however small, is unconstitutional.

Justice Douglas said, that the vice in any such aid is that "the state is lending its assistance to a church's efforts to gain and keep adherents."

The Baltimore case was argued for the Murrays by Leonard J. Kerpelman and for the city by City Solicitor Francis B. Burch; his deputy, George W. Baker Jr., and Attorney General Thomas B. Finan of Maryland.

Henry W. Sayer 3d of Philadelphia represented the Schempps. The state's case was argued by Philip H. Ward 3d of Philadelphia and John D. Killian 3d, Deputy Attorney General.

Mrs. Murray was in the courtroom today with a younger son, 8-year-old Garth. She said they had had stones thrown at their home because of the litigation and that despite today's victory, they were going to leave Baltimore.

June 18, 1963

Freedom of Religion

It is to protect freedom of worship that the Supreme Court once again has ruled against official school prayers. That is the meaning of this week's decision that Bible reading and recitation of the Lord's Prayer in Maryland and Pennsylvania public schools were unconstitutional. Last June the Court held that reading the State Regents' prayer aloud in New York public schools violated the Constitution. These decisions together should now result in ending religious exercises where practiced in many school districts across the country.

In his opinion for the 8-to-1 majority, Justice Clark pointed out Monday that "In the relationship between man and religion, the state is firmly committed to a position of neutrality." Justice Goldberg, in a concurring opinion, emphasized the fact that neutrality is mandated by the Constitution. And neutrality means favoring neither religion nor non-religion.

The First Amendment is a two-edged protection for freedom of worship. It forbids the Government from establishing an official religion; it also forbids the Government from prohibiting the free exercise of religion. These two aspects are indivisible and they insure for religion in this country both its individuality and its freedom. Freedom of religious practice can be observed in homes and churches under family and self-chosen guidance.

The Supreme Court has outlawed neither God nor the Lord's Prayer; to say it has is completely to distort the truth. Far from interfering with freedom of religion, the Supreme Court decision helps guarantee it.   June 19, 1963

SUPPORT GROWING FOR PAROCHIAL AID

By GENE CURRIVAN

A drive for legislation to provide state funds for parochial schools is gaining momentum throughout the nation.

The traditional argument that direct aid is prohibited by the constitutional provision for separation of church and state appears to be overshadowed increasingly by the economic argument that it may be cheaper to aid parochial school pupils now than take on the full cost burden if those schools are forced to close.

Connecticut and Rhode Island this year have agreed to provide direct aid to parochial schools, following the example set last year by Pennsylvania. Similar legislation failed this year in seven states, but proponents are still pushing the idea in at least 22 states.

The Pennsylvania law was challenged several days ago in a key test case in the United States District Court in Philadelphia by six major organizations. The American Jewish Congress, involved in the Pennsylvania case, also plans to bring suits in Rhode Island and Connecticut.

The mounting legislative campaign, bolstered by a recent Supreme Court decision permitting textbook loans to nonpublic schools, has been characterized as "unprecedented" by Joseph B. Robison, director of the Congress' Commission on Law and Social Action.

"The drive is unusual," he said "not only in the amount of pressure generated but also in the kinds of demands made.

"The stress is no longer on such fringe benefits as free buses and textbooks but on outright financing—the payment of tax-raised funds directly into the treasuries of the schools," Mr. Robison said.

"In most of the states in which the legislatures have completed their work, these proposals were defeated," he said. "Notable were Michigan, where a well-publicized, hotly debated drive for various forms of 'parochiaid' was defeated, and New York where the Legislature rejected a variety of proposals — passing only one, which was then vetoed by Governor Rockefeller."

At Grass Roots Level

But the mounting drive "is very hopeful for the future of our schools," according to the Rev. C. Albert Koob, head of the National Catholic Educational Association in Washington. "The interest is considerable and it is mostly at the grass roots level—and spreading fast."

Earlier this year, Msgr. James C. Donohue, a director of the United States Catholic Conference who speaks for the bishops, said that about two million Roman Catholic elementary school pupils would be dropped in the next six years unless there was a vast upsurge in public support. This would represent about half the current enrollment.

In New York state, where all bills failed, the state aid advocates saw future hope in Governor Rockefeller's support for a constitutional amendment that would permit aid to sectarian institutions of higher learning. The present Blaine Amendment precludes state aid to any type of religiously affiliated schools.

Pennsylvania set the pace last year with an appropriation of $4.6-million from the proceeds of harness racing for nonpublic schools and is now seeking $45-million that would dip into cigarette tax revenues. The state's House of Representatives passed the latest measure, but there was doubt about Senate passage even before the Federal Court suit was filed.

"I don't think you can get $45-million out of this Senate for a program that is under legal challenge," said State Senator Preston B. Davis, chairman of the Education Committee. "The parochial school system is doomed because of spiraling costs. The question is can we help them out during this phasing-out period?"

State Representative Martin P. Mullen, chairman of the Appropriations Committee, who has threatened to block any new taxes required to balance the budget unless the bill is passed, argued that the taxpayers would save "tremendous sums of money" by keeping nonpublic schools open instead of forcing the pupils into the public school system.

Mr. Mullen said four Catholic schools closed last year for financial reasons, 10 more will close in September, and 35 to 45 are expected to close over the next three years unless substantial tax aid is given.

The bill provides for nonpublic educational services in four instructional subjects — modern languages, mathematics, physical education and physical science.

The Connecticut bill, which anticipated a constitutional challenge, will pay $6-million over two years, provides for payment of 20 per cent of salaries of teachers who teach nonreligious subjects.

The state also will pay for textbooks on secular subjects in the amount of $10 for each pupil from Grades 1-8 and $15 for each pupil from Grades 9-12.

Furthermore, to induce nonpublic schools to take disadvantaged children, the state will pay 50 per cent of teacher costs in nonreligious subjects where classes have a one-third enrollments of disadvantaged children and 60 per cent of teachers in classes having a two-thirds enrollment of disadvantaged children.

During debate in the Connecticut House, Representative Thomas J. Donnelly, Republican, lamented "the unseemly spectacle of my church scrambling for public funds."

The Connecticut Civil Liberties Union has already announced plans for a suit.

The bill allows for a test of its constitutionality in that payments will not be made until the second year.

Rhode Island came up with $375,000 for part payment of teachers salaries in Grades 1-8. The bill provides for underwriting 15 per cent of salaries of those teaching secular subjects and who receive a minimum of $4,000 a year but not more than the maximum in the public schools.

Gov. Richard B. Ogilvie of Illinois asked unsuccessfully for state grants totaling $32-million for nonpublic schools. The bill was sponsored by Representative Edward J. Copeland, Republican of Chicago, who is of the Jewish faith. The measure asked for $60 for each elementary grade pupil and $90 for each high school student. It passed the House, but failed in the Senate, where there is considerable opposition to the Governor's revenue program.

In Michigan, a bill that would pay up to 75 per cent of salaries of teacher of secular subjects failed by a narrow margin. It would have provided $44-million for 1970-71.

The opposition was composed mostly of the 70,000-member Michigan Education Association, Protestant Church groups and the American Civil Liberties Union. The Catholic proponents were aided by Dutch Reform Church groups in western Michigan working through the Michigan Association of Non-Public Schools.

The Missouri legislature killed a series of bills that would have provided for textbooks, scholarships, busing, driver education and classes for the handicapped. The Catholic groups in Missouri are trying to get a foot in the door rather than go all out for broad-based aid.

State aid bills enacted this year, besides, those in Connecticut and Rhode Island, were a text book rental measure in Indiana and a transportation bill in Minnesota. Bills for a wide variety of state aid were defeated in Illinois, Michigan, Montana, Missouri, New Mexico, New York and West Virginia.

June 16, 1969

COURT BARS ROLE IN CHURCH DOGMA

By FRED P. GRAHAM

Special to The New York Times

WASHINGTON, Jan. 27 — Courts in the United States may not undertake to judge whether or not a religious body has violated its own beliefs, the Supreme Court declared today.

Thus, the Justices ruled, it is unconstitutional for civil courts to award church property to dissident congregations on the ground that the parent church has lost the faith.

The decision appeared to doom a spate of court suits that have recently been brought by conservative church congregations claiming the right to take their local property and to leave the parent church organizations. These suits have alleged that the parent churches have embraced innovations that violate church dogma.

Today's unanimous decision overturned a ruling of the Supreme Court of Georgia, which had upheld a jury's finding that the Presbyterian Church in the United States—usually called the Southern Presbyterian Church—had abandoned some of its traditional tenets of faith.

As a result of the Georgia ruling, the breakaway Hull

Memorial and Eastern Heights Presbyterian Churches of Savannah had been granted title to their church properties. Today's decision reversed that ruling.

"First Amendment values are plainly jeopardized when church property litigation is made to turn on the resolution by civil courts of controversies over religious doctrine and practice," Justice William J. Brennan Jr. wrote in the Court's opinion.

He ruled that the Georgia courts had breached the separation between church and state that the First Amendment requires when they permitted a jury—which was dominated by Baptists and included no Presbyterians—to consider whether the Southern Presbyterian church had violated its tradi-

tional beliefs. The jury heard testimony from theologians and concluded that it had.

The congregations of the two local churches had voted overwhelmingly to pull out of the parent church in 1966, accusing it of "revolutionary, fundamental, unlawful and radical diversion from the Presbyterian faith."

Specifically, they objected to the parent church's support of civil rights activities, civil disobedience tactics and Vietnam war dissent. They also complained that the general church had modified the doctrine of predestination and had approved the ordination of women as ministers.

They argued that the parent church was no longer the church that they had joined when the local units were

formed decades ago. Since the local people had financed the purchase of the property, they demanded the right to pull out and worship according to the original beliefs.

When the parent church indicated that it would send new pastors to take over the church property, the local groups brought suit to establish their ownership of it.

Although courts have traditionally upheld the parent church in such disputes without considering the doctrinal issues, the Georgia courts ruled the opposite in this case because the Southern Presbyterian Church was found guilty of a "substantial abandonment" of its original faith.

In reversing that decision, the Supreme Court ruled today that civil courts would have to

"determine matters at the very core of a religion" to decide whether there had been a substantial departure from dogma.

The ruling will affect only hierarchical denominations that give the parent body control of local church affairs. These include the Episcopalians, Lutherans and Methodists.

It will not affect such non-hierarchical churches as Baptists, Quakers, Christians, Unitarians and Jews. Local branches of these churches retain local autonomy and can depart with their property at any time.

Charles L. Gowen of Atlanta argued for the Southern Presbyterian Church. Owen H. Page of Savannah argued for the local churches.

January 28, 1969

Niebuhr Is Critical of President's Sunday Services

Theologian Says Nixon Undermines Separation of Church and State

By EDWARD B. FISKE

Reinhold Niebuhr, the theologian and social philosopher, has accused President Nixon of undermining the separation of of church and state by holding Sunday morning worship services in the East Room of the White House.

Writing in the current issue of Christianity and Crisis, a biweekly journal of liberal religious and social comment that he helped found more than two decades ago, the 77-year-old Protestant thinker said:

"By a curious combination of innocence and guile, he [Mr. Nixon] has circumvented the Bill of Rights' first article. Thus he has established a conforming religion by semi-officially inviting representatives of all the disestablished religions, of whose moral criticism we were naturally so proud."

Dr. Niebuhr also accused the President of giving semiofficial support to the religious attitudes of Billy Graham, the evangelist, who is a personal friend of Mr. Nixon and who preached at the first service, on Jan. 26.

The "Nixon-Graham doctrine of the relation of religion to public morality and policy" precludes criticism on religious

grounds of public policies, Dr. Niebuhr charged.

'Complacent Conformity'

"It was this type of complacement conformity that the Founding Fathers feared and sought to eliminate in the First Amendment," he said.

Dr. Niebuhr, a former professor at Union Theological Seminary, is widely regarded as the most prestigious living Protestant thinker. He now lives in retirement in Stockbridge, Mass.

Thus far Mr. Nixon has held 10 Sunday morning services in the East Room of the White House. Other preachers have included Terence Cardinal Cooke of New York; the Rev. Norman Vincent Peale, pastor of the Marble Collegiate Church in Manhattan, and Dr. Paul S. Smith, president of Whittier College, Mr. Nixon's alma mater.

There has been little comment one way or another about the services from prominent religious leaders. White House officials, however, said that mail has been overwhelmingly sympathetic to the idea.

Presidents Eisenhower and Kennedy held occasional religious services in the White House, but Mr. Nixon is the first to make them a regular affair. Administration officials have said that the reasons for doing so have included security considerations and Mr. Nixon's desire to bring together members of the official family.

'A Heady Mixture'

In the article, Dr. Niebuhr said that Thomas Jefferson and the other Founding Fathers included a prohibition against a national established religion at the head of the Bill of Rights because they knew from experience that "a combination of religious sanctity and political power represents a heady mixture for status quo conservatism."

He observed that a conflict has existed since Old Testament times between those who regard religion as an ally of ruling powers and those who see it as a potential critic, and he charged that the White House services have encouraged the former and evoked a "new form of conformity" from participants.

Without specifically mentioning his name, Dr. Niebuhr cited a comment by Rabbi Louis Finkelstein, chancellor of Jewish Theological Seminary, after he preached at the White House on June 29.

The rabbi expressed the hope that future historians "may say that in a period of great trial and tribulations, the finger of God pointed to Richard Milhous Nixon, giving him the vision and wisdom to save the world and civilization, and opening the way for our country to realize the good that the century offered mankind."

"It is wonderful what a simple White House invitation

will do to dull the critical faculties, thereby confirming the fears of the Founding Fathers," Dr. Niebuhr said.

The theologian said that Mr. Nixon and Mr. Graham "have many convictions in common, not least of all the importance of religion."

He continued that their view of the relation of religion to public affairs "regards all religion as virtuous in guaranteeing public justice."

"It seems indifferent to the radical distinction between conventional religion — which throws the aura of sanctity on contemporary public policy, whether morally inferior or outrageously unjust—and radical religious protest, which subjects all historical reality...to the 'word of the Lord,' i.e. absolute standards of justice," he declared.

The theologian also said that the "Nixon-Graham doctrine" falsely assumed that "a religious change of heart, such as occurs in an individual conversion, would cure men of all sin."

He questioned whether the late civil rights leader, the Rev. Dr. Martin Luther King Jr., would have been invited to preach because "established religion, with or without legal sanction, is always wary of criticism, especially if it is relevant to public policy."

The White House said it would have no comment until it had seen the Niebuhr article.

August 7, 1969

HIGH COURT, 8 TO 1, FORBIDS STATES TO REIMBURSE PAROCHIAL SCHOOLS; BACKS COLLEGE-LEVEL HELP, 5 TO 4

By FRED P. GRAHAM
Special to The New York Times

WASHINGTON, June 28 — The Supreme Court declared unconstitutional today state programs that reimburse Roman Catholic and other church-related schools for instruction in nonreligious subjects.

With only one Justice — Byron R. White — dissenting, the Court's eight other Justices ruled that direct financial aid of this type involved "excessive entanglement between Government and religion."

However, at the same time the Court upheld by a 5-to-4 vote the Federal Higher Education Facilities Act of 1963, under which $240-million in Federal funds has been paid for the construction of academic buildings on the campuses of private colleges — including church-related colleges.

Provision Is Voided

The Court struck down only one minor feature of the United States law—a provision that after 20 years the colleges could use the buildings for any purposes, including religious ones.

If such buildings were to be converted into chapels or other religious structures, "the original Federal grant will in part have the effect of advancing religion," the Court held.

It therefore declared that feature of the law unconstitutional under the First Amendment's prohibition against any official "establishment of religion."

Chief Justice Warren E. Burger wrote the majority opinion in the state-aid case and the prevailing opinion in the Federal-aid decision.

Division in Voting

The latter opinion was joined by Justices John M. Harlan, Potter Stewart and Harry A. Blackmun, but Justice White, who provided the fifth vote in favor of the law, filed a separate concurring opinion. The dissenters in the United States case were Justices Hugo L. Black, William O. Douglas,

William J. Brennan Jr. and Thurgood Marshall.

The decision on direct state aid to parochial schools, which invalidated state laws in Rhode Island and Pennsylvania, marked the first time that the Supreme Court had struck down a law on aid to church schools.

In a series of decisions that began in 1947, the Court upheld such indirect forms of aid as the use of Government-owned buses to transport students to parochial schools and the lending of state-purchased books to parochial students.

This encouraged 36 of the 50 states to enact aid programs that benefit parochial school students in various ways, ranging from busing and free lunches, books and counseling services to the direct salary supplements of parochial school teachers that were declared unconstitutional today.

Further litigation will be required to disclose how many of these programs will fall under the principles announced today.

However, the Americans United for Separation of Church and State—a group that has been active in court challenges against these programs—asserted in a statement that similar salary-supplement laws of Ohio, Connecticut, New Jersey and Illinois will be struck down as a result of today's decision.

Chief Justice Burger took great pains to point out why the "entanglement" between church and state in the state-aid program was enough to invalidate them, while the Federal program could stand.

A key point, he said, is that pre-college church schools are more involved in religious indoctrination than colleges are. Noting the "skepticism of the college student," he held that "there is substance to the conclusion that college students are less impressionable and less susceptible to religious indoctrination" than are elementary and high school students.

He also found fewer entanglements between church and state in the "one-time, single-purpose construction grant" than in continuing salary-supplement programs. Finally, he said, colleges normally do not draw

major support from one area, so that bitter state political battles are not likely to erupt over aid to colleges.

A Shift in Emphasis

On the other hand, a major reason for the Court's ruling against the state laws was their "divisive political potential." Mr. Burger's opinion noted that political pressures for increased state aid to hard-pressed parochial schools could be expected to continue.

The opinion stated that political division along religious lines was an "evil" that the First Amendment was designed to avoid, and it left no doubt that the Supreme Court hoped to put an end to the spreading tendency toward political battles in state legislatures over aid to parochial schools.

Both decisions today marked a shift in the high court's emphasis in cases on aid to church schools.

Previously, the Court had emphasized a "child benefit" theory, which held that aid programs might be constitutional if they benefited primarily the student in the parochial school and not the school. Since most aid programs basically assist the children, aid programs tended to proliferate.

In 1970, the Court hinted at a new approach, when it upheld the New York law that granted real estate tax exemptions to church property. The major rationale of the decision was that if church property were taxed, the church and state might become embroiled in battles over tax assessments, and that excessive "entanglements" were avoided by the tax-exemption system.

This test was used in both decisions today.

Justice White's View

Among the potential "entanglements" that Chief Justice Burger cited were the "comprehensive, discriminating and continuing state surveillance" of parochial schools that would be necessary to see that teachers receiving state funds were not teaching religion or that the money was not otherwise being used to propagate a faith.

Justice White, the swing man in upholding the Federal law and the lone dissenter to the state ruling, said that he would uphold them all on the theory that aid to a separable

secular function of a church-related school was not unconstitutional. The fact that religious interests "may substantially benefit" from the aid does not matter, he said.

Although Justice White said that both the Rhode Island and the Pennsylvania laws were constitutional, he dissented only to the Rhode Island decision because of a quirk in the disposition of the appeal in the Pennsylvania case.

In it the Supreme Court reversed the Pennsylvania courts because they had thrown out the suit challenging the law without a trial.

Justice White disagreed with the Supreme Court's further finding that the Pennsylvania law was unconstitutional, but he did not dissent because he felt that there should be a trial to consider if the law operated in an unconstitutional way by allowing religious schools to use public funds for religious purposes.

Justice Brennan, the only Roman Catholic on the Court, stated that all three laws were unconstitutional. He deplored what he saw as the secularizing impact of public assistance on church schools.

By accepting Government funds, Justice Brennan said, Roman Catholic teachers "surrender their right to teach religious courses" and promise not to inject religion into their secular courses.

He insisted that church schools and colleges properly attempt to proselytize, and said that there was no way to separate out the religious and secular functions. Thus, if a school or college was found to be a "sectarian" institution, he would deny it any direct aid.

In a final dissent written by Justice Douglas and signed by Justices Black and Marshall, it was argued that the only difference between the state laws, which were struck down, and the Federal program, which was not, was the theory that "small violations of the First Amendment over a period of years are unconstitutional while a huge violation occurring only once is de minimus."

The Rhode Island law paid up to 15 per cent of the salary of teachers in private schools, provided the teacher taught only "secular subjects." About 250 teachers in nonpublic schools had applied for the grants. All of them were in

Roman Catholic schools.

The Pennsylvania law granted $20-million a year from taxes on cigarettes and horse racing to pay for salaries of teachers, textbooks and instructional materials for courses in mathematics, modern foreign languages, physical sciences and physical education.

The challenge to the Federal law arose out of grants to four Connecticut colleges to build libraries and science, arts and language buildings. The colleges were Annhurst College in Woodstock, Fairfield University and Sacred Heart University in Fairfield and Albertus Magnus College in New Haven.

Edward Bennett Williams of Washington argued for the Connecticut colleges and for the Rhode Island plan. F. Michael Ahern, Assistant Attorney General of Connecticut, argued in behalf of the United States law. Charles F. Cottam of the Rhode Island Attorney General's office argued to uphold his state's law. Daniel M. Friedman of the Solicitor General's office also argued to uphold the United States law.

William B. Ball of Harrisburg argued in support of the Pennsylvania law. Henry W. Sawyer 3d of Philadelphia argued for the taxpayers who challenged it. Leo Pfeffer of New York, special counsel of the American Jewish Congress, argued for the taxpayers who challenged the Federal statute and the Rhode Island law.

Milton Stanzler of Providence also argued against the constitutionality of the Rhode Island law.

June 29, 1971

COURT, 8 TO 1, BARS OHIO TUITION PLAN

By FRED P. GRAHAM
Special to The New York Times

WASHINGTON, Oct. 10—The Supreme Court struck down, 8 to 1, today an Ohio plan for direct tuition grants to parents of children in private and parochial schools. The plan had been considered a testing ground for new methods of public aid to church-related schools.

Acting summarily without hearing arguments, the Court affirmed a three-judge Federal District Court's ruling that the 1971 Ohio law was a violation of the principle of separation of church and state.

[In New York, the state Attorney General, Louis Lefkowitz, said that he would study the Court's decision before deciding whether it would affect an appeal that his office has planned of a Federal appeals court ruling last week. That ruling was against private school tuition refunds for poor parents and state-supported maintenance allowances for inner-city private schools.]

Because the Supreme Court ruled today without full arguments or a written opinion, its decision does not automatically rule out all of the various techniques that are not being considered to channel public funds to hard-pressed parochial schools.

But it does appear to rule out tuition subsidies to parents, which the Ohio Legislature tried after the Supreme Court ruled out direct payments to church-related schools when it struck down Pennsylvania and Rhode Island salary supplement plans in 1971.

The Court gave no reasons for its action in the Ohio case. Justice Byron R. White, the lone dissenter in 1971 when the Court ruled out salary supplements to sectarian schools, said the Court should have agreed to hear the case.

Under the Ohio law, $90 a year went to parents of private school students as reimbursement for tuition payments. The three-judge court decision that was affirmed today said, "One may not do by indirection what is forbidden directly."

The lower court concluded that the law violated the First Amendment's prohibition against any public "establishment of religion" because the "effect of the scheme is to aid religious enterprises."

The other states most likely to be affected are Connecticut, Maryland and Illinois, which have also adopted grant systems. New York's Legislature has approved grants for low-income families earning under $5,000, and tax credits for families up to $25,000, and both have been challenged in court.

Tax Credits Likely

Tax credit schemes are now likely to become the focus of new aid efforts, although critics of parochial school aid say they are only another way of reimbursing parents for payments to church schools.

Last week the House Ways and Means Committee approved a $200-a-year tax credit for parents of students in private and church-related schools, and both President Nixon and Senator George McGovern, the Democratic nominee, have campaigned in support of aid of this type.

If Congress should pass such a law the Supreme Court would be expected to give it a full hearing before ruling on its constitutionality.

The action today came as the Supreme Court held its first day of arguments in the new Court term. The Court also issued rulings on more than 800 petitions for review that had accumulated during the summer recess.

It agreed to hear a different type of challenge to state aid to private education—Mississippi's system of lending textbooks to students in all-white academies that have sprung up as public schools have been required to integrate.

Lower courts held that the 32-year-old textbook plan long predated desegregation, that it was not crucial to the establishment of the white academies and that 90 per cent of the students had stayed in public schools. Negro parents contended that the effect of the program was to encourage efforts to avoid integration.

The Court agreed to take another look at the increasingly active area of sex discrimination when it granted the appeal of a woman Air Force lieutenant and her husband, who contend that military rules discriminate against married servicewomen.

First Lieut. Sharron A. Frontiero of Maxwell Air Force Base, Ala., challenged the rule that automatically grants housing supplements and medical benefits to the spouses of servicemen — assuming that they are dependent upon the male service member—while denying similar benefits to husbands of servicewomen unless the men actually receive more than half of their income from their wives.

Lieutenant Frontiero's husband, Joseph, is a student who was denied benefits because most of his income came from veterans' benefits.

In an appeal brought by the American Civil Liberties Union, she asserted that the different treatment of men and women was arbitrary and unreasonable. The Government replied that it was logical to presume that wives were dependent upon servicemen husbands but not to presume that husbands were dependent upon wives in services.

The Court declined to review the appeal of a former Salvation Army officer, Mrs. Billie McClure of Atlanta, who tried to sue the Salvation Army on grounds that it had discriminated against her by paying her less than it paid male officers.

Lower courts had ruled that Mrs. McClure's suit under the Civil Rights Act's equal employment provisions on the ground that she was a voluntary minister and not an employe of the Salvation Army.

Lefkowitz Sees 'Difference'

New York State Attorney General Louis Lefkowitz said yesterday there may be "a major difference" between the provisions of the Ohio statute and the two New York provisions for aid to poor parents with children in private schools that a Federal appeals court struck down last week.

He said that the present plans were to go ahead with his intention to appeal last week's ruling, but he stressed that "as a lawyer it's hard for me to comment on the Supreme Court decision without having seen it."

Last week, a special three-man Federal panel struck down a new state statute that would have granted private school tuition refunds up to $50 for each child to parents earning than $5,000.

The appeals court also ruled out a state plan to provide up to $4-million in maintenance assistance for dilapidated private schools — most of them church-run — in poor communities.

The Attorney General said that the New York statute, with its limitation of tuition refunds to poor parents, might offer an arguing point that was not covered by the Supreme Court in yesterday's ruling.

The appeals court tentatively upheld a third part of the disputed state statute, to grant income tax relief pegged to private school tuition costs for parents earning more than $5,000.

The Committee for Public Education and Religious Liberty, which initiated the suits against the state statute, hailed yesterday's Supreme Court ruling, but said it would in turn press its intention to appeal last week's tentative upholding of the state tax relief provisions.

The American Jewish Congress also praised the Supreme Court's position as "a victory for religious freedom and the constitutional principle of separation of church and state."

But a spokesman for the National Society of Hebrew Day Schools here said the decision "shuts the door on the availability of educational options for the disadvantaged, the poor and the middle class."

Rabbi Bernard Goldenberg echoed the charge frequently made by Roman Catholic educators that the constitutional ban on state support of religious schools favors the well-to-do.

October 11, 1972

Carter's Evangelism Putting Religion Into Politics for First Time Since '60

By KENNETH A. BRIGGS

Jimmy Carter's open espousal of his Christian beliefs in the 1976 Presidential campaign has raised the issue of religion's place in politics more arrestingly than it has been raised in any Presidential race since John F. Kennedy's in 1960.

In Mr. Kennedy's case the question was whether a Roman Catholic could be elected and what the consequences would be for relations between church and state.

The church-state concern has re-emerged with Mr. Carter's candidacy, and in addition the question for the 51-year-old Southern Baptist is whether a deeply committed evangelical Christian can appeal to an overtly more secular culture with his frank admission of conservative Protestant piety.

Mr. Carter began to speak of his faith in the campaign for the North Carolina primary, on March 23, and remains the only candidate in this Presidential campaign to do so. His showing in the primaries last week in New York and Wisconsin appeared to support the view that his openness on religion has not hurt him.

And the nation's religious climate suggests that the former Georgia Governor's stance of evangelical theology is not only widely shared but is also growing more rapidly than any other Christian perspective.

Many Share His View

The Rev. Dean M. Kelley, author of "Why the Conservative Churches Are Growing," estimated in a telephone interview the number of Christians who readily identify with Mr. Carter's evangelical outlook at 40 million. Others put it as high as 50 million.

In addition, as Mr. Kelley and others point out, millions more Christians and non-Christians are sympathetic to the candidate's theology because it evokes elements of a widely held faith in a personal God and a nation richly blessed.

The current evangelical movement, whose most celebrated spokesman is the Rev. Billy Graham, grew out of earlier stages of fundamentalism. It inherited some of the biblical and moral views of fundamentalism but has generally developed a more relaxed, open spirit toward both religion and the world.

The Southern Baptist Convention, whose ranks include Mr. Carter and Mr. Graham, is the largest single evangelical church, with 12.7 million members and an average yearly growth rate of 250,000.

Though a broad range of churches define themselves as "evangelical," the phenomenon is more a religious state of mind than a strictly identifiable branch

of Christianity. Other Christians, including Roman Catholics and some members of main line Protestant groups, embrace basically the same outlook on the need for personal faith, Biblical teaching and evangelism.

"Every indication is that evangelicalism is skyrocketing," says Gerald Strober, who is co-author of a book, "Religion and the New Majority," subtitled "Billy Graham, Fundamentalism and the Politics of the 70s," in 1972. "Nothing is stopping it."

The book contends that Mr. Graham speaks the language of the new or "silent" majority of voters, the same group to which Mr. Carter would presumably appeal.

The former Governor's style of subjective, fervent faith has also frequently won enthusiasm among blacks, from whom he has drawn sizable support. His most eloquent testimony to his beliefs during the New York campaign came in a black Methodist church in Buffalo. He is comfortable in such settings.

Mr. Strober cites such indication of the vitality of evangelicalism as upward spiraling enrollments at conservative seminaries and ballooning sales of evangelical books.

Mr. Graham's latest book, entitled "Angels," for example, has astonished its Doubleday publishers. Since being introduced in September, 1.3 million copies have been placed in print. "The Living Bible," a biblical paraphrase by Kenneth Taylor, has sold 19 million copies in three years.

Dr. Martin Marty, a University of Chicago historian, believes the Carter theology has "a huge constituency" and would prove a possible stumbling block only for a small minority of "semi-secularized" voters.

He divides the nation's religious map into five districts: the Baptist-dominated South, the Methodist-oriented mid-South, the heavily Lutheran upper Midwest, Mormon Utah and the non-geographical urban "pluralist" community. Mr. Carter would presumably have trouble only in the last area because of its secularist tendencies, Dr. Marty believes.

Carter's Decision

Mr. Carter says his decision to talk about his convictions in the midst of the campaign came after prayerful thought.

"When the media began to emphasize my beliefs," he said in an interview on his last day of campaigning in New York, "I did not know how to deal with it; whether to answer the questions or say I didn't have a comment."

"I decided to tell the truth," he continued, "not to conceal it but reveal it. If there are those who don't want to vote for me because I'm a deeply committed Christian, I believe they should vote for someone else."

Like Mr. Kennedy in 1960, Mr. Carter is apparently appealing to the nation's sense of fair play to eliminate religious identification as a negative bias. While it is not at all certain that the subject would come close to raising the same concern that it did in 1960, it has already drawn widespread attention.

Last week President Ford's campaign director, Stuart Spencer, said that Mr. Carter's beliefs could become a factor in a race between the two men. Mr. Ford is an Episcopalian.

Among the other Democratic candidates, Senator Henry M. Jackson is an Episcopalian, Representative Morris K. Udall is a former Mormon and Gov. George C. Wallace of Alabama is a United Methodist. Ronald Reagan is a member of the Christian Church but has been attending a Presbyterian Church, according to an aide.

President's Beliefs

A Carter-Ford race would match two candidates with similar religious beliefs. Mr. Ford is known to have become strongly evangelical in recent years. His son attended Gordon-Conwall Seminary in Massachusetts, a leading evangelical school, and he is a close friend of the Michigan evangelist preacher Billy Zeoli. The difference between the two men thus far is that Mr. Ford's beliefs have been muted to a far greater degree than Mr. Carter's.

However, Mr. Ford shows signs of seeking to keep his religious identity clear. For instance, recently he made a point of stopping at Wheaton College, in Wheaton, Ill., the nation's most prestigious evangelical college and Billy Graham's alma mater, an action regarded by some observers as not at all accidental.

'Conversion Experience'

Many political observers say that Mr. Carter's decision to explicate his faith during the North Carolina primary campaign contributed to his victory. The state is heavily Baptist.

As he explained it, the salient features of Mr. Carter's spiritual biography emerged. Born in the rural community of Plains, Ga., he spent his formative years in a distinctly Baptist culture, a mixture of revivalist religion, traditional folkways and prevailing mores.

But not until after his defeat in his first attempt to become Governor in 1966 did he have what Baptists term a "conversion experience." Mr. Carter has not disclosed details, but he says he came away from it with "an inner peace and inner conviction and assurance that transformed my life for the better."

He began reading the Bible avidly, and still does. Like many Christians, he balks at a literal view of the Scriptures, an article of faith among the fundamentalists.

Asked on a television interview if he agreed with St. Paul's admonition that wives be "subject to their husbands," Mr. Carter tactfully explained that he had tried to accept that teaching but could not.

He believes in the power of prayer, recalling that he "spent more time on my knees the four years I was Governor in the seclusion of a little private room than all the rest of my life put together." But he disavows all contentions that his prayer life has experienced the miraculous.

There has been no serious challenge to Mr. Carter's sincerity or his spiritual credibility. Most uneasiness appears to stem from a fear that an evangelistically minded President might use his power to advance his beliefs or violate the separation of church and state.

Nixon and Graham

Interest in religion's role in politics was generated during the Nixon Administration when President Nixon held regular Sunday morning services in the White House and frequently consulted with Mr. Graham. Public debate over this and other forms of civil religion has particularly stirred those worried that public officials would manipulate religious symbols and language for personal advancement.

Mr. Carter's supporters say that Baptists have been in the forefront of struggles to maintain a wall of separation between church and state, and that the candidate's record shows nothing that could raise any objections on this score.

"I've never tried to use my position as a public official to promote my beliefs, and I never would," Mr. Carter said.

He has said that he believes personal example is the best way to influence others and that matters such as abortion and premarital sex should not be legislated against, though he opposes both personally.

Mr. Carter also rejects any suggestion that he has a messiah complex.

"I don't think God is going to make me President by any means," he said at a recent news conference. "But whatever I have as a responsibility for the rest of my life, it will be with that infinite personal continuing relationship."

In a talk to a Buffalo congregation, he said, "I believe I can be a better President because of my faith." He said he did not ask God, "Let me succeed," but, "Let me do the right thing."

Mr. Kelley believes that Mr. Carter, "like Billy Graham, speaks in the inherited idiom that is the closest to a common explanation of the meaning of life that America has."

This view, Mr. Kelley said, "resonates" with the vast majority of the public.

April 11, 1976

ARCHBISHOP ASSERTS CHURCH IS NEUTRAL IN WHITE HOUSE RACE

Says Statements on Abortion by Roman Catholic Hierarchy Show No Preference for President

By PHILIP SHABECOFF
Special to The New York Times

WASHINGTON, Sept. 16—The chief spokesman for the nation's Roman Catholic hierarchy said today that the church leadership was "absolutely neutral" in the Presidential contest and stressed that the hierarchy's recent statements on abortion indicated no preference for either candidate or party.

Archbishop Joseph L. Bernardin of Cincinnati, president of the National Conference of Catholic Bishops, said at a news conference here, "It is not our job to endorse candidates or oppose candidates."

Archbishop Bernardin also said that the hierarchy had not developed its position on abortion "in the context of what is sinful or what is not sinful." Accordingly, he added, all voters should draw their own conclusions on the abortion issue "and vote as their conscience dictates."

Bishops' Statements Criticized

The bishops apparently called the news conference to answer a storm of criticism that followed their meetings with Jimmy Carter, the Democratic Presidential nominee, and President Ford, the Republican nominee, after which they expressed "disappointment" with Mr. Carter's stand on abortion and said they were "encouraged" by Mr. Ford's.

The criticism came from Catholic as well as non-Catholic groups and, among Catholics, from members of the clergy as well as the laity. Much of the reaction was critical of what was widely taken to be an effort by the hierarchy to use partisan politics to achieve its goals on the abortion issue.

Polls Discount Issue

Recent public opinion polls, including one taken by The New York Times and CBS News, suggest that abortion is not a partisan political issue, not even among Roman Catholics. The Times/CBS poll showed that Mr. Carter's margin over Mr. Ford was greater among Catholics who favored an anti-abortion amendment than those who opposed it.

Those familiar with the internal politics of the Roman Catholic Church in the United States believe that the bishops had staked a great deal of prestige and authority on achieving their goal of a constitutional amendment to limit abortion. These observers said that the hierarchy's control of church and secular matters was being seriously challenged and that a defeat on the abortion issue would be damaging to the bishops' authority.

The news conference today and the disavowals by the bishops might be, among other things, an indication of the internal church problems the bishops are facing.

Archbishop Bernardin said, "We have gotten a considerable amount of mail, some of it supportive and some of it not supportive." Much of the mail, he added, "expressed concern that we have endorsed one candidate over another. We have not done this."

Mr. Ford had said he was opposed to abortion on demand except in certain specified conditions, and would like to minimize the use of Federal funds for abortion. He also said he would uphold existing laws governing abortion but favored a constitutional amendment that would give the states the right to decide whether to permit abortion. That right was taken from the states by a Supreme Court ruling in 1973.

Mr. Carter's views on abortion are similar to Mr. Ford's, with one major exception: He does not support a constitutional amendment of any kind to overturn the Supreme Court ruling.

The Roman Catholic church is seeking a constitutional amendment that would, according to a position paper handed out at the news conference today, "correct the tragic errors of the Supreme Court on abortion." The church's position has been generally understood to mean a virtual ban on legal abortions.

The recent statements by the bishops were widely regarded as an endorsement of Mr. Ford's position on abortion and a rejection of Mr. Carter's. A number of critics, including some within the Catholic clergy, also said they regarded the statements as an effort to sway the Catholic vote in the Presidential election.

Women's groups have criticized the bishops for their statements on the ground that they were using their political power to curtail individual rights. The bishops have also been denounced by non-Catholic religious groups for allegedly seeking to interfere with constitutional guarantees of religious freedom.

In addition, a national organization of Roman Catholic priests has expressed concern that the abortion issue has been stressed by the hierarchy "to the neglect of other important social issues." The Rev. Timothy S. Healy, president of Georgetown University, warned in a speech this week that the church was in danger of being identified with one political party.

September 17, 1976

CHRISTIANITY IN CITIES.

No more vital subject, in its bearing upon American life, can be discussed than the social and religious position of the masses in our great cities. How are the masses of people who own no homes, who move every month or every year, whom nobody is interested in, who never see a clergyman unless at a marriage or a funeral, to feel the sunshine which the Gospel of the CHRIST and a professedly Christian civilization ought to bring to them? This is the question which comes to the minds and hearts of the clergy, the philanthropists, the large-minded and large-hearted people who constitute the Christian forces of the hour. By so much as Christian influences are superior to the ordinary social and personal influences, by so much are they to be prized and sought as agencies not only in maintaining social order and the amenities of life, but in reaching down to the convictions which rule conduct and control the duties to GOD and man. It is an excellent thing for men to be won to Christian discipleship, but this means, in its relation to the masses in our cities, something more than simply a religious belief. If the masses are ever to be won to cleaner, purer, brighter lives in our large cities, it will not be by sermons alone, nor by liturgical services alone, nor simply by industrious visiting from house to house, nor by any process short of that which recognizes men and women as personal wholes. No doubt, many individuals are disagreeable ; no doubt, the bars of access to many are such that one cannot easily leap over them ; no doubt, the forces of resistance are strongest in cases where beneficent and up-lifting work most needs doing ; whether one labors for the CHRIST or for humanity, the point of chief resistance is the point of duty, and the personal resistance to that species of religious effort in which the heart is larger than the creed is just the sort of resistance which most needs to be overcome.

This question of the masses is often looked at as if it were something less broad than our common humanity. The rich patronize Christianity ; the poor use it to help out their present necessities ; the middle class are indifferent to it. But Christianity never recognizes classes, whether in city or country, and it is the broad Christianity that integrates all classes which is the need of the hour. It is easier to theorize than to be practical on this point. Had we a national establishment, as in England, some of the worst types of class Christianity would disappear. The divisions between Christians would bring less harm to religious work than they do now, because they would be insignificant in influence. Where the reaching a city multitude is left entirely to voluntary effort, it is next to impossible that the heathenism of our cities shall be effectually dispersed by either social or Christian methods. The Roman population is reached by better methods than the Protestant, but the Protestant temper could never be controlled by the Roman agencies. Yet worse than the religious divisions is the growing pessimism of the people at large. The Pastors of churches and the kind-hearted persons who assist them with money or with personal service seldom have more than the ghost of an idea of the actual spiritual condition of the people of the respectable class who almost never darken the doors of houses of worship, and whose interests are almost entirely included within the limit of each day's activity. It is here that the issue is to be met, and it is here that the Christianity of the day is on trial. It is not whether this or that religious body shall have most converts. It is whether, in the terrible and remorseless grind in which the souls and bodies of men are worn out, any voice of the CHRIST or of His human representatives shall be heard.

The murmur of the city is the murmur of life. By day, by night, hour by hour, the hum is heard. No hour is without its pain, its agony. No moment is without its witness to the surrender of life. It is the constant struggle to live, to bear burdens, to withstand temptations. Life in its glory and in its shame, life in its strength and in its weakness, is strangely blended. More and more our great cities present conditions which Christianity has never been called upon to meet before. It is the increasing heathenism of an outwardly Christian civilization which has to be met at our very doors. The problem is here. It faces us on the street. It starts up in empty churches. It glares upon us along the avenues of crime. The murmur of the city is the murmur of its unconsecrated, unchurched, unreached, unresting masses, and there is not a problem of modern society which does not have its roots in the question whether Christianity has the will to conquer the practical difficulties which beset our latest and ripest civilization. It is a question of will, not of power ; a question of the amount of consecrated purpose which exists in our Christianity as a whole, not of denominations or individuals alone, a question which can never be decided by the clergy without the people, nor by the people without the clergy. Trinity Parish, in this City, has given a living example of what can be done with money and men when both are rightly directed. The example of the Rev. EDWARD JUDSON, son of the great Baptist missionary to Burmah, giving up a suburban parish in the prime of life that he may throw his whole energy into a People's Church on the West Side, is another indication of a movement toward the religious education of the masses in individual minds and hearts. There are instances in every respectable religious communion as marked as those here mentioned, in which individuals have felt themselves to be called of GOD to this work. It is the will of the individual that becomes the will of the multitude, and, if the heathenism of our cities is ever to be overcome, the victories will always be at the hands of individuals whom GOD has touched. Pet theories about churches or services or vestments are useless. Christianity is too broad to be *doctrinaire*. It always works with the best common sense of the world. Here is its human method ; here is its centre of practical influence. Earnestness and common sense are its avenues to the multitude, and its secret on the human side is the winning of one man. It is one man at a time, and until, in the aggregate, the one man is the Christianized multitude. The will to do is from above ; the way to do is the way that seems best, and this is the divinely human method for meeting the religious and social problems of our great cities.

October 23, 1881

LABOR AND RELIGION.

PROF. RICHARD T. ELY DESCRIBES HOW THEY MIGHT BUT DO NOT UNITE.

The Baptist ministers, at their weekly meeting yesterday, enjoyed an hour of good advice from Prof. Richard T. Ely of Johns Hopkins University, who read them a paper on "The Church and the Workingmen." Prof. Ely is a specialist in sociology, and in his studies he has profited by association with the labor leaders, who have kept him abreast of current thought and tendencies on their side on industrial questions. On the other hand, his normal associations with scholars and churchmen have enabled him to absorb the purely philosophical view of sociology. The paper which he read yesterday embodied the conclusions with which such mastery of his subject equipped him. The fact ought first to be recognized, he said, that the relations of the church to workingmen were not what they should be. Existing influences estranged the workingmen from the church. One special cause for such estrangement was that workingmen found that religion was rarely a guide to conduct in business or social life. They did not find churchgoing employers better than non-churchmen. Churchmen did not sell superior goods or deal by more honest methods than other persons in trade. This opinion was not held solely by workingmen, but by men of education and fortune. From the bottom to the top of the social ladder the great complaint against the church was that it was too easily satisfied with things as they are and too much inclined to let sin and abuses go unrebuked.

The speaker believed that within the church there was room for all reforms. In his opinion, however, the church had failed to recognize the fact that it was primarily concerned with the things of this world. People go to the Bible and construe teachings intended to apply to this earth as applicable to a future existence. Consequently by common assent the church was left to deal with dogma and the future, while the world retained to itself the guidance and control of temporal affairs. The church ought to fit men to do their present tasks well, and the future, while the promises of immortality were not to be undervalued, might in great measure take care of itself. Christ's teachings all dwelt on the present. It was deplorable that the schools of theology had not trained preachers to work for the world and that the problems of sociology should be left to so few and such poor instructors.

Some of the evils which the church should seek to correct were those of excessive working hours for men ; of child labor, especially among corrupting influences ; of the labor of women under conditions harmful to the family ; of seven days of labor every week. Workingmen had repeatedly tried to interest the clergy in these reforms, but with discouraging results. The school, he said, should be improved in all respects to fit children for practical life. There ought to be ample playgrounds in all the cities, in order that a proper channel might be furnished for the movement of the animal spirits of youth, which are now apt to be diverted toward evil. Provision should be made for the removal of children from the control of unfit parents. Official corruption should be denounced from the pulpit. There ought to be a Saturday half-holiday. That country in which there were the fewest hours of work was most dreaded in trade competition, and that country in which labor was most degraded was not dreaded at all. Prof. Ely said that the half-holiday reform had not been fairly tried here. Naturally the first effect of relaxation in anything manifested itself in excesses, but this only afforded the clergy better opportunities than ever to teach the workingmen how to use their leisure. There ought to be more just distribution of wealth, and the pulpit should make unrelenting war on the jugglery that would have people believe that labor gets nine-tenths of the wealth of the country. Lastly, there ought to be less optimism about our affairs, less spread-eagleism, and more repentance for actual sins and for the supremacy of corruption in our municipal Governments.

When the paper was finished a score or more of the ministers asked questions of Prof. Ely. He said in reply to some of them that the remedies for these evils could be furnished by Legislatures, by individuals, by associations, and by the churches. He did not believe that legal institutions were as good as human nature would warrant. With regard to the differences of classes he thought the chasm in this country deeper and wider than in England, where some of the best minds had brought the interests of the masses to the sympathetic attention of the classes. In practical work in this country he thought that nothing was to be gained by shutting the eyes to the fact that classes exist. The clergy ought to concern themselves with social questions as if they were a part of the Gospel. By so doing they might do much for the desired reforms, for the workingmen as a class were reasonable and their leaders on the whole were sincerely and unselfishly devoted to the cause of improving their kind. Everything that Prof. Ely said was most attentively heard, and he was rewarded at the close with a rousing vote of thanks.

November 20, 1888

THE PROBLEMS OF CITY CHURCHES.

At a conference of the Baptist ministers of Chicago a few days ago a prominent and evidently courageous member made the startling statement that " unless the church becomes a continuous vaudeville it cannot hold its congregation." Chicago experience seems to show that this generalization is warranted by the facts. Concerts, popular lectures, stereopticon entertainments, and the like are gradually taking the place of the customary Sunday services, and still more radical departures from the established order of things are said to be in contemplation. Ministers of the old school view these proceedings with consternation; but the advocates of such methods of holding their flocks together vigorously defend them, and seem to have the best of the argument, since they are keeping their churches full and paying expenses, whereas those who adhere to the old methods find that the number of their empty pews is steadily increasing. It is reported that some of the Chicago churches have adopted the vaudeville idea, but are keeping their arrangements profoundly secret until the second week in January, when a concerted effort for church rehabilitation is to be made.

These are matters concerning which lay opinion cannot be expected to carry much weight. The Baptist ministers are evidently confronted by a condition and not a theory, and are trying to do the best they can. In the spirit of helpfulness, however, we venture to suggest that perhaps the trouble is chiefly in the pulpit, and results from a mistaken idea of the best way in which to make its teachings impressive and effective. It is also possible, from the lay point of view, that congregations find the continuous pastoral relation a trifle monotonous, and that however deep their attachment to their pastors, it is asking a good deal of intelligent people to expect them to be profoundly interested in listening to them week after week and year after year, until every phase of their thought, every habit of expression, every inflection, every oratorical trick, and every characteristic mannerism can be anticipated. The ministers lay great stress upon the superior attractions of the theatres. We will not discuss the questions of taste or of morals involved in this popular preference; but it is pertinent to ask, How attractive would a theatre be to the throngs which visit it if it had but one actor, however clever, and kept one piece on the boards, year in and year out, with the same songs and everything as nearly unchanged as possible? Comparatively few people see a play or any other entertainment twice, unless at long intervals. Even the vaudeville has to change its programme frequently to attract paying audiences. We do not know how the deadly monotony of the pastoral function can very well be avoided, but perhaps the matter is worth thinking of.

To the lay intelligence the difficulty which the churches in large cities are experiencing is perfectly intelligible. Congregations may be divided into two general classes—those who are religious and go to church because it is a place of worship and instruction, and those who maintain a church connection because it is socially good form to do so, but find it difficult to become really interested in the services. For the sheep of the flock who not only do not go astray, but who could not be driven or enticed away, the churches as conducted in the usual manner are perfectly satisfactory; but for sheep possessed of a wandering propensity it looks as if the folds could be made attractive only by means which cannot fail to be distasteful to the devout. The second phase of the difficulty is that the church accommodations exceed the requirements of the devout by about as 16 to 1, and that fixed charges and running expenses can be met only by attracting and holding large and liberal congregations, which must be attracted and held by other means than the devout are likely to find edifying. That every one should attend church regularly and devoutly may be true enough; but that the masses do not, and will not under present conditions, is sufficiently obvious to be extremely disquieting to those who have the welfare of the church and of the human race at heart. What will bring the irreligious within the good influences of church association and keep them there is so different from what those with pronounced religious tastes and tendencies consider legitimate church work that the conscientious minister is often forced to decide whether he shall make the spiritual or the temporal welfare of his church a first consideration. It is a hard choice in most cases, no doubt, but it seems to be the one which is forced upon the Baptist denomination in Chicago, as, indeed, it is to a greater or less extent upon Protestant churches generally in all large cities. The logical solution of the problem would seem to be to make the churches as attractive as possible, and maintain within them a nucleus of holiness which, always sufficiently in evidence to make its influence felt, need not, and perhaps should not, interfere with anything innocent and proper which will attract those who are needed to fill the pews and help swell the church revenues. This, at least, is a business view of the question, and the modern city church has to be managed on business principles.

December 11, 1900

EPISCOPALIANS DEFEND ORGANIZATION OF LABOR

Essential to the Working People, a Committee Finds.

CRITICISES THE CAPITALIST

Says He Has Taught Laborers to Despise Order and Break Law—Employment of Children Denounced.

BOSTON, Oct. 19.—In the House of Bishops of the Episcopal General Convention to-day, Bishop Henry C. Potter of New York, Chairman of the Standing Committee on the Relations of Capital and Labor, presented a lengthy report, which touched upon certain evils the committee found, and pronounced the organization of labor to be essential to the well-being of the working people.

" We are agreed," the report says, " in the conviction that the causes of the violence of the past three years in Pennsylvania, in Colorado, and in Illinois are not so much economical as moral. The strike commonly begins in distrust. The reason at the heart of it is that the master has as little confidence in the good-will of the men as the men have in the good faith of the master.

" The laborer has learned from the capitalist to despise order and break law. He has learned from the churchman to pursue the dissenter with menace and violence. The recent tragedies in Colorado do not follow at a far distance the massacres which, in the sixteenth century, ensued upon the withdrawal of Holland from the ecclesiastical union.

" While, then, we condemn the tyranny and turbulence of the labor union, and call upon the law to preserve the liberty of every citizen to employ whom he will and to work for whom he will, we deprecate the hasty temper, which, in condemning the errors of the unions, condemns at the same time the whole movement with which they are connected. The offenses of the union are as distinct from the cause for which the organization of labor stands as the inquisition is distinct from the Gospel.

" In the face of a prejudice and a hostility for which there are serious reasons, we are convinced that the organization of labor is essential to the well-being of the working people. Its purpose is to maintain such a standard of wages, hours, and conditions as shall afford every man an opportunity to grow in mind and in heart. Without organization the standard cannot be maintained in the midst of our present commercial conditions.

" This report is designedly general in its terms, but there is one matter which we are constrained to commend in particular to the consciences of Christian people. The employment of children in factories and mills depresses wages, destroys homes, and depreciates the human stock. Whatever interferes with the proper nurture and education of a child contradicts the best interests of the Nation. We call, then, on Christian employers and on Christian parents to endeavor after such betterment of the local and general laws as shall make the labor of children impossible in this Christian country."

The report is signed by Henry C. Potter, William Lawrence, Charles P. Anderson, R. H. McKim, George M. Hodges, C. D. Williams, Samuel Mather, and Jacob Riis.

The report was accepted, and a resolution that the commission be continued was adopted by the House of Bishops.

October 20, 1904

TAINTED MONEY.

DR. GLADDEN'S book, "The New Idolatry and Other Discussions," (McClure, Phillips & Co.,) is an appeal to the American conscience. The famous motto, "The end justifies the means," may not be that of the Jesuits; but it cannot be denied that it is followed by many business men of the United States. And their end is the getting of money. This end, and this motto, form the new idolatry which Dr. Gladden fights. To him its spread is terrifying, its hold over its votaries threatening to the Nation. His campaign against this new-old worship of the golden calf is not a thing of to-day; he began it ten years ago. But recent events have caused him to take it up energetically again—if he ever dropped it—with what result cannot yet be told; quite probably with none, from a worldly point of view.

The worship of Mammon, "the least exalted spirit that fell from Heaven," Dr. Gladden reminds us that Milton calls him, has "to a very large extent supplanted the worship of God. It is not a mere lip service; it is a living allegiance. It is by their works that the devotees prove their faith. The evidences of this devotion are visible on every side. * * * What is it

that dulls the sense of honor and the impulse of probity and makes men faithless to their trusts?" Even the churches are tainted with the belief in the value of money simply as money. "How often have I heard men at the head of great Christian enterprises say, 'The one thing we need is more money!' With the crowd about us all the while falling prostrate before Mammon, it is hard for us to keep from going down with the rest. * * * It is a great error to turn the emphasis of our appeal toward the resources of multimillionairism. 'A little that a righteous man hath is better than the riches of many wicked.'" That is the argument that, in one form or another, runs through the sermons and essays that make up this book—for "some true things need to be said over many times," Dr. Gladden remarks.

Mr. Rockefeller's gift to a foreign missionary started the present discussion of "tainted money;" Dr. Gladden promptly took the ground that Standard Oil money should not be accepted by a Christian Church, but his colleagues did not agree with him. But he stands up for his belief unabashed. His logic is good, too:

Money that has been gained by nefarious methods is often brought to the door of the church, and those who bring it seldom fail of a warm welcome. * * * Of course the pulpit of this church is not likely to discuss the kind of iniquity by which this money was

gained, nor anything near akin to it. It would be extremely ungrateful—it would indeed be dishonorable—for this pulpit to touch on such matters. Having sought and welcomed these liberal donations, it is simply the dictate of ordinary decency to refrain from criticising the financial methods of the donor. This pulpit, then, will have no message respecting wrongs of this particular kind. And inasmuch as it would seem rather inconsistent to attack other closely related social wrongs and avoid these, this pulpit will probably abstain from all reference to public evils. It will probably confine itself to what is known as "the simple Gospel." The kind of preaching which Isaiah and Jeremiah and Amos and Paul and James practiced will not be heard from this pulpit. * * * Similar results must appear in the life of a college built on such foundations, or largely dependent on resources of this character. * * * It would be utterly dishonorable for an institution thus largely befriended to enter into a thorough investigation of the methods by which its endowments were accumulated. The teaching might deal, in an abstract way, with social subjects, but it could not examine historically and scientifically certain burning questions of its own neighborhood and generation. But this is not all. An institution thus allied must needs pay honor to those whose benefactions it is sharing. The whole world will see who these scholars and leaders of the people delight to honor. So it is that public opinion is formed, and that men who are the pirates of industry and the spoilers of the State are advanced to the front rank in modern society.

January 13, 1906

THE ETHICS OF WAGES.

Prof. Ryan's Significant Book—What a "Living Wage" Is and the Moral Obligation to Pay It—Connection with the Tariff Controversy.*

Written for THE NEW YORK TIMES SATURDAY REVIEW OF BOOKS by

EDWARD A. BRADFORD.

ETHICS and economics are strangers rather than enemies. It is because economics takes no cognizance of morals that it justifies many things which are unmoral. Men who would indignantly refuse to buy stolen goods fail to perceive any reason why they should pay any higher wages than they agree to pay. If the bargain is free, is it not fair? Is it not a hardship to the worker to withhold employment which the laborer desires at the agreed terms? What other way can there be of fixing wages except the time-tried and universally accepted method of competition? If an employer should pay more than the market price for labor how could he hope to survive in his own struggle for existence against those whose labor cost is less, and whose goods are therefore cheaper? And what would become of the trade of a nation whose

employers should by any chance agree generally among themselves to pay not the market price for labor, but what the laborer "ought" to receive? Would not the production of that nation decrease and the cost of its production increase? And what other way is there of settling what the laborer "ought" to receive except to make a bargain about it? There can be no doubt what answer orthodox political economy makes to such questions. From Adam Smith down there is an unbroken line of authority in support of what may be called "wage slavery." The slavery is by deliberate choice, to be sure—the choice between unavoidable alternatives—but it is under the compulsion of an economic duress hardly distinguishable from the highwayman's pistol.

How does this system, so buttressed by practice and authority, work? At the date of the census of 1890, in fifty leading industries, 51 per cent. of 757,865 adult male employes received under $12 weekly. An American family cannot be supported suitably upon $600, and each of those men had a natural right to be the head of a family. In the census of 1900 an even more careful inquiry placed the wages of 69 per cent. of adult males at under $12.50. We lack exact figures for comparison with the Nation's earlier years, but we can infer the result from the method in which wage bargains were customarily made. As to this it is possible to cite the testimony of a patriarch, Mr. Stephen A. Knight, who gave his experience to the international gathering of the cotton trade a few days ago. Said he:

A mother with several children suggested to the proprietor of the factory that the pay seemed small. The proprietor replied, "You get enough to eat, don't

you?" The mother said, "Just enough to keep the wolf from the door." He then remarked, "You get enough clothes to wear, don't you?" to which she answered, "Barely enough to cover our nakedness." "Well," said the proprietor, "we want the rest." And that proprietor, on the whole, was as kind and considerate to his help as was any other manufacturer at that time.

It must therefore be taken as established that since the establishment of the factory system down to the present era of unexampled prosperity the wage system has resulted in underpayment of a majority of workers. There are two million men unable to supply their physical wants, or keep themselves as well as good employers keep the cattle from which they are desirous of getting the best results. There are 2,000,000 children struggling for their bread, and reducing their parents' wages by competition. And in the anthracite strike negotiations the operators declared that they preferred boys to men at 5.9 cents per hour, and could not afford to pay more to either. Is it the last word of this century that there is no better way than this?

Mr. Ryan declares that morally there ought to be, and that economically there is, a better way. There is a certain parity of argument between his reasoning and that of Henry George's "Progress and Poverty." Just as all have a right to share in the profits from land, nature's common gift to all, so Mr. Ryan argues that the sacredness and dignity of the individual soul created by God give a right to decent support from

* A LIVING WAGE. Its ethical and economical aspects. By John A. Ryan, S. T. L., Professor of Ethics and Economics in the St. Paul Seminary. With an introduction by Dr. Richard T. Ely. Pp. 331. New York; The Macmillan Company. $1.50

the goods of the community in which the laborer lives and to which he contributes his efforts. If there were a universal strike employers would gladly pay a living wage to procure resumption of work. It is the need of the laborer, and the economic might of stored capital possessed by the employer, which alone explain a wage system so severe in operation as we have seen. But the need of labor is proof that the laborer renders a social service, and so is worthy of his hire in proportion to the cost of indispensables of existence, including the right to rear a family in comfort. Mr. Ryan ranks this right ahead of the right of capital to interest or of the employer to profit. The obligation of supporting the willing laborer is upon the community, and more particularly upon that part of the community whose acquisition of goods and opportunities of living exclude him from access to possessions of his own. Their wealth and his need are correlative, and their claim to profits or interest or unequal enjoyment is inferior to his by as much as the right to existence takes precedence of every other right. The employer is no more justified in using his superior economic strength to reduce wages than he would be justified in using physical strength to exclude one starving from food. Neither economic force nor physical force is any determinant of rights. And let not the smug buyer of bargains think that the duty of the employer to waive profits and the loan capitalist to waive interest in case of underpayment of labor exhausts the duty to maintain a living wage standard. The duty of the landlord and the capitalist is secondary. The primary duty is divided between the employer as the paymaster of society and the consumer, whose payments supply the wage fund. Consumers are morally bound to do what they legally can by directing their purchases toward employers who are fair to their employes and to merchants whose goods are produced under humane conditions. Consumers are absolved from this duty only when their duty to themselves overrules their duty to the wage earner, and it is to be reckoned in the calculation as the basis of the obligation—just as it is in the case of the capitalist and the employer —that what is matter of slight importance to the buyer may in the aggregate turn the scales of life and death among the wage earners. "Among 10,000,000 well-to-do persons the number of yearly deaths is probably not more than 100,000; among the highest class of wage earners the number is probably not less than 150,000, and among the poorest, or those in poverty, the number is probably not less than 350,000." The prevention of disease and the reduction of mortality are the ultimate objects of the duty inculcated upon each class of the community in any way concerned.

"Finally, the State is morally bound to compel employers to pay a living wage, whenever and wherever it can, with a moderate degree of success, put into effect the appropriate legislation." In this appeal to a higher law—if it is possible to use the phrase without offense—Mr. Ryan places himself on the platform on which Secretary Shaw is seeking the nomination, and may seek the Presidency. It is but a few days since Mr. Shaw addressed the Missouri League of Republican Clubs and propounded an entirely novel theory of protection. Originally, declared Mr. Shaw, we protected our industries in their infancy, not foreseeing that we should thereby create a standard of living 50 per cent. above any other country, and 100 per cent. above the world's average. Therefore, contended Mr. Shaw, we must preserve the tariff system to protect not our industries but our standard of living. Here we have the economist and the moralist reaching the same destination by routes as different as possible, and each unconsciously. We prefer the moral to the political argument. There are fewer gaps in it, if it be admitted at all that morals may properly influence economics. It is a fatal objection to the protective system that it is subject to the reproach implied in the underpayment of wage earners as above set out. The capitalist is protected rather than the laborer.

***

It may be doubted whether protection is as beneficial to wage earners as trades unions. The National income resembles a field which may be planted to produce food or flowers, or either in varying proportions. The National income is adequate to provide each head of a family $864, but less than $600 is received. The harvest field provides orchids for a few and scarcely feeds the multitude. Accumulation of wealth and capital benefits the many very little, for they are accumulated rather than distributed, and distribution is in every way to be desired. The Administration of which Mr. Shaw is a member has begun the regulation of prices at the wrong end. If it be conceded that any price should be regulated, the price of labor is eminently suitable for dictation as to what should be paid by all protected by the tariff. Then perhaps many doubting Thomases would perceive new virtues in a system now composed mostly of extortion and ill-distribution of benefits. The trusts, good and bad trusts alike, exercise a species of eminent domain comparable to that which is held to justify the regulation of what rates railways may charge by way of tax upon the community. Similarly all protected industries, having been protected in order that they may raise wages, should be compelled to raise them. They even ought to do so in enlightened self-interest, first because the community is ripe for revolt against an extortion which is not justified by the realization of industrial benefits claimed for it, and, secondly, to preserve themselves from the ills of overproduction and the disappearance of their market. Prices are at their maximum, and whenever that is observed what is called underconsumption is close at hand, and upon the heels of underconsumption comes reaction and prostration. Now there is properly no such thing as overproduction. Even the resources of modern civilization are inadequate to the production of more goods than are wanted. Underconsumption is not the result of overproduction, but of unsatisfied wants, and wants are unsatisfied because of underpayment of wages to producers, in order that capitalists may exploit labor.

tion is close at hand, and upon the heels of underconsumption comes reaction and prostration. Now there is properly no such thing as overproduction. Even the resources of modern civilization are inadequate to the production of more goods than are wanted. Underconsumption is not the result of overproduction, but of unsatisfied wants, and wants are unsatisfied because of underpayment of wages to producers, in order that capitalists may exploit labor.

There is, therefore, moral and economic basis for a lawful minimum wage rate. It is no more an interference with individual liberty regarding paying or receiving wages than are laws regulating sanitation or hours of labor. And specifically there is nothing novel about a regulation of wages by law. Until 1813 there were such laws upon the British statutes, and they exist now in some British colonies. If politicians and moralists and workingmen should unite upon such a campaign there would be a new turn given to an old issue. Sooner or later protection must be mended or ended, and if it is to survive it must do more for the common people than leave them to the tender mercies of a "free" wage contract.

***

This inadequate summary of an interesting argument will do good if it attracts attention to what it is a pity cannot be called a Christian theory of wages. It is more properly to be called a Roman Catholic system of political economy, although we are only able to allude approvingly to the cogent citations from the Fathers which show that they long ago had well considered a topic which may yet become burning with us. As an alternative to Socialism, as an antidote to Anarchism, as a stimulator of thought, the book seems to us well described in Dr. Ely's words —"a meritorious performance."

May 19, 1906

THE SPIRIT OF DISCONTENT.

Prof. Rauschenbusch on the Problems of Christianity in the Social Crisis —Books by Dr. Bussell and Mr. Tenney.*

Written for THE NEW YORK TIMES SATURDA REVIEW OF BOOKS by

JOSEPH O'CONNOR.

IT is an old story that as civilization advances and material wealth increases and concentrates, the disadvantages of poverty become more burdensome and the inequalities in society tend to discontent and danger; and so it has been held that the growth of great fortunes leads either to the utter degradation of the poor or to a reaction against the methods by which such fortunes are accumulated. The Western world was never so prosperous as it is to-day, and, broadly speaking, its peoples were never so near to the mastery of nature's resources and forces, and so potent in the creation of wealth; and yet they have seldom been more restless, more dissatisfied with social and economic conditions, or more convinced of the necessity of change in the distribution and the use of wealth. It is the opinion of Prof. Rauschenbusch that the spirit of discontent is so general that "a desperate grapple between the vastness and the free sweep of overconcentrated wealth on the one side" and "the independence, intelligence, moral vigor, and political power of the common people on the other side" is at hand. This is what he calls the "social crisis," threatening "social revolution." There be those who believe that the betterment of society is to come through the influence of religion leading and lifting men to loving brotherhood; those who think it is to come through the evolution of the altruistic and social elements in humanity and the modification or obliteration of individualism; those who look for it through political reform; those who are content to wait for it with patience, and those who would hasten it as the quick result of controversy, if not strife.

A distinguished Catholic priest, discussing this subject, said: "If I did not believe in God and the immortality of the soul, in a Providence overruling all things for good, and the world wherein all the wrongs of this world are to be righted, I should be a Socialist, or even an Anarchist, and strike here and now for a fair share of the material means of happiness." He meant that faith in religion enabled him not only to trust in the Lord's purpose, but to await the leisure of the Lord's way even in bringing righteousness to prevail on earth. This attitude the militant Socialist despises, and he regards the promises of religion as delusions which soothe men into the endurance of wrong in the only world and the only life to which man is born. The author of "Christianity and the Social Crisis" believes it is the business of religion to strive for the realization of the higher socialism on earth and in time. He was a pastor among the working people on the west side of New York City for eleven years before he entered on his professorship, and there the natural chivalry of his nature was quickened through his daily experience with the poor, and the sense of obligation grew upon him—that it is the mission of religion not only to deal with the regeneration of the individual, but to strive directly and immediately for the regeneration of society. Hence this argument that Christianity must act one way or another to sway the result in the "social crisis" of our time.

It is the purpose of the reviewer to indicate the drift of the discussion rather than give opinions of his own or pause to question judgments that may touch upon his or some other reader's sensibilities or traverse their convictions. It is enough to feel that the book was bravely written to free an honest man's heart; that conscientious scholarship, hard thinking, and the determination to tell the truth as he sees it, have wrought it out and enriched it; that it is written in a clear, incisive style; that stern passion and gentle sentiment stir at times among the words, and keen wit and grim humor flash here and there in the turn of a sentence; and that there is a noble end in view. If the hope be too

*CHRISTIANITY AND THE SOCIAL CRISIS. By Walter Rauschenbusch, Professor of Church History in Rochester Theological Seminary. Cloth, 12mo. Pp. xv.-429. New York: The Macmillan Company.
CHRISTIAN THEOLOGY AND SOCIAL PROGRESS. The Bampton Lectures for 1905. By F. W. Bussell, Brasenose College, Oxford, Rector of Sisland, Norfolk. Cloth, 8vo. Pp. xi.-343. New York: E. P. Dutton & Co. $3.50.
CONTRASTS IN SOCIAL PROGRESS. By Edward Payson Tenney, A. M., Sometime President of Colorado College. Cloth, 8vo. Pp. xvi.-415. New York: Longmans, Green & Co. $2.50.

confident, if there be once in a while a step taken beyond the line of justice into indignation, if a quaint old prejudice, or even animosity bustles to the front in an emergency—no matter. It is a book to like, to learn from, and, though the theme be sad and serious, to be charmed with.

***

In the Days of the Prophets. The author, in tracing the relations of Christianity to the social crisis, goes back to Judaism, and especially to the greater Hebrew prophets. The old law, as he interprets it, had in it manifest sympathy for the poor and respect for their equal humanity; for the land belonged to Jehovah, the national God; it was held for clan or family; every seventh year the fields lay fallow, and their untilled product belonged to all; the poor had the privilege of gleaning and the wayfarer could pluck and eat grain or fruit if hungry; the laborer was paid at sundown, and there was rest on the seventh day; no interest was charged among brethren; and the fiftieth year was the time of jubilee—a fresh start in life. But the prophets supplemented the law and taught righteousness as the condition of divine favor—not merely the righteousness of individuals, but the righteousness of the nation. Their ideal was such moral perfection in the people as would insure prosperity and happiness to them as a nation, because living in loyalty to divine precept, they deserved it; and though at first the promise was for the Jews and looked to immediate fulfillment, the vision widened under the influence of misfortune to the conception of an era of a general and a far-off peace. The prophets were no mere dreamers or theorists, but statesmen anxious as to the actions and the faith of Israel; and their standard was ethical and moral. They were the pessimists of seasons of prosperous depravity, and the optimists of ages of suffering and captivity, since they stood for the ideal that condemned the nation in successful evil and sustained it in hapless righteousness, and had faith that such an ideal is to prevail. It was characteristic of the Jewish teaching of common happiness and prosperity based on common morality, says the author, that it dealt with the present life and made no promise as to another.

The spirit of the prophets, so we are told, passed on into Christianity; and so Christ, when He spoke of coming to preach the kingdom of heaven, was understood as promising an earthly community in harmony with the thought of God. Some of His followers conceived of that kingdom as coming in His lifetime and as having the attributes of human power and glory, and after His death they had faith that this kingdom was close at hand. That belief sustained the primitive Christians and persisted for generations; but gradually the spiritual and typical interpretation of the kingdom of heaven became common, and the ideal of a realization of the Christian teachings and aspirations on earth faded. Among the Jews who became Christian this dream of the kingdom of heaven on earth was the strongest influence, and their life tended toward brotherhood in all things. Among Christian communities of other nationalities the strongest influence was the idealization of this view, the hope of immortality, and a kingdom of heaven in eternal happiness hereafter. In the lapse of ages this ideal shaped Christianity, and the conception of human life as an earthly pilgrimage became dominant. The author doubtless holds to the belief in immortality as the noblest element in Christianity; but he regards the comparative neglect of the ideal of a kingdom of heaven in this world and the duty of working for its establishment, as a misfortune in the career of the Christian Church; and in interpreting its history, though not denying its vast influence in the development of modern civilization, he is less inclined to glory in what it has accomplished than to regret its lost opportunities. In early Christianity there was the social hope as well as the individual hope, and the former seemed the more potent, verging in apocalyptic vision at times toward political triumph. In a word, historical Christianity was begun as a great revolutionary movement, and, after three centuries of obscurity and persecution, rose to be the dominant power in civilization and the guiding force in the Roman Empire. Its triumph came at a time of national decay, but when the empire was overthrown and the old civilization was shattered by the barbarians it remained unbroken and became the master influence in the creation of a new civilization.

***

Religion and Social Reconstruction. It is the opinion of many that religion has constituted the civilization of Christendom in accordance with its own principles, and the opinion of others that it has failed because of inherent unfitness for the task; but the author, conceding that the good results of Christianity are everywhere manifest, and conceding also the various evils in modern society, still asserts the duty and the power of Christianity to bring to pass the kingdom of heaven in this life, and he discusses in detail the reasons why religion has never undertaken the work of social reconstruction. In the early centuries public agitation against political abuses was practically out of the question; the expectation of the second coming of the Lord made any immediate temporal reform seem worthless; the evils of the heathen world were so great that the task of overcoming them looked hopeless, and the divinities of Greece and Rome were so identified with the life of the people and the ceremonial of the State that a Christian could not mingle in civil affairs without seeming to acquiesce in the service of demons. Later the faith in a future life, though indirectly influential on society, lessened interest in social reform, and the distinction between spirit and matter implied something of contempt for material things. Asceticism influenced religious people to turn from marriage and to despise property, and so the Church overflowed in charity, but did nothing in the way of abolishing the sources of pauperism. Monasticism led to the foundation of many ideal communities that helped the poor and the sick, gave good counsel, provided hospitality for the traveler, reclaimed wild places, fostered learning, and gathered the finest natures into a communistic colony; but the monasteries withdrew from active social life the men most needed and cut them off from family life. Moreover, so runs the argument, the growth of sacramentalism, dogma, and church organization diverted religious enthusiasm, and the subservience of the Church to the State brought its mission into an inferior position and weakened the spirit of democracy within it. The process of reasoning can only be hinted at, not even sketched, and, though it is ingenious, the reviewer cannot help thinking that the most obvious explanation of the failure of Christianity, in so far as it may have failed, is in persuading men created with strong individual and social tendencies to live up to its ideals.

***

Church and Society in the Middle Ages. It is worth while, in passing from Prof. Rauschenbusch's interpretation of the religious life of the Middle Ages, to note that of the Rev. F. W. Bussell in "Christian Theology and Social Progress." It is a learned and interesting but very difficult book; and its thesis seems to be that Christianity is essential to modern society, because it is the source of democracy, and without it democracy cannot survive against the forces of State autocracy and scientific fatalism. The Bampton lecturer says in substance that the Church in the Middle Ages was busy in all human affairs, since religion was regarded as embracing science, art, social life, government, jurisprudence, letters, philosophy, agriculture, and the embellishments and comforts of home, within its sphere. In an age of strife it elevated a supreme power purely moral in its censures, which often spoke from exile and nearly always in defenselessness. In an era of tyrannical power it asserted the democratic basis of all human authority and raised the elective principle against hereditary right. In times of serfdom and violence it emphasized the law of brotherhood, the equality of man, and the imperishable value of the individual. When Princes claimed irresponsible power it maintained the rule of law, the delegation of office from the people, and the responsibility of the ruler to his subjects, and while criticised for sacrificing present interests to the eternal, it brought its own system of government close to perfection.

Prof. Rauschenbusch is hopeful as to the influence of Christianity in regenerative work now because he thinks that many of the causes of failure hitherto have passed away. Agitation for social reform does not challenge martyrdom; the hope of an immediate millennium no longer deters Christians from their wider mission; the State is not regarded as allied with demons and the moral power of religion may co-operate with it; there is no excess of other-worldliness and the longing to die and go to heaven is not to-day a test of spiritual life; the ascetic and monastic ideal is disappearing and Christianity is praised because it makes men and nations prosperous and wealthy; ceremonialism is slowly dying out and in the Protestant churches sacramentalism is at an end; Christianity cares less about dogmas and is free to consider ethical and social problems; Christianity has ceased to be churchly and religion is less an institution and more a diffused force than ever; there is a tendency to the separation of the Church from the State; its organization is changing from monarchy to democracy; there is a growth of general intelligence, and while Christianity is fitter than ever for its social mission, the world is calling for its aid in influencing the social crisis.

"It rests upon us to decide if a new era is to dawn in the transformation of the world into the Kingdom of God, or if Western civilization is to descend to the graveyard of dead civilizations, and God will have to try once more." In this rapid summary the reviewer has laid no stress upon certain incidental passages in criticism of the Catholic Church, and yet they have a curious significance in relation to the general argument. It is an appeal to Christianity, and yet somewhat out of harmony with the great majority of Christians. Can there be union on so difficult an issue? Perhaps it is only fair to quote in suggesting the doubt what the author says about condemning the men of the past:

> If I had known St. Francis, I hope I should have had grace enough to become a Franciscan friar and serve the Lady Poverty. If destiny had put me in the chair of St. Peter, I hope I should have made a good fight against the encroachments of the secular power on the sacred heritage of Christ and the vicar of Christ. But being a twentieth century Christian I hope I shall do nothing of the kind.

Duty of Churchmen to the Present Crisis. The fifth chapter of the book is given to the discussion of "The Present Crisis," dwelling on the actual evils and the evil possibilities of the time. Such a review of social and economic conditions has been taken often in recent years, and it need only be said that the author sketches the dark side of the industrial age with many original, shrewd, and suggestive touches. He does not profess to consider the whole of our life and civilization, but so much of it as calls for betterment and seems to threaten the future. The trend of his argument is socialistic, and yet it has this distinguishing characteristic—that it foresees and avoids the usual socialistic conclusion against marriage, and regards the family as the true unit in society. He holds approximate equality to be the only foundation of political democracy, and the sense of equality to be the only basis for Christian morality. He thinks that we are at a point in history when the decline of our civilization is to begin or a forward movement in the intellectual, social, and moral life of mankind hitherto without a parallel. "It is either a revival of social religion or the deluge."

The sixth chapter considers "The Stake of the Church in the Social Movement." In the opinion of the author it must act for the masses or against them, and if it acts against them it loses its character as a religion fit for them, and compels distrust and hostility. In the great forward movements of humanity he declares religion has been a driving force, and the great forward movements of religion have usually come at the call of a great historical situation. He cites the Reformation as a classical illustration and characterizes the popular view of it as a restoration of evangelical doctrine on the basis of the open Bible as misleading. Luther, in his opinion, stood for the smoldering anger of northern nations at Italian domination in other matters than religion, but he ceased to be the leader of a nation, disavowed the cause of the people, allied himself with Princes, and became the leader of a sect. When the Lutheran Reformation became narrowly religious "it became scholastic and spiny, quarrelsome, and impotent to awaken high enthusiasm and noble life," and so "the scepter of leadership passed to Calvinism and to regenerated Catholicism." In the author's opinion the continuous influence of Calvinism lay in the fact that it fused religious faith with the demand for political liberty and social justice. This means that it is the mission of religion to be in the thick of the struggle for the betterment of the world not only through the individual, but through organized effort. It is the fate of the Church to rise or fall with society.

***

Individualism and Socialism Both Essential. The closing chapter of the book bears the title "What to Do." It argues that society must be taken as it is, and no thought of reversion to old conditions considered. Let each contribute to the social movement a regenerated personality, the betterment of himself. Let the ministry lift social questions to a religious level by faith and insight. Let the supremacy of life over property be asserted. Let religious sentiment protect good customs and create good customs and convictions. Let Christianity scrutinize all claims to property and detect wherein public rights are betrayed. Let the spell of lies protecting social wrongs be broken, and distinctions drawn between eternal rights and those institutions that stand merely for modes of progress, have changed with environment and ought to change again. Let the Church recognize the communism inherent in the State and in society and co-operate with it.

The reviewer sympathizes with the book, for personal and impersonal reasons, and he has no doubt that if every, or even any great, religion were to take its purpose and policy to heart much good would come of the crusade; but not, perhaps, the ultimate good aimed at. What the great creeds have done and failed as yet to do Prof. Tenney has set forth in "Contrasts in Social Progress"; and achievement seems slow and consummation far off. And so the sadness of doubt remains. The Jewish prophets could not convince the Jewish nation, nor would their triumph have availed with other nations unconvinced; Christianity has wrought for nearly 1,900 years, and the Kingdom of Heaven is not yet at hand; Socialism is an old ideal, seeming close at times to realization, yet still, like the sailor of the Celtic legend, pursuing a vanishing island paradise. And why? Simply because few men can live up to the ideals of the creed they profess; nor do those who have ideals without a creed attain to them.

Even belief in Christianity has not made Christendom a veritable republic of God, because it has not made the masses of professing Christians ready for it or worthy of it. Socialism has failed hitherto because in nearly all Socialists the sources of conviction are selfish, not altruistic; and in the innermost heart of a Socialist leader the spirit of personal greed and ambition may have a home. Everywhere in human life we see two forces at work—individualism and Socialism; and they are the master elements in man's nature. He is an individual, and individuality is his highest possession—commensurate with life and hoped for as a survival after death in immortality. But he is a social being who must have companionship and to whom society brings security, power, pleasure, and every opportunity for the exercise of his noblest faculties. He may die for his country, but he would not surrender his personality in any cause. Is not any movement, then, which tends to the elimination of either individualism or Socialism, at strife, not merely with the nature of things, but with the essence of manhood? Somewhere between these impulses there is a point of balance, relation, and consequent harmony and righteousness, never yet determined, though its determination is the key to the mystery of the best attainable for humanity in our world at least. Individualism and Socialism tend to overpass this point of balance unconsciously, and they will tend to overpass it consciously; so that when the intellectual difficulty is solved, and we know how far each may safely go, the moral difficulty will remain—that we may not abide by what we know to be the best good.

J. O'C.

Rochester, N. Y., May, 1907.

DENOUNCES PASTORS CONTROLLED BY RICH

Preacher Often Told to be Silent on Business Morality, Dean Mathews Declares.

Special to The New York Times.
CHAUTAUQUA, N. Y., July 28.—Materialism in the Church has its most dangerous aspect in the domination of the Church by men of wealth, according to Dean Shailer Mathews of the University of Chicago Divinity School, who lectured at Chautauqua Assembly today. This control the speaker thought not universal, although dangerous enough to demand the attention of thoughtful Church workers.

"The materialistic dangers," said he, "which assail the Church are too obvious to demand detailed description. There are; however, two which are particularly fatal to the special purposes of the Gospel.

"The first danger is that the preacher may be controlled by men whose ideals are materialized by the standards of an unethical commercialism, and who would lose money by a genuine Christianization of the law. This control is sometimes explicit, and the preacher is bidden to keep silence on the larger question of business morality and confine himself to the sort of sins of which church attendants are seldom guilty. There is, for instance, little opposition to the pastor's denouncing saloons or red-light districts, except in those rare instances in which the property devoted to immoral purposes is in the possession of a member of his congregation.

"There is, however, frequent objection to outspoken frankness concerning the rights of laboring men, and those who are being crushed in the war of competition.

"A more subtle and widespread danger than this, however, is the time-serving spirit which creeps in upon the Church because of its relation with men of wealth. In too many cases a church will have among its attendants those whose business ethics are notoriously bad. The minister who preaches to a congregation thus leavened with corruption, does not need to be a conscious sycophant or time-server to find himself avoiding subjects which would tend to alienate such persons."

Dr. Mathews also spoke of ministers who try to "reform people surreptitiously," and also those who are satisfied with the attempt to "amuse a congregation into righteousness."

July 29, 1909

Churches Unite in Great Publicity Campaign

Plan to Cover the Country Next Year in Discussions of Modern Problems

WHEN the Presbyterian Church instituted its Department of Church and Labor it was taking a radical step, and was starting the way for all sorts of innovations. Other churches dealt with the social problems of the day through committees, but the Presbyterians decided that the matter called for more vigorous handling than that. The result has been not only the remarkable success of the department, but the drawing up of a plan by the Home Missions Council for work along the same lines that shall bring before the churches of all Protestant denominations the vital economic questions of the day. This plan is nothing more nor less than a great campaign of advertising, conducted just as well-regulated business houses would run their publicity departments.

The Home Missions Council represents practically all the Protestant denominations in this country, with a membership of 18,000,000. Hitherto the work of the Home Missions has been chiefly with the folk on the frontier or hidden away in the mountains, but all that is changed. The Home Mission people announce that they are going to concern themselves with the questions "social, racial, economic, and religious" right at our doors. They are going to make the Protestant churches a force in the world's life. They are going to take a long step toward fellowship with the "unchurched millions," and they believe that they will be met half way.

The idea is to present to churches and people, by means of newspaper, magazine, and billboard advertising and the distribution of literature, such topics as the labor question, the immigration problem, the negro problem, the conditions of life in the city, the village, and the town. Experts will prepare the material that is used, and the methods of setting the facts before the public will be in accord with the strictest business principles. No pains will be spared to make the advertising attractive. The country must listen, whether it will or no, for it will be attacked on all sides.

Early in January a series of one-day publicity campaigns will be held in the large cities of the country. The stations of the campaign will be about 200 miles apart, so that by inviting ministers and church workers within a radius of 100 miles the whole country will be covered. The entire day will be spent in the consideration of modern problems, set forth by men of National reputation in their special fields. In the evening there will be popular mass meetings in the largest halls available. The appeal will be made not only to church members, but to the public at large, and there will be nothing sectarian about the matter.

The man at the head of the work is the Rev. Charles Stelzle, the present head of the Presbyterian Department of Church and Labor. He has been described as the "livest wire in present-day organized Christianity," and a better phrase could hardly be devised. Mr. Stelzle knows what he is talking about, for he was born in a tenement, went to work at eight in a sweat-shop and now has his machinist's certificate hanging over his desk in the Presbyterian Building. He looks like a labor leader of the John Mitchell type. He doesn't believe in handling topics with gloves and he can be depended on to keep his audience interested—to say the least. As he talks his listener cannot help drawing a mental picture of some smug and self-satisfied audiences before which this man must often have appeared and to which he now plans to carry his aggressive message. It is safe to say he will give them a much-needed electric shock. He is no sentimentalist and hits from the shoulder. His motto is "To interpret the Church to the workingmen, to interpret the workingmen to the Church, and to interpret employer and employee to each other through education, inspiration, mediation, evangelism and twentieth century methods of Christian work."

What is more, he does it:

At the recent Presbyterian General Assembly in Kansas City he held a church and labor mass meeting that was attended by over 10,000 persons, more than half of them workingmen. It was the largest meeting in over 100 years of the church's history. Mr. Stelzle is under no delusions as to the workingman's attitude toward the Church; he knows perfectly well that the two have drifted far apart, but he believes and feels he has demonstrated that they can be brought together again. For as a result of this Kansas City meeting he has had invitations from trades-unionist leaders in every part of the country to come and address workingmen under the auspices of the Central Labor bodies. The unions offer to bear all the expenses. So far the attendance at these meetings has run from 1,000 to 10,000.

If this is not proof of the workingman's readiness to co-operate with the Church when it comes to him in a way he feels to be friendly, what could prove it?

Further, an exchange has been organized between the Ministers' Associations and the Central Labor Unions, each sending delegates to the other for the discussion of the relation of Church and labor. In some cases the ministers have been made chaplains of the labor unions. Among the churches that have been interesting themselves in labor matters in this way the increase in the labor membership has been from 10 to 40 per cent. Mr. Stelzle holds that while there is still considerable alienation of the workingman from the Church there is no class of men among whom there is a more conspicuous movement toward the Church. "The question of the Church and the workingman," he says, "is no longer a problem, but an opportunity."

"Now, to hold the cities is to hold the Nation, and the Church will keep on losing ground in the cities unless it sits down to honest study of these problems. More dangerous than any opposing religious system is the Church's apparent failure to recognize the influence of the social and physical conditions which affect many of those whom we are seeking to win. These conditions have more to do with their alienation from the Church than is generally supposed. The dirty slum, the dark tenement, the unsanitary factory, the long hours of work, the lack of a living wage, the back-breaking labor, the want of money to pay doctors in time of sickness, the poor and insufficient food, the lack of leisure—all these weigh down the hearts of thousands and thousands in our great cities.

"To such men and women, what does it matter whether the doors of the Church are open or closed?

"What do they care for flowery sermons or fine orations?

"What meaning can the Fatherhood of God and the brotherhood of man have for them?

"They ask, 'Where is God,' and they say, 'What does man care?'"

"The hell in the future does not interest them. Their hell is here and now. It is in meeting the needs of these people that the test of the Church comes. It is to help the Church in its task that we are organizing this campaign."

The Presbyterian Department of Church and Labor, which sets the pace for the whole of this new movement, says that "the labor question is fundamentally a moral and religious question. Therefore the Church has a most important part in the solution of this world problem. And because it is a world problem it must be studied in the most comprehensive manner. No little two-by-four scheme will solve this question." The office of the new movement becomes a clearing house for the most exact information affecting every phase of the problem. From all over the world suggestions and statements arrive. Out they go, carefully digested and systematically tabulated, to clergymen and workers all over the country. Instead of the usual spectacle of each church working separately, making its individual blunders and achieving its individual successes, the whole thing is on business principles. All pull together and profit by the experience of the others.

There are no less than thirty divisions of social questions on which information can be had, and all of these are subdivided again and again. Taking the subjects alphabetically, they are: Advertising—how to get your church before the people you are trying to reach; child welfare; Christian workers for the city; city problems; the Church and the masses' clubs; deaconesses; educational classes; evangelism; fraternal delegates, church and labor; general methods—the bookkeeping of the church; immigration; the institutional church; industrialism; labor; labor unions—these last two with fifty sub-heads between them; lecture courses; the life of the working people; literature; music; philanthropy; poverty; self-help; social centres; social reform; Socialism—with twenty sub-divisions; the Sunday question; temperance, and workingwomen. To these the Negro question has been added, and if you want to know what the Church may do about any or all of them the information is yours without money and without price.

All these topics will receive treatment in the course of the big advertising campaign.

October 31, 1909

RABBIS WARN JEWS AGAINST SOCIALISM

DUE TO INDUSTRIAL STRIFE

BALTIMORE, April 16.—The inroads of Socialism among the working class of Jews was deplored in reports and speeches made at the conference of American rabbis here to-day. A committee which investigated this subject last year made a report in which it was said that the tendency to break from the synagogue and all forms of religion was growing less among the working classes than some time ago, although Rabbi R. J. Coffee of Pittsburgh said he was convinced that more than ever before Socialism is being embraced as a creed by Jewish working-men who are dissatisfied with existing conditions.

The committee suggested that open conferences be held to study the relation of laboring people to the synagogue, so that the problem could be met and dealt with by the congregations.

The report of the committee which investigated the attitude of the Jewish industrial classes toward the synagogue and their religion said that "the industrial conflict has aroused in some Jews an antipathy for religion, especially the synagogue as the institution of religion, because it is believed that the synagogue has become the bulwark of the rich, the defender and advocate of the modern taskmaster. It is distressing to observe that our altars, always regarded as the unifying and pacifying influence par excellence, have lost their hold on so many of our working people."

The committee, however, finds that "the working people are becoming less violent in their opposition to the synagogue and less denunciary in their criticism of religion than a few years ago."

April 17, 1912

BOLSHEVIKI BORE INTO THE CHURCHES

Civic Federation Committee Says They Are Using Religion to Spread Propaganda.

MEETING ENDS IN TURMOIL

Speaker's Demand for Recognition of Lenin Brings Cries of "Put Him Out!"

Successful efforts have been made by the Socialists, Communists and other subversive elements to gain a foothold in the Presbyterian, Episcopal and Methodist Churches, according to report presented yesterday to the National Civic Federation by Everett P. Wheeler, Chairman of its Committee on Socialism in the Churches, at the twenty-first annual convention of the Civic Federation at the Hotel Astor. The report says indications point to the same tendency in the Roman Catholic Church, while there is unmistakable evidence of the activities of these elements in such nonsectarian religious bodies as the Y. M. C. A., the Y. W. C. A., and even the Red Cross.

Mr. Wheeler's report was presented at the fourth session of the convention, which ended in a turmoil when Abraham Lefkowitz, appearing in response to an invitation to the American Labor Alliance, advocated the resumption of trade with Soviet Russia, and then, speaking only for himself, urged the recognition of the Bolsheviki by the United States Government. Instantly there were dozens of cries of "Put him out!" No attempt was made to eject him, however.

Investigations Cover Ten Months.

The activities of revolutionary and radical groups in the churches, according to Mr. Wheeler, have been the subject of an investigation by his committee, covering ten months. Specific information on the subject was ready for submission to the Executive Council of the Civic Federation. Meanwhile it was deemed proper to make certain general observations to acquaint the members of the federation with the principal findings of the committee.

Quasi-political parties and economic groups that formerly tried to spread their revolutionary doctrines by propaganda among workers were now seeking to reach the American people through instrumentalities that create public opinion.

"It is, therefore, not surprising that the Socialist, communist and other submersive elements," says the report, "have made a determined effort to gain a foothold in the schools, colleges, newspapers and churches."

The report says it is a matter of satisfaction that the great majority of the clergy, priests and rabbis of the Catholic, Protestant and Jewish faiths, as well as Christian and Jewish religious organizations, themselves are loyal to the institutions and laws of this country, and are exerting a powerful influence for right throughout the nation.

"It is, however, a matter of concern to the committee that there is a small but active and well-organized element in the churches," the report continues, "which appears to be impatient with the slow and orderly process of political and economic evolution, and has espoused Marxian doctrines as supplying the only solution for existing problems."

Instances Cited in Report.

As a typical instance of the foothold gained in the Presbyterian Church by these elements, the report cites the Labor Temple, Fourteenth Street and Second Avenue, described as a "regularly constituted Presbyterian church, known as the American International Church."

248

Among the speakers that have been permitted to use the church are William D. Haywood, Ralph Chaplin and others of the I. W. W.; Henry Jaeger, Algernon Lee, Gregory Zilboorg, Norman Thomas and others of the Socialist Party, and such independent radicals as Elizabeth Gurley Flynn and Arthur Giovaniti.

"A similar tendency has been noted in certain Episcopal churches," continues the report. "For example, a public forum, analogous in many ways to the Labor Temple, is conducted in the Church of the Ascension at Tenth Street and Fifth Avenue.

"It should be noted that a certain group of Episcopal clergy and others have organized themselves into the Christian Socialist League of America, which is frankly the exponent of Marxian socialism and carries on an extensive propaganda in church organizations and in theological seminaries."

While the Methodist Church does not tolerate "conspicuous centres," such as have been found in the Presbyterian and Episcopal Churches, the report shows that "there are among its clergy men who have espoused radical and some revolutionary doctrines."

The fact that the Roman Catholic Church "is steadfast in its support of law and order" is recognized in the report, which alleges, however, that "there are to be found certain priests whose viewpoints on social and economic questions meet with the hearty support and applause of the radical and revolutionary elements in our country." Certain of these priests are in important positions in church organizations and speak with apparent authority on economic and social questions.

"There have in recent years been established a number of organizations within the churches of an interdenominational character," continued the report, "with the avowed purpose of spreading socialism in the churches as well as to disseminate propaganda with the view of impelling the Church to adopt a definite policy on certain social and industrial questions. If these may be mentioned the Christian Socialist Fellowship, which was organized in Louisville, Ky., in 1911, and the Christian Socialist League of America, which has already been referred to."

Create Propaganda in Churches.

The leaders of these various organizations, according to the report, are avowed members of the Socialist Party, and their organizations are created for propaganda in the Church. The report adds:

"The committee has also found unmistakable evidence of the activities of the same elements in such non-sectarian religious bodies as the Y. M. C. A., as well as in such philanthropic organizations as the Red Cross, which are supported largely by the churches."

The question of permitting unrestricted utterances by all kinds of radicals at the forum of the Labor Temple has been taken under advisement by the Church Extension Committee of the Presbytery of New York, according to Dr. David W. Wylie, Secretary of the General Assembly Board of Elections of the Presbyterian Church.

"The churches should not be used for propaganda by the radicals," said Dr. Wylie, "and about two weeks ago the Church Extension Committee of the Presbytery decided certain changes should have to be made in the conduct of the forum at the Labor Temple."

February 16, 1921

DENY CHURCH AIDS REDS.

Two Presbyterian Clergymen Attack Federation Committee's Report.

In a letter addressed to the members of the National Civic Federation the Rev. Henry Sloane Coffin, President of the Church Extension Committee, and the Rev. William Adams Brown, Chairman of the Sub-Committee on Home Missions of the Presbyterian Church, denied the Federation Committee's charge that a vast majority of speakers at the Labor Temple conducted by the Presbyterian Church had been identified with one or another of the radical and revolutionary groups.

Dr. Coffin and Dr. Brown said that of the seven advertised Sunday meetings one was a Sunday school, four were religious services conducted in English and foreign languages, one a lecture upon some great spiritual teacher, and one a public forum. They said they were convinced the lecturer was in no sense a teacher of radical or seditious doctrine, adding that the forum was presided over by a staff member of the Presbyterian Church.

February 25, 1921

CLERGY DEFY EMPLOYERS.

Special to The New York Times.

PITTSBURGH, June 6.—In reply to a series of communications from the office of the Pittsburgh Employers' Association, designed to persuade influential business men to withhold financial support from certain Christian organizations because ministers failed to keep within a "neutral zone" in sermons and other addresses, the Pittsburgh Ministerial Union today adopted resolutions expressing resentment against the attempt to dictate to the pulpit. The resolutions, presented by the Rev. Dr. F. R. Johnston, follow in part:

Whereas, the Secretary of the Pittsburg Employers' Association has issued communications with the purpose of dissuading men from furnishing financial support to certain Christian organizations because ministers have not limited their message to a so-called "neutral zone"; and,

Whereas, this involves the dictation to religious bodies as to what fields of thought and human service they may enter.

Whereas, the Church, whenever true to its mission, has zealously guarded its absolute freedom to proclaim the full Gospel of Jesus Christ without dictation from any external authority; and,

Whereas, the Pittsburg Employers' Association represents itself as speaking for the employing group—an assumption which we are convinced is contrary to fact;

Resolved, That we, the Pittsburgh Ministerial Union, resent this attempt of a commercial organization to prescribe limits within which alone the Church and other religious organizations may move; that we reaffirm the historic right and the duty of the Church to proclaim the whole truth in Christ as revealed in the Scriptures and as applied under the Holy Spirit to every relationship in life; that we deny to any political, commercial, industrial, or any other group or agency the right to set any restrictions on the freedom of the Christian Church or its agencies to apply the spirit and standards of the Kingdom of God to the whole of life; that we declare it our solemn duty and purpose to defend this liberty of the Gospel.

June 7, 1921

DEPLORES SOCIAL CHURCH.

Bishop Freeman in Yale Lecture Criticizes Secular Intrusions.

Special to The New York Times.

NEW HAVEN, Conn., April 20.— The Right Rev. James E. Freeman, Bishop of the Episcopal Diocese of Washington, D. C., today criticized the growing tendency to discuss political and social questions from the pulpit and the increased social and recreational activity carried on in connection with the Church as perils that today threaten the larger efficiency of the Christian ministry.

In the course of the sixth Lyman Beecher lecture before the convocation of the Yale Divinity School Bishop Freeman said:

"Nothing is more to be deplored than the tendency to convert the Christian pulpit into a rostrum for the discussion of political themes. The very fact that the clergy themselves have a particularly inaccurate knowledge of these weighty subjects precludes the discussion of them. It is the policy of the Christian pulpit to deal with principles rather than policies."

He said that the "institutional agencies" of the Church, developed within the last half century, have diverted the interest and enthusiasm from religion to pastimes and recreations. This trend, he said, had placed the Church at a disadvantage by putting it in competition with secular agencies.

Most deplorable of all, it has shifted the emphasis from a concern for souls to a concern for bodies," he said.

April 21, 1928

FINDS CHURCHES FIT INTO SOCIAL STRATA

3-Year Study of Protestantism in Cities Shows Its Fortunes Vary With Neighborhoods.

TYPES LIKENED TO STORES

'Great Downtown Pulpits' Are Compared to the 'Attractive Windows' of Big Shops.

CENTRALIZATION IS URGED

'Social Engineering' Such as Public Utilities or Catholics Carry On Suggested as 'Strategy' Goal.

Under the title "The Strategy of City Church Planning," suggested principles whereby Protestant churches may progress are published today by the Institute of Social and Religious Research, headed by John R. Mott, chairman of the International Missionary Council and also of the World Committee of Young Men's Christian Associations.

Under the direction of the institute 994 urban churches throughout the country have been studied for the last three years by Ross W. Sanderson, executive secretary of the Baltimore Federation of Churches.

The detailed findings make up more than 200 pages of a published report, with the result summarized by Mr. Sanderson as follows: "The statistics of urban white Protestant churches in America closely reflect the social trends in their environment. This is the rule: In general, as goes the neighborhood, so goes the church." He records it as a "a bit of a shock, even to the expectant mind," to find the facts support "in such convincing detail" the contention that the churches do not transform the life of the community, but are themselves "a function of the environment."

In a footnote Mr. Sanderson explains that he is speaking of church progress in terms of attendance and church prosperity, "as distinct from the meaning of religion for the changing city."

Churches in Social Strata.

"Actual Protestantism," he continues, "is made up of churches which are ranged in a number of sharply contrasting social strata. On Madison Avenue in New York or adjoining the Gold Coast in Chicago churches may make valiant efforts to draw the poor as well as the rich. Always such efforts, however sincere and democratic, are reported with a certain wistfulness. Fifth Avenue is one thing, Second Avenue is another.

"In the Roman Catholic churches, with a worship which is high drama to be witnessed by rich and poor occupying a common abject level in the presence of a deity so transcendent as to make all human distinctions irrelevant, there is the appearance of less class distinction. At the same time there is not likely to be any such social fellowship as is char-

acteristic of Protestant churches."

The survey found no proof of the assertion that the workingman is deserting the church.

"That in many churches the workingman would doubtless feel strange is equally plain," Mr. Sanderson continues, "but the same is true of many stores and other institutions. In many churches, moreover, the man of wealth would feel equally strange. Churches differed no more than the homes of their members. Whether or not such inequalities are desirable is not here under consideration. The data convince the makers of this study that economic cleavage within the church is a phase of economic cleavage within society."

Churches Compared to Stores.

The detailed sections of the study examine the factors which determine the success of churches having neighborhood parishes and those having scattered parishes—that is, with more than half of the members living more than a mile from the church building. The report concludes:

"The church is affected by the same factors of population, economic status, topography and transiency as affect retail trade distribution. The great downtown pulpits and the high-priced music of the centrally located churches are the ecclesiastical equivalent of the vast stocks and the attractive windows of the high-priced shops or the great department stores."

Mr. Sanderson closes his summary of the study as follows: "The final question is: How can a divided Protestantism, at the end of four centuries of decentralization, accomplish in its own way that sort of social engineering which the public utilities find it easy to undertake and continue through their monopolistic control of particular functions and which the Roman Catholic Church steadfastly performs on the basis of ecclesiastical authority?"

November 30, 1932

DEFENDS THE WORK OF RADICAL MINISTRY

Rev. J. P. Jones Retorts to Dr. Peale, Saying the Sermon on Mount Is Their Guide.

The Rev. John Paul Jones, president of the Ministers Union of America, in a sermon in Brooklyn yesterday morning, warned against "the common and fatal tendency to identify the Kingdom of God with the social scheme beneficial in the main to the class in power."

The Rev. Mr. Jones is pastor of Union Church, Eightieth Street and Ridge Boulevard, Brooklyn, composed of members of a Presbyterian and a Reformed Dutch church which merged a few years ago. He is a member of the editorial council of the Presbyterian Tribune. Yesterday he replied to a sermon preached a week ago by the Rev. Dr. Norman Vincent Peale, of the Marble Collegiate Reformed Church,

Twenty-ninth Street and Fifth Avenue, in which Dr. Peale had said:

"We want it known that a noisy radical minority, made up of largely theoretical student types who know little or nothing of the practical world of hard day-by-day living, do not reflect or represent the mature judgment of the Christian Church."

The Rev. Mr. Jones is head of an organization of about 100 composing the Ministers Union of America, whose sympathies are with workingmen.

"The Christian fellowship astonished the world and won its early converts through the power of a new venture of the spirit," the Rev. Mr. Jones declared. "The Christian declaration of independence through which the new spirit was set forth is the Sermon on the Mount.

"In the preaching of the Kingdom of God, which is the attempt to apply the principles of the Sermon on the Mount to the fellowship of human life, this means that the preachers themselves also stand in need of making preparation such as they are urging upon their listeners."

March 16, 1936

Conservative in Everything Except Industrial Democracy

RIGHT REVEREND NEW DEALER: John A. Ryan. By Francis L. Broderick. 283 pp. New York: The Macmillan Company. $5.95.

By GEORGE N. SHUSTER

THIS very careful review of the life and writings of a priest who will keep a place in the history of social reform is also a chronicle of that part of the recent American past which paradoxically explains the present because it fought hard for things which now seem commonplace. Father Ryan (1869-1945) had grown up on a Minnesota farm in circumstances which bred the conviction that a man must always be a Democrat and never succumb to the blandishments of Republicanism. Later he followed the great Democratic Presidents into war as cheerfully as he supported them in times of peace. But he played no role in politics save that perhaps he may have strengthened the fibre of Frances Perkins's Christian soul. His function was to associate moral theology with a deep concern for welfare economics.

In a period when that was

Mr. Shuster, since his retirement as president of Hunter College, has been serving as assistant to the president of Notre Dame.

not easy, he advocated the minimum wage, abolition of child labor, proper work conditions for women and social insurance, finding himself therefore in the company of social reformers whose zeal for all good causes was not greater than their indifference to the Catholic Church. Inside this communion he was conservative, upon occasion very conservative, about everything except what he called in one of his best books "Distributive Justice."

NO whiff of modern speculative theology was about Father Ryan. Thus his restatement of older views that in a Catholic State non-Catholic groups could justly be proscribed, since no one can claim a right to be in error, caused a very considerable uproar which has only recently been calmed in part by other theologians. He took the doctrine from standard manuals, merely denying that it had any relevance for the United States. It has been argued that he was persuaded that since the social gospel he preached was novel and indeed unwelcome in influential Catholic circles he had better be ultra-orthodox in every other respect. But this all who knew him well would think improbable.

He served his cause quite fearlessly. One of his greatest

early successes was a long debate with Morris Hillquit about socialism. This is still a model of mutual courtesy, of a genuine confrontation of issues, and of a far-sighted appraisal of the changes through which the social order was passing. Mr. Broderick cites an intriguing comment that "Ryan won all the economic points and Hillquit all the religious ones." Not a few people thought that more buckshot should have been fired at Hillquit, and some of them kept badgering Father Ryan after he settled down at the Catholic University in Washington to become one of the dullest and yet most influential professors that seat of learning has known.

On the whole things went surprisingly well. Commissioned by a committee of the hierarchy in 1919 to draw up a Bishops' Program of Social Reconstruction, "he produced a document which went far toward bestowing on industrial democracy the blessing of the Church. The newly established National Catholic Welfare Conference gave him command of its Social Action Department and he made the most of the opportunity. When the Great Depression came he was in the forefront of those who assailed the economic policies of President Hoover and then welcomed the New Deal. As a

result he was a target for extremists of one hue or other inside and outside the Catholic Church, but the pertinent bishops supported him without flinching. It is true that he did not become a bishop. He had to settle for non-signorial honors, but, as his biographer makes amply clear, even these were more than he really wanted. His views of social reform had to a great extent prevailed. He was widely traveled and what he said and wrote found its audience. Sometimes he had a rousing day, as when a torrent of abusive letters poured in after an attack on Father Coughlin. But the thing which really counted was that he happened to be a good, solid, square-shooting priest who helped turn the face of American Catholicism toward the future. It is this simplicity and singleness of purpose which Mr. Broderick has now revealed in a book which sedulously respects the documentation and only seldom ventures an eccentric judgment. Inevitably, no doubt, there is more than a bucket-full of comment on ecclesiastical and academic politics but these were part of the hero's life and to Mr. Broderick's credit it may be said that he seldom allows them to befog the reader's vision.

April 14, 1963

Catholic Hierarchy Urges Capital Be Subordinated to Human Welfare

In what was hailed by the Catholic press as the most important pronouncement on social questions by the American hierarchy since 1919, the Archbishops and Bishops of the Administrative Council of the National Catholic Welfare Conference made public yesterday in Washington a statement on "The Church and Social Order" which called for the subordination of economic power to human welfare, both individual and social.

The statement was released first to the Catholic press by the conference news service and was made available to the secular press in New York by The Catholic News, a religious weekly.

Under the general headings of "Ownership," "Property and Labor," "Security," "Wages" and "Establishment of Social Order," the statement discussed the whole range of social organization in the United States and called for a return to Christian principles in our economic dealings.

It reaffirmed the position of the church on ownership of private property, denounced the principle of supply and demand as applied to labor, called for not only a living wage but a security wage to

provide against the future for the workingman, called for a stabilization of wages and prices, and establishment of a social order on a "via media" between the economic individualists on the one hand and the Communists and Socialists on the other, both of whose theories of the use of property, it declared, resulted only in harm to the public generally.

One solution it saw leading to reform of our present system was the formation of guilds or vocational groups "which will bind men together in society according to their respective occupations, thus creating a moral unity." Before this social reform can be accomplished, however, the statement said, "there must be a reform of morals and a profound renewal of the Christian spirit which must precede the social reconstruction."

"We must bring God back into government," the statement said in its introduction, "we must bring God back into education; we must bring God back into economic life; we must bring God back indeed into all life, private and public, individual and social. The truth of God, the law of God, the justice, mercy and charity of God must, by

conscious effort and willing submission be made to permeate all our social intercourse and all our public relations."

The position of the State in the reorganization of the social structure, the statement declared, must be more than that of a "mere policeman or umpire," but it should not go to the length of totalitarianism "in the way of economic planning and direction."

Although administrative measures were not mentioned specifically in the statement, it was recalled that in 1935, after the Supreme Court had declared the National Recovery Act unconstitutional, a statement by the social action department of the National Catholic Welfare Conference urged passage of a constitutional amendment which would revive the NRA on a broader basis, with labor as well as capital represented on the code authorities. The 1935 statement also urged the inclusion of farmers and the professions in such "occupational group organization"—the same phrase used now—for economic self-government in collaboration with political government.

Coming only a brief time after the encyclical of Pope Pius XII "To the Church in the United States," which expressed the hope that the American people might "untie the knotty and difficult social question" of unemployment and distress by application of the teachings of the Gospel, the document might be regarded as a reply to the challenge there expressed.

In the present emergency in the world, the statement says, it is the duty of the church to "recruit and

train leaders from within the various ranks of society who know the mentality and aspirations of their respective classes and who with kindly fraternal charity will be able to win both their minds and their hearts" and bring about a rebirth of Christian principles in economic dealings.

Frequent citations are made in the statement from the famous encyclical of Pope Pius XI "Quadragesimo Anno" (Forty Years After), the "Rerum Novarum" and the "Divini Redemptoris."

The pronouncement of twenty-one years ago to which the present statement is compared was the "Bishops' Program of Social Reconstruction," setting up the present National Catholic Welfare Conference for promotion and coordination of Catholic action in the United States.

The following, comprising the administrative board and assistant bishops of the conference, were listed as signers of the statement: Archbishops — Samuel A. Stritch, Chicago (chairman); John Gregory Murray, St. Paul; Joseph F. Rummel, New Orleans.

Bishops—John Mark Gannon, Erie; Hugh C. Boyle, Pittsburgh; Francis C. Kelley, Oklahoma City-Tulsa; John B. Peterson, Manchester; Edwin V. O'Hara, Kansas City; John A. Duffy, Buffalo; Edward F. Hoban, Rockford; Emmet M. Walsh, Charleston; Karl J. Alter, Toledo; Charles Hubert LeBlond, St. Joseph; Francis P. Keough, Providence; Walter A. Foery, Syracuse; Bartholomew J. Eustace, Camden.

February 9, 1940

BETTER CHURCHES PROTESTANT AIM

Table of Methods to Adjust Church Strategy to Changes Set Up After Survey

Fewer and better Protestant churches manned by personnel trained to cope with recurring social problems in the light of world needs are being urged upon urban Protestant leaders as a result of findings in several recent church surveys in widely separated cities in the United States.

A program of action based on trends discovered under war conditions, some of the underlying causes of which have not been removed, has begun to take shape for the nation's urban Protestant churches. A table of suggested methods of adjusting church strategy to changing social environments in urban areas, virtually all of which are in operation, has been made up for consideration in new areas as well as in those surveyed. More than thirty general and specific objectives have been set.

The methods and objectives have been prepared under the direction of Dr. H. Paul Douglass, director of the Committee for Cooperative Field Research of the Federal Council of the Churches of Christ in America.

Adjustments Found

Adjustments found in the surveys include relocating, federating, merging, forming new churches by using older ones as nuclei; transfer of field and property to other denominations or churches, developing larger parishes, encouraging multiple constituencies, joint use of property by two or more churches; use of "adjunct institutions" such as neighborhood houses or Christian centers; branch and community churches

General objectives include overcoming of handicaps of underlying subnormal conditions; more adequate meeting of social and community changes, accepting responsibility to minister to specific social conditions, seeking to increase Christian solutions for emergent ethical issues.

Among twenty-five specific objectives for urban Protestant churches in addition to setting up continuous research, which has started in some cities, bringing more people into church membership and restoring vitality to Sunday Schools, are that the churches create an agency for continuous cooperative planning; maintain proper balance between central and peripheral churches; adopt common policy for organizing new churches, with special reference to suburbs; adapt churches to suburban expansion; devise church programs to match the special needs of neighborhoods; continue emergency ministries in war housing projects; take advanced ground on the relations of racial groups and churches; maintain solidarity in spite of theological divergencies, pool Christian resources to serve the neediest in the community; develop a religious master plan for the metropolitan community and make common cause with constructive secular community planning movements.

The surveys have been in progress for two and a half years in different parts of the country, including New England and mid-Western areas, with the aid of a limited research service and skeleton staff maintained by the Federal Council of the Churches of Christ in America, the Home Missions Council of North America and cooperating denominations. Such collaboration has depended in most cases upon requests for aid from councils of churches.

One of the latest of these surveys, which arrived here in printed form last week, was in the San Francisco Bay area, being the last of five projected on the West Coast.

Purpose of Studies

The purpose of the five studies, as set forth in the first, which was made in San Diego, Calif., early last year, was described in part as an "attempt to outline in some general fashion what would seem to be the wise strategy in the immediate future for ecumenically minded churches as they seek to deal with social change." The other three studies were made in the late winter and spring of 1945 in Los Angeles, Seattle, Washington and Portland, Ore.

Special attention was emphasized on possible population trends for the post-war period; which war emergency churches should be continued as permanent churches; what was to be their status; prospects for self-support and for acquiring adequate buildings, and the meaning of proportionately larger growth of urban centers to the rural population and churches especially in areas adjacent to larger cities.

For San Diego, the conclusion was reached that "while the population is likely to level off or even decrease for a few years," it was not expected to revert to the 1940 level. Churches were found to be gaining, but less rapidly than population, while Sunday schools were falling off "dangerously."

The San Francisco report, which runs to 113 pages, included in its recommendations, with minor adaptations to the area, the schedule of recommended objectives from the Committee for Cooperative Field Research, directed by Dr. Douglass. A total of 676 churches of all faiths and denominations was studied. It was found that "not only is there a wide diversity of denominations but the denominations which are nationally committed to cooperation are not relatively so strong on the Coast as they are in many smaller communities. Consequently their leadership and action does not assure the solidarity of the religious forces to the extent that it does in other sections of the country." "Yet," the report continued, "more denominations cooperate than elsewhere." It included in its recommendations a welcome to and the assimilation of returning Japanese-Americans.

November 17, 1946

NEW STRATEGY SEEN IN CHURCH BUILDING

Population Shifts Cause Need for Structures Outside Cities, Methodist Official Says

BUCK HILL FALLS, Pa., Dec. 10 (AP)—A new strategy in church building will be required in the next decade to meet the shifting spiritual needs of the country, Dr. Earl R. Brown, home missions executive secretary of the Methodist Church, said today.

In a speech to the meeting of the board of missions and church extension, Dr. Brown predicted the Methodist Church would spend upward of $100,000,000 in new structures during the period of church readjustment.

He emphasized the population transfers which have created new communities around such cities as Philadelphia, Detroit, Cleveland, Chicago, Los Angeles, Portland, Houston, St. Louis and New Orleans.

Other areas requiring new church facilities are in agricultural districts adjoining Government irrigation and reclamation projects; city areas where foreign groups have been supplanted by a new generation and northern communities that have been enlarged by Negro groups from the South, Dr. Brown said.

In the cities the church's biggest problem, Dr. Brown added, is that resulting from the population movement to the suburbs, leaving the old churches surrounded by new religious groups or industrial growth.

In rural areas a noticeable back-to-the-farm movement, spurred by returned veterans, has found churches unable to cope with the increased population, Dr. Brown said.

In all these areas the Board of Missions and Church Extension is facing numerous requests for assistance in building new churches, he added, and it will be up to the church to provide it.

Church officials announced the resignation of Dr. Channing A. Richardson, for eighteen years superintendent of the department of city work in the division of home missions. A former resident of Wisconsin, he will make his home in California.

December 11, 1946

RED INFILTRATION FOUND IN RELIGION

Special to THE NEW YORK TIMES.

WASHINGTON, Nov. 22—American Communists have "dug into" some religious groups and are still "at it," the House Committee on Un-American Activities asserted today.

In a pamphlet not prepared as an official report to the House, but directed rather to the public, the committee, headed by Representative J. Parnell Thomas, Republican, of New Jersey, declared:

"The Communist party of the United States assigns members to join churches and church organizations, in order to take control where possible, and in any case to influence thought and action toward Communist ends.

"It forms 'front organizations' designed to attract 'fellow travelers' with religious interests."

The document, the second in a projected series of five dealing with what was called "the Communist conspiracy" in this country in its relation to various fields, was prepared in question-and-answer form.

It specified the Young Men's Christian Association, the Young Women's Christian Association and "church groups such as the Epworth League" as among those which the Communists were declared to be attempting to infiltrate. Methodist circles were quick to point out that the Epworth League was dissolved on Dec. 31, 1940.

Also listed was The Protestant, a religious publication, and the Federation of Social Action. Both have headquarters in New York.

"Better Stay on Alert"

The text carried these passages: Q.—"Do you mean that every Epworth League or Y. W. C. A. is a Communist hide-out?"

A.—"Of course not. But we do mean that Communists do dig into such groups any way and any time they can. We do mean they have dug into such groups, and are at it today. We do mean that if you want to keep your own organization fit for your own family's membership, you had better stay on the alert."

Although the document asserted that "unfortunately" there were Communist clergymen in the United States, only two persons were accused by name as such in the same context. These were the Rev. Claude C. Williams and the Rev. Eliot White, both Protestants.

The committee declared that religion itself was "not under any sort of investigation," and added that the reason for publication of the pamphlet was "to help you protect your religion and faith from Communist attack by showing you exactly what the Communists are up to."

It went on to assert that Communist propaganda sometimes was surreptitiously introduced into certain church publications, and that Communist speakers sometimes went before church groups.

"Only a few months ago," it added, "the legislative secretary of the Communist party addressed a conference of 100 ministers in Washington, D. C.

Speaking of clergymen alleged to be "open" Communists, the pamphlet termed these not as important as "the others who have joined the Communist fronts which the Attorney General and this committee had declared to be subversive."

"Joiners" Are Attacked

"Do you mean," ran a question at this point, "that just because a clergyman joins or sponsors one or two Communist fronts for one reason or another, he is playing Stalin's game in America?"

"No," read the answer, "We are talking about those clergymen who have over a period of years consistently followed the party line and joined not one or two fronts, but ten, twenty or thirty. These are the core of agents the party depends on in the religious field."

The pamphlet characterized "Marxism-Leninism" as a positive "Communist faith," headed by Marshal Joseph Stalin of the Soviet Union, which would "never accept as final anything else than the complete end of religion," and was implacably arrayed alike against the Catholic, Protestant and Jewish faiths.

"The long and short of it," the committee concluded, "is just this: You cannot be a Communist and believe in God. You cannot believe in God and have a peaceable life under communism."

Today's publication by the committee was entitled "100 Things You Should Know About Communism and Religion." The first of the series, which was issued in June, was titled "100 Things You Should Know About Communism in the U. S. A."

Charges Are Scouted

The Rev. Jack R. McMichael, secretary of the Methodist Federation for Social Action, yesterday termed the Thomas Committee's charges "ridiculous and untrue." He declared that the federation was a democratic fellowship of more than twenty Methodist bishops, 5,571 pastors, church men and church women founded in 1907 on "the original source of the Social Creed of the Methodist Church and churches."

Kenneth Leslie, founder and editor of The Protestant, a bimonthly religious magazine, said:

"The Protestant is under attack by the political agents of cartels because we have broken the smooth face of the Christian Front against the Soviets.

"We used the phrase 'Christian-Communist two-way bridge,' meaning that ideas must come from both sides to make a common understanding.

"If the ministers of one church can bring its Christian influence bear on fascism, the ministers of other churches can bring their Christian influence to bear on communism."

Raymond L. Dickinson, executive vice president of the Y. M. C. A., declared:

"We have had no evidence here in New York of any Communist infiltration. Although we are constantly watching, it has been no problem for us so far."

November 23, 1948

Methodists Revise Economics Stand

By GEORGE DUGAN
Special to The New York Times.

SAN FRANCISCO, May 6—A major revision of the social creed of the Methodist Church was approved overwhelmingly here today at the closing business session of the denomination's Quadrennial General Conference.

The new section of the creed was hailed by its supporters as a vehicle for silencing forever charges that the church endorsed a communistic way of life.

Prior to today's change, a section had declared that the church favored "the subordination of the profit motive to the creative cooperative spirit." It was this phrase that was interpreted by some persons as condemnation of private enterprise and an endorsement of a socialistic form of life.

The new section, approved in a burst of applause, says:

"We stand for the principle of the acquisition of property by the Christian processes, and in the right of private ownership thereof with full acknowledgment of stewardship under God and accountability to Him for its use.

"We espouse no particular economic system, and refuse to identify Christianity with any economic order. We approach every economic order in the commands of our Christ and judge its practices by the Christian gospel."

The social creed revision was brought to the floor of the conference by its committee on the state of the church. In presenting the change to the delegates Charles C. Parlin of the Newark, N. J., area of the church and committee chairman, emphasized that the revision was a "clarification" of a section that had been misunderstood by some persons.

The creed revision was one of more than 100 legislative items passed in the final hours of the two-week long session.

Another report also brought by the committee on the state of the church and approved after a brief debate, contained long statements on the attitude of the church toward war and peace, international affairs, Soviet-United States relations and civil liberties.

Excerpts From the Report

Excerpts of these follow:

ON THE CHURCH AND WAR: Regarding the duty of the individual Christian, opinions sincerely differ. Faced by the dilemma of participation in war, he must decide prayerfully before God what is to be his course of action in relation thereto. What the Christian citizen may not do is to obey men rather than God, or overlook the degree of compromise in our best acts, or gloss over the sinfulness of war."

ON THE REJECTION OF PREVENTIVE WAR: "We reaffirm the conviction that war is not inevitable * * * We rejoice that responsible statesmen recognize this fact, and we call on all Methodists to support this stand by holding steady in goodwill and faith."

ON THE UNITED NATIONS: "In spite of tensions within the United Nations, we believe that it must be kept united. We reject the proposal that the world should be split politically, as it is now ideologically, into two blocs. If the United Nations is to serve the interests of peace, it must not become the instrument of any bloc of nations. Regardless of difficulties that may be encountered in arriving at agreements or securing unanimity, the United Nations should be maintained for all nations * * * We call for revision of the United Nations Charter in such manner as to enable that body to enact, interpret, and enforce world law against aggression and war."

ON SOVIET-UNITED STATES RELATIONS: "We should not charge the entire Russian people with being Communist. There are still many millions of Christians in Russia. They are not materialists for they believe that the Eternal Spirit, the God and Father of our Lord Jesus Christ, is the ultimate reality. Despite severe repressions, churches and cathedrals are open and people worship in them, traditional scriptures of the Old and New Testaments are used, and Christian hymns are sung. We should make every effort to communicate with these people and send a message of Christian fellowship and good will."

ON CIVIL LIBERTIES: "In this time of fear, areas of freedom of speech and thought are being narrowed all over the world * * *. In some lands, thought control uses the techniques of absolute censorship * * *. In other lands the techniques are those of social rejection, calling of names, demands for 'loyalty oaths, denial of employment, irresponsible accusations, and assertion of 'guilt by association' * * *. Our role is not to suppress ideas, but to open channels of communication, so that men can come to know the thoughts of their neighbors, and so that the best thoughts of all men can come to be possessions of all mankind."

The conference also reaffirmed its opposition to universal military training, the appointment of an Ambassador to the Vatican, and the liquor traffic.

A Board of Social and Economic Relations, designed to serve the Methodist Church in such fields as labor, race and community betterment, was established today by the Conference.

Membership of the new board, regarded by many delegates as the church's answer to the Methodist Federation for Social Action, will include six Bishops and clerical and lay representatives chosen from the church at large.

Yesterday the conference formally requested the unofficial federation to drop the word "Methodist" from its name and to vacate its headquarters in the New York offices of the church. The federation had long been under fire for alleged "'leftist" tendencies.

In an action dealing with a specific problem in the field of racial discrimination, the conference urged this morning that all Methodist schools of theology admit qualified students without regard to race or color, "except in those instances where state laws would force an undue hardship upon the institution involved."

Late last night a more general statement had been approved by the delegates, asserting that "there is no place in the Methodist Church for racial discrimination or racial segregation" and proposing that the church "seek to free itself utterly from racial discrimination and segregation."

May 7, 1952

CHURCHES COUNCIL SETS SOCIAL CODE

Adopts Christian Precepts Opposing Collectivism and Backing Free Enterprise

By GEORGE DUGAN

A declaration of Christian principles and their relation to social and economic life was adopted yesterday by the policy-making General Board of the National Council of Churches of Christ in the U. S. A.

The 4,000-word declaration included thirteen "norms for guidance" in applying these principles to daily life. It rejected the socialization of production and gravely warned against the dangers of "collectivism." At the same time, it approved the democratic way of life and praised a responsible free enterprise system.

The document, which had been debated and revised many times in the last two years, was approved by a vote of 77 to 4. It is the National Council's first major statement on social and economic issues since its formation in 1950.

The interchurch organization represents thirty Protestant and Eastern Orthodox communions with a total membership in excess of 35,000,000 persons. The board meeting was held at the Brick Presbyterian Church, Park Avenue and Ninety-first Street.

Opposition to the document was spearheaded by a laymen's group within the council that contended, in essence, that the church should hew closely to the spiritual goals of religion and refrain from speaking out on political, social and economic issues that might tend to divide churchgoers.

The pronouncement, in rejecting socialized production, declared that "in some situations Christians have had the misconception that the one sure road to economic justice is the socialization of all major means of production."

"During periods of exploitation of large classes of the population and also in times of depression and unemployment," it said, "it was understandable that some Christians and others concerned about the welfare of the victims of the situation should regard every move toward increasing social control as an advance.

"Today we have enough knowledge of what happens under a thoroughgoing collectivism to realize that uncritical recourse to the state to remedy every evil creates its own evils. It may easily become a threat to freedom as well as to efficiency.

"The union of political and economic power is a dangerous road, whether it leads toward complete state control of economic life or toward control of the state by private centers of economic power. A wide distribution of centers of power and decision is important to the preservation of democratic freedom."

The declaration warned, however, against "another misconception" held by some Christians "that a maximum of individual economic freedom will by itself create the economic conditions that contribute to a good society."

"On the contrary,' it asserted, "the weight of evidence shows that some use of government in relation to economic activities is essential to provide the environment in which human freedom can flourish."

Answer to Totalitarians

In discussing the role of the church in its relation to society, the document made it clear that "from the Christian standpoint free democratic institutions are clearly superior to any form of totalitarianism." It added:

"But our way of life has been challenged by totalitarian philosophies and practices, especially communism, which are competing with it for the loyalty of men around the world."

The document was presented to the Board by Charles P. Taft, Cincinnati lawyer and chairman of the 121-member General Committee of the Department of the Church and Economic Life of the National Council. Mr. Taft described it later as a guide for denominations and local councils of churches.

The general board also adopted a resolution urging its constituent members to heed the call of President Eisenhower to pray for peace on Sept. 22.

A statement on the use of the hydrogen bomb was referred back to a committee for further study.

The board will meet again on Nov. 22 in Boston on the eve of the four-day third general assembly of the National Council.

September 16, 1954

RECTOR DESCRIBES 'SLUM CHURCH' JOB

Must Supply Food and Advice as Well as Solace, He Tells Episcopalian Bishops

By GEORGE DUGAN
Special to THE NEW YORK TIMES.

EL PASO, Tex., Jan. 10 — A description of how the Protestant Episcopal Church could minister to "depressed" urban areas was presented here today to a special meeting of the House of Bishops by the 34-year-old rector of Grace Church in Jersey City.

Describing his parish as a "slum church" in an area of "unbelievably bad" housing, the Rev. C. Kilmer Myers told the Bishops that the focal points of his ministry were the "kitchen in the rectory and the altar in the church."

The Rev. Mr. Myers emphasized that when parishioners lived in basements "crawling with rats" under sanitary conditions "so foul that children die," the church must become a "Christian home" rather than a community social center.

According to the youthful rector, a parish house in a slum area must be open at all times, whether for food, advice or spiritual solace.

Must Sacrifice Privacy

The minister in such an area, he added, must resolve to live with his people as well as to minister to them. He also must be willing to sacrifice his personal privacy, suffer an "occasional robbery," and be prepared to celebrate services ranging from Solemn High Mass to "revival meetings during Lent."

Grace Church in Jersey City, the Rev. Mr. Myers explained, is served by a three-man team of rectors that in itself forms the basic "Christian community."

Formerly a strong parish in a once-wealthy neighborhood, Grace Church gradually succumbed to population shifts and in 1949 when the team took over there were practically no worshipers.

"The three of us," the clergyman commented, "literally prayed and rang the bell alone."

The Rev. Mr. Myers emphasized that the parish is "completely interracial."

Bishop Conkling Speaks

Another speaker, Bishop Wallace E. Conkling of Chicago, warned his fellow-churchmen against permitting a downtown parish that is "going to seed" to "get away from us."

"We must overcome the idea," he said, "that the Episcopal Church is just a church for nice people."

He deplored the "old theory" that the "best people go to the mother church in a city and the less privileged can find their worship in neighborhood chapels."

In the same vein, Bishop Norman B. Nash of Massachusetts said that the "dreadful truth" is that the Protestant Episcopal Church ministers mainly to the "upper classes."

"We are losing out," he declared, "with the people at the bottom of the social structure."

A proposal that the House elect a Suffragan Bishop for the armed forces was defeated late this afternoon when a commission report opposing such a move was unanimously approved by the assembled Bishops.

In "reluctantly" coming to this conclusion, the report recommended, instead, that both the clergy and laity assume individual responsibility for the spiritual welfare of the Church's men and women in the armed forces.

It also proposed that every parish conduct "constant prayer by name" for those in military service and that every congregation pray regularly for a just peace.

Thirteen nominees were proposed for election as missionary Bishops in Puerto Rico, Utah and North Dakota. The election will be held Friday morning.

January 11, 1951

CHURCH IS FIGHTING CRISES IN 11 CITIES

Episcopal Council Gets Data on 5-Year Program Aimed at Typical Problems

ONE PARISH IN NEW YORK

Special to The New York Times.

GREENWICH, Conn., April 27 —The National Council of the Protestant Episcopal Church learned here today about a new counter-attack on the menace of paganism in American cities.

The Right Rev. Frederick J. Warnecke, Bishop of Bethlehem, Pa., and vice chairman of the council's division of urban-industrial church work, told the quarterly session of the council in Seabury House of an effort being made in eight states from Texas to New England.

Eleven parishes, each presenting a different though typical problem, were selected for treatment on a program financed by the $125,000 grant of an anonymous fund. The money is to be distributed evenly over a period of five years, the first of which has now ended. All of the parishes share in the cost and some are paying 100 per cent.

St. Peter's Church, 346 West Twentieth Street, in the Chelsea district of New York, defined by Bishop Warnecke as a "historic church in a chronic problem area," has received a Spanish-speaking staff member to cope with "the heavy influx of Puerto Ricans" in the neighborhood.

At Roxbury Crossing, Mass., a trained social worker skilled with children was assigned to St. John's Church, "a poor to middle income parish with many critical problems."

Salesmanship Is Involved

Far removed was the case of Christ Church in downtown Cincinnati where a new $1,500,000 sanctuary is being built to handle a "massive program." Here the question is one of salesmanship—how can that church not alone survive but succeed?

"Plans are under way," said the Bishop, "for a market research analysis, religion potential surveys and similar emphases, led by competent sales and promotion executives."

Bishop Warnecke related that in Austin, Tex., St. David Church, for many years a powerful parish, has found itself "with certain symptoms of impending crisis since 1950." While the members are tackling the issue along at least five lines, the grant is to concentrate on "a specific attempt to win people in the immediate service area."

Special cases arouse the interest of the committee. Thus in Reno, Nev., where Trinity Church has faced "an increasing demand for the church's ministry by people whose marriage is in difficulty," pastoral counselling services have been established with emphasis on sound home life.

At Schenectady, N. Y., virtually everyone in St. Paul's Church is a union member employed by General Electric or in the family of one. The new rector, the Rev. William S. Van Meter, was for five years deputy commissioner of labor in Oregon and now spends two days a week on research consultant work for the council.

Other Problems Summarized

The remaining five parishes and their problems are:

¶St. Mary's Church, Braddock, Pa., one man serving a complex of three small industrial towns.

¶St. Mark's Church in Chicago, a transitional inner city type of area with a parish in the crisis stage. A competent social worker will be assigned June 1.

¶St. Stephen's Church, Wilkes-Barre, Pa., one of five cooperating parishes in a community with a weakening economy. Maximum strength is sought through a pooling of effort while each year concentration will be on one aspect. This year it is to be youth work.

¶Memorial Church of the Advocate in Philadelphia, "an old church with a building which would probably cost $10,000,000 to reproduce, finds itself in a critical struggle for existence." A tonic is sought in community service and personal evangelism.

¶Memorial Church in Baltimore, an older area fringed with sharply differing neighborhoods. The parish, to survive, is becoming increasingly involved in civil affairs. A public health nurse has been added to the staff.

April 28, 1955

PROTESTANTS LOSE STRENGTH IN CITIES

But Despite 'Alarming' Flight to Suburbs, Report Cites Urban Opportunities

By GEORGE DUGAN
Special to The New York Times.

CLEVELAND, Nov. 2—Protestantism in the United States is fleeing to the suburbs at an "alarming" rate.

This "critical" tendency of Protestant churches to disappear from the "heart" or inner areas of large cities was high-lighted today in a commission report prepared for delegates attending a four-day National Conference on the Churches and Social Welfare.

The meeting is being held under the auspices of the National Council of the Churches of Christ in the U. S. A.

According to the report, modern transportation has whisked churches away from the city's heart "with the blighted central sections left behind and never revisited by the higher-income Protestant groups who have moved to self-sufficient, self-controlled out lying communities."

This "circle of blight," the report declared, has steadily widened, making congested slums of former "fair neighborhoods."

'Acres of Blight Segregated'

"Many of these heavily overpopulated acres of blight are segregated by poverty, social class, race, and politically, from the communities where the better established American Protestant denominations are strong," it added.

Fifty years ago, the report said, one typical large city maintained 278 Protestant churches in its inner area that served a population of 1,196,805 persons. Today, ninety-one churches remain, but the population is 1,125,683.

The report was far from pessimistic, however. It went on to assert that "at this time prospects for successful Protestant work in the left-behind areas of our cities are better than ever before."

Challenge of the City

Protestant evangelical effort in the city's heart, the report declared, is face to face with a ready-made challenge, namely, the influx of Negroes, low-income Southern whites from rural areas, Puerto Ricans and Mexicans.

In view of this challenge, it added, "large sections of American cities which were thought to be lost to Protestantism are now available for successful Protestant Christian effort."

The commission report was prepared under the aegis of the Rev. Dr. Neil E. Hansen, director of the Chicago City Missionary Society, and the Rev. Dr. David W. Barry, director of the New York City Mission Society.

November 3, 1955

'Social Pressures' Found Undermining Religion in Suburbs

Special to The New York Times.

GARDEN CITY, L. I., July 17 —Organized religion in the suburbs is in danger of "betraying its heritage by becoming the handmaiden of secular pressures," a group of Long Islanders was warned today.

Dr. Dan W. Dodson, director of New York University's Center for Human Relations and Community Studies, gave the warning at a one-day institute on "religion in suburbia" held at Adelphi College.

The pattern of suburban growth since World War II has had an impact on institutions of religion that is just beginning to be assessed, Dr. Dodson said. While suburbanites have raised church attendance to a new high, he argued, it is doubtful religious feeling had correspondingly increased.

Suburban churches and synagogues, he said, have become social centers complete with recreation and social halls, kitchens and after-school classrooms.

Dr. Allyn P. Robinson, director of the Greater New York area of the National Conference of Christians and Jews, said that many social problems were masked behind religious issues. He encouraged clergymen not to minimize their religious differences, but to recognize social problems as such and to work harmoniously towards solving them.

July 18, 1958

Presbyterians Push Integration in City

By JOHN WICKLEIN

In the November issue of Harper's, a leading churchman declared that the Protestant attitude toward cities was summarized in Ogden Nash's couplet:

The Bronx?
No thonx.

But the Rev. Dr. Wendell Q. Halverson, who has just been installed as administrative head of the Presbytery of New York, says that as far as Presbyterians here are concerned, that's nonsense.

The Presbytery, which recently passed its 220th year in the city, has called on 30,000 active members to raise $5,000,-000 to spread its work, chiefly through missions to Puerto Ricans, Negroes and other low-income groups.

"We're going to stay in the city," said Dr. Halverson. "And to do that, we've got to take a multi-lingual, multi-racial attitude. There can't be a church for Negroes, one for Puerto Ricans and one for Anglo-Saxons."

On April 12, the integrated Sound View congregation will dedicate a new church in the Clason Point section of the Bronx. The church has three ministers: Anglo (the church's term for Continental-born white), Negro and Puerto Rican.

Dr. Halverson, who is 42 years old, left a large pastorate in a Chicago suburb to become administrative officer for his denomination in Manhattan, the Bronx and Staten Island. His main job here, he feels, is to see that all sixty-two of the Presbytery's churches become racially and culturally integrated in practice as well as in policy.

Four years ago, the national governing body of the church required that every Presbyterian agency adopt a policy of an inclusive church. The Presbytery of New York is following that precept.

The churches have got to integrate, Dr. Halverson said, both to carry out their Christian commitment to brotherhood and to remain in the city in the face of these facts:

More than 55 per cent of the city's 960,000 Protestant church members are non-white. Of this total, 440,000 are Negroes and 90,000 are Spanish-speaking people, mostly Puerto Ricans.

The non-white majority is increasing steadily. As the incomes of the white become higher, many of them move away from the city. In their places come Negroes and Puerto Ricans.

Concern Shown

Realizing this situation, leaders of many denominations have shown concern for improving their ministries to "the inner city." The Presbyterian Progress Program is only one of such campaigns.

But in the eyes of the Rev. Dr. Truman B. Douglass, a Congregational leader, none of the denominations has gone far enough toward meeting the needs of cities.

Protestantism, he declared, has virtually been giving up in the cities.

The old ways are changing, Presbyterian leaders here insist. There is no anti-urban bias in their denomination, they say, because it grew up in a commercial city—Geneva.

In its roots, Dr. Halverson acknowledged, Presbyterianism was a middle-class entity. But today, in New York, he said, it ministers more to the extremes of the rich and poor, rather than to the people in the middle, who have pretty much taken to the suburbs.

To meet the challenge of this change, he would like the church to try a new approach to urban work—a "peripatetic ministry."

Instead of putting so much energy into the upkeep of buildings, Dr. Halverson would rather see twenty-five or thirty clergymen assigned to one central church. They would fan out to minister to the divers communities that exist in any one section.

One of the large Madison Avenue or Fifth Avenue churches could be used as the "cathedral church" for many groups meeting in living rooms and store-front chapels under the guidance of one of the roving ministers.

"We could have one man working in a housing development," said Dr. Halverson, "calling on six to eight groups of from fifteen to twenty people each, and that way localize the ministry.

"It's a known fact that people join face-to-face groups within a church, rather than the whole church. Its growth depends on people finding themselves in face-to-face groups that have meaning for them.

"Now fifteen to twenty people can't maintain a church, but sixty face-to-face groups can. And they can all get together for worship in the larger parish—the central church."

The larger parish idea has been tried in the rural field, with specialist ministers. In addition to his outlying church group, each minister of the central church has a specialty—Christian education, fund-raising, counseling, the Sunday school or something else.

A pilot project for the adoption of the "larger parish" idea in the city began yesterday. The Presbyterian Church of the Sea and Land opened a store-front chapel for Spanish-speaking residents of the Lower East Side.

There were more worshipers than seats at the service conducted by the Rev. Juan E. Mercado, director of Spanish work for the Presbytery.

Second Church Chapel

The Rev. David W. Romig, minister of the church, and the Rev. John D. Cato, his assistant, built the 8-by-16-foot chapel in the old store at 191 Henry Street themselves. They also have converted another store to a chapel at 176 Madison Street a few blocks away. It will be used by the English-speaking congregation while their 1819 church at Henry and Market Streets is being renovated.

Foreign-language groups and chapels within established churches can be only a step on the way toward total integration of whole congregations, the General Presbytery of New York believes. But that, Dr. Halverson admits, poses deep emotional problems that won't be solved by saying to white people: "You're going to accept Negroes and Puerto Ricans as brothers and friends, and that's all there is to that."

Many Presbyterian ministers are ready to accept integration, he said, but many parishioners are not. "We are going to overcome that," he said, "by constantly preaching the gospel of love."

In the past, rather than extend the fellowship when minority people began appearing at services, many white parishioners transferred to more segregated congregations.

This happened at the St. Augustine Presbyterian Church in the Bronx. In the middle Thirties, Negroes began moving from Harlem into the Morrisania area around the church, at Prospect Avenue and 165th Street.

The newcomers attended Sunday services at St. Augustine, and a few asked to join the church. Not one was accepted. They were made to know that while they were welcome to attend worship services, they could not become members.

As the area's white population diminished, so did the membership of the church. By 1938, the white congregants had abdicated and merged with another white congregation a mile away.

The dozen Negroes who had been attending services got permission from the Presbytery to rebuild St. Augustine. The little group chose for their pastor a Negro graduate of Union Theological Seminary who had just been ordained as a Presbyterian minister. His name is Edler G. Hawkins.

Last April the 50-year-old Mr. Hawkins, who is still pastor of St. Augustine's, was elected Moderator—head of the governing body—of the Presbytery of New York. His church has grown to a thousand members, and he has added a communion of

The New York Times

STORE-FRONT CHAPEL: Rev. Juan E. Mercado, the director of Spanish work for the Presbytery of New York, conducting service yesterday in chapel for Spanish-speaking people at 191 Henry Street. Chapel was opened by the Presbyterian Church of the Sea and Land. At the right is the Rev. David W. Romig, pastor of the Church of the Sea and Land.

Spanish-speaking people. An assistant, Domingo Rosado, conducts services in Spanish.

"We have a sprinkling of whites in the congregation," Mr. Hawkins said recently. "But the white population does not find it easy to be a minority. The climate has to be created where it becomes as natural for whites to find fellowship in a Negro congregation as it is for the Negroes to find fellowship in a white congregation."

The Spanish-speaking population of Morrisania has been rising steadily since the mid-Forties. Today the distribution is about 58 per cent Negroes, 32 per cent Puerto Ricans and 10 per cent "Anglos" and other peoples.

Hopes for Union

"Someday we hope we will have a united, English-speaking congregation of Negroes, Puerto Ricans and "Anglos," Mr. Hawkins said. "But now, the older Puerto Rican folk feel the need to communicate in Spanish, and so we hold a separate service for them on Sunday afternoons."

About eighty adults have joined the church as members of the Spanish-language group.

The two peoples have begun to cross cultural lines in the church's youth groups, choirs and women's groups, the minister said. But full integration, he believes, will take a generation to accomplish.

How long will it be before continental whites mingle freely with Negroes in his church and other churches of the Presbytery?

"Being realistic," he replied, "because of the attitudes that exist, I don't think this will happen for a long time."

Dr. Halverson's idea for a peripatetic ministry could help to create true integration, Mr. Hawkins said.

"We're hoping this church might be a demonstration that these groups can work out relationships in community as well as church life," said Mr. Hawkins.

Dr. Halverson hopes the churches of the Presbytery may someday become examples of united fellowship for all the churches in the country.

"Four years ago, the Presbyterian church nationally declared that this must be an inclusive church.* In the 'inner city' of New York we have the means and the peoples to make it so, and we should be glad of the opportunity."

Or, to return to Ogden Nash, the leaders of the Presbytery are determined their churches' approach to the city shall be:
The Bronx? Give Thonx!

January 26, 1959

METHODISTS LOSE STRENGTH IN CITIES

Rejection of Non-Whites Is One Cause, Study Shows —Church Fights Trend

By JOHN WICKLEIN

The Methodist Church, the largest Protestant denomination in the country, is dying out in the cities.

Methodist congregations, while increasing elsewhere, are dwindling in inner urban areas because most have refused to accept as members any but whites of the upper and middle class. And this is a vanishing breed in the cities.

These ideas are the consensus of Methodist leaders in four Northern cities studied last week.

A bishop in Boston said that if a city church did not serve the low-income people of its immediate areas, but ministered only to an élite who drive to it from the suburbs, it had no right to exist.

A director of church planning in Detroit asserted that the biggest inner-city problem was not racial integration, but class integration, a problem that exists within the Negro group itself.

The pastor of a successfully integrated church in Chicago put it another way. The difficulty of the churches, he said, is in welcoming people who are different from the members of the congregation—different in social or economic status or in

Reynolds, Photography, Inc.

WHILE PARENTS WORSHIP at St. James Methodist Church on the South Side in Chicago, children are provided for in nursery there. Membership, white and Negro, has been increasing under the guidance of the Rev. E. Jerry Walker, former advertising man.

ethnic background.

The director of the Mayor's Commission on Human Relations in Pittsburgh, a Methodist layman, went a step further.

"The key to the city problem," he said, "is the increase of the Negro population.

"Methodist churches are going to have to decide to serve these people or get out of the cities."

For Methodists, the church leaders pointed out, this is harder than for many national denominations. Although its churches are not segregated by church law, its conferences are. In most areas white church conferences overlap Negro conferences, so that churches within a mile of each other may find themselves in separate regional organizations.

This arrangement is insisted upon by members from the South, where half of the 10,-000,000 Methodists, Negro and white, live.

In the individual churches, the pastor may welcome to membership anyone he wants to, regardless of race.

Official Is Worried

But one official, the Rev. Dr. Robert A. McKibbin, director of the Board of Missions' Department of City Work, is worried that the policy is not being put into practice.

While the nation has become urban, Dr. McKibbin said, the denomination has stayed rural. Nearly 60 per cent of the nation's population lives in metropolitan areas; only 40 per cent of all Methodists live there. This contrasts with 73 per cent for Episcopalians and 62 per cent for Presbyterians.

The Department of City Work has begun a long-range program to make rural and suburban members support city churches in meeting the needs of the people.

To begin it, Dr. McKibbin invited editors of national Methodist publications and others to visit three cities—Boston, Pittsburgh and Detroit —in which church organizations have made strong and varied efforts to revive themselves. He also pointed out as excellent and difficult the integration work of several churches in Chicago, a city that has suffered from racial tensions for years.

In Boston, five churches died in ten years, leaving only five surviving in the inner city. And until two years ago the death of all but one of the survivors was being predicted freely by outsiders who studied their situation.

At that time the national Board of Missions proposed that three churches in the South End, a slum area of three-quarters of a square mile, combine into a parish under the administration of Morgan Memorial, a long-established social service institution run by the denomination.

The idea was to develop a "social-gospel" type of ministry, in which the pastors and church workers went into the area to serve the needs of the people, rather than sit in the large, old, decaying churches and wait for the people to come to them.

The three ministers agreed, and the churches — Morgan Memorial's Church of All Nations, Tremont Street Church and Union Church — combined in the South End Methodist Parish.

At their head, as coordinator, was placed a fourth minister, the Rev. John E. Barclay.

Mr. Barclay, who is on the Mayor's Committee for Urban Renewal, feels rehabilitation of the low-income people of the South End as a personal responsibility.

The area, which begins just a few blocks south of Boston Common, is a disorganized community, producing disorganized lives, he said. About 46,000 people are jammed into the section, and there is one barroom for every 220 of them.

Victory Over the Devil

Mr. Barclay is pressing for stronger state laws to clean up prostitution in the area. When the Church of All Nations was built a number of years ago, Morgan Memorial bought up the buildings of a red-light district surrounding the site and used the bricks to construct the sanctuary. "A victory of God over the Devil," says the minister.

Ministers of the parish work as members of city and private social service agencies that abound in the area, rather than have the churches set up separate agencies.

In an area where the attitude of the people is "nobody cares what you do around here," they feel their responsibility is primarily to raise the spiritual and moral level of the community.

They try to do this by visiting people of all races and economic classes and inviting them to come into an integrated fellowship. The area is predominantly Negro, but there are also people of Puerto Rican, Chinese and Irish background, among others.

Strength in Diversity

The parish thinks it will survive in the city, because its churches do not have to depend on a dwindling core of white people for support; they are drawing their support from people of all races in their immediate areas.

On Palm Sunday the Church

of All Nations will take in thirty-six new members, bringing its active membership to 540. One of these members is coming in after sixty-four visits — most of them outdoors or in jail — from Mr. Barclay.

The man, whose name is Dominic, sells fruit from a pushcart under the elevated tracks. The minister, in passing the spot every day, had come to know him, and in time suggested he join the church.

The old man, who speaks little English, said no, because he would have to come to classes for instruction, and it would embarrass him if he didn't understand.

Mr. Barclay, who speaks some Italian, said "All right, I will come here and instruct you at your pushcart."

So the daily instruction began, until one day Mr. Barclay found the man and his pushcart gone.

He asked at the police station, and the sergeant said, "Didn't you know, Reverend — Dominic stabbed a man yesterday."

The minister went to the jail to ask Dominic why he had done it.

"Because this man tried to make me buy his paper bags to put fruit in," said the old man. "And he put his hand in his pocket as if he had a gun, and I got scared and grabbed the lettuce knife and did it."

The minister convinced the judge to give Dominic a suspended sentence and release him in his custody. On Palm Sunday Dominic will become a member of the parish.

Although he respects Mr. Barclay's point of view, the minister of the most successfully integrated church in Chicago believes another approach is better.

The minister, the Rev. E. Jerry Walker, is a former advertising executive. He took up the pastorate of the St. James Church five years ago because he didn't feel that advertising gave him full satisfaction.

"Everything a church does," he said, "has to stem from the spiritual ministry of the church. If the church doesn't emphasize the spiritual, it is no different from any social agency. The church stands for something. Let the people adapt to it."

In the St. James area, near the University of Chicago on the South Side, people of all classes, white and Negro, have done that.

The minister, who is married and has three children, came to the church when it was still the white "cathedral" church of Chicago Methodism. But it had only 150 members, and the trend was gently down, as the area became increasingly Negro and the former upper-middle-class people who lived there fled to the suburbs.

He immediately arranged for a Y.M.C.A. outpost program for white and Negro children in the huge parish house. Within two months the first Negro adult applied for membership.

The word got out; the wife of a prominent member told the minister's wife that if he en-

gaged in any such foolishness as "mixing the races" most of the big-money pledges would be canceled, and the church would die on the spot.

Mr. Walker asked the Negro applicant to be patient and continue to come to services. In the meantime, the minister decided, he would begin putting the Christian gospel of brotherhood in force at the church, first through the children.

He would invite children from the neighborhood, then 80 per cent Negro, to come to Sunday school. The white Sunday school teachers, who had twenty-five children to teach in seventy-five rooms, voted down the idea.

Mr. Walker tacked with the wind: he brought the Negro children into a Sunday Afternoon Club, recruiting teachers from among their parents.

As the white commuters from the suburbs got used to seeing these teachers at services, the animosity died; in November, 1954, these teachers and the first applicant, who had stuck it out, were taken into membership.

The tide turned; St. James was not going to die. Mr. Walker has since added new white members, as well as Negroes, from various economic backgrounds.

The membership stands at 690. No longer is the church a white island in the midst of Negro homes. And no longer do neighborhood children throw bricks through its stained-glass windows, for now they feel it belongs.

Racial integration has succeeded at St. James, its minister believes, precisely because the church has not looked upon itself as a social institution.

The attitude at St. James is exceptional, and the majority of the people in Chicago will have nothing to do with it.

"I certainly am pleased with what you are doing," a white matron from an outlying area told the minister. "But I hope you keep it down there."

Methodist leaders in the city have no intention of keeping integration "down there." In some places, the policy leads to violent opposition from the white community.

No area is worse than that around the South Deering Methodist Church. There, in the Trumbull Park Homes, race rioting broke out five years ago, and race tensions have continued since.

The troubles began when Negroes were admitted to the Trumbull Homes, near a previously all-white community of small one-family homes that included the South Deering Methodist Church.

Shortly after that, the church building burned down. The denominational conference decided that to live up to the Christian ethic, the church, when it was rebuilt, had to integrate. It assigned a new young minister, the Rev. David K. Fison, who left a suburban resort community to take on the job.

Bombs Were Exploded

Mr. Fison began calling on Negroes in the housing development; white residents of the community began threatening

his life. During church services, now held in a park building, aerial bombs were exploded to disrupt the prayers and hymns.

And in 1957, when the first Negro family came into the congregation, crowds of white residents gathered outside to bait the members as they emerged and pelt the Negroes with rocks. The membership dropped to fourteen.

A Neighborhood Improvement Association was formed, with funds supplied by White Citizens Councils in the South. It set up a "rival" Protestant church with a former minister of South Deering Methodist, whose orders had been withdrawn.

It publishes a bi-monthly hate sheet in which it reviles Mr. Fison as "The Python." Through a real estate owner in the group, the association evicted him and his family from his home.

The Methodist conference bought him another house, which was stoned. Until a couple of months ago a police car stood twenty-four-hour guard outside the Fisons' door.

With the help of outside Methodist sources he has built a small, modern church — with a police tricycle parked in front of it day and night to protect the builders and building.

The Methodist approaches to problems in Pittsburgh and Detroit are civic and interdenominational.

In Pittsburgh the denomination draws heavily on the services of three laymen who are leaders in urban redevelopment. They are George Culbertson, director of the Mayor's Commission on Human Relations and chairman of the Pittsburgh Conference's Board of Missions; Robert Pease, director of the Urban Redevelopment Authority and head of the conference's urban committee, and Herbert Dunsmore, chief of the Allegheny County Bureau of Environmental Health and a member of the urban committee.

Their work in the much-heralded Pittsburgh redevelopment has brought a rebirth of planning within the church.

For instance, the urban committee pointed out to sixteen inner-city churches that most of them could no longer survive individually; some would have to merge, others would have to integrate.

Since Pittsburgh has a large and increasing Negro population, integration is extremely important, according to Dr. Ernest V. May, head of the conference Board of Missions.

In Detroit in the last fifteen years, fifty-four churches of all denominations have closed their doors or moved to the suburbs.

The Methodists are working with the Detroit Council of Churches to stem the exodus and minister to the Protestants — old residents and the new low-income groups — who are left.

The council tries to keep one denomination from competing with another — setting up no more than one new church for every 2,500 additional people in a given area.

EXTREMISTS TRY TO CURB CLERGY

Moves to Ban Social Issues Causing Protestant Rift

By JOHN WICKLEIN

Protestant leaders in the Midwest and in Texas believe a concerted effort is being made by extreme economic and religious conservatives to keep ministers and church councils from speaking out on social issues and force them to "stick to the Gospel."

The effort, they say, has intensified in the six weeks since an Air Force training manual drew attention to long-standing assertions by ultra-conservatives that Communists had infiltrated the major Protestant denominations and their federation, the National Council of Churches.

The council protested the manual, and the Defense Department withdrew it with apologies. The withdrawal incensed fundamentalists. They insisted in rallies that the charges were true, and demanded that the publication be reinstated.

This week-end the Rev. Dr. Roy G. Ross, general secretary, sent a letter to all members of Congress stating that the council and its thirty-three constituent bodies "are and always have been unalterably opposed to communism."

But the council "insists not only on the right, but also on the duty of the churches and of religious communions and their members to study and comment upon issues, whether political, economic or social, which affect human relations," he went on.

It is on this point that liberal and moderate ministers run into violent disagreement from fundamentalist clergy. The conservatives insist that the church "preach the Bible and teach Sunday school," and keep out of social and political debates.

"The basic issue in the present controversy is still the old fundamentalist-modernist argument," the Rev. Dr. Roe Johnston, minister of the First Presbyterian Church in Indianapolis, said in an interview last week.

"The fundamentalists have found a new club in these Communist charges, and it gets them more publicity than they ever had before, and so they are going to flail away."

Ministers such as Dr. Johnston, a former football star at Annapolis, are not afraid to speak strongly on social issues. But many others, according to

executives of local church councils, are afraid that if they do they will be attacked as Communist sympathizers or undercut financially.

Intimidation Seen

A Chicago denominational official saw the attacks as attempts at intimidation in the manner of the late Senator Joseph R. McCarthy, Republican of Wisconsin, with guilt by association as the chief weapon.

"If we lose the freedom of the pulpit," he said, "then we're gone."

He noted that the attackers had not been able to name any incumbent official of a major denomination or the National Council as a Communist.

That moderate and liberal clergymen have genuine fears for this freedom was indicated in interviews last week in four areas, where pressure from ultra-conservative clergy and laymen had been reported—Cincinnati, Indianapolis, Chicago and Houston.

The pressure, these men agreed, stems from two sources:

¶ Wealthy laymen in and out of mainline denominations who object to social, economic and political pronouncements by local ministers, denominational leaders and officers of the National Council.

¶ Theological conservatives who object to liberalism in matters of belief, which predominates within the major denominations affiliated with the council.

The efforts of the one group, according to local church council executives, reinforce the efforts of the other.

Those opposing the council have found guidance in the nightly broadcasts of Fulton Lewis Jr. For the last three weeks the commentator has devoted a third of his daily broadcasts on 310 stations across the country to attacks on the council and liberal clergy leaders.

Lewis Often Quoted

Midwestern ministers say Mr. Lewis is the source most frequently quoted to them when their parishioners ask questions such as, "What are you going to do about the Communists in our denomination?"

Mr. Lewis was asked whether he was making his attack on the council as a kind of crusade.

"Yes, I am," he replied. "I think that the National Council of Churches in many of its functions is a very fine organization. But it should not, however, be represented as the spokesman for 38,000,000 Protestants when it is not the spokesman."

This objection was also heard across the Midwest from supporters of the council. At the council's headquarters here, James G. Wine, associate general secretary, said the organization was aware of the criticism.

"Certainly we do not speak for 38,000,000 people," he said. "No one could. And you'll note that pronouncements adopted by our General Assembly always say the delegates 'urge' the churches to do thus and so, never that they have to do it."

Mr. Lewis said he wanted to stress "that the Air Force manual told the truth and should

never have been repudiated."

The council, he said, "should not speak out on political issues, and so far as they speak out on social issues, it should be from a religious standpoint."

Would Withhold Funds

He has suggested his listeners write to J. Howard Pew, former president of the Sun Oil Company and head of the United Presbyterian Foundation, for a report Mr. Pew wrote opposing the council's participation in "current secular affairs."

Mr. Pew, in a speech in Chicago a week ago, warned his denomination that men of wealth would continue to withhold contributions to the corporate church until it stopped making pronouncements on social issues, such as civil rights and collective bargaining. He has been supported by Gen. Robert E. Wood, former head of Sears, Roebuck & Co., and other affluent laymen.

In an interview Mr. Pew said:

"I would be just as much opposed to their making these pronouncements if they were enunciating my philosophy. These people do not have the knowledge and the competence in these areas. They should stick to ecclesiastical subjects."

The local minister, he said, has a responsibility in ethical and moral considerations that does not apply to the corporate church.

The Rev. Dr. Eugene Carson Blake, chief executive officer of the United Presbyterian Church disagreed with Mr. Pew.

"In all my ministry," he commented, "I have never been criticized for 'meddling' in political affairs by any church member who agreed with the views expressed.

"The stake that the Protestant churches have in this whole business is to keep themselves free to teach and preach the Gospel. Those who are pressing the church to keep out of economic and political areas, whether they know it or not, are attempting to make in this country a tame, kept church such as all totalitarian states attempt."

Support for slanderous accusations against liberal churchmen "normally comes from people who combine conservative theology with conservative economics and politics, specifically including we thy men of the far right," he declared.

He said he would not put it past the Communist party to try to push this kind of confusion in the Protestant churches.

Raises Red Connection

"If there are Communists in this thing," he said, "I am sure they are using these extreme anti-Communists as their unwitting tools to try to destroy the Protestant churches, which have always been implacable foes of the Communist party and ideology."

Dr. Blake and other major denominational officials listed these fundamentalists as chief sources of attacks on the more liberal clergy:

¶ Maj. Edgar C. Bundy of the Air Force Reserve, chairman of the Church League of America in Wheaton, Ill., a lecturer and pamphleteer. He led the group in the Illinois department of the

American Legion that condemned the Girl Scout handbook as "un-American."

¶ Myers G. Lowman of Cincinnati, executive secretary of Circuit Riders, Inc., organized in 1951 by thirty-three Methodist laymen to oppose "socialism and communism" in the Methodist Church.

¶ The Rev. Carl McIntire of Collingswood, N.J., funder of the American Council of Churches, a small schismatic group, and editor of The Christian Beacon, which is devoted to attacks on the National Council.

¶ Verne P. Kaub of Madison, Wis., organizer of the American Council of Christian Laymen and a pamphleteer, who supports Mr. McIntire.

¶ The Rev. Billy James Hargis of Tulsa, Okla., president of The Christian Crusade, lecturer and radio speaker. His pamphlet, "The National Council of Churches Indicts Itself on 50 Counts of Treason to God and Country," was cited as source material in the Air Force training manual.

Heavy Financial Backing

All these men have said they draw financial support from contributors to their organizations, or from lecture fees.

Church council executives say the major costs of their operations—the distribution of pamphlets and air time for radio program—are underwritten by two independent oil operators in Dallas and a Philadelphia industrialist. Attempts to reach these men and their business offices for confirmation have proved unavailing.

The five appear to have strong financial backing. Several weeks ago a small radio station in Illinois was offered $5,000 a week to broadcast Mr. McIntire's "Reformation Hour." The clergyman is heard on ninety stations across the country.

After 1936, when the Presbyterian Church in the U. S. A. withdrew his ordination, Mr. McIntire concentrated his attack on that church. Later he shifted to attacks on the Roman Catholic Church, and more recently to the National Council.

Material used over the years by the five anti-liberals was quoted freely in the Air Force manuel as proof that Communists were a guiding force in the council and major denominations.

Their chief sources of "documentation" are quotations from one another, information against clergymen in the "raw" files of the House Committee on Un-American Activities, unevaluated testimony (sometimes their own) before that committee, and writings by them inserted in the Congressional Record by ultra-conservative Senators and Representatives.

Omission in Charge

A charge circulated by these men and Mr. Lewis is that Bishop G. Bromley Oxnam spoke at a dinner of the Congress of American-Soviet Friendship.

Omitted from the charge is the fact that the time was Nov. 8, 1942, when the United States was officially allied with the Soviet Union, that those present included Owen D. Young, the late Cordell Hull, Lord Halifax, Edward Stettinius Jr. and Senator Kenneth McKellar, Democrat of Tennessee, and that sponsors of the congress included Senator Leverett Saltonstall, Republican of Massachusetts, and Christian A. Herter, now Secretary of State.

Charles P. Taft of Cincinnati, brother of the late Republican Senator Robert A. Taft and an Episcopal layman active in the National Council, called the charges "chiefly an anti-intellectual attack."

"They don't want to discuss the 'Communist conspiracy' on any intellectual basis," he said, "because they don't show at all that ministers preach Communist doctrines. They always merge proposals for social welfare with communism, with an anti-intellectual refusal to make a discrimination between them. In a sense, it is the same sort of anti-intellectual attack that Senator McCarthy made on proposals for social welfare."

Churchgoers in Houston, Tex., seemed by far the most disturbed over the charges of communism. A council official described it as a "disaster area" for old-line Protestantism.

This may be because the area mixes religion with conservative economic and social thought: A car parked outside a large fundamentalist church has a sticker that reads "Constitution Party—Repeal the Income Tax"; a lighted sign in front of an insurance company division office says, "Joy shall be in heaven over one sinner that repenteth."

Independent, emotional-appeal churches are springing up all over the city in attractive contemporary buildings containing church schools, nurseries and air-conditioning.

At one, the Berachah Church, Major Bundy last Sunday, drew 4,000 persons to four rallies against the National Council.

"Moderns and liberals hate the word fundamentalist, because it deals with the fundamental teachings of the Bible and because it means the fundamentals on which this country was founded," he told them.

Refers to Professor Here

Churchmen who do not agree with his definition of fundamentals, he implied, are soft on communism.

He said a retired professor at Union Theological Seminary in New York had been identified as a Communist. He charged that the professor had been active in the National Council, which was not true.

"The National Council of Churches is on the same block in New York City as Union Theological Seminary and Columbia University," Major Bundy observed, and added: "Birds of a feather, eh?" His audience laughed.

But officials of the Greater Houston Council of Churches think the situation is serious.

"There is a readiness of the people in this Bible Belt to accept these charges," the Rev. Virgil E. Lowder, executive director, said. "Most pastors are being pretty cautious about saying anything in rebuttal, for fear of reprisals."

The council decided it had to reply, and it did in a television talk by the Rev. John D. Craig, a Presbyterian minister and former president of the Houston Association of Ministers.

"Of course the Communists have tried to infiltrate the churches, just as they have tried to infiltrate the business and professional groups," Mr. Craig declared. "But they have not been successful in the churches, because it is too hard for them to pretend to be Christians."

Criticism of the church councils comes from persons within as well as outside old-line churches.

W. Hume Everett, Houston division attorney for the Ohio Oil Company, has written to all vestrymen of St. John the Divine Episcopal Church asking them to withhold contributions from the local, state and national councils so long as they speak out on social affairs.

"They don't speak for me," he said in an interview.

"They support, without exception, all socialistic laws. The primary purpose of the local, state and national councils is not to promote the love of Jesus Christ but more government control."

Mr. Everett said he knew and had worked with Major Bundy.

"Bundy advises people to leave their churches, but I want to work inside the church. I want to persuade the pastors to leave us poor, dumb laymen

to take care of politics, and take care of the spiritual guidance that will help us do this."

Widening Effects

The attack has had an effect in other cities.

In Wichita, Kan., the board of deacons of the largest American Baptist Church in the country voted to cut off the church's $33,000 contribution to the denomination in protest against its membership in the National Council.

While a reporter was in local church council offices in the Midwest, phone calls came in from ministers and laymen asking about the Communist charges and what would be done about them. Ministers reported their congregants confused and disturbed by the issue.

"This is the first time I've seen our clergy angry," the Rev. Laurence T. Hosie, executive secretary of the Greater Indianapolis Church Federation, said. "The whole American concept of the right to differ within your loyalty to the country is being challenged here."

The Indiana Area of the Methodist Church reported that Communist charges concerning the authors of the Revised Standard Version of the Bible had led members of the Central Avenue (Indianapolis) Methodist Church to ask the minister to stop using it. The members said they did not want any "Red-oriented scripture."

American Legionnaires in a Presbyterian church were reported to have asked that funds be withheld from the denomination until it dropped its affiliation with the National Council.

The Legion, which has its national headquarters in Indianapolis, has taken no official stand on the Air Force manual, but the charges have been discussed at meetings in local posts.

Neil E. Wetterman, Americanism chairman of the Legion's Hamilton County (Cincinnati) Council, said the manual "certainly is an important part of the education concerning Communist infiltration, and we will be using it in lectures before the Kiwanis, P. T. A. and church groups."

He said he had used pamphlets by Mr. Lowman for ref-

erence when his committee had been asked if a person was a "good individual to have as a speaker."

The Circuit Riders pamphlets, which Mr. Lowman says are devoted exclusively to listings of "subversive affiliations" of clergymen and laymen, are distributed widely in and outside the Methodist denomination.

Church leaders in Cincinnati, Mr. Lowman's home, say he has been able to keep the issue alive in the area.

In an interview Mr. Lowman said he was glad the manual issue had come up.

"I think this controversy is the best thing that ever happened for conservative religion in this country," he said. "It's brought it down to a matter of survival for the National Council of Churches."

He said his only concern was that church facilities not be used for subversion or socialistic purposes.

"My position is that the National Council of Churches and its program addresses itself in the main to the grievances and the animal appetites of man," he went on. "The program goes under the fancy title of 'social gospel.'

"We are for a minister speaking out on any issues except the promotion of socialism, communism or pro-Communist activities."

Last year Mr. Lowman was paid $4,500 by the Georgia Commission on Education as a "secret investigator" in its efforts, according to Gov. Marvin Griffen, "to keep our educational institutions free and segregated."

Mr. Lowman has attacked leaders of the Greater Cincinnati Council of Churches as subversive. In 1952 he applied for a job as public relations director of the council. He was refused.

The Rev. Raoul C. Calkins, district superintendent of the Cincinnati area of the Methodist Church, commented:

"The whole implication that within Protestantism there is a lack of loyalty to the United States and a tendency to be loyal to communism is just ridiculous and unfounded."

March 28, 1960

Churches in Rockland County Suburb Seek Relevance to Problems of Contemporary Life in Community

By PAUL L. MONTGOMERY

Special to The New York Times

SPRING VALLEY, N. Y., Jan. 31—The churches in this town of 7,000, like hundreds of others in the metropolitan area, are seeking to break the pattern that has so often made religion in the suburbs a subject for satire.

The community, which is 25 miles from New York City, has

emerged from the rural fringe into the suburbs in the last 10 years.

For the town this has meant confrontation on short notice with problems like civil rights and crowded schools—problems that seemed part of the remote and complicated life of the big city only a few years ago.

Stimulus to Activity

For the churches the change

has meant a growing involvement in the community and its problems and an attempt to avoid the much-criticized aloofness of the suburban churches from real contemporary issues.

Recently, for example, the congregation of the Reformed Church here discussed at its annual meeting the adoption of an open-housing covenant. It was the first time the Reformed

Main Street is the heart of Spring Valley, N. Y., a town of 7,000 persons 25 miles from Manhattan. It has 15 churches and 10 synagogues.

The Rev. David W. Jenks is pastor of Reformed Church.

churchgoers, acting as a congregation, had considered a civil rights matter. The covenant is expected to be adopted.

A charge often made against houses of worship in the suburbs is that it is difficult to distinguish them from country clubs.

Critics have said the suburban church is little more than an exclusive institution, turned in on itself and divorced from the traditional missionary concerns of Christianity in the world.

Many church executives feel that the entrance of the churches into the Negro campaign for equality and the increasing identification of the suburb with the concerns of its metropolitan area can serve to revitalize the suburban church.

The churches of Spring Valley, in their attempt to escape the image of religion in the suburbs, are finding this to be true. A word frequently heard in conversations with ministers here, as in the church at large, is relevance.

There are really two Spring Valleys. One is the town itself, a pocket of narrow streets and wooden buildings settled in a hollow of the Ramapo Hills. The other is the outlying blanket of modern homes—ranging in price from $17,000 to $35,000— that covers the apple orchards and cow pastures and woodlands of the recent past.

A problem familiar to central city areas—urban blight—is incipient in the village. Shopping centers in the modern fringes have reduced the importance of the antiquated town.

The churches, which are in the town but draw most of their congregations from the outskirts, have had to take an interest in planning and urban renewal to preserve their place in the community.

There are 11 Protestant, two Roman Catholic and two Eastern Orthodox churches in the town. Of the 15, however, the only additions since the community's growth began have been the African Methodist Episcopal Zion Church, a Negro denomination, and the Assemblies of God, a Pentecostal group.

The number of synagogues has increased from three to 10 over the same period. A recent survey of one new housing development showed 28 Jewish families, one Roman Catholic family and one Protestant family moving into it.

The Rev. David W. Jenks, the soft-spoken, 50-year-old pastor of the Reformed Church, is one of the clergymen who is attempting to make his church relevant to the town and its problems.

His church, a traditional brick structure, is on Church Street, a block away from the village's main thoroughfare. It will be a century old next year. Recently a $125,000 renovation providing a refurbished sanctuary and new meeting and Sunday school rooms was completed.

Much of Mr. Jenks's drive for relevance in his 350-member congregation is directed toward civil rights, a problem that is increasingly acute in the town.

Ten years ago there was only a handful of Negroes in Spring Valley. Now the northern part of the village is predominantly Negro, largely as a result of an urban renewal project in Nyack, six miles away. That project removed many lower-class houses and forced Negroes to look elsewhere for homes.

There is rarely a Sunday when Mr. Jenks does not refer outspokenly to racial issues in his sermon. "If our church is going to discriminate, then it cannot be the church of Jesus Christ," he said in a recent sermon.

It was primarily because of his prodding that the open-housing covenant got through the consistory and came up before the annual meeting. Last summer he and his wife participated in the March on Washington. He has encouraged church members to write to their Congressman about the Civil Rights Bill.

Mr. Jenks says there have been some "strained relations" with the congregation because of his stand but no outright defections. He adds that "a fair portion" of the membership feels strongly on the side of integration.

On a recent Sunday there were 100 persons at the morning worship service, including three Negroes.

Mr. Jenks acknowledged that the percentage of Negroes in his congregation is far less than the proportion of Negroes in the town's Protestant population. "We have not kept pace with the Negro growth," he says, "but we are trying."

February 1, 1964

CHURCH COUNCIL ASKS U.S. TO HALT VIETNAM BOMBING

By GEORGE DUGAN
Special to The New York Times

MADISON, Wis., Dec. 3—The National Council of Churches proposed today that the United States halt the bombing of North Vietnam long enough to create more favorable circumstances for peace negotiations.

It suggested that efforts also be made to "induce" the North Vietnam Government to stop sending military personnel and materiel into South Vietnam.

In a message to churches that accompanied a policy statement, the council asserted that unilateral action by the United States in Southeast Asia would not lead to peace and urged joint efforts by the United Nations and its "concerned" members.

The Council's action was approved by its policy-making general board and thus became a formal pronouncement of the organization, the first to be made on the Vietnam war by a major United States religious body.

Vote Is 93 to 10

The vote was 93 in favor of the policy statement and 10 opposed, with 6 abstentions.

The national council is a federation of most of the larger Protestant and Eastern Orthodox churches in the country, with a combined membership of about 40 million persons. The statement will serve as a guide to its 30 member denominations in considering the moral implications of the Vietnam conflict.

"We believe that a solution of the problem in Vietnam can be essentially advanced only when action is moved from the battlefield to the conference table," the policy statement declared. "We pray that this may be speedily accomplished."

The message to the churches voiced confidence in the willingness of the Administration to negotiate unconditionally for peace in Vietnam.

It also commended the Government for its "restrained policy even though great pressure has had to be resisted against the escalation into an all-out war."

"We believe," the message declared, "that if the United States follows a unilateral policy in Vietnam, no conceivable victory there can compensate for the distrust and hatred of the United States that is being generated each day throughout much of the world because we are seen as a predominantly white nation using our overwhelming military strength to kill more and more Asians."

The policy statement directed these additional recommendations to the Administration:

¶That it insist on strict adherence to the policy of avoiding the bombing of centers of population in North Vietnam.

¶That it request the United Nations to begin negotiations wherever and whenever possible for a cease-fire agreement under United Nations supervision.

¶That it urge the United Nations to convene "as soon as possible" a peace conference on Vietnam.

¶That it favor the "phased withdrawal" of all United States troops and bases from Vietnam territory "if and when they can be replaced by adequate international peace-keeping forces."

¶That it make available immediate reconstruction assistance and long-range economic development programs for Southeast Asia.

The policy statement also suggested that the national council increase "high-level" dialogue between Asian and United States Christians and place in the "crisis area" a representative to serve as a "Christian presence" authorized to interpret Asian points of view to United States churches.

The special message, written and introduced to the board by the Rev. Dr. Eugene Carson Blake, chief administrative officer of the United Presbyterian Church, directed council officials to take the initiative in seeking through the World Council of Churches, in cooperation with the Roman Catholic Church, a "mobilization" of the worldwide Christian community in developing and supporting a "just alternative" to war.

Later, Dr. Arthur S. Flemming, a vice president at large of the national council who is president of the University of Oregon, told the board that "what we have done here will be used as a basis for dialogues throughout the country."

He described the action as a "genuine contribution toward the working out of a solution to a serious matter."

December 4, 1965

Churches Flex Their Economic Muscle

By EDWARD B. FISKE

When most clergymen quote the Biblical saying "where your treasure is, there will your heart be also," the odds are overwhelming that an appeal for money is not far away.

In the last two years, however, this favored text of fund raisers has been applied to a new area: social action.

An increasing number of churchmen have begun to argue that if the churches are genuinely committed to racial justice and other social ideals, they will make sure that their treasures will not be used to perpetuate social injustice — even at the cost of an occasional bargain.

The result is a new ethical dilemma: how far should religious groups go in using their vast economic power to pursue ethical goals?

The issue has been raised most recently by a group of Protestant churches that announced its intention to withhold proxies on more than 30,000 shares of Eastman Kodak Company stock in order to question the company's repudiation of a job training program for Negroes in Rochester.

The churches participating are the Protestant Episcopal Church, the United Church of Christ, the United Presbyterian Church in the U.S.A., and the Methodist Church. They took the action in support of a militant civil rights organization known as FIGHT (Freedom, Integration, God, Honor — Today).

'Unauthorized' Agreement

After extensive negotiations FIGHT and a Kodak assistant vice president signed an agreement last December that provided for the training and employment of 600 Rochester Negroes. Two days later, however, the company said that the agreement was "unauthorized" and therefore not binding. It explained that it could not "discriminate" by having an exclusive recruiting program with only one organization.

The churches have made plans to attend the annual shareholders' meeting in Flemington, N.J., on April 25 to challenge the company's actions.

Officials admit that the action will be largely symbolic, for the total number of outstanding Kodak shares is more than 80 million. Still, they are hopeful that using their holdings to call attention to the issue could force Kodak to reconsider its position.

Some of the same churches have been involved in a similar protest against renewal of a $40-million loan to the Government of South Africa by a consortium of American banks.

By far the most sophisticated example of economic protest by religious groups is Project Equality, which was launched two years ago by the National Catholic Conference for Inter-Racial Justice, but now draws more than three-quarters of its support from Protestant, Jewish and Orthodox groups.

The assumption of Project Equality is that religious groups can use their spending power to demand not only fair prices and high quality merchandise, but fair employment practices on the part of the suppliers as well.

After first surveying their own employment practices to insure that they are not discriminating against minority groups, the participating religious bodies, such as local diocese and presbyteries, ask firms with whom they have business dealings to affirm their willingness to maintain equal employment opportunities.

These suppliers are then asked to submit annual reports with statistical data on their employment practices. Cooperating firms are listed in a booklet that is distributed on a confidential basis to purchasing agents of religious institutions.

Policy Revised

The project directors have dis-

262

covered that the withholding of business from firms that discriminate in employment can have rapid effect. A Connecticut bank, for instance, was quick to revise its policies when faced with the withdrawal of deposits from a Catholic lay organization.

Project Equality is now operating in 10 areas, including St. Louis, Detroit and Connecticut. Officials estimate the buying power of the participating religious groups at $2-billion.

So far the project has been directed primarily at the groups themselves and firms that supply goods or services. The archdiocese of Detroit, for instance, awarded a contract for contribution envelopes to the second lowest bidder re

cently when the lowest one refused to cooperate. Subsequent stages call for concentration on firms engaged in church construction, insurance, banking and real estate.

Mathew H. Ahmann, executive director of the conference, said that the project is not a boycott. "It is educational rather than punitive in purpose," he stated recently. "We're not telling anyone how to run their business; we're only saying what our policies are as consumers."

Some churchmen regard the use of church resources as a weapon for social gains as dangerous.

The Rev. John L. Reedy, editor of the Ave Maria Press in South Bend, Ind., for instance, fears that the use of temporal instruments

to achieve spiritual goals can easily lead to abuses.

"Churches aren't at home with this sort of method and can easily foul up their own purposes," he said. "The power that is used to promote equal employment today might easily be used to enforce censorship tomorrow."

He then added, "What does the liberal who backs Project Equality say to someone else who thinks that Catholic hospitals should boycott pharmaceutical firms that manufacture birth control pills?"

"We must," he said, "find some way of responsibly confronting the fact that when churches don't recognize their economic power, they simply re-enforce the status quo."

April 16, 1967

Presbyterians Approve Creed for Social Action

By LAWRENCE E. DAVIES
Special to The New York Times

PORTLAND, Ore., May 22—The 179th general assembly of the 3.3 million-member United Presbyterian Church in the U.S.A. approved today the first major doctrinal changes since American Presbyterianism was established in 1706.

The more than 800 commissioners adopted "The Confession of 1967" by a standing vote following a last-ditch floor fight.

The confession makes social action officially a part of basic church doctrine. It also rejects any thought that the Bible is "inerrant" and thus immune from criticism in the light of new knowledge.

"The Confession of 1967," adopted without change in wording, becomes a part of the Book of Confessions, in which it joins the Westminster Confession of Faith, dating to 1647, and seven other creedal statements including the Shorter Catechism. It eliminates the Larger Catechism, which had been a part of the church's constitution.

Obligation Assumed

It places upon members of the United Presbyterians an obligation to work for racial integration, peace and the elimination of poverty.

Later, after prolonged debate, the General Assembly adopted a "declaration of conscience" toward the war in Vietnam. It urged that the Government again consider "cessation of bombing as one tangible evidence of our desire to negotiate."

The issue of the Confession of 1967, the most eagerly awaited one to come before the General Assembly, was introduced by Richard D. Shewmaker of St.

Louis, chairman of the committee on bills and overtures, in a majority report favored by 19 of the 23 committee members.

A minority report of three members (one committeeman abstained) was offered by the Rev. Raymond N. Ohman of Philadelphia. This report restated the argument that the General Assembly would be acting unconstitutionally in approving the doctrinal changes.

According to this argument, the church constitution permitted the amending or altering of the three former doctrinal symbols — the Confession of Faith and the Larger and Shorter Catechisms — but made no provision for "total deletion" of any of them.

Mr. Shewmaker took the position that the General Assembly was "the highest court of the church — the highest legislative body — and the decision is ours." Moreover, he added, dictionaries give as definitions of the word "amend" to "delete as well as add to."

Mr. Shewmaker told the commissioners that while a committee that held hearings on the confession had received more than 1,100 communications, there was possibly only one that raised the question of legality. He asked what the significance of that was.

The way had been previously prepared for General Assembly action when 165 of the 184 presbyteries voted for the constitutional and creedal changes.

The 4,500-word confession has been in preparation since the Presbyterian Church in the U.S.A. and the United Presbyterian Church of North America merged in 1958.

After adopting the new confession the General Assembly defeated the first attempt to start amending it. The commissioners by a standing vote decreed "no action" on an overture from the Washington City (D. C.) Presbytery that would have stricken from the confes-

sion a phrase in connection with the quest for peace.

The confession called for the pursuit of fresh and responsible relations across every line of conflict, "even at risk to national security," to reduce areas of strife and broaden international understanding.

Mr. Shewmaker told the General Assembly that the press and government officials had sometimes given "careless reading" to the words "even at risk to national security." The phrase, he said, had "nothing to do with individuals" but applied to the nation.

"It means," he said, "it is the duty of the nation, acting under God, to risk its national security at times in laying aside selfishness" and seeking peace and justice.

It was disclosed last week that a Pentagon official had circulated a memorandum among military agencies and defense industries denying that adoption of the confession would jeopardize the security clearance of church members.

One passage in the confession objected to by fundamentalists who hold the Bible to be "inerrant" is the following:

"The Scriptures, given under the guidance of the Holy Spirit, are nevertheless the words of men, conditioned by the language, thought forms, and literary fashions of the places and times at which they were written. They reflect views of life, history and the cosmos which were then current.

"The church, therefore, has an obligation to approach the Scriptures with literary and historical understanding. As God has spoken His word in diverse cultural situations, the church is confident that He will continue to speak through the Scriptures in a changing world and in every form of human culture."

The Rev. Dr. Eugene Smathers, the new United Presbyterian moderator, presided during the hour and a half of discussion that preceded the vote.

After the approval of the

confession by a vote of about 4 to 1, the commissioners stood in the arena of Memorial Coliseum and sang the 17th-century hymm "Now Thank We All Our God."

Then the General Assembly adopted a motion by the Rev. Dr. Arthur C. Cochrane of Dubuque, Iowa, that the body "humbly commend this our Confession of 1967 to other Christian churches — Roman Catholic, Orthodox and Protestant—for their prayerful consideration and study, that, if need be, this our confession may be corrected out of God's mouth, the Holy Scriptures; and that this our confession of reconciliation in Christ, or some such confession, may be the confession of the one, holy, catholic church of Jesus Christ in this land."

The confession has drawn heavy criticism from fundamentalist groups.

Declaration on Vietnam

In its declaration on Vietnam, the assembly said that in light of the "increasing cost and peril of our present course of escalation," the nation had an obligation as the stronger power "to act first, taking initiatives that will create a climate of trust leading finally to the negotiating table."

Besides a possible halt to the bombing, it further sought exploration of "other alternatives, such as a purely defensive war behind a fortified demilitarized zone in South Vietnam, with the subsequent pacification of the South Vietnamese countryside."

"Just as our present policy of escalation involves risks," the declaration continued, "so also does a policy of de-escalation. We believe it is a risk we must take for the sake of the future of mankind."

The assembly also spoke out for continued affirmation of the "morality of dissent," saying that "increasing numbers of citizens, including some in high office, are equating dissent with disloyalty."

May 23, 1967

263

YOUTHS CRITICIZE SYNAGOGUE'S ROLE

Failure to Deal With Social Issues Laid to Institutions

By IRVING SPIEGEL

A group of Jewish college students has attributedd the alienation of the current generation from Jewish cultural and spiritual life to the failure of the synagogue to deal with such social issues as poverty, civil rights and peace.

The answers came during an informal interrogation of the students last week at the annual convention of Conservative Judaism's college group known as Atid (the Hebrew word for "future") at the Statler Hilton Hotel.

The meeting was held with the session of the United Synagogue Youth, whose members are teen-agers affiliated with Conservative synagogues. Participating were 2,000 youths from various parts of the country and Canada.

Those who were questioned described themselves, despite their criticism of the synagogue as an "in" rather than an "out" group in terms of their commitment to Jewish religious life.

They are affiliated with Conservative congregations, but they were outspoken in their criticism.

Failure to Lead

For instance, Martin Lasker, a student at the University of California, Los Angeles, said the synagogue "may talk social action, and in some cases act social action, but only after someone else does something about it."

As an example, he referred to a rabbi who was asked by college students whether the spiritual leader should counsel college youngsters on the draft.

"Regardless of our views," Mr. Lasker said, "he was more concerned with what the congregation or the community would say were he engaged in such work."

Miss Judy Lechner, a student at Trenton State College in New Jersey, charged that the synagogue "had abdicated the central role it can play in the area of the poverty program," saying that the houses of worship "have not actually participated in the community grass roots areas, like the Quakers who work in the slums."

Other students noted that Jews who wanted to participate in programs of social action involved themselves with other community agencies that dealt specifically with such programs. Miss Marsha Greenfield, a student at Barnard said:

"You go to the synagogue for a dance or to pray, but you never consider going there to carry out social action activities."

Question Dollar Values

Still other students held that their alienation from Jewish life stemmed from too much emphasis placed on dollar values by Jewish institutions.

Criticism was voiced against congregational lay leaders for spending large sums on the construction of lavish buildings. One student said such buildings were "seldom used except during the Jewish High Holy Days when a smaller building could have been constructed and the remaining money sent to aid Negroes in the South or Harlem or other worthy programs."

Many agreed with Miss Sanday Braun, a Barnard College student, on what they described as the gap existing between Jewish parents and their children.

"Our parents," Miss Braun said, "live an assimilated rather than a Jewish life while expecting us to acquire a substantive Jewish education by merely sending us to religious and Hebrew school. They want their children somehow to acquire an understanding and love for Judaism by themselves and to live a Jewish life without a contribution on their part."

January 2, 1968

Hillel Leader Finds Confusion Over Role of Jews in New Left

By IRVING SPIEGEL
Special to The New York Times

GROSSINGER, N. Y., Dec. 18 —The executive head of a Jewish campus movement at 270 colleges cautioned the Jewish community today against "confused judgments" over the character and number of Jewish college youths in the New Left.

Rabbi Benjamin M. Kahn, national director for B'nai B'rith Hillel Foundations, said that many Jewish leaders had shown an "excessive preoccupation" with the issue. "This has been compounded by their inadequate understanding of the attitudes and convictions" of Jewish youths who are attracted to radical student movements, he asserted.

While Rabbi Kahn did not identify what he called "the confused critics" of the Jewish

campus community, in recent months a number of national Jewish groups have publicly expressed concern about Jewish participation in campus rebellions.

Rabbi Kahn discussed the subject at the annual conference of Hillel Foundations directors.

He cited studies by his organization indicating that Jewish students in the New Left, while highly visible in its leadership and constituting perhaps one-third of its ranks, generally made up "not much more than 5 per cent" of Jewish student enrollments.

The estimated Jewish enrollment at American colleges this semester is 350,000.

December 19, 1968

Social Action for the Parish

A quiet revolution is underway in certain parish churches.

In Boston, 28 Protestant and Roman Catholic churches and synagogues have banded together, hired an executive director and launched an extensive ghetto housing program.

Eight churches on the South Side of Chicago — two Roman Catholic and six Protestant — have joined forces to form Christian Action Mission: a cluster of churches that operates an employment center and provides legal aid services, tutoring and other assistance to ghetto residents.

In New York the Episcopal diocese is working on a reorganization plan whereby churches would function not only by themselves but as members of cooperative "inter-parish" councils with 10 or 12 others.

These and similar developments are evidence of a major structural revolution now under way among Protestant churches throughout the country. In many cases they lead to alliances with Catholic churches and synagogues.

The revolution results from an increasing belief that the place where most people have their only contact with religion—the local parish church—has become out of date in its present form. It aims not at eliminating the local church entirely, but at supplementing it through the formation of such clusters of churches as those described above.

The new development fundamentally grows out of the increasing concern among religious leaders in recent years to involve churches in social problems, including such complex social change as community organization projects, in which ghetto residents are organized to be aware of and to defend their interests.

Many church leaders have discovered, however, that the local parish has severe drawbacks as an instrument for social change, including the fundamental drawback of isolation.

For one thing, those individuals interested in working through churches on issues such as housing or poverty are likely to be spread out among various churches, and most social problems today are simply too complex for even the most dedicated handful of individuals in a single church to handle.

"An isolated structure like the local parish is simply unsuited for confronting social evils that require allied action," said Charles V. Willie, an active Episcopalian layman and chairman of the Department of Sociology at Syracuse University.

To overcome these liabilities, an estimated 100 clusters of churches have now been formed throughout the country. Typical, for instance, is the situation in Portland, Ore. There 82 members of the Greater Portland Council of Churches have formed five clusters, and William B. Cate, executive director of the council, said last week that plans are being made to "blanket the area" with such alliances.

Mr. Cate said that the primary benefit of the clusters has been to permit churches to cooperate on such issues not only across denominational lines, but with secular agencies such as the Urban Coalition.

"The old style of getting away from the world to be with God all by yourself just doesn't appeal to the young person today," said Mr. Cate.
—EDWARD B. FISKE

October 13, 1968

Church Unit Sells Shares Of Dow Chemical Stock

WORCESTER, Mass., June 10 (AP)—Acting in opposition to the use of napalm in the Vietnam war, the Massachusetts Conference of the United Church of Christ today divested itself of Dow Chemical Company stock.

Dow makes napalm, a jelly-like incendiary substance.

The conference said it lost $15,000 in the transaction, having bought the stock for $131,475 and receiving approximately $116,000 in the sale. A spokesman said the money was reinvested in 2,000 shares of International Telephone and Telegraph stock.

The stock sale was authorized by the executive committee of the Congressional Fund, an investment fund of the conference.

June 11, 1969

QUAKERS ASSAIL NIXON WAR STAN

Philadelphia Friends Rejec References to Heritage

By DONALD JANSON
Special to The New York Times

PHILADELPHIA, April 7 — The Philadelphia Yearly Meeting of the Religious Society of Friends, long the country's leading Quaker organization, rebuked President Nixon today for coupling references to his Quaker heritage with a defense of his Administration's war policy in southeast Asia.

Charles K. Brown 3d, clerk of the 291-year-old Philadelphia Yearly Meeting, released a copy of a letter sent to the President at the conclusion of the meeting's annual session on Saturday.

It noted that, in an interview with C. L. Sulzberger of The New York Times on March 9, Mr. Nixon had labeled himself a "deeply committed pacifist" because of his Quakerism and had simultaneously defended his commitment to a strong military posture abroad.

"This is not our understanding of the Quaker peace testimony," the letter said. "In 1660 Friends wrote to King Charles of England: 'We utterly deny all outward wars and strife and fighting with outward weapons, for any end, or under any pretense whatsoever; this is our testimony to the whole world."

The letter pointed out that the current faith and practice of the Philadelphia Yearly Meeting and many other Quakers throughout the world states. "If we are true to our faith, we can have no part in war."

"No official body of the Religious Society of Friends has ever repudiated this position," the letter stated.

The letter said that Quakers here realized that their pacifism was a minority view in the United States that the official leader of the armed forces would have difficulty following, but urged the President to make no "further distortion" of the Friends' "historic and deeply felt conviction."

Quakerism consists of autonomous regional annual gatherings called yearly meetings. The largest in the United States is the Philadelphia Yearly Meeting, started by William Penn in 1681. It takes in parts of Pennsylvania, New Jersey, Delaware and Maryland and has a membership of 16,300.

Practices Weakened

In one of three references to his Quakerism and pacifism

265

in the interview, Mr. Nixon had told Mr. Sulzberger: "I rate myself as a deeply committed pacifist, perhaps because of my Quaker heritage from my mother."

Religious leaders have called Mr. Nixon a "birthright Quaker" rather than a practicing Quaker.

He is a member of the East Whittier Meeting, near Los Angeles, where he attended Sunday school. California Quakerism bears more resemblence to orthodox American Protestantism than to the pacifistic Quakerism of the Philadelphia area and England, where it was founded by George Fox in the mid-17th century.

When Quakers moved west from the East Coast in the 19th century, they often set up churches open to all Protestants in a new town. The exposure to other religious strains weakened traditional Quaker practices, and the forceful clerical leadership of most Protestant denominations became the mode in western Quakerism.

Mr. Nixon has never become a worshiper at the Washington Friends Meeting in the capital as was Herbert Hoover, the only other Quaker President. Mr. Nixon has attended Congregational, Methodist, Presbyterian and interdenominational services in his adult years.

The traditionally pacifistic Friends are now in a minority even within the society. Some 80 per cent of the 120,000 Quakers in the United States today, particularly in the West, are not pacifistic. The California Yearly Meeting has stopped contributing to the Philadelphia-based American Friends Service Committee, the pacifistic service organization that won the Nobel Peace Prize in 1947 and has been a leading force in antiwar activities.

Nonpacifist "fighting Quakers" contend that they, too, uphold the traditional Quaker peace testimony but prefer an "active" search for peace rather than doctrinaire opposition to war in any form. Many agree with Mr. Nixon that military strength is necessary to the preservation of peace.

The President traces his Quaker ancestry to 1690, when ancestors left County Kildare in Ireland for religious freedom in Pennsylvania. The family gradually moved West. Quakers founded Whittier in 1887. Mr. Nixon's mother, Hannah, a traditionally pacifistic Quaker, arrived there a decade later. His father, a Methodist, turned Quaker following marriage.

April 8, 1971

Report Says 10 Churches' Investments Abet 'Immoral Acts' of Arms Industry

By DOUGLAS ROBINSON

A unit of the National Council of Churches has accused 10 Protestant denominations of complicity through their stockholdings in the "irresponsible, immoral and socially injurious acts" of 29 corporations holding military contracts.

Among the churches with military stockholdings, according to a report on religious investment practices, are those that have been in the forefront of the criticism of the Vietnam war and of the growing militarism in the United States.

The report, prepared by the Corporate Information Center of the National Council, is to be made public Friday. It shows that the 10 denominations, plus the National Council itself, have almost $203-million invested in companies that last year provided more than $10-billion worth of war matériel ranging from guns to missiles.

Religious involvement in the military field, the report says, gives a "moral aura of legitimacy" to such investments and is a "factor of far greater significance than the actual dollar amounts invested."

Frank P. White, director of the Corporate Information Center, said under questioning that the report did not imply that churches were being "hypocritical" in their investment policies.

"Generally, the reason that investment ethics has not kept pace with policy is quite simple —no one has thought much about it," he said.

"Aside from the newness of the issue, there are some process questions involved," he said. "Most investment committee men historically have been and still are top corporate and financial executives."

"To ask these people to begin to prescribe moral sanctions against peers and competitors or for that matter their own companies is troublesome to say the least," he said.

Questioning Urged

The 50-page report, entitled "Church Investments, Technological Warfare and the Military - Industrial Complex," urges clergymen and laymen to "ask how the moral and economic wealth of the churches and other institutions is used" and then to "assume a leadership role by providing an example of corporate social responsibility."

To date, the report says, "ethical and moral concerns have not been expressed through the investment policies and responsibilities of the church."

Mr. White said the report did not recommend that churches sell their defense stocks, although he conceded that action "might be the end result."

"Selling stock obviously negates your right as a stockholder to speak to management about policies with which you disagree," he said. "Many churches can petition and interview management, and there are proxy proposals that can be submitted after further study."

"Our report only recommends that the churches begin to look seriously at their military holdings," he maintained. "They must decide for themselves what to do about the situation."

The churches examined in the report are the United Methodist Church, the Christian Church (Disciples), the United Presbyterian Church, the American Baptist Convention, the Lutheran Church in America, the Protestant Episcopal Church, the United Church of Christ, the Church of the Brethren, the Presbyterian Church in the United States and the Unitarian Universalist Association. Among the 29 corporations named were the American Telephone and Telegraph Company, Standard Oil Company (New Jersey), the Ford Motor Company, the United Aircraft Corporation, Litton Industries, Inc., the General Electric Company and the International Business Machines Corporation.

$1.5-Billion Invested

Others were the Lockheed Aircraft Corporation, the Westinghouse Electric Corporation, Honeywell Inc., the General Motors Corporation, TRW Inc., the RCA Corporation and Texas Instruments Incorporated.

Mr. White said that the 10 churches, on a national denominational basis, had investment portfolios totaling $1.5-billion.

He estimated that the nation's three major religions, Protestant, Roman Catholic and Jewish, had about $22-billion invested in the stock market on a national, regional and local basis. The figure also includes religious agencies.

The report says that, in addition to the churches and agencies that have taken antiwar stands, others have come out against "national priorities that divert vital resources into implements of war and away from tools of peace."

The churches, the report continues, have ignored ethical and moral concerns and, "instead, like other investors, have placed themselves in a position of complicity with the irresponsible, immoral and socially injurious acts of the corporations represented here."

"Instead, the churches are providing an important amount of economic support for the military-industrial complex and the war in Southeast Asia. Instead, they are assisting in the manufacture and use of weapons of mass human and environmental destruction," the report says.

Unlike other investors, the report says the church "with its tradition and unique role as a moral leader in society, has a special obligation to question that complicity."

The study dealt with the top 60 military contractors, which

Military Stocks Held by Churches

Following is a table showing the value of stockholdings of 10 major Protestant denominations and the National Council of Churches in 29 companies that are among the prime 60 defense contractors, according to a unit of the council:

Church	No. of cos. Invested	Mkt. Value (1970)	% of Total Portfolio
United Methodist Church	23	$59,751,899	14.1
Christian Church (Disciples)	21	8,690,821	41.4
United Presbyterian Church	18	57,871,157	12.8
American Baptist Conv.	14	30,556,371	10.5
Lutheran Church in America	11	7,741,698	8.8
Protestant Episcopal Church	10	29,891,430	10.9
United Church of Christ	10	2,903,267	5.4
Church of the Brethren	9	801,199	N/A
Presbyterian Church in the United States	7	1,450,521	N/A
Unitarian Universalist Asso.	6	2,812,979	11.5
National Council of Churches	5	332,831	11.7

account for about 65 per cent of all such contracts. The churches had investments in 29 of these corporations.

The report shows that in 1970, a bad earnings year, income from these investments was more than $6.2-million and the total number of shares amounted to almost two million.

According to the report, the leading religious investor in military hardware was the United Methodist Church with market value investments totaling $59,751,899. The second highest was the United Presbyterian Church with $57,871,157.

Major Investors

Other major investors included the American Baptist Convention with $30,556,371; the Protestant Episcopal Church, $29,891,430, and the Christian Church (Disciples), $8,690,821.

The National Council of Churches, which, along with several of the denominations mentioned in the report, finances the work of the Corpo-

rate Information Center, has a military investment of $332,-831, according to the report.

The report says that many of the corporations mentioned in the study also produce a variety of consumer goods and services, but that "in volume of business or dollar amounts they are undeniably major corporations in the military field."

In an interview, Mr. White said the report on corporate investment by churches in the military field was the first in a series of similar studies on other investment areas that include pollution, foreign investments and minority hiring policies.

The center was established 10 months ago as an outgrowth of a small staff studying church investments. It is part of the Office of Resource Studies of the Division of Christian Life and Mission of the National Council of Churches. The defense contract report is not a policy paper of the National Council, but a study publication of the center.

The 29 corporations named in the report, their total defense business for 1970 and the percentage of their total sales constituted by defense contracts are as follows:

The American Telephone and Telegraph Company, $931,233,000, 5.5 per cent.
Standard Oil Company (New Jersey), $229,188,000, 1.4 per cent.
The Ford Motor Company, $345,877,000, 2.3 per cent.
The United Aircraft Corporation, $873,793,000, 37.5 per cent.
Litton Industries, Inc., $543,053,-000, 22.5 per cent.
The General Electric Company, $1,000,452,000, 11.5 per cent.
The International Business Machines Corporation, $256,052,-000, 3.4 per cent.
The Lockheed Aircraft Corporation, $1,847,738,000, 72.9 per cent.
The Westinghouse Electric Corporation, $417,655,000, 9.7 per cent.
Honeywell Inc., $397,928,000, 20.7 per cent.
TRW Inc., $179,067,000, 11.3 per cent.
RCA Corporation, $262,805,000, 8.1 per cent.
Texas Instruments Incorporated, $190,540,000, 23 per cent.
The International Telephone and

Telegraph Corporation, $217,-325,000, 3.4 per cent.
The General Motors Corporation, $385,738,000, 2.1 per cent.
Uniroyal, Inc., $115,253,000, 7.4 per cent.
E. I. du Pont de Nemours and Company, $161,671,000, 4.4 per cent.
Mobil Oil Corporation, $165,596,-000, 2.2 per cent.
FMC Corporation, $140,911,000, 10.6 per cent.
General Telephone and Electronics Corporation, $107,715,000, 3.1 per cent.
The Magnavox Company, $95,225,-000, 19.3 per cent.
Goodyear Tire and Rubber Company, $103,522,000, 3.2 per cent.
The Chrysler Corporation, $92,-033,000, 1.3 per cent.
The City Investing Company, $92,-469,000, 18.3 per cent.
Texaco Inc., $85,583,000, 1.3 per cent.
The Olin Corporation, $247,654,-000, 22 per cent.
The Sperry Rand Corporation, $398,888,000, 22.7 per cent.
Tenneco Inc., $248,944,000, 9.8 per cent.
The Standard Oil Company of California, $140,347,000, 3.4 per cent.

January 5, 1972

THE MINISTRY AS A PROFESSION

SAYS MINISTRY HAS RETROGRADED

Annual Report of Carnegie Foundation Says Low Educational Standards Are Evident.

PARTLY DUE TO MANY SECTS

Report Praises Training Demanded of Catholic Priests, Who Succeed, It Says, Where Protestants Fail.

Some caustic comments on the standard of training of the average minister of the day are made in the last annual report of the Carnegie Foundation for the Advancement of Teaching. It is stated that the demoralization due to low educational standards is more evident among the clergy than in the professions of law and medicine, and that much of the delay in religious progress is due to the fact that "men who assume, as representatives of the Christian denominations, to take the place of religious leaders, are unprepared for such leadership, are untrained in the fundamentals of theology, in the elements of learning, in knowledge of mankind, in the interpretations of life from the religious rather than from the denominational standpoint."

The report declares that "the profession of the preacher has not kept pace with the enormous advance in popular education. A hundred years ago ministers were the educated men of their communities, and their power was in proportion. In the interval the congregations have risen enormously in the scale of general education. With this rise the law and medicine have kept pace to a considerable extent. The

ministry has relatively retrograded. The standards of admission to it have not kept pace with the general progress."

Part of this trouble is explained by the existence of so many sects. A comparison is struck between the divisions among physicians, all of whom base their practice on the same fundamental sciences, and the schisms among the clergy, all of whom appeal to the Bible. But it is pointed out that "the medical sects have one enormous advance over religious sects. The better representatives of all medical sects have gathered themselves into one society for the betterment of their common standards, a thing which is scarcely to be hoped for in the near future among religious sects."

The report notes the common complaints of recent years of the weakening of church ties, particularly among Protestants, and suggests that one of the most evident factors is "the inefficiency of the ministry, due in the main to low standards of admission. In the Protestant churches, where the power of authority has largely passed away, the work of the church depends on the quality of the religious leadership of the preacher. The efficiency of this leadership is low.

"In the small towns one finds the same conditions as exist among lawyers and physicians. Four or five ministers eke out a living where one or two at most could do the work efficiently. Like the doctors of the villages, these men concern themselves with chronic cases and specific remedies, while the great problems of the moral health go untouched."

A word of praise is bestowed on the "long and severe training" the Roman Catholic Church demands of her priests, although it is suggested that the kind of education may be open to criticism.

"To it," says the report, "is due in very large measure the enormous moral power of the Roman Catholic Church throughout the world, particularly among the great masses of working people in the cities, where Protestantism has been so markedly ineffective, partly at least because of defects that an adequate education would go far toward remedying."

The economic difficulties of the Protestant bodies are recognized. The multiplication of sects and church building, it is admitted, is one cause of the introduction into the ministry of a large number of ill-trained men. At the same time it is contended, it has "brought down the financial recompense of the minister to a very low basis—the basis, indeed, of the inefficient man."

Granting the place in the life of the preacher of altruistic motives, the report urges that once the Roman Catholic solution of the economic difficulty—the institution of celibate priests supported by the Church—is dismissed, the efficiency of the preacher must have a direct relation to the quality of his financial support. Of this it says:

"The recovery of this support at this time, its uncertainty, the uncomfortable attitude of begging for oneself which many preachers have to assume, particularly in small communities, all operate powerfully to turn away able and serious men from this profession. A community which would support in comfort and dignity two able religious leaders will pay a bare living to five denominational preachers. And it is quite true in the ministry as in any other profession that taken by and large, one decently paid man is worth many ill-paid and inefficient men. * * * Meagre as are the salaries paid, they are in many cases equal to the services rendered. In this situation the public is profoundly interested."

In conclusion the report declares:

"The raising of the efficiency of the profession of the ministry rests largely in the hands of the preachers themselves, just as the raising of the profession of the law rests with lawyers and the raising of the profession of medicine with physicians. That the effort presents for any particular Christian organization serious social, administrative, and economic difficulties cannot be denied. That the advancement of religious influence in the lives of men rests in large measure on this effort seems equally clear."

August 8, 1909

PRESBYTERIANS OPEN DRIVE FOR RECRUITS TO MINISTRY

Increasing Shortage of Pastors Leads to a Campaign for Vocational Guidance of the Young— Loans Available, Salaries Advanced

FACED with a shortage of ministers, which is becoming more serious every year, the Prebyterian Church of this country has entered upon an active campaign to recruit new candidates for the pastorate to serve its numerous congregations. It aims to carry its appeal to the young men and young women who are about to choose a profession, to impress them with the desirability of entering the religious field and to acquaint them with the opportunities that are to be found in it.

A recent study of the Presbyterian field revealed that there were 2,114 vacant churches last year. Of these more than 400 offer an average salary of $2,000 a year, while more than 1,000 pay slightly less. Sixty per cent. of Presbyterian ministers are now supplying 80 per cent. of the churches, and in order to man all the vacant pulpits within the next fifteen years, taking into consideration the death and retirement of old ministers by that time, the Presbyterian Church will need a total of 1,900 more clergymen than it is ordaining at the present time, or an average of 126 more every year.

The shortage is in part accounted for by the fact that of the total number of vacant churches 1,364 have a membership of less than twenty-five, whereas in order to obtain the permanent services of a pastor at least sixty supporting members are necessary.

The Young Not Attracted.

Of 667 different ways of earning a living enumerated in the last United States Census report the ministry appears to be among those receiving the least attention. It is said that a recent inquiry made among 500 members of a graduating class in a large Eastern university disclosed that only three of the total number of seniors were planning to enter the ministry. The class contained ten sons of clergymen. In another instance, where 25,914 high school boys and girls were invited to express their vocational preferences, only ninety-three boys and eight girls indicated a desire to take up religious activities. Only one girl wanted to be a deaconess, fourteen boys thought of missionaries' careers, 636 boys were interested in law, 521 in education and 417 in medicine.

This lack of interest in religious professions contrasts with the membership progress of the Presbyterian Church. Within the last century the Church has grown 629 per cent., slightly faster than the population of the country. But it takes now more than twice as many members as it did in 1896 to contribute one candidate for the ministry. Thirty-four per cent. of the additions to the ministry are from other denominations, and even with this increase from outside the net gain in the Presbyterian ministry is less than one-tenth of 1 per cent. of the net gain of the Presbyterian membership.

Even evangelical revivals seem to fail to influence the situation. It has been found that the maximum influence of a revival lasts only about three years and that each peak of religious enthusiasm created by a revival is followed by a period of recession. According to the figures compiled by its authorities, the Presbyterian Church last year had less than half the number of candidates for the ministry, less than half the number of seminary students and less than half the number of seminary graduates that it had in 1896, while the number of candidates necessary to result in one ordination has increased 50 per cent. over that needed in 1896.

The unwillingness of young people to embrace religious careers is usually explained by the comparatively small returns which such careers offer. On the other hand, it has been said that not all of the members of other professions are qualified for the work which brings in a larger remuneration. Some authorities assert that of the number of those who labor with their hands or brains only one-fourth have found their right place, and that the remaining three-fourths of the workers of the world are occupying positions for which they are not properly fitted.

Salaries Increased.

In view of these facts, the Presbyterian Church feels that it is vitally concerned in making its opportunities known to those naturally adapted for the ministry. With that aim in view, it is endeavoring to raise the remuneration paid to pastors. Within the last ten years the average salary of the pastor has risen from $900 to more than $2,500 a year, exclusive of parsonages supplied. Another inducement offered to the prospective minister is the Sustentation Fund to the amount of $15,000,000 which is now being raised by Presbyterians under the chairmanship of Will H. Hays, for the purpose of supporting men and women who have given the best of their lives to the cause of serving Christianity.

The authorities in charge of the Presbyterian drive believe, however, that too much emphasis is placed upon the economic side of the contemplated career and not enough on the spiritual side. It is the object of those who are engaged in the campaign to impress upon young minds that no profession should be chosen for selfish or purely commercial motives, and that they will fall short of the realization of the highest ideals of their callings if they disregard the teachings of religion. For this reason the Church has abolished the distinction that used to be made between secular and sacred work. It regards all work as sacred in so far as it puts upon the worker the obligation to perform his duties in the best manner acceptable to God and man.

The Presbyterian Church feels that if the vocational guidance work is left entirely to the school under the present conditions of the separation of the Church from the State, the religious emphasis and the opportunites for purely religious service may not receive the attention which they should. But even with the public schools cooperating, there is still a tremendous field for vocational guidance work to be done directly by the Church and under the leadership of the minister.

Loans to Students.

The vocational guidance program laid out is intended to supplement the work of the public schools in preparing the boys and girls of tomorrow for the tasks which they are to take up in their mature life and to present for the consideration the ministerial field, which as a rule is not stressed in general vocational guidance work.

The minister, the teacher, the Parent Association, the Young People's Society, the Sunday School, in fact every organization or individual active in the Church has a suitable share in the work. The first step is the taking of a survey by the local church of all the educational work done by the public schools and other agencies. Instruction is provided concerning opportunities in the professional fields. The Christian appeal is added. The teachers are requested also to make a careful survey of all pupils, from junior high school up, ascertaining their interests and abilities and making records of their intelligence tests.

Special self-analysis blanks are provided for this purpose. These blanks are carefully studied and leaders are invited to interview the young people and enlighten them on the opportunities and responsibilities of the professions in which they show a special interest. When these students enter college they are to be followed up by the pastor, who is to act as their adviser during their college career. Those who show an inclination for pastoral work are helped with loans made by the Church and if any of the young men enter the ministry and serve at least five years they are relieved of the obligation to repay the loan.

May 17, 1925

CLERGY CHANGING, PROTESTANTS FIND

By GEORGE DUGAN

Mr. Protestant Minister of 1955 is the best-educated preacher in American history. Yet, never before has he had to face such a multiplicity of problems.

Chief among these are:

• How can he remain a "general practitioner" of religion in a specialized world? Can he be at the same time a preacher, pastor, counselor and administrator?

• What is his role in an era of swiftly changing community life?

• How can he minister to churchgoers who are daily confronted with major controversial issues?

In addition to these are the traditional headaches of the Christian ministry: Too much desk work, the preparation of denominational reports, parish "screwballs," skirmishes among parishioners and the recruitment and training of lay leadership.

And always there is the constant battle to allot time for his family and himself.

To find out what manner of clergyman is facing these problems while serving Protestant churchgoers today, the Russell Sage Foundation and Union Theological Seminary began last year what is probably the most exhaustive survey of the parish ministry in history.

Professor Conducts Study

Dr. Samuel W. Blizzard, a 40-year-old Presbyterian clergyman on leave from his post as associate professor of sociology and rural sociology at Pennsylvania State University, was named to head the study.

Dr. Blizzard's qualifications were virtually tailor-made. In addition to his sociological attainments, he served Presbyterian churches in Roselle, New Jersey and Long Green, Maryland.

He holds degrees in theology from Princeton Seminary and the

Hartford (Conn.) Seminary Foundation.

His headquarters are at Union Seminary, Broadway and 120th Street, where he will serve for the next two years as Visiting Professor of Social Science.

Dr. Blizzard started his survey by sending out more than 1,600 detailed questionnaires to the alumni of five theological seminaries.

These were Union (interdenominational), Garrett Biblical Institute, Evanston, Ill. (Methodist), Butler University School of Religion, Indianapolis (Disciples of Christ), Virginia Theological Seminary, Alexandria (Protestant Episcopal), and Louisville Theological Seminary in Kentucky (jointly administered by Northern and Southern Presbyterians).

The questionnaires also went to a group of representative clergymen from rural and urban areas selected by denominational leaders.

10-Page Questionnaire

Each minister received a ten-page, legal-size document containing sixty questions with ample space for comment. Questions ranged from the size of his church to his personal problems as a pastor.

Salary information was not requested because, as Dr. Blizzard put it, "it might scare away some respondents." (Other studies have brought out that ministerial salaries are inadequate—with a few outstanding exceptions.)

A foreword to the questionnaire promised that all information would be treated confidentially. It made it clear that the purpose of the study was to "find out how ministers function as pastors of churches in the United States."

Astonishingly, 1,150 replies were received from ministers in forty-seven states representing twenty-two denominations. Their answers filled some 10,000 pages of careful documentation.

With negligible exceptions, according to Dr. Blizzard, every respondent "knew his problem, was not overwhelmed and exhibited a strong desire for self-understanding."

It will take at least another year to tabulate all of the findings in book form. There is sufficient data on hand now, however, to paint a fairly clear picture of how Mr. Protestant Minister is facing up to his problems in the parish ministry.

In summing up his survey, Dr. Blizzard observed that the Protestant minister has been traditionally known as a "preacher."

Preaching Role Declines

However, he noted, the complexity of American society today is causing htis role to assume a "declining importance."

"It is being relegated to a less important position," he commented, "and the roles of pastor, counselor, organizer, administrator and promoter are coming to occupy the resulting void.

"The demands of the religious public and the response of parish ministers as they restudy their Christian vocation may very well change the 'face' of the parish ministry as a profession."

"The rapid shift that is being made from the life of the village and the countryside to the urbanized mass society is an increasingly important social fact for the church and the Protestant minister.

"Clergymen being trained in the seminaries in the current decade walk out to face a different world than did those of a previous generation.

"Therefore, the parish minister must re-examine the way he functions, the roles he plays, and the methods he uses to make the theology of the church meaningful in terms of the problems and aspirations of the people he serves."

In commenting on this aspect of the survey, Dr. Reinhold Niebuhr, vice president of Union Seminary, had this to say:

"A minister is not only a preacher of the Gospel, but he is a community leader and a teacher of social ethics who must try to do his part in guiding his congregation through the complex social and moral issues of our day."

April 4, 1955

MINISTER'S DUTIES OVERFILL HIS DAYS

Family Man in Modest Home Busy on Constant Round for Church and Town

---

HIS READING IS PROBLEM

Like Most of the Protestant Clergy, He Is Alone on Job —Savings Are Slender

---

By GEORGE DUGAN

The typical Protestant minister in the United States is 40 to 45 years old, lives in a medium-sized Midwest city, has two children, a car and a rather slim bank account.

He dresses modestly, dwells in a comfortable six-room house, and smokes a pipe on occasion.

His wife is his greatest boon and comfort, but he seldom has enough time to relax with his family.

This portrait of a pastor was deduced from an exhaustive survey of the Protestant clergy now being conducted here by Dr. Samuel W. Blizzard. Visiting Professor of Social Science at Union Theological Seminary.

Sixteen hundred detailed questionnaires were sent to graduates of five seminaries over the country. Of these, 1,150 came back, carefully filled out.

Mr. Protestant Minister is "a joiner," sometimes because he feels it to be his duty, but mainly because he likes people.

He belongs to his local service club (Rotary, Kiwanis, Lions) and the ministerial association and he is active in community projects.

Few Gaps for Reading Time

What and when to read, the Rev. Mr. Minister frankly admits, is a problem that can't be licked.

Here is his "must" reading list: the Bible, professional books and magazines bearing on his "trade," sermon volumes and devotional literature, current "provocative" books on theology, and Biblical interpretation.

From here on, his reading is on a catch-as-catch-can basis. But he does his level best to read regularly one newspaper of national coverage, his local daily and one news magazine. When time permits he tries to keep aware of what is going on in current fiction and in literature generally.

The Blizzard survey emphatically laid at rest the old saw that all a minister has to worry about is his Sunday sermon. That problem is usually reserved for Saturday.

Here is a typical day in the life of an average Protestant clergyman:

Breakfast at 8 A.M., correspondence, telephone calls, parish business from 9 until 11 A.M., then a private counseling session with a parishioner followed by an organizational luncheon meeting.

In the afternoon comes a hospital call and several pastoral visits, two of which were canceled the day before because of a funeral. Back in his study he puts the finishing program touches on a scheduled evening forum in the church, hoping he will have time for pre-dinner devotions with his family, then off to the evening meeting.

If he's lucky, there will be time for reading before lights-out.

Do-It-Yourself Rule Applies

Statistically, Dr. Blizzard's 1,150 clergymen disclosed the following information:

Seven out of nine of the ministers queried served one-pastor churches. In other words, most Protestant preachers have no ministerial help—they are the masters of their ships, with no first mates.

Ninety-six per cent of the ministers interviewed were married. More than one-third had two children, one out of nine had four children and two out of nine had three children.

A majority of those interviewed—56 per cent—ministered to congregations of fewer than 500 members.

Out of the entire 1,150 respondents, only thirteen served churches with more than 2,000 members.

Nearly two-thirds of the clergymen had Sunday schools, or church schools, with a membership up to 400. But only twenty-nine pastors could claim a church school enrollment in excess of 1,000.

Half of the preachers got along with no office help and 20 per cent managed with part-time secretarial assistance. Here is where the shoe pinched hardest when letters had to be answered, reports prepared and the weekly bulletin turned out.

Nine per cent performed their own building maintenance chores and 54 per cent had the benefit of only part-time help.

One minister from a small church in Ohio had this comment to make:

"In addition to the matters covered in the questionnaire, I would like to mention the fact that I feel that there are a good many ministers who feel rather lost. I'm among them. We simply cannot see where we are going in the church.

"Our churches are successful. We gain more members, we have more at church, we have bigger budgets, we have more activities, we have better Sunday school materials, and so on. But we can't see that we are making much of a difference in our communities or in the lives of the individual members of our communities. This disturbs me."

April 5, 1955

3 Faiths Find Lag
In Clerical Students

By JOHN WICKLEIN

Is the post-war surge of religious feeling coming to an end? There are signs that it is. One is that the nation's Protestant, Catholic and Jewish leaders find they are unable to attract enough youths to religious vocations.

It is feared that the popular interest in religion may dissipate before it can be captured and transformed into meaningful gains for the faiths.

The Protestant denominations are hardest hit and most worried. Enrollments in their seminaries across the country showed a drop in the last year of 5.3 per cent, or 1,125 students from the 1959 total of 26,365.

Jewish seminary enrollments appear to be faltering, and could go either way in the next few years.

The Roman Catholic major seminaries are better off, showing a slight increase. But the hierarchy is concerned that priestly and other religious vocations are not keeping up with the rise in the Catholic population.

From interviews in the last three weeks here and in other centers of religious activity, a key word in the problem appears to be "relevance." Youths in colleges seem less certain that the organized religious life has meaning in a world overwhelmed by science, politics and the atomic bomb.

Says Answers Are Lacking

James P. Doyle, a third-year student at Union Theological Seminary who will take a United Presbyterian pulpit this June, noted that seminarians in his denomination had dropped 12 per cent in one year.

"There's a feeling that we're over the hump in the surge of piety, the 'upsurge' in religious feeling," he said. "The people have been seeking something in the church, prompted by the total anxiety of the world situation. They haven't found the answers to this problem in the mainline, orthodox Protestant churches.

"In this way, Protestantism has failed. The decline in popular interest in Christianity has already affected enrollment in the seminaries."

Dr. Hubert C. Noble, general director of the National Council of Churches Commission on Higher Education, does not think there has been a slackening of interest in religion among students on the campuses, the pool from which ministerial candidates must come.

Yet, there has been a decline in pre-theology students in college, while the general enrollment has gone up sharply.

"For the students, there's no question of interest in the Christian faith, but a feeling that the church isn't representing it adequately," Dr. Noble commented. "It's a question of relevance of the church to world affairs. The churches must make the students feel the ministry is a place where they can make their lives count for something."

An enrollment survey just completed by the American Association of Theological Schools shows evidence of a disturbing trend, according to Dr. Jesse H. Ziegler, associate director. Interviewed in the association's headquarters at Dayton, Ohio, he said:

"It should be pointed out that neither a decline in total autumn enrollment in 1960 of 5.3 per cent nor a decline in five years of 4 per cent may be cited as evidence that professional education for the ministry is about to fold up.

"But neither is it safe to say that these declining enrollments are some fluke and lack significance for the churches."

Major denominations showing drops in enrollment in the survey included the American Baptist Convention, the Southern Baptist Convention, the Disciples of Christ, the American Lutheran Church and the (Southern) Presbyterian Church, U. S.

Protestant worry over the supply of ministers reflects a gnawing concern, increasing in the last few years, that the nation is entering a post-Protestant era.

The Catholics reported growth twice that of Protestant denominations last year. A Lutheran study shows that 1,000,000 secularists are being added each year to the 66,000,000 who now have no church affiliation.

Protestants See Decline

There are indications that the Protestants are not even keeping up with the general population increase. How, then, their leaders ask, can they hope to maintain the position of Protestantism, much less improve on it, if they cannot produce the ministers to guide the work?

The rational answer is that they cannot—which is why so many churchmen have turned this year to trying to solve the problem of recruitment. They have asked themselves: Why has not the interest in church vocations kept up with church membership, which still appears to be rising?

After suggesting the reason of relevance, Protestant leaders interviewed offered several others, some of which Catholic and Jewish clergymen thought had meaning for them, too. The reasons included:

¶The kind of dedication demanded by the ministry is now demanded by science. The nation's plea for scientists since sputnik went into orbit in 1957 has "called" many who would otherwise be entering seminaries. Science has almost been made a religion of its own, particularly by philosopher physicists relating it to the ethical problems.

¶The churches' recent emphasis on the "ministry of the laity" has backfired. The student asks: "If I can be a full-time servant of the Lord in any profession, I choose and still earn my $15,000, why should I go into the ministry?"

¶The costs of theological school education are rising rapidly, as they are in other postgraduate schools. But far more fellowships are available to professional school students than to theological. Earlier marriages are increasing the financial burden of completing a course of study that takes a man three years beyond the bachelor's degree.

¶Theological schools are over the post-Korea boom in G. I. students, and they have smaller college classes on which to draw.

Some theologians also suggested that Bible colleges, with ordination courses totaling three to five years, might be drawing off students looking for a "short cut to the ministry."

But the Rev. Terrill B. Crum of Providence, secretary of the Accrediting Association of Bible Colleges, said he saw no evidence of this. Bible colleges are moving toward a seven-year course of study, he pointed out. The enrollments of the thirty-seven accredited schools in the association went up 3 per cent last fall to 10,102, he said, but over the last ten years they have not kept up with the increase in population.

"The failure to grow more rapidly," he said, "is due to a strong counselling trend in the high schools which often emphasizes the material benefits and prestige of other vocations."

Since the churches almost always trail industry in salary brackets and fringe benefits, anyone entering the ministry has to do so in the spirit of service and sacrifice. A man getting out this year from Union Theological, for instance, can expect to receive no more than $4,500 plus a house to live in.

Poor Recruitment Seen

These reasons all are important, said Dean Liston Pope of Yale Divinity School, but from a practical standpoint "the most important single reason for the drop in enrollments is poor recruitment in the churches."

Many denominations recognize this, and recently some have set up full time recruiting offices.

The United Presbyterian Church, disturbed by a five-year decline, has been making an intense effort to "get through" to qualified college people, according to the Rev. Dr. Lewis A. Briner, secretary of the General Division of Vocation and Ministry.

Last summer, to stress the church's relevance, the denomination took fifteen student prospects to observe its ministers' work with narcotics addicts in the Chicago slums. Thirty others were sent to a seminar with scientists at Los Alamos, entitled "The Christian Faith in a Nuclear Age."

The denomination also encourages career days in high schools, with rabbis, priests and ministers to tell pupils the challenges and responsibilities of religious vocations.

One look at the statistics convinces Presbyterians that a major effort is needed. The 9,000 active ministers do not fill present pulpits, and new churches are being established at a rate of seventy-five a year.

Last year the denomination graduated about 400 for the ministry. But 360 of these went to fill posts of pastors who had died or retired, leaving only forty to provide for national expansion.

In 1955 the Methodist Church, which with 10,000,000 members is the largest Protestant denomination in the country, realized that bad times were coming for ministerial recruitment. The Methodist Board of Education, in Nashville, began a program that so far has been able to buck the national trend.

The needs are emphasized by recruiting officials, denominational magazines, conferences and a "Ministry Sunday"—to be held this year on May 21—in which the choice of the ministry as a profession is encouraged by pastors and youth leaders in the local churches.

"We still haven't solved our manpower problem," the Rev. Dr. Gerald O. McCulloh, director of theological education, remarked. "We have to get it over to the families that our needs continue to exceed our supply, even though the enrollments are going up."

Similar programs have been instituted by the Southern Baptist Convention, the Disciples of Christ, and other church groups.

Other denominations besides the Methodists have been able to increase enrollments over a five-year period, the A. A. T. S. survey showed. Among them, in order of percentage increase, were the Unitarian, Congregational, United Lutheran and Protestant Episcopal churches. The best known interdenominational seminaries have also been holding their own, and report applications are up to normal for this fall.

Shortage of Rabbis

Within all three of the country's major Jewish movements —Orthodox, Conservative and Reform—there is a shortage of rabbis. But since the war they have experienced such an expansion of congregations, with synagogues springing up in the suburbs and across the country, that their leaders have come to accept the shortage as a continuing fact. There just are not enough seminaries, they point out, to supply the demand from the new pulpits.

Annual reports indicate that enrollments in the rabbinical schools, which have shown unprecedented increases in the last fifteen years, may be leveling off. But so far only the officials at Yeshiva University, an Orthodox institution here, have decided that heavy pump-priming is necessary.

The student body at the university's Rabbi Isaac Eichanan Theological Seminary slid from 160 in 1956 to a low of 92 in 1958, and moved back last fall to 111.

"This spring," a Yeshiva official remarked, "we're interviewing at the college level every student who qualifies, to ask him, 'Why don't you consider entering the rabbinate?'

"A real problem is that the financial situation is becoming more acute. If a student is on the ball, he has a tremendous opportunity to get arts and science fellowships, but not for the theological courses."

For this reason, he said, Yeshiva has decided to set up a special fellowship program for rabbinical students and provide low-cost apartments for those who are married.

Once a student is graduated, his financial burden is not so severe as that of his Protestant contemporary: rabbis taking first pulpits can expect to be paid between $6,000 and $7,500.

But seminarians of both groups said they seldom heard salaries discussed as a consideration.

"You go into the ministry to contribute something, not to receive," one of them commented.

Recruiting Efforts

All three branches of Judaism rely heavily on campus religious agencies, summer Hebrew camps and young people's groups in the synagogues to attract candidates for the rabbinate. All three will probably have to increase their recruiting efforts if the rise in interest in temple life continues.

For the Roman Catholics, the problems are different, but the shortages are great. There is no drop in vocations, nor any signs that they will decrease in the future. But the number of persons baptized in the faith is increasing far more rapidly than the number of priests and sisters to minister to them.

"We're running as fast as we can, and falling behind," Martin Stevens, a Catholic writer, commented in The Priest.

In 1958, he noted, 1,088 priests were ordained, a net increase of 336 when the number who died that year is subtracted. The same year, the Catholic population increased by 1,460,126. If the new priests were sent out to minister to the new Catholics, there would be one for every 1,436 parishioners.

In the last ten years the Catholic population has risen 40 per cent, to more than 40,000,000. The number of priests has risen at about half that rate, to 54,000. The imbalance has caused many bishops, especially in the South and West, to draw on seminaries in Ireland.

Graduates 'Borrowed'

Others have to "borrow" graduates from areas, such as the Archdiocese of Boston, that produce an excess of priests. Still other bishops are looking hopefully to seminaries, such as

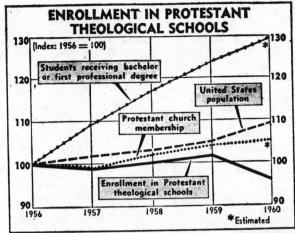

ENROLLMENT IN PROTESTANT THEOLOGICAL SCHOOLS

The New York Times — April 16, 1961

ENROLLMENT OFF: Protestant seminaries showed a 5.3 per cent drop between fall of 1959 and fall of 1960. Latest statistics on degrees and churches are for 1959.

St. Philip Neri, set up there by Richard Cardinal Cushing, for men deciding to enter priesthood late in life.

Because of the church's need to maintain its school system, its vocational problem has a dimension not found among most other religious groups. Teaching sisters are in shorter supply, relatively, than priests. In the ten years after 1950, students under Catholic instruction increased from 4,500,000 to 8,500,000, while the number of teaching sisters increased only from 80,000 to 96,000.

This means that the Catholic schools have had to draw more and more upon lay teachers, at a far greater cost, since teaching sisters, in accordance with their vows of poverty, take no pay for their work.

Between 1959 and 1960, the latest years for which statistics are available, sisters in all orders increased only 3,600, to a total of 168,527.

To many Catholic officials concerned with vocations, the central question is one of motivation: How are young men and women moved to accept the call to a religious life?

In the board room of the National Catholic Welfare Conference in Washington recently, three Catholic educators—two priests and a brother—sat around a table and discussed the question.

The Rev. John P. McCormick, rector of the Theological College of the Catholic University of America, remarked, "I've found there are more drop-outs in recent years."

Worldly Attractions

The short, partly bald priest sat back, puffed on a pipe, and

thought about the reasons for a moment. "The attractions of the world, I guess—big wages; automobiles," he went on. "Boys get a job during the summer with a big check. It's a temptation for them if they aren't strong in their vocations."

Brother Bertrand Leo, a slim, wryly humorous man who is director of De La Salle College, nodded. "You have to give them the hard pitch today, as far as their joining a religious order." His order, the Brothers of the Christian Schools, trains teachers for Catholic high schools and colleges. "I don't think you can appeal to material aims to bring young men into the religious life—you have to appeal to idealism. That way, you get the best men."

Father McCormick agreed. "If they're looking for an easy job or monetary returns, they're in the wrong pew."

"I think a vocation is a mysterious thing," said the Rev. William P. Ryan, master of studies and the Dominican House of Studies. "It's a question of Christ saying 'I have chosen you, you have not chosen me.' All the gimmicks, the films, the brochures and so on, are means of aiding this call."

Prodding is Defended

Brother Leo said that he thought some of this outside prodding was necessary, however. Getting young men away for a week-end at a retreat house is an excellent way to cut out the distractions of their daily lives and help them make a final decision, he declared.

"There is a tendency today for brothers, priests and sisters to recruit directly for the vocations—what with recruiters

for big business going to every campus," he stated. "We feel that we should be very direct in recruitment and come right out and ask: 'Did you ever think of the priesthood?'"

With the realization over the last few years that vocations were falling far behind, direct action has become more and more the watchword in Catholic dioceses. The method used is the decision of the bishop.

In New York Cardinal Spellman, responding to several years of decline in candidates for parish priest, began a "crash program" of recruitment two years ago. The program, which lasted ten months, was aimed at the parents, who are held responsible for the early guidance of children in the direction of church vocations.

The Paulist Press prepared ten illustrated booklets, to be distributed one each month to every adult parishioner leaving mass. The booklets provided information and exhortation on vocations in the priesthood and sisterhood. Pastors were asked to back up the messages in sermons on the Sundays the booklets were handed out.

Increase in Freshmen

The saturation program appears to have succeeded. Last September, the freshman class at Cathedral College numbered 145, an increase of fifty-two over the year before. It was the largest class in eight years.

Msgr. Thomas A. Donnellan, who instituted the program, said that there had also been a "decided increase" in women's vocations in the last year.

Today fourteen dioceses across the country have begun similar adult education efforts. The hope, which appears far from realization, is to increase men's and women's vocations in a percentage exceeding the continuing increase of Catholics.

In 134 major seminaries across the country about 15,000 young men are studying for the priesthood, an increase of 17 per cent in five years.

Three of these students, interviewed at lunch in the Catholic University seminary, said that they thought interest in vocations was picking up among boys coming along behind them.

Milam Joseph, a first year theology student from Dallas, commented that he thought a boy in high school wasn't "kidded" so much as in the past for saying he wanted to become a priest.

"You used to think about it and keep it to yourself," he added concerning his own experience. "Now people think about it and go discuss it with other fellows in their class."

April 16, 1961

Nation's Clergymen Still on Church-Mouse Pay

By GEORGE DUGAN

Despite such gradual improvements as rising salaries, new pension systems, medical programs and eligibility

for Social Security, clergymen remain the nation's least affluent professional men.

The Protestant minister whose congregation could include a $75,000-a-year doctor,

a $50,000-a-year businessman, and a host of other churchgoers whose salaries far outstrip his own, may still be clothing his children in hand-me-downs and relying

on donations of food and housing.

The problem of adequate subsistence is not confined to Protestant clergymen, but extends also to rabbis and, to

The Ministry as a Profession

and those of the Eastern Orthodoxy.

Although this old paternalistic attitude toward clerical support is slowly giving way to a more professional approach—in a change welcomed by ministers—recent statistics put the median salary for the clergy of 15 Protestant denominations well below that of other professionals.

According to the National Council of Churches, this ministerial median is just under $7,000 a year. New York State regards a salary of $6,000 a year for a family of four as inadequate to provide proper medical care. It makes such families eligible for Medicaid, the program financed by the state, local and Federal Governments to furnish such service for those unable to pay for it.

The United States Department of Labor reports that the median for salaried professionals in all fields is close to $11,000 a year. The same Federal agency set $5,839 as the minimum adequate to support a city worker's family of four.

In the words of the Rev. Keith Wright, director of church ministry studies for the National Council, there is still a "cultural lag" in churchgoing when it comes to paying the man in the pulpit. Despite recent improvements, he said, the church is still a "very non-professional employer."

Too often it places the a different degree, to priests of the Roman Catholic Church clergyman in a special category, supposedly free from the economic desires and worries of other persons, mainly because he is a minister of the gospel.

The Rev. Dr. Ross P. Scherer, a former associate of Mr. Wright at the National Council, has compiled a chart showing median salaries after 15 years in the pulpit, when, presumably, a clergyman should be at his peak.

Southern Church at Top

The top median after 15 years was paid by the Southern Presbyterian Church — $7,852. In descending scale came the United Church of Christ, $7,845; the Episcopal Church, $7,820; the Disciples of Christ, $7,812; the Southern Baptist Convention, $7,785; the United Presbyterian Church, $7,777; the Lutheran Church in America, $7,623; and the American Lutheran Church, $7,257.

In the last 10 years, Dr. Scherer said, average ministerial salaries in the American Baptist Convention have risen from $3,903 to $5,759. And the Presbyterians and the Episcopalians have made a good professional start in establishing a minimum salary scale for their ministers.

Recently, clergymen were brought into Social Security. If they seek exclusion because of religious scruples or conscientious objection to what they might consider an infringement of government in the area of church-state separation, they must ask for an exemption in writing.

Poor salaries also drew the attention last fall of Dr. Nathan M. Pusey, the president of Harvard University, who told the triennial general convention of the Episcopal Church that a third of its congregations had fewer than 100 communicants. As a consequence, he said, the average salary of Episcopal ministers is about $6,000.

A Minister's View

One Presbyterian minister, the Rev. Mr. J. B., a Phi Beta Kappa graduate of the University of Pennsylvania and Princeton Theological Seminary, recently expressed some of the dissatisfaction felt by a man trying to raise five children on a minister's salary. He said:

"I've lived through the greatest economic boom ever known to mankind and I haven't got a red cent to show for it."

Mr. B. is the pastor of an "inner city" church in an East Coast metropolitan area. He gets $10,000 a year, plus manse. Three months ago, his salary was increased by $500.

The minimum in his Presbytery, or local governing unit, has been set at $5,200, plus housing allowance. He considers himself better off than many of his colleagues, but still way behind men in other fields with a comparable educational background.

Mr. B. doesn't think he will ever get out of debt. Two daughters are in college; one receives $1,400 a year in scholarship help, the other $1,200.

His teen-aged son has a part-time job outside high school hours. The two youngest daughters are in grade school.

Budgeting is "for the birds," he says, because "you never know what the next day will bring."

Clothes are a problem, especially with two daughters in college. Now, the youngest girls must be content with hand-me-downs.

Mr. B. is community-minded and this means cash for luncheon meetings and $2 and $3 contributions to worthy causes.

Food is a major item. Mr. B. has never attempted to estimate his outlay, but he describes it as "frightening."

He is frequently called upon to be the host at committee meetings, which involves putting out snacks and liquid refreshment. On New Year's Day the B.'s hold an open house for church members, a "smorgasbord" that starts the New Year with a debit of $30 to $40.

Wife Teaches School

Heat, telephone and car expenses all come out of his salary.

On the credit side, Mrs. B. teaches school. She earns almost enough for the B.'s to break even on the college bills.

A friendly doctor in the congregation takes care of Mr. B.'s personal ills, but not those of the rest of the family.

"All of us, except the dog, wear glasses," the minister said recently in explaining other costs. And the youngest child is undergoing teeth-straightening, at the cost of a borrowed $950.

Mr. B. officiates at weddings and conducts funerals free for members of his congregation. He estimates his yearly income in this category at $150. This is a little above the average for all Protestant ministers.

Occasionally he will pick up $20 to $25 in speaking engagements at nearby colleges or in other pulpits.

He gets a month for vacation and his denomination takes care of his pension.

No Expense Accounts

In an interview Mr. Wright, the National Council official, said:

"People somehow think that the cost of being a minister doesn't increase along with everything else. They expect him to be a community leader, good fellow, and a joiner. But they forget that extra-pulpit obligations are more often than not out-of-pocket expenses for the average clergyman."

For instance, Mr. Wright said, the business-man-in-the-pew can lean heavily on a fat expense account for lunches, a privilege the minister doesn't have.

And in making his pastoral rounds to shut-ins, the sick and bereaved, he added, the pastor "can just about operate a motorcycle on the money he gets to run his car."

The Rev. William A. Tieck, minister of St. Stephen's Methodist Church in the Bronx, earns $6,500 a year. This is the minimum for Methodist clergymen in this area. It is also the minimum for Presbyterian ministers in the New York Presbytery. Mr. Tieck is single, and says it would be "rough" to raise a family on his salary.

Mr. Tieck has four earned degrees in philosophy. He says he is "disturbed but not chagrined" at his earnings. He has no car and about one-third of his income goes for Federal, state and local taxes.

Priests Fare Better

Parish priests in the Roman Catholic Church fare better economically than their Protestant counterparts. They are free of heavy family responsibilities and their financial needs are almost entirely taken care of by their congregations.

They live, eat and sleep in rectories while collecting from $100 to more than $200 a month for purely personal expenses including clothes, and usually a month-long vacation.

They are sometimes given cars by their parishioners as an expression of appreciation for their priestly duties.

The salary of a priest is established by his bishop and varies from diocese to diocese. In New York, parish pastors receive $225 a month, with a small travel allowance for home visits, retreats or meetings connected with their work. An assistant gets $150 to $175.

Ten years ago, pastors made $135 and assistants $110.

Offerings for weddings and baptisms range from $10 to $50, depending on the circumstances of the donor. These go into the parish treasury. Last year, a typical suburban church in New Jersey took in $780 from these sources.

The Administrators

Stipends for special masses and funerals usually are given to the officiating priest. These are in the $1 to $10 range.

Members of religious orders are supported by their communities. Whatever they may earn in teaching or in other fields reverts to the order to which they owe allegiance.

Cardinals, archbishops and bishops in the Roman Catholic Church receive no set salary. All of their expenses are met by the sees they administer.

As administrators they control the purse strings with complete authority over the total resources of their dioceses.

They can write checks for any worthy cause they wish, and frequently do. The late Cardinal Spellman gave away thousands of dollars of archdiocesan money by simply writing a check.

But all prelates are required by canon law to make out wills, leaving the financial resources of their sees to their successors.

Cardinal Spellman's personal estate amounted to "not more than $30,000" when it was probated last December. This figure did not take into account the value of the almost priceless collection of Roman Catholic memorabilia that the cardinal had collected over the years and left intact to the archdiocese.

A similar arrangement exists in Eastern Orthodoxy for archbishops and bishops. But, unlike the Roman Catholic rule requiring celibacy, Orthodox

272

priests may marry. In so doing, however, they relinquish their chances to become a bishop and must rely on wages paid by their congregations, as in Protestantism.

Statistics on Rabbis

Statistics comparable to those for Protestant ministers may be applied to rabbis.

The spokesman for one of the major rabbinical organizations in this country said the other day that no full-time rabbi gets less than $5,000 a year, with pension rights added.

Like most Protestant clergymen, a rabbi is hired by the congregation and can be dismissed by it. His employer fixes his salary.

Also, as in Protestantism, the choice pulpits are in major metropolitan areas. Some plush synagogues and churches in New York, Chicago and Boston pay their clergy salaries ranging from $20,000 to $40,000 a year. For them, the economic squeeze is no worse nor better than for other professionals.

Despite their economic prob-

lems most clergymen accept their lot in the philosophical manner of Mr. Tieck, who says:

"Many of us are plowing rock, but we have faced up to a situation where a man doesn't stay in the kitchen unless he can stand the heat."

February 18, 1968

Pastors Leaving Church for Better Way to Serve

By EDWARD B. FISKE

The Protestant minister, once an unchallenged symbol of the divine presence in human society, is experiencing a crisis of identity marked by a radical transformation in the nature and purpose of his work.

Eager to apply religious beliefs to social problems but frustrated at opposition by laymen, young clergymen are fleeing the neighborhood church in increasing numbers.

At Union Theological Seminary the portion of seniors planning to take jobs in neighborhood churches has dropped from 53 to 20 per cent in the last two years.

While clergymen in the past provided well-defined and needed services to their parishioners, many ministerial tasks, such as counseling or work with the aged, have largely become the domain of trained lay specialists.

"The contemporary clergyman is in a state of enormous frustration and upheaval," said Jeffrey K. Hadden, a sociologist who has done extensive research on the role of the minister. "He doesn't know what he's doing or who he is."

New emphasis on the importance of laymen in the church has reduced the distinctiveness of the minister's role even in such traditional priestly activities as preaching and teaching.

Oiling the Machinery

Clergymen complain that they spend much of their time simply oiling ecclesiastical machinery or serving as "jack of all trades but master of none." When they seek out such new roles as trying to help solve urban problems, they frequently find themselves inadequately trained.

As a result, increasing numbers of young ministers are developing specialties ranging from youth work to welfare activities.

Others are taking up "nonprofessional" ministries where they emulate the "worker-priests" of Paris and earn their livings in secular jobs and perform sacerdotal functions on the side.

Still others are foresaking

ordination entirely and seeking to develop new ministries as theologically trained laymen.

The changing role of the Protestant minister today is closely linked to a revolution in the neighborhood church.

In the past the local church was the center of all religious activities in a community. The minister, in turn, was a spiritual figure with certain clearly defined tasks, including preaching, administering the sacraments, visiting the sick and counseling parishioners.

Today's mobile society, however, presents different circumstances. Breadwinners work in one place, sleep in another and vacation in still another. Important decisions affecting business, politics and the other great issues of the day are generally in a context more wide-ranging than the local residential area.

The Distant Pulpit

Ministers thus complain that the neighborhood pulpit has difficulty reaching into "where the action is."

"The local pastor ends up being a chaplain to men's families but not to them," said the Rev. Dr. Edgar W. Mills, director of the Ministry Studies Board in Washington.

The problem of identity is exacerbated by conflicts between ministers and local congregations over what they are supposed to do. These are particularly acute when it comes to social action.

Large numbers, probably a substantial majority, of Protestant clergymen agree with the Rev. Dow Fitzpatrick, the pastor of the 2,800-member First Methodist Church in Evanston, Ill., who maintains that social action is integral to the work of the ministry.

"A minister has both the right and the obligation to go outside his church to seek to influence morality," the 51-year-old minister said in an interview. "The great issues today are moral issues, and they are tied to our very survival."

Such clergymen frequently find, however, that the local church, which is in many ways a mirror of stable middle-class values, is not an effective institution through which he may bring about social change.

Recent sociological research has indicated that Protestant laymen as a group not only tend to oppose church involvement in social issues but also

are no more sympathetic than the public as a whole to social justice in general.

Mr. Hadden, for example, found in two national studies that 45 per cent of regular churchgoers "basically disapprove of the civil rights movement in America" and that three-quarters would be upset if their minister were to take part in a civil rights demonstration.

Opposition Found

The Rev. Robert P. Barnes, 35, rector of St. John's Episcopal Church in Frankline, Mass., said that he had encountered opposition from his parishioners over offering church facilities to nonreligious community groups.

He said his congregation tended to think of his responsibilities as primarily directed toward them. He added, however, that he thought of the church "as having a role in the whole community."

One result of such conflicts is that young ministers are seeking positions outside the parish.

The American Association of Theological Schools reported last fall that although enrollment in seminaries was up 3.9 per cent over 1966, the percentage of students in the bachelor of divinity programs that are the principal source of parish ministers was down. Only 17 per cent of the first-year students at Yale Divinity School this year indicated an interest in the parish. Nine years ago the figure was 45 per cent.

As an alternative to traditional parish work, both seminary graduates and experienced clergymen are seeking a variety of new and specialized forms of ministry.

These include social work, medical services, chapels in shopping centers and ministries in coffeehouses, skiing resorts and other vacation areas.

In some cases such clergymen perform essentially traditional tasks, such as counseling and religious education, and only the context is different. In others, however, the ministers are opening up whole new areas of activity.

Clusters in Queens

The Rev. Scott I. Paradise, for example, directs the Boston Industrial Mission. Its goal, the 38-year-old Episcopalian said, is to "open discussions with

engineers and scientists of the research and development industry of the human and social implications of what they're doing."

Numerous clergymen have turned their attention to transforming existing parishes into more effective means of serving a community.

The Rev. Theodore Erickson is directing the formation of two clusters of churches in the South Ozone Park and Richmond Hill sections of Queens for Metropolitan Urban Service Training, an ecumenically sponsored training institute in Manhattan.

Under the plan the churches are to pool their resources and permit ministers to specialize in such fields as preaching and counseling. They will then apply these skills to several congregations instead of doing a variety of jobs for a single church.

"We hope that this kind of transcongregational structure will help end the problem of ambiguous clergy roles by letting each minister do what he's best at," Mr. Erickson said.

Use Laymen's Talents

He added that another prime goal was to provide a more effective mechanism than the local parish for making use of the talents of laymen.

Among the most radical experiments are those that blur the traditional distinction between laymen and clergy.

Clergymen who enter "nonprofessional" ministries take secular jobs and seek to apply their theological training in situations previously occupied only by laymen.

Such ministries are known as "tent-making" ministries because St. Paul supported himself as a tent-maker.

James Liebig, 39, for instance, is a former plant manager of an automotive products firm in Chicago who will graduate next month from Yale Divinity School. He hopes to return to industry as a layman and take a position where he can be instrumental in forming "the social conscience of a corporation in an urban situation."

For the last three years the Episcopal Diocese of Idaho has been training laymen who have full-time jobs to serve as part-time priests during evenings and on weekends. The first eight graduates will be ordained this spring.

Despite the widespread dissatisfaction and frustration, many clergymen continue to find the local pastorate personally rewarding.

'Whine and Whimper'

The Rev. David B. Watermulder, minister of the Bryn Mawr Presbyterian Church near Philadelphia, expressed annoyance at clergymen who "whine and whimper about the great problems today."

"I talk with professional people in medicine, education and politics who have precisely the same frustrations," he said.

Most church leaders believe

that the local church will continue to function in more or less its present form, but many add that it may cease being the norm.

"The local church is a viable structure in our time, but it has to be seen as merely one specialized ministry among many," said the Rev. Gerald J. Jud, an official of the United Church of Christ.

Some defenders of the parish ministry argue that the solution to the clergyman's identity problem lies in a new relationship to the laity.

The Rev. George A. Pera, minister of the First Presbyterian Church in Greenwich, Conn., said the clergyman must be regarded not as a "holy man" who performs the church's ministry, but as a theologically trained "catalyst" who assists laymen in seeking out their own forms of Christian service.

Parishioners Assist

In his church he has begun to call upon laymen who have faced certain problems, such as the loss of a job or a major

operation, to assist him in aiding other church members facing similar crises.

Another clergyman who agrees that the key to the work of the minister in the future may be the layman is the Rev. Robert A. Mackie, rector of St. John's Episcopal Church in Winthrop, Mass.

"I can go out and picket till the cows come home, but that really won't mean a whole lot," he said. "I'm not really doing my job unless I get the people aware of their own responsibilities."

April 26, 1970

Clergymen, Citing War and Poverty as Issues, Seek State and National Offices

By DOUGLAS ROBINSON

An increasing number of clergymen are seeking national or statewide elective office this year in what appears primarily to be their growing impatience with the continued fighting in Vietnam and with the pace of antipoverty efforts.

At least 12 clergymen, including four Roman Catholic priests, have made known their intention of running for office. Six of these men live in the New York metropolitan area, the remainder are scattered across the country.

Eleven of these candidates are members of the Democratic or Liberal parties and one is a Republican. Two are seeking seats in the United States Senate, one is running for Governor and the rest are aiming at the House of Representatives.

3 Incumbent Clergymen

Although there is nothing new about clergymen serving in Congress, they have always been in an almost miniscule minority. The nine seeking election to the House for the first time this year compares with three clergymen now serving there, including the Rev. Adam Clayton Powell Jr., Democrat of Manhattan.

Roman Catholic priests in Federal elective posts or even running for them have been a rarity. Records show only one priest as having served in the House — the Rev. Gabriel Richard of Detroit, who was elected in 1822 as a delegate from the Territory of Michigan. He served one term.

This week, the American Bishops of the Roman Catholic Church, meeting in San Fran-

cisco, accepted a recommendation by a pastoral committee that urged heads of dioceses to "discourage any priest from seeking public office."

One priest, the Rev. Louis R. Gigante of the Bronx, who is running for the Democratic nomination in the 16th Congressional District, said he agreed with the Bishops' resolution "in principle," but he indicated he would not give up his campaign.

'Politicians Deserted Us'

"I've been saying all along that it is unusual for a priest to run for office," he said. "I'm running for Congress because the politicians have deserted us."

Father Gigante is an assistant pastor at St. Athanasius Church in the poverty-ridden Hunts Points section and the first Roman Catholic priest to run for Federal office in the history of New York State.

Other Catholic priests running for national office include the Rev. Joseph R. Lucas, one of 13 candidates for the Democratic nomination in Ohio's 13th Congressional District, and the Rev. Robert F. Drinan, a Jesuit who is campaigning for the Democratic nomination in Massachusetts' 3d District.

Father Lucas, an associate professor of philosophy at Youngstown State University, is seeking the seat held for 36 years by Representative Michael J. Kirwan, a Democrat who is retiring.

The clergyman, who insists that his status in the church would not be altered by his election, said his campaign had not brought any public reaction

from his superiors. Among his campaign positions are withdrawal from Vietnam, curtailment of spending for the military and reapportionment of taxes.

Father Drinan, who is dean of the law school at Boston College, is challenging Representative Philip J. Philbin for the Democratic designation.

Runs as Republican

The fourth Roman Catholic is the Rev. John J. McLaughlin, an associate editor of the Jesuit magazine America. Father McLaughlin is actively seeking support for the Republican Senatorial nomination in Rhode Island. If he wins election, he will be the first priest to serve in the Senate.

If he gets the nomination, the clergyman will run against Democratic Senator John O. Pastore. He opposes the Senator's vote for the Safeguard antiballistic missile system.

Two more clergymen are seeking office in New York. They are the Rev. Dr. Donald S. Harrington, the Liberal party candidate for Governor, and the Rev. George D. McClain, the Liberal party's choice to run from the 16th Congressional District, which includes all of Staten Island and part of Brooklyn.

Dr. Harrington, who is also his party's state chairman, is rector of the Community Church, 40 East 35th Street. He sees his political activities as a "vital complement" to his ministerial role. There are indications that Dr. Harrington might withdraw from the campaign later and allow the Liberal party endorsement to go

to another candidate.

The Rev. McClain, who was not available for an interview, is a Methodist minister and is on the staff at Shalom House, an ecumenical community center in the Stapleton area of Staten Island. The 31-year-old clergyman has been active in the antiwar movement.

Students 'Dig' Campaign

In upstate New York, The Rev. Harvey H. Bates, chaplain of the United Christian Fellowship at Syracuse University, is preparing to wage a primary fight in the 34th District against Representative James M. Hanley a Democrat. Mr. Bates, a graduate of Union Theological Seminary, said his congregation of university students "dig the idea" of his running for office.

Farther north, in Buffalo, the Rev. Hugh G. Carmichael, an Episcopal minister, is candidate for the Democratic nomination from the 41st Congressional District. His opponent in the primary will be Representative Thaddeus J. Dulski.

Mr. Carmichael is canon of St. Paul's Cathedral and vicar of St. Thomas Church and has been active in civic affairs for three years in Buffalo. He said that his church superiors had given him the permission to enter the campaign.

In Hartford, the Rev. Joseph Duffey is seeking the Senate nomination against Senator Thomas J. Dodd. Mr. Duffey is not a practicing minister. He was a Congregational minister a few years ago in Danvers, Mass., but is now director of the Center of Urban Studies at the Hartford Seminary Foundation.

Mr. Duffey is national chairman of Americans for Democratic Action. "I am not running as a clergyman," he said. "I am running as a father, as a citizen and as a Democrat."

In the South, the Rev. Andrew Young, a black minister in the United Church of Christ and former executive vice president of the Southern Christian Leadership Conference, is running for the House in Georgia's Fifth District, a district that is split between Atlanta and its suburbs.

In Maryland, the Rev. Thomas B. Allen is vying for the Democratic nomination from the Eighth Congressional District against Representative Gilbert Gude.

Mr. Allen, who has gained attention for opening a swimming program in which black children are bused to suburban public and private pools, was rector of St. Luke's Episcopal Church in Bethesda for 12 years. He now gives guest sermons in suburban Maryland and, in his campaign, is emphasizing withdrawal from Vietnam.

In California, the Rev. Dr. Stuart McClean, a Presbyterian clergyman, is opposing Representative Charles S. Gubser in the Democratic primary in the state's 10th District, which includes Santa Clara County.

April 21, 1968

Seminaries Turn Pragmatic

By EDWARD B. FISKE

Most graduates of Protestant and Roman Catholic seminaries in this country begin their ministerial careers with solid grounding in classical disciplines like theology, church history and Biblical exegesis. But can they run a local church?

An increasing number of theological educators are regretfully concluding that the answer is no. "Just talk to any group of ministers about their education," said A. Lee Schoemer, one of the architects of the new Inter-Met Seminary in Washington. "You'll find that they learned most of their basic skills after they got into a church."

The result is a growing trend toward increased professionalism in Christian theological education and a wide range of efforts to distinguish the training of ministers for local churches from the production of scholars in the field of religion.

The efforts range from attempts to upgrade traditional "field work" programs through better supervision to new degree programs designed exclusively for the production of parish clergy. "The idea is to put the same amount of energy into professional excellence that has always been put into scholarly excellence," said Marvin Taylor of the American Association of Theological Schools.

Beginning of the Trend

The trend began in the mid-nineteen-sixties, when the Claremont School of Theology and the University of Chicago Divinity School instituted Doctor of Ministry degrees. These programs, which would not qualify a student for a teaching career, were intended to provide a higher level of professional training than the standard three-years bachelor (or master) of divinity degree given by most seminaries.

Mr. Taylor estimated that about half of the approximately 100 accredited members of the association now either have such programs or are planning to begin them.

Some seminaries, notably Claremont and Chicago, offer the D. Min. degree as a first degree after college. Others, such as Princeton Theological Seminary, offer it as an advanced degree for clergymen who want to do an additional year or so of study after they have been out on the job for awhile.

Catholics have a different degree system, but they are moving in the same direction. The Diocese of Brooklyn, for instance, recently adopted a policy whereby priests must spend a full year working in a parish after completing their classroom work before they are eligible for ordination.

And in addition to developing a new kind of professional degree, theological educators are devising new structures for the training of pastors.

Some are essentially an extension of the traditional idea of field work, in which a student learned ministerial skills and then went out to a church or a related institution to try them out. The Vincentian Fathers, for instance, are now strongly encouraging their seminarians to use their summers and even year-long internships to work in a variety of practical jobs.

The United Theological Seminary of the Twin Cities, a United Church of Christ seminary in Brighton, Minn., requires first year students to spend half their time in congregations, denominational offices and community agencies and has introduced courses in fields such as organization development.

Union Seminary in Richmond, drew up a list of "competencies" needed by parish ministers and has now redesigned all of its courses in light of these objectives. Students in a course in New Testament exegesis, for instance, are evaluated not only on their skill in interpreting the Bible but on their ability to relate the passages they translate to present-day problems.

18 Weeks of Church Work

The Perkins School of Theology, a Methodist seminary in Dallas, now requires all of its future ministers to spend at least 18 weeks working in a local church under the guidance of carefully selected pastors. Small groups of students and supervisors meet periodically to reflect on the implications — theological as well as others — of what they are doing.

James M. Ward, acting dean at Perkins, said that this concept differed substantially from traditional field work, which was generally thought of as "practicing" what was learned in the classroom. "Our conviction is that in-service training is fundamental to the learning process in the first place," he stated.

The most radical effort thus far is Inter-Met, an ecumenically sponsored Protestant experiment whose full name is Inter-Faith Metropolitan Theological Education, Inc.

Inter-Met, which began operating this year with 13 students, including two Jews and a Catholic, has no campus. Students take jobs in local churches and then make contracts with local professors—with the seminary acting essentially as a broker—for instruction in fields such as theology and church history.

In another departure from tradition the foundation-supported Case Study Institute in Cambridge, Mass., has begun developing a theological equivalent of the case method used at the Harvard Business School. Owen Thomas, one of the leaders, said that cases had already been developed in areas such as parish administration and social issues and that "we're trying to get into fields like theology as well."

Theological educators also recognize that one area for potential growth is the part-time, or "non-stipendiary," minister who holds down a secular job and then works in a church in the evenings or on weekends.

Training programs for such clergymen are almost entirely geared to the new thinking about on-the-job learning. In the Episcopal Church, for instance, there are at least 26 such programs with somewhat more than 100 candidates, typically organized around the local cathedrals.

While Christian seminaries are moving toward practical experience in the training of future pastors, Jewish institutions seem to be in the opposite direction. Especially in the Reform movement, their curriculums are becoming more heavily oriented toward classical disciplines.

Rabbinical Students Stand

Rabbi Eugene Borowitz of Hebrew Union College-Jewish Institute of Religion in New York said that this was occurring because rabbinical students were dissatisfied with the way Jewish life was structured. "They are saying 'You teach us about classical Judaism and we'll try to create new structures to express it'," he said.

Not all of the Christian efforts at a higher level of professionalism are successful. Chicago, for instance, has pulled back its program, partly for financial reasons and partly because the faculty was more interested in a program that would serve future scholars.

Leaders of all the seminaries agree that a major problem—perhaps the key one—is the development of capable supervisors. "You're wasting your efforts unless the student gets excellent guidance while he is performing ministerial tasks and reflecting on it later," said Msgr. John J. Egan, a professor of pastoral theology at Notre Dame.

Several educators note that the trend toward in-service training seems like a throw-back to the days when clergymen were trained through an apprentice system. They note that it was only in the 19th century that theological education took up the model of the Western university.

Others, though, argue that it differs from both. "What we're trying to do now is much more sophisticated," said Mr. Taylor. "We're trying to find new ways of using academic institutions."

January 8, 1973

EPISCOPAL VESTRIES GIVE VOTE TO WOMEN

Practically all Episcopal churches in New York yesterday announced either that their vestries had already authorized women to vote, or else that popular votes are to be taken at Parish meetings one week from today to authorize them to do so. From the chancel of the Church of the Incarnation, Madison Avenue, and Thirty-fifth Street, it was said yesterday that the vestry has acted favorably.

Heavenly Rest, Grace, St. Thomas, St. Andrew's, Calvary, Holy Trinity, St. James, and other parishes are said to favor the vote by women, and it was said yesterday at Christ Church, Seventy-first Street and Broadway, that the matter would be passed on by the vestry on Wednesday night. St. Mary the Virgin, Holy Communion, and St. Edward the Martyr parishes are said to have different parish foundations, and that further action by them will be necessary before the women may vote. Trinity Parish has not yet determined its course.

The persons to be voted for on Advent Monday, Nov. 29, are wardens and vestrymen. These form the governing body of the parish, including of course the rector. Privilege of voting does not, it is said, imply also the right to be voted for, so that wardens and vestrymen, and delegates to conventions will be men as heretofore. E. L. Tefft of Christ Church, speaking yesterday of the women voting, said:

"Since 90 per cent. of the workers in our churches are women, and almost that large proportion make up the congregation, it is high time women had voice in the management of parish affairs. If I had my way I would let them serve on vestries. Perhaps if they did needed reforms in the conduct of business affairs would follow."

November 22, 1915

BAPTISTS ADMIT WOMEN.

Dr. Porter Warns Southern Body It Means Start on "Down Grade."

JACKSONVILLE, Fla., May 18 (Associated Press).—Change in the constitution of the Southern Baptist Convention to admit women to membership on the Executive Committee and various boards was adopted today after a spirited discussion. Dr. J. W. Porter of Louisville, Ky., opposed the change, quoting the Apostle Paul's abjuration of women speaking in the church.

"We have started on the down grade," he declared, "and the time will come when a woman will preside over this convention."

Dr. Porter deprecated the "feminist movement," and said many leading workers of the Women's Missionary Union are opposed to women taking part in the convention.

Dr. W. J. McGlothlin of Greenville, S. C., Dr. A. J. Barton of Alexandria, La., and others pointed out that women already had been admitted to the convention and to its routine committees, and argued that they should be placed on its important boards and committees. The Apostle Paul, Dr. Barton declared, said nothing against women taking part in the practical affairs of the churches.

Recommendations of the Education Board, presented by the Rev. J. W. Gillon of Mayfield, Ky., Chairman, termed Darwinism "not science at all, but theory," and recommended that "Christian scientists" be sought "who will prepare text books for all departments of science which will rightly relate science to the Bible, and set forth the fact that the majority of the greatest men of science have repudiated Darwinism except as an "unproved working hypothesis." The report, which was adopted, complained that "text books cannot be found for the departments of science free from erroneous statements with reference to evolution."

May 19, 1922

METHODISTS ACCEPT WOMAN AS PREACHER

Miss Puera B. Robison the First of Her Sex to Be So Honored in the East.

The first woman anywhere in the East to be accepted as a local preacher in the Methodist Episcopal Church was received yesterday afternoon at the sixty-eighth session of the Newark (N. J.) Annual Conference, which began Wednesday in St. Luke's Church, Clinton Avenue and Murray Street, Newark. She is Miss Puera B. Robison, a teacher of the Bible in the Hackettstown Collegiate Methodist Institute, Hackettstown, N. J. She is about 30 years old. Miss Robison will be ordained by Bishop Luther B. Wilson, who is presiding at the conference, Sunday afternoon.

The candidate was accepted unanimously in an executive session of the conference. She was not present at any time, but she was recommended for ordination by the Conference Board of Examiners on Ministerial Qualifications, of which the Rev. Dr. Harry Y. Murkland, pastor of the First Church, Orange, N. J., is the Chairman. Dr. Murkland announced that Miss Robison had passed high in all the conference examinations. He said she had asked ordination because she spent her Summers laboring among the mountain whites of the South, and as the missionaries were scarce it would make her of added usefulness inasmuch as she could officiate at baptisms and funerals, could perform the marriage ceremony and could assist in the administration of the Holy Communion.

March 27, 1925

Ask Equal Voice In the Churches

Women Want More Active Part, Federal Council Survey Discloses

A feeling of dissatisfaction among Protestant church women over their inability to have official voice in the governing bodies of the church is reported in a study just completed of the woman's status in the churches. The report is based on questionnaires sent to over 1,000 women leaders in ten denominations, and was prepared at the request of the Women's Cooperating Commission of the Federal Council of Churches.

Miss Inez Cavert, research assistant of the council, undertook the study a year ago, when leaders expressed concern that younger women were drifting away from the church into activities where they would obtain greater responsibilities.

Dr. Mary E. Woolley is chairman of the commission which requested the study, and Miss Anna E. Caldwell its secretary.

"There is a wide variation of practice in including women on boards," Miss Caldwell explained. "Large churches are less likely to have women in important positions, and smaller churches where there are fewer women to take up the responsibility customarily have more women on their boards. The study shows that the objection to women is based on tradition, and is not a matter of denomination."

Majority Want Representation

In her questionnaires to women, Miss Cavert asked for frank opinions on the question.

Of those replying, 71.4 per cent think that women should be represented on at least some of the boards, while a few others would have them serve where there is a scarcity of men.

Sixteen per cent either say that women should not serve or express the fear that the men will drop out if the women are included. Of the remainder, 7.1 per cent think that church women are satisfied, either with their present representation or "to let the men do it."

In the Friends Church where women share equally in church work, the women commented that they were satisfied with their status. Among the Methodist Episcopal women, 89 per cent said that at least a minority should be women.

"Close behind are the Southern Methodists—87 per cent," the report states. "The Disciples, Northern Baptists and Congregationalists are close together, as might be expected: 74.4 per cent, 73.1 per cent, and 72 per cent, respectively.

"Of the Presbyterians, 65.1 per cent are convinced that there should be at least a minority of women on the boards of the church; an additional 10 per cent would have women on some but not all of the boards, and 8 per cent would have them serve if there is a real lack of men; while 16.8 per cent consider that it should be left to the men.

Lutheran Women Approve

"Slightly over half of the United Lutherans approve of women on church boards, while 37.5 per cent definitely disapprove. The Episcopalians give the smallest positive vote for the service of women on church boards—45.3 per cent. But an additional 11 per cent would have them eligible to serve if men are really lacking, or would have them regularly members of some, but not all, governing bodies."

An outspoken minority commented that boards of both men and women may be all right in theory, but do not work out well in practice. "Locally, we had peace and harmony when the men attended to business," one wrote, "but trouble began when two women were added to the board."

Comments of those approving the inclusion of women were equally varied. The change was described as "salutary" for church affairs by a Baptist. An Episcopal woman wrote:

"The men welcome the women's assistance as there are certain parish interests which concern the women more than they do the men. The interest of the men has certainly increased since we have had women on the vestry."

Others reported that the admission of women improved the church's finances and that women's assistance was found "very valuable" and "strengthened the program." It is "taxation without representation" when women raise the money that is spent by men without consultation, some complained.

Women are in the majority both in membership and attendance, they raise a larger share of the budget, they have more time to give to church work than the men, they know far more about the missionary work, and frequently local needs as well—these are some of the reasons advanced by those favoring greater representation.

"The present attitude toward women," Miss Cavert said, "often means a real loss to the church, for the different groups frequently work alone with little or no real understanding of each other's special tasks. The theory that 'women will work anyway' apparently does not hold good with the younger women."

November 24, 1940

Woman Named Temple Cantor, Perhaps First in Jewish History

Young Mother of 4 Selected Unanimously by Board of Long Island Congregation

Special to The New York Times.

MASSAPEQUA, L. I., Aug. 2 —A young matron of this commuting village on the south shore of Long Island has been appointed cantor of Temple Avodah, a Reform congregation at Oceanside.

A spokesman for the School of Sacred Music of Hebrew Union College-Jewish Institute of Religion said she might well be the first woman cantor in 5,000 years of Jewish history. A cantor is a ritual singer, not part of a choir, who assists the rabbi with services in a synagogue.

The new cantor, Mrs. Sheldon Robbins, will sing her first service on Sept. 15, the eve of Rosh ha-Shanah, or Jewish New Year, one of the two holiest days of the Hebrew calendar. She was appointed by unanimous vote of the board of trustees of the temple last night.

Mrs. Robbins learned all the principal services by heart long ago. She was born in Greece of Russian parents thirty-one years ago. She received religious education in Danzig, Poland, and was soloist in the choir of the German synagogue in that city for six years.

With her parents, she fled the Hitler invasion of Poland in 1939 and emigrated to Australia, where she continued studying music. In 1943 there, she met and married Mr. Robbins, then with the United States Air Force, and returned with him to the United States in 1944. He is now an inspector for the New York Health Department.

Mrs. Robbins has been leading

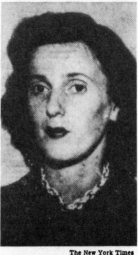

The New York Times

Mrs. Sheldon Robbins

soprano with the fifteen-voice choir of Temple Avodah since it was organized in 1952. The temple has always had male cantors, but when a vacancy occurred recently it took the unusual step of naming a woman. The con-

gregation numbers 200 families.

The spokesman for the School of Sacred Music, founded in 1947 as the first training school for cantors in this country, said today there was no religious law, merely a tradition, against women becoming cantors.

Women always have had a subordinate place in synagogue services. They may not take Bar Mitzvah, the rite of confirmation of boys at the age of 13, and may not participate in men's morning prayers or group services called a minion. In June, the Conference of American Rabbis decided to study for one year the controversial question of ordaining women as rabbis of Reform congregations.

Women have never been considered as possible rabbis or cantors in Orthodox or Conservative temples, where even choirs are not permitted. Reform congregations are self-governing in such matters, Herbert Weisberg, president of Temple Avodah, pointed out.

Mr. and Mrs. Robbins have four children: Jacqueline, 9; Sandra, 6; Stephen, 5; and Judd, 18 months. The family lives at 421 Charles Avenue here. Mrs. Robbins carries on all the duties of a housewife in addition to her singing.

August 3, 1955

Methodists Accept Women in Clergy

By GEORGE DUGAN
Special to The New York Times.

MINNEAPOLIS, May 4— Methodist women won today the right to full clergy privileges in their church.

The Quadrennial General Conference turned down a compromise proposal that would have permitted only unmarried women and widows to serve as full-fledged ministers.

The vote came quickly after a full afternoon of vigorous debate, sparked with friendly and sometimes humorous debate.

According to the best available statistics, there are about fifty women from the laity who have been ordained as preachers in the Methodist Church. They can administer the sacraments and preach in pulpits assigned to them by district superintendents.

They have not had the right to "demand" an assignment from their Bishops, however, as is the right of a fully ordained male clergyman. Nor could they participate in ministerial pension

plans, not being full-fledged members of a Methodist "conference."

For more than a year the Woman's Division of Christian Service of the church's Board of Missions has been conducting an informational campaign on the local level to acquaint women with the issues. The Quadrennial Conference has 2,716 memorials, or resolutions, before it on this one subject. Membership of the woman's division is 2,000,-000.

This afternoon a conference committee on the ministry, which considered the memorials, presented its report. The result: A 40-to-32 division in recommending that full clergy rights be granted only to unmarried women and widows who are ministers.

A minority report urging the church to retain its present policy also was introduced. It was signed by nine members of the full committee of eighty-three.

The committee recommendation was presented by the Rev. Dr. R. Marvin Stuart of Palo Alto, Calif., a subcommittee chairman.

The minority report was introduced by the Rev. Dr. J. Dewey Muir of Jacksonville, Ill.

Women's Rights Emphasized

As debate progressed, it became apparent that neither report was satisfactory to many delegates. Several made it crystal clear that practical or not, women's rights were at stake.

Mrs. Henry Ebner of Atlantic City, a lay preacher, cast her lot with the minority.

"How would you like a woman Bishop?" she asked the delegates.

At this point, a vote on the minority report was called for. A show of hands was so close that a head count was demanded. The minority report was defeated by 425 to 310.

With the minority report out of the way, events moved rapidly.

A substitute for the majority report was moved by the Rev. Dr. Zach T. Johnson of Wilmore, Ky. He recommended that the church's "Book of Discipline," which governs the work and activities of the denomination, be amended by deleting a paragraph limiting pastoral duties of women to "lay" preaching assignments.

The substitute was approved by another head count of 389 to 297. Then, by an overwhelming show of hands, final approval was voted.

Full ministerial rights have been granted to women by two other major religious denominations in this country. Both the Congregational Christian Churches and the Disciples of Christ list women among their ordained ministers.

At its last general assembly, the Presbyterian Church in the U. S. A. voted to accept women as ministers.

May 5, 1956

Rising Voices of Women

St. Paul ordered women to "keep silence in churches." Tertullian in the 2nd century called them "the gate which opened the way to the devil." St. Thomas, whose theology was better than his biology, explained the birth of a female child as a generative mistake.

The result is that women are now strictly second-class citizens in the Roman Catholic Church—as well as in Anglican, Greek Orthodox and the majority of Protestant denominations. They have little voice in the government of the churches and few rights in the most crucial area of all: ordination to the ministry.

A movement has now developed in both Catholic and Protestant circles, however, to re-evaluate woman's role.

The latest development comes this week when Harper and Row will publish a new volume entitled "The Church and the Second Sex." In it one of the few female Catholic theologians, Mary Daly, takes aim at ecclesiastical anti-feminism in general and Canon Law 968, which limits ordination to males, in particular.

Traces Mysogyny

Complaining that the Catholic church talks boldly about the nobility of women, but lags far behind society as a whole in doing anything about it, she argues, "There will be no genuine equality of men and women in the church as long as qualified persons are excluded from any ministry by reason of their sex alone."

Dr. Daly, who holds a theological doctorate from the University of Fribourg and is the first woman theologian to teach at Boston College, traces ecclesiastical misogynism to the inferior status of women in Jewish and Greek society and to the traditional image of God as a stern father figure of judgment.

Exclusion of women from the priesthood was justified on the grounds that the priest is the imitator of Christ, who was male. Furthermore, it was said if Jesus had wanted female priests he would have chosen some female disciples.

Today most theologians reject such reasoning. The prominent Swiss theologian Hans Küng, for instance, believes that there are "no dogmatic or biblical reasons" why women should not be ordained. "It is entirely a matter of cultural circumstances," he said.

Despite changes in modern theology, ordination of women is hardly a serious immediate possibility in the Catholic Church. The New Catholic Encyclopedia, for instance, does not even discuss the matter in its article on women in the church.

Lesser changes, however, are evident. Pope Paul VI began this year to appoint women as members of the Sacred Congregations.

In other religions there are also some glimmers of possible changes. Although Reform Jews in this country have actively discussed the possibility of having female rabbis for more than a decade, actual change is most evident among Protestants.

Modern Movement

Nearly 80 of the more than 250 Protestant denomina- tions in the U.S. now ordain women. The Unitarians and Congregationalists pioneered in the 19th century. The Presbyterian Church in the U.S.A. and the Methodist Church launched the modern movement when they changed their rules in 1956.

The major Protestant non-ordainers of women are the Lutherans and Episcopalians.

The latter became the best-known holdouts in 1955 when the Right Rev. James A. Pike, then Bishop of California, tried to ordain a female deacon, Mrs. Phyllis Edwards. He failed.

Last September, however, the church's General Convention, its highest policy-making body, set machinery in motion to permit women delegates at its next meeting in 1970. In New York women have been permitted to serve on the vestries, or governing boards, of local parishes since 1965.

This summer the Lambeth Conference, the decennial meeting of the worldwide Anglican Communion, is expected to take up the issue of ordaining women. A change could come then.

—EDWARD B. FISKE
March 24, 1968

LUTHERANS VOTE TO ORDAIN WOMEN

Denomination Is 7th Major One in the U.S. to Do So

By GEORGE DUGAN
Special to The New York Times

SAN ANTONIO, Tex., Oct. 24 — The 2.6-million-member American Lutheran Church approved today, 560 to 414, the ordination of women to the ministry. It was the seventh major American denomination to do so.

Exactly one week ago the House of Deputies of the Episcopal Church, meeting in triennial general convention in Houston, narrowly defeated a move to permit the ordination of women to the priesthood and the episcopacy.

The 700 priests and lay persons in the Episcopal house debated the issue for four hours. But there was almost no debate here today when the Lutherans acted on the fourth day of their week-long biennial convention.

Last July, the 3.2-million-member Lutheran Church in America, meeting in Minneapolis, approved by voice vote the ordination of women. Thus, of the three major Lutheran bodies in the United States, only the second largest and the most conservative, the 2.8-million-member Lutheran Church-Missouri Synod, bars women from the pulpit.

Other major Protestant bodies now permitting the ordination of women are the United Presbyterian Church, the United Methodist Church, the United Church of Christ, the Disciples of Christ and the American Baptist Convention.

Influential Statement

Looming large in influencing today's vote was a statement approved by the faculty of the Luther Theological Seminary in St. Paul two years ago. It made these points:

¶The New Testament does not confront the question of ordination of women and therefore does not speak directly to it. On the other hand, nothing in the New Testament speaks decisively against it.

¶Although the ordination of women raises new and difficult questions, there is no decisive theological argument against the ordination of women.

¶The practical objections, however serious, do not by themselves settle the questions for Lutherans. As long as no decisive Biblical or theological objections are raised, the ordination of women remains a possibility.

¶The most serious objection is the ecumenical, that Lutherans ought not unilaterally in in the present divided state of Christendom, make decisions that affect all Christian churches. But, inasmuch as other churches have already ordained women to the ministry, and since some churches that do not ordain women are open to discussion of its possibility, the exact weight of this objection is difficult to assess.

The Lutheran churches of Norway, Denmark, Sweden and Czechoslovakia ordain women. Their decisions were made fairly recently, all within the last 20 years.

But in this country, the Lutheran churches until now had opposed any effort to ordain women.

The Break in the U.S.

The break here came when most of the major Protestant bodies agreed to give women a vote and a voice in policy making.

At its recent meeting in Houston, the Episcopal Church agreed to permit women to serve as fully accredited members of the heretofore all-male House of Deputies and permitted women to be ordained as deacons, but not as priests.

Many observers believe that the future of Lutheran unity is at stake in the decision that was made here today by the nearly 1,000 delegates—equally divided among clergy and laity. The favorable action, it is believed, will move the American Lutheran Church closer to the Lutheran Church in America and away from the Lutheran Church-Missouri Synod.

October 25, 1970

Young Women Challenging Their '2d-Class Status' in Judaism

By ENID NEMY

A small but increasing number of young women, stimulated by the feminist movement, are questioning their rôle, and what they describe as their second-class status, in Conservative and Orthodox Judaism.

"There's a new category of single young Jewish women and Jewish society hasn't thought of ways to cope with this," said Barbara Gingold, a 25-year-old editor of the Jewish Student Press who was brought up in a Conservative household. "It's that business of a nice Jewish girl going to school and getting married . . . some synagogues haven't even thought it out, they have only family memberships."

Individual synagogue membership for single women, still denied in some Conservative and Orthodox congregations, is but one of the objectives of the women, who are committed to seeking change from within, rather than accommodating themselves to the more églitarian Reform branch of Judaism.

"Most of us have had these feelings of being left out but we never conceptualized them," said Deborah Weissman, a graduate of Barnard College now working on her master's degree at New York University. "The women's movement galvanized us."

Miss Weissman, who is Orthodox, belongs to a woman's group studying the Talmud, a legal and literary encyclopedic commentary on the Bible.

'A Wall Built Up'

"Jewish law is not a static thing . . . it's really a process of development . . . rabbis in every generation have reinterpreted things," she said. "The trouble is that recently, as reaction to widespread assimilation, they feel there has to be a wall built up. The majority of the Orthodox community has become very stultified and that's what I'm objecting to."

Earlier this year, a "Call for Change" was issued by Ezrat Nashim, a group of 14 young women of Orthodox and Conservative backgrounds. (Conservative Judaism stands somewhere between Reform and the traditional Orthodox practices.) The women, many of them well versed in the history, tradition and ethics of Judaism, believe that the Jewish tradition regarding women, once far ahead of other cultures, "has now fallen disgracefully behind in failing to come to terms with developments of the past century."

The Ezrat Nashim manifesto, presented to the annual convention of the Rabbinical Assembly in March, asked that women be allowed full participation in religious observances, be permitted and encouraged to attend rabbinical and cantorial schools and perform these functions in synagogues, take part in decision-making bodies and assume leadership roles in synagogues and the community.

Other requests included recognizing women in Jewish law, as witnesses, allowing them to initiate divorce, and counting them in the 'minyan,' the quorum of 10 men required in order to hold a religious service.

'Separate but Equal'

"The social position and self-image of women have changed radically in recent years," the statement read. "It is now universally accepted that women are equal to men in intellectual capacity, leadership ability and spiritual depth . . . to educate women and deny them the opportunity to act from this knowledge is an affront to their intelligence, talents and integrity.

"It is not enough to say that Judaism views women as separate but equal, nor to point to Judaism's past superiority over other cultures in its treatment of women. We've had enough of apologetics."

The declaration received what was termed "significant support" from many of the more than 500 Conservative rabbis at the conference, and from a good number of their wives, according to several of the women who were present.

"When tradition is incompatible with a sense of self, with some of your basic ethics, then you have to go back and examine the tradition," said Paula Hyman, a 25-year-old graduate student at Columbia University who is one of the spokeswomen for the group.

Miss Hyman, who was raised in a Conservative environment and has degrees from both Radcliffe College and the Hebrew College in Boston, considers herself professionally committed to Judaism and to living a Jewish life but said "there is a conflict between the way we are educated and the kind of role we are allowed in the Jewish community."

Although a woman has just been ordained a rabbi in Reform Judaism and another is studying in the Reconstructionist branch (the Reform and Reconstructionist congregations are considered more modern, liberal arms of the religion) there have, as yet, been no women studying for the rabbinate in Conservative and Orthodox seminaries.

However, the Conservative Jewish Theological Seminary would not summarily reject the idea today, according to Dr. Gerson D. Cohen, the chancellor-elect.

"It would have to be a decision of a multiple nature," he said.

"I, for one, would urge serious consideration if a woman applied who was qualified academically, characterologically and religiously, and I would urge the faculty and my colleagues in the Rabbinical Assembly to consider it."

Historically and traditionally, women were not counted, and could not actively participate in religious services of Judaism because they were not obligated to perform certain daily rituals and only those with obligations could take part. Women were freed from obligation because of their duties as homemakers and mothers.

The women who are challenging this concept are doing so on the basis that

women today have the same education and careers as men; that men should play an equal role in child raising, and that the obligations once imposed are ignored by many men.

"As I have a stronger Jewish education than my husband, he would consider it an anomaly for him to participate in services and not me," said Miss Hyman, whose husband, Stanley Rosenbaum, is a "strong supporter of feminism in general."

The minyan is still an all-male quorum in Orthodox synagogues and a matter of the individual rabbi's discretion in Conservative congregations. (One Conservative rabbi is said to have refused to hold services for a congregation of 38 women and seven men because he would not consider women as part of the quorum of 10.)

"The Rabbinical Assembly recently issued a statement that counting women for a minyan was not beyond Conservative perimeter, but we don't have a hierarchy and the commission does not decree that it must be done by all congregations," said Rabbi Judah Nadich of the Park Avenue Synagogue.

Dr. Nadich, who is also president of the Rabbinical Assembly, pointed out that in his synagogue, both men and women participate in what was once considered the male honor of an "Aliyah," being called to the reading of the Torah, the first five books of the Bible.

It was also his personal view, he said, that women should be given the same rights and powers to initiate divorce now inherent in men, and that women should also be able to serve as witnesses in a Jewish court of law.

"It is time to restore the status of women in Judaism at least to the level of women in other cultures today," Dr. Nadich said.

Although women in Conservative congregations sit in the same section as male worshipers, Orthodox congregations separate the sexes by seating women in separate sections.

"Women really have the better seats," said one rabbi.

"That's so the serious business of religion can take place downstairs and women can gossip upstairs," said one young woman bitterly.

Until recently, Orthodox women were members of a synagogue only through their husbands, but in some congregations, such as Kehilath Jeshurun on East 85th Street, women are now recognized as members. A married couple, however, has only one vote, although the vote can be that of the woman. Nor can women run for office.

Haskell Lookstein, the associate rabbi, said he believed in separate but equal status for women and would not be in favor of women presiding as functionaries at services.

"It's against Jewish law and tradition for women to function together with men at a service," said Rabbi Lookstein, who is 40 years old. "I believe in equality of value but not equality of function.

"Judaism places the primary function of a woman as a home function, not a public function . . . to the extent that women become public personalities first, rather than home personalities, the role of women will be changed for the worst. I don't think a woman concerned with her public performance can be the same kind of mother and wife she can be otherwise."

Rabbi Lookstein said he believes, however, that within the next decade women will be more active in Orthodox Jewish life in a corporate sense.

"We will see women trustees and women officers, but I don't think there will be any change in religious functionaries," he said. "I don't see any clamoring for women's rights in ritual and services."

A Rabbi Sees Change

But Dr. Irving Greenberg, a 39-year-old Orthodox rabbi at Riverdale Jewish Center, said he has noted a change in many of the young women of his congregation.

"Five years ago, young women were satisfied with their role," he said. "In the last couple of years, there's been a definite consciousness changing."

He characterized the current feminine challenge of traditional precepts as "significant."

"At one time most people who felt strongly about such things checked out of the religion," he said. "Now we have people who are not leaving but are committed to the orthodox experience and are challenging from within . . . they are ahead of their time, but I think they are the spearhead."

The movement, as small as it might be presently, was important, Dr. Greenberg said, "because they are demanding not only cosmetic changes but fundamental changes . . . I think it has to come . . . when you put women on a pedestal, it may be a form of patronizing and not taking them seriously.

"I hope they want not just equality but equality where that is in order, and uniqueness and distinctiveness where that is in order," he continued. ". . . not to do things like men but the development of a specific women's expression and experience . . . that they are looking for new active feminine religious forms."

A Unique Contribution

Miss Weissman also voiced the hope that women would have a unique contribution to make to religious services.

"During the transitional period, religious services should be opened up in every respect to men and women," she said. "But maybe, after a period, it would be more appropriate for women to create their own forms of religious expression."

Miss Weissman said she believes that much of the opposition to date has been on emotional rather than religious grounds.

"There is a feeling within the Orthodox, that if they bend, they'll break," she said. "I don't share that feeling. What we are calling for is not reform, but opening up of participation to all people, men and women.

"I think what we are doing is for the benefit of the community. Today, so many young people reject tradition . . . so many young women are interested and, if they are rejected, the community is cutting off a source of leadership."

To Mrs. Sandy E. Sasso, a 25-year-old student at the Reconstructionist Rabbinical College in Philadelphia, the time has come to abandon "the dual standard" in Judaism.

"I do not want to judge history negatively, or annul 2,000 years of tradition, but today we have to do something," she said. "Outside society is changing and the role of women is changing and we have to keep up."

June 12, 1972

Where Sisterhood Isn't Powerful

By Dan Herr

CHICAGO—Among American Catholics there may be almost as many theories about the critical state of their church as there are communicants. I say almost because some care so little they may not even be aware their church is in trouble. But for the rest, pious folk as well as scholars, the causes cited for current problems have ranged from the papal encyclical Humanae Vitae to the quality of the hymns being sung at Sunday mass.

I suggest, however, that in the search for reasons, too little attention has been given to the changing role of nuns in the contemporary church. Probably because of the age-old repression of women, most Catholics have not fully appreciated the contribution of nuns in the history of the church. Some pay lip service to "the good nuns" but just as many seem to blame most of their adult problems—from acne to sexual frustration—on the nuns who taught them in parochial schools. The attitude toward nuns by Catholics, male and female, has tended to be patronizing. Even when credit is given for the accomplishments of nuns, it is often begrudging and minimal.

The strength of the Catholic church in America is due more to nuns than any single group, and under "single group" I include the hierarchy, the clergy and the laymen. Catholic church history has never been too popular a subject with American Catholics but when future, non-sexist, historians probe further into the church of the 19th and early 20th century, perhaps long-overdue recognition will be given to the American nuns—their common sense, their hard work, their vision.

To them must be credited the success of the parochial school system, which is undoubtedly the most important factor in the quality—and quantity, too, for that matter—of American Catholicism. Catholic higher education for women resulted from their efforts, as did a still vital chain of hospitals, and institutions of specialized care for the young, the aged, the homeless. Progressive movements in the church, particularly social action, would never have outgrown the theory stage without them.

So what happened? Many American sisters simply got fed up with their second-class citizenship, fed up with a lack of appreciation of their essential role in the life of the American church, fed up with seeing reforms change the superficialities of their lives but not the basic inequalities. In less than a decade, the number of American nuns dropped from 181,000 to 130,000, and the decline has by no means stopped.

Even more disturbing for the future has been the decrease in the number of women entering religious life—in most religious orders only a handful compared to a steady onrush of applications in the 1950's. Many of those who have stayed understandably seem to have lost something of their one-time enthusiasm. Today, the distinction between the nun and the mature single woman in the world is subtle. Some argue that the only major difference is in the realm of security and other material benefits and that the nun's life may even be preferred.

Fortunately, for the future of the Catholic church in America, there is a solution—and as far as I can see, the only solution. There is a way of recapturing the spirit of dedication that built the church in America. There is a way of once more making American nuns the dynamic center of a revitalized church. The way, of course, is ordination of women. (Not that all nuns, anymore than all women, want to be priests—they want to be able to be priests.)

I submit that not until women are given their rightful place in the church will we be able to once again expect from nuns the zeal, the leadership, the inspiration, that proved so fruitful in the past. All other attempts at solving the problems of the American Catholic church are bound to fail unless the basic problem is met. Unless the men who run the church are completely blinded to what is happening or are too warped by their sexist prejudices, ordination of women cannot be long delayed.

Dan Herr is president of The Thomas More Association.
September 2, 1976

Conservative Jews Vote to Allow Women in Minyan

By IRVING SPIEGEL

In a radical break with rabbinical tradition, Conservative Judaism will allow women to be counted in the minyan—the quorum of 10 or more adult Jews required for communal worship.

"The change of status in women is one of the welcome

Every act of sanctification requires not less than ten.
—Talmud Tractate Brakhot 21b

revolutions of our day," remarked Rabbi Judah Nadich, president of the 1,100-member Rabbinical Assembly, the Conservative rabbinical body. "It is time that the status of Jewish women in Jewish religious and legal life should be heightened."

By a vote of 9 to 4, the Committee on Jewish Law and Standards voted a resolution last Wednesday that "men and women are to be equally included in the count of a required quorum for Jewish public worship."

The dissenting minority felt that the tradition of excluding women from a minyan—which derives from rabbinical interpretation of the Talmud — should be maintained. The minority contended, according to Rabbi Seymour Siegel, chairman of the committee, that "most synagogues were not ready for

such an innovation and the institution of the new norm might disrupt the unity of the congregations."

The committee, composed of leaders of the Rabbinical Assembly and the United Synagogue of America, the congregational arm of Conservative Judaism, is the official body of the movement in matters of Jewish law and practice. The two other principal branches of Judaism— the Orthodox and the Reform —are unaffected by the actions of the Conservative body.

Details of the historic action were explained yesterday at the Park Avenue Synagogue, 50 East 87th Street, by Rabbi Nadich, spiritual leader of the congregation, and by Rabbi Siegel, who is professor of theology at the Jewish Theological Seminary of America.

Rabbi Siegel, who led the fight for the resolution, said the "changing role of women in society now makes it advisable, in view of the majority of our committee, to afford equality to women."

The ruling, he explained, is not obligatory or binding on Conservative rabbis throughout the country. He said the rabbi of a congregation was the "mara d'atra" —the final authority—on matters relating to Jewish law, including the minyan.

A Talmudic tractate records that "every act of sanctification requires no less

than ten," he noted, and the tractate did not specify males.

However, he added, the Code of Jewish Law, codified in the 16th century by Rabbi Joseph Karo, interpreted the Talmudic text as applying to 10 males or more.

The Talmud is a repository of views of Jewish scholars and sages on Biblical texts.

According to 2,000-year-old tradition, observed by the Orthodox, women are separated from men in religious worship. A woman may not be counted in the minyan, is not accepted as a witness in Jewish court and may not be granted a divorce without her husband's permission.

Rabbi Siegel said that the ruling followed animated debate over a period "of several years." He said rabbis and women representing the feminist movement with Conservative Judaism had participated in various discussions.

Rabbi Siegel and Rabbi Wolfe Kelman, executive vice president of the Rabbinical Assembly, predicted that the liberalized ruling would be followed by most Conservative rabbis. Rabbi Kelman said that before the ruling "less than 10 per cent of Conservative synagogues were asking women to be members of a minyan."

Rabbi Kelman said that his rabbinical body would conduct "an exhaustive study in the immediate future" to determine how many Conservative congregations would follow the ruling.

In this city, Rabbi Kelman said that about six Conservative synagogues, headed by

the Park Avenue synagogue, have been counting women in a minyan. In 1955, Conservative Judaism's religious law committee ruled that women could be summoned by rabbis for a reading from the Torah. Rabbi Kelman said that 500 Conservative synagogues were now following this practice.

The Park Avenue synagogue began permitting women to be counted in a minyan and also to be summoned to the altar for Torah readings a year and a half ago.

Commenting on Conservative Judaism's ruling, Rabbi Israel Klavan, executive vice president of the Rabbinical Council of America, the leading Orthodox body, said that "Orthodoxy holds that the richness of Judaism's heritage, its tradition, forecloses such drastic changes in religious practice."

Reform Judaism makes no distinction between men and women and even has ordained women as rabbis. The Orthodox adhere to a strict observance of religious laws. Conservative Judaism has tempered its observance of these laws with a tradition of rabbinical reinterpretation and, like Reform, conducts confirmation services for girls who reach the age of 13, the age at which Judaism consider adulthood to have been reached.

Reform Judaism, a radical departure from both Conservative and Orthodoxy, stresses the need for adjustment to contemporary needs.

September 11, 1976

Group of Jewish Women Opposes Masculine Terminology in Liturgy

By GEORGE DUGAN

A task force on equality of women in Reform Judaism began a campaign yesterday to eliminate masculine terminology in Jewish liturgy.

The group's prime ammunition was a mimeographed glossary of substitute words for "Lord," "Father," "King," "Master," "His" and other terms held to be masculine. "God" was regarded as permissible and nonsexist.

For "Lord" the glossary suggested "God," "Almighty," "Blessed One" or "Creator."

"Father" could also become "God," and "King" and "Master" simply "Ruler," it was suggested.

The glossary was prepared by a special liturgy committee of the New York Federation of Reform Synagogues, an arm of the Union of American Hebrew Congregations. The task force met at Hebrew Union College-Jewish Institute of Religion, 40 West 68th Street.

Call to Worship

The call to worship, a prayer said at every Jewish service, reads, "Praise ye the Lord our God, to whom all praise

is due." The women would simply drop "the Lord our."

In the First Commandment, which reads, "Thou shalt love the Lord thy God with all thy heart," the women proposed the deletion of "the Lord."

Edith J. Miller, chairman of the liturgy committee and assistant to the president of the Union, told the group that "we can no longer accept the use of masculine terminology on the basis that it is 'generic' and covers all humankind."

"We want language which utilizes words encompassing male and female, together and as one," she said.

Change From Within

Cecile Fallon, moderator of yesterday's meeting and regional administrator of Catholic Charities' Community Life Center in Patchogue, L.I., described the task force as "made up of well-educated, hardworking female congregants who wish to change things from within, because we want our daughters to remain Jewish."

"They will not work for a community and pray, using a liturgy that systematically excludes them," she said.

Mrs. Fallon, who is Jewish and is married to a Roman Catholic, thanked the college for the use of its facilities and said: "In recognition of the differential in attendance today, the men's room on this floor becomes the women's and the women's room upstairs becomes the men's."

Rabbi Chaim Stern, editor of the Reform movement's yet to be published new High Holy Day Prayerbook, was an invited guest.

In an interview, he said he had "no quarrel with the women in principle," but described his "problem" as one of "practical application."

According to Rabbi Stern, "Lord" and "King" are archaic words with no "reference to reality." He described them as nonmasculine because "here we have no lords, no kings."

September 13, 1976

More Women Entering Ministry But They Still Meet Resistance

BY ELEANOR BLAU

Parishioners more often comment to the Rev. Sue Ellis Mellrose on how well her voice carried rather than on what she said in her sermon.

Clergymen interviewing Marilyn Owen Robb as a candidate for ordination "spent an hour and a half of their hour" discussing her relationship with her estranged husband and never once brought up theology.

A couple told the Rev. Nancy Grissom Self that they simply would not feel "as married" if a woman performed the ceremony.

Although the percentage of women in major Protestant seminaries has leaped from about 3 to 35 in the last decade and hundreds of women have been ordained, women ministers are still viewed as no more than curiosities, it seems, in many churches.

Male Pastors Move On

"There have been a few breakthroughs, with women appointed to significant parishes, but it's an uphill fight," reports Sidney Skirvin, dean of students at Union Seminary, which has achieved a commitment it made four years ago to increase women's enrollment to 50 percent.

For the most part, women who find parish work become assistant pastors or serve at rural churches. The same is true for men just out of seminaries, but they move on more easily to become senior pastors in large cities with higher pay.

Virtually all the major denominations have made commitments to women's equality in the last few years and have set up task forces to try to help realize that goal.

The highly publicized controversy over

Associated Press

Although the number of women in the clergy continues to rise, some still face problems of acceptance.

the ordination of women in the Episcopal Church, now beginning also among Roman Catholics, has helped draw attention to the issue in Protestant churches, most of which now ordain women. Attitudes seem to be changing, but slowly.

Complicating the situation is a generally tight job market. "With the increased enrollment of women in seminaries comes the question 'What are we going to do with them?' observes Bernice Fjellman of the National Council of Churches' commission on women in ministry. "In many cases there is innuendo—the blame for the oversupply seems to be on the women."

the oversupply seems to be on the women."

"As a Presbyterian, I think the situation is bleaker," says the Rev. Barbara Roche, discussing the job outlook for women in her financially pressed denomination.

Miss Roche, who is director of student services at the Pacific School of Religion, where 40 per cent of the 200 seminarians are women, observed that the situation varies according to the denomination, depending on financial conditions, general attitudes and method of hiring.

"It's more sunny for the Methodists—they haven't suffered as much financially and are seriously committed to placing women," said Miss Roche. In that denomination, appointments are made by a bishop rather than by the local parish, where much of the resistance to women ministers rests.

Among Baptists, "the resistance is terrible," Miss Roche reported, and seminary graduates who are Lutherans "are pioneers—it's going to be rough."

Most of the increased seminary enrollments and the denominational studies of women's role in the church have had some impact in the last five or six years.

"The big difference is in women's perception of themselves as professionals," says the Rev. Dr. Barbara Zikmund, who teaches at the Chicago Theological Seminary. "They are openly saying, 'I want to be a pastor. I like to preach.'"

Some continue to seek the roles sought by women seminarians earlier—in counseling, campus ministry and as hospital chaplains, for example—or outside the institutional church in, say, women's centers.

Teaching Jobs Turned Down

But the increasing number of women who want parish work are refusing the once traditional dumping ground for women graduates—as teachers of Christian education. And most people in the field agree that it is only a matter of time — and visibility — before women ministers are generally accepted.

The Rev. Ann Suzedell of Milton, Mass., a United Church of Christ minister, has found that most of the prejudice against women is based on ignorance. "They've never seen a woman in the pulpit or a woman serving communion," she said.

"They can't imagine you in the role. But when they see it works, the resistance quickly fades."

Miss Suzedell, who will soon take a new position in Greenwich, Conn., felt better about job hunting the second time than she did the first.

A woman graduate fresh out of a seminary, she explained, tends to be defensive and angry when interviewers ask irrelevant questions they would not ask of a man. Now, she says, "I tend to be more composed about the basis for some of these questions. The less defensive you are, the more you can try to get to the fear behind the questions they're asking."

Program for Women Seminarians

Defensive replies are one of the problems tackled in Training Women for the Ministry, a two-year-old experimental program for seminarians in the Boston area.

The program, which includes role-playing, is conducted by a three-member teaching team that, among other things, examines the traditional authoritarian image associated with male pastors.

"We try to show that you can also get things done by helping other people make decisions," says Nancy Richardson, one of the teachers. "This is training for a different style of ministry."

As Dr. Zikmund observes, "Instead of falling into the old patriarchal models, a lot of women—perhaps because they haven't seen themselves in positions of authority—are approaching ministry with an openness that is revitalizing. They have no habits, and nobody has any agenda to lay on them."

Other developing programs for women in the ministry include a six-week residential seminar at Grailville, a religious community of women in Loveland, Ohio, and a program at the Harvard Divinity school that seeks to determine where black women ministers might serve.

Black women, a small minority among women seminarians, find particularly strong resistance in black parishes in major churches, although not in independent denominations, according to the Rev. Elenora Giddings Ivory, head of the program, whose grandmother and grandfather were pastors in a Pentacostal church.

If the increased number of women ministers has only begun to have impact on local parishes, it is felt with buoyancy and relief among women still in seminaries and those already ordained.

"There's a great feeling of support," says the Rev. Joan Fersborg, director of admissions and registrar at Yale Divinity School. The United Church of Christ minister, ordained in 1954, remembers when women constituted 10 percent, not 30 percent, of the school's student body. "There were no women on the faculty," she said, "and no place for us to live on campus, and it never occurred to any of us to ask why."

Miss Suzedell, who graduated from Union two years ago, recalls being warned there against the "Queen Bee Syndrome" in which a woman, once she gets to the top of her profession, does not help other women, sometimes even trying to keep them away.

She will be glad when the ranks of women are fuller. "It would be nice to be just ordinary and not holding the torch," she said.

September 11, 1976

Ordination of Women as Priests Authorized by Episcopal Church

House of Deputies Decides to Concur With Resolution Passed by Bishops

By ELEANOR BLAU
Special to The New York Times

MINNEAPOLIS, Sept. 16—The Episcopal Church approved today the ordination of women to be priests and bishops.

The historic step was taken when the House of Deputies, a lay and clerical body, voted to concur with the resolution approved yesterday by the House of Bishops.

That resolution adds to the church canons a stipulation that the ordination requirements apply equally to women and men.

The 2.9-million-member Episcopal Church is the American part of the worldwide Anglican Communion. Several other Anglican bodies have already approved women's ordination in principle or in practice.

In the two previous conventions in which the issue came to a vote, the deputies acted first and defeated it, precluding any vote by the bishops.

A majority of the bishops, however, were known to favor women's ordination

and it was among the deputies that the real battle this time was waged and won.

Both orders approved the measure. In the clerical order the vote by diocese was 60 to 38, with the delegations from 16 other dioceses equally divided. The lay vote was 64 to 37, with 12 dioceses divided.

When the vote is by orders—with lay and clergy votes recorded separately—an even split in votes within a diocese is counted as entirely negative.

The Rev. Alison Cheek, one of the 15 women "irregularly" ordained to the priesthood, said, "I am very happy for my sister deacons." Asked what was the next step, Mrs. Cheek said, "I think that now sexism in the church goes underground a little and that we will need to support very much our sisters who live in dioceses where their bishops will not ordain them."

Mrs. Cheek said she thought the action "frees up" bishops of the 15 to recognize their priesthood, but did not know

if this would happen. The Rev. Carter Heyward, another of the 15, commented, "This has not been an event here; it has been part of a process that has been going on for decades."

It was not clear what would be the reaction of all those opposed to women's ordination. Some have made a point in recent days of saying they would remain in the church no matter what happened.

After the vote, the Rev. Kenneth E. Trueman of the Milwaukee Diocese rose to say he could not in conscience support the deputies' action nor did he recognize the authority of the convention to rule on the matter. He would, however, remain loyal to the church, he stressed. The move parallels a statement made in the House of Bishops yesterday and signed by 37 members of that house.

However, Canon Albert J. duBois, a spokesman for an umbrella group that he said represented 400,000 Episcopalians, said yesterday that his people would find themselves "separated" from the church if it approved the resolution that was voted tonight. It would be the church, not its critics, who would be "voting themselves into schism," he said.

Obviously in a mood to get the issue settled one way or another, the deputies turned down by substantial majorities efforts to postpone consideration of the resolution or to amend it.

One amendment would have stipulated that the resolution would not affect the final authority of a diocesan bishop or his policy-making standing committee.

This would have reflected Presiding Bishop John M. Allin's compromise suggestion that women be ordained in areas that would accept them.

The other would have permitted women's ordination by changing the church constitution. Since such a change requires approval by two successive conventions, this would have delayed the matter until 1979.

Although none of the deputies rose to further amend the resolution, scores rose when it was announced that debate would begin.

"If there are any left in their seats, they may be excused," quipped the Rev. John B. Coburn, outgoing president of the house.

The two-hour debate, in which speakers were limited to two minutes each, repeated arguments that have been heard many times in recent years.

Women's ordination is a "moral issue, the issue of liberation," declared Canon Allan Wentt, a black delegate from Columbus, Ohio. It would certainly be "ironic," if blacks joined forces with those who would keep women "spiritually and emotionally enslaved," Canon Wentt said.

A repeated argument of speakers opposed to women's ordination was that Christ appointed only men to be his apostles. Others pointed out that, as Mrs. Nancy Moody, a delegate from Marion, Ind., put it, "Our Lord was male and so also must be those who stand in his place at the altar."

Replying to this argument, another woman delegate said, "Of course Jesus did not appoint women to be his apostles. At that time and at that place it would not have made sense. Women had no status in church or society. They could not have been effective teachers or preachers."

Before the vote was taken, the committee that had recommended the resolution appealed for reconciliation whatever the outcome. Delegates then stood in silent prayer for five minutes at the committee's request.

September 17, 1976

USE OF THE MEDIA

CHURCHES' BILLBOARD PLEAS

Stirring Up New Rochelle Worshippers in Novel Ways.

New Rochelle, Larchmont, and the Pelhams are aroused over their churchgoing campaign. Yesterday at nineteen Protestant and four Catholic Churches counts were made of attendance, and also of the numbers of men. Red and blue signs on billboards and housetops urging church attendance stare at one from many angles. Oddly, yesterday, in the churches themselves the preachers, as far as heard, refrained from mentioning the campaign in their sermons. The campaign, they said, is for outside. Once in, the sermons contain the Gospel in the usual form.

Several weeks ago the Rev. W. W. T. Duncan, pastor of St. John's Methodist Church, New Rochelle, went to the Rev. Dr. Charles F. Canedy, rector of Trinity Episcopal Church, as the oldest New Rochelle minister resident, and asked what he thought of a churchgoing campaign for Lent. The Trinity man said he thought well of it. So the campaign was formed. Nineteen Protestant churches went in—six Episcopal, three Methodist, three Baptist, three Lutheran, one African, and four Presbyteran. The Blessed Sacrament and St. Gabriel's Roman Catholic Churches are not formally joined, but are known to be sympathetic, or at any rate to be working on the same lines.

The campaign is to end at Easter, and counts are being made of numbers attending. Invitations, signed by representatives of all the churches, have been sent out by the thousands.

The campaign has an Executive Committee, consisting of the Rev. R. G. McGregor, Presbyterian, Chairman; the Rev. B. T. Marshall, Presbyterian; the Rev. Dr. C. F. Canedy, Episcopal, and the Rev. W. Wofford T. Duncan, Methodist. At the close of the campaign a full report is to be made. So far as could be discovered by visits to most of the churches yesterday conditions were much as they have been.

March 11, 1912

WOULD USE MOVIES TO FILL THEIR PEWS

The New York Conference of the Methodist Episcopal Church gave its approval yesterday to several essentially modern methods of drawing people to church. Among them were:

Holding moving-picture performances in the churches or the church buildings.
Utilizing brass bands or orchestras to draw the general public.
Conducting gymnasiums in connection with the churches, to interest young people.

It was at the first annual "church efficiency" conference of the New York Conference, held yesterday at Grace Methodist Episcopal Church, in West 104th Street, that these methods were described. The Rev. Dr. Christian F. Reisner, the pastor of Grace Church, was the prime mover in calling the conference together, and the clergymen present were called on for definitions of the term "church efficiency." Dr. Reisner described it as "delivering the goods."

Among the speakers at the day's sessions was the Rev. C. C. Marshall, the pastor of the Metropolitan Temple, in Fourteenth Street, where moving pictures have been a feature for some time. Replying to the critics of this new method of attracting a congregation, he said:

"I remember when an organ was brought into a little country church for the first time a lot of people criticised that 'innovation' adversely. They said the devil had been brought into the church with the organ, and I've read that the same thing was said in olden days when a printed Bible was used for the first time. As for the 'innovation' of the movies, I see no reason why a congregation should not be instructed in the Bible by sight as well as by hearing."

His experience has proved, went on Mr. Marshall, that the old methods did not get as good results as showing religious pictures and then preaching on them. Moreover, he believed in presenting moving pictures for sheer recreation. If it was said that the pictures were shown "merely to draw a crowd," surely a clergyman had a better chance to teach when his church was crowded than when its pews were empty.

The clergymen yesterday had a movie show of their own at the evening session of their conference. "The Birth of a Nation" was presented in full in the auditorium of the church, accompanied by an orchestra.

October 13, 1915

Griffith to Advise Church on Films.

It was learned yesterday that D. W. Griffith, the motion picture producer, is to become the advisor of the Methodist Church in its plan to spread its religious and moral teachings by use of the screen. Mr. Griffith, who arrived in New York from Hollywood, Cal., on Friday, expects to go to the Centenary Celebration and meeting of the Methodist Church to be held in Columbus, Ohio, beginning June 20, where he will confer with the church's committee in charge of motion picture activities.

The producer's immediate business in New York is the presentation of his latest photoplay, "Broken Blossoms," which opens at the George M. Cohan Theatre on Tuesday evening.

May 11, 1919

PRESS AGENTS OF CHURCHES

Expert Organizers of Publicity Are Now Employed by Both Catholics and Protestants

"SWEET are the uses of publicity." Thus, with apologies to Shakespeare might the Catholic Church which has followed in the footsteps of the Protestant denominations and every other sort of denomination, religious and otherwise, explain its entrance into the lists of newspaper space fillers.

Never before has there been such an influx of press agents into newspaper offices. They come with all sorts of material, representing all sorts of organizations and munitioned with all sorts of stories. The type of press agent usually varies with the organization he or she represents. The society woman's charity bazaar representative may be a débutante who is anxious to show her friends that she can do other things besides go to dinner parties and dance, or she may be the society woman herself calling in state and speaking with authority. The organization for the Upkeep of Songless Canaries has a different type of press agent. He may be a man filled with an irrepressible yearning to let the world know what it is losing by not lending its ear to the distress of these poor victims of chance. The more serious organizations like the Food Relief and Flood Relief and Flu Relief groups employ specialists in their publicity campaigns. Not a few of these specialists are brisk, business-like, square-heeled young women. They breeze into the offices, leave behind them reams of typewritten material out of which a conscientious editor lifts a may lift a paragraph or two and disappear—only to breeze in again the day after with a "new angle." There are hundreds of this type busily coming and going among the newspaper offices.

Nurtured by the War.

Essentially the species, if not a war product, is one which the war has mightily increased. Liberty Loans had to be advertised throughout the country. Publicity did that. Five times, at short intervals, the newspapers of the nation stepped into line and "put across" to the man at the breakfast table, at his office, in the factory, in the mines, in every phase of commerce and industry, in fact, the need of digging down deep into his pocket and "coming across." It worked. Beautifully and efficiently. The man behind the campaign had a genius for organization. Not only did he have a staff of press agents working immediately under him in a central office, but he decentralized the system so that every type of industry in the country had its own special group of publicity workers. In this manner, more than in any other, were the heads and directors of movements of every type introduced to and made cognizant of the value of concentrating on publicity so-called "drives." The observing were not slow in applying this knowledge to other fields. Various relief organizations sprang up as a direct result of conditions brought on by the war. The salary of a competent press agent was the first item of expense considered. The greater the acquaintance of the press agent among the editors of the papers the higher he came. Naturally so. The man or woman who was known and liked in a newspaper office quite logically stood more chance of putting over his idea than the individual who was comparatively unknown. In the first place, he knew how to get in and who to go to—

in the second he had a better chance of being listened to.

Along with the relief organizations press agents came those who represented patriotic societies. These, too, had their legitimate pleas for space. These, too, had a message to deliver to the public at large. In very many cases they succeeded.

It was not long before the churches began to consider the question of hiring press agents. With every group of individuals interested in getting at the public funds or public sympathy, employing a person who knew the ropes, the churches without press agents were at a serious disadvantage in competitive propaganda. The churches fell into line.

Perhaps the Protestant churches got started first. The Y. M. C. A. and the Y. W. C. A. had for a long time maintained a publicity staff. Theirs, to be sure, was not essentially a church program, but an educational one. Nevertheless, they formed the nucleus for the spread of the idea of organized church publicity.

Expert Publicity.

The term publicity is used in the broadest sense of the term. The churches have always maintained a staff of workers who let their own congregations know what was happening in the denominations as a whole. The Methodists knew for instance how many missionaries their church had sent to Siam. But the Baptist or the Episcopalian did not know about the Methodists' work in Siam. The business and the duty of the special press agent was to spread to the world at large the knowledge which had been confined to those especially concerned. Naturally they worked through the medium through which the world at large gained most of its information, that is, the newspapers. If the press agent was efficient the trick could be done. In any number of cases it has been done.

A short time ago the different denominations of the Protestant Church in an effort to co-ordinate their activities organized themselves into a body called the Inter-Church World Movement. One of their first steps was the employment of a large well-paid publicity staff whose business it was to keep the editors of the papers in the country informed on matters important to them —the Church.

There is an interesting sidelight on this work. Several months ago they decided to stage a Biblical pageant in Madison Square Garden. Heretofore the Church had made no appeal to the readers of the dramatic sections of the paper. As a matter of fact, it was not unknown that some of the denominations were very much averse to the staging of the spectacle, religious as it professed to be. Whether or not the regular staff did not feel capable of handling this special job, or whether they felt it was without their sphere is not known. At any rate, they hired two experienced theatrical press agents in New York to do their work. The senior member of the staff has had several productions on Broadway, had been associated with a particularly well advertised and picturesque stage personality and certainly was not generally suspected of churchly leanings. The junior member is a young woman who by her tact and ability had made herself what is so essential toward success in this business, a welcome visitor in editorial offices. She does not spend her Sundays in church. As a matter of fact, the Sabbath of her ancestors is held sacred on Saturdays.

The Goal of Success.

But—and here is the point of the whole matter—the people in charge of the pageant wanted to make a success of it, monetarily as well as popularly; they thought the best way to do it was to conduct an efficient publicity campaign, and they were quite ready to confess that it was a job for experts.

When the five weeks' run of the pageant had been completed the scrap book of the play showed that they had managed to corrall over five hundred columns of newspaper space. That much was pasted on the leaves of the book. It was impossible to give an accurate estimate of the amount of space actually given them, because a good deal of the material had been syndicated over the country and had not been turned in by the clipping bureaus. Few avenues of approach, to the mind of the editor, had been neglected. Every possible phase of the question, from the labor to the dramatic, had been exploited. The whole campaign was conducted on a dignified, efficient basis that grew out of years of experience in press work. The Inter-Church World Movement was satisfied with the results.

Perhaps the greatest factor in the publicity service for the Catholic Church in this country is the organization known as the Knights of Columbus. They are quite frank in admitting that "the biggest and most practical human lesson learned from the war is that nothing requiring organized effort can succeed without publicity, and plenty of it." The author of these words is John B. Kennedy, the head of the publicity staff of the Knights of Columbus in this city. "Without the aid of the press," he goes on to say in an article written on this subject, "the war relief agencies would have been helpless because fundless."

Mr. Kennedy is fully appreciative of that when he speaks about the birth of the Catholic press work.

K. of C. Publicity.

"Joseph C. Pelletier of Boston, Supreme Advocate of the Knights of Columbus," he says, "had the inspiration for a nation-wide press bureau—the first of its kind under Catholic auspices. This was in the Summer of 1918, when the war was at its height. The Knights of Columbus War News Service was formed, and the operations of this bureau have demonstrated two things—that the editors of the country were glad to receive authentic information from a Catholic source (a fact which thousands of well-informed Catholics had doubted), and that this information could be disseminated by the most approved modern methods at a cost singularly small when compared with the costs of operation of other organizations.

"That word—'organization'—is the answer to the question of why the Church and its various subsidiaries met with success in their undertakings.

"There are about 13,000 parishes in the Catholic dioceses of this country, and each parish is now being made a radiating point for Catholic activity, Catholic publicity.

"Last week in Washington the Catholic press of the country held its annual convention. Seventy Catholic editors, representing a combined circulation of approximately five million readers, considered the program of activity their papers and magazines will push during the coming year. It is a program which comprises the entire public work of the Catholic Church—education, social welfare and propaganda.

"The aim of the Church is simply to make the maximum contribution in its power to the national welfare, and a part of this contribution is the clear and authentic pronouncement of Catholic principles.

"The Church realizes that it is not sufficient to preach from Catholic pulpits.

"There are minor reasons why Catholic press work should be done. News supposedly emanating from the Vatican and other exclusively Catholic sources is often garbled or totally incorrect and misleading. Catholic publicity will rec-

285

tify such errors, and the editors of the country will be for it; they want news, and truth is an indispensable component of real news.

" That is why the Catholic Church has taken up the trumpet, why she will speak through the press, not for her own glorification—otherwise she would long ago have formed her publicity organization—but for the propagation and application of American ideas.

" In some quarters it has been rumored that a great Catholic daily newspaper would be established; but this is hardly probable. The press of the country has a place for everything that is news—and the Church will always be an active source of news."

This is the brief set forth for the organization of a Catholic publicity bureau by one of its members. The same statements modified to suit its own peculiar conditions may doubtless be applied to every other organization employing a press bureau.

From the point of view of efficiency of the organization, it is worth while. From the point of view of the validity of news, it may be less valuable. It is no secret that a reporter on being sent out to cover an assignment is apt to turn for the information first to the press agent who is in charge of that specific matter. It is no secret, either, that the expression of the press agent who is paid to get the activities of the movement to which he belongs into print may be biased and highly colored. A considerable proportion of the news in our papers at the present time con-

sists of printed material which has either been sent out or brought around by a member of the species, which is today legion.

Some of the material they offer is good and can hold its own with the best that comes through the regular channels of newspaper work. Some of it is simply bad and finds its level in the waste-basket. Some of it has to be sifted to find the grain of wheat in the chaff. Some of it has to be scrutinized with a trained, selective eye and have its poison of pure propaganda neutralized.

But it is eloquent testimony to the real place of the publicity expert that his specialty finds the " praise agent " as indispensable as does the theatrical manager or the street railway corporation.

February 1, 1920

SKY SIGN TO MARK BROADWAY CHURCH

Union Methodists Hope 25-Foot Sparkler Will Outshine Gum, Cabaret and Movie Ads.

WILL SHOW GREAT CLOCK

Brilliant Cross to Surmount Stars and Stripes and Congregation's Flag.

The biggest electric church sign in the United States is being made for the Union Methodist Episcopal Church, Forty-eighth Street just west of Broadway. It will aim to outshine all the advertisements of plays, movies, cabarets, gums, prohibition and other joys. It will be twenty-five feet high, and will cost $5,000.

The big sign will stand eight feet out from the church building, so it can be seen from both sides. Dr. Benson has had the exterior of the church thoroughly cleaned, and has placed boxes of flowers in the windows.

At the top of the sign will be a brilliant cross, of white nitrogen lamps, six feet tall and four feet wide. Under the cross will be an American flag with the red, white and blue in lamps, and under the Stars and Stripes will be placed the Church flag, white field with a blue square with a red cross in one corner.

Under the Church flag in immense letters in transport lights will be the legend: " Union Church and Social Centre. Always Open."

Beneath the cross will be a great clock that will ring a chime at each half hour. The clock will be lighted from the inside and it will be the only big public clock in that vicinity.

The sign will be visible from Fifth to Eleventh Avenue and far up and down Seventh Avenue and Broadway. The cross will be level with the roof of the church.

Union Church is not an imposing structure, but the idea is to make it, not in architecture but in its service to the city, a Cathedral for Methodism. However, there will be no Methodist propaganda, the denomination not even appearing on the sign. The Rev. Dr. John G. Benson, the new pastor, is on duty from 11 o'clock in the morning to 11 o'clock at night every day.

The Methodist Board of Home Missions has purchased for the church the two apartment houses adjoining it and is converting them into a transient home for girls, to accommodate sixty-five. It is to be for girls who are stranded in New York. The property cost $88,000.

Miss Grace Ferry of St. Paul, Minn., will arrive today to take charge of the home and all the welfare work for young women. She was a teacher but gave much of her time to social service in St. Paul. She is being brought here by the Centenary Conservation Committee of the Methodist Church.

Dr. Benson has built dormitories at the back of his church to house twenty boys, and already he has six living there. He will build two more stories on that side of the church and arrange dormitory room for one hundred more boys and young men.

Dr. Benson has made a " survey " of his neighborhood. Ten thousand persons were visited. The pastor thinks it is the most fertile field in the city, although most of his parishioners will be transients. He had already organized " absentee membership " by persons in all parts of the country who promise to visit the church and its homes when in this city.

Bishop Luther B. Wilson will dedicate the sign and open the home for girls on Oct. J. The temporary home for boys will be opened Sept. 1.

August 27, 1920

RADIO TO BROADCAST SERVICES IN CHURCH

Washington Installation Will Make Sermon and Music Audible Over a 200-Mile Radius.

Special to The New York Times.

WASHINGTON, Dec. 31.—Marking an advance in the utilization of scientific devices by the church of today, the Church of the Covenant, one of the leading Presbyterian churches of Washington, of which the Rev. Dr. Charles Wood is pastor, will tomorrow broadcast over a radius of about 200 miles around Washington, the morning, afternoon and evening services of the church.

At the afternoon service Senator Borah of Idaho will deliver an address on "Disarmament?—and the Conference." In the evening a chorus choir of 150 voices, sustained by an octette of soloists, will sing. This, together with the organ music and congregational singing, in addition to Dr. Wood's sermon, will be made distinctly audible to the great audience of "listeners-in" within the radius of sound extending over the District of Columbia and into Virginia, West Virginia and Maryland.

The installation of the "wireless service" at the Church of the Covenant was made under the auspices of the Christian Endeavor Alumni Association of the District of Columbia.

January 1, 1922

ADVERTISE CHURCHES BEST IN NEWSPAPERS

Chicago Federation Tells Its Members How to Get the Most Effective Publicity.

Special to The New York Times.

CHICAGO, Jan. 1.—Suggestions on church publicity in news articles and in paid advertising in the newspapers are given in the findings of the committtee representing the Chicago Church Federation as the result of the National Publicity Conference held here on Oct. 31, which was attended by more than 400 ministers and laymen from eleven States. The findings are in manuscript, but will soon be published. Some extracts follow:

" The most effective way to reach the crowd and interest them in the church is through the daily newspaper in cities of 650,000 and over.

" The newspaper welcomes news, but is shy on propaganda.

" The newspaper is more interested in what you do than in what you say, especially if you do something to help another person or the community as a whole.

" It pays to serve the newspaper even at one's inconvenience. One minister said he postponed a funeral and a wedding to furnish an interview requested by his daily paper.

" Get on good terms with the newspaper by occasionally furnishing news which does not especially concern you or your particular church.

" You can create news. Preach on matters current in the press. The Salvation Army painted flowers on beer mugs, which proved popular and were pictured in the press.

" Get the facts in correct detail to the newspaper office and trust the editor to give it the right form.

" It pays in dollars to advertise. One metropolitan church increased its loose collections to $22,000 in two years, certain other smaller churches showing a proportionate increase.

" Advertising lifts the standard of preaching and service in order to make good and come up to advertising.

" Magazines spend large sums in taking advertisements in the daily newspapers. It pays or they would not do it.

" Advertising must be consecutive, persistent, prepared for, distinctive. If a minister does not know how to advertise let him learn how or let him get the help of an advertising man.

" Don't expect the newspaper to take the trouble which belongs to you.

" Write or, better, typewrite your news, giving proper initials and locations. Omit eloquence and exhortations, and, above all, be on time."

January 2, 1923

RISE OF RADIO CREATES NEW CHURCH PROBLEM

Some Ministers Fear Broadcasting of Church Services Will Decrease Attendance—Most Observers Think Radio "Sells" Religion

EVERY churchgoer with a radio set has a practical choice to make when Sunday comes around. "Shall I put on my best clothes and go to church or shall I keep my slippers on and attend service in my easy chair?"

Now that a considerable section of every congregation in the country has a radio set, the question of the effect on the Church commands the attention of religious leaders all over the country. That the effect of radio on religion will be profound is deemed certain, but just what the effect will ultimately be is still a matter of conjecture.

For the Catholic Church the question has no immediate importance because Church discipline compels physical attendance at mass. But for the Protestant denominations it has become an outstanding issue. Some ministers have met it one way, others in another, some have not yet met it at all.

There has been, naturally, considerable apprehension among Protestant leaders about the radio. If the congregations of the future can get a sermon, music—in fact, all the audible part of the whole religious service—simply by turning a button in their own homes, will they make the physical exertion of going to church any more? That small oval, perched on a pulpit like a darkened reading lamp, which has brought hundreds of thousands of listeners into the range of the speaker's voice, might reduce church ritual to a mere talking into an intrument in a church full of empty pews, or even talking into a radio disk among the upholsterings of some broadcasting studio. Furthermore, what effect might radio have on the rural chapel if all the facilities of the powerful metropolitan church were thus placed at the easy disposal of people in the outlying parish?

The more progressive elements in New York's Protestant churches have taken the bull by the horns, and during the past year or so have incorporated radio into their program of action. This same decision has been made in other cities throughout the country, of course, but it is in New York and vicinity that the outstanding experiment has been made.

Two Broadcasting Methods.

In New York two distinct methods have been employed—one, that of broadcasting sermons directly from churches during the regular Sunday morning service; the other, broadcasting an auxiliary religious program, held specially in a broadcasting studio, or in a Y. M. C. A., in the afternoon, so as not to conflict with the Sunday morning services. This distinction is worth bearing in mind, for it reflects a difference of opinion on the subject of radio even among those who favor its use. The services sent out through WJZ belong largely to the former type; those through WEAF, to the second. Despite the difference in technique, both methods represent a positive effort to make use of radio as an instrument to further religion.

An inquiry into the results of this use of the radio has brought to light interesting facts and opinions from persons who are in close touch with the situation. Two questions were asked:

First, How has the radio affected interest in religion?

Second, How has radio reacted on church attendance?

The response to the first question has

been affirmative. In the words of those interviewed, the radio has "sold" religion to the community on a broader scale than ever before.

The radio has sold religion by bringing it to hundreds of thousands who otherwise would not have been reached at all. Upon this, all the clergymen agreed. It has forced religion upon the attention of many who never go to church—both those who could not and those who would not. In the latter case, it has been largely a matter of the line of least resistance. The broadcasting stations have cooperated fully with the churches to avoid any competitory feature at the time. Fans who tuned up on Sunday morning and afternoon had to get religion, if they got anything.

Morris Chair Services.

In this latter case it has sometimes made a revolutionary change in the immediate background of the theme. As Heywood Broun expressed it once, it was the "first time in his life that he had been able to go to church, smoke a cigarette while listening to the sermon, and throw in an occasional cussword when the minister said something he didn't like." This is certainly different from the old conventional setting for religion; but many of the clergy don't seem particularly worried. They prefer to have people listen to sermons, even flavored with tobacco smoke, than not at all. In fact, it was an Episcopalian rector, a representative of a Church supposed to be the acme of traditionalism, that mentioned this incident as an example of the advantages of radio.

"The radio has shown itself to be a beneficial factor in religious life," said the Rev. William B. Millar, Secretary of the New York Federation of Churches. As the central organization of Protestant Christian Churches in New York, the federation has had charge of the broadcasting of religious programs from station WEAF since the feature was introduced a year ago. "There has been a marked increase in interest in religion recently. True, there have been contributing causes, such as the Modernist-Fundamentalist controversy. But radio undoubtedly had a large share.

"The function of radio, as I see it, is to supplement the churches, to get to an element in society which they cannot reach. It has possibilities within the church, of course; our radio 'normal school' course for Sunday school teachers illustrates this point. But its chief value, I believe, is to bring religion to people who either can not or will not attend church."

He reached into his desk. "Here are dozens of letters from people whose religious life has been brightened by the radio. The most appealing is the story of the 'shut-ins,' that large body of invalids, cripples and aged. The radio has brought comfort to the sick bed, the invalid's chair and the dreary retreat of the infirm. Here is one letter from a man who had been paralyzed for five years. He is just recovering use of his left arm. He encloses $5 to help defray expenses of the work. All this, of course, is primarily humanitarian.

Conversion by Radio.

"But we have reason to believe that radio is helping to spread religion." He produced letters telling of people who had been "brought to church" by the radio.

"I even know of one conversion by radio. A man in Brooklyn listened in one afternoon. We happened to sing his favorite hymn. He was converted on the spot. The psychology of such occurrences is interesting. It is a matter of emotional shock. That song over the radio brought back a flood of strong emotional associations, the impact of which aroused him and changed his life. I know of a number of instances where the radio has revived an interest in religion which had slumbered for years.

"The letters commenting on our services at WEAF have brought out an-

other interesting trend in the popular attitude toward religion. They show a marked swing away from controversial themes and back toward the gospel. The people are wearying of debates over theological issues. Our speakers are intrusted to keep off these fields."

Asked what he meant by "the gospel," he replied, "the teachings of Christ."

The question arose of the "satisfactoriness" of radio sermonizing from the personal viewpoint of the preacher.

"It affects different men differently," he explained. "I have seen eminent speakers, men accustomed to large metropolitan audiences, grow confused at the sight of the broadcasting disk. I recall one distinguished preacher who had all he could do to get through with his sermon, even though he read it. He said the nervous strain was worse than a year of ordinary sermons. Some become panicky when they see that oval and know they've got to keep going in front of it. All, however, complain of the absence of the stimulating effects of a visible audience. There is nothing to inspire you in a studio.

"It obliges a speaker to be pithy, however. Our first instruction to our sermonizers is to be pointed."

For this reason E. H. Felix of Station WEAF believes that the radio spells the deathknell of long-winded sermons, that it will improve religion as a "sales product."

Sermons Must Be Short.

"Judging from results thus far," he said, "the radio will force preachers to speed up their sermons. Unless a speaker can get right into his subject and keep it interesting he cannot expect to hold a radio audience. The tenure over these invisible hearers is fragile. In church the disgruntled hearer has to face the moral disapproval of the congregation and his own sense of shame if he leaves before time. At the radio set all he has to do is turn a button and he is free. Once gone he seldom returns. Long sermons are taboo over the radio."

A radio studio "church service" in itself is an interesting sight to the uninitiated. Every Sunday afternoon the choir of the Federation of Churches comes to the broadcasting rooms of station WEAF. The outer compartment might be the reception room of a club—oil paintings on the wall, several bronze statuettes, soft chairs and sofas, a writing table, all in the glow of subdued indirect light-bowls against the ceiling.

The only hint of the purpose of the room is a large perforated area at one corner from which may issue voices, or music. This is connected with the broadcasting studios. The studios themselves adjoin—cozy, quiet, like a small music room in a well equipped private home.

You have a peculiar mixture of sensations as you enter. You feel the intimacy of it all, yet you cannot escape that consciousness of man's mastery over the elements which it involves.

The first hour is devoted to familiar hymns. Then the preacher begins. He may stand facing a disk on a pedestal level with his mouth, or he may sit at the library table and talk into an apparatus which at first glance would be mistaken for a small library reading lamp.

Broadcasting from a church has much less of the unusual. The writer inspected the pulpit at the West End Presbyterian Church. A small pedestal, with the disk, is placed immediately in front of the pulpit. A casual visitor would hardly notice it.

Station WJZ has broadcast Sunday morning services alternately from three large New York churches: St. Thomas's Episcopal Church on Fifth Avenue, the West End Presbyterian Church at 105th Street and Amsterdam Avenue and the Grace Methodist Episcopal Church.

"Religious broadcasting has become an established feature of our station," S. H. Hawkins of WJZ said. "We do not intend to give it up."

What, however, has been the effect of all this on attendance in the churches?

Experience for the past year indicates that in New York broadcasting has had no appreciable effect upon church attendance. So far as the churches in this city are concerned—both those which broadcast their services and those which do not—the fears of those who anticipate an emptying of pews have not materialized.

Reports from the staff of two large metropolitan churches in which Station WJZ has placed radio dials, as well as scattering reports from the others, fail to reveal either a marked diminution or increase in attendance. If a few of the more indolent parishioners remained at home in their armchairs on Sunday mornings, their places were taken by others who became interested in the preacher through the radio. In New York the radio has worked both ways and the pull in each direction has been about equal.

In the outlying districts, however, there is evidence to show that there has been a tendency toward a dwindling of congregations. In the absence of any other outstanding cause during the past twelve months, this has been laid, by some, to the radio.

Rev. Wilbur Caswell, associate to the rector of St. Thomas's, said that clergymen complain the radio is stealing some of their hearers; that their congregations is more inclined to remain at home and listen to one of the leading pulpit orators in New York than to make the physical exertion of going to church in their own district, where, at best, they could hear a service of inferior quality compared with that of the big metropolitan cathedral.

One country church has this dilemma in a unique manner. According to Dr. Caswell, a little Episcopal chapel in Maryland actually rigged up a radio horn in its pulpit one Sunday morning, got in tune with the cathedral in Washington and the congregation sat in silence while the services of the great church came to them through the instrument. When the preacher in Washington announced a hymn, the congregation got out its hymn books and sang, too.

The incident suggests the question, Is this a forecast of the rural church of tomorrow? Will the devotional feature of religious activities become centralized in a large metropolitan centre, with the country parishes becoming only provinces of "ministration," presided over by pastors whose sole duty will be that of making pastoral calls and officiating at marriages?

City and Country Competition.

Precisely to what extent the radio has already reacted upon the country churches is impossible, of course, to measure this early. But it is possible to say that if the present drift continues the smaller chapels are likely to be confronted with a situation which may cause them some embarrassment. Either they must devise some method of effectively competing with the metropolitan institutions or they may have to yield to them in this one department of religious activities.

As a sect, the Jews have not gone in for broadcasting on any regular basis. Individual rabbis have, however, spoken on religious subjects several times from the studios of Station WJZ.

One Easter service was broadcasted from St. Patrick's Cathedral and Station WJZ always picks up the Christmas chimes service. A priest at St. Patrick's ventured the opinion that the Catholic Church might be able to use the radio to broadcast services of an educational nature, primarily designed for non-Catholics. But he did not see how the radio could be of value to the Church in its regular mass.

"The Catholic Church requires of its parishioners actual physical attendance at mass every Sunday, and at masses on five or six feast days during the year," he explained. "Attendance over the radio would not answer."

He was careful to add, however, that the Catholic Church does not oppose the radio, which it regards as a great scientific achievement.

NEWS STYLE URGED FOR 'LIVE' SERMONS

Dr. Coffin Tells Clergymen Picturesqueness Will Save Them From Being Boresome.

NOISE IN PULPIT DECRIED

Oxford Minister Stresses "Healing Spirit of Silence" and Pleads for Unity of Worship.

Sunday sermons can be made more interesting by studying the style of the newspapers, the Rev. Dr. Henry Sloane Coffin told clergymen yesterday at the annual conference of ministers on church work at the Union Theological Seminary. He urged ministers to devote more attention to the use of symbolism and picturesqueness in their sermons, citing many examples of "symbolic flavor" in the Bible.

"The clergymen can learn a great deal from the press in making their sermons picturesque, concrete and interesting," Dr. Coffin declared. "If the style of the newspapers were adopted, there would be many less boring sermons preached. A paper like THE NEW YORK TIMES, for example, lends flavor and interest to its news through the use of pictures and concreteness."

Some religions are of little value to the world, he continued, pointing to Mohammedanism as acting as a deterrent to human progress. A true religion, he added, supplied a means to life and power to live.

Protestant Christianity had been unable to adjust itself to current life, the Rev. Dr. Joseph R. Sizoo of Washington, D. C., told the clergymen. He added that "the cynicism which has drenched the modern world has crippled nothing so severely as religion."

"The Christian religion is suffering today from a discipleship which has lost faith in its enterprise," he continued. "We sing very loudly and lustily the hymns of conquests, but often it is only whistling to keep up our courage. The Christian religion is the religion of love, and yet it is love that the world needs today."

The Rev. Frank R. Barry, Vicar of the University Church of St. Mary the Virgin, Oxford, England, declared that symbolism, rather than definition or logic, was the best medium to convey religion through the Christian church. He asserted that public worship must be considered as a conscious art.

"Too often the mental gymnastics we demand from our congregation leaves them completely baffled," he continued. "The whole service should be made a complete unit of worship. Worship should be treated as the culmination of all the arts, for if public worship goes, the whole Christian line caves in.

"The mystical intuitions of the people are being starved and inhibited too often in our preaching. We tolerate too much noise. Many clergymen take the attitude that a moment not filled with sound is a moment wasted. But in this busy age there is nothing that the people need more than the healing spirit of silence."

Paul S. Leinbach of Philadelphia, editor of The Reformed Messenger, was elected chairman of the committee on resolutions by the delegates. Others on the committee include Roy Gilmour Pavy, Westfield, Mass., Congregationalist; George S. Duncan, Washington, D. C., Presbyterian; William J. Ducker, Elloree, S. C., Lutheran; William J. Doherty, London, Ont., Anglican; C. Everard Deems, New Brunswick, N. J., Baptist, and Charles I. Stephenson, Rushville, Ind., Disciples of Christ.

June 27, 1931

RADIO AND TELEVISION

Bishop Fulton J. Sheen Preaches Absorbing Sermons in 'Life Is Worth Living' Series

By JACK GOULD

A remarkably absorbing half hour of television, successfully refuting many of the preconceived notions of what constitutes model programming, is being presented by the Most Rev. Fulton J. Sheen, Auxiliary Bishop of the Archdiocese of New York, at 8 o'clock Tuesday evenings over the DuMont Network and WABD.

Bishop Sheen appears in front of the cameras for the full thirty minutes and, in effect, delivers what could be construed as a straight sermon, which heretofore has been regarded as one of the traditional "don'ts" of broadcasting.

Yet such is the forcefulness of Bishop Sheen's personality and the persuasiveness of his words and philosophy that a viewer, regardless of his individual faith, finds himself not only paying attention but doing some serious thinking as well.

The Bishop's program, which is entitled "Life Is Worth Living," is presented from the stage of the Adelphi Theatre. The clergyman speaks from a setting of a study especially designed for the program by Jo Mielziner of the Broadway theatre. Attired in the vestments of his office, the Bishop is on his feet throughout the program and eschews the use of either a prepared manuscript or notes.

To avoid a static quality that might come from unrelieved preaching, Bishop Sheen employs a blackboard to illustrate his thesis of the evening and he moves about the study at frequent intervals. But it is the substance rather than the form that makes "Life Is Worth Living" a unique presentation. Bishop Sheen not only has something to say but he has the gift for saying it well.

While Bishop Sheen's point of view reflects the doctrines of the Roman Catholic Church, he is not using television for proselytizing or sectarian ends. A member of the Protestant or Jewish faiths can draw strength and inspiration from his words just as easily as a Catholic.

As he explains on the air, the purpose of Bishop Sheen's talks is not complicated: it is merely to induce the television viewer sitting at home to have a love of God. His appeal is to reason, not emotion. This week he drew on the work of scientists, including their development of the atomic bomb, to underscore that today's world is not a product of chance but of a master plan.

In likening the scientists to "proof readers of nature," Bishop Sheen emphasized that atomic fission of itself was nothing new; it always has existed in the sun. The construction of the infinitesimal atom, he noted, was comparable to the construction of the solar system. This similarity between the smallest and largest things known to man, he contended, was evidence of God's work.

In his television sermon, however, Bishop Sheen by no means is always of a serious mien. He quips about his television "opposition" on Tuesday evenings, which is the Milton Berle show; he tells amusing stories on himself and he is not averse to an outright joke. Admittedly, his humor at times may be a trifle self-conscious and occasionally he succumbs to an overly theatrical touch, but this does not detract from a viewer's larger reward, which is a stimulating association with an alert and perceptive mind.

"Life Is Worth Living" is produced by the Rev. Edwin B. Broderick, director of television and radio for the New York Archdiocese, who has some refreshing views of his own on the subject of television. Only this week he stressed that Catholics should not create the impression that their sole function is monitoring programs with a view to criticizing bad taste. An equal responsibility is to applaud the good programs and urge constructive use of the medium. With "Life Is Worth Living" Father Broderick is practicing what he is preaching.

February 22, 1952

VIDEO DEPARTURE

Bishop Sheen's Program To Be Sponsored

By JACK GOULD

LAST week's announcement that Bishop Fulton J. Sheen's television program will be presented this season under commercial sponsorship represents a new departure in broadcasting. It will be the first program of a dominantly religious character to be financed by an advertiser who intends to use a portion of the time on the air for direct selling of his product.

Under the arrangements approved by Bishop Sheen, the Admiral Corporation, a manufacturer of television sets, will pay approximately $1,000,000 to sponsor the program on a coast-to-coast network for a period of twenty-six weeks. The program, entitled "Life Is Worth Living," is scheduled to resume over the DuMont facilities at 8 P. M. Tuesday, Nov. 18.

The figure of $1,000,000 includes a donation that will be made to Mission Humanity, Inc., of which Bishop Sheen is national director. Mission Humanity is a member of the voluntary agencies of the United Nations and distributes funds to hospitals, leprosaria, dispensaries, homes for the aged and orphanages, without regard to race, creed or color.

In addition, Bishop Sheen will donate his personal fee to Mission Humanity, which last year aided more than 50,000,000 persons in nearly every country throughout the world.

Problems

According to a spokesman for the DuMont network, there will be two commercial announcements on the program, one at the opening and one at the close. The initial announcement will be institutional in character. The second, according to the spokesman, will be "a typical, hard-selling commercial" running for about a minute and a half.

The decision of a prelate of a major faith to accept commercial sponsorship on television focuses renewed attention on the problems of religious broadcasting that long have been in the making. They are problems that have their roots perhaps in economic and practical considerations, but none the less lead to results that can only be regarded as disturbing.

The truth is that while religion is one of the mainstreams of American life it is not so treated by radio and TV. As a general rule the religious program is shunted about in marginal time periods. The good time is simply sold out to sponsors and the religious group must be satisfied with what is left.

In addition, the only realistic way that a religious program—and for that matter most other forms of public service programming—can achieve an audience of outstanding size is to obtain a sponsor. That way the affiliated stations of networks will agree to carry the program; otherwise they are inclined to pass it up. To say of any sustaining or noncommercial program that it is carried "by a network" may be highly misleading; actually, it may be carried by only a handful of stations.

Advantages

Under his contract with the Admiral Corporation, Bishop Sheen undoubtedly is going to have the largest regular audience of any prelate in history. That an immense portion of the population should be exposed to an inspirational message is certainly a goal of which religious leaders of all faiths can approve.

Coincidentally, there is another practical advantage. With taxes what they are today, all charitable organizations have difficulty in raising funds. Through commercial sponsorship of Bishop Sheen's program, Mission Humanity, Inc., will have a new source of income for its fine work.

But there are other values which must enter into a consideration of sponsored religious broadcasting. In this column's opinion, which admittedly may be only a minority and personal viewpoint, the strange and unique economics of television must not become an excuse for altering basic precepts that were valid long before there was any TV and will be valid long afterward.

The modern world is so fraught with materialistic considerations that, perhaps more than ever before, the clergyman represents a world apart from mundane economics. In the sight of Bishop Sheen on television, quietly, humanly and interestingly asserting eternal truths, there was conveyed to a viewer some of the solace and repose that comes from entering a house of worship.

Oasis

Indeed, "Life Is Worth Living" was a half-hour oasis that afforded a pause and a moment for individual contemplation free from all the desperately urgent salesmanship so common to TV. It was an invitation to the spiritual plane that allowed a personal reexamination of one's heart and mind. That experience is not something to be made to serve as a cue for a "typical, hard-selling commercial."

But the question goes even deeper. The cause of an ever-widening spiritual understanding will not be most nobly served if it is necessary for the churches to adopt the techniques of the marketplace in order to make themselves heard.

Stimulation of the national faith is not a task to be burdened by matters of contracts, options and sponsors. Let the philosophy of the popularity rating take hold in the field of religion and the possibilities for abuse are truly awesome.

Broadcasting must not put the cart before the horse in religious broadcasting. It is not for the churches to adapt themselves to the habits of television; it is television which must adapt itself to the needs of the churches.

If all faiths are to be equally and fairly served, the religious broadcast must be removed from the realm of commercial sponsorship. Individual stations must recognize that it is not a nuisance but a privilege to help strenghen the country's spiritual fiber.

The true significance of the decision to sponsor Bishop Sheen is the sad fact that many men of goodwill should have felt that it was necessary. It never should have been. He and the leaders of other faiths should be seen and heard from coast to coast as a matter of course.

October 26, 1952

RADIO, TV, FILMS PREACH TO MASSES

Director of National Council Agency Says 'Millions' of Nonchurchgoers Listen

By GEORGE DUGAN
Special to The New York Times.

CINCINNATI, Feb. 5—The Protestant churches are preaching the gospel to "millions" of non-churchgoers each day of the year by modern techniques of mass communication.

This is a conservative estimate of the influence of a comparatively new form of religious ministry, that of radio, television and the motion picture.

It was made here today by the Rev. Dr. S. Franklin Mack of New York. He is executive director of the Broadcasting and Film Commission of the National Council of the Churches of Christ in the U. S. A.

The council represents thirty Protestant and Eastern Orthodox denominations in the country. Its Division of Christian Education is holding a week-long annual convention here.

On March 1, according to Dr. Mack, the Broadcasting and Film Commission will be asked to approve a 1955 budget of $1,400,000, third largest of all arms of the council. Only the Division of Christian Education and Church World Service, relief agency of the council, have larger budgets.

Famous Preachers Heard

The top radio stars of the national council include the Rev. Dr. Norman Vincent Peale of the Marble Collegiate Church in New York, and the Rev. Dr. Ralph W. Sockman, minister of Christ Church, Methodist, also in New York.

The Peale program appears on 100 stations over the National Broadcasting Company network. Dr. Sockman's voice is heard from 118 stations on the same network.

The Rev. Dr. John Sutherland Bonnell of the Fifth Avenue Presbyterian Church in New York is on fifty-eight stations of the American Broadcasting Company.

Both N. B. C. and the Columbia Broadcasting Company are programming a growing number of television shows on religion or some aspect of it. The national council's top TV show is a dramatized series of thirty-minute films on Christian living, entitled "This Is the Life." It is telecast over 235 stations.

All the network shows of the national council are on a sustaining basis. The council also supervises the production of many radio transcriptions, spot announcements and films for church use.

It operates radio workshops and television institutes and maintains a consultation service for local churches, ministerial associations, and individuals.

Mail Response Stressed

According to Dr. Mack, "it can be said with confidence that any pastor appearing once on a local television station can be assured of an initial audience in excess of the aggregate audience in the pews of his church in a year's time."

"Most of these listeners will be people who would never hear him otherwise," Dr. Mack said. "Half or more would be people who do not habitually attend any church or synagogue."

He added that the mail response indicated that at practically any hour of the day or night there were people listening to radio and watching television who were "in the market" for what the church has to offer.

In the area of broadcasting and films, the council actually has two agencies at work. One is the commission, with headquarters in New York and Hollywood. The other, devoted largely to planning educational audio-visual materials for such uses, is the Department of Audio-Visual and Radio Education with headquarters in Chicago.

The newest council venture in TV programming is a series of "person - to - person" appearances of outstanding Christian spokesmen, Dr. Mack said. This will be started Oct. 1.

February 6, 1955

Color TV Commercials to Promote Religion

Protestant Council Stresses Theme of 'God Is Alive'

The National Council of Churches will sponsor a series of six color television spot announcements in Columbus, Ohio, to attract more churchgoers.

The campaign, the first of its kind for a religious organization, has as its official slogan: "Keep in circulation the rumor that God is alive." It will begin next month.

The spots will be made available to councils of churches in all of the major sections, including New York. Local stations will donate time for the announcements on a sustaining, or public service basis and use them throughout the day, including prime-time periods.

The spots are done in a low-pressure, entertaining style with more emphasis on getting viewers to "think about God" than on supporting a particular denomination. Each appears in 20- and 60-second versions.

Officials of the Roman Catholic Diocese of Columbus, after viewing the spots last week, announced that they would help publicize them as an "ecumenical gesture."

Three of the spots deal explicitly with the campaign's official slogan. In one, the nine words "crawl" up over the screen in brightly-colored letters torn from magazines. In another the viewer watches an antique bottle wash up on a beach with the words inscribed on a note inside. One spot opens with several pairs of elderly women's hands busily at work on a quilt. There are then shots of the six women's faces—among them a Chinese, a Negro and an Italian, all gay and intent on an unknown project.

The viewer's curiosity about what is going on is satisfied only at the end when the nine words are discovered sewn into the quilt.

The spots were developed by the Division of the Radio and Television of the United Presbyterian Church in the U. S. A. at a cost of $41,000, including distribution expenses. They were

In one of the items in the TV series, women are shown lettering the theme onto a quilt

produced by Miss Nancy Carter, a staff member of the division, and by Dennis Wheeler, an independent film maker and graphic designer.

Bouncy and upbeat musical effects were created for the announcements by Fred Karlin, a free-lance composer and conductor.

A Brief Tag Line

In one spot, for instance, two boys — one white, the other Negro—are shown meeting in Washington Square Park, playing, fighting, then making up. To follow this rapidly changing still-photograph sequence musically Mr. Karlin employed a ukulele, bass guitar, toy piano, bongoes and a bouncing rubber ball.

That the message also has religious significance is suggested only by the brief identification of the National Council of Churches at the end.

The Rev. William F. Fore, executive director of the N.C.C. Broadcasting and Film Commission, said that the cost of spot was "quite low" compared with that of their commercial counterparts.

Mr. Wheeler, a Roman Catholic, said that the spot announcement would seek to "stimulate the viewer to think about where he stands with God." He explained that he had

tried to do this by means of color, suspense and graphic symbols that might take on "personal significance for each viewer."

An announcer is heard on only two of the six spots. One of these shows a young girl chasing an elusive butterfly. Throughout the chase the form of a butterfly can be seen on the screen, and the announcer suggests that some things—like the love of God—"may be right there all the time."

The series of television spots was created after the success of a similar series of radio "commercials" done for the Presbyterian church by the comedian Stan Freberg two years ago. Market research indicated that listeners showed unusually high recall of the message content.

Mr. Freberg, who also is a writer and advertising man, produced three one-minute disks that resulted in discussion over church use of advertising. There were some complaints that the spots impaired the dignity of the church, but other observers said they made people aware that a life without God was distorted.

The Rev. Dr. Richard R. Gilbert, executive director of the Presbyterian agency that produced both the radio and television spots, defended them

against the criticism that nothing theologically significant can be said in 20 seconds or a minute.

"Most of Jesus' parables were about 30 seconds long and said one thing," he commented. "We're also borrowing the simile technique used in these short parables: God is like this or like that."

Dr. Gilbert said that although the "alive" campaign was decided upon before the recent interest in the so-called "death of God" theologies, the theme was inspired by the same question raised by the new theologians: How present is God in human life and affairs? The "God is dead" theologians maintain that God is no longer part of human experience and that Christianity cannot now afford the luxury of reference to a divine being.

Dr. Gilbert said there were good historical precedents for the use of modern mass media by the church. When St. Paul preached in the market squares of Rome at the crossroads of the ancient world, Dr. Gilbert explained, he was coming as close as he could to the same techniques.

The stations that will carry the spots in Columbus beginning Feb. 21 are WBNS-TV, WLW-C and WTVN-TV

January 23, 1966

REDEFINED VALUES IN RELIGION URGED

Interfaith Meeting Stresses Social Issues' Relevance

By EDWARD B. FISKE
Special to The New York Times

BUCK HILL FALLS, Pa., Jan. 19—Leaders of an interfaith organization dedicated to "selling" religion through mass media discovered this week that their knowledge of marketing had to some extent outdistanced their understanding of the product.

The organization is Religion in American Life, which is supported by 33 Protestant, Jewish, Roman Catholic and Orthodox groups.

Its purpose is to stress the values of religion for individuals and society by means of advertising and printed promotional materials. The current campaign theme, "God's work must truly be our own," is a familiar sight on billboards and subway cards and in television and newspaper advertising.

This week the organization, which was founded in 1949 and has an annual budget of $200,-000, held its second two-day consultation here on "the relevance of religion in American life."

About 60 representatives of the sponsoring groups, which include most major Protestant denominations, agreed that Americans were receptive to religious ideas if they were expressed in specific and pragmatic terms.

Next year's campaign will thus emphasize the application of religion to such problems as world tensions, racial injustice, anxiety, divorce and addiction to drugs and alcohol.

There was also general agreement, however, that words such as "faith" and "religion" and even "God" had lost much of their meaning today and that religious groups must make serious efforts to redefine the spiritual values that they hope will be applied to these social issues.

Participants in the conference noted that religion in American life campaigns since 1949 have closely reflected developments in American religious thinking.

The first slogan was "Find yourself through faith. Come to church this week." During the so-called "religion boom" of the nineteen-fifties its advertisements emphasized the themes of church attendance and how faith can solve problems for individuals and families.

In recent years, however, the advertisements have begun to deal with themes such as race relations, and the emphasis has shifted somewhat from what faith can do for the individual to how the worshiper can use his faith to serve others.

In a paper for the conference the Rev. Dr. Martin E. Marty, a church historian, described the change as a movement away from the goal of producing "warm bodies for the movement."

While endorsing the policy of relating religion to specific issues, however, many delegates frankly questioned whether the religious institutions to which they belonged were capable of meeting this challenge.

Some, for instance, suggested that the effort to make religion "relevant" could cause it to lose its distinctiveness. "Let's not become so secular that we forget that there is another realm," said the Rev. Walter D. Wagoner of the United Church of Christ.

January 22, 1967

Vatican Bids Church Use Media and Curb Secrecy

By EDWARD B. FISKE

The United States Catholic Conference made public yesterday a set of Vatican guidelines calling for more effective use of the mass media by church spokesmen and a minimum of secrecy in the conduct of church affairs.

The 20,000-word document, which was prepared at the request of the Second Vatican Council of 1962 to 1965, quotes Pope Pius XII in describing the media as "gifts of God" and says that failure to use them to convey the church's message amounts to "burying the talent given by God."

It says secrecy should be restricted to "matters that involve the good name of individuals or that touch upon the rights of people whether singly or collectively."

'Rumor Is Unloosed'

"When ecclesiastical authorities are unwilling to give information or are unable to do so," it declared, "then rumor is unloosed, and rumor is not a bearer of the truth but carries dangerous half-truths."

The document was accompanied by a 1,500-word commentary by the Most Rev. John L. May, Bishop of Mobile, chairman of the conference's communications committee.

Bishop May hailed the Vatican document as "an expression of the church's coming of age, at least conceptually, in regard to the world of modern communications."

He endorsed the idea that secrecy, while sometimes necessary, should be "strictly limited" and added:

"Without at all imputing motives, one must acknowledge that secrecy is a matter on which churchmen have sometimes exhibited an excessive and ill-advised caution, which in particular cases may have done more harm than good."

Openness an Issue

Lack of openness in the management of church affairs has been an issue in the American Roman Catholic Church. Various lay and clergy groups have objected to the fact that the bishops hold their semi-annual meetings behind closed doors and that statements of church finances are not generally available.

The document released yesterday was entitled the Pastoral Instruction for the Application of the Decree of the Second Vatican Ecumenical Council on the Means of Social Communication. It has been under preparation for six years by an internal commission appointed by Pope Paul VI.

The instruction puts modern communications media in a theological context by asserting that they are one means by which men can assert "creative power" given to them by God.

It condemns state control or censorship of information media and asserts that "freedom of speech for individuals and groups must be permitted so long as the common good and public morality be not endangered."

Right Held Limited

It adds, however, that the right to information is "not limitless" and must be reconciled with other rights such as that of "privacy which protects the private life of families and individuals." It also warns that "the reporting of violence and brutality demands a special care and tact."

The new instruction says that comparable principles apply within the church and that "individual Catholics have the right to all the information they need to play their active role in the life of the church."

"The normal flow of life and the smooth functioning of government within the church require a steady two-way flow of information between the ecclesiastical authorities at all levels and the faithful as individuals and as organized groups," it states.

"On those occasions when the affairs of the church require secrecy, the rules normal in civil affairs equally apply. On the other hand, the spiritual riches which are an essential attribute of the church demand that the news she gives out of her intentions as well as or her works be distinguished by integrity, truth and openness."

In other sections, the document emphasizes that advertising must "respect the truth" and not "affront human dignity or harm the community" and opposes monopolies in the dissemination of public information.

It also urges assistance for developing countries in establishing communication centers.

June 3, 1971

Varieties of Religious Spokesmen Seeking More Out of TV Shows

By C. GERALD FRASER

It is an index to the atmosphere in religious television programming that many who have a hand in the making say that the ideal program would not mention God, synagogues, churches or temples. It would not preach, shout or deliver sermons. The ideal program, they say, would be nonreligious in appearance and project an ethical, moral, social, humanistic and subliminal religious message.

Religious programing on television is both near and far from that ideal. It includes spot announcements, hour-long specials, sermons, sermonettes after midnight, sign-on prayers before dawn, cartoons, interviews, evangelists, Sunday school classes, Bible classes and documentaries. But in spite of this range and variety, practically no one is really happy about the situation.

Various religious spokesmen believe that more could be done. They would like to see religion and religious topics integrated into the regular programming day, and not kept primarily for Sunday morning.

They would like to see the stations assign reporters to cover the religious beat just as a reporter, say covers the consumer beat. They would like, in short to see religion treated like an ordinary subject rather than a special one.

What happens is that the networks give the "major faiths" free time and absolve themselves of their "public service" commitments. Local stations both give and sell religious time. Their religious programs are produced under the aegis of the news and public affairs departments.

The law does not require television stations to broadcast religious programs. If they do not do so, however, the Federal Communications Commission takes what one of its spokesmen called a "hard look" at that station's capacity to meet license requirements—requirements that call for some kind of public service programing.

Broadcasters, networks and local station owners are wary of religious programing because they prefer to avoid dealing with both religious sects and cults, who may want free time and, on the other hand, groups of atheists who may question the propagation of any religion on the public airwaves.

"The media world is full of paradoxes," the Rev. William B. Gray has written, "but consider this one: television's best, in some cases its only, religious programing arrives on Sunday morning. And where is the audience most likely to understand and respond to these offerings? Attending church services, of course.

"Television, the clergy sometimes feel," he continued, "gives low-response periods to religion simply to keep license challenges and complaints from the devout to a minimum. Adding to the problem is the general apathy in the land toward religion. This translates into a small pool of potential viewers. Though surveys show that a high percentage of the public says it believes in God, all polls point to a declining interest in organized religion."

Mr. Gray is director of the office of communications for Trinity Church Parish here.

On Sunday morning in New York, most channels pile up their religious programs, presenting most of their regular offerings, from dawn with a wake-up sermonette or sign-on prayer through noon or early afternoon.

WCBS-TV runs three half-hour programs back to back from 9:30 A.M., starting with "The Way to Go" and then the network's two long-standing prize-winners: "Lamp Unto My Feet" and "Look Up and Live."

WNBC-TV presents from 8:30 to 9:30 A.M. the "Maryknoll World," "TV Sunday School," "The Jewish Scene" and at noon, "First Estate: Religion in Review."

WNEW-TV's two regular religious programs are at 6:30 A.M., a half-hour gospel program with the Rev. Cleophus Robinson, who wears the big rings, and then the hour-long "Wonder Window." a sort of progressive Sunday school.

WABC-TV offers three straight hours including programs sponsored by the Lutherans, Seventh Day Adventists and Roman Catholics from 7:30 to 10:30 A.M. The ABC network's half-hour religious program, "Directions," comes on at 1 P.M. 39 weeks a year.

The largest number of Sunday religious programs are on WOR-TV. The variety of cartoons, evangelists, Sunday masses and interviews runs from 7:30 A.M. to 1 P.M.

The program of the Christo-phers, a Catholic adult education organization, "Davey and Goliath" — a children's animated cartoon feature — and Oral Roberts, all on WOR-TV, are also on WPIX-TV Sunday mornings.

WPIX-TV also presents three half-hour shows at 9 A.M. Mondays, Wednesdays and Fridays. Each program is devoted to Jewish, Catholic or Protestant affairs. Two shows after midnight, Calvary Baptist Church's "Encounter" and the Paulist Fathers' "Insight" are also broadcast each week.

Church and Society

The network programs, said the Rev. William McClurken of the Broadcast and Film Commission, are "a far cry from a lot of religious programing you can see on local stations. Theirs is much more preachy. The type of stuff we do is much more informational and discusses where the church is today and what the needs of society are.

"We'd just as soon that people not be aware that it's a religious program. We have more of a concern to reach a larger audience, many of whom are on the periphery of the church.

"We don't feel you have to shout religion from the rooftops."

According to the Broadcast Institute of North America, during 1972-73, there were 178 syndicated religious programs provided by 63 sponsoring producers. The 178 included religious series, 5-minute to 15-minute segments, spot announcements, dramas and documentaries and specials usually linked to religious holidays.

Dr. Ben Armstrong, executive secretary of the National Religious Broadcasters, said in a telephone interview that there were two basic types of religious programs: the public service program and the evangelical programs.

"Public service," he said, "tends to be more general in outlook, tends to be ecumenical, easy going, without too much bite in it or incisive content. They don't ask for people to make a decision for Christ, don't ask for money . . . they tend to relate to problems such as race, poverty, ecology and that kind of thing.

"The second type is in its ascendancy in New York, the evangelical programing," he said. In this category he placed the "main line denominations which have large evangelical segments within their framework." These include the United Methodist Church, and the Lutheran Church in America.

There are also, he continued, organizations outside the framework of the organized church. He cited the Billy Graham organization as one example. But these groups, tend to cooperate with church groups.

Independent Groups

Operating independently are groups such as Dr. Rex Humbard's Cathedral of Tomorrow, which is seen over 200 to 300 stations a week, he said.

The final category are those in opposition to organized churches of which, he said, Dr. Carl McIntyre is an example. Dr. Armstrong said these groups tended to be ultra-conservative.

Most syndicators also tend to do one specific type of program. Howard Coleman of the Lutheran Church in America's Commission on Press, Radio and Television, said his church produced the animated cartoon "Davey and Goliath" for syndication as a sustaining program. It is a 15-minute show for children from 10 to 12 years old. "Each show is complete, and there's a small point that's made," said Mr. Coleman.

He estimated that the Lutheran Church had spent $1.7-million on the show in its 13 years and now has an audience of about 1.7 million viewers. The Lutherans are now experimenting with a one-minute spot announcement. If it is successful, he said, they will expand that.

There is one religious broadcasting network, the Christian Broadcasting Network, based in Portsmouth, Va. It calls itself nonprofit and interdenominational. The president and founder is the Rev. Dr. M. G. (Pat) Robertson. Dr. Robertston's network has 16 television station affiliates and owns and operates three UHF channels—one each in Portsmouth, Atlanta and Dallas.

The Christian network's owned and operated stations sell commercial time. They carry religious programs on about half of their on-the-air hours, and they carry them on prime time between 8 and 11 P.M.

Eldon Wyant, the programing coordinator, said the network sought to use radio and television to broadcast gospel —the salvation method of Jesus. "We are," he said, "within the new charismatic renewal movement."

September 23, 1974

CHAPTER 3

Toleration and Intolerance

Comparative religion students from Stephen Wise Free Synagogue attend a demonstration of the mass at St. Paul the Apostle Roman Catholic School in New York City.

Manning/NYT Pictures

A NOTE OF WARNING.

It is well to have a candid foreigner assume now and then the friendly office of pointing out the perils that lie in our way as a nation, and pry gently into the weak places of our armor, just to show that we are not invulnerable. We are apt in our complacency and confidence to overlook or to underrate dangers that appear quite formidable to the distant looker-on, or it may be that our insidious enemy is so entangled with us in relations of friendly alliance that we have not the moral independence to grapple with him. In the December number of the *North American Review*, just issued, we find in the opening pages a somewhat startling contribution by Mr. JAMES ANTHONY FROUDE on "Romanism and the Irish Race in the United States." It is more startling, however, in the suggestions which the title raises than in its actual substance. It is to be followed by at least one more article on the subject, and we may hereafter be treated to a sensation of genuine alarm; but so far we find it impossible to be scared by any prospect that is set before us.

Mr. FROUDE assumes, rather than states, that the Irish race and the Roman Catholic religion are making such strides in this country as seriously to threaten the integrity of our free institutions. Some things which he does state as a basis for disquieting inferences are undeniably true. We have now something like six millions of Irish citizens, all acquired in the last thirty years or so. Owing to their faithful devotion to the Roman Catholic authority and the vigilant care of the Church to keep them in a state of obedience, they have failed to fuse into the mass of citizenship. They stand as distinctly defined in the body politic as though they were separated from the rest of the nation within actual territorial limits. It is equally true that the Romish Church, whose authority over them is stronger than that of any secular authority, is hostile to free institutions. Of this there can be no question,

for the Church makes no secret of her pretensions, and they are in terms contradictory to the principles of freedom on which our national fabric rests. The ultramontane doctrine which now prevails through all the vast hierarchy of Rome, is that the Pope should have supreme authority in the domain of conscience. To that the action of nations as well as of men should be submissive. Allegiance to no earthly Government can come athwart the obligation to submit to GOD's vicegerent. The subjection of the national power to the head of the Church is a principle never abandoned. Essential to our republican institutions is freedom of worship and belief, liberty of discussion, and the independence of the individual in all that pertains to his personal interests and claims. All these the Romish Church denies and never fails to suppress where it has the power.

While this is true, are we really in danger from Romanism and the multiplication of the race in our population which is its obedient instrument? The Irish constitute less than one-seventh of our population even now, and Mr. FROUDE himself says that, from various causes, "the immigration from Ireland has almost ceased." Increase of population from foreign sources certainly has not ceased. Germans come to us in greater numbers than the Irish, and are scarcely less prolific. They are in little danger of being used to promote the designs of Rome upon the institutions of freedom. We are drawing sturdy elements from Great Britain and Scandinavia, and the small number of immigrants from the Southern Catholic countries add little or nothing to the organized power of Romanism. The bulk of our increase in population, which goes on with a steady pace, is now non-Irish and non-Catholic, and it is not easy to see how it can result in increase of peril in that direction. The English writer's remarks about the tendency toward conversion from Protestantism to Romanism, on account of the unsettling of

faith and a lack of unity and positive authority among the opponents of the latter, are far more applicable in his own country than in this. There is little indication here of the disposition of unhappy and perturbed souls to seek repose in the bosom of Rome.

But we are reminded that our own principles make us powerless to contend against an organized and aggressive minority. We believe in liberty, and must allow it, even when used against the very life of free institutions; while the enemy we have to deal with does not believe in it and is under no such restraint. We cannot resort to repressive measures, and the divided and demoralized forces of Protestantism have not the faith and the zeal to pursue the conflict in the arena of sentiment and opinion. Just here is where the alarmist argument will fail. The fact is that American sentiment and opinion will persist in regarding the contest as purely political and not religious. The people may not agree in any well-defined religious belief, or accept the guidance of any single religious authority, but they have an abiding faith in political liberty and the authority of the National Constitution and Government. They may not resist Catholic encroachment because of a burning zeal for Protestantism, but they will defend the stronghold of their liberties, which has cost them so much. Mr. FROUDE speaks of the Irish vote turning the scale among political parties, but the fact is that one party enjoys pretty much all the accession of strength that it can give already, but does not use it for the promotion of the designs which there is supposed to be so much reason to dread. The moment it attempted to do so, it would find itself in a hopeless minority. What we have to fear from the Irish vote is rather the mismanagement and corruption in cities that comes from the control of the ignorant and vicious by unscrupulous demagogues for their own purposes, than the supremacy over the nation or the people of "the woman of the seven hills."

November 21, 1879

THE UNPOPULARITY OF JEWS.

Prof. Adler Tells of Some of the Causes and Offers a Remedy.

Prof. Felix Adler, President of the Ethical Culture Society of the City of New-York, spoke before the Russian-American Hebrew Association at the Hebrew Institute, East Broadway and Jefferson Street, last evening. The large hall was entirely filled, and Prof. Adler commanded close attention from his listeners throughout his address.

Prof. Adler first spoke upon the anti-Semitic movement in Germany, stating its causes, and later upon the anti-Semitic tendency in this country, its causes, and its remedies.

"The name 'Anti-Semitic movement,'" he said, "was given instead of 'Anti-Jewish movement' as an especial stigma upon the race, to indicate that through all the ages the race of the Jews remained unchanged, and that there could be no assimilation of the Jews with the Aryan and other races. This purity of descent was the

boast of the Jews and the reproach of their enemies.

"But, in fact, the assertion is untrue. Jews intermarried with natives of Palestine, with the people of Alexandria, and, during the Middle Ages, with those of Spain and France. They are the product of a commingling of races. It is false that they cannot commingle. They are closely associated in thought to-day with the best thought of other races, and take the same stand in letters and sciences."

Prof. Adler attributed the anti-Semitic movement in Europe partly to religious prejudice and gave this as a chief cause for the expulsion of the Jews from Russia. The awakening of a strong national feeling, too, helps on this feeling and causes hostility toward all elements foreign to the people of the State. This national feeling, he said, is strongest in those nationalities where the people do not yet know themselves.

"In England alone," Prof. Adler continued, "I have not seen a trace of Jewish opposition because she is sure of herself. Then there are economic reasons. The Jews possess more comfort in life than the Prussian officers, who live on the dignity of their offices. The Jews take the best seats in theatres and cafés, and are given audiences while the titled officers wait in the ante-rooms."

The opposition to Jews in the United States, however, Prof. Adler said, he did not deem so

serious. It is not due, in his opinion, to any religious prejudice, nor is it due to any insolent nationalism.

"It is certain social defects which grate upon Americans. It is the lack of nerve and modesty and the push of the Jews that render them unpleasant. Their many sterling virtues cannot outweigh their few defects, and, while a great majority of the Jews may be modest, the failings of one will counterbalance in public estimation the modesty of the many. There is a tendency to loudness in speech, to showiness in dress, and to put themselves forward which grate upon our more quiet and taciturn companions.

"We must endeavor to remedy these defects by adapting ourselves to the manners of the people among whom we live."

Prof. Adler recommended the establishment of debating clubs where parliamentary rules prevail and quietness in dress is cultivated by the refinement of those in charge. Also the organization of political clubs, which should build up societies that would prove strong in bringing about municipal reform, and render the influx of Russian Jews a benefit rather than a menace to public welfare.

May 29, 1893

CRITICISES THE JEWS.

Pastor Lynch Declares They Are Ungrateful for American Privileges.

The Rev. Frederick Lynch, pastor of the Pilgrim Church, Madison Avenue and 121st Street, preached last night on "Christians and Jews in New York City: A Warning." In part, he said:

"Our Hebrew friends our continually complaining of being treated as a race apart and yet they often seem to be doing their best to separate themselves from the rest of the community and to segregate their interests. We have as much admiration for them as has any man, we have been their best friend, have defended them, have worshipped with them, have preached tolerance and charity and fairmindedness toward them, have resented all outbursts of race prejudices among Christians, and condemned them as petty and medieval.

"Yet we must confess that sometimes we are tempted to lose patience and to feel with the recent Court pastor of Berlin, that they bring the ire of every nation they enter upon their heads by their immediate attack upon all its most sacred institutions and their universal insistence on remaining a race within a race.

"Nowhere has the Jew been more fairly treated than in New York. So fairly has he been treated that the city has become in many senses his own, and before long it may be a question of Christian privilege in New York rather than Hebrew. This is bad for the city and the country. If New York is ever to be a righteous city and saved from the evil in it, it has got to be by the efforts of a homogeneous society of all good people acting together.

"The papers have recently been full of meetings being held in New York by Hebrews, to organize a strong society to look after Jewish exiles and their interests. We have heard much of another society, the Jewish Community. We have watched these meetings with great interest and have been greatly vexed to observe that so little has been said about being American citizens, or what they would do for New York as a whole. One or two men, who are Americans first and Jews second, honored friends of ours, leaders of the Jews to whom we wish they would listen, did raise their voices. But it has been Jews and Jewish rights and Jewish protection and Judaism. There is no such thing as Jewish rights in this country, nor Irish rights, nor Japanese rights, but only American rights."

He went on to condemn bills, which, he said, the Jews were introducing at Albany to conduct secular business on Sunday, as selfish, and as tending to break down the great American institution of Sunday for the benefit of a few.

April 19, 1909

SECT WAR IN PITTSBURGH.

Catholics Abandon Their Annual Parade Because of It.

Special to The New York Times.

PITTSBURGH, Sept. 21.—Intense religious rancor has resulted in the abandonment of Pittsburgh's annual procession of Holy Name societies. Last Fall 40,000 Catholics marched in the parade. Bishop Canevin of Pittsburgh to-day issued a statement in which he said:

"When the procession might be regarded as an ostentatious display of numerical strength to challenge the intolerant and evil-minded, or represented as a disguised political demonstration, then Christian charity and prudence counsel us to pause and forego our plans for this year rather than exasperate still more minds already excited and unbalanced by the fever of anti-Catholic prejudice and rancor.

"In these days of excited bigotry, when the entire Catholic Church is condemned for the crimes and scandals of a few degenerate members, considerations of charity, truth, justice, or peace do not restrain the malignity of distempered zealots and anti-Catholic politicians in their efforts to incite intolerance and destroy the peace and confidence which fellow-citizens and neighbors ought to cherish toward one another."

It is said that in at least three contests for public office in Allegheny County this Fall the fights will be conducted along denominational lines. Recently a riot provoked by an address on Martin Luther was the subject of an Aldermanic investigation.

September 22, 1913

JEWS DENOUNCE "PROTOCOLS OF ZION"

PUBLIC STATEMENT.

NEW YORK, Nov. 30, 1920.

A conference to discuss the widespread campaign of secret anti-Jewish propaganda in the United States was called by the American Jewish Committee. This conference was participated in by the foremost national Jewish organizations, and authorized the issuance of a public statement in which the so-called "Protocols of the Learned Elders of Zion" now being circulated in large numbers by secret agencies are condemned as a forgery, and the charge that Bolshevism is part of a conspiracy of Jews and Freemasons to secure world domination is denounced as a malicious invention inspired by foreign reactionary forces for the purpose of breeding suspicion and hatred of the Jews and Freemasons in the United States in order to discredit free government in the eyes of the European masses and thus facilitate the restoration of absolutism in government."

The signatories of the declaration, which is addressed "To Our Fellow-Citizens," include the following representative Jewish organizations: The American Jewish Committee, the Zionist Organization of America, the Union of American Hebrew Congregations, the Union of Orthodox Jewish Congregations, the United Synagogue of America, the Provisional Committee for an American Jewish Congress, the Independent Order of B'nai B'rith, the Central Conference of American Rabbis, the Rabbinical Assembly of the Jewish Theological Seminary and the United Orthodox Jewish Rabbis of America. The complete address follows:

Text of the Address.
To Our Fellow-Citizens:

During the war, by secret agencies, a document variously called "The Protocols of the Elders of Zion," "The Protocols of the Meetings of the Zionist Men of Wisdom" and "The Protocols of the Wise Men of Zion," was clandestinely circulated in typewritten form, among public officials and carefully selected civilians, for the purpose of giving rise to the belief that the Jews, in conjunction with Freemasons, had been for centuries engaged in a conspiracy to produce revolution and anarchy, by means of which they hoped to attain the control of the world by the establishment of some sort of despotic rule. Some months ago this document was published in England. More recently it has appeared in print in the United States and thousands of copies have been circulated with an air of mystery among legislators, journalists, clergymen and teachers, members of clubs, and indiscriminately to the general public. The London Morning Post has given out a series of articles as a commentary upon The Protocols, in which the charge of an unholy conspiracy between Jews and Freemasons is elaborated, and Bolshevism is characterized as a movement of, for and by the Jews and is declared to be a fulfillment of The Protocols. These articles, whose authorship is not disclosed, have now appeared in book form under the title "The Cause of World Unrest." During the past six months there have been sent forth weekly in Henry Ford's organ, The Dearborn Independent, attacks of extraordinary virulence upon the Jews. These assaults upon the honor of the Jewish people are all founded on The Protocols and on the discredited literature of Russian and German anti-Semitism, inspired by the minions of autocracy. Parrot-like, they repeat the abominable charges that can only appeal to the credulity of a stunted intelligence—charges long since conceded to be unfounded by all fair-minded men. Ford is employing his great wealth in scattering broadcast his fulminations, regardless of consequences.

When the Jews of the United States first learned of these malevolent prints, they deemed it beneath their dignity to take notice of them, because they regarded them as a mere recrudescence of medieval bigotry and stupidity, showing upon their face their utter worthlessness. These publications have, however, been put in circulation to such an extent that it is believed that the time has come, humiliating though it be to them, for the Jews to make answer to these libels and to the unworthy insinuations and innuendoes that have been whispered against them.

Protocols a Forgery.
Speaking as representatives of the Jewish people, familiar with the history of Judaism in its various phases and with the movements, past and present, in Jewish life, we say with all solemnity:

(1) The Protocols are a base forgery. There has never been an organization of Jews known as The Elders of Zion, or The Zionist Men of Wisdom or The Wise Men of Zion, or bearing any other similar name. There has never existed a secret or other Jewish body organized for any purpose such as that implied in The Protocols. The Jewish people have never dreamed of a Jewish dictatorship, of a destruction of religion, of an interference with industrial prosperity or of an overthrow of civilization. The Jews have never conspired with the Freemasons, or with any other body, for any purpose.

From the time of the destruction of the Temple at Jerusalem by Titus, the Jews have had no political state.

For centuries they were forced to wander from land to land, to flee for refuge wherever they might find it against bitter persecution. They were pent up in ghettoes, were deprived of even the shadow of civil or political rights, and were made the objects of every possible form of discrimination. It is little more than fifty years since the Jews of Western Europe became politically emancipated. Until the outbreak of the World War the Jews of Eastern Europe, constituting a majority of all the Jews of the world, were not even permitted to exercise the rights of citizenship in lands where they and their ancestors had dwelt for generations. The great mass of Jews were hampered in every way in their efforts to earn a livelihood. Far from desiring to govern the world, they were content with the opportunity to live. Numerically they constitute less than 1 per cent of the population of the earth; and more than one half of them are on the verge of starvation. The suggestion that, in their feebleness, they have been planning in secret conclave to seize absolute power and to dominate the 99 per cent non-Jews upon the globe is a ridiculous invention than which even madness can conjure nothing more preposterous.

Questions Unanswered

Where is the habitat of these so-called Elders of Zion, by whatever name they may be called? Who are these hidden sages? Whence do they come? What is the nature of their organization? The distributers of the protocols are silent on that subject. Whence come these pretended protocols? There have been various versions. One Serge Nilus, of whose identity little is known, a Russian mystic and an ardent supporter of Czarism, claims to have received them in Russia, in 1901, in manuscript form, from a Russian officeholder, who stated that the manuscript had been originally obtained by a lady, whose name is not given, and who, he said, obtained them in a mysterious way. In what language they were written is not stated. Where that manuscript now is does not appear. Nilus asserts that he submitted the protocols to one of the Russian Grand Dukes, who, after examination, returned them with the despairing message, "Too late." Apparently there was no room for them in the Russian archives, and they suggested no task for the Czar's ubiquitous police to perform. In 1905 Nilus published at Tsarskoe Selo a second edition of a mystical book entitled "The Great in the Little," the first edition having been published in 1901. Into this later edition he incorporated for the first time the protocols, which he claimed to have had in his possession for four years. In January, 1917, he published another book under the title "It Is Near, at the Door," purporting to foretell "the coming of the Anti-Christ and the Kingdom of the Devil on Earth." In his book he announces that he had only then learned authoritatively from Jewish sources (what they were is not explained) that these protocols were nothing other than a strategic plan for the conquest of the world, of putting it under the yoke of Israel, "the struggler-against-God," a plan worked out by the leaders of the Jewish people during the many centuries of their dispersion, and finally presented to the Council of Elders by the Prince of Exile, Theodor Herzl, at the time of the first Zionist Congress summoned by him at Basle in August, 1897. He declared that the protocols were signed by the Zionist representatives of the thirty-third degree of initiation; that they were secretly removed from the complete file of protocols that pertained to the first Zionist Congress; that they were taken from the secret vaults at the main Zionist office, which, it is said, "at present is located in French territory."

No Signatures to Protocol.

The protocols as published bear no signatures. The identity of the Zionist representatives by whom they are claimed to have been signed is left untold. The location of the main Zionist office and of the secret vaults from which the protocols were secretly removed remains a secret. It is, however, a matter of history that the first Zionist Congress was publicly held by Jews who came from various parts of Europe for the purpose of considering the misery of their brethren in Eastern Europe and of enabling them to find shelter in the Holy Land. Theodor Herzl was a distinguished journalist, a man of true nobility of character. He presided at the Congress, all of whose deliberations were held in the light of day. The insinuation that there was a thirty-third, or any other, degree of initiation in this organization is merely a malicious effort to bring the Jews into parallelism with the Free Masons and thus to subject them to all the fanciful and fantastic charges that have from time to time been laid at the door of Free Masonry, oblivious of the fact that fifteen Presidents of the United States, including Washington, and many of the leading statesmen of Europe and America, have been members of that order.

Nilus and his associates belonged to the Russian bureaucracy. In 1905, through the Black Hundreds that body sought in every way to crush the Jews and to prevent the liberalization of the Government. The time was propitious for the perpetration of a political forgery by a Government that habitually resorted to the employment of agents provocateurs, a Government which only a few years later, against the protest of the enlightened clergy of the world, ineffectually sought to convict Mendel Beilis on the charge of ritual murder. It is significant that one of his prosecutors has been active in distributing manuscript copies of the protocols throughout the United States.

What an Analysis Shows.
Irrespective of this history, bristling with suspicion, an analysis of The Protocols shows that on their face they are a fabrication and that they must have emanated from the bitter opponents of democracy. They are replete with cynical references to the French Revolution, and to the conceptions of liberty, equality and fraternity. They uphold privilege and autocracy. They belittle education. They condemn religious liberty. They assert that political freedom is an idea and not a fact, and that the doctrine that a government is nothing but a steward of the people is a mere phrase. These are the very doctrines that one would expect from the protagonists of autocracy. Nothing can be more foreign to Jewish thought and aspiration than these brutal theories of reaction. That the Jews, whose very life has been a prayer for the blessings of liberty and equality, should hold them in contempt is unthinkable.

The document throughout is farcical in its absurdities. In the Russian original there is a passage, significantly omitted from the translation, to the effect that the Jews are the descendants of the Lost Tribes of Israel and the British Government is violently attacked for its liberalism. If climax there be to all this folly, it lies in the idea set forth in The Protocols that "the world ruler is to spring from the dynastic roots of King David," and that "the King of Israel will become the real Pope of the Universe and the Patriarch of the International Church," whatever that may mean.

It is needless, however, to elaborate, when one considers that the editor of The London Morning Post, in his introduction to "The Cause of World Unrest," himself doubts the genuineness of The Protocols, and that the anonymous author of that book, after using them as his text, is unable to give them any higher certificate than that they may or may not be genuine. Indeed, he goes so far as to say:

"We have said that this document flashes a blaze of light, and so it does, but whether this document is genuine or not, whether the blaze of light is true or false, can only be judged by internal evidence and probabilities. We may say at once that Nilus advances nothing in the nature of real evidence to prove the document, and that his account of how it came into his hands consists of assertion only, without evidence to support it."

Indicts an Entire People.

And yet a document, thus discredited by its sponsors, is made the basis of an indictment against an entire people.

(2). The contention that the genuineness of "The Protocols" is established by the outbreak of Bolshevism in Russia twelve years after their publication, and that Bolshevism is a Jewish movement, is absurd in theory and absolutely untrue in fact. As well might it be said that a forged deed is genuine because twenty years after its date a relative of the person whose name is forged is falsely charged with being a disturber of the peace.

To say that the Jews are responsible for bolshevism is a deliberate falsehood. The originators of bolshevism were exclusively non-Jews. While it is true that there are Jews among the Bolshevists, notably Trotsky, they represent a small fraction of the Jews and of the followers of Bolshevism. Lenin, who belonged to the Russian aristocracy and has not a drop of Jewish blood in his veins, was the creator as he has been the motive power of the Soviets. Tchicherin, who has conducted their foreign affairs, Bucharin, Krassin and Kalinin, all non-Jews, are, with Lenin, the brains of the Communist Party.

The Bolshevist Cabinet, known as the People's Commissars, consists of twenty members, of whom Trotsky and Sverdlov are the only Jews, and they are Jews merely by birth. Of the Central Committee of the Communist Party, including Trotsky, there are four Jews out of thirteen. The so-called Extraordinary Commission, whose function it is to suppress opposition to the Bolshevist regime from within, is directed by a triumvirate consisting of a Pole and two Letts, none of whom is of Jewish origin. Although Trotsky is the head of the War Department, his General Staff is composed exclusively of non-Jews.

In "The Cause of World Unrest" a list of fifty names is given, most of whom are classified as Jews and Bolshevists, in order to establish the thesis that "nearly all of the Bolshevist leaders are Jews." An examination of the list shows that ten of the Jews included in the list are the leaders of the anti-Bolshevist movement in Russia; that a number of those who are classified in the list as Jews are not Jews at all; that a large proportion of those classified as Jews are men who are so obscure and hold positions so inconspicuous that whether or not they are Jews is not only uncertain but unimportant. They are certainly not leaders.

Foes of Bolshevism.

On the other hand, the leaders of the Mensheviki, who are the sworn foes of Bolshevism, are to a large extent Jews. Among the chiefs of the Constitutional Democratic Party of Russia, who are strongly opposed to the Soviets, are Vinaver, Sitosberg, Pasmanik, Kaminka, Landau, and Friedman, all prominent Jews. Among the leaders of the Peoples Socialist, the Socialist Revolutionary, and the Menshevik section of the Social Democratic parties, bitter opponents of the Bolsheviki, are a large number of Jews. The leading anti-Bolshevist newspapers, which of necessity are published outside of Russia, have Jews upon their editorial staffs. An overwhelming majority of Russian Jews have been ruined by the coercive measures of the Soviets. They have submitted to the confiscation of their property and are undergoing unspeakable hardships. The Orthodox Jews, whose numbers preponderate, remaining loyal to the faith of their fathers, regard the Bolsheviki as the enemies of all religion, and, therefore, hold the doctrines of Bolshevism in abhorrence. With comparatively few exceptions the Jews are looked upon by the Bolsheviki as belonging to the hated bourgeoisie and as favoring capitalism. The Zionists, who constitute a numerous and important element of the Jews of Russia, have been denounced by the Soviets as counter-revolutionary, and many of them have been cast into prison and threatened with death—Zionists, we repeat, who are the followers of Herzl.

If the Jews are to be condemned because of a Trotzky, who has never in the slightest degree concerned himself with Judaism or the welfare of the Jews, then there is not a people that has ever lived that might not with equal right be condemned because in its membership there were men who are alleged to have advocated hateful doctrines. The Jew has traditionally stood for religion, law, order, the family, and the right of property. It is, therefore, the height of cruelty to charge him with responsibility for Bolshevism, when its doctrines, should they prevail, would inevitably lead to the destruction of Judaism. It is especially a brutal charge when one considers all that the Jew has suffered from the oppressive and discriminatory laws of Russian autocracy and from its effort to suppress every aspiration that the Jew had for freedom.

Tribute to Patriotism.

It is a great tribute to the patriotism of the Russian Jews that, in spite of the indignities that they had to undergo, hundreds of thousands of them fought under the banner of the Czar, loyally and gallantly, and in large numbers laid down their lives in the Allied cause. The rosters of the army and navy of the United States contain the names of tens of thousands of Jews born in Russia who served so faithfully under our colors that they gained the unqualified approval of their officers, and proportionately many of them were awarded decorations of honor by a grateful country.

We have refrained from commenting on the libels contained in The Dearborn Independent. Ford, in the fullness of his knowledge, unqualifiedly declares the Protocols to be genuine and argues that practically every Jew is a Bolshevist. We have dealt sufficiently with both of these falsehoods. It is useless in a serious document to analyze the puerile and venomous drivel that he has derived from the concoctions of professional agitators. He is merely a dupe.

What is the motive of those who have set in motion this new onslaught of anti-Semitism? It is the motive that again and again has actuated autocracy and its adroit supporters—that of seeking a scapegoat for their own sins, so that they may be enabled under the cover of a false issue to deceive the public.

It is an attempt to drive into the solidarity of the citizenry of our country that has been its pride and its strength the wedge of discord, by arousing suspicion and inciting overt acts not only against those of Jewish origin but also against Freemasons, in the hope of discrediting free government in the eyes of the European masses and thus facilitate the restoration of absolutism in government.

Manufactured in Russia.

The protocols were manufactured in Russia under the bureaucracy, and the ammunition with which the campaign is conducted has been furnished out of the arsenal of imperialistic Germany and by those who are seeking to restore the Hapsburgs, the Hohenzollerns, and the Romanoffs on their former thrones. Ancient hatred and unreasoning prejudice and a failure to understand and know what the Jew really is, are likewise responsible for the readiness with which these falsehoods have been accepted by those who are ever willing to believe evil of their fellow-men.

We have an abiding confidence in the spirit of justice and fairness that permeates the true American, and we are satisfied that our fellow-citizens will not permit the campaign of slander and libel that has been launched against us to go unreproved. There is enough for all of us to do in the great task of building up our common country and of developing the principles on which it is founded. Let not hatred and misunderstanding arise where peace and harmony, unity and brotherliness, are required to perpetuate all that America represents and to enable all men to know that within her wide boundaries there is no room for injustice and intolerance.

[Signed.]

THE AMERICAN JEWISH COMMITTEE.

By LOUIS MARSHALL, *President.*
CYRUS ADLER,
JULIUS ROSENWALD,
Vice Presidents.
ISAAC W. BERNHEIM, *Treasurer.*
SAMUEL DORF,
ABRAM I. ELKUS,
ALBERT D. LASKER,
IRVING LEHMAN,
A. C. RATSHESKY,
HORACE STERN,
CESAR S. STRAUS,
CYRUS L. SULZBERGER,
MAYER SULZBERGER,
ISAAC M. ULLMAN,
A. LEO WEIL,
Executive Committee.

THE ZIONIST ORGANIZATION OF AMERICA.

By JULIAN W. MACK, *President.*
JACOB DE HAAS, *Secretary.*

THE UNION OF AMERICAN HEBREW CONGREGATIONS.

By J. WALTER FREIBERG, *President.*
GEORGE ZEPIN, *Secretary.*

THE UNION OF ORTHODOX JEWISH CONGREGATIONS.

By HERBERT S. GOLDSTEIN, *Secretary.*

THE UNITED SYNAGOGUE OF AMERICA.

By ELIAS L. SOLOMON, *President.*
CHARLES I. HOFFMAN, *Secretary.*

THE PROVISIONAL ORGANIZATION FOR AMERICAN JEWISH CONGRESS.

By NATHAN STRAUS, *President.*
MORRISS ROTHENBERG, *Chairman Executive Committee.*
STEPHEN S. WISE,
BERNARD G. RICHARDS, *Secretary.*

THE INDEPENDENT ORDER OF B'NAI B'RITH AND THE ANTI-DEFAMATION LEAGUE.

By ADOLF KRAUS, *President.*

THE CENTRAL CONFERENCE OF AMERICAN RABBIS.

By LEO M. FRANKLIN, *President.*
FELIX A. LEVY, *Secretary.*

THE RABBINICAL ASSEMBLY OF THE JEWISH THEOLOGICAL SEMINARY.

By MAX D. KLEIN, *President.*
SAMUEL FREDMAN, *Secretary.*

THE UNITED ORTHODOX JEWISH RABBIS OF AMERICA.

By M. S. MARGOLIS, *President.*

The American Jewish Committee.

The American Jewish Committee, 31 Union Square West, New York, is a national organization instituted in 1906 and incorporated by an act of the New York State Legislature in 1911, "to prevent the infraction of the civil and religious rights of Jews in all parts of the world; to render all lawful assistance and to take appropriate remedial action in the event of threatened or actual invasion or restriction of such rights, or of unfavorable discrimination with respect thereto; to secure for Jews equality of economic, social and educational opportunity; to alleviate the consequences of persecution and to afford relief from calamities affecting Jews wherever they may occur." Its officers are:

President, Louis Marshall; Vice Presidents, Cyrus Adler and Julius Rosenwald; Treasurer, Isaac W. Bernheim; Executive Committee: Cyrus Adler, Philadelphia, Chairman; Isaac W. Bernheim, Louisville; Samuel Dorf, New York City; Abram I. Elkus, New York City; Albert D. Lasker, Chicago; Irving Lehman, New York City; Louis Marshall, New York City; A. C. Ratshesky, Boston; Julius Rosenwald, Chicago; Horace Stern, Philadelphia; Oscar S. Straus, New York City; Cyrus L. Sulzberger, New York City; Mayer Sulzberger, Philadelphia; Isaac M. Ullman, New Haven; A. Leo Weil, Pittsburgh.

ISSUE A PROTEST ON ANTI-SEMITISM

A Notable Document Signed by Distinguished Americans, Led by President, Put on Record.

WHOLLY OF CHRISTIAN ORIGIN

Originated by John Spargo, Leaders of Thought Readily Signed It, Some of Them Adding Personal Comment.

BENNINGTON, Vt., Jan. 16.—A protest against anti-Semitic propaganda in the United States, bearing the signatures of President Wilson, William H. Taft, Cardinal O'Connell and 116 other widely known men and women of Christian faith, was made public here tonight by John Spargo, Socialist author. It exhorts particularly those who are "moulders of public opinion—the clergy and ministers of all Christian churches, publicists, teachers, editors and statesmen—to strike at this un-American and un-Christian agitation."

"We regret exceedingly," the protest says, "the publication of a number of books, pamphlets and newspaper articles, designed to foster distrust and suspicion of our fellow-citizens of Jewish ancestry and faith—distrust and suspicion of their loyalty and their patriotism."

A new and dangerous spirit, it asserts, is being introduced into the national political life by these publications, challenging and menacing American citizenship and American democracy. Men and women of Jewish faith, it declares, should not be required alone to "fight this evil, but that it is in a very special sense the duty of citizens who are not Jews by ancestry and faith."

Probably no similar document ever bore such a distinguished array of signatures. It is said to be quite unprecedented for such a memorial to bear the signatures of the President of the United States and the Secretary of State, as this does. In making it public Mr. Spargo also let it be known that no Jewish person or organization had anything to do with the preparation or publication of the protest.

"A single citizen, a non-Jew, acting upon his own initiative and responsibility, and without consultation with anybody," he said, "wrote the brief protest and invited other distinguished citizens, non-Jews like himself, to sign it. All the work connected with the protest and all the expense involved, therefore, represent the contribution of an individual citizen to the defense of American ideals. Neither directly nor indirectly did any person of Jewish ancestry or faith, or any Jewish organization, contribute as much as a postage stamp to the cost of the undertaking."

President Wilson's Opinion.

So far as the President's signature is concerned, it was learned that when the protest was submitted to Mr. Wilson by its originator there was no thought in his mind that the President would himself desire to sign the document. At most the originator believed and hoped that Mr. Wilson might send some word of sympathetic approval of the protest. The President, however, preferred to sign the document and personally requested that his name be attached. President Wilson wrote:

I have your letter of Dec. 22 and am heartily in sympathy with the protest against the anti-Semitic movement. I beg that you will add my name to the signatures.

With best wishes, sincerely yours,
WOODROW WILSON.

Ex-President Taft responded with great readiness and since then has spoken on the subject in a public address.

President-elect Harding, while preferring to avoid the creation of a troublesome precedent for himself by signing the memorial, which would make it difficult for him to refuse to give his name to other memorials for worthy causes in the future, took pains to make plain his emphatic disapproval of the anti-Semitic agitation. In a personal letter to the originator of the protest he wrote:

I am sure you can understand why, at the present time, I am seeking the avoidance of undue publicity and reluctant to make public statements relating to any of our pending problems. I am no less sure that you already know, and that the American people already believe, that I am giving no sanction to anything so narrow, so intolerant or so un-American as the anti-Semitic movement. I have been preaching the gospel of understanding and good-will, and no one who believes in these things and hopes for the concord of America can be interested in any movement aimed against any portion of our American citizenship. Very truly yours,
WARREN G. HARDING.

Mr. Lansing on the "Protocols."

The protest also bears the signatures of Secretary of State Colby and former Secretaries of State Lansing and Bryan. Secretary Colby cabled from South America his desire to be included among the signatories. Ex-Secretary Lansing in sending his adhesion to the protest explained that he had made a personal examination of the much discussed "protocols," and reached the conclusion that they were "forgeries circulated for malicious purposes." In his letter he wrote:

I remember that they were brought to my attention while I was Secretary of State, that I examined them and returned them to the division having charge of such matters with a statement that there was no evidence as to their authenticity, and that personally I considered them to be without the least foundation in fact, but forgeries circulated for malicious purposes. My examination took place certainly over a year ago, and it is possible that it was over two years ago—I am unable to say which. They are, in any event, entirely without evidence to support them. If I can do anything further to aid in this justifiable campaign against the enemies of the Jewish race in this country I will be glad to serve.

Cardinal O'Connell's Letter.

Cardinal O'Connell, in joining the protest, wrote as follows:

My attention has been brought to what would appear to be an organized campaign against the Jews in America. Such a campaign is entirely at variance with America's best traditions and ideals, and its only effect can be the introduction of religious tests to determine citizenship and a reign of prejudice and race hatred wholly incompatible with loyal and intelligent American citizenship. To discriminate against any race or religion is utterly un-American; and I, therefore, wish to register my protest against any campaign against the Jews or any other religious groups constituting the great citizenship of this country.
WILLIAM (Cardinal) O'CONNELL, Archbishop of Boston.

The other signatures include such eminent representatives of the Protestant churches as Dr. Lyman Abbott, Dr. Robert E. Speer, President of the Federal Council of Churches; Bishop Williams of Michigan, Bishop Brewster of Maine and Bishop Brewster of Conn.; such eminent dignitaries of the Catholic Church as Archbishop Hayes and Bishop O'Connell, and other religious leaders so diverse in their general views from these two groups as Commander Booth of the Salvation Army, the Revs. John Haynes Holmes and Jesse H. Holmes, President of the National Federation of Religious Liberals. Others are Dr. Nicholas Murray Butler, of Columbia University; Dr. John Grier Hibben, of Princeton University, and President Hopkins of Dartmouth College; the Rector of the Catholic University of America, Dr. Shahan; James M. Beck, John G. Agar, Paul D. Cravath, George Wharton Pepper, Judge Gray, and former Attorney General Wickersham, eminent lawyers and jurists; Jane Addams, Charles Dana Gibson, William Sergeant Kendall, the portrait painter; Judge Lindsay, Dorothy Canfield Fisher, the novelist; William Fellowes Morgan, R. Fulton Cutting, and Darwin P. Kingsley, men connected with large financial enterprises; Dr. DuBois, the radical negro editor; Henry C. Ide, the veteran diplomatist; former United States Senator Beveridge and John Spargo, the Socialist.

Following is the text of their protest, with the full list of signatures:

The undersigned, citizens of Gentile birth and Christian faith, view with profound regret and disapproval the appearance in this country of what is apparently an organized campaign of anti-Semitism, conducted in close conformity to and co-operation with similar campaigns in Europe. We regret exceedingly the publication of a number of books, pamphlets and newspaper articles designed to foster distrust and suspicion of our fellow-citizens of Jewish ancestry and faith—distrust and suspicion of their loyalty and their patriotism.

These publications, to which wide circulation is being given, are thus introducing into our national political life a new and dangerous spirit, one that is wholly at variance with our traditions and ideals and subversive of our system of government. American citizenship and American democracy are thus challenged and menaced. We protest against this organized campaign of prejudice and hatred, not only because of its manifest injustice to those against whom it is directed, but also, and especially, because we are convinced that it is wholly incompatible with loyal and intelligent American citizenship. The logical outcome of the success of such a campaign must necessarily be the division of our citizens along racial and religious lines, and, ultimately, the introduction of religious tests and qualifications to determine citizenship.

The loyalty and patriotism of our fellow citizens of the Jewish faith is equal to that of any part of our people, and requires no defense at our hands. From the foundation of this Republic down to the recent World War, men and women of Jewish ancestry and faith have taken an honorable part in building up this great nation and maintaining its prestige and honor among the nations of the world. There is not the slightest justification, therefore, for a campaign of anti-Semitism in this country.

Anti-Semitism is almost invariably associated with lawlessness and with brutality and injustice. It is also invariably found closely intertwined with other sinister forces, particularly those which are corrupt, reactionary and oppressive.

We believe it should not be left to men and women of Jewish faith to fight this evil, but that it is in a very special sense the duty of citizens who are not Jews by ancestry or faith. We therefore make earnest protest against this vicious propaganda, and call upon our fellow citizens of Gentile birth and Christian faith to unite their efforts to ours, to the end that it may be crushed. In particular, we call upon all those who are moulders of public opinion—the clergy and ministers of all Christian churches, publicists, teachers, editors and statesmen—to strike at this un-American and un-Christian agitation.
Signed:

WOODROW WILSON.
WILLIAM HOWARD TAFT.
WILLIAM CARDINAL O'CONNELL.
LYMAN ABBOTT,
   Editor The Outlook.
JANE ADDAMS, *Social Worker.*
JOHN G. AGAR, *Lawyer.*
NEWTON D. BAKER,
   Secretary of War.
RAY STANNARD BAKER, *Author.*
CHARLES A. BEARD,
   Author and Educator.
JAMES M. BECK, *Lawyer.*
BERNARD I. BELL,
   President St. Stephen's College.
ARTHUR E. BESTOR,
   President Chautauqua Institution.
ALBERT J. BEVERIDGE,
   Former U. S. Senator.
W. E. B. DUBOIS,
   Editor The Crisis.
MABEL T. BOARDMAN,
   Commissioner D. of C.
EVANGELINE BOOTH,
   Commander Salvation Army.
BENJAMIN BREWSTER,
   Bishop of Maine.
CHAUNCEY B. BREWSTER,
   Bishop of Connecticut.
JEFFREY R. BRACKETT,
   Social Worker.
HORACE J. BRIDGES,
   Ethical Teacher.
WILLIAM JENNINGS BRYAN,
   Ex-U. S. Secretary of State.
HENRY BRUERE,
   Financial Expert.
NICHOLAS MURRAY BUTLER,
   President Columbia University.
BAINBRIDGE COLBY,
   Secretary of State.
GEORGE W. COLEMAN,
   President National Council of Forums.
ALICE B. COLEMAN,
   (Mrs. George W.),
   Club Worker.
PAUL D. CRAVATH, *Lawyer.*
GEORGE CREEL,
   Former Chairman U. S. Committee on Public Information.
SAMUEL McCHORD CROTHERS,
   Clergyman.
R. FULTON CUTTING, *Financier.*
OLIVE TILFORD DARGAN, *Poet.*
CLARENCE DARROW, *Lawyer.*
JAMES R. DAY,
   University Chancellor.
HENRY S. DENNISON,
   Manufacturer.
JAMES DUNCAN,
   First Vice President A. F. of L.
ROBERT ERSKINE ELY,
   Director Civic Forum.
CHARLES P. FAGNANI, *Theologian.*
W. H. P. FAUNCE,
   President Brown University.
DOROTHY CANFIELD FISHER,
   Novelist.
IRVING FISHER, *Economist.*
JOHN FORD, *Jurist.*
RAYMOND B. FOSDICK, *Lawyer.*
ROBERT FROST, *Poet.*
JAMES R. GARFIELD, *Lawyer.*
H. A. GARFIELD,
   President Williams College.
LINDLEY M. GARRISON,
   Former U. S. Secretary of War.
JOHN PALMER GAVIT,
   Editor New York Evening Post.

HERBERT ADAMS GIBBONS,
Historian.
CHARLES DANA GIBSON, *Artist.*
FRANKLIN H. GIDDINGS,
University Professor.
MARTIN H. GLYNN,
Ex-Governor New York.
GEORGE GRAY, *Jurist.*
EDWARD EVERETT HALE,
University Professor.
JAMES HARTNESS
Governor of Vermont.
PATRICK J. HAYES,
Archbishop of New York.
JOHN GRIER HIBBEN,
President Princeton University.
JOHN HAYNES HOLMES,
Clergyman.
JESSE H. HOLMES,
*President National Federation of
Religious Liberals.*
HAMILTON HOLT,
Editor The Independent.
ERNEST MARTIN HOPKINS,
President Dartmouth College.
FREDERIC C. HOWE, *Publicist.*
HENRY C. IDE, *Diplomatist.*
INEZ HAYNES IRWIN, *Author.*
WILL IRWIN, *Author.*
GEORGE R. JAMES, *Capitalist.*
DAVID STARR JORDAN, *Scientist*
WILLIAM W. KEEN,
Professor of Surgery.
PAUL U. KELLOGG,
Editor The Survey.
WILLIAM SERGEANT KENDALL,
Artist.
GEORGE KENNAN, *Journalist.*
HENRY CHURCHILL KING,
President Oberlin College.
DARWIN P. KINGSLEY,
*President New York Life Insurance
Company.*

W. P. LADD,
Dean Berkeley Divinity School.
IRA LANDRITH,
Prohibition Advocate.
FRANKLIN K. LANE,
*Former U. S. Secretary of the In-
terior.*
ROBERT LANSING,
Former U. S. Secretary of State.
JULIA C. LATHROP,
*Chief Children's Bureau, U. S. Dept.
of Labor.*
BEN B. LINDSEY,
Juvenile Court Judge.
CHARLES H. LEVERMORE
Peace Advocate.
FREDERICK LYNCH, *Clergyman.*
EDWIN MARKHAM, *Poet.*
Mrs. EDWIN MARKHAM, *Writer.*
DANIEL GREGORY MASON,
Musical Composer.
JOSEPH ERNEST McAFEE,
Religious Publicist.
J. F. McELWAIN, *Manufacturer.*
RAYMOND McFARLAND,
Principal Vermont Academy.
ALEXANDER R. MERRIAM
Theologian.
E. T. MEREDITH,
*Secretary U. S. Dept. of Agricul-
ture.*
JAMES F. MINTURN, *Judge.*
JOHN MOODY, *Financial Expert.*
WILLIAM FELLOWES MORGAN,
Financier.
CHARLES CLAYTON MORRISON,
Editor The Christian Century.
PHILIP STAFFORD MOXOM,
Clergyman.
JOSEPH FORT NEWTON,
Clergyman.
D. J. O'CONNELL,
Bishop of Richmond.
MARY BOYLE O'REILLY, **Publicist.**

GEORGE WHARTON PEPPER,
Lawyer.
LOUIS F. POST,
Assistant Secretary of Labor U. S.
THEODORE ROOSEVELT,
Member of New York Legislature.
CHARLES EDWARD RUSSELL,
Publicist.
JACOB GOULD SCHURMAN,
Educator.
VIDA D. SCUDDER,
University Professor.
SAMUEL SEABURY, *Jurist.*
THOMAS J. SHAHAN,
*Rector of the Catholic University
of America.*
CHARLES M. SHELDON,
Editor The Christian Herald.
EDWIN E. SLOSSON,
Associate Editor The Independent.
PRESTON SLOSSON, *Journalist.*
JOHN SPARGO, *Author.*
ROBERT E SPEER,
*President Federal Council of
Churches.*
CHARLES STELZLE,
Religious Publicist.
PAUL MOORE STRAYER,
Clergyman.
MARION TALBOT, *University Dean*
IDA M. TARBELL, *Author.*
HARRY F. WARD,
Theological Professor.
EVERETT P. WHEELER, *Lawyer.*
GAYLORD S. WHITE, *Social Worker.*
GEORGE W. WICKERSHAM,
Ex-Attorney General of U. S.
CHARLES DAVID WILLIAMS,
Bishop of Michigan.
CHARLES ZUEBLIN,
Writer and Lecturer.

January 17, 1921

BARS PILGRIM PAGEANT.

Archbishop Messner Objects to Spectacle in St. Paul as Non-Catholic.

ST. PAUL, Minn., April 30.—A statement that a pageant, "Landing of the Pilgrims," which had been arranged for presentation in Milwaukee by the Sane Fourth of July Commission, was "exclusively a glorification of the Protestant pilgrim," was made here today by Archbishop Messner of Milwaukee, in explanation of his order forbidding Catholic school children to take part.

The Archbishop's objections, when communicated to the Milwaukee committee arranging the Independence Day celebration, caused the Pilgrim pageant to be deleted from the program.

"The spectacle will in no way make a recognition of the Catholic faith, and I forbade Catholic children taking part in a demonstration, partially religious in character, which does not give a fair consideration to their belief," the Archbishop said.

May 1, 1921

KU KLUX MUST GO, SAYS DR. STRATON

Pastor of Calvary, However, Wins Applause by Praising Their Ideals.

HITS ALL SECRET BODIES

Denounces World and "Yellow Journalism," "Green Sectarianism" and "Blackguardism."

Condemning the methods but not the motives of the Ku Klux Klan, the Rev. John Roach Straton, pastor of Calvary Baptist Church, declared in a sermon there last night that there was no room for the man in the mask in America. Dr. Straton added that he believed there was no place in this country for any secret society, either Protestant, Catholic, Jewish or negro, and pleaded for the elimination of racial and religious predjudice and a united country.

Dr. Straton also denied that Calvary Church was a "Klu Klux Klan nest," as stated in The World, and charged The World with "yellow journalism," yellow being one of the hues in the subdivisions of his sermon, the other colored subdivisions being "white Klu Klux Klanism," "green sectarianism," a reference to Irish Catholics, and "general blackguardism," which referred to his charge that the articles connecting Calvary Church and the Klan had been inspired by a minority faction within the church.

At least 2,000 persons heard the sermon and half that number were unable to gain entrance to the church. Dr. Straton announced that he would preach next Sunday evening on "How to Fight the Negroes, Foreigners, Catholics and Jews in the More Excellent Way."

Objects to "Color Scheme."

"My friends, I do not like the color scheme of today," Dr. Straton said, leading up to a finish reminiscence of the Rev. William A. Sunday and George M. Cohan. "White Ku Klux Klanism, green sectarianism, yellow journalism and general blackguardism are equally distasteful to my eye and heart.

"But I will tell you a color scheme that I do like—The Red, White and Blue. I love this glorious flag of our republic which tonight adorns this pulpit and which, thank God, untarnished and unashamed, now floats around the world. Yes, we all love the flag and we need to rally around it, all of us, Jews and Catholics and Protestants and white and black alike. We need to salute it afresh and to pledge anew our loyalty and love."

As Dr. Straton ended, he grasped the fringe of one of the flags draped on opposite sides of the pulpit and spread its folds before the congregation. The response was immediate. The members of the congregation rose applauding, and joined in singing "America," after which they stood while the organ played the national anthem. Dr. Straton then dismissed them with a brief prayer for the United States.

Dr. Straton started with the statement that the sermon was caused by the accusations of The World against the church. He denied The World's story that Klan leaflets had been distributed at a service and produced a statement signed by all the ushers and deacons of the church to show that such a distribution would have been impossible without their knowledge.

Dr. Straton said he had written The World to learn the basis of its original story, but had received no reply. He added that his only information was from a World reporter, who told him that two men called at The World office and gave The World two copies of the Klan leaflet, which they said they had received with church calendars in Calvary Church. Dr. Straton said that it was possible that these leaflets might have been handed out in the church by some designing or malicious person, but, if that were so, it was without his knowledge or any of his church officers.

Referring to the connection of the Rev. Dr. Oscar Haywood, national lecturer of the Klan, Dr. Straton said that Dr. Haywood's connection with the church was only nominal and had resulted from the consolidation of the Collegiate Baptist Church, of which Dr. Haywood was pastor, with Calvary Church. Dr. Straton read the resolution appointing Dr. Haywood the church evangelist, which specified that he should receive no pay and act only outside New York City. Dr. Straton said

Dr. Haywood's connection was merely a courtesy extended to help him in his evangelistic work.

"I believe that Dr. Haywood will see the incongruity of his present activities with a continuance of his nominal title in connection with our church," Dr. Straton said. "Dr. Haywood undoubtedly has a sense of humor and I think he will be what is popularly called 'good sport' enough to relieve his church of any possible embarrassment because of present conditions. If later Dr. Haywood decides to give up the Klan work, as I sincerely hope he will do, I will be the first to welcome him back to his old relationship."

"Tempest in Hootch-Pot."

Referring to the articles in The World, which stressed Dr. Haywood's connection with Calvary Church in support of its charge that the church was a "Klan nest," Dr. Straton said he considered it all a "tempest in a hootch-pot," and said he came out long ago in opposition to the Klan, once in a letter to The World, commending its exposure of the Klan, and once in an address in Tennessee. Dr. Straton then declared he would call The World to the "mourners' bench," and said:

"If The New York World does not wish to stand convicted of the worst sort of yellow journalism, then, as one who has been its friend in the past, I would say that it ought frankly and openly to correct the injustice it has done this church. There have been in recent times some things that have grieved the friends of The World. The printing of statements which Rudyard Kipling was alleged to have made to a correspondent of The World, and which were calculated to stir up bitter feeling between America and England, and which were later repudiated as absolutely false by Kipling, was a distinct jar to thoughtful friends of The World.

"May I say further that the bitter and, as some of us think, often unfair war which The World has waged against the Prohibition Amendment to the Constitution of the United States has been deplorable for a paper of its standing. How can it reconcile consistently its warfare upon the lawlessness of Ku Kluxism with giving aid and comfort to the lawlessness of the rabid liquor nullifications of today?

"Can it be that this present fight is another case of what might be called newspaper 'alcoholic poisoning,' leading to the marring of moral ideals, the vitiating of high vision, and the jaundicing of judgment, which things usually characterize all alcoholics? Is it a tempest in a teapot, or will we have to call it 'a tempest in a hooch pot?' I wish to say also in this connection that, in my judgment, The World's recent editorial excusing the disgraceful riot by Irish revolutionists upon the streets of New York last Sunday night was most unfortunate.

"My reference to The World's Irish mob editorial naturally leads our thoughts to another tendency that is endangering American unity, fraternity and progress and peace. I will have time to touch but briefly upon this, but I wish to say that I thank God that I am free from racial or sectarian prejudice, bigotry or bitterness. As a Baptist, I cannot forget that Roger Williams suffered amid the snows of Rhode Island for the great principle of religious liberty, and the Baptist people have always stood for the right of every man to worship God according to the dictates of his own conscience. In fact, my friends, that has been one of the very greatest services rendered by the Baptist denomination to the world.

Recalls Police Shake-Up.

In connection with his remarks on "green sectarianism," Dr. Straton acknowledged Mayor Hylan's order to Police Commissioner Enright to give him a little police attention and expressed the hope that it would be as effective as the attention he, Dr. Straton, had given the police. "You may recall that a couple of years ago I found conditions so viciously immoral and lawlessness so flagrant in dance halls and cabarets that it was evident that this was the connivance of grafting police officials. I felt impelled by a sense of duty to make public my findings. These disclosures resulted not only in the conviction of the proprietors of the places I named, but led also to a tremendous shake-up in the police department.

"Mayor Hylan is a good man in some ways, but he lacks gumption. In the South we define gumption as one-third Bible teaching, one-third practical experience and one-third common sense. Put a teaspoonful on a hound's nose and it will prevent him from barking up the wrong tree."

Dr. Straton condemned the Klan for its persecution of negroes. "It is a shame to have taken these simple-minded children of the human race from Africa and enslaved them in the past and now to terrorize and intimidate them," he said. "So sure as God is in his Heaven, he will send vengeance upon us as a people if we practice injury and wrong upon the defenceless and the poor."

Dr. Straton also condemned the persecution of Jews and mentioned the use of the boycott by the Klan in Texas as one unworthy weapon. "I wish to warn you here tonight that God has definitely warned all people against persecuting the Jews," he continued. "He promised Abraham that He would not only bless him, but that He would bless them that blessed him and curse them that cursed him. And one of the most interesting and significant facts of world history and one of the surest proofs of the truthfulness of the Bible is the fact that no race or nation has persecuted the Jewish people without suffering for it. Look at the Italian city republics. Yes, look at bleeding, starving Russia today. It was in Russia that the Jews were most unjustly treated. It was there that they were robbed and massacred literally, in the course of the years, by the millions, and Russia is the one great nation which suffered worst through the World War, while America, which has been more just to the Jews than any other nation, is today the most prosperous and blessed among the peoples of the whole earth."

Says Klan Has Good Men.

Dr. Straton said he intended to be both frank and fair in discussing the Klan. "I recognize for one thing," he said, that there are good men in the ranks of the Ku Klux Klan and that many of them are actuated by the highest and noblest motives. I believe, however, that such men have acted on sentiment in connecting themselves with this organization, and they have not thought the proposition through to its logical and inevitable results. The ideals of the Ku Klux Klan, as stated in their literature, and by their lecturers, beyond any question are fair and good enough. But they fail to see that their ways are necessarily contrary to our American principles. I believe, therefore, to put it concisely, that their motives are good and their methods are bad, their principles are virtuous, but their practices are vicious. I think recent history in this country today, to which I shall refer, will support me in this contention.

"They profess, for example, that they have no prejudice against the negroes, the Jews and the Catholics. Yet the very manner of this profession and the way in which they organize and conduct themselves arouse instant suspicion and antagonism in the ranks of all those classes of our citizens, and lead inevitably to counter-organizations and reprisals. These things, of necessity, tend to break up the unity and peace of American life and to engender bitterness and strife.

"There is no place in America for the man in the mask. In the very nature of the case he cannot be anything except a menace. The very weakness of human nature makes inevitable abuses and excesses, if the man in the mask should succeed in supplanting the orderly administration of law. The Ku Klux Klan people themselves are claiming that some of these outrages in the West and South are perpetrated by groups of men who mask themselves but are not really members of the Ku Klux Klan, though they pose as such. Even this admission proves the utter impossibility of doing any real good by Ku Klux methods.

"Oh, my friends, the folly and the shame of it all! We must come back in this country of ours to oldtime Americanism and to oldtime Christianity, all down the line. These things, in the past, enabled us to become the strongest and most successful nation of the earth and to lead the whole world with righteousness and power, and we do not need anything better than these simple but sturdy old-fashioned things. We do not need here any 'Invisible Empire.'"

K. of C. Plans Campaign.

In answer to attacks by the Ku Klux Klan upon Catholicism, the local Knights of Columbus will send a force of speakers through the State to defend their religion, it was announced yesterday after a meeting of the New York Chapter of the Knights, comprising forty-two councils in Manhattan and the Bronx, in the Hotel Astor. The following resolution was passed with a chorus of "ayes."

"The New York Chapter, Knights of Columbus, heartily condemns the activity of the notorious Ku Klux Klan as vicious, dangerous and un-American, and it is hereby resolved that we pledge our support and assistance to other organizations and individuals, in conjunction with legally constituted authority, to suppress the activities of the Ku Klux Klan."

Frank W. Smith, Chief Clerk of Special Sessions, proposed the resolution, after reading aloud and condemning as vicious and uncalled for an attack upon President Harding printed in Colonel Mayfield's Weekly, of Temple and Houston, Texas, in its issue of Nov. 25, 1922, criticising the President's appointment of a negro as Collector of Customs at New Orleans.

The announcement of the anti-Klan speaking crusade was made by Walter A. Lynch, Chairman of the Chapter's Committee on Catholic Interests.

Dr. Hillis Defends Klan.

The Ku Klux Klan was defended by the Rev. Newell Dwight Hillis, pastor of Plymouth Church, Brooklyn, in a sermon yesterday. Dr. Hillis said many criminal charges had been brought against the Klan, but that so far no newspaper had found proof against the Klans of any crime north of Mason and Dixon's line, nor had any crime on the part of the Klan been established in any court of law.

December 4, 1922

BAR CATHOLIC BOOKS FROM HIGH SCHOOL

Red Robe Riders and Ku Klux Sisters Force Removal to Belleville Library.

BOARD HEEDS PROTESTS

The little town of Belleville, N. J., was stirred yesterday when news spread that the Belleville Board of Education on Monday evening had voted to take the Catholic Encyclopaedia out of the Belleville High School and place it in the Public Library.

This action followed protests by fifteen residents. The encyclopaedia had been donated a week ago by Belleville Council, Catholic Daughters of America. When George R. Gerard, Superintendent of Schools, tried yesterday to obey instructions, he found that a volume had been stolen.

Among the protestants were persons who said they represented the Junior Order of United American Mechanics, the Patriotic Sons of America and the Ladies of the Grand Army of the Republic.

Two letters were received by David Clearman, President of the Board, objecting to the books. One was signed "Belleville Chapter, No. 3, Royal Riders of the Red Robe." The other was signed "The Keeper of the Sacred Seal of Martha Washington, Council No. 9, Ladies of the Invisible Empire." Both had been mailed in Belleville and bore the return address, "Box 118, Portland, Oregon." The letter from the "Royal Riders" read:

"We, the Royal Riders of the Red Robe, hereby and herein raise voice in protest against the acceptance of nineteen volumes of the Catholic Encyclopaedia presented to the Belleville High School, inasmuch as this would be an intermingling of Church and State, something to which we are absolutely opposed.

"And be it further resolved that we will strenuously oppose any action toward the acceptance of these books, as the same are unfit for use in our public schools."

Henry Snyder, a trolley conductor, said he represented the Belleville Council, Junior Order of United American Mechanics. He demanded that the books be removed.

John Maher, the only Catholic among the five members of the board, said he did not think the board was doing wrong when it accepted the gift, and pointed out that Catholics help to support the public schools. He then moved that the books be returned to the donors. This was amended by a non-Catholic board member so that it ordered the books removed to the town library. In that form the motion carried.

March 21, 1923

SIFT RELIGIOUS BIAS AGAINST CATHOLICS

Test Is Made in Fairfield, Conn., by Social Service Group in Plan to Promote Understanding.

15 PERSONS QUESTIONED

Priest Finds Experiment Showed "Marked Misunderstanding" About Catholic Doctrines.

Protestant prejudice against Catholics was made the subject of a study at Fairfield, Conn., it is reported in the current issue of The Commonweal, a Catholic weekly review, to enable a non-sectarian organization which is working for a better understanding between different religious groups to determine how best to proceed with its task.

The study was made by the Inquiry, an independent social service group which has headquarters at 129 East Fifty-second Street, as a result of a dinner last March attended by twelve Catholics, Protestants and Jews. Fairfield was chosen because, it was said, there was no bitter feeling between Protestants and Catholics there, but the study revealed, according to an analysis of it by Father J. Elliot Ross of Yale in The Common-

weal, that "there was mutual suspicion and a marked misunderstanding of some of the main doctrines and practices of Catholicism on the part of even some of the more intelligent representatives of the Protestant group."

The study was made, it was disclosed, in eight meetings held in Fairfield homes attended by fifteen persons, all members of the Congregational Church. The group included two school teachers, a physician and his wife, a farmer, a county judge, the local librarian, the matron of a women's home, an insurance agent and his wife, a business man and his wife, and the wife of an army officer.

Three Tests Given to the Group.

Three tests were given to the group, and they were reported in a pamphlet entitled "The Fairfield Experiment," published by the Inquiry. One test listed nineteen different situations in which Protestants might show their willingness or reluctance to deal with a Catholic. Another consisted of more than fifty words bearing on religion which the group was to scratch if they had a disagreeable connotation and the third test consisted of forty-one statements which Protestants and Catholics were alleged to make against each other and which were to be marked as justified, probably justified, doubtful, probably unjustified and unjustified. The situations test was taken by seven members, with the following result:

	Refus-al.	Hesita-tion.	Willing-ness.
Contract marriaeg with a Catholic	5	1	1
Vote for Catholic as President of the United States	3	2	2
Employ Catholic as nurse for your children	2	4	1
Appoint one as guardian of your child	2	4	1
Vote for one as member of school board	2	3	2
Approve of the election of one as member of the United States Supreme Court	3	1	3
Accept one as employer or foreman over you	1	4	2
Engage one as private secretary	2	2	3
Vote for one as first selectman	0	4	3
Approve of one as librarian	1	2	4
Approve of one as day school teacher	1	2	4
Select one as intimate friend	0	3	4
Vote for one as member of Library Board	0	3	4
Select one as Fourth of July main orator	0	2	5
Invite one to your church to give address at religious service	0	1	6
Pray with a Catholic	0	1	6
Admit and welcome one to sacrament in your church	0	0	7
Discuss religious differences with one	0	0	7
Recognize one as Christian	0	0	7

In the second test, on words bearing on religion, the words most frequently scratched were Ku Klux Klan, parochial, nun, confessional, Knights of Columbus, holy orders, crucifix, His Holiness, high mass, inquisition, Vatican, convent. Eleven of fifteen persons scratched Ku Klux Klan, ten scratched parochial school and the remainder were scratched by from seven to nine persons.

In the third test, on the statements, general agreement, it was reported, was found in believing that "Catholics were too superstitious," that "they believe in the infallibility of the Pope, although many Popes have led wicked and immoral lives"; that "they deny the validity of legally contracted marriages between Protestants and Catholics," &c. But there was "fairly unanimous disbelief" reported on the statements that "Catholic churches are full of rifles" and that "Catholics hope to establish the Pope in Washington."

November 29, 1927

CATHOLIC PREJUDICE CALLED LESS IN TEST

Experiment Indicates Greater Willingness to Cooperate Than a Protestant Group.

ANALYSIS BY FATHER ROSS

Yale Man Finds Greatest Conflict on Politico-Moral Questions—Notes Some Faults in Method.

A group of Catholics who lent themselves to a series of tests to determine the relative measure of prejudice that exists between Protestants and Catholics and to find ways to combat it "showed on the whole about two and one-half times as great a willingness to cooperate with Protestants" as did a group of Protestants who submitted to similar tests, according to an analysis of the tests made by Father J. Elliot Ross of Yale. The study was made by the Inquiry, an independent, non-sectarian social service organization, 129 East Fifty-second Street, as a

result of a meeting of Catholics, Protestants and Jews last March.

The study among the Protestants was made in Fairfield, Conn., at eight meetings held in homes. The result of the tests was reported in a pamphlet entitled "The Fairchild Experiment," which was a reprint of the report published in the Commonweal. The report on the experiment with the Catholic group is issued in a pamphlet by Father Ross entitled "A Sequel to the Fairfield Experiment—How Catholics See Protestants."

Members of Catholic Group.

Of the twenty-one Catholics who took part in the test, seven were men. In the group there were a physician, a manufacturer, three business men, two professors in nonsectarian universities and the personnel officer of a large employer. Three of the men were converts and one had been a student for the Baptist ministry, according to Father Ross's report.

The "religious distance test" included the same type of questions for both Catholics and Protestants. Catholics were asked whether they would vote for a Protestant President and Protestants were asked whether they would vote for a Catholic President. The entire list of nineteen questions asked the Catholic group follows:

WOULD YOU BE WILLING TO

Pray with a Protestant?
Admit and welcome one to sacrament in

your church?
Vote for one as President of the United States?
Approve the election of one as member of the United States Supreme Court?
Employ one as nurse for your children?
Accept one as employer or foreman over you?
Contract marriage with one?
Discuss religious differences with one?
Vote for one as member of school board?
Vote for one as member of library board?
Approve of one as day school teacher?
Approve of one as librarian?
Appoint one as guardian of your child?
Engage one as private secretary?
Recognize one as Christian?
Select one as intimate friend?
Invite one to your church to give address at religious service?
Select one as Fourth of July main orator?
Vote for one as Mayor (first selectman)?

Each refusal counted two points and each hesitation counted one. Willingness counted as nothing.

Scores in the Tests.

Father Ross points out that the seven Protestants who took the test made a score of 83 out of a possible 266, or about 30 per cent. Describing the results in the Catholic group, he says:

"In the Catholic group twenty-one persons took the test, and so their total score should be divided by three for the sake of making a genuinely fair comparison. Thus divided, the total Catholic score was 36."

The Catholic score was a little more than 13 per cent. Continuing, Father Ross comments:

"This particular Catholic group, therefore, showed on the whole about two and one-half times as great a willingness to cooperate with Protestants in these specified ways as did the Fairfield group to cooperate with Catholics. But no general conclusions should be drawn from this, as another Catholic group might have

303

had a very different reaction. In spite of the effort to make the personnel in this group correspond fairly well with that of a Fairchild, it must be admitted that the individuals had probably had more contact with Protestants than the Fairchild members had had with Catholics."

Word Reaction Test.

In a "word reaction test" a different list of words was submitted to each group and the members were asked to consider each word not more than five seconds and indicate those that suggested "a disagreeable association." Because the lists were different, a comparison of the results from the Catholic group with the results from the Fairfield group was impossible. The following is a list of the words submitted to the Catholic group:

Parson,	Birth Control,
Unitarianism,	Ne Temere Decree,
Torquemada,	John Wesley,
The "Open Bible,"	Pope Alexander VI,
Gallicanism,	Pilgrim Fathers,
Anti-Saloon League,	Quirinal,
Private Judgment,	Priesthood of the Believer,
Evangelist,	"Filioque,"
Ancient Order of Hibernians,	Puritanism,
Y. W. C. A.,	Peter's Pence,
Mental Healing,	The Republican Party,
Sunday School,	Inquisition,
Celibacy,	Catholic Socialism,
Laicism,	W. E. Gladstone,
Erasmus,	The Ark and the Dove,
Methodism,	Psycho-Analysis,
The Man Christ Jesus,	John Calvin,
Avignon,	The Lord's Table,
Woman Preacher,	Hersey,
'ussolini,	Revival,
ıblic School,	Dwight L. Moody,
ivine Right of Kings,	Missioner,
Vicar of God,	Bismarck,
Preaching Friars,	George Tyrrell,
David Livingstone,	Uniats,
Jesuit,	Fish,
Christian Endeavor,	Y. M. C. A.,
Justification by Faith,	John Roach Straton,
Georgian Chant,	Feminism,
Martin Luther,	Tolstoy,
Anglo-Catholic,	Harry Emerson Fosdick,
Lord's Day Alliance,	Savanarola,
Americanism 100%,	Mary Baker Eddy,
Index Expurgatorius,	Christian Imperialism,
Personal Liberty,	Fundamentalism,
Bishop Manning,	Trapist,
Christian Science,	Judge Ben Lindsey,
Confessional,	Sectarian,
"The Mayflower,"	Married Priesthood,
Concordat,	British Empire,
French-Canadians,	Father Mathew Society.
Eighteenth Amendment,	

Father Ross reports the following results:

"The highest number of persons scratching any one word was eleven, and the word receiving that distinction was 'Anti-saloon League.' This is significant when taken in conjunction with the results of the third test, to be commented on shortly. It is interesting that the next highest score was on a word implying a practice sanctioned for some of the Roman Catholic Uniate Churches—'married priesthood.' 'Woman preacher,' 'Martin Luther,' and 'John Roach Straton' were tied with nine votes each. 'The Eighteenth Amendment,' 'Inquisition' and 'Judge Ben Lindsey' each had seven votes. 'The Ancient Order of Hibernians' evoked more antagonism than the 'Y. M.' or 'Y. W.,' being scratched by six persons as compared with four for the others. 'The Mayflower' was not scratched at all, whereas 'The Ark and the Dove' was scratched by two.

"The words that were queried, as indicating that the persons did not know the meaning, are almost as significant as the ones scratched. Among these was 'The Ark and the Dove,' so that it may be necessary to tell Catholics that these were the boats in which the first Maryland colonists came over. 'Torquemada,' 'Ne Temere,' 'Filioque,' 'Gallicanism,' 'contemplative communities' and 'laid' were likewise questionmarked.

"The third test was what was called at Fairfield 'an anthology of hate'," continues the report. 'It consisted of twenty-three assertions supposed to be made by Catholics about Protestants. As the leader of the Fairfield group said, the assertions put into the mouths of Catholics were considerably milder than those put into the mouths of Protestants and presented to the Fairfield group. Each person was asked to mark the assertions accordingly whether he believed them justified, probably justified, uncertain, probably unjustified or unjustified."

Questions Put to One Group.

The list of questions submitted to the Fairfield group follows:

CATHOLICS SAY OF PROTESTANTS THAT

They discriminate against Catholics in a political way.

They attempt to proselytize among poor Catholics, particularly Italians and Mexicans.

They support all manner of outrageous publications against Catholics, such as the old Menace.

They form bitterly unfair anti-Catholic organizations, such as the Know-Nothings, A. P. A., Guardians of Liberty, Ku Klux Klan.

They are puritanical and attempt to regulate other people's business by law, for instance, prohibition and Sunday observance.

They profess the American principle of separation of Church and State, yet speak of this country as Protestant.

They look upon the public schools, supported by the taxes of Catholics as well as their own taxes, as belonging exclusively to themselves.

They attempt to make the public schools Protestant by having a distinctly Protestant translation of the Bible read in class

They discriminate against Catholice in business.

They have attempted to keep Catholics out of the United States through legislation directed at the European Catholic countries

They bring political and economic pressure to bear upon Catholics to contribute to distinctly Protestant undertakings such as the Y M C A.

They seem to imply that Catholics are not Christians.

They are intolerant of Protestants who become Catholics.

They control the press of the country and do not give a reasonable amount of space to Catholics and Catholic activities.

They look upon Catholics as socially inferior

They do not accept the whole Bible.

They undermine the real authority of the Scripture.

They deliberately use terms offensive to Catholics, such as Romanist and Papist.

They have no fixed body of religious or moral belief.

By letting "conscience be their guide" they can reason conscience into making anything seem right.

While remaining political constitutionalists they are religious anarchists.

Supposedly for freedom, but notoriously intolerant.

By supporting divorce with right to remarry are really believers in legalized free love.

Statements of Protestants.

PROTESTANTS SAY OF CATHOLICS THAT

In Politics

They are seeking a political strangle hold on the country.

They are clannish and stick together against Protestants in politics.

When once in power they will not give "heretics" a look-in.

They talk "toleration" when Protestants are in a majority and "intolerance" when Catholics are in a majority.

They are mostly wets and seek to nullify the Eighteenth Amendment.

They hope to establish the Pope in Washington.

They are seeking to get control of the public schools.

They deny the validity of marriages between Protestants and Catholics, though legally contracted.

They believe in the infallible authority of the Pope, even though he may be notoriously wicked or immoral.

They are torn by a dual allegiance and can not be loyal to America and to the Pope.

Their church cellars are full of rifles.

Their whole system is autocratic and fundamentally opposed to democracy and Americanism.

Roman Catholicism is essentially the product of Italian culture, and hence unfitted to American needs.

Economically

Catholic countries are less prosperous than Protestant nations.

Catholics are clannish and stick together in business against Protestants.

It is often impossible for a capable Protestant to get a job where Catholics are in control.

They wring money out of the poor to support their various institutions.

They are always begging money, even from Protestants.

They sell the consolations of religion (e. g. indulgences) at a fixed price.

The Catholic Church tends to keep the people poor.

In Educational and Intellectual Matters

They are too superstitious

They are generally low in intelligence.

They believe everything priests tell them.

They are kept in ignorance by the priests.

Priests are usually ignorant.

They have no real liberty as to what they can read or think. Everything is censored.

Their policy of indoctrinating the young children makes against the fullest intellectual and spiritual development of the latter.

As the Catholic service is mostly in Latin the people do not for the most part know what is going on.

The Catholic Church is usually opposed to new scientific theories.

Catholic leaders are afraid to let Catholics mingle with non-Catholics since they might be led away from the faith by the greater intelligence of the latter.

Catholics furnish much more than their quota of insane.

They are opposed to all progressive measures making for popular liberty and enlightenment.

Morally.

They tend to be deceitful and tricky and cannot be trusted.

They do not believe it wrong to lie to Protestants.

They consider celibacy a higher state than marriage.

Priests and nuns are often immoral.

Catholics celibate priests are always urging large families for other people, even when the latter cannot afford them.

They take an unreasonable attitude against birth control.

They allow Protestant Missions and Community Houses to support and help their uncared for young.

Catholics furnish much more than their quota of criminals.

Their confessional system makes them less scrupulous about wronging any one.

Catholic institutions are scandalously administered.

They put the will of the Pope above conscience.

They extol the sanctity of marriage in theory, but willingly annul marriages when it serves their purposes to do so.

In Latin countries they contribute to illegitimacy through high marriage fees.

They believe that the end justifies the means.

Religiously.

They are tawdry in their church decorations.

They do not admit the direct approach of the believer to God.

They are not allowed to read the Bible.

They are idolators and worship images and pictures.

They believe that Protestants will go to hell.

When they have been to mass on Sunday they can do anything they like the rest of the day.

Too many fake miracles, bleeding tongues, liquefactions, "showers from Saint Teresa," &c.

Catholicism encourages too much formalism and "hocus-pocus."

Results of "Anthology."

Giving the results on the "anthology of hate" test, Father Ross made this report:

"At Fairfield the average score was 17, or 21 per cent. of the total possible score; in the Catholic group it was —3, out of a possible +46. The Protestant group, therefore, showed itself more than five times as willing to believe the much stronger assertions presented to it as the Catholic group was to believe the much milder assertions presented to it. But the same caution must be kept in mind here as in regard to the first test, that the wider experience of the Catholic group tended to soften their judgment of Protestants."

It was concluded that the greatest cause of friction between Catholics and Protestants in the United States was the "question of relations between Church and State." The group, according to Father Ross, tried to "clarify its own conception of the American principle of separation of Church and State."

"After considerable discussion," he continued, "it was decided that this principle implied not only freedom of worship and no established church, but also from the standpoint of the State freedom from ecclesiastical interference in purely political matters, and from the standpoint of the Church a corresponding freedom from interference by the tSate in purely ecclesiastical affairs.

"The greatest difficulty was felt to hinge upon questions that were not purely political, and not purely religious, but politico-moral matters. In order to clarify its own stand on such questions, the group then elaborated the formula to carry the implication that no Church should take action in an organized way on a political question or politico-moral question, unless inaction would mean a compromise of principle.

"The only specific example of such inaction being a compromise of principle that occurred to the group was the complete yielding by the Church and by the family of practically all right to determine the primary education of their children, as was demanded by the Oregon school law. Prohibition was accepted as an example of a politico-moral question where inaction would not be a compromise of principle, because upright men equally zealous for temperance might differ as to the advisability of attempting to achieve temperance in this particular way."

The Inquiry undertook the investigation to determine how best to proceed with its work for a better understanding between different religious groups.

BANS SHAKESPEARE PLAY

Boston Schools End Reading of 'The Merchant of Venice'

BOSTON, June 22 (AP).—Classroom reading of Shakespeare's "Merchant of Venice" was banned today in Boston public schools as a result of complaints that the character of "Shylock" was offensive to the Jewish race.

The Schools Committee decided that students could select the play for voluntary reading but prohibited classroom discussion.

Leading the fight for restriction, Maurice Tobin said that "if any other racial group were subjected to the same embarrassment that the Jewish people are in the book they certainly would also protest."

Mr. Tobin said "The Merchant of Venice" had been banned in schools of about 100 other cities.

June 23, 1937

FORD REPUDIATES BIAS AGAINST JEWS

Anti-Semitism Is 'Weakening National Unity,' He Writes B'nai B'rith Leader

Henry Ford repudiated anti-Semitism in a letter made public here yesterday.

He wrote it on Jan. 7 to Sigmund Livingston of Chicago, founder and national chairman of the Anti-Defamation League of B'nai B'rith, saying "I consider it of importance that I clarify some general misconceptions concerning my attitude."

Previously Mr. Ford's personnel chief, Harry H. Bennett, had invited the national director of the Anti-Defamation League, Richard E. Gutstadt, to call at the Ford office in Detroit. Mr. Bennett explained that Mr. Ford was "highly indignant" over the charges of anti-Semitism that have followed him through the years, and with renewed intensity recently.

Found Ford Very Pleasant

Mr. Ford was introduced and Mr. Gutstadt says he found him "very pleasant."

Thereafter Mr. Bennett took charge and arranged for the letter. He told Mr. Gutstadt that B'nai B'rith had been picked as the recipient because of its outstanding position in Jewish organizational life. It is one of the oldest and largest Jewish fraternal bodies in the United States, with some 900 branches and a membership of

FORD LETTER SCORING ANTI-SEMITISM

Ford Motor Company
ROUGE PLANT
DEARBORN, MICHIGAN

January 7 1942

Mr Sigmund Livingston
160 North LaSalle Street
Chicago, Illinois

Dear Sir:

In our present national and international emergency, I consider it of importance that I clarify some general misconceptions concerning my attitude toward my fellow-citizens of Jewish faith. I do not subscribe to or support, directly or indirectly, any agitation which would promote antagonism against my Jewish fellow-citizens. I consider that the hate-mongering prevalent for some time in this country against the Jew, is of distinct disservice to our country, and to the peace and welfare of humanity.

At the time of the retraction by me of certain publications concerning the Jewish people, in pursuance of which I ceased the publication of "The Dearborn Independent," I destroyed copies of literature prepared by certain persons connected with its publication. Since that time I have given no permission or sanction to anyone to use my name as sponsoring any such publication, or being the accredited author thereof.

I am convinced that there is no greater dereliction among the Jews than there is among any other class of citizens. I am convinced, further, that agitation for the creation of hate against the Jew or any other racial or religious group, has been utilized to divide our American community and to weaken our national unity.

I strongly urge all my fellow-citizens to give no aid to any movement whose purpose it is to arouse hatred against any group. It is my sincere hope that now in this country and throughout the world, when this war is finished and peace once more established, hatred of the Jew, commonly known as anti-Semitism, and hatred against any other racial or religious group, shall cease for all time.

Sincerely yours,

Henry Ford

more than 150,000 adult Jews.

One visit by Mr. Gutstadt was sufficient. Mr. Livingston did not have to appear in the matter.

He received a letter in which Mr. Ford declared anti-Semitism was "prevalent" and was 'weakening our national unity" and that "I do not subscribe to or support, directly or indirectly, any agitation which would promote antagonism against my Jewish fellow citizens."

Further, Mr. Ford "strongly urged" his fellow-citizens to give no aid to any such movement, and concluded with "my sincere hope" that "now in this country, and throughout the world when this war is finished, hatred of the Jew and hatred against any other racial or religious group shall cease for all time."

Made Retraction in 1927

The present repudiation of anti-Semitism is Mr. Ford's most forthright declaration since June, 1927. Then, facing a $1,000,000 libel suit, he addressed a letter to the late Louis Marshall, "retracting" the all-out attacks on the Jews conducted under his name since 1920 in his own magazine, the Dearborn Independent.

"I deem it my duty as an honorable man," Mr. Ford wrote in 1927, "to make amends for the wrong done to the Jews as fellow-men and brothers, by asking their forgiveness for the harm I have unintentionally committed, by retracting so far as lies within my power the offensive charges laid at their door by these publications and by giving them the unqualified assurance that henceforth they may look to me for friendship and good-will."

January 12, 1942

Vatican Justifies Views of Prelates On Curbing Protestant Minorities

Special to THE NEW YORK TIMES.

ROME, July 20 — The Vatican said today that an address by Alfredo Cardinal Ottaviani here, March 2, supporting the Spanish Bishops' position favoring restriction of Protestant minorities in Roman Catholic countries in the face of criticism by some French and United States Catholics, was not official or semi-official but was nevertheless "unexceptionable."

The Vatican's statement was elicited by a request from THE NEW YORK TIMES for an authoritative clarification of the speech in view of apparently conflicting interpretations given to it in Spain and in the United States.

[A controversy has waged in Catholic circles for many months over the Spanish Bishops' position that Spain, as a Catholic country, should not grant freedom of propaganda to other religions. Cardinal Ottaviani created a furor by his speech siding with the Spanish Bishops. Some prelates in the United States are said to have sent protests to Rome against the Cardinal's statement.

[In a dispatch from Madrid ecclesiastical circles there were cited as authority for the statement that the Ottaviani speech conveyed the Vatican's approval of the Spanish position.

[Apprised of this, a spokesman for critics here insisted that the Cardinal had spoken only in his personal capacity, neither officially nor semi-officially. While upholding the view held in the United States on this, the Vatican statement also stressed the "unexceptionable" quality of the Cardinal's statement.]

The Vatican pointed out that the Cardinal's statement was based largely on Papal texts, such as encyclicals and allocutions. Cardinal Ottaviani is a well-known Catholic jurist and expert on ecclesiastical law. That his arguments and conclusions were in line with Vatican doctrine was indicated by the fact that a summary of the speech was published by L'Osservatore Romano, the Vatican newspaper.

Spanish Circles See Approval

Special to THE NEW YORK TIMES.

MADRID, July 9 — Spanish ecclesiastical circles said today that the doctrinal stand taken by the Roman Catholic Episcopacy of Spain on what it considered the duties and obligations of a Catholic state toward religion in general and the Protestant minorities in particular had been confirmed by the Vatican.

That stand, which would confine Protestant religious activities to the interior of places of worship and forbid proselytizing and all external signs of worship, had been criticized as too "rigid" and "quite behind the times" by some Catholic circles in the United States and France.

The Vatican approval of the Spanish position and disapproval of the United States position, it has become known, was conveyed indirectly through the lecture delivered March 2 at the Pontifical University of St. John Lateran in Rome by Alfredo Cardinal Ottaviani, pro-secretary of the Congregation of the Holy Office and author of what the Italian Episcopacy considers fundamental works on Public Ecclesiastical Law.

On the subject of Protestant propaganda in Catholic countries, Cardinal Ottaviani clearly sided with the Spanish and Italian authorities who have attempted in past years to restrict it within their national territories. He said that Protestant propaganda had found its "strongest allies and supporters among the Communists."

Cardinal Quoted on Tolerance

According to the official text of the lecture—which is not generally known in its entirety—published by the Pontifical University last March, Cardinal Ottaviani said:

"The [Roman Catholic] Church, too, recognizes the necessity with which rulers in some Catholic countries may be faced of granting —because of grave reasons—a degree of tolerance to the other cults.

"But tolerance is not a synonym for freedom of propaganda [by non-Catholics] which foments religious discord and alters the secure and unanimous possession of [Catholic] truth and of religious practice in countries such as Italy, Spain and others.

"* * * Unfortunately, in the U. S. A., where many dissident brethren [Protestants] are unaware of the situation, both in its juridical and actual aspects, existing in our countries, there are those who show a zeal similar to that of the Communists in protesting against the alleged intolerance shown in the missionaries sent to 'convert us.'

"Believers overseas who collect the funds for their missionaries and for the neophytes they have won over do not know that the majority of the 'converts' are authentic Communists who couldn't care less for religious questions, except as a means to stir up trouble for the Catholics. What Communists want first and foremost is to use the funds sent from beyond the Atlantic. I believe that if [Protestant] believers knew all this they would think twice before sending money that eventually ends by encouraging communism."

Two Main Themes Developed

In his lecture, Cardinal Ottaviani developed two main themes: the duty and obligations of the state toward religion in nations with a Catholic majority, and in nations with a Catholic minority.

In countries where Catholics are a minority "the exclusiveness of the mission of the Catholic Church is not recognized," the Cardinal said.

"In such a case the church is content to advance its claims in the name of that tolerance, of that equality, and of those common guarantees by which the legislation of those countries is inspired."

The Cardinal made it clear that even in overwhelmingly Catholic states, the so-called "intransigent stand" as ennunciated in principle by Catholic doctrine, might be juridicially applied in varying degrees tempered by social—as distinct from religious—concepts such as the "rights of man." In this, therefore, the Cardinal acknowledged some of the views expounded by "liberal catholicism."

Since the Pope himself is the Prefect, or head of that Congregation, which is considered the most important of all the Vatican departments because it deals with questions of faith and morals vital to catholicism, the view of the Spanish bishops is that Cardinal Ottaviani would not have discussed without first having obtained papal assent so important and delicate a questions as that of the rights of Protestants in Catholic and non-Catholic states.

Controversy Started in February

The controversy originated from tatements made by Pedro Cardinal Segura y Saenz, Archbishop of Seville, in a pastoral letter dated Feb. 20, 1952. In it, the Cardinal expressed his concern for what he thought was the excessive tolerance shown by the Spanish Government toward the Protestant minority living in Spain.

Some Catholic circles in the United States criticized Cardinal Segura's position as anachronistic but the Spanish Episcopacy strongly upheld Cardinal Segura's position.

In discussing the purely doctrinal aspect of the Church-State issue, Cardinal Ottaviani echoed the views of the Spanish episcopacy, not—as he indicated—because they were a specifically Spanish interpretation of Catholic doctrine, but because they were the orthodox interpretation given to it by the Vatican itself through solemn papal pronouncements in the past.

Consequently, he deplored the views of what he called "liberal Catholicism," as expressed by some United States circles inasmuch as, in his opinion, they represented a departure from the true Catholic theological path.

Jesuit Calls Views Personal

The Rev. John Courtney Murray, S. J., Professor of Theology and Editor of Theological Studies at Woodstock (Md.) College, and one of the leading Catholic scholars in the United States, said yesterday:

"Cardinal Ottaviani was speaking only in his purely personal capacity. His statement was neither an official nor a semi-official utterance. It was just the statement of a private theologian —one of very considerable reputation, of course—speaking on his own authority.

"It is still entirely possible and legitimate for Catholics to doubt or dispute whether Cardinal Ottaviani's discourse represents the full, adequate and balanced doctrine of the church."

July 23, 1953

NEW PHASE NOTED IN ANTI-SEMITISM

American Jewish Committee Finds More Subtle Tactics Being Used in Campaigns

The American Jewish Committee reported yesterday that organized anti-Semitism in this country had changed its tactics radically in the last seven years. The committee stressed the need for vigilance "against malicious movements striving to foment racial and religious discord."

The statements were made in a report on "Anti-Semitic Activity in the United States: A Report and Appraisal." Founded in 1906, the American Jewish Committee is devoted to combating bigotry, protecting civil and religious rights of Jews and advancing human rights.

The report held that "many of these movements have now abandoned their former overt appeals to bigotry in favor of more subtle tactics to which the public must be alerted."

In pointing to the change of tactics, the report said:

"To achieve a proper perspective, it is necessary to understand that many anti-Semites have abandoned their former brash and obvious tactics. The more skillful hate-mongers and cunning publicists have now developed a sense of public relations. They exploit legitimate issues, toning down, if not eliminating, open anti-Semitism. They aim to win the support of respectable elements."

Ultra-Nationalism Pushed

The anti-Semites today, the report said, have learned "how to salt public debate with hate propaganda," adding that "ultra-nationalists" groups offered convenient platforms for this strategy.

Among the themes falsely stressed by the ultra-nationalists are extreme isolationism, opposition to foreign aid, unreasoning hostility to the United Nations, condemnation of both major political parties and agitation for "a realignment of political forces," it was explained.

"While some of the ultranationalist groups espouse retrogressive economic reforms," the report said, "and others have political aims, all favor extremist techniques in combating communism—free-swinging, wild-accusation tactics which indiscriminately charge liberals with being Communistic. Ultra-nationalists are now appealing to the American people on this basis, equating everything they oppose with communism, subversion, and a newly invented phenomenon—'creeping socialism.'

"There is much room in the market-place of the ideas for opposing viewpoints on a multitude of issues—national and international, political, social and economic. That is the glory of the American democracy, but the public must be shown how to recognize and reject the ideological counterfeiters who would pass on as legal tender their hollow coins of bigotry."

April 1, 1954

CATHOLIC STRESS ON MARY SCORED

Presbyterian Report Asserts Devotion Widens Breach With Other Christians

By GEORGE DUGAN
Special to The New York Times.

LOS ANGELES, May 21—The increasing emphasis of the Roman Catholic Church on the role of the Virgin Mary has "widened the breach" between that faith and "all other Christian communions," it was declared here today.

An official commission of the Presbyterian Church in the U. S. A. is scheduled to present a long statement on Monday to the 167th General Assembly of the Presbyterian Body for final approval. In it the church's Permanent Commission on Interchurch Relations asserted that the devotion of Roman Catholicism to Mary "now equals, and even exceeds, the devotion to Christ Himself."

The commission commented on what it described as the "development of the Marian cult." It declared that "in the figure of the Virgin the Church of Rome has created a semi-divine female being who becomes virtual head of the Church, the hope of all who are distressed and the Sovereign Overlord of all that occurs in history."

The statement was the outgrowth of a request made last year in Detroit by the 166th Presbyterian General Assembly. The assembly sought an exposition of the issues involved in the Roman Catholic Church's observance of a "Marian Year" during 1954 and its relation to "Christ's place in the Christian religion."

The request was referred to the permanent commission for "consideration and report" in 1955.

Named to Prepare Report

The Rev. Dr. Jonn A. Mackay, a former moderator of the church and president of Princeton Theological Seminary, was selected by the commission to prepare the report. Early last March, Dr. Mackay's statement was approved by the commission.

The Mackay statement said that "today the Roman communion stands alone, in proud yet tragic isolation, from all other Christian churches." It then declared:

"The glory of Christ's Headship in His Church, His undying concern for the members of His body and for all human beings, is both tarnished and challenged by the new status accorded to the Virgin. The meaning of Christ's Kingship for life and history becomes emptied of all true significance."

Singling out Our Lady of Fatima as the "concrete symbol of this new and exalted status of Mary," the statement said the "Fatima cult" provided "a moving, pictorial and allegedly historical basis for the idea, so assiduously inculcated, that the Virgin Mary is that member of the celestial family who is most sympathetically and potently related to the problems of our disordered world."

"Because of that," it said, "and in virtue of her God-given office as Mediatrix, she is the one most capable of achieving the solution of man's problems today."

Our Lady of Fatima, according to Catholics, appeared on a Portuguese plateau in 1917, the year of the Russian revolution, bearing a "peace plan from heaven."

'Special Interest in Russia'

The Presbyterian statement noted also that the Virgin of Fatima had expressed a "very special interest in the conversion of Communist Russia."

Thus, the statement continued, "Russia has accordingly been consecrated to Mary." It added:

"Mariology, that is the theology of Mary, is of a very organic kind and is still in the making. It is not determined by any reference to the Bible or to Christ. The doctrine of Mary is founded upon the sole authority of the Roman Catholic Church.

"Doctrinally speaking, the theology of the Virgin has passed through three distinct stages. In the first stage, the doctrine of Mary was an integral part of the theology of Christ. In the second stage, it was an appendix to the theology of Christ. In the third stage, the stage which has now been reached, Marian theology forms a completely independent chapter of Christian theology.

"Honors bestowed upon the Virgin Mary in the course of Christian history have closely paralleled, and in some instances duplicated, honors paid to Jesus Christ.

Process Still Continues

"This process, which still continues, has been equally true in liturgical practice and in theological concept. Episodes in the life of Christ, festivals held in honor of Christ, mysteries relating to the person and work of Christ, have all been duplicated by episodes, festivals and mysteries connected with the Virgin Mother. The Feast of Christ the King has been paralleled by the Feast of the Queenship of Mary. The Sacred Heart of Jesus is now paralleled by the Most Pure Heart of Mary."

The statement emphasized that "nothing is more distasteful than to subject to unfavorable analysis developments which occur in another Christian communion."

"Only when such developments affect the very core of the Christian religion, especially the doctrine, so foundational in New Testament Christianity, of the perfect Saviourhood and the complete Lordship of Jesus Christ, can such a course be justified," it said.

"It is because the Permanent Commission believes that an issue of this kind has been created by the cult whose chief contemporary emblem is 'Our Lady of Fatima' that it essays to make some pertinent observations. This it desires to do in charity but with candor."

May 22, 1955

CATHOLIC SOCIETY DEFENDS MARIANS

A recent Presbyterian declaration that the Church of Rome had "created a semi-divine female being" in the figure of Virgin Mary was criticized yesterday by the Catholic Theological Society of America as a "distortion of Catholic devotion to Mary."

At the close of the tenth annual convention of the society at the Commodore Hotel, 168 priest-theologian members of the group's total membership of 550 in this country and Canada issued a statement. It expressed "regret and sorrow" at Presbyterian assertions that "the development of the Marian cult has widened the breach between the Roman Catholic Church and all other Christian communions."

The Catholic group said it felt bound in conscience to reply to the Presbyterian statement approved by the General Assembly of the Presbyterian Church in the U. S. A. last May 23 in Los Angeles. In that statement, the Presbyterian Assembly asserted that the Virgin Mother had become "virtual head" of the Catholic Church and contended that the devotion by Catholics to Mary "now equals, and even exceeds, the devotion to Christ Himself."

The Catholic society declared: it is not true that in the mind and heart of Catholics Mary takes the place of Christ; it is not true that Catholics think of Mary as a "semi-divine" being; it is not true that the cult of Our Lady of Fatima symbolizes any "new and exalted status of Mary."

June 30, 1955

Tensions Inside the City

PROTESTANT AND CATHOLIC: Religious and Social Interaction in an Industrial Community. By Kenneth Wilson Underwood. 484 pp. Boston: The Beacon Press. $7.50.

By CONSTANCE McL. GREEN

THIS study by Kenneth Underwood is a careful analysis of the way in which churches and people of the Protestant and Roman Catholic faiths respond to each other in the give-and-take of everyday life in an American industrial city—in business dealings, in labor relations, in neighborhood associations, in the schools and in recreational and political activities. Through this intensive examination of a particular city the author seeks to illuminate a vitally important aspect of all American culture.

In choosing for this purpose "the most Catholic city in America," as Catholics have labeled Holyoke, Mass., he might be accused of taking an extreme example and thereby exaggerating the significance of religious cleavages in modern America. "Paper City," the name he adopts for Holyoke, has a long history of religious conflict, unadmitted or open. Indeed, this tension dates back virtually to the founding of the town in 1850 and represents today not a recent flare-up but a steady evolution. "Roman Catholic-Protestant relations," a Paper City industrialist observed, "are woven into the

Mrs. Green is the author of "Holyoke, Massachusetts" and is now working under a Rockefeller grant on a history of the District of Columbia.

whole warp and woof of our life."

The author, Associate Professor of Social Ethics and Public Affairs at Wesleyan University, makes no attempt to justify his choice on grounds of typicality, but he notes "that the decisions men face in this city about the relations of their own religious group to other faiths, to social stratifications and to economic and political associations contain the same basic issues with which other men wrestle in our nation and our civilization as they seek to develop significant and creative relationships between the various organizations and interests of their common life."

Moreover, an extraordinary episode that in the fall of 1940 focused the attention of religious leaders throughout the nation upon this city of 55,000 souls provides a dramatic introduction to the community problems with which the book deals. The factual, detailed account of "the Sanger incident" alone should stir the interest of every thoughtful American, for the pressure brought by Roman Catholics upon members of a Protestant congregation led to the rescinding of permission to use the church for a lecture on birth control.

Margaret Sanger, sponsored by the New England Mothers' Health Council, was to speak in favor of a petition for state legislation that would permit doctors to give married women information on planned parenthood. The entire story as it unfolds has shocking aspects and far-reaching implications, which a good many Catholics perceived quite as clearly as did the Protestants.

The last ironic twist lies in the fact that the city's one organization to offer its rooms for the meeting was the C. I. O. Textile Workers Union, at that time an organization upon which conservative Protestants looked with distrust. In the cramped little offices of the Textile Workers Union the meeting took place.

THIS episode serves as an effective introduction to the tensions that prevail in Paper City—but it is only an introduction. The intelligent Protestant must find much of what follows a profoundly disturbing analysis of the shortcomings of American Protestantism. The analysis is convincing not only because of its thoroughness and its dispassion but because the analyst is himself manifestly aware of the values inherent in the Protestant ethic.

This study, with its criticism of the vague and diffuse thinking of Protestant denominations, comes from a Congregationalist, a man trained in the Yale Divinity School. When he points to the confusions and timidity that mark Protestantism in Paper City, no one weighing his evidence could attribute to him baseless religious hostility. His findings should force every Protestant to re-examine and define his religious beliefs.

"Protestant and Catholic" is a sociological study "in depth," though it employs little or none of the sociological jargon. The result is a readable text, requiring, to be sure, concentrated attention, but it is well worth the effort.   February 2, 1958

PRESIDENT SCORES 'VIRUS OF BIGOTRY'

Warns It Must Be Stemmed as Peril to Freedom

President Eisenhower declared yesterday that freedom and decency could be destroyed everywhere if Americans ignored "the virus of bigotry" or permitted it "to spread one inch."

The President's message was one of several from various quarters expressing concern over bigotry as shown in recent anti-Semitic vandalism.

It was addressed to the National Conference of Christians and Jews in reply to a telegram last Thursday from Dr. John Sutherland Bonnell, pastor of the Fifth Avenue Presbyterian Church; the Rev. John A. O'Brien of Notre Dame University and Rabbi Maurice N. Eisendrath, president of the Union of American Hebrew Congregations.

The clergymen, who serve as co-chairmen of the Commission on Interreligious Relations of the conference, had voiced concern over the threat of religious bigotry in politics and the anti-Semitic outbreaks.

The President's reply follows:
"We deeply regret that the virus of bigotry seems to be ever present in the body politic. We cannot ignore it nor can we allow it to spread one inch. For when it becomes rampant it can cause the destruction of freedom and decency everywhere.

"In this age, when so much is expected and required of America, we can ill afford to waste a single day combating bigotry or prejudice at home. United in a common purpose, in free and responsible teamwork between those of all races, of all faiths and of all nationalities, we will continue seeking to advance the general welfare of all our people and our neighbors abroad."

The rash of anti-Semitic activities caused concern throughout the country.

Representative John W. Lindsay, Republican of Manhattan, urged the Civil Rights Commission to inquire into the desecration of synagogues and churches. Addressing the House, he deplored the incidents as "harbingers of racial and religious hatred."

Rockefeller Decries Acts

In Albany, Governor Rockefeller and the Senate joined yesterday in condemning the demonstrations. The Governor sent a telegram to an emergency meeting of the American Jewish Congress here in which he said:

"The recent outbreak of vandalism of synagogues and churches is shocking. Every thinking person is indignant at these shameful acts and those responsible for these depredations in various parts of the world."

Leaders of three faiths addressed 400 persons attending the emergency session in Stephen Wise Free Synagogue, 30 West Sixty-eighth Street. They were the Most Rev. Philip J. Furlong, Auxiliary Roman Catholic Bishop of New York; the Right Rev. Horace W. B. Donegan, Protestant Episcopal Bishop of New York, and Dr. Joachim Prinz, president of the American Jewish Congress.

Bishop Furlong declared that there must be a consciousness that each one is his brother's keeper "and that the brotherhood of man is so basic that civilization will perish without it."

Bishop Donegan observed that "any person who is anti-Jewish in his acts or feelings is at the same time anti-Christian."

Dr. Prinz warned against dismissing vandalism as a "fad like the hula hoop or rock 'n' roll."

The Senate unanimously adopted a resolution deploring the desecrations. It proposed a review to determine whether state laws were adequate to prevent future incidents. The resolution was sent to the Assembly.

Theobald Pledges Action

At City Hall, Mayor Wagner told twenty-five spokesmen for nationality groups and foreign-language publications that the city was deeply concerned and deplored the descrations. He asked that they cooperate with the Commission on Intergroup Relations and the Police Department to work out "a concrete program."

Superintendent of Schools John J. Theobald promised that the city's public schools would give added emphasis to their programs in human relations. After meeting with his board of superintendents, Dr. Theobald scheduled a meeting for tomor-

row to discuss the program.

Among incidents yesterday, eighty-seven headstones and markers in the Baron Hirsch Cemetery, Graniteville, S. I., were found smeared with yellow paint. Vandals had defaced a three-acre section of Staten Island's largest Jewish burial ground with swastikas and German terms for death and fatherland.

The term "Feuhrer" also was found. Paint had been daubed over the Star of David, Jewish religious symbol, on the headstones.

The Suffolk County police said burglars, apparently youngsters, had broken in to the Port Jefferson, L. I., elementary school on Scraggy Hill and Belle Terre Road during the night, stolen $85 from the principal's desk and painted a swastika on a wall.

Acts of vandalism continued in other cities.

A swastika was found painted on the Hillel Foundation building at the University of Pennsylvania in Philadelphia. The

foundation is a Jewish reigious and cultural organization.

Student Admits Vandalism

In Columbus, Ohio, an Ohio State University student admitted painting the Nazi symbol on the door of the Hillel Foundation there. In Los Angeles vandals broke into an elementary school, tore up an American flag and scrawled swastikas over a music room.

Other incidents of similar character were reported at a synagogue and school in Omaha, Neb., and in La Crosse, Wis., and Lowell, Ind. The St. Louis police searched for pranksters who daubed two swastikas on the front doors of the Bethesda Lutheran Church in suburban Pine Lawn.

In Washington, Bernard Abrams, national commander of the Jewish War Veterans, addressed a telegram to Secretary of State Christian A. Herter urging a commission "to conduct searching analysis into current manifestations of Nazi and Fascist resurgence."

January 13, 1960

SOME BIAS NOTED IN RELIGION TEXTS

Study at Yale Shows Books Distort Views on Jews— Fair Portrayals Cited

By IRVING SPIEGEL

A seven-year study of Protestant teaching materials, made at the Yale Divinity School, disclosed a number of them contained negative and distorted references to other faiths, the American Jewish Committee heard yesterday.

However, the study also found that some Protestant denominations portrayed other religions positively.

Major findings were an-

nounced at the fifty-third annual meeting of the committee at the Commodore Hotel by Frederick Greenman, chairman of the agency's executive board.

The committee cooperated with Yale, and also with St. Louis University, Southern Methodist University and the Dropsie College for Hebrew and Cognate Learning, where similar studies are in progress.

The study was supervised by the Rev. Dr. Bernard E. Olson of the Yale Divinity School. He reported that references to Jews or Judaism ranged from 44 per cent of the lessons of one denomination to 66 per cent of lessons in another.

'Convenient Whipping Boy'

He cited the danger that a Jew was sometimes used as "a convenient whipping boy simply because he is there in the Biblical material and therefore suggested to the [religious text]

writer as the most immediately relevant object of criticism."

"This can be especially harmful to good intergroup relations," Dr. Olson reported, "because the part that church-school literature plays in building up attitudes of friendliness or antipathy in growing children and adults must be recognized."

The study showed that in relating the Crucifixion one denomination cautioned its students: "Feelings of hate and acts of violence [against the Jew] have a long history. Their roots are deep and widespread."

The text added:

"There is one branch among these roots which it is especially important for Christians to discover; and strange as it seems, this branch grew from the old story of Salvation.

"In that great story the Jewish people were accused of having killed the Son of God.

Such an accusing attitude toward the Jewish people is surely not a fitting part of the Christion Gospel."

Forty-three per cent of the lessons of one denomination and 36 per cent of the lessons of another contain variations of the generalization that the Jews crucified Jesus, according to the study. At the same time the study showed that in all the curriculums but one it was found that the charge was repudiated.

The study indicated that there was anti-Catholic bias, but stressed that all groups studied condemned anti-Catholicism, and were "capable of varying degrees of self-criticism in respect to prejudice against Catholics."

The research for the study was supervised by a faculty committee headed by Dr. Paul Vieth, Horace Bushnell Professor of Christian Nurture.

April 23, 1960

LUTHERAN POINTS TO CATHOLIC GAINS

Cleric Tells Church Council to Emulate Creative Social and Political Approach

By GEORGE DUGAN
Special to The New York Times

MILWAUKEE, Feb. 5—Protestants were cautioned here tonght against "begrudging" the Roman Catholic Church what was described as its growing influence in American society.

The warning was voiced by

the Rev. Dr. Robert E. Van Deusen, Washington representative of the National Lutheran Council. The council, representing eight separate Lutheran bodies with a total membership of 5,000,000, will end its four-day annual meeting at the Astor Hotel tomorrow.

Dr. Van Deusen told the delegates that Protestants would be well advised to study the reasons for the increasing significanec of the Catholic Church while reappraising their own approach to social and political problems.

"In areas such as effective public relations, encouragemento able men and women to enter public life, and creative approach to social issues," he de-

clared, "wholesome growth should not be envied but emulated."

The Lutheran official said that sometimes "it becomes necessary to oppose the tendency of the Roman Catholic Church to use social, economic and political pressure to force its own standards of moral judgment on all of society."

"But when we difer," Dr. Van Deusen asserted, "we should do so as friends and fellow Christians, expressing our convictions honestly and openly. We must remember that Protestants and Roman Catholics are common contenders against the secularism of our times, and that at the deepest level, we are Christian brothers."

Dr. Van Deusen cited press,

radio and television coverage of the death of Pope Pius XII and the election and coronation of Pope John XXIII as one of the ways in which the growing influence of the Catholic Church was revealed during 1958.

As another indication of the growing influence of the Catholic Church, Dr. Van Deusen pointed to the recent success of Roman Catholic candidates at the polls.

Two states — Pennsylvania and California — elected Catholic Governors for the first time. Also, four new Catholic Senators were chosen.

"This means that the day is rapidly passing when it is a political liability to be a Roman Catholic," Dr. Van Deusen observed.

February 6, 1959

CATHOLIC TREND TO LIBERTY SEEN

Important Opinion in Favor of Religious Freedom Is Noted by World Council

By A. M. ROSENTHAL
Special to The New York Times.

GENEVA, March 3—Important opinion is building up within the Roman Catholic Church in favor of the principle of religious liberty and the trend is of 'momentous" significance, according to a report published today by the World Council of Churches.

The council is the world's largest non-Catholic church organization and the report, published from its headquarters here, is the first part of a study on religious liberty conducted by a special commission.

The theme of the ninety-five-page report is that more and more Roman Catholic theologians are pronouncing themselves in favor of religious liberty and that this "increasing stream" holds out hope of new understanding within the Christian world.

The report says many Roman Catholics still believe in restricting the freedom of non-Catholics.

Emphasis of the Study

But the whole emphasis of the study is that "inside the orthodoxy of the Roman Catholic Church" the principle that freedom to accept the tenets of other faiths is compatible with Catholicism is gaining strength, has not been officially condemned and is supported by important members of the hierarchy.

"Once this Roman Catholic opinion ceases to be only one of several admitted within the Catholic orthodoxy and becomes the official attitude of the Church itself, a practical agreement with the Roman Catholic Church on the real exercise of religious liberty in all countries will be possible," said the study. "And we sincerely hope that time is not so far away as many fear.

"It is most unfortunate that the question of religious freedom has so frequently been treated in a general atmosphere of suspicion and distrust, so far as the doctrine of the Roman Catholic Church is concerned.

"Too many Protestants seem to believe that all Roman Catholics (even those who defend religious liberty) are of bad faith. * * * As for Roman Catholics, many of them also seem to think that Protestants raise the question of religious liberty merely as a pretext to attack the Catholic Church."

Author of Report Named

The report was written for the council—which is composed of 172 Anglican, Protestant and Orthodox member-churches—by Dr. A. F. Carillo de Albornoz.

A representative of the council here said that Dr. Carillo is a Spaniard who is a lay member of the Protestant Episcopal Church in the United States.

At its Geneva headquarters a representative of the council said that its published studies did not necessarily mirror the opinions of the organization. Dr. Carillo is a research associate of the council's Study of Religious Liberty.

The chairman of the special commission making the study is the Rev. Dr. Alford Carleton, executive vice president of the American Board of Commissioners for Foreign Missions of the Congregational Christian Church of the United States.

The commission membership includes two of the World Council's six presidents — Bishop Sante Uberto Barbieri, Methodist, of Argentina, and Archbishop Iakovos, Greek Orthodox, of the United States.

Dr. Carillo said in his report that the common interpretation of the Roman Catholic attitude toward religious liberty was this:

On matters of policy, Catholics ask for religious freedom where they are in the minority and oppose it when they are in the majority. On matters of doctrine, Catholics believe that where the principles of the Church can be applied, "error" must not be free to be propagated. Where Catholics cannot "prudently" impose their principles, "freedom of error" can be provisionally tolerated as the lesser evil. This is called the doctrine of "thesis and hypothesis."

Growing Opposition Seen

The report says that although many Catholics defend this doctrine, more and more theologians in the Church are disturbed by it and oppose it.

Large parts of the report are devoted to quotations from Catholic laymen and clergymen, including Cardinals, in defense of the principle of freedom of religious practice for non-Catholics.

The report says that these Catholics believe that there has been no decisive statement against religious freedom by the Church.

The report recalls the statements of nineteenth-century Popes against religious freedom. But it says that these were directed against "absolute freedom" and were conditioned by events of the time and so were "without eternal validity."

The theory of religious liberty held by many Roman Catholics today, says the report, is not a matter of opportunism or a "tactical variant" on the old position of thesis and hypothesis.

It is "another radical and irreducible doctrinal position which is very sincerely and fiercely fighting the old one," the report declares.

Dr. Carillo said there was no decisive Catholic Church proclamation in favor of religious freedom as yet, perhaps because the Church "does not consider the actual controversy among Roman Catholic theologians as sufficiently ripe for making a final decision."

March 4, 1960

Christian Beliefs on the Death of Jesus Assayed

Survey Finds Jews Blamed by 69% of Churchgoers

By IRVING SPIEGEL

Sixty-nine per cent of "church-oriented Christians" still believe that Jews are the group "most responsible" for the death of Jesus, a study by the Survey Research Center of the University of California disclosed yesterday.

The report was based on a preliminary test in which members of Protestant congregations replied to questionnaires on their attitudes toward Jews. The findings were reported by Benjamin R. Epstein, national director of the Anti-Defamation League of B'nai B'rith, at its 51st annual meeting, held at the Savoy Hilton Hotel.

The university's survey research center is conducting a five-year analysis of anti-Semitism in the United States that was underwritten by the league at a cost of $500,000.

Mr. Epstein told the session that "one of the root causes of anti-Semitism through the centuries has been religious teachings" and he cited in particular the Crucifixion as attributed to "the Jews."

The belief that the Jewish people have responsibility for the death of Jesus is "still distressingly alive and cruel," Mr. Epstein declared.

The test findings by the research center listed the following items:

¶81 per cent of the adult Christian church members studied believed that Pontius Pilate wanted to spare Jesus from the Cross. More than 48 per cent thought that he failed to spare Jesus because "a group of powerful Jews wanted Jesus dead."

¶69 per cent of the total chose Jews as the group "most responsible" for crucifying Jesus.

¶19 per cent believed that Jews have been persecuted because "God is punishing them for rejecting Jesus." And 15 per cent were undecided on this.

¶45 per cent held that "Jews can never be forgiven for what they did to Jesus until they accept Him as the True Saviour." But 18 per cent were uncertain about it.

A spokesman for the Protestant Council of New York, representing some 1,700 churches, withheld comment pending a study of full findings.

The late Pope John XXIII was responsible for the deletion of certain invidious references to Jews in Catholic liturgy. A statement clarifying Judaism's relationship to Christianity is expected to be presented at the third session of the Vatican Council next September.

Mr. Epstein, in reporting on the attitudes of churchgoers toward Jews, said that 84 per cent in Fundamentalist churches blamed the Jews for the death of Jesus compared with 55 per cent of large, liberal congregations.

"But the report indicated that all groups tended to remember Judas as a Jew, not as a Christian, and the sinister connection was reinforced by the similarity of the words 'Judas' and 'Judaism,'" he added.

Noting that Christian leaders had repeatedly stressed that Christianity owed "a profound debt to Judaism for its origins and tenets," Mr. Epstein commented:

"I think that Jews have every right to call upon Christian leaders and friends and expect that they themselves will increasingly seek to rectify the centuries-old injustice and barbarism of anti-Semitism."

February 2, 1964

JESUITS FIND BIAS IN CATHOLIC BOOKS

St. Louis University Report Examines Attitudes on Jews and Protestants

By IRVING SPIEGEL

A major study by Roman Catholics of their textbooks on religion has found that the books still sometimes convey distorted and negative attitudes toward Jews and Protestants.

However, the study showed that these books were "overwhelmingly positive" toward racial and ethnic groups where religion was not involved.

The three-year study was made by St. Louis University, a prominent Jesuit institution.

Its findings were made public jointly here yesterday by the Rev. Paul C. Reinert, president of the university, and Morris B. Abram, newly elected president of the American Jewish Committee, at the committee's annual meeting at the New York Hilton.

Sixty-five volumes widely used in parochial schools were analyzed in the study. They included seven basic religion series, two church histories, one guidance series, four supplementary volumes and accompanying teachers' guidebooks.

Crucifixion Stressed

The study cautioned against generalizations and oversimplifications of other religions. It said that negative comments regarding Protestants and Jews dealt particularly with historic conflicts.

For Protestants, for example, these themes are doctrinal differences with the Roman Catholic Church and the Reformation conflict.

For Jews, they stress the rejection of Christianity, the Crucifixion and the Pharisees.

The report cited the following excerpt as a "negative distortion" of the Crucifixion:

"The chief priests took up a cry that put a curse on themselves and on the Jews for all time. . ."

The references to the Pharisees as the "temple gang" and as "racketeers selling sheep and doves in the building" were also criticized.

Future textbook authors were urged to "explain the true significance of the Crucifixion. Jesus suffered and died for the sins of all and for the salvation of all. The only disposition proper at the foot of the Cross is sorrow for one's own sins; there is then no need to accuse others."

Positive references to Jews, the report noted, abound in comments on the Old Testament as a heritage of the Roman Catholic Church.

For example, one text states: "Catholics of the world, regardless of their nationality, are all spiritually Semites, we are all children of Israel."

Some Recommendations

The study offered the following recommendations that would avoid portraying distortions in teachings about Jews.

¶"Set forth the continuity of the Old and the New Testament, the unity of the divine work of Salvation. In discussions of the Old Testament, stress the existing law of love, also.

¶"Show Jesus as He lived in His own country and among His Jewish people, with His Mother Mary, the Jewish Maiden, His apostles and disciples—Jewish friends. Picture Jesus as the true 'Israelite' (John 1:47) who came 'not to destroy the law but to fulfill It' (Matthew 5:17)."

¶"Give a true picture of Judaism in the days of Jesus with its tense atmosphere of expectancy, pointing out the fact that there were some digressions (not universal) and note also the rich participation in religious worship without overemphasizing the extremes in the law.

"It is necessary to avoid this same warping of the truth in speaking of present-day Judaism. To try to inculcate love for Christianity by denigrating (so it seems at times) would be as shameful as it is incorrect."

¶"Refrain from making negative value judgments in the treatment of the Jewish people, those of the time of our Savior as well as those regarding present-day Jews. God alone knows the secret yearnings of the individual (Catholic, Jew, other Christian or Gentile)."

The report gave the following as a textbook distortion about Protestants:

"Protestantism granted concessions in an attempt to attract all who lacked courage to live up to the high standard proposed by Christ and the Church. Protestantism today is rapidly deteriorating, while the unchanging spiritual Church has grown ever stronger with the years."

The study said various Reformation leaders have been described as "obstinate heretic," "self-satisfied monarch," "positively immoral," "drunken brewer," "adulterous tyrant."

The report urged that Catholics discard the apologetic approach toward Protestants and stress the positive virtue of love of God and neighbor.

The study was written by Sister Rose Albert Thering, who received the cooperation of the American Jewish Committee. The committee also cooperated in a seven-year self-study of Protestant textbooks completed at Yale University Divinity School last year.

A Jewish self-study has been completed at Dropsie College for Hebrew and Cognate Learning. Its findings will be made public soon.

The St. Louis University study comes at a time when the Ecumenical Council, at its next session in September in Rome, is expected to act on a statement defining Catholic-Jewish relations and absolving the Jewish people from the guilt of the Crucifixion.

Last Thursday, at the dinner session of the American Jewish Committee, Cardinal Spellman voiced his regard for the Jewish people, stressing that anti-Semitism "can never find a basis in the Catholic religion."

May 3, 1964

CUSHING PRESSES FOR STRONG STAND ABSOLVING JEWS

Leads International Effort at Vatican for a Forthright Draft on Crucifixion

SEVEN OTHERS JOIN PLEA

Council Supports Formation of Deacons' Order to Aid Where Priests Are Few

By ROBERT C. DOTY
Special to The New York Times

ROME, Sept. 28 — Richard Cardinal Cushing, Archbishop of Boston, led today a broad international effort by Roman Catholic prelates to obtain a strong declaration by the Ecumenical Council that the Jews bear no special responsibility in the Crucifixion.

During today's session, the Council approved by a vote of 1,903 to 242 a proposal for re-establishment of a permanent order of deacons.

These lesser priests would carry out some sacramental functions in areas where there is a shortage of ordained priests.

Vote Looms on Celibacy

The Council action opens the way for votes tomorrow on the revolutionary proposal that married men, or young men not required to pledge celibacy, should be admitted to the order of deacons. Council conservatives are expected to resist strongly this dilution of the church's rule of absolute celibacy for the clergy.

In his plea, Cardinal Cushing urged that the Church declare itself strongly against the "iniquity" of anti-Semitism. He suggested that, in the recent past, "not many Christian voices were lifted" against the crimes committed against the Jews.

The charge that Pope Pius XII should have spoken out forcefully against the Nazi genocide of the Jews, presented in Rolf Hochhuth's play "The Deputy," has produced worldwide debate on the role of the wartime Pontiff.

Amended Draft Sought

The Boston churchman and seven other Cardinals — two from the United States, and one each from Austria, Canada, France, West Germany and Italy—urged the current session of Ecumenical Council Vatican II to amend and strengthen in liberal terms the present draft declaration on the attitude of the church toward the Jews. Four other prelates of lesser rank also supported the move.

The opposition in the opening debate on the draft was limited to statements by a Cardinal from Antioch, Syria, speaking for four other Middle Eastern prelates, and by Ernesto Cardinal Ruffini of Palermo, Sicily, a member of the church's ultraconservative wing.

The heart of the issue is a statement on the role of the Jews in the Passion of Christ on the cross. A draft submitted to the Council last year made it clear that neither in Christ's time nor today did the Jews, as a people, have any special guilt in a sacrifice that was an atonement for the sins of all mankind.

Liberal Victory Forecast

For reasons that have never been officially explained, but probably for a combination of political and conservative theological considerations, this was changed to a more lukewarm

311

exoneration of "the Jews of today."

Interpreting both the texts of the speeches today and the evident mood of the Council majority, qualified experts foresaw the final approval of a statement that would probably be more positive in its condemnation of anti-Semitism generally and of the Crucifixion-guilt theory than even the draft introduced last year but since diluted.

"In this declaration," Cardinal Cushing said, his strong, nasal voice and Boston-accented Latin evincing conviction, "in clear and evident words, we must deny that the Jews are guilty of the death of our Saviour except insofar as all men have sinned and on that account crucified Him, and, indeed still crucify Him.

"And especially," he went on, "we must condemn any who would attempt to justify inequities, hatred or even persecution of the Jews as Christian actions."

Urges 'Humble' Confession

In a final passage, noted by all who have followed recent public discussions of the attitude of the church, officially, toward the persecution of Jews during the World War II, Cardinal Cushing said:

"I ask, venerable brothers, whether we ought not to confess humbly before the world that Christians, too frequently, have not shown themselves as true Christians, as faithful to Christ, in their relations with their Jewish brothers?

"In this our age," he declared, "how many have died because of the indifference of Christians, because of silence! There is no need to enumerate the crimes committed in our own time. If not many Christian voices were lifted in recent years against the great injustices, yet let our voices humbly cry out now."

Cardinal Cushing urged that the Council statement be made "more positive, less timid, more charitable," with greater emphasis on the special reasons for love between Christians and Jews because of their common religious patrimony of the Old Testament.

Aquinas Position Cited

Albert Cardinal Meyer, Archbishop of Chicago, stressed this theme of common heritage. He also recalled the statement of St. Thomas Aquinas, author of much of the church's theological interpretation, that no Jew, even in Christ's time, was formally guilty of deicide — the killing of God — because the Jews did not know of the divinity of Christ.

Text of Cushing's Address

Special to The New York Times

ROME, Sept. 28—*Following, in unofficial translation from the Latin, is the text of a speech today by Richard Cardinal Cushing, Archbishop of Boston, to the Ecumenical Council in St. Peter's Basilica:*

The declaration on the Jews and non-Christians is acceptable in general. Through this Ecumenical Council the church must manifest to the whole world, and to all men, a concern which is genuine, an esteem all embracing, a sincere charity—in a word, it must show forth Christ. And in this schema "De Ecumenismo," with its declarations on religious liberty and on the Jews and non-Christians, in a certain sense it does just that. I would propose, however, three amendments specifically on the Jews.

First: We must make our statement about the Jews more positive, less timid, more charitable. Our text well illustrates the priceless patrimony which the new Israel has received from the law and the prophets.

And it well illustrates what the Jews and Christians share in common. But surely we ought to indicate the fact that we sons of Abraham according to the spirit must show a special esteem and particular love for the sons of Abraham according to the flesh because of this common patrimony. As sons of Adam, they are our brothers: As sons of Abraham, they are the blood brothers of Christ.

Rejection a Mystery

The fourth paragraph of this declaration should manifest this and our obligation of special esteem, as a conclusion which logically flows from the first section.

Secondly: On the culpability of the Jews for the death of our Saviour. As we read in sacred scriptures, the rejection of the Messiah by his own people is a mystery: a mystery which is indeed for our instruction, not for exaltation.

The parables and prophecies of our Lord teach us this. We cannot judge the leaders of ancient Israel—God alone is their judge. And most certainly we cannot dare attribute to later generations of Jews the guilt of the crucifixion of the Lord Jesus or the death of the Saviour of the world, except in the sense of the universal guilt in which all of us men share.

We know and we believe that Christ died freely, and he died for all men and because of the sins of all men, Jews and gentiles.

Therefore, in this declaration, in clear and evident words, we must deny that the Jews are guilty of the death of our Saviour except insofar as all men have sinned and on that account crucified Him and, indeed, still crucify Him. And especially, we must condemn any who would attempt to justify inequities, hatred or even persecution of the Jews as Christian actions.

No Rationale for Hatred

All of us have seen the evil fruit of this kind of false reasoning. In this august assembly, in this solemn moment, we must cry out: There is no Christian rationale—neither theological nor historical—for any inequity, hatred or persecution of our Jewish brothers.

Great is the hope, both among Catholics and among our separated Christian brothers, as well as among our Jewish friends in the New World, that this sacred synod will make such a fitting declaration.

Thirdly and finally: I ask, venerable brothers, whether we ought not to confess humbly before the world that Christians too frequently have not shown themselves as true Christians, as faithful to Christ, in their relations with their Jewish brothers? In this our age, how many have suffered! How many have died because of the indifference of Christians, because of silence! There is no need to enumerate the crimes committed in our own time. If not many Christian voices were lifted in recent years against the great injustices, yet let our voices humbly cry out now.

Joseph Cardinal Ritter, Archbishop of St. Louis, called approval of an improved text "an opportunity to repair the injuries of past centuries."

He criticized both the style and the content of the present version, apparently arbitrarily redrafted by the Council Coordinating Commission from the more comprehensive text submitted by Augustin Cardinal Bea, head of the Vatican Secretariat for the Promotion of Christian Unity.

Heart of Matter Evaded

Because of certain omissions, he said, the text does not go to the heart of the Jewish problem and offers "offensive ambiguities" because "in some places what is not said is more eloquent than what is said."

Other spokesmen for a stronger version of the declaration were Achille Cardinal Liénart of Lille, France; Joseph Cardinal Frings of Cologne, Germany; Giacomo Cardinal Lercaro of Bologna, Italy; Paul-Emile Cardinal Leger of Montreal; Franziskus Cardinal Konig of Vienna. Also, the Most Revs. Lorenz Jaeger, Archbishop of Paderborn, Germany, and Philip Pocock, coadjutor of Toronto; and the Most Revs Peter Nierman, Bishop of Groningen, the Netherlands, and Jules Daem, Bishop of Antwerp, Belgium.

Ignace Cardinal Tappouni, Syrian Patriarch of Antioch, who spoke for Patriarchs from Egypt, Syria, Iraq and Lebanon, asked that the entire declaration be "deleted" from the acts of the Council as "inopportune."

Arab Protest Forecast

This echoed objections voiced by Catholic prelates from Arab countries at the 1963 Council session that Arab governments would tend to regard as a pro-Israeli act the approval of a declaration favorable to the Jews.

"If this document is insisted on," Cardinal Tappouni said, according to an official Council paraphrase, "it will cause most serious difficulties for the hierarchy and the faithful in many localities. The Council will be accused of favoring specific political tendencies."

In the opinion of informed observers, Cardinal Tappouni's statement constituted no more than "pro forma" opposition. He was held to be too thoroughly aware of the prevailing sentiments of the Council to have any serious hope of obtaining withdrawal of the document again this year.

September 29, 1964

Council Votes Exoneration Of Jews on the Crucifixion

Special to The New York Times

ROME, Nov. 20—The Roman Catholic hierarchy approved today on the first reading a text offering friendship and mutual respect to non-Christian peoples and specifically denying any special Jewish guilt in the Crucifixion of Jesus.

The document, the subject of two years of behind-the-scenes maneuvers by supporters and opponents, was passed at the final business meeting of the current session of the Ecumenical Council by a vote of 1,651 to 99, with an additional 242 conditional affirmative votes.

This action meant that the text, as drafted by the Secretariat for Christian Unity, would remain the approved basis for a final version to be submitted for definitive action to the fourth session of the Council next year.

A Community of All Peoples

Dealing broadly with all of the approximately two billion non-Christians of the world, the text holds that "one is the community of all peoples, one their origin, for God made the entire human race live on all the face of the earth."

[Leaders of 14 major Jewish organizations in the United States said the Council's statement would contribute to the elimination of anti-Semitism. Page 9.]

In its most debated passage, the text declares Christianity's basic origins are in the Judaic Old Testament and states:

"All that happened to Christ in His passion cannot be attributed to the whole [Jewish] people then alive, much less to those of today. Besides, the church held and holds that Christ underwent His passion and death freely, because of the sins of all men and out of infinite love."

This formal exoneration of the Jews for Christ's passion is expected to serve ultimately as a mandate for the removal from Catholic educational and liturgical texts of all references to the Jews as a deicide people.

This allegation, based on a misunderstanding of events at the time of Christ and compounded by medieval anti-Jewish measures based on it, has been identified in scientific surveys as a significant source of anti-Semitism.

The declaration begins with a recognition that even the most primitive of men reach out toward God, and with respect for even that rudimentary religious feeling.

It recognizes all that is "true and holy" in such great religions as Hinduism and Buddhism. Pope Paul VI will have an opportunity to give tacit expression to this doctrine when he visits Bombay, India, between Dec. 2 and 5 during the International Eucharistic Congress there.

Speaking next of the Moslems, the text expresses "esteem" for their adoration of "the one God," for their submissiveness and obedience to His decrees as they are understood and for the honor they give to Christ as a prophet, if not the son of God, and to the Virgin Mary.

The text urges forgetfulness of past hostilities between Moslem and Christian and mutual understanding in the future.

In the section on the Jews, the text says the church acknowledges "with a grateful heart" the fact that "the beginnings of her faith and her election were already among the patriarchs, Moses and the prophets."

It notes that Christ, the Virgin, the Apostles and most of the early Disciples "sprang from the Jewish people." Even though a large part of the Jewish people do not accept the Gospel, it is stated, "they remain most dear to God for the sake of the Patriarchs."

An earlier version, arbitrarily

redrafted between the 1963 and 1964 sessions by the Council's Coordinating Commission, stated a hope for reunion of the Jews with Christianity in terms that were widely and resentfully interpreted in Jewish circles as a call to present-day conversions.

Augustine Cardinal Bea, the liberal German Jesuit who heads the Secretariat for Christian Unity, announced that it had been decided that the declaration, when it is enacted next year, should be attached as an appendix to the main schema of the Council, "De Ecclesia" ("Of the Church").

It would have been desirable, he said, if the declaration could have been formally promulgated before the Pope's coming voyage to India. But, he added, "This, alas, is not to be."

This was the only reference to the troubled history of the declaration. A first, liberal version was prevented from coming to the floor in 1963 by opposition of bishops from Arab countries, who convinced the Vatican Secretariat of State that a declaration favorable to the Jews would provoke Arab reprisals against Catholicism.

Between sessions, this current of opinion produced a watered-down version that was rejected, largely on the impetus of the United States hierarchy, in preliminary debate two months ago.

Dr. Joseph I. Lichten, director of the Department of Intercultural Affairs of the Anti-Defamation League of B'Nai Brith, said tonight that the preliminary vote alone represented a significant milestone "in Catholic-Jewish cooperation, which is already so vivid and friendly in the United States."

November 21, 1964

COUNCIL POSITION DEBATED BY JEWS

Some Welcome, Some Reject Statement on Crucifixion

By IRVING SPIEGEL

The Ecumenical Council's preliminary adoption of a statement exonerating the Jewish people as a whole of the Cruxcifixion of Jesus brought divergent reactions yesterday from Jewish spokesmen.

At the same time, the Union of American Hebrew Congregations, a Jewish reform group, announced it had started a series of programs involving Christian and Jewish lay and spiritual leaders designed to "translate into action the new Christian attitudes and desires regarding contact with Jews."

The disagreement on the proposed Roman Catholic doctrinal change was voiced in a debate on the theme by four religious and lay leaders at a meeting sponsored by the American Jewish Congress in Stephen Wise House, 15 East 84th Street.

Rabbi Emanuel Rackman, professor of political science at Yeshiva University, who is prominently identified with Orthodox Judaism, said: "Jews have had no part to play in the Vatican Council deliberations, because the Catholic Church does not regard us as equals. Not until it does can there be worthy discussion. What is needed is not discussion, but the negation of any attempt to convert each other."

While the statement "does indeed speak of a common patrimony and recommends mutual knowledge, respect and fraternal dialogue," he said, "not once does it accord Judaism recognition as an equal, nor, for that matter, does it do so for the

other non-Christian religions."

Shad Polier, chairman of the governing council of the American Jewish Congress, expressed hope that the statement would "mark not the end, but the beginning of a process that would eliminate anti-Semitism."

Mr. Polier said the significance of its adoption "lies in the implicit undertaking by the church that, through the daily teachings in its schools, in the sermons of its priests throughout the country and in the revision of textbooks and other church documents, its communicants will be taught that anti-Semitism is incompatible with Catholicism and is contrary to the basic tenets of that religion."

Rabbi Morris N. Kertzer, spiritual leader of the Larchmont Temple, Larchmont, N. Y., well known in American Reform Judaism, praised the efforts of American Catholic leaders "who stood up in St. Peter's and told their Roman and other colleagues that the Church in America has learned the lesson of democracy."

Leo Pfeffer, chairman of the Political Science Department of Long Island University and special counsel to the Congress, termed the statement "not an act for the preservation of the Jews, but [one] for the preservation of the Catholic Church."

At the annual meeting of the board of trustees of the Union of American Hebrew Congregation at 838 Fifth Avenue, Irvin Fane, chairman of the board, said the Ecumenical Council's action "will not alone serve to wipe out centuries of injurious teachings about Judaism and Jews."

Rather, he said, the highest bodies of official Christendom must give a "more accurate and truthful representation of the place that Judaism and the Jewish people play in the history of the world and in the history of Christianity."

November 23, 1964

DECLINE IS FOUND IN ANTI-SEMITISM

Racial Concept Discarded in U.S., Survey Discloses

By IRVING SPIEGEL
Special to The New York Times

MIAMI BEACH, Dec. 3—A survey of public opinion polls issued here today shows that American attitudes toward Jews and Judaism have changed drastically in the last quarter of a century.

Today, a majority of Americans view Jews as individuals rather than as members of a "racial" group, and Judaism is widely considered as one of the major religions in this country. Many hostile stereotypes about Jews have "very nearly disappeared," according to the study.

The survey found that overt anti-Semitism had gone through a "massive decline." However, the survey warns that latent prejudice could be stirred up by upheavals and crises in American society. It has been estimated that there are 5.5 million Jews in the United States.

These findings are embodied in a study of public opinion polls sponsored by the American Jewish Committee in the period from 1937 to 1962.

Board Opens Meeting

The survey was made public by the committee at the opening of its annual national executive board meeting, the agency's top policy planning board, at the Fontainebleau Hotel.

The committee also announced that it had established an extensive cultural and religious community service program for the 625,000 Jews throughout South America.

Harris Berlack, chairman of the agency's committee on foreign affairs, said the program, styled as "a cultural peace corps," would cooperate with existing Jewish organizations to develop libraries and other resources devoted to strengthen every phase of Jewish living.

Mr. Berlack cited the lack of qualified rabbis, teachers, social workers and other skilled Jewish personnel in South America.

The survey was conducted by Charles Herbert Stember, professor of sociology at Rutgers University, with the cooperation of the Rutgers Research Council. Social scientists from Harvard, Columbia, Brandeis, Cornell, the University of Chicago, New York University, Vanderbilt University and the University of Michigan are contributing evaluative papers on the survey.

Dr. John Slawson, executive vice president of the American Jewish Committee and also a prominent social scientist, said that the study on the papers would be published in 1965 as "Jews in the Mind of America."

In contrast to the late thirties and early forties when anti-Semitism was at its peak, Dr. Stember found that the negative stereotypes about Jews have "very nearly disappeared." These stereotypes included such notions that "Jews as a group are clanish, dishonest, unscrupulous or excessively powerful in business and finance."

In an interview, Dr. Slawson said that "one of the great advances these polls have disclosed —and this is one of the most promising aspects—is that Jews are being more and more seen as distinct individuals rather than a special kind of people with fixed qualites."

In his survey, Dr. Stember points out that the waning of the "race" concept about Jews has helped to reduce other fixed notions.

On the question of association with Jews, Dr. Stember's survey cites these findings in current attitudes:

¶Most Americans are against restrictive quotas on admission of Jews to colleges, in contrast with their wide approval of the idea in the nineteen-forties.

¶Most non-Jews have indicated a willingness to have their children associate with Jewish children.

¶The majority of Americans in business and industry are willing to work in association with Jews.

¶Sentiment against marriage with Jews has waned between 1950 and 1962. "Acceptance of Jews as marriage partners increased at about the same rate as did acceptance of Jewish employes, fellow students and neighbors," the report said.

December 4, 1964

INTERFAITH AMITY NOTED IN SUBURBS

Study Finds Rapport Among Christians and Jews

By IRVING SPIEGEL

A spirit of friendship and cooperation between Christians and Jews has been found to be developing in middle-class suburbia. Barriers are disappearing as the groups relate to each other increasingly at work and in community effort.

In a 5-year study conducted by the American Jewish Committee of a large mid-Western upper middle-class suburb, almost half the Christians questioned had an attitude of "don't care" about how many Jews lived in their neighborhood.

The study was made public yesterday by Dr. John Slawson, social scientist and executive vice president of the committee, which opened its 58th annual meeting at the Americana hotel. The study, whose author is Dr. Benjamin B. Ringer, associate professor of sociology at Hunter College, was conducted under the direction of Dr. Marshall Sklare, the committee's director of scientific research.

The 'Lakeville' Story

The study was based mainly on interviews in depth with Christians and Jews living in "Lakeville," a fictional name given to the Midwestern community, whose population of 26,000 is about one-third Jewish.

The spirit of cooperation, the study showed, was particularly evident when Jews and Christians worked together for common goals, such as improvement of schools, more playgrounds and parks. They mingled comfortably in parent-teacher associations and similar groups.

However, the study also found that older members of the community tended to direct their resentments over cultural and social changes in the suburb toward Jewish newcomers. Such changes included overcrowding of schools and new home designs.

High 'Acceptance Level'

The study indicated that four out of five non-Jews in Lakeville were willing to live among Jews, although the degree of the "acceptance level" varied within the group.

Twenty-three per cent of the non-Jews said they would prefer Jews to remain in the minority—not more than about 30 per cent of the community population.

Twenty-five per cent said they would accept a situation in which there were as many Jews as non-Jews, and about 43 per cent were in the "don't care" group.

The study described these types of non-Jewish attitudes toward Jews in Lakeville:

¶"The exclusionist — considers Jews a 'racial' or biological type and is opposed to them as a group." He would tend not to accept Jewish neighbors.

¶"The exemptionist — is willing to tolerate Jews when they remain in a very small minority as non-Jewish Jews."

¶"The pluralist—is the individual who finds differences in people challenging rather than threatening. He is attracted and stimulated by Jews because he believes their 'differences' can be rewarding. He prefers an equally balanced neighborhood where no one group is dominant."

¶"The egalitarian—emphasizes the similarities underlying group differences and believes in relating to people as individuals rather than as members of a group. He seems to be generally indifferent to the number of Jews in his neighborhood and maintains a 'live and let live' attitude which fosters congeniality and acceptance."

The study covered a broad cross-section of established Jewish residents and newcomers from German and East European backgrounds of diverse social and economic classes. It will be published early next year by Basic Books.

The American Jewish Committee, which will meet here through next Sunday, is devoted to safeguarding the civil and religious rights of Jews in this country and throughout the world. Its headquarters are at the Institute of Human Relations, 165 East 56th Street.

May 20, 1965

Catholic Books Stress Jewishness of Jesus

School Texts Portray Him as Living by the Hebraic Law

By IRVING SPIEGEL

New Roman Catholic textbooks that are being distributed in increasing numbers in parochial schools portray a positive image of Jews and reject the principle of collective Jewish guilt for the Crucifixion of Jesus.

Two of the books shown here yesterday offer colorful, simple presentations written in language suited to 6-year-olds. The Jewishness of Jesus is unmistakably emphasized by illustrations and the use of Hebraic lettering. The child who reads the books soon gets used to the idea that Jesus worshiped in synagogues, learned the Jewish Scriptures and lived according to the Jewish law.

The new textbooks reflect the spirit of the statement on the Jews that was approved in principle at the third session of the Vatican Council last year.

The statement stressed the Jewish roots of Christianity and pointed up the fact that Jesus, His mother and other members of His family, His apostles and original disciples were Jews. It repudiated anti-Semitism and asserted that the Jews in general, past or present, bore no collective guilt or responsibility in the death of Jesus.

The statement was recently revised to take into consideration the wishes of the Council Fathers who voted for it Juxta modum (with reservation) but was reported to have been left intact in its essential elements. It will be reconsidered at the fourth and last session of the Council next September, but according to its rules may not be changed in substance until then.

Ralph Friedman, chairman of the American Jewish Committee's executive board, who displayed the books, said they represented "still another dramatic turning point in the historic perception by Christians of their fellow Jews and provide a basis of promising new understanding between Catholic and Jewish people."

The committee, long active in promoting interfaith cooperation, is holding its annual meeting at the Americana Hotel.

The two new textbooks were prepared by the Pope Pius XII Religious Education Center of Monroe, Mich., and published by Allyn & Bacon of Boston. Rabbi Marc H. Tanenbaum, director of the committee's Department of Interreligious Affairs, serves as Jewish consultant to the center, which is headed by Sisters Mary Johnice and Mary Elizabeth. Both books carry the imprimatur of Richard Cardinal Cushing of Boston.

The books, the first of an eight-volume "Bible, Life and Worship Series," are "The Lord Jesus," and "Come Lord Jesus."

Rabbi Tanenbaum said yesterday that 120,000 copies of "The Lord Jesus," published last year, had been distributed in parochial schools throughout the country.

"Come Lord Jesus" is having an initial printing of 40,000 copies for distribution in parochial schools in New York, Philadelphia, Wilmington, Detroit and in Canada.

One section of "The Lord Jesus," in dealing with the Crucifixion, reads:

"Jesus knew that His Father had sent Him to make up for the sins of all men . . . Jesus went to the garden with His Apostles. He prayed: 'Father, Your will be done. I will suffer and die to save men.'"

The section then adds: "While Jesus was praying, the soldiers came to arrest Him. Jesus let the soldiers take Him to Pilate. Pilate said that Jesus must suffer and die on the cross."

Survey of Textbooks

Last year, St. Louis University, a major Jesuit institution, released a study of Catholic religious textbooks, sponsored by the Jewish committee. The study reported that there was a strong tendency in some of the books to place upon Jews "exclusive and collective responsibility for the Crucifixion of Jesus."

One illustration in "The Lord Jesus" shows Jews at prayer in a synagogue. The caption, in Hebrew, says "This is a Jewish synagogue. Jesus worshipped in a Jewish synagogue."

Another picture in the same book shows Jesus being held up to women of Jerusalem by an elderly Jew. In the background is the Jewish Torah, the all-embracing document that governs Jewish religious life.

The Hebrew caption reads: "And the Glory of Israel Thy People."

Jesus is shown in another illustration as a Jewish child speaking in a synagogue of the first century before a Jewish congregation against the background of the Star of David. The caption, written in Hebrew, says: "And all who listened to Him marveled."

First to Have Them

Rabbi Tanenbaum, who worked in close cooperation with the Pope Pius XII Religious Education Center, said that this was the first time that Catholic textbooks in this country had had Hebrew captions and illustrations.

He said that the books, both in themselves and "as symbols of a large process of interreligious understanding, are significant contributions to the reduction of ancient barriers of misunderstanding and mistrust" between Christians and Jews.

Mr. Friedman said that at least six major publishing companies were either revising their religious texts, or preparing new material, in the light of the recommendations in the study.

He said that 17 Protestant denominations were undertaking an examination of current educational publications, with special attention to Judaism and Jewish-Christian relations, Catholicism, Catholic-Protestant relations and racial questions.

These undertakings by all faiths, Mr. Friedman said, "are concrete expressions of the spirit reflected in the Vatican Council's declaration on non-Christians, including the Jews."

The American Jewish Committee, founded in 1906, is devoted to safeguarding the civil and religious rights of Jews throughout the world.

May 22, 1965

THIRD OF U.S. HELD NOT ANTI-SEMITIC

Study Says Another Third Has a 'Negative Image'

By IRVING SPIEGEL
Special to The New York Times

WASHINGTON, April 19 — One of every three Americans is "virtually free" of anti-Semitic beliefs, one has a "negative image of Jews" and the third is indifferent to the problem of anti-Semitism, a major study reported today.

The comprehensive analysis of attitudes on anti-Semitism, conducted by the Survey Research Center of the University of California, also found that "simplistic beliefs, ignorance and low tolerance for social and political diversity go hand in hand with anti-Semitism."

"Given a crisis situation and political leadership, they [anti-Semites] constitute a threat to the whole country, not just to Jews," the study said.

"An anti-Semitic candidate with a promised economic solution during a crisis period might gain the votes of all those susceptible to political anti-Semitism—the 25 per cent who said they would vote for an anti-Semitic candidate, the more than a third who said the candidate's anti-Semitism wouldn't matter, plus uncountable fellow travelers who made up the indifferent majority."

The study, made public at a news conference, was financed by a grant from the Anti-Defamation League of B'nai B'rith, which is holding its annual meeting at the Shoreham Hotel.

2,600 Interviews Held

Dr. Charles Y. Glock, director of the Survey Research Center, said that the survey was based on 2,000 interviews, representing a national cross section of the population. Each interview lasted 75 minutes.

The project was started in 1965 and was completed recently. It will be published as a book, entitled "The Tenacity of Prejudice," by Harper and Row in the fall.

While negative attitudes toward Jews "remain deeply ingrained and widely accepted," the study found, "overt anti-Jewish discrimination is low." It warns, however, that "to focus solely on discrimination would minimize it."

Mrs. Gertrude J. Selznick and Stephen Steinberg, the behavioral scientists who directed and prepared the report, used questions based on three criteria for the "continued viability of anti-Semitism:"

1. The acceptance of anti-Semitic beliefs and stereotypes.
2. The acceptance of social club discrimination.
3. The acceptance of political anti-Semitism.

The social scientists found that 37 per cent of the population held negative images of Jews based on "old canards that Jews control international banking, engage in shady business practices, are too powerful, clannish or ambitious."

Other Findings Given

The study also showed that:

¶More than 25 per cent defended the right of social clubs to exclude Jews. Another 29 per cent, while opposed in principle, would do little or nothing to combat social club discrimination practice. Thirty-six per cent were firmly opposed, and 10 per cent had no opinion.

¶Only 5 per cent said that they would vote for an anti-Semitic candidate, but more than a third said the candidate's anti-Semitism would make no difference to them.

¶Sixteen per cent, who rejected all three of the sociologists' criteria for anti-Semitism, constitute "the small minority which can be described as principled and consistent opponents of anti-Semitism."

Education was stressed as "the factor most powerfully related to prejudice." But although anti-Semitism was found to be typically low among college graduates, the college-educated with high income and high occupational status were cited as heavy supporters of social club discrimination.

Religious Groups Evaluated

Among religious groups, liberal Protestant denominations —Unitarian, Congregationalist, Episcopalian—were found to be lower in anti-Semitism (24 per cent) and higher in college attendance (52 per cent) than either Roman Catholics or conservative Protestant denominations—Presbyterian, Methodist, Baptist, Lutheran, Evangelical and Reform, Disciples of Christ, and sects.

Catholics were rated 35 per cent on anti-Semitism and 21 per cent on college attendance. Conservative Protestants were rated 46 per cent on anti-Semitism and 23 per cent on college attendance.

In the analysis of Negro attitudes, the study reported that 91 per cent of the American

Negro population was opposed to social club discrimination against Jews.

It also found that 89 per cent of Negroes were against anti-Jewish employment discrimination—19 per cent more than the figures for whites. More Negro citizens than white—68 per cent against 51 per cent—said they would not be "disturbed if a Jew was nominated for President."

However, concerning Negro attitudes toward Jews in the economic sphere, the study found that anti-Semitism among young Negroes was 30 to 45 per cent higher than among whites.

April 20, 1969

Jewish Activists See Ranks Growing

By MICHAEL T. KAUFMAN

Since its founding in the summer of 1968, the Jewish Defense League has withstood the criticism of most major Jewish organizations and has pursued its vision of militant preparedness with karate classes and neighborhood patrols.

The group, which sees itself as a spearhead of active resistance to anti-Semitic attack, now stands accused by three Arabs of having directed the assault against them in their offices near the United Nations last Friday.

A flyer left in the offices explaining that the attack was in retribution for the killing of Israeli schoolchildren by Palestinian guerrillas ended with the phrase "Never Again." The words, referring to murders of six million Jews in World War II, serve as the motto for the Jewish Defense League.

Asked whether the league took credit for the attack, the organization's founder, Rabbi Meir Kahane, replied: "If we did, we'd be open to all sorts of problems. We obviously can't." An investigation of the assaults is being conducted by the New York police.

Anti-Semitism 'Exploding'

Rabbi Kahane, a 39-year-old Orthodox rabbi with a degree in international law, to hasten the growth of the league, has left his job as a columnist for the Jewish Press, a weekly English-language newspaper, to devote most of his time to organizing chapters.

In his speaking engagements throughout the country, Rabbi Kahane starts in a quiet voice, explaining his view of the position of American Jews. Anti-Semitism, he says, is "exploding" and the traditional Jewish organizations, he maintains, have failed to protect American Jews, particularly those middle-class and lower-class Jews who, he believes, are vulnerable to

The New York Times
Rabbi Meir Kahane, Jewish Defense League founder.

attack from black militants and radicals of the left.

His voice rises to a homiletic crescendo. By the time he ends his address his voice is booming, "Never again."

The league claims a membership of about 7,000, with chapters in Boston, Philadelphia, Montreal and Los Angeles. There are adult and youth divisions. Riflery practice and karate instruction are held regularly.

Last year, the group opened Camp Jedel in Woodbourne, N. Y., a Catskill Mountain resort. About 50 youths have been trained there in the martial arts. In many cities the group has organized patrols to escort Jews who feel that they are being harassed. Other members ride through some poor neighborhoods to keep an eye on businesses owned by Jews.

A New York rabbi who said he had no sympathy for the group, noted that the league's organizational work had enabled it to unite people quicker

than any other group. "They can get 50 people out in the garment center almost instantly, or 70 college students," he said. "They work very efficiently on the phone and they have people responsible for mustering units of several dozen men."

In addition to its activities in the Jewish neighborhoods, the league has organized some large demonstrations. One of them, at the Metropolitan Museum of Art was to protest what the group called an anti-Semitic introduction in the catalogue of the "Harlem on My Mind" exhibition. In another protest, 40 members bearing sticks and chains lined the front of Temple Emanu-El on Fifth Avenue, to block James Forman, a black activist, from demanding reparations from the congregation, following rumors that he would make such an attempt.

During last fall's mayoral campaign, the group sponsored advertisements opposing the reelection of Mayor Lindsay, saying that he was indifferent to anti-Jewish hate.

Partly as a result of such tactics the group has come under repeated attack from major Jewish organizations. Rabbi Maurice N. Eisendrath, president of the Union of Hebrew Congregations, has called the league's patrols goon squads. And the Anti-Defamation League referred to the league as "a group of self-appointed vigilantes whose protection the Jewish community does not need or want."

Rabbi Kahane says those criticisms of his organization are from wealthy Jews. "How can a rich Jew or a non-Jew criticize an organization of lower- and middle-class Jews who daily live in terror?", he once asked. "The Establishment Jew is scandalized by us, but our support comes from the grass roots."

May 25, 1970

Jews Fear Anti-Zionism of New Left

By LINDA CHARLTON

Hostility to Israel in the New Left has aroused increasing concern among many American Jews, some of whom are convinced that such animosity is a convenient mask for a resurgence of anti-Semitism.

In private argument and public debate, in magazines such as Commentary and Trans-action, and at seminars, conferences and cocktail parties, the question of whether the anti-Israel, pro-Arab feelings of some radicals can be equated with traditional forms of anti-Semitism is being worried over by a growing number of Jews.

Some Jews contend that for many in the New Left, anti-Zionism is a purely political position reached on the basis of an anti-imperialist question that assumes Israel to be a client and a supporter of the United States. But others maintain that such political attitudes can be legitimately construed as anti-Semitism, whether or not they are expressed intentionally.

And still other Jews point to instances in which anti-Zionism has been used as a transparent code for anti-Jewish feeling—when "Zionist" stands for "Jew" and is used in the classical manner, as a term of abuse in itself.

Antagonism to Israel is most visible in articles appearing in radical and underground publications, and on college campuses where more and more Arab students have been appearing as speakers. But it also surfaced last week at a Central Park rally marking the 25th anniversary of the dropping of the atomic bomb on Japan.

Paul O'Dwyer, a leading figure of the "liberal left," and a gun-runner for Israel in the nineteen-forties, was virtually booed from the speakers' platform by about 100 young people in the audience who said they opposed his pro-Israel position.

"If my position in relation to Israel makes it impossible for me to speak to you about peace, then I shall reluctantly have to leave this platform," Mr. O'Dwyer said. The booing continued and Mr. O'Dwyer left.

THE BLACK PANTHER SATURDAY AUGUST 30, 1969 PAGE 20

ZIONISM (KOSHER NATIONALISM) + IMPERIALISM = FASCISM

By Field Marshall, D.C.

Workers World—8

Israel Fronting for U.S. in New Attack on Arab People

Samples of anti-Zionist and pro-Arab material from radical publications. Upper left, cartoon from S.N.C.C. Newsletter depicts President Gamal Abdel Nasser and Muhammad Ali, or Cassius Clay. At upper right, a figure marked "World Zionism" drinks from bottles bearing dollar signs, held by figures marked West Germany, France, Britain and U.S. Imperialism. This cartoon and the headline at top are from The Black Panther. The text and drawing of a guerrilla at bottom are from Workers World, biweekly that is published here.

To counter the anti-Israel campaign some young Jews have formed campus-based, left-oriented groups that are specifically pro-Israel. And worried Jewish community organizations, such as the Anti-Defamation League and the American Jewish Committee, are watching anti-Israeli activity carefully, compiling file folder after file folder of material, trying to assess its meaning.

Richard Cohen, the associate executive director of the American Jewish Congress contends: "We don't think there is any valid or real difference between anti-Israel sentiment and anti-Semitism. Anti-Zionism is a cover for anti-Semitism."

Mr. Cohen said in an interview that he would not call every critic of the legitimacy of Israel's policies anti-Jewish. But, he added:

"Because we believe that Israel is essential to the survival of the Jewish people in a post-Auschwitz world, to propose that this Jewish state be either obliterated or revised into a so-called nonsectarian state is ultimately anti-Semitism because it would tend to very seriously wound and injure and diminish the possibility of Jewish continuity."

Tension Between the Faiths

'Old Venom' Cited

Another authority who argues that the anti-Israeli sentiment on the left that surfaced after the Six-Day War in 1967 is the same old venom in new bottles is Moshe Lazar, the chairman of the romance languages department at the Hebrew University in Jerusalem and an authority on anti-Semitism in the Middle Ages.

"After Auschwitz and Buchenwald, overt anti-Semitism was no longer fashionable in most intellectual circles," said Professor Lazar in an interview here. "Now it is expressed in anti-Zionist propaganda, which they find more acceptable."

The sort of material that, in the view of Hans Morgenthau, the political scientist, tends to "stir some of the entrenched anti-Semitic prejudices that have been popularized through the ages," can be found in almost every issue of the publications of the cluster of groups sheltering under the umbrella term of "the New Left."

A target now in these publications is Israel; the word "Jew" is rarely used and the term "Zionist" is substituted. But sometimes, as in an article in The Black Panther, the militant black party's weekly newspaper, that referred repeatedly to a slumlord as a "racist Zionist," it seems an interchangeable code word.

One of the earliest expositions of the radicals' vision of the Middle East appeared in the June-July, 1967, issue of the newsletter of the Student Nonviolent Coordinating Committee, which actually appeared in early August, 1967. The two-page spread of text, photographs and drawings contains little that has not reappeared, basically unchanged, in innumerable radical publications since then.

One cartoon shows Moshe Dayan — the eyepatch is unmistakable — epauletted with dollar signs. Another shows Muhammad Ali (Cassius Clay, the boxer), and President Gamal Abdel Nasser of the United Arab Republic throttled with a noose held by a hand decorated with the Star of David. A dollar sign centers the star, and an arm and curved sword labeled "Third World Liberation Movement" are raised to slash the rope.

A Parallel to Nazis Drawn

There are photographs of slaughtered bodies, captioned: "Gaza Massacres, 1956," and "This is the Gaza Strip, Palestine, not Dachau, Germany." This parallel between Israel and Nazi Germany, a staple of Soviet anti-Israel propaganda, is the most shocking aspect of the anti-Israeli rhetoric to many Jews.

Similarly, in a series on "Zionism vs. Socialism" in the March, 1970, issue of The Long Beach (Calif.) Free Press, Mike Klonsky, a leader of the RYM-II faction of the Students for a Democratic Society, equated the "continuous attacks on the Arab people" by Israel with "The German Fascists who committed genocide against the Jews."

And a recent issue of The Black Panther devoted its entire back page to a cartoon depicting "Israel: The Zionist Puppet State of Imperialism." Israel, shown as an eyepatched pig labeled "World Zionism," is sucking greedily at nursing bottles filled with dollar signs that are held by a cluster of smiling pigs labeled "U.S. Imperialism, West Germany, France and Britain."

Another 1970 issue of the Panther weekly newsletter contained an article entitled "Will Racism or International Proletarian Solidarity Conquer?" by Connie Matthews, who is described as the international co-ordinator of the party.

It was a "Zionist judge, Judge [Monroe] Friedman" who sentenced Huey P. Newton, Miss Matthews wrote, and another "Zionist judge," Julius J. Hoffman, who "allowed the other Zionists to go free but has kept Bobby Seale in jail and sentenced him to four years for contempt charges."

Beyond that, she charged: "The other Zionists in the Conspiracy 8 trial were willing and did sacrifice Bobby Seale and his role . . . to gain publicity. We once again condemn Zionism as a racist doctrine."

"Fire!" the now-defunct publication of the Weatherman faction of S.D.S., wrote in August, 1969, of "The almost universal collaboration of organized Jewry with the Nazis . . . and the general absence of resistance" and charged that Israel has "proved incapable of even one humane gesture" toward the Arab population.

A 1969 series, "History of the Middle East Liberation Struggle," in New Left Notes, an S.D.S. publication, links Israel's beginnings with "leaders in developing world imperialism like the Baron Edmund de Rothschild," and characterizes its founding as having taken place on the basis of "The complete relocation of thousands of people of color."

Defamation of Israel is accompanied by the glorification of the Arab-guerrilla cause. In the March, 1970 issue of "Militant," the publication of the Young Socialist Alliance, a Trotskyite-Marxist group, a recitation of the disavowals by various guerrilla groups of responsibility for the explosion aboard a Swissair jet was followed by:

"The truth, though, is that if in fact a Palestinian individual or organization had anything to do with the crash of the Swissair liner, the 47 people who died were as much the victims of imperialism as . . . the 400 Vietnamese men, women and children of Songmy and the six million Jews of Central and Eastern Europe."

Israel Linked to U.S.

This paragraph also demonstrates a basic equation underlying much of the hostile rhetoric. Israel, since its 1967 victory over the Arabs, is identified by the radical left with the United States and with all the sins — imperialism, exploitation and oppression of the "Third World" — of which the United States is accused and, indeed, convicted by them.

A matching factor is the identification of black militant groups, in particular the Black Panthers, with the Arab cause. And at least in part because of the pervasive influence of the Panthers in the New Left, Dr. Amitai Etzioni of Columbia University said in an interview that one's attitude toward Israel now "serves as a test in the left-liberal camp."

But Dr. Etzioni described the "mechanical positions" of the New Left as "stupid, not anti-Semitic," the result of "simple-mindedly projecting on the Middle East, hawk and dove positions that have nothing to do with the Middle East."

Dr. Etzioni, for many years an Israeli citizen who served with the armed forces there, maintains that the left's traditional sympathy with what it saw as the underdog contributed to the upsurge of anti-Israel feeling since David beat Goliath in June, 1967:

"If the Israelis hadn't won so easily," he said, the New Left "would love them better."

Among those who feel that criticism of, even hostility to, Israel is a political phenomenon and not some fugitive, mutant strain of anti-Jewish feeling are some prominent intellectuals of the New Left.

Dr. Noam Chomsky, the Massachusetts Institute of Technology linguist, said in an interview recently that it was "obviously perfect nonsense" to equate criticism of Israel with anti-Semitism, either the specific criticism of Israeli policy and attitude that he and others such as I.F. Stone, for years an Israel supporter, have made, or the virulent attacks in the radical press.

In an article replying to attacks on his position, Dr. Chomsky wrote: "It is quite impossible to identify a definite New Left doctrine" vis-a-vis Israel, except for "the Black Liberation movement, whose attitude about the Middle East must be interpreted in terms of domestic American problems and developments."

Dr. Chomsky added: "To the extent that there is anti-Israel feeling in the New Left, it is in part in reaction to the behavior of the American Jewish community, to its extolling of the martial and chauvinistic elements in Israeli society, which are by no means dominant there."

One aspect of the New Left attitude that is particularly distressing to many American Jews, and one most likely to split the generations sharply, is the fact that many young radical activists are Jewish, and hence participants in what their elders may see as anti-Semitism. The suggested explanations for this vary, too.

Josh Muravchik is a 22-year-old 1970 graduate of City College who was a founder of the Youth Committee for Peace and Democracy in the Middle East, a campus-based group that he described as a "'left' organization that believes that radicals should support Israel." Mr. Muravchik sees a subtle, perhaps unacknowledged anti-Semitism in the participation of young Jews who are active in the radical left.

"Anti-Israel new-leftism has become for many young Jews a modern means of 'passing,'" he says.

Richard Cohen described such Jewish involvement in anti-Israel activity as having "a number of reasons — an insane kind of self-hatred that has characterized Jewish anti-Semitism for a long time, the need to identify with the majority, to rebel against your parents."

Jerry Rubin, the "Chicago Conspiracy" defendant and one of the most prominent of the Jewish radicals, explained his own anti-Israel, pro-Arab position, in blunt terms in an interview last year. It began, he said, with a disillusioning visit to Israel: "So here I came for idealism and I got — America. I became anti-Israeli and pro-Arab."

"Inevitable Conclusion"

Michael Spiegel, then a national secretary of S.D.S., said in an interview last year that Jewish members of the organization, "At first, coming from middle-class Jewish backgrounds . . . are shocked by the prospect of anti-Zionism. But when they think about it, they come to the inevitable conclusion."

Another hypothesis was put forward by Bertram H. Gold, the executive vice president of the American Jewish Committee. Mr. Gold says the willingness of young American Jews to become involved may be traceable, in part, to their own lack of a sense of "being Jewish."

The holocaust that consumed six million Jews in Europe is not seared into the memory of a generation born after World War II, he maintains. Nor, Mr. Gold says, can they remember, as their parents can, when anti-Semitism was almost commonplace, if not respectable, in this country; when universities had Jewish quotas for both students and faculty and hotels displayed signs that said, "No Dogs or Jews Allowed."

On the whole, he said, the young radicals "don't know what anti-Semitism is."

August 14, 1970

Taboo on Anti-Semitism Seen Waning

By IRVING SPIEGEL

Norman Podhoretz, the social and literary critic, said yesterday that for the first time in a generation Jews in the United States were confronted with open anti-Semitism because of a sharp weakening of a "long-standing taboo" against it.

Mr. Podhoretz, the editor of Commentary, cited three developments as examples of the breaking of this taboo. He spoke at a luncheon of the 65th annual conference of the American Jewish Committee at the Waldorf-Astoria Hotel, where 500 delegates have gathered for the conference ending today.

Mr. Podhoretz cited the spread of "anti-Zionist" sentiment among intellectuals since the six-day war in June, 1967, between Israel and the Arab states, the "surfacing" of anti-Semitism among "militant, black separtists" since the New York City teachers strike of 1968 and the frequent expressions of resentment in the literary community concerning the "dominance" of Jews in American cultural life.

Cites Resentment

He said the nation's literary community resented the prominence of Jews in the arts, particularly the areas of literature music, the theater and films.

"Anti-Zionism," he said, "has served to legitimize the open expression of a good deal of anti-Semitism which might otherwise have remained subject to the taboo against anti-Semitism that prevailed in American public life from the time of Hitler until the six-day war."

Mr. Podhoretz said the New York teachers' strike "brought black anti-Semitism into widespread public view and exposed in certain elements of what blacks themselves like to call the white power structure, an apparent readiness to purchase civil peace in the United States—I do not say social justice—at the direct expense of the Jews."

Mr. Podhoretz contended that this inclination was exemplified by the drive to "replace the merit system in civil service employment and university admissions by a system of proportional representation according to race or ethnic origin."

"If such a replacement," he added, "should be effected, Jews would be seriously affected."

A special report, prepared by Prof. Sidney Goldstein of Brown University, prominent sociologist and director of the Population Studies and Training Center at the university, indicated that Jews in the United States were migrating "in increasing numbers away from northeastern centers of Jewish population, particularly New York, Pennsylvania and New Jersey."

The trend, the study said, was to areas without large, long-established Jewish communities. Contributing to this movement, the study said was the location of plants in various parts of the country that offer executive posts to Jews.

May 16, 1971

Report by Anti-Defamation League Sees Examples of New Kind of Anti-Semitism

By IRVING SPIEGEL

The Anti-Defamation League of B'nai B'rith asserted yesterday that American Jews were becoming increasingly concerned over a new kind of anti-Semitism expressed by individuals and institutions.

The conclusion is based on a three-and-one-half-year study made by Arnold Forster, the league's associate director and general counsel, and Benjamin R. Epstein, its national director. The findings were made public at a news conference at the 61-year-old human-rights agency's headquarters at 315 Lexington Avenue.

In their analysis, Mr. Forster and Mr. Epstein concluded that the "major difference between anti-Semitism today and the traditional kind is that the new anti-Semitism is not necessarily deliberate in character and is more often expressed by respected individuals and institutions here and abroad—people who would be shocked to think themselves or have others think them, anti-Semites."

In asserting that "hostility and insensitivity to Jews and Jewish concerns were displayed by 'respectable' elements in the American media, clergy and government" before the recent Arab-Israeli conflict, the study cited the following as examples:

¶A sermon by the Very Rev. Francis B. Sayre Jr., Dean of Washington's National (Episcopal) Cathedral who called the Israelis "oppressors" and "used language which, deliberately or not, revived the central theme of anti-Semitism — that the Jews collectively are guilty of having killed Jesus." (The league also charged that Dean Sayre "equated the willful murder of Israeli athletes by Arab terrorists in Munich with the accidental deaths of villagers during Israeli self-defense raids against terrorists' bases in Lebanon.")

¶An address before the Association of Arab University Graduates by the Rev. Daniel J. Berrigan, the Jesuit priest, who "castigated Israel in New Left terms."

¶Rowland Evans and Robert Novak, the columnists, "consistently hostile" to Israel since 1967, "frequently echoed the main themes of pro-Arab propaganda" — that Israel's war successes made further United States arms aid unnecessary; that Jewish pressure groups control the Government's Middle East policy.

¶The American Friends Service Committee (Quakers), "long admired for humanitarianism, published a pro-Arab document entitled 'Search for Peace in the Middle East,' which repressed facts and distorted history to reach a slanted and one-sided set of conclusions."

¶"A segment of the press led by The Christian Science Monitor defended and justified the Arab attack and 'swallowed whole' the Arabs' propaganda claim that they were merely attempting to reclaim Arab territories."

Fulbright Accused

John Hughes, editor of The Christian Science Monitor, reached by telephone at his offices in Boston, said, "We try to be even-handed and, in the course, we incur the hostility of both sides."

Mr. Evans, reached by phone in Washington, said, "It is too bad that reporters or columnists who attempt to report objectively on the highly emotionalized Middle East so often are attacked by friends of Israel for being anti-Israel or even anti-Semitic."

John A. Sullivan, executive secretary of the American Friends Service Committee, rejecting the league's charge, said that his agency's report "is a balanced study and tries to present both Arab and Israeli viewpoints." It was first studied by Jews and Arabs here and in the Middle East, he said.

The study criticized Senator J. W. Fulbright, Democrat of Arkansas, chairman of the Senate Foreign Relations Committee, for his "false charge that the Israelis control Mideast policy in the Congress contrary to our interests."

The document also listed a number of cartoon books that

gave "negative images of Jews," among them, "We Wish You a Kosher Christmas," "My Son, the Santa Claus," "Fanny Hillman: Memoirs of a Jewish Madam," "How to Be a Jewish Madam," "It's Fun to be Jewish" and "Loxfinger."

Mr. Forster said in an interview that the forthcoming American Broadcasting Company television production of "The Merchant of Venice," starring Lord Olivier, did not lessen the impact of anti-Semitism.

Mr. Forster, who has seen the production, said at no time was "the viewer permitted to forget the Jewishness of Shylock." He said, "It pervades the entire play, and if the Jew is not being excoriated for his evil and unprincipled ways, the stage settings and props constantly remind the viewer this play is about Shylock—a Jew."

The production is scheduled to be shown on the evening of March 16.

A spokesman for the American Broadcasting Company said no comment would be issued concerning the charge.

Mr. Epstein and Mr. Forster asserted that the possibility of a major outbreak of anti-Semitism did not exist "but holds a potential for the future."

The study will be published next month as a book, titled, "The New Anti-Semitism" (McGraw Hill).

March 6, 1974

Chairman of Joint Chiefs Regrets Remarks on Jews

By JOHN W. FINNEY
Special to The New York Times

WASHINGTON, Nov. 13—Gen. George S. Brown, chairman of the Joint Chiefs of Staff, expressed regret today for comments that he made a month ago in which he suggested that Israel had undue political influence in Congress and that Jews controlled the newspapers and banks in this country.

In statements issued through the Defense Department, General Brown said that his comments were "unfortunate," "ill-considered," "unfounded," and "all too casual" and did not represent his convictions.

The White House, in what amounted to a reprimand to the nation's top military officer, said that President Ford felt "very strongly" that General Brown's comments were "ill-advised and poorly handled." Ron Nessen, the Presidential press secretary, said that Mr. Ford also wanted it emphasized that the comments of General Brown "in no way represent his views or the views of any senior officials of his Administration, military or civilian."

Despite General Brown's apologies, which stopped short of a direct retraction, it appeared that he was enmeshed in a major personal controversy as a result of comments that he made Oct. 10 at Duke University but that went unreported nationally until a Duke law student provided a tape recording of his statements to The Washington Post.

In response to a question after a speech on international law before Duke law students, General Brown said that if there was another Arab oil embargo, the American people might "get tough-minded enough to set down the Jewish influence in this country and break that lobby."

General Brown went on to say, however, that the Jewish influence "is so strong, you wouldn't believe, now."

"They own, you know, the banks in the country, the newspapers," he said. "Just look at where the Jewish money is."

At least for the moment, there appeared to be no inclination within the Administration to dismiss General Brown. However, because of the protests made by Jewish groups, it was apparent that his political standing, particularly on Capitol Hill, was seriously injured, and perhaps his future as Chairman of the Joint Chiefs was in jeopardy.

He took over that post last July after serving as Air Force Chief of Staff.

Mr. Nessen, while emphasizing the President's disapproval of the general's statements, said that he had "not heard of any plans for him not to remain in office."

Pentagon Statement

At the Pentagon, a spokesman said that Defense Secretary James R. Schlesinger "continues to have confidence" in General Brown and "realizes this was a very unfortunate misexpression of the general's opinions."

Various Jewish groups, however, demanded General Brown's resignation. The Jewish War Veterans said that if President Ford did not dismiss him, it would work through Congress to secure his dismissal.

The Anti-Defamation League of B'nai B'rith told Mr. Ford that General Brown's remarks were "not only false but contemptible, and have an illiterate odor of prejudice and malice" and that the general should be dismissed immediately.

Rabbi Arthur Hertzberg, president of the American Jewish Congress, sent a telegram to Mr. Ford saying that the general's remarks demonstrated "a degree of ignorance and susceptibility to classic anti-Semitic propaganda that cast grave doubts on his ability to serve in his presently critically important position."

Investigation Asked

The telegram asked the President to investigate General Brown's statements and "determine whether it is fitting for him to serve in his present career."

Elmer R. Winter, president of the American Jewish Committee, welcomed General Brown's action in repudiating some of his remarks but expressed concern that "he has not yet withdrawn his reckless canard about 'Jewish control.'"

Senator William Proxmire, Democrat of Wisconsin; Representative Bella S. Abzug, Democrat of Manhattan—and Representative Elizabeth Holtzman, Democrat of Brooklyn, all issued statements charging General Brown with anti-Semitic statements and demanding his dismissal.

In a transcript provided by the Pentagon today, the general said at Duke:

"Now, in answer to the question would we use force in the Middle East, I don't know—I hope not. We have no plans to. It is conceivable, I guess. It would be almost as bad as the seven days in May. You can conjure up a situation where there is another oil embargo, and people in this country are not only inconvenienced and uncomfortable, but suffer.

"They get tough-minded enough to set down the Jewish influence in this country and break that lobby. It is so strong, you wouldn't believe, now.

"We have the Israelis coming to us for equipment. We say we can't probably get the Congress to support a program like this. And they say don't worry about the Congress. We will take care of the Congress. This is somebody from another country, but they can do it. They own, you know, the banks in this country, the newspapers. Just look at where the Jewish money is."

General Issues Statement

This afternoon, the general issued a statement in which he said that his "remarks might mistakenly lead to the wholly erroneous inference that American citizens and groups do not enjoy in this nation the privilege of expressing their views forcefully."

"What are called pressures lies at the very heart of democracy," he said. "We in Defense know that. We experience pressures from contractors, pressures from those opposed to defense expenditures, pressures from foreign governments.

"Moreover, my improper comments could be read to suggest that the American Jewish community and Israel are somehow the same. Americans of Jewish background have an understandable interest in the future of Israel—parallel to similar sentiments among other Americans, all of whom at one time or another trace their descent to other lands.

"I do in fact appreciate the great support and the deep interest in the nature of our security problems and our defenses that the American Jewish community has steadily demonstrated, and I want to reemphasize that my unfounded and all-too-casual remarks on that particular occasion are wholly unrepresentative of my continuing respect and appreciation for the role played by Jewish citizens, which I have reiterated to the Jewish War Veterans."

November 14, 1974

Vatican Offers a Guide to Bolster Links With Jews

By KENNETH A. BRIGGS

A long-awaited Vatican statement on ways to improve Roman Catholic-Jewish relations is being made available today.

The guidelines, as they are called, were prepared by the church's Commission on Relations With Judaism to carry out the "Declaration on the Jews" issued in 1965 by the Second Vatican Council.

Like the declaration the guidelines reassert the church's condemnation of anti-Semitism and call for a sweeping action to eliminate all forms of discrimination against Jews that might be found in the church's worship and teaching.

The guidelines call for dialogue, affirmation of a joint Biblical and theological heritage and emphasis on "common elements of the liturgical life" as means for improving relations between Catholics and Jews.

Among other things, they appeal for Catholic respect for the Jew's "faith and his religious convictions," warn against comparing the Old Testament unfavorably with the New Testament, stress that "it is the same God" who speaks through Abraham, Moses and Jesus, and urge a common quest for social justice.

The guidelines were to be officially released at a news conference today, but news services reported the details a day in advance.

In response the International Jewish Committee on Interreligious Consultations predicted in a statement that the guidelines would "encourage better understanding" and applauded their stand on anti-Semitism. But it noted regretfully that the text failed to include a reference to Israel and left unanswered the question whether Jews were to be viewed as needing conversion to Christianity. The committee spoke on behalf of the World Jewish Congress, the Synagogue Council of America and the American Jewish Committee.

Rabbi Marc Tanenbaum, secretary for interreligious affairs for the American Jewish Committee and co-secretary of the joint committee, said in a separate statement that "no self-respecting Jew" could live "in good conscience" with portions of the guidelines, particularly those that "imply a religious 'second class' status in the family of faith communities."

Rabbi Tanenbaum singled out for special criticism the "assertion of a conversionary intention" that assumes "that Judaism is inadequate as the source of truth and value to the Jewish people."

'Will Open New Doors'

The Rev. Edward Flannery, director of the secretariat on Catholic-Jewish relations for United States bishops, denied that the guidelines impugned the integrity of Judaism and said the document "will open new doors and give impetus to the course of the relations between the faiths."

"In clear and firm tones it repudiates not only anti-Semitism but also that anti-Judaism which characterized so much of traditional Christian thinking about Jews and Judaism," he said. "It recognizes the richness and ongoing vitality of Judaism. In this way it solidifies the basis for genuine dialogue between the church and the synagogue."

The declaration by Ecumenical Council Vatican II, called "Nostra Aetate" ("In Our Time"), was regarded as a major accomplishment of the three-year session. Four drafts were needed before final approval came on Oct. 28, 1965. One of the declaration's central convictions is that blame for the death of Jesus cannot be placed upon "all the Jews then living, without distinction, nor upon the Jews of today."

The effort to erase all such blame has taken concrete forms in the absence of guidelines. The United States Conference of Bishops established the secretariat for Catholic-Jewish affairs in 1967. Twenty-five dioceses across the nation have instituted similar offices to deal with the matter, while other dioceses include it under the general office of ecumenical relations.

A set of guidelines was adopted by the Vatican Secretariat for Promoting Christian Unity in 1969 but did not win approval of the church's Secretary of State. That plan, which was leaked to the press, stirred controversy because of its inclusion of an explicit recognition of Israel and a strong position against proselytizing.

Both items have been seen as critical to the future of relations between the two faiths. Many Jews regard acknowledgement of Israel as an implicit sign of respect for the Jewish faith. Likewise, recognition that Judaism is complete unto itself is understood as recognition by Christians that further conversion is unnecessary.

The guidelines—their formal title is "Guidelines and Suggestions for Implementing the Conciliar Declaration 'Nostra Aetate'"—assert the promise that the 2,000-year history of Jewish-Christian interaction has too often been marked "by mutual ignorance and frequent confrontation." The document also says Christians must "strive to acquire a better knowledge" of Judaism, especially the "essential traits" by which Jews "define themselves."

The task of improving relations is set forth in the areas of liturgy, dialogue, education and social action.

In the area of dialogue, the statement says there is still a "widespread air of suspicion" that must be confronted through respect for religious liberty and understanding of the Jew's uniqueness.

The liturgy section calls on the church to regard the Old Testament as valuable in itself apart from the New Testament and urges that homilies based on "passages which seem to show the Jewish people as such in an unfavorable light" not be "distorted."

Special Sensitivity Urged

Moreover, special sensitivity toward Judaism is counseled in the field of religious education. In the preparation of catechisms, history books and media reports, the statement says, Judaism at the time of Jesus should be viewed as a "complex reality" in which He took part; the concept of collective guilt on the part of Jews for His death should be expunged, and Judaism should be understood as a continuing, vital tradition after the destruction of Jerusalem in A.D. 66.

Further research on delicate theological issues is also encouraged, and the need for joint social action is underscored. Joint prayer and meditation are suggested.

In an introduction, John Cardinal Willebrands, president of the Commission on Relations With Jews, said they were a "first step."

"This document," he said, "invites the whole Catholic Church to an effort of comprehension and cooperation which will be the best guarantee that all hatred of Jews will be rooted out, both racial and religious."

January 3, 1975

Extent of Anti-Catholicism Is Debated; Issue Linked to Abortion and School Aid

By ELEANOR BLAU

After Dr. Kenneth C. Edelin was convicted in Boston last February of manslaughter in an abortion operation, a spokesman for the American Roman Catholic hierarchy said that much of the news coverage of the event had been marked by "innuendo and unfounded accusation directed against the Catholic community."

Similar criticisms were widespread among diocesan newspapers and individual Catholics. They said the general assumption seemed to be that Catholics (who were predominant on the jury) were not capable of making fair decisions—even though, it was noted, the trial involved alleged manslaughter of a fetus, not the abortion itself.

Aside from the question of the validity of these assertions, the reaction brought into focus a feeling among some Catholics that anti-Catholicism was on the rise.

'Liberal Elites' Blamed

The Rev. Andrew M. Greeley, a sociologist who is program director of the National Opinion Research Center of the University of Chicago, says he finds anti-Catholicism among people he describes as "liberal élites" who stereotype as racists all "hard hats" or "white ethnics"—terms he says are euphemisms for Catholics.

Michael Novak, the author, says he first noticed anti-Catholicism two or three years ago in politics, where, he says, Catholics are associated with "the machine" in contrast to non-Catholic reform forces identified with "morality."

The Rev. Virgil C. Blum, president of a two-year-old organization called the Catholic

League for Religious and Civil Rights, contends, among other things, that pro-abortion forces openly encouraged hostility against Catholics.

Father Blum, who is on leave as professor of political science at Marquette University, says he also finds anti-Catholicism reflected in a United States Supreme Court decision in 1973 that rejected New York State aid to private, principally Catholic, elementary and secondary schools. He contended that, at the same time, the Court supported state assistance to a Baptist college in South Carolina and other private colleges and universities that, he said, "happen to be Protestant."

Others cite the prevalence of Polish or Italian jokes, and cartoons and antireligious parodies in recent publications.

The league, modeled in part after the Anti-Defamation League of B'nai B'rith and said to have 13,000 members, maintains that it has persuaded six advertisers to stop placing ads in the National Lampoon because the magazine published what Father Blum called "scurrilous" attacks on Catholics, Protestants and Jews.

However, others in the Catholic community dispute these assertions and insist that anti-Catholicism has decreased steadily, particularly since the election of John F. Kennedy as President in 1960.

John Deedy, managing editor of Commonweal, views claims of anti-Catholicism as "the manifestation of a kind of inferiority complex" and suggests that a few vocal spokesmen inadvertently have created the impression that the claims are more widespread than they really are.

Discounting the abortion controversy as a manifestation of anti-Catholicism, Msgr. George Casey, who writes for a diocesan publication in Boston, remarked:

"There are civil libertarians and women who think the church is trying to shove its doctrine down other people's throats. We were a little rugged and they retaliated."

Donald J. Thorman, publisher of the National Catholic Reporter, says he sees no rise in anti-Catholicism and that most of what he does perceive is among Catholics themselves who are anti-institutional.

And an official of the United States Catholic Conference, the action arm of the church hierarchy, says those who accuse others of anti-Catholicism ought to be more certain that is what they are talking about. "For example, I'm not sure all hard hats can be called Catholics," said the official, who did not want his name used.

At any rate, the issue of anti-Catholicism has been widely discussed within the Catholic community. And, whether they are talking about bigotry or about a mistaken notion that bigotry exists, spokesmen agree that a major element is the church's involvement over the last decade in the controversial abortion and school aid issues.

"Catholics feel beleaguered because whenever they speak out against abortion they are identified as Catholics," the official said. Many Catholics—and non-Catholics — complain that valid arguments regarding the "pro-life" and parochial school aid positions have been obscured or distorted because the two issues are labeled publicly as "Catholic" even though they have many non-Catholic supporters.

'Tag-Line' Opposed

Mr. Novak says the Catholic label extends beyond those issues. "I'm described as a Catholic philosopher and I find that obnoxious," he said. "Sidney Hook isn't described as a 'Jewish philosopher.' That tag-line is always there, and I think, that's discrimination."

No one is comparing the situation to blatant episodes of anti-Catholicism in the past, such as the burning of a Boston convent in the period of the Know-Nothing party in the mid-19th century.

"It's subtle, it has a different form, just as anti-Semitism has a different form," Mr. Novak said.

Father Greeley contends that it is not religious bigotry; the notion of the "Catholic ethnic superpatriot racist" is "not against the Pope, or against doctrine," he says. "It's against people who happen to be Catholics."

Father Greeley attributes the increase in anti-Catholicism to a kind of "hydraulic" scapegoat effect. When one prejudice goes down—namely anti-black sentiment—another goes up, he said.

Rabbi Marc H. Tannenbaum, director of interreligious affairs of the American Jewish Committee, says he thinks there is some validity to complaints that abortion and parochial school aid have not always received fair hearings. But he warned that recent comparisons of this situation to more successful efforts on behalf of Jewish causes could foment anti-Semitism "in less friendly hands."

April 11, 1975

Anti-Catholic Feeling Among Jews

By Andrew M. Greeley

CHICAGO—While the general relationship between American Roman Catholicism and American Judaism is excellent—perhaps better than that between the two historic offshoots of the Sinai religious tradition anywhere else in the world—there are still some moderately critical flashpoints that may flare up when some Jewish intellectuals—probably a small minority—engage in behavior that many Jewish nonintellectuals also engage in.

The white ethnic, blue-collar, racist, hardhat, chauvinist hawk image has become a favorite whipping boy for the national news media, élite and popular. This Catholic ethnic inkblot was not created by Jews; nonetheless, many of those in both the university and the media worlds who propagate it are Jewish. One has the impression that some of them rather enjoy flailing away at the white ethnic bigot.

There is still substantial discrimination against Catholics, particularly practicing ones, at the upper levels of America's élite culture. In the national media, certain governmental agencies, many if not most of the great national foundations, and in the finest elite universities, discrimination is rife. It is justified by the viciously bigoted argument of Catholic intellectual inferiority, an argument that simply does not admit of refutation even if you have overwhelming data to disprove it. Some Jews aid and abet the myth of Catholic intellectual inferiority. One is hard put to find Jews, so many of whom have been vigorous in their criticism of racism and sexism, who raise much in the way of objection to anti-Catholic nativism.

Many of the new generation of Catholic ethnics who are now showing up at the best graduate schools of the country are no longer disposed to take a stand of apology and shame over the past and their own heritages. They don't really feel inferior; they don't feel that being Polish, Italian, or Irish is second-rate or mediocre.

When they learn from a bright, arrogant young faculty member that the conventional wisdom of the liberal upper academy views them and their people with scarcely veiled contempt, they are not likely to accept it. And when that smart, arrogant, articulate, junior faculty member turns out to be Jewish, he runs the risk of stirring up needless anti-Jewish sentiment.

There is a propensity for many non-Catholic scholars to ignore the impressive economic and educational achievements of American Catholics. Many Jews tend to ignore, deny, or minimize the immense importance that the Catholic parochial schools have made to the success and self-confidence of the ethnic immigrants. They overlook completely the fantastic popularity of the inner-city Catholic schools to members of the black community.

Black enrollment in Catholic schools, for example, most of it non-Catholic, goes up each year by as much as 70,000 to 80,000 students. It is the only educational alternative, the only option for freedom of choice available to most inner-city blacks. Such a service deserves to be recognized. Presumably Catholics do not expect and will not get gratitude from the Jewish community for this important social service, but it is time to end the pretense that the service is not occurring.

It is worth observing that the correlation between Catholic school attendance and the absence of anti-Semitism is even stronger now than it was when we first studied it ten years ago. There seems to be no more effective way of reducing anti-Semitic feelings than to support Catholic schools.

The Rev. Andrew M. Greeley is director of The Center for the Study of American Pluralism.

Why is it that all of our issues are relatively less important and seem to make no major claim at all on moral concern? Justice for the people of Israel is supremely important, but justice for the Catholics in the nasty little colonial regime in the north of Ireland is not. Freedom for Soviet Jews is of capital concern, but freedom for the Catholic captive nations is not.

There is a strong and powerful anti-Catholic feeling in the Jewish community. The empirical evidence shows it, the impressions of many Catholics indicate it, and not a small number of Jews will acknowledge it—though usually off the record. Catholics have acknowledged the existence of anti-Jewish feelings in the latest years since the Vatican Council and have worked against them—though perhaps not effectively enough. As far as I can see, there has been no reciprocity at all from the Jewish side.

June 19, 1976

A phrase in Andrew M. Greeley's article "Anti-Catholic Feeling Among Jews," on the Op-Ed page Saturday, contained a transcribing error that originated in his manuscript. The phrase should have read: "There are still some moderately critical flash-points that may flare up when some Jewish intellectuals—probably a small minority—engage in behavior that many non-Jewish intellectuals also engage in."

June 25, 1976

Readers Answer Father Greeley

To the Editor:

I do wish Father Andrew Greeley were a little more restrained in his prose, that he would give a little more consideration to the effects of what he writes. Without doubt, today Jewish-Catholic relations are better than they have been in 2,000 years. Then Father Greeley makes gratuitous charges about Jewish intellectuals and their supposed anti-Catholicism, thus feeding the remnant of anti-Semitism among Catholics and anti-Catholicism among Jews. As a scholar and a priest, I think that he ought to be more responsible than that.

Certainly there are differences of points of view between the Catholic and Jewish communities, such as the question of aid to parochial schools and the abortion issue. Flinging wild charges of prejudice is not going to help the dialogue that is needed to resolve these issues. They will only be resolved by mutual understanding and sympathy. Acting like a bull in the china shop, as Father Greeley has done, will resolve nothing.

THE REV. JOHN P. MAHONEY, O.P.
New York, Conn.
The writer is chairman of the department of religious studies at Albertus Magnus College.

■

To the Editor:

As a Yale-educated Irish Catholic, I find Andrew Greeley's remarks about anti-Catholicism among academic Jews, however much it may be true, a convenient escape from the more painful issue of the tyranny of Rome.

Jewish intellectual achievement has not come about through fighting anti-Semitism. That achievement embodies an age-old respect for and a nurturing of the life of the individual mind. The reason why the admittedly towering achievements of Europeans and Americans of Catholic background in all areas of civilized life are frequently not seen as Catholic achievements is because the Church has made it all too tempting and in some cases advisable for these people to become ex-Catholics. What does this have to do with Jews or Judaism? ANTHONY SCULLY
New York City

To the Editor:

Greeley's piece will undoubtedly arouse an outpouring of indignation. His accusations of "powerful anti-Catholic feeling in the Jewish community," of contempt of Catholic ethnics on the part of "smart, arrogant, articulate" Jewish intellectuals, and of the propagation of anti-Catholic stereotypes by Jews in the "university and media worlds" will surely stamp him as an anti-Semite in the minds of many Jews and non-Jews alike.

I know Father Greeley, and I know he is not an anti-Semite, but he has only himself to blame for that inevitable impression, for his polemic is couched in language that is intemperate, reckless, and calculated to incite people less thoughtful than he to precisely the kind of mindless stereotyping that he decries.

Most readers are probably unaware that Father Greeley's criticisms of the Catholic Church and its hierarchy have been far sharper and more merciless than his *J'Accuse* against the Jews. He has been devastating in his condemnation of his own Church and its bishops for a variety of alleged failings. I do not doubt that a very genuine sense of grievance, not anti-Semitism, motivated Greeley's criticism of the Jews.

Unfortunately, in his Op-Ed piece he resorts to exaggerations and half-truths which destroy his credibility, and only exacerbate the residual hostility that is the legacy of an unhappy and sometimes bloody past.

It is simply not true that Jews will not acknowledge the existence of anti-Catholic feeling in the Jewish community. At a recent encounter between representatives of the Vatican and international Jewish organizations that took place in Jerusalem in March, the major Jewish paper that was the subject of the four-day consultation urged "a re-examination of the image of Christianity in traditional pedagogy and folk culture, which still tends to be defensive and hostile."

There is a demagogic quality to Greeley's complaint that Catholic issues seem less important to Jews than their concern for Israel and Soviet Jewry. In their anguish over real threats to Israel's existence, Jews have not denigrated the suffering of other imperiled nationalities. Indeed, they have been disproportionately in the forefront of virtually every humanitarian cause—whether for domestic civil rights or international justice.

The truth is that American Catholics have not made the plight of Catholics in Northern Ireland and of the captive nations, the two issues mentioned by Greeley, a burning question of conscience for their own faithful. Why they have failed to do so, I do not know, but it is a cheap shot to accuse American Jews of failing to give sufficient moral weight to Catholic concerns which have not visibly agitated the Catholic community itself.

I am not aware of "empirical evidence" of "powerful anti-Catholic feeling in the Jewish community." I tend to doubt that there is any such evidence. But what I find most distressing of all in Greeley's polemic is the implication that American Catholics (over 40 million) are an endangered species—outsiders in a society that is controlled by a Jewish elite. No amount of anti-Catholic sentiment among Jews—which, to whatever degree it exists, is to be deplored and uprooted—can change the fact that such a charge is dangerous nonsense.

There is ample "empirical evidence," stretching back 2,000 years, that Catholic anti-Semitism (and not least among the Catholic captive nations) has had the most horrendous consequences for Jews in the form of pogroms and bloody persecution, which were usually grounded in the myth of Jewish elites who deviously manipulate the fate of nations. It requires an incredible insensitivity to this history to resort to such rhetoric in our own day.

RABBI HENRY SIEGMAN
New York City
The writer is executive vice president of the Synagogue Council of America.

■

To the Editor:

In reference to Andrew M. Greeley's appeal for Jewish examination of their anti-Catholic feelings, it is my belief that the Catholic Church at this time instead of worrying about how others feel cannot afford to waste any energy on anything other than its own rehabilitation.

Recently good friends invited me to the confirmation ceremonies of their 10-year-old son in their church. The distributed text, now in English, made the usual derogatory remarks about Jews around Christ. It occurred to me that the Church does not have the grace to spare its ten-year-olds from the burden of hate and prejudice.

My friend was visibly embarrassed; we will remain close and true friends but I resent that the equality of our relationship is now upset by the guilt and shame that he now bears.

We are too close in time to the Inquisition to spend much time and energy on the prejudice of Jews.

ROBERT SEIDENBERG, M.D.
Syracuse, N. Y.

∎

To the Editor:

Andrew Greeley's column is hogwash. I have worked for Jews most of my life. I have worked side by side with Jews most of my life. I have had Jews work for me for a large part of my life. This is the first I've heard that they didn't like me because I attended mass most Sundays. Perhaps the intellectual Father Greeley travels in the wrong circles.

JOHN J. READY Jr.
West Caldwell, N. J.

∎

To the Editor:

Father Andrew Greeley's piece alleging anti-Catholic prejudice among Jews hurts because it comes from an admired academician, a sociologist who might be expected to measure his words. I have lived more than 40 years in professional academic and intellectual Jewish circles and have never encountered the attitudes he ascribes to us. He offers no evidence other than the report of an anti-Catholic putdown by some young snit on the college campus. I do not doubt that there are some brash, prejudiced, and loose-tongued Jews in the academic world, but we certainly hold no monopoly on that type of individual.

Permit a personal reflection: My own outlook has in great part been molded by Catholic intellectual influences such as Jacques Maritain and Teilhard de Chardin, and I have been informally educated by Jesuits at Xavier, Creighton and John Carroll. I respond with joy to every evidence of burgeoning Catholic liberalism just as I respond with sorrow to the factual history of Church violence, cruelty and persecution of my people, and with deep distaste for the remaining pockets of ignorance and malice.

Indeed, until now, Andrew Greeley himself has been one of the contemporary writers I have most admired. Let us have chapter and verse, Father Andy, or let us have an apology.

RABBI ARTHUR J. LELYVELD
Cleveland

The writer, president of the American Jewish Congress from 1966 to 1972, is president of the Central Conference of American Rabbis.

July 1, 1976

THE ECUMENICAL MOVEMENT

POPE TO SUMMON COUNCIL TO SEEK CHRISTIAN UNITY

By PAUL HOFMANN
Special to The New York Times.

ROME, Jan. 25—Pope John XXIII announced today that he would call an ecumenical council aimed at seeking unity between the Roman Catholic Church and other Christian communities throughout the world.

It will be the first ecumenical council, or general conference of the church, since the one of 1869-70, which proclaimed the infallibility of the Pope.

The announcement, termed "epochal" by priests here, came at the end of week-long prayers in the churches of Rome for Christian unity. The occasion was the nineteenth centenary of the Apostle Paul's Epistle to the Romans.

The Pontiff's first objective appeared to be a "dialogue" with Eastern Orthodoxy on the chances of a reunion.

Bid to Anglicans Foreseen

Healing of the 900-year-old split between Rome and the Christian East could not but have a profound impact on general East-West relations, prominent Roman Catholics here said. They conceded that the proposed church assembly would at best mark a first step in that direction.

Roman Catholic overtures for unity with the Church of England and other Christian communities in the West may also be expected, it was predicted here, although it was granted that the possibilities of union with these denominations were more remote than with the Eastern Orthodox Christians.

Pope John's announcement evidently came as a surprise even to most of the twenty Cardinals who were the first to hear it. It came after a pontifical mass in the Basilica of St. Paul Outside the Walls shortly after noon.

The Pontiff's words to the members of the Sacred College were described as his most important pronouncement since his election three months ago.

The Pope also announced that a general revision of church legislation would be promulgated. The Code of Canon Law of 1917 will be brought up to date and the law of the Eastern Church in communion with Rome, which is being codified, will soon be promulgated as a separate statute.

Speaking as Bishop of Rome, he mentioned "the grave problems related to spiritual assistance of the population," a Vatican communiqué said. The Pope also "underlined the daily increasing perils threatening the spiritual lives of the faithful—notably, the errors that are infiltrating their ranks at various points and the immoderate attractions of material goods, which have increased more than ever with technical progress."

The Pontiff said that as head of the Roman diocese he would hold a synod or regional assembly of the Roman clergy for discussion of pastoral problems in this rapidly growing city and its surroundings.

The Vatican press office said later:

"The celebration of the ecumenical council, in the thinking of the Holy Father, not only is aimed at the edification of Christian people but also is intended to be an invitation to the separated communities to search for the unity for which so many souls in all parts of world yearn today."

Neither a date nor a place for the momentous assembly was mentioned. It was thought that an ecumenical council, even in an era of rapid worldwide communications, required such thorough preparation that it would not be convened before late this year, or more likely next year. It was assumed that Rome would be the scene.

1,800 May Vote

Under canon law, all Cardinals and residential patriarchs, primates, archbishops and bishops and the abbots and superiors general of certain orders are entitled to participate and vote in an ecumenical council. This group, according to Vatican data, totals nearly 1,800 churchmen.

In addition, many of the nearly 900 titular Archbishops and Bishops are expected to be invited. These prelates in various church posts bear the honorary titles of early Christian dioceses now extinct. Leading theologians may also be asked to attend, but may not vote.

Unofficial Vatican sources said it was "highly probable" that some churchmen not in communion with the Holy See would be invited by Pope John to attend as observers.

It was thought that some non-Catholic Christian leaders had already been confidentially sounded out, and that at least a few had indicated that they would accept an invitation. More such feelers will be put out in coming months, it was predicted.

It was recalled that the Greek Orthodox Patriarch of Istanbul had recently sent a personal letter to Pope John. The contents were not disclosed. It was suggested that the Pontiff had been encouraged by this message to go on with his plans for an ecumenical council.

Served Long in Mideast

The new Pope is understood to be convinced that the time has come for a move for reunion, above all between Rome and the Eastern Christians. During his nineteen years as papal envoy to Bulgaria, Greece and Turkey, Pope John, then Archbishop Angelo Giuseppe Roncalli, traveled widely in the Balkans and Middle East, learned their languages and gained first-hand knowledge of the problems and personalities of the Eastern Churches. He has remained a friend of several Orthodox prelates.

The Orthodox and Roman Catholic Churches regard each other as schismatic. Their split goes back to the shift of power in the ancient Roman Empire from Rome to Byzantium, and it became definitive in the eleventh century.

The Eastern Orthodox churches, according to Roman Catholic sources, number between 130,000,000 and 150,000,000 communicants. Most of them live in the Balkans, the Middle East and the Soviet Union. Flourishing Orthodox communities exist also in the American Hemisphere.

Ecclesiastics here voiced the hope that a world-wide move for Christian unity would strengthen religious faith everywhere, especially behind the Iron Curtain.

Comments were cautious regarding possible unity talks between Roman Catholics and Protestants. The Roman Catholic Church so far has not participated in ecumenical conferences promoted by Protestant churches, and it was felt here that the Vatican would carefully weigh whether it should invite Protestant churchmen to the proposed council.

All authorities consulted here made it emphatically clear that the Vatican was expecting the Eastern Christians and Protestants to "return to the common home"—that is, to recognize the primacy of the Pope.

The ecumenical council would examine ways to make such a return easier, these sources explained. They said the church could not renounce its dogmas, because they are held to have been defined by divine inspiration, but it could introduce changes in canon law, liturgy and church discipline.

Among precedents mentioned was that of the late Pope Pius XII in waiving the rule of celibacy for married German Lutheran pastors who had embraced the Roman Catholic creed and were allowed to continue in the ministry.

January 26, 1959

Across the Fence of Faith

AN AMERICAN DIALOGUE: A Protestant Looks at Catholicism and a Catholic Looks at Protestantism. By Robert McAfee Brown & Gustave Weigel, S. J. Foreword by Will Herberg. 216 pp. New York: Doubleday & Co. $2.95.

By STRINGFELLOW BARR

THIS book is a landmark in America's progress toward religious maturity. In it a Protestant theologian, Robert McAfee Brown of Union Theological Seminary, looks at Catholicism; a Roman Catholic theologian, Gustave Weigel, S. J., looks at Protestantism, and a Jewish theologian supplies a wise foreword. The entire book is highly readable; and it would be a healthy thing if millions of Americans, regardless of their religious faith or their lack of it, would read "An American Dialogue." In an important sense, the book fails; but it could at least remind us how much more significant it is to fail at some things than to succeed at others—as, for example, to succeed in electing or defeating a Presidential candidate because of his religion.

The book fails because it does not achieve true dialogue. Or, rather, the dialogue it does achieve occurs less between Mr. Brown's Part I and Father Weigel's Part II than inside each part, especially inside Part I. Mr. Brown traces Catholic-

Mr. Barr, Professor of Humanities at Rutgers, contributed to the recent symposium, "American Catholics: A Protestant-Jewish View."

Protestant relations through warfare and mutual torture, through mutual polemics, and then in America through studied indifference, through superficial agreement, to power-bloc jockeying in politics and publicity. And now both sides are beginning to try really to understand. To help this new dialogue bear fruit, Mr. Brown suggests six excellent ground rules, his most excellent one based on the highly Platonic insight that true dialogue, as distinguished from mere dispute, is like prayer.

HE then uses the history of the American Roman Catholic community to explain some of its striking traits and produces statistical evidence against the Protestant bogy that the Catholic community is outgrowing the Protestant. After demolishing a few more Protestant stereotypes, he gently suggests to the Catholics some of the facts which helped cause them. After examining how much Protestants and Catholics have recently begun to learn from each others' scholars, he nevertheless points out how deeply the problem of authority separates them.

In Part II, Father Weigel first expresses the puzzlement the Protestant scene causes the Catholic. He discusses generously, but pungently, Protestant piety and Protestant morality. He analyzes "the Protestant stance": the Protestant's empiricism, his skepticism, the voluntarism his skepticism breeds and his naïve modernity. He ob-

serves the Protestant's fear that the Catholics will take over and speculates that the Protestant really fears Protestantism may die and that perhaps the Protestant would like to persuade Catholics to practice birth control to rid himself of a deep insecurity on the subject.

On the question of church unity, Father Weigel feels certain that Catholics cannot invite Protestants to ecumenical discussion, nor can the Protestant invite the Catholic. When a certain point is reached, "no dialogue is possible. But two sets of monologue for mutual information are possible." These monologues could be para-ecumenical; they might be pre-ecumenical, they could reduce hostilities.

While Father Weigel has faithfully and provocatively carried out his assignment as implied in this book's subtitle, Mr. Brown has gone somewhat beyond the subtitle to the title itself. Partly, his intellectual stance tends to be Platonic where Father Weigel's tends to be Aristotelian. But partly, he has heightened the reader's sense of dialogue by quoting Catholic theologians in Europe.

HE urges Protestants to read "Tolerance and the Catholic," by a group of French Catholics; Father Louis Bouyer's "The Spirit and Forms of Protestantism"; Father George Tavard's "The Catholic Approach to Protestantism"; Father Yves Congar's "Divided Christendom."

And he quotes Father Maurice Villain as saying that "The way of achieving deeper comprehension will not come conceptually but spiritually." Father Villain also holds that, ever since the Council of Trent, both Roman Catholic and Protestant theology have been constructed polemically, and he urges that his own church rethink its position as if there had been no heresy.

Perhaps it is natural that Europe should be so far ahead of us: their dialogue was largely born out of the agony of persecution, out of torture and death. For the most part, we Americans have been too fat to engage in good dialogue. Moreover, as Mr. Herberg points out, our talents have gone into "interfaith cooperation" rather than understanding each other's religious beliefs.

I wish I thought this book would provoke another dialogue: a discussion between American Catholics and some of the European Catholics Mr. Brown quotes, and dealing with the Roman Catholic Church's relations with their "separated brethren." Good dialogue can be just as contagious as polemic has been, just as prayer can be as catching as blasphemy. Even we Americans, we cooperative activists, are ripe for more dialogue, or the book I am discussing would not have been written; nor, if written, published. Instead, here it is; a real conversation has started; and that is always a mystery and a miracle.

September 18, 1960

EPISCOPAL LETTER PRESSES FOR UNITY

By GEORGE DUGAN
Special to The New York Times.

DETROIT, Sept. 29 — The bishops of the Protestant Episcopal Church called on their 3,500,000 constituents today to shun parochialism and to work with patience and sacrifice for the end of a divided Christendom.

Their plea was the main thesis of a pastoral letter issued at the end of the church's twelve-day triennial general convention here in Cobo Hall.

The letter was read by the Right Rev. Angus Dun, Bishop of the Diocese of Washington. Bishop Dun, widely regarded as one of the denomination's leading religious statesmen, will retire next May.

Leader in Ecumenicalism

He has long been an advocate of the ecumenical movement that in essence strives to overcome the traditional divisions of Christianity. The major ecumenical bodies are the World Council of Churches and the National Council of Churches, both of which include Protestant and Eastern Orthodox bodies in their memberships.

The pastoral letter hailed the work of both of these bodies in advancing cooperation but expressed "grief" that the Roman Catholic Church was not a member of the World Council.

"But we can rejoice," it added, "that that communion is increasingly represented by officially approved 'observers' at major meetings of the council and that there are many evidences of the seriousness and respect with which it views this organ of the ecumenical movement."

Earlier this month it was announced in Vatican City that the Roman Catholic Church, for the first time, would send official observers to the General Assembly of the World Council in New Delhi, India, Nov. 18 to Dec. 6.

Church Ready to Talk

The pastoral letter noted that for the last seventy-five years the Episcopal Church has "publicly and officially" expressed its readiness for reunion talks with other Christian bodies.

In the last twelve days the church formally extended the hand of friendship to sister bodies here and overseas. It also agreed to discuss a merger with the Methodist Church, the United Presbyterian Church and the United Church of Christ.

The letter acknowledged that the Episcopal Church and Anglicans over the world were "but a small part of the whole number of Christ's people."

"We would not overwhelm you with figures," it said, "but when we look at them it is plain, without minimizing one whit the heritage and the mission God has committed to us, that Christ's cause in America and overseas is in many hands besides ours."

The letter warns that "there have been so many Episcopalians concentrated in Detroit that we can almost think the world is made up of Episcopalians."

Patience Is Advocated

But in the long view of the future the pastoral declared: "We urge patience, for centuries of division and misunder-

standing are not soon overcome. We urge restraint, for there will be inevitable strain within our own corporate life and in that of others with whom we seek unity. We urge humble sacrifice, for obedience is costly and treasures shared in love mean change for all.

"Above all, we urge deep awareness that we are committed to the one great church and that we are called to be faith-

ful to it. We, your bishops, call you therefore to work and to pray without ceasing until by God's grace and in His time the division by which we dishonor our one Lord are done away."

The letter will be sent in printed form to all of the nearly 7,000 Episcopal Churches over the country. It must be read in all pulpits within a month of its receipt.

The pastoral letter was writ-

ten in almost its entirety by Bishop Dun. He was assisted by a committee composed of the Right Rev. Stephen F. Bayne Jr., executive officer of the Anglican Communion; the Right Rev. Robert F. Gibson Jr., Bishop of Virginia; the Right Rev. Henry I. Louttit, Bishop of South Florida, and the Right Rev. Frederick J. Warnecke, Bishop of Bethlehem, Pa.

September 30, 1961

COUNCIL APPROVES TEXTS ON HEALING CHRISTIAN SCHISM

By ROBERT C. DOTY
Special to The New York Times

ROME, Oct. 5—The Roman Catholic hierarchy approved today the most liberal, fraternal and conciliatory expressions of its will to reunify Christianity since before the great Protestant schism of the 16th century.

The bishops and higher prelates of the church, assembled in the Ecumenical Council, gave formal expression to the spirit of Christian unity that has gradually replaced in modern times the centuries of Catholic anathema leveled against all outside the Roman communion.

Catholic and Protestant experts agreed that the ultimate goal of a single Christian church probably was still generations away. But, they said, the four Council votes today sounded a very "positive tone" for future Catholic-Protestant dialogue.

The votes technically were preliminary but in fact were decisive.

Fault on Both Sides Noted

The texts approved acknowledged that both Catholics and Protestants had been at fault in the creation of past divisions.

They recognized the possibility of merit and, technically, of salvation outside the Catholic fold.

And they exhorted all Catholics to recognize and work actively for the ecumenical spirit — the drive toward Christian unity.

With a maximum of only 57 dissenting votes on each poll taken, the more than 2,100 Fathers of the Council present approved four sections of the schema "De Ecumenismo" ("Of Ecumenism or the Goal of Christian Unity"). These actions vir-

tually reversed the violent anti-Protestant tone of the Council of Trent, the church's formal reaction to the Reformation, which was held between 1542 and 1563.

The Council of Trent listed a number of Protestant doctrinal heresies and fostered an "anathema sint" ("let him be cursed") position against all who professed them.

Application Has Varied

The practical application of this official stand has varied from the violence of the Inquisition of the 17th and 18th centuries to the de facto accommodations between Catholics and Protestants of the last 150 years.

The latter attitude has been reflected in encyclicals by modern popes, but has never been as formally ratified as it was today.

The texts approved speak of "fault on both sides" in past schisms, of "reverence and love" for the separated brethren, of the "many and precious Christian elements" outside the "visual boundaries" of the Catholic church and of God's use of other churches as a means of salvation.

None of these texts constitute a denial of the conclusions of the Council of Trent. Heresy is still heresy. It is a fundamental tenet of the church that its "magisterium"—its teaching authority in its formal expression in pope or council—cannot err.

But the bishops and theologians of the church, under the impetus of ecumenism, have shown, in the opinion of most qualified Catholic and Protestant observers, a will and a skill to adapt past decisions of the church to changing conditions without denying them.

Thus, the texts voted still identify the fact of the original separation from the Catholic church as "sin." But they add that persons born into separated-church communities cannot be blamed for the "sin" and that the Catholic church "embraces them in brotherly reverence and love."

Basic Position Undiluted

Similarly, the statement that there is merit and salvation outside the "visible limits" of the Catholic church does not dilute the basic Catholic assertion that salvation is to be found only within the church.

But, by referring to the "visible limits" of the church it seemed to imply that there was a continuing mystical bond among Christians within the theoretical "invisible" limits of the church.

Another recurring theme of the four texts is a spirit of self-examination and criticism among Catholics, a recognition that, however right and infallible church doctrine may be, there have been lapses from perfection in its expression.

"Although the Catholic church is endowed with revealed truth and the means of grace," one passage stated "its members do not all live with the proper fervor, so that the face of the church is less resplendent before the separated brethren and . . . the unification of the Kingdom of God is retarded."

The Catholic faithful are exhorted to refrain from "words, judgments and deeds" that do not accurately reflect the true beliefs of separated Christians and that would render relations with them more difficult.

Sanction is specifically given for meetings among experts of Catholic and Protestant communities to explain and explore their respective points of view and achieve "truer knowledge and higher estimation" of each other.

Move for Converts Goes On

At the same time, it is stated that nothing in the ecumenical movement can interfere with the church's active efforts to obtain individual converts from other faiths.

The four sections expressing these views were given interim approval by more than 2,000 "placet" ("it-pleases") votes in each case, while the "non placet" ("it-does-not-please") ballots numbered 16, 30, 57 and 50.

Commenting on the negative votes, a clerical expert on the American Bishops' press panel quoted an American Bishop, whom he did not identify, as having said that there was a "hard core" of about 30 to 50 prelates who expressed general discontent with the very idea of the Council itself by automatic

votes against every proposition.

But the balloting today reinforced the clear indications from the first three weeks of this, the third, session of Ecumenical Council Vatican II that the progressive majority of the world's Cardinals, Patriarchs, Archbishops and Bishops were proceeding firmly on the course of modernizing the church set by the late Pope John XXIII in summoning the Council in 1962.

This has been manifested, with the quiet, implicit approval of Pope Paul VI, in such actions as the approval of the principle of collegiality—collective authority—of the Bishops under the Pope. It has also been evinced in debates on religious liberty and on a new liberal Catholic attitude toward the Jews.

Despite the spirit manifested today, the Catholic church has still made no move to join the World Council of Churches, in which most of the world's other Christian bodies meet to discuss church matters.

Responding to a question on this, the Rev. Thomas Stransky, an American Paulist priest of the Council Secretariat for Christian Unity, said the Catholic view was that there was no theoretical obstacle to Catholic adherence to the world council since one of the council's tenets was that each member could observe its own ecclesiology — theory of its church.

Only a minority, he said, would contend that the Catholic doctrine of "magisterium" — infallibility of teaching — would be compromised by accepting a position of equality with others.

But he questioned whether the world council, representing about 400 million Protestants, was ready to welcome a church of a half-billion Catholics.

As a practical matter, he said, there was much that could be done short of membership in the world council in the way of cooperation on such questions as Christian evangelism and aid to refugees.

The Rev. Dr. Eugene R. Fairweather, professor of divinity at the University of Toronto and an official Anglican (Episcopalian) observer at the Council, stressed the "very positive tone" of the texts voted on ecumenism.

October 6, 1964

World Jewish Congress Cancels Plan for Role at Vatican Council

By GEORGE DUGAN

Dr. Nahum Goldmann, president of the World Jewish Congress, has canceled representation of the congress at the Vatican Council, which is scheduled to begin in Rome on Oct. 11. The council will consider the entire field of Roman Catholic practice and doctrine.

Dr. Goldman's decision, it was learned yesterday, was made in deference to what was described as the Jewish consensus that it would be improper to participate in a gathering of such a nature as the council.

Some weeks ago it was announced that Dr. Chaim Wardi, a member of the Israeli Ministry of Religions, had received a leave of absence to attend the Vatican Council as an unofficial observer representing the World Jewish Congress. It was this appointment that was canceled by Dr. Goldmann.

The congress, which has its headquarters at 15 East Eighty-fourth Street, seeks to safeguard the rights, status and interests of Jews and Jewish communities over the world. It represents Jewish groups in the United Nations and other world bodies on matters of concern to Judaism.

The congress has been the only Jewish body so far to consider sending observers to the council. However, a hundred observers representing Protestant-

ism and Eastern Orthodoxy are expected to attend. About 3,000 Bishops of the Roman Catholic Church from over the world will be delegates.

The issue of Jewish representation at the Rome meeting has been generating friction in this country for some time.

On July 11 the Rabbinical Council of America unanimously adopted a resolution in Miami calling on Jewish secular bodies to shun gatherings such as the Vatican Council.

The resolution read as follows:

"The Rabbinical Council of America views with grave alarm recent press releases which attribute to the World Jewish Congress and Dr. Nahum Goldmann, its head, efforts with respect to representation in world Christian theological conferences.

Variance of Reform Rabbis

"The Rabbinical Council of America reaffirms its previous position that no secular agencies or their leaders have the authority to make representations on behalf of the religious Jewish community and fears that such actions may jeopardize and impair improving Christian-Jewish relations."

Rabbi Bernard Twersky, public relations officer of the Rabbinical Council, said yesterday that Jewish opinion over the world has been almost unanimous in its feeling that Jewish involvement in the religious councils of another faith was "inadvisable."

On July 21 the Rev. Dr. William F. Rosenblum of Temple Israel, New York, a Reform rabbi, took issue with the Miami

resolution. The Rabbinical Council represents the Orthodox branch of American Judaism.

Dr. Rosenblum called the Orthodox action "a startling and striking example of isolationism . . . in an era when our various religions are seeking ways to get together."

He praised recent modifications in the Roman Catholic liturgy that referred to Jews and added that the best way to continued improvement "is to keep in touch with the church and not to withdraw from contact."

But yesterday another Reform rabbi, the Rev. Dr. Louis I. Newman of Temple Rodeph Sholom, took Dr. Rosenblum to task. In his sermon at the temple, 7 West Eighty-third Street, Dr. Newman called Dr. Rosenblum's statement "unjustified."

"It is irrelevant and obtuse," he asserted, "to say that the Rabbinical Council has furnished a 'startling and striking example of isolationism' in issuing a resolution of caution against involvement in a Catholic Church council by any Jewish leader in any country before the mature opinion of the Jewish people is obtained.

"If Catholic ecclesiastical authorities wish any information, suggestion or comment from Jewish religious spokesmen they are well aware of the organizations and individuals to whom they can quickly turn.

"Whenever Christian authorities, whether Catholic or Protestant, are ready to lessen or to eliminate those incitements to religious prejudice which eventuate in hatred and violence it will be found that Jewish authorities, duly designated by stable and wise public opinion in Jewry, will be glad to cooperate, approve and applaud.

"This is a time for watchful

waiting, and every preacher, writer or lay reader in Jewry must act with restraint, not with the enunciation of 'obiter dicta,' such as we have recently read."

That the Vatican Council may turn out to be the most significant gathering in the history of the Roman Catholic Church is the opinion of Augustin Cardinal Bea, president of the Vatican Secretariat for Promoting Christian Unity, and the Rev. Thomas F. Stransky, a Paulist priest who is a permanent staff member of the secretariat.

Succession of Councils

Cardinal Bea's comments will appear in the Aug. 11 issue of America, a Jesuit weekly published here. Father Stransky's remarks were made at a press interview on Thursday in the Paulist Communications office, 411 West Fifty-ninth Street.

In the 2,000 years of Christian history only twenty "ecumenical," or world-wide, councils have been held. The nineteenth was the Council of Trent in the sixteenth century and the twentieth was the First Vatican Council that came to a premature close in 1870 when the Piedmontese army invaded the Papal States. Its sole accomplishment was to proclaim papal infallibility.

The Second Vatican Council, as the twenty-first will be officially called, will convene in two sessions: Oct. 11 to mid-December, and from shortly after Easter (April 14, 1963) to about the middle of June.

It will review every phase of church life, including doctrine, liturgy, law, missions, the sacraments and the training and discipline of the clergy. Christian unity will be discussed at length.

July 29, 1962

PRELATES ADOPT LIBERTY DECREE

Freedom of Conscience Is Backed by 1,954-249 Vote of Ecumenical Council

By ROBERT C. DOTY
Special to The New York Times

ROME, Nov. 19—The Roman Catholic world hierarchy voted overwhelmingly today for the adoption of a positive concept of religious liberty as church doctrine to replace the negative one of "toleration."

Ending three years of sometimes bitter controversy in Ecumenical Council Vatican II, the prelates approved, by 1,954

votes to 249, a declaration affirming that no man may be coerced to act against his conscience or prohibited from following its dictates except by the demands of public order.

These immunities are recognized as inherent personal rights implicit in Scripture. The drafting commission, resisting efforts by conservatives to define religious liberty as only a "civil right," explained that this would make it subject to the whims of civil authority.

"We claim in the text that man enjoys immunity from external coercion, and this in virtue of his very nature," said the Most Rev. Emile-Joseph de Smedt, Bishop of Bruges, Belgium, spokesman for the commission in presenting the final draft. "The basis of this right is the dignity of the human person endowed by God according to his image with

free will and personal responsibility."

The practical consequences of the declaration are obscure. The right of states, acting for "peculiar" historical reasons, to grant a special status to one religion —as in Italy, Spain and Britain — is still recognized. The new view may make the lot of non-Catholic missionaries easier in some parts of South America. Theoretically, it should swing church influence behind a relaxation of Spain's restrictions on the opening of Protestant churches.

Assuredly, it eliminates one more obstacle to dialogue and to the still remote but potential union between Catholic and non-Catholic Christians.

For many centuries the Roman Catholic Church, like some Protestant sects, denied rights to other faiths wherever it had the power to enforce its will.

In 1888 Pope Leo III pub-

lished an encyclical declaring the principle of "toleration." This stated that the ideal situation would be the exclusive triumph of the "one true faith" everywhere, but, as a practical matter, it recognized that a pluralistic society demanded Catholic toleration of other beliefs.

The new declaration renews the assertions that Catholicism is the "one true faith" and that every man has the duty to follow it to the limit of his understanding. But now the church specifically rejects any effort to coerce man to embrace this "duty," not because such an effort is objectively impractical but because it is morally unacceptable.

The 249 negative votes today apparently represent the hard core of conservatives who have argued the traditional thesis that "error has no rights."

In deference to conservative opinion, the drafters put into the final version a reaffirmation of the concept of "one true church" that all Catholics hold

327

but that progressives thought was inopportune and "unecumenical" in a document on religious liberty. This failed of its purpose, for 25 more prelates voted against the final version than opposed the earlier draft in October.

The Council heard today the results of balloting Wednesday on the last few sections of the massive schema on the church in the modern world. These showed that the Most Rev. Philip M. Hannan, Archbishop of New Orleans, a former paratroop chaplain, had failed to muster sufficient support to force amendment of sections on war and peace that, he argued, took an unrealistic view of current realities.

He sought recognition of the "necessity" of a resort to arms to redress violated rights and of the role of Western nuclear stockpiles in deterring aggression.

on the modern world, on missionary activity, and on priestly life and the ministry remaining on the agenda, the Council went into recess until Nov. 30.

With debate ended 10 days ago and only the final redrafting and voting of the schemata

November 20, 1965

On 'the Post-Christian Era'

By JOHN COGLEY

The religious scene in recent years has resounded with ecumenical chant and interfaith harmony. But here and there a discordant note is still heard and nowhere more sharply than in the current issue of Judaism, a quarterly published by the American Jewish Congress. (The A.J.C. of course does not necessarily endorse the views of contributors to Judaism.)

"Judaism in the Post-Christian Era" is the title of a challenging article written by Prof. Eliezer Berkovits of the Hebrew Union College in Skokie, Illinois.

Professor Berkovits begins his argument by stating flatly that a "phase in world history" that might have been called the Christian Era has come to an end. That Era, he holds, began not with the birth of Jesus but with the conversion of Constantine in the 4th century. From that time forward Christianity became a conquering religion, using the sword to convert ("baptism or death") and persecuting, suppressing or actually exterminating other religions as it broadened its conquests.

Pattern Followed

Other ideologies and secular movements now follow the pattern established by the early aggressive Christianity, according to Dr. Berkovits. The sword of Constantine has been passed on to new hands. "The Soviets are holding it mightily in their grip; Red China has taken possession of it; the dark millions of Africa are acquiring it; hundreds of millions of Moslems, Buddhists and Hindus have learned to wield it."

This situation more than anything else, in Professor Berkovits' view is responsible for the ecumenical movement,

especially among Roman Catholics. After sixteen centuries of Christian dominance, the Catholic Church especially, but also other Christian churches, is finally ready to champion humane ideals of religious toleration that were realized by the heathen Romans, 2,000 years ago and upheld by Judaism and the secularistic forces of the past four centuries.

The primary explanation for contemporary ecumenism and the spirit of toleration for other religions now flowering in Christianity, then, is that the Church is exhausted and no longer enjoys its old dominance. "When the Church leaders speak of freedom of religion," Dr. Berkovits says, "they mean 'first of all freedom for Christians to adhere to their faith in Communist lands." Similarly, support for civil toleration is primarily motivated by a desire to propagate the Christian faith among Muslims, Buddhists, Hindus and other peoples.

Question of Stance

The question now facing Judaism, the professor holds, is what stance it should take in confronting this "morally and spiritually bankrupt civilization and religion."

He argues that those in the Jewish community who have been participating in the interfaith dialogue recommended by the Vatican Council and approved by other Christian religious groups are at best ill-advised.

The professor describes his co-religionists who go along with ecumenism as either Jews without memory, Jews for whom Judaism is strictly a matter of public relations, or as confused and spineless Jews. "For Jewry as a

whole," he states, "an honest fraternal dialogue with Christianity is at this stage emotionally impossible." The events of Buchenwald and Auschwitz are too close. Perhaps in a hundred years, he holds, Jews may be ready for theological dialogue with Christianity — but even that possibility is dependent on Christian behavior in the meantime.

Aside from the emotional block, Dr. Berkovits cites philosophical, theological and practical reasons why a Jewish-Christian confrontation is unwise at this time.

PHILOSOPHIC: The realm of thought is universal. There is no more reason for a Jewish - Muslim, Jewish - Hindu, Jewish - Existentialist, or Jewish-atheist dialogue. Christian philosophers, like Paul Tillich or Jacques Maritain, have been welcomed by Jews to the general philosophic conversation, but there is no reason why Christian theological thinkers should be singled out for special attention.

Theological: Theological dialogue is pointless. Judaism is Judaism because it rejects Christianity, and Christianity is Christianity because it rejects Judaism, and that is all there is to that. Whatever remains in Christianity that is authentically Jewish is acceptable to Jews, but nothing else.

Christians and Jews do not have the Old Testament nor even the God of the Old Testament in common, according to the professor. In the first place, the Old Testament is not an "incomplete" Bible to the Jewish believer. Therefore it is something different to him than to one who believes its prophesies were fulfilled by the events recounted in the New Testament.

Again, the God of Abraham and Isaac is a triune Deity to the orthodox Christian— Father, Son and Holy Spirit— but to the Jewish believer the

whole notion of Trinity is blasphemous.

Practical: A Christian-Jewish dialogue, like a Roman Catholic-Protestant dialogue suggests that there were misunderstandings, distortions and mutual injuries committed in the past which now will be repented. In the case of the Jews and Christians, however, the persecution and repression were one-sided. "We reject the idea of inter-religious understanding as immoral," Dr. Berkovits writes boldly, "because it is an attempt to whitewash a criminal past."

No Common Front

The appeal to form a common front with Christians against irreligion and secularism leaves Dr. Berkovits utterly cold. He argues that Judaism, less encumbered by dogmas than Christianity, should work out its own unique response to the challenge of the age. To join forces with Christianity would only weaken its doctrinal position.

"Moreover, the Jewish religious position has the advantage of not being compromised by sins of the past —colonialism in Africa, for example, or the religious wars and the persecution of religious wars and the persecution of religious dissenters that must be laid at the doorstep of organized Christianity.

"It would seem then that, on the whole, we have to go our own way," Dr. Berkovits writes. "We who were there when the Christian era began; we in whose martyrdom Christianity suffered its worst moral debacle; we in whose blood the Christian era found its end—we are here as this new era opens. And we shall be here when this new era reaches its close — we, the *edim*, God's own witnesses, to the *am olam*, the eternal witnesses of history."

April 3, 1966

Orthodox Priest Says Most Christians Are Slow in Adjusting to Ecumenism

By JOHN COGLEY

The vast majority of Christians are still simply unprepared to adjust to the ecumenical climate in Christianity, according to the Very Rev. Alexander Schmemann, dean of St. Vladimir's Orthodox Theological Seminary, Tuckahoe, N. Y.

Father Schmemann told an ecumenical workshop meeting last week at Trinity College in Washington, a Roman Catholic women's school, that as a consequence the "ecumenical avantgarde" is in danger of being cut off from the body of their churches.

He pointed to his own religious tradition, the Eastern Orthodox, as a prime example of unknown religious territory for millions of American Protestants and Roman Catholics.

"We lost you and you lost us," he told the interfaith gathering. As a result, he added, little is known of the Orthodox Church, though a greater awareness of it would help the ecumenical movement by putting things "in perspective."

Father Schmemann is a priest of the Russian Orthodox Church, one of 20 Orthodox bodies in the United States that have a total of about 3.2 million members. More than half, 1,735,000, belong to the Greek Orthodox Archdiocese of North and South America, presided over by Archbishop Iakovos, whose headquarters are at 10 East 79th Street, Manhattan.

Isolation Decried

At a recent meeting here of his church's lay and clerical leaders, Archbishop Iakovos struck out against the Orthodox community's habitual isolation from the mainstream of American religious life. The time has come, he said, for full participation in interfaith activities.

The Orthodox should make their voice heard in the United States and break with the patterns of nationalistic isolation that has effectively cut them off from other religious com-munities, he said at the St. Moritz Hotel, where he announced the formation of a new charitable organization.

Father Schmemann sounded a similar note at the Catholic-sponsored workshop but insisted that ecumenism was a two-way street. Until the pontificate of Pope John XXIII, the relationship between Orthodoxy and Protestantism was notably more cordial than that between Orthodoxy and Roman Catholicism.

From the beginning, the Orthodox were active in the the Protestant-inspired World Council of Churches. They have been increasingly so since the Council's organizing meeting in Amsterdam in 1948 and now practically every major world division of Orthodoxy is represented in the organization.

Roman Catholic participation, once strictly forbidden by Vatican directives, is still confined to observers at World Council meetings and a few semi-official joint efforts.

Nevertheless, there are probably stronger theological links between Orthodoxy and Roman Catholicism than between Orthodoxy and Protestantism, though these links have frequently been weakened by the stresses of historical disagreement and the vanity of prelates.

Father Schmemann said last week that in spite of their long estrangement, it was time to remember that Orthodoxy and Roman Catholicism are two halves of the same church.

In the bmeginning, the priest said, the Christian Church was given its "shape" by the contours of the Greco-Roman world. Orthodoxy, in the Greek mode, and Catholicism, in the Roman mode, coexisted fraternally for 1,000 years, observing "unity in diversity and diversity in unity."

There was ample room for theological divergence in such an arrangement, he pointed out. But despite disagreements, neither half of the Church broke from the other. Rome and Constantinople respected each other's differences.

How It Happened

Rome, he reminded his audience at the Catholic women's college, freely accepted the doctrinal teachings hammered out at the great ecumenical councils held in Nicea, Chalcedon, Ephesus and other Eastern centers.

The Church in the West as a distinct entity, Father Schmemann said, followed only after these councils. "It followed creatively and constructively—but nevertheless it followed," he said.

Thereafter, he said, the "psychology of 50 per cent" developed. Each of the halves began to see itself as the whole Church. After the Pope's legates excommunicated Michael Cerularius, Patriarch of Constantinople, and the Patriarch in turn excommunicated the legates in 1054, the break was complete.

Both of these excommunications were penitently "assigned to historical oblivion" by Pope Paul and the Ecumenical Patriarch Athenagoras, who holds the place of honor among the Orthodox patriarchs, near the end of the Vatican Council last fall.

Most of the present difficulties separating the Orthodox and the Roman Catholics, Father Schmemann said, can be traced to the separate acts of the churches since the distant days of their loose union.

Infallibility Disputed

A major point of dispute is the doctrine of papal infallibility as defined by the First Vatican Council in 1870. The Council defined the Pope as infallible in matters of faith and morals when he intends to bind the whole Church to his teaching.

The Pope's power, the Council stated, comes from his own authority and not from the consent of the Bishops or of the whole Church.

The Orthodox Churches conceivably might again grant primacy of honor to the Patriarch of Rome as the successor of Saint Peter, Father Schmemann indicated. As such and as the spokesman for the whole Church, the Pope's solemn doctrinal pronouncements might be regarded as infallible under certain special circumstances.

But the infallibility would never be regarded as deriving from the Pope's personal authority but only from the "consent of the Church," the priest insisted.

The stark papalism of 1870 was tempered somewhat at the Second Vatican Council with the definition of episcopal collegiality—the idea that all the bishops share in the ruling authority over the Church under the direction of the Pope.

But the change, though promising, was not significant enough to obliterate the theological problem created for the Orthodox by the definition of papal infallibility at the earlier ecumenical council of the Roman Catholic Church.

The Orthodox put heavy emphasis on the work of the Holy Spirit in the Church and considerably less on the pronouncements of their hierarchy, Father Schmemann said. "The Holy Spirit," he said, "is continuously active in the Church" — and his activity does not depend on the approval of bishops.

This point, too, was dealt with at the Vatican Council. The fathers of the council granted that charisms, or special gifts of the spirit, are bestowed without regard to position in the Church. However, as bishops, they reserved the right to "test the spirit"—that is, to determine whether any supposed charismatic gift should be acknowledged by the Church.

In their emphasis on the teaching that the gifts of the spirit might be showered on anyone, however lowly or powerless, Father Schmemann added, the Orthodox have more in common with certain forms of Protestantism than with Catholicism. "Here, we feel closer to Quakers than to Roman Catholic or Anglican theologians," the priest said.

June 26, 1966

FORDHAM NAMES LUTHERAN CLERIC

He Joins Theology Faculty as a Permanent Member

By EDWARD B. FISKE

The Rev. Dr. Robert L. Wilken, a Lutheran church historian, has been named to the theological faculty of Fordham University, a Jesuit institution.

In announcing the appointment yesterday, the Rev. Christopher F. Mooney, chairman of the theology department, said, "As far as I know, this is the first time that a non-Catholic has been given a permanent position on a Catholic theological faculty."

Dr. Wilken, a 30-year-old member of the Lutheran Church-Missouri Synod, currently teaches early Christian history at the Lutheran Theological Seminary in Gettysburg, Pa. His appointment as assistant professor of patristic theology at Fordham becomes effective in September.

Patristics is the study of the early centuries of Christianity, when doctrines that are now considered orthodox, such as the Trinity, were still being formulated.

Father Mooney and other Protestant and Catholic educators interviewed yesterday could think of no instances where Protestants are permanent members of Catholic theological faculties or where Cath-olics hold permanent positions at Protestant seminaries or divinity schools.

Several Catholic universities, including Fordham, have had, however, Protestant and Jewish visiting professors of theology. Catholics and Jews likewise have served as visiting professors in a number of Protestant seminaries, including the Yale Divinity School.

Some Protestant divinity schools, such as Harvard and the University of Chicago, have also set up revolving chairs whereby a succession of Catho-

329

lic and Jewish scholars teach on a regular basis.

Rabbi Irwin M. Blank of Temple Sinai, Tenafly, N.J., is currently a visiting professor of Hebrew Literature at Fordham. The Jesuit institution is also involved in a program whereby it shares professors and facilities with Union Theological Seminary.

In noting the ecumenical significance of Fordham's appointment, Father Mooney described it as "an effort towards mutual understanding and clarifying of the differences that still divide us."

He said he hoped to name another Protestant to his staff "in the near future."

'Common Ground' Cited

Dr. Wilken said in an interview yesterday that he had accepted the post "for the adventure of it" and because he wanted to "see the Roman Catholic Church at close range."

"The vitality of American Christianity can be seen as much in the Roman Catholic Church as anywhere," he said. "Moreover patristics, because it deals with the earliest Christian traditions, is an area where a common ground can be found rather quickly.

The Rev. Albert L. Schlitzer, chairman of the theology department at Notre Dame, said yesterday that inter-faith faculty appointments were "the coming thing." He indicated that he, too, was looking for a Protestant faculty member.

"No one can have the entire statement of the truth of revelation," he said. "Truth is so many-sided that even heresy can offer helpful insights."

Dr. Wilken, who is an associate editor of the Lutheran theological journal Una Sancta, is a native of New Orleans and holds a doctorate in early Christian history from the University of Chicago. In 1963 he engaged in post-doctoral studies at the University of Heidelberg.

January 4, 1967

Primitive Christian Rite Revived by Group Here

By PAUL HOFMANN

Twenty-five men and women have been breaking bread, pouring wine and singing hymns under a glass chandelier in the faded but still genteel dining room of an East Harlem brownstone one night a month in a re-enactment of the Last Supper of Jesus.

The agape (Greek for love feast) meals are meant to revive an observance practiced by primitive Christians.

The participants in the rite and related liturgical experiments salute one another with "Shalom!" and preface toasts with the same word, which in Hebrew means "peace."

Three maverick Roman Catholic priests, a Presbyterian woman minister, other clergymen, Catholic and Episcopal sisters, Puerto Ricans and Negroes from the neighborhood and suburbanites from New Jersey attended an agape last Friday night at Emmaus House, 241 East 116th Street, between Third and Second Avenues.

The Rev. David Kirk, coordinator of the year-old Christian interfaith group, stuck the emblem of the antiwar movement into the lapel of his dark street suit, sat at the head of a U-shaped table, and opened Emmaus House's fourth monthly agape (pronounced AHG-uh-pea) with the first of several toasts.

"Shalom! To those working for peace, for mediation in Vietnam, those who are in jail for peace, those who are actively demonstrating or not demonstrating," he said.

Father Kirk, who was called "Dave" by all present, is a 32-year-old Alabamian who 12 years ago was baptized into the Melchite Byzantine Rite, one of the various Eastern branches of Catholicism that have their own traditions and liturgy, but are in communion with the papacy. He studied for the priesthood in Rome and was ordained in Jerusalem in 1964.

"Shalom! To effective justice!" said the Rev. Lyle Young, a 46-year-old former Anglican missionary in New Guinea who has become a Roman Catholic priest and wants to join the Melchites.

"Shalom! To the Beatles who have helped us in our liturgy," said the Rev. Richard Mann, 28, an Australian who is a member of the Congregation of the Blessed Sacrament, wears open shirts and sandals and says his order's superiors "don't want me.'

Ceremony Explained

The Rev. Letty M. Russell, a Presbyterian of the East Harlem Protestant Parish, said: "Shalom! To the 12 long days of Christmas."

The Lord's prayer was recited jointly, and Father Kirk said: "God. we believe that You are present in the world in many ways and many places. You are present in our homes, our places of work, our jails, our courts, our schools . . . where men are breaking down barriers of fears, selfishness and hate."

Then, the participants in the agape passed around two large loaves of bread, drank red wine from paper cups, and dined on salad, beef Stroganoff and noodles, ice cream and coffee.

Earlier, Father Kirk had explained to a visitor that "we are holding agape with the connotations of the Lord's Supper without specifically taking communion."

Miss Russell added: "People attribute to the agape whatever they want, and for me it isn't different from communion. For Catholics it's different, a kind of celebration."

Friday's agape had been preceded by an hour of conversation and hymn-singing around of bowl of sauterne punch in a hall adjoining the second-floor dining room. On previous Sundays, services had been held by priests in the dining room, which is decorated with ikons, graffiti, an abstract painting and a photograph showing the late Pope John XXIII receiving African pilgrims.

Would Avoid Gawkers

However, Father Kirk said that the next Sunday service would be transferred to the apartment of one of the group's members because "we don't want to attract curious people who want to see underground masses—we aren't an underground church."

He said Emmaus House had evolved from formalized Melchite liturgy into group devotions where bread and wine were passed around and the "kiss of peace" exchanged. Father Mann said the group had on occasion borrowed music from the Beatles.

The Roman Catholic Archdiocese of New York officially ignores Emmaus House. "I have heard of its existence," the archdiocese's director of information, Msgr. Thomas J. McGovern, said yesterday. "It is not related with us."

The Melkite Apostolic Exarchate, which embraces all of the about 50,000 Melchite Catholics in the United States, considers Father Kirk a priest "on private projects," according to a listing in the 1967 Catholic Directory. "I don't think anything is changed in his status," an official of the exarchate in West Newton, Mass., said on Friday.

"We bypass a lot of structures," Father Kirk told a visitor before the agape. "We are seeking a style of life that's real to us."

Neighborhood Services

He, Father Young and Father Mann live in Emmaus House. The house—which is named for the town near Jerusalem where the risen Jesus, according to Christian belief, appeared to two disciples—often gives shelter also to temporary guests.

Other members of the group of two dozen or so Christians

The New York Times

Shalom, the Hebrew word for peace, and the Jerusalem Bible are adjuncts of the bread and other things used in re-enactment of the Last Supper one night a month in Harlem.

live in the neighborhood, and still others come regularly from distant places in the metropolitan area.

Members of Emmaus House offer some neighborhood services, like remedial reading, sympathize within antiwar and radical leftwing activities and have linked up with the Shalom movement in the Netherlands, which promotes frequent Catholic-Protestant agapes.

Miss Russell is co-coordinator

of a new sponsoring group, Emmaus, Inc., which aims at developing the East Harlem center into a "clearing house for ecumenical information" and starting related programs.

Father Kirk said that Emmaus House had been bought with funds provided by private backers and that all members of its staff were working without salaries.

The biggest recent contribution, he reported, was a $1,000

check from the Rev. Malcolm Boyd, the Episcopal priest who wrote, "Are You Running With Me, Jesus?" and has occasionally caused controversy by acting as a nightclub entertainer and taking other unconventional attitudes.

A board of advisors of Emmaus House includes noted progressive Catholic and Protestant theologians and civil rights and antiwar advocates.

January 7, 1968

Papal Infallibility Dogma Assailed Here

By GEORGE DUGAN

The Vatican's recent reaffirmation of papal infallibility has placed future ecumenical conversations between Roman Catholics and other Christian bodies in "dire jeopardy," according to Canon Walter D. Dennis of the Cathedral Church of St. John the Divine (Episcopal).

Also, Canon Dennis said in his sermon yesterday, the Vatican action will in all probability deal a "death blow" to the Anglican-Roman Catholic dialogue movement.

The dogma of infallibility, first promulgated in 1870 by the first Vatican Council, means that the Pope cannot err or teach error when he speaks on matters of faith and morals ex cathedra, or "from the chair" of St. Peter.

Dogma Invoked Once

In the 103 years since Vati-

can I, the dogma has been invoked only once—in 1950—when Pope Pius XII declared that the Virgin Mary was assumed bodily into heaven.

Canon Dennis emphasized that he was not indulging in "a kind of pathological no-popery prejudice—a diseased state of mind from which I sincerely believe myself to be entirely free."

"From my view," he said, "Popes have often spoken excellently in the past and I hope and believe, they will in the future. It is the faulty logic of the theory of infallibility, not the institution of the papacy as such, which I am criticizing.

"In trying to establish a criterion by which we can detect the authoritative from the non-authoritative, is it necessary to resort to a dogma of the infallible? This is the question. I believe not."

Even in the Roman Catholic Church, Canon Dennis said, "it would be universally agreed that most of the Popes never spoke infallibly at all, but indeed it is quite possible for a Pope to be a good and great Pope yet never speak infallibly."

"The values of the papal office cannot be comprehended exclusively under the heading of infallibility," Canon Dennis said.

"Thus John XXIII, almost certainly the greatest Pope for many centuries, who in a few swift years brought the papacy to a height of prestige perhaps unknown since the days of Innocent III in the 13th century, never put forth any infallible utterance whatsoever. This didn't stop him from being universally acknowledged as a supremely great Pope.

"Evidently the Pope is armed with better and more effective weapons than infallibility. So why then is this questionable dogma reasserted at this time unless it is a signal to end serious ecumenical encounter? It may very well be that the Roman Curia has decided ecumenical dialogue has reached its outer limits."

In reaffirming papal infallibility, the Vatican document did not point to any theologian as a target for censure.

But, a Vatican spokesman indicated at the time that it was aimed principally at the Rev. Dr. Hans Küng, a Swiss professor at Tübingen University in West Germany, whose recent book, "Infallible? An Inquiry," analyzed the dogma and found it nearly meaningless. The volume is under investigation by the Vatican.

July 16, 1973

Lutheran-Catholic Accord Voted

By EDWARD B. FISKE

A joint commission of United States Roman Catholic and Lutheran theologians issued a study yesterday declaring that papal primacy—a major issue in the Protestant Reformation of the 16th Century—need no longer be a "barrier to reconciliation" of their churches.

In a 5,000-word "Common Statement" the scholars envisioned a time when Lutheran and Catholic churches would be part of a single "larger communion" — autonomous but linked by common recognition of the Pope in Rome as a visible symbol of their underlying unity.

The statement, whose formal title is "Ministry and the Church Universal: Differing Attitudes Toward Papal Primacy," was adopted by the 26-member Lutheran-Roman Catholic Consultation in the United States.

The commission, which comprises 13 Roman Catholics and 13 Lutherans, was appointed in 1965 by the National Committee of the Lutheran World Federation and the Committee for Ecumenical and Interreligious Affairs of the National Conference of Catholic Bishops. The Lutheran delegation includes representatives of all major branches of Lutheranism in this country.

The document, the fruit of nine years of theological dialogue, represents the first time since the Lutheran Reformation of the 16th Century that an officially sanctioned group of Roman Catholic and Lutheran scholars has expressed agreement on crucial aspects of papal authority.

It is likely to be regarded as a major ecumenical landmark because, while it is in no way binding on any of the churches involved, it would seem to eliminate—at least on the theological level—a major obstacle to Christian unity.

"It is now up to the churches to indicate how far they want to go in implementing it," said the Rev. George A. Lindbeck, a theologian at Yale University and one of the Lutheran members of the commission.

The document leaves for further study the relatively limited but controversial issue of papal infallibility. However, in light of the consensus achieved thus far, the scholars involved are hopeful that agreement can be reached on this matter as well within two to three years.

The joint commission is one of numerous groups engaged in theological dialogue in this country and elsewhere. The American Catholic hierarchy in the United States for instance, is now involved in separate dialogues with representatives of the Episcopalian, Presbyterian, United Methodist, Desciples of Christ and Orthodox churches.

Last December, in a similar ecumenical advance, the Anglican-Roman Catholic International Commission, which represents Anglicans and Catholics on a worldwide basis, released a report declaring that they had reached "basic agreement" on the nature of the Christian ministry.

The Lutheran-Roman Catholic discussions in this country headed by the Rev. Paul C. Empie, retired general secretary of the national committee, and the most Rev. T. Austin Murphy, Auxiliary Catholic Bishop of Baltimore.

The commission has already produced statements of consensus on the Nicene Creed, baptism, the ministry and the eucharist, and in 1970 it became the first of the dialogue groups to take up the question of papal primacy. This is generally regarded as perhaps the most difficult issue dividing Catholics and other Christians.

The scholars reported that, after seven semiannual meetings and the production of 30 research papers, they were able to achieve "a convergence in the theological understanding of the papacy."

The basic elements of this consensus, they said, are that the visible unity of Christians is desirable, that all Christians have an obligation to seek this unity, and that "a special responsibility for this may be entrusted to one individual minister, under the Gospel."

They further agreed that the Bishop of Rome "can in the future function in ways which are better adapted to meet both the universal and regional needs of the church in the complex of modern times."

The text of the document makes it clear that this "convergence" was possible because recent Biblical and historical scholarship by Catholics and Lutherans has shed new light on old controversies and made possible "a fresh approach to the structure and operations of the papacy."

In the past, for instance, the document declared, Catholics taught that Jesus conferred papal status on St. Peter and that, in effect, "the papacy has remained substantially the same through succeeding centuries." Lutherans, on the other hand, it noted, "minimized Peter's role in the early church" and described the papacy as a later invention.

However, on the basis of historical and scriptural studies, the scholars concluded that neither of these positions was correct.

They declared that a "Petrine function"—or ministry expressing the "oneness of the church" —is implicit in the New Testament, but also asserted that its form has evolved over the centuries and that continuing evolution and reform is possible.

"There is a growing awareness among Lutherans of the necessity of a specific ministry to serve the Churches' unity and universay mission, while Catholics increasingly see the need for a more nuanced understanding of the role of the papacy within the universal church," they said.

The report envisions a situation in which Catholic and Lutheran churches would function as "sister churches" with close sacramental and other ties. It pictures the Roman Pontiff as an expression of the "Petrine function" for both Lutherans and Catholics, but leaves open the question of how he would fulfill this role—whether symbolically, as a spokesman on moral and social issues, or with specific areas of authority.

"Perhaps this might involve a primacy in which the Pope's service to unity in relation to Lutheran churches would be more pastoral than juridical," it declared.

However, the document does specify several forms of "renewal" that would have to take place within the papacy before it would be acceptable to Lutherans as well as Catholics.

These are acceptance of diversity within the church, a "collegial," or consultative style of operation, and the principle of "subsidiarity," which means that decisions that can be made at a local or regional level "ought not to be referred to church leaders who have wider responsibilities." The renewed papacy, it said, must also be "commited to Christian freedom."

The scholars noted that several related isues, notably Catholic teachings about papal infallibility, have yet to be discussed.

March 4, 1974

Protestants and Catholics Get a Common Catechism

By KENNETH A. BRIGGS

An extensive statement of agreed-upon beliefs, the first document of its kind written jointly by Roman Catholics and Protestants since the 16th-century Reformation, will become available here this spring.

Called "The Common Catechism: A Book of Christian Faith," and aimed primarily at adults, the German version has circulated widely in Europe for the last two years. It is being published in English for the first time by Seabury Press of the Episcopal Church.

Though approved as official teaching by no Roman Catholic or Protestant church body, the 720-page document represents a landmark in the process of developing an ecumenical theology that began in large measure with the Second Vatican Council's spirit of reconciliation.

Technically, the statement does not fit the conventional definition of "catechism." In its original usage, the term applied to the body of teaching used to instruct new Christians. Through the ages, catechisms have also borne the stamp of ecclesiastical legitimacy and been written in a "dogmatic" question-and-answer format.

A spokesman for the National Council of Catholic Bishops said that the hierarchy in the United States, while not actively promoting the statement, would not discourage its use as a study guide.

Forty Lutheran, Reformed and Roman Catholic theologians worked over a five-year period to produce the statement. Heading the project were Dr. Lukas Vischer, a Protestant and head of the World Council of Churches' Faith and Order Secretariat, and the Rev. Johannes Feiner, a former member of the Vatican's Pontifical Theological Commission.

The document adopts what is known in theological circles as an "apologetic" approach— that is, it tries to explain the faith by taking into account the doubts and challenges to Christianity posed by the contemporary world.

Recognizing and assessing such factors in modern thinking as science, Marxism and existentialism, and their impact on religious thought, the document "answers" in terms of Christian beliefs.

In the course of this dialogue, the document spells out broad areas of ecumenical agreement on such matters as the nature of God, the meaning of Jesus' life and the validity of certain moral stances.

The final portion of the document outlines issues that block Christian unity, such as the debate over the doctrine of papal infallibility and the definition of the sacraments.

Emphasis on Unity

But the clear premise in the statement is that no obstacle remains insurmountable, mirroring a growing sense of confidence among many Christians that the long-separated churches can deal effectively with the most important concerns.

"The various branches of the Christian church are no longer interested in what divides them," the editors write in an introduction, "but instead in how they are to understand, present and live the Christian faith in the world of today."

The statement brings considerable Biblical historical and theological resources to bear on the central questions, and is careful to delineate the different views that have grown up between the churches.

At some points, the statement underlines matters that are considered open to wide interpretation; at others, it makes firm declarations.

Understanding the doctrine of Jesus' resurrection, for example, is said to have been a "permanent problem" since the "European enlightenment of the seventeenth and eighteenth centuries" raised questions

about the credibility of the Biblical text and introduced a scientific world view.

But, more affirmatively, the statement says that Jesus' "word, his life, his death and his resurrection open the way for us to God," adding, "Anyone who believes in Jesus must accept this claim or else he does not believe in Jesus."

Each main section of the statement was originally drafted by a Roman Catholic or a Protestant and each side responded to the other. The final project involved shaping these views into a commonly acceptable form.

The concept of God relies heavily on seeing God as an agent in history who gives meaning to mankind. God's love "gives both man and mankind courage to engage in historical action and then to entrust the future of man and his world to that love," the statement says.

Jesus' life is examined from the standpoint of the Gospels, St. Paul's writings and creeds and traditions. Built on the orthodox conviction that Christ was both fully man and fully God, the statement traces the development of the dogma that developed about Christ over the centuries. March 17, 1975

Southern Baptists and Catholics Find Ties

By KENNETH A. BRIGGS

Every third Thursday, the Rev. C. Brownlow Hastings and six other Southern Baptist ministers drive a few miles from downtown Atlanta to a secluded Trappist monastery. There, with three Roman Catholic monks, they spend the day reading the New Testament in Greek.

For three years, since the first such session, the monthly routine has been what Dr. Hastings, a church official, calls "one of my most satisfying experiences."

It also represents the kind of easy communication between members of the two powerful religious groups that was virtually unknown a decade ago.

History of Antipathy

A heavy overlay of distrust and antipathy has, in fact, darkened relations between them for most of the nation's history. Significantly, the legacy of this feuding has been injected into the current Presidential campaign, particularly in terms of the impact of Jimmy Carter's Southern Baptist identity among Roman Catholics. Recent polls have found concern by Catholic voters about the religion of Mr. Carter, the Democratic candidate.

Much of the consequent discussion has centered on the images each religious group has held of the other. Despite efforts to erase the past, the negative notions die hard.

Baptists and Catholics, usually isolated from one another, have viewed each other across a solid barrier of disagreement, confusion and animosity.

To a Catholic, the Baptist was often portrayed as a fanatical follower of a

superficial, revivalistic faith who has strayed from the historic church. Moreover, the stereotype was of a straightlaced moralizer for whom the Bible was almost an object of worship.

Another Stereotype

Many Baptists, on the other hand, were reared to regard Catholics as puppets of the Pope for whom personal faith in Jesus Christ counted less than reliance on church formulas for salvation. Furthermore, Catholic belief in the intercessory role of the Virgin Mary and the saints often looked like idolatry to Baptists.

Meanwhile, each church proudly held itself up as the true way. Generally, neither Baptist nor Catholic could imagine being the other.

Though these impressions remain, especially in Baptist rural areas and Catholic urban areas, the ecumenical age, among other things, is bringing about a transformation of attitudes.

Baptists and Catholics are now going on spiritual retreats together, working on joint projects in such areas as evangelism, examining differences on issues like abortion and the meaning of conversion, and, perhaps most importantly, just getting to know one another.

'Brothers and Sisters'

"We are movingly encountering each other as brothers and sisters in Christ," says Bishop Bernard F. Law of the Springfield-Cape Girardeau, Mo., diocese, who was a priest for many years in Mississippi. "We simply were not able to do that previously."

According to Bishop Law, who has attended several regional conferences sponsored by the two churches in recent years, certain stereotypes begin to crumble as lay people and clergymen exorcise the demons of the past.

Southern Baptists often say they come away surprised by the Catholic commitment to Bible reading, prayer and personal faith in Jesus Christ, hallmarks of Baptist tradition.

Catholics report being amazed to find Baptists who do not believe that being "saved" implies spiritual development ends there but rather, as one priest put it, "that there is need for continual forgiveness and growth," a sound Catholic concept.

"Catholics are learning that the term 'born again' doesn't have to be an expression of arrogance," a Catholic observer says. "It doesn't necessarily mean the person thinks everything is just fine and that he thinks he's got a place staked out in heaven."

Factors in Change

Several factors have made these first steps possible. The Second Vatican Council's emphasis on interchurch relations and its declaration on religious liberty was a major development. Another has been the gradual openness of Southern Baptists toward relations with other churches.

"Ecumenism itself is still a dirty word in some places in the church," says Dr. Claude Broach, director of the Catholic-Baptist Ecumenical Institute in Winston Salem, N.C., "primarily because it implied a move to homogenize all Christians into one."

333

But leaders of the Southern Baptist Convention have been able to convince many of their co-religionists that conversations could be held with other churches without risking theological compromise.

"We have been able to develop unity," says Dr. Hastings, who has become the Southern Baptist observer at most large Catholic gatherings, including the Synod of Bishops in Rome, without having to resolve all the doctrinal differences that have come down over the years."

Wide Differences

In practice, the churches are poles apart. For example, Catholicism works within a highly complex hierarchy, while among Baptists each church is autonomous. Baptists treat baptism as an initiation for those old enough to "believe," while Catholics baptize new born infants.

The greatest differences arise over their respective concepts on the meaning of salvation. This issue, perhaps more than another other, has led to the deepest levels of suspicion.

In the main, Baptists understand salvation as an initial conversion or "born again" experience in which the person feels a commitment to Christ. "In our evangelical tradition," Dr. Broach explains, "it simply signifies your personal decision to be a Christian."

While some say the moment was a dramatic, even supernatural, experience, most, including Jimmy Carter, describe it as an outwardly unspectacular but inwardly peaceful sense of resolve. At that time, according to Baptist thinking, God confers forgiveness and grace.

Stress on Sacraments

Catholics, by comparison, hold that the sacraments are the vehicles of grace and that the baptized infant has already received the fruits of salvation that are strengthened over the years through continued participation in the sacraments.

Do Catholics have something akin to conversion experiences? Participants in the Catholic-Baptist dialogues conclude that many do, though not in "conversion" terms Baptists would find familiar.

At a recent dialogue in California, for instance, a bishop outlined his confirmation and decision to become a priest in a way that reminded Baptists of their own moments of decision.

The two traditions disagree sharply on a number of issues, among them abortion and aid to private schools. As perhaps the nation's staunchest defender of church-state separation, Southern Baptists vigorously oppose Government support of private schools. On abortion, though Southern Baptists are generally opposed as individuals to the practice they have as a convention refused to back an amendment that would prohibit abortion, mirroring Jimmy Carter's own stated position.

Ambassador to Baptists

The Rev. Will Steinbacher, a Jesuit priest who works with the Glenmary Missioners, a mission agency to the rural South, says that "while Catholics frequently don't talk about their experiences, they've often had them."

Father Steinbacher, in an attempt to create better interfaith understanding, became the official Glenmary ambassador to the Southern Baptist Convention and spent three years traveling throughout five Southern states meeting with church groups, attending worship and listening to problems.

He left this summer, replaced at his Newnan, Ga., residence by another priest with the same mission. He says that he came to respect Southern Baptist integrity and adds that he was received with "warmth and acceptance." Father Steinbacher's initiative is one of many efforts being made to open channels of communication between groups.

The Ecumenical Institute, a joint program of Wake Forest University in Winston-Salem and Belmont Abbey, a nearby Catholic college, has brought scholars, clergymen and the laity to yearly conferences since 1969.

Ministerial associations in most Southern communities now include Catholic priests.

So far, the dialogues been aimed at mutual understanding rather than finding theological harmony.

Local Church Efforts

In addition to the more orchestrated regional endeavors, local churches have undertaken interchurch retreats, evangelistic projects and social projects.

One example of cooperation comes from the southern Louisiana town of Jennings. As as result of growing sensitivity and closer ties, the First Baptist Church two years ago sponsored a youth evangelism campaign with the two local Catholic churches and is planning a retreat to help Catholics become more effective law ministers.

The pastor of the First Baptist Church, the Rev. Lawrence Baylot, says that the area is the "heart of antagonism" and that until recently the two groups remained far removed. But, through the ministerial association, "Catholics and Protestants began to share our concerns and found them to be the same," he said. Then we started to pray about it."

'Inner Circle' of Agreement

"We found an inner circle of things we agree on," Mr. Baylot says. "We all have a firm conviction that Jesus Christ is the answer. We don't discuss things like sacraments. We just put that aside."

These developments are enormously significant to those who lived among a minority of Catholics in an atmosphere that eyed them with hostility.

"If clergy get together it means a lot," says Bishop James D. Niedergese of the Nashville diocese where Catholics number 60,000 in a population of 2.6 million. "We've started getting rid of erroneous ideas."

Bishop Niedergeses grew up in a small Tennessee town and remembers insults hurled at him for being Catholic. He is indictative of many newly appointed bishops who are acutely aware of the need to reach across church lines.

"Catholics don't believe everybody who's non-Catholic will go to hell," he says, citing what he says has been a commonly held assumption. "And we don't worship statues, we use them as visual aids. Things are being understood much better now."

September 19, 1976

THE RELIGION OF BLACK AMERICANS

THE COLOR LINE IN CHURCH.

BLACK MINISTERS NOT WANTED IN CONVENTION.

CHARLESTON, S. C., July 12.—The committee appointed by the clerical and lay delegates who withdrew from the Diocesan Episcopal Convention in Charleston last May have completed their statement of the cause which led to the withdrawal. It is signed by ex-Secretary C. S. Memminger, Edward McCrady, Jr., W. St. J. Jervey, W. C. Benet, and C. G. R. Drayton, and will make a pamphlet of about 60 pages. The committee begin by sketching the history of the dividing question during the last 12 years, and

contend that it shows that the position of the laity with regard to the admission of colored clergymen to the diocesan conventions differs from that of many of the clergy, not in principle, but in expediency. In 1885 the question took the shape of an assertion of the right of all clergymen on the Bishop's list to seats in the convention, independent of the action of that body, and by virtue of the clergyman's office. The subject was avoided the next year, but came up again in the convention last May, not as a matter of principle only, but as involving the question of the admission of colored clergymen to the church councils. The Bishop having ruled, notwithstanding the refusal of the convention to confirm the report of the committee on the clergy list, that the convention was duly organized for business, and having ignored the

refusal of the convention to sustain his ruling, the dissidents had no choice but to submit, protest, resort to parliamentary expedients, or withdraw with dignity. They accordingly withdrew from the convention. It is recognized by the committee, however, that the point to be determined is whether the admission of colored clergymen to the convention was contemplated in the constitution of the church. They contend that it was not and that it is the first attempt in the history of the church to make a church other than a national church—that is the church of a race.

They believe the seating of colored clergymen in the convention to be not only unconstitutional but dangerous, and in this relation recall the resolution of Mr. Prentiss in 1875, asserting the right of exclusion, the resolutions of the standing committee on the Saltus case in 1876, recognizing the differences of the two races brought together in the diocese, and the report of the Sewanee Conference in favor of a missionary organization because of the peculiarity of the relations between the two races. It is argued that there is no danger whatever to any of the social barriers between the races if the colored people be taken into councils and churches as the equals of the whites, but the committee are confident that the actual and practical result would be to force negro social equality upon the people. The duty and responsibility of the church in the Southern States in regard to the colored people is fully recognized, but there is no call "to take them into our councils." In conclusion the committee give their reasons for holding that there was no legal convention

in 1887. They claim that the election of a standing committee and the attempted alteration in the constitution were "void and of no effect, even had the illegality of the Bishop's ruling not otherwise vitiated its proceedings."

The importance of the congregations represented by the dissidents who withdrew from the convention is shown in an unmistakable way. Those who withdrew represented more than half of all the persons connected with the church and more than half of all the communicants. They represented also parishes which pay nearly two-thirds of the convention expenses, more than two-thirds of the Bishop's fund, and nearly two-thirds of the contributions to missions. The committee say that in withdrawing

from the convention they did not withdraw from the church. It is for the laity to determine what their future course shall be. They will not impair their connection with the church by withdrawing from union with the convention. They can if they choose send deputies with instructions to abandon the position which has been taken, and in admitting the colored element to the church councils "brave the dangers" from which the dissidents shrink. But if the laity desire that the right to pass upon the clergy list shall be abandoned they must choose to represent them other deputies than those who withdrew from the convention of 1887.

July 13, 1887

COLORED BRETHREN BARRED.

Admission to Council of the Federation of Churches Refused.

The Rev. R. A. Motley, pastor of Salem Afro-American Baptist Church, Jersey City, yesterday denounced the Federation of Churches for refusing to admit colored ministers to their council. Mr. Motley said he had attended a meeting of the council on Wednesday night, and was denied recognition. He said that when he asked the reason the Rev. Dr. Charles Herr, pastor of the First Presbyterian Church, said it was because there was an objection on the part of white people to receiving calls from colored people.

"I have been a minister for twenty-four years," said Mr. Motley, "and have frequently been called on to pray at the bedside of white persons who were dying. In all that time I never heard of any objections to my ministrations, and I can see no reason why the colored people should not be considered in any work intended to evangelize Jersey City."

Dr. Herr confirmed Mr. Motley's statement as to his remarks in reply to that gentleman at the council. He said the colored ministers and churches could not be admitted to the Federation without giving them some sort of social recognition. He thought that if the colored ministers wished to participate in the evangelization of the city they should work independently in their own field.

January 11, 1901

METHODISTS VOTE TO ABOLISH COLOR LINE

General Conference Amends Constitution.

MEANS COLORED BISHOPS

All Discussion of Heresy Is Dropped and the Theological Schools Are Exonerated.

LOS ANGELES, Cal., May 28.—The Methodist General conference to-night voted by a practically unanimous vote to amend the church constitution so as to provide for the election of bishops of other than the white race.

The matter came from the Committee on Episcopacy as the result of memorials from several annual conferences favoring the election of colored Bishops to preside as General Superintendents. Chairman J.

N. Buckley presented the report of the committee.

The report read, in part, as follows:

"The General Conference shall not change or alter any part or rule of our government so as to do away with Episcopacy, nor destroy the plan of our itinerant general superintendency, but may elect a Bishop or Bishops for work among particular races and languages or for any of our foreign missions, limiting their Episcopal jurisdiction to the same, respectively.

"Resolved, second, that if this report is adopted, thereafter the above proposed amendment to the Constitution be submitted to the General Conference in order to ascertain whether the legal constitutional vote of two-thirds of the members present and voting shall be given, and,

"Resolved, third, if such should be the result, the Bishops shall be requested to submit the proposition to the members of the annual Conference, and of the lay electors at the Conference which shall meet in the years 1907 and 1908 for adoption of the same amendment to the Constitution."

A motion to make the report a special order of business for to-night prevailed.

The heresy question, over which a heated debate was expected, proved to be a very small matter after all. It was dismissed

with a report brought in by the Committee on Education, the conference adopting its recommendations without a ripple of excitement. There was no debate except a brief speech by Dr. Munhall, who is credited with being the leader of the forces opposed to the so-called higher criticism in theological colleges. Dr. Munhall merely stated his opposition to Bible criticism, and declared himself favorable to the report as presented.

The recommendations of the Committee on Education on this particular point were that in the absence of sufficient proof against the Faculties of certain universities these institutions be exonerated on all the charges of heresy. The report recommended also that since there is some unrest and a disposition to fear that heresy will develop, the Directors should exercise care in the selection of instructors, appointing none concerning whose soundness of doctrine there is any question. Professors were cautioned to instruct their students to preach none but established doctrines. The report was passed by a large vote.

The Conference voted against the recommendation of the Committee on Temperance providing for a special department of temperance work and authorizing collections for its maintenance.

May 29, 1904

METHODISTS ADOPT RACE EQUALITY PLEA

From a Staff Correspondent.
Special to THE NEW YORK TIMES.

ATLANTIC CITY, N. J., May 7.—Emphasizing its stand for racial equality, the thirty-first general quadrennial conference of the Methodist Episcopal Church voted here today that it would never meet again in a city where the color line was drawn in hotels, restaurants and other public places.

Despite warnings that adoption of the resolution might end all hope of the eventual reunion with the Methodist Episcopal Church South, which has long been a subject of prayer and negotiation, the measure was adopted by a close vote.

Embarrassments complained of during the conference here, where some of the Boardwalk hotels have refused to receive Negro Bishops and delegates, served to bring the question to the fore. The place for the next general conference may not be decided for another two years.

Dr. Ernest F. Tittle of Evanston, Ill., widely known as a liberal, led the lively debate which preceded passage of the resolution. He urged the Methodist Church to align itself with the Federal Council of Churches and the Congregational Church, which have opposed racial discrimination against delegates to their conferences.

"I believe there are cities which would be glad to entertain us under these conditions," Dr. Tittle said. "If there are not, it would be much better for us not to meet at all, and if we do not meet for this reason we will be doing the cause of racial equality more good by not meeting than we could by meeting."

During the meeting here most of the Bishops and delegates, including Hindus, Japanese and Chinese, have been staying at a beach-front hotel, but the two Negro Bishops and the Negro delegates have been registered at a hotel on a side street. Some of the Oriental delegates have complained privately that they were segregated in the Boardwalk hotel.

The resolution, which was passed by a vote by show of hands, was as follows:

"Be it provided that no conference shall hereafter meet except in cities where there is no segregation of special racial groups, no discrimination in hotels, elevators and restaurants, and where there have been specific instructions given to all hotel employes to treat the representatives of every race with equality and courtesy."

May 8, 1932

The Strange Case of Father Divine and His Followers

GOD IN A ROLLS ROYCE. The Rise of Father Divine, Madman-Menace or Messiah. By John Hoshor. 272 pp. New York: Hillman-Curl, Inc. $2.50.

MR. HOSHOR has become greatly worked up over Father Divine. He doesn't know whether the little Negro is a "madman-menace or a messiah," and his book reflects his confusion. He seems on the whole to tend to the more respectful view. His argument is that if all a man's friends and associates call him a bum he shortly becomes a bum, and that there is no good reason why the opposite should not be true. It would be interesting to observe Mr. Hoshor's conduct toward a dog with a good name.

The book is interesting despite inept handling. The saga of the smart little black man with a good head for figures who has convinced some 5,000 persons that he is God is one of the stranger yarns of our time. Father Divine has not only convinced 5,000 persons that he is God: he has set them working for him. He has shown them that material possessions are of no value and that they are better off without them. He has persuaded those who suffer from cancer, tuberculosis and other ills that they will live happily forever. He has made the prosperous believe that they will be happier poor. He has persuaded many, by casual-seeming inference, that he killed King George of England because the King failed to answer a letter. And he has convinced thousands of the most physically minded citizens in America that they must love no one but God.

According to those expert reporters, St. Clair McKelway and A. J. Liebling, Father Divine now owns twenty-five restaurants, a half-dozen grocery stores, ten barber shops, ten cleaning and pressing establishments, between twenty and thirty huckster wagons, a small coal business, 1,000 acres of farming land, two weekly newspapers, a garage full of cars, trucks and buses, an airplane, many dozens of shoe-shine boxes, and considerable quantities of cash. He operates, in addition to his main Heaven, three apartment houses, nine private houses, and between fifteen and twenty flats, all made into dormitories. His income is supposed to be about $20,000 a week.

Mr. Hoshor is weak on Father Divine's present state of glory, tending to pass on such irresponsible exaggerations as that the leader has 2,000,000 followers as an "intelligent" estimate, and that he is negotiating to buy whole villages in the neighborhood of New York for his followers to live in. He is a better reporter on the beginnings in telling of how, in his words, "the little acorn became a tree."

Father Divine once made the claim in response to a formal inquiry that he had been born mature and with the title of Major. His birthplace, he said, was Providence. Mr. Hoshor says that he was born in the Fort section of Savannah, along about 1882. He was given the name of George Baker—his father's name was Joseph, and his mother was called Mary.

Baker's history really starts with his meeting with Father Jehovia. At the time of this meeting Baker was an odd-job man who took care of Baltimore lawns and hedges for 50 cents a day.

Jehovia came to Baltimore in 1906 with the message that the body is the temple of the living God, and that he had God within him. Baker heard Jehovia and was impressed. He took to calling himself The Messenger and he ranged the South preaching the message Jehovia had brought, that the body is God's temple and that God lives in man.

In 1915 when he came to Prince Street, Brooklyn, he had twelve disciples.

Another pupil of Jehovia had established here. This pupil called himself "The Rev. St. Bishop, The Vine." He was also known, according to Mr. Hoshor, as God Number One and he had as auxiliary Gods Joe World, Steamboat Bill, Saint Peter, &c. It has been suspected that Baker had "The Vine" in mind when he took Devine, and then "D-i-v-i-n-e," as his name.

Devine left the city for Long Island and created so great a sensation with his community of workers, and his holiday guests, at Sayville, that a determined effort to run him out of town was made. A judge, with little law on his side, sent Devine to jail and, though he had seemed in perfect health, died two days later.

This accident of death was all the little Negro needed for his ascension to Harlem. Converts flocked to him, ready to give up all that they had and to enter into his service, and the era of great prosperity has resulted. The saga isn't ended yet.

As has been intimated, this is not a good book on Divine. But it has so much of interest in it that perhaps its faults of omission deserve to be forgiven.

ROBERT VAN GELDER.

August 30, 1936

RACIAL AMITY PLAN SENT TO CHURCHES

Declaring that this is "a day of deadly peril," partly due to "racial tensions," the Federal Council of Churches of Christ in America issued yesterday a message outlining thirteen things churches and their members can do toward averting the peril.

The suggestions are designed for use by church groups in preparation for "Race Relations Sunday," Feb. 10, sponsored by the race relations department of the council, at 297 Fourth Avenue.

The message, which was sent to 140,000 churches of the twenty-five communions in the council, asserts that in the matter of racial tensions, "we are dealing with a situation of world-wide scope and, as war becomes more destructive, of literally terrifying possibilities."

Suggestions for Churches

The message sets forth "What the churches can do," under seven heads, as follows:

"Demonstrate in practice and policy their belief in the worth and dignity of every human being.

"Include in services to returning war personnel all veterans of whatever race, creed or national origin.

"Open membership and fellowship, with no barriers on account of race or national origin.

"Have persons of different racial and national origin teach in church schools and lead in other church activities.

"Sponsor study groups, forums, fellowship in worship and other interracial means through which men learn cooperation in meeting common needs and mutual interests.

"Give support to the doctrine of brotherhood, by standing against discrimination on account of race, creed or national origin in employment, education, housing, recreation, etc.

"Urge our Government, by petition and other means, to stand for independence or self-government of colonial peoples within a fixed term wherever practicable and in the meantime insist upon genuine international trusteeship through the United Nations Organization."

Suggestions for Individuals

The declaration offers the following six suggestions for individual Christians:

"Examine own heart and mind for lurking prejudice and hostility toward persons of other racial or cultural groups; and refrain from judgment about them without understanding the facts involved.

"Practice in daily contacts personal beliefs in the human value and dignity of each person.

"Enlist for definite tasks to promote interracial brotherhood in the organizations and activities of your own community.

"Become informed and active in legislation for permanent fair employment practices in your State and the nation.

"Work to see that policies and practices of racial segregation are removed from the armed services of our nation.

"Keep in touch with agencies that are working in the field of better race relations, to keep informed on the question through their literature and programs. Consult the Social Action Department of your church denomination."

January 13, 1946

Negro, White Baptists Meet in Joint Session First Time in History to 'Practice Good Will'

SAVANNAH, Ga., Nov. 12 (AP) —Negro and white Baptists of Georgia met in a one-hour joint session today for the first time in their history to hear an appeal that the two races "practice a spirit of good will."

The white Baptists adjourned their convention to go to the Municipal Auditorium and occupy special seats in the balcony as their leaders presented a program before the Negro convention.

The Rev. Leander Asberry Pinkston, Negro president of the General Missionary Baptists Convention yielded the gavel of his group after stating the joint session marked a "spirit of good will" between the two races.

Dr. Drederick E. Smith of Bremen, chairman of the special committee from the white convention, explained that "we have come to have fellowship with you."

Dr. J. C. Wilkinson of Athens, immediate past president of the convention, declared in the principal address that "your convention and my convention have got to work together."

Dr. Roland Smith, editor of the State paper for the Negro group, responded for his race with a declaration: "This marks a moment of progress" and that Negroes and whites "must live together in Georgia and the South as friends."

November 13, 1946

Legal Fight on Negro Pupils Ends After Excommunication Threat

Special to THE NEW YORK TIMES.

ST. LOUIS, Sept. 21 — Archbishop Joseph E. Ritter today warned Roman Catholics protesting the admission of Negro children into parochial schools with white pupils here that they will be excommunicated automatically from the Church if they persist in plans to bar the Negroes by civil action against the Archbishop.

The caution, contained in a pastoral letter read at all masses throughout the archdiocese, is believed to be the first such general warning in its history.

In sequel to the reading of the pastoral letter about 500 parents agreed at a meeting tonight to drop all consideration of legal action.

The meeting voted, however, to ask the intercession in the dispute of the Apostolic Delegate to the United States, the Most. Rev. Amleto Cicognani.

John P. Barrett, chairman of the protest group, told the meeting that the attorneys retained last week had advised that, since the Archbishop was titular "owner" of the schools, nothing could be done legally about what he chose to do with them.

In a resolution Mr. Barrett was asked to write to the Apostolic Delegate at Washington. The resolution stated that the group desired to know "whether we are sinning against our church in a matter of faith and morals" and asked the Apostolic Delegate "to intercede, either for or against us."

It was agreed the group would continue to meet and function under the name of Catholic Parents Association of St. Louis and St. Louis County and leave up to each individual member the decision on whether to withdraw his children from the Catholic school in protest.

Cheers greeted the suggestion of one man that "we move our children out of the schools and let the colored children have them."

Before the meeting Mr. Barrett said:

"I personally will not take any action that will jeopardize my religion or that of anyone else."

Those in the protesting group were reminded in the pastoral letter that "the equality of every soul before Almighty God" and "obedience to ecclesiastical authority" are fundamental principles of the Catholic faith to which they have a filial obligation to cooperate with their Bishop, clergy and fellow Catholics.

"We realize that many of these good people are being misled," the Archbishop explained.

Stating that the decision for a public caution was made after "mature deliberation," his letter continued:

"The policy of admitting Negro children to Catholic schools with white pupils is one which we consider our right and duty as chief pastor of this archdiocese, regardless of race or nationality."

The penalty of excommunication is incurred automatically, the Archbishop explained, should an individual or group of individuals, with full knowledge of the violation of canon law, interfere in the administrative office of the Bishop by going to authority outside the church.

Msgr. Charles H. Helmsing, archdiocesan secretary and an expert in canon law, explained that "while the penalty lasts, it means that the Catholic is excommunicated from holy communion and other sacraments of the church, and from all his rights as a member of the church."

Stating that the penalty applied to all participants as well as to leaders and pointing out that the late Pope Pius XI termed racism as practiced by the Nazis a heresy, he added:

"The crime of trying to impede the lawful authority of the Bishop in matters of faith and morals in the administration of the diocese has the grave penalty of excommunication which can only be lifted by the Holy See, if the criminal is repentant."

While Negro students have attended some elementary parochial schools with white students here since about 1937, the policy was broadened this month to admit Negroes to diocesan high schools. About 100 Negroes are attending Catholic schools with white students.

September 22, 1947

End of Racial Segregation Asked by Churches' Council

By GEORGE DUGAN
Special to THE NEW YORK TIMES.

CINCINNATI, Dec. 3—A statement condemning racial segregation in all its ramifications and calling upon the churches of this country to press for the extension of full social, economic and political rights to every citizen without discrimination as to race, color, creed or sex was overwhelmingly adopted here today by the Federal Council of the Churches of Christ in America.

The statement on human rights was described by council officials as the most comprehensive document of its kind ever to be acted upon by the organization in its forty-year history. The interchurch body, representing twenty-three Protestant denominations and four Eastern Orthodox groups, ended its three-day biennial session this afternoon.

Following adoption of the human rights statement the council unanimously elected as its president Bishop John S. Stamm of Harrisburg, Pa. He is senior bishop of the Evangelical United Brethren Church, and succeeds Charles P. Taft of this city. Mrs. Mildred McAfee Horton, president of Wellesley College and wartime head of the Waves, was elected vice president, also by unanimous vote. Mrs. Horton is the first woman elected to a major office in the council.

It is "a Christian duty," the council declared in its statement, to oppose the denial of freedom, justice and security to any individual, and added:

"The flagrant violation of human rights in our generation has outraged every Christian feeling and has impeded the achievement of world order."

In a sweeping survey of the entire social, economic and political scene in this country, the council listed nearly a score of specific areas, demanding "social safeguards" based on non-segregation and non-discrimination.

They included the right to educational and professional training; the right to "wholesome" living space; the right to an adequate standard of living; the right of every employable person to work under decent conditions, and the right of all persons to organize into labor unions and "corporate enterprises."

Also, the right to the use of transportation on the basis of full equality; the right to receive equal services from businesses and persons serving the public; the right to participate fully in any branch of the Government, and the right to organize for peaceful political activity.

Defining a responsible society as one where "those who hold political authority or economic power are responsible for its exercise to God and the people whose welfare is affected by it," the document listed four "freedoms" which it described as "basic human rights due every person," as follows:

Freedom of religion and conscience; freedom of speech, press, inquiry and study; freedom of peaceable association and assembly, and freedom from arbitrary arrest, police brutality, mob violence and intimidation.

The hour-long debate on the human rights statement was notable for its good humor and marked absence of any rancor whatsoever. The attitude of several delegates from the South was expressed by the Rev. Dr. J. McDowell Richards, president of Columbia Theological Seminary, at Atlanta, Ga., who told the delegates that while he would not vote in favor of the statement he would not oppose it.

A resolution calling on the United States to refrain from forming a military alliance with the Franco regime in Spain was approved in principle and referred to the council's Department of International Justice and Good Will for study and report to the executive committee.

December 4, 1948

337

CHURCH PUTS BAN ON SEGREGATION

Southern Presbyterian Body Adopts Proposal to Open Membership to All

By GEORGE DUGAN

Special to The New York Times.

MONTREAT, N. C., May 29—The Southern Presbyterian Church called upon its 3,776 local churches tonight to open their membership rolls to all individuals regardless of race.

The historic action, approved by a vote of 236 to 169, came when the General Assembly of the Presbyterian Church in the United States endorsed a series of recommendations prepared in a report presented by its Council of Christian Social Relations.

In a floor debate that was notable for its obvious sincerity, opposition delegates warned that the move would cause "disruption" within the church and that by opening church portals to Negroes, white members would leave by another door. Others held that the action was "hasty" and "unwise" at a time of great tension in the South.

Delegates favoring the action noted that the "only division the Scripture knows is the difference between saints and sinners and believers and unbelievers."

In the "fellowship of faith," they said, "we worship, work, and live together, regardless of color."

Others approved recommendations urged that all of the church's institutions of higher education be operated on a non-segregated basis. They affirmed that "enforced segregation of the races is discrimination which is out of harmony with Christian theology."

The report noted that of 116 white, church-related colleges representing twenty Protestant denominations in sixteen Southern states and the District of Columbia, six reported enrollment of Negro students. Of these six, two operate on a segregated basis. The four non-segregated colleges are in Texas, Missouri, and West Virginia.

All four of the theological seminaries supported by the Presbyterian Church in the United States receive Negro students.

"Since segregation of the white and Negro people continues to diminish," the report declared, "it is time to determine the church's relation to this trend. This state of flux is due to two dynamic forces at work, the Federal Constitution and the Christian conscience, the one legal and the other spiritual, the one finding expression in statutes and court decisions, and the other in personal conduct, in the voice and policies of the church.

"If it be judged that segregation is not merely the separation of two peoples, but the subordination of one people to another, we can, on good evidence, observe that the courts have shown more sympathy toward the Negro than has the church. The church would then find itself in the embarrassing position of having to adjust its sense of morality to measure up to the mores of the state."

A supplementary recommendation from the council, based on the decision of the United States Supreme Court outlawing racial segregation in the public schools, called on the churches to "consider thoughtfully and prayerfully the complete solution of the problem involved."

It urged "all our people to lend their assistance to those charged with the duty of implementing the decision, and to remember that appeals to racial prejudice will not help but hinder the accomplishment of this aim."

Montreat, where the assembly is holding its annual meeting, is a quiet mountain retreat in the Blue Ridge Mountains of the Appalachian range. It is the home of the evangelist Billy Graham.

May 30, 1954

Vatican Commends New Orleans Prelate

By PAUL HOFMANN

Special to The New York Times.

ROME, Oct. 17—The Vatican commended publicly today the Archbishop of New Orleans for his measures against the racial discrimination practiced by some Roman Catholics in Louisiana.

It urged Roman Catholic Americans to join the fight against "inhuman" racial prejudice.

The action by some parishioners of the St. Cecilia Mission at Jesuit Bend, La., to bar a Negro priest from saying mass and some incidents at near-by Belle Chasse and Myrtle Grove were branded in an editorial in today's Osservatore Romano, the Vatican newspaper, as "sacrilegious."

The unusually emphatic editorial was unsigned, but it was understood to have been written by L'Osservatore's editor in chief, Count Giuseppe Dalla Torre, on direct instructions from the Vatican Secretariat of State.

"The news of racial discrimination in the Archdiocese of New Orleans struck all Catholics with painful amazement," L'Osservatore said.

It voiced "Christian pride" in the decision taken by the Most Rev. Joseph Francis Rummel, Archbishop of New Orleans, to suspend religious services at the Jesuit Bend mission and to impose church censures on the Catholics of the communities of Belle Chasse and Myrtle Grove.

To prevent colored priests from preaching the word of God and celebrating the Divine sacrifice, L'Osservatore declared, is a blasphemous crime that calls for prayer. It noted that Jesus Christ said of those who crucified Him, "Father, forgive them for they know not what they do."

Fortunately, L'Osservatore added, only "a few people out of their minds" among Roman Catholics were guilty of racial prejudice and the American Roman Catholic hierarchy and many of the faithful were active in the fight against discrimination and segregation.

The newspaper noted that racial prejudice in the United States had, "unfortunately, caused many crimes."

It cited specifically the "wolf whistle" trial at Sumner, Miss., deploring that "a crime against an adolescent victim remained unpunished."

The reference was to the acquittal by a jury of two white men accused of slaying Emmet Louis Till, 14-year-old Chicago Negro, after he had allegedly insulted the wife of one of the men with a "wolf whistle" at her. The trial was in September.

Today's editorial asserted that the fight against racial prejudice must be supported by all citizens who want to rid the "gentle and generous" civilization of the great American nation of a "stain."

Archbishop Gratified

Special to The New York Times.

NEW ORLEANS, Oct. 17—Archbishop Rummel said today:

"I am surprised that this incident has attracted the attention of the L'Osservatore Romano. I feel gratified over the reaction it expressed to the steps I had to take."

He added that he hoped it would make those responsible for the action he had taken "reflect seriously about the change of conduct they should take in their attitude toward their fellow Catholics of the colored race and especially toward a priest, regardless of race, color or nationality."

October 18, 1955

Presbyterians Ask Churchgoers to Aid Housing Bias Fight

By GEORGE DUGAN
Special to The New York Times.

PHILADELPHIA, May 30—The General Assembly of the Presbyterian Church in the U. S. A. called today on Christian churchgoers whose homes were up for sale to make them available to "all qualified purchasers without regard to race."

The recommendation was approved by an overwhelming vote of the 910 commissioners, or delegates. It was believed to be one of the strongest and most specific proposals on race relations ever made by a major Protestant body. The General Assembly speaks in behalf of 2,700,000 Presbyterians from coast to coast.

The church assembly also urged the United States Government to continue negotiations aimed at eliminating weapons of mass destruction.

It further reaffirmed its support of Federal contributions to education that would be applied exclusively to help tax-supported public schools.

The appeal to homeowners was part of a long report from a standing committee on social education and action. This was adopted at the closing business session of the assembly.

It urged homeowners to obtain recent studies of the effect on property values when nonwhites bought into white residential areas. "Values do not necessarily decline, and, in fact, rise after such purchases," the report noted.

At the same time, the assembly urged officials of local churches to weld their parishioners in "covenants of open occupancy." These agreements, it was asserted, should be designed to "stem the tendency toward panic selling and stabilize their neighborhoods on a nonsegregated basis."

Another section of the report called on churchgoers to participate in and "prayerfully support" responsible persons and organizations that have "sought through the courts by legal means to secure Constitutional rights for all citizens." This was interpreted by many commissioners as an extension of the church's hand of fellowship to the National Association for the Advancement of Colored People.

The report also urged Christians, individually and corporately, to "help bear the burdens of their fellow-men under persecution by sending gifts of money to Church World Service for the relief of persons designated as 'political refugees in our own country.'" Church World Service is an interdenominational relief agency representing most of the major Protestant denominations. The phrase "political refugees" referred to persons persecuted for racial reasons.

Political Action Urged

In other actions, the assembly:

¶Called on church members to regard service in a political party as "an effective method for Christians to witness and work for good government."

¶Urged the Congress to review and debate proposals for foreign aid without acrimony and partisan maneuvering so that decisions would be made on the basis of human welfare.

¶Called on the churches to work in helping to formulate public policies in such areas as housing, health, education, police protection, courts, social security and public welfare programs.

¶Commended so-called "inner-city" churches, such as the East Harlem Protestant Parish in New York, for "bringing the Gospel to unchurched people of low income families and for their work in witnessing the Gospel to the whole life of a community."

During debate on the report, one commissioner asked for an expression of opinion on the "significance and import" of the document.

The Rev. Dr. Eugene Carson Blake, chief administrative officer, replied that the report

The Rev. Dr. Eugene Carson Blake, chief administrative officer of Presbyterian Church in U. S. A. He will help implement church recommendation on housing.

"speaks for the whole church, but does not bind anybody's conscience."

He added that "this is not a papal pronouncement—if it were it would not be Presbyterian."

The assembly will meet next year in Omaha, Neb.

May 31, 1956

NEGRO CATHOLICS GAIN

5% Rise Reported in Year—530,000 Counted in U. S.

WASHINGTON, March 20 (*AP*)—A Roman Catholic bishops' organization reported today an increase of 5 per cent in the last year in the number of Catholic Negroes in the United States.

The count is given in the annual report of the Commission for Catholic Missions Among the Colored People and Indians. It said 530,000 of the country's 16,000,000 Negroes were Catholic. This was reported as a rise of 90 per cent in the last twenty-five years.

Catholic Indians, the report said, number 110,000 of a total of nearly 400,000.

Francis Cardinal Spellman, Archbishop of New York, is chairman of the missions commission.

March 21, 1957

Catholics Appeal for Desegregation

Papal Stand Cited

By JOHN W. FINNEY
Special to The New York Times.

WASHINGTON, Nov. 13—The Roman Catholic Bishops of the United States called today for decisive but prudent action to eradicate racial segregation.

The prelates appealed to "responsible and sober-minded Americans of all religious faiths, in all areas of our land;" to "seize the mantle of leadership from the agitator and the racist."

"It is vital that we act now and act decisively," they declared. "All must act quietly, courageously and prayerfully before it is too late."

They cited the writings of the late Pope Pius XII to support integration.

The Bishops spoke for the Catholic Church as a whole in the United States.

The Bishops took a firm moral stand against compulsory racial segregation in a special statement drafted at their annual meeting here. The statement was signed by the twelve episcopal members of the administrative board of the National Catholic Welfare Conference—the bishops' coordinating agency—and approved by those attending. Of the 220 Catholic bishops in the United States, 210 were at the meeting.

Their stand was based on the moral principle, which they noted was embodied in the Declaration of Independence, that "all men are equal in the sight of God."

"Men are unequal in talent and achievement," they said, but "discrimination based on the accidental fact of race or color cannot be reconciled with the truth that God has created all men with equal rights and equal dignity."

The statement said enforced segregation could not be "reconciled with the Christian view of our fellow man" for the following two reasons:

1. "Legal segregation, or any form of compulsory segregation, in itself and by its very nature imposes a stigma of inferiority upon the segregated people."
2. "It is a matter of historical fact that segregation in our country has led to oppressive conditions and the denial of basic human rights for the Negro."

While the statement offered no specific "concrete plans," it did present a philosophy of prudent action to take into account the deep-rooted problems underlying segregation.

"We may well deplore a gradualism that is merely a cloak for inaction," they said. "But we equally deplore brash impetuosity that would sacrifice the achievements of decades in ill-timed and ill-considered ventures.

November 14, 1958

Congregationalists Report 49% Ready To Accept Negroes

By JOHN WICKLEIN

Only 12 per cent of surveyed white Congregational Christian churches in metropolitan areas have accepted Negro members, and only 49 per cent show a willingness to accept them.

The situation, disclosed yesterday by the denomination, was discovered in a two-year interview survey of 1,054 congregations with 528,800 members. It was the first such study any major church has made and released for publication.

As a result of the findings, the church's Board of Home Missions has voted to finance a campaign to put into practice the denomination's publicly stated policy of "a nonsegregated church in a nonsegregated society."

The board adopted a resolution to give money to any congregation whose financial support was jeopardized by its moves to integrate.

In addition, the home missions agency appropriated $2,500 for the work of the racial relations division of the National Council of Churches, an interdenominational group. It also appropriated $2,500 for the legal defense fund of the National Association for the Advancement of Colored People.

"The diligent efforts of the N. A. A. C. P. in this area," the board asserted, "are in behalf of the civil rights and freedom of all Americans."

The Rev. Truman B. Douglass, executive vice president of the Board of Home Missions, said that this was the first time that a denominational integration drive had been backed by cash to the individual churches.

The money will come from the reserve funds of the board, with help from the regional conference of which the local church is a member.

The denominational agency, whose headquarters are at 287 Fourth Avenue, also wants to do some experimental things, its executive said.

For instance, if a church in a rapidly changing community needs an associate pastor of another race, the board will help support that man to give the church an interracial status.

In the South, it would give financial aid to white conferences that took Negroes on their staffs to help coordinate activities with Negro conferences in the same geographical areas. This, Dr. Douglass said, would be a first step toward integration of the churches themselves.

South Also Surveyed

Interviewers for the Board's survey reached 70 per cent of the churches in the "standard metropolitan areas" of thirty-eight states—South as well as North. These urban areas, which include at least one city of 50,000 or more people, were chosen for the survey because most racial problems arise within them. Including rural areas, the denomination reports a total of 5,544 churches and 1,392,600 members.

The interviewers talked to the minister and at least one layman officer of each church. They learned that 27 per cent of the congregations had admitted members of at least one minority group—Negro, Oriental, Spanish-speaking, or Indian-American.

This is a "modest gain" over the situation of twelve years ago, Mr. Douglass said. At that time, he said, a less thorough study showed that about 17 per cent of the Congregational Christian churches could be classified as racially inclusive in this respect.

"Church bodies," Mr. Douglass declared, "are prone to make grandiose proclamations of high ethical purposes through their general assemblies and then assume that because brave words have been spoken something significant has been done.

"This study tries to find out how far the 'non-segregated church' resolutions adopted by Congregationalists have been implemented. Such self-examination requires a measure of courage."

'Good Start' Made

Mr. Douglass said he was encouraged to think that a good start had been made toward the inclusion of minority groups, especially in the East and in the West. In those areas, 32 per cent and 28 per cent of the churches, respectively, had classified themselves as racially inclusive in membership.

The Midwest had 21 per cent of such churches, and the South, 19 per cent, but almost all the Southern churches were from Washington north.

Many of the survey's findings were disheartening, Mr. Douglass said. Among them, he said, were these:

• "In a period when events in the realm of human relations move with lethal swiftness, the churches proceed with glacial slowness."

• The extent of integration in the churches compares unfavorably with accomplishments by other institutions and governments.

• A large number of lay officers said their pastors would have more support for programs of desegregation in the community than in their own churches.

"Surely," said Mr. Douglass, "there is cause for disquietude in every indication that church people are more willing to accept a desegregated society than a desegregated church."

Dr. Herman Long, the board's secretary for race relations, who directed the study, called this its "most negative finding."

Mr. Douglass also found it disturbing that 51 per cent of the lay respondents from the Midwest believed that there were legitimate exceptions in community life that permitted segregation without violating the Christian commitment to brotherhood.

"It is alarming that what has been considered the 'Southern pattern' may be also the Midwestern pattern," he said.

The church leader was asked whether he thought the white conferences and churches in the South felt that they ought to integrate.

"I think that in the conferences, and even in the individual churches, the majority think integration is the Christian thing to do," he replied. "But they are baffled about how to do it, because of the racial tensions. I can say for certain that there is none of this hooey about 'God wouldn't have created all these separate races if he didn't want to keep them apart.' "

38% Have Policy

Among all the churches in the survey, only 38 per cent had adopted a racial policy, despite General Council pronouncements dating to 1944. Of those that had adopted a policy, 72 per cent were for racial inclusiveness and 28 per cent were restricted.

Ministers of all the churches were asked candidly whether they thought their churches were racially inclusive, policy or no. Forty-nine per cent replied that their churches were inclusive in actuality; 51 per cent said that they were not.

"This is probably the best approximation to reality which we were able to obtain," Dr. Long said in his report.

He said that minority-group membership findings could be summed up this way:

• The metropolitan Congregational churches appear to be strongly middle, upper middle and upper class in character (81 per cent).

• They contain about 528,800 members, among whom are 14,127 persons of Negro, Oriental, Spanish-speaking and other minority-group background.

• Minority members amount to 2.7 per cent of the total, and at least one of the principal groups is found in about 3 of every 10 churches.

"In general," said Dr. Long, "acceptance of minority persons into membership has been accompanied by a wholesome effect and only minor losses in members."

January 5, 1959

Churches of South Beset By Segregation Dilemma

By JOHN WICKLEIN

The churches in the South today are faced with their greatest dilemma since the dispute over slavery. The current crisis is similar to that at the time of the Civil War. Then the question was: "Is slavery Christian?" Today the question is: "Is segregation Christian?"

Those who would desegregate the churches do not look ahead of their parishioners in the fight. They find the opposition from their own churches and from the community intense. Some are dismissed for their views—as was the Rev. Robert B. McNeill, a Presbyterian minister in Columbus, Ga., on June 7.

Southern white church members, individually and in lay groups, have overwhelmingly supported the policy of "white only" for their churches. When the mass of churches in this churchgoing region is considered—estimates run as high as 100,000—there are next to no integrated congregations.

The Southern Regional Council, a church-supported lay group working in the field of race relations, has reports of no more than twenty Protestant churches within the eleven-state bounds of the old Confederacy that have one or more members of a second race. About three-quarters of these are affiliated with the liberal American Unitarian Association, among the smallest national denominations represented in the South.

Some Integrated Churches

Church leaders estimate that in the entire seventeen-state area where segration has some sanction in law, there are only a couple of hundred integrated churches. And this includes border states that are moving toward Northern patterns on race.

("Northern patterns," however, do not imply massive integration of the churches. It is estimated that throughout the North only 10 to 12 per cent are integrated. This, however, is still five times the percentage estimated in 1947.)

A hundred years ago white church leaders contended that slavery was compatible with their Christian convictions. Today no major denomination in the South and few leading churchmen assert that segregation can be reconciled with their religion.

And therein lies the dilemma: If Southern white churchmen follow their conviction and work for integration, they are damned at home; if they compromise their conviction and condone segregation, they are damned in the nation and the world. Many clergymen have made the difficult choice, and placed themselves in the forefront of groups acting to end the "peculiar institution" of twentieth-century America.

"Very few people in the South are taking a public position for integration, but in every instance where some people have taken leadership ministers are part of this leadership," said Dr. Herman Long, head of the Congregational Christian department of race relations, with offices at Fisk University, Nashville.

Usually the ministers are far to local congregations as a source of aid and comfort. They do find hope in some larger units of church life. All the major denominations in the South have adopted policies supporting the Supreme Court's mandate for integrating the schools; almost all have condemned segregation as morally wrong.

Similar Statements

Similar policy statements have been approved in many church regional organizations, by ministerial associations and by women's and young people's groups.

Although there are exceptions, the laymen's groups have been more conservative. This is thought to be partly because the men feel more vulnerable to reprisal from segregationists, especially in their jobs and businesses.

The larger denominations support a number of agencies working directly in the South for the cause of racial equality, both in church and out.

At regional-group levels, interracial meetings and religious retreats are held. In some national denominations, such as the Protestant Episcopal and the Presbyterian (both Northern and Southern) church conferences and jurisdictional areas are integrated.

In other denominations, such as the Methodist Church and the Congregational Christian Churches, white and Negro conference areas are kept separate.

Indication of Gap

This itself is an indication of the gap between national pronouncement and local practice. The dualism is not necessarily hypocritical, because the people at home often take violent exception to policy statements approved at a convention held far from their precincts and in the limelight of national publicity.

The largest Protestant denomination in the region, the Southern Baptist Convention with 9,000,000 members, has voted to stand with the Supreme

Court's decision on school integration. Yet at the local level its churches have done next to nothing to promote integration and much to continue segregation.

At the convention's recent annual gathering in Louisville, Ky., its outgoing president, former Representative Brooks Hays of Arkansas, was assailed by Deep Southerners for proposing a high-level conference between white and Negro Baptist leaders to "conduct a comprehensive examination" of the race problem.

Watered-Down Version

The convention finally endorsed a watered-down form of the proposal. But it elected as its new head the Rev. Ramsey Pollard, a Knoxville minister considered to be far "safer" on the race question than the moderate Mr. Hays.

One of the strongest voices heard from Southern white Methodists, the second largest white church group in the region, is that of the Methodist Laymen's Union in Birmingham, Ala. This group was formed specifically to insure that the Central Jurisdiction of the denomination, containing all the Southern Negro Methodist congregations will not be integrated with the white conferences it overlaps.

In the Roman Catholic Church, the Council of Bishops nationally and several bishops in Southern dioceses have condemned segregation as morally wrong and sinful.

Catholic bishops in four border cities—St. Louis, Louisville, Washington and Wheeling, W. Va.—integrated their parochial schools before the Supreme Court decision in May, 1954. A few other bishops have acted since.

In theory, all Catholic churches are integrated; in practice they are not. Negro members attending masses, which by church law are open to all, normally seat themselves at the rear. Almost nowhere do they participate in all church activities.

Yet the fact that many Catholic masses are interracial has spurred a number of white Protestant leaders to offer Negroes the opportunity to come freely to services even though the congregation will not extend them the hand of fellowship.

As in other areas of Southern life, the sentiment among white churchmen against integration increases as the percentage of Negroes in the population increases. Church opposition to "mixing" is most vocal in Alabama, with South Carolina and Mississippi close behind.

Interracial churches are rare to nonexistent; where they do exist, their members try hard to keep the fact quiet for fear their lives may be threatened or their sanctuaries bombed. White ministers do not sit in the same associations with Negro ministers on a local level.

White parishioners who exclude Negroes from membership do so primarily for social reasons. The one most often offered is that close contacts in the social milieu of church life,

especially among the young, would lead inevitably to mixed marriages. Many white churchmen are determined to prevent "mixing" even at the expense of having their actions denounced by Northern liberals as lacking in Christian charity.

"Just People"

"Segregation is maintained by older folks who too often dominate our churches," a white clergyman said at a conference in Gatlinburg, Tenn. "Young people don't agree with their parents, and would welcome integration. Young people go away to school in the North, and find the Negroes in their classes are just people."

John Marion, a Virginian who directs United (Northern) Presbyterian Church work in race relations from his office in Nashville, thinks a big change in attitude on race is taking place in church rank and file. Many will not admit it even to their neighbors, he says, because of fear.

"Their consciences are troubling them," Mr. Marion said, "and that's significant. Many of them think they are alone. If they were guaranteed no reprisals, I think many would express opinions that would amaze you."

Threat from Outside

The opposition to church integration that comes from outside the churches is rougher, more deeply grounded in prejudice and hate. It is the threat in the night from these people—often members of the more rabid White Citizens Councils or the Ku Klux Klan—that non-segregationist ministers fear even more than loss of their pulpits.

A prominent Congregational layman in New Orleans said that one Sunday recently a white couple walked down the aisle of a Negro church and asked the minister if they might become members.

The minister, surprised, made an appointment to talk to them about it, and then went directly for advice to another minister in town who was white.

"If I take them in," he said "it would cause a stir. What should I do?"

The white minister looked at him solemnly. "If a Negro couple walked down the aisle in my church on Sunday, I'd just pack up and leave town."

The thought seems ludicrous, but its implication for liberal and moderate ministers in the South are serious. Yet the number of these is increasing, as young men return home to pulpits from the integrated, modern theological seminaries maintained by the major denominations of the region.

Quote the Bible

Clergymen who openly espouse segregation are usually drawn from fundamentalist groups (independents Baptists and others) who believe the Bible demands that the race be kept apart. But the mainstream of Southern church leadership finds no Biblical justification for segregation.

Ideally, the majority believes with Paul:

"There is neither Jew nor Greek, there is neither slave nor free, there is neither male or female; for you are all one in Christ Jesus."

There are ministers and laymen who believe this, yet do nothing to make it a fact of Southern life.

Last year a confidential poll by Pulpit Digest indicated that four out of five Protestant ministers in the South favored integration of the public schools. Some of them have had the temerity to speak out on this and other racial issues, but most of them have not. A number of those who have taken pulpit stands for integration have been dismissed for doing it.

Still, the white liberal ministers of the South are the most powerful and respected group working in the white community to bring the races together in a single fellowship of man.

Responsibility of Whites

Although Negro church leaders have done much to end segregation, the responsibility in race relations falls more heavily on the white ministers. They, as respected mentors of the controlling majority, are in a better, safer and stronger position to ease racial tensions in the area than any other leaders in the South.

Harold C. Fleming, director of the Southern Regional Council, said in Atlanta that there was no organized force of comparable size doing as much for racial amity and integration as the churches. Potentially, he said, it is a tremendous force, if it can be brought down to the local level.

"The difference between integration in Louisville and Little Rock was leadership," he said. "The same thing is true in churches."

Mr. Fleming said the denominations had provided a professional corps of people working to ease racial tensions—"Dr. A. C. Miller of the Southern Baptists here, to name only one."

The amount of money they put into it, he said, "is inadequate compared to the amount they put into other church activities, but it helps."

The big problem in local churches, Mr. Fleming believes, is to close the gap between clergy and lay leaders.

New Group of Ministers

"Theological seminaries have been breeding a new group of ministers who see race in a new and progressive way," he said.

"But the laymen haven't been subjected to the new ideas; their frame of reference is traditional customs. Some leading laymen have stretched themselves beyond the traditional patterns—they go to conventions and vote for liberal moves they would never approve in their own home towns."

The purpose of this series of articles was to find whether the churches and denominations of the South wanted to end or continue segregation in their own communions and in the community.

The information was derived over a six-week period from research and personal interviews with fifty-three ministers, laymen, church workers and edi-

The Religion of Black Americans

STRESSES CHURCHES: Harold C. Fleming, director of the Southern Regional Council. He said churches have power for promoting racial amity and integration that will be great if it is used on local level.

tors in ten communities across the South. This article considers the church and segregation generally; later ones will discuss Protestant efforts for desegregation in Atlanta, Protestant segregationist sentiment in Birmingham and Montgomery, Ala., and the Roman Catholic drive to integrate the Archdiocese of New Orleans.

If religious leaders decide they do want to end segregation, how can they bring that about?

'Played by Ear'

"If anything has to be played by ear, this is it," said the Rev. Dr. Dow Kirkpatrick, minister of a large Methodist church in Atlanta. "I'm very proud of our Southern ministers—they've been as liberal as any minister in the North on this issue.

"I've preached strong sermons on race and I've had objections. And I've also preached on liquor and had objections. A minister has to feel the tenor of his church and lead in the best way he can."

This, Dr. Kirkpatrick said, may be through direct attacks on segregation (if a man dares), through indirect preaching on brotherhood, or through talks behind the scenes with his parishioners.

He and other Southern liberals think more of this last kind of leadership is taking place in Southern churches than most people believe. Many ministers feel that quiet persuasion, away from the intimidating glare of publicity, can bring about a change to an interracial church much faster than any other method.

And an interracial church, they say, will mean an interracial society—church membership is so widespread in the South that the church is society.

Wants Schools Open

There is no Christian basis for separation of men on an artificial basis of color, Dr. Kirkpatrick declared.

"But that is not to say integration is practical," he added. "The church is not ready to prefer integration to segregation at this point, but only to accept enough integration to keep the schools open."

This is the point where many of Dr. Kirkpatrick's fellow ministers feel they can and should take their stand. Ministers have found they can speak forthrightly on keeping the schools open, if they speak in a group.

Preserving the public schools makes sense to a lot of segregationists, even if that means some integration will be necessary.

President Eisenhower, on March 22, 1956, asked ministers to urge their congregations to keep the schools open in the face of integration.

"Frankly," he said, "I believe that the pulpits do have a very great deal of responsibility here."

"Now let's don't try to think of this as a tremendous fight that is going to separate Americans and get ourselves into a nasty mess. Let's try to think of it as how we can make progress and keep it going and not stop it. Now that, I believe, the pulpits can help on."

Surprisingly, the first national denomination to support the Supreme Court's decision was the (Southern) Presbyterian Church in the U. S. Its vote, at the 1954 convention, was taken early because its meeting happened to come just after the May 17 decision was handed down.

Adopted Two Statements

The group has since adopted two statements backing racial equality that are considered to be the most liberal of any approved by a predominantly Southern church.

But it was the Richmond (Va.) Ministers Association that started a trend that was to create great interest throughout the South and in the nation.

For two years after the court decision the Byrd machine, the Virginia Legislature and the Richmond newspapers had been building a program of "massive resistance" to integration of the schools.

On Jan. 28, 1957, the ministers of Richmond decided the state had gone too far in restricting the rights of citizens, white and Negro, to discuss the issue, and in depriving the Negro of his constitutional rights.

In paid advertisements in the Richmond papers, it published a manifesto, signed by fifty-nine of its members, scathingly criticizing the then Gov. Thomas B. Stanley and the Legislature.

It declared the public schools must be preserved, and that it would be possible to establish an educational system in the spirit of the court's decision and satisfactory to citizens of both races.

"Wherever possible and as rapidly as possible, social customs violating the dignity of

the Negro should be eradicated," the statement declared. "The passing away of these irritating customs does not involve intermarriage or amalgamation of the races; it declares a wholesome respect for all people and evidences common courtesy."

Poll by Papers

The newspapers jumped on the statement editorially; they took a poll of ministers in Richmond to see if it represented a majority. Of 430 questioned, 216 said they favored the step, fifty-six were opposed and 158 had "no comment."

The day the statement was adopted, the Rev. Dr. Joseph S. Johnston, a Methodist minister, was elected president of the association. He has since become president of the Virginia Council of Churches, which has also adopted a policy against segregation.

"Nearly everything in the Richmond statement has since been accomplished by the courts," Dr. Johnston said. "The massive resistance laws have been struck down."

The Richmond document was the forerunner of racial manifestoes. The ones signed by Atlanta ministers in the last two years, urging that Georgia schools be kept open despite integration, are the most widely known. But ministerial groups have taken similar stands in Gainesville and elsewhere in Georgia; in Houston and Dallas, Tex., and in other states where school-closing laws are at issue.

No Integration Seen

Although integrated schools will come, Dr. Johnston said, integration of churches in Richmond isn't likely. Negro and white housing areas are separate, he pointed out, and most Negroes would not want to come long distances to white churches even if these churches made them welcome.

Richmond ministers, he said, as many others in the South, worry about the white-engendered breakdown of communication between the races that has occurred since the Supreme Court decision. Often the churches provide the only existing bridge between the two groups. The ministers association, Dr. Johnston said, is the only major interracial organization in the city.

In the opinion of the Rev. Dr. Samuel Proctor, a Negro who is president of Virginia Union College in Richmond, none of the white ministers is leading a drive for desegregation.

"As pastors in big middle-class churches," he said, "they are caught in the same dilemma as everyone else in the South—they can't integrate their churches."

The Rev. Dr. E. D. McCreary Jr., a 40-year-old Richmond pastor and a Negro, pointed out that whites were welcome in Negro churches.

Sees Disparity

"But there is a great disparity in training of the average Negro minister and the average white minister," he said. "The average white person wouldn't be interested in going

to a Negro church, because of the intellectual level."

This is being rectified, he said, by institutions such as the new federated theological center for Negroes being set up in Atlanta with the help of the Sealantic Fund.

Dr. McCreary, who has run for the state Legislature in opposition to the Byrd machine, feels that for a minister—white or Negro—preaching and counseling on the moral issues involved are more important than working actively in politics and social affairs.

"In some instances," he said, "the minister must get out and work—that's my role, for instance. But mostly, ministers should work to change the thought patterns that lie behind the legal victories for segregation."

The Rev. Dr. Martin Luther King Jr., a symbol of moderate, enlightened Negro leadership for integration, believes segregation would fall swiftly if the churches ever took a forthright stand against it.

The 30-year-old pastor from Montgomery, Ala., was interviewed while on a tour to raise funds for a movement of passive resistance to segregation.

The custom would fall even sooner, he said, if church work were backed with stronger national leadership to win the hearts of men to the cause of integration.

Just as the President hopes the ministers will heed his call to help prepare the way for school integration, so Negro ministers hope he will assume the moral leadership of the nation on the issue. This plea from Negro leaders recurred in interviews across the South.

The President has said repeatedly that racial equality will be won not in the legislatures, but in the hearts of men. Negro religious leaders agree, except that they think that having the law on their side since 1954 has been a great psychological boon. They have the law; now they want the President to use the vast influence and prestige of his person and office to help win the people.

"It is one of the great tragedies in this period of transition," Dr. King said, "that the most powerful person in our country has not made a public statement endorsing the Supreme Court's decision on integration.

"I think that if President Eisenhower had appealed to the conscience of the people, there would not have been the opposition to the decision that subsequently developed.

"I very definitely feel that the President should state not only that integration is the law of the land, but that segregation is morally wrong."

No Comment on Ruling

The President has been asked at news conferences whether he agrees with the Supreme Court that separate is not equal and that the schools should be integrated. He has replied that he would not comment on the court's decision, but would continue to support it as the law of the land.

A member of the White House staff was asked why the President had not denounced segregation.

"People who know the President personally," he replied, "suggest that the President has two reasons for not saying flatly 'This is wrong.':

"1. He feels he is President of 180,000,000 people.

"2. All his closest friends — bridge-playing, golfing and hunting—are from the Deep South.

"They must hammer him continually on this, and yet he has done many concrete things to uphold the law of the land."

The White House official pointed out that the President had acted forcefully when any clear-cut test on the issue arose, such as his "lonely decision" to send troops to Little Rock in the school integration crisis there.

'Service of Reconciliation'

In response to a letter from the President, the Right Rev. Robert R. Brown, Protestant Episcopal Bishop of Little Rock, arranged a city-wide "service of reconciliation" on Oct. 11, 1957. In it, at the President's request, ministers urged the 6,000 people who came to the churches to "disregard the incitement of agitators."

Aside from this and similar action, the integrated Little Rock Ministerial Association as a group took little leadership in the crisis. Fundamentalist ministers outside the group were much more vocal. One of them declared:

"There are enough God-fearing citizens in Arkansas to rise up and get these troops out of here."

The White House officer thinks President Eisenhower's actions on Little Rock spoke for themselves.

"The President is not a man to stand up on a platform and issue bitter pronouncements," he said. "If you asked him, he would say 'I do what is best for the country'."

Negro religious leaders and white liberal ministers say they wish the President would make a pronouncement, not bitterly, but calmly, that segregation is undemocratic and un-Christian. This would give them a plank to cling to, in addition to the national church pronouncements, in a sea where rafts are few.

July 5, 1959

METHODISTS VOTE INTEGRATION PLAN

By GEORGE DUGAN
Special to The New York Times

PITTSBURGH, May 1 — The quadrennial general conference of the Methodist Church overwhelmingly approved here today a plan to abolish its all-Negro, nongeographic Central Jurisdiction within four years.

The vote of the nearly 900 delegates, representing 10 million members of the denomination, was interpreted as a resounding victory for Charles C. Parlin of New York. The lawyer is one of six presidents of the World Council of Churches.

Mr. Parlin, as chairman of the Methodist Commission on Inter-Jurisdictional Relations, shepherded its plan through nine hours of debate that began yesterday morning.

When the final vote was taken, it became apparent that advocates of immediate abolition of the Central Jurisdiction had suffered a severe setback.

They were led by Chester A. Smith of Peekskill, N. Y., and the Rev. Dean E. Richardson of Buffalo. They contended that the church could not afford even a moment's delay in ridding itself of what had become a symbol of segregation.

Will Absorb Conferences

The nongeographic Negro jurisdiction is one of the church's six administrative arms. It includes about 90 per cent of Methodism's 370,000 Negroes. The five other jurisdictions are the Northeastern, South Central, Southeastern, North Central and Western.

In substance, the plan provides for transferring the Central Jurisdiction's 17 annual Negro conferences, or governing units, into the five geographic jurisdictions. Either the jurisdictions or the Negro conferences may take merger steps on their own initiative.

If the Central Jurisdiction is not eliminated by this process within four years, a proposal asking for its outright abolition will be presented to the next quadrennial conference in Dallas in 1968.

This afternoon, 125 pickets marched around the civic arena where the conference was in session, protesting what they held to be a compromise solution to the issue.

Later they quietly entered the auditorium and took seats in the balcony. Members of a group called Methodists for Church Renewal, they announced that their intention was to hold an all-night prayer vigil beginning at midnight.

After the vote today, Mr. Parlin told the delegates that they had taken a "giant step" and vowed that "this quadrennium will see the end of the Central Jurisdiction."

Handicap Is Charged

He then called the delegates' attention to this paragraph in the preamble to the plan:

"The Central Jurisdiction is an undeniable handicap to the Methodist Church in the proclamation of the Gospel to all peoples. It is considered by many as both a fact and a symbol of racism within the church. It is incompatible with the basic principle of equality. This plan of action is likewise based on the belief that there is urgency, and a conviction that the Methodist Church is determined to eliminate the Central Jurisdiction in a fair and orderly manner and at as early a date as possible."

While much of the long debate yesterday and today involved technicalities of procedure, it was clear that the plan's opponents remained unconvinced, despite the preamble.

They viewed it as a compromise that placed the Methodist Church on the side of gradualism in the civil rights struggle.

Further Integration Seen

It is expected that, under the plan, the Northeastern, North Central and South Central Jurisdictions will move quickly to assimilate Negro conferences. It is also expected that they will go further and integrate Negro and white churches into the same regional conferences.

Negro churches in the Western Jurisdiction have already become part of the regional conferences.

But the Southeastern Jurisdiction presents a more difficult problem. It includes Georgia, Alabama, North and South Carolina, Mississippi, Tennessee, Florida, Kentucky and Virginia.

There seems little doubt that it will accept Negro conferences, but it is unlikely that Negro and white churches will be placed in the same conferences.

Opponents of the plan asked immediate abolition of the Central Jurisdiction by constitutional amendment. Mr. Parlin, however, argued that such a procedure would result in a chaotic situation, with many Negro conferences lost in an administrative muddle.

The 36-member Commission on Inter-Jurisdictional Relations included not only Negro representatives but also John C. Satterfield of Yazoo City, Miss., secretary of the Coordinating Committee for Fundamental American Freedoms, which is opposing the civil rights bill in Congress.

In its concluding paragraph the plan offered these words of advice:

"Carrying through the plan will require the action by and cooperation of all jurisdictions and their annual conferences. For all there will be a change in the status quo and from all will be required concessions and sacrifices. The concessions and sacrifices required of all must be accepted gladly as essential to the achievement of the inclusive church, for which we pray and must now work. The commission believes that the best interests of the church demand that the Central Jurisdiction be eliminated without delay and that the plan of action proposed is as fair as can be worked out."

May 2, 1964

CARDINAL'S OFFICE PICKETED ON COAST

Special to The New York Times

LOS ANGELES, June 15—A score of pickets paced in front of the Roman Catholic Chancery office today as part of a wave of protests against James Francis Cardinal McIntyre on the racial question.

The 77-year-old head of the Los Angeles Archdiocese continued to maintain silence on the criticism from both clergy and laity. Other clergymen, however, spoke out in his defense.

The Cardinal has been accused of opposing positive enunciation of the church's precepts on racial equality, particularly with respect to the campaign to repeal a California law prohibiting discrimination in real estate transactions. His critics say that the Cardinal has disciplined priests who spoke out for racial equality and has impeded the Catholic Human Relations Council, a lay organization promoting racial equality.

A number of well-informed Catholics say, however, that the racial controversy is just a convenient point of leverage for the expression of long-smoldering dissatisfaction of more liberal Catholic clergy and laity over the Cardinal's general conservatism.

June 16, 1964

DADDY GRACE, 78, EVANGELIST, DIES

LOS ANGELES, Jan. 12 (AP) —Charles Manuel Grace, picturesque Negro evangelist and church founder, died today in Metropolitan Hospital. He had suffered a heart atttack Friday and a stroke Sunday. Daddy Grace, as he was known to adherents across the nation, was 78 years old.

He claimed that his church, the House of Prayer for All People, had a membership of 3,000,000 persons in more than sixty cities.

"I am all people's man," he told his flock. "I am the boy friend of the world!"

He looked and lived the part. He painted his houses of worship—and his fingernails—red, white and blue. He wore a mustache and cutaway coats. Some

Associated Press

Charles Manuel Grace

of his coats were green, with trousers to match. His fingers were jeweled and his hair flowed over his shoulders.

Relatives said the religious leader had built 350 houses of prayer in the last thirty years. He also acquired many other properties in major cities, including the Grace Hotel-Apartments and a $450,000, eighty-five room mansion here. In 1953 he bought a twenty-room mansion in Montclair, N. J., for $72,000.

Daddy Grace's visits to his communicants were occasions for rejoicing. They showered him with dollar bills, scattered roses in his path and fanned him with palm leaves. Commodities, even toothpaste, in packages bearing his name enjoyed widespread sales.

Large Newark Following

In Charlotte, N. C., where he founded his church in 1926, baptizing new members in a mudhole, there is a congregation of more than 13,000. The church cafeteria offers Grace coffee from his Brazilian plantation and eggs from his hatchery near Havana. A beauty parlor at the church sells Grace cold cream.

The evangelist had a large following in Newark, N. J., where he alternated two brass bands at his services at the former Savoy Theatre. One band played blues, the other more lively tunes. After the blowing of a whistle, Daddy Grace would appear on a throne carried by two men.

Several times he proved as persuasive in court as he was in the pulpit. In 1934 he was indicted on income tax charges after having paid $41 tax on $190,000 income. The case was thrown out of court.

Two sisters, Mrs. Sylvia Gomes and Mrs. Louise Grace, of New Bedford, Mass., flew here today. They said the body would be taken to New Bedford for burial.

January 13, 1960

Man of Myth and Fact
Elijah Muhammad

ONE night a year after the start of the Great Depression, an out-of-work sharecropper's son named Elijah Poole turned up for a secret meeting in a musty basement in Detroit. He had gone to hear an ex-convict itinerant silk merchant turned prophet, who went under the name W. D. Fard.

Man in the News Fard, who was also known as F. M. Ali, Professor Ford, Mr. Wali Farrad, and Wallie Ford, had appeared in the Detroit streets earlier in the year.

Telling strange tales of Africa and Allah and the evil ways of the blue-eyed white man, he had attracted a few followers from the disadvantaged Negro community. They became known as the Temple of Islam.

As Elijah Poole tells the story of that night in 1930, he recognized instantly that Fard was "the second return of the son as prophesied." He became Fard's lieutenant in the burgeoning movement.

In 1934 W. D. Fard disappeared and has not been heard of since. Yesterday, Elijah Poole, now 67 years old and known as Elijah Muhammad, the Messenger of the Temple of Islam, was greeted by a roaring crowd of 6,500 at the 369th Regiment Armory in Harlem.

At Center of Rebellion

Elijah Muhammad's movement, the Black Muslims, has come to be the center of what is sometimes called the Black Man's rebellion in mid-century America. Existing alongside civil rights organizations calling for integration, his iron-disciplined legions pray for total separation from the "white devils" that have kept them down for so long.

His followers, who dress in neat, dark business suits or white floor-length gowns and veils, have established mosques, schools and their own businesses in the major cities. Their number has never been officially announced; claims run from 50,000 to 250,000.

An elite corps of black Puritans, they renounce alcohol, drugs, tobacco, gambling and sexual immorality. They are enjoined never to carry weapons, not even nail files, and always to be polite and pay their bills. Cleanliness in dress and housing is heavily stressed.

They eat one meal a day--never including pork -- and face east five times a day to pray to Allah.

A Status of Divinity

To them, the frail, delicate-boned Elijah Muhammad has the status of divinity. His words are at the center of their belief; his picture is on their walls.

When his thin, high voice intones the traditional beginning to his speeches a wave of excitement passes through their ranks.

"As - Salaam - Alaikum (Peace Be Unto You)," he begins. "In the name of Allah, the most Merciful God, to whom all holy praises are

The New York Times

To his followers, divine
(Mr. Muhammad at rally here)

due, the Lord of all the worlds; the most Merciful Father and life-giver to the lost-found, mentally dead so-called Negroes here in the Wilderness of North America."

In the life of Elijah Muhammad, as in the obscure background of his movement, myth and fact are intertwined. It abounds in mysterious strangers, prophetic voices and conflicting stories. All of this, apparently, he does not discourage.

Elijah Poole was born in Sandersville, Ga., on Oct. 7, 1897. His father, Wali Poole, was a Baptist preacher who scratched out a living for his 13 children by farming a

white man's land.

At the age of 16, having completed the fourth grade, he left home and took a succession of temporary jobs. At 22 he married the former Clara Evans, and in 1923 they moved with their two children to Detroit.

He was bitter when he left Georgia, and his bitterness grew as jobs became scarce in the North. "I saw enough of the white man's brutality in Georgia to last me for 26,000 years," he once said. His meeting with W. D. Fard was a fateful one. Fard, he said, "took me out of the gutters in the streets of Detroit and taught me knowledge of Islam."

With Fard's disappearance in 1934 Elijah Muhammad assumed leadership of the movement, which by then had grown to 8,000.

His succession was disputed by others in Detroit and he moved the organization to Chicago, where the Temples of Islam multiplied.

Elijah was in jail for draft-dodging from 1942 to 1946, but he directed the movement from prison and took up the reins again when he was released.

The movement has mushroomed in the last six years. Its principal teaching — the establishment of a separate nation for Negroes—is widely discussed and its newspaper, "Muhammad Speaks," widely read.

Asthma and bronchitis have compelled Elijah to move to Phoenix, where he lives in a small, two-bedroom house with a staff of three. His public appearances are rare.

June 29, 1964

Key Man of the South— The Negro Minister

He is traditionally a spokesman as well as a pastor, and the civil-rights movement enhances both roles.

By C. ERIC LINCOLN

ONE of the most maligned institutions in America has been the Negro church, one of the most caricatured professions the Negro ministry. Today, however, the Negro minister is teaching America to perceive him in a new light. The civil-rights movement at the grass-roots level is largely in the hands of ministers, and the ministers themselves have found a new dignity which lifts them above the stereotype of pompous behavior, fried chicken and expensive automobiles with which they were once identified.

The Negro minister has had to come a long way. During the slave period, Negro ministers were rare, for any form of black leadership was considered inimical to the interests of the slavocracy. At first slaves were admitted to the galleries of white churches; later, it was not unusual for white preachers to preach carefully selected sermons to gatherings of slaves. In a few places, Negro exhorters or self-styled preachers were permitted to hold services in the presence of the white overseer or some other white man designated to monitor the meetings.

However, most religious services led by early Negro preachers were clandestine, held deep in the swamps and forests to escape detection. It was at such secret meetings that the "freedom spirituals" denying the permanency of slavery, and promising deliverance by a just and avenging God, were developed. It was here, too, that the dual role of the Negro preacher as a spiritual leader and as a protest leader was first developed.

Freedom from bondage brought with it the freedom to choose a profession, at least theoretically, and the ministry was the profession most readily available to Negro men. Between the end of the Civil War and the turn of the 20th century, certainly more Negroes went into the ministry than into any other profession.

UNTIL fairly recently it was only required that a preacher "know his Bible" better than his congregation and be able to preach and pray in an "arousing" manner in order to found or lead a church. Frequently, the first re-

C. ERIC LINCOLN is a professor of sociology at Clark College in Atlanta, Ga. and author of "The Black Muslims in America."

quirement was readily waived if a man could "preach the Word with force and conviction" and set the congregation to "shouting" with his imagery and showmanship. God would tell him what to say, as he told Moses in Egypt and countless other prophets in Hebrew history.

Booker T. Washington was fond of telling the story of a Negro farmer, who was plowing in the field one day when he suddenly exclaimed: "Lord, this sun is so hot, this grass is so tall and this doggone mule is so stubborn, I b'lieve I hear you calling me to preach!" With that he left mule and plow standing in the field and went off to found a church.

Free-wheeling preaching begot a free-wheeling response like that in a Baptist church I knew as a boy in north Alabama. Every Sunday night Aunt Sally Rogers (who was older than anyone could remember) would "get happy" and "walk the benches"; this frail little woman of 90 pounds or so would climb to the backs of the pews and walk them rigidly from the rear to the front of the church and back again, singing and shouting and flinging aside those who got in her way.

Down in front of those churches of a generation or so ago was the "moaners' bench," where confessed sinners sat through the long revival meetings hoping to be touched by the Spirit and cleansed of their sins. Amid much preaching and singing, praying and shouting, the sinners were usually delivered of their burdens, and with shouts of ecstasy and tears of joy on all sides they were received into the fellowship of the church.

PROBABLY every Negro who grew up in the South before the last World War knows from personal experience the meaning of the knotted handkerchief. Women like my grandmother would tie a quarter in one corner of their Sunday handkerchief for church dues, and fifteen cents in the opposite corner for burial insurance. And nothing on earth save "good preaching" and good singing at the village church could unknot the 25-cent end of that handkerchief. Occasionally at the Sunday night services my grandmother would even put her "insurance money" into the collection plate and "trust the Lord to take care of her" until she could catch up on her insurance. But the insurance man never got what belonged to the church.

THE Negro's preoccupation with church dues and insurance was, of course, a reflection of the precarious circumstances in which he lived. As late as 1940, the total income of many Southern Negro families did not exceed five or six dollars a week, very often considerably less. As a consequence, the emphasis of the living was directed largely toward preparation for dying, and in this preparation the minister played a part of great importance. Faithful membership in his church would assure a better life "over Jordan."

But the minister was deeply concerned with his members' lives this side of Jordan, too. Despite his professional shortcomings and his frequent inclination to make the church organizations instrumental to his personal aggrandizement, he was the most important leader in the community, and sometimes the only one. The Negro community looked to him as their spokesman before the mysterious white world, and trusted him to keep their affairs in order.

Today, the number of Negroes entering the ministry is diminishing in relation to other professional interests (although, except for teaching, it probably remains the largest single profession among Negroes). At the same time, the quality of this training is fast improving. Dr. Harry Richardson, president of Atlanta's Interdenominational Theological Center, the largest predominantly Negro seminary in the country, says that "Negro youth are now deliberately choosing the ministry rather than being pushed into it by lack of opportunity in other fields." In some Negro denominations today the minister must have at least a college degree, with further training in a seminary — although this rule is far from universal and most Negro pastors are still concentrated in denominations where a minister need only be "called of God" in order to preach.

THE "typical" Southern Negro minister is probably as elusive as the "typical" anything else, but in order to take a closer look at the role of the contemporary Negro minister in the South, I followed the Reverend A. S. Dickerson through his ministerial paces for several days. Mr. Dickerson, whose given names are Adolphus Sumner, is pastor of Central Methodist Church in Atlanta. His church has about 1,500 members, and is located in an urban-renewal area near downtown Atlanta.

Pastor Dickerson is 50 years old and was born in a small town in western Georgia. Ordained in 1937, he has advanced until he is now head of one of the largest churches in his conference. He holds or has held many important positions on the various boards or committees of his conference, and has had a term on the trustee board of a church-related Negro college in Atlanta, a few blocks from his church. Mr. Dickerson is better educated than most Negro ministers, holding advanced degrees from Atlanta University and Boston University. He met his wife, Virginia, in "church work," and they own their own home.

TWO services are held each Sunday morning at Central Methodist Church, one at 8:15 and another at 10:45. Mr. Dickerson's assistant, the Reverend W. H. McIver, officiates at the early service. I attended the 10:45 service on two successive Sundays, and both times the sanctuary was almost filled, with 400 or 500 worshipers. Some of the women wore furs and jewelry. Others dressed quite plainly. I learned later that many of the older members who moved away after the neighborhood began deteriorating still come back for Sunday services, although they are less active in weeknight activities.

The church service was more or less routine, the order of worship being taken from the "Official Methodist Hymnal." The sermon preached on my first visit, "The Will to Overcome," was forcefully presented, yet with a certain dignity and restraint. On this visit there was no "shouting" or weeping. However, on the next Sunday during Communion, as the congregation began to sing "Let Us Break Bread Together," a large woman in the choir became overwrought and began to scream and wave her arms. She was restrained, but only after her outburst had started a chain reaction of shouts and sobbing throughout the church.

IN some class-conscious Negro churches, it is no longer "acceptable" to "shout." I asked Mr. Dickerson whether "shouting" occurred frequently in his church. He said that the practice, while acceptable, was diminishing.

Following his sermon, Pastor Dickerson talked briefly with his congregation about civic issues and their responsibilities as citizens. Two items claimed his attention in particular. One was the necessity of restraint and nonviolence in the continuing fight for first-class citizenship. "First-class citi-

zenship we *must* have and we *will* have," he asserted, "but not at the expense of law and order."

The second item was a coming referendum to decide whether Atlanta was to make the sale of mixed drinks legal, or whether liquor sales would be restricted to package stores. Of this he said, "The way you vote is your business, isn't it? That is the American way. But *do vote*, and vote responsibly! It is your duty. If you want to be citizens, you must exercise the responsibilities of citizens."

MR. DICKERSON'S week is hectic. He is a part-time chaplain at the Atlanta Federal Penitentiary, and on Monday I accompanied him there. As we made our way to the chaplain's office he was sought out by a succession of prisoners who wanted variously to share a joke with him, make an appointment or just shake hands. All the prisoners who sought to speak with him that day were white.

Next day, Mr. Dickerson was one of a handful of Negro ministers and educators asked to meet with members of the Emory University Medical School faculty to discuss ways of improving the health of indigent mothers and their children. Some of the ministers present suspected a ruse to make birth control mandatory for Negro mothers (who constitute about 80 per cent of the indigent cases). Mr. Dickerson thought not, but he suggested that any board selected to oversee the matter, and the team of doctors who would administer any proposed program, should have "effective representation" from Negro professionals from the beginning.

Tuesday night there was choir rehearsal. Central Methodist has only two choirs, although some Negro churches have as many as six or seven, for the numerous choirs not only provide a popular outlet for church participation, but they compete with each other in raising money to augment the church treasury. On Wednesday night there was Mid-Week Prayer Meeting, the Young Adult Fellowship and a rehearsal of the Senior Choir.

Thursday afternoon, I went calling with Pastor Dickerson for a glimpse of the people who make up his parish and their ways of life. One call took us to the home of an elderly widow a block or two from the church. On the way, Mr. Dickerson explained that he did not ordinarily telephone before calling, as he did not like his parishoners to feel

special preparations were necessary for a visit from the pastor.

THE widow was obviously pleased to receive us. In a room filled with old clocks, pictures, statuary and bric-a-brac from bygone times, she waved me to a chair half hidden under a profusion of old magazines and newspapers. She and Mr. Dickerson shared an ancient piano bench.

"Reverend," she exclaimed, recovering from her surprise, and trying valiantly to conceal a wad of snuff in her bottom lip, "Reverend, I *knowed* you were coming to see me! My rheumatism's been bothering me so, and that ol' landlord done been acting so mean — threatening to put me out and all, I just had a feeling that you were coming to see me! Bless the Lord, you don't forget me!"

The minister listened pa-

Negro Churches

At present there are about ten million Negroes in racially distinct denominations. More than half of these belong to two Baptist "conventions," and practically all of the others are Methodists of one kind or another. Although Catholicism is making some solid gains, and a few Negroes are embracing other ways of faith such as Unitarianism, Christian Science, Bahaism and the doctrines of the Black Muslims, it is still a popular saying that "if a Negro does not belong to a Methodist church or a Baptist church, somebody has been messin' with his religion." — C. E. L.

tiently to her troubles, and before leaving, offered prayer. As we stood up to go, from somewhere in the folds of her ancient gingham, the old lady produced a handkerchief carefully knotted at opposite corners. "Reverend," she said quietly as she fumbled with one of the knots, "if I don't make it to church Sunday, I want you to have my dues." She unfolded two worn one-dollar bills and handed them to her pastor.

Another call was at the home of a prominent businessman in a meticulously kept neighborhood which had been the show place of black Atlanta 15 years ago. The spacious homes were set discreetly back from the gracefully curving

street on which they bordered. The dogwoods and azaleas offered a variety of color, and the lush green lawns were neatly clipped. We stopped before a large ranch house which easily dominated the street. The front door was open, but no one answered the bell. The pastor left his card.

FRIDAY night is "Fun Night" at the Central Methodist Church, providing an opportunity for the minister to meet the young people of his congregation in a relaxed atmosphere. There are games and group singing and refreshments, but no dancing. Adults attend Fun Night, too, and the pastor enters enthusiastically into the spirit of the evening.

On Saturday Mr. Dickerson prepares his sermon, and "tries to do a little reading and meditation." In his busy week he manages to find time for a full share of civic responsibilities, to teach a class at the Interdenominational Theological Center, and to carry a fairly heavy counseling load, lending a hand to those in trouble whether or not they belong to his church.

"My people, like all people, have problems," he reflects. "Families are broken, teenagers get into trouble, somebody's furniture is set out on the street. I have to go and do what I can do to help them. This is my job. I wouldn't change it."

Like almost every other effective Negro minister in the South today, Mr. Dickerson is active in the civil-rights movement, although he does not consider himself to be a "professional" civil-rights leader. A few months ago when Negro leadership in Atlanta met in a series of day-long "summit conferences" to formulate means of coordinating an attack on remaining segregation in Atlanta, he was prominently involved, although he shies from publicity.

"Whenever it is possible," he explains, "I prefer to meet the white man in quiet negotiation. I do not mean that we should talk merely for the sake of talking. Conversation is not a reasonable substitute for action. But we should go into the streets only as a last resort, and once there we should conduct ourselves reasonably; but we ought to be prepared to stay until the job is done. Above all things, we should remember that the white man, too, is a personality, a personality we no more wish to destroy than to have our own personalities destroyed."

Here Dickerson represents a growing feeling among responsible Negro clergymen that the Negro minister must assume some responsibility for protecting society from the consequences of the white man's bias and helping the white man toward a kind of self-reclamation.

In Atlanta there is a strong Republican tradition among Negroes, and they have labored tirelessly for a two-party system in Georgia. Mr. Dickerson has no political ambitions of his own, but he works hard in the Fulton County Republican Club, "not just for the sake of party partisanship, but in or-der that all our people may be freed eventually from the tyranny of a single party."

His colleagues in the ministry hold Pastor Dickerson in high respect, as does the white establishment with which he is in constant contact. It is not a patronizing attitude with the latter. Warden David Heritage of the Atlanta Federal Penitentiary called Dickerson "as able a chaplain as I have seen without regard to race. And a good man." When Mr. Dickerson was named chairman of a grievance committee dealing with a civil-rights issue, a Negro service station attend-ant said: "I ain't a-tall wor-ried. So long as Reverend Dickerson is going to be the one to talk to them white folks, you don't have to worry about getting sold out."

THERE are still Negro ministers in the South and elsewhere who belong to the stereotype of ill-prepared, money-grubbing, chicken-eating, women-chasing, gold-toothed frauds, but they are, as I have said, a vanishing breed. Here and there a Baptist congregation still shows its "appreciation" of its minister by giving him a new Cadillac and a "love offering" of several thousand dollars a year, but such behavior is fast becoming obsolete.

When the Negro's only sense of prestige and dignity was derived vicariously through the person and status of his minister, it was understandable and perhaps even pardonable. When Negroes were hungry, they fed the preacher; when ragged, they clothed him with expensive suits; while they walked, they bought the pastor a big car.

But times have changed. Every man is now in search of his own dignity, and he expects his minister to lead him in finding it. Those unprepared to lead are on their way out.

July 12, 1964

The Clergy Heeds A New Call

By JOHN COGLEY

SANTA BARBARA, Calif. **W**HAT patrols Southern streets in bands, wears hoods, carries crosses—and is not the Ku Klux Klan? According to a recent editorial in Commonweal the answer is obvious—nuns. The Commonweal writer recalled that when two Roman Catholic sisters joined a civil rights picket line in Chicago in 1963, their pictures appeared on front pages from coast to coast. Two years later, the participation of nuns in street demonstrations has almost ceased to be newsworthy. Not only in Alabama but in sympathy marches across the nation, the sisters, in common with Protestant deaconesses and conventionally dressed churchwomen of all faiths, have joined Protestant, Jewish, Orthodox and Roman Catholic clergymen and lay leaders in public demonstrations of support for Negro rights.

The participation of the clergy and other religious leaders in the Alabama marches was the most telling expression of massive white middle-class support that the Negro Revolution has received since it got under way with the Montgomery bus strike a decade ago. To be sure, hundreds of clerics and seminary students showed up for the Washington march in the summer of 1963. But the recent demonstrations were the first in which church leaders in force ventured to move into hostile and actually dangerous territory in support of the cause.

The clergy involved were not all young insurgents, either. Among those who responded to Martin Luther King's appeal for clerical marchers in Selma last month were a number of middle-aged bishops, distinguished divinity-school professors and sedate denominational chiefs. Within hours

JOHN COGLEY, a former editor of Commonweal, is on the staff of the Fund for the Republic in Santa Barbara.

after the first telephone calls were made, they arrived in Selma from all parts of the nation, not knowing quite what to expect but ready for anything.

The Rev. Dr. Martin Marty, a Lutheran theologian who teaches at the University of Chicago's Divinity School and is an editor of the Christian Century, was one of those who volunteered to round up candidates for the trip South. "I had no trouble," he said. "Just about everyone was willing. Piggy banks were raided and people borrowed money, but somehow airline tickets were purchased. Classes and rectory appointments were canceled, and off we went. We did not know what awaited us. I don't know how anyone else felt, but I for one was scared. Still, that is why I went. I don't believe in safe gestures. A man who is an editor of the Christian Century and a professor at the university, like me, doesn't have to fear economic reprisals for marching in Chicago or Washington. But Selma was different. There was an element of physical danger there. It was a time to stand up and be counted."

Hundreds of other clergymen agreed after watching television reports from Alabama. The time had come, they were convinced, not only to pray but to act for civil rights. They acted by praying and singing liberation hymns, not within the comfortable confines of their own churches but on the streets of a beleaguered, tense city under the gaze of the network cameras and the hostile taunts of white churchgoers. And within days the clergy-in-the-streets movement spread all over the nation.

After the death of the Rev. James Reeb, the minister who was murdered in Selma, memorial marches were hastily organized in dozens of American communities, with local clergymen and church leaders of all persua-sions playing a leading role. In many towns bearded rabbis and Orthodox priests marched beside bearded beat-niks and exuberant collegians. Catholic monks marched with Protestant ministers, and sophisticated new-school theologians joined with lusty Bible-thumpers as all held hands and sang the stirring anthem of The Movement, "We Shall Not Be Moved." Theological differences and ancient hostilities faded but theological "concern" grew in a new version of Brotherhood Week, as they publicly demonstrated for a common Protestant - Catholic-Orthodox-Jewish-humanist ideal of liberty, fraternity and equality.

TAKE our town — Santa Barbara. Calif. Only a few years ago the city received national attention and a dubious reputation for being a center of John Birch Society activities and bitter ultraconservatism. But the death of Mr. Reeb was solemnly marked here as elsewhere by an inter-racial memorial parade down the city's main thoroughfare, a civic ceremony at the City Hall, and a solemn religious service at the Franciscan Mission, which is the historic symbol of the whole community.

Marching with clergymen from most of the Protestant denominations in the area were white-robed Holy Cross Fathers from the Episcopal mountaintop monastery which overlooks the city, dozens of brown-robed friars from the Santa Barbara Mission seminary, and 60 Sisters of the Immaculate Heart, a California order of teaching nuns. The sisters carried colorful homemade banners with the words "No More Segregation," "Love," or "Freedom Now" and quoting antiracist phrases from Pope John's encyclicals.

Most of the marching nuns were young. Some were new to convent life. A few

The Religion of Black Americans

still wore the schoolgirl costume of the postulant. "This," one of these aspiring nuns said, "is really the first time I have ever appeared in public identified as a sister—what a wonderful way to begin the new life."

The memorial service for the slain Unitarian minister at the Mission was typical of the new look in America's religious life. First, the marchers gathered on the broad steps of the Mission church, the nuns and friars outnumbering the laity. There they were led in the singing of rhythmic gospel hymns and songs of social protest by a Protestant Negro veteran of the civil-rights movement. Then, inside the Roman Catholic Church, a memorial mass was said, with the eulogy of Mr. Reeb delivered by the Franciscan pastor.

In the congregation were representatives of Mr. Reeb's own faith, including the local Unitarian minister. Protestants of the various denominations with their pastors, and Jews, as well as agnostics and nonbelievers who were drawn to the church for this special occasion. As the Roman Catholic mass progressed, most of them joined with the friars in singing Martin Luther's "A Mighty Fortress Is Our God" and the familiar Protestant doxology, "Praise God From Whom All Blessings Flow."

Thus the service became not only an example of admiration for the kind of religious "involvement" symbolized by Mr. Reeb, and of unity in the civil-rights movement, but a moving expression of the ecumenical spirit.

IT is hard to separate these two developments—ecumenism and the struggle for human equality — in contemporary American religion. For as the ecumenical movement has grown in significance, so has religious involvement in the civil-rights movement. One has fed on the other.

Most of the churches in recent years have been seeking for a new relationship not only with each other but with the world outside the sanctuary. The Vatican Council is only the most dramatic example of this. The theological enterprise in all the major faiths of America, in fact, has been largely a matter of establishing the social "relevance" of religion to the life men are called upon to live in the contemporary world. Participation in the struggle for Negro rights, then, has provided an ideal outlet for religious leaders seeking to be closer to those of other faiths and to

work with them in a common cause.

Practically no religious body within the bounds of respectable orthodoxy is not on record now as denouncing pride of blood and proclaiming universal human brotherhood, though all are bedeviled by the problem of the faithful (and frequently their pastors as well) talking one way and acting another. There is general agreement among them that the churches of America have not led as they should have in practicing the brotherhood they all preach.

Many of the faithful are still not used to nuns and members of the clergy who have lifted a page from the radical movement's book and have taken to dramatizing the antiracist position of their churches on the streets of the nation. Millions of churchgoers were delighted to see the religious "concern" expressed publicly, but even more were shocked by it.

The latter cannot all be put into the same prosegregation bag. For there are churchgoers who are not opposed to integration but believe that clerical participation in The Movement is undignified and unfitting. Moreover, they will tell you, it verges on a dangerous admixture of religion and politics. They feel that the churches should confine themselves to proclaiming general moral statements and that the actual working-out of these statements in the political arena is the prerogative of the laity.

Other churchgoers, both North and South, are frankly or secretly opposed to racial integration and support the American version of *apartheid*. These people tend to dismiss the procivil-rights clergy simply as the victims of political naiveté and susceptibility to the "propaganda" of Negro leaders and "liberal do-gooders." For them, the sight of marching nuns and parading parsons constitutes a kind of scandal and "perversion" of religion to crassly "political" purposes.

The Gallup poll found that 32 per cent of white Americans approved the clergy's participation in the marches, 56 per cent disapproved and 12 per cent had no opinion. Protestants tend to be more disapproving than either Catholics or Jews. Sixty per cent of the Protestants polled disapproved, whereas 44 per cent of the Catholics (who are largely based in the North) disapproved and 40 per cent positively approved. Though no further figures are cited, the poll stated that persons of the Jewish faith expressed

a higher degree of approval than either Protestants or Catholics.

RELIGIOUS participation in the drive for equality is not new, of course. Dr. King is, after all, a minister of the Gospel and his movement has had an evangelical aspect from the beginning. For many years, too, all the major denominations have been hearing strong minority voices within their own walls demanding that they abandon segregation themselves and rouse the consciences of their members against the evils of racism in the secular society. But, in spite of these efforts, there is solid reason for organized religion to have a bad conscience in the matter.

Racial discrimination in America could not have persisted so long had the churches taken a stand earlier. And there is still a sting in the charge that the most segregated hour in American life, in the North as well as the South, is 11 o'clock on Sunday morning.

When the Negro author Louis Lomax points out in parish halls that brothels were desegregated long before houses of God were opened to all, and as a matter of fact are still ahead, his audiences have no choice but to admit the truth of the blistering charge. Only a few years ago Dean Liston Pope of the Yale Divinity School declared that "the church has lagged behind the Supreme Court as the conscience of the nation on the question of race, and it has fallen far behind trade unions, factories, schools, department stores, athletic gatherings and most other human associations, as far as the achievement of integration in its own life is concerned"—and there was no one to contradict him.

THERE is, then, a feeling of guilt hanging over many of the older clergy and lay leaders. But they are determined to make up for past failures by assisting the drive for equality in the present hour of crisis, even to the point of becoming a "spectacle before God and man." This resolution on the part of church leaders was first tested during a National Conference on Religion and Race, a meeting held in Chicago in January, 1963.

The conference, which was initiated by a 31-year-old layman, Mathew Ahmann, executive director of the National Catholic Conference for Interracial Justice, was ultimately carried out under the joint sponsorship of agencies of the National Council of Churches of Christ, the Synagogue Council of America and

the National Catholic Welfare Conference. It turned out to be a historic assemblage, the effects of which will be felt for years to come.

The three-day meeting—the first of its kind—was attended by 657 delegates, most of them highly influential leaders in their synagogues, churches and denominations.

Before they left Chicago, the delegates issued "An Appeal to the Conscience of the American People." In it they described racism as the nation's "most serious domestic evil." They unequivocally endorsed recent Supreme Court decisions against segregation and the nonviolent protests then taking place. They acknowledged that "patterns of segregation" remain entrenched in all sections of the country.

In their appeal the delegates asked Americans "to seek a reign of justice in which voting rights and equal protection of the law will be everywhere enjoyed; public facilities and private ones serving a public purpose will be accessible to all; equal education and cultural opportunities, hiring and promotion, medical and hospital care, open occupancy in housing will be available to all."

Finally, they called upon the American people "to work, to pray and to act courageously in the cause of human equality and dignity while there is still time, to eliminate racism permanently and decisively, to seize the historic opportunity the Lord has given us for healing an ancient rupture in the human family, to do this for the glory of God."

Then they went home.

For a while it seemed as if nothing much had come out of their meeting, despite the courageous and humble admissions of past failures and the high resolution to do better. But when young Mr. Ahmann and others went to work two years later to round up clergymen to go to Selma, the determination and enthusiasm of the closing hours of the Chicago meeting were revived.

THE climax now being reached by the civil-rights movement coincides with a general ferment in the various faiths. Not for generations has organized religion in America been more vital than it is today, though it is a period of reassessment and reevaluation. Especially in the Roman Catholic and other hierarchical churches, it is also marked by a "crisis of obedience'' among the young. Obedience to the Spirit seems more important to them than conformity to convention and tradition. This ''crisis'' was dramatized by the participation in the Alabama demonstrations of many young priests and nuns who came despite the disapproval of the local Catholic bishop.

Only five years ago, the leaders of The Movement, given the fact of the local bishop's objection, could not have expected so many who live under the Catholic vow of obedience to answer the call for clerical volunteers. The word would in all likelihood have come down from on high that priests and sisters ''are out of place in these demonstrations—their place is at home doing God's work,'' and that would have been enough.

Actually these were the words which Archbishop Thomas J. Toolen of the Roman Catholic diocese of Mobile-Birmingham used to express his displeasure with the invasion of Northern clergy into his domain in March. But in spite of Archbishop Toolen's disapproval, the Catholic clergy and relig-

ious impenitently moved into his diocese in no smaller number than the less restricted members of the Protestant clergy. They did not seek Archbishop Toolen's permission, though it is customary for visiting priests and religious to defer to the local bishop. The canon law of the Roman Catholic Church, however, does not precisely provide for picketing or demonstrating clergy. So on the technical grounds that the case was not covered by specific legislation, clearances from the local chancery office were not sought.

Archbishop Toolen, 79 and a native of Baltimore, has been the bishop of the Alabama diocese since 1927. It is clear that he sees the situation with the eyes of a Southerner and an old-school conservative churchman. It was no great surprise then that he spoke out against the visiting Catholic clergy, as his Southern counterparts in other faiths spoke snappishly of ''interference'' from ''do-gooders'' and ''interlopers'' among their own denominational brethren.

''I do not believe that priests

are equipped to lead groups in disobedience to the laws of the state,'' Archbishop Toolen told a St. Patrick's Day audience tartly. Martin Luther King is ''dividing the people,'' he added. These demonstrations, the elderly prelate concluded, are ''not helping things at all . . . There are crazy people on both sides. As good citizens we should try to control them.''

This was the kind of advice and paternal direction that the younger clergy, Protestant and Catholic, or spirited nuns and other churchwomen who took part in the Selma demonstration, are simply no longer ready to take, whether it comes from bishops, shocked members of the laity or angry trustees. They tend, rather, to go along with Msgr. Josiah Chatham, a Jackson, Miss., pastor, who called Dr. King ''one of the truly great men of this age'' and who praised the clergy of all faiths who ''have come into our Southland to prod our Southern conscience.''

The South, said Monsignor Chatham, has a ''clear vocation'' to confess . . . ''to repent, to die to its sin, to rise and,

having risen, to lead America out of the poisonous fogs of hypocrisy, brutality and injustice which envelop much of this nation as they envelop us.''

Dr. King himself, speaking of the massive display of religious ''concern'' at Selma, declared that ''it has identified the Church with the struggle in a way that has not existed before and has made it clear that civil rights is, at the very bottom, a moral issue.''

SELMA was a high moment in America's religious history as well as in its eternal search for freedom. It was a new beginning for a movement that may roll faster than even the civil-rights struggle itself —a movement to relate religious doctrine to life, to bring noble ideals and abstract professions of brotherly love down to earth where—these pioneer demonstrators showed — they have always belonged. ''God's work''—as Archbishop Toolen calls it, as President Kennedy once reminded us—is the work of man, on earth. It is to be done wherever fear or hatred, suspicion or prejudice thrive.

May 2, 1965

New Orleans Prelate Is Named To Head Chicago Archdiocese

Pope Picks Archbishop Cody, a Leader in Integration— He Is Due to Be Cardinal

By NAN ROBERTSON
Special to The New York Times
WASHINGTON, June 16—Pope Paul VI today appointed Archbishop John Patrick Cody of New Orleans as Archbishop of Chicago, the biggest see in the United States with 2.3 million Roman Catholics.

Archbishop Cody has been a strong advocate of racial justice in the largest Catholic diocese in the South. He was characterized by Catholic officials here as conservative on theology.

The announcement came simultaneously today from the Vatican and the Apostolic Delegate to the United States in Washington, the most Rev. Egidio Vagnozzi, who said he expected Archbishop Cody to get the red hat of a Cardinal soon.

The newly appointed prelate is 57 years old. He fills the post left vacant by the death last April 9 of Albert Gregory Cardinal Meyer. His elevation to the rank of Cardinal is not automatic, but traditional for the spiritual leader of the largest diocese in any country.

In Chicago, Rabbi Seymour J. Cohen, president of the Synagogue Council of America, welcomed Archbishop Cody ''as a powerful impetus to all who labor for improvement of the position of the Negro in our country.''

Archbishop Cody came to New Orleans in November, 1961, as archbishop coadjutor. His Superior, Archbishop Joseph Francis Rummel, was ailing, near-

ly blind and facing an explosive racial problem.

Integration of all parochial schools was ordered, and it was up to Archbishop Cody to carry out the edict. In the ensuing controversy, three segregationists were excommunicated and Archbishop Cody was widely criticized by segregationists as an outsider who had forced the issue.

'Center of Communications'

Archbishop Vagnozzi, who presided at today's press conference in the Vatican delegation's stone palazzo on Massachusetts Avenue, called Chicago ''next to New York, the most important and most influential See in the United States.''

"It is the center of communications, even from a Catholic point of view, and of missionary dioceses," he said.

Chicago's Archbishop rules over 457 parishes, 437 grade schools, 90 high schools, six colleges and universities and 22 hospitals. The Archdiocese covers Cook and Lake counties, an area of 1,411 square miles.

In Catholic population, the New York archdiocese ranks second, with 1.8 million persons, and Boston third, with 1.7 million.

There are 45,000 Negro Catholics in Chicago, and it was hinted in Washington today that Archbishop Cody might name a Negro auxiliary bishop by next year.

The speculation here was that Archbishop Cody would be elevated to cardinal at the next consistory of the College of Cardinals in Rome, perhaps following the fourth and final session of the ecumenical council, which begins Sept. 14.

There are now five United States cardinals.

Indirect Backing Seen
Special to The New York Times

ROME, June 16—Archbishop Cody's selection by the Pontiff from the three candidates submitted—the other names are never revealed—constituted at least indirect papal endorsement of his stand on segregation, in the opinion of observers here. The Pope has made several statements condemning racial discrimination.

Archbishop Cody's choice as head of the Chicago Archdiocese followed a long process of winnowing by United States bishops and Vatican officials.

Members of the United States hierarchy are normally asked to submit lists of names of prelates they consider eligible for major appointments. The leading candidates in this poll are studied by the Apostolic Delegate to the United States, and the confidential assessments of bishops in neighboring dioceses are solicited.

From this information, the Apostolic Delegate submits three names to the consistorial congregation in Rome, together with a detailed analysis of each. After review by the curial body, the names are then submitted to the Pope for final selection.

Hailed in Chicago

CHICAGO, June 16 (AP)— Mayor Richard J. Daley and leaders of many faiths expressed pleasure today at the appointment of Archbishop Cody as Archbishop of Chicago.

"All Chicago joins me in extending congratulations to you on your appointment as Archbishop of Chicago," Mayor Daley said in a telegram to the prelate. "We look with great expectation to your coming to our city."

Dr. Donald E. Zimmerman, executive of the Presbytery of Chicago of the United Presbyterian Church, said:

"We congratulate Chicago Roman Catholics on the appointment of Archbishop Cody. He will find here an uncommon foundation for the further pursuit of genuine ecumenical dialogue and action. We welcome him to the fraternity of those who are committed to turning the face of this city in the direction of the Kingdom."

June 17, 1965

Dr. King Condemns 'Blatant Hypocrisy' Of White Churches

Special to The New York Times

GENEVA, July 17—The Rev. Dr. Martin Luther King Jr. said in a prepared sermon today that the American Negro was "usually greeted by a cold indifference or blatant hypocrisy" when he called on the "so-called white churches."

"One of the shameful tragedies of history is that the very institutions which should remove men from the midnight of racial segregation participate in creating and perpetuating the midnight,"

Dr. King said in the sermon that was recorded yesterday in Chicago.

More than 400 delegates to a World Conference on Church and Society saw only an empty pulpit as Dr. King's voice rang through St. Peter's Cathedral.

Dr. King's appearance was to have been a major highlight of the two-week conference organized by the World Council of Churches.

But the United States civil rights leader canceled his visit because, he said, the riots in Chicago required his presence there.

The theme of his sermon was that the world is in a moral and social darkness with many people failing to find the guidance they look for in the church.

"In the terrible midnight of war," Dr. King said, "men have knocked on the door of the church to ask for the bread of peace, but the church often disappoints them."

"Millions of Africans, patiently knocking on the door of the Christian church where they seek the bread of social justice have either been altogether ignored or told to wait until later, which almost always means never," he said.

Dr. King said that "those who have gone to the church to seek the bread of economic justice have been left in the frustrating midnight of economic deprivation."

"If the church does not recapture its prophetic zeal it will become an irrelevant social club without moral or spiritual authority," he warned.

July 18, 1966

Five Denominations Of Protestants Said To Ignore Negroes

Special to The New York Times

WASHINGTON, Oct. 19—The head of the Rockefeller Fund for Theological Education said today that five influential Protestant denominations in the United States, were ignoring their Negro congregations.

The Rev. Dr. C. Shelby Rooks, executive secretary of the fund, said that the American Baptist Convention, the Episcopal, the Methodist, the United Presbyterian Churches, and the United Church of Christ had "virtually excluded Negroes from the centers of denominational power and decision making."

Dr. Rooks said that he could cite only five denominations because Negro membership in other predominantly white denominations was so small that few generalizations of importance could be made about them.

Speaking before a group of Negro leaders of the United Church of Christ here, Dr. Rooks, himself a Negro, said that the five denominations had never had a "clear, conscious, or positive denominational attitude or strategy toward Negro members, clergy or churches."

"No Negro, so far as I know, is pastor of a major white church," Dr. Rooks said.

He said that Negroes made up only 2 per cent of the United Church of Christ membership and contributed only 1 per cent of its income.

Dr. Rooks is an ordained minister of the United Church of Christ. He took it to task because only about 3 per cent of its pulpits are filled by Negroes.

October 20, 1966

Pastor Active in Rights Is Asked To Quit Swarthmore, Pa., Pulpit

Special to The New York Times

SWARTHMORE, Pa., Nov. 21 — The pastor of the fashionable Swarthmore Presbyterian Church has been asked to resign because of civil rights activity and what was called his failure to preach more sermons on "peace of mind" and the "joy of salvation."

He is the Rev. Dr. Evor Roberts, a 47-year-old clergyman who has been pastor of the church for the last eight years. Dr. Roberts had picketed during racial demonstrations in nearby Chester and he participated in the Montgomery, Ala., civil rights march last spring.

He was asked to resign by a special counseling committee set up with the aid of the Philadelphia Presbytery.

The committee was named eight months ago at the joint request of Dr. Roberts and the church session, its governing body of ruling elders.

At that time the session had questioned the effects of the minister's civil rights activities on church membership and contributions by the congregation.

Similar problems have arisen in a number of Protestant churches in both the North and the South.

Six years ago the church listed 1,850 members. Its membership today is 1,604.

The committee's report was made public at yesterday's worship service.

"If Dr. Roberts had balanced his sermons by more frequent references to peace of mind, the joy of salvation, the love of God, the therapy of faith, etc.," it said, "many of the problems would have been minimized and never have arisen to the surface of the relationship between pastor and people."

The committee said it had wondered "to what extent—if at all—these difficulties would have arisen, had not the moderator by spoken word and personal action taken a strong stand on the civil rights issue."

Many worshipers wept as they heard the report read and their pastor's reply.

Dr. Roberts said he was "deeply distressed" that the problem had not been solved "without a tearing of the fabric of the congregation's life."

He said he had asked himself "if you think that I have been a faithless shepherd to you, that I have not cared for you or about you, that I have been lured away to other interests, other causes."

Referring to his participation in the Chester demonstrations two years ago, he reminded his parishioners that he had told them from the pulpit what he was doing and why.

Dr. Roberts quoted from the church's Book of Common Worship that instructs pastors to be "concerned for the work of the kingdom beyond your own parish."

"Perhaps," he said, "even those who have opposed me will admit that I have shown some concern for the welfare of my brethren in other churches, some of those brethren having a skin not the color of most of you."

He told the congregation that he has not yet resigned, but was accepting the committee's recommendations and would seek a new call.

The committee report declared that the basic difficulty lay in the "difference in the understanding of what the church of Jesus Christ is doing and what it ought to be doing." The committee said this difference was highlighted by two concerns—"civil rights and the statistical trends of the Swarthmore church."

It dismissed other criticisms, including contentions that "he is not warm enough, he does not make enough pastorals calls, his sermons are not spiritual enough, his sermons frequently fail to comfort and generally disturb because they are on controversial topics and he changes the order of the worship service without notice or preparation."

A minister in the Presbyterian Church cannot be dismissed by the congregation, but only by the vote of the presbytery, the denomination's area governing unit.

Swarthmore is a well-to-do community in the western suburbs of Philadelphia. Its most notable landmark is Swarthmore College, founded by the Quakers in 1864.

The committee report said that in six years the number of pledging units at the church had dropped from 778 to 546, but in the same period the per capita pledge had risen from $154 to $207. A pledging unit is a single pledge that could come from a family or an individual.

"The per capita increase, when compared with the decrease in pledging units," it declared, "poses a thorny dilemma that defies off-hand or unstudied explanation."

It continued:

"We feel, that the minister has sometimes been lacking in tact and diplomacy, that he should have recognized the deteriorating situation and taken a more active hand in trying to do everything in his power to correct it.

"He should have recognized that his first and major responsibility was to the membership of the congregation that called him. He should have consulted with the entire session, taking the elders into his confidence in everything concerning the Swarthmore church."

November 22, 1966

Negro Clergymen Form National Unit To Work in Ghettos

Special to The New York Times

DALLAS, Nov. 3—A group of Negro clergymen set themselves up today as the National Committee of Negro Churchmen, dedicated to "giving black people more control over their own destinies."

The Rev. Calvin Marshall, spokesman for the group, hailed the action "as a symbol of the end of the era in which predominantly white denominations would determine the nature of church activities in Negro ghettos."

"The era of welfare colonialism is over," he declared. "If white Christianity feels any sort of obligation to do anything about the ghettos, it will now have to work through the people who live there."

The committee was formed on an ad hoc basis in July, 1966, to issue a statement interpreting the meaning of black power.

Subsequent statements on issues such as the crisis in the cities have involved approximately 700 Negro churchmen.

This week, about 75 Negro clergymen met for three days at St. John's Baptist Church here to draw up a formal constitution.

At the closing session this morning the group elected Bishop Herbert Bell Shaw of the African Methodist Episcopal Zion Church in Wilmington, Del., as its president. The Rev. M. L. Wilson, pastor of the Convention Avenue Baptist Church in Harlem, was named chairman of the board.

An executive director will be appointed later.

The delegates approved an Economic Redevelopment Corporation, which leaders said would be the principal operating arm of the new organization.

November 4, 1967

Storefront Churches Draw Harlem Newcomers

The New York Times (by Don Charles)

Bishop George Wiley addressing his congregation in the Mount Hebron Apostolic Temple.
Some seek in smaller churches something more personal.

By EARL CALDWELL

It was near 11 A.M. and the music from the shabby little storefront churches scattered along Eighth Avenue in Central Harlem drifted out into the empty street.

There was the Second Tabernacle Baptist Church, Mount Hebron Apostolic Temple and Mount Sharion Baptist. And across the street there were the United Pentacostal Church and the Church of God.

In the block between 133d and 134th Streets there were five of the little churches, which because of their smallness attract Harlem newcomers, people who have trouble adjusting to the big, established churches.

A neatly dressed Negro woman who said that her name was Mrs. McKee wandered into Mount Hebron Apostolic Temple.

A Significant Service

"I'm from Salem Methodist Church," she told the small congregation after the service. "But it's too large for me. I want to dress myself in Jesus; I want personal baptism, and I heard you before when I passed by and today I thought that I'd come in."

There were only about a dozen people in the little church, and Bishop George Wiley listened as each of the guests introduced himself to the regular members of Mount Hebron Temple.

He welcomed Mrs. McKee and promised her that he would baptize her again.

Around the corner on Seventh Avenue at 129th Street,

Dr. Roy Nichols sat in his office at Salem Methodist Church, one of Harlem's larger congregations, and talked about "the smaller sidewalk churches."

"They render a significant service," he explained. "Many people come here [to Harlem] from a rural background and they cannot adjust to the larger church.

They need a small setting, and the sidewalk church provides that."

Dr. Nichols did not call them storefront churches. "They don't like that," he explained. "It's something of a stigma for them, and they are trying to get away from it."

The differences between a

Carrying her Bible and a Sunday paper, a parishioner leaves the Mount Hebron Apostolic Temple.

small storefront church like Mount Hebron and a larger Harlem church, such as Salem Methodist Church, are many.

Salem has 2,650 members on its rolls, and yesterday at the 11 A.M. service there were more than 1,000 persons in attendance.

Dr. Nichols's sermon reflected the church's concern with the community's social problems. He talked about education in Harlem schools, and he condemned the recent attacks on school officials.

"We're losing the battle for education," he told his congregation, "because there is not much work going on in the schools."

He discussed the community's need for more adequate and prepared teachers, for discipline in the schools and for parents to provide an atmosphere conducive to learning in the homes.

Stay After Service

In his sermon, Bishop Wiley concentrated on the salvation of the individual. "Get right with God," he warned his small congregation. "You need him, he doesn't need you."

At Mount Hebron most of the worshipers were older women and younger children whom they had brought along. In contrast, Salem Methodist was filled with families, husbands and wives and many teen-aged youths who had stayed over after Sunday School.

After the service, nearly half the members of the congregation adjourned to the social activity area, where they chatted over a home-cooked dinner.

"A lot of the people like to

Marguerite B. Smith and William Lester sharing a hymnal during services at Salem Methodist Church

stay around after church," Dr. Nichols explained. "Some of them stay here for hours, just talking and socializing with one another."

Inside the Mount Hebron storefront church there were only rows of plain wooden folding chairs and the plain pulpit that Bishop Wiley used sparingly while delivering his sermon from the aisle.

Salem Methodist had rows of new pews in the main auditorium and a balcony that seated about 500 persons. In addition, the church had just completed a major construction project in which it built an $800,000 community center.

Salem also makes a strong appeal to its younger membership. It has a special children's choir, it offers scholar-

ship help to any member attending college and it sponsors a wide range of activities that vary from a Boy Scout troop to a bowling league for teen-agers.

But Salem is not considered a "rich" church in the community.

Drives a Cadillac

"More than 80 per cent of our people live right here in Central Harlem," Dr. Nichols said. "And we have one lawyer and one doctor and a handful of schoolteachers. The rest are just average wage earners in the low-income bracket."

But it is Bishop Wiley from the storefront church and not the minister of Salem Methodist who drives a Cadillac.

"His people want him to

drive a Cadillac," another minister explained. "They helped him buy it, but actually the car is more of a church bus than his personal car. If you watch, you will see that he rides members of his congregation around in the car. They use it for church meetings in other areas of the city and out of town. Things like that."

Many of the worshipers at the storefront church are people who live next door or on the same block. In being new to the city, some have not yet been able to find jobs or make friends in the community. So they come to the little church to find the personal relationships that they left behind.

"Some of the people in those little churches go there because they don't think that they have the clothes or the prestige to

go to a big church," a member of a larger church explained. "They don't feel embarrassed down there. They feel more at home."

'Robe and Everything'

The storefront church has its own way of making its members feel that they are part of the church.

One is with music.

At Mount Sharion there were 12 persons in the choir, three ushers, five church officers and less than a dozen "just plain members."

"If you want to sing, you sing. You're a part of the choir. Reverend Sawyer [the minister at Mount Sharion] sees to that," a member of the church said. "You're in the choir and you get a robe and everything, just like everyone else."

Many persons who join the storefront churches when they arrive in New York leave them once they become settled in the community. But others stay on for years.

Nondenominational Churches

For the most part, these sidewalk churches do not become involved in social problems although their ministers often deliver stern lectures against the evils of narcotics, liquor and gambling.

Unlike the larger churches in Harlem, the storefront church generally does not belong to any denominational organization and does not demand that its pastor be an ordained minister.

But like the larger churches, many of them also have grand plans that they hope to implement some day.

Each Sunday at Mount Sharion they take a special collection for the "building fund," and on one wall in the church there is a picture of a neat little church. Over the picture of the new church is written "Mt. Sharion Baptist Church Building Fund $125,000." On Sunday, the building fund reported donations of $71.

January 29, 1968

Negro Priests Assail Catholic Church as Racist

Special to The New York Times

DETROIT, April 18 — A group of Negro Roman Catholic priests today called the Catholic Church in the United States "primarily a white racist institution" and called for changes in church thinking and action.

The denunciation came in a statement of the "Black Catholic Clergy Caucus," made up of priests attending the Catholic clergy conference on the interracial apostolate in the Sheraton Cadillac Hotel.

The conference is considered unofficial by the Catholic hierarchy, but Detroit's Archbishop, the Most Rev. John F. Dearden,

spoke to the group.

The conference amounts to a lobbying effort designed to obtain the support of Bishops for church programs to help ease racial problems. It was attended by 387 persons, including 58 Negro priests. Conference officials said that of 11,000 priests in the United States only 170 were Negro. Of the Negroes, 120 are actually engaged in conference work, the officials said.

The black caucus statement said:

"Because of its past implicit

and active support of prevailing attitudes and institutions of America, the church is now in an extremely weak position in the black community. In fact, the Catholic Church is rapidly dying in the black community. In many cases, there is a serious defection, especially on the part of black Catholic youth."

The statement demanded the following:

¶That there be "black priests in decision-making positions on the diocesan level and, above all, in the black community."

¶That every effort be made

to recruit Negroes for the priesthood.

¶That dioceses "provide centers of training for white priests intending to survive in black communities."

¶That within the framework of the United States Catholic Conference "a black directed department be set up to deal with the church's role in the struggle of black people for freedom."

¶That Negroes, married and single, "be ordained permanent deacons."

¶That each diocese allocate substantial sums to set up programs for black leadership training.

April 19, 1968

Jewish Community Is Debating Black Anti-Semitism

By HENRY RAYMONT

Confronted by racial and religious hatred brought to the surface by the city's school crisis, a shocked Jewish community is debating what to do about it.

Fed by black extremist propaganda, an impression has developed among some Jews that anti-Semitism, which seemed safely out of the way after World War II, is on the increase and must be vigorously countered.

Other Jews, however, while equally distressed by recent anti-Semitic outbursts, fear that an overly defensive reaction might bring on a backlash and hasten the political anti-Semitism that all Jews seek to avoid.

Jewish community leaders, intellectual journals and religious and secular organizations are not only debating the magnitude of anti-Semitism among Negroes and hostility directed by Jews against blacks, but also the way in which public officials, private foundations and public-minded citizens are responding to the problem.

Typical of some Jewish opinion on this point was a recent editorial in Reconstructionist, the publication of the Jewish Reconstructionist Foundation, an organization that stresses a flexible interpretation of the traditions of Judaism. The editorial said:

"Extremism, which is of the very essence of rapid change, is bound to seek scapegoats and the Jews are ready victims—not alone because of inherited prejudices but because Jews have had to move into those exposed positions in society which were available to them—that is, not already pre-empted by the establishments."

The debate, which reflects the mood of fear and frustration increasingly pervading the Jewish community at large—in synagogues, community centers and social clubs—is concentrated in these general themes:

¶That anti-Semitic utterances and literature employed by a handful of black power extremists in the school dispute is tolerated by too many Negroes as a convenient weapon in their competition for jobs held by Jews in the teaching, school administration and social welfare fields.

¶That public officials and non-Jewish civic leaders did not speak out soon and vigorously enough at the first signs of anti-Semitic propaganda during last fall's series of teachers' strikes.

¶That by using anti-Semitism as a political strategy, black power extremists may be finding unwitting allies among politicians eager to maintain racial peace in the cities, even at the expense of working class and Jewish interests.

Jewish concern received perhaps its strongest expression in a report on the school dispute issued last week by the Anti-Defamation League of B'nai B'rith. Warning that anti-Semitism had reached "a crisis level" in the city's schools, the report concluded that the incitement against Jews was allowed to gain momentum "by the failure of New York City public officials to condemn it swiftly and strongly enough, and to remove from positions of authority those who have utilized anti-Semitism."

On Friday, Bernard Botein, the retired justice who headed the Mayor's Special Committee on Racial and Religious Prejudice, which a week earlier had completed a two-month study of hate literature circulated in the schools, added the contention that "continued silence" by most white Christian and Negro leaders was adding to the rising tide of anti-Semitism in the city.

Reaction Called Late

In an interview, Will Maslow, executive secretary of the American Jewish Congress reflected the opinions of those who believe that the intrusion of anti-Semitism into the school dispute could have been arrested if community leaders had reacted earlier.

Mr. Maslow, who attended several private meetings with Jewish leaders and the Mayor on the issue, said:

"What appalled most of the leaders of the Jewish community was the utter silence of the Christian community and Negro leadership in the face of flagrantly anti-Semitic utterances and articles. For example, it would have been tactically wise and expedient for the Ocean Hill school board to have denounced the black anti-Semites; instead they kept quiet."

After an initial criticism by some Jews that he had not acted quickly enough, the Mayor has moved firmly against what he perceives as anti-Semitism. As a result, Jewish criticism of the Mayor has become considerably muted and in some instances has turned to praise.

Among the steps Mr. Lindsay has taken in addition to appointing the Botein committee on Oct. 30, was his ordering of prompt investigation of suspicious synagogue fires; his appearing frequently before synagogue congregations to discuss forcefully the anti-Semitism issue; his requesting that the Board of Education "take appropriate action" against two black teachers, Leslie R. Campbell and Albert Vann, for alleged anti-Semitic remarks, and his denouncing the introduction to a catalogue published for the Metropolitan Museum of Art's "Harlem on My Mind" exhibition as "racist" and most particularly anti-Semitic.

Mayor Defended

In answer to criticism that the Mayor could have acted sooner, an aide said yesterday:

"The Mayor has been an effective fighter for civil liberties and civil rights all of his life, has taken the lead in condemning, most outspokenly — publicly and privately — and in acting courageously to combat racism in all of its evil guises, antiwhite, anti-Semitic and antiblack. Most of the people of the Jewish community, the black community and the entire city acknowledge his courage and leadership in this sensitive area."

Some Jewish leaders have also been encouraged of late by denunciations of anti-Semitism by some leading voices in the black community. The Amsterdam News, for example, devoted a front-page editorial last week to a condemnation of bigotry in all forms.

But the Mayor's position has created some other problems, even as he has earned renewed respect for his recent forthright stand on anti-Semitism. When the Mayor spoke out against Mr. Campbell for reading "an obviously anti-Semitic" poem over radio station WBAI, for example, Mr. Vann assailed him for attempting to "appease the powerful Jewish financiers of the city."

Remarks such as Mr. Vann's cause fear and anger in portions of the Jewish community. Other Jews, however, regard anti-Semitic expressions by Negro militants as manifestations of hostility toward all white people, or as rhetorical devices that provide emotional release.

"What I feel strongly that many people are missing," said Dore Schary, national chairman of the Anti-Defamation League, "is the fact that the black power movement is continuing an old American tradition in fighting for its rights by using stereotypic concepts.

"This stereotype came as a result of our polyglot heritage. They were used by the Irish and the Italians against the WASPS, and now they are being used by some black extremists against the Jews. It is deplorable, but we should not over-react and become hysterical."

Earl Raab, a California sociologist, is one who takes sharp issue with those who would explain Negro anti-Semitism as expressions of hostility toward white men or as rhetorical weapons.

"That is an exact and acute description of political anti-Semitism," he asserted. "'The enemy' becomes the Jew, 'the man' becomes the Jew. The villain is not so much the actual Jewish merchant on the corner as the corporate Jew who stands symbolically for generic evil. 'Don't be disturbed,' the Jews are told, 'this is just poetic excess.' But the ideology of political anti-Semitism has precisely always been poetic excess, which has not prevented it from becoming murderous."

Mr. Raab's analysis was presented in an article in the January issue of Commentary, an independent monthly of literature and political opinion published by the American Jewish Committee.

The article, "The Black Revolution and the Jewish Question," has stimulated debate among Jews because of a suggestion that anti-Semitism is evolving as a political stategy of the black power movement in the big cities to force the "white Anglo-Saxon Protestant Establishment" into concessions at the expense of Jewish interests.

'A Classic Marriage'

"There is the possibility," Mr. Raab wrote, "of a classic marriage, a manipulative symbiosis, between the privileged class and the dis-privileged mass—in this class a WASP class and a black-man—in these cities: the kind of symbiosis which existed in the nineteen-twenties between respectable Republican leaders and the Ku Klux Klan, and which permitted a temper of repression and bigotry to flourish.

"The anti-Semitic ideology developing in the black movement would be eminently suited to such purposes. Some have suggested that the edges of this possibility are actually peeking out in New York City. Certainly, whatever the outcome, this face of the black expressive movement is there for the Jewish community to contemplate with justified concern."

Another article in the same issue of Commentary, "The New York School Crisis," by Maurice J. Goldbloom, echoed Mr. Raab's concern about a potential alliance between the political establishment and black militants. It said:

"There is a widespread movement now afoot to ally the bottom and top layers of American society against those in the middle—and especially against the organized workers. This strategy has implicit assumptions; it stems from the belief on the one side that the first enemy of the man at the bottom is the man one step up, and on the other that the discontents of the most wretched can effectively be appeased without any expense of those at the top."

Crisis Confronts Jews

Norman Podhoretz, editor of Commentary, said the Raab and Goodbloom articles represented "the beginning of a far-ranging public debate of the most serious crisis confronting American Jews since World War II."

Elaborating on Mr. Raab's brief reference to New York, Mr. Podhoretz said it was an allusion to the drive by city authorities, the Urban Coalition and the Ford Foundation on behalf of school decentralization and wider control of antipoverty programs by Negroes.

"Perhaps unwittingly, this effort to weaken the influence of teachers and professional social workers is directed against the working class and also against the Jews, the two groups that happen to be predominantly on the Democratic side of party politics."

Rabbi Richard L. Rubenstein, a chaplain at the University of Pittsburgh who participated in the 1965 Freedom March to Montgomery, Ala., was one of the first members of the Jewish community to discuss the thesis of an Establishment-black militant coalition at the expense of other groups. In an interview recently, he said:

"This inevitable process has been aided by the decision of the Ford Foundation to lend its prestige and financial aid to the movement for neighborhood control of schools. Jews are the easiest and most convenient group to sacrifice before the pressure of black power takeover. The non-Jewish white community has more to gain by satisfying Negro rather than Jewish interests when they conflict."

Thesis Rejected

Most Jewish leaders identified with the civil rights movement as well as non-Jewish members of the Establishment reject this thesis, contending that the assumption of an inevitable clash of Negro-Jewish interests is a fallacy.

But a number of civic leaders have said lately that potential group frictions had been overlooked in formulating school decentralization plans.

One of these was Francis Keppel, president of the General Learning Corporation and former United States Commissioner of Education. Mr. Keppel participated in drafting the Ford Foundation's school decentralization plan. Asked to evaluate the decentralization experiment in the light of Jewish-Negro tensions, Mr. Keppel said:

"I confess not to color blindness but to insufficient acuity on anti-Semitic prejudice. We were quite aware of the racial problem, that was obvious enough. But on the other one, perhaps we didn't give it enough thought.

"Personally, I don't think I was sensitive enough to the prejudice issue. In formulating plans for greater community control in schools we made a conscious choice—that professional administrators and teachers would have to adjust to the need for more local involvement. We felt it was in the interest of the community as a whole. But we had not counted on the fallout of prejudice it produced."

Calls Articles Hindsight

Referring to the Commentary articles, he remarked cheerfully:

"If those social science fellows were so right and smart about what we did wrong, why didn't they say so at the time?"

Another attitude of the Establishment was expressed by a prominent lawyer with a distinguished record in the foreign service, who requested anonymity. Deploring some recent denunciations of anti-Semitism as "just exacerbating the situation," he declared:

"I think the Jewish community is making a mistake. I may not be an over-all judge of anti-Semitism, but several of my most valued partners are Jewish. Anti-Semitism has been on the wane ever since World War II, but this great furor has just been overemphasized by the Jewish community."

David Rockefeller, president of the Chase Manhattan Bank and a member of the executive committee of the National Urban Coalition, also expressed surprise over the intensity of the conflict touched off by the decentralization plans. The Urban Coalition is an organization that has enlisted some of the nation's most prominent businessmen in programs designed to correct society's injustices against the black poor.

"I wish I had known that the emotions would be so overheated and the tensions so great," he said. "The whole school strike has become based on a struggle between two groups that have been most subject to discrimination. That they should now be attacking one another is both ironic and tragic."

Dialogue Is Sought

Numerous attempts at establishing a dialogue are under way through such agencies as the American Jewish Committee and the National Conference of Christians and Jews, but in an atmosphere clouded by the volatile pronouncements of some black separatists and a passionate anti-Negro backlash shaping in the Jewish community, particularly within the lower middle-class.

Liberal Jewish leaders, notably Arthur J. Goldberg, who is now president of the American Jewish Committee, and Mr. Schary are using their influence to counsel prudence.

In a series of recent speeches before Jewish community groups, they have strongly cautioned against allowing exaggerated fears of anti-Semitism to disrupt the traditional Jewish support for Negro rights, including the idea of wider local controls for schools and welfare programs.

Similarly, Murray Gordon, a national vice president of the American Jewish Congress, has expressed fear that "over-reaction" will create a deep cleavage in the Jewish-Negro liberal coalition that for decades had been working toward elimination of the nation's racial problems.

"What troubles me deeply," he declared, "is that denunciation and over-reaction will keep us from dealing with the real causes of racial hatred—the slums of the ghettos, educational and job opportunities. Maybe I'm wrong, but I still tend to regard the recent outbursts as insults and not as threats, and that American society is strong enough to absorb them without any need for us to lose a proper sense of priorities with which to respond to the urban crisis as

But differences in emphasis and strategy have emerged between the liberal leaders of some of the major Jewish organizations and their professional staffs—generally made up of social scientists and researchers.

For example, in a recent letter circulated to the membership of the American Jewish Committee, Mr. Goldberg stressed that Negro anti-Semitism was still confined to an unrepresentative minority and that Jews must continue an unrelenting support for the civil rights movement.

But just a few weeks earlier, Bertram H. Gold, executive vice president of the A.J.C. and a social psychologist, cautioned the organization's annual meeting:

"Jews are beginning to feel that their national leadership is more concerned with bettering intergroup relations than protecting the interests of the Jewish community. Though we must reject demands for withdrawal from the civil rights struggle, the committee's leadership would not be fulfilling its functions if we were to ignore the legitimate demands for greater power by the Negro community at the expense of hard-won gains made by individual Jews."

Talk of retrenchment by Jews is viewed with concern by such Negro moderates as Whitney M. Young Jr., director of the National Urban League, Roy Wilkins, director of the National Association for the Advancement of Colored People, and Bayard Rustin, director of the A. Phillip Randolph Institue, all of whom have sharply condemned recent outbursts of anti-Semitism.

Mr. Rustin said in an interview that "nothing could be more terrifyingly dangerous for the Negro" than attempts to divide the liberal Catholic-Jewish-Protestant coalition that has fought for civil rights legislation.

"Negro leaders have a moral obligation to fight against anti-Semitism," he asserted. "Jews have been in the forefront of the civil rights fight and probably made more of a contribution than any single group. We cannot be timid and we cannot be silent. Negro children who themselves have been brutalized by racism ought not to be further brutalized by teaching them anti-Semitism and religious prejudice."

January 26, 1969

Black Power Drive Brings Change to Churches

By EDWARD B. FISKE

Fifteen black seminarians at the Colgate-Rochester Divinity School locked themselves in an administration building last month and gained promises by the administration to let them name nine Negro trustees.

Alongside the stubby wooden cross at the Blue Hill Soul Center in the Roxbury section of Boston are a crutch and a short rope in the shape of a noose.

"The noose is the evil that blacks have endured, and the crutch is how we've had to hobble along in the absence of power to deal with it," said the Rev. Virgil Wood, pastor at the center.

These and dozens of similar incidents are the visible signs of changing attitudes among the two million Negroes in predominantly white Protestant and Roman Catholic churches.

Hundreds of black lay-

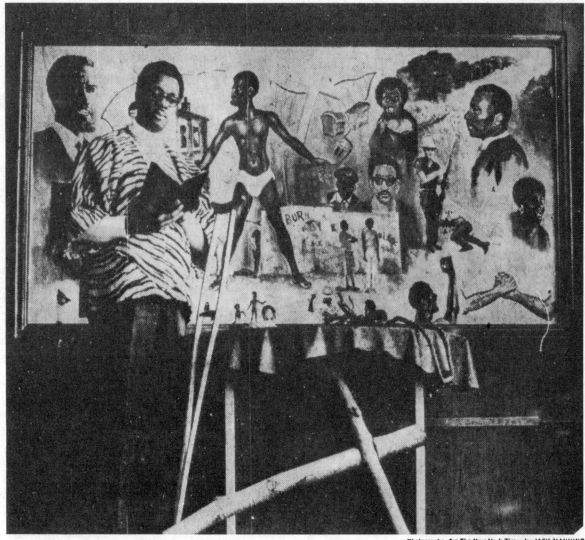

The Rev. Virgil Wood, pastor of Blue Hill Soul Center, with noose and crutch, symbols of evil and lack of power. Painting shows black heroes Malcolm X, H. Rap Brown and the Rev. Dr. Martin Luther King Jr. and scenes of violence.

men, clergymen and nuns have banded together in national caucuses to push for increased decision-making power in their particular churches. Many are experimenting with African liturgical forms and talking of interfaith alliances dubbed "soul ecumenism."

Even more fundamentally, Negro scholars are actively reshaping basic Christian teachings into theologies of black power. In most cases this is accompanied by a new-style Messianism that regards black religion as essential not only to the self-respect of Negroes but to the integrity of white Christians.

"Black theology is the only genuine manifestation of Christianity in America today," said the Rev. James H. Cone, a 30-year-old Methodist theologian who will join the faculty of Union Theological Seminary next fall. "White theology is basically racist and non-Christian."

In all-black churches, such as the African Methodist Episcopal Church, which have the allegiance of the majority of the country's black Protestants, such ideas have not taken root, largely because of a tradition of conservative leadership and the fact that they are already self-sufficient.

Many Whites Sympathetic

For their part, white church leaders have generally reacted with sympathy to the new black awareness. Edwin R. H. Espy, general secretary of the National Council of Churches, for instance, said that it was "certainly healthy that black thinkers are thinking in terms of theologies that are relevant to their experience."

He added, however, that "we should distinguish between Christian teachings and the failure of many in the churches to live up to them."

Like the black power move-

ment in general, the changes in Negro religious attitudes reflect growing black self-consciousness and an intensified search for identity. Vincent Harding, Negro historian, has termed this search "a quest for a religious reality more faithful to our own experience."

It represents an effort by black churchmen both to contribute to the black power movement by giving it a religious dimension and to retain a leadership role in the Negro community.

"The black church, like any other institution in the black community, will rise or fall on the basis of its capacity to understand the voice of black power," said the Rev. Metz Rollins, executive secretary of the National Committee of Black Churchmen, which was founded two years ago to spur black consciousness in the churches.

Like Negro leaders in other fields, black churchmen begin with the assertion that in

their institutional behavior the major denominations are as "racist" as other institutions, especially in their personnel policies.

For instance, C. Shelby Rooks, executive director of the Fund for Theological Education, complained recently in an issue of Christian Century that there were only 300 black students in 95 fully accredited seminaries and that only 39 black Americans received doctoral degrees in all seminaries and graduate departments in this country and Canada from 1953 to 1968.

Figures in the area are generally imprecise, but a New York Times survey of 11 major Protestant denominations, including several with large Southern constituencies, showed that Negroes made up an average of 2 per cent of the communicants.

In these denominations, slightly less than 2 per cent of the clergymen are black, but the number of Negroes in board positions averaged 5 per cent and the number of officials listed in last year's Yearbook of American Churches averaged 3 per cent.

The survey also disclosed no blacks held top church executive positions in this country and fewer than a dozen were in major secondary posts. Almost all of the latter were in the fields of race relations and urban affairs, such as Leon Modeste, director of an emergency urban program for the Episcopal Church.

Some recent efforts have been made to correct the situation. The Most Rev. Harold R. Perry, for instance, became two years ago the first black Catholic bishop in this country in modern times. About 4 per cent of all Catholics are Negroes, and the number of black priests is fewer than 1 per cent.

Several Protestant denominations have also channeled $700,000 in unrestricted funds into the Interreligious Foundation for Community Organization, which is run by the Rev. Lucius Walker, a Negro, with an integrated board of directors.

Even so, black leaders such as the Rev. Gayraud S. Wilmore Jr., director of race relations work for the United Presbyterian Church, still complain that church integration has been bogged down in white cultural perspectives.

"Everything black was subordinate and inferior and would have to be given up for everything white," he said.

Black students in the major seminaries, for instance, complain that their liturgy and preaching courses are designed for white churches.

Priorities Different

"It is a crime against black and white religion as well that no seminary's black students dare to preach in class as they do in their black congregations," the Rev. Henry H. Mitchell, a California Baptist pastor, said.

Negro Catholic priests also argue that their church's view of sexual morality and strict laws against the baptism of divorced persons reflect white values that are fundamentally unworkable in the black community.

"Illegitimate children and divorce are not taken with the same alarm as they are in white culture," said the Rev. Rollins Lambert, one of the few black Catholic pastors.

There is also a general consensus among black religious leaders that whites have tailored their doctrinal teachings to the shape of an oppressive social and economic class.

Dr. Wilmore, for instance, described the Christianity that was passed on to the Negro as "deliberately adulterated, defused, shorn of its most relevant and immediate ethical insights and implications for revolution."

Specifically, black theologians charge that white Christianity distorted the Gospel by emphasizing its otherworldliness and individual morality at the expense of social justice.

"The white Jesus is a pale effeminated figure who walks around gardens praying and smelling flowers," the Rev. Jesse Jackson, a 27-year-old civil rights worker in Chicago, said. "Ours is the guy who identified with lepers and stopped people from laughing at prostitutes. He's a cat who had a great capacity to redeem folks no matter what their past."

Black theologians also charge that whites have undermined the Christian concept of love by disassociating it from justice and power. On this point there is considerable criticism of the Rev. Dr. Martin Luther King Jr. on the ground that he falsely identified a secular tactic — nonviolence — with Christian love.

Black historians have also been harsh on their own past leaders for acquiescence in watering down the Gospel.

Joseph R. Washington Jr. of Albion College, for instance, wrote that the Negro church "has served as a cut-rate social outlet, selling itself for quantity rather than quality, offering cheap white medicine in colored doses of several hours of relief for a week-long headache."

In an effort to gain more decision-making power, black churchmen have organized national caucusses in 12 major churches as well as the National Committee of Black Churchmen and a National Black Sisters Conference in the Catholic Church.

Strategy Papped

All of these organizations are only a year or two old and most are still in the process of drawing up objectives and strategy.

The Black Caucus of the Unitarian-Universalist Association, however, which claims the allegiance of three-fourths of the estimated total of 1,200 black Unitarians, forced the denomination last year to give it control of a $1-million budget for social action over four years.

Black Methodists for Church Renewal, which lists 600 members, received grants of $35,000 from two divisions of the United Methodist Church and has begun to press for programs in the fields of new ministries, poverty and liberation move-

ments in southern Africa.

Black students at the Andover-Newton Seminary in Boston organized a Consultation on the Black Church last fall that drew 200 black seminarians, and black student groups have been set up in all of the major white seminaries to work for more black faculty members, courses aimed at storefront ministries and more recognition of black church history and liturgy.

There is also a growing consensus that such activities need a theological undergirding.

"The fact that I am black is part of my ultimate reality," Dr. Cone said. "Unless I accept this I cannot love either God or my neighbor."

Books dealing with such themes are beginning to appear. The Rev. Albert B. Cleage Jr., pastor of the Shrine of the Black Madonna in Detroit, for instance, has published a series of sermons entitled "The Black Messiah."

In the sermons he argues that Jesus was a "revolutionary black leader" and that blacks must seek "not the Resurrection of the physical body of Jesus but the Resurrection of the Black Nation which He started."

In "Black Theology and Black Power," which will be published next month by the Seabury Press, Dr. Cone provides a systematic overview of a "theology of black power."

Just as the so-called "theologies of hope," now popular in theological circles, begin with the presupposition that hope is the central motif of Christianity and then treat each doctrine in this light, so Dr. Cone begins with the assumption that Christianity is "overwhelmingly" a religion of and for the oppressed.

In this context, God, for instance, thus becomes not a static Greek "prime mover" or "creator" but "one who acts, moves and goes about correcting wrongs."

"The basic question is not whether God is omnipotent or transcendent," Dr. Cone said in an interview. "It's whose side is he on."

Dr. Cone argues that even white theologians must begin to think black.

"In America blacknesss is the overriding symbol of oppression," he said, "so theology must be done in black terms."

Such thinking has invariably led to reworking of the liturgy and other symbols of the Christian faith. Dr. Cleage, for instance, has placed a painting of a Black Madonna at the front of his sanctuary.

Mr. Wood's congregation has sponsored a Black Passover with "soul food that tells our story," and Mr.

Jackson is leading his followers in a "black Easter" celebration that seeks to "resurrect" Marcus Garvey, Malcolm X and other black heroes in the mind of Negroes.

The new religious black power movement is not without its problems. The number of qualified black theologians is still small, and no one has come up with a definitive theological approach to the morality of violence.

There are also sharp differences over how to interpret black church history. Preston N. Williams, of Boston University, for instance, has argued that white influences are not entirely negative and even "provided the black man with new elements for creating a meaningful religion."

Little Talk of Schism

Thus far there has been little talk of schism, though Mr. Rollins declared that "the seeds are there." Dr. Wilmore argues that the main threat is "possible heresy" resulting from interest in Malcolm X and other non-Christian black religious forces.

"We're alienated from white Christian experience," he said. "Maybe we're alienated from Christianity entirely."

The militant black religious leaders have little contact with white liberals, largely because preoccupation with race problems leaves little time for such issues as Vietnam, birth control and celibacy which are given priority by many white reformists.

The black radicals, however, are also not bothered by what whites consider burning theological problems, such as the "death of God" and the meaning of life.

"These are the questions of an affluent society," Dr. Cone said. "Whites may wonder how to find purpose in their lives, but our purpose is forced on us and laid out for us."

So far most black religious spokesmen have spoken of a period of some form of separatism followed by eventual integration. "An interim goal," Dr. Harding said, "Is now to make white men invisible' while black men are brought into the light."

They argue, however, that if it comes, integration will have to be a two-way affair.

"To compensate for the generations of brainwashing the Negro has undergone and to validate the equality of identies and cultures in a dramatic way," Mr. Mitchell said, "the white man will have to become integrated into black culture."

April 4, 1969

2 Episcopal Bishops Here Given Negro Demand for $500-Million

By C. GERALD FRASER

Two of the nation's most influential Episcopal bishops were confronted yesterday by a representative of the National Black Economic Development Conference who demanded $500-million as reparations due Negro Americans who have been persecuted, exploited and killed.

James Forman, the representative, also called for black people to disrupt "selected" church-sponsored agencies and stage sit-in demonstrations in black and white churches to support the demand.

Mr. Forman said Negroes were "the most oppressed group" of people inside the United States, suffering "the most from racism, exploitation, cultural degradation and lack of political power."

Sitting beside Mr. Forman at a news conference in the Episcopal Church Center, at 815 Second Avenue, were two Episcopal bishops, the Right Rev. J. Brooke Mosley, deputy for overseas relations, and the Right Rev. Stephen Bayne, first vice president of the church's executive council.

The bishops said they agreed that their denomination and others were racist, and that the half-billion dollar demand was just.

"Your're not wrong in asking," Bishop Mosley said, "you're asking the wrong people."

Bishop Bayne commented that the Episcopal Church was a "tiny, powerless agency."

The two bishops met with Mr. Forman in the absence of the Presiding Bishop, the Right Rev. John E. Hines, who was said to be out of the country.

Mr. Forman, who is also director of international affairs for the Student Nonviolent Coordinating Committee, said he would take the conference's demands to all "white Christian churches and Jewish synagogues."

What the bishops did object to was what Bishop Mosley called Mr. Forman's "declaration of war."

He said: "I think you could get a lot more if you went at it another way . . . you are going to weaken one of your best allies."

The Episcopal Church at present spends $3-million on community organization and cooperative programs.

The bishops repeatedly said that the $500-million demand was "unrealistic" as presented. The bishops doubted that "total control" of the money would be placed in the hands of Negroes if they did get the money.

The nine nonprofit projects, which the money purportedly would be spent on are the establishment of: a Southern land bank, publishing industries, television networks, a communications and community organization training center, a black labor strike fund, a black university, an International Black Appeal (for fund-raising), a research skills center, and assistance to the National Welfare Rights Organization.

"The Manifesto" was drawn up at a National Black Economic Development Conference in Detroit, April 25-27. It was sponsored by the Interreligious Foundation for Community Organization, which is made up of 23 national religious agencies and local community groups.

May 2, 1969

Churchmen Critical of Forman's Militant Tactics

By EDWARD B. FISKE

Protestant church leaders reacted with cautious opposition yesterday to the tactics of black militants that caused the cancellation of a communion service on Sunday at the Riverside Church.

At the same time many expressed sympathy with the militants' demands of increased efforts by the church in the field of race relations, and several endorsed the idea that American Negroes were entitled to some form of reparation for injustices resulting from the slavery period.

"The question of reparations is a very serious issue that white America has to face, and we haven't done it," said the Rev. Jon L. Regier, head of national missions work for the National Council of Churches.

"If we agree there is guilt on the part of whites, then we must agree that efforts at restitution are valid. The only question is how to do it."

The national and local church leaders were responding to the action of James Forman, the 40-year old representative of the National Black Economic Conference who read a series of demands in the Riverside Church during last Sunday's 11 A.M. service and caused the service to halt abruptly.

Privileges Demanded

The demands included rent-free space in the church, unrestricted use of the church's FM radio station 12 hours a day and on weekends, and the payment of 60 per cent of the yearly income from the church's investments.

The Rev. Ernest T. Campbell, senior minister of the church, denied Mr. Forman permission to read his statement during the service. The minister, his assistants, the choir and organist, and most of the 1,500 in the congregation walked out after the opening hymn when Mr. Forman forced his way to the altar area and began speaking.

All of the Protestant leaders interviewed yesterday either opposed the tactics of disrupting worship or took a neutral position.

The most vigorous criticism came from the Right Rev. Horace W. B. Donegan, Episcopal Bishop of New York, who said that the "record of the churches is clear in terms of our black brethren."

"While we acknowledge with regret the unhappy existence of racism in some places within the Christian body, the leadership of our church has been with the black people and all oppressed minorities all along the way," he said.

Police Action Feared

Bishop Donegan warned that the time may come when "existing law-enforcing agencies may have to be called upon for the purpose of safety."

"We do not wish to take such a step and will seek every way not to do so," he said, "but the rule of law is for protection of persons against the rule of irrationality and unreason."

The Rev. Dan B. Potter, executive director of the Council of Churches of the City of New York, the former Protestant Council, said that "the wires have been burning here," with calls demanding vigorous opposition to the tactics of Mr. Forman.

"I don't think that's the way," he said of Mr. Forman's interruption of a service. "There is an orderly procedure, and it ought to be attempted first. Only after it fails would a procedure like this, in my opinion, be condoned by the churches."

Not 'Right or Proper'

The Rev. Edwin H. Tuller, executive secretary of the American Baptist Convention, with which the Riverside Church is affiliated, said that he was not familiar with details of the incident but added: "I do not think it is right or proper for a group to disrupt a worship service."

Most of the churchmen agreed with th militants that churches had not lived up to their professed ideals in race relations.

The Rev. Robert P. Johnson, the first Negro stated clerk of the Presbytery of New York City, said that the action Sunday "presents those of us who are in the churches with a dramatic and forceful display of the gap between the secure members of society and the desperate members."

He rejected the concept of "reparations" on the grounds that it is "predicated on the war image" and took a neutral position on the question of tactics. "I'm not issuing a carte blanche for their tactics," he said, "but neither am I issuing a condemnation."

New Militancy Examined

The clergymen cited a number of reasons for the new militancy against the churches, including an alleged contrast between the churches' words and performance on racial matters and the belief that the churches, especially because of their tax exemptions, have substantial resources that could be put into Negro hands.

Several also expressed the belief that churches were a visible target because they had large grass-roots constituencies, especially among middle-class whites.

"I don't see how the churches can expect to avoid what every-

358

one else is getting," said Mr. Tuller.

Mr. Campbell said that leaders of the church would be meeting shortly to discuss the incident but that no public announcement would be made beforehand.

He repeated his earlier statement that the concept of restitution had validity but added, "Somewhere along the line we have to have a statute of limitations."

Among the reactions from outside the churches was a statement by Corliss Lamont, chairman of the National Emergency Civil Liberties Committee, who called the disruption "an outrageous violation of freedom of assembly and freedom of worship."

"We cannot permit the churches of America to become victimized by pressure groups of any kind,' he declared. "It is time for all Americans, black and white, young and old, to rededicate themselves to preserving the Bill of Rights in every field of thought and action."

Support From Negroes

Meanwhile, the Ad Hoc Committee of Black Churchmen met here yesterday and issued a three-page statement supportin in principle all the demands of the National Black Economic Development Conference, as outlined Sunday by Mr. Forman.

The statement, which was signed by 35 members, made no specific mention of the tactics used, saying only that a variety of methods were available.

The statement said that by paying reparations, the churches would "demonstrate to other American institutions the authenticity of their frequently verbalized contrition."

The signers included the Rev. Dr. Charles S. Spivey Jr., executive director of the department of social justice of the National Council of Churches, and J. Metz Rollins, executive director of the National Committee of Black Churchmen.

May 6, 1969

CATHOLICS REJECT FORMAN DEMANDS

Episcopal Council Also Gives Manifesto a Cool Reply

The Roman Catholic Archdiocese of New York rejected yesterday the so-called "Black Manifesto" of the National Black Economic Development Conference demanding $500-million in "reparations" to American Negroes from the nation's churches and synagogues.

In a four-page statement, the archdiocese denounced the rhetoric of the manifesto as "closely joined to political concepts which are completely contrary to our American way of life."

The concept of "reparations" for centuries of injustice to blacks was called "highly controversial" in the unsigned statement, which was released by Msgr. Thomas J. McGovern, director of the archdiocesan bureau of information.

In another reaction to the manifesto, the executive council of the Protestant Episcopal Church issued a nine-point response to the manifesto last night that, a spokesman for the council said, "rejected the rhetoric of the manifesto but turned the church's attention to the problems and needs" to which the manifesto pointed.

The Episcopal council's response came after a two-hour discussion of the manifesto at a regular meeting in Greenwich, Conn.

The statement issued by the council declared, in part: "We recognize the continuing poverty and injustice and rascism in our society to which it [the manifesto] speaks, but do not accept the manifesto as it is presented."

The statement cited efforts by the Episcopal Church in helping to fight poverty and injustice, and it promised to increase further the church's efforts. A resolution "in specific terms" will be voted on today, a church spokesman said.

The manifesto and its demand for "reparations" was presented by James Forman, the chief spokesman for the National Black Economic Development Conference.

On May 1, Mr. Forman brought manifesto to the Episcopal Church Center at 815 Second Avenue. As part of the over-all "reparations" demand, he asked from the Episcopal Church $60-million plus 60 per cent annually of all the income from the church's assets.

On May 4, Mr. Forman read the demands of the manifesto at a service at Riverside Church. When he walked to the chancel to address the congregation, the service was canceled by the minister, the Rev. Dr. Ernest T. Campbell.

On May 9, Mr. Forman delivered what he said was a "bill" asking $200-million from the Catholic Church at the headquarters of the New York Archdiocese. He met for two hours with a committee of chancery officials headed by Msgr. Joseph R. O'Brien, the vicar general.

The church was asked to list its assets for the Economic Development Conference.

One of those who accompanied Mr. Forman to the meeting, the Rev. Metz Rollins, executive director of the National Committee of Black Churchmen, said afterward that they had been assured that a recommendation would be made to Cardinal Cooke that "he give us a hearing."

Yesterday's statement made no reference to the May 9 meeting or to the possibility of Mr. Forman's meeting with the Cardinal.

The statement observed that Mr. Forman's public pronouncements "have caused all of us to reflect deeply upon some of the frustrations and aspirations of the black people," but that in view of the manifesto's rhetoric, its "manner of presentation and other substantive considerations, we do not endorse the 'Black Manifesto' or its demands."

The archdiocese, the statement said, has always been concerned with providing services to "alleviate suffering" and with working for the "renewal of society."

Neither Mr. Forman nor any of his associates could be reached immediately for comment on the statement.

Last night at Riverside Church, 500 members of the congregation, most of whom were white, met to discuss the manifesto. Speakers for and against it were applauded, but the loudest applause was in response to a strong condemnation of the manifesto.

White Protestant churchmen have generally favored the "reparation" ocncept, while deploring the use of what they describe as disruptive tactics. A number of churches and denominations, conceding that they have not done enough for the poor, have indieated they will commit more money for this purpose. However, in most instances it does not appear that the funds will go to Mr. Forman.

Support From Blacks

The United Presbyterian Church in the U.S.A. voted last Tuesday to set up the machinery for a campaign to raise $50-million for use "in depressed areas for deprived people," and to give $100,000 to the Interreligious Foundation for Community Organization. The foundation is a coalition of 10 Protestant denominations that—with some Jewish and Catholic support—channels money from churches to groups of poor people.

The foundation has agreed to help the Economic Development Conference raise $270,000 for operating expenses through contributions from churches, but it has stated that it will forward only those funds specifically designated for the conference.

Among black churchmen, the tendency has been toward full support for the manifesto. The National Committee of Black Churchmen hailed Mr. Forman last week as "a modern-day prophet."

The black caucus of the United Methodist Church—Black Methodists for Church Renewal—announced plans yesterday to seek $300-million from the 10.3-million-member denomination for black economic development.

The reference in the statement of the archdiocese to "political concepts" expressed in the manifesto is apparently directed at the document's preamble, which is couched in fiery language.

The preamble characterizes the United States Government as "this racist, imperialist government that is choking the life of all the people around the world."

Calling the nation "the most barbaric country in the world," the preamble adds that "we have a chance to help bring this government down."

Referring to the "power structure" of the United States the preamble goes on to say, "these ruthless, barbaric men have systematically tried to kill all people and organizations opposed to its imperialism."

. In another development yesterday, Mr. Forman, who is under a court order barring him from causing any disturbance at the Riverside Church, served a subpoena on the trustees of the church, asking to examine many of its financial records of the last three years.

A motion by the church for a more binding restraining order against Mr. Forman is scheduled for argument this morning in State Supreme Court.

May 22, 1969

Mormons Reaffirm Curb on Negroes

By WALLACE TURNER

Special to The New York Times

SAN FRANCISCO, Jan. 8 —The top leadership of the Church of Jesus Christ of Latter-day Saints (Mormon) has re-emphasized its religious policy that bars Negroes from priesthood in the church. The policy was affirmed in a statement distributed to Mormon leadership around the world.

A copy of the statement, issued Dec. 15, was received here today. It was directed to "general authorities, regional representatives of the twelve, stake presidents, mission presidents and bishops" —the men who control the religious organization, which says it has 2.8 million members.

Mormons believe, the statement said, that "each citizen must have equal opportunities and protection under the law with reference to civil rights."

"However," it continued, "matters of faith, conscience, and theology are not within the purview of the civil law. The First Amendment of the Constitution specifically provides that 'Congress shall make no law respecting an establishment of religion, or prohibiting the free exercise thereof.' "

The statement said the church's position "has no relevancy whatever to those who do not wish to join the church." It continued:

"Those individuals, we suppose, do not believe in the divine origin and nature of

the church, nor that we have the priesthood of God. Therefore, if they feel we have no priesthood, they should have no concern with any aspect of our theology on priesthood so long as that theology does not deny any man his constitutional privileges."

Of those receiving the statement, "general authorities" refers to the church's top officers, including the 12 apostles and the president, and his counselors. The regional representatives report from their regions to the general authorities; stake presidents are the administrative heads of collections of congregations in a locality, and bishops are the heads of congregations.

Except to confirm that the copy was genuine, spokesmen for the church would not comment on it. Top church leaders were not available for comment. The leaders were attending their customary Thursday meeting in the church's Salt Lake City temple.

Knowledgeable sources outside the church said the statement had been produced for local church leaders to read to congregations in explaining the church's dispute with Stanford University over cancellation of further athletic competition.

Loss of Eternal Role

Negro athletes at different schools for the last several years have protested taking part in contests with teams from Brigham Young University, the Mormon school at Provo, Utah. Stanford canceled its athletic relationship with Brigham Young last fall on the ground that the Mormons were

prejudiced against Negroes.

There are said to be about 200 Negro members in the Mormon church. Except for the Negroes, all male Mormons are expected to become members of the priesthood orders.

The priesthood orders are at the core of the religious practice established on the teachings and revelations that Mormons believe Joseph Smith Jr., the prophet, received from God. For example, not to belong to the priesthood during life will diminish the role in the celestial kingdom of eternity, the Mormons teach.

While there is no question that the church rigorously withholds the priesthood from Negroes, the reasons for its action are unclear, and unofficial explanations vary.

David O. McKay, who is now infirm at 96 years of age, is the Mormon president. His two chief assistants are Hugh B. Brown, first counselor, and N. Eldon Tanner, second counselor. Their signatures were on the statement distributed to church leaders.

Some years ago Mr. McKay said in a letter that insofar as he knew, the ban on Negro priesthood members derived from a paragraph in the book of Abraham, a part of the Mormon "pearl of Great Price," which is a collection of some of Joseph Smith's translations of hieroglyphics found on papyrus inside a mummy's wrappings.

The phrase occurs in the first chapter of the book of Abraham. It follows a narrative in which the Egyptian Pharaoh is described as "descendant from the loins of Ham," through a daughter of Ham who "settled her sons" in Egypt so that "from Ham sprang that race which preserved the curse in the land."

Curse on Pharaoh

The passages praise the Pharaoh as righteous, wise and just but note that he was "cursed . . . as pertaining to the priesthood." The next paragraph notes that the Pharaoh was "of that lineage by which he could not have the right of the priesthood."

The Mormons' position on Negroes has disturbed Mormon liberals for decades and has been the reason for many serious internal conflicts. In 1963 Mr. Brown said he considered the disputes over the Negro issue to be the most serious area of conflict since the Mormons were required by United States Government pressures to abandon their practice of polygamy.

In the late 19th century, the Mormons cited the constitutional protections of religious practice as they did in the statement issued last month. Then the United States Supreme Court upheld the jailing of Mormon elders convicted of violating Federal laws by living with plural wives and replied that religious freedom guarantees had to be fitted into the fabric of life.

The church abandoned polygamy in an "official declaration" on Oct. 6, 1890.

The papyri from which the prophet said he translated the book of Abraham were thought for decades to have been lost in the Chicago fire of 1871. But in 1968 they turned up in a storage room of the Metropolitan Museum in New York and were turned over to the Mormons, who now preserve them in their extensive archives.

Non-Mormon Egyptologists for decades have scoffed at the prophet's translations and have contended that the papyri are common burial documents, not a record of the Hebrew imprisonment in Egypt, as the Mormons are taught.

January 9, 1970

Negro Heads Southern Presbyterians

By ELEANOR BLAU

Special to The New York Times

LOUISVILLE, June 16 — The Presbyterian Church in the United States elected today the first black moderator in the 113-year history of the largely Southern denomination

He is the Rev. Dr. Lawrence W. Bottoms, a minis-

ter in Decatur, Ga., who was the first black moderator of a presbytery, or a regional unit, in Louisville, in 1963.

Before he was chosen on the first ballot, the 66-year-old Dr. Bottoms predicted that his election would provide "an opportunity to stand

with all minorities and take their burden upon the shoulders of this assembly."

The office is the highest and most symbolic of the 900,000-member church. The moderator presides at the annual General Assembly, the governing body of the de-

nomination, and speaks during the year for the church.

Dr. Bottoms was born in Selma, Ala., graduated from Geneva College in Beaver Falls, Pa., and attended the Reformed Presbyterian Seminary in Pittsburgh. He also studied at Atlanta University.

From 1951 to 1973, he was a staff associate on the denomination's Board of Church Extension and its successor, the Board of National Ministries. In that capacity, he was secretary for Negro work for the denomination for about nine years.

The election of Dr. Bottoms by the Southern Presbyterians came a day before a significant joint session with the Northern counterpart, from which the Southerners separated 113 years ago at the start of the Civil War.

The purpose of the joint session is to consider steps that could lead to uniting the Southern body and the larger United Presybyterian Church, which has a national membership of three million.

The two denominations have been working on a possible merger plan for five years, and a revised version is up for preliminary consideration by the governing General Assemblies of the churches.

Dr. Bottoms will succeed the Rev. Charles E.S. Kraemer of Richmond.

The church has 7,000 black members, about 1 per cent of the membership in its 4,000 churches in the Southern and Border states.

In an interview after his election Dr. Bottom said, "I think this is a breakthrough in the experience of the Presbyterian Church in the United States in a sharing of decision-making and planning with minorities."

Asked why a breakthrough had come at this time, he replied, "There's a change going on in the South, caused by industrialization, commercialization, secularism and bureaucracy." The church, he asserted, is becoming involved in this change.

Dr. Bottoms said he hoped to work on behalf of minorities, "not only blacks but others, women." He noted that when he was with the Negro work division, about 20 years ago, "we were instrumental in getting the church to raise a million dollars for new Negro churches in changing areas." As a result, he said, black membership in the denomination rose from 3,000 to its present level.

On another matter, he said white churches in suburban areas have a "strong mission opportunity" with middle-class Negroes concerning "black crime, black anger and black desperation."

June 17, 1974

CHAPTER **4**

The Frontiers of Faith

Members of the International Society For Krishna
Consciousness at a festival in West Virginia.

Donaldson/NYT Pictures

GOD AND EVOLUTION

Charge That American Teachers of Darwinism "Make the Bible a Scrap of Paper"

By WILLIAM JENNINGS BRYAN

I APPRECIATE your invitation to present the objections to Darwinism, or evolution applied to man, and beg to submit to your readers the following:

The only part of evolution in which any considerable interest is felt is evolution applied to man. A hypothesis in regard to the rocks and plant life does not affect the philosophy upon which one's life is built. Evolution applied to fish, birds and beasts would not materially affect man's view of his own responsibilities except as the acceptance of an unsupported hypothesis as to these would be used to support a similar hypothesis as to man. The evolution that is harmful—distinctly so—is the evolution that destroys man's family tree as taught by the Bible and makes him a descendant of the lower forms of life. This, as I shall try to show, is a very vital matter.

I deal with Darwinism because it is a definite hypothesis. In his "Descent of Man" and "Origin of Species" Darwin has presumed to outline a family tree that begins, according to his estimate, about two hundred million years ago with marine animals. He attempts to trace man's line of descent from this obscure beginning up through fish, reptile, bird and animal to man. He has us descend from European, rather than American, apes and locates our first ancestors in Africa. Then he says, "But why speculate?"—a very significant phrase because it applies to everything that he says. His entire discussion is speculation.

Darwin's "Laws."

Darwin set forth two (so-called) laws by which he attempts to explain the changes which he thought had taken place in the development of life from the earlier forms to man. One of these is called "Natural Selection" or "Survival of the Fittest," his argument being that a form of life which had any characteristic that was beneficial had a better chance of survival than a form of life that lacked that characteristic. The second law that he assumed to declare was called "Sexual Selection," by which he attempted to account for every change that was not accounted for by Natural Selection. Sexual Selection has been laughed out of the class room. Even in his day Darwin said (see note to "Descent of Man" 1874 edition, page 625) that it aroused more criticism than anything else he had said, when he used Sexual Selection to explain how man became a hairless animal. Natural Selection is being increasingly discarded by scientists. John Burroughs, just before his death, registered a protest against it. But many evolutionists adhere to Darwin's *conclusions* while discarding his *explanations*. In other words, they accept the line of descent which he suggested *without any explanation whatever* to support it.

Other scientists accept the family tree which he outlined, but would have man branch off at a point below, or above, the development of apes and monkeys instead of coming through them. So far as I have been able to find, Darwin's line of descent has more supporters than any other outlined by evolutionists. If there is any other clearly defined family tree supported by a larger number of evolutionists, I shall be glad to have information about it that I may investigate it.

The first objection to Darwinism is that it is only a guess and was never anything more. It is called a "hypothesis," but the word "hypothesis," though euphonious, dignified and high-sounding, is merely a scientific synonym for the old-fashioned word "guess." If Darwin had advanced his views as a *guess* they would not have survived for a year, but they have floated for half a century, buoyed up by the inflated word "hypothesis." When it is understood that "hypothesis" means "guess," people will inspect it more carefully before accepting it.

No Support in the Bible.

The second objection to Darwin's guess is that it has not one syllable in the Bible to support it. This ought to make Christians cautious about accepting it without thorough investigation. The Bible not only describes man's creation, but gives a reason for it; man is a part of God's plan and is placed on earth for a purpose. Both the Old and New Testament deal with man and with man only. They tell of God's creation of him, of God's dealings with him and of God's plans for him. Is it not strange that a Christian will accept Darwinism as a substitute for the Bible when the Bible not only does not support Darwin's hypothesis but directly and expressly contradicts it?

Third—Neither Darwin nor his supporters have been able to find a fact in the universe to support their hypothesis. With millions of species, the investigators have not been able to find *one single instance* in which one species has changed into another, although, according to the hypothesis, *all* species have developed from one or a few germs of life, the development being through the action of "resident forces" and without outside aid. Wherever a form of life, found in the rocks, is found among living organisms, there is no material change from the earliest form in which it is found. With millions of examples, nothing imperfect is found—nothing in the process of change. This statement may surprise those who have accepted evolution without investigation, as most of those who call themselves evolutionists have done. One preacher who wrote to me expressing great regret that I should dissent from Darwin said that he had not investigated the matter for himself, but that nearly all scientists seemed to accept Darwinism.

The latest word that we have on this subject comes from Professor Bateson, a high English authority, who journeyed all the way from London to Toronto, Canada, to address the American Association for the Advancement of Science **the 28th day of last December.** His speech has been published in full in the January issue of Science.

Professor Bateson is an evolutionist, but he tells with real pathos how every effort to discover the origin of species has failed. He takes up different lines of investigation, commenced hopefully but ending in disappointement. He concludes by saying, " Let us then proclaim in precise and unmistakable language that our faith in evolution is unshaken," and then he adds, " our doubts are not as to the reality or truth of evolution, but as to the origin of species, a technical, almost domestic problem. Any day that mystery may be solved." Here is optimism at its maximum. They fall back on faith. They have not yet found the origin of species, and yet how can evolution explain life unless it can account for change in species? Is it not more rational to believe in creation of man by separate act of God than to believe in evolution without a particle of evidence?

Fourth—Darwinism is not only without foundation, but it compels its believers to resort to explanations that are more absurd than anything found in the " Arabian Nights." Darwin explains that man's mind became superior to woman's because, among our brute ancestors, the males fought for the females and thus strengthened their minds. If he had lived until now, he would not have felt it necessary to make so ridiculous an explanation, because woman's mind is not now believed to be inferior to man's.

As to Hairless Men.

Darwin also explained that the hair disappeared from the body, permitting man to become a hairless animal because, among our brute ancestors, the females preferred the males with the least hair and thus, in the course of ages, bred the hair off. It is hardly necessary to point out that these explanations conflict; the males and the females could not both select at the same time.

Evolutionists, not being willing to accept the theory of creation, have to explain everything, and their courage in this respect is as great as their efforts are laughable. The eye, for instance, according to evolutionists, was brought out by " the light beating upon the skin;" the ear came out in response to " air waves;" the leg is the development of a wart that chanced to appear on the belly of an animal; and so the tommyrot runs on ad infinitum, and sensible people are asked to swallow it.

Recently a college professor told an audience in Philadelphia that a baby wiggles its big toe without wiggling its other toes because its ancestors climbed trees; also that we dream of falling because our forefathers fell out of trees 50,000 years ago, adding that we are not hurt in our dreams of falling because we descended from those that fell and were *not killed.* (If we descended from animals at all, we certainly did not descend from those that were killed in falling). A professor in Illinois has fixed as the great day in history the day when a water puppy crawled upon the land and decided to stay there, thus becoming man's first progenitor. A dispatch from Paris recently announced that an eminent scientist had reported having communicated with the soul of a dog and learned that the dog was happy.

I simply mention these explanations to show what some people can believe who cannot believe the Bible. Evolution seems to close the heart of some to the plainest spiritual truths while it opens the mind to the wildest of guesses advanced in the name of science.

Guessing Is Not Science.

Guesses are not science. Science is classified knowledge, and a scientist ought to be the last person to insist upon a guess being accepted until proof removes it from the field of hypothesis into the field of demonstrated truth. Christianity has nothing to fear from any *truth;* no *fact* disturbs the Christian religion or the Christian. It is the unsupported *guess* that is substituted for science to which opposition is made, and I think the objection is a valid one.

But, it may be asked, why should one object to Darwinism even *though it is not true?* This is a proper question and deserves a candid answer. There are many guesses which are perfectly groundless and at the same time entirely harmless; and it is not worth while to worry about a guess or to disturb the guesser so long as his guess does not harm others.

The objection to Darwinism is that it is *harmful,* as well as groundless. It entirely changes one's view of life and undermines faith in the Bible. Evolution has no place for the miracle or the supernatural. It flatters the egotist to be told that there is nothing that his mind cannot understand. Evolution proposes to bring all the processes of nature within the comprehension of man by making it the explanation of everything that is known. Creation implies a Creator, and the finite mind cannot comprehend the Infinite. We can understand some things, but we run across mystery at every point. Evolution attempts to solve the mystery of life by suggesting a process of development commencing " in the dawn of time " and continuing uninterrupted up until now. Evolution does not explain creation; it simply diverts attention from it by hiding it behind eons of time. If a man accepts Darwinism, or evolution applied to man, and is consistent, he rejects the miracle and the supernatural as impossible. He commences with the first chapter of Genesis and blots out the Bible story of man's creation, not because the evidence is insufficient, but because the miracle is inconsistent with evolution. If he is consistent, he will go through the Old Testament step by step and cut out all the miracles and all the supernatural. He will then take up the New Testament and cut out all the supernatural—the virgin birth of Christ, His miracles and His resurrection, leaving the Bible a story book without binding authority upon the conscience of man. Of course, not all evolutionists are consistent; some fail to apply their hypothesis to the end just as some Christians fail to apply their Christianity to life.

Evolution and God.

Most of the evolutionists are materialists; some admitting that they are atheists, others calling themselves agnostics. Some call themselves " Theistic Evolutionists," but the theistic evolutionist puts God so far away that He ceases to be a present influence in the life. Canon Barnes of Westminster, some two years ago, interpreted evolution as to put God back of the time when the electrons came out of " stuff " and combined (about 1740 of them) to form an atom. Since then, according to Canon Barnes, things have been developing to God's plan but without God's aid.

It requires measureless credulity to enable one to believe that all that we see about us came by chance, by a series of happy-go-lucky accidents. If only an infinite God could have formed hydrogen and oxygen and united them in just the right proportions to produce water—the daily need of every living thing—scattered among the flowers all the colors of the rainbow and every variety of perfume, adjusted the mocking bird's

throat to its musical scale, and fashioned a soul for man, why should we want to imprison God in an impenetrable past? This is a living world. Why not a living God upon the throne? Why not allow Him to work now?

Theistic evolutionists insist that they magnify God when they credit Him with devising evolution as a plan of development. They sometimes characterize the Bible God as a " carpenter god," who is described as repairing his work from time to time at man's request. The question is not whether God could have made the world according to the plan of evolution—of course, an all-powerful God could make the world as He pleased. The real question is, Did God use evolution as His plan? If it could be shown that man, instead of being made in the image of God, is a development of beasts we would have to accept it, regardless of its effect, for truth is truth and must prevail. But when there is no proof we have a right to consider the effect of the acceptance of an unsupported hypothesis.

Darwin's Agnosticism.

Darwinism made an agnostic out of Darwin. When he was a young man he believed in God; before he died he declared that the beginning of all things is a mystery insoluble by us. When he was a young man he believed in the Bible; just before his death he declared that he did not believe that there had ever been any revelation; that banished the Bible as the inspired Word of God, and, with it, the Christ of whom the Bible tells. When Darwin was young he believed in a future life; before he died he declared that each must decide the question for himself from vague, uncertain probabilities. He could not throw any light upon the great questions of life and immortality. He said that he " must be content to remain an agnostic."

And then he brought the most terrific indictment that I have read against his own hypothesis. He asks (just before his death): " Can the mind of man, which has, as I fully believe, been developed from a mind as low as that possessed by the lowest animal, be trusted when it draws such grand conclusions?" He brought man down to the brute level and then judged man's mind by brute standards.

This is Darwinism. This is Darwin's own testimony against himself. If Darwinism could make an agnostic of Darwin, what is its effect likely to be upon students to whom Darwinism is taught at the very age when they are throwing off parental authority and becoming independent? Darwin's guess gives the student an excuse for rejecting the authority of God, an excuse that appeals to him more strongly at this age than at any other age in life. Many of them come back after a while as Romanes came back. After feeding upon husks for twenty-five years, he began to feel his way back, like a prodigal son, to his father's house, but many never return.

Professor Leuba, who teaches psychology at Bryn Mawr, Pennsylvania, wrote a book about six years ago entitled " Belief in God and Immortality " (it can be obtained from the Open Court Publishing Company, Chicago), in which he declared that belief in God and immortality is dying out among the educated classes. As proof of this he gave the results which he obtained by submitting questions to prominent scientists in the United States. He says that he found that more than half of them, according to their own answers, do not believe in a personal God or a personal immortality. To reinforce his position, he sent questions to students of nine representative colleges and found that unbelief increases from 15 per cent. in the freshman year to 30 per cent. in the junior class, and to 40 to 45 per cent. (among the men) at graduation. This he attributes to the influence of the scholarly men under whose instruction they pass in college.

Religion Waning Among Children.

Any one desiring to verify these statistics can do so by inquiry at our leading State institutions and even among some of our religious denominational colleges. Fathers and mothers complain of their children losing their interest in religion and speaking lightly of the Bible. This begins when they come under the influence of a teacher who accepts Darwin's guess, ridicules the Bible story of creation and instructs the child upon the basis of the brute theory. In Columbia a teacher began his course in geology by telling the children to lay aside all that they had learned in Sunday School. A teacher of philosophy in the University of Michigan tells students that Christianity is a state of mind and that there are only two books of literary value in the Bible. Another professor in that university tells students that no thinking man can believe in God or in the Bible. A teacher in the University of Wisconsin tells his students that the Bible is a collection of myths. Another State university professor diverts a dozen young men from the ministry and the President of a prominent State university tells his students in a lecture on religion to throw away religion if it does not harmonize with the teaching of biology, psychology, &c.

The effect of Darwinism is seen in the pulpits; men of prominent denominations deny the virgin birth of Christ and some even His resurrection. Two Presbyterians, preaching in New York State, recently told me that agnosticism was the natural attitude of old people. Evolution naturally leads to agnosticism and, if continued, finally to atheism. Those who teach Darwinism are undermining the faith of Christians; they are raising questions about the Bible as an authoritative source of truth; they are teaching materialistic views that rob the life of the young of spiritual values.

Christians do not object to freedom of speech; they believe that Biblical truth can hold its own in a fair field. They concede the right of ministers to pass from belief to agnosticism or atheism, but they contend that they should be honest enough to separate themselves from the ministry and not attempt to debase the religion which they profess.

And so in the matter of education, Christians do not dispute the right of any teacher to be agnostic or atheistic, but Christians do dispute the right of agnostics and atheists to use the public school as a forum for the teaching of their doctrines.

The Bible has in many places been excluded from the schools on the ground that religion should not be taught by those paid by public taxation. If this doctrine is sound, what right have the enemies of religion to teach irreligion in the public schools? If the Bible cannot be taught, why should Christian taxpayers permit the teaching of guesses that make the Bible a lie? A teacher might just as well write over the door of his room, "Leave Christianity behind you, all ye who enter here," as to ask his students to accept an hypothesis directly and irreconcilably antagonistic to the Bible.

Our opponents are not fair. When we find fault with the teaching of Darwin's unsupported hypothesis, they talk about Copernicus and Galileo and ask whether we shall exclude science and return to the dark ages. Their evasion is a confession of weakness. We do not ask for the exclusion of any scientific truth, but we do protest against an atheist teacher being allowed to blow his guesses in the face of the student. The Christians who want to teach religion in their schools furnish the money for denominational institutions. If atheists want to teach atheism, why do they not build their own schools and employ their own teachers? If a man really believes that he has brute blood in him, he can teach that to his children at home or he can send them to atheistic schools, where his children will not be in danger of losing their brute philosophy, but why should he be allowed to deal with other people's children as if they were little monkeys?

We stamp upon our coins "In God We Trust"; we administer to witnesses an oath in which God's name appears; our President takes his oath of office upon the Bible. Is it fanatical to suggest that public taxes should not be employed for the purpose of undermining the nation's God? When we defend the Mosaic account of man's creation and contend that man has no brute blood in him, but was made in God's image by separate act and placed on earth to carry out a divine decree, we are defending the God of the Jews as well as the God of the Gentiles, the God of the Catholics as well as the God of the Protestants. We believe that faith in a Supreme Being is essential to civilization as well as to religion and that abandonment of God means ruin to the world and chaos to society.

Let these believers in "the tree man" come down out of the trees and meet the issue. Let them defend the teaching of agnosticism or atheism if they dare. If they deny that the natural tendency of Darwinism is to lead many to a denial of God, let them frankly point out the portions of the Bible which they regard as consistent with Darwinism, or evolution applied to man. They weaken faith in God, discourage prayer, raise doubt as to a future life, reduce Christ to the stature of a man, and make the Bible a "scrap of paper." As religion is the only basis of morals, it is time for Christians to protect religion from its most insidious enemy.

Dr. Henry Fairfield Osborn, paleontologist, President of the American Museum of Natural History, and Dr. Edwin Grant Conklin, Professor of Zoology at Princeton University, will answer Mr. Bryan in next Sunday's NEW YORK TIMES.

February 26, 1922

ATTACKS W. J. B.

Preacher Says Bryan's Article on Evolution Works Injury to Bible—God Infinitely Grander Than Occasional Wonder-Worker

By HARRY EMERSON FOSDICK, Professor at Union Theological Seminary and Preacher at the First Presbyterian Church, New York.

THE editor of THE TIMES has asked me to reply to Mr. Bryan's statement on "God and Evolution." I do so, if only to voice the sentiments of a large number of Christian people who in the name of religion are quite as shocked as any scientist could be in the name of science at Mr. Bryan's sincere but appalling obscurantism.

So far as the scientific aspect of the discussion is concerned, scientists may well be left to handle it. Suffice it to say that when Mr. Bryan reduces evolution to a hypothesis and then identifies a hypothesis with a "guess" he is guilty of a sophistry so shallow and palpable that one wonders at his hardihood in risking it. A guess is a haphazard venture of opinion without investigation before or just reason afterward to sustain it; it is a jeu d'esprit. But a hypothesis is a seriously proffered explanation of a difficult problem ventured when careful investigation of facts points to it, retained as long as the discovered facts sustain it, and surrendered as soon as another hypothesis enters the field which better explains the phenomena in question.

Every universally accepted scientific truth which we possess began as a hypothesis, is in a sense a hypothesis still, and has become a hypothesis transformed into a settled conviction as the mass of accumulating evidence left no question as to its substantial validity. To call evolution, therefore, a guess is one thing; to tell the truth about it is another, for to tell the truth involves recognizing the tireless patience with which generations of scientists in every appropriate field of inquiry have been investigating all discoverable facts that bear upon the problem of mutation of species, with substantial unanimity as to the results so far as belief in the hypothesis of evolution is concerned. When Darwin, after years of patient, unremitting study, ventured his hypothesis in explanation of evolution—a hypothesis which was bound to be corrected and improved—one may say anything else one will about it except to call it a "guess." That is the one thing which it certainly was not. Today, the evolutionary hypothesis, after many years of pitiless attack and searching investigation, is, as a whole, the most adequate explanation of the facts with regard to the origin of species that we have yet attained, and it was never so solidly grounded as it is today. Dr. Osborn is making, surely, a safe statement when he says that no living naturalist, so far as he knows, "differs as to the immutable truth or evolution in the sense of the continuous fitness of plants and animals to their environment and the ascent of all the extinct and existing forms of life, including man, from an original and single cellular state."

The Real Situation.

When, therefore, Mr. Bryan says, "Neither Darwin nor his supporters have been able to find a fact in the universe to support their hypothesis," it would be difficult to imagine a statement more obviously and demonstrably mistaken. The real situation is that every fact on which investigation has been able to lay its hand helps to confirm the hypothesis of evolution. There is no known fact which stands out against it. Each newly discovered fact fits into an appropriate place in it. So far as the general outlines of it are concerned, the Copernican astronomy itself is hardly established more solidly.

My reply, however, is particularly concerned with the theological aspects of Mr. Bryan's statement. There seems to be no doubt about what his position is. He proposes to take his science from the Bible. He proposes, certainly, to take no science that is contradicted by the Bible. He says, "Is it not strange that a Christian will accept Darwinism as a substitute for the Bible when the Bible not only does not support Darwin's hypothesis, but directly and expressly contradicts it?" What other interpretation of such a statement is possible except this: that the Bible is for Mr. Bryan an authoritative textbook in biology—and if in biology, why not in astronomy, cosmogony, chemistry or any other science, art, concern of man whatever? One who is acquainted with the history of theological thought gasps as he reads this. At the close of the sixteenth century a Protestant theologian set down the importance of the Book of Genesis as he understood it. He said that the text of Genesis "must be received strictly"; that "it contains all knowledge, human and divine"; that "twenty-eight articles of the Augsburg Confession are to be found in it"; that "it is an arsenal of arguments against all sects and sorts of atheists, pagans, Jews, Turks, Tartars, Papists, Calvinists Socinians and Baptists"; that it is "the source of all science and arts, including law, medicine, philosophy and rhetoric," "the source and essence of all histories and of all professions, trades and works," "an exhibition of all virtues and vices," and "the origin of all consolation."

One had supposed that the days when such wild anachronisms could pass muster as good theology were passed, but Mr. Bryan is regalvanizing into life that same outmoded idea of what the Bible is and proposes in the twentieth century that we shall use Genesis, which reflects the pre-scientific view of the Hebrew people centuries before Christ as an authoritative textbook in science, beyond whose conclusions we dare not go.

Martin Luther and Bryan.

Why, then, should Mr. Bryan complain because his attitude toward evolution is compared repeatedly, as he says it is, with the attitude of the theological opponents of Copernicus and Galileo? On his own statement, the parallelism is complete. Martin Luther attacked Copernicus with the same appeal which Mr. Bryan uses. He appealed to the Bible. He said: "People gave ear to an upstart astrologer who strove to show that the earth revolves, not the heavens or the firmament, the sun and the moon. Whoever wishes to appear clever must devise some new system, which of all systems is, of course, the very best. This fool wishes to reverse the entire science of astronomy, but sacred Scripture tells us that Joshua commanded the sun to stand still, and not the earth."

Nor was Martin Luther wrong if the Bible is indeed an authoritative text book in science. The denial of the Copernican astronomy with its moving earth can unquestionably be found in the Bible if one starts out to use the Bible that way—"The world also is established, that it cannot be moved" (Psalm 93:1); "Who laid the foundations of the earth, that it should not be moved forever" (Psalm 104:5). Moreover, in those bygone days, the people who were then using Mr. Bryan's method of argument did quote these passages as proof, and Father

Inchofer felt so confident that he cried, "The opinion of the earth's motion is of all heresies the most abominable, the most pernicious, the most scandalous; the immovability of the earth is thrice sacred; argument against the immortality of the soul, the existence of God, and the incarnation should be tolerated sooner than an argument to prove that the earth moves."

Indeed, as everybody knows who has seriously studied the Bible, that Book represents in its cosmology and its cosmogony the view of the physical universe which everywhere obtained in the ancient Semitic world. The earth was flat and was founded on an underlying sea (Psalm 136:6; Psalm 24:1-2; Genesis 7:11); it was stationery; the heavens, like an upturned bowl, "strong as a molten mirror" (Job 37:18; Genesis 1:6-8; Isaiah 40:22; Psalm 104:2), rested on the earth beneath (Amos 9:6; Job 26:11); the sun, moon and stars moved within this firmament of special purpose to illumine man (Genesis 1:14-19); there was a sea above the sky, "the waters which were above the firmament" (Genesis 1:7; Psalm 148:4) and through "the window of heaven" the rain came down (Genesis 7:11; Psalm 78:23); beneath the earth was mysterious Sheol where dwelt the shadowy dead (Isaiah 14:9-11) and all this had been made in six days, each of which had had a morning and an evening, a short and measureable time before (Genesis 1).

Are we to understand that this is Mr. Bryan's science, that we must teach this science in our schools, that we are estopped by divine revelation from ever going beyond this science? Yet this is exactly what Mr. Bryan would force us to if with intellectual consistency he should carry out the implications of his appeal to the Bible against the scientific hypothesis of evolution in biology.

The Bible's Precious Truths.

One who is a teacher and preacher of religion raises his protest against all this just because it does such gross injustice to the Bible. There is no book to compare with it. The world never needed more its fundamental principles of life, its fully developed views of God and man, its finest faiths and hopes and loves. When one reads an article like Mr. Bryan's one feels, not that the Bible is being defended, but that it is being attacked. Is a 'cello defended when instead of being used for music it is advertised as a good dinner table? Mr. Bryan does a similar disservice to the Bible when, instead of using it for what it is, the most noble, useful, inspiring and inspired book of spiritual life which we have, the record of God's progressive unfolding of his character and will from early primitive beginnings to the high noon in Christ, he sets it up for what it is not and never was meant to be—a procrustean bed to whose infallible measurements all human thought must be forever trimmed.

The fundamental interest which leads Mr. Bryan and others of his school to hate evolution is the fear that it will depreciate the dignity of man. Just what do they mean? Even in the Book of Genesis God made man out of the dust of the earth. Surely, that is low enough to start and evolution starts no lower. So long as God is the Creative Power, what difference does it make whether out of the dust by sudden fiat or out of the dust by gradual process God brought man into being? Here man is and what he is he is. Were it decided that God had dropped him from the sky, he still would be the man he is. If it is decided that God brought him up by slow gradations out of lower forms of life, he still is the man he is.

The fact is that the process by which man came to be upon the planet is a very important scientific problem, but it is not a crucially important religious problem. Origins prove nothing in the realm of values. To all folk of spiritual

insight man, no matter by what process he at first arrived, is the child of God, made in His image, destined for His character. If one could appeal directly to Mr. Bryan he would wish to say: let the scientists thrash out the problems of man's biological origin but in the meantime do not teach men that if God did not make us by fiat then we have nothing but a bestial heritage. That is a lie which once believed will have a terrific harvest. It is regrettable business that a prominent Christian should be teaching that.

One writes this with warm sympathy for the cause which gives Mr. Bryan such anxious concern. He is fearful that the youth of the new generation, taught the doctrine of a materialistic science, may lose that religious faith in God and in the realities of the spiritual life on which alone an abiding civilization can be founded. His fear is well grounded, as every one closely associated with the students of our colleges and universities knows. Many of them are sadly confused, mentally in chaos, and, so far as any guiding principles of religious faith are concerned, are often without chart, compass or anchor.

Danger of Materialistic Teaching.

There are types of teaching in our universities which are hostile to any confidence in the creative reality of the spiritual life—dreary philosophies which reduce everything to predetermined mechanical activity. Some classrooms doubtless are, as Mr. Bryan thinks, antagonistic, in the effect which they produce, alike to sustained integrity of character, buoyancy and hopefulness of life and progress in society. But Mr. Bryan's association of this pessimistic and materialistic teaching with the biological theory of evolution is only drawing a red herring across the real trail. The distinction between inspiring, spiritually minded teachers and deadening, irreligious teachers is not at the point of belief in evolution at all. Our greatest teachers, as well as our poorest, those who are profoundly religious as well as those who are scornfully irreligious, believe in evolution. The new biology has no more to do with the difference between them than the new astronomy or the new chemistry. If the hypothesis of evolution were smashed tomorrow, there would be no more religiously minded scientists and no fewer irreligious ones.

Heart of Problem.

The real crux of the problem in university circles is whether we are going to think of creative reality in physical or in spiritual terms, and that question cannot be met on the lines that Mr. Bryan has laid down. Indeed, the real enemies of the Christian faith, so far as our students are concerned, are not the evolutionary biologists, but folk like Mr. Bryan who insist on setting up artificial adhesions between Christianity and outgrown scientific opinions, and who proclaim that we cannot have one without the other. The pity is that so many students will believe him and, finding it impossible to retain the outgrown scientific opinions, will give up Christianity in accordance with Mr. Bryan's insistence that they must.

Quite as amazing as his view of the Bible is Mr. Bryan's view of the effect of evolution upon man's thought of God. If ever a topsy-turvy statement was made about any matter capable of definitive information, Mr. Bryan's statement deserves that description, for it turns the truth upside down. He says: "The theistic evolutionist puts God so far away that He ceases to be a present influence in the life * * * Why should we want to imprison God in an impenetrable past?" This is a living world. Why not a living God upon the throne? Why not allow Him to work now?" But the effect of evolution upon man's thought of God, as every serious student of theology knows, has been directly the opposite of what Mr. Bryan supposes. It was in the eighteenth century that men thought of God as the vague, dim figure over the crest of the first hill who gave this universal toboggan its primeval shove and has been watching it sliding ever since. It was in the eighteenth century that God was thought of as the absentee landlord who had _ilt the house and left it—as the ship-wright who had built the ship and then turned it over to the master mariners, his natural laws. Such ideas of God are associated with eighteenth century Deism, but the nineteenth century's most characteristic thought of God was in terms of immanence—God here in this world, the life of all that lives, the sustaining energy of all that exists, as our spirits are in our bodies, permeating vitalising, directing all.

The idea of evolution was one of the great factors in this most profitable change. In a world nailed together like a box, God, the Creator, had been thought of as a carpenter who created the universe long ago; now, in a world growing like a tree, ever more putting out new roots and new branches, God has more and more been seen as the indwelling spiritual life. Consider that bright light of nineteenth century Christianity, Henry Drummond, the companion of D. L. Moody in his evangelistic tours. He believed in evolution. What did it do to his thought of God? Just what it has done to the thought of multitudes. Said Drummond: "If God appears periodically he disappears periodically. If he comes upon the scene at special crises, he is absent from the scene in the intervals. Whether is all-God or occasional-God the nobler theory? Positively the idea of an immanent God, which is the God of evolution, is infinitely grander than the occasional wonder-worker who is the God of an old theology."

Mr. Bryan proposes, then, that instead of entering into this rich heritage where ancient faith, flowering out in new world views, grows richer with the passing centuries, we shall run ourselves into his mold of medievalism. He proposes, too, that his special form of medievalism shall be made authoritative by the State, promulgated as the only teaching allowed in the schools. Surely, we can promise him a long, long road to travel before he plunges the educational system of this country into such incredible folly, and if he does succeed in arousing a real battle over the issue we can promise him also that just as earnestly as the scientists will fight against him in the name of scientific freedom of investigation so will multitudes of Christians fight against him in the name of their religion and their God.

March 12, 1922

BRYAN LOSES FIGHT TO BAN DARWINISM IN CHURCH SCHOOLS

Presbyterian Assembly Defeats His Anti-Evolution Resolution After a Hot Debate.

MILD SUBSTITUTE ADOPTED

Commoner Angry When J. W. Baer Remarks He Has Been "Mistaken Before.'

BUT HIS 'DRY' PLEDGE WINS

Assembly Adopts Proposal Applying to All Ministers and Church Members.

Special to The New York Times.

INDIANAPOLIS, May 22.—After one of the hottest debates in its history, the Presbyterian General Assembly defeated William J. Bryan's anti-evolution proposal today and adopted a mild substitute, which fell far short of the wishes of the fundamentalists who backed Mr. Bryan.

The Commoner, however, had the satisfaction of winning an earlier fight for a demand that a strict total abstinence pledge should be required of all Presbyterian ministers, officials and members of churches and all teachers and students in Presbyterian colleges and schools.

Debate on the evolution issue began when the Committee on Education presented its report and Mr. Bryan offered the following resolution:

"Resolved that no part of the Educational Fund of the Presbyterian Church of the United States of America shall be paid to any school, college, university or theological seminary, that teaches, or permits to be taught as a proven fact, either Darwinism or any other evolutionary hypothesis that links men in blood relationship with any other form of life."

Substitute Adopted.

The substitute resolution which the Assembly finally adopted was offered by John Willis Baer, of Pasadena, Cal., Chairman of the Committee on Education, of which Bryan is a member. It read:

"Resolved, That Synods and Presbyteries within whose bounds Presbyterian supported academies, colleges and training schools are located are hereby instructed to exercise careful oversight over the instruction given in such institutions, and that Synods and Presbyteries withhold their official approval from such academies, colleges and training schools where any teaching or instruction is given which seeks to establish a materialistic evolutionary philosophy of life which disregards or attempts to discredit the Christian faith."

It looked for a time as if Mr. Bryan's resolution might go through. He spoke to it for an hour, repeating his familiar anti-evolution arguments, with some variations. His speech was punctuated with applause, and at times the Assembly became so unruly that Moderator Wishart had to appeal to the Commissioners to act with "decorum," reminding them that they were "a court of Jesus Christ."

There were numerous amendments, amendments to amendments, motions to refer back to the committee and motions to lay the whole matter on the table.

"Don't put it on the table. Let's fight it out!" called out one commissioner, and that proved to be the prevailing spirit.

Opponents' Main Argument.

Mr. Bryan's opponents presented as their main argument that to pass the Commoner's resolution would be to say to the world that the Presbyterian Church believed a man could not be a Christian if he was an evolutionist.

When Mr. Bryan realized that he was defeated he sank into his chair and looked so pale as to appear almost ill.

In presenting the Committee on Education's report Chairman Baer asked that two members of the committee be heard on resolutions they had submitted to the committee, but which the latter preferred should be presented direct by the movers to the assembly.

The first was introduced by the Rev. Dr. Thomas V. Moore of San Francisco. It called upon "all those in places of responsibility and authority in our State educational institutions to give all diligence to the end that our young men and women shall be safeguarded while pursuing other studies against attacks upon the Christian religion and that the sovereign right to religious faith on the part of all young men and women, not only of our own but also of other nations attending our State-supported institutions, shall at all times be respected."

This was passed without debate, and then Mr. Bryan's resolution was presented and its author made his principal argument.

The first commissioner to speak against the Bryan resolution was the Rev. Dr. Murray S. Howland of Buffalo, N. Y., who offered the following substitute:

"Whereas, the teaching of science and its philosophy has in some colleges been of a character to unsettle the faith of the students; and,

"Whereas, there are many devout men and women of unquestioned Christian character and faith possessing accurate scientific knowledge who believe in evolution, finding it not unsettling but confirmatory to their faith in Christianity; be it

"Resolved, That this general assembly enjoins all officers and trustees of colleges under the Board of Christian Education to secure that the teachings of evolution in their institutions be of such a character as to show that it is not subversive of the Christian faith."

When this had been defeated the Rev. Dr. Edward H. Pence of Portland, Ore., the commissioner who seconded the nomination of Mr. Bryan for moderator, moved the following resolution, which was beaten after a long debate:

"Resolved, That the resolution be referred back to the committee with instructions to prepare and submit a statement of the form of evolution intended, drawing the distinction between one form which affirms or implies the conclusions of a material philosophy, to wit:

"That man was evolved with all his mental, moral, spiritual content, to his consciousness of self and God, by the operation of laws inherently within a form from which he came, and the acknowledgment of possibilities, or even probabilities, that a physical organism may have been evolved by forces and processes implanted by God, sacred, because so chosen and used by Him, and that this organism did not and could not have become human until, by creative fiat of God, he breathed into it the inherent parts which constituted man as the potential son of God.

The final vote on the Bryan resolution, taken after three hours of debate, was a rising vote, and it was so evident that Mr. Baer was the victor and Mr. Bryan the loser that no count was demanded.

Moderator Wishart, in a voice filled with emotion, called on Mr. Baer to pray, and the Californian prayed that, now that the issue had been settled, all bitter feelings might die away.

Bryan and Baer at Odds.

In his final summing up Mr. Bryan protested against a statement made by Mr. Baer, who had remarked:

"The gentleman is as honest as any

man can be, but he is mistaken, as he has been before."

"I object to the statement that I have been mistaken several times. I don't want my democracy to figure here," Mr. Bryan exclaimed.

"Did you do more than I did to put across prohibition?" he shouted to Mr. Baer. "Did you do more than I did to put across women's suffrage? Did you do more than I did to put across the election of Senators by direct vote of the people? Did you do more than I did to levy an income tax so that those who had wealth would have to pay for it?"

Then, turning from Mr. Baer to the audience, he exclaimed:

"There has not been a reform for twenty-five years that I did not support, and I am now engaged in the biggest reform of my life. I am trying to save the Christian Church from those who are trying to destroy her faith."

Yells and screams interrupted the Commoner and Dr. Wishart pounded his gavel and pleaded for "Christian decorum."

"We have preachers in this audience who don't believe in the virgin birth," Mr. Bryan went on. "We have preachers in this audience who don't believe in the resurrection of Christ's body. We have preachers in this hall who don't believe in the miracles."

Mr. Bryan blamed all this disbelief on the belief of these preachers in evolution.

"A professor in Ann Arbor University told his class that thinking men of today did not believe in a personal God," Mr. Bryan declared. "The world needs Christ; he is our only hope."

The report on the ten anti-Fosdick overtures is due tomorrow.

The Assembly, previous to the fight on evolution, passed the following unanimously, without debate:

"Resolved, That, in accordance with the declared policy of this Church, no part of the Educational Fund of the Presbyterian Church in the United States of America be given to any school, college, university or theological seminary that employs any teacher in any grade who is not a member in good standing of some branch of the Christian Church and personally interested in the spiritual welfare of students."

Mr. Bryan's defeat came at the end of a day in which he had been unusually prominent. By special request of the Moderator he led the noon devotional exercises, the Commissioners all remaining. He waxed so warm in his defense of the Christian religion that the Commissioners applauded. He sat on the platform all day by invitation of the Moderator, and his entrances were greeted each time with applause.

Smith Urged to Veto Dry Repeal Bill.

Among the resolutions passed on recommendation of the Committee on Temperance were:

"Resolved, That we deplore the action of the Legislature of New York State, which has passed a bill repealing its State prohibition laws; that we urge the Governor of said State not to sign this bill and that the Stated Clerk be instructed to telegraph this action to Governor Alfred E. Smith of New York.

"That we commend the President of the United States for his stand for law enforcement and for his support of the Eighteenth Amendment and with him we commend Federal Prohibition Commissioner Roy B. Haynes and all Governors of States and others in positions of authority who are using their influence for the strict enforcement of the amendment.

"That we send greetings to Hon. Gifford Pinchot, Governor of Pennsylvania, and urge him to continue the fight for the enforcement of prohibition in his State.

"That this Assembly respectfully urge the President and Congress to use all the powers of the Federal Government to prevent the use of foreign flags for the protection of the rum-laden vessels that anchor beyond the three-mile limit and openly conspire with smugglers to violate the Eighteenth Amendment and the law enacted for its enforcement.

"We affectionately urge all our people, especially ministers and elders, to discourage by precept and example the use of tobacco in all forms.

"This Assembly approves control and oversight of the motion picture industry by Federal, State and local authority in such a manner that each shall supplement the other."

Rumors of a stormy session of the Committee on Education yesterday, when Dr. William P. Merrill, pastor of the Brick Church of New York, faced Mr. Bryan and demanded a retraction of a statement the Commoner was re-

ported to have made about Merrill's mother in a sermon Sunday night, were confirmed today after Dr. Merrill had joined the evolutionists in opposing Mr. Bryan's resolution.

Newspaper accounts of Mr. Bryan's sermon at Westminister Presbyterian Church Sunday night quoted him as saying that one of the most prominent ministers in the Assembly, who had filled one of the most prominent churches in the   Sunday morning, had told him his mother became an agnostic before her death.

Mr. Bryan is reported to have repeated the statement yesterday afternoon in the meeting of the Committee on Education, naming Dr. Merrill as the minister referred to.

When the New York preacher heard of the statement he asked and obtained permission to face Mr. Bryan before the committee and deny the allegation.

Reports from the committee room say that Mr. Bryan did not recognize Dr. Merrill when he first appeared and said the man he said in mind was another person. Dr. Merrill is quoted as replying that "Mr. Bryan's imagination has been substituted for his memory both as to the man he had in mind was another to have said."

"Steam Rolled," Bryan Declares.

INDIANAPOLIS, Ind., May 22 (Associated Press).—Mr. Bryan declared tonight that his resolution had been steam rolled by a machine-ridden convention, dominated by a minority group of clever politicians who are lacking in frankness.

"I have had experience enough in politics to know a machine when I see it, and the machine in control of this assembly works perfectly," his statement said. "The so-called liberals have everything their own way. I found this out as soon as I arrived. * * *

"My protest is against a lack of frankness, but frankness can hardly be expected from people who know they are in the minority and yet want to control the church and its policy. They have used the same tactics that politicians use under the same circumstances."

May 23, 1923

BRYAN WILL DEFEND ANTI-EVOLUTION LAW

Will Act as Counsel in Case to Test Constitutionality of the Tennessee Statute.

MEMPHIS, Tenn., May 12.—William J. Bryan was asked in a telegram sent today by the World's Christian Fundamental Association to act as counsel for the association in the case of J. T. Scopes of Dayton, Tenn., charged with teaching the theory of evolution in violation of the Tennessee State law. The case is designed to test the constitutionality of the Tennessee statute.

Mr. Bryan, telegraphing from Pittsburgh, said he would be pleased to represent the association in the prosecution, provided his acceptance was agreeable to the legal department of the State.

PITTSBURGH, May 12.—William J. Bryan announced today that he had accepted an invitation to aid in defending the State law prohibiting the teaching of evolution in public schools of Tennessee. He made the announcement in an address before the Pittsburgh Presbytery, in which he defended the passage of the law.

"I have been asked to help in the fight to preserve the integrity of that law, and I have wired that I am going to do it," he said.

May 13, 1925

DENIES EVOLUTION REPUDIATES BIBLE

NASHVILLE, Tenn., June 21 (AP).—The theory of evolution in no way conflicts with the divine creation of man as related in the Bible nor repudiates the biblical story of creation, Clarence Darrow, lawyer of Chicago, engaged in the defense of Professor John T. Scopes at Dayton, said in a letter to Noah H. Cooper of Nashville in answer to a questionnaire sent by Mr. Cooper.

Mr. Darrow in his reply denied that he had laid the Leopold and Loeb crime to Nietzsche or any such philosophy.

"As to the Loeb-Leopold case, I did not ask for justice and mercy," he declared. "I did say their crime grew from heredity and environment. I did say that they had been carefully trained, but if one were wise enough to know the end from the beginning some other sort of training might have prevented the act.

"I did say, in answer to something the State had said, that I thought their lives would be perfectly safe if Jesus was to pass upon them, and I still think so. I likewise think that he would not have believed in a law making it a criminal offense to teach evolution in the public schools.

"If evolution is contrary to the teaching of the Bible as to the origin of man, then astronomy and geology are likewise in conflict, and these also should be barred from the public schools. If it should be a crime to teach evolution, then it should be a crime the same whether in public or private schools; whether on the platform or in newspapers or books.

"I believe that if the theory of evolution is wrong free discussion and investigation will show it, and that it will likewise show that it is not inconsistent with any real religion.

"I believe that the business of public schools should be to educate pupils."

June 22, 1925

SCOPES GUILTY, FINED $100, SCORES LAW; BENEDICTION ENDS TRIAL, APPEAL STARTS; DARROW ANSWERS NINE BRYAN QUESTIONS

FINAL SCENES DRAMATIC

Defense Suddenly Decides to Make No Plea and Accept Conviction.

BRYAN IS DISAPPOINTED

Loses Chance to Examine Darrow and His Long-Prepared Speech Is Undelivered.

HIS EVIDENCE IS EXPUNGED

Differences Forgotten in the End as All Concerned Exchange Felicitations.

Special to The New York Times.

DAYTON, Tenn., July 21.—The trial of John Thomas Scopes for teaching evolution in Tennessee, which Clarence Darrow characterized today as "the first case of its kind since we stopped trying people for witchcraft," is over. Mr. Scopes was found guilty and fined $100, and his counsel will appeal to the Supreme Court of Tennessee for reversal of the verdict. The scene will then be shifted from Dayton to Knoxville, where the case will probably come up on the first Monday in September.

But the end of the trial did not end the battle on evolution, for not long after its conclusion William Jennings Bryan opened fire on Clarence Darrow with a strong statement and a list of nine questions on the basic principles of the Christian religion. To these Mr. Darrow replied and added a statement explaining Mr. Bryan's "rabies." Dudley Field Malone also contributed a statement predicting ultimate victory for evolution and repeating that Mr. Bryan ran away from the fight.

The end of the trial came as unexpectedly as everything else in this trial, in which nothing has happened according to schedule except the opening of court each morning with prayer. It was reached practically by agreement between counsel in an effort to end the case, which showed signs of going on forever, although all the testimony offered before the jury took only two hours.

Young Scopes, in his shirt sleeves, his collar open at the neck, his carrot-colored hair brushed back, stood up before the bar with a gold epauletted policeman beside him, and Judge Raulston had pronounced sentence before his counsel could suggest that Mr. Scopes might have something to say.

"Oh," exclaimed Judge Raulston. "Have you anything to say, Mr. Scopes, as to why the Court should not impose punishment upon you?"

Scopes Calls Statute Unjust.

Mr. Scopes, who is hardly more than a boy and whose pleasant demeanor and modest bearing have won him many friends since this case started, was nervous. His voice trembled a little as he folded his arms and said:

"Your Honor, I feel that I have been convicted of violating an unjust statute. I will continue in the future, as I have in the past, to oppose the law in any way I can. Any other action would be in violation of my ideal of academic freedom, that is, to teach the truth as guaranteed in our Constitution, of personal and religious freedom. I think the fine is unjust."

No one had expected such a quick ending. Mr. Darrow came into court full of the pleasant anticipation of another "go" at Mr. Bryan, whom he questioned to the delight of hundreds the day before. But the court had no sooner opened than Judge Raulston cided that there would be no furt ir questioning, and then ordered _r. Bryan's testimony expunged from the record.

Mr. Bryan, who had contented himself with the thought that he would have an opportunity to put Mr. Darrow on the stand and tear into him, was somewhat chagrined at this turn of the case, and announced that he would have to appeal to the fairness of the press to give prominence to the questions which he would have asked Mr. Darrow.

"I had not reached the point where I could give my statement to answer the charges made by the counsel for the defense as to my ignorance and bigotry," he said, bitterly.

Sparrow Poses as Dove of Peace.

But before the day's session was over a dove of peace hovered over the court room in the form of a frightened sparrow, which had strayed in through an open window, and everybody exchanged felicitations except Mr. Bryan and Mr. Darrow. Judge John Raulston declared that the Word of God, "given to man, that man may use it as a waybill to the other world," was an indestructible thing, and prayed God that he had decided right the questions raised in the trial. A minister pronounced a benediction and court adjourned.

The general gratification of the people at the end of a good show was shown by their applause whenever any member of either side, or the visiting spectators, rose to thank Dayton for its hospitality and kindness. And there was a further manifestation of the remarkable change in sentiment which has taken place since this trial began.

The defense faced a unitedly hostile audience when they started. There were clamors against Clarence Darrow, the agnostic, and resentment that outsiders should come in and tell Tennessee how to run its schools.

The tide turned when Dudley Field Malone made his first speech and won the hearts of Dayton, for Tennesseans love a fiery speaker, and rounded, eloquent periods delight them. Mr. Darrow ended by winning their respect by his courage in the face of hostility, and when today both sides spoke briefly their appreciation of courtesies, and Mr. Bryan defended his position, it was a repudiation of Mr. Bryan's charges by Mr. Malone and the denunciation of bigotry by Mr. Darrow that won the most fervent applause.

That does not mean that the majority was with them. It was not. But they had caught the fancy of the crowd, which has learned a lot about evolution from the scattered fragments presented to them. Many people of the State crowded around Mr. Darrow after court was over to thank him for his defense of Mr. Scopes and to say that they were ashamed of the Anti-Evolution law.

There was no doubt that the ruling of the Court against further examination of counsel on either side was as much a disappointment to Mr. Bryan as it was to Mr. Darrow. Mr. Bryan was obviously full of wrath at the position in which he had been placed, with no opportunity of justifying himself on the court record, and Mr. Darrow had come into court with the pleasant anticipation of learning what else Mr. Bryan knew about the Bible.

There was a council of war by the forces of the State last night, and whatever desire Mr. Bryan had of going on with his examination so that he could rip into Mr. Darrow and his colleagues, and brand them as agnostics or infidels, was suppressed by Attorney General Stewart, who has maintained an indignant, though dignified, opposition to the events of the last few days. He was anticipated, however, by the Court.

"Since the beginning of this trial the Judge of this court has had some big problems to pass upon," said Judge Raulston as soon as court opened. "Of course, there is no way for me to know whether I have decided these questions correctly or not until the courts of last resort speak. If I have made a mistake, it was a mistake of the head and not the heart.

"There are two things that may lead a Judge into error. One is prejudice and passion, and another is an over-zeal to be absolutely fair to all parties. I fear that I may have committed error on yesterday in my over-zeal to ascertain if there was anything in the proof that was offered that might aid the higher courts in determining whether or not I had committed error in my former decrees. I have no disposition to protect any decree that I make from being reversed by a higher court, because, if I am in error, I hope to God that somebody will correct my mistake.

"I feel that the testimony of Mr. Bryan can shed no light upon any issues that will be pending before the higher courts. The issue now is whether or not Mr. Scopes taught that man descended from a lower order of animals. It isn't a question of whether God created man as all complete at once, or it isn't a question as to whether God created man by the process of development and growth. Those questions have been eliminated by this Court, and the only question we have now is whether or not this defendant taught that man descended from a lower order of animals.

"As I see it, after due deliberation, I feel that Mr. Bryan's testimony cannot aid the higher court in determining that question. If the question before the higher court involved the issue as to what evolution is, or as to how God created man, or created the earth, or created the universe, this testimony might be relevant, but those questions are not before the Court, and so, taking this view of it, I am pleased to expunge this testimony given by Mr. Bryan yesterday from the records of this court, and it will not be further considered."

"Of course I am not at all sure that Mr. Bryan's testimony would aid the Supreme Court, or any other human being," said Mr. Darrow, "but he testified by the hour there and I haven't got through with him yet."

General Stewart objected to an argument, and Mr. Darrow took an exception from the Court's ruling, announcing that he would try to get from the Supreme Court a writ certifying the testimony. Then Mr. Darrow threw up his hands and ended the case.

"We have all been here quite a while, and I say it in perfectly good faith, we have no witnesses to offer, no proof to offer on the issues that the Court has laid down here," he said, "that Mr. Scopes did teach what the children said he taught, that man descended from a lower order of animals. We do not mean to contradict that and I think to save time we will ask the Court to bring in the jury and instruct the jury to find the defendant guilty. We make no objection to that and it will save a lot of time and I think it should be done."

Hays Again Offers Proof.

Arthur Garfield Hays then made again his offer of proof for the record.

"We offer to prove by Mr. Bryan that the Bible was not to be taken literally," he said, "that the earth was a million years old, and we had hoped to prove by him further that nothing in the Bible said what the processes were of man's creation. We feel that the statement that the earth was a million years old, and nothing said about the processes of man's creation, that it was perfectly clear that what Scopes taught would not violate the first part of the act."

All Mr. Hays's arguments brought nothing but exceptions, and then Mr. Bryan rose to his feet, a great weariness in his voice and with the look of a tired and disappointed man.

"At the conclusion of your decision to expunge from the testimony the testimony given by me upon the record I didn't have time to ask you a question," he said. I fully agree with the Court that the testimony taken yesterday was not legitimate or proper. I simply wanted the Court to understand that I was not in position to raise an objection at that time myself, nor was I willing to have it raised for me without asserting my willingness to be cross-examined. Now the testimony has ended and I assume that you expunge the questions as well as the answers."

"Yes, sir," said Judge Raulston.

"That it isn't a reflection upon the answers any more than it is upon the questions," continued Mr. Bryan in his dispirited voice.

"I expunge the whole proceedings," said the Court.

"Now, I hadn't reached the point where I could make a statement to answer the charges made by the counsel for the defense as to my ignorance and bigotry," said Mr. Bryan, turning to glare at Mr. Darrow, who hunched up his shoulders and said:

"I object, your Honor! Now, what's all this about?"

"Why do you want to make this, Colonel Bryan?" asked the Court.

"I just want to finish my sentence."

"Why can't he go outside on the lawn?" growled Mr. Darrow.

Judge Raulston said he would hear what he had to say, and Mr. Bryan continued:

"I shall have to trust to the justice of the press which reported what was said yesterday to report what I will say, not to the Court, but to the press, in answer to that charge scattered broadcast over the world, and I shall also avail myself of the opportunity to give to the press, not to the Court, the questions that I would have asked had I been permitted to call the attorneys on the other side."

"I think it would be better, Mr. Bryan," said Mr. Darrow, "for you to take us out also with the press and ask us the questions, and then the press will have both the questions and the answers."

"The gentleman who represents the defense not only differs from me," continued Mr. Bryan, "but he differed from the Court very often in the matter of procedure. I simply want to make that statement, and say that I shall have to avail myself of the press without having the dignity of its being presented in this court, but I think it is hardly fair"—his voice rose as he lifted his clenched hand—"to bring into the limelight my views on religion and stand behind a dark lantern that throws light on other people but conceals themselves. I think it is only fair that the country should know the religious attitude of the people who come down here to deprive the people of Tennessee of the right to run their own schools."

"If your Honor please," interrupted Mr. Malone, who manages to get into every argument, "I wish to make a statement if statements are in order."

"If your Honor please," added Mr. Malone, who has taken joy in standing up for the religious principles of all those on the side of the defense, "the attorneys for the defense are hiding behind no screen of any kind. They will be happy at any time in any forum to answer any questions which Mr. Bryan can ask along the lines that were asked him yesterday."

Attorney General Stewart, whose Fundamentalism has been the cause of much embarrassment to him all during the case, stopped fidgeting and suggested that the jury be brought in and the case ended. Mr. Darrow and Mr. Stewart, with Judge Raulston, then agreed that the jury be brought in and instructed by both sides to bring in a verdict of guilty.

When the jury were present Judge Raulston charged them that all they had to do was to determine whether or not Mr. Scopes taught that a man descended from a lower form of animals and that if they so found beyond a reasonable doubt they should bring in a verdict of guilty.

"May I say a few words to the jury," said Mr. Darrow. He stood before them, as plain a looking person as any one among them, his suspenders standing out against his shirt, his arms folded so that he grasped his shoulders, and smiled benignantly at them.

"We are sorry we have not had a chance to say anything to you. We will do it some other time," he said. "Now, we came down here to offer evidence in this case and the Court has held under the law that the evidence we had is not admissible, so all we can do is take an exception and carry it to a higher court to see whether the evidence is admissible or not. As far as this case stands before this jury, the Court has told you very plainly that if you think my client taught that man descended from a lower order of animals you will find him guilty, and you heard the testimony of the boys on that question and heard read the books, and there is no dispute about the facts.

"Scopes did not go on the stand, because he could not deny the statements made by the boys. I do not know how you may feel, I am not especially interested in it, but this case and this law will never be decided until it gets to a higher court, and it cannot get to a higher court very well unless you bring in a verdict. I do not want any of you to think we are going to find any fault with you as to your verdict.

"We cannot explain to you that we think you should return a verdict of not guilty. We do not see how you could. We do not ask it."

"What Mr. Darrow wanted to say to you was that he wanted you to find his client guilty," said Mr. Stewart to the Judge, "but did not want to be in the position of pleading guilty because it would destroy his rights in the Appellate Court."

Bryan's Speech Is Undelivered.

And that's all there was to that. Mr. Bryan did not get his chance to make the summing up he had been working on so long, the speech that was to rival his "Cross of Gold" speech of many years ago, which made him a candidate for the Presidency. He knew he would not get this into the records soon after court opened, and it was one of his great disappointments. He is said to have been writing it for three months. He never would have gotten a chance to make it even if the verdict of guilty had not been found by agreement because the defense had planned to let the State open the summing up, and then refuse to argue, which would have shut off anything except the verbal onslaught of Sue Hicks, who was scheduled to talk first for the prosecution.

After Mr. Scopes had been found guilty and fined, Judge Raulston set bail in $500, which was furnished by The Baltimore Sun. The case will come up before the State Supreme Court in September, and Judge Raulston allowed thirty days for preparation of the appeal.

Then followed the felicitations, started by Mr. Malone, who said:

"Your Honor, may I at this time say on behalf of my colleagues that we wish to thank the people of the State of Tennessee, not only for their hospitality, but for the opportunity of trying out these great issues here."

He was applauded liberally by the crowd. One of the visiting spectators got up to thank Dayton for its hospitality. Gordon McKensie of the prosecution, thanked the defense for bringing into Tennessee new ideas.

"We have learned to take a broader view of life since you came," he said. "While much has been said and much written about the narrow-minded people of Tennessee, we do not feel hard toward you for having said that, because that is your idea. But we people here want to be more broad-minded than some have given us credit for, and we appreciate your coming and we have been greatly elevated, edified and educated by your presense, and should the time ever come when you are back near the garden spot of the world we hope that you will stop off and stay a while with us here in order that we may chat about the days of the past when the Scopes trial was tried in Dayton."

Dr. John R. Neal of the defense spoke, and then Mr. Bryan rose again and said the people would decide this issue.

"I don't know that there is any special reason why I should add to what has been said, and yet the subject has been presented from so many viewpoints that I hope the Court will pardon me if I mention a viewpoint that has not been referred to," he said. "Dayton is the centre and seat of this trial largely by circumstance. We are told that more words have been sent across the ocean by cable to Europe and Australia about this trial than has ever been sent by cable in regard to anything else doing in the United States. That isn't because the trial is held in Dayton. It isn't because a school teacher has been subjected to the danger of a fine of from $100 to $500, but I think it illustrates how people can be drawn into prominence by attaching themselves to a great cause.

"Causes stir the world, and this cause has stirred the world. It is because it goes deep. It is because it extends wide and because it reaches into the future beyond the power of man to see. Here has been fought out a little case of little consequence as a case, but the world is interested because it raises an issue, and that issue will some day be settled right, whether it is settled on our side or the other side. It is going to be settled right. There can be no settlement of a great cause without discussion, and people will not discuss a cause until their attention is drawn to it, and the value of this trial is not in any incident of the trial, it is not because of anybody who is attached to it, either in an official way or as counsel on either side.

"Human beings are mighty small, your Honor. We are apt to magnify the personal element and we sometimes become inflated with our importance, but the world little cares for man as an individual. He is born, he works, he dies, but causes go on forever, and we who have participated in this case may congratulate ourselves that we have attached ourselves to a mighty issue.

"Now, if I were to attempt to define that issue I might find objection from the other side. Their definition of the issue might not be as mine is, and, therefore, I will not take advantage of the privilege the Court gives me this morning to make a statement that might be controversial, and nothing that I would say would determine it.

"I have no power to define this issue finally and authoritatively. None of the counsel on our side has this power, and none of the counsel on the other side has this power. Even this honorable Court has no such power. The people will determine this issue. They will take sides upon this issue, they will state the questions involved in this issue, they will examine the information—not so much that which has been brought out here, for very little has been brought out here, but this case will stimulate investigation and investigation will bring out information, and the facts will be known, and upon the facts as ascertained the decision will be rendered, and I think, my friends and your Honor, that if we are actuated by the spirit that should actuate every one of us, no matter what our views may be, we ought not only desire but pray that that which is right will prevail, whether it be our way or somebody else's."

Darrow Makes Final Retort.

His words brought a last retort from Mr. Darrow. He thanked Dayton for its hospitality and courtesy and liberality and thanked the Court for not sending him to jail, which aroused laughter.

"Of course there is much that Mr. Bryan has said that is true," he continued. "And nature—nature, I refer to—does not choose any special setting for mere events. I fancy that the place where Magna Charta was wrested from the barons in England was a very small place, probably not as big as Dayton. But events come along as they come along.

"I think this case will be remembered because it is the first case of this sort since we stopped trying people in America for witchcraft, because here"—and he thundered out the last words—"we have done our best to turn back the tide that has sought to force itself upon this modern world of testing every fact in science by a religious dictum. That is all I care to say."

Judge Raulston was moved to join the proceedings.

"I recently read somewhere what I think was a definition of a great man, and that was this: That he possess a passionate love for the truth and has the courage to declare it in the face of all opposition. It is easy enough, my friends, to have a passion to find a truth, or to find a fact, rather, that coincides with our preconceived notions and ideas, but it sometimes takes courage to search diligently for a truth that may destroy our preconceived notions and ideas.

"The man that only has a passion to find the truth is not a complete and great man; but he must also have the courage to declare it in the face of all opposition. It does not take any great courage for a man to stand for a principle that meets with the approval of public sentiment around him, but it sometimes takes courage to declare a truth or stand for a fact that is in contravention to the public sentiment.

"Now, my friends, the man—I am not speaking in regard to the issues in this case, but I am speaking in general terms —that a man who is big enough to search for the truth and find it, and declare it in the face of all opposition, is a big man.

"Dayton has been referred to, that the law—that something big could not come out of Dayton. Why, my friends, the greatest Man that has ever walked on the face of the earth, the Man that left the portals of Heaven, the Man that came down from Heaven to earth that man might live, was born in a little town, and he lived and spent his life among a simple, unpretentious people.

"Now, my friends, the people in America are a great people. We are great in the South, and they are great in the North. We are great because we are willing to lay down our differences when we fight the battle out and be friends. And, let me tell you, there are two things in this world that are indestructible, that man cannot destroy, or no force in the world can destroy.

"One is the truth. You may crush it to the earth, but it will rise again. It is indestructible, and the causes of the law of God.

"Another thing indestructible in America and in Europe and everywhere else, is the Word of God, that He has given to man, that man may use it as a way-bill to the other world. Indestructible, my friends, by any force because it is the Word of the Man, of the forces that created the universe, and He has said in His Word that 'My word will not perish,' but will live forever.

"I am glad to have had these gentlemen with us. This little talk of mine comes from my heart, gentlemen. I have had some difficult problems to decide in this lawsuit, and I only pray to God that I have decided them right.

"If I have not the higher courts will find the mistake. But if I failed to decide them right, it was for the want of legal learning and legal attainments, and not for the want of a disposition to do everybody justice."

The meeting was about to break up when Arthur Garfield Hays rose and called out to the Judge, laughingly:

"May I, as one of the counsel for the defense, ask your Honor to allow me to send you the 'Origin of Species' and the 'Descent of Man,' by Charles Darwin?"

There was a roar of laughter as the Judge said he would be glad to receive them.

"We will adjourn," said the Court, "and Brother Jones will pronounce the benediction."

Benediction was pronounced, and it was followed by a rush to the doors.

July 22, 1925

Text of Bryan's Nine Questions on Religion And Darrow's Replies to the Commoner

Special to The New York Times.

DAYTON, Tenn., July 21.—The text of the nine questions which William Jennings Bryan asked Clarence Darrow this evening and Mr. Darrow's replies to them was as follows:

I—The Existence of God.

Q.—Do you believe in the existence of God as described in the Bible?

A.—I do not know of any description of God in the Bible, although we are informed in one part of it that He is a spirit. If Mr. Bryan would describe what he means by God I could probably tell whether I believe in his God. The question of what is meant by the Word was directly put by counsel for the defense, and one of counsel for the State, in Mr. Bryan's presence, said he believed God was like man, and was a magnified picture of a man. I do not believe in this kind of God. As to the origin of the universe and what is back of it I do not pretend to know. I haven't the intimate acquaintance with it that Mr. Bryan says he has.

II—The Bible.

Q.—Do you believe that the Bible is the revealed will of God, inspired and trustworthy?

A.—I think that there is much of value in the Bible. I do not believe that it was written or inspired by God. I believe it should be taken as every book and the portions of every great book made sublime by great figures of speech, may be called inspired. I might even say this of Mr. Bryan's book "In His Image," if I could find any such portion.

III—Christ.

Q.—Do you believe in the supernatural Christ, foretold in the Old Testament and revealed in the New Testament?

A.—I do not believe any supernatural Christ was foretold in the Old Testament and revealed in the New. I believe that the Christ that was prophesied in the Old Testament was a great Jew who should deliver the Jews from their physical bondage and nothing else.

Mr. Darrow answered questions 4, 5, 6 and 7 collectively.

IV—Miracles.

Q.—Do you believe in the miracles recorded in the Old and New Testaments?

V—Reasons Asked.

Q.—If you believe in some, but not all of them, please name a few of those which you accept and those you reject, with the reasons for same?

VI—Virgin Birth.

Q.—Do you believe that Christ was conceived of the Holy Ghost and born of the Virgin Mary as recorded in Matthew and Luke?

VII—The Resurrection.

Q.—Do you believe that Christ rose from the dead, as described in the four Gospels?

A.—As to Questions 4, 5, 6 and 7, I do not believe in miracles. I believe that the universe acts and always has acted in accordance with immutable law, and whatever may be back of the Universe has never violated these laws.

VIII—Immortality.

Q.—Do you believe in the immortality of the soul?

A.—I have been searching for truth of this all my life with the same desire to find it which is incidental to every living thing. I have never found any evidence on the subject.

IX—Origin of Man.

Q.—If you believe in evolution, at what point in man's descent from the brute is he endowed with hope and promise of a life beyond the grave?

A.—I have no knowledge on the question of when man first believed in life beyond the grave. I am not at all sure whether some other animals have not the same hope of future life. The origin may have arisen in vivid dreams concerning the return of the dead, or, for all I know, from actual evidence of the return of the dead.

July 22, 1925

CARDINAL DOUBTS EINSTEIN.

O'Connell Warns New England Catholics Against Relativity.

Special to The New York Times.

BOSTON, Mass., April 7.—Declaring that he had never yet met a man who understood in the least what Dr. Albert Einstein was driving at in his theory of relativity, and that he doubted if Dr. Einstein himself really knew, Cardinal O'Connell today warned members of the New England Province of Catholic Clubs of America not to be misled by false philosophy.

"I have my own ideas about the so-called theories of Einstein, with his relativity and his utterly befogged notions about space and time," the Cardinal said. "It seems nothing short of an attempt at muddying the waters so that, without perceiving the drift, innocent students are led away into a realm of speculative thought, the sole basis of which, so far as I can see, is to produce a universal doubt about God and His creation.

"The outcome of this doubt and befogged speculation about time and space is a cloak beneath which lies the ghastly apparition of atheism."

April 8, 1929

RELIGION AND SCIENCE

—— By Professor Albert Einstein ——

EVERYTHING that men do or think concerns the satisfaction of the needs they feel or the escape from pain. This must be kept in mind when we seek to understand spiritual or intellectual movements and the way in which they develop. For feeling and longing are the motive forces of all human striving and productivity however nobly these latter may display themselves to us.

What, then, are the feelings and the needs which have brought mankind to religious thought and to faith in the widest sense? A moment's consideration shows that the most varied emotions stand at the cradle of religious thought and experience.

In primitive peoples it is, first of all, fear that awakens religious ideas—fear of hunger, of wild animals, of illness and of death. Since the understanding of causal connections is usually limited on this level of existence, the human soul forges a being, more or less like itself, on whose will and activities depend the experiences which it fears. One hopes to win the favor of this being by deeds and sacrifices, which, according to the tradition of the race, are supposed to appease the being or to make him well disposed to man. I call this the religion of fear.

This religion is considerably stabilized—though not caused—by the formation of a priestly caste which claims to mediate between the people and the being they fear and so attains a position of power. Often a leader or despot, or a privileged class whose power is maintained in other ways, will combine the function of the priesthood with its own temporal rule for the sake of greater security; or an alliance may exist between the interests of the political power and the priestly caste.

A SECOND source of religious development is found in the social feelings. Fathers and mothers, as well as leaders of great human communities, are fallible and mortal. The longing for guidance, for love and succor, provides the stimulus for the growth of a social or moral conception of God. This is the God of Providence, who protects, decides, rewards and punishes. This is the God who, according to man's widening horizon, loves and provides for the life of the race, or of mankind, or who even loves life itself. He is the comforter in unhappiness and in unsatisfied longing, the protector of the souls of the dead. This is the social or moral idea of God.

It is easy to follow in the sacred writings of the Jewish people the development of the religion of fear into the moral religion, which is carried further in the New Testament. The religions of all the civilized peoples, especially those of the Orient, are principally moral religions. An important advance in the life of a people is the transformation of the religion of fear into the moral religion. But one must avoid the prejudice that regards the religions of primitive peoples as pure fear religions and those of the civilized races as pure moral religions. All are mixed forms, though the moral element predominates in the higher levels of social life. Common to all these types is the anthropomorphic character of the idea of God.

Only exceptionally gifted individuals or especially noble communities rise *essentially* above this level; in these there is found a third level of religious experience, even if it is seldom found in a pure form. I will call it the cosmic religious sense. This is hard to make clear to those who do not experience it, since it does not involve an anthropomorphic idea of God; the individual feels the vanity of human desires and aims, and the nobility and marvelous order which are revealed in nature and in the world of thought. He feels the individual destiny as an imprisonment and seeks to experience the **totality of existence as a unity full of** significance. Indications of this cosmic religious sense can be found even on

"What a Deep Faith There Must Have Been * * * to Unravel the Mechanism of the Heavens in Long Years of Lonely Work!"

earlier levels of development—for example, in the Psalms of David and in the Prophets. The cosmic element is much stronger in Buddhism, as, in particular, Schopenhauer's magnificent essays have shown us.

The religious geniuses of all times have been distinguished by this cosmic religious sense, which recognizes neither dogmas nor God made in man's image. Consequently there cannot be a church whose chief doctrines are based on the cosmic religious experience. It comes about, therefore, that we find precisely among the heretics of all ages men who were inspired by this highest religious experience; often they appeared to their contemporaries as atheists, but sometimes also as saints. Viewed from this angle, men like Democritus, Francis of Assisi and Spinoza are near to one another.

How can this cosmic religious experience be communicated from man to man, if it cannot lead to a definite conception of God or to a theology? It seems to me that the most important function of art and of science is to arouse and keep alive this feeling in those who are receptive.

Thus we reach an interpretation of the relation of science to religion which is very different from the customary view. From the study of history, one is inclined to regard religion and science as irreconcilable antagonists, and this for a reason that is very easily seen. For any one who is pervaded with the sense of causal law in all that happens, who accepts in real earnest the assumption of causality, the idea of a Being who interferes with the sequence of events in the world is absolutely impossible. Neither the religion of fear nor the social-moral religion can have any hold on him. A God who rewards and punishes is for him unthinkable, because man acts in accordance with an inner and outer necessity, and would, in the eyes of God, be as little responsible as an inanimate object is for the movements which it makes.

SCIENCE, in consequence, has been accused of undermining morals—but wrongly. The ethical behavior of man is better based on sympathy, education and social relationships, and requires no support from religion. Man's plight would, indeed, be sad if he had to be kept in order through fear of punishment and hope of rewards after death.

It is, therefore, quite natural that the churches have always fought against science and have persecuted its supporters. But, on the other hand, I assert that the cosmic religious experience is the strongest and the noblest driving force behind scientific research. No one who does not appreciate the terrific exertions, and, above all, the devotion without which pioneer creations in scientific thought cannot come into being, can judge the strength of the feeling out of which alone such work, turned away as it is from immediate practical life, can grow. What a deep faith in the rationality of the structure of the world and what a longing to understand even a small glimpse of the reason revealed in the world there must have been in Kepler and Newton to enable them to unravel the mechanism of the heavens in long years of lonely work!

Any one who only knows scientific research in its practical applications may easily come to a wrong interpretation of the state of mind of the men who, surrounded by skeptical contemporaries, have shown the way to kindred spirits scattered over all countries in all centuries. Only those who have dedicated their lives to similar ends can have a living conception of the inspiration which gave these men the power to remain loyal to their purpose in spite of countless failures. It is the cosmic religious sense which grants this power.

A contemporary has rightly said that the only deeply religious people of our largely materialistic age are the earnest men of research.

November 9, 1930

PROFESSOR EINSTEIN'S "COSMIC RELIGION": A SYMPOSIUM

Eight Ministers Define Religion in the Light of the Scientist's Statement That "the Only Deeply Religious People of Our Largely Materialistic Age Are the Earnest Men of Research"

IN an article published in THE NEW YORK TIMES Magazine last Sunday Professor Albert Einstein stated his view of "religion and science." He wrote that there are three stages of religious development—the first, that of primitive peoples: the "religion of fear"; the second, the religion which finds its source in the social feelings: the "moral religion" and the third, the "cosmic religious sense," "which recognizes neither dogmas nor God made in man's image."

Defining the "cosmic religious sense," Professor Einstein says that "the individual feels the vanity of human desires and aims, and the nobility and marvelous order which are revealed in nature and in the world of thought. He feels the individual destiny as an imprisonment and seeks to experience the totality of existence as a unity full of significance." He concluded: "A contemporary has rightly said that the only deeply religious people of our largely materialistic age are the earnest men of research."

In view of the interest aroused by Professor Einstein's article, THE TIMES asked several New York ministers to comment upon it, and, in their statements, to reply to the following questions:

1. *What is your definition of religion?*

2. *Do you believe that the highest form of religion is the cosmic religion, as defined by Einstein?*

The replies of the clergymen follow:

"WE ARE CITIZENS OF INFINITE SPACE"

By the Rev. ROBERT NORWOOD,
Rector, St. Bartholomew's Church.

THERE is, of course, nothing new in Professor Albert Einstein's observations on religion and science. The fact is, any kind of relationship in terms of one's devoted best is religious. I suspect that few thinkers now stress the so-called supernatural element in religion, for how can one be related to that which is beyond experience? It is only as we know that we can enter into eternal life. So Jesus taught.

Real knowledge leads us into cosmic freedom, for we cannot be free if we are imprisoned on a planet. As we know ourselves to be citizens of infinite time and space, we share with all true pioneers of man that ecstasy which I am sure Dr. Einstein would describe as cosmic. Paul re-garded the cosmic mind as identical with eternal life. For that reason the supernatural element in religion is bound to disappear. There is nothing above nature, for it reveals God in whom "we live and move and have our being," as certain also of our own poets have said.

I see no reason why any one should quarrel with this Einstein statement. Since relations are progressive, if they are sincere, man steps from glory to glory as he passes on his way into the deepening fellowship of the spirit. I am disposed to challenge the statement that "the only deeply religious people of our largely materialistic age are the earnest men of research," if by that we limit ourselves to either the scientist or the philosopher. We must not narrow the word. All friendship is the expression of research in terms of personality, and the exploration of the human heart is as heroic as the patient study of this planet and its surrounding space throbbing with the rhythms of that heart. The religion of the future will be a fellowship of mankind following the torch of truth and singing a Te Deum as it goes on its appointed way.

"RELIGION—A QUEST FOR THE ULTIMATE"

By the Rev. DANIEL A. POLING.
Editor-in-Chief of The Christian Herald.

ANOTHER has said "Religion—any religion—is man's quest for God." Man's search for God is man's search for the answer to his being. What am I? What is my origin? What is my destiny? Where am I bound? Professor Einstein is correct when he writes, "the most varied emotions stand at the cradle of religious thought and experience."

But fear is not the final answer to the question, "What is the origin of religion?" Religion is born rather in the eternal query, "What is man?" Professor Einstein has given a generally true picture of the progress of the human race from its conception of a tribal diety who must be bribed or appeased to a Heavenly Father whose love is as great as his power. But does not the distinguished scientist fall into an error common to humbler mortals when he affirms that "the ethical behavior of man requires no support from religion" and that "the churches have always fought against science and persecuted its supporters"? Is not Professor Einstein too general to be accurate? Is not his endorsement of a "contemporary" who declares "the only deeply religious people of our largely materialistic age are the earnest men of search" —is not his endorsement of this statement a departure from his usually scientific spirit and method? He is at least a victim of overstatement.

Professor Einstein's brilliant contribution to current religious discussion should be reassuring to every leader of religious thought in every faith. It emphasizes again the timeless fact that man is indeed incurably religious. The greatest scientist of the age has his "cosmic religious experience." To him it is "the strongest and noblest driving force" behind his life. As he describes his faith in the "rationality of the structure of the world" and the longing of great minds to know the truth, one senses the same ecstasy that sent Livingstone into Africa and Grenfell to Labrador; the same profound and purposeful emotion that shone from my mother's eyes as she taught me the prayers of my childhood. Religion is a cosmic experience to Professor Einstein, and his experience by whatever name will enrich the race. But to him and to us all, religion "pure and undefiled" is man's quest for the ultimate.

To those whose faith centres in the Man of Galilee, in His will and His way, religion is more than a quest of God; it is finding God in Jesus. For them Jesus voiced the answer to man's long search when he said, "I am coming that they might have life and that they might have it more abundantly."

"COSMIC RELIGION IS NOT RELIGION"

By the Rev. IGNATIUS W. COX, S. J.,
Professor of Philosophy, Fordham University.

IN requesting a statement on the religious views of Dr. Albert Einstein, THE NEW YORK TIMES asked me to answer two questions. This I shall do in the order they were proposed. "What is your definition of religion?" I hold the following statements as expressing the nature of religion: Historically, the term religion means the intellectual grasp by man of a bond between him and a Supreme Being of superlative excellence, upon whom man knows himself to be physically dependent

An emotional consciousness, called religious emotion, is a consequence of, but not antecedent to, the understanding of the above truth. Religion, therefore, is a moral bond supervening upon the physical bond of man's dependence upon God.

Such a moral bond presupposes certain truths to which intellectual assent is given and entails certain duties arising from these truths. Theoretic religion is the sum of truths defining our relations to the Supreme Being; practical religion is the sum of our duties toward God arising from these truths. Hence religion, looked at objectively, is the totality of these truths and duties. If the truths defining our relations to the Supreme Being are known solely by the light of reason, religion is natural; if the truths are the result of a special manifestation of God to man, the religion is supernatural.

Dr. Einstein makes religion solely a matter of emotion, and this is incorrect. Spiritual emotions presuppose acts of knowledge and religious emotions are spiritual. An irrational animal is incapable of religious emotion. Dr. Einstein is again wrong when he says that in primitive peoples "it is fear that awakens religious ideas." This is not the case in the Aetas of the Philippines, the inhabitants of Terra del Fuego, the Veddahs of Ceylon, the pigmies of Africa, the Semangs of Malacca, the Andaman Islanders. It is arbitrary and contrary to fact to say that all religions are founded on emotions. The religion of the Jewish people, cited by Dr. Einstein, was a supernatural religion, and not founded on an emotion, but on the intellectual grasp of a supreme, personal, intelligent being, distinct from man and the universe, a being upon whom man depended and toward whom man had duties. In fact, Dr. Einstein gave no definition of religion in his article.

What definition would be applicable to the first two divisions of religion he gives and his cosmic religion? The first two have this in common: they are founded on the acknowledgment of a personal God; his cosmic religion is based on no such acknowledgment. Indeed, in the words of the distinguished doctor, cosmic religion is "essentially" different from the first two. In that case it ceases to be religion. Things that essentially differ cannot be the same.

The second question proposed was this: "Do you believe with Einstein that the highest form of religion is cosmic?" I do not. Cosmic religion is not religion because it does not admit the existence of a supreme personal God, distinct from the universe. Cosmic religion is not moral because Dr. Einstein does not believe in human freedom, since Dr. Einstein claims that man "acts in accordance with inner and outer necessity." I think that cosmic religion is atheism, euphemistically called religion. Many sincere admirers of Dr. Einstein would doubtless be pleased to have the illustrious scientist answer a question, which would throw a flood of light on his whole position: "Doctor, are you not an atheist in this meaning of the term, one who does not admit the existence of a personal God distinct from man and the universe?"

"EINSTEIN EXCLUDES, I WOULD INCLUDE"
By RABBI NATHAN KRASS
of Temple Emanu-El.

I HAVE very little fault to find with Einstein's declaration that the cosmic religious sense as manifested by Kepler, Newton, himself and the other earnest men of research is indicative of the fact that in the deepest sense there is no conflict between science and religion.

But Einstein delimits religion. He excludes. I would include. He avers that the believers in the religion of fear, the devotees of the social-moral religion, the people of faith whose God is anthropomorphic and anthropopathic, dishing out destinies, rewards and punishments, are not in reality deeply religious. I think they are profoundly, mystically, most intimately, most naïvely, yet most genuinely, religious. Their ways may not be, and actually are not, my ways of religious experience, but inasmuch as they do have those experiences, fearing, revering, loving, striving to be morally and spiritually like the anthropomorphic God whom they worship, they are religious. I do not exclude them because they have no cosmic religious sense. I do include Einstein and all other noble-minded men and women who wholeheartedly dedicate their lives to the quest of the good and the true, and, I may add, the beautiful. Because beauty in its essence is the artistic expression of a genuine religious feeling.

We must look in life for the higher synthesis and in a neo-Hegelian sense envisage the great variety of religious experiences, with their multifarious contradictions, conflicts and illogicalities, as the cosmic content of man's unquenchable yearning for contact with eternality and infinity. Hence we must include all, even the crudest expressions of this yearning, in the category of religion. If exclude I must, then out goes the scoffer who sneers at and scorns what others hold sacred. But I am confident that my God, who is infinitely better than I am, would include even him!

"THE LIFE OF GOD IN SOULS OF MEN"
By the Rev. S. PARKES CADMAN
Pastor, Central Congregational Church, Brooklyn.

I SHOULD hesitate to ascribe all the motive forces of human beings to "feeling and longing." The noblest displays of human activity are traceable, in my judgment, to that superior guidance and strength which plays a major part in man's spiritual development.

Doubtless fear had much to do with the awakening in him of religious ideas. Their primitive stages were profoundly influenced by his dread of natural events which he could not understand, and his personalization of those events or of their reactions in himself, in deities which he worshipped. These processes are still observable in backward peoples.

But I find it difficult to concede so large a place to fear as that assigned by Professor Einstein. In the transition from polytheism to monotheism other and finer elements assumed an importance which should be considered. These are indicated in the professor's comments upon the domestic relationships to which he attributes the social or moral ideal of God. Yet neither Judaism nor Christianity sustains his interpretations of their origin. They claim to have been founded upon a divine revelation which has generated humanity's virtues and repressed its vices. The prophets and apostles of the Bible are practically a unit in this claim. Plainly, they believed they shone in a borrowed light and also that the Father of lights was its source.

As I read Professor Einstein's article I wonder if he has sufficiently safeguarded it against the assumption that the psychological description of any given human experience is the final explanation of that experience. Take prayer as the test. It implies the reality of a Supreme Being with whom we may make definite contact. The contact is made by those who definitely believe that man's spiritual life is as completely controlled by certain laws, or known ways of operation, as his physical life. Countless myriads pray for the same basic reason that they eat. Praying and eating renew the life to which they respectively minister.

Spiritual and Physical.

Nobody repudiates food because he does not understand the physiology of eating. Nobody repudiates prayer solely because it is addressed to an invisible objective. If it connects its devotees with a larger, purer life, there is no danger of its disappearance. The objection that this beneficial result is due to a self-induced state of mind is not serious. Provided that state of mind elevates and energizes the soul, surely prayer makes a difference and is as valid in the spiritual realm as hygienics and proper diet are in the physical realm.

Certainly I cannot admit that the essentials of a spiritual faith are limited to "exceptionally gifted individuals or especially noble communities." The history of religion justifies St. Paul's magnificent paradox that God chose the weak and despised things of this world to confound the mighty and the popular things. Many of the purest examples of "the cosmic religious sense" were raised out in the very dust by a regenerating strength foreign to them and to their surroundings. There is a universal note in righteousness which places its practice at the disposal of the poor, the obscure and even the intellectually unprivileged.

Science, like religion, is by no means "such stuff as dreams are made of." Both have great realities to express. As I see it, their work is complementary, not antagonistic. All knowledge meets at the top. But few there be that scale that height. Meanwhile, the churches familiar to me do not stress penalization or reward as the required stimuli for just and equitable deeds. Personally I have no objection to Professor Einstein's assertion that "the cosmic religious experience is the strongest and the noblest driving force behind scientific research." Be it so—since the professor is here relating his experience, allow me to add mine, that religion is the very life of God in the souls of men. The numerous superfluities attached to it do not for a moment prevent me from holding that Christianity is for me eternal life lived here and now, under the eye of God and for the service of my fellow-men. Nor can I conceive any state of society, however scientific or cultured, which can dispense with religion, so understood, without incurring grave and irreparable loss.

"VITAL RELIGION IS A RELATION TO GOD"

By the Rev. A. EDWIN KEIGWIN,
Pastor, West End Presbyterian Church.

PROFESSOR EINSTEIN'S article is an interesting and stimulating treatment of a vital and mysterious subject. No doubt it will clarify many minds as to certain phases of religion and accomplish even larger good.

Of course, the treatment is not exhaustive. Indeed, the mystery can never be solved by proof, argument and thinking. Vital religion, being something entirely beyond all our solutions, can be grasped only by faith. While the article leaves much to be desired, it goes about as far as a scientific discussion should be expected to go.

A "cosmic religious experience" is considered, but no notice is taken of a personal religious experience, which is the kind of which the Bible mostly treats. The author limits the former to "only exceptionally gifted individuals," but the latter is not so limited, since it has been and still is enjoyed by countless men and women of the lowly as well as the gifted class. As between the two, therefore, it would seem that the latter approaches more nearly the heart of the subject. Vital religion is, beyond all else, an inner conscious, personal relation to God. Ever since the dawn of the Reformation this view of religion has gained ground, becoming more and more clear-cut with the passing years. Certainly this was Jesus's view, and it would be presumptuous indeed to assume to know more about religion than Jesus did.

If, as Professor Einstein frankly admits, "a cosmic religious experience is hard to make clear to those who do not experience it," much more is it difficult to "communicate from man to man" (as he puts it) "a definite conception" of a personal religious experience, or direct illumination from God. And this was precisely the difficulty that confronted the writers of the Old and New Testaments. But for their confidence that the Holy Spirit who moved them to write would also give insight to those who read, the prodigious effort would probably not have been undertaken.

"I assert," says Professor Einstein, "that the cosmic religious experience is the strongest and noblest driving force behind scientific research." This is an impressive and moving assertion. And with equal conviction I would assert that the personal religious experience is the strongest driving force behind the individual and the social trend upward and onward. And the emotion awakened by this driving force of which I speak is not fear but trust in God and love for God and for mankind.

"INTELLECTUAL AND SPIRITUAL MIRACLE"

By the Rev. JOHN HAYNES HOLMES,
Minister, the Community Church.

PROFESSOR EINSTEIN has given a noble interpretation of religion. His statement of the relation between science and religion is one so clear, so wise, so instinct with the essential genius of a great mind, that it should end forever the futile discussions which have so long thrown this subject into confusion. If a humble learner can without impudence endorse a consummate master of human knowledge, I gladly take this opportunity to endorse this great savant's presentation of religion.

When Professor Einstein declares that the highest form of religion is that cosmic religion which strives to comprehend and enter into communion with the vast harmony of the illimitable universe, he is stating what is to my mind the constant character of all religion. even the most primitive. I have long since come to think of religion, in all its forms, as in essence man's ultimate reaction upon the cosmos.

The human race has come to consciousness in its cosmic environment as a child comes to consciousness in its nursery. Like the child, man, conscious of his world, straightway proceeds to make contact with it. His first and last question has always been, what is this world which rings me 'round, this life in which I live and move and have my being? The answer to this question constitutes Science. But in this question—saturating it as light saturates the sky, or water the sea—is that more ultimate question which man has always asked of the universe, What can I do with it?

The Nature of Religion.

The answer to this question constitutes religion, which is none other than man's use of the best knowledge he can get to fulfill the best dream he can conceive. This is surely what Professor Nathaniel Schmidt means when he says in his recent book, "The Coming Religion," that religion is "man's consciousness of some power in nature determining man's destiny, and the ordering of his life in harmony with its demands." It is precisely this which Professor Einstein has in mind in his beautiful adjustment of mind and spirit, science and religion, to the apprehension of the cosmic reality of being.

From the standpoint of such exalted faith, all attempts to define God, to picture his appearance, to establish his will for humankind, of course become ridiculous. It is this fact which makes the accessories of religion—churches, creeds, rites of worship, codes of law—at the best so trivial and at the worst so blasphemous. Professor Einstein is aware of what Herbert Spencer so well termed "the impiety of the pious," and thus assumes that attitude of humble agnosticism which alone befits the truly reverent soul. This is the reason why churches, theologies, rituals are of no fundamental importance and thus tragically in the way when they usurp so central a place in spiritual experience as to become tests of faith or dividing lines of loyalty.

But not all men can survive in the rarefied atmosphere which Professor

Einstein breathes. Most of us walk on lower levels, and thus "are bound," as John Fiske expressed it, "to conceive of the Eternal Reality in terms of the only reality we know, or else refrain from conceiving it under any form whatever." This reality is of course ourselves, and thus deliberately we personalize the universe by a great act of the creative imagination. Our mistake is not in formulating conceptions of God, the soul, &c., but in dogmatizing them into theologies which we presume to substitute for science, instead of recognizing them as poetry which we may use to glorify science. Science deals with facts, religion with uses, poetry with the symbolic expression of the two. In Einstein's transcendent mind these three are miraculously synthesized into a unity which constitutes one of the intellectual and spiritual miracles of history.

"SAINTS GO FURTHER THAN SCIENTISTS"

By the Rev. HARRY F. WARD,
Professor of Christian Ethics, Union Theological Seminary.

PROFESSOR EINSTEIN'S article should have been called "The Religion of Science." Once again he has placed the world in his debt—this time by his clear and forceful statement of the fact that the sacrificial labors of the creative scientist derive from and are supported by a passionate faith in the orderliness and rationality of the universe. This "cosmic religious experience" is indeed a high religion. Its value to mankind, however, depends upon the removal of the limitations with which Professor Einstein has surrounded it. If, as he seems to indicate, it is to be the privilege of the favored few, it will only give us again another priestly class guarding the mysteries or proclaiming the authoritative revelation until they corrupt themselves along with the society they dominate.

The point at which Professor Einstein invites this repetition of history is where he separates "the cosmic religious experience" from the needs of the millions by denying its support to man in his struggle to develop ethical behavior. He does this by a strange inconsistency. Having discriminated between fear religions and ethical religions, he then turns round and confuses them by assuming that the only support religion can give to ethical behavior is through fear of punishment and hope of rewards after death. As a matter of fact, the most ethical of all religions, that of Jesus (not official Christianity), makes exactly similar assumptions about the moral aspect of the universe that the religion of science makes about its physical aspect. From them it derives the same support for the effort to realize the moral possibilities of man that the scientist gets in his effort to satisfy the insatiable intellectual hunger of the human animal.

Interdependent Problems.

Here is where the saints and the prophets of an ethical religion go further than the creative scientists, with whom, as Professor Einstein points out, they have kinship. To the scientist's deep faith in the rationality of the structure of the world" they add an equally deep faith in the morality of the universe. Both of them, of course, recognize its irrational and immoral aspects. It is their faith that in both realms orderliness is basic and can be made to prevail.

The intellectual problem and the moral problem, the need to understand the universe, along with man's part in it, and the need to order human ways and works in justice and fraternity, are interdependent. To separate them by claiming the support of a cosmic faith for one and denying it to the other is fatal. It is harder to get order out of the conflicting impulses and passions of men than to discover the orderliness of the physical universe. If the lonely scientist needs the power of a "cosmic religious sense," how much more do the common people require its equivalent? If they cannot get it, then in the end the scientist and the civilization he makes possible are destroyed by the anarchic passions of the mob. Unless his religion becomes also an ethical religion, throwing both its method and its cosmic faith into the struggle to create the Great Society, the scientist will finally find himself degraded to the function of providing the crowd with creature comforts and the means of destruction.

November 16, 1930

SCIENCE STUDENTS CALLED AGNOSTIC

Says Many Believe Science and Faith Incompatible— Poor Teaching Blamed

By JOHN WICKLEIN
Special to The New York Times.

HOBOKEN, N. J., Dec. 25— Sixty-five per cent of the students at Stevens Institute of Technology have put aside their religious beliefs because they think such beliefs are incompatible with science, according to the Rev. Theodore R. Smith Jr.

Mr. Smith, interdenominational religious adviser on campus, based his statement on a survey he made at the school over the last three years.

Of a total of 1,100 students, he said yesterday, no more than fifty take part in the programs of the three campus religious organizations — the Newman Club for Roman Catholic students, the Stevens Christian Fellowship for conservative Protestants and the Christian Roundtable for moderate and liberal Protestants.

Forty-five per cent of the students indicated they had a Catholic background, 45 per cent Protestant and 10 per cent Jewish. The percentage of students who have turned from these backgrounds, Mr. Smith found, is higher at Stevens, a science and engineering school, than at a liberal arts college where he formerly did counseling.

Lack of Proofs Felt

"Many fellows enter the field of science," the Methodist minister said, "thinking they have to be completely objective. They feel they will have to give up religion because it can't be proved or disproved."

Half of the members of this fall's freshman class of 370 have indicated they have no religious preference or belief, Mr. Smith said. He said he thought that students who lived by the rule of "prove it or throw it out" could never be true scientists.

"Even in science," he said, "there are a number of presuppositions that can be neither proved nor disproved. For instance, the idea that we live in an orderly universe. That can't be proved."

The religious conflicts in scientific students' minds usually stem from poor Sunday school teaching early in life, Mr. Smith has found.

Mr. Smith, who is a metallurgical engineer as well as an ordained minister, insists the modern concepts of religion and science are not incompatible.

Calls Science an Ally

"I feel that science is the ally of faith and not the enemy," he said.

"There's a kind of religious schizophrenia here," Mr. Smith remarked. "Some of them see no disparity between the scientific approach to the truth in the realm of science and the strictly dogmatic approach to truth in religion.

"The temptation of the scientist today is the same as the temptation of the priests in former times—to regard their discipline as infallible. The students who fall in with this tend to make science into a new religion. They cannot be true scientists."

Rather than any one of these approaches, Mr. Smith prefers a more liberal one that permits a student to find out if the "seeming disparities" between science and religion can be resolved.

"Science," he said, "must put to the student a challenge to rethink the things, in religion and elsewhere, that he has formerly accepted as true just because someone told him they were true."

December 26, 1960

SHEEN DENOUNCES PSYCHOANALYSIS

He Recommends Confession of Sin as 'Key to Happiness of the Modern World'

Psychoanalysis in general and "Freudian" psychoanalysis in particular were attacked yesterday by Msgr. Fulton J. Sheen, Professor of Philosophy at the Catholic University of America in Washington.

In a sermon at solemn mass in St. Patrick's Cathedral, he assailed psychoanalysis as "a form of escapism" that produced "morbidity and disintegration" and failed to relieve "the unresolved sense of guilt of sin" from which "most people who consult psychoanalysts are suffering." His topic was "Psychoanalysis and Confession."

Contrasting psychoanalysis with the Catholic practice of confession of sin, he said: "There is no morbidity in confession. You don't look so much on your sins as you look upon your Saviour, who restores you to relationship with the Heavenly Father. Psychoanalysis gives no norms or standards. There are no more disintegrated people in the world than the victims of Freudian psychoanalysis. Confession gives you the standard of Christ, the perfect personality."

The preacher singled out for special condemnation, a psychoanalytic method he described as "transfer of the affection to the analyst."

"This method," he charged, "is only used when the patient is a young and very beautiful woman. It is never found to work among the ugly or the poor."

Since Freudianism is based on "materialism, hedonism, infantilism and eroticism," Msgr. Sheen continued, the patient who consults a "Freudian" analyst can expect "to have him angry with you if you avow long 'arid wastes' of purity." He also charged that "most psychoanalysts cater only to the rich."

Declaring that the modern need is for "psychosynthesis," he said: "People need to be put together. Confession gives you the model person on whom you can be conformed. Confession is no longer an apologetic problem. We Catholics believe in confessing our own sins to a priest, who is the representative of Christ. Others cry out everybody else's sin. Not to be conscious of sin is the unforgivable modern sin. Confession is the key to happiness of the modern world."

March 10, 1947

PSYCHIATRIST QUITS IN CATHOLIC CLASH

Dr. Frank J. Curran Resigns St. Vincent's Post Because of Msgr. Sheen's Views

Dr. Frank J. Curran has resigned as chief psychiatrist of St. Vincent's Hospital, Seventh Avenue and Eleventh Street, because of the failure of the Roman Catholic Archdiocese of New York to clarify or repudiate an attack made on psychiatry by Msgr. Fulton J. Sheen, Professor of Philosophy at the Catholic University, Washington.

Dr. Curran, a Catholic, submitted his resignation on May 27 in a letter to the hospital. Copies also were dispatched to high officials of the archdiocese, including Cardinal Spellman. Dr. Curran withdrew at the same time from posts he held in the archdiocese, among them that of psychiatric expert in the archdiocesan matrimonial court and that of psychiatric consultant in the Chancery Office.

Dr. Curran, confirming his resignation last night at his home,

500 West End Avenue, said his action was the result of a sermon by Msgr. Sheen in St. Patrick's Cathedral on March 9 in which the priest assailed psychoanalysis as a "form of escapism" that produced "morbidity and disintegration."

The physician said that Msgr. Sheen's remarks, thus far uncorrected or unrepudiated, had interfered seriously with his work and that of other psychiatrists throughout the country.

Noting that the Catholic Church made use of the value of psychiatric treatment and that it sponsored and supported the teaching of psychiatry at the Catholic University in Washington, Dr. Curran declared he was dismayed that the church had taken no action to offset a widespread opinion that it condemned the entire field of psychiatry.

Patients Stopped Visits

In his letter to St. Vincent's, Dr. Curran asserted that "as a result of the newspaper publicity given to Msgr. Sheen's speech, private patients of mine as well as hospital patients of St. Vincent's stated that they could no longer come for psychiatric treatment or even consult a psychiatrist because they would be committing a sin if they did."

The letter added that "if Monsignor Sheen was misquoted, he could rectify this easily by giving another statement to the press."

"If, however," the letter went on, "he was not misquoted, then

he has made statements which are not true to fact and therefore, in the interests of truth, as well as in the interests of Catholic patients who might now or later require psychiatric help, his superiors should take action in the matter.

"In the opinion of many Catholics, Msgr. Sheen represents the mouthpiece of the Catholic Church in the United States, not only because of his weekly sermons at St. Patrick's Cathedral but because of his nation-wide broadcasts.

"For this reason, unless someone in authority in the Catholic Church gives a contrary opinion, most Catholic and non-Catholics believe that his speeches are authoritative and represent Catholic dogma."

Says Church Approves

Dr. Curran said last night that nearly 50 per cent of his patients were referred to him by Catholic priests. He also declared Catholic priests who are physicians are being trained in psychiatry with the approval of the church.

Any Catholic in the city who wants to be married and has ever had psychiatric treatment must be examined by a psychiatrist and be judged mentally and emotionally competent before the ceremony can be performed, Dr. Curran explained.

Dr. Curran, who said he was considering an offer to establish a psychiatric clinic at an East Coast university, established the department of psychiatry at St. Vincent's last fall at the request of

the archdiocese, he said. He is 42 years old and was senior psychiatrist at Bellevue Hospital from 1934 to 1945.

Msgr. Walter P. Kellenberg, secretary to Cardinal Spellman, refused last night to comment on Dr. Curran's resignation.

Sees Dispute Enlarged

Dr. Bernard L. Pacella, a consulting psychiatrist for St. Clare's Hospital and associate research psychiatrist at the New York State Psychiatric Institute, commented last night:

"In my own work with the priests with whom I have had contact their own personal views have been in accord with scientific psychiatry and psychoanalysis."

Dr. Pacella, a Catholic, also remarked that, "I'm uncertain whether Monsignor Sheen's views necessarily represent the official views of the Catholic Church. My opinion is that Monsignor Sheen was expressing his own views on the matter. I think the whole matter should be dropped. The controversy has been needlessly enlarged."

Dr. Thomas W. Brockbank, director of the Catholic Charities Guidance Institute, said last night that in his sixteen years of association with that institution he had never "had any difficulty with or criticism from the hierarchy of the Archdiocese of New York."

"We have always got along well with the hierarchy," he said. "There has never been any conflict about our work."

July 20, 1947

Of Faith and Neuroses

PSYCHOANALYSIS AND RELIGION. By Erich Fromm. Dwight Harrington Terry Foundation. 119 pp. New Haven: Yale University Press. $2.50.

By H. A. OVERSTREET

THIS is a daring book to have cast into the midst of the world's excitements, for it will itself breed new excitements. It asks a question about which there cannot help being furious disagreement: Are religion and psychoanalysis compatible? Freud, in his book "The Future of an Illusion," seemed to assert that the two were not compatible. Msgr. Fulton Sheen, in his book "Peace of Soul," makes the same assertion, although for quite different reasons. On the other hand, there have been strong voices proclaiming that the two are not foes but friends. What shall we believe?

In these distinguished lectures Erich Fromm (German-born psychoanalyst, member of the Bennington College faculty, author of "Escape From Freedom" and other books) attempts a fresh approach. To set up alternatives of either irreconcilable opposition or identity of interest, he holds, is quite

Emeritus Professor of Philosophy at the College of the City of New York; Mr. Overstreet wrote "The Mature Mind."

fallacious. The whole issue is far more complex. Before we can say that psychoanalysis is or is not a foe of religion, we need to know what kind of religion we are talking about— also what we understand by the psychoanalytic function.

Defining religion as "any system of thought and action shared by a group which gives the individual a frame of orientation and an object of devotion," he agrees that there is no one without a religious need. However, this does not tell us anything about how the individual satisfies the need. He may worship animals, trees, idols. "The question is not religion or not, but what kind of religion: whether it is one furthering man's development, the unfoldment of his specifically human powers, or one paralyzing them."

Scratch the surface of modern man, he asserts, and we discover any number of primitive religions. Usually we call them neuroses; but we might call them ancestor worship, totemism, fetishism, ritualism, the cult of cleanliness, and so on. They are all doing a thriving business among us.

THE author chooses to concern himself with two major

kinds of religion: authoritarian and humanistic. Authoritarian religion (following the Oxford Dictionary's definition of religion as such) is "recognition on the part of man of some higher unseen power as having control of his destiny, and as being entitled to obedience, reverence, and worship." With such religion, the author holds, psychoanalysis can have nothing in common; for the precise object of psychoanalysis is to free the individual of dependence upon irrational authority and from the tensions that such dependence breeds.

On the other hand, with humanistic religion psychoanalysis has everything in common. Exactly as in the great humanistic religions of Lao-tse, Buddha, Isaiah, Jesus, so in psychoanalysis, the aim is to free the individual from his various enslavements so that he is able "to see the truth, to love, to become free and responsible, and to be sensitive to the voice of his conscience."

The real conflict today, as the author sees it, is not between belief in God and atheism, for "many who profess the belief in God are in their human attitude idol worshipers or men without faith, while some of the most ardent 'atheists' * * * have exhibited faith and a profoundly religious attitude." The real conflict is between genuine re-

ligion and idolatry. "Today it is not Baal or Astarte but the deification of the state and of power in authoritarian countries and the deification of the machine and of success in our own culture which threatens the most precious spiritual possessions of man."

In this brief volume Fromm has, I think, put his finger on quite the central issue of religion. It is, therefore, a book not to be missed by those interested in man's spiritual growth. The central issue of religion, he holds, is not "Do we or do we not believe in God?" but "What kind of human beings are we expected to be?"

Are we expected to be creatures submissive to a divine fiat—creatures, therefore, who will inevitably develop the neurosis-breeding traits that go with such submissiveness? Or are we expected to be individuals free to develop our best human powers, so that we can understand ourselves, our relation to our fellow-men, and our position in the universe?

"Man's aim in humanistic religion is to achieve the greatest strength, not the greatest powerlessness. * * * The prevailing mood is that of joy." To which, according to Fromm, the psychoanalyst says a fervent Amen.

October 29, 1950

SEMINARY SETS UP PSYCHIATRY STUDY

Dr. Earl Loomis Jr. to Begin New Program at Union Theological July 1

By STANLEY ROWLAND Jr.

A new program of religion and psychiatry will be instituted this summer at Union Theological Seminary. It will be made possible by a grant of $200,000 from the Old Dominion Foundation for an initial period of five years.

Dr. Earl A. Loomis Jr. will become director of the program and Professor of Psychiatry and Religion on July 1.

Last August Dr. Loomis became chief of child psychiatry and development in the Department of Psychiatry at the University of Pittsburgh School of Medicine. A lecturer in psychoanalysis, he is a member of the Philadelphia Psychoanalytic Society and the American Psychoanalytic Association.

A minister will be appointed to work with Dr. Loomis in the new program at the seminary, Broadway and 120th Street. The main purpose is "to strengthen the training of prospective ministers for their tasks by introducing them to the understanding of human behavior afforded by contemporary psychodynamics," according to a seminary announcement.

Classrooms and Clinics

The new program will include classroom instruction at the seminary and experience for prospective clergymen in New York hospitals and clinics.

The venture is part of a recent trend toward cooperation between religion and psychiatry.

As modern psychology developed, the care of the soul, or psyche, was frequently taken from the church to the office of the psychiatrist or psychoanalyst. Hostility grew between the fields. It was caused partly by misunderstanding, partly by contradictory assertions about the nature of man. The theologian started with God and the psychiatrist started with man and often seemed to deny God.

Many came to believe that religion and psychology were incompatible; that to believe in the findings of one field was to deny the validity of the other. This idea is still held, but not so widely as it was twenty or thirty years ago.

Signs of Rapprochement

In announcing the new program at Union Theological Seminary, Dr. Henry P. Van Dusen, its president, gave three indications of a rapprochement between psychiatry and religion:

1. Psychiatry challenges religion to a radical re-examination of its understanding of the human spirit and its traditional methods of ministering to the spiritual life of man.
2. Not a few psychiatrists appear to be moving toward a more positive attitude toward religion and the church. Many are turning toward the clergy as possible collaborators.
3. The theologians, having once looked askance at psychoanalysis, are now coming to see fruitful possibilities in the interchange between the disciplines of theology and psychiatry.

"These and other factors," Dr. Van Dusen asserted, indicate a need for prospective clergymen to be instructed in the insights of contemporary psychiatry."

February 6, 1956

RELIGIOUS THOUGHT

THE PHILOSOPHY OF KIERKEGAARD

EITHER/OR. By Soren Kierkegaard. Translated by David F. Swenson, Lillian Marvin Swenson and Walter Lowrie. 2 vols. 387 and 304 pp. Princeton: Princeton University Press. $7.50.

KIERKEGAARD'S THE CONCEPT OF DREAD. Translated with Introduction and Notes by Walter Lowrie. 154 pp. Princeton: Princeton University Press. $2.

TRAINING IN CHRISTIANITY. AND THE EDIFYING DISCOURSE WHICH ACCOMPANIED IT. By Soren Kierkegaard. Translated with an Introduction and Notes by Walter Lowrie. 275 pp. Princeton: Princeton University Press.

FOR SELF-EXAMINATION AND JUDGE FOR YOURSELVES! AND THREE DISCOURSES, 1851. By Soren Kierkegaard. Translated by Walter Lowrie. 243 pp. Princeton: Princeton University Press. $2.50.

KIERKEGAARD'S ATTACK UPON "CHRISTENDOM," 1854-1855. Translated with an introduction by Walter Lowrie. 303 pp. Princeton: Princeton University Press. $2.50.

SOMETHING ABOUT KIERKEGAARD. Revised Edition. By David F. Swenson. Edited by Lillian Marvin Swenson. 259 pp. Minneapolis: Augsburg Publishing House. $2.50.

By RICHARD McKEON

IN an essay on Kierkegaard written fifteen years ago, Professor Swenson complained that the great Danish philosopher and theologian was not available in English and was all but unknown to the English-speaking world. Since 1935 all of his major works have been translated; they have already introduced into the idiom of poets, moralists and theologians terms and dialectical distinctions which fit the latest intellectual fashions. For Kierkegaard, a hundred years ago, laid the foundation of his philosophy in "existential" thinking; and the "existence philosophy" or phenomenology, which reached its fullest development between the two wars in the works of Husserl and Heidegger, is only now coming to broad attention in England and America. Word from liberated France indicates that the philosophy of Heidegger has captivated the young intellectuals there; cultural contacts with Latin America have disclosed to us the prevalence of existential philosophy as a prominent reaction to Positivism and Neo-Scholasticism; and enthusiasts have found suggestive analogies to existential philosophy in the anti-intellectualism of North American pragmatism and in its emphasis upon the individual.

THE form and much of the content of Kierkegaard's voluminous literary output are conditioned by his search for adequate determinations of existence. Existential thinking, as opposed to objective or abstract thinking, takes into account the peculiarities of the thinker as a means of attaining understanding of things. Truth is subjective, and any statement of truth reflects the person of the writer while expressing its object more or less adequately. Many of Kierkegaard's works were, therefore, published under pseudonyms, and the variety of points of view they present as stages toward a grasp of the truth create a gallery of fictitious authors, all distinct, yet all Kierkegaard, and all absorbed in the final stage of his philosophy as expressed in books published under his own name.

The objective thinker fails to attain a truth separated from himself, and he creates a philosophy which he cannot live, for he abstracts thought from the concrete particularities of thinker and subject matter and cuts the thinker off from what he seeks to apprehend. The existential thinker, on the other hand, recognizing that all thought, interest and decision are rooted in personal experience, seeks to understand himself in the concrete process of thinking and as influenced by uncertainties and passions. Truth for Kierkegaard is not something changeless and apart, but, as he says in "The Concept of Dread," "truth exists for the particular individual only as he himself produces it in action." Three main stages on the way of life the esthetic, the moral and the religious are reflected in Kierkegaard's works. Only his religious works express doctrines which he thought proper to appear under his own name, but the esthetic and the moral are absorbed into the religious, and the religious "does not abolish the esthetical but dethrones it."

ALL of the stages of thought and all of the complexities of personal expression are reflected in "Either/Or," the literary masterpiece published in 1843, when Kierkegaard was 30 years old. Kierkegaard appears neither as editor nor as author of the work: its editor, "Victor Eremita," presents papers written by two anonymous authors, designated by the letters A and B, which he has happened on accidentally. The essays of A, which constitute the first volume, set forth the esthetic point of view, while those of B in the second volume transcend and include the esthetic in the moral point of view. The esthetic point of view is presented not merely by setting forth striking insights into the nature of music and poetry or by achieving the lyrical beauty of poetry in the language used by A and the factual concreteness of a short story in the statement of his arguments, but also by supplying moral motive in his concern with the esthetic. A's lengthy study of Mozart's Don Juan turns on the nature of the sensual and seduction; his discerning essay on the motive of ancient and modern tragedy depends on the argument that subjectivity, which is prominent in the modern world, was unknown in antiquity; three literary heroines are studied as victims of "deception"; and the famous "Diary of the Seducer," with which the first volume closes, is a long expression of the conviction of the seducer that his plot (nothing as gross as a physical act since "love has its own dialectic") was lived poetically.

THE second volume consists of two long letters by B: marriage is defended in the first as the most concrete manifestation of life and possessed therefore of esthetic validity, and personality is analyzed in the second as an equilibrium between the esthetic and the moral, in which, far from being destroyed, the esthetic is preserved and ennobled. The religious is adumbrated, even in this either-or of the esthetic and the moral, in a short sermon by a country parson, included in B's letters, which brings God into relation with man by meditation on the happiness implied in the thought that as against God we are always in the wrong. By the device of this sermon the two volumes close with words expressive of a kind of transcendental pragmatism: "only the truth which edifies is truth for you."

Non-rational processes assume great importance in Kierkegaard's philosophy; edification is essential to truth; esthetic, moral and religious problems center about the states of deception, guilt and sin, and they are

explained by the passion of fear, dread and despair. Kierkegaard intended at first to publish "The Concept of Dread," which appeared in 1844, under his own name, but since it contained so intimate a confession of his "stern upbringing from innate dread to faith," it was issued as the work of Vigilius Haufniensis (the Watchman of Copenhagen).

It is, as the author reiterates, a psychological study of dread, applied to the unfruitful problem, as it would seem to modern temperaments, of original sin and on the unpromising assumption that man is a synthesis of soul and body constituted and sustained by spirit. Yet the examination of contradictions found in the historical conception of original sin leads Kierkegaard to a dialectical elucidation of guilt and innocence by means of dread which is, while consistent with innocence, the presupposition of sin, and thence to the differentiation of "objective" dread which reflects the sinfulness that came into the world with Adam's sin and "subjective" dread which is the possibility of freedom. Spirit synthesizes body and mind and brings the determination of time into relation with future and eternity; and dread is turned finally on the consequences of sin when the dread of good is distinguished from the dread of evil. Like St. Augustine, Kierkegaard is able to find flashes of profound psychological insight into moral and religious purposes in the dialectical exploration of doctrinal points and biblical incidents.

KIERKEGAARD'S religious "Discourses" had from the first been published under his own name and after 1848, when his writings concentrated upon Christian themes, the method of "indirect communication" and the pseudonyms were abandoned. However, "Training in Christianity," written in 1848 and published in 1850, was published as the work of "Anti-Climacus," although Kierkegaard's name appeared as editor, for this examination of faith and its object reflected and affected his personal relations to Bishop Mynster, since it turned on the argument that the relation of man to Christ is not a dilemma between doubt and belief but between "offense" and belief, and it led to the sharp separation of "Christendom," as instituted in the official Church, from "Christianity." This theme reappears with specific application to Lutheran Protestantism in "For Self-Examination," which was published under Kierkegaard's name in 1851 and in "Judge for Yourself!" which was published twenty-one years after his death. It takes its most striking form in "Attack Upon 'Christendom,'" a series of articles which Kierkegaard was engaged in publishing at the time of his death, in protest against a eulogy of Bishop Mynster in a memorial sermon as "one more link in the holy chain of witnesses for the Truth stretching all the way from the days of the Apostles to our own times," on the grounds that the established Church falls far short of Christianity and its ministers from the Christian ideal of witnesses to the Truth.

THE philosophy of Kierkegaard is so complicated by the circumstances that affected it and the pseudonyms that participate in its expression that the reader stands in need of such aid and introduction as the late Professor Swenson sought to supply. "Something About Kierkegaard" is a collection of essays and lectures, somewhat repetitious at points, but animated not only by veneration for Kierkegaard, but also by profound understanding of the philosophic sources and implications of his dialectic. They afford helpful guidance both to the fraternity of authors which Kierkegaard created for his works and to the intricacies of doctrinal continuity and opposition contained in those works.

THE significance of Kierkegaard must be sought, however, not merely in his works but, as he himself would doubtless have put it, "in our times." The growing vogue which he enjoys is not indication that many people are now prepared to follow the way he pointed back from the esthetic and from speculation to Christianity, but it is, rather, an echo sounded by each of his three stages in contemporary anti-intellectualism. Poets may find in his nice oppositions of motives and emotions the materials for poetic constructions that have vague ethical overtones, but instead of following the strenuous dialectic which the oppositions imply, they conceive of poetry as simple oppositions coexisting in a historical character or event. Moralists welcome an analysis of doubt and resolution, but they turn the conception of dread (now become a staple of moral philosophy) to dubious metaphysical perplexities about time and being or about times and characters. Theologians repeat somewhat more timidly the certainty that Christianity has not been realized as a prelude to advocating broader adherence to their own particular sects.

Kierkegaard liked to compare his method and mission to the inquiry of Socrates and the demon that inspired him. In considering the influence of Kierkegaard, it is well to remember that the Socratic method influenced Xenophon as well as Plato and it led to the formation of schools of skeptics, hedonists and mystics, for although Kierkegaard's philosophy might conceivably contain a concrete formulation of some of the troubles which his times, like ours, glossed over in philosophies which not even philosophers live, his doctrines have in their turn inspired bizarre simplifications and aggravations of the confusions of contemporary life and thought which are stated as their solutions.

A Faith--and a Literary Program

EXISTENTIALISM. By Jean-Paul Sartre. Translated by Bernard Frechtman. 92 pp. New York: Philosophical Library. $2.75.

WHAT IS EXISTENTIALISM? By William Barrett. 63 pp. New York: Partisan Review. 50 cents.

By GRANVILLE HICKS

THE influence of Marxism, so strong in American intellectual life in the middle Thirties, declined in the later years of the decade and was largely obliterated by the Soviet-German pact of August, 1939. Five years later, when Paris was liberated, Americans began to hear about the Existentialists and the part they had played in the resistance movement. The intellectuals, who abhor an ideological vacuum, were immediately on the alert. Existentialism appeared to be both a faith and a literary program. Perhaps this was the long-awaited post-war, post-Marxist movement—about which all intellectuals could argue and to which some would presumably be converted.

The self-appointed interpreters have done their best, in all sorts of periodicals from the most recondite to the most popular, and Existentialism has been widely discussed, but it has not become more than an object of curiosity. In part the explanation seems to be that there are two Existentialisms. One is a philosophy that has a worthy lineage and that concerns itself with profound and often rather technical problems, and the other is an attitude toward life, or perhaps one should say a mood. Both the philosophy and the attitude are in a general way understandable; what is obscure is the connection between them.

Jean-Paul Sartre, acknowledged leader of the movement and by all accounts a power in French literature and perhaps in French politics as well, has been adequately represented in this country as spokesman for the Existentialist mood. He lectured here in 1946; his two plays have been produced; one of his novels recently appeared in translation and another is to be published in the fall. "L'Etre et Le Néant," however, his major exposition of Existentialism as a philosophy, has never been translated, and we have had to learn about his theories at second hand.

The little volume that is pretentiously entitled "Existentialism" does not do much to remedy the situation. It is simply a transcript of a lecture delivered by M. Sartre in Paris in 1945, a lecture that he evidently prepared with the critics of Existentialism very much in mind. (The volume contains some of the discussion that followed the lecture, including an argument between M. Sartre and a Marxist named Naville.) Moreover, it is rather less formally expository than one would expect even a polemic to be. Reading it, indeed, I feel as if I had caught fragments of some harangue in passing through a crowded room. I can tell that the speaker feels deeply about something, and he seems to believe that his remarks are coherent, but the essential clues are missing.

Sartre's manner is urgent and even belligerent. He strikes leftward at the Communists, who charge him with fostering quietism, and rightward at the Catholics, who accuse him of dwelling on human degradation. He insists that the Existentialist choice is not an arbitrary one, and that there is an Existentialist basis for judging human conduct. He denounces all determinists as cowards. What he is for is defined almost entirely in terms of what he is against.

SARTRE distinguishes between Christian and atheist Existentialists, identifying himself with the latter group. There can be, he maintains, no such thing as the idea of man, since there is no divine mind in which that idea could have its abode. The basic fact for the individual is his own existence: in the familiar phrase, existence precedes essence. But if there is no idea of man, no divine pattern to which life must conform, the individual is fully responsible for every choice he makes. He makes himself, in short, and he cannot escape responsibility for the result.

The Existentialist mood, as conceived by M. Sartre, is expressed in certain key words. Because of his complete responsibility, man feels anguish. Because there is no God, he suffers from forlornness. Because he has no general truths to rely on, he feels despair. But M. Sartre's insistence on anguish, forlornness and despair does not lead him to resignation and passivity. On the contrary, he preaches what he calls involvement—that is, participation in human affairs—as the only way in which men can realize themselves.

HERE, then, are some of the characteristic themes of Existentialism as revealed in M. Sartre's polemic. To understand what lies behind them, we cannot do better than to read William Barrett's pamphlet. Barrett begins, of course, with Kierkegaard's revolt against the Hegelian system, but he sees Kierkegaard's philosophy as only one element in a widespread movement. "It requires," he writes, "only a rapid glance over the philosophy of the last hundred years to discover in its development a remarkable enlargement of content, a progressive orientation toward the immediate and qualitative, the existent and factual." In this "search for the concrete" not only Nietzsche and Dilthey but James, Bergson, Dewey, and Whitehead have played their parts. Sartre's Existentialism, however, derives directly from Otto Heidegger, who flourished in the Twenties and subsequently became a Nazi, and it is to Heidegger that Mr. Barrett devotes most of his attention.

Although Mr. Barrett's pamphlet is not easy reading, it gives the layman a clearer conception of Existentialism as a philosophy than he could possibly get from Sartre's lecture. We see what problems preoccupy the Existentialists—the problem of being, for instance, and the problem of time—and how they and their forerunners have approached these problems. Barrett not only places Existentialism in the history of philosophy; he relates it to the period in which it developed, and his comments on Existentialism as a phase of Romanticism are particularly suggestive.

It is not enough, however, to deal with Sartre's Existentialism as a philosophical phenomenon. There is the Existentialist mood, which Sartre discusses in his lecture in terms of anguish, forlornness and despair, but has elsewhere described as nausea. Is this mood to be regarded as a logical deduction from certain philosophical principles, or should it be understood as, at least in part, the product of a general crisis in Western civilization and of certain specific crises in the life of the French nation? Are not the critics with whom Sartre spars in this lecture right in asserting that his talk about responsibility reduces itself to a justification of arbitrary — and often violent — action? If so, his experiences during the German occupation may help to explain his fondness for acts that at any cost proclaim the survival of individual freedom. And certainly his participation in the resistance movement helps us to understand his concern with involvement, which is one of the more attractive but not one of the more logical aspects of his doctrine.

Mr. Barrett takes cognizance of the Existentialist mood in a preface and an epilogue that have as their theme Dostoevsky's Underground Man, who "vomits out the state, nature, all logic and common sense." The Underground Man, Mr. Barrett suggests, is a natural Existentialist. Existentialism is an affirmation of the importance of uncomfortable facts, the facts that the systematic philosopher overlooks. That is the source of its appeal to the Underground Man, who feels that his world is full of uncomfortable facts and who is himself an uncomfortable fact. Sartre's characters—and presumably Sartre himself—do not feel as they do because they are Existentialists; they turn to Existentialism because it provides a justification for their feelings.

We have found a connection between Existentialism as a philosophy and Existentialism as a mood, and if it seems rather tenuous, that may explain Existentialism's failure to catch on in America. Although we can understand Existentialism as a mood, it is not really our mood, and therefore we can be objective about the problem it poses. Furthermore, we can be objective about the solutions of those problems that are offered by Existentialism as a philosophy. We can see that they may turn out to be important, but we cannot get excited about them. It is a safe bet that there will be no Existentialist riots in New York City.

August 17, 1947

ALL SARTRE'S WORKS BANNED BY VATICAN

Special to The New York Times.

ROME, Oct. 30—By a decree of the Supreme Congregation of the Holy Office all of Jean Paul Sartre's works have been placed in the Vatican's index of forbidden books. The decree, which bears yesterday's date, was approved today by the Pope and ordered published. It appeared this afternoon in the Vatican newspaper Osservatore Romano.

The Congregation of the Holy Office made no mention in its decree of the reasons for which M. Sartre's works have been thus condemned. Osservatore Romano was equally silent on this subject.

The condemnation of M. Sartre caused no surprise in Catholic circles.

It was recalled that in November, 1946, the St. Thomas Aquinas Institute of Philosophy met in Rome to examine existentialism in the light of Catholic doctrine. It drew a sharp line between existentialism, according to the ideas of its founder, Soren Kierkegaard, in the nineteenth century and the Sartre brand of existentialism. M. Sartre was held to have distorted and debased existentialism in his quest of popularity.

It was recalled also that the Pope, speaking to members of the St. Thomas Aquinas Institute on that occasion, said: "We have no intention of dealing fully with existentialism. But we ask: has philosophy any road open to it except despair if it does not find its solutions in God, in personal eternity and immortality?"

October 31, 1948

Christian View of Existentialism

EXISTENCE AND THE EXISTENT. By Jacques Maritain. Translated by Lewis Galantiere and Gerald B. Phelan. 149 pp. New York: Pantheon Books. $3.

by PAUL RAMSEY

The word "existentialism," M. Sartre remarked recently, "no longer signifies anything at all." This is not because it means nothing but because it means too much. There is no existentialism, there are only existentialisms. Here now is a Christian version of existentialism from the point of view of the "existentialist intellectualism" of Thomas Aquinas.

The author, Jacques Maritain, universally recognized as the leading Roman Catholic philosopher of our time, recently relinquished his position as French Ambassador to the Vatican in order to teach philosophy at Princeton University. The reader will not find here Thomist doctrine dissected like a corpse by a professor of anatomy. Rather it is vividly presented by a philosopher unusually sensitive to the main currents of his time.

Many non-Catholics have learned to admire Maritain's understanding of the crisis of our civilization, his defense of democracy, just law and human rights, yet they have been unable to follow him into the more obscure realms of logic and metaphysics. They will find the present volume a masterly combination of penetration and pertinence in these matters.

Disclaiming any intention of rejuvenating Thomism by verbal artifice, the author nevertheless believes Thomism "the only authentic existentialism." He claims prior right to use the word, at the same time crediting modern existentialists with having evoked consideration of neglected aspects of the thought of Thomas Aquinas by reminding his disciples of the great lesson of anguish.

Moreover, existentialism of the Sartre school represents for him the completion of a certain cycle in modern thought. It makes plain the fruitlessness of the initial decision taken more decorously by other philosophers: "Manage at all cost to make atheism livable." It brings "being," and consequently the being of God back into the main stream of modern thought. It is concerned with individuality and liberty. And its notion of anxiety is "a truth which modern philosophy was unable to understand and which has disorganized it."

The final chapter, which should perhaps be read first, appeared last spring in The Sewanee Review under the title "From Existential Existentialism to Academic Existentialism." Maritain praises the "first existential generation of Kierkegaardians for distinguishing between two fundamentally different attitudes of mind. The first he calls "the posture of cause-seeking, the sapiential mien, the bearing of Minerva confronting the cosmos"; the second, a "posture of saving my uniqueness, the imprecatory mien, the bearing of Jacob wrestling with the angel." But today, he holds, existentialism has become a philosophic rather than a religious protest, and hence is worthless.

Other chapters on the nature of being, moral action, personal existence and the relation of human freedom to the Free Existent (God) carry forward the thesis that there is a "great zeal for being which animates Thomistic thought." This zeal for being makes Thomism "desperately necessary," yet "foreign and intolerable to the emptied, exasperated, ailing reason of our time." Being, or the "act of existing," Maritain describes as a "mysterious gushing forth" or "victorious thrust" by which the humblest thing triumphs over nothingness. In contrast, modern forms of existentialism define "ex-istence" in post-Kantian fashion as "standing outside oneself"—a capacity peculiar to self-conscious persons. Doubtless the word should not be used in both senses, whichever be its correct meaning.

Therefore, the central concern of Thomistic "existential intellectualism" is still metaphysical. Not unexpectedly, Maritain finds his greatest point of contact with the other schools of existentialism in his analysis of moral action. For ethics does business with deeds, not with "the existence exercised by ideas."

On the level of ordinary mortality, where no refinement of theory can take the place of prudence and rectitude; in the lives of the saints, in the supreme Christian virtue of charity—in all this "morality hangs upon that which is most existential in the world." For by love a person attains the supreme level of existence, which is "self-mastery for the purpose of self-giving."

Dr. Ramsey is an Associate Professor of Religion at Princeton University.

January 23, 1949

The Why Of Man

THE COURAGE TO BE. By Paul Tillich. 197 pp. New Haven: Yale University Press. $3.

THE THEOLOGY OF PAUL TILLICH. Edited by Charles W. Kegley and Robert W. Bretall. 370 pp. New York: The Macmillan Company. $5.50.

By W. NORMAN PITTENGER

PAUL TILLICH, Professor of Philosophical Theology at Union Theological Seminary in New York, is a distinguished German-American scholar who has been in this country since the early Thirties. As Theodore M. Greene of Yale University remarks in his essay on "Tillich and Our Secular Culture"—one of the essays in "The Theology of Paul Tillich"—this German émigré thinker is "the most enlightening and therapeutic theologian of our time." Each of the books under review, in its different way, demonstrates the accuracy of Mr. Greene's claim.

"The Courage To Be" contains Tillich's recent Terry lectures at Yale. The topic is courage, understood as "an ethical reality, but • • • rooted in the whole breadth of human existence and ultimately in the structure of being itself." "The Theology of Paul Tillich" is the initial presentation in a new series called The Library of Living Theology, designed to give the reading public a critical introduction to the work of important thinkers of our day.

Each volume in the series will contain an autobiographical sketch by the subject of the study, a series of descriptive and critical essays, and a concluding "answer" by the man under consideration.

In his Terry lectures, Tillich is concerned with "courage as the universal and essential self-affirmation of one's being" as an "ontological concept." After a historical sketch of the varying meanings of "courage," he turns to an analysis of anxiety, which for him is the condition which courage meets. Anxiety, as we experience it existentially, appears as "anxiety of fate and death," "anxiety of emptiness and loss of meaning" and "anxiety as guilt and condemnation."

Such a situation is found in all men; but in some it is found in a pathological form—these are the neurotic, who because they do "not succeed in taking • • • anxiety courageously upon [themselves] can succeed in avoiding the extreme situation of despair by escaping into neurosis." The neurotic "affirms himself but on a limited scale." "He affirms something which is less than his essential or potential being." A brilliant analysis of this neurotic escape follows.

IN succeeding chapters Tillich points out the ways in which through "participation" and through "self-realization" man may be able to find courage to be. Finally, the supreme sort of courage, which is discovered when man "accepts his acceptance" is defended as the final solution to man's anxiety. This bare outline can give no idea of the brilliance, the wealth of illustration and the aptness of personal application which makes the reading of these chapters an exciting experience.

Even in the last section, where Tillich shows how "theism," in the sense of *a* God, must be transcended in commitment to God as being itself, the profundity of thought and pointedness of illustration may be noted—although some will find it difficult to follow the author at this point.

In the study of Tillich's theology, the introductory sketch is of particular interest. Here Tillich traces the development of his thought. His primary concern has always been with the meaning of human existence, especially with the meaning of that existence in the world situation in which man today finds himself. Hence, he is not only a theologian but an interpreter of culture. Man is related, inevitably, to the "Unconditioned"—that which is his "ultimate concern"; but he is also a sharer in the life of his own time, which suggests that every interest which is natural to him as man must be understood and related to his existence.

"What am I?" has as its immediate corollary, "What is this world, this history, this culture, in which I am placed?" Even those who cannot share

Tillich's Christian faith can profit by his penetrating analysis of the human situation. This explains why Tillich is the apologist par excellence for our time.

Of the several essays in description and criticism, the ordinary reader will find those of Walter Marshall Horton, Greene, George F. Thomas and A. T. Mollegen most readily understandable. Horton places Tillich in the theological and philosophical stream; Greene discusses Tillich's contribution to an understanding of our times; Thomas outlines the main emphases in Tillich's "system"; and Mollegen treats of the place of Christ in the thought of Tillich.

Other essays are more directly philosophical and theological. Noteworthy among them are David Roberts' discussion of the doctrine of man presented in Tillich's writings and Dorothy Emmet's analysis of his theory of knowledge. A chapter by Edward Heimann of the New School is interesting for its critical analysis of Tillich's social views.

ALL in all, this is an admirable beginning of an important new series. We may regret that more adequate attention was not given to Tillich's conception of the "theonomous" and his doctrine of the "daemonic." They are among his most significant contributions to our understanding of existence and of culture. And more might have been said about his significant contribution to the understanding of religion, psychology, sociology and medicine as these bear on man's "health" or his "salvation." Fortunately in the Terry lectures Tillich himself gives a very valuable outline of his views on these subjects (chapter 3).

We can be grateful for this excellent introduction to the thought of a man who, as some of us think, is the most germinal thinker of our day not only as a theologian but as a student and critic of culture, and a prophetic voice speaking with compelling power to our generation. One may hope that many will come to know more of this man who has been, over the years, a master of thought and a generous and helpful teacher.

Mr. Pittenger is Professor of Christian Apologetics at the General Theological Seminary.

January 4, 1953

A Pastor's Prescription

THE POWER OF POSITIVE THINKING. By Norman Vincent Peale. 276 pp. New York: Prentice-Hall. $2.95.

By GEORGE R. STEPHENSON

AS minister of New York's Marble Collegiate Church, Norman Vincent Peale, author of "A Guide to Confident Living," has had wide experience with all sorts of people in all kinds of trouble. Out of his experience he has evolved simple rules for overcoming problems of everyday living. His new book is a practical guide to the application of these rules to particular situations. His recommendations include the use of counseling, the cultivation of relaxation, the memorization and repetition of Biblical texts, the affirmation of positive thoughts, and drawing upon "the Higher Power."

There is no problem, difficulty, or defeat, the author claims, that cannot be solved or overcome by faith, positive thinking, and prayer to God. In citing proofs of his claim, he tells how people he knows have turned troubled minds into peaceful ones, improved their health, stopped worrying, increased their energy, and have become successful and popular.

Mr. Peale says that he does not ignore or minimize hardships and tragedies. In spite of this statement, these problems seem too easily solved, the success a bit too automatic and immediate, the answers a little too pat, and the underlying theology a shade too utilitarian.

October 26, 1952

Mr. Stephenson is rector of St. Peter's Episcopal Church, Gulfport, Miss.

EDUCATOR DECRIES DR. PEALE'S VIEWS

'Positive Thinking' Opposed by Church Council Leader as 'Easy' Optimism

By GEORGE DUGAN
Special to The New York Times.

CINCINNATI, Feb. 7—A top-ranking Protestant educator said here today that he took a "negative" view of the Rev. Dr. Norman Vincent Peale's "Power of Positive Thinking."

The remark was made by the Rev. Dr. Paul Calvin Payne of Philadelphia. He is chairman of the Division of Christian Education of the National Council of the Churches of Christ in the U. S. A. He spoke at a press interview at the annual meeting of the division.

Dr. Payne also is general secretary of the Board of Christian Education of the Presbyterian Church in the U. S. A.

Dr. Payne brought into the open a controversy seething within Protestantism for months.

Dr. Peale is the pastor of the Marble Collegiate Church in New York. He is the author of a book entitled, "The Power of Positive Thinking." It has topped the general best seller list in The New York Times Book Review for 118 weeks.

Every Sunday Marble Collegiate Church is packed. Closed circuit television pipes his sermons to worshipers in separate auditoriums. His weekly radio and television shows are heard and seen by millions.

In essence, Dr. Peale maintains that a simple but sincere belief in the power of God and the efficacy of prayer can improve an individual's earthly lot.

Dr. Payne voiced the attitude, until now unspoken, of many church leaders. He took issue with what he described as the "easy optimistic sentiments" expressed by Dr. Peale.

The Presbyterian educator asserted that Christianity required "heroic commitment to great causes and ideas."

He also advocated higher taxes to improve the public school system. He predicted that "if our great industrial society continues to build armor to the neglect of brains, our civilization will collapse."

Dr. Payne declared that "the public school teacher should be able to realize that in the classroom she can make the greatest witness as a Christian."

"In high schools where religion comes naturally into discussions," he asserted, "the teacher ought to fee free and the preachers and others ought to let her be free, to deal easily with Christianity, Judaism or any other religion."

Similar views were expressed at the press interview by the Rev. Dr. Gerald E. Knoff, executive secretary of the Division of Christian Education of the National Council.

He asserted that to deal with everything but religion in the modern educational system "creates the impression that religion is some form of minor hobby like stamp collecting."

February 8, 1955

Theatre: Beckett's 'Waiting for Godot'

Mystery Wrapped in Enigma at Golden

By BROOKS ATKINSON

DON'T expect this column to explain Samuel Beckett's "Waiting for Godot," which was acted at the John Golden last evening. It is a mystery wrapped in an enigma.

But you can expect witness to the strange power this drama has to convey the impression of some melancholy truths about the hopeless destiny of the human race. Mr. Beckett is an Irish writer who has lived in Paris for years, and once served as secretary to James Joyce.

Since "Waiting for Godot" has no simple meaning, one seizes on Mr. Beckett's experience of two worlds to account for his style and point of view. The point of view suggests Sartre—bleak, dark, disgusted. The style suggests Joyce—pungent and fabulous. Put the two together and you have some notion of Mr. Beckett's acrid cartoon of the story of mankind.

•

Literally, the play consists of four raffish characters, an innocent boy who twice arrives with a message from Godot, a naked tree, a mound or two of earth and a sky. Two of the characters are waiting for Godot, who never arrives. Two of them consist of a flamboyant lord of the earth and a broken slave whimpering and staggering at the end of a rope.

The Cast

WAITING FOR GODOT, a tragicomedy in two acts by Samuel Beckett; staged by Herbert Berghof; presented by Michael Myerberg, by arrangement with Independent Plays, Ltd.; scenery by Louis Kennel; costumes by Stanley Simmons; production supervisor, John Paul. At the John Golden Theatre.

Estragon (Gogo) .... Bert Lahr
Vladimir (Didi) .... E. G. Marshall
Lucky .... Alvin Epstein
Pozzo .... Kurt Kasznar
A Boy .... Luchino Solito de Solis

Since "Waiting for Godot" is an allegory written in a heartless modern tone, a theatregoer naturally rummages through the performance in search of a meaning. It seems fairly certain that Godot stands for God. Those who are loitering by the withered tree are waiting for salvation, which never comes.

The rest of the symbolism is more elusive. But it is not a pose. For Mr. Beckett's drama adumbrates — rather than expresses—an attitude toward man's experience on earth, the pathos, cruelty, comradeship, hope, corruption, filthiness and wonder of human existence. Faith in God has almost vanished. But there is still an illusion of faith flickering around the edges of the drama. It is as though Mr. Beckett sees very little reason for clutching at faith, but is unable to relinquish it entirely.

Although the drama is puzzling, the director and the actors play it as though they understand every line of it. The performance Herbert Berghof has staged against Louis Kennel's spare setting is triumphant in every respect. And Bert Lahr has never given a performance as glorious as

his tatterdemalion Gogo, who seems to stand for all the stumbling, bewildered people of the earth who go on living without knowing why.

Although "Waiting for Godot" is an uneventful, maundering, loquacious drama, Mr. Lahr is an actor in the pantomime tradition who has a thousand ways to move and a hundred ways to grimace in order to make the story interesting and theatrical, and touching, too. His long experience as a bawling mountebank has equipped Mr. Lahr to represent eloquently the tragic comedy of one of the lost souls of the earth.

•

The other actors are excellent, also. E. G. Marshall as a fellow vagrant with a mind that is a bit more coherent; Kurt Kasznar as a masterful egotist reeking of power and success; Alvin Epstein as the battered slave who has one bitterly satirical polemic to deliver by rote; Luchino Solito De Solis as a disarming shepherd boy—complete the cast that gives this diffuse drama a glowing performance.

Although "Waiting for Godot" is a "puzzlement," as the King of Siam would express it, Mr. Beckett is no charlatan. He has strong feelings about the degradation of mankind, and he has given vent to them copiously. "Waiting for Godot" is all feeling. Perhaps that is why it is puzzling and convincing at the same time. Theatregoers can rail at it, but they cannot ignore it. For Mr. Beckett is a valid writer.

April 20, 1956

"A Fierce but Eloquent Prophet of the Lord"

THE DEATH OF GOD: The Culture of Our Post-Christian Era. By Gabriel Vahanian. 253 pp. New York: George Braziller. $5.

By ROBERT E. FITCH

WE have heard before about Christian pessimism. Usually it designates a somber view of man's sinfulness and depravity, but the author of this book has a new twist. He is a Christian pessimist who is pessimistic about Christianity.

The modern legacy of Christianity is its "self-invalidation." If in our culture God is dead, then that fact is to be imputed to the "delinquency of Christianity," rather than to atheistic aggressions. The difficulty is that a religion is significant only as it is bound to a culture, but the interplay of religion and culture calls for compromises that put religion into bondage. Hence the present "desuetude of Christianity." Paul Ramsey in a preface to this book explains that we are now in the second phase of the period post-mortem Dei: the first

Mr. Fitch, a writer and teacher in the fields of philosophy and religion, is the author of "The Decline and Fall of Sex" and the recent "Odyssey of the Self-Centered Self."

phase was anti-Christian; ours is post-Christian.

In elaborating this thesis Gabriel Vahanian, Assistant Professor of Religion at Syracuse University, takes up first "The Religious Agony of Christianity" and then "The Cultural Agony of Christianity." Of the nine essays making up the book, one was published in Theology Today, and four were published in The Nation. Obviously the author knows how to speak to diverse audiences. But everywhere his message has to do with the "dishabilitation" of the Christian tradition, with its replacement by bourgeois religiosity and a theology of "immanentism," and with the desperate effort of Western culture to shake off the "crippling shackles" of a superannuated piety.

The quality of mind which enters into this book is unique and fascinating. The author is by origin a French Calvinist, who has studied in his native land as well as in this country. He has translated some Karl Barth, and holds for himself a Barthian philosophy of culture. He has also published some of his own poetry, and, as a writer of prose, retains the best of the Gallic graces — lucidity, elo-

quence, persuasiveness, even passion. But this particular Calvinist is more the critic and brilliant impressionist than the systematic theologian.

His comments on contemporary literature are provocative. He dissects Graham Greene, Bernanos, Samuel Beckett; discusses the Christ-figure in fiction; has a word for Sartre and for Salinger, for Maritain and for Tillich, and for the "vestigial Christian" Bultmann. He also gives us the gist of the difference between Job and MacLeish's character, J. B.

Job's predicament is that, though he believes in God, he acts at times as if he doubted. But he cannot be convinced by his doubt. At the end, his tragedy comes to the point: Without God, man would be nothing. J. B.'s predicament is that he does not believe in God, but acts as if he does or wishes he did. At the end of his tragic life he clearly states that without man there would be no God. And in his final essay he explodes the existentialism of which he is in part the representative.

One question haunts me as I read Vahanian: is it true, what he says? Is God any more dead today than he was in the eighteenth century, when many

eminent minds were busy composing his funeral oration? If Christianity is being done to death now, then does the guilt lie with "bourgeois religiosity," or with the super-subtle sophistication of religious issues which is complacently shared both by theists and by atheists among the intelligentsia? Must all acculturation of religion be "deleterious"?

When, after taking Protestantism apart in three propositions, he also assures us that "Rerum Novarum," Pope Leo XIII's encyclical on the social order, was another surrender to this world, and that "Christianity never actually existed even during the Middle Ages," I begin to wonder if there ever was a truly Christian era to which our own era could be "post."

Certainly what is said in this book is true as far as it goes; only it does not go so far as the author thinks it does. In particular he is blind to the ways in which Christianity has been able to transcend as well as to criticize and to transform the culture to which it has accommodated itself. But Vahanian is not a historian. He is a fierce but eloquent prophet of the Lord, and, with his sense of high drama, worth the watching and the hearing.

August 6, 1961

'New' Theologians See Christianity Without God

The 19th century German thinker Friedrich Nietzsche shocked the philosophical world with his famous cry, "God is dead." Today that same cry is being heard in theological circles as well.

A group of radical Protestant thinkers—variously known as "atheistic," "death of God" or "new" theologians—has arisen to assert that Christian thought must now proceed without any reference to God.

They say that the word "God" is meaningless and that even if there once was a God, He no longer speaks to man. True Christianity, they say, is an affirmation of the secular world in the style of the man Jesus, and has no relation to traditional church practices such as worship, the sacraments and prayer.

It is too early to predict whether these thinkers will, or indeed could, foster a major theological school.

They have made it clear, however, that for a new generation of theologians the two schools that have dominated Protestant thought for the last century—liberalism and neo-orthodoxy—are no longer viable.

"We may not like it, but the radical theologies are meaningful to our times, and they pose the basic theological questions of the day," said one churchman.

3 Key Theologians

There are three principal "death of God" theologians: Thomas J. J. Altizer of Emory University in Atlanta; William H. Hamilton of the Colgate Rochester Divinity School in Rochester, and Paul Van Buren of Temple University in Philadelphia.

Dr. Altizer is a layman with an Episcopalian background; the latter two have been ordained as a Baptist and Episcopalian clergyman, respectively.

They have written only a handful of books, and the movement has so far progressed mainly through articles and personal correspondence. There is now of establishing a journal dedicated to radical theologies.

A committee will meet in New York this week to lay plans for a three-day meeting of radical theologians sometime during the current academic year. It is expected that about 40 persons — primarily young scholars and students—will attend and that the papers presented at the conference will be published.

The three principal new theologians, all of whom are in their early forties, come from widely varying backgrounds and find their common strands largely in what they deny from previous traditions. They share two main ideas.

First, the radical theologians assert the unreality, or "death," of God for modern man. Talk of a divine or other wise supernatural force is meaningless

Dr. William H. Hamilton

and irrelevant, they say, because such "God-language" is not related to contemporary experience.

Dr. Hamilton spelled out this theme in a recent article in The Christian Scholar:

"It used to be possible to say: 'We cannot know God but He has made himself known to us,' and at that point analogies from the world of personal relations would enter the scene and help us out. But somehow, the situation has deteriorated: as before, we cannot know, but now it seems that He does not make himself known, even as enemy."

The second common strain is an affirmation of the secular world as the source of spiritual and ethical as well as physical standards. In different ways, the radical theologians look to the historical figure of Jesus as one who makes a claim upon men and guides them to a secular salvation.

"In almost every field of human learning, the metaphysical and cosmological aspect has disappeared and the subject matter has been 'limited' to the human the historical, the empirical," wrote Dr. Van Buren in his book, "The Secular Meaning of the Gospel."

"Theology cannot escape this tendency if it is to be a serious mode of contemporary thought," he continued, "and such a 'reduction' of content need no more be regretted in theology than in astronomy, chemistry or painting."

The consequence of these two ideas—the rejection of God and the acceptance of the world—is what the Rev. Dr. Langdon Gilkey of the University of Chicago Divinity School, a leading critic of the new theologies, has called "the most fundamental possible break with the long tradition of Christian theological discourse."

In a recent paper, he said this "new wind" in theology represented "a definite new movement," although "what it has to say is less clear than that it is new."

Though the three leading radical theologians unanimously reject any system in which a deity serves as the fulfiller of human needs and a solver of human problems, they differ greatly in their reconstructions of nontheistic faiths.

Dr. Hamilton, for instance, begins with the problem of the existence of evil and suffering, which, in "The New Essence of Christianity," he says can "dry up in man any capacity or wish to call out for the presence of God."

'At the Disposal of Man'

For him faith in God is but a hope for the future. In the present it dissolves into love of man, and the Protestant is defined not as a forgiven sinner but as one "beside the neighbor, beside the enemy, at the disposal of the man in need." The example for such an ethic of self-giving is the worldly Jesus.

Dr. Van Buren, on the other hand, has been trained in the philosophical methods of linguistic analysis and begins with the problem of speaking "meaningfully" about a God for whom no sensory "verification" is possible.

With talk of anything transcendent ruled out, Dr. Van Buren builds an ethical faith around Jesus of Nazareth.

In many ways the most radical of the new theologians is Dr. Altizer. His approach is neither ethical nor analytical, but mystical. He rejects not only the Christian tradition but much of the Western culture to explore Eastern and primitive religious phenomena.

The task of the theologian, he says, is to affirm—and even "will"—the death of God. Dr. Altizer regards Jesus as a somewhat Nietzschian figure who was "free of history," and he looks forward to liberation from the absence of the sacred to its opposite through a dialectical movement of history.

Theories Helpful

Many theologians who challenge the conclusions of the radical theologies nevertheless admit that they must be taken seriously. Some even find them helpful.

The new theologians are widely regarded as an expression within the church of the secular mind with which theology must deal if it is to communicate at all.

The radical thinkers self-consciously accept this role, and though their terms so far have been conditioned largely by the European theologies they reject, they regard their ideas as quite American. "We are the most profane, the most banal, the most utterly worldly of places," in Theology Today.

Theology of the last century was primarily concerned with

whether one could make sense of the idea of God, and it dealt with this question mainly by asserting a continuity between secular culture and deity.

This liberal theology broke down when World War I and other events dampened its optimism, and the last half century has been largely dominated by the neo-orthodoxy of the Swiss theologian Karl Barth and others. Neo - orthodoxy makes a sharp distinction between God and man and emphasizes the limitations on what man can accomplish or know apart from divine revelation.

"Now that mankind is learning to live with the bomb and developing some self-confidence, it is the unanswered 19th century questions about the existence of God, not the 20th century ones about how to speak of Him that are important," said one theologian. "The new theologies, if inadequate as systems, have at least focused on the right questions."

Criticism of the radical theologians has been leveled at many aspects of their thought, but several main themes have emerged.

First, it is argued that while they have obviously touched some nerves in their cultural analysis, their theological reconstructions have so far been limited to the single doctrine of God and are therefore of minimum value to the theological discipline as a whole.

'Jesus-Language'

Critics have also challenged the new theologies for merely substituting "Jesus - language" for "God-language." Dr. Gilkey, for instance, has accused them of performing a "slight of hand in pretending that there is no contradiction between accepting the lordship of Jesus and at the same time affirming the standards and ways of the modern world."

A frequent question put to the new theologians is why they choose to remain in the Christian church and to accept Jesus rather than some other figure as a model. In the current issue of Christian Century Dr. Hamilton answered:

". . . because there is something there, in his words, his life, his way with others, his death, that I do not find elsewhere. . . . There may be powerful teaching elsewhere, more impressive and moving deaths. Yet I have chosen him and my choice is not arbitrary nor is it anxiously made to avert the atheist label. It is a free choice, freely made."

In an interview last week, Dr. Hamilton said he recently had sensed "considerable support not only from scholars and students but from pastors as well" for the new theologies.

October 17, 1965

'God Is Dead' Debate Widens

By JOHN COGLEY

The clearest thing about the small but much-publicized "God is Dead" movement in Protestant theology is its catchy, provocative title. After that, all is subtlety, the specialized technical language of the academy, professional abstruseness and lay bafflement.

The movement has been taken by some to mean the propagation of old-fashioned cracker-barrel atheism in poly-syllabic terms. As such it has angered many church folk who feel that the idea of proponents of atheism drawing salaries from theological schools is an abomination. There have been demands from benefactors and alumni that the leading "Death of God" theologians be fired from their teaching posts, though the authorities have stoutly resisted the pressure.

Dr. Thomas Altizer, a leading figure in the movement who is a professor of Bible and religion at Emory University in Atlanta, Ga., has said that after the first national publicity about the movement he was bombarded by letters and telephone calls, a good percentage of them highly critical.

One Emory Medical School alumnus, Dr. Robert Shumate of Columbus, Ga., published an advertisement in The Atlanta Journal and Constitution suggesting that other alumni write to the president of Emory and "tell him why you, like me, are not donating to the 25 million dollar building fund."

The urbane spokesman for evangelical Christianity, *Christianity Today*, said editorially:

"No one will deny these men the right to be atheists. but (we say it reverently) for God's sake let them be atheists outside of institutions supposedly training men to spread the Gospel that God is alive and that faith in His Son means life from the dead."

Christian Atheists

Some of the "God Is Dead" professors do not shrink from describing themselves as atheists, a flamboyant touch that makes for headlines if not always for serious communication. They also go out of their way to establish that they are Christian atheists and indicate that they are atheists precisely because they are Christians. However confusing this might appear, their reasoning, based on dialectic and paradox, is considerably more complex than they are sometimes credited with.

Dr. Altizer, writing in The Christian Advocate, gives some indication of the circuitous pathways of his thought when he says:

"We cannot open ourselves to a new form of faith while remaining bound to the primordial

---

'GOD IS DEAD'

The following ritual was presented during a chapel service at a small denominational college in the South. It was designed to explore in liturgical form the experience of the "death of God." The reaction, according to a campus reporter, "ranged from tears to a new enthusiasm for theology."

Reader:
He was our guide and our stay
He walked with us beside still waters
He was our help in ages past

Chorus:
The lengthening shadow grows formless
The lengthening shadow grows formless

Reader:
Now the day is over
Night is drawing nigh
Shadows of the evening steal across the sky

Chorus:
He is gone. He is stolen by darkness
He is gone, He is stolen by darkness

Reader:
Now we must wonder
Was He only our dream.
A dream painted across the sky?

Chorus:
And in the beginning our fear created him
And in the beginning our fear created him

Reader:
Did we create Him in our image?
Did we surround Him with hosts because
We were alone?

Chorus:
Our imaginations rescued us from the deep
Our imaginations rescued us from the deep

Reader:
Space has stretched beyond Him.
It is very cold here
And from time there comes no warmth

Chorus:
The universe is too vast for him
The universe is too vast for him

Reader:
Beyond the stars, more stars
Beyond the skies, more skies
Above our dreams, more dreams

Chorus:
Heaven is empty
Heaven is empty

Reader:
Only his footsteps remain
Only stained glass and arched hopes
Only wasted steeples and useless piety

Chorus:
There is silence along the forest path
There is silence along the forest path

Reader:
Why is there no dawn?
Why do our dead only die?
Why do our living only live?

Chorus:
Your God is Dead
He died in the darkness of your image
He died because he grew ill from your
    dreams of salvation
He died because you held his hand too
    tightly
God is Dead

God who has once and for all revealed his Word; we will never pass through a new reformation until we liberate ourselves from the God of our Christian past . . . If faith is now confronting a world in which God is dead, and if this world is present both inside and outside of faith, then faith can speak to this world only by speaking the word of God's death."

Of this kind of talk Dr. John C. Bennett, president of the Union Theological Seminary in New York, has said:

"It is hard to take them seriously as theologie at all except as they are protests against the unreality of much 'God talk.' When they say in effect: 'God is dead; long live Jesus,' they would project a kind of Christian thinking that cannot last very long. It would be a miracle if the secular man who cannot believe in God is long able to affirm the centrality of Jesus and to speak of the resurrection in any sense."

Dr. Martin E. Marty, Lutheran theologian of the University of Chicago divinity school. though he

begins his treatment of the phenomenon with a weary "Ho hum, do we have to go through all that again?." acknowledges that the "God Is Dead" theologians have their finger on the "hot button."

"They know," he writes, "that we in the West and in the world are passing through an epochal religious crisis; they see the old falling apart and want to be part of the new . . . Most Protestant thinkers are dealing with the themes which the 'Death of God' men have taken up. But they handle them in different ways." Better ways. or at least more comprehensible ways, according to Dr. Marty.

No one interested in achieving "conceptual propriety" would fall back on a term like "death of God," in his view. As a metaphor it is razzle-dazzle but also confusing, misleading and misplaced. Nevertheless, the "Death of God" professors "have hold of a big and important issue, one about which many theologians are nervous, Protestant and Roman Catholic alike."

The issue, which has long been a conversational staple in university dining halls, is that the "God"

of the catechisms and the philosophical formulations is "dead," in the sense that the conventional ecclesiastical language and the theological categories that describe Him have become meaningless to modern men. The God "up there" somewhere in outer space is "dead" to the modern believer who would no more look for Him in the wild blue yonder than the first Soviet astronauts did.

The God who presided over secular culture and a Church-dominated "Christendom" for centuries was "dead" when men began to take human affairs into their own hands. The God whose official representatives presumed to regulate science and limit research was "dead," when the arts and sciences declared their autonomy from theological dictatorship.

The resulting "religious crisis," now reaching a climax. cuts through almost every area of modern life.

Modern Problem

Dr. Altizer once put it this way: "It is not possible for any responsible person to think that we can any longer know or experience God in nature, in history, in the economic or political areas, or in anything which is genuinely modern, whether in thought or in experience."

Not all the critics of "God Is Dead" would disagree with this analysis. Yet many are convinced that it is not the living God who is "dead" but an immature concept of Him that held on through centuries while mankind moved toward true belief in this world and in human possibility—a movement with still a long way to go.

Dr. Harold A. Bosley, a New York Methodist minister, for example, said recently that the word "God" has been cheapened by so much misuse that it is understandable that the new theologians no longer find it capable of interpreting the ultimate meanings of life which they find and are trying to describe. "I honor them for their humility even as I question the necessity or the finality of the position they take."

Dr. Bosley added, however, that in his view the "death" theologians are missing an essential point. "It is the contention of religious thinkers like Tillich, Whitehead, Wieman, and many others, that the more we investigate and attempt to think about our experiences of meaning, the more certainly we are led to the conviction that there is an essential unity in the separate meanings of life, and this unity they call God."

January 9, 1966

MEETING DEBATES 'ABSURD' CONCEPT

Relevance of Idea in Modern Theater Is Explored Here

By RICHARD F. SHEPARD

Is meaninglessness meaningful? Is the absurd serious?

That the answer is a resounding yes and no, was indicated Monday night in a nonconsensus, by a theologian, a psychoanalyst, a critic, an Off Broadway producer and two poet-playwrights. Their topic was: "The Idea of the Absurd from Kierkegaard to 1966."

The occasion was a symposium following the annual meeting of the Foundation for the Arts, Religion and Culture, whose members are distinguished people who favor rapprochment of pulpit, palette and performing arts on the way toward a new interpretation of our age.

About 200 people gathered in the auditorium of the United Engineering Center, First Avenue and East 47th Street, to see two short, way-out French films and to hear the discussion that followed.

Defining the Terms

Stanley R. Hopper, the foundation's new president who is dean of the Graduate School and professor of philosophy of letters at Drew University, gave an introductory discourse on Kierkegaard, Sartre and Heidegger. After the first film—a cartoon about a man bedeviled by a large and menacing letter "A"—he said, "Wouldn't it be wonderful if I could tell you what it was about?"

The panel consisted of Robert Lowell and Ronald Ribman, playwrights and poets; Roger Shinn, dean of instruction at Union Theological Seminary; Leslie Farber, a psychoanalyst and chairman of the Association of Existential Psychology and Psychiatry; Sidney Lanier, a former Episcopal minister who is now president of the American Place Theater, and Elizabeth Hardwicke, who is an author, drama critic and the wife of Robert Lowell. Mr. Lowell and Mr. Ribman were last-minute volunteer substitutes for Edward Albee, who was ill.

The theater of the absurd and theater in general pushed Kierkegaard into the conversational background, despite his credentials as a founding father more than a century ago of a philosophical system that has given rise to the concept of the absurd.

Last or First?

Mr. Howell commented that he had been reading the record of the great Soviet purge trials of the mid-nineteen-thirties.

"The trial of Bukharin is much more absurd than Iones-co," he said.

Miss Hardwicke called the theater of the absurd "a deterioration of bourgeois drama."

"It can't deal with politics or wars," she said. "I can't imagine it dealing with Vietnam. It is the final gasp of family drama."

Mr. Lanier and Mr. Hopper agreed, but really disagreed. Now that all the props are down, they replied, the theater of the absurd is meaningful because it is necessary to start from the bottom up. This theater is either the last of the old or the first of the new.

Mr. Farber said that existential psychiatry was designed to "tackle the absurdities indigenous to my own profession," which, he said, needs the same soul-searching that religion and philosophy do.

"I think there's a great deal that's funny about my field, far more than The New Yorker has even touched," he said.

Mr. Shinn observed that "theology has always had a vested interest in foolishness. Ionecso is basically a moralist."

Mr. Ribman said that the anti-hero was the hero of today and that anybody writing about someone of heroic proportions would be laughed off the stage.

"It's possible that this is a legitimate way to produce tragedy, through laughter," he added. "The audience will laugh until it finally realizes that what is going on is horrible.'"

February 9, 1966

AN 'OBITUARY' FOR GOD

The following, written by Anthony Towne, is a satirical comment on the 'God Is Dead' movement. This shortened version of an "obituary," written in the style of The New York Times, was excerpted from a longer article that appeared in Motive, a Methodist student publication (Box 871), Nashville, Tenn.

Special to The New York Times

ATLANTA, Ga., Nov. 9—God, creator of the universe, principal deity of the world's Jews, ultimate reality of Christians, and most eminent of all divinities, died late yesterday during major surgery undertaken to correct a massive diminishing influence. His exact age is not known, but close friends estimate that it greatly exceeded that of all other extant beings.

The cause of death could not be immediately determined, but the deity's surgeon, Thomas J. J. Altizer, 38, of Emory University in Atlanta, indicated possible cardiac insufficiency. Assisting Dr. Altizer in the unsuccessful surgery were Dr. Paul van Buren of Temple University, Philadelphia; Dr. William Hamilton of Colgate-Rochester, Rochester, N. Y., and Dr. Gabriel Vahanian of Syracuse University, Syracuse, N. Y.

Word of the death, long rumored, was officially disclosed to reporters at five minutes before midnight after a full day of mounting anxiety and the comings and goings of ecclesiastical dignitaries.

In Johnson City, Tex., President Johnson was described by aides as "profoundly upset." He at once directed that all flags should be at half-staff until after the funeral. The First Lady and the two Presidential daughters, Luci and Lynda, were understood to have wept openly. Both houses of Congress met in Washington at noon today and promptly adjourned after passing a joint resolution expressing "grief and great respect for the departed spiritual leader." Senator Wayne Morse, Democrat of Oregon, objected on the grounds that the resolution violated the principle of separation of church and state, but he was overruled by Vice President Hubert Humphrey, who remarked that "this is not a time for partisan politics."

Plans for the deity's funeral are incomplete. Reliable sources suggested that extensive negotiations may be necessary in order to select a church for the services and an appropriate liturgy. Dr. Wilhelm Pauck, theologian of Union Seminary in New York City, proposed this morning that it would be "fitting and seemly" to inter the remains in the ultimate ground of all being. Funerals for divinities, common in ancient times, have been exceedingly rare in recent centuries.

Reaction from the world's great and from the man in the street was uniformly incredulous. "At least he's out of his misery," commented one housewife in an Elmira, N. Y. supermarket. "I can't believe it," said the Right Rev. Horace W. B. Donegan, Protestant Episcopal Bishop of New York. In Paris, President de Gaulle in a 30-second appearance on national television, proclaimed "God is dead! Long live the republic! Long live France!" News of the death was included in a one-sentence statement, without comment, on the 3d page of Izvestia, official organ of the Soviet Government. The passing of God has not been disclosed to the 800 million Chinese who live behind the bamboo curtain.

Public reaction in this country was perhaps summed up by an elderly retired streetcar conductor in Passaic, N. J., who said: "I never met him, of course. Never even saw him. But from what I heard I guess he was a real nice fellow. Tops." From Independence, Mo., former President Harry S. Truman, who received the news in his Kansas City barbershop, said: "I'm always sorry to hear somebody is dead. It's a damn shame." In Gettysburg, Pa., former President Dwight D. Eisenhower released through a military aide the following statement: "Mrs. Eisenhower joins me in heartfelt sympathy to the family and many friends of the late God. He was, I always felt, a force for moral good in the universe. Those of us who were privileged to know him admired the probity of his character, the breadth of his compassion, the depth of his intellect. Generous almost to a fault, his many acts of kindness to America will never be forgotten. It is a very great loss indeed. He will be missed."

From Basel, Switzerland, came word that Dr. Karl Barth, venerable Protestant theologian, informed of the death of God, declared: "I don't know who died in Atlanta, but whoever he was he's an impostor."

Dr. Altizer, God's surgeon, in an exclusive interview with The Times, stated this morning that the death was "not unexpected." "He had been ailing for some time," Dr. Altizer said, "and lived much longer than most of us thought possible." He noted that the death of God, had, in fact, been prematurely announced in the last century by the famed German surgeon, Nietzsche. Nietzsche, who was insane the last 10 years of his life, may have confused "certain symptoms of morbidity in the aged patient with actual death, a mistake any busy surgeon will occasionally make." Dr. Altizer suggested, "God was an excellent patient, compliant, cheerful, alert. Every comfort modern science could provide was made available to him. He did not suffer —he just, as it were, slipped out of our grasp."

March 6, 1966

NEW THEOLOGIES FOUND UNRADICAL

Scholar Sees No Challenge in 'Death of God' View

The trouble with the so-called "death of God" theologies is that they aren't radical enough, a Presbyterian scholar believes.

The contention was made in an article in the March 23 issue of the Christian Century by the Rev. Dr. William M. Alexander, associate professor of religion and philosophy at St. Andrews College, Laurinburg, N. C.

In the article Dr. Alexander discounted as "trivial" the usual objection to the new atheistic theologies—namely, that they deny most of the fundamentals of the Christian faith.

The so-called "death of God" theologians about whom Dr. Alexander wrote are a small but controversial group of thinkers who argue that belief in God is no longer meaningful or relevant in today's society. In different ways, each theologian looks to the man Jesus as a guide to achieving a secular salvation for individuals and for society.

Expressions of Optimism

The important point to make about these "radical" theologies, Dr. Alexander said, is that they are really nothing more than theological expressions of the traditional American optimism and belief in human progress.

"The early Christian gospel came as a radical attack on the culture of its age," he said. This gospel was truly "radical" then, and is just as radical today, because it expressed God's "inescapable judgment on human activity and pretension," he added.

The new "death of God" theologies, on the other hand, cannot be considered radical because they do nothing to challenge traditional liberal optimism, he argued.

"The new American gospel comes as a palliative justification of national illusions, so that it is now possible to find religious support for our oldest national mythology."

Emory Theologian Is Target

Although no names were mentioned in the article, Dr. Alexander directed much of his criticism at the work of Dr. Thomas J. J. Altizer of Emory University in Atlanta.

Dr. Altizer, whose style is highly mystical, has written that the task of the theologian today is to affirm the death of God as a "historical event" in order that history may then move forward to a new era in which the sacred will again be felt in a new form.

In his article, Dr. Alexander said American culture had been characterized by "belief in the illusion that [Americans] have escaped the prejudices and limitations of their past and are not subject to the historical limitations of the culture they left behind."

Affluence and power, he said, have led to the dogma that "history has not essentially affected this nation—or if it has, it has been a history which we ourselves created de novo."

The consequence is that "we can be contemptuous of history" and "rejoice in death as the clearing away of obstacles to progress," he continued.

"We Are Not Almighty"

Dr. Alexander stated that this optimism, however, is illusory.

"As a nation we are now beginning to be introduced by Vietnam to the suspicion that we are not almighty, that our ultimate destiny as a nation might be death," he said. "And this suspicion will be reinforced by fresh evidence from other Vietnams to come."

In such a situation—where the reality of death is replacing the myth of progress—the truly "radical" message, he stated, is not a reassertion of traditional optimism but "the prophetic message that God is not only life but death."

To assert, as Dr. Altizer and others do, that God is dead is merely "to indulge in the optimism of a false hope and sentimental religion," said Dr. Alexander. "That is so because the judgment of a God who is dead can be avoided and his death surmounted..."

On the other hand, he said, to assert that the traditional Christian God is alive and standing in judgment over human life is truly radical because it alone constitutes a departure from American "mythology."

March 27, 1966

The Role Of Man

THE SECULAR CITY. By Harvey Cox. 276 pp. New York: The Macmillan Company. Paper, $1.45.

By FREDERICK BUECHNER

IF the cry of the 19th century was that God was in His heaven and all was right with the world, or at least soon would be, the antiphonal response of the 20th tends to be that God is not in His heaven or anywhere else and nothing much is right with the world or shows any signs of becoming so. In their marvelous simplicity, both views have great appeal: whether humanity is moving irresistibly up toward the stars or inexorably down into the abyss, the individual can rest easy because there is really not much for him to do.

In "The Secular City," Harvey Cox attacks both the political apathy and many of the cliches of that brand of 20th-century disillusionment which regards the modern city, Technopolis, as both symbol of and accessory to man's dehumanization and the loss of meaning, purpose and value in his life. Technopolis is above all a *secular* city in that it tears down, together with its outmoded buildings, all the outmoded myths and meanings and cults that marked man during the "religious" stage of his history, and thus sets him free to build something new in their place.

WITH insight, erudition and wit, Mr. Cox examines such phenomena of secularity as the bankruptcy of traditional religion, the breakdown of the Puritan sex ethic, the growth of the Organization, and the anonymity and unceasing mobility of urban man, and sees them as cause not for despair but for only slightly qualified rejoicing. He interprets secularization as the sign of man's coming of age and advocates that instead of panicking and characteristically trying to arrest the process, the church should become the avant-garde in helping it along. The church should follow Jesus's example by exorcising the cultural demons that still possess many an unwitting Technopolitan and prevent him from realizing his full humanity.

Although Mr. Cox warns against equating secularization with the Messiah and recognizes, without dwelling upon them, the perils that it involves, he does not hesitate to make as his central point that the Secular City is really the contemporary embodiment of much that the Biblical symbol of the Kingdom of God points to. And by the time he is through, it is hard not to agree with a great deal of what he says as well as to applaud the liveliness and clarity with which he says it. A new order of things is breaking in upon the world—secularization happens as much in spite of as because of man—and men are called to participate in it by leaving all earlier values and loyalties behind in order to meet as brothers on the ruins of many of the old barriers that once kept them apart.

The church's mission, as Mr. Cox sees it, is to reconcile people not by converting them but by liberating them to live with each other as human beings despite the ideologies, theologies and politics that divide them. In doing this, the church becomes God's partner in redeeming history.

It should be said that even though much of "The Secular City" could have been advanced by any academic humanist of liberal persuasion and theological sophistication, whether a believer in God or not, in his last chapter Harvey Cox states unequivocally that for him the God of Biblical faith is "real" and not "just a rich and imaginative way man has fashioned for talking about himself."

Yet it is where this impressive book deals directly with God that, for me, it impresses least. It is difficult to quarrel with the assertion that God comes to us today in events of social change and that we speak of Him best, whichever of His names we use or do not use, in the language of political action. Certainly the prophetic tradition of the Old Testament supports such assertions as does much of what Jesus teaches in the New. But it seems to me no less certain that even in the Secular City man speaks of God and to God, and God speaks to man, in other ways as well: through the myths and symbols and rituals of earlier generations which Mr. Cox tends to dismiss too cavalierly as "adolescent" and "immature." But this is after all peripheral to the important thesis that he is advancing and detracts little from the power and timeliness of the work as a whole.

Mr. Buechner, School Minister at Phillips Exeter Academy, is the author of several novels. His most recent work is "The Magnificent Defeat," a volume of meditations.

March 6, 1966

'We Are a Problem to Ourselves'

By JOHN COGLEY

Dr. Martin E. Marty, the aphoristic young Lutheran pastor who does double duty as a professor at the University of Chicago Divinity School and as an editor of The Christian Century, has said that contemporary theologians can be divided into two groups: those who are indebted to Dietrich Bonhoeffer and acknowledge the debt, and those who are indebted to him and don't acknowledge it.

Bonhoeffer, who was still in his 30's when he was executed by the Nazis in 1945, was an Evangelical clergyman who studied at Union Theological Seminary in the 1930's. He was invited to stay in New York but elected to return to his native Germany and oppose Nazism from within.

One of the most influential of his utterances has turned out to be this paragraph written in prison:

"Honesty demands that we recognize that we must live in the world as if there were no God. And this is just what we do recognize—before God! God himself drives us to this realization—God makes us know that we must live as men who can get along without Him."

These words have become a basic text for the God-Is-Dead theologians, who unfortunately are being widely misunderstood as they try, against the odds of spectacular publicity, to explain what they mean.

'Secular City' Idea

Bonhoeffer's ideas also play a significant part in the now flourishing "Secular City" thesis proposed by the young Harvard theologian, Harvey Cox.

Dr. Cox's book was within the past year has become a kind of bible for socially concerned activists in both Protestantism and Roman Catholicism.

Its underlying theme, that this world is worth the mightiest effort and full measure of spiritual energy of the religious person is congenial not only to contemporary Christian theology but also finds strong support in traditional Jewish thinking.

Certainly Dr. Cox has the ear of the young. His influence has been compared favorably with that exercised by Reinhold Niebuhr a generation ago. Dr. Niebuhr liberated Christian theology from social irrelevance; Dr. Cox, many believe, is liberating social activism from theological irrelevance.

In spite of the present ferment in Catholicism, oddly enough, there have been no outstanding American Catholic contributions to the intellectual development of the "secular city" theme.

Many Invitations

The Catholic intelligentsia have generally accepted the Cox thesis, however, holding that it is quite compatible with their own best traditions. Dr. Cox, a Baptist, receives numerous invitations to Catholic campuses, and has admitted to being surprised to find himself a culture hero among young priests, seminarians, and nuns.

In Commonweal, Thomas Merton, a famous Catholic cleric of another generation, recently offered his reaction to the new Christian "secularism."

Father Merton's fame originally derived from the drama inherent in his turning his back on the "world" and entering a Trappist monastery.

He is now 51 years old. In 1949 his book, "Seven Storey Mountain," was a best seller. An autobiographical account of a Columbia student's conversion from "worldliness" to Catholicism, it traced the spiritual road that led triumphantly from Nick's Bar in Greenwich Village to the Trappist monastery in Gethsemane, Ky.

Father Merton may not have intended it to be such, interpreted as a glorification of uncompromising otherworldliness. It suggested to many that the highest exercise of the Christian calling was to turn one's back on what Dr. Cox was to call the "secular city."

Present Position

In his Commonweal article, the Monk, whose later writings have focused on peace and civil rights, stated his present position on the "world." He wrote:

"As long as I assume that the world is something I discover by turning on the radio or looking out the window I am deceived from the start. As long as I imagine that the world is something to be 'escaped' in a monastery—that wearing a special costume and following a quaint observance takes me 'out of this world,' I am dedicating my life to an illusion.

"Of course, I hasten to qualify this . . .In a certain historic context of thought and of life this kind of thought and action once made perfect sense. But the moment you change the context, then the whole thing has to be completely transposed. Otherwise you are left like the orchestra in the Marx Brothers' "Night at the Opera," where Harpo had inserted 'Take Me Out to the Ballgame' in the middle of the operatic score."

In general, he approves of the present social activism among the religiously committed.

He added, however: "The stereotype of world-rejection is now being suddenly replaced by a collection of equally empty stereotypes of world affirmation in which I, for one, have very little confidence. They often seem to be gestures, charades, mummery designed to make those participating in them feel secure, to make them feel precisely that they are 'like participating' and really doing something."

Father Merton concluded: "The world itself is no problem, but we are a problem to ourselves because we are alienated from ourselves, and this alienation is due precisely to an inveterate habit of division by which we break reality into pieces and then wonder why, after we have manipulated the pieces until they fall apart, we find ourselves out of touch with life, with reality, with the world and most of all with ourselves."

June 12, 1966

'God Is Dead' Doctrine Losing Ground to 'Theology of Hope'

By EDWARD B. FISKE

A doctrine largely ignored by Christian thinkers for 1,800 years has replaced the "death-of-God" theologies as the most avant garde issue in both Protestant and Roman Catholic theological circles.

The doctrine is that of eschatology, which seeks to interpret what will happen when, according to Christian belief, Christ returns to initiate the Kingdom of God.

In recent years the most controversial subject among Christian theologians has been the challenge of the death-of-God theologies, which have asserted that God is irrelevant to contemporary life.

Now, however, a movement known as the "theology of hope" has become the central issue in theological debate. Adherents regard it as an answer to the same doubts about the existence of God that led to the death-of-God phenomenon.

New York churchmen will have their first opportunity to confront one of the leading proponents of the theology of hope tomorrow when Jürgen Moltmann, a 41-year-old German Protestant who is now a visiting professor at Duke University, lectures at Union Theological Seminary.

In the early church, eschatology was central to belief, for Christians expected the imminent end of the world and the appearance of the new heaven and a new earth prophesied in the Book of Revelation.

When it became clear that the end was not near, however, eschatology was demoted to a relatively obscure place in Christian thought. The theology of hope is one of the few movements since then that have revived the original concern with the future.

The movement developed during the past several years among young Catholic and Protestant theologians in Europe, but only recently has become widely known in this country. Other leading proponents include Johannes B. Metz, Wolfhart Pannenberg and Gerhard Sauter.

Differ in Specifics

Although the various members of the theology-of-hope movement differ in specifics, their basic approach can be seen in the writings of Dr. Moltmann, who teaches at the University of Tubingen and whose book "The Theology of Hope," was published in English last November by Harper & Row.

His fundamental assertion is that eschatology, seen as the direction in which mankind is moving, is the criterion by which all Christian teachings are to be defined.

Dr. Moltmann holds that God is to be regarded not as a supreme and static being but as the One who is coming to man. God's most important characteristic in this theory is not that He acted in the past, but that He has promised to act in the future.

The Bible and Jesus Christ thus are significant not as examples of divine revelation in the past but because they point to continuing revelation in the future. The church is not the community of those already saved but of those "seeking a communion with the coming Lord."

Hope Held Basic

"From first to last, and not merely in the epilogue, Christianity is eschatology," said Dr. Moltmann.

For the German theologian, the primary religious experience for the individual is not faith or love but hope. The implication of this focus on the future, however, is not withdrawal from the world in the hope that a better world will somehow evolve, but radical and revolutionary involvement in order to participate in its coming.

A central theme in Dr. Moltmann's theology is the Resurrection of Christ, which many other theologians now regard as a myth. Another is the Exodus, or the movement from slavery to freedom.

In such thinking, Dr. Moltmann and other members of the theology-of-hope movement were greatly influenced by the neo-Marxist German philosopher Ernst Bloch, whose works have not yet been translated into English and who thus looms as a sort of mystery man behind the phenomenon.

Dr. Bloch, whose major work, "The Hope-Principle," was written in the early nineteen-forties, regards hope as the definitive characteristic of man and puts forward an openended and atheistic view of history.

American scholars generally point to at least three reasons for the widespread attention that the theology of hope is now attracting.

The first, they say, is the problem of how to speak of God in an age when evil is widespread and when men tend to experience the world in scientific and technological rather than religious terms.

There is a consensus among theologians that although the "death of God" theologians were helpful in defining the problem of speaking about God in such an age, their contribution to solving this problem is proving to be minimal.

The theology of hope attempts to deal with this difficulty by asserting that God does not come into human affairs from above or from an outside point. Rather, He acts upon history out of the future toward which mankind is moving. According to Dr. Moltmann, God is to be found in the interaction of present human activity with past "promise" and future "possibility."

Critics have charged, however, that this does not solve the problem because it is just as easy to assert a future atheism as a present one.

Harvey Cox, a prominent American theologian who says that he has been greatly influenced by the theology of hope, adds that it is not necessary to exclude God's involvement in the present in order to assert hope for the future.

"I still want celebration of the secular today," he said. "A stern, Puritanical march toward the future leaves no room for enjoying the here and now."

A second reason frequently suggested for the current attention that is being given to the theology of hope is the widespread disillusionment among liberals with the capacity of traditional democratic institutions to solve such problems as racial and economic injustice or the war in Vietnam.

In accepting the Marxist tenet that the task of philosophy is not only to interpret the world but to change it, Dr. Moltmann argues that the Christian is in a unique position to change society because he approaches it not merely in terms of how it exists now but in terms of "what it is promised to be."

'Factors of Instability'

The theology of hope, he says, introduces "factors of instability" into contemporary institutions. Because his point of reference includes future as well as present "reality," the Christian is free to work within institutions and, if necessary, to seek to transform them.

The Rev. H. Richard Shaull of Princeton Theological Seminary is among those who have asked whether such motifs of hope as the Resurrection and the Exodus are specific enough to provide content and direction to revolutionary social change.

Langdon Gilkey, a theologian at the University of Chicago Divinity School, also argued that Dr. Moltmann's emphasis on the future disregards the extent to which any revolution is grounded in the past and the present.

"If he's cutting God off from the past, then he is cutting God off from revolution as well," he said in an interview.

A third reason for the popularity of the theology of hope, according to scholars, is the apocalyptic, or future-oriented, mood of contemporary society.

"The mark of 'modern' times is the persistent quest for something 'new,' a desire expressed in social, political and technological revolution," said Father Metz, a Catholic theologian at the University of Münster in Germany.

In a recent interview, Dr. Moltmann agreed with commentators that the theology of hope is particularly suited to American philosophy, which has often emphasized evolution and openness to the future.

"Europe thinks of itself as having no future, America as having no past," he said.

Theologians unanimously agree that it is too early to predict the effect that the theology of hope will have on contemporary American theology. For one thing, most scholars are only now beginning to read the writings of its proponents.

The Rev. Dr. Martin E. Marty of the University of Chicago Divinity School believes, however, that Mr. Moltmann's work "is a theology that could make a difference in a revolutionary world."

"It could help inform and inspire an uncertain Church," he said. "It could force a rethinking of the basic Christian promises and mandates; it could free people from the dead hands of dead pasts."

March 24, 1968

Reinhold Niebuhr Is Dead; Protestant Theologian, 78

By ALDEN WHITMAN

The Rev. Reinhold Niebuhr, the Protestant theologian who had wide influence in the worlds of religion and politics, died last evening at his summer home in Stockbridge, Mass., after a long illness. He was 78 years old.

Mr. Niebuhr had been under orders from his doctors in recent years to cut down on his sermons and lectures.

Throughout his long career he was a theologian who preached in the marketplace, a philosopher of ethics who applied his belief to everyday moral predicaments and a political liberal who subscribed to a hard-boiled pragmatism.

Combining all these capacities, he was the architect of a complex philosophy based on the fallibility of man and the absurdity of human pretensions, as well as on the Biblical precepts that man should love God and his neighbor.

The Protestant theology that Mr. Niebuhr evolved over a lifetime was called neo-orthodoxy. It stressed original sin, which Mr. Niebuhr defined as pride, the "universality of self-regard in everybody's motives, whether they are idealists or realists or whether they are benevolent or not."

It rejected utopianism, the belief "that increasing reason, increasing education, increasing technical conquests of nature make for moral progress, that historical development means moral progress."

As influential as he was in the disputatious world of religion, it was in the arena of practical politics that the effects of his thought were most apparent to the general public. He was the mentor of scores of men, including Arthur Schlesinger Jr., who were the brain trust of the Democratic party in the nineteen-fifties and sixties. George F. Kennan, the diplomat and adviser to Presidents on Soviet affairs, called Mr. Niebuhr "the father of us all" in recognition of his role in encouraging intellectuals to help shape national policies.

In addition to Mr. Kennan and Mr. Schlesinger, the "all" included such well-known intellectual movers and shakers as Paul H. Nitze, Dean Acheson, McGeorge Bundy, Louis J. Halle, Hans J. Morgenthau and James Reston.

"I suppose the thing Niebuhr has done for me more than anybody else," Mr. Reston once said, "is to articulate the irony of our condition as a country in the world today."

Mr. Niebuhr advocated "liberal realism."

"The finest task of achieving justice," he once wrote, "will be done neither by the Utopians who dream dreams of perfect brotherhood nor yet by the cynics who believe that the self-interest of nations cannot be overcome. It must be done by the realists who understand that nations are selfish and will be so till the end of history, but that none of us, no matter how selfish we may be, can be only selfish."

"The whole art of politics consists in directing rationally the irrationalities of men," Mr. Niebuhr said. He thought of intellectuals as a "collective leaven" in a democratic society, men and women who could apply their learning to the practical problems of power and social justice. To them Mr. Niebuhr often served as an adviser, as when he lectured to the Policy Planning Staff of the State Department.

Mr. Niebuhr was himself active in politics, as a member first of the Socialist party, and then as vice chairman of the Liberal party in New York.

Active in Ad Hoc Groups

He was an officer of Americans for Democratic Action and active in numerous committees established to deal with specific social, economic and political matters. He was a firm interventionist in the years before United States entry into World War II. He was equally firm in opposing Communist goals after the war, but at the same time he was against harassing American Communists.

Much of Mr. Niebuhr's political influence was subtle, embodied in a virtually continuous outpouring of articles on topics ranging from the moral basis of politics to race relations to pacifism to trade unionism to foreign affairs. He did not offer pat solutions, but what he called "Christian realism," which emphasized the importance of arriving at approximate, rather than absolute, answers to public questions. Public morality, he argued, differed from private morals in this respect.

Mr. Niebuhr had been associated with Union Theological Seminary, Broadway and 121st Street, since 1928. He was, successively, associate professor of the philosophy of religion (1928-30); William E. Dodge Jr. Professor of Applied Christianity (1930-55); and Charles A. Briggs Graduate Professor of Ethics and Theology from 1955 to his death. He was vice president of the seminary after 1955.

Hundreds of seminarians jammed lecture halls for his courses, and thousands of laymen heard him preach or lecture. He spoke at many colleges across the country, preached at scores of churches, large and small, and appeared on innumerable public platforms. He was a sparkling talker, exerting a magnetism that kept his listeners excited and alert through lengthy and profound expositions.

Mr. Niebuhr possessed a deep voice and large blue eyes. He used his arms as though he were an orchestra conductor. Occasionally one hand would strike out, with a pointed finger at the end, to accent a trenchant sentence.

He talked rapidly and (because he disliked to wear spectacles for his far-sightedness) without notes; yet he was adroit in building logical climaxes and in communicating a sense of passionate involvement in what he was saying.

Many who heard him lecture on secular matters were incredulous when they found that he was a clergyman, for he wore his erudition lightly and spoke in common accents. When he preached, one auditor recalled, "he always seemed the small-town parish minister, able to relate the Christian faith simply to contemporary problems."

A high forehead and premature baldness, except for a ring of hair above his ears, made Mr. Niebuhr appear taller than his 6 feet 1 inch. His frame was large and his hands were big-knuckled.

Office Filled With Books

He looked outsized in his snug office on the seventh floor of the seminary, which he occupied during his teaching years. Its walls were so hidden by books, mostly on sociology and economics, that there was space for only one picture, a wood engraving of Jonah inside the whale. On his desk, amid a wild miscellany of papers, was a framed photograph of his wife and children. When students dropped in, as they frequently did, he liked to rock back in his swivel chair, cross his legs, link his hands on top of his head and chat.

In those informal moments he was a gay and witty talker, tossing off ideas in virtually every sentence and drawing upon a seemingly inexhaustible store of quotations from books he had read. Some students were disquieted by his eyes.

"He didn't really look at you," one of them recalled, "so much as measure you."

Mr. Niebuhr had an easy way about him, one that dispelled barriers of communication. He was "Reinie" to friends and acquaintances; in public references he preferred "Mister" to the honorific "Doctor." His highest earned academic degree was Master of Arts, which he received from Yale in 1915, but he collected 18 honorary doctorates, including a Doctor of Divinity from Oxford.

Mr. Niebuhr's diversions were few. He was fond of walking on Riverside Drive with his wife and his large black poodle, but the family conversation was mostly about religion. Mrs. Niebuhr was a lecturer on that subject at Barnard College for a number of years. Otherwise Mr. Niebuhr worked from 7:30 A.M., when he had breakfast, until he retired at midnight.

His writing appeared in the most diverse publications. For several years in the nineteen-thirties he edited and contributed to The World Tomorrow, a Socialist party organ; from the forties on he edited and wrote for Christianity and Crisis, a biweekly magazine devoted to religious matters. In an ecumenical spirit, he wrote for The Commonweal, a Roman Catholic magazine; for Advance and Christian Century, Protestant publications; and for Commentary, a Jewish publication.

Because Mr. Niebuhr did not employ Biblical citations to support his political attitudes, some associates were skeptical of the depth of his faith.

"Don't tell me Reinie takes that God business seriously," a political co-worker once said.

The remark got back to Mr. Niebuhr, who laughed and said: "I know. Some of my friends think I teach Christian ethics as a sort of front to make my politics respectable."

Troubled agnostics, Catholics, Protestants and Jews often came to him for spiritual guidance. Only half facetiously, one Jew confessed: "Reinie is my rabbi."

Men and women of other faiths felt equally close to him, for he did not seek to convert so much as to counsel.

Frankfurter an Admirer

Among Mr. Niebuhr's admirers was Supreme Court Justice Felix Frankfurter. After listening to one sermon, the late Justice said:

"I liked what you said, Reinie, and I speak as a believing unbeliever."

"I'm glad you did," the clergyman replied, "for I spoke as an unbelieving believer."

Although Mr. Niebuhr was acclaimed as a theologian, the closest he came to systematizing his views was in his two-volume "The Nature and Destiny of Man," published by Scribner's in 1943. He began an "intellectual biography" issued in 1956 by saying:

"I cannot and do not claim to be a theologian. I have taught Christian Social Ethics for a quarter of a century and have also dealt in the ancillary field of apologetics. My avocational interest as a kind of circuit rider in colleges and universities has prompted an interest in the defense and justification of the Christian faith in a secular age . . .

"I have never been very competent in the nice points of pure theology; and I must confess that I have not been sufficiently interested heretofore to acquire the competence."

There was, nonetheless, a Niebuhr doctrine. In its essence it accepted God and contended that man knows Him chiefly through Christ, or what Mr. Niebuhr called "the Christ event." The doctrine, in its evolved form, suggested that man's condition was inherently sinful, and that his original, and largely ineradicable, sin is his pride, or egotism.

"The tragedy of man," Mr. Niebuhr said, "is that he can conceive self-perfection but cannot achieve it."

He argued also that man deluded himself most of the time; for example, he believed that a man who trumpeted his own tolerance was likely to be full of concealed prejudices and bigotries.

Mr. Niebuhr asserted that man should not passively accept evil, but should strive for moral solutions to his problems. He urged man to take advantage of his finitude, to deal realistically with life as it is and to have Biblical faith.

In the ceaseless battle between good and evil, man must "recognize the heights," for there is "no sinful life in which there is not a point where God's grace may find lodgement."

"The Christian faith cannot deny that our acts may be influenced by heredity, environment and the actions of others," he once wrote. "But it must deny that we can ever excuse our actions by attributing them to the fault of others, even though there has been a strong inclination to do this since Adam excused himself by the words, 'The woman gave me the apple.'"

Mr. Niebuhr also insisted that

"when the Bible speaks of man being made in the image of God, it means that he is a free spirit as well as a creature; and that as a spirit he is finally responsible to God."

In struggle for the good, institutional change is likely to be more effective than a change of heart, Mr. Niebuhr suggested. He decried clergymen who offered salvation on what he considered simplistic terms.

Billy Graham, the evangelist, and the Rev. Dr. Norman Vincent Peale, the expositor of "the power of positive thinking," were among the clergymen Mr. Niebuhr contradicted. Their "wholly individualistic conceptions of sin," he said, were "almost completely irrelevant" to the collective problems of the nuclear age.

Mr. Niebuhr objected especially to the notion that religious conversion could cure race prejudice, economic injustice or political chicanery. The remedy, he believed, lay in societal changes spurred by Christian realism. In this sense, man could be an agent in history by coming to terms with it and working to alter his environment.

Mr. Niebuhr's own life illustrated his beliefs. He was born June 21, 1892, in Wright City, Mo., the son of Gustav and Lydia Niebuhr. His father was pastor of the Evangelical Synod Church, a German Lutheran congregation, in that farm community. At the age of 10 Reinhold decided that he wanted to be a minister because, as he told his father, "you're the most interesting man in town." At that point his father set about teaching him Greek.

From high school Reinhold went, with his brother Richard, to Elmhurst College in Illinois, a small denominational school, and from there, after four years, to Eden Theological Seminary near St. Louis. After the death of his father in 1913, Reinhold was asked to take his pulpit in Lincoln, Ill. He declined in order to enter Yale Divinity School on a scholarship. He received his Bachelor of Divinity degree there in 1914, and his Master of Arts a year later.

Only Pastorate in Detroit

Upon his ordination by the Evangelical Synod of North America, he was sent to his first and only pastorate, the Bethel Evangelical Church of Detroit. He remained there 13 years, nurturing the congregation from 20 members to 650, and becoming the center of swirling controversy for his support of labor, and later for his espousal of pacifism.

"I cut my eyeteeth fighting Ford," Mr. Niebuhr said in recollection of his Detroit years. Whereas Henry Ford was usually praised in those days for his wage of $5 a day and the low price of his automobiles, he was condemned by Mr. Niebuhr as ravaging his workers by the assembly line, the speedup, periodic layoffs for retooling and by summary dismissal of men in middle age.

"What a civilization this is!" Mr. Niebuhr said. "Naive gentlemen with a genius for mechanics suddenly become arbiters over the lives and fortunes of hundreds of thousands."

Mr. Niebuhr not only preached against what he regarded as Mr. Ford's callousness, but he also wrote stinging articles in The Christian Century that were read by Mr. Ford, among others. Mr. Ford was neither amused nor converted. Mr. Niebuhr emerged as a public champion of social justice and as a Socialist.

A Socialist Without Marx

Recalling this phase of his career in after years, the clergyman said:

"Mr. Ford typified for my rather immature social imagination all that was wrong with American capitalism. I became a Socialist in this reaction. I became a Socialist in theory long before I enrolled in the Socialist party and before I had read anything by Karl Marx.

"I became the prisoner of a very cute phrase which I invented, or it seemed to me at least to be cute. That phrase was, 'When private property ceases to be private, it no longer ought to be private.'

"The phrase, which was prompted by the unprivate character of these great motor companies, does not seem to be so astute in the light of subsequent history in which justice was achieved by balancing various types of collective power."

For a number of years Mr. Niebuhr preached what was termed "the social Gospel," a jeremiad against the abuse of laissez faire industrialism. He was a much-prized speaker at labor and liberal gatherings and on college campuses.

He castigated capitalists not only for their inhumanity to man but also for their spiritual blindness. He called for labor brotherhood, and racial and religious brotherhood as well.

At the same time, he tolled the doom of capitalism. "Capitalism is dying and it ought to die," he said in 1933. He was then teaching at Union Theological Seminary and agitating for the Socialist party. He was a founder, in 1930, of the Fellowship of Socialist Christians, whose membership included Paul Tillich, the theologian.

All during the thirties, however, Mr. Niebuhr was reassessing his ethical, social and political beliefs. He had never been a thoroughgoing Marxist, an advocate of class struggle and revolution; and now he turned from Socialism. He was never a Communist; indeed, he was a vigorous critic of the Soviet Union for the "brutality" of its economic system.

Mr. Niebuhr's dispute with Socialism, and his ultimate break with it, was on religious and ethical grounds, and later on realistic grounds. It was idolatry, he thought, to suggest that human beings could blueprint and bring forth the Kingdom of God on earth. He also had mounting doubts about the inevitability of progress.

In 1939 Mr. Niebuhr was invited to deliver the Gifford Lectures at Edinburgh University. This offered him a further opportunity to refine his views, which came more and more to be centered on man's pretensions about himself.

"A Christian justice will be particularly critical of the claims of the self against the claims of the other, but it will not dismiss them out of hand," he said. "A simple Christian moralism counsels men to be unselfish. A profounder Christian faith must encourage men to create systems of justice which will save society and themselves from their own selfishness."

Although Mr. Niebuhr recanted his Socialism, he did not lessen his interest in social change. Instead, he saw it in a different light—as a continuous adjustment of tensions between power groups in society. Nor did he diminish his concern for the plight of minorities and the rights of labor. Their cause, he contended, was part of a grander social adjustment within the general framework of American capitalism.

At the outset of World War II Mr. Niebuhr favored American intervention.

"The halting of totalitarian aggression is a prerequisite to world peace and order," he declared. He headed the Union for Democratic Action, a committee formed in 1941 by liberal former pacifists to encourage participation in the war.

In the war period Mr. Niebuhr worked with the World Council of Churches' Commission on a Just and Durable Peace. He also joined the Liberal party in 1944, and was an untiring spokesman for the anti-Communist left.

Mr. Niebuhr was a member of the American Academy of Arts and Letters, a group of 50 distinguished Americans. He received the Presidential Medal of Freedom in 1964.

Mr. Niebuhr's principal writings were "Does Civilization Need Religion?" (1927); "Leaves From the Notebook of a Tamed Critic" (1929); "Moral Man and Immoral Society" (1932); "Reflections on the End of an Era" (1934); "An Interpretation of Christian Ethics" (1935); "Beyond Tragedy" (1937); "Christianity and Power Politics" (1940); "The Nature and Destiny of Man" (1941-43); "The Children of Light and the Children of Darkness" (1944); "Discerning the Signs of the Times" (1946); "Faith and History" (1949); "The Irony of American History" (1952); "Christian Realism and Political Problems" (1953); "The Self and the Dramas of History" (1955); "Pious and Secular America" (1958); "The Structure of Nations and Empires" (1959); and "Man's Nature and His Communities" (1965).

He leaves his wife of 40 years, the former Ursula Keppel-Compton; a son, Christopher Robert of Albany, and a daughter, Mrs. Elizabeth Sifton of Brooklyn.

June 2, 1971

A Consideration of Faith After Auschwitz

By RICHARD L. RUBENSTEIN

There is a potentially irreconcilable conflict between the Judaeo-Christian image of the Biblical God as the just Lord of history and the terrible events of the twentieth century. The problem is especially urgent within Judaism. The traditional Jewish doctrine of the chosen people, no matter how interpreted, is difficult to maintain in the face of Auschwitz. If history expresses God's purposeful activity, especially toward his elect community, God himself must be regarded as ultimately responsible for the death camps. Contemporary Biblical faith, whether Jewish or Christian, must either assert that God had his mysterious reasons for permitting Hitler's genocidal activities or that faith must see its image of God dissolve together with Auschwitz's other victims.

Until recently, few establishment theologians acknowledged that Auschwitz in any way constituted a challenge to traditional formulations of religious belief. Only after the issue had been widely discussed within academic departments of religion did the establishment theologians attempt a response. The most conservative Christian response was that the camps were part of God's continuing punishment of the Jews for their rejection of Jesus.

Establishment Jewish theologians have tended to ignore the problem al-

Richard L. Rubenstein, author of "My Brother Paul," is professor of religion at Florida State University.

together or to dismiss it by denying its novelty. They regard Auschwitz as but a contemporary exemplification of the perennial problem of reconciling unmerited human suffering with a just God. Jewish thinkers have also tended to see the death camps as the latest in a long series of anti-Semitic onslaughts. Many Jewish thinkers reacted with hostility and, I believe, without comprehension when Hannah Arendt, the pre-eminent social theorist, suggested that the Nazi extermination project was entirely without precedent, that Auschwitz was strictly a twentieth-century phenomenon. They failed to recognize the extent to which death camps are as much an expression of the innate potentialities of a technologically competent civilization as are jets and computers. At Auschwitz human beings were subjected to an unprecedented assault by uniformed technocrats who utilized sophisticated techniques of psychological manipulation first to strip their victims of dignity and then to exterminate them with an extraordinary economy of means.

Unless a believer is prepared to regard the Lord of history as the ultimate technocrat for whom mass population elimination is simply a problem of bureaucratic manipulation awaiting solution, neither the previous experience nor the value structures of Judaism and Christianity offer any means of comprehending Auschwitz. The incredible transformations thrust upon us by our own inventiveness have profoundly altered contemporary sensibility. There is a radical hiatus between traditional forms and contemporary culture in politics, art and the new life styles. It ought not to be surprising that the same chasm between the old and the new is becoming manifest in religion.

It is my conviction that the Biblical God has ceased to be credible after Auschwitz and that a religious situation of great fluidity is developing under the impact of contemporary technology. In this new situation, some Christians have found renewed meaning in the Redeemer whose awesome sufferings are a prelude to mankind's victory over death. Many Jews have elected continued submission to a God who inflicted extermination upon them rather than suffer the loss of an inherited system of belief which once infused their lives with meaning. By contrast, a growing number of both Jews and Christians are finding nontheistic forms of religion, often based on ancient pagan or Asian models, increasingly relevant to their life experience and their values. This writer has found the ancient earth gods and the realities to which they point extremely meaningful. It is my faith after Auschwitz that we are children of Earth, that all of us are destined eventually to be consumed by our original progenetrix, that we have nothing to hope for beyond our bodily lives, and that our religions with their impressive rituals are but the distinctive ways we share and celebrate a condition entirely enclosed within the fatalities of an absurd earthly existence.

March 4, 1972

Faith After Auschwitz

To the Editor:

Richard L. Rubenstein ("A Consideration of Faith After Auschwitz," Op-Ed March 3) has, for a professor of religion, a rather obtuse concept of G-d.

One would assume from his article that he regards the Almighty as a puppeteer or baby-sitter for mankind. He is very wide of the mark if he believes this to be Judaism's attitude.

In the Jewish ethic man is not the blind, dumb executor of G-d's will but is endowed with freedom of choice and is thus regarded as a partner to the Almighty. It, therefore, follows that man cannot shift the responsibility for his evil to G-d.

It is sheer hypocrisy to deny Him when disaster befalls us if it is we who have abrogated our part of the contract. We have been blessed with exact guidance as stated in the Torah. "There is life and there is death, there is blessing and there is curse, there is good and there is evil, there is light and there is darkness"; it is for us, as free human beings, to choose.

The leaders of Nazi Germany, the Western democracies and the rest of the world had this freedom of choice.

Germany chose unrivalled bestiality, the rest of the world chose silence. The question remains: "Where was man?"

Esther Jungreis
North Woodmere, L. I., March 8, 1972
The writer survived Bergen Belsen.

•

To the Editor:

As a Christian I recommend that Mr. Rubenstein take a longer and closer look at his fellow Jews. The majority of the young American Jews today are not turning their backs on the God of their forefathers. Quite to the contrary, they are taking a deeper and more meaningful interest in their being Jewish than was the case with their parents. They are proud, and quite rightfully so, of their religious, social and intellectual heritage and its contributions to Western civilization which was founded on Judaeo-Christian moral values.

The God of the Jews, who is also the God of us Christians, is not dead. He is alive and vital in the hearts and souls of the vast majority of the Jews with whom I come in contact. Auschwitz and Belsen did not destroy their faith but only strengthened it.

Thomas Michael Desmond
Massapequa, L. I., March 5, 1972

To the Editor:

Hitler and Auschwitz were not the first great horrors of human history. The Crusaders, the Mongols, Chmelnitzki, World War I were only less modern in their procedures of murder.

Denying the worth of religion demeans the deaths of the six millions to meaninglessness, whereas faith can leave them the dignity of dying for something beyond themselves. If it is man's greatest tragedy, so it is God's.

(Rabbi) Morrison D. Bial
Summit, N. J., March 4, 1972

•

To the Editor:

In the organic, interrelated nature of One World, neglect and evil may be practiced in one part of the world organism and another part may suffer as the innocent victim. But the opposite is also true—somewhere in the world a good is discovered and people in other parts of the universe benefit. It is part of the oneness of the world, combined with human freedom.

So why blame God? Quite the contrary. He is to be praised for His patience with His children.

(Rabbi) Bernard Mandelbaum
New York, March 6, 1972

March 23, 1972

18 Christian Leaders Attack 'Debilitating' Secular Influences

By KENNETH A. BRIGGS

Eighteen leading Protestant, Roman Catholic and Orthodox thinkers have signed an appeal urging Christians to abandon secular influences that are "false and debilitating" to the church's work.

Among these, they said, is the concept that religious thought must pass the test of scientific rationality, that all religions are the same, that religion is a manmade creation and that Jesus can be described in purely human terms.

Such "false" concepts—and the answers to them—were detailed in "An Appeal for Theological Affirmation," composed by the ecumenical group last weekend at a conference at the Hartford Seminary Foundation. The appeal is considered a major theological statement and is expected to provoke prolonged discussion and debate.

One aim of the conference was to address Christians who may be, in the words of one participant, Prof. George Forrell of the University of Iowa, a Lutheran author, caught between "the 'with-it' theology and the madness of fundamentalist fads."

"Lots of people find both alternatives useless," Dr. Forrell said. "They want an assertion of the reality of Christian experience."

In terms of pure theology, the declaration's thrust is toward conventional emphasis on God as a transcendent reality and Christ as a divine figure. But translated into social and political terms, the document defines a liberal view toward the church's involvement in such issues as war and race relations.

The primary need, as interpreted by the group, is to reclaim the faith from those who would attempt — in the language of the document—to "exploit the tradition without taking the tradition seriously."

The document was drawn up by a group of influential theologians, writers and scholars who had been invited to the conference by its principal organizers, Prof. Peter Berger of Rutgers, a Lutheran who is a noted sociologist of religion, and the Rev. Richard J. Neuhaus, associate editor of the religious journal Worldview and pastor of St. John the Evangelist Lutheran Church in Brooklyn.

Those participating included the Rev. Gerard Sloyan, a Catholic who is chairman of the department of religion at Temple University; the Rev. Avery Dulles, a Jesuit theologian, of Catholic University in Washington; the Rev. William Sloane Coffin Jr., a Presbyterian, chaplain of Yale University; and Dr. Lewis Smedes of the Christian Reformed Church, who is dean of the Fuller Seminary in Pasadena, Calif., a major evangelical school.

The clear design of the conference was to rebuke what Mr. Neuhaus called the "hopeless effort" by elements of the church to be "acceptable to the culture" by borrowing too heavily from secular attitudes and behavior. Such an effort, according to many at the conference, has led to "capitulation" to and "captivity" by essentially nonreligious forces.

The document is written in the form of 13 "theses." Underlying the document is the view that much of the church has lost touch with transcendence —the idea of God as an all-powerful creator who exists beyond the world.

"The central issue," Dr. Berger said, "is the loss of transcendence. This is not an obscure point argued by theologians, but a condition of everyday life. In this loss, there is an incredible irony. For a substantial portion of the churches not only don't provide help—but actually celebrate the loss.

"It is an evil of considerable dimensions. We must reaffirm what Christianity is all about—transcendence."

The participants stressed a number of what they considered to be profoundly disturbing signs in religious thought. They particularly criticized efforts to make the church too "relevant" or faddish and what they regarded as a tendency to reduce religion to worldliness.

The document argues that Christian truth is not bound by a strict code of scientific rationality. It also insists that salvation may bring human fulfillment, but ultimately, it contends, salvation cannot be found on human level, but only with God.

While the exact targets of the attack on secularism are alluded to only indirectly, they were generally understood by the signers to be those Christians who, in the opinion of the conferees, have drunk too deeply of humanistic ideals and who have leaned too far toward non-Christian doctrines.

Parts of the document that treat of social problems affirm the need to "denounce oppressors," to free the oppressed and to "heal human misery." But it cautions the church against setting its social-justice programs soley by reference to secular programs.

"Sometimes the church's mission coincides with the world's programs," it says. "But the norms for the church's activity derive from its own perceptions of God's will for the world."

Other participants at the conference included:

Dr. Elizabeth Ann Bettenhausen, a national staff officer for the Lutheran Church in America.
Dr. Neal Fisher of the United Methodist Church board of global ministries.
James N. Gettemy, president of Hartford Seminary Foundation and a United Church of Christ clergyman.
Prof. George Lindbeck, a Lutheran specialist in Catholicism at Yale University.

Prof. Ileana Marculescu, faculty of Union Theological Seminary.
Prof. Ralph McInerny, a Catholic faculty member at Notre Dame University.
Prof. Richard Mouw, a philosopher at the Christian Reformed-related Calvin College.
lege.
The Rev. Carl Peter, systematic theologian at Catholic University of America.
The Rev. Alexander Schemann, faculty of St. Vladimir's Orthodox Theological Seminary.
The Rev. George H. Tavard, Catholic theologian on faculty of Methodist Theological School in Ohio.
Prof. Richard Wilkin, a Lutheran faculty member at Notre Dame University.

January 28, 1975

Theologians Plead for Social Activism

By KENNETH A. BRIGGS

An ecumenical group of 21 Boston area theologians, teachers and laymen released yesterday a sweeping theological statement that attacks what the group sees as escapist tendencies in recent religious thought and calls on Christians to recognize God's active concerns for the world.

In a four-page, 1,500-word document called the "Boston Affirmations," the group decried what it called a widespread "retreat from these struggles" by the church and suggested that spiritual renewal could be found in suffering on behalf of the poor and oppressed.

This declaration enlivens an ongoing theological dispute between those who are committed to a basically action-oriented perspective and those who argue for a stronger spiritual view of the faith. In part, the controversy has arisen from the activism among churches in the 1960's and the subsequent turn toward conservative theology among many Christians.

Among those who helped produce the statement over the last year were Prof. Harvey Cox, the Harvard theologian; Max Stackhouse of Andover Newton Theological School, a social ethicist, and Norman Faramelli, co-director of the Boston Industrial Mission, under whose auspices the statement evolved.

The group consists of six Episcopalians, four Presbyterians, three Roman Catholics, three members of the United Church of Christ, two Baptists, two Lutherans and a Methodist. Five of the signers are women.

Their deliberations began following a statement produced in January 1975 by another group in Hartford, Conn. The Hartford "appeal" urged Christians to reject "false and debilitating" secular ideas that had allegedly crept into the church.

The Boston response, issued on the eve of the Epiphany, the traditional celebration of Christ as the light of the world, challenged the implicit assumption at Hartford that social action should be subordinated to more "spiritual" concerns.

Among other things, the Boston document rejected the idea that God could be placed "in a transcendent realm divorced from life" and said that "those who authentically represent God" would assert God's presence "in the midst of political and economic life."

"Our main concern," Professor Cox said in an interview, "was to anchor social concern in the Biblical message and in the central tradition of the church."

Taken together, the Hartford and Boston statements represent the classic lines of debate between pietists, who focus on doctrine and personal salvation, and social activists, who understand faith as developing out of engaging in struggles for justice.

These emphases often overlap, of course, as when the Hartford appeal, oriented toward transcendent themes, also notes the need to "denounce oppressors" and when the Boston document makes personal faith the basis for social action.

But the main thrust of each document was to underscore what was believed to be lacking in the other position. The current exchange has already engendered the liveliest theological controversy in recent years and is expected to heat up further now that the Boston text has been released.

Debt to Hartford Group

Mr. Faramelli said the Boston group was indebted to the Hartford group for emphasizing that "there is a spiritual dimension that goes beyond this world."

"But I'm afraid," he continued, "that their desire to talk about piety and transcendence divorces them from human experience and historical phenomena."

The Boston statement, the outcome of a dozen revisions by Mr. Stackhouse, draws heavily from the concepts and language of "liberation" theology.

It rests on the conviction that there is often a false separation between thought and action, faith and works, doctrine and service.

It further implies that salvation is not simply a personal matter between the individual and God but requires compassionate involvement in the struggle for such things as alleviation of poverty, the equality of women and medical care for the sick and elderly.

"We cannot," the statement says, "stand with those secular cynics and religious spiritualizers who see in such witnesses no theology, no eschatological urgency and no Godly promise or judgment."

"In such spiritual blindness, secular or religious, the world as God's creation is abandoned and the church is transmuted into a club for self- or transcendental awareness."

Most of the signers have been long active in ecumenism and social action and many had known each other through this work. Collectively, they represent a liberal outlook that has fallen into some disfavor in the recent reaction against the social involvement of church people in the 1960's.

The Hartford conclave was convened by two Lutherans, the Rev. Richard Neuhaus, a Brooklyn pastor and editor of Worldview magazine, and Peter Berger, a sociologist. The participants were drawn mainly from conservative and evangelical traditions and included both Catholics and Protestants.

They insist that social involvement is not a modern extracurricular Christian activity but is at the heart of the Bible's message.

"There is a widespread notion that such concerns are not really theological but a cultural accretion of some modern thinkers and religious activists," Mr. Stackhouse said in a separate statement. "This false impression has, we acknowledge, been compounded by the failure of some church leaders to state the foundations for what they have been trying to do."

Under separate headings, the Boston document declares that a trinitarian God underlies all life, that humanity ignores this source of life, that God "delivers from oppression and chaos" and that "God is known to us in Jesus Christ."

It also notes the contributions of various church traditions and specified areas such as the arts, the "halls of justice" and social sciences where God is working to transform the world.

Mr. Faramelli said the Boston group had rejected the idea of attacking the Hartford appeal directly and decided instead to formulate a positive statement of beliefs. He said the final text represented a consensus, though individual members did not necessarily think the document was inclusive enough.

Professor Cox, for example, said he would have preferred more emphasis on Christ and mention of the Holy Spirit and the Resurrection.

Omitted from the document were precise definitions of the significance of Christ, the authority of the Bible and the nature of salvation.

Spokesmen for the group said the goal was to spell out these themes in the realm of action rather than in formal, theological terms.

"In working out this statement," Mr. Stackhouse said, "we intentionally chose social metaphors to express the core of biblical and theological tradition. We did this because the mood of much contemporary piety specifically ignores the social implications of the faith."

The participants were:

Norman Faramelli, Episcopalian, Boston Industrial Mission.
Harvey Cox, Baptist, professor of theology, Harvard Divinity School.
Mary Roodkowsky, Roman Catholic, lay chaplain at Harvard and Radcliffe.
Dave Dodson Gray, Episcopalian, member of adult education department, Massachusetts Institute of Technology.
Jeanne Gallo, Catholic, Sister of Notre Dame, lay educator, part-time worker, Boston Industrial Mission.
Robert Starbuck, United Church of Christ, social ethicist, Andover Newton Theological School.
Preston Williams, Presbyterian, social ethicist and former acting dean, Harvard Divinity School.
Max Stackhouse, United Church of Christ, professor of social ethics, Andover Newton Theological School.
Scott Paradise, Episcopalian, co-director, Boston Industrial Mission.
George Rupp, Presbyterian, professor of theology, Harvard Divinity School.
Liz Dodson Gray, Episcopalian, member of adult education department, Massachusetts Institute of Technology.
Ignacio Casteura, Methodist, student, Harvard Divinity School, faculty, Evangelical Seminary in Mexico City next academic year.
John Snow, Episcopalian, professor of pastoral studies, Episcopal Theological School.
Mary Hennessey, Catholic, co-ordinator, Boston Theological Institute.
Constance Parvey, Lutheran, associate pastor, University Lutheran Church in Cambridge.
Joseph Williamson, Presbyterian, pastor, Church of the Covenant in Boston.
Paul Santmire, Lutheran, chaplain and part-time faculty, Wellesley College.
Richard Snyder, Presbyterian, director Inter-Seminary Training for Ecumenical Mission.
Moises Mendez, Baptist, graduate student, Harvard Divinity School.
Eleanor McLaughlin, Episcopalian, professor of church history, Andover Newton Theological School.
Jerry Handspicker, United Church of Christ, professor of pastoral studies, Andover Newton Theological School.

January 6, 1976

ST. MARK'S CHURCH CUT OFF BY BISHOP FOR DANCE RITUALS

Deprived of Episcopal Ministration Until Dr. Guthrie Heeds Superior's Counsel.

OFFICIAL CITES CANON LAW

Registrar of the Diocese Quotes Authority for Dr. Manning's Ban on Eurythmics.

RECTOR WITHHOLDS REPLY

In the Meantime Another "Special Service" at St. Mark's Is Announced for Sunday.

Bishop William T. Manning has deprived the Church of St. Mark's-in-the-Bouwerie of the ministrations of the Bishop's office as the result of the service last Sunday at which six young women, bare of foot, executed a religious dance in honor of the Virgin Mary.

Until the rector, Dr. William Norman Guthrie, sees fit to heed the admonition and counsel of his Bishop, the parish is to remain "without episcopal visitation and ministration." A visit to St. Mark's which the Bishop had set for June 11 is summarily canceled.

Official notice has been sent to Dr. Guthrie of the Bishop's disciplinary measure in a letter, the contents of which the Rev. Dr. George F. Nelson, Registrar of the diocese, made public yesterday. Dr. Nelson draws attention to the fact that Dr. Guthrie has been placed "under discipline" for his "unauthorized and unlawful" acts as rector of St. Mark's. The Registrar also draws attentions to several quotations from the constitution and canons of the Protestant Episcopal Church, which the diocesan authorities believe, have bearing on the case.

The Bishop's Letter.

Bishop Manning's letter is as follows:

Diocesan House,
416 Lafayette Street,
New York, March 26, 1924.

The Rev. W. N. Guthrie, D. D., rector St. Mark's Church, New York City:

My Dear Dr. Guthrie: In December last I requested and entreated you to refrain from certain unauthorized and unlawful acts, and on the 14th of March, 1924, I solemnly counseled and admonished you that at or in connection with the approaching Feast of the Annunciation, and at or in connection with what you have denominated Indian Day, May 11 and May 18, the Sunday nearest the full moon of May, and not merely on those occasions but in general at all other times, you were neither to use nor permit to be used in St. Mark's Church or at any place within your spiritual jurisdiction as rector of St. Mark's: (a) any forms of worship composed in whole or in part out of American aboriginal material or out of Buddhist literature or any non-Christian form of worship; or (b) any

eurythmic, or other dancing in the church building or in connection with divine worship.

I asked your assurance that it was your purpose to follow my admonition and submit to my counsel in these matters.

On the 20th of March you declared to me in writing your purpose on Sunday, the 23d of March, to proceed with a service which you had announced in honor of the Blessed Virgin Mary which, under the name of the eurythmic ritual, included dancing. I warned you on the 21st of March that such service was unauthorized and unlawful.

You further declared to me in writing, on the 22d of March, that what you were proposing to do on Sunday, the 23d, was in no sense a service or an additional service or a special form of worship, but strictly a religious pageant.

On Sunday, the 23d of March, Evening Prayer not being said, you used and permitted to be used in St. Mark's Church in the afternoon and again in the evening a service or a special form of worship not contained in or selected from the Book of Common Prayer nor authorized by this Church or by the Bishops of this Church or the Bishop of this diocese, which you described in your printed announcement as an office and eurythmic ritual in honor of the Blessed Virgin Mary for the Feast of the Annunciation and also as a festal service in which service or special order of worship, in disregard of my counsel and admonition, you used and permitted to be used eurythmic or other dancing in the said church.

Now, therefore, in consequence of your unauthorized and unlawful action, and your disregard of my official counsel and admonition I hereby notify you that I decline to visit the parish and congregation of St. Mark's, and that my visitation of St. Mark's Church announced for Wednesday, June 11, 1924, is canceled and that the Parish of St. Mark's will remain without Episcopal visitation or ministration so long as you refuse to follow my said admonition and to act in accordance with my said counsel.

Dated at the Cathedral of St. John the Divine in the City of New York, on Wednesday, the 26th day of March, in the year of our Lord 1924.

Yours very truly,
WILLIAM T. MANNING.
Bishop of New York.

Dr. Guthrie Will Consult Vestry.

Dr. Guthrie has not yet received the Bishop's letter. He is again away "somewhere in New Jersey." An official at St. Mark's last night informed him by telephone of the contents. He then made the following comment:

"I am not prepared to say anything about the Bishop's letter until I return to town. As I have pointed out before the matter concerns St. Mark's as a corporation. It will be therefore necessary for me to get in touch with my wardens and vestry to see if the Bishop's communication calls for any further action on the part of the church."

One who is in close touch with the rector took the matter lightly and described the Bishop's action as very mild in the circumstances. "It just amounts to being cut off the Bishop's visiting list," he said, "and that's all there is to it."

The Rev. Dr. John A. Wade, rector of St. John the Evangelist, who witnessed and approved the dancing at Dr. Guthrie's church last Sunday, laughed when he was informed that the action of the Bishop was merely that of declining episcopal visitation or ministration to St. Mark's.

"I hardly think that that will end the matter," he said. "I am not authority on the church law, but I doubted if the Bishop had authority to forbid the dancing. He certainly has all the right in the world to decline to visit St. Mark's."

The Rev. Eliot White of Grace Chapel said last night that in the absence of the rector, the Rev. Dr. W. Russell Bowie, in Boston, he did not care to comment upon Bishop Manning's letter. He said he was present at last Sunday's service at St. Mark's and had found the services seemly, decent and dignified. He would not comment on Bishop Manning's prohibition of the dance services.

Action Mild, Says Vestryman.

Vestryman George Jay Smith of St. Mark's, commenting on the Bishop's letter, said last night:

"I have not seen an official copy, but, if the summary I have heard is correct, I agree with other comment that the Bishop's action is very mild. The point of it all, in my opinion, is that it does not appear that the future progress of St. Mark's on the lines which Dr. Guthrie has laid down will be hindered. I see no reason for any alarm at the nature of the communica-

tion, and I should judge that it now settles the matter, at any rate so far as St. Mark's is concerned.

"Of course, I am only expressing my personal belief. I should not like to speak in behalf of St. Mark's until a vestry meeting has been held."

Questioned as to the statement in the Bishop's letter that Evening Prayer had not been said, Mr. Smith said:

"I do not quite understand this. To the best of my knowledge Evening Prayer was said. The assistant pastor, the Rev. Edward S. Cosbey, read many prayers in the usual order of service. But I am not well versed in the canons and Bishop Manning may have in mind some particular prayer."

The quotations from the canons and constitution of the Church are interpreted as a reply to Dr. Guthrie's statement in church last Sunday, preceding the service, that the ritual was classified as a pageant and, therefore, did not require the Bishop's sanction.

Canon Law Quoted.

Attention is drawn to the law governing the services of the church: to Canon 21, which deals with the spiritual control of a parish; to the vows of a priest on ordination; to the constitution of the Church as contained in Article 10, and finally, to Canon 18, which says that if the Bishop has declined to visit a parish, the minister or vestry may apply to the Presiding Bishop to appoint five Bishops in neighboring dioceses to settle differences amicably. The quotations are as follows:

"1. On any day, when morning and evening prayers shall have been said or are to be said in the church, the minister may, at any other service for which no form is provided, use such devotions as he shall at his discretion select from this book, subject to the direction of the ordinary.

"For days of fasting and thanksgiving, appointed by the civil or ecclesiastical authority, and for other special occasions for which no service or prayer hath been provided in this book, the Bishop may set forth such form or forms as he shall think fit, in which case none other shall be used."

2. Canon XXI, which reads as follows: "The control of the worship and the spiritual jurisdiction of the parish are vested in the rector, subject to the rubrics of the Book of Common Prayer, the canons of the Church and the godly counsel of the Bishop."

3. The vow made by every priest at his ordination, which is as follows:

"Will you reverently obey your Bishop and other chief ministers who, according to the canons of the Church, may have the charge and government over you, following with a glad mind and will their godly admonitions, and submitting yourselves to their godly judgments?

"Answer. I will so do, the Lord being my helper."

"4. The constitution of the Church, Article X, which is as follows:

"The Book of Common Prayer and administration of the sacraments and other rites and ceremonies of the Church, together with the Psalter or Psalms of David, the form and manner of making, ordaining and consecrating bishops, priests and deacons, the form of consecration of a church or chapel, the office of institution of ministers and articles of religion, as now established or hereafter amended by the authority of this Church, shall be in use in all the dioceses and missionary districts of this Church. No alteration thereof or addition thereto shall be made unless the same shall be first proposed in one triennial meeting of the General Convention and by a resolve thereof to send within six months to the Secretary of the convention of every diocese, to be made known to the Diocesan Convention at its next meeting, and be adopted by the General Convention at its next succeeding triennial meeting by a majority of the whole number of bishops entitled to vote in the House of Bishops, and a majority of the clerical and lay deputies of all the dioceses entitled to representation in the House of Deputies voting by orders. Provided, however, that the General Convention at any meeting shall have power to amend the Table of Lessons and all tables and rubrics relating to the use of the psalms by a majority of the whole number of bishops entitled to vote in the House of Bishops, and by a majority of the clerical and lay deputies of all the dioceses entitled to representation in the House of Deputies voting by orders.

"And provided, further, that nothing in this article shall be construed as restricting the authority of the bishops of this Church to take such order as may be permitted by the rubrics of the Book of Common Prayer or by the canons of the General Convention for the use of special forms of worship."

"5. Canon 18, as to the visitation of parishes by the Bishop, of which Subsection II. of Section II. reads as follows:

"If a Bishop shall for three years have declined to visit a parish or congregation, the minister and vestry (or the corporation), or the Bishop, may apply to the presiding Bishop to appoint the five Bishops in charge of dioceses who live nearest to the diocese in which such church or congregation may be situated as a council of conciliation, who shall amicably determine all matters of difference between the parties and each party shall conform to the decision of the council in the premises; provided, that in case of any subsequent trial of either party for failure to conform to such decision, any constitutional or canonical right of the defendant in the premises may be pleaded and established as a sufficient defense, notwithstanding such former

decision; and, provided, further, that in any case the Bishop may at any time apply for such council of conciliation.'

St. Mark's issued an announcement yesterday of another ritualistic service on Sunday next. This will consist of "The Devotion of the Catholic Creeds," with extracts from the Apostles' and Nicene Creeds. The service is to be "ritually interpreted" by responses from the congregation, while the erector will present a "Litte Litany of the Life of Our Lord."

The substance of this office, as explained in a foreword by Dr. Guthrie,

will be the rendering of the Credo from Beethoven's Missa Solemnis. This is to be sung by a choir of eight solo voices selected for the occasion.

The ritual service will take place in the afternoon. In the morning Dr. Guthrie will introduce his subject by preaching on "Why Should the Creeds be Reverenced and Used in Devotion Today."

The Bishop's letter, it was said at St. Mark's last night, will not cause alteration in the plans for this service.

March 27, 1924

Hymns Sung in Jazz Form At Another Boston Service

Special to The New York Times

BOSTON, April 25 — Teenagers danced the frug and the watusi, and hymns were set to a rock 'n' roll beat at a religious service here last night. Contemporary jazz was played at a second service.

The two unusual services were held coincidentally at churches in the Back Bay area.

About 1,100 teen-agers attended the rock 'n' roll service of the United Church of Christ, Congregational denomination in Old South Church.

At the same time, about 700 worshipers—most of them in their twenties and thirties—attended a service in jazz at Emmanuel Church, Episcopal.

About 45 minutes of rock 'n' roll music preceded the Old South Church service. During the service rock 'n' roll tunes were used with religious lyrics substituted for the original words. The original title of one of the hymns was "My World Is

Empty Without You, Babe."

The Rev. Dr. Frederick M. Meek, senior minister, said the congregation — composed of young people's groups from 39 New England churches — "participated reverently."

"There was a section in which the young people formed a procession down the center aisle to lay objects on the communion table to symbolize the bringing of their whole selves to God," Dr. Meek said.

"One brought a Bible as a symbol of religion," he said. "Another brought a loaf of bread and a coke, signifying eating; another brought a pool cue and a ball, which signifies playing."

At one point involving audience response, one of the four teen-agers helping to conduct the service called: "Praise His name with rock 'n' roll for the Lord takes pleasure in His people, He wants to see them happy." The response was, "Praise His name with lots of dancing."

Twelve teen-agers then danced the frug and watusi in the aisle.

The service was conceived and written by Eugene Langevine, a graduate student at Harvard Divinity School who is also a probation officer in the Quincy District Court.

The Rev. A. L. Kershaw, the rector of Emmanuel Church, described the service there as "an ancient service in contemporary music."

The general format of a regular service was followed. The only sermon, however, was a "sermon-dance" by Ann Tolbert of Wheaton College in Norton. In the dance, which lasted less than five minutes, Miss Tolbert interpreted her feeling of love and of reaching for God.

The congregation sang hymns in jazz form. Herb Pomeroy and his sextet of jazz musicians and a choral ensemble led by Diane Cullington took part in the liturgy.

The jazz service was composed by Ed Summerlin with liturgy by William R. Miller, a poet. It was based on a service written in 215 A.D. by Hippolytus.

April 26, 1966

And Now Even Prayers Are Pop

By JULIUS DUSCHA
SAN FRANCISCO.

DICK GREGORY welcomed the audience of the hungry i night club to "the church" and put a slice of bread on his bar stool in case "the reverend" was in the mood for miracles. A three-man combo played a jazz processional, the lights dimmed and a spotlight searched out a slight, diffident man in a clerical collar who had stepped on stage to say his prayers.

"It's morning, Jesus," he

JULIUS DUSCHA is Associate Director of Stanford's Professional Journalism Fellowship Program.

began as bearded Peter Yarrow of the Peter, Paul and Mary trio softly played a guitar. "I've got to move fast . . . get into the bathroom, wash up, grab a bite to eat, and run some more . . . Are you running with me, Jesus?"

The man in the clerical collar was the Rev. Malcolm Boyd, an Episcopal priest who has been banished by two bishops, described by another bishop as "spokesman for the alienated generation," labeled by critics as "the espresso priest" and a "disturber of the peace," and included in a Life magazine list of the 100 most influential young men and women in the United States.

Father Boyd prefers to think of himself as a latter-day Luther or a more worldly Wesley trying to move organized religion out of "ghetto-ized" churches into the streets, the business offices, the union halls, the CORE chapters, the theaters and even the night clubs where the people are. His efforts are considered by sympathetic churchmen to be part of the secularization of the church that began at the end of World War II and has included such activities as the worker-priest movement and the involvement of clergymen in civil-rights protests and on the side of union members in labor disputes.

FOR a month this fall Father Boyd, an intense, 43-year-old man of medium height, nervously shared the stage of the hungry i with comedian Gregory. Wearing a wrinkled clerical suit, he stood at a lectern improvised

from a music stand and read from his best-selling book of "pop" prayers, "Are You Running With Me, Jesus?"

Father Boyd would be an unlikely night-club entertainer if he wore no clerical collar. Most of his hair is gone and what remains is graying. The glare of the spotlight makes him squint. He has something of a Bob Hope nose, an open face and a boyish grin. He reads his prayers with considerable feeling but at the end of his act he is snappish when answering questions from hecklers. He does not suffer fools gladly even when they have paid $3.50 ($4 on Fridays and Saturdays) to pray with him.

He is an angry man and his prayers are written in jarringly modern language because he says he feels "there is something phony about praying to God in Old English." He also likes to shock people. His subjects are as contemporary as racial relations and traffic jams but he is also deeply concerned with the loneliness and mystery of life and man's inhumanity to man. The German massacre of Jews during World War II is a frequent subject of his anguish.

"I oppose the Dale Carnegie approach to religion," Father Boyd says. "In my prayers I'm relating to a great deal of suffering and pain in the world. I don't feel this is a very happy culture, whether you're on the top or on the bottom."

"What was Hiroshima like, Jesus, when the bomb fell?" he asks. "Blacks and whites make me angry, Lord," he confesses in another prayer. "I got very mad at a white guy today, Lord, when he came out with all the old clichés . . . And the other day I got mad at a Negro. He was so ashamed of being a Negro that he had stopped being human."

MOST audiences applauded between the prayers, and when they didn't Father Boyd became concerned that the silence was due only to a false piety. But once he finished his praying, which was much like a poetry reading in a Greenwich Village coffeehouse, and sat on a bar stool to answer questions, the audiences had no inhibitions.

Hey, father, do you think the Catholic church is really in favor of peace in Vietnam? "Well, baby, I don't know what the Catholics think in Vietnam." Are you doing your job? "Completely. We've got to get with it. We need some armpit theology." What are your ulterior motives? "If you mean, do I want to sprinkle everyone with holy water?— no. The population explosion, black and white, hunger— these are my concerns."

Clergymen who infiltrated the hungry i audiences wrote to Father Boyd. The Rev. James Clark Brown, of San Francisco's First Congregational Church, said: "You were on, man . . . It was the most effective and, for my money, gutty evangelism I've observed in a long time." The Rev. H. T. Knight, assistant minister of St. Luke's Church in San Francisco, commented: "I had read the book, but the prayers moved me even more in the setting last night. What a fantastic opportunity to reach so many people who would never go near a church at the 'holy hour' Sunday morning."

THE contrapuntal performance of Boyd and Gregory was the provocative idea of Enrico Banducci, owner of the hungry i ("We forgo capital letters so as not to appear ostentatious") who in the early nineteen-fifties provided a platform for Mort Sahl and helped to launch a new school of stand-up social commentators. "I was not out to save souls," Banducci said. "I just thought it would be a good business marriage." And it

It's bumper to bumper, and the traffic is stalled. . . . If I could have anything in the world right now, it would be a road stretching out ahead, empty, all other cars gone, and a beautiful freeway for miles and miles, just for me, and then *home*.... Jesus, thanks for sweating it out with me out here on this highway.

•

The masks are on parade tonight, Jesus. The masks are smiling and laughing to cover up status anxieties and bleeding ulcers. Tell us about freedom, Jesus.

•

Look up at that window, Lord, where the old guy is sitting. . . . There is nothing for him to do. He doesn't have any money; all he has is time.... I just wanted to let him know somebody understands he's alive and he's your brother, so he's not alone or lost. Does he know it, Jesus?

•

This young girl got pregnant, Lord, and she isn't married. There was this guy, you see, and she had had a little too much to drink. . . . What am I going to tell her, Jesus? How can I help her understand the nature of the love she's looking for?

•

Help us really to dig in, Jesus, and be with you. After all the poor fiction and cheap Biblical movies which have turned your life and death into almost bizarre superstition, Jesus, it's hard for me to see your cross as it really was.

•

I know it sounds corny, Jesus, but I'm lonely. . . . It's getting dark again, and I'm alone; honestly, Lord, I'm lonely as hell.

•

Who am I in this great big rut? . . . I'm sick of this same-old-thing jazz and the laughs that don't make me laugh any more. . . . I need freedom. . . . I want to get close to life, feel it and smell it, sweat over it, and maybe even pick my spot to die.

was. Banducci had no trouble meeting Father Boyd's weekly salary of $1,000, which the priest said he would donate to civil-rights organizations.

The engagement was a personal success for Father Boyd, too. It led to seven minutes on the Huntley-Brinkley show, an interview with Johnny Carson, photos and articles in newspapers and magazines, increased sales of his book, a new record album made with guitarist Charlie Byrd and offers from Basin Street East in New York, the Cellar Door in Washington and the Happy Medium in Chicago.

Father Boyd disdains clergymen who notch conversions on I.B.M. cards ("On a good day I experience conversion three times, but I can go five weeks without it"). He does, however, display favorable letters as evidence of his hungry i success. "Please, sir," wrote a student, "keep telling people of a human Jesus, and of the basic dignity of all men and perhaps some day people will stop looking upward for guidance and will begin looking inward." And a postcard read: "I want to apologize for giving you a hard time

Wednesday night. I had too much to drink."

Before Father Boyd left San Francisco for a speech to the American Jewish Congress in Detroit and appearances this fall on campus religious programs in the South and East, he lingered late one afternoon in a North Beach bistro and talked over two bull shots (gin and hot bouillon), borscht and *cannelloni*. The conversation was a public confession.

HE began life in New York City as the child of a prosperous investment banker, but the marriage broke up by the time of the Depression and he went with his mother to Denver, where he graduated from high school in 1940. Bronchial trouble kept him out of military service during World War II and led him to the University of Arizona. An indifferent student, he graduated in 1944 with a major in English and a minor in economics.

From Arizona he went to Hollywood and a $50-a-week job with an advertising agency. After directing a homemakers' hour on radio, he moved to Republic Pictures where he made arrangements for radio appearances by the studio's stars. By 1949 he was in New York and associated with Mary Pickford and Buddy Rogers in a venture organized to package television programs.

Two years later, in 1951, he was in a hotel room in Tucson, Ariz., spending a weekend with the Bible. Shocking his friends and amazing Hollywood—he had seemed to be only starting a promising career—he decided to enter the Divinity School of the Pacific in Berkeley, Calif.

"I wanted to face myself. I wanted to live with myself," Father Boyd explained. "There was no moment of revelation. God does not speak in an echo chamber. I just pictured myself in an ivy-covered church, administering communion."

Three years as a seminarian were followed by a year at Oxford University. In England he discovered an Episcopal mission ministering to the needs of workers in Sheffield and the forgotten residents of slums. From England he went to an ecumenical institute in Geneva and on to Union Theological Seminary in New York, "where every question was asked." Then he was back in Europe at the Taize community in France, learning first hand about the worker-priest movement.

HIS first and, as it turned out, only church was in Indianapolis. There in 1957 he took charge of a 150-member, all-white parish in a neighborhood that had become largely Negro, and there he

Dick Gregory) and to an appointment as field secretary of the Episcopal Society for Cultural and Racial Unity.

From 1961 to 1963 he served as a chaplain on the Wayne State University campus in Detroit. While there he wrote five plays about race problems (one was performed on a television network) and at one point took up modern dance when an essay of his on Christianity was being choreographed. But his writing got him into trouble, too, and Michigan Bishop Richard Emrich denounced him for using the words "damn" and "nigger" in his plays.

Early in 1964 Father Boyd found friendly shelter when Suffragan Bishop Paul Moore Jr. of Washington, D. C., took him under his wing and made him assistant pastor of the all-Negro Church of the Atonement. From this base Father Boyd has traveled to as many as 125 campuses in a year and has become an unofficial chaplain-at-large to college students.

HIS prayers, which so many readers have found unsettling, have provided him with the security that comes to few clerical iconoclasts. More than 60,000 copies of his book of prayers have been sold, continued good sales are expected as the Christmas season approaches, and a sequel, "Free to Live, Free to Die," will be published next spring. In addition, a million copies of a paperback edition of "Are You Running With Me, Jesus?" are scheduled to be printed next year.

Father Boyd is a spectacular example of the church's new thrust into secular life

became aware of the depths of the race problem when he traded altars one Sunday with a Negro priest and "the biggest question in my parish was whether they would receive the chalice from a nigger's hand."

In 1959 he became chaplain at Colorado State University and received nationwide attention as well as his first ecclesiastical rebuke when he moved his ministry off the campus into the Golden Grape Coffee House and student beer joints. Newspapers and magazines found "the espresso priest" great copy, but Colorado's Bishop Joseph Minnis decried "priests going into taverns and drinking and counting it as ministry."

Father Boyd got the message and in 1961 went on a Freedom Ride with 26 white and Negro priests from New Orleans to Detroit, where they attended an Episcopal conference. The Freedom Ride was the beginning of Father Boyd's intense commitment to the civil-rights movement, a commitment that has taken him to Alabama and Mississippi, to Watts, to an arrest in Chicago (when he first met

Father Boyd received only a $250 advance on his first prayer book, which his publishers thought might sell 4,000 copies over a two-year period. Now he hopes to earn $100,000 from the book and the paperback rights to it in the next decade.

A compulsive, nonstop talker, Father Boyd has little time for anything but his prayers, his lectures and his writing. He generally eats only one meal a day, usually steak. The rest of the time he subsists on coffee. Although the jacket of "Are You Running With Me, Jesus?" displays a picture of him with a cigarette, Father Boyd has not smoked for three years. A bad back has made him a bit stooped and to help his back he lies on the floor with his feet in the air at least an hour a day.

He has never married and one senses that he has only time for himself and his career. He reviews films for The Christian Century and other church magazines and he has acquired the journalist's habit of reading newspapers and magazines rather than books. But he is always

66He is an angry man and his prayers are written in jarringly modern language because he says he feels there is 'something phony about praying to God in Old English.'**99**

ready for an interview and quite aware of what publicity can do for him and his views of the church's role in society.

TO those sympathetic to efforts to modernize the substance and form of religion, Father Boyd is a spectacular example of the church's new thrust into secular life. Robert McAfee Brown, a professor of religion at Stanford University, believes that Father Boyd is "a significant catalyst of ferment within the church" even though "he is a nuisance to the structure of the church."

Neither Father Boyd nor any of those who approve of his unorthodox methods believe that he succeeded in getting people out of the hungry i and into Grace Cathedral on Nob Hill. Realists among the clergy feel that the church represents a minority view in a culture no longer Christian and that the church's job is to join with other forces in society to preserve the dignity of life.

In San Francisco, for example, there is a night ministry sponsored by some of the Protestant churches. Clergymen walk the streets of the city's Tenderloin, sometimes talking people out of suicide, sometimes just speaking with bartenders, pimps and prostitutes. Two years ago in California ministers of all faiths fought against Proposition 14 to repeal open-housing legislation. Despite the united clerical opposition, the referendum carried. This year ministers joined the strikers in the vineyards of California.

BUT is Jesus running with the secular trend in organized religion? And where should the line be drawn between secularism and entertainment or sensationalism? Traditionalists look on Father Boyd's hungry i engagement as a kind of self-aggrandizing sensationalism embarrassing to the church. But his defenders see nothing very different in his efforts from the Rev. Billy Graham's carefully organized and highly theatrical crusades, which Father Boyd's fundamentalist opponents accept.

Father Boyd himself believes he is being heard by people who are listening to no other voices of the church. He does not think all clergymen ought to move out of their churches into night clubs, but he is planning two or three night-club engagements a year and hopes that his example will encourage other churchmen to become as involved in life as he feels himself to be.

"I think," he says, "that the church must take total risks. I don't feel I'm controversial. I think the Gospel is controversial."

November 13, 1966

Liturgies Embracing More Pop Art Forms

By EDWARD B. FISKE

The floral decorations at a "Mary's Day" mass last week at Immaculate Heart College in Los Angeles were displayed in 76 deep oil cans as a symbol of "Christian involvement in the world."

An Ash Wednesday service this year began with the reading of New York Times headlines. "'Bootblacks Hurt as 35c Shine Cuts Business,'" said the clergyman. "'Army Opposition to Mao Reported.' This is the day the Lord has made."

At a recent outdoor vesper service traditional music gave way to a tape-recorded anthem that included disconnected bits of electronic music, newscasts, strange clanging sounds and a commercial for a detergent.

Earlier that afternoon the congregation had put together a 12-foot-high assemblage of old tires, beer cans, a hockey glove and other pieces of junk.

Such far-out liturgical innovations are part of a growing interest in pop art and other contemporary forms that has led to the modification or replacement of traditional liturgies in scores of churches and educational institutions over the country.

The results range from religious "happenings" to theological interpretations of the cartoon Peanuts, a "Missa Bossa Nova" and a pop art chapel designed to destroy itself.

To some churchmen these new liturgical forms constitute a crass attempt to increase attendance and to make religion superficially relevant by diluting the Gospel with secular values. L'Osservatore Romano, the official Vatican newspaper, described pop art in general as an expression of the "total and general defeat of culture."

Others argue that the church has always used contemporary art forms to express itself and that Bach in his day was considered as far out as the hippy.

The liturgical use of junk and other pop forms, they say, is a hopeful sign that churches—long criticized as being too otherworldly— are now succeeding in giving profound religious meaning to the ordinary and the commonplace in human life.

From congregations the use of pop and folk forms draws mixed reactions. "I don't feel like I've been to church," a worshiper commented after listening to a folk-rock group called the Drunken Lords sing at St. James's Episcopal Church, at 71st Street and Madison Avenue. But another worshiper said: "I suppose some people are shocked by it, but I think that

anything that drags people into church is O.K."

The best-known example of the new marriage of piety and pop is "Mary's Day," an annual festival at Immaculate Heart College that Gerald Huckaby, an associate professor of English, has described as a "celebration of ourselves, of the world, of the products and processes by which we live."

This year's theme was "Survival With Style." The celebration began Wednesday evening with the mass and a soup-and-bread dinner symbolizing the college community's concern for the poor.

The next morning participants wound their way through a 50-by-60 foot "Survival" maze made out of seven-foot walls of brightly decorated paper boxes. On the boxes were phrases and quotations such as "I Must Be What I Am" and "Get With the Action."

Messages on Plates

In a noontime procession there were hundreds of balloons, miniskirts and blue felt pennants on which students had pasted words and pictures from newspapers and magazines.

The Ash Wednesday service using newspaper headlines took place at Western Maryland College, in Westminster, Md. A jazz combo led by Ed Summerlin, a saxophonist, provided the music while dancers moved down the aisles and hurled paper plates at the congregation.

Random sentences from the Bible, newspaper ads and books were pasted on each plate, and the worshiper who caught a plate was instructed: "Sometime, during the next four minutes, stand up and read."

The Rev. Roger E. Ortmayer, the National Council of Churches official who led the service, explained that "the content of this new-style prayer book is not the point so much as the fact that the people participate in the service and make interesting sounds."

The Rev. James M. Boyd, chaplain at Drew University, organized the vesper service on the campus of the Methodist institution, at which the junk assemblage and pop anthem were part of a "celebration of creation."

"It's a way of saying that the ordinary and the imperfect can be made beautiful, and the God we worship is a nitty-gritty God who is involved in everything," he said.

Several religious happenings have been staged, including a "Eucharistic happening" at St. Clement's Episcopal Church in Manhattan.

A jazz band was perched high above the congregation, which moved among a series of booths to participate in the various elements of the service. The Rev. Eugene A. Monick Jr., the rector, called the occasion "an experiment in worship without direction."

Barton Benes, a young artist who spent a year at the New York Theological Seminary, is

among those who have used pop art to express religious themes.

A Smokehouse Chapel

Leaving the meat hook in place, he turned a smokehouse in Princeton, N. J., into a private chapel equipped with a tin can cross and an aluminum foil ceiling that crackles when candles are lighted.

"I left the bug nests, and the chapel has already begun to destroy itself with spider webs," he said. "It's esthetically exciting and leaves you questioning."

The best-known religious pop artist is Sister Mary Corita of Immaculate Heart College, whose serigraphs, or silk-screen art, combine scraps of handwritten texts, colors and shapes in cheerful celebration of ordinary experience.

A blown-up wrapper from Wonder Bread, for instance, serves as the vehicle for a Ghandi quotation: "There are so many hungry people that God cannot appear to them except in the form of bread."

Another of Sister Corita's works sums up the concept of Mary's Day: "Mary does laugh and she sings and runs and wears bright orange. Today she'd probably do her shopping at the Market Basket [a local supermarket]."

Still another serigraph based on a quotation from Sam Eisenstein, a California poet, is entitled "Mary Is the Juiciest Tomato of Them All."

Opinions clash on the meaning of this new interest in popular art forms, but many agree with the lay Roman Catholic theologian, Daniel Callahan, that it is part of "the big drive for relevance." He says that "folk and jazz masses especially are attempts to reach contemporary men in thoroughly contemporary forms."

Churches have been dabbling in jazz liturgies for more than a decade. The Washington Square Methodist Church, for example, conducted a nationally televised jazz service on New Year's Eve, and Duke Ellington has performed his compositions in churches.

Recently, however, jazz has largely given way to the teenage genre of folk music and rock.

More than 150 Roman Catholic parishes and other institutions in Chicago now use folk music, and records in the field include a "Rock and Roll Mass" and a "Missa Bossa Nova."

A recent Vatican pronouncement was initially interpreted as banning such new forms, but subsequent statements indicated the warning was directed only at "abuses." One of Italy's top "rhythm bands" recently performed during a mass in a church near Udine, in Northern Italy.

Synagogues have shown little interest in pop art, but some have begun to use folk music. Rabbi David Hartman of Montreal, who has experimented with Hasidic folk songs, said

they "make worship and learning a vital thing."

The search for new liturgical forms also extended to electronic and random music.

"Anthem Number Two" by David Ahlstrom and Roger Ortmayer, for instance is based on the theme, "now is the time for the word." It lasts 4 minutes and 1 second, and requires singing and speaking voices operating "all at different tempos, different rhythms."

Turn to New Media

Mr. Summerlin, a Methodist who spends most of his time working with the new liturgies, conducts choirs of "nonmusicians" in anthems of clicks, sighs, and other vocal effects.

Churches such as St. Clement's have been involved with the theater for many years, and now other churches and religious groups are turning to new "multimedia" techniques of expression.

The Rev. Ronald Schlegel, pastor of St. Philip's Lutheran Church in St. Louis, for example, has preached "visual/-verbal" sermons. In one, a piece of sculpture was covered with balloons, which were popped during the sermon as an expression of how God "shatters contemporary secular patterns which separate us from the love of God."

Most churchmen involved in the use of pop religious forms see parallels between trends in contemporary art and contemporary religion. For example, Robert Rambusch, an Episcopal layman in New York, believes that both are involved in a "search for identity."

Pop art, which began to flower five years ago, focuses on the banal and the commercial aspects of the contemporary environment, such as Andy Warhol's painting of the Campbell's soup can. It has been variously regarded as surrender to debased realism and as a satirical protest against commercialism.

The happening incorporates elements of theater, music and art to create an open-end situation in which colors, sounds and events are left to chance and improvisation. It emphasizes spontaneity, viewer participation, and total involvement of the senses.

Comparable developments have taken place recently in religious thought, where there has been great emphasis on the "secular world," including concern for social issues such as civil rights.

Where God Works

For example, Harvey Cox, a theologian at Harvard Divinity School, has had great influence in both Catholic and Protestant circles with his assertions that instead of being rejected as a producer of evil, the modern city should be affirmed as the place where God is at work.

Whereas the pop art school in general takes a pessimistic view of life, religious pop art asserts that the ordinary and the commercial must be celebrated as part of God's creation.

The Rev. Alvin A. Carmines, assistant pastor at Judson Memorial Church, described a Thanksgiving Day service last fall in which the congregation carried forward pieces of junk at the offertory.

"The old tire or broken TV tube are symbols of brokenness," he explained, "but they are also signs that religious experience must be at the center of life."

The Rev. Daniel Berrigan, a Jesuit priest whose writings have been used extensively by Sister Corita, said that liturgical use of junk expressed "the highly provisional character of life." He added: "It forces religion—which tends to grow roots—to take the ordinary seriously, to assimilate and celebrate it and then to move on."

B. J. Stiles, editor of the Methodist student magazine Motive, suggested that the new liturgies, especially religious happenings, represented a "resurgence of emotion in worship."

"Religion has become too verbal and rational," he said. "But the young person today is no longer interested in intellectual games over whether God is dead or alive. He wants religion to be an extension of his feelings and his social concerns."

Others, however, view the new liturgies as too worldly to be useful to religion. The Rev. Carl F. H. Henry, editor of the fundamentalist Protestant weekly, Christianity Today, said in an interview: "The junk assemblage and other pop art forms glorify the natural and don't call for a new spiritual birth. Thus it's impossible for them to express the core of the Gospel message."

Some feel that in embracing the new pop forms the churches may misuse the arts.

The Rev. Howard Moody of Judson Memorial Church, for example, observes that religion has traditionally tended to become "imperialistic" and insist that something has to have religious significance before it could be accepted as legitimate.

One controversial figure on this point is Robert Short, a University of Chicago Divinity School student who has written a best-selling book, "The Gospel According to Peanuts," which is based on the comic strip.

In the Peanuts cartoons Mr. Short finds illustrations of religious themes such as original sin and salvation. "It uses cultural language that people can understand—like the parables of Jesus," he said.

Another much-disputed figure is the Rev. Malcomb Boyd, the Episcopal chaplain-at-large to the nation's colleges who read prayers and answered questions at the hungry i, a night club in San Francisco.

Father Boyd, whose theology is considerably more orthodox than his methods, says his act is "a way to reach people who would never go near a church."

Mr. Summerlin, however, said Father Boyd "is circumcising the night club and trying to impose his clerical collar on something that should be accepted in its own right."

Numerous clergymen have found religious meaning in recordings by the popular folk-rock group Simon and Garfunkel. Paul Simon, who writes many of their songs, agreed in an interview that this was legitimate.

"The general outlook of some of the songs concerns morality and love," he said. "The problem is that some religious people are like English majors and can find religious significance in 'Ba Ba Black Sheep.'"

A Matter of Seriousness

One advertisement for their records says, "They get to the fundamentals, love, justice, beauty, salvation."

Most churchmen, including critics of pop religious forms, agree that churches must employ contemporary artistic forms. Mr. Henry, for example, acknowledges that "there may be room for folk music in some churches."

The differences occur over the question of how seriously one should take the message that accompanies some of the new forms. Should the churches, for instance, accept the preoccupation with the mundane that pop art necessitates?

The Rev. Dr. Martin E. Marty, a church historian at the University of Christian Divinity School, is among those who see validity in these messages.

He says: "The here and now people are protesting the exhaustion of old theological forms and seeking a new sense of joy and contagion."

Conceding that religious pop art is "candidly ephemeral and self-defeating," he adds: "But it is helping to enlarge our vocabulary for a new language of worship if it ever comes into being. We're all a little jazzier than we thought we'd be."

May 15, 1967

Home Masses, Authorized and Unauthorized, Growing

By EDWARD B. FISKE

A priest in a light gray sport coat and maroon tie lifted a goblet and said, "The blood of Christ."

He sipped from the goblet and handed it to a man standing at his right. He in turn passed it to a woman in a blue jumper, and when all 16 persons at the table had drunk, they bowed their heads in prayer.

"The mass is over," said the priest. "Go in peace." A guitar sounded. The tiny congregation began singing a jaunty folk song, and the hostess appeared with coffee and cakes.

The scene was the dining room of a private home in northern New Jersey on a recent Saturday evening, and the occasion was one of the rapidly increasing number of home masses being conducted by Roman Catholic laymen and priests.

No one has precise statistics, but estimates of the number of home masses held every year range from several hundred to more than a thousand in the New York area alone.

Half a dozen parishes in Westchester County, for instance, sponsor them as part of their regular programs. At least 12 priests in Bergen County are known to be available to groups of lay-

men seeking to hold home masses on an unauthorized basis.

In practically all cases, home masses grow out of a search for a more "personal" or "intimate" form of worship than is available in large Sunday masses in local parishes.

"We were missing the warmth," said one participant in the New Jersey service. "We wanted an experience that was personal and where we could feel like we were part of it."

The development of home masses follows in the wake of the Ecumenical Council's call for a greater "sense of community" in the celebration of the mass.

Authorized by Archdiocese

The Archdiocese of New York has authorized—though not actively pushed—home masses for the last three years. It grants permission routinely, and this summer it will publish a set of guidelines to aid participants.

Two weeks ago the Archdiocese of Newark, which had previously approved home masses only for the sick, gave priests what amounted to carte blanche to conduct them as long as certain safeguards were observed, such as the use of communion wafers rather than leavened bread.

Last Tuesday evening the

Rev. Edward J. O'Brien, the 31-year-old assistant pastor of Holy Name of Mary parish in Croton-on-Hudson, N.Y., conducted an authorized mass in the home in Croton of Mr. and Mrs. Lawrence H. Keon, members of the parish.

Attired in full mass vestments, Father O'Brien stood behind an altar that had been set up on a narrow table in the hall.

The 45-minute service began at 8:30 when two Maryknoll seminarians broke out guitars and began singing "We are one in the Spirit." The 13 adults sitting around the small living room joined in. High-pitched voices of an equal number of children could be heard from the hall, where they were squatting on the stairs.

During the offertory some of the children presented crayon drawings they had made with such phrases as "I love You God." At communion the adults filed by and received the host from the celebrant.

Father O'Brien said that he regarded such home masses as primarily educational. "We felt that the people weren't getting the full meaning of the Sunday mass and that having home masses would help get it across."

Frank P. McGurk, a 33-year-old engineer who was

attending his first home liturgy, agreed afterward that it was a good idea. "You feel more a part of it," he said. "You can feel this way in church, too, but it's easier here."

The mass in the Keon home varied little from the ordinary Sunday service. In other cases, however, the liturgy of home masses undergoes radical change for its new setting.

Innovations in Ritual

Most home masses include "dialogue homilies," or discussions, in which both priest and laymen participate, rather than homilies by the priest alone. Many of the masses violate canon law or other regulations on a number of counts. Among the innovations are these:

¶The wearing of simple clerical collars or street clothes rather than mass vestments by the celebrant.

¶The use of regular bread, often baked by the hostess, instead of unleavened wafers.

¶The distribution of both the bread and wine to laymen, rather than the bread alone.

¶The use of unauthorized and frequently original texts in the canon, or central section of the mass.

Unauthorized masses, which appear to outnumber legal ones, are frequently held to celebrate special occasions, such as a first communion, an engagement or the return of a son from Vietnam. Sometimes they are spontaneous, such as one that was held in Manhattan during a party attended by a number of priests.

"We used table wine in wine glasses," said one participant. "There was a guitar, and the priest was without vestments, and during the offertory a girl got up and did an interpretative dance."

'Underground Churches'

In a few cases the home mass movement leads to the formation of what are coming to be known as "underground churches," groups which meet on a regular basis and constitute, in effect, a substitute for normal church experience.

In most cases, however, those who participate in home masses also attend their parish services on Sundays. They share secrecy with the "underground churches" because of fear that pastors will undertake disciplinary measures against the priests involved.

One regular group met recently in a fourth-floor walkup apartment in Lower Manhattan. The 14 participants, including some prominent laymen, began arriving at 8 o'clock on a Monday evening and spent about an hour chatting over cocktails.

They then sat in a circle in the living room, and a man read from the Gospel of John. The priest, a member of a major religious order, offered a commentary on the passage, and the participants discussed it for 20 minutes.

After prayers and unaccompanied singing, the priest poured some red wine into a brandy sniffer, took two small loaves of French bread from a folding table before him and began the Eucharistic celebration with the words, "We are here to recall that Christ freed us by His resurrection."

Later, the hostess on this occasion remarked, "When we first began meeting, we thought of keeping everything simple, like having only Cokes or beer beforehand. Then we decided that was silly. We usually drink Scotch in our living room, and we wanted it to be just the way we live."

Participants in the various forms of home liturgies frequently note that the early Christians celebrated the Eucharist within the context of a meal and that they normally met in homes.

This return to ancient forms, however, contains some potentially far-reaching implications.

The Rev. Robert Ledogar, a Maryknoll liturgical specialist, observed in an interview that the early Christians thought of the Eucharist primarily as a communal meal in remembrance of the death and resurrection of Christ.

During the Middle Ages, however, the emphasis on feast and community gave way almost entirely to a concept of the mass as ritualistic participation in the sacrifice by which Christ redeemed man from sin.

"Now the sacrifice idea is breaking down, and people are taking up the idea that Christ is present not only in the host and chalice but in the community itself," Father Ledogar said.

In addition to encouraging a new understanding of what the Eucharist is, home liturgies also serve to break down the distinction between the clergy and the laity.

"It's an egalitarian process," said Robert Rambusch, a New York layman who is active in national liturgical affairs. "The laity are writing their own services and taking communion with their own hands. It's no longer the infantile sort of thing where you open your mouth and the priest drops the host in like a mother robin feeding her young."

Both participants and critics of unauthorized home masses agree that they run the risk of being divisive, elite groups. Some regular groups have consequently taken steps to minimize this, such as asking the host on each occasion to invite friends who have not attended before.

John Scanlon, a Brooklyn layman, also warned that those who become involved in home masses tend to be the most articulate and best-educated laymen. "It would be a shame if these masses drained off the energies of people who have the ability to change the church itself," he said.

Many persons look to the home mass movement to produce modifications of the local parish structure. Though few expect large parishes to disappear, many priests and laymen believe that the church will eventually have to offer smaller groups for Catholics who prefer this sort of an experience.

The Rev. Gabriel Moran, a theologian at Manhattan College, is among those who believe that small communities can crystallize around a variety of groupings, including vocations.

The important thing is not taking a ritual from another age and putting it into homes," he said. "What counts is developing new communities and new liturgies out of where people actually are."

May 20, 1968

NEW FAITHS FOR AMERICA

BLAVATSKY, THE MAHATMA

THE MAJORITY OF HER FOLLOWERS NEVER SAW HER.

Nothing in Her Appearance to Indicate the Powers She Professed to Possess—Could Have Earned a Living as an Exhibit—Cigarette Smoking Was Her Only Weakness, Her Admirers Claim—Born in Russia, She Left Blavatsky Immediately After Marrying Him.

The Theosophists have been brought prominently before the public again by the discharge of teachers from the Wilson Industrial School and Mission for Girls because they were believers in the doctrine of Karma and members of the society founded by Blavatsky.

It is impossible to dissociate Theosophy and Blavatsky. A thought of one brings a thought of the other. It was in her mind that the whole scheme of the doctrine of reincarnation, on which Theosophy is based, originated. She was the great Mahatma of the following which she

H. P. Blavatsky

drew about her, their high priestess, the principal writer and teacher on the occult subjects on which Theosophists live and grow fat.

To the great majority of the thousands of her followers Blavatsky in the flesh was unknown. She is to them as a saint is to a follower of the Church, a priestess gifted above all others in unveiling the mysteries of life and death. Blavatsky is the shrine at which the Theosophist worships.

The human mind naturally conceives its own pictures, and these pictures are generally drawn on lines that have come to be accepted impulsively as appropriate to the subject. Probably most persons who never saw Blavatsky or her photograph have formed a mental picture of her in which she appears to them as a mysterious, spirituelle esoteric she, from her personality radiating the powers to penetrate into the impenetrable which Theosophists profess to believe she possessed.

The picture of Blavatsky is from her favorite photograph, and indicates the character of the woman to an unusual degree. Posed with head settled down between outstretched arms, with a cigarette poised between her fingers, those who knew her best see her as they best knew her. It is a picture that may shatter ideals, but it is a picture true to life, showing her as she sat a thousand times in her parlors in this city and elsewhere, enlightening circles of her followers as to the mysteries which she claimed it had been given to her to solve.

It is no exaggeration to say that the Blavatsky's body—not her astral body, but her anatomical and physical structure—was bulky enough to have made it possible for her to earn a living as an exhibit had she not chosen an easier and more profitable path. She was a tremendously heavy woman.

Theosophists declare that all the stories which have gained currency affecting the moral character of the Blavatsky, such as touched on her relations with men and accused her of drinking intemperately and being addicted to opium, are slanderous, and have gained circulation only through the enemies of the "cult." Several "exposures" of her character have been attempted, but as they were based on charges affecting her early life in Russia, the proof was not forthcoming, and the confidence of her followers in her was not shaken. The constant smoking of cigarettes, they say, was her only weakness. That the Blavatsky was not a woman of the kind that church people would tolerate as a teacher for their children, however, is certain.

Probably no woman ever led a less prosaic existence than did the Blavatsky. Helena Petroma was her maiden name, and she claimed descent from the royal family of Russia. She was born in Ekaterinoslaw, Russia, in 1831, when a terrible scourge of cholera was sweeping that land. She received little education, but her followers relate that, as a child and as a girl, she "showed abnormal psychic powers" and startled the natives. She must have been much slimmer then than in later years, for it is said she could ride the wildest horse in a man's saddle, and used to stay in the field for weeks with her father's regiment.

She began to travel about the Continent when fourteen years old, and when she returned to Russia, in 1848, she married Gen. Nicephore Blavatsky. The story is that she married him because her friends dared her to, and that immediately after the ceremony she broke a candlestick over his head and ran away, never to see him again. But she kept his name.

Then she began globe trotting, and, according to her own accounts, visited about every civilized and uncivilized country. She returned to Russia in 1858 with very much developed "psychic powers," and she let the forces play again to the astonishment of the natives.

She started out globe trotting again and, according to her followers, something happened wherever she went that they now regard as due to her presence. There were earthquakes and gunpowder explosions, in which pretty nearly everybody except herself was killed, and her escapes, she asserted, were due to the assistance of "unseen beings who were men living on the earth, but possessed of developed senses that laughed at time and space" and apparently at earthquakes and explosions. There were and are many "beings," not "unseen," who laughed at her assertions.

During all this time she dabbled in Spiritualism, or, rather, started a few crusades against it, and had a finger in about all the other "isms" with which she came in contact. She was then developing Theosophy and tried unsuccessfully to establish it in many lands. Success did not attend her efforts until, in 1875, she came to this "imperial city of an empire State," as the political orators say during campaigns. Here she founded the Theosophical Society and induced wealthy followers to print its literature and spread its doctrines.

In 1878 the Blavatsky, with Col. Olcott and a few others, left New York and went to India to start a society and a magazine in Bombay devoted to the scheme. Theosophists regard India as the great happy hunting ground of their Mahatmas. In 1885 she returned to London, where a society had been started, and began to publish another magazine. She remained in London until she died, and her rooms became the Mecca toward which all the other prominent Theosophists traveled to gather inspiration to carry on the work.

June 8, 1893

KRISHNAMURTI ENDS HIS AMERICAN VISIT

Hindu Philosopher Sailing, Says Chase for Gold Keeps People Here From Religion.

FINDS AMERICANS ARE KIND

He Declares We Are Concerned Only With Surface Things—Mrs. Besant to Lecture Abroad.

Jeddu Krishnamurti, the young Hindu who arrived last August with Mrs. Annie Besant and was acclaimed by the 100,000 Theosophists in the United States as "the Bringer of the Word," sailed yesterday on the Republic of the United States Lines without ceremony or farewell speeches.

While visitors were below in the cabins the young Hindu reclined on a deck chair, wearing a gray lounge suit, tan shoes and spats. He was reading "Elmer Gantry" when reporters discovered him.

Asked what he thought of the book Krishnamurti replied: "I think it is quite a good book, but it rather characterizes one man than any class of people."

In speaking of his stay in America he said he had been living on the estate of 900 acres near Santa Barbara, Cal., which had been purchased by Mrs. Besant and himself, and had enjoyed his visit. He intends to return there early next year to hold Theosophist conferences similar to those which have been held at Doorn, Holland, for some years. After a month in England with Mrs. Besant, who accompanied him on the Republic, Krishnamurti said he was going to Holland.

"What are your views about America?" he was asked.

"I think the Americans are very kind and I like the country, but there is too much excitement everywhere. Religion does not attain its proper growth here, and there is no time for deep thinking to get at the root of things. Americans who have lots of dollars think only of having a good time and spending money. They do not understand that one can enjoy one's self in this world of ours without any of those luxuries that are purchased by dollars.

"There is too much tendency to show off and too much striving for popularity among the wealthy here," he said. "The chase for gold has taken the people away from religion founded on basic philosophy. The American people are concerned with surface things and the churches never answer the question, 'Why do we live?'"

Mrs. Besant said she would deliver a series of lectures before returning to America.

April 30, 1927

Call it the neo-sacred, I Chingism, witchery, Teilhardism . . .

There's a New-Time Religion on Campus

By ANDREW M. GREELEY

DURING a recent unpleasantness between the University of Chicago and its Students for a Democratic Society the normal, decorous quiet of the Social Science Building was rent one fine afternoon by ear-piercing sounds. Secretaries, research assistants and even a few faculty members dashed to their of-

ANDREW M. GREELEY, a Roman Catholic priest, is program director at the National Opinion Research Center of the University of Chicago and a lecturer in sociology at the university.

fice doors to discover who was being murdered. Three young women dressed in shabby and tattered garments were standing in front of the Sociology Department office shrieking, "Fie on thee, Morris Janowitz! A hex on thy strategy!" WITCH (Women's International Terrorists Corps from Hell) had come to put a curse on the Sociology Department.

So far, nothing seems to have happened to Professor Janowitz or the Sociology Department. But if it does, there's going to be an awful lot of frightened people along the Midway.

(I offered to sprinkle holy water on the departmental office; but, while social science seems ready for witchcraft, it is not yet ready for exorcism.)

WITCH is only one manifestation —though a spectacular one—of a resurgence of interest in the occult on the college campuses of the country. Although some observers of WITCH's "hexing" dismiss it as a form of "guerrilla theater," the WITCHes themselves elaborate a quasi-scholarly explanation of how they continue a neolithic religion that worshipped the great earth mother goddess until it

was replaced by Christianity. One suspects that the WITCHes are but first cousins of the California Druids who also claim to be carrying on a tradition from the neolithic underground—thus confounding those of us who thought that the only Druids left in the world were Irish Monsignors.

WITCH is a combination of the put-on and the serious, the deliberately comic and the profoundly agonized, of the bizarre and the holy. The same is true of the other manifestations of the neo-sacred now observable around the country:

New Faiths for America

- Prof. Huston Smith of M.I.T. describes an experience with a seminar of some of the best students in the institution. "I cannot recall the exact progression of topics, but it went something like this: Beginning with Asian philosophy, it moved on to meditation, then yoga, then Zen, then Tibet, then successively to the 'Bardo Thodol,' tantra, the kundalini, the chakras, the *I Ching* [*ee-ching*, a book presenting an ancient Chinese divination device which enables one to make decisions — a sort of pre-I.B.M. computer], karate and aikido, the yang-yin macrobiotic (brown rice) diet, Gurdjieff, Maher Baba, astrology, astral bodies, auras, U.F.O.'s, tarot cards, parapsychology, witchcraft and magic. And, underlying everything, of course, the psychedelic drugs. Nor were the students dallying with these subjects. They were on the drugs; they were eating brown rice; they were meditating hours on end; they were making their decisions by *I Ching* divination, which one student designated the most important discovery of his life; they were constructing complicated electronic experiments to prove that their thoughts, via psychokinesis, could affect matter directly.

"And they weren't plebeians. Intellectually they were aristocrats with the highest average math scores in the land, Ivy League verbal scores, and two to three years of saturation in M.I.T. science."

- A certain Catholic university discovered that it had a coven of warlocks on campus (warlocks, for the uninitiated, are male witches). As the dean of the institution put it, "We've really become progressive around here. A couple of hundred years ago we would have burned them at the stake. Twenty-five years ago I would have expelled them. Now we simply sent them all to psychiatrists."

- At a Canadian university, the student body was given a chance to recommend courses of its own choosing to be included in the curriculum. The majority of the courses chosen had to do with astrology, Zen, sorcery and witchcraft.

- In most of the élite universities in the country, horoscopes and the prediction of the future by the use of tarot cards are widespread. Not all the students, not even a majority, are engaging in such divination. But a minority is and the majority does not ridicule their efforts. On the contrary, one has the impression that the majority reacts the same way it reacts to the S.D.S.: "We understand why they want to do it, even if we are not yet ready to do it ourselves."

- Catholic girls' colleges seem to be particularly disposed to producing groups of young women who make decisions by use of the *I Ching*.

- In a number of colleges, particularly in California, semi-monastic cults have arisen composed of young people who subsist on vegetarian diets, take vows not to cut their hair and spend long hours in contemplation.

- A thin network of students has formed a loose "community" to support one another through the stresses of graduate school, a community which does not take spatial separation to be a very serious problem in the providing of mutual support. One leader of the "community" describes quite bluntly what the "community" is about: "You might say we're forming a new religious cult."

- In the hills of Sonoma, Calif., there flourishes an institution called the "Six-Day School," composed largely of Berkeley dropouts, who learn about political pacifism, astrology, vegetarian dieting, mysticism and magic, during the course of their stay at the school—which usually exceeds six days. One group last year left Sonoma to proceed to Mount Shasta, there to await the end of the world.

- A bookstore just off Harvard Square, clearly doing an excellent business, announces itself as 'The Sphinx—Occult Books.'

- The White Brotherhood, a medieval Catharist sect made up of those in direct contact with "the spirit" (who has revealed to them that they are among the 144,000 white-robed martyrs of the Book of Revelation) is spreading at West Coast universities from Seattle to San Diego. Interestingly enough, the brotherhood is being spread by the same messengers who propagated it in the 13th century—wandering poets and minstrels, or, as they used to be called, troubadours and meistersingers.

I REMARKED in one of my classes that I had been able to locate almost every kind of offbeat religious behavior on our campus save for spiritualistic seances and wondered why someone hadn't thought of hunting up a medium. Several members of the class promptly assured their confreres that I hadn't looked very far; spiritualism was alive and well in Hyde Park.

Perhaps the most puzzling aspect of the new pursuit of the sacred is that it is so funny and yet so serious. Students cannot talk about it without laughing and yet they must interrupt their laughter to protest that they respect the goals of new devotees of the sacred. However, the puzzle is less difficult when one understands that the cultists are engaging in a form of *drama*—partly, one suspects, under the influence of their cousins, the hippies. Drama about the sacred is *liturgy*; and liturgy, as J. Huizinga pointed out in his famous book, "Homo Ludens," is sacred play.

The sacred by its very nature has large components of the playful and the comic close to its core. Only with the Reformation did the idea that the sacred was grimly serious finally triumph in the Western world. Catholic clerics will probably admit, now that the venerable Solemn High Mass has fallen into disuse, that they frequently found it hard to keep a straight face during its complex ceremonies. The new manifestations of the sacred, like the Solemn High Mass, are simultaneously much in earnest and a hilarious put-on. To put a hex on the Sociology Department is comic; but it is also a tentative assertion that there are powers in heaven and on earth which may transcend sociology departments.

Let us, first of all, make all the proper qualifications. Only a minority of students is engaged in the pursuit of the bizarrely sacred. Such a pursuit is not new among young people but is a continuation of the interest in the occult and the mystical which has persisted for some time. It is

a form of romanticism which has recurred in one fashion or another periodically in years gone by. It is experimental and does not indicate any return to the organized churches; as one student said to me, "Who in the world would expect to find anything sacred in the churches?"

The evidence for this resurgence of interest in the sacred is "impressionistic" and not yet based on the kind of "hard" empirical data that so delight the heart of the social scientist. Nevertheless, with all these qualifications, it still does seem there has been a very notable increase, however temporary, in interest in the sacred and particularly the bizarrely sacred among students on the college and university campuses in the last few years. Furthermore, the "return of the sacred" has happened exactly where one would least expect it—among the élite students at the best colleges and universities in the land, precisely those places where secularization would presumably have been most effective and most complete.

WHAT the hell is going on? God is dead, but the devil lives?

One of the things that strikes an interviewer who talks to students about the "return of the sacred"—even though they may themselves not be involved in witchcraft, astrology, or the *I Ching*—is that they resolutely refuse to dismiss as foolish those who are so involved. The first reason that young people give for the "return of the sacred" is the failure of science. One graduate student said to me, "Let's face it, science is dead. While the newspapers and magazines were giving all the attention to the death of God, science was really the one that was dying."

The extent and the depth of the revolts against positivism come as a considerable shock to those like myself whose training in the positive sciences took place in a time when they were totally unquestioned at the great universities. During the last winter quarter I put a statistical table on the blackboard and proceeded to explain the implications. One of my students respectfully but pointedly observed, "Mr. Greeley, I think you're an empiricist. In fact, at times I even think you are a *naive* empiricist." The accusation didn't surprise me because I guess I am an empiricist, but the tone of it did, for it was a tone of voice that used to be reserved for the accusation of being a "clerical Fascist."

The student then went on to deliver a fierce harangue against "the epistemology of science," and to assert that the "imperialism" of science by which it claimed to be the only valid form of human knowledge and the only valid rationale for organizing society was completely unsatisfactory to his generation. A number of other students rose to offer vigorous support to this position.

After class I pondered the matter in some confusion and returned the following session to ask if there was anyone who disagreed. Would no one

rise with the appropriate quote from Kaspar Naegele to defend empiricism, positivism and rationality? The class was completely silent, until one young woman remarked, "I think we all agree with what was said in the last class." At the beginning of the nineteen-sixties when I was in graduate school, such thoughts would have been "thinking the unthinkable."

The young people seem to be angry at science for its failures. A coed observed, "Science hasn't ended war, it hasn't ended injustices, and it doesn't respond to most of man's needs. Why should we take it seriously?" And another joined in: "Pure rationalism just isn't rational because man is more than reason and religion knows that even if positive science doesn't." And a third coed concluded, "Science was something that we had to work through our system. It only started with people like Darwin and it's not surprising that for a while everybody thought it was the only thing that mattered. It's just now that we've come to know better."

OTHER students explained the return to the sacred as a reaction to the failure of the university administrations and faculties to live up to their own rationalist and scientific principles. A young man put it this way: "When we see the utter incapacity of the rationalists to engage in rational discourse with us, we begin to rediscover the legitimacy of emotions. From these it is just a short step to the legitimacy of the sacred."

The rhetoric of the return to the sacred is not so very different from the rhetoric of the radical political movements. Words like "honesty," "integrity," "fidelity," "love," "openness" and "community" abound. The hippy culture with its emphasis on drugs stands midway between the two, bridging the gap between and pervading both other movements with its influence. Yet the movements are distinct. The hippies and the radicals may frequently use religious terminology and even respond to "religious needs," but their concerns still tend to be this-worldly. The neo-sacralists, on the other hand, are willing to accept as a working possibility a world which, if it does not completely transcend the present world, at least to some extent stands beyond it.

It is precisely this "standing beyond" which young people relate to the second reason for the return to the sacred: The sacred seems to provide an avenue for personal efficacy. As a male undergraduate described it, "Why use the *I Ching* in a world where you have the I.B.M. 360? The answer is easy. You can't understand the 360 and you don't have much control over it. The *I Ching* says that there are powers that stand beyond and are more powerful than the 360, powers with which in some way you can enter into a meaningful relationship when you can't do it with the 360." And one of his friends added, "Most of us realize that other people make our decisions for us quite arbitrarily. Whether I go to Vietnam or not, whether I get killed there or not doesn't depend at all on who I am or what I think. I'd sooner feel that my future was being shaped by the stars or by the turn of the cards because these would represent powers that would be more concerned about me than would either my draft board or the Pentagon."

I pressed these two young men to question whether they really did think that there was something beyond that made itself known through the movements of the stars or the turn of the cards. One of them shrugged uncomfortably. "I'm not sure," he said, "but I like to think so." And the other commented, "It's like the conclusion of Arthur Miller's 'Death of a Salesman.' In death, somebody did 'notice' Willy Loman. When someone turns the cards for you, you feel at least here you are being noticed."

The theme that religion is a response to alienation and to a feeling of unimportance against the larger society is widespread in the students' comments. "Religion makes you feel like you're a *person*." A woman undergraduate told me, "It makes you feel that you are important and that what you do does matter and you can have influence on others." Students are further impressed by the enthusiasm and confidence of the cultists. "They really believe that what they say is *true*," observed one young man to me. "They really believe that they do have the answer and that they do know what is ethically right and ethically wrong. It's hard to avoid being affected by their enthusiasm after you've been in a school that really isn't sure what is true or what is right or wrong."

L**IKE** the radicals and the hippies, the neo-sacralists are in desperate search for something to belong to. The religious groups are *communities*, places where one are more than just an I.B.M. file card. A young woman put it this way: "If you get into a group like that, you at least know that somebody will notice the difference if you're murdered. Around this university, you could be dead in your room for days and nobody would ever know the difference." And another commented, "We don't have to worry anymore, at least not very much, about where our food and housing is going to come from so we worry about ourselves and about finding ourselves. The only place where we are going to find ourselves is in deep relationships with others and that means either religion or sex and maybe both." The religious communities that grew up around the various cults of the sacred are felt to provide opportunities for meaningful intimate relationships over against the depersonalizing formalism of the academic and governmental bureaucracies. "You're a *person* in the group even if you don't want to be. You're forced to face yourself and discover who you are."

The quest for community in small groups makes the neo-

sacralists quite conscious of the relevance to their quest of T-groups (T stands for training), encounter groups, and the whole bag of group-dynamics tricks. Just as for some students group dynamics or sensitivity training become almost a religion, so for others already involved in quasi-religious behavior, sensitivity training and its cousins become an important means of religious growth. One girl told me how delighted she was to be part of a T-group which included two people who were on drugs and two others who were making their major decisions by means of horoscopes. It was, she noted, a fascinating experience.

Underlying the other three explanations the young people offer for the return to the sacred is a fourth: the sacred provides meaning. "In one way," a charming young woman said to me, "the sacred is even better than drugs, because when you're on drugs the world looks beautiful to you only if you're on a trip and ugly when you're not on a trip. But religion has persuaded some people that the world is beautiful most of the time despite the ugliness we see. That's terribly important."

One of her male classmates chimed in, "What we're really concerned about is whether anything is real, I mean, whether it is *really real*. Is there something that is so powerful that it can even make *us* real?" And an older graduate student (a clergyman, I suspect, but nowadays it's hard to tell) pointed out, "And Mircea Eliade [professor of history of religions at the University of Chicago and one of the world's most distinguished experts on the sacred] tells us that this is exactly what the sacred is, the *really real*."

Some of those who have kept an eye on WITCH argue that its principal contribution is to give its members some sense of what it means to be a woman, even if it is a bizarre concept of womanhood. Full meaning involves not only understanding what the world is all about or at least understanding whether the world has anything in it that is "really real," but it also involves having some sense of what you are all about and whether there is a possibility that you are "really real." The religious experience in the final analysis is seen as "ecstatic," that is to say, that it, like sex, takes a person out of himself and brings him into contact not only with other human beings but with the "creative powers" which presumably underpin the cosmos.

M**Y** very unsystematic survey of student opinion on the neo-sacred leads me to conclude that what is going on is authentically, if perhaps transiently and bizarrely, religious. Personal efficacy, meaning, community, encounter with the ecstatic and the transcendental, and the refusal to believe that mere reason can explain either life or personhood—all of these have traditionally been considered religious postures. An anthropologist visiting the secular

university campus from another planet could not help but conclude that there was a lot of very interesting religious behavior going on and he would probably feel that it was very primal and primordial, if not indeed primitive religious behavior.

Do these students believe in God? I have the impression that most of the young neo-sacralists would not understand the question or at least would find it premature. They don't believe in the God they left behind in their parish congregations. But they are frankly experimenting—as a part of a self-conscious "psychosocial moratorium"—with the "experience of the sacred" to see whether there is anything there which could add depth and richness to their lives. Most of them seem to hope, at times rather foriornly, that they will be able to find something or Something. But they are not ready to give it or It a name just yet.

T**HE** new religious enthusiasts clearly owe a major debt of gratitude to the hippies. Indeed, one might even consider them to be merely one wing of the hippie movement. Both emphasize the prerational if not the antirational. The quest for the spontaneous and the "natural" in the two dissenting groups is a protest against the "hang-ups" of a society that is viewed as overorganized and overrationalized but less than human. Both are a search for "experience"—and for a specific kind of experience—one that "takes one out of oneself." Both have, as noted, a strong comic element about them—an irresistible urge to "put on" the rational society.

Both the neo-sacralists and the hippies are communitarian, seeking experience and vitality from intimate friendships, friendships which in many instances are strongly at odds with the conventions of the large society. The two groups are further linked by their longing for the mystical and the reflective, again because these activities are seen as a means of standing apart from the rest of society, which has so little time for anything else but activity. The ceremonies, the rituals, even the *vestments* of the two groups also represent a common revolt against the sober and somber garb of the suburban businessman and his daily schedule. (Long hair used to be important but now that even the suburban executive is wearing sideburns and maybe a goatee, we might expect the deviants to imitate Buddhist monks and shave their heads.)

So the new search for the sacred shares with the hippies an "acted out" rejection of the rationalized bourgeois society, a rejection that is also a put-on of that society. The hippies were the first to become concerned with the mystical and the occult. But many of the new religious enthusiasts are not hippies in the ordinary sense and most of them are not willing to go the "drug route" with the hippies. Some say quite frankly that they view religion as a substitute for drugs and one that is much less dangerous. One

hesitates to say it, but the neo-sacralists appear to be much more "respectable" than the hippies.

But the important difference, I think, is that the religious cultists are seeking for something that hippies refuse to be hung up on; they seem to be looking for what the sociologists would call a "meaning system" or an "interpretative scheme." The hippies put on life because they think life is a put-on and ought not to be taken seriously. Those who are engaging in the quest for the sacred are, with a greater or lesser amount of explicit acknowledgment of the fact, looking for an explanation for life and for themselves. They're not sure they'll find it; they're not even sure that the search is anything more than a joke. But they'd like to think it just might be.

I**T** might be pertinent to ask why we are so surprised about the return of the sacred. The non-rational has been with man a long time and so has the supernatural and even the superstitious. Was it not unduly naive of us to assume that it would disappear so quickly? Astrology has always been a rather successful industry. Superstition is widespread in the general population. More than two-fifths of the American population go to church every week as do almost half the college students in the country. The limited amount of longitudinal research done on religious beliefs and behavior shows very little change in the last two decades. If the sacred and the superstitious still permeate the larger society, why are we so surprised that they have been tenacious enough to reassert themselves on the college campus?

Students themselves will cheerfully admit that their lives are not at all free from superstitious behavior even if they don't take the sacred or the supernatural very seriously. As one girl said to me, "I always wear the same sweatshirt every time I take an exam and I know other people who simply refuse to go into an exam unless they've had a shower beforehand. When you ask us why we do these things, the only response we can come up with is, why not? Sure, it might not make any difference, but then again it might, and there's no point in taking any chances." One is reminded of the famous agnostic prayer which is addressed "To Whom it may concern."

My friend, Peter H. Rossi, chairman of the Department of Social Relations at Johns Hopkins University, summarized only half-facetiously the relationship between agnosticism and superstition: "I'm not sure that I believe in good spirits but I have the uncanny feeling that there might be evil spirits."

W**ILL** the interest in the sacred on the college campus survive? For some individual students, it is clearly nothing more than an experiment which is part of their youthful "psychosocial moratorium," a part of their quest for personal identity. If the data on graduate student church attendance are to be believed, the moratorium will end not so much with agnosticism or even a new form of religion for most students, but rather with a return to some form of traditional religion. (A recent survey of graduate students showed that about 40 per cent of the students at the 12 major arts and science graduate schools in the country were regular church-attenders.) Witchcraft, astrology and divination, if they lose at all, are likely to lose to the traditional religions.

Yet some of the present concern about the sacred is likely to continue influencing the traditional church system within—perhaps even leading to the formation of new religious sects. Like most everything else on campus, the return to the sacred, while it is communitarian, is profoundly anti-organizational. Whatever of the present commitment to the sacred survives is likely to be informal and casual but such groups as the Druids and WITCH could conceivably grow much larger.

The students, in any event, have little doubt that the sacred will continue to interest them and that it will continue to fascinate their successors on campus. As one undergraduate male argued, "The interest in the sacred is rooted in a kind of existentialist dissatisfaction with the way

things are and since the way things are is not likely to change for a while, there is no reason to think the sacred is going to go away either."

Certainly the dissatisfaction with the failures of positive science does not seem to be reversible and one is inclined to suspect that it will be a fairly long time before the argument that religion or the supernatural or the sacred are' not "scientific" will be persuasive. Not everybody will be religious; but neither will religion be in full retreat, and some of the more bizarre, primitive, and superstitious forms of the religious are likely to enjoy a respectability for a number of years to come.

Max Weber, the founder of modern social theory, anticipated the rise of new prophecy (or the resurgence of old ones) as long ago as the first decade of the present century and anticipated it precisely as a revolt against the rationalism of the "spirit of capitalism." He wrote: "In the field of its highest development, in the United States, the pursuit of wealth, stripped of its religious and ethical meaning, tends to become associated with purely mundane passions. which often actually give it the character of sport. No one knows who will live in this cage in the future, or whether at the end of this tremendous development en-

tirely new prophets will arise, or there will be a great rebirth of old ideas and ideals, or, if neither, mechanized petrification, embellished with a sort of convulsive self-importance. For of the last stage of this cultural development, it might well be truly said: 'Specialists without spirit, sensualists without heart; this nullity imagines that it has attained a level of civilization never before achieved.' "

MOST of the contemporary manifestations of the sacred on the college and university campus are a form of withdrawal from the larger society—if not positively destructive in their view of said society. Yet the constructive element is not completely absent. I remarked a few weeks ago to my seminar on the sociology of religion that I thought most of the new religious forms offered personal redemption but despaired of social redemption. One young woman raised her hand. "Mr. Greeley," she asked, "have you ever heard of a book called 'The Phenomenon of Man' by a man named Teilhard de Chardin?" I admitted that I had. "Well," she said, "I was deeply impressed by that book because even though there is so much wrong with the world right now, I think Teilhard is right when he says that we're on the verge of a great leap

into a much better form of human life, that we are moving into the noosphere and that we are traveling toward an omega point. I think there's a lot of us that feel that we can have a faith in the sacred which will help us to create a better world."

I admitted to being something of a Teilhardist myself and conceded that there might be some of what she described in the student quest for the sacred, but insisted that I didn't see much of it and that I felt the "return of the sacred" assumed largely that the world was unredeemable and discriminating.

That was a mistake, for all kinds of hands rose up in the seminar room and all kinds of students rose up to assert their faith in the possibility of a Teilhardist-like vision of evolution toward the omega point.

I still can't quite figure out the meaning of that experience, but I must say I never expected to encounter a classroom of Teilhardists at the University of Chicago. Such people are necessarily a minority—a very small minority —of the whole student population, or indeed of the whole population of the world. There are not very many Teilhardists around. But it wouldn't take very many . . . ∎

June 1, 1969

SCIENTOLOGY WINS APPEAL ON METER

Judge Scores Use of Device but Upholds the Cult

Special to The New York Times

WASHINGTON, July 30 — A Federal judge condemned today the use of an electrical gadget purported to be a cure-all, but he permitted the Church of Scientology to continue to use the instrument in its religious practices.

District Judge Gerhard A. Gesell's decision held that the founder of the cult, L. Ron Hubbard, "first advanced the extravagant false claims that various physical and mental illnesses could be cured" through the use of the instrument, called the E Meter. The judge said the claims were "quackery."

But in a 14-page decision on the case, which has dragged through the courts for eight years, Judge Gesell said Scientology did indeed meet the qualifications of being a

religion and that, therefore, it was entitled to protection under the First Amendment.

With the religious issue established, Judge Gesell went on to state that the adherents of Scientology were entitled to continue to use the E Meter, which the Food and Drug Administration had sought to prohibit.

Intrusion on Religion Cited

"If a church uses a machine harmless in itself to aid its ministers in communicating with adherents, the destruction of that machine intrudes on religion," the judge said.

"A decree of condemnation will therefore be entered, but the church and others who base their use upon religious belief will be allowed to continue auditing practices [the use of the e meter] upon specified conditions which allow the Food and Drug Administration as little discretion as possible to interfere in future activities of the religion."

The judge ordered the F.D.A. to return to their owners 100 E Meters and two tons of printed matter that the agency had seized in 1963 on condition that "the device may be used or sold or distributed only for use in bona fide religious counseling."

Only ministers of Scientology will be permitted to use the devices, Judge Gessell ruled, and they must file with the F.D.A. an affidavit "stating the basis on which a claim of bona fide religious counseling is made."

"The effect of this judgment will be to eliminate the E Meter as far as further secular use by Scientologists or others is concerned," the decision added.

Proponents of Scientology maintain that by monitoring an individual's answers to questions, the meter enables the counselor to identify areas of emotional stress and to facilitate the person's progress toward self-knowledge and other forms of spiritual growth.

The Rev. Arthur J. Maren, a minister of the Church of Scientology, said his church "was pleased" with Judge Gessell's decision, but "less pleased" with some of the comment made about the value of the E Meter.

A spokesman for the Food and Drug Administration said the agency's lawyers were studying the decision and were undecided on an appeal.

July 31, 1971

The Jesus Movement Spreading on Campus

By DOUGLAS E. KNEELAND

Special to The New York Times

PALO ALTO, Calif., Dec. 25 —A new interest in religion, which in some ways resembles the rise of radicalism in the late nineteen-sixties, is taking root on many of the nation's recently becalmed college campuses.

Some of the fascination is intellectual and is reflected in increased enrollment in religion classes. Some of it represents a personal search for human and spiritual values and may draw the seeker to Eastern as well as Western theologies.

But campus observers in many parts of the country agree that the most visible manifestation of this is in the rapid spread of nondenominational, Fundamentalist, evangelical Christianity.

Just as the radicals gained adherents because of the wide disenchantment among the young with existing political and economic institutions, the Christian movement is attracting many who are disillusioned with the established churches and the quality of American life, including some facets of the so-called counterculture.

Both movements have been nourished by a pervasive sense of malaise, by a conviction that old ways have failed and by a search for truth. But, while the growing Christian movement comes at a time when the radicals are in decline on campuses, there is little evidence that the constituencies overlap, that many frustrated political activists are seeking solutions in the spiritual.

The Christians, as they prefer to be called, who make up what is known on campuses as the Jesus Movement, tend to resent being identified as "Jesus freaks," a term usually applied to street people who have frequently dropped out of the drug scene and occasionally out of radical politics to commit their lives to Christ.

"Most of the Jesus people I know seem to come out of the mainstream of life," said Jerry A. Irish, a professor of religion at Stanford University here, which has a large contingent of new Christians. "I think an awful lot of them are right out of middle-class and upper-middle-class homes."

"I think there's more going on in theology," he went on. "I think it's an authority structure in a society that's at a loss for authority structures.

There's a real authoritative simplicity about the evangelical Christian position that's very appealing.

Sense of Community

"Another factor is that it's a kind of discipline in a society that doesn't take discipline very seriously.

"A third thing is community —there's a real sense of community among people who are part of this movement."

Shaking his head thoughtfully, he added, "The only time that it scares me is when it's so clearly a kind of Linus blanket."

The Rev. David Roper, a minister at the Peninsula Bible Church, a nondenominational, evangelical institution that has 15 young internes working with Stanford students, took a somewhat different view.

"One thing is the disenchantment of kids of late with science," he said. "They're hungry for something that's real. There's still a lot of skepticism there, but I see a lot of kids responding to Jesus."

Sipping coffee at a local restaurant, the baldish, serious minister marveled at the growth of the Jesus Movement at Stanford in the last year or so.

"Sometimes it reminds me of a story they tell about the French Revolution," he said with a trace of wonderment in his voice. "You know about the woman who saw a man running after a mob and called out to him, 'Don't follow them. They'll lead to destruction. And the man answered, 'I have to. I'm their leader.'"

Forthright About Beliefs

"These kids are aggressive, they're forthright about their religion, they're unashamed."

Still pondering the sudden upsurge in the movement, he added, almost as an afterthought:

"I suppose it has something to do with the climate of despair."

The young Christians themselves, from one end of the country to the other, tend to explain their commitment in open, simple terms.

"Freshmen year I saw that what I thought was Christianity was really only 'churchianity,'" said Mark Hoffmann, an earnest, short-haired senior at Stanford who majors in biology. "After I had an intellectual understanding of where I was at and what the alternatives were, I realized in my own mind that I needed Jesus. Two guys who knew Him personally told me what knowing Him meant and then I took the step to go to Him and say, 'Lord, I need you.'"

"I have a real hang-up about the term 'Jesus freak,' because it denotes someone easy to explain away," said Kathleen Polasowski, a junior majoring in social studies at Wayne State University in Detroit. "I've been committed to Christ for two years. The movement will grow. It's really beautiful. We praise God for His goodness."

And at Boston University, which has a small but enthusiastic chapter of the Campus Crusade for Christ, one of several evangelical bodies that are actively engaged in spreading the movement across the nation, Joseph Battaglia, a fully committed member, explained:

"When one comes into a commitment with Jesus Christ, it's total. And when one's life is transformed through this total commitment, you've got to believe He's true. The present Jesus Movement bears this out, because people are committing their lives to Him."

There is no question that the movement is growing rapidly, but total numbers across the nation are almost impossible to obtain. Like the radicals before them, the new Christians usually start out with small, extremely dedicated groups such as the one at Boston University, which has about 15 members. By fervent proselytizing and by the example of their own lives, these groups frequently expand dramatically in a few months.

As with the radicals in their formative years, the movement's development seems to be spotty and somewhat unpredictable. Reports by campus correspondents of The New York Times from a score of colleges indicate that at some schools the movement has become perhaps the single most visible force on campus, while at others it has not arrived or is in an early stage where its impact has been negligible.

Large Massachusetts Group

At Amherst, Mass., for example, Campus Crusade for Christ has six full-time staff workers and more than 300 active members out of 24,000 undergraduates at the University of Massachusetts. At Amherst College, the Crusade claims only about a dozen members out of 1,200 students, while at Smith in nearby Northampton it reports 40 members out of an enrollment of 2,400.

The new Christian group at Wayne State in Detroit is estimated at only 50 out of 35,000 students, while at the University of Michigan in Ann Arbor, which has a student body of similar size, several hundred are reported to be in the Jesus Movement. On the Ann Arbor campus, the largest group is said to be the Word of God Community, which started with a prayer meeting of 10 people in 1967 and now has a membership of about 400, more than half of them Roman Catholics.

And so it goes around the country. Dartmouth and Brown in the Ivy League have small but deeply committed groups. The University of Chicago reports no apparent Jesus Movement, but the University of Illinois has well over 100 of the new Christians. At the University of Minnesota, the number is estimated at 200 and at the University of Colorado in Boulder a member said that there were "maybe 75 committed Christians when I got here three years ago; now there are several hundred."

Influence Seems Large

Again, as with the radicals, the new Christians' influence may often appear to be out of proportion to their numbers. Two hundred or 300 active new Christians may represent a small percentage of students on a campus, but, in a year when most students are shunning movements of any kind, they loom large by comparison.

At Stanford, for instance, most persons close to the movement place the number of committed new Christians at about 300 out of more than 11,000 graduate and undergraduate students, but this probably makes them the largest cohesive group on campus. They publish a mimeographed newspaper, The Fish, and meet in 20 separate Bible study groups, an increase of 16 in the last two years. Most of them also attend Seminar 70, a cluster of Bible seminars held each Sunday morning in campus classrooms.

On a recent rainy Sunday at final examinations, more than 160 straggled into a large lecture hall, wet and bedraggled, but greeting one another with cheerful smiles and friendly hugs.

In a few minutes, a guitarist started picking and singing, "Sing that sweet, sweet song of salvation and let the people know that Jesus lives."

Soon the room reverberated with:

And when you know a wonderful secret
You go out and tell it to your friends,
That a life that's filled with Jesus
Is like a street that never ends.

After another song and some announcements, the meeting broke up into seminar groups in smaller classrooms to take up such subjects as "Mere Christianity," "The Gospel of Matthew," "A Song for You," "Christology," and "The Joy of Discovery."

Forty-eight youths crowded into the "Joy of Discovery" class, described as "a workshop in Bible study designed to help you develop a lifetime habit of exploring the Book." It was taught by David Wilbright. Before beginning the class, he asked, as is the custom at all the seminars, if anyone had any problems to share with the group.

407

Hey, Pray for Her

A slender, dark-haired girl volunteered that she was soon getting married and that she had found herself becoming so self-centered that she had resented when her parents asked her to paint the bathroom.

"I just want to stand in the forgiveness of the Lord," she said.

"Hey, Mary, pray for her," Mr. Roper said softly.

"Let peace and calm come into her life," Mary prayed.

In the "Christology" seminar, Jack Crabtree, a 1971 Stanford philosophy graduate who is a Peninsula Bible Church interne, was discussing the Atonement. Declaring that Jesus died on the cross to expiate the sins of man before

and since, he went on to say that God had been impressed.

"He said, man, that's a quality sacrifice," the slim, young lecturer said, his eyes shining behind his glasses. "I like what you did. That's my Son, man. That's a quality sacrifice."

Waiting a moment for it to sink in, he added, "That's pretty exciting."

Most of the new Christians seem to agree, but there are others in the campus religious community across the nation who are not so excited about the whole Jesus Movement and its scorn for traditional churches, its total acceptance of the Bible as the given word of God, its every real belief in the presence of the Holy Spirit and its joyful

expectation of the Second Coming.

Some Couples Break Up

"I had a student in this office who had come down from a Jesus high," said B. Davies Napier, dean of the chapel and a professor of religion at Stanford. "He said it was like having been on a drug high for a number of months. He thought it was fraudulent."

"Another tragedy from my point of view," he went on, "is the number of couples who are breaking up, where one member gets picked up by the 'Jesus freaks' and the other can't accept it."

Dean Napier's criticism, though harsher than most, was typical of the attitude of many campus ministers.

For the last decade or more, large numbers of them had been preaching social activism, the importance of the church's reaching out beyond its doors to play a role in the community. Now, with traditional churches barely holding their own at most schools and admittedly being in some difficulty, they are worried by the great growth of the apolitical, Bible-oriented Jesus Movement, which shuns social involvement.

"The Jesus Movement is not going to lift a finger to change the status quo," Dean Napier said disapprovingly. "They're waiting for the Second Coming and Christ is going to take care of all that."

December 26, 1971

Young Ascetics Honor Lord Krishna

By JON NORDHEIMER
Special to The New York Times

MOUNDSVILLE, W. Va., Sept. 4—On the crown of a lovely green hill in the West Virginia countryside, under the aluminum roof of an open pavilion, the faithful gathered this week to chant the name of Lord Krishna and kneel at the feet of their spiritual master, a wrinkled brown man named A. C. Bhaktivedanta Swami Prabhupada.

Hare Krishna Hare Krishna Krishna Krishna Hare Hare; Hare Rama Hare Rama Rama Rama Hare Hare.

It was the opening of a seven-day festival at a communal farm celebrating the birth of Lord Krishna nearly 5,000 years ago, and the chanters were members of the Hare Krishna sect, a small ascetic band of young mendicants in flowing robes who are appearing in increasing numbers on the streets of large American cities from Times Square in New York to Ghiradelli Square in San Francisco.

The meeting was the first such national gathering and drew several hundred members. In addition, it also attracted individuals who apparently came here in expectation of a religious awakening.

Prabhupada (Pra-VOO-pada), as he is called by his followers, came to the United States from India in 1965 to spread the word of Krishna, the peripatetic god of the ancient Vedic scriptures that constitute the basis of most of the Hindu religious cults.

In the ensuing years he has shaped a hard-core group of about 1,000 United States devotees—the worldwide number is placed at more than 3,000—who have renounced the material world in the

hope of finding spiritual redemption at death. Consequently, the members exhibit the enthusiasm of Jesus Freaks, the abstinence of monks and the persistence daily discourses the spiritual mentor conducted on the grassy hilltop, "and yet no man has seen the inside of an eyelid, which is closest to the eyes."

Most of the devotees are in their late teens or 20's, and share a background in the upper middle class and the drug culture. Many are former Jews and while there are those who have been lured from a temporal life of intellectual achievement and status, the majority appear to be young people who had grown disillusioned after extensive experimentation with drugs and the hippie cult.

"Hippies are our best customers," remarked 24-year-old Dharmaraj Das, while awaiting the arrival of Prabhupada at the cult's 350-acre farm in the hilly wedge of West Virginia that separates Pennsylvania and Ohio "They are frustrated because they have learned that a life of illicit sex and drugs is not the way to spiritual consciousness."

Purity of mind and body is the path to spiritual awakening, according to the cult's saintly Prabhupada, and devotees accept rigid rules of conduct that reject not only the materialism of their city-suburban background, but also the sense gratification and free expression of the youth culture.

The Four Regulative Principles, for example, condemn "illicit sex." All sexual contact, including kissing, is considered illicit unless it is performed by married couples once a month at the optimum

time for procreation. Intercourse is to be attempted only after each partner performs several hours of repetitive chanting to cleanse the mind.

The consumption of meat, fish and eggs is forbidden.

No intoxicants of any kind are allowed, and that includes coffee and tea. The final restriction is against gambling, which is extended to outlaw all "mental speculation," a dictum that denies the devotee the privilege of opinions, whether they be his own or those advanced by other philosophers or spiritual leaders.

"The rigidity of behavior and thought control has a purpose," observed Prajapati Das, a former social worker from Dallas.

"The regulations control activity," he explained. "The control of activity reduces tensions, freeing the senses. The heightening of the senses enlarges the mind, and leads to a greater consciousness."

The control and discipline of the initiates is absolute, and outsiders struck by the hierarchical structure of the cult and its élitism, its attitude toward women and children, and its rejection of ideas find it difficult to fathom why it should attract men and women of inquiring minds.

Response by Leader

The response by Prabhupada is that man in his imperfect state cannot recognize God, and only after he has freed himself of sin and has become submissive can he develop the spiritual attitude to follow Krishna.

"I f you begin to give service to the Supreme Lord then you can begin to know Him," Prabhupada has writ-

ten. "Your service begins with the tongue. How? By the tongue you can chant Hare Krishna and by the tongue you can taste Prasadam, spiritual food."

The initiates are expected to turn all their worldly goods over to Prabhupada and submit to the labors he and his assistants request of them. Except for the communal farm, where about 35 members live and work, most of the devotees dwell in theurban temples, chanting on the streets for donations.

The four divisions of the Hindu caste system are accepted as the law of God, and there is a yearning to reach the level of Brahmana—the intellectual—in this life or the next life as the soul transmigrates, hopefully toward eternal reunion with Krishna in a spiritual corner of the universe called Viakunta.

Inside the movement there are three areas of endeavor. The Brahmacharis, or bachelors, are the foot soldiers; the Grihasta are householders whose marriages have been arranged by the godbrothers with the approval of Prabhupada on the basis of spiritual compatibility, and the Sannyasis, the highest order, are men who have renounced all family ties to wander from temple to temple to spread the word of Krishna.

"This is a movement of intelligent men," explained Ruganuba Das Goswami, a 32-year-old Sannyasi who was a New York City social worker named Robert Corens until he was enlisted by Prabhupada six years ago. "We have plenty of educated men who have been searching for God for years and discovered Him in Krishna. They have to be intelligent to reach a point where they ask 'Why?' They see order in the universe and realize wherever there is order there is meaning."

And intelligent men recognize, he continued, that the material world's only rewards are disease, suffering, aging and death. "We are not these bodies—that is the first basic lesson of Krishna consciousness," he said. "We understand that we have an eternal relationship with God and once that is developed then peace and prosperity will follow."

Prabhupada, in an interview, mixed maxims and analogies to press the same point.

"What happens in this world is of no consideration," he said as he sat cross-legged on an oilcloth floor in one of the commune's dwellings. "This life is an opportunity to make your next life—behave like a human being and you can go back home to Krishna. Act like an animal and you will become an animal in the next life."

'Diamond Is a Diamond'

He said that the low number of devotees he has gained in this country after six years of effort did not distress him. "If you sell diamonds you cannot expect to have many customers. But a diamond is a diamond even if there are no customers."

The presence of several hundred devotees at the commune for the week-long festival troubled some of the neighboring farmers. One man chased an orange-robed Sannyasi off his property with a shotgun and battered his young assistant when he caught them bathing in his creek. But the rest of the community hardly blinked.

The festival also drew parents of the devotees who came for a rare moment of contact with a daughter or a son. "From a parent's point of view, the Hare Krishna movement is fantastic," smiled a middle-aged woman who said she was from upstate New York where her husband is a professor of medicine at of a sidewalk Salvation Army drumbeater.

The Hare Krishnas stalk the city streets in groups ranging from six to a dozen, thumping drums and ringing bells, chanting in the belief that the souls of the non-believers they pass will be elevated simply by hearing the divine name of Krishna.

The men, their heads shaved except for a top knot of hair, wear dhotis (long loincloths) of burnt orange and pale yellow. The women are dressed in saris. All wear the mark of Krishna—a daub of white clay or some other material that streaks down their forehead to a point between the eyes.

Look of Rapture

And all display the beatific look of rapture as the chanting rises in volume and intensity, accompanied by dancing and rhythmic hand clapping.

Members of the sect dwell in city temples to which they have been assigned by Prabhupada, who himself resides in a former Methodist church in Los Angeles from where he directs the operations of the International Society of Krishna Consciousness. They sojourned here in buses and vans with bright Hare Krishnas emblazoned on the sides; some hitchhiked and some came by commercial transport for thousands of miles to praise Krishna at his festival of birth and to listen raptly to Prabhupada preach the wisdom of 5,000 years of succession through disciples.

"Men doubt what they cannot see," he intoned as the faithful pressed around the the University of Rochester.

"First Steve [her son] was into radical politics, then into drugs and the whole hippie scene, and then a Jesus Freak," she said. "One year he spent in Mexico looking for a perfect Stone Age cave for a commune, and spent another year following a crazy old man who thought he was the incarnation of Elijah. All those years he rejected his parents, but one of the first rules of the Krishna people is reconciliation with the family."

A retired chemical engineer from Maryland and his wife pointed out their 21-year-old daughter to another visitor.

"That baby she's carrying is my grandson," said the man. "I don't know what's' going to become of him."

The Hare Krishnas preach that women have a natural propensity for child-rearing and caring for the home, but also advise against strong emotional attachments inside a family. It is recommended that children should be sent by the time of their fifth birthday to the cult's school in Dallas.

James Hammond, a college student from Maine who came to the festival to explore Krishna consciousness further, had his doubts. "It seems young people do things like this in a fit of depression," he remarked . "I get skeptical when I see all these people who've done all these depressing things in drugs get caught up in stuff like this. You keep hearing the same old clichés about how high they are on it and how rewarding it is, and the next time you see them they're into something else."

How many devotees dropped out of the movement if not publicly discussed by the leaders, who call the process "blooping."

"Bloop," explained Rasananda Das, an intense 29-year-old former medical student named Hyman Zuckerman, "is the sound the soul makes as it falls into the pool of materialism."

September 6, 1972

Guru's Followers Cheer 'Millennium' in Festivities at Astrodome

By ELEANOR BLAU
Special to The New York Times

HOUSTON, Nov. 11—Maharaj Ji, the young Indian guru whose followers say he is god, talked about inner peace and accepted a golden swan in the Astrodome last night in the finale of what was billed as "the most significant event in human history."

While thousands of devotees chanted his praise, electronic fireworks burst on a scoreboard screen of the mammoth stadium, which is used more often for football and baseball games. Quotations from the Bible, the Koran and Maharaj Ji himself lit up two other screens. And a group called Blue Aquarius blared its big-band sounds, led by a brother of the guru in a glittering silver suit.

Earlier in the evening, Rennie Davis, the former antiwar activist, told the assemblage: "All we can say is, honestly, very soon now, every single human being will know the one who was waited for by every religion of all times has actually come."

The three-day event, called "Millennium '73," was said to herald "a thousand years of peace for people who want peace." The idea was that peace could come to the world as individuals experienced inner peace or "knowledge" of a source of energy inside them. To do this, they would have to use techniques taught by "disciples" of the guru, who is said to be 15 years old.

Size of Crowd

Mr. Davis, who coordinated the extravaganza, conceded at a news conference that followers had overestimated the expected turnout. "I thought [an overflow of] 100,000 would fill the parking lot," he said.

The police put the turnout at 10,000; followers put it at 25,000. The audience filled less than a quarter of the Astrodome, which was said to have cost $75,000 in rent. The maximum capacity of the stadium is 66,000.

Mr. Davis insisted that the size of the crowd was unimportant. "There's much more going on than meets the eye," he said.

Most of the spectators appeared to be followers of the movement, which claims six million to eight million members, including more than 40,000 in the United States. Nearly all of those who said they were not devotees were nevertheless acquainted and impressed with the guru's teachings.

"I'm interested in peace," explained Charley Price of Austin, who is 26 years old. "This seems to be where it's at. I feel the energy." And he added what many of the young followers told a visitor: "It's not something I think, it's something I feel."

Kathryn Barkley, who lives in a Los Angeles ashram, or spiritual center for devotees, said her participation was "just another step" in the peace activities she had engaged in since her graduation from Stanford in 1969.

Miss Barkley, the wife of Anthony J. Russo Jr., a defendant in the Pentagon papers case, said that although he was not a follower of the guru, "he sees the changes in me. Anger doesn't happen to me any more," she said. "There is no anxiety. There are changes in my tone of voice, my eyes."

One prominent figure in the peace movement of the nineteen-sixties, Jerry Rubin, showed up at the Astrodome, apparently at the urging of Mr. Davis, and was heard to remark, "I don't like this movement." He looked somber and declined to elaborate.

Most Are Young

A majority of the spectators appeared to be in their 20's, white and middle class. Most of those interviewed appeared to have had at least some college education. Their religious backgrounds varied widely and they came from many parts of the United States as well as about 30 other countries, some on chartered flights.

Many replied to questions by quoting Maharaj Ji or imitating his style of parable. "It's like this," more than one devotee responded when

The New York Times/Sam Pierson

Guru Maharaj Ji gesturing from his blue Plexiglas throne on the opening night of "Millennium '73" last week in the Houston Astrodome.

asked about the special knowledge. "I can tell you about an orange, I can describe it to you, but you won't know what it tastes like until you bite into it."

Or, as the guru himself put it during one of his three satsangs, or spiritual discourses, at the Astrodome: "Try it, you'll like it."

Although Maharaj Ji stops short of saying that he is divine, most of his followers say unreservedly that he is the lord of the universe, god incarnate, the one "perfect master" on earth at a given time.

The plump young man, who looks older than 15, but whose voice sounds teenaged, seemed to compare himself to Christ and Buddha during the satsangs. He remarked at one point that it was unnecessary to conjecture about whether God had, say, a long beard, "when we can see God face to face."

But at a news conference,

Maharaj Ji, asked if he were a messiah, responded, "Please do not presume that. I am humble servant of God, trying to establish peace in the world."

Why then did his followers call him the lord? "Why don't you do me a favor," the youth replied. "Why don't you ask them?" Asked why he did not sell his Rolls-Royce and other expensive gifts from devotees and give the money to the poor, he said, "If I give it for food to the people in the evening they will only be hungry the next morning."

Regarding reports that he had an ulcer, he said, "Ulcer is not the thing. This body has been born out of dust and will return to dust. When Jesus was nailed to the cross, He bleeded."

Addressing his disciples, he referred to an incident in which money and watches were seized by Indian customs agents, a year ago. He

said, "People think I'm a smuggler. Well, I'm a smuggler, you betcha. Oh, boy, it's too big. I smuggle peace and truth from one country to another."

Alluding to other critics, including groups from the Hare Krishna and Jesus movements who passed out literature outside the Astrodome, Maharaj Ji remarked, "Many people say, 'You're a fake.' you know what I say? I smile. Because they don't know what they're talking about. Probably they're drunk or something." He added, "When the Antichrist comes they won't know. Gonna be too professional."

Last July, at the start of a United States tour by the guru, his promoters said they would disclose plans here for a divine city organized by an arm of the guru's Divine Light Mission, a tax-exempt organization that coordinates activities, including a monthly magazine, chiefly through membership donations.

The only plans announced here were that the city would include a 144,000-seat hall for satsangs, built between two mountains. Spokesmen said the site had not yet been chosen. Everything would be free, with service replacing money as a basis of exchange.

The guru sat on a throne of blue Plexiglas on the top, seventh level of a 35-foot-high stage made of translucent white plastic that glowed from internal lighting. On a lower level, in smaller orange thrones, were members of his "holy family" — three brothers and his mother.

In contrast to the grandiose words of his followers, the young guru spoke simply. "This life is a big car," he told the devotees, or premies, last night. Just as cars need filters to keep dirt out of the fuel, he said, so cluttered minds need filters.

Grateful premies presented him with "a golden sculpture of the swan of truth uplifting the earth" as well as a marble plaque showing a lion and a lamb together. Blue Aquarius played a medley of tunes from the nineteen-sixties and songs with words such as "He's so funky, the lord of humanity."

Mr. Davis told reporters at one point that he could imagine how outsiders might regard the event. "Flashing lights, a huge stage, a kid talking not like Jesus but with parables about autos instead of a [fisherman's] net. It's not really a very good show," he said. "It's too hokey."

As for himself, he said, "I'm blown out. Here's the lord of the universe speaking from the stage of the Houston Astrodome saying, 'Here is peace.'"

November 12, 1973

Alan Watts, Zen Philosopher, Writer and Teacher, 58, Dies

Special to The New York Times

MILL VALLEY, Calif., Nov. 16—Alan Watts, the philosopher whose writings influenced the beat and hippie generations and helped popularize Zen Buddhism in the United States, died today at the age of 58.

A family physician said Mr. Watts had been under treatment for a heart ailment and died of natural causes in his sleep early in the morning at his Mill Valley home near San Francisco. He also maintained

a houseboat residence in nearby Sausalito, where he lived for many years.

Mr. Watts was said by friends to have been tired after a recent European lecture trip. He had been scheduled to give a lecture in Palo Alto tomorrow.

The family said the body would be cremated and services would be private, but that there would be a memorial observance later.

Virtually Cult Figure

By ALDEN WHITMAN

The road to Zen Buddhism began for Alan Wilson Watts when he was 12 years old and read the novels of Sax Rohmer, the creator of Dr. Fu Manchu. The exploits of this fictive inscrutable Chinese detective inspired the boy to an interest in the Far East and, ultimately in Indian and Chinese and Japanese mystical philosophy.

As an expounder of Zen in the West, Mr. Watts was virtually a cult figure in the nineteen-fifties and early sixties, when Zen achieved a certain popularity in the United States among the "beat generation." He was nonetheless critical of

what he considered the beats' ego-conscious interpretation of the philosophy, which led, he said, to self-justification.

"Zen is above all the liberation of the mind from conventional thought," Mr. Watts asserted," and that is something utterly different from rebellion against convention, on the one hand, or adapting foreign conventions, on the other."

Attempting to describe his definition more precisely, he wrote:

"The Westerner who would know Zen must first make his peace with his Judeo-Christian conscience so that he can take it or leave it without fear of rebellion or the itch to have status.

"Otherwise, his Zen will be either 'beat' or 'square,' the one just a noisy revolt against society, the other (as in Japan) just a new kind of stuffy traditionalism and respectability. The real Zen of the old Chinese masters was *wu-shih,* or 'no fuss.'"

'Spiritual Entertainer'

Mr. Watts believed that the "main assistance we can derive from Eastern man's experience is in methods for changing human consciousness so that the individual can actually *feel* his identity as an organism-environment (or man-universe), instead of a lonely ego sealed in a bag of skin." He also believed that drugs could be helpful in facilitating a changed consciousness, and he is said to have experimented along these lines in recent years.

In his autobiography, "In My Own Way," published last year by Pantheon, Mr. Watts characterized himself as a "spiritual entertainer" whose function was to enliven the theory and practice of all religions. He was not, he emphasized, concerned with dogma.

Critics of Mr. Watts—and there were many—deplored some of his interpretations and reproached him for his admitted disinclination to practice any of Zen's formal disciplines, especially the ascetic ones. He, however, was not abashed, saying that he was "an intellectual, a Brahmin, a mystic and also somewhat of a disreputable epicurean who has three wives, seven children and five grandchildren.

Enrolled at Seminary

A Kentishman, Mr. Watts was born in Chislehurst, England, on Jan. 6, 1915, and educated at King's School, Canterbury. After failing to obtain an Oxford scholarship, he started a first-hand search for mystical experiences, first among theosophists and gurus and then among London Buddhists. Meanwhile, he had begun to write about Eastern culture, and his first book, "The Spirit of Zen," appeared in 1936. It was quickly followed by "The Legacy of Asia and Western Man."

Coming to the United States in 1939, Mr. Watts enrolled at the Seabury-Western Theological Seminary in Evanston, Ill., and earned a Master of Sacred Theology degree. He was ordained in the Episcopal Church, and served as Episcopal chaplain at Northwestern from 1944 to 1950, when he left the church. His books in those years were "The Meaning of Happiness" and "Behold the Spirit."

In the succeeding years Mr. Watts lectured widely at such institutions as Harvard, Columbia, Chicago, Brandeis, Wesleyan and California. He was also frequently a radio and television speaker—his New York radio outlet was WBAI-FM. He continued, moreover, to produce magazine articles and books, including "The Supreme Identity," "The Wisdom of Insecurity," "Myth and Ritual in Christianity," "The Way of Zen" and "Best Zen, Square Zen and Zen."

Popularized Concepts

The last two books and "Psychotherapy East and West" were especially influential in popularizing Mr. Watts's Zen concepts. Like his other books, they were noteworthy for their literateness, wit and lucidity. He was also adept at the composing of haiku, a 17-syllable poem that is a literary expression of Zen. "A haiku," he said, "is a concrete image of a moment in life."

In recent years Mr. Watts helped run encounter programs, especially those promoted by the Esalen Institute in California. He also lectured, having just completed a European tour; and, of course, he maintained his literary output, mostly in the form of articles.

Mr. Watts leaves his third wife, Mary Jane; two daughters, Joan and Ann, from his first marriage; and five children of his second union—Tia, Mark, Richard, Lila and Diane. Five grandchildren also survive.

November 17, 1973

Sun Myung Moon, Prophet to Thousands

By ELEANOR BLAU

His face is everywhere, it seems.

Gazing benignly from billboards, subway stations, construction sites and glossy leaflets distributed by polite but persistent young followers, the color photo of a Korean man in a business suit has become a familiar sight to many New Yorkers in recent weeks.

He is the Rev. Sun Myung Moon, and he will deliver his message this Wednesday night in an admission-free program at Madison Square Garden. "He is God's prophet," explained one of the 1,000 followers who have been brought here from abroad to help in the $350,000 effort to arrange and publicize the event.

Actually most, if not all, of his followers consider the 55-year-old Mr. Moon the Messiah returned. They say fellow members of the movement exhibit a "loving" attitude they never encountered before. They believe Mr. Moon can save the world.

Critics of the church give different acounts. They question the wealth of his Unification Church and the motives of his fiercely anti-Communist stance.

Former members tell of a highly disciplined, hierarchical and fanatic organization in which overworked members are never alone, eat poor food, "don't have time" to think for themselves and are told they will die or suffer torment if they leave.

Parents of some followers level charges similar to those that have been made against the Children of God and other sects that have sprung up in recent years — that the group alienates its members from their families, telling them anyone opposed to the movement is influenced by Satan.

Clergymen of various Christian denominations charge that Mr. Moon falsely represents himself as a Christian. And in South Korea, where his Unification Church is one of the most controversial sects, reliable sources insist, among other things, that he has been arrested several times for sexual misconduct and that followers have countered criticism with violence.

Charges Vigorously Denied

Spokesmen for the movement vigorously deny all the charges and compare the criticism to that leveled against Jesus Christ.

"Absolutely vicious, unfounded," declared Col. Bo Hi Pak, Mr. Moon's chief associate and translator. "They try to twist the truth around. Why was Jesus Christ persecuted? This is a good analogy."

Mr. Moon's theology, spelled out in his "Divine Principle," holds that God intended Adam and Eve to marry and have perfect children, thereby perpetuating a "kingdom of God on earth." But Eve was seduced, literally, by Satan and, thus tainted, brought Adam into sin.

God wanted Jesus Christ to find a perfect mate and have perfect children, according to Mr. Moon, but, again, man failed him, crucifying Jesus and thus aborting his mission. That interpretation, in particular, infuriates those who say Mr. Moon only pretends to be Christian.

"The heart of Christianity is that Christ died for the sins of the world," says the Rev. Paul Moore, pastor of the Manhattan Church of the Nazarene, who plans to demonstrate at Madison Square Garden Wednesday with a dozen other clergymen. "He denies the basic tenet of Christian faith."

Tours Since 1972

Mr. Moon has been conducting increasingly publicized speaking tours in this country since 1972, a year after, he says, God told him to take his message to America.

Mr. Moon, who refuses these days to meet with reporters, addresses audiences in Korean, sometimes gesturing and shouting to emphasize a point and pausing for translation by Colonel Pak, a former Korean Army officer who was military attaché in Washington from 1961 to 1964.

The president of the Unification Church in the United States, 29-year-old Neil A. Salonen, says membership has doubled in the last year, apparently in part because of aggressive college campus recruitment.

Mr. Salonen reported that there were more than 25,000 members in this country, of which at least 500 were in New York. The largest bodies of followers are in South Korea and Japan—each with more than one million, he said.

Member Total Disputed

A State Department spokesman said, however, that Mr. Moon's Korean following was much smaller than that and that the Unification Church in Korea officially claimed only 320,000 members. Colonel Pak puts the worldwide total at "more than two million," or a million fewer than Mr. Salonen estimates.

Mr. Salonen disparages recent reports in the secular and religious presses that Mr. Moon is "worth $15-million."

"It is true that the movement throughout the world probably is worth far more than that," he said in an interview, stressing that the funds were held by the church, not Mr. Moon.

Nevertheless Mr. Moon is board chairman of various businesses in South Korea, and Colonel Pak acknowledged that Mr. Moon derived income from them.

They include the Tongil Industrial Company, Ltd., a shotgun manufacturing plant near the outskirts of Seoul; the Korea Titanium Company, producers of paint and coating materials; the Ilwha Pharmaceutical Company, specializing in ginseng tea; Ilshin Handicraft Company, which produces stone vases, and the Tonga Titanium Industrial Company.

Most or all employes are church members who live together in regimented style and receive token wages.

There are also businesses in Japan and a few in the United States, including a printing company in San Francisco, home-cleaning services in many states and a teahouse in Washington.

Mr. Salonen says the church in this country makes far more money from street sales of peanuts, candles, flowers and dry-flower arrangements than from businesses.

People who have left the movement confirm the efficacy of street soliciting. "I used to make over $100 every single day selling and just asking for money," recalled Laura Laufer of Providence, R.I.

Church property here includes a 22-acre estate overlooking the Hudson River at Tarrytown N.Y. The tax-exempt estate, reported to have cost $850,000, is said to be used as an international training center and as the headquarters for Mr. Moon, his wife and seven children. Mr Moon has spent most of the last three years in this country and has a permanent resident visa.

There also is a 255-acre estate farther up the Hudson at Barrytown, purchased from the Christian Brothers for an un-

disclosed sum, and 26-acre property in Irvington, said to cost $625,000.

Mr. Moon's personal life-style is something of a mystery. He appears in public only at well-orchestrated programs, such as the Madison Square Garden event. He dresses conservatively and works long hours, followers say.

He seemed stiff and polite in an interview he granted two years ago. During that New York visit, his rather mild appearance, at Alice Tully Hall, contrasted with a more fiery style the next year at Carnegie Hall.

Committed members of the church live communally in centers, of which there are eight in the metropolitan area, including a town house at 18 East 71st Street and houses in Brooklyn and Queens and on Long Island.

Pre-marital sex, drugs and smoking are taboo. A typical day includes prayer, calisthenics, singing, pep talks and long hours peddling on the streets. Members say the movement has altered their lives profoundly.

"I'm a lot happier and I have a sense of purpose about my life," said Andy Wilson, 23, at the Brooklyn center. Mr. Wilson, who studied biochemistry and was graduated magna cum laude from Harvard two years ago, explained that he could

never satisfactorily combine science and helping people" and that this was the first religion he had found that "had a lot of logic to it."

According to Mr. Moon's associates, he was born in what is now North Korea, raised as a Presbyterian and received a revelation at the age of 16, when Jesus Christ appeared to him and told him he had a great mission.

During nine years of prayer and study, the associates say, Mr. Moon discovered "the process and meaning of history, the inner meanings of the parables and symbols of the Bible and the purpose of all religions." He also studied engineering.

He was arrested and tortured by the Communists, according to his associates, served in a labor camp, was freed by United Nations forces in 1950 and founded his church four years later.

Some of Mr. Moon's early acquaintances in Korea insist that his first arrest by the Communists involved charges of "disrupting social order"—specifically, promiscuous sex. The second arrest is said to have been for remarrying without divorcing his second wife.

His present wife is his fourth, according to sources in Seoul—not his second, as reported by church spokesmen.

A third jailing occurred in July, 1955, also reportedly for "causing social disorder" and bad morals. Newspapers at the time reported that the charge involved ritual sexual intercourse with women in the church.

Colonel Pak angrily denied these charges in an interview, saying that the 1955 arrest was for alleged evasion of military service and that he was cleared in a trial.

Nevertheless Pak Chong Gu, chief evangelist of the Unification Church in Seoul, admitted in a recent interview there: "It is true that Teacher Moon was tried on moral charges. But he was eventually acquitted, and that proves his innocence."

Mr. Moon teaches that the "last days" are upon us and that the Messiah or "third Adam" will be known soon. The "Divine Principle" does not state precisely that Mr. Moon is that "third Adam," but it does say, for example, that Messiah will come from Korea.

Colonel Pak said the movement had no ties with the Government of President Park Chung Hee, other than the Little Angels, a dancing and singing group founded by Mr. Moon that represents South Korea in some of its appearances.

September 16, 1974

Gallup Poll Indicates 32 Million Believe in Astrology

"Our business is growing by leaps and bounds," said Lester Cherubim president of Time Pattern Research Institute in West Caldwell, N. J., which casts astrological reports by computer for people according to their exact time and place of birth.

Mr. Cherubim, whose company sends out between 60,000 and 100,000 reports a year, is one of some 32 million adults in the United States who, according to a Gallup poll released yesterday, say they believe that stars influence people's lives and foretell events.

From 300 Places

The survey indicated that 22 per cent of the nation's adult population believe in the practice. It also showed that twice as many women as men hold the belief. As many churchgoers as nonchurchgoers believe in astrology, according to the poll.

About 24 per cent said they read an astrology column reg-

ularly, and 77 per cent of the 1,536 adults interviewed said they knew which astrological sign was associated with their birthday. More than 90 per cent of those under 30 years of age could identify their sign, the survey found.

The poll, taken from Oct. 3 to 6, was based on answers from people in more than 300 localities around the country to the following questions:

"Do you happen to read any astrology column regularly? Do you happen to know under which sign you were born? Do you believe in astrology?"

Recently, 186 prominent scientists issued a statement calling astrologers charlatans and asserting that there was no rational basis for belief in the practice. Many signers of the statement, which was drafted by Dr. Bart J. Bok, former president of the American Astronomical Society and professor emeritus of astronomy at the University of Arizona, were astronomers or astrophysicists.

Eighteen signers were Nobel Prize winners.

A professional astrologer, R. Donald Papon, director of the Academy of Mystic Arts in New York, said recently that "1,250 out of 1,500 daily newspapers carry an astrology column, and six universities, including the New School, have had academic courses in astrology."

Like Weather Forecast

Asked why so many people put their faith in astrology now, Julienne P. Sturm, founder and president of the International Society for Astrological Research based in Montclair, N.J., said, "It is the result of a search for meaning in life."

"Knowing where your stars are," she said, is like having a "weather forecast" of "problems with your life."

Mr. Cherubin agreed that people were looking for answers for their lives "during times of stress," but said that

anything short of an astrology report based on the exact time and place of birth was worthless. Newspaper astrology, he said, is a "fraud."

Dr. Stephen A. Appelbaum, a psychoanalyst and psychologist at the Menninger Foundation in Topeka, Kan., said the current interest in astrology was a "part of that movement which has to do with the paranormal—it links up with the renewal of interest in Eastern religions and mystical traditions of the East."

Seeking Magic

Dr. Appelbaum said he had been investigating this renewed interest for the last two years. He remarked that turning to astrology was part of a rejection of "the rules by which Western civilization lives." And if those rules can be broken, he added, "then anything might come true that we all wish would come true —including that you're not going to die."

Dr. Oliver Quentin Hyder, a psychiatrist who is the medical director of the Christian Counseling and Psychotherapy Center in Manhattan, said that the reason more people were turning to astrology was that "men and women are seeking something magical in their nitty-gritty daily details and pressures."

Asked why so many church members believed in the ancient practice, he said, "It is really a religious search, but if they do not find their spiritual needs being met by a personal faith in Jesus Christ, then they turn to something else."

"It is clear from Deuteronomy 18 that astrology is a sin," he said. Deuteronomy 18:10 reads: "There shall not be found among you any one that maketh his son or his daughter to pass through the fire or that useth divination or an observer of times or an enchanter or a witch."

"The whole system of astrology is self-destructive," Dr. Hyder added. "Imagine if every decision of your life is made by a flip of a coin. That's how much chance you have of making a right decision using astrology."

October 19, 1975

Despite Rigors, Buddhism Continues to Win Adherents in U.S.

By KENNETH A. BRIGGS

Seated on small cushions, the 10 newcomers to the Zen Studies Center at 223 East 67th Street wrestled themselves into the full lotus position, or a variation thereof, and listened to their instructor, a black-robed lay monk with a shaved head.

"At the beginning, sitting like this feels horrible," said the teacher, Don Scanlon, a longshoreman and former prizefighter. "But as it is said, 'No pain, no gain.'"

If the newcomers are typical of hundreds of students around the country entering introductory classes in Buddhism, many will be prepared to endure the muscle aches that go with learning the basic principles and will develop a lasting interest in what is rapidly becoming a distinctve form of American religion.

Buddhism has existed here among Asian-Americans for decades. General interest was aroused during the 1960's when gurus flocked to this country, and many college students became enchanted, at least superficially, with Far Eastern religions.

No Longer Just a Fad

But only in the last few years has American Buddhism evolved as a solid religion. In the view of observers Buddhism has gone beyond faddishness and has acquired traits of an indigenous religious form with staying power, to the extent that world Buddhism is taking it very seriously.

"The spirit of Buddhism is in America now," said Heng Ju, a student of the religion who recently returned from a tour of the Far East. "People are starting to recognize that fact."

The Buddha taught that one could attain truth by ridding oneself of earthly craving, and that failure to do so results in endless deaths and rebirths. Buddhism posits no gods or dogma; rather, it urges its subjects to reach the state of illumination through human powers of self-examination.

Great stress is placed upon meditation, which highlights self-control, self-discipline and moral purity. As such, Buddhism provides a pathway to truth rather than a body of truths that depend on divine authority. Zen refers to a particular meditative method that developed most fully in Japan.

Among the signs of how far Buddhism has grown as a serious, permanent feature of America's religious landscape are the following:

¶The presence of large study and meditation centers made up almost entirely of native-born adherents who in some cases have already devoted several years to the discipline.

¶The establishment on the East and West Coasts, where the new movements are concentrated, of a number of lavish retreat centers costing millions of dollars and providing a base for expansion.

¶A vigorous effort at translating Chinese, Japanese and Tibetan Buddhist texts into English at such places as the Nyingma Tibetan Institute in Berkeley, Calif., and the Center for the Study of World Religions at the State University at Stony Brook on Long Island.

¶The cultivation of a corps of native-American Buddhist masters. The Gold Mountain Monastery in San Francisco, for example, includes 20 such monks fully ordained in one of the most orthodox of Zen schools.

Observers of the trend estimate that tens of thousands of Americans, mostly young people, have seriously taken up Buddhist pursuits in the last decade. Many were initially drawn to the popularized methods of meditation that accompanied the social protest, religious and drug experimentations of the 1960's.

Eyes on America

Gradually, however, the interest has settled into more conventional patterns of discipline and philosophy. Buddhist masters say that Americans are good students, though impatient, and that the surge of interest in Buddhism here could rejuvenate the tradition in large areas of Asia, including Japan, where it has been in decline.

"Everybody is watching the American movement," said Eido Roshi, a Zen master at the Zen Studies Center, one of three Zen centers in New York. "If it does well, it could have a revitalizing influence."

The Zen Studies Center is now spending $2.5 million to build a retreat monastery on a 1,400-acre tract in Livingston Manor, in the Catskills.

Financing for such costly expansion comes from various sources. The Nyingma Tibetan center, for example, reports most of its income is derived from gifts under $100. Other center, such as Gold Mountain, have received large gifts from single donors. As they have grown, most groups have begun to incorporate systematic fundraising.

The San Francisco Zen Center, which consists of three facilities—a city center, a farm and a retreat in Santa Cruz—has a total of 150 residents, 100 of whom have already spent at least six years there. The center reports a waiting list of one year for applicants.

Many of those seeking enlightenment are motivated by some of the reasons that led Buddhism's founder, Siddartha Gautama, on his religious quest 2,500 years ago: boredom and disillusionment with affluence. The Buddha (the word is Sanskrit for an "enlightened one") was the son of a rajah; many of his American followers also come from well-to-do backgrounds and are rebelling against materialism.

The 250 'Precepts'

Three monks at the Gold Mountain Monastery exemplify the radical change in life style that often accompanies the search. Before receiving Chinese names from their Zen master, they were known as Stephen Lovett, who is a Harvard graduate from Lowell, Mass.; Christopher Clowery, a Chinese scholar from Toledo, Ohio, and Richard Josephson, a native New Yorker whose pleasure-seeking had led him to life as a surfer in Hawaii.

Now they are, respectively, Heng Kuan, Heng Sure and Heng K'ung, and they dress in the peasant style of ancient monks, wear black-knit skullcaps over shaved heads and meditate up to 14 hours a day.

Explaining the growth of Buddhism, Heng Sure, who is preparing for full ordination, which includes acceptance of 250 "precepts," or moral laws, says: "Energy in this country has turned inward. People realize that you can't really change anything without changing yourself first."

Heng Sure first came across Eastern religion in an article on yoga in an encyclopedia. In high school he was in an experimental program in Chinese, which spurred his interest in the language and people.

Like many other devotees of Buddhism, he had also come into contact with the writings of the late Buddhist scholar, Dr. D. T. Suzuki of Columbia University, who was largely responsible for introducing the religion to this country.

Some Explanations

The three monks, in an interview, put forth several explanations for the current enthusiasm for Buddhism, its inherent democracy ("a real do-it-yourself religion," said one); an interest among Americans who believe the mind is the last frontier, the attractiveness of a religion that is concerned with the unconscious mind and a vision of wholeness; and the willingness of Americans to accept the physical and psychological rigors involved in study and practice.

The Sino-American Buddhist Association, which sponsors the Gold Mountain Monastery and an institute for translation, recently purchased a 240-acre residential community near Eukiha, Calif., from the state for $6 million. The organization plans to turn it into a Buddhist center for 10,000 people, with facilities for retired people and the handicapped.

"Buddhism has experienced a natural growth," says Nancy Wilson Ross, author of two books on the subject. "Like psychoanalysis it tries to move you from adolescent dependence to the realm where life is up to you. I think young people are ready for that."

February 4, 1976

Religious Movements In Contemporary America

Edited by Irving I. Zaretsky and Mark P. Leone.
900 pp. Princeton, N.J.: Princeton University Press. $25.

Thirty scientific observers of the American religious scene have combined their efforts and the result, amazingly enough, is rich and readable, a guidebook to a colorful country fair of faiths. Along the midway we can sample spiritualist sermons, Afro-American rituals, urban witches, black Jehovah's Witnesses (yes, there are many), tongue speaking, Hare Krishnas, scientology (where the occult, psychoanalysis and science fiction meet), Mormons, Pentecostals and many more. Do not be misled by the claim of the writers that they have restricted the study to "marginal" movements. Such groups are always important as well as interesting. Not only do "marginals" give clues about future developments in religion, they also help us see where the whole society may be heading.

Fortunately, although the articles are nearly all written by scholars, the language, with a few exceptions, is comprehensible and clear. Where technical terms appear they are usually explained. Among these my own favorite is "ideolect," which is the ideological equivalent of a "dialect." It is a variant, even eccentric, but clearly identifiable expression of a religious belief system. Apparently America today is absolutely rife with ideolects. In fact it is precisely the vast multiplication and growing acceptance of such adaptations that seems to be the single most important key to the American religious horizon today. Although people still leave religious movements to start their own, a time-honored American procedure, even more people seem to be restyling existing religious teachings to their own needs. Consequently it is becoming ever more difficult to predict in advance what someone believes on the basis of his or her affiliation.

In two of the book's better essays Janet L. Dolgin and Mark P. Leone

---

Harvey Cox is the author of "The Secular City" and "The Seduction of the Spirit."

show how and why this process has markedly altered Mormonism, a religious group, which although it appears rigidly dogmatic to outsiders, exhibits an enormous variety of "ideolects" within. But this same tendency seems to hold across the board. As the introduction to the final section puts it, "The new religious movements emerging in America are built on an ability to allow their faithful to revise their lives continually and on an ability to revise themselves as religious movements." If this sounds like a modern echo of the reformation notion that the church is, or should be, "semper reformanda," always reforming itself, then the spirit of the reformers may be alive and well today, though quite possibly not where the reformers expected it to be. In any case, the capacity for selective appropriation, reimaging and demythologizing—once the domain of "modernizing" theologians—seems now to have been democratized: all exegesis to the people!

Neo-oriental and mystical groups naturally receive a lot of attention. What does the current American fascination with them actually mean? For Raymond Prince, a Magill University psychiatrist, these movements represent a kind of "cocoon work." They provide opportunities for middle-class young people, sated with structure and organization, to retreat temporarily to a mini-world where nonacquisitive values, communal feelings and mystical experiences are cultivated. Unlike their insect analogs, however, these human larvae have no clearly modeled adult stage toward which they are developing. So what happens? Prince hopes for a change in the larger society itself which will generalize some of the values the young people find at the margin.

Other contributors however, including Dick Anthony and Thomas Robbins—who have a marvelous essay on the Meher Baba movement—see it a bit differently. Instead of inducing large scale change, they believe these movements may in fact be "cooling people out," providing them with a compensatory community of feeling and affect which, ironically, may enable them to turn the wheels in the big impersonal bureaucracies even more efficiently. Less committed to the goals of success and accomplishment, supplied with feeling and affect elsewhere, these gentle devotees may provide pliant, nonabrasive human material for the soul-less, overorganized society. "Baba Lovers," many of whom were once drop-outs and heavy drug users, nearly always return to work and school and family life. The values of the movement allow them to move back into roles and niches they once left in despair.

June Macklin, in another essay, finds that spiritism has much the same conventionalizing influence on Mexican Americans. Far from pulling them out of the mainstream, it pushes them in. Instead of striking a blow at the technological colossus, spiritism and neo-oriental mysticism may be making it even more secure. "Those hearing the spirits admonish them to be patient, to work hard, to delay gratification, to get an education, to be optimistic and make an effort," writes Macklin, "could become the technocrats of tomorrow."

The prospects of this paradox are stunning. What if out of the Zen centers, Buddhist mountain retreats, meditation halls and mystical ashrams of America there now begins to stream forth a new army of inwardly tranquil white collar key punch operatives? What began as a revolt against the automated culture could end up by making it more efficient. Then, yet more ironical, Christianity, which with its desacralized nature and centered selves helped spawn Western technical civilization, but which has never been completely comfortable with it, would find itself once again on the margin. Someday a few decades hence a future group of scholars might decide to study those little groups of Christians who, feeling alienated from the great Karmic machine culture around them, seem on the edge of hatching something new.

For me the most engaging dimension of this book is its *tone*. In the past, when anthropologists, linguists, sociologists and psychiatrists have written about religion, especially about marginal groups" one could almost hear the sneer coming through the typewriter. Regardless of what informants told them about faith and what it meant to them, the investigators always knew better. They saw religion as a buttress for the status quo, a haven for the maladjusted, a compensatory mechanism for misfits. Religion was always consequence, epiphenomenon or symptom.

But in these essays a different posture appears. The book is dedicated, interestingly, not to some senior scholar but to "the members of the religious groups" themselves. This note recurs. University of Minnesota anthropologist Luther P. Gerlach, for example, declares that although in his previous research among the Digo people of the Kenya coast he was still mired in the traditional condescending "scientific" attitude, his further reflection and research, especially on North American and Haitian Pentecostals, has caused him to question it. The "game," as he describes the conventional know-it-all approach in the study of religion, "is facilitated by the shared assumption of the social science community that there is in fact no 'supernatural' or at least that we cannot use supernatural cause to explain events. What, we can wonder, would happen," he then asks, "if our scholarly paradigm was based on or at least admitted the existence of God, spirit forces, or the like?"

I wonder too. Indeed in reading Gerlach's article and many of the others in this volume, I asked myself if Carlos Castaneda's discovery in the Mexican desert—that there are more ways to perceive reality than the one provided by social science—may begin dawning on more people. If it does, and if the freshness and self-critical openness of the essays in this book indicate that a new breeze is blowing, then the long-stymied conversation between theology and social science may begin anew. Frustrated once by the haughty triumphalism of theology and then by the arrogance of social science, it can proceed only if all participants agree they will not try to reduce the other's world to the terms of their own, that there is more than one way to see a blackbird, listen to a prayer or symbolize a cosmos.

December 22, 1974

Suggested Reading

Bibliographies

Burr, Nelson R. *A Critical Bibliography of Religion in America*. 2 vols. Princeton, N.J.: Princeton University Press, 1961. (Part One, pp. 3-84 on bibliographical guides.)

Handlin, Oscar, et al. *Harvard Guide to American History*. Cambridge, Mass.: Harvard University Press, 2 vols., rev. ed. 1974.

Vollmar, Edward R. *The Catholic Church in America: An Historical Bibliography*. 2nd ed. New York: Scarecrow Press, 1963.

Studies of Religion in America

Ahlstrom, Sydney E. *A Religious History of the American People*. New Haven: Yale University Press, 1972.

——, ed. *Theology in America: The Major Protestant Voices from Puritanism to Neo-orthodoxy*. Indianapolis: Bobbs-Merrill Co., 1967.

Baird, Robert. *Religion in America*. 1844. Critical abridgement with introduction by Henry W. Bowden. New York: Harper & Row, 1970.

Bestor, Arthur Eugene, Jr. *Backwood Utopias: The Sectarian and Owenite Phases of Communitarian Socialism in America, 1663-1829*. Philadelphia: University of Pennsylvania Press, 1950.

Blau, Joseph L. *Judaism in America: From Curiosity to Third Faith*. Chicago: University of Chicago Press, 1976.

——. *Modern Varieties of Judaism*. New York: Columbia University Press, 1966.

——, and Salo W. Baron. *The Jews of the United States, 1790-1840. A Documentary History*. 3 vols. New York: Columbia University Press, 1966.

Braden, Charles S., ed. *Varieties of American Religion*. Chicago: Willett, Clark and Co., 1936.

Brauer, Jerald C. *Protestantism in America: A Narrative History*. Rev. ed. Philadelphia: Westminster Press, 1965

Clark, Elmer T. *The Small Sects in America*. Rev. ed. New York: Abingdon-Cokesbury Press, 1949.

Clebsch, William A. *From Sacred To Profane America: The Role of Religion in American History*. New York: Harper & Row, 1968.

Ellis, John Tracy. *American Catholicism*. 2nd ed., rev. Chicago: University of Chicago Press, 1969.

Frazier, E. Franklin. *The Negro Church in America*. New York: Schocken Books, 1964.

——. *The Negro in the United States*. New York: Macmillan Co., 1949.

Gaustad, Edwin S. *Historical Atlas of Religion in America*. New York: Harper & Row, 1962.

——. ed. *Religion in America*. Two reprint series. I. 38 titles, 1969. II. 40 titles, 1972. New York: Arno Press.

——. *A Religious History of America*. New York: Harper & Row, 1966.

Glazer, Nathan. *American Judaism*. Chicago: University of Chicago Press, 1957.

Glock, Charles Y. and Robert N. Bellah. *The New Religious Consciousness*. Berkeley: University of California Press, 1976.

Handlin, Oscar. *Adventure in Freedom: Three Hundred Years of Jewish Life in America*. New York: McGraw-Hill Book Co., 1954.

Holloway, Mark. *Heavens on Earth: Utopian Communities in America, 1680-1880*. 2nd ed. New York: Dover Publications, 1966.

Hudson, Winthrop S. *American Protestantism*. Chicago: University of Chicago Press, 1961.

——. *Religion in America*. New York: Charles Scribner's Sons, 1965.

Marty, Martin E. *Righteous Empire: The Protestant Experience in America*. New York: Dial Press, 1970.

Mead, Frank S. *Handbook of Denominations in the United States*. 5th ed. Nashville, Tenn.: Abingdon Press, 1970.

Mead, Sidney E. *The Lively Experiment: The Shaping of Christianity in America*. New York: Harper & Row, 1963.

Moberg, David O. *The Church as a Social Institution: The Sociology of American Religion*. Englewood Cliffs, N.J.: Prentice-Hall, 1962.

Olmstead, Clifton E. *History of Religion in the United States*. Englewood Cliffs, N.J.: Prentice-Hall, 1960.

Pfeffer, Leo. *Church, State and Freedom*. Boston: Beacon Press, 1953.

Smith, Hilrie Shelton, Robert T. Handy, and Lefferts A. Loetscher. *American Christianity: An Historical Interpretation with Representative Documents*. 2 vols. New York: Charles Scribner's Sons, 1960-63.

Smith, James W., and A. Leland Jamison, eds. *Religion in American Life*. 4 vols. Princeton, N.J.: Princeton University Press, 1961.

Sontag, Frederick, and John K. Roth. *The American Religious Experience: The Roots, Trends, and the Future of American Theology*. New York: Harper & Row, 1972.

Sweet, William W. *The Story of Religion in America*. New York: Harper & Brothers, 1950.

Washington, Joseph R., Jr. *Black Religion: The Negro and Christianity in the United States*. Boston: Beacon Press, 1964.

Weigle, Luther A. *America Idealism*. New Haven: Yale University Press, 1928.

Zaretsky, Irving and Mark P. Leone. *Religious Movements in Contemporary America*. Princeton: Princeton University Press, 1974.

Index

Hallinan, Paul J., 85
Halverson, Wendell Q., 256-57
Hamilton, William, 385
Hardwicke, Elizabeth, 387
Hare Krishna Movement, 408-9
Hargis, Billy James, 259
Harner, Nevin C., 23
Harrington, Donald S., 274
Harvard University, 41
Harvard Zionist Society, 132-33
Hayes, Patrick J., 66, 76-78
Hebrews, *See* Jews
Heyrman, Donald, 101
Himmler, Heinrich, 139
Hines, John E., 52, 53
Hitler, Adolf, 135-37
Hochhuth, Rolf ("The Deputy"), 93
holocaust, 142-44, 155-57, 159, 393-94
Holy Bible, *See* Bible
homosexuals, 56-57
Hoover, Herbert, 139-40
Hopper, Stanley, 387
Hoshor, John (*God in a Rolls Royce*), 336
hotels, Bibles in, 15
Howard, Murray Shipley, 31
Hrbek, George, 54
Hughes, Edwin Holt, 43, 139-40
Hungary, 71
hungry i night club, 397-401

Ickes, Harold, 139-40
Illig, Alvin, 100
Indians, 2-3
Institute for Freedom in the Church, 98
Institute for Propaganda Analysis, 43
intermarriage, *See* marriage, intermarriage
Israel: criticized, 317-20; David Ben-Gurion, 149-50; and the New Left, 317-18; proclaimed, 145, 146; Zionism rebuked, 147; *see also* Zionism
Italian immigrants, 69

Jackson, Jesse, 357
jazz, 25, 397, 400
Jehovah's Witnesses: described, 165-67; flag salute, 210; vs Roman Catholics, 209
Jenks, David W., 261
Jesus Christ: death of, 310, 312-13; Jewish roots of, 315; *The Man Nobody Knows* (Barton), 21
Jesus Movement, 407-8
Jewish Defense League, 316
Jews: anti-semitism, 148-49, 297, 301, 305, 306, 308-9, 314-16, 319-20, 354-55; apostasy report, 153; appeal for exiles, 137-38; bias against, in religious texts, 309; blacks and, 354-55; centers for, 128; and Christians, 132-33, 297, 314, 328; and Christian Sabbath, 201-2; concentration camps, 142-44, 155-57, 159, 393-94; denunciation of Hitler, 135; discrimination vs., 134-25; East Side, 128; education for, 126, 158-59; endangered existence, 144; in Europe, 134-35; faith after Auschwitz, 393-94; famous American, 151-53; and Felix Adler, 124; fund-raising, 55; George S. Brown, 320; German prison state, 140; Hasidim, 150; Hebrew Anarchists, 127; holocaust, *See* concentration camps; immigration curb, 134; intermarriage, 132-33, 149, 160, 161, 162; and Jesus Christ, 311-13, 315; and Kehillah, 131; life among poor, 127; "The Merchant of Venice" (Shakespeare), 305, 320; Nazis, 135, 138-39; New York community, of, 130; Orthodox, 131; *"Our Crowd": The Great Jewish Families of New York* (Birmingham), 122-23; persecution of, 135-36, 138-41, 155-57; and politics, 131, 248, 264; Reform, 160-61; rivalry among, 150; and Roman Catholics, 85, 311-13, 321-24, 327; Russian, 125-26; socialism, 248; and swastika, 136-37; theologians, 155-57; tradition, 160-61; in United States, 132, 133, 147; unpopularity of, 296; woman cantor, 277; World War II refugees, 140-41; and young people, 154, 159, 162, 264; *see also* Judaism; rabbis; Zionism
Jews and Americans (Malin), 151-53
Johann, Robert, 90-91
John XXIII (Pope): elevated to Papacy, 81-83; praised, 331; Vatican Councils, 86-89, 324-25
Jones, John Paul, 250
Judaism, 134, 154: of Jesus, 315; revival of, 148; women's role, 279-80, 281-82; youth's criticism of, 264
Judson Memorial Church, 401

Kahane, Meir, 316
Kahn, Benjamin, 264
Kamphoefner, Henry L., 45
Kavanaugh, James (*A Modern Priest Looks at His Outdated Church*), 102
Kegley, Charles and Robert Bretall, (*The Theology of Paul Tillich*), 382-83
Kellogg, John Harvey, 49
Kennedy, Eugene C., 113
Kennedy, John F., 103, 223-32, 240
Kierkegaard, Soren, 380-81, 382, 387,
King, Martin Luther, 342, 348-49, 350
Kirk, David, 330-31
Kirkpatrick, Dow, 342
Knorr, Nathan, 165
Krishnamurti, Jeddu, 403
Krol, John J. Cardinal, 88, 95-96, 112-13
Ku Klux Klan, 301-2, 341

labor: and Episcopal Church, 243; and Roman Catholic Church, 71-72; and religion, 242
La Guardia, Fiorello, 71-72